Adapted Physical Activity, Recreation and Sport

Dedicated to my parents, Ivalene and Robert Sherrill, of Logansport, Indiana

Adapted Physical Activity, Recreation and Sport

Crossdisciplinary and Lifespan

Fifth Edition

Claudine Sherrill
Texas Woman's University

WCB
McGraw-Hill

Boston, Massachusetts   Burr Ridge, Illinois   Dubuque, Iowa
Madison, Wisconsin   New York, New York   San Francisco, California   St. Louis, Missouri

WCB/McGraw-Hill

A Division of The **McGraw·Hill** *Companies*

ADAPTED PHYSICAL ACTIVITY, RECREATION AND SPORT:
CROSSDISCIPLINARY AND LIFESPAN

Credits appear on page 696, and on this page by reference.

 This book is printed on recycled paper containing 10% postconsumer
waste.

234567890 QPK QPK 9021098

ISBN 0-697-25887-4

Publisher: Ed Bartell
Project editor: Theresa Grutz
Production editor: Debra DeBord
Production supervisor: Janice Roerig-Blong
Visuals/design freelance specialist: Mary Christianson
Art editor: Joyce Watters
Photo editor: Rose Deluhery
Marketing manager: Pamela S. Cooper
Copyeditor: Wendy Nelson
Cover design: Kay Fulton
Cover illustration: © Gary Phillips
Compositor: Shepherd, Inc.
Typeface: 10/12 Times Roman
Printer: Quebecor Printing Dubuque, Incorporated

Library of Congress Catalog Card Number: 96-85402

http://www.mhcollege.com

BRIEF CONTENTS

CONTENTS

PART III

INDIVIDUAL DIFFERENCES, WITH EMPHASIS ON SPORT

P R E F A C E

This fifth edition has been revised extensively to stay abreast of the rapidly expanding knowledge base of adapted physical activity as a profession and an academic discipline. This textbook is designed to develop the beginning-level knowledge and skills of both undergraduate and graduate students who aspire to meet individual needs in physical education, recreation, sport, fitness, or rehabilitation settings. Although the emphasis is on cooperative home-school-community physical education programming for infants, toddlers, children, and youth, this textbook also addresses the competencies of professionals in other settings who work with people of all ages.

NCPERID Standards and Competency Test

Study of this text and use of the multiple-choice questions in the teacher's manual and computer test kit will enable professionals to meet the personnel preparation standards established by the National Consortium for Physical Education and Recreation for Individuals with Disabilities (NCPERID) in 1995 and to pass the new NCPERID National Competency Examination. This optional examination, which has been widely publicized, was developed to assure high-quality performance in school-based adapted physical activity service delivery for individuals from birth to age 21. The author of this textbook is a life member and past president of NCPERID.

Comprehensive, Multipurpose Resource

This textbook is designed to guide study in the basic adapted physical activity course as well as in such specialized courses as (a) assessment, (b) curriculum, instruction, and pedagogy, (c) administration, including consulting, (d) disability sport, and (e) individual differences, including disabilities. The content is purposely broad to afford professors the freedom to select content that meets individual needs and interests. It is not necessary to cover all chapters in every course. The teacher's manual explains how the textbook can be used with different course outlines.

The intent is to save the student both money and time by including all of the essentials of adapted physical activity in one book that can be kept as a reference for on-the-job use. The content can be surveyed rapidly in beginning courses and read again for in-depth competency development in advanced courses. Over 600 photographs and line drawings make the book interesting and user-friendly.

The Role of This Text in Infusion

Adapted physical activity attitudes, knowledge, and skills must be *infused* into all regular education courses. After university students are introduced to the content of this text in a basic course, their competencies should be further enhanced by a teacher-training *infusion model* in which individual dif-ferences are addressed in every course. *A goal is for this textbook to be used as a resource in every class.* To achieve this, adapted physical activity proponents must share this text with regular education colleagues and emphasize infusion of content into daily lesson plans.

The PAP-TE-CA Model Refined

The content of this text is based on the belief that both regular and adapted physical activity personnel need competencies in seven areas:

P   Planning
A   Assessment
P   Prescription/Placement
T   Teaching/Counseling/Coaching
E   Evaluation
C   Coordination of Resources and Consulting
A   Advocacy

I call the knowledge comprising these areas the PAP-TE-CA model. It would be helpful if this acronym spelled something meaningful, but we shall have to settle for its spirited rhythm. It is a mnemonic device that effectively assures memory of the services that guide competency development.

In this fifth edition, I have reorganized the content in Part I of the text so as to present PAP-TE-CA roles, functions, and competencies in order. This should make the learning of adapted physical activity service delivery easier. Advocacy (Chapter 4) is, however, still presented first because of my belief that this remains our most important service: advocacy at international, national, state, and local levels, and, most essential, advocacy that regular physical educators in our neighborhood schools assume their responsibility for active, healthy lifestyles for all children.

Practical Knowledge Emphasized

Part II of this fifth edition is extensively revised to focus on physical activity goals and the knowledge that professionals must have to enable individuals of all ages to achieve these goals. Each chapter has been revised to increase the emphasis on assessment and pedagogy specific to a goal. Content on self-concept and attitudes, which previously was in Part I, is now in Chapters 8 and 9.

New Chapters in the Fifth Edition

All chapters in Parts I and II have been revised extensively, but the following chapters are new:

Chapter 3   Teamwork, Communication, Adaptation, and Creativity
Chapter 5   Philosophy, Planning, and Curriculum Design

Organization of the Fifth Edition

This textbook's 27 chapters are organized into three sections:

Part I Foundations

Part II Assessment and Pedagogy for Specific Goals

Part III Individual Differences, With Emphasis on Sport

Parts I and II are completely rewritten for this edition; Part III is updated. Part I combined with either Part II or Part III makes an excellent introductory course. The choice depends on whether the professor wishes to emphasize assessment and pedagogy (Part II) or individual differences and sport (Part III). Extra credit for optional reading or oral reports of unassigned chapters is encouraged.

Part I focuses first on an understanding of adapted physical activity, individual differences, and home-school-community teamwork; then introduces advocacy as the first of the PAP-TE-CA services to be taught; and then concludes with sequential coverage of philosophy, planning, curriculum design, assessing, prescribing, writing the IEP, teaching, evaluating, and consulting. Part I thus gives an overview of how regular and adapted physical educators can work together to meet individual needs of students.

Part II presents in-depth coverage of each of 10 goals of adapted physical activity (e.g., self-concept, inclusion and social competence, motor skills and patterns). Each chapter relates to a selected physical education goal. The university student is taught to assess present level of performance, then to write specific objectives based on assessed needs, and then to adapt and create pedagogy so as to help individuals achieve these objectives. This section, in conjunction with Chapter 6 on assessment, can easily serve as the textbook for an assessment course. Likewise, it can serve as a textbook for a curriculum, instruction, and pedagogy course, when combined with Chapters 5 and 7.

Part III presents in-depth coverage of infants, toddlers, and early childhood (Chapter 18), followed by chapters on the disabilities recognized by Public Law 101-476, the Individuals With Disabilities Education Act (IDEA) of 1990. Sport terminology from the worldwide Paralympic movement is used to designate disabilities, and sport classifications used by the International Paralympic Committee (IPC) and its constituent organizations are described. Special Olympics and Deaf Sport are also given strong coverage.

Emphasis on Sports for Individuals With Disabilities

Whereas some authors develop separate chapters and books on sport for athletes with disabilities, this text treats sport as an integral part of adapted physical activity. Over 150 pages of text on sport have been included in this fifth edition, as well as outstanding photographs of athletes with disabilities in competition.

Pedagogical Devices

This text offers numerous pedagogical devices designed to help students blend theory with practice. These include the following:

- *Chapter objectives to guide study*
  Objectives at the beginning of each chapter can be the basis for written assignments or used as essay questions on an examination. An objective can be assigned to a student who prepares an oral report for class, makes a tape recording or videotape, or develops a slide presentation.

- *Learning activities embedded in each chapter*
  These activities are designed to ensure that practicum experiences supplement classroom theory. Use of these activities works especially well in contract teaching.

- *Subject index that can be used as a dictionary for looking up spellings of words*
  The subject index can also be used as a testing device. A card for every word in the index is made and color-coded (if desired) by chapter. Students randomly draw cards from the stack for a particular chapter and talk or write for 60 sec on the subject drawn. The subject index can also be used in studying for the final exam; students should be able to spell and discuss every word in the index from the chapters they have covered.

- *Name index for becoming familiar with authorities in adapted physical activity and related disciplines*
  The name index can be used the same way as the subject index. Emphasis on learning names (i.e., primary sources) is probably more appropriate for graduate than for undergraduate students.

- *Numerous photographs and line drawings*
  Approximately 250 photographs and 340 line drawings enrich the text. Test questions can be drawn from figure captions, since these descriptions provide double emphasis of facts.

- *American Psychological Association (APA) format*
  Adherence to APA writing style provides a model for students who wish to acquire research and publication skills.

- *Appendixes on definitions, prevalence, and incidence*
  Appendix A presents definitions of disabilities as stated in the United States federal law. The prevalence and incidence statistics in Appendix B are helpful in preparing term papers and in documenting the need for adapted physical activity service delivery.

- *Appendixes on sources of information*
  Appendixes C, D, and E provide readers with over 100 addresses to write for additional information.

- *Appendix on the history of adapted physical activity, recreation, and sport*
  Appendix F presents a chronology of more than 100 events, beginning in 1817 with the establishment of the first residential schools in the United States, including dates for the initiation of services, enactment of legislation, and formation of organizations.

- *References to reinforce understanding of primary sources*
  The reference list at the end of each chapter provides direction for persons who wish to get more in-depth coverage through additional reading. Students should be encouraged to learn the names of journals and to stay abreast of new issues as they are published.

ACKNOWLEDGMENTS

To the many individuals and agencies who shared in this adventure, a heartfelt thank you. I am especially grateful to *Julian Stein,* who served as major reviewer and advisor for the first edition and who has been my mentor for many years; and to *Janet Wessel* of *I Can* and the *ABC* curriculum, whose work forms the basis of the PAP-TE-CA service delivery model in this textbook.

To Creators of Our Knowledge Base

I am indebted to the many persons who are creating the adapted physical activity knowledge base and to the editors of the journals that disseminate this knowledge. Work that appears in the *Adapted Physical Activity Quarterly* and *Palaestra: The Forum of Sport, Physical Education, and Recreation for Those With Disabilities* significantly affects my thought, creativity, and commitment. My thanks to the editors of these journals for their service and scholarship: *Geoffrey Broadhead,* Kent State University; *Greg Reid,* McGill University; and *David Beaver,* Western Illinois University. Writers who particularly have stimulated my thinking are Terry Rizzo, Walter E. Davis, Allen Burton, Dale and Beverly Ulrich, Gail Dummer, Ted Wall, E. Jane Watkinson, Martin E. Block, Patricia Krebs, Karen DePauw, Trevor Williams, and Greg Reid.

To My Students

Most important, I thank my students at the Texas Woman's University, who keep me involved in research and practicum experiences, and the parents who trust us with their children. Each edition brings new students as well as memories of past ones who have shared and grown with me and significantly affected the contents of this book. I wish I could mention all their names, but a few will have to do: Karen DePauw, Nancy Megginson, Abu Yilla, Luke Kelly, Jim Rimmer, Sarah Rich, Boni Boswell, Wanda Rainbolt, Jo Ellen Cowden, Garth Tymeson, Jim Mastro, April Tripp, Ellen Kowalski, Carol Pope, Ron Davis, Leslie Low, and Lisa Silliman-French.

To My Support Network and Photographers

For her photography, assistance with the many aspects of production, and overall support, I thank *Rae Allen.* For their help with photography in this fifth edition, I thank *Deborah Buswell, Joe Nolan,* and *Mary Carol Peterson.* I am grateful also to the outstanding staff of McGraw-Hill Higher Education, whose editing, production, and marketing excellence makes them the leaders in creating a knowledge base for adapted physical activity. A special thanks to *Theresa Grutz.*

To My Resource Persons

Special recognition is extended to *Wynelle Delaney,* DTR, who coauthored Chapter 16, "Adapted Dance and Dance Therapy"; *James Rimmer,* who offered suggestions for improving Chapter 13, "Fitness and Healthy Lifestyle"; *Jeff Jones, Carol Mushett, Dr. Ken Richter, Kim Grass, Ruth Burd,* and *Duncan Wyeth,* who shared their expertise on cerebral palsy sports; *Patricia Krebs* and *Cindy Piletic,* who assisted with the chapter on mental retardation; *Charles Buell, Harry Cordellos, Rosie Copeland,* and *James Mastro,* who taught me about blindness and visual impairments; *David A. Stewart* and *Gina Olivia,* who reviewed the chapter on deaf and hard-of-hearing conditions and offered valuable suggestions; *Abu Yilla, Pam Fontaine,* and *Don Drewry,* wheelchair athletes who shared their knowledge; *Inge Morisbak* of Norway, who helped with winter sports; and *Terry Rizzo* and *April Tripp,* who assisted with content on attitudes and social acceptance.

To My Role Models

Acknowledgments can be complete only if they extend backward in time to those persons who sparked the initial enthusiasm in teaching and writing: *Dr. Harry A. Scott* of Teachers College, Columbia University, who spoke of competency-based teaching in the early 1950s; *Dr. Josephine Rathbone,* also of Teachers College, who instilled in me a deep concern for the right of all persons to efficient and beautiful bodies; and *Dean Anne Schley Duggan,* Texas Woman's University, who taught me to hear the different drummer and to keep step to the music—however measured or far away.

Claudine Sherrill

PART

I

Foundations

C H A P T E R

1

Active, Healthy Lifestyles for All

FIGURE 1.1   Holistic model to guide understanding of purpose, goals, domains, and outcomes of lifespan adapted physical activity.

ADAPTED PHYSICAL ACTIVITY MODEL

PURPOSE

| To remediate psychomotor problems and reinforce psychomotor strengths, thereby facilitating self-actualization |

ILLUSTRATIVE GOALS

Self-concept, body image

Social competency, inclusion

| Physical and motor fitness | Motor skills and patterns | Skills in sports, dance, games, and aquatics |

INTERACTING DOMAINS FOR EMPOWERING CHANGE

Cognitive   Affective   Psychomotor

OUTCOMES OR BENEFITS

Active, healthy lifestyle at all ages

Self-actualization

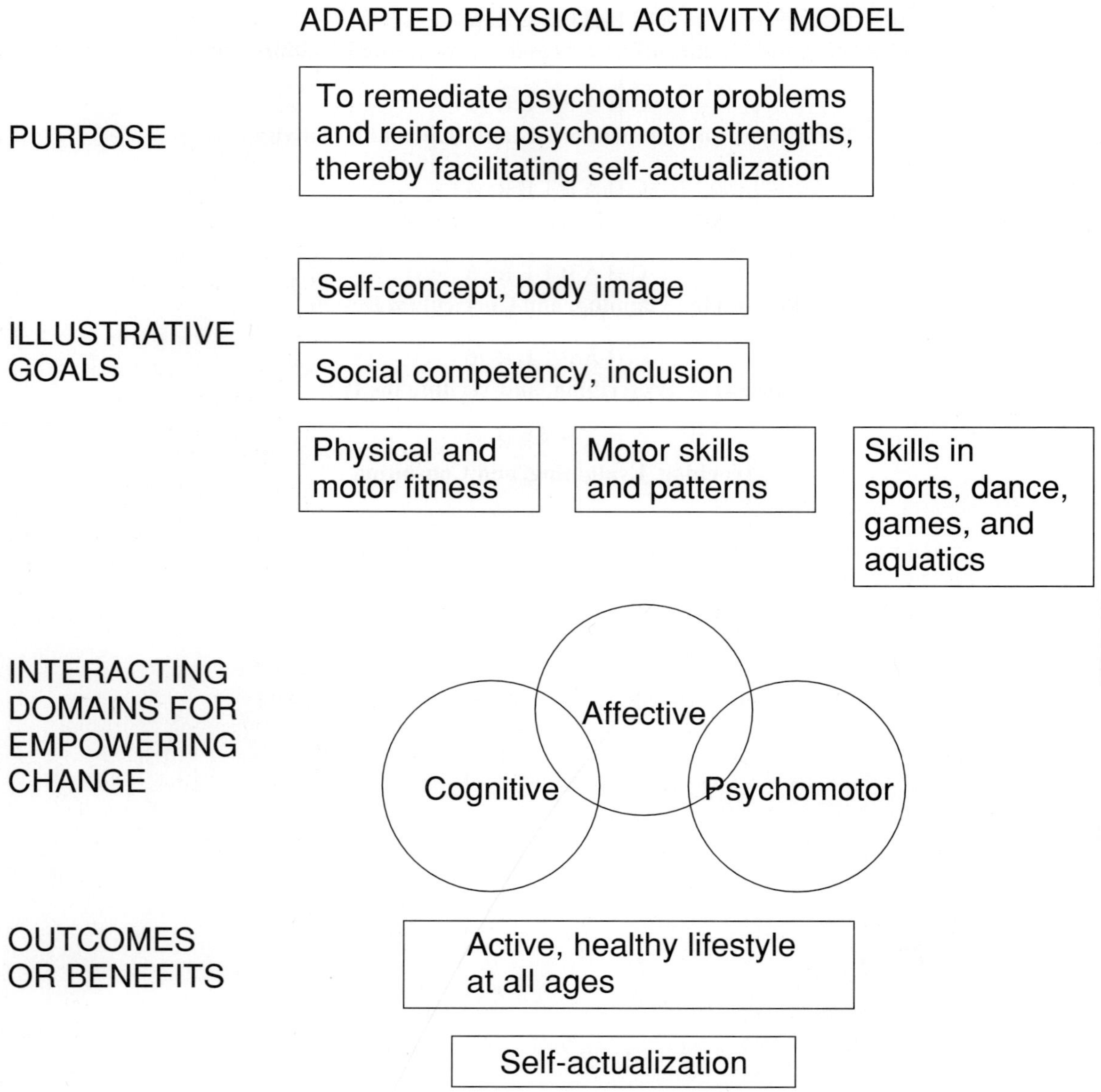

After you have studied this chapter, you should be able to do the following:

1. Understand the many meanings of adapted physical activity and discuss how and why meanings change.

2. Understand the purpose, goals, domains, and outcomes of adapted physical activity and communicate these to others.

3. Critically think about who needs adapted physical activity and why.

4. Identify and discuss basic terms (e.g., *psychomotor problems, self-actualization, adaptation, ecosystems, service delivery, support services, IEP, disability, individual differences*).

5. Differentiate between such concepts as *adapted* and *adaptive; interdisciplinary, crossdisciplinary*, and *multidisciplinary*.

6. Consider ways generalists and specialists can work together to achieve active, healthy lifestyles for all.

7. Appreciate the history of adapted physical activity, and use your understanding of the past to critically think about the present and future.

8. List and discuss adapted physical activity organizations.

9. Critically think about zero-reject and zero-fail principles, basic beliefs, and ethics.

10. Critically think about standards, job functions, and competencies, and assess yourself in relation to these, set goals, and develop a personal learning plan.

In physical activity, everyone fails at one time or another—by coming in last on the relay team, by missing the basket or field goal that would have tied or won the game, by choking and struggling in the swimming pool, by letting days go by with no vigorous exercise. Some people, however, fail more than others, and these failures affect all aspects of their lives. Failure often results in labels, such as *clumsy, awkward, fat, lazy, disabled.*

How long does a label, once internalized, endure? What effect does a label have on growth and development? In particular, how does failure affect body image and self-concept? What causes failure? How does failure, real or perceived, make people feel different? How do individual differences affect social acceptance and inclusion? This book is about individual differences that interfere with the achievement of physical activity goals and aspirations and the variables associated with success and failure.

Psychomotor Problems and Strengths

Psychomotor problems are specific limitations, barriers, constraints, weaknesses, or delays in self/environment interactions that prevent goal achievement and self-actualization. Figure 1.1 presents some of the goals that must be achieved in order to maintain an active, healthy lifestyle. These goals involve behaviors in all three behavioral domains because it is not possible to separate one domain from another.

The term *psychomotor problems* is really an abbreviation for *integrated cognitive-affective-psychomotor problems.* **Cognitive domain goals** include intellectual skills necessary for learning play and game behaviors and sport rules and strategies, for using perceptual-motor function, and for thinking and moving creatively in order to overcome various barriers. **Affective domain goals** include feelings, attitudes, intentions, values, interests, and desires. Among these are self-concept and body image, social competency and inclusion, and fun/mental health. **Psychomotor domain goals** include sensorimotor function, physical and motor fitness, motor skills and patterns, and skills/participation habits in sports, dance, and aquatics.

Psychomotor problems are offset by psychomotor strengths, abilities, competencies, or affordances in self/environment interactions that promote an active, healthy lifestyle and self-actualization. Good assessment and programming focus on both strengths and weaknesses. We change psychomotor behaviors by addressing specific variables in individual performance and in the environment (both social and physical).

Many professions are interested in concurrently remediating psychomotor problems and reinforcing strengths. Among these are physical education, recreation, special education, occupational therapy, physical therapy, and sports medicine. The purpose, goals, and domains in Figure 1.1 are important to all of these professions. A trend, which influences the content of this book, is the growing ability of these professions to share concerns and work together. Learning cooperation begins early in undergraduate professional preparation and entails understanding and respecting the integrity and separateness of one another's professions. The specific nature, purpose, and goals of various professions are continuously changing, but most professions support self-actualization as a desirable long-range outcome.

Self-Actualization: Purpose and Outcome

Figure 1.1 indicates that self-actualization is the purpose, and therefore the desired outcome, of helping individuals with psychomotor problems. The term **self-actualization,** as used in this text, is defined as making actual, or realizing, all of one's psychomotor potentialities. This term comes from the self-actualization theory of Abraham Maslow (1908–1970), which strongly influences all of the helping professions (see Figure 1.2). Self-actualization, explained in more detail in Chapter 5, means different things to different professions. However, there is agreement on the following:

1. Self-actualization is a lifelong process that begins with dependence and other-directedness in infancy and progresses to independence and inner-directedness.

2. Self-actualization increases as time-competence improves. Time-competence is the ability to use time wisely, to link time usage to goals, and to tie past, present, and future together in meaningful continuity.

FIGURE 1.2 "What an individual *can* be, he *must* be. He must be true to his own nature. This need we may call self-actualization."—Abraham Maslow (1970, p. 46)

3. Self-actualization increases as self-concept, self-esteem, and body image improve.

4. Self-actualization is closely associated with **empowerment,** the process by which individuals gain control over their lives, a sense of having power equitable with that of others, and a feeling of responsibility for self, others, and environment. Empowerment occurs through the efforts of both self and others. Professionals help individuals to empower themselves.

With regard to empowering an active, healthy lifestyle, the following self-actualization indicators are helpful in assessment and programming:

1. Feels good about self and has confidence in movement abilities.
2. Demonstrates positive attitudes toward physical activity.
3. Possesses knowledge, skills, and fitness for goal achievement.
4. Has friends with whom to share exercise and physical activity.
5. Finds or creates time for exercise and physical activity.
6. Has the creativity to solve problems and reach goals.

Individuals with psychomotor problems that interfere seriously with goal achievement and self-actualization need particular help with self-concept, self-esteem, and body image.

Self-concept refers to all the opinions, feelings, and beliefs that a person holds about self. The self contains many dimensions (e.g., scholastic, behavioral, physical appearance, athletic, social, global), and persons typically feel better about some dimensions than about others. **Self-esteem,** one aspect of self-concept, is global good feelings about oneself. **Body image** refers to opinions, feelings, and beliefs about the total body and specific parts. This book emphasizes self-concept, self-esteem, and body image. See Chapter 8 for more details.

The Role of Physical Education

Of all the helping professions, physical education is the only one recognized by federal law as a direct service area for individuals with psychomotor problems (called disabilities in the law). Federal law defines **physical education** as follows:

(i) The term means the development of:
  (A) Physical and motor fitness;
  (B) Fundamental motor skills and patterns; and
  (C) Skills in aquatics, dance, and individual and group games and sports (including intramural and lifetime sports).
(ii) The term includes special physical education, adapted physical education, movement education, and motor development. (20 U.S.C. 1401 [16]) (*Federal Register,* August 23, 1977, p. 42480)

Figure 1.1 uses the components of this definition as goals, but adds other goals important to an active, healthy lifestyle and self-actualization. Federal law requires that individuals, ages 0–21 years, who meet *special education criteria* indicating that they are disabled in physical education, receive *individualized instruction adapted to their special needs.* This adapted instruction must be delivered in the mainstream (regular physical education setting) unless proof is provided that the student cannot benefit from mainstream instruction.

Physical education thus includes adapted physical education. This has not always been true (see the section on history later in this chapter). Today adapted physical education can occur in either a mainstream or a nonmainstream setting. The meaning of adapted physical education has changed drastically since the 1950s, when it was associated with instruction in a separate class placement. Today, adapted physical education is much broader than instruction. It involves many services, such as assessment, goal setting to promote inclusion, and advocacy for the rights of people who are different from the majority.

This text emphasizes that physical education services must extend beyond students covered by law (designated as special education) to anyone with a psychomotor problem that seriously interferes with goal achievement and self-actualization. Many such individuals need adaptation and individualization as much as or more than special education students do. Moreover, such services may be needed throughout the lifespan.

Central Themes in This Text

The title of this text emphasizes five interrelated themes of great importance. Following are basic definitions that are expanded upon throughout the text.

Adapted physical activity is the umbrella term for services that promote an active, healthy lifestyle by remediating psychomotor problems that interfere with goal achievement and self-actualization. Adapted physical activity services are delivered in both mainstream and nonmainstream settings by **generalists** (physical educators, recreators, coaches, classroom teachers) and **specialists** (adapted physical educators, therapeutic recreation specialists, special educators, occupational therapists, physical therapists). In the United States, adapted physical activity has been associated mainly with physical education instruction. This concept is broadening, however, as employment practices change.

Recreation is included in the title of this textbook for many reasons. Most importantly, recreation emphasizes a mental process (a continuous creation or *re*-creation of beliefs, attitudes, and intentions) that assures fun, enjoyment, and meaningfulness. Recreation generally is associated with use of leisure time and reminds us that one purpose of adapting physical activity is to help individuals develop the attitudes, appreciations, and habits that contribute to an active, healthy lifestyle and rich, satisfying leisure. The profession of recreation and leisure studies does not use the term *adapted recreation;* neither does this text.

Sport is included in the title in recognition of the right of all persons to engage in competition. While sport can be developmental, recreational, or competitive, the term increasingly refers to competition in both disability and able-body (AB) sport. Athletes and coaches in the disability sport movements (e.g., Paralympics, Special Olympics, Deaf Sport) have contributed significantly to adaptation theory and practice. Sport is woven into this book throughout and has particularly strong coverage in Chapter 2 and in the chapters on individual differences in Part 3. Athletes with disabilities and sports personnel associated with them do not use the term *adapted sport;* neither does this text.

Crossdisciplinary refers to the integration of knowledge from many academic disciplines in the creation of a distinct, unique body of knowledge that focuses on the identification and remediation of psychomotor problems. Adapted physical activity is also **multidisciplinary** (individuals from many professions participate in service delivery) and **interdisciplinary** (individuals from many different professions interact in service delivery and share knowledge and skills). The term used in federal law is *multidisciplinary,* but this text extends beyond federal law to focus on knowledge needed by all professionals who cooperate in service delivery.

Lifespan in the title reflects the need to adapt physical activity for persons of all ages. Whereas *adapted physical education,* when associated with the requirements of federal law, can be made available to students from birth to age 21 years, *adapted physical activity* extends beyond the law to address psychomotor problems of all age groups.

Adaptation

Adaptation is the process that professionals use to achieve goals and assure outcomes through various kinds of service delivery (teaching, coaching, sports medicine, rehabilitation, fitness and leisure counseling, recreation programming). **Adaptation** means modification, adjustment, or accommodation in accordance with formal and informal assessment data about both an individual and the environment. Adaptation is similar to, but broader than, the concept of individualization. Adaptation is a complex process that requires considerable knowledge about the ways individuals and the environment change each other. This knowledge is crossdisciplinary (integrated from many academic fields), which is the reason why the title of this book includes the term *crossdisciplinary.*

A large body of knowledge that has evolved and is continuing to grow is called **adaptation theory** (Kiphard, 1983; Sherrill & DePauw, 1997). Use of this theory guides service delivery practices directed toward providing optimal physical activity experiences for all individuals, regardless of the extent of their diversity.

Illustrative Adaptations

Some individuals learn best in one-to-one or small-group situations. Adaptations in class size or in organization of space into stations is helpful. Using partners or peer teachers is another adaptation. When students in the mainstream have movement or learning problems that limit their functional abilities, it is necessary to adapt goals, objectives, pedagogy, and grading practices.

Individualizing warm-up exercises, expectations, and equipment is adaptation. Each student, for instance, should be taught to aspire to a different number of bent-knee sit-ups, depending upon his or her abdominal strength. Individuals with low strength execute their sit-ups with hands on their thighs, while the more athletically inclined undertake the traditional sit-up, with hands clasped behind the neck. In learning racket games, awkward students use shorter rackets, while the better coordinated begin with rackets of standard length.

The official rules of such games as volleyball and softball are adapted, and learning—not recreation or competition—is the main goal. For example, in classes based upon the principle of success, pupils are not all required to stand behind the baseline when they serve a volleyball. Each stands at a point on the court where she or he is most likely to get the ball over. Well-coordinated students accept the official rule of hitting the ball one time, while the less athletic may volley it multiple times. In softball, an inning may be played by time rather than by three outs. The pressures inherent in striking out are thereby deemphasized so that equal turns at bat and optimal skill development are possible.

The well-skilled athlete can learn and practice official rules in after-school athletic programs or in league play. The instructional period in a model physical education program is a time when games and exercises are modified in accordance with individual differences. All students are accepted for what they are—awkward, uncoordinated, obese, skinny, or gifted. Students must have no doubt about what is more important to the teacher—the game or the individual. When teaching is based upon the concept of individual differences, students seldom fail.

FIGURE 1.3 The ecosystem of an individual, showing the influence of persons in the family, community, neighborhood, and school or work site.

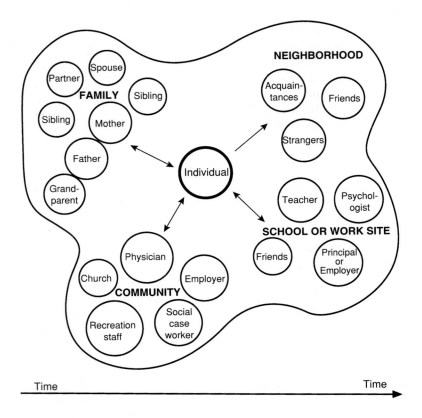

Ecosystem Considerations

Central to understanding adaptations is the concept of an ecosystem (see Figure 1.3). An **ecosystem** is an individual in continuous interaction with his or her environment. This process includes everyone who influences an individual throughout the lifespan as well as the barriers and affordances (bad and good things, respectively) in the physical environment. It is not enough to assess and change an individual. The entire ecosystem must be addressed. The adapted physical activity knowledge base pertains to changing individuals without psychomotor problems (i.e., changing their beliefs, attitudes, intentions, practices) as well as individuals with psychomotor problems.

Individual differences in this text always refers to the individual as part of an ecosystem. The concept of ecosystems has its roots in human ecology theory, dynamical systems theory, and various other interactionist theories (Boss, Doherty, LaRossa, Schumm, & Steinmetz, 1993; Davis, 1983; Davis & Burton, 1991; Davis & Rizzo, 1991; Vermeer & Davis, 1995).

Changing or adapting ecosystems is guided by a process called **ecological task analysis** (ETA). This process requires brainstorming about all of the variables in the ecosystem that affect success in learning a particular task. Analyzing a task in this way enhances the discovery of adaptations that will maximize the possibility of success. *Ecosystem* and *environment* are sometimes used as synonyms, but this is an error. An ecosystem encompasses both the individual and the envi-

ronment in continuous interaction. Chapter 3 focuses on ecological task analysis as a part of adaptation theory.

What Is Adapted Physical Activity?

Adapted physical activity has many meanings, but its central focus is on individual or ecosystem differences that cause psychomotor problems anytime during the lifespan. Some of the definitions of adapted physical activity follow:

Service delivery to remediate psychomotor problems

An academic specialization, discipline, or subdiscipline

A crossdisciplinary body of knowledge

A profession in which specialists have specific competencies

A philosophy or set of beliefs that guides practices

An attitude of acceptance that predisposes inclusive behaviors

A dynamical system of interwoven theories and practices

An advocacy network for disability sports and other rights

A process and a product (i.e., programs in which adaptation occurs)

Because this is a textbook for professionals learning to deliver adapted physical activity services in mainstream and nonmainstream settings, the following discussion focuses on adapted physical activity as service delivery, with three components: believing, doing, and knowing.

The Believing Component

The believing component of adapted physical activity is an attitude, a way of teaching in both integrated and special class environments, that is reflected in the beliefs and practices of professionals who adjust learning experiences to meet individual needs and assure optimal success. An **attitude** is an enduring set of beliefs charged with emotion that predisposes a person to certain kinds of behaviors. Attitudes typically involve feelings about people, especially people who are different, and how they should be treated and/or educated. The adapted physical activity attitude embraces individual differences and enjoys the challenge of helping persons achieve self-actualization through exercise and sport. Like birthdays and other good things, individual differences are celebrated!

The Doing Component

The doing component of adapted physical activity is more than instruction. It is a *comprehensive service delivery system* designed to ameliorate problems within the psychomotor domain (see Figure 1.4). A **service delivery system** is a classroom, school, agency, or community model used to individualize the provision of services to people with different needs. The term evolved out of federal legislation in the 1970s and is widely used in special education and the helping professions. A service delivery system is a way of matching individuals to services, rather than associating one set of services with regular physical education and another set of services with adapted physical education.

The services delivered depend on the philosophy of the school system, residential facility, or agency that employs the professional. Typically, however, these services are

P Planning Services
A Assessment of Individuals/Ecosystems
P Prescription/Placement: The IEP
T Teaching/Counseling/Coaching
E Evaluation of Services
C Coordination of Resources and Consulting
A Advocacy

An acronym to help remember these services is *PAP-TE-CA.* These services, with the exception of the last two, are the same as those comprising the widely used Achievement-Based Curriculum (ABC) model, on which I CAN is based (Wessel, 1977; Wessel & Kelly, 1986). The ABC and I CAN models were developed to guide personnel preparation and service delivery that would result in quality physical education for all students.

The PAP-TE-CA model emphasizes that advocacy, the coordination of resources, and consulting are umbrella services that must be added to the ABC or I CAN models to assure differently abled persons fair opportunity for self-actualization through physical activity (see Figure 1.4). The adapted physical activity PAP-TE-CA model also stresses the importance of counseling skills in teaching and coaching persons with psychomotor problems. Coaching has been added to extend the model's applicability to sport and recreation programs.

FIGURE 1.4 Services included in the adapted physical activity delivery system: the PAP-TE-CA Model.

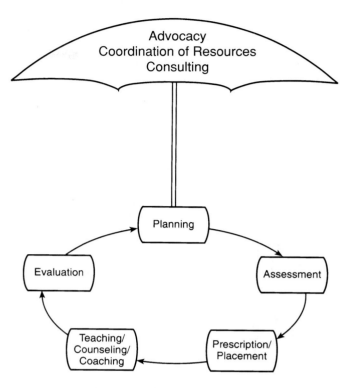

The Knowing Component and Core Areas of Knowledge

The knowing component of adapted physical activity focuses on problems within the psychomotor domain in individuals who perform below age-level expectations and/or need help in overcoming aspirational, attitudinal, or environmental barriers. Central to gaining this knowledge is emphasis on problem-solving skills (Hogan, 1990).

The core areas of knowledge in adapted physical activity that enable professionals to deliver services and to understand individual differences are these:

1. Individual differences in human growth, development, and function, including ecosystem influences and the neurological bases of motor function.
2. Attitude, interpersonal relations, consulting, and communication theory.
3. Law, human rights, and advocacy theory.
4. Scientific foundations of adaptation, including biomechanics, exercise physiology, and motor control theory.
5. Psychosocial foundations of adaptation, including self-actualization, self-concept, motivation, social competence, and behavior management theory. This area also includes theories and approaches to normalization, integration, inclusion, and least restrictive environment.
6. Service delivery theory, including the traditional bodies of knowledge taught in assessment, curriculum, instruction, and evaluation courses.

7. Counseling theory, weaving together sport psychology, rehabilitation counseling, and movement therapy.

8. Adaptation, creativity, and individualization theory, based on a thorough understanding of movement, fitness, sports, games, dance, and aquatics. Illustrative of evolving theory in this area is work on ecological task analysis (Davis & Burton, 1991) and perceptual-motor learning (Burton & Davis, 1992). This area also encompasses the disability sport movement, including sport classifications and the design and adaptation of equipment.

9. Philosophy, history, and problem solving in relation to every core area, with emphasis on the great thinkers and researchers as models for helping to clarify and shape personal philosophy and understand current issues and emerging trends.

This textbook is designed to develop beginning-level knowledge and skills in each of these areas. Much research is needed to develop theories, principles, and models in each area. A trend of the 1990s is a new emphasis on **theorizing,** the process of identifying related facts, concepts, and statements and synthesizing them into conceptual frameworks or theories that help individuals to become better teachers and service providers (Reid, 1989).

How Does *Adapted* Differ From *Adaptive?*

Some persons confuse the terms *adapted* and *adaptive*. These words should not be used interchangeably. **Adapted** can be a verb denoting the process of modifying (e.g., they *adapted* the activity, equipment, or facilities) or an adjective referring to a program or service delivery outcome (e.g., *adapted* games were used; the program was *adapted*). In contrast, **adaptive** is an adjective that describes behaviors, skills, or functions and appears in the official definition of mental retardation.

Adapted physical activity is the name of the profession, academic discipline, and system delivery system that this book describes. Major organizations that professionals join are the **International Federation of Adapted Physical Activity** (IFAPA) and the **Adapted Physical Activity Council** of the American Alliance for Health, Physical Education, Recreation and Dance (AAHPERD). The major research journal that professionals use is the *Adapted Physical Activity Quarterly* (APAQ).

The term *adapted* was first recommended in 1952 by AAHPERD, then called the American Association for Health, Physical Education, and Recreation (AAHPER). This recommendation marked a major policy change in that *corrective* and *modified* were the predominant terms for individualized assessment and programming at that time. The decision to change terminology to *adapted* was strongly influenced by the widespread acceptance of the work of Jean Piaget (1896–1980), of Switzerland, who was considered the world's greatest child psychologist. Piaget based his developmental theory on the concept that *adaptation* is the fundamental process of change that enables individuals to interact effectively with the environment (Piaget, 1962).

In contrast, the term *adaptive* originated with pioneer social competency research in the 1930s (McGrew, Bruininks, & Thurlow, 1992). Since 1959, official definitions of mental retardation have emphasized adaptive behavior levels. The term **deficits in adaptive behavior** is defined as "significant limitations in an individual's effectiveness in meeting the standards of maturation, learning, personal independence, and/or social responsibility that are expected for his or her age level and cultural group" (Grossman, 1983, p. 11). The most recent definition of mental retardation lists 10 **adaptive skill areas:** communications, community use, functional academics, home living, health and safety, leisure, self-care, social skills, self-direction, and work (American Association on Mental Retardation, 1992).

In summary, education and service delivery are *adapted,* but behaviors are *adaptive.* Other areas besides mental retardation sometimes use the concept of adaptive behaviors because the concept offers a good framework to guide assessment and programming. Adapted physical activity aims to dually remediate deficits in adaptive behavior and enhance strengths in adaptive behavior.

Good Service Delivery Is Adapting

Adapting is a desirable practice in all settings: mainstream and nonmainstream, school and nonschool. It is important for both **generalists** (regular physical educators, community recreators) and **specialists** (adapted physical educators, special educators, therapeutic recreators) to become skillful in adaptation. This is why undergraduates in almost all generalist professional preparation programs take courses in adapted physical activity and engage in practicum experiences that expose them to a wide variety of individual differences (Connolly, 1994).

Today all professionals in the mainstream are expected to address the needs of individuals who formerly were labeled disabled, handicapped, or health-impaired and placed in separate settings. Likewise, professionals are expected to cope with diversity associated with different cultures, value systems, languages, ethnic groups, and socioeconomic levels (see Figure 1.5).

Often the range of individual differences in mainstream settings is too large for one professional to manage. Schools, agencies, businesses, and industries are therefore increasingly employing specialists to dual- and team-teach and to serve as consultants. Adapted physical activity (APA) specialists are typically individuals with master's or doctoral degrees in adapted physical activity (or education) with particular expertise in psychomotor problem solving.

Generalists must know when to request the help of an adapted physical activity specialist. One purpose of this text is to familiarize generalists and specialists with ways they can help each other. Some programs lag behind others; when specialists are needed, generalists need to convince administrators to employ them. The future will bring new employment trends, just as the past (legislation and changing attitudes) has brought new understandings of integration, inclusion, and least restrictive environments.

Good Teaching Is Adapting

Good teaching involves adapting goals, content, and pedagogy to individual needs so as to minimize failure and preserve ego strength. In a sense, *all good physical education is adapted physical education.* The larger the class size and the more varied the abilities of the students, the more adaptation is needed. However, having special education students in class does not necessarily mean additional adaptation demands.

Many students with disabilities participate successfully in regular physical education. An individual in leg braces may be able, without adaptations, to engage in swimming, gymnastics, or archery. A pupil with an arm amputation may be a star soccer player or excel in baseball, basketball, or football. Disability therefore should not automatically be equated with adapted physical education services. Any student who routinely performs below average should be provided these services.

Good teaching requires that generalists and specialists work together. Although all physical educators are expected to practice adaptation, at least one adapted physical education specialist is needed in every school district or city to supplement and complement the efforts of generalists, to serve as consultants and administrators, and to provide direct instruction for students with severe psychomotor problems who require more help than full-time mainstream placement can afford. Of particular importance is providing units of instruction in wheelchair or other specialized sports that will enable students to recreate and compete in nonschool activities designed to challenge abilities different from the norm.

Regular physical educators should be well acquainted with adapted physical education specialists in their city and feel comfortable in asking for help. This is so important that federal law includes provision of support services.

Support Services

Support services are supplementary human and nonhuman resources and aids in regular physical education or community settings that serve a wide range of individual differences. **Human support services** are (a) consultants (adapted

physical educators) who visit on a regular basis and sometimes dual- or team-teach and (b) extra classroom personnel with specialized training. Illustrative of these are adult aides, peer or cross-age tutors, athletes and role models with disabilities, coaches of disability sport teams, special educators, and other specialists. **Nonhuman support services** include computer and electronic technology, videocameras and monitors, transportation devices for lugging equipment around, and special equipment like sports wheelchairs, ball-pitching machines, stationary bicycles, and portable swimming pools. Of particular importance is equipment that will enable teaching in small-group stations within a large-group setting.

Physical educators must sometimes negotiate with principals for support services. Such negotiation is called **advocacy,** which means action aimed at promoting, maintaining, or defending a cause. Advocacy is one of the competency areas covered in this text.

The Individualized Education Program (IEP)

The **IEP** is a written document, required by law, to certify that a student meets criteria for inclusion in one of several disability categories for whom federally funded special services are available. Based on multidisciplinary assessment and parent agreement, the IEP specifies the services that a student must receive in each school subject in which she or he is declared disabled. Federal law requires that all services be delivered in the regular education setting unless assessment data indicate that the student cannot benefit from regular classroom involvement or proof is provided that the presence of the student seriously interferes with the learning or welfare of other students.

Under law, many students with disabilities do not qualify for adapted physical education services in either mainstream or nonmainstream settings. The following are some of the reasons:

1. Some students with disabilities have average or above-average skills and do not need adapted services.
2. Services are linked to the availability of money, which fluctuates with good and bad economic times and influences the number of students targeted for help.
3. Services are influenced by attitudes of decision makers concerning the importance of various kinds of physical education, and many people in power assign low priority to physical education.

This text emphasizes that adapted physical education service delivery should extend beyond law to encompass all students who need help, not just those with an IEP that specifies services. More information about the IEP process is provided in Chapters 4 and 6. Regular physical educators have many students with disabilities in their classes and need to acquire competencies for helping them achieve goals. Following is basic information about disability.

Disability: Definition and Guidelines

Disability is a controversial term with many meanings. This text uses the World Health Organization (1980) definition: the loss or reduction of functional ability and/or activity. Synonyms for disability abound. In the United States, prior to 1990 legislation, disabilities were called handicaps.

The Individuals with Disabilities Education Act (IDEA) of 1990 prescribed *disability* as the most appropriate term for use in special education assessment and placement practices. *The law uses the term* disability *as a diagnostic category that qualifies students for special services.* Table 1.1 presents a list of these diagnostic categories. (See Appendix A for definitions of these categories.) Unfortunately, the use of categories contributes to the misconception that whole persons are disabled and therefore must be treated differently than others. Following are some guidelines to combat misconceptions.

Think of Specific Problems, Not Disabilities

Today we recognize the importance of identifying specific problems that interfere with achievement of physical education goals. The term *individual differences* is not meant as a synonym for *disability*. *Individual differences* refers to specific problems that a person with or without a disability may have. Individual differences may also be strengths. Good teaching creates a balance between the attention given to weaknesses (constraints) and strengths (affordances). This is a form of adaptation that contributes to good self-concept.

Use Person-First Terminology

Good service delivery emphasizes person-first attitudes and terminology. This means that we say **individuals with disabilities** rather than "disabled persons." This practice recognizes that a disability is only part of a person's constellation of strengths and weaknesses. Good teaching also avoids language that equates individuals with their condition (e.g., *the re-*

Table 1.1 **Diagnostic categories recognized by federal law.**

1. Autism
2. Deaf-blindness
3. Deafness
4. Hearing impairment
5. Mental retardation
6. Multiple disabilities
7. Orthopedic impairment
8. Other health impairment
9. Serious emotional disturbance
10. Specific learning disability
11. Speech or language impairment
12. Traumatic brain injury
13. Visual impairment including blindness

tarded, the disabled). The *Publication Manual of the American Psychological Association* (1994) recommends that these guidelines be followed in both speaking and writing.

Be Sensitive to Disability Language

Good service delivery is sensitive to the language of people with disabilities. The worldwide Paralympic sports movement (comparable to the Olympics for athletes without disabilities) supports the use of such terms as *disability sport, wheelchair sport,* and *blind sport*. Referring to disability sport as "disabled sport" or "adapted sport" is not acceptable. Likewise, *disability community* is more acceptable than *disabled community*. Special Olympics involves sport only for individuals with mental retardation, whereas Paralympics encompasses sport for many groups.

Avoid Thinking of Characteristics

Good service delivery avoids associating lists of characteristics with particular disabilities. Every human being, with and without disabilities, is appreciated as different, even though some persons might be assigned to the same diagnostic category for special education funding purposes. **Assessment** is the process by which specific strengths and weaknesses are identified and analyzed. Skills in this area are so important that an entire chapter in this book focuses on assessment (see Chapter 6). Moreover, Chapters 8 through 17 all include sections on assessment. This book avoids reference to characteristics because assessment cannot be nonbiased when professionals associate lists of characteristics with specific conditions.

Philosophy and Ethics: Basic Beliefs

A **philosophy** is a system of values and beliefs that guides behaviors. Derived from the Greek word *philosophia,* the literal meaning of *philosophy* is "love of truth" and "the search for what is right." Philosophy in adapted physical activity evolves from ethics and moral reasoning, personal conscience, and concern for law and human welfare. Ethics represent the moral dimension of a profession (Singer, 1993). Specifically, **ethics** refers to critical thinking about what is good or right and the derivation of moral principles to guide action. Ethics are especially important in a democratic society where everyone votes

FIGURE 1.6 A normal curve is a mathematical model that shows where 100 or more students will score if given a standardized test. Along the baseline are standard deviation marks that divide the curve into 3%, 13%, and 68% areas.

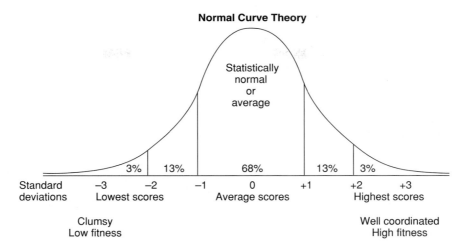

and makes decisions about how resources are used and minority groups (persons who are disabled, ill, aged, poor, migrant, ethnic, etc.) are treated.

Of particular importance in adapted physical activity is philosophy about individual differences. An important part of the adapted physical activity profession is advocacy to help the public make ethical decisions about treatment of people who are different from the norm. Remember that individual differences philosophy refers to the individual as part of an ecosystem. Changing individuals means changing entire ecosystems. This requires hard decisions about how to utilize resources.

Individual differences relate to the **normal curve distribution** in that **different** is defined in terms of distance from a statistical average (mean). Normal curve theory indicates that 68% of the population can be conceptualized as average or normal on a specific ability or skill (see Figure 1.6). The law of normal distribution predetermines that the other 32% will be divided evenly between the two extremes of below average (clumsy or low fitness) and above average (extraordinarily coordinated or high fitness).

Governments make political and economic decisions about what percentage of individuals in the lowest 16% have access to special services that cost extra money. Adapted physical activity professionals advocate for special help for any student whose test scores repeatedly fall below the mean (50th percentile) or whose performance looks clumsy to an expert observer.

Individual differences philosophy is closely associated with the zero-reject and zero-fail principles. The **zero-reject principle** emphasizes the right of all individuals, regardless of severity of problems, to high-quality physical education instruction and recreation programming. The **zero-fail principle** captures the idea of success-oriented programming, with adaptations so all individuals can fulfill their psychomotor potentials.

Consider the following beliefs that are associated with individual differences philosophy. Can you add to this list? How can these beliefs be used to guide service delivery?

1. All individuals at all ages *can benefit* from physical activity in many goal areas in all three domains.
2. All individuals at all ages *can learn* when adaptations are incorporated into instruction.
3. All individuals at all ages *deserve access to high-quality physical education instruction* that will enhance their self-esteem, contribute to good health, and carry over into their use of leisure time.
4. All individuals at all ages *deserve access to recreational and competitive sports, dance, and aquatics activities* in both mainstream and nonmainstream settings in which they can succeed.

Past, Present, and Future

A characteristic of a scholarly discipline is a "substantial history and a publicly recognized tradition exemplified by time-tested works" (Nixon, 1967, p. 47). Adapted physical activity meets this criterion. Its beginnings in the Western hemisphere can be traced to the early 1800s. An understanding of history helps us to think critically about the present and the future, to expect pendulum swings, and to appreciate the agents and processes of change. The following sections provide background information central to critical thinking about issues and concerns described throughout this text.

Crossdisciplinary Knowledge Roots

Today's adapted physical activity knowledge base is a cross-disciplinary blend of

1. medical gymnastics, which has evolved into sport and exercise science, fitness training, physical therapy, and sports medicine;
2. special education, which originally stressed sensorimotor and perceptual-motor training but today emphasizes behavior management, cognitive psychology, and IEP-driven service delivery;
3. lifespan human growth and development;

1 Active, Healthy Lifestyles for All **11**

4. social sciences, which provide knowledge about attitude change and inclusion strategies; and

5. sports, dance, and aquatics instruction and leisure studies adapted to individual needs.

Adapted physical activity leaders have integrated knowledge from these areas into university course work and have begun to develop theories (e.g., theories of adaptation, individual differences, and ecological task analysis) to guide research and practice. The history of adapted physical activity is therefore complex. Most prominent are its roots in medicine and special education. The medical emphasis dominated until special education legislation in the 1970s mandated physical education instruction for all children, including those with mental retardation.

Medical Roots

Swedish medical gymnastics, an exercise system created by Per Henrik Ling (1776–1839) of Stockholm, is the forerunner of corrective and remedial physical education in the 1920s to the 1950s and adapted physical education thereafter. Ling is therefore recognized as the father of adapted physical activity. Medical gymnastics was brought from Sweden to the United States by Nils Posse around 1885, introduced into the Boston public schools, and systematically integrated into the teacher-training programs of Amy Morris Homans (1848–1933). Homans, perhaps best known as having been the chair of the Physical Education Department at Wellesley College, is recognized annually at special events at AAHPERD and other conferences.

Physicians, physical therapists, and physical educators with special interest in exercise, posture, and fitness promoted Swedish and other medical exercise systems from the 1900s through the 1930s. Illustrative of textbooks with a medical emphasis that shaped early adapted physical activity history are *Exercise in Education and Medicine* (1909, 1915, 1923) by R. Tait McKenzie, professor at McGill University in Canada until 1904 and at the University of Pennsylvania thereafter, and *Corrective Physical Education* (1934, followed by seven later editions) by Josephine Rathbone, who was a professor at Teachers College, Columbia University, in New York City. McKenzie was a physician, whereas Rathbone was a dual PE/PT specialist, a combination popular in the 1920s to the 1950s. Both Canada and the USA give annual R. Tait McKenzie Awards at their national conventions in recognition of McKenzie's leadership.

Special Education Roots

Special education has multiple roots, one for each type of disability. However, contributions to adapted physical activity have been particularly strong in the areas of deafness, blindness, and mental retardation. Persons with these disabilities were first served in residential facilities, and pedagogy evolved to meet their special needs out of the sensorimotor training emphasis of the early 1800s.

Jean-Marc Itard (1775–1839), a French physician, is often recognized as the father of special education and the founder of sensorimotor theory. Itard is known for his attempt to educate Victor, a 12-year-old boy found naked, wild, and nonverbal in 1800. Although Victor, the "Wild Boy of Aveyron," remained functionally retarded, Itard and his followers believed that Itard's innovative sensorimotor training caused some improvement. Itard's system was brought to the United States around 1860 by his protégé, Edouard Seguin, who helped found the American Association on Mental Deficiency (AAMD), the oldest organization in the United States pertaining to special education. Today this organization, now called the American Association on Mental Retardation (AAMR), publishes excellent journals and offers many services.

The Council for Exceptional Children (CEC), which today is the major special education association, was founded in New York in 1922. By then, many individuals formerly educated in residential schools were attending classes in special education public schools in their home communities. However, special education did not evolve as a strong profession until federal legislation of the 1960s and 1970s. Many adapted physical education specialists maintain dual membership in CEC and the Adapted Physical Activity Council of AAHPERD.

Stages of Adapted Physical Activity History

Adapted physical activity has survived many name changes and philosophical differences. In the United States, this service delivery system seems to have evolved through five stages.

Stage 1, Medical Gymnastics: Before 1900

Prior to the 1900s, all physical education was medically oriented and preventive, developmental, or corrective in nature. The physical education curriculum was comprised primarily of what we know today as gymnastics, calisthenics, body mechanics, and marching or military-like exercise drills. University physical educators were generally *physicians* who applied known principles of medicine to the various systems of exercise. The purpose of physical training (or physical culture, as the profession was called then) was to prevent illness and/or to promote the health and vigor of the mind and body.

Stage 2, Transition to Sports: 1900–1930

The gradual transition from medically oriented physical training to sports-centered physical education occurred in the early 1900s. Factors influencing this change were (a) the introduction of sports into American culture and, subsequently, the physical education curriculum; (b) the application of psychological and sociological theory to education, resulting in the conceptualization of the *whole child;* (c) the trend away from medical training as appropriate teacher preparation for physical educators; and (d) the advent of compulsory physical education in the public schools.

State legislation making physical education mandatory in the public schools increased the number of students to be taught and brought new problems. What, for instance, would be done if a student were ill or disabled, or lacked the physical stamina to participate in the regular curriculum? The solution was to divide physical education into two branches: (a) *regular* and (b) *corrective* or *remedial*.

Stage 3, Corrective Physical Education: 1930–1950

Between the 1930s and the 1950s, both regular and corrective physical education served mostly what are known today as normal students. Assignment to physical education was based on a thorough medical examination by a physician, who determined whether a student should participate in the regular or the corrective program. Corrective classes were comprised primarily of limited, restricted, or modified activities related to health, posture, or fitness problems. In many schools, students were excused from physical education. In others, the physical educator typically taught several sections of regular physical education and one section of corrective physical education each day. Leaders in corrective physical education continued to have strong backgrounds in medicine. Persons preparing to be physical education teachers generally completed one university course in corrective physical education.

Veterans returning from World War II were instrumental in initiating a name change. They pointed out that amputations and spinal cord injuries could not be corrected. They also emphasized the potential of sports in rehabilitation and started various wheelchair sports.

Stage 4, Adapted Physical Education: 1950–1970

During the 1950s and 1960s, the population served in public school corrective/adapted physical education broadened to include persons with all disabilities. Instrumental in this change was the trend away from residential school placement. This resulted in increased enrollment of students with disabilities, particularly mental retardation, in the public schools. The values that such children and youth could derive from participation in sports, dance, and aquatics adapted to their special needs were increasingly recognized. The following definition evolved in the early 1950s:

> Adapted physical education is a diversified program of developmental activities, games, sports, and rhythms suited to the interests, capacities, and limitations of students with disabilities who may not safely or successfully engage in unrestricted participation in the vigorous activities of the general physical education program. (Committee on Adapted Physical Education, 1952, p. 15)

This definition was viable throughout the next two decades because adapted physical education teaching practices paralleled the special education procedure of segregating students with disabilities in separate classes and/or special schools. During this era, many names were proposed (*special, developmental,* and *remedial*) and used in textbook titles.

Through the efforts of President John F. Kennedy, his sister Eunice Kennedy Shriver, and his brother Senator Edward Kennedy, physical educators became increasingly aware of mental retardation. Special Olympics was created in 1968. The human rights movement of the 1960s led to federal legislation that addressed inequities in public school education and prohibited segregation.

Stage 5, Adapted Physical Activity: 1970–Present

Since 1970, countries throughout the world have passed legislation to guarantee rights to persons with disabilities. The United Nations designated 1981 as International Year of the Disabled. This stage marked the shift from educating persons with disabilities in separate or special settings to an emphasis on least restrictive educational environments and integration. The concepts of service delivery systems and IEPs emerged in conjunction with federal legislation.

Physical educators became seriously interested in individual differences and the development of an adapted physical activity knowledge base. Specialists emerged when colleges and universities began offering graduate degrees in adapted physical activity in the 1970s. Professional organizations were created, and a new profession was born.

Many individuals provided leadership for this new profession. Chief among these were Julian Stein in the United States and Patricia Austin in Canada. As director of the AAHPERD Office on Programs for the Handicapped/Disabled from 1966 to 1981, Stein influenced teacher education through numerous publications, active involvement in legislation, and extensive consultation and demonstration teaching. At the University of Alberta in Edmonton, Canada, Austin pioneered in establishing exemplary teacher education and service delivery programs. Information about other important leaders and developments appears in such sources as Sherrill (1988), Sherrill and DePauw (1997), and the 1986 history issue of *Adapted Physical Activity Quarterly* (Volume 3(2), April). Appendix F of this text provides a detailed chronology of events important in the history of adapted physical activity. Photographs of important leaders representing different periods in history appear in Figure 1.7.

Models That Guide Professional Preparation

Analysis of the stages of adapted physical activity history reveals that the emphasis in professional preparation has gradually changed over the years. First, the **medical or categorical model** dominated, with major attention given to symptoms and characteristics that would facilitate diagnosis, prescription, and correction of conditions. Second, the **educational model** was initiated in the 1970s to ensure that teachers developed the competencies necessary to implement new laws that stressed assessment and individualized education programs (IEPs). The educational model was also called the **competency or generic model** because the recommended competencies matched generic (general) job functions required to deliver services to all students and did not relate to specific categories of conditions. Third, the **individual differences or social minority model** evolved as approaches became life-span- and community-based, and leaders sought to achieve equal rights and opportunities for various social minorities.

Combinations of all three models are used in professional preparation today, but the trend is toward expansion of the individual differences or social minority model, which has its roots primarily in the social sciences of psychology, sociology, and ecology. This model posits that people who are different from the norm compose social minorities that share common problems of social acceptance, inclusion, and access to certain rights. Thus, the knowledge base that has been developed about gender, ethnic group, and poverty marginality applies to individuals with disabilities. This knowledge base is called **individual differences theory.**

Professional Organizations

The first adapted physical activity organization in the United States was created in 1905 as a special interest group within the Association for the Advancement of Physical Education,

FIGURE 1.7   Outstanding leaders in adapted physical activity history.

R. Tait McKenzie
Stage 2

Josephine Rathbone
Stage 3

Julian Stein
Stages 4–5

Patricia Austin
Stages 4–5

Janet Seaman
Stage 5

the forerunner of AAHPERD. The first chair was Rose Posse, wife of Nils Posse (then deceased, who had brought medical gymnastics to the United States around 1885). Later this structure became the Therapeutics Section of AAHPERD. This group merged with the Adapted Physical Education Academy of AAHPERD in 1985 to become the Adapted Physical Activity Council (APAC).

APAC

Today APAC is a part of the American Association for Active Lifestyles and Fitness (AAALF) of AAHPERD. Dr. Janet Seaman, a well-known leader in adapted physical education (Seaman & DePauw, 1989; Seaman, 1995) is executive director of AAALF. Professionals should affiliate with both APAC and AAALF when they join AAHPERD.

NCPERID

The National Consortium for Physical Education and Recreation for Individuals with Disabilities (NCPERID) was founded in 1973 in Minneapolis. This organization serves primarily as an advocacy body for supportive federal legislation and for quality control in professional preparation.

Adapted Physical Education National Standards, which specifies standards to guide teacher training, was published by NCPERID (1995).

IFAPA and NAFAPA

In 1973, the International Federation of Adapted Activity (IFAPA) was founded in Quebec, Canada. IFAPA now has regional affiliated organizations in all parts of the world. The first of these was founded in Europe. The official journal of IFAPA is the *Adapted Physical Activity Quarterly* (APAQ), which began publication in 1984. The organization of the North American Federation of Adapted Physical Activity (NAFAPA) was finalized in 1994 after several years of effort. Dale Ulrich, of Indiana University, was elected its first president.

Adapted physical activity thus can trace its organizational history in the United States back to 1905. It existed before many other professional organizations were founded, namely, those for recreation (1906), occupational therapy (1917), physical therapy (1921), and special education (1922). The future of adapted physical activity depends on society's commitment to a philosophy of healthy, active lifestyles for all and to the zero-reject and zero-fail principles. Organizations strive to help the public understand the role and scope of a profession and the importance of the services it delivers. Concurrently, organizations help their members become the best they can be by offering services like conferences, workshops, and presentations. Addresses of professional organizations appear in Appendix D.

Standards, Job Functions, and Competencies

An important role of professional organizations is to specify standards of knowledge and skill that qualify individuals to be employed as professionals. Generally these standards are enforced by national or state certification and accreditation policies, but new professions like adapted physical activity require many years to establish methods of quality control. Standards provide specific criteria for judging competencies to perform job functions or tasks. The remainder of this chapter aims to acquaint readers with standards, job functions, and competencies so that regular and adapted physical activity personnel can know what to expect of one another.

With current integration and inclusion trends, the range of individual differences in most physical activity settings is too large for one professional to manage. Generalists must possess some adapted physical activity competencies because adaptation is the key to good teaching and good service delivery, but generalists must also know when to take the initiative in requesting support services. The following sections will increase awareness of the roles and responsibilities of generalists and specialists and of standards and competencies that must be met.

Standards

The National Consortium for Physical Education and Recreation for Individuals with Disabilities (NCPERID, 1995) published 187 pages of standards to guide competency development in 15 areas related to school-based service delivery for individuals from birth to age 21. These areas are

1. Human development
2. Motor behavior
3. Exercise science
4. Measurement and evaluation
5. History and philosophy
6. Unique attributes of learners
7. Curriculum theory and development
8. Assessment
9. Instructional design/planning
10. Teaching
11. Consultation
12. Program evaluation
13. Continuing education
14. Ethics
15. Communication

As you study this textbook, be aware of mastering content related to each of these areas. In Chapter 1, for example, you have read a lot about history and philosophy, unique attributes of learners, ethics, and communication. This textbook, how-

ever, extends beyond the NCPERID school-based standards to lifespan needs and to professional roles beyond teaching.

Job Functions or Roles

Services that professionals perform depend upon the job function or role for which they are employed. Broad categories of job function are (a) direct service delivery, (b) related services delivery, (c) administration, (d) research, and (e) university professor. **Direct service delivery** refers to face-to-face contact with students or clients aimed at assessment and/or achievement of specific performance goals and objectives. Adapted physical activity is classified by law as a direct service. **Related service delivery** refers primarily to various kinds of therapy that are needed in order to benefit from instruction. **Administration,** defined differently at various job sites, usually includes responsibility for assessment, curriculum development, consulting, program evaluation, and supervision of staff. **Research** is the creation of knowledge, usually by testing theory or generating theory. **University professor,** within the adapted physical activity context, usually means involvement in teacher training.

This textbook is concerned primarily with direct service delivery and ways that consultants can help direct service providers. Figure 1.8 presents a structure of knowledge model that shows how core areas of knowledge lead to philosophy, which in turn influences job functions, services to be delivered, and competencies needed. Services are sometimes called "specific job functions." This text aims to develop competencies in seven specific job functions known by the acronym *PAP-TE-CA* (see Figure 1.4).

Adapted Physical Activity Competencies

Competencies are abilities adequate to perform specific job functions or services. The word is derived from the Latin *competere,* meaning "to meet" or "to agree"; this emphasizes that competencies must be linked to specific job functions. Competencies encompass philosophy, attitudes, knowledge, and skills, because these components are all necessary to the performance of specific job functions. Many lists of adapted physical activity competency guidelines have been developed (see Sherrill, 1988, Appendix). Additionally, Jansma and Surburg (1995) have developed competencies to guide doctoral study. However, the PAP-TE-CA model competencies that follow are the first to address all aspects of lifespan service delivery and to include philosophy and attitudes as central to adequate job performance. Use the PAP-TE-CA competencies to evaluate yourself and others and to set personal learning goals.

PAP-TE-CA Model Competencies

A **competency** is a philosophy, attitude, knowledge, or skill that is adequate and suitable to perform a specific job function or task. Study of this textbook will result in the competencies necessary to (a) perform the job functions indigenous to direct service delivery, (b) conduct research to further the knowledge base of adapted physical activity, and (c) serve as a leader and professional educator in in-service and college and university settings.

FIGURE 1.8 A structure of knowledge model for the adapted physical activity specialization and/or courses that focus on direct service delivery.

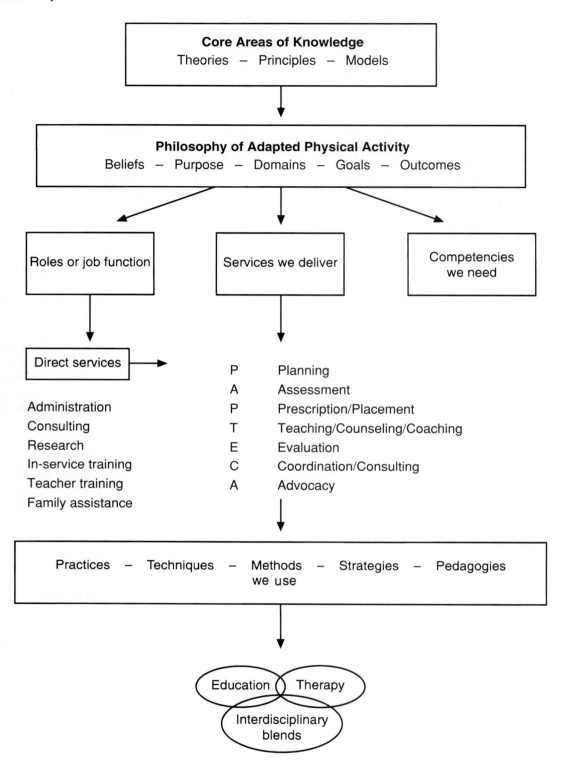

Competencies Related to Advocacy, Ethics, and Philosophy

1.1 Philosophy that supports
    1.11 The right of all persons to (a) high-quality physical education instruction and (b) lifespan sport, fitness, and recreation
    1.12 Assessed individual differences (not characteristics of people with disabilities) as the basis for adapted physical activity
1.2 Attitude of accepting and appreciating individual differences
1.3 Knowledge of
    1.31 Individual differences associated with normal curve theory and with various disabilities: myth and reality
    1.32 State and local physical education requirements and indicators of high-quality instruction
    1.33 Laws that eliminate barriers and protect rights
    1.34 Lifespan sport, fitness, and recreation opportunities in a variety of settings
    1.35 Theories, models, and strategies relevant to acceptance and appreciation of individual differences
1.4 Skill in
    1.41 Increasing comfort and communication among people with limited exposure to individual differences
    1.42 Applying attitude and behavior management theories to promote acceptance and appreciation of individual differences
    1.43 Using advocacy strategies in the 5 L model (Look at me, Leverage, Literature, Legislation, Litigation)
    1.44 Working with the press and media

Competencies Related to Coordination of Resources and Consulting

2.1 Philosophy that supports
    2.11 Resource utilization as a means of learning and personal growth as well as improving service delivery to others
    2.12 Multidisciplinary, interdisciplinary, and crossdisciplinary cooperation
    2.13 Partnerships between persons with and without disabilities in promoting lifespan sport, fitness, and recreation
    2.14 Partnerships between generalists and specialists
    2.15 Partnerships between families, schools, and communities
2.2 Attitude of self-confidence in human relationships
2.3 Knowledge of
    2.31 Many types of resources (e.g., organizations, athletes with disabilities, special educators, related services personnel, parents)
    2.32 Many types of settings for learning about and using resources
    2.33 Models, theories, and practices that impact on resource coordination

2.4 Skill in
    2.41 Locating, contacting, and establishing rapport with resources
    2.42 Bringing resources together (e.g., planning meetings or introducing people to each other)
    2.43 Communicating and public relations
    2.44 Working with administrators and parents

Competencies Related to Planning and Instructional Design

3.1 Philosophy that supports critical thinking about
    3.11 The nature of adapted physical activity (APA); its philosophy, goals, and characteristics; core areas of knowledge; job roles and functions; service delivery; eligibility requirements for APA services
    3.12 The nature of human beings, the values of physical activity, and the rights of individuals and families
    3.13 Desirable student, parent, teacher, and administrator behaviors
    3.14 APA theories, models, principles, and practices
    3.15 Law, the role of government, morality, and personal ethics
3.2 Attitude of responsibility for critical thinking as the basis for
    3.21 Planning APA learning experiences for self and others
    3.22 Decision making in all aspects of direct service delivery
    3.23 Evaluating effectiveness
3.3 Knowledge of planning for (a) individual students; (b) classrooms, schools, and school districts; (c) communities; and (d) organizations and agencies
3.4 Skill in
    3.41 Decision making regarding variables to be assessed, procedures to be followed, and resources to be used
    3.42 Prioritizing and establishing goals
    3.43 Writing behavioral objectives to achieve goals
    3.44 Matching activities to objectives
    3.45 Calculating instructional time for objectives and activities
    3.46 Writing instructional units and lesson plans
    3.47 Addressing transitional education concerns and monitoring systems that maximize active lifestyles
    3.48 Creating behavior management plans

Competencies Related to Assessment

4.1 Philosophy that supports assessment as the key to individualizing and adapting
4.2 Attitude of commitment to assessing both individuals and environments (i.e., ecosystems)
4.3 Knowledge of
    4.31 Instruments and protocols for assessing performance in goal areas

4.32 Scientific and psychosocial foundations that relate to assessment (e.g., biomechanics, exercise physiology, motor learning, human development, sport sociology)

4.4 Skill in

4.41 Using various types of assessment

4.42 Interpreting assessment data

4.43 Decision making based on data collection and interpretation

4.44 Making referrals for further assessment

Competencies Related to Prescription

5.1 Philosophy that supports

5.11 Individualized education programs (IEPs) as vehicles for curricular prescription for people with and without disabilities

5.12 Exercise prescriptions as guides for fitness training

5.13 Lesson plans as means of achieving prescribed objectives

5.2 Attitude of accountability

5.3 Knowledge of

5.31 Parts of an IEP and of procedures in the IEP process

5.32 Parts of an exercise prescription

5.33 Parts of a lesson plan and of environmental variables to be manipulated

5.34 Exercise indications and contraindications for specific conditions

5.35 Models that guide school district decision making

5.36 Support services and placement options

5.4 Skill in

5.41 Making decisions about placements and services

5.42 Writing IEPs, exercise prescriptions, and lesson plans

Competencies Related to Teaching, Counseling, and Coaching

6.1 Philosophy that supports

6.11 Adaptation, creativity, and individualization as theories that guide instruction

6.12 Counseling as an integral part of teaching and coaching

6.13 Self-concept, self-actualization, and empowerment as central constructs

6.14 Humanistic and behavior management teaching practices

6.15 Inclusion, normalization, and least restrictive environment (LRE) strategies

6.16 Transition strategies

6.2 Attitude of celebrating individual differences and lifespan ability to learn and change

6.3 Knowledge of

6.31 Adaptation, creativity, and individualization theories, models, processes, principles, and pedagogy

6.32 Scientific and psychosocial foundations of adaptation (e.g., biomechanics, exercise physiology, motor learning and control, human

development, psychology, sociology, behavior management)

6.33 Assessment, curriculum, instruction, and evaluation practices that contribute to good teaching

6.34 Counseling theory, weaving together sport, psychology, rehabilitation counseling, and movement therapy

6.35 Pedagogy related to different teaching styles

6.36 Pedagogy related to different goals and objectives

6.37 Pedagogy related to different instructional settings and curricular models

6.38 Individual differences in growth, development, and function that impact on teaching, counseling, and coaching

6.4 Skill in

6.41 Adapting instruction for individual differences (age, performance) and for achievement of specific goals

6.42 Using ecological and traditional task and activity analysis

6.43 Motivating students and athletes to personal bests and managing individual and group behaviors

6.44 Socializing persons into active, healthy lifestyles and sport

6.45 Applying knowledge in all aspects of teaching, counseling, and coaching

Competencies Related to Program Evaluation

7.1 Philosophy that supports continuous evaluation as an integral part of service delivery

7.2 Attitude of

7.21 Striving for personal best while accepting that the best can always be improved

7.22 Seeking ways to improve and being open to ideas for change

7.3 Knowledge of

7.31 Instruments and protocols for program evaluation

7.32 Evaluation theories, models, principles, and strategies

7.4 Skill in

7.41 Using evaluation instruments and protocol and, when necessary, developing new ones

7.42 Applying evaluation theories, models, principles, and strategies

Competencies Related to Research

8.1 Philosophy that supports research as the method of choice for improving service delivery and for creating the knowledge base of a profession and discipline

8.2 Attitude of responsibility for

8.21 Reading research to stay abreast of new knowledge

8.22 Conducting research to contribute to the knowledge base

8.23 Ethical behaviors in conducting and applying research

8.3 Knowledge of

8.31 Journals and books that publish research

8.32 Meetings where research is presented

8.33 Research methods and strategies, including statistics

8.34 Computer- and hand-search techniques for locating research

8.35 Topics on which research is needed

8.4 Skill in

8.41 Locating, reading, understanding, and applying research

8.42 Reviewing research related to selected topics

8.43 Conducting and reporting research

Competencies Related to Staff Development and Continuing Education

9.1 Philosophy that supports adapted physical activity training for professionals and parents

9.2 Attitude of helpfulness in assisting adults to achieve personal goals in relation to adapted physical activity competencies

9.3 Knowledge of

9.31 Content in adapted physical activity textbooks and journals

9.32 Roles, service delivery areas, specific job functions, and competencies

9.33 Best practices and models of direct service delivery

9.34 Pedagogy for adult education

9.4 Skill in

9.41 Motivating adults to accept personal responsibility for learning

9.42 Helping adults acquire favorable attitudes about individual differences

9.43 Individualizing content and learning experiences for adults

References

American Association on Mental Retardation. (1992). *Mental retardation: Definition, classification, and systems of supports* (9th ed.). Washington, DC: Author.

American Psychological Association. (1994). *Publication manual of the American Psychological Association* (4th ed.). Washington, DC: Author.

Boss, P. G., Doherty, W. J., LaRossa, R., Schumm, W. R., & Steinmetz, S. K. (Eds.). (1993). *Sourcebook of family theories and methods: A contextual approach.* New York: Plenum.

Burton, A. W., & Davis, W. E. (1992). Issues related to balance in adapted physical education: Assessment and intervention strategies. *Adapted Physical Activity Quarterly, 9*(1), 14–46.

Committee on Adapted Physical Education. (1952). Guiding principles for adapted physical education. *Journal of Health, Physical Education, and Recreation, 23,* 15.

Connolly, M. (1994). Practicum experiences and journal writing in adapted physical education: Implications for teacher education. *Adapted Physical Activity Quarterly, 11*(3), 306–328.

Davis, W. E. (1983). An ecological approach to perceptual-motor learning. In R. L. Eason, T. L. Smith, & F. Caron (Eds.), *Adapted physical activity: From theory to application* (pp. 162–171). Champaign, IL: Human Kinetics.

Davis, W. E., & Burton, A. W. (1991). Ecological task analysis: Translating movement behavior theory into practice. *Adapted Physical Activity Quarterly, 8*(2), 154–177.

Davis, W. E., & Rizzo, T. (1991). Issues in the classification of motor disorders. *Adapted Physical Activity Quarterly, 8,* 280–304.

Federal Register, August 23, 1977, PL 94-142, the Education for All Handicapped Children Act.

Grossman, J. J. (1983). *Classification in mental retardation.* Washington, DC: American Association on Mental Retardation.

Hogan, P. I. (1990). Problem-based learning and personnel preparation in adapted physical education. *Adapted Physical Activity Quarterly, 7*(3), 205–218.

Jansma, P., & Surburg, P. (1995). PhD competency guidelines and adapted physical education professional preparation in the United States. *Adapted Physical Activity Quarterly, 12,* 307–322.

Kiphard, E. (1983). Adapted physical education in Germany. In R. Eason, T. L. Smith, & F. Caron (Eds.), *Adapted physical activity: From theory to application* (pp. 25–32). Champaign, IL: Human Kinetics.

Maslow, A. (1970). *Motivation and personality* (2nd ed.). New York: Harper & Row.

McGrew, K. S., Bruininks, R. H., & Thurlow, M. L. (1992). Relationship between measures of adaptive functioning and community adjustment for adults with mental retardation. *Exceptional Children, 58*(6), 517–529.

National Consortium for Physical Education and Recreation for Individuals with Disabilities. (1995). *Adapted physical education national standards.* Champaign, IL: Human Kinetics.

Nixon, J. (1967). The criteria of a discipline. *Quest, 9,* 42–48.

Piaget, J. (1962). *Play, dreams, and imitation in childhood.* New York: W. W. Norton.

Reid, G. (1989). Ideas about motor behavior research with special populations. *Adapted Physical Activity Quarterly, 6*(1), 1–10.

Seaman, J. A. (Ed.). (1995). *Physical best with individuals with disabilities: A handbook for inclusion in fitness programs.* Reston, VA: American Alliance for Health, Physical Education, Recreation and Dance.

Seaman, J. A., & DePauw, K. P. (1989). *Adapted physical education: A developmental approach.* Mountain View, CA: Mayfield.

Sherrill, C. (Ed.). (1988). *Leadership training in adapted physical education.* Champaign, IL: Human Kinetics.

Sherrill, C., & DePauw, K. P. (1997). Adapted physical activity and education. In J. D. Massengale & R. A. Swanson (Eds.), *History of exercise and sport science* (pp. 39–108). Champaign, IL: Human Kinetics.

Singer, R. N. (1993). Ethical issues in clinical services. *Quest, 45*(1), 88–105.

Vermeer, A., & Davis, W. E. (Eds.). (1995). *Physical and mental development in mental retardation.* Basel, Switzerland: Karger.

Wessel, J. (Ed.). (1977). *Planning individualized education programs in special education.* Northbrook, IL: Hubbard.

Wessel, J., & Kelly, L. (1986). *Achievement-based curriculum in physical education.* Philadelphia: Lea & Febiger.

World Health Organization. (1980). *International classification of impairments, disabilities, and handicaps: A manual of classification relating to the consequences of disease.* Geneva, Switzerland: Author.

2

Celebrating Individual Differences and Appreciating Disability Sport

FIGURE 2.1   Two models that guide teaching/coaching practices. The medical model guided service delivery in the 1970s and 1980s. The social minority model is recommended for the 1990s.

Categorical or Old Medical Model	Individual Differences or Social Minority Model
• Disability is equated with being defective, inferior, or less than.	• Disability is equated with being different; different is *not* less than; it is simply being different.
• Individuals have common anomalies and deficits that guide treatment.	• Individuals have only one commonality (social stigma), and it should be eliminated.
• Terminology tends to be negative (e.g., *defects, deficiencies*).	• Terminology tends to be positive or neutral with person-first emphasized.
• Programming is based on defects, problems, or characteristics.	• Programming is based on individual assessment data, personal strengths, and weaknesses.
• Purpose is to give advice, prescription, or remediation.	• Purpose is to empower individual to assume active role in self-actualization.
• Graphics are passive.  	• Graphics are active. 

After you have studied this chapter, you should be able to do the following:

1. Understand and apply the concepts of celebrating individual differences, establishing equal-status relationships, and modeling inclusive behaviors.

2. Discuss the eight disabilities most common in the public schools from a lifespan perspective, and find examples of persons of all ages with these disabilities in your community. Critically analyze the wide range of individual differences in persons with disabilities.

3. Apply guidelines for interacting with and speaking and writing about persons with disabilities.

4. Understand the values, benefits, and outcomes of sport and physical activity and relate these to different needs, aspirations, and ecosystems.

5. Appreciate the many forms of disability sport and differentiate among Special Olympics, Paralympics, and Deaf Sport.

6. Understand sport classification as the major adaptation that separates disability sport from able-bodied (AB) sport. Critically analyze various approaches to fairness in sport competition.

7. Be an intelligent spectator at various disability sport events, and use the knowledge you gain to enhance your teaching and counseling competencies.

8. Take pride in the Paralympic movement and help others to understand the tremendous variety of summer and winter Paralympic sports that should be introduced to children and youth at an early age.

9. Understand the importance of involving athletes with disabilities as major resources in instructional and recreational settings and enlisting their help in achieving transition goals for individual students.

Duncan Wyeth, a leader in cerebral palsy sports, provided the ideas for Figure 2.1, which presents old and new ways of thinking about disability and individual differences. Wyeth is one of a growing number of individuals with disabilities who are advocating that disability is simply difference, neither good or bad, and only a part of the total person. Like many others, Wyeth believes that stigma is the main experience that separates individuals with disabilities from others. In all other ways, each individual with a disability is unique, different from everyone else, and this is good. Individual differences are to be celebrated!

Stigma is the label or category assigned by others to indicate an undesirable deviation from the standard or norm. The stigma may be a conscious or an unconscious labeling, but it inevitably results in discriminatory or special treatment. Examples of **stigmatization** are being ignored, being excluded from certain groups and programs, or being considered child-like and incapable of self-determination and self-governance. The only way to eliminate stigma is to cease thinking of disability as an undesirable difference and instead consider it neutrally as a uniqueness that is neither good nor bad. Acquiring an attitude of acceptance and appreciation of individual differences is an important competency.

The purpose of this chapter is to promote critical thinking about all kinds of individual differences, especially in regard to sport. First, case studies are presented of eight individuals with different kinds of disabilities. Each values sport for different reasons, and this focuses our attention on the wide variety of goals that physical activity instruction and participation can achieve. Second, the chapter presents guidelines for interacting, speaking, and writing about people with disabilities. This knowledge is essential to forming equal-status relationships with individuals with disabilities, attending disability sport events, and learning to use the resources of athletes with disabilities in delivering adapted physical activity services. Last, the chapter provides basic information on the

ways various sports have been adapted to promote fair competition and introduces the differences among Special Olympics, Paralympics, and Deaf Sport.

Celebrating individual differences means listening to people who are different, respecting their beliefs, promoting their empowerment, and enjoying equal-status relationships. A logical learning progression is to achieve these goals with persons of your own age before testing your abilities with children and youth. It is hoped that, concurrent with studying this chapter, readers will create practicum experiences for themselves in local disability sport, attend several different kinds of disability sport events, get to know athletes and coaches, and seek to develop equal-status relationships with several adults with different kinds of disabilities.

Equal-Status Relationships

A central premise of this chapter is that physical activity personnel who have experienced equal-status relationships with adults with disabilities and who have attended a variety of disability sport events are better qualified to teach children and youth than are professionals without such experience. **Equal status** describes bidirectional interactions with persons of approximately the same age who learn to respect and care about each other as they facilitate each other in contributing equally toward the achievement of common goals and the sharing of mutual interests (Sherrill, Heikinaro-Johansson, & Slininger, 1994). A good example is an able-bodied coach working with an elite adult athlete with disabilities. In such a relationship, both individuals contribute equally, although in different ways, to the good feelings associated with winning events and/or achieving personal bests.

Knowledge about disability sports and adaptation theory enables professionals to motivate children to aspire to become athletes, to determine the specific sports best suited to different abilities, and to make community contacts essential to sport involvement and lifespan active, healthy living. Interacting with elite adult athletes with disabilities is the best way for professionals to learn the skills, rules, and strategies of sports to be taught and practiced in school and recreation center settings (see Figure 2.2). No activity affords better information about empowerment than involvement as a spectator or volunteer in sport events that are properly conducted. Moreover, seeing their teachers and coaches in equal-status relationships gives students a powerful message. They learn by example that individual differences can enrich lives and that inclusion is ethically good and right. They also realize that inclusion is a two-way process, a mutual concern, that individuals with and without disabilities must work together to achieve. There are many kinds of inclusion, just as there are numerous varieties of individual differences. People with disabilities must reach out and include able-bodied peers in disability sport, and vice versa.

Individuality and Uniqueness Expressed Through Sports

This chapter now presents accounts of several individuals who have overcome various psychomotor problems. The role of physical activity and sport in expressing individuality and uniqueness is explored, as is the personal meaning of feeling different.

Asthma and Health Problems: Case Study 1

• *I was a sickly child, missing approximately 1 week of every 6 weeks of school because of various combinations of asthma, colds, and respiratory illness. My earliest memories center on looking out the windows at the other kids, engaged in fast, wonderful, vigorous games, and wanting desperately to be with them and like them. I was skinny and unfit. Exercise almost always made me wheeze, and I hated my lungs and what I perceived to be an inefficient body that wouldn't let me do and be what I wanted. I read a lot and made good grades, but I didn't feel good about myself.*

By high school, I seemed magically to have outgrown my asthma. Physical education became my favorite class, and the after-school sports program was my life. I felt suddenly alive, really alive. My mind and body were finally working together, and I believed I could do everything. I never achieved the skill level of my friends who had rich, active childhoods, but I made up for this with enthusiasm and extra effort. I felt like my PE teacher liked me for myself, not because I made good grades or was one of her best athletes. She spent a lot of time talking with us kids. We all had a lot of problems, but we would never have gone to the school counselor.

When it was time to enter college, I agonized over whether to major in physical education or medicine. Physical education won. I loved the active life (sports, aquatics, primitive camping), and somehow I felt that PE had made me a happy, whole, integrated person. PE had also helped me to make friends and feel that people cared about me. I worshiped my PE teachers and wanted to be just like them: to help others as they had helped me.

When I got to college, I found out I wasn't as good (skill wise) as other PE majors. I made As on knowledge tests and Cs on skill tests. Amount of effort didn't seem to matter, especially

in hand-eye coordination activities. Field hockey provided some success, primarily because I trained so hard I could run longer and faster than my peers. But I wanted to be with my friends and play on the varsity basketball, volleyball, and softball teams!

I discovered that self-esteem is multidimensional. I felt good about myself as a studious, fit individual, but I mourned the highly skilled athlete that day by day I failed to become. It often seemed that I loved physical education more than any of my athlete friends did. They took for granted what I wanted so much. •

These words, from the author of this textbook, illustrate that sports and games can be meaningful to persons who are not well skilled and/or who have health and fitness problems. Physical education can accomplish many goals. Chief among these is the opportunity to share the fun and excitement of the sport setting and to be with peers perceived as popular, healthy, and happy. Persons who miss school frequently and/or lack the stamina to engage in vigorous activities often feel left out. Physical education, if properly conducted, provides an environment in which meaningful contacts are made with significant others. These contacts should lead to shared after-school and weekend experiences in sports. The process of making and keeping friends, and thereby feeling included rather than excluded, is called **social competency** in this text. This goal requires that teachers play an active role in helping students to care about each other and to structure their leisure to include physical activity with friends.

Asthma, diabetes, obesity, cancer, cardiovascular disorders, seizures, and similar problems are called **other health-impaired (OHI)** conditions and are covered in Part 3 of this book. Federal legislation defines OHI conditions as "Limited strength, vitality, or alertness due to chronic or acute health problems which adversely affect a child's educational performance" (*Federal Register,* September 29, 1992). **Acute** means rapid onset, severe symptoms, and a short course; **chronic** means of long duration. Asthma, for example, is a chronic condition that is typically *managed* by medication and healthful living practices (e.g., balanced diets and regular eating, sleeping, and exercise practices). Occasionally, however, an acute episode (i.e., an asthma attack) may occur. How individuals cope with acute and chronic OHI conditions varies widely.

Conditions like asthma, diabetes, obesity, and cardiovascular disorders require individualization in regard to exercise. Both perceived and real limitations must be addressed, and students often need extra help in achieving physical education goals and in developing attitudes and habits conducive for lifelong health and fitness. Typically, however, school district budgets are too limited to classify students with these problems as needing special education and thereby justify extra money for special programming. The knowledge and creativity of the regular physical educator determine the extent that special needs are met. In such cases, regular physical educators are said to be delivering adapted physical education services.

Clumsiness: Case Study 2

• *In about the third grade, I could neither catch nor throw a ball with the proficiency that would enhance my self-concept. By the time I finished third grade, I had come to detest that ball because it was the source of all those feelings of inadequacy, which, at the time, mattered most. One day, after an eternity of missed catches, inaccurate throws, strikeouts, and being chosen last (or being told by the team captain to play in the outfield because the ball seldom got that far), I managed to get that damned ball when nobody was looking. Intent upon punishing that ball for all it had done to me, I took it to the farthest corner of the playground and literally buried it. For a while, I felt good because I knew my spheroid enemy, in its final resting place, couldn't hurt me any more. Unfortunately, our class soon got a new ball. (Eichstaedt & Kalakian, 1987, p. 89)* •

These memories come from Leonard (Lennie) Kalakian, professor of physical education at Mankato State University in Minnesota, who has coauthored an excellent adapted physical education textbook: *Developmental/Adapted Physical Education: Making Ability Count.* In a telephone interview, Dr. Kalakian said:

> Yes, I was a clumsy child. It took me a long time to find a sport I was really good at, but eventually I became an All-American Gymnast. Obviously, sport and movement were very important to me. When it came time to enter the university, I majored in physical education.

Clumsiness, or physical awkwardness, is the inability to perform culturally normative motor activities with acceptable proficiency (Wall, 1982). The prevalence of clumsiness for regular education students who have no sensory, motor, emotional, or learning problems is estimated at 10 to 15%. Prevalence of clumsiness for special education students is much higher.

Clumsiness is related to perceptual-motor function, sensory integration, and information processing. A clumsy individual may demonstrate an acceptable level of proficiency in a **closed skill** (one done in a predictable environment that requires no quick body adjustments) but perform miserably in an **open skill** (one done in an unpredictable, changing environment that requires rapid adjustments). Thus, clumsiness is typically evidenced in activities of balance, bilateral coordination, agility, and ball handling, particularly in game settings.

Clumsiness is caused by both human and environmental constraints (limitations). Among these are insufficient opportunities for instruction and practice; delayed or abnormal development of the nervous, muscular, or skeletal systems; genetically imposed body size and motor coordination limitations; and problems related to space, equipment, surfaces, noise, visibility, weather, allergens, improper clothing, and rules or instructions.

The effect of clumsiness on an individual's mental health depends largely on the personal meaning of sport and movement. How significant others in the ecosystem view sport and value physical prowess affects how clumsy persons feel about themselves. If, for example, the father or mother is an athlete, expectations are probably high that a child will do well in sports. If one's best friend is on a team, achieving similar status may be terribly important. Attitudes toward self, based largely on perceived competence and beliefs about what significant others hold important, predispose individuals toward active or passive lifestyles. This, in turn, may help to decrease or increase clumsiness.

Clumsiness is particularly debilitating because it is a global manifestation that is easily identified but poorly understood. Everyone can pick out "the clumsy kid" in an activity; typically, such persons endure a lot of teasing. No one wants them on their team. The teacher may repeatedly single them out for special help. The ecosystem of clumsy children is different from that of classmates; thus, clumsiness is a psychosocial problem as well as a physical one. Some children, like young Lennie, express their individualities and uniqueness through action. They keep trying new activities until they find one compatible with their body build and motor coordination. Others withdraw and seek success and self-esteem in other areas.

For clumsy students, the development of positive self-concept is an especially important goal. Through individual and small-group movement activities and counseling, students learn to accept limitations that cannot be changed and to adapt the environment so as to make the most of their strengths. Achievement of this goal requires small class sizes so teachers can work individually with students.

Clumsiness is a disability in most physical education classes, yet is not defined as a disability in special education legislation. However, the syndrome of *developmental coordination disorder* (DCC) has recently been recognized by several organizations (Henderson, 1994) and is the theme of Volume 11 (1994) of the *Adapted Physical Activity Quarterly.* Adapted physical activity professionals need to consider what is a disability in a movement setting and should not be governed by eligibility criteria derived by special educators for classroom academic work.

Learning Disabilities: Case Study 3

Learning disabilities (LD) is the special education condition most prevalent in the United States. Almost 45% of the students receiving services have a specific learning disability. By definition, these students have normal or better intelligence quotients (i.e., they are not mentally retarded). Students with LD are identified on the basis of significant discrepancies between intellectual abilities and academic achievement. Specific problems are diagnosed in the ability to listen, think, speak, read, write, spell, or do mathematical calculations. Typically, students with LD demonstrate an uneven learning profile: They are good in some subjects and bad in others.

Don, a high school counselor, was diagnosed as having a learning disability in the fourth grade. Subsequently, he received individual assistance with math and other problems in a resource room for 3 years. He recalls:

• *I was the fourth boy in a family where education was really important. My father was a university professor, and my mother was a librarian. I don't remember being different until the second or third grade. I loved to read, and it was easy for me, but there were crazy little discrepancies in my learning pattern. Like I didn't memorize the alphabet until I was 7 years old. I just couldn't remember the sequence. My parents thought I would never learn to tie my shoes. I'd watch and I'd listen, but I just couldn't make my fingers do what I wanted.*

But math was what made my life really miserable. In the fourth grade, we started having story problems. You know, things like: "Your car is going 50 miles an hour. It takes 5 hours to drive from Dallas to Austin. How many miles will you drive?" The longer and more complex those sequences got, the more I was lost. In the fourth grade, I brought home a D in arithmetic. Everything else was Bs and Cs, but my parents had a fit. They said my IQ was 125 and I wasn't trying. The school gave me a bunch of tests and assigned me to a resource room 1 hour a day. Although I hated to admit it, I was having trouble remembering and dealing with sequences in my other classes also. Like in gym, this teacher would tell us we were going to work in stations. Then he'd talk on and on about what to do at each station. By the time he finished, I'd have forgotten where to start. I just followed whoever was next to me and copied them.

Everybody kept telling me to try harder, to concentrate, to have a better attitude. I was so humiliated and so hurt, mainly because my parents didn't believe in me. I made up my mind that I would conquer math if it killed me. I quit going out to play after school. All I can remember in junior high and high school is studying. I managed to get dismissed from the special education roll and maintain a C average in math, but only with extraordinary effort.

I used to have terrible migraine headaches and feel so tense all the time. I was so scared I wouldn't have the grades to get into college. Life just wasn't much fun. No, I wasn't very good at PE, but I wasn't bad either, considering I never practiced. I never had a weight problem, so PE just wasn't very important to me. No one in my family cared much about sports. Looking back, I know I missed a lot. •

Analysis of this passage shows that physical education has not been very meaningful in Don's life. As an adult, he has no physical activity leisure skills and interests. He eventually learned relaxation and stress reduction techniques in course work to become a counselor but remains unaware that this learning could have been part of regular PE instruction made available to students with special tension control needs.

The many individual differences among students with LD allow for few generalizations. Although many have average or better intelligence, some have borderline IQs (in the 70 to 90 range) that further intensify learning problems and stress. Some are hyperactive, have attention deficit disorders, and display perceptual-motor problems. Others do not. Many are deficient in balance, fine motor coordination, and agility stunts involving total body coordination. Listening and thinking deficits affect all areas of life, especially social relations. Students with LD often need extra help in developing appropriate play and game behaviors and in acquiring the social competency for acceptance.

Mild Mental Retardation: Case Study 4

• *Eric Tosado is an 18-year-old middle-distance runner from Puerto Rico. Handsome, tall, and slender, Eric easily passes for normal, as do many persons with mild mental retardation. He reads at about the sixth-grade level, attends high school, works part-time, and has many friends. Eric competes in both able-bodied (AB) track and Special Olympics. He has over 50 trophies from various AB road races and is a gold medalist in the 1,500-m and 3,000-m events of the International Summer Special Olympics Games. Although Eric is a special education student, he has never thought of himself as handicapped in sports. For many years, he avoided Special Olympics because he didn't want to be associated with "the retarded movement." Eric says, "But I love to run so much that I thought, why lose an opportunity to compete? I'm good in able-bodied competition, and I often win local-type races. Teachers kept telling me I could be the best in the world if I entered Special Olympics. It was a way to test myself in international competition, to have opportunities I couldn't find elsewhere. And now I am so glad I made the choice. There's no reason a person can't compete in both AB road races and Special Olympics." Eric's gold medalist times were 4:14.3 in the 1,500 m and 9:38 in the 3,000 m. About the role of sports in his life, Eric says:*

> It's hard to grow up mentally retarded. A lot of people tease you when you have trouble in studies. Once, when I was little and was upset, a teacher said, "Let's go out and run." He told me I was good at running, and this made all the difference in my life. It's really important to feel good at something. It helps you accept the bad stuff you can't change. Running makes me feel good physically, but competing and winning is what makes me feel good mentally. •

Eric clearly expresses his individuality and uniqueness in both AB sport and Special Olympics. Strongly motivated to train hard and perform well, he is an excellent role model for persons who aspire to become runners. Like many persons with mild disability, Eric is intensely aware of the *stigma* (i.e., undesired differentness) of mental retardation (MR) and thus reluctant to be associated with activities for the MR population. In sociological terms, he is coping with **role ambiguity:** whether to pass for normal or to take advantage of opportunities offered to persons with MR. Good counseling can help Eric to realize that he can be himself and do what he wishes; it is not necessary to choose between roles.

Mental retardation is a condition of impaired intellectual and adaptive behavior function that is documented by a score of 70 or less on a standardized intelligence test and an assessment of personal and vocational independence. Approximately 3% of the world's population is mentally retarded, and most of these individuals pass as normal once they have left school. Approximately 90% of all MR conditions are classified as mild. By adulthood, persons with mild MR typically function academically somewhere between the third and sixth grades. Cognitively, their greatest deficits are in the areas of abstract thinking, concept formation, problem solving, and evaluative activity.

Severe Mental Retardation: Case Study 5

• *In the same school with Eric, the same age, and also classified as mentally retarded, is a boy we shall call Juan, who has Down syndrome. Approximately 10% of all persons with mental retardation are born with this chromosomal abnormality, which has distinct physical features (see Figure 2.3). Juan has close-set, almond-shaped, slanting eyes, a flattening of the bridge of the nose, and an abnormally small oral cavity. He is not as tall as other boys of his age and has short limbs with small, stubby fingers and toes. He appears loose jointed because ligaments are lax and muscle tone tends to be poor. Juan has an intelligence quotient of about 45, functions at the first-grade level, and will probably always need to live and work in a sheltered environment. Like Eric, Juan is a special education student and eligible for Special Olympics.* •

In physical appearance, intellectual functioning, and motor ability, however, Eric and Juan are totally different. Whereas Eric can pass for normal, except when called on to read or to do abstract thinking, Juan has been treated as special since birth. There are real problems in assigning both boys the same diagnostic label: mentally retarded. This is why federal law now requires that an individualized education program (IEP) be developed separately for each student. Each person, regardless of label, has distinctly different needs. No two persons with Down syndrome are the same, even though the syndrome causes similar physical appearance. Likewise, no two persons with MR are the same.

Whereas appropriate physical education goals for Eric may be physical fitness, leisure-time skills, positive self-concept, and social competency, Juan probably needs help primarily in play and game behaviors, perceptual-motor function, and sensory integration. Special attention will probably be important for him to master the mental operations needed to understand game formations, rules, and strategies and to appreciate the differences between cooperation and competition. He will also need continued guidance on what to watch for during demonstrations, how to listen to instructions, and how to integrate information from all the senses into meaningful wholes.

Through Special Olympics, many persons have developed good attitudes toward mental retardation. Special Olympics, however, is only one of many sport organizations

FIGURE 2.3 Persons with Down syndrome have distinct features.

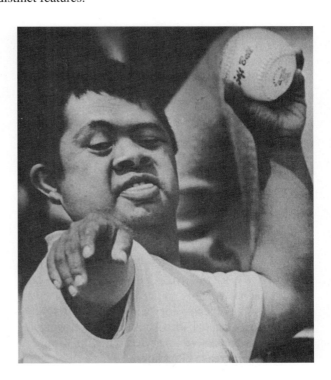

designed to serve persons who are differently abled. Only persons with mental retardation are eligible to participate in Special Olympics. Therefore, physical educators need to know how to match disabilities with organizations. More about these organizations appears in Part 3 of this text.

Cerebral Palsy: Case Study 6

Cerebral palsy (CP) is a group of neuromuscular conditions caused by damage to the motor areas of the brain. There are many types of CP and many degrees of severity, ranging from mild incoordination to muscle tone so abnormal that a person cannot use a manual wheelchair and must therefore ambulate in a motorized chair. More information on CP is presented in Chapter 25.

CP is the most common orthopedic disability seen in the public schools. Because of the many individual differences within CP, a classification system is necessary for describing persons and assessing their abilities. The U.S. Cerebral Palsy Athletic Association uses eight such classifications.

• *Nancy Anderson, a world-class athlete in her middle thirties, is a Class 2 CP, which means that she uses a wheelchair for daily living activities. She can take a step or two, with assistance, to transfer from wheelchair to bed or toilet but is unable to ambulate on crutches. Nancy's motor problems are expressed largely as athetosis (involuntary, purposeless, repeated movements of head and limbs), but she also has spasticity (abnormal muscle tightness and exaggerated reflexes). She thus lacks motor control for participation in sports unless rules and equipment are adapted. This combination of motor problems also makes fine motor coordination like writing difficult, but Nancy uses a word processor and types approximately 24*

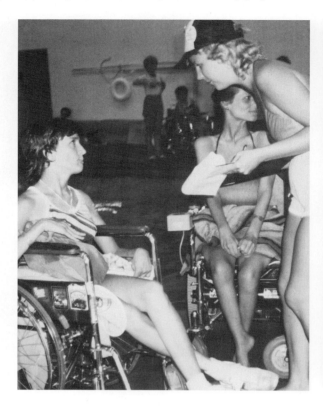

words a minute. She feeds herself but needs a helper to cut up food. Through speech therapy, Nancy has learned to talk, but experience is needed to understand her speech. Nancy has a bachelor's degree from Michigan State University, lives independently in her own apartment, and writes professionally. Her passion, however, is sports.

Nancy was introduced to swimming at age 3 by her parents. In the beginning, she simply did exercises in the water to increase range of motion and strength, but eventually, Nancy learned to swim. After introduction to CP sports competition, Nancy began to train seriously, and today she is a top U.S. swimmer in her classification (see Figure 2.4). Illustrative of her times are 1:00.1 in the 25-m free stroke and 1:02.4 in the 25-m back stroke. CP sports rules mandate different distances for swimming and track for each classification. These are the distances appropriate for a Class 2 CP.

Nancy also competes in field events (shot put, club throw, discus) and boccia, a team sport that involves throwing balls at a target ball. She wheels a 60-m dash in 34.01 sec and completes the 100-m dash in 1:00.54. She sees sports as a means of expressing her competitiveness and takes advantage of every opportunity to excel.

Nancy expresses her philosophy in the following song, which is featured in a commercial videotape of athletes with disabilities:

LOOK AT ME

In the beginning, no one thought I could.
In the beginning, I wondered if I should.
But in the beginning, I just knew I would—

If I really tried my best,
Put myself through every test
Never settled for any less—
My Personal Best.

CHORUS:
Look at me—I'm going stronger, faster, farther
than they thought I could.
Look at me—I'm going stronger, faster, farther
than some wished I would.
Look at me—I'm going stronger, faster, farther
than I dreamed I could
Wait and see—I'll better my best yet.
(Reprinted with permission from Nancy Anderson and Terry N. Terry, THE MESSAGE MAKERS, Lansing, Michigan.) •

Spinal Cord Injury: Case Study 7

• *Rick Hansen, a Canadian, is one of the best-known spinal-cord-injured athletes in the world. Not only is he an international-level competitor, but Rick is acknowledged as a creative and courageous advocate for wheelchair sports. The first to wheel around the world (24,901 miles through 34 countries), he has generated millions of dollars for wheelchair sports, raised awareness levels, and stimulated research and action to enhance the lives of individuals with disabilities (see Figure 2.5). The Rick Hansen Centre at the University of Alberta, Edmonton, Canada, a major wheelchair sports training and research facility, is but one of his many contributions.*

Rick was a teenager with three obsessions: fishing, hunting, and sports. His life changed drastically at age 15, when a ride in the back of a pickup truck ended in an injury to the

FIGURE 2.5 Rick Hansen, of Canada, wheeling on the Great Wall of China during his Man in Motion tour.

spinal cord at thoracic segments 10 and 12. The result was flaccid paralysis of the hip, leg, and foot muscles, loss of sensation from about the waist down, and changes in bladder, bowel, and sexual function. This condition is variously called a spinal cord lesion, a lower motor neuron disorder, and paraplegia. Flaccidity refers to loss of muscle tone, loss of or reduction in tendon reflexes, atrophy (wasting away) of muscles, and degeneration of muscle tissue.

After the accident, Rick spent approximately 7 months in hospitals and rehabilitation centers to learn how to handle all of the changes in his body. This included mastering wheelchair techniques, learning to use leg braces and crutches, and going to the bathroom in a different way. It also included much loneliness, self-evaluation, and periodic depression. Because Rick was younger than the average person who sustains spinal cord injury, there were few persons his age to socialize with in the rehab centers.

Making the transition from rehab center to home also was hard, however. His was the only wheelchair in the small rural town, and he opted to ambulate on crutches and braces for many months. Returning to the gymnasium was the hardest of all. Rick stated:

> *. . . going back into the gym was devastating. I avoided it as long as I could. Then one day I screwed up my courage and peeked through the door. There they were: Bob Redford and the volleyball team. Same coach, same guys, only now I was on crutches and out of it. It was going to be awful. (Hansen & Taylor, 1987, p. 40)*

This first experience ended with Rick rushing out of the gym, jumping into his car, and driving out into the country for a long cry. Looking back, Rick says he underestimated his friends. After initial shyness, his friends were fine. Rick, however, had to learn to cope with new experiences, allow persons to help him

with things he couldn't handle, and become creative in devising alternative ways to achieve goals and meet needs. The following passage illustrates his growing acceptance of self and his understanding of the importance of adapting:

> *There's nothing wrong with being carried down a bank by your friends so you can go swimming. What's wrong with taking your clothes off and going in shorts and letting people see that you've got skinny legs? It's no big deal. I had to realize that there weren't too many things I used to do that I couldn't do again, but that some of it wouldn't be the same. All I really had to do was adapt. (Hansen & Taylor, 1987, p. 43)*

As might be expected, Rick became involved in wheelchair basketball, then track, and later marathoning. He won the Boston marathon, completing the course in 1 hr, 48 min, and 22 sec, as well as other marathons and races throughout the world. He discarded the crutches and braces (a slow, inefficient method of ambulation for most persons with spinal cord injuries) and made life in a wheelchair adventurous and self-actualizing. He completed a degree in physical education at the University of British Columbia, married a physiotherapist named Amanda Reid, and developed into the mature, creative individual who today serves as a model for thousands of others who are learning to problem solve and move in alternative ways. •

Sport is the way both Rick Hansen and Nancy Anderson express their individuality and uniqueness. These elite athletes both use a wheelchair and have many commonalities: a love of competition, a willingness to train hard, good self-esteem, tremendous perseverance, and a strong commitment to become the best they can be. Their conditions and movement capacities, however, are very different. Nancy has an upper motor neuron disorder that manifests itself in spasticity and athetosis. Rick has a lower motor neuron disorder that manifests itself in flaccidity and loss of sensation. Nancy's total body is involved; Rick has perfect control of his upper extremities. Nancy is dependent upon others for transportation; Rick can drive anywhere in a car adapted with hand controls and brakes. Rick was socialized into sport before his injury. Because Nancy's condition was congenital, no one expected her to become an athlete and she was not socialized into sport in the ways her peers were.

Is Nancy more like you or Rick? Is Rick more like you or Nancy? On what bases would you make such comparisons: gender, method of ambulation, speech fluency, creative writing ability, amount of travel, interest in basketball versus swimming? Professionals learn not to categorize human beings as disabled and nondisabled but rather to celebrate and appreciate their many similarities and differences as human beings.

Deafness: Case Study 8

Persons who are deaf or hearing impaired also demonstrate individual differences in motor performance and fitness. Disability for a deaf person is primarily environmental and depends on the two-way interactions possible in a given setting. Because most hearing people cannot use sign language, the world is divided for a deaf person. There is the deaf community, where people share a common language, similar values, and positive attitudes toward deafness; here, one is free of disability. Then there is the hearing world, which is uncertain and unpredictable for a deaf person; sometimes, one is disabled there and sometimes not.

There is much controversy in educational circles concerning the best school placement for students who are deaf or hearing impaired: separate classes where sign language is used, mainstream classes, or some combination. The question is similar to that addressed in bilingual education: Can children be taught better in their native language, or should they be exposed only to English? The issue is complicated for students who are deaf because their primary language at home probably depends on whether or not their parents are deaf. The sensitive physical educator must be aware of this citizenship in two worlds and the inherent problems.

Dr. David Stewart, a professor in the College of Education at Michigan State University and author of *Deaf Sport: The Impact of Sports Within the Deaf Community* (1991), was born deaf (see Figure 2.6). The cause of his deafness is unknown, although genetics is suspected. An operation for otitis media at age 4 improved his ability to hear for a while, but his hearing has progressively deteriorated since that time, and he is now profoundly deaf. Dr. Stewart has written about himself and the importance of sports:

• *I am bilingual in American Sign Language and English and proficient in the use of various forms of English signing. I am culturally Deaf and socialize within the Deaf community. I have a hearing wife and three hearing daughters and spend much time socializing with hearing members of society. I rely heavily on sign interpreting at meetings. In noisy environments with individuals who do not sign, I generally resort to writing or to slow, exaggerated spoken conversations. I have a 95-decibel hearing loss in both ears; yet, I can use the phone with amplification if I am talking about a familiar topic with people I know. My preference is to use a Telecommunication Device for the Deaf (TDD). I empathize with other deaf individuals dealing with the challenges of a hearing and speaking society. I sympathize with hearing individuals who spend much time trying to understand the various ramifications of deafness. If someone were to ask what my biggest asset in communication is, I would respond that it is my ability to respond to a wide range of communication demands. I do not impose my communication standards on others, and I accord full respect to those with whom I communicate.*

My confidence in deafness as a facilitator of a treasured lifestyle is a result of many years of interacting in both the Deaf and hearing communities. In particular, my involvement in sports has been critical. When I was 14 years old, I had a keen interest in becoming a basketball player because a lot of my friends were interested in that sport. I followed them to my first basketball practice in high school. I didn't have a clue what the coach was saying or what was expected of me. The techniques for doing lay-ups and for following through on a shot went right past me. Because I was a fast learner, I remember saying to myself that, if only the coach would take me aside and explain a few things, then I would fit right into the team picture. I didn't realize at that time that I should have confronted the coach with my own strategies for becoming a good basketball player. Instead, I found other interests and let a chance to obtain a lifelong skill disappear.

Confronting a coach and putting forth my own objectives for learning and playing a game was a skill I learned many

years later, when I became involved with other deaf athletes in various deaf sport activities. Within deaf sport, communication is not a special consideration, and objectives for participating in sport are clearly focused.

Many deaf persons gravitate toward deaf sport activities because communication is restricted in hearing sports. In addition, the bond forged through a commonality of experiences in deafness increases the likelihood of obtaining social gratification in deaf sport. Hence, the deaf are a linguistic and cultural minority. •

Many students who are deaf participate in integrated physical education. They have a right to full understanding of class instructions, officiating calls, and comments from team members. A certain degree of maturity is required, however, to confront the individual in authority with the idea that he or she is not getting the lesson across. Sometimes, pretending to understand or somehow fading into the background is easier. The physical educator must create an environment of open, honest, and effective communication. The presence of an interpreter is just as important in physical education as in classroom subjects. To learn, one must understand.

Knowing that opportunities for full participation and socialization in after-school hearing sports may be limited for students who are deaf or hearing disabled, physical educators should be knowledgeable about deaf sports and able to refer students. The choice of whether to participate during leisure time in deaf or hearing sports or both belongs to the student, and the decision should be treated with respect and dignity. Sports are more than motor skills and fitness; they are a vehicle for making and keeping friends. This requires equal access to communication in all class and after-school activities.

Today, an increasing number of hearing persons are enrolling in sign language courses. Dr. Stewart points out that he is proficient in American Sign Language and various forms of English signing. How much do you know about the different kinds of sign language? See Chapter 26 for further information.

Ideas to Consider About Individual Differences

The preceding case studies were presented to stimulate critical thought about individual differences. Among the ideas you may wish to consider are (a) how the personal meaning of physical activity varies from person to person; (b) how goals of adapted physical activity are illustrated in these accounts; (c) how the persons served by adapted physical education may differ from those served by special education; (d) how misleading it is to lump all persons with disabilities into a category called "handicapped," "disabled," or "impaired"; (e) how a health impairment like asthma, diabetes, and obesity can be just as disabling as mental retardation and cerebral palsy; (f) how a person with a disability may feel more similar to you and me than to other persons with a disability; (g) how labeling a condition as disabling and providing federal and state monies for special services relates to politics—who decides what condition gets the money and how; (h) how much you can learn by becoming personally acquainted with persons of your own age who have disabilities; and (i) how the persons described in this chapter are similar or different from other individuals with disabilities that you have known.

In this section, you have been introduced to several kinds of individual differences: asthma and other health impairments, clumsiness, learning disabilities, mental retardation, cerebral palsy, traumatic spinal cord injury, and deafness. If you wish to know more about these or other specific conditions, check the index at the end of the book for the page numbers in Part 3 of the text where the conditions are described in detail. The index can also serve as a spelling aid and guide for assessing your vocabulary in relation to adapted physical activity.

Guidelines for Interacting

The best way to learn about individual differences—and, thus, to prepare to teach adapted physical activity—is to become personally acquainted and closely associated with several persons with disabilities. Through interactions, you clarify your beliefs concerning individual differences and refine your philosophy with regard to service delivery. The following guidelines may be helpful in the early stages of getting acquainted:

1. Remember that each person who is disabled is different, and no matter what label is attached for the convenience of others, is still a totally "unique" person.

2. Remember that persons with disabilities are persons first and disabled individuals secondly. These persons have the same right to self-actualization as any others—at their own rate, in their own way, and by means of their own tools.

3. Remember that persons with disabilities have the same needs that you have to love and be loved, to learn, to share, to grow, and to experience, in the same world you live in. They have no separate world. There is only one world (see Figure 2.7).

4. Remember that persons with disabilities have the same right as you to fall, to fail, to suffer, to decry, to cry, to curse, to despair. To protect them from these experiences is to keep them from life.

FIGURE 2.7 Joannie Hill, Denton State School teacher, demonstrates comfort in giving and receiving love. Persons with severe mental retardation often rely on touch and physical closeness to communicate feelings.

5. Remember that only those with disabilities can show or tell you what is possible for them. We who love them must be attentive, attuned observers.

6. Remember that persons with disabilities must do for themselves. We can supply the alternatives, the possibilities, the necessary tools—but only they can put these things into action. We can only stand fast, be present to reinforce, encourage, hope, and help, when we can.

7. Remember that persons with disabilities, no matter how disabled, have a limitless potential for becoming—not what we desire them to become, but what is within them to become.

8. Remember that all persons with disabilities have a right to honesty about themselves, about you, and about their condition. To be dishonest with them is the most terrible disservice one can perform. Honesty forms the only solid base upon which all growth can take place. And this above all—remember that persons with disabilities need the best you possible. In order for them to be themselves, growing, free, learning, changing, developing, experiencing persons—you must be all of these things. You can only teach what you are. If you are growing, free to learn, change, develop, and experience, you will allow them to be. (Buscaglia, 1975, pp. 19–20)

Only by interacting on an authentic and equal-status basis can professionals acquire the attitudes and knowledge to help children and youth accept and appreciate individual differences. Find some persons with disabilities on your campus or in your community, explore areas of mutual interest, and discover some things that each of you can do better than the other. Have long talks, do activities together, and perhaps you will become friends.

If we believe in the right of persons with disabilities to participate fully in society, we must be their friends.

Approximately 10% of the world's people have disabilities. Do 10% of your personal friends have disabilities? As models for children and youth, what is our responsibility?

Guidelines for Speaking and Writing

Traditionally, textbooks have presented physical, mental, social, and emotional characteristics for each disability. This practice is changing. By definition, a **characteristic** is a highly stable quality, a constituent or trait, that is difficult or impossible to change. The purpose of education is change. Therefore, we should focus on assessing and describing specific, observable behaviors rather than characteristics. **Behaviors** are actions that change constantly in relation to internal and external variables. We should not assume that certain categories of people will evidence the same behaviors. We should assess carefully and list only what we see.

The following are some criteria to guide writing and speaking about differently abled persons (Research and Training Center on Independent Living, 1990):

1. Do not refer to a disability unless it is crucial to the story.
2. Avoid portraying persons with disabilities who succeed as superhuman. This implies that persons who are disabled have no talents or unusual gifts.
3. Do not sensationalize a disability by saying "afflicted with," "victim of," and so on. Instead, say "person who has multiple sclerosis," "person who had polio."
4. Avoid labeling persons into groups, as in "the disabled," "the deaf," "a retardate," "an arthritic." Instead, say, "people who are deaf," "person with arthritis," "persons with disabilities."
5. Use person-first terminology. Say, "people or persons with disabilities" or "person who is blind," rather than "disabled persons" or "blind person."
6. Avoid using emotional descriptors, such as "unfortunate," "pitiful," and so on. Emphasize abilities, such as "uses a wheelchair/braces," (rather than "confined to a wheelchair"), "walks with crutches/braces" (rather than "is crippled"), "is partially sighted" (rather than "is partially blind").
7. Avoid implying disease when discussing disabilities. A disability such as Parkinson's disease might be caused by a sickness but is not a disease itself; nor is the person necessarily chronically ill. Persons with disabilities should not be referred to as "patients" or "cases" unless they are under medical care.

Terminology Issues

Numerous terms have evolved to describe individual differences. Professionals use words carefully because they know words have the power to hurt people or make them angry, particularly when reference is being made to an undesired differentness.

Semantics (the study of the meaning of words) is important in deciding which terms are best under various circumstances. Language not only is a means of communication, but it shapes the way persons perceive and experience the world. The meaning of words not only varies by country and culture but from person to person within the same family or social group.

The connotation of words also changes with time. For example, persons with mental retardation were once called *feebleminded* and classified by school personnel as *idiots* (severe), *imbeciles* (moderate), and *morons* (mild). Official terminology then shifted to *trainable* (severe or moderate) and *educable* (mild). In the 1980s, the categories of *profound, severe, moderate,* and *mild* were used to describe severity of mental retardation, but now the trend is toward differentiating only between mild and severe conditions. Who knows what tomorrow will bring? Persons with physical disabilities were designated by federal legislation as *crippled* for many years, while persons with learning disabilities were called *brain-injured*. Changes in terminology are typically launched by either professional organizations or legislation.

World Health Organization Definitions

As world events bring professionals from many countries together, international definitions are supplanting those of legislation and tradition. Today, a growing number of persons are accepting the definitions of the World Health Organization (1980):

Impairment—any disturbance of, or interference with, the normal structure and function of the body

Disability—the loss or reduction of functional ability and/or activity

Handicap—a condition produced by societal and environmental barriers

Analysis of Meanings

Of the preceding terms, *impairment* is the broadest and most neutral. Nevertheless, several synonyms have been proposed (limitation, challenge, inconvenience, disadvantage) as persons seek to describe themselves and others in a positive way. Advocates of individual differences theory support the phrase *differently abled* as a means of emphasizing differences (the full spectrum of abilities) rather than limitations.

The term *disability* evokes mixed feelings because the Latin prefix *dis-* means apart, asunder, aside, or away and connotes negation, lack, or invalidation. Words that begin with *dis-*—disaffirm, disbelief, discontent, dishearten, disown—all convey a negative feeling. Some persons remember that, in Latin mythology, Dis is the god of the underworld, the equivalent of Pluto in Greek mythology. Still others confuse *dis-* with *dys-,* which means "diseased," "difficult," "faulty," or "bad" (e.g., *dysentery, dysmenorrhea, dyslexia, dysplasia*). In spite of these problems, disability seems to be the word of choice among athletes with impairments. References to *disability sport* and the *disability sport movement* are common.

Handicap, the most controversial of these words, is defined in dictionaries as a race or contest in which, to equalize chances of winning, a disadvantage is imposed on superior contestants or an advantage is given to inferior ones. Handicap is derived from the Anglo-Saxon phrase *hand-n-cap,* which, according to dictionaries, originally referred to drawing lots from a cap before horse races. Today, several sports (e.g., golf, bowling) use handicaps to help equalize competition. Some persons, however, insist that the word *handicap* evolves from the cap in the hand of a beggar. Such widely differing views show the importance of integrating semantics into the adapted physical activity knowledge base.

Social Psychology Perspectives

The varied use of *handicap* is also illustrative of how professions define words differently. The World Health Organization, by defining this term as "a condition produced by societal and environmental barriers," supports the social psychology viewpoint. Beatrice Wright, a leading scholar in the psychosocial aspects of disability, emphasizes that it is not the condition that handicaps an individual but the personal meaning attached to the condition. Personal meaning comes largely from the way persons are treated by society, especially significant others. Every differently abled person can describe architectural, attitudinal, and aspirational barriers that must be overcome daily. According to Wright (1983):

> If people with a disability are unable to participate in some activities that are highly valued, their space of free movement is restricted. Part of the restriction may be due to the physical limitation itself. A person who is deaf may not enjoy nuances of music. A person with limb or heart impairments may avoid walking more than modest distances. However, part of the restriction has its source in socially derogatory attitudes—attitudes that say, in effect, "You are less good, less worthy because of the disability. It is something to be ashamed of, to be hidden, and made up for." Devaluation is expressed sometimes subtly, sometimes bluntly, and sometimes viciously. (p. 17)

The Role of Law and Economy

In sharp contrast to the sociology view, the federal law used *handicapped* to describe special education students until 1990. During that year, an amendment called Public Law 101-476, the Individuals with Disabilities Education Act, was passed that legally changed the terminology to *disabled*. The federal law (see Chapter 4) officially defines several categories of disabilities (e.g., mental retardation, learning disabilities, orthopedic impairments, and deafness).

Gradually, the terms *special education* and *disabled* have come to mean the same thing. This is very confusing inasmuch as assessment procedures often identify a student as needing special education in some areas and not others. A child disabled in reading and spelling may not be disabled in math and physical education, or vice versa. *Disability* thus is a relative term that changes with federal legislation and school policy. When the economy is good and ample money is available for education, a definition may be broad so that all persons with special needs can be declared eligible to receive help. When money is tight, eligibility criteria are narrowed so that only students with the most severe conditions are diagnosed as disabled.

A healthy way to think of handicaps and disabilities is that we all have some. Depending upon our needs, interests, goals, and aspirations, any mental or physical limitation can be perceived as a handicap. If one aspires to be outstanding in any area of endeavor, possessing only average abilities is a handicap. Short stature, if it prevents one from making the varsity basketball team, is a disability. Asthma and other respiratory problems are disabilities if one desires to socialize but cannot breathe when friends smoke. Finger dexterity becomes a disability if the time required to type school assignments is so great that it eliminates recreation.

Exceptional and Special: Varied Meanings

The terms *exceptional* and *special* are also used to denote persons who are different. Dictionary definitions indicate that *exceptional* means uncommon, rare, or forming an exception, and *special* means (a) distinguished by some unusual quality, uncommon, noteworthy, or (b) particularly favored or loved, as a special friend. *Exceptional* encompasses giftedness as well as undesired differentness and derives its popularity from the name of the professional organization to which most special educators belong: the Council for Exceptional Children. *Special* not only connotes special education eligibility but also evokes an image of Special Olympics (sports training and competition for persons with mental retardation) in many persons' minds. The common term *special populations* can refer to any group with special needs (e.g., the aged, the disadvantaged or poor, the disabled, juvenile delinquents).

Characteristic: A Frequently Misused Term

Characteristic refers to a highly stable individual quality, a constituent or trait, that is difficult or impossible to change. The opposite of a *characteristic* is a **variable,** something that can be changed, such as a specific behavior or environmental factor. In the educational context, where emphasis is on facilitating change, the focus should be on behaviors rather than characteristics.

Historically, the term *characteristic* and its various synonyms (e.g., *attribute, distinguishing feature*) have been misused in much special education and adapted physical activity literature. Teachers have been encouraged to memorize lists of physical, mental, social, and emotional characteristics that presumably capture the uniqueness of specific disability categories, like mental retardation and blindness. Today, this practice is believed to cause misconceptions, prejudice, and discrimination. The trend is away from generalization and categorization. Federal law now requires assessment to determine individual strengths and weaknesses and supports service delivery that enables the achievement of personalized goals and objectives.

Technology and pedagogy are becoming increasingly sophisticated, so that, if money is available, almost every aspect of structure and function can be changed. For example, surgery can modify the facial features of individuals with Down syndrome, cleft palate, and other anomalies; hormone therapy can help dwarfs and others with short stature grow; computers can read words aloud for persons with blindness; and artificial limbs can enable individuals with disabilities to achieve the same speeds and distances as nondisabled peers. The term *characteristic,* as used in the past, appears to be outdated, inappropriate, and dehumanizing. *When describing a disability, think of individuals and specific behaviors that express uniqueness.*

Labeling Issues

In general, slogans like "Label jars, not people" and "Labeling is disabling" summarize good practices in relation to individual differences. The implications of labeling are so vast that some sources include entire chapters on labeling theory. A major problem in calling persons "disabled" is that it lumps them together in a single category that emphasizes an undesired difference. This takes away from their individuality and humanity (see Figure 2.8). None of us likes to be remembered by or categorized on the basis of one strength or weakness. We want to be thought of as whole people, constantly changing, with many individual differences. For an excellent review of research on labeling, see Davis & Rizzo (1991).

Labels contribute to negative self-concept. The following poem expresses the feelings of a 6-year-old boy who is just becoming aware of his differentness:

LABELS

There are labels in my shirts;
    They tell me front and back,
My "P.F. Flyers" make me run faster on the track.
    "Billie the Kid" made my pants
And "Bonnie Doon" my socks.
    Momma says "Mattel" made my brightly colored blocks.
There are labels on most all things,
    And that is plain to see.
But Momma, why's there a label on me?

Contributed by Jean Caywood
Physical Education Instructor
Plano, Texas

Appreciating Disability Sport

Appreciating disability sport means getting involved as a spectator, fan, coach, athletic trainer, or advocate who helps to raise money for sport programs and to increase others' awareness of and commitment to disability sport. It also means developing the skills and knowledge to provide appropriate sport training and competition to children, youth, and adults in school and community programs.

The federal requirement, from 1990 onward, of *transition services* in the IEPs of special education students aged 16 and over creates the opportunity to prescribe disability sport training as part of public school services. The purpose of **transition services** is to assure that students have the competencies to become fully involved in community programs when they leave school. In particular, students in wheelchairs need special sport training to participate in community activities like wheelchair basketball and tennis, to make transfers and safely use swimming pools and other community facilities, and to know how to find the resources and programs to enable lifespan sport involvement.

Disability Sport Terminology

Disability sport, not *disabled sport,* is correct terminology. It is also appropriate to say *wheelchair sport, deaf sport, CP sport,* and the like. **Disability sport** originally referred to sport conducted by disability sport organizations (DSOs). Today the term is broadening to encompass mainstream and reverse mainstream sport that includes athletes with and without disabilities (Brasile, 1990; Lindstrom, 1992; Sherrill & Williams, 1996).

FIGURE 2.8 Persons with disabilities want to be known by name. These international-level athletes represent five disability groups. They have little in common except love for sports and exceptionally high skill.

Mainstream sport refers to activities, events, and settings in which individuals with and without disabilities train, recreate, or compete with each other. In these sports the number of individuals without disabilities is larger than the number with disabilities, whereas in **reverse mainstream sport** the opposite is true. Individuals without disabilities competing in wheelchairs or while wearing blindfolds are examples of reverse mainstream sport.

Able-body (AB) sport originally meant sport exclusively for athletes without disabilities (i.e., able-bodied). Individuals without disabilities are called ABs. Today **able-body sport** means sport predominantly for ABs, because laws and human rights policies prevent the exclusion of athletes with disabilities who meet performance criteria.

Special Olympics refers to a worldwide sport movement for athletes with mental retardation (MR). These athletes might have a second disability, but the major eligibility criterion is MR. No one can be a Special Olympian without MR. Special Olympics, founded in Chicago in 1968, is the oldest and largest sport organization for individuals with MR. However, a second organization, founded in Europe in 1986, officially represents the MR condition in the Paralympic movement. This organization is the International Sports Federation for Persons with Mental Handicap (INAS-FMH).

Paralympics refers to the worldwide sport movement for elite athletes with disabilities, which parallels the Olympics in that international Summer and Winter Games are held alternately every 2 years. The Paralympic Games are conducted in the same year and country as the Olympics. The Paralympics is governed by the International Paralympic Committee (IPC), just as the Olympics is governed by the International Olympic Committee (IOC). The IPC includes representatives from all of the international DSOs that conduct two or more Olympic sports, except for the organization for deaf sports (CISS), which withdrew in 1994.

Deaf sport refers to sport governed by the Comite International des Sports des Sourds (International Committee of Sports of Silence) and national affiliates for athletes with a hearing loss of 55 decibels or greater in the better ear. Summer and Winter World Games for the Deaf are held in the year after the equivalent Olympic Games. Deaf sport may also be defined as sports offered by the deaf community, which considers itself a cultural and linguistic minority, not a disability group. The deaf community does not apply the principle of person-first terminology (e.g., individuals with deafness) because they see *deaf* as an adjective similar to *American* or *Canadian*. Such phrases as *deaf sport, deaf people,* and *deaf education* are therefore acceptable.

Wheelchair sports refers to sports conducted in wheelchairs for athletes with spinal paralysis (e.g., spinal cord injury, spina bifida, postpolio) or lower limb amputations. The term evolved out of sports conducted at the Stoke Mandeville Sports Centre in Aylesbury, England, the birthplace of international competition for individuals with spinal cord injuries (SCI). The governing body for wheelchair sports is the International Stoke Mandeville Wheelchair Sports Federation (ISMWSF). The Centre was founded in 1944 by Sir Ludwig Guttmann, a neurosurgeon, now called the father of wheelchair sports (see Figure 2.9). The term was also popularized by the wheelchair basketball movement, which was initiated by World War II veterans in the United States in the 1940s.

The traditional use of the term *wheelchair sport* to encompass only athletes with spinal paralysis and lower limb amputations is confusing in that athletes with CP and other locomotor limitations also compete in wheelchairs. Many sport organizations thus conduct wheelchair sport events and use the term *wheelchair sports* in ways that depart from the traditional definition (Sherrill, 1986).

Sport classification is an assessment and programming system, based on functional and/or medical capabilities, used to assign athletes to events or heats that provide optimal success and fair competition. Sport classification also enhances communication about individual differences. Classification has long been used in AB sport, especially in competition where body weight makes a difference (e.g., wrestling, boxing, judo, weight lifting). Whereas AB sport uses classifications for some activities, disability sport applies classification procedures in all forms of wheelchair and blind sport.

Classification is the major adaptation that separates disability sport from AB sport. The purpose of classification is to provide an equitable starting point for training and competition and to ensure fairness. DSO leaders (Richter, 1994; Riding, 1994) distinguish between *equity/equitable* (fairness) and *equality/equal* (exactly the same). In the disability sport context, these words should not be used interchangeably. Individual differences are so great that it is not possible to provide each competitor with exactly the same opportunity. The alternative is the achievement of fairness to the greatest extent possible.

Functional ability (capability) refers to residual potential in a specific sport after impairment imposes limitations. Functional ability does not mean skill or fitness performance but rather the underlying abilities. In disability sport, functional

FIGURE 2.9 Sir Ludwig Guttmann, the father of wheelchair sports.

ability is innate capacity that cannot be altered by training, practice, or motivation. To assure fairness in track and field events, CP sport uses eight classifications. Paralympic competition, however, specifies four classes for track and seven classes for field. In the United States, three classes are used in wheelchair basketball; the rest of the world uses eight (see Figure 2.9).

Sport Classification for Fairness

Sport classifications are important to teachers and coaches in schools in that they provide insight into ways to adapt physical education. DSOs have conducted considerable research about what distances, times, and events are appropriate for each classification. Some of this information is presented in Part 3 of this text. More detail is easily available by writing DSOs or contacting local sport clubs. Professionals who apply this information enable students to more easily make the transition from school physical education to competitive and recreational activities in the community. This enhances fairness of opportunity. This text recommends that IEPs specify the student's functional classification and that programming be linked to sport class.

Sport classification may be medical or functional, general or sport-specific, and integrated or disability-specific. To be an intelligent spectator of disability sport, one must know what classification system is guiding the competition. To be a good professional, one must be able to communicate with students and parents about classification and teach activities appropriate to

33

FIGURE 2.10 Medical and functional classifications for wheelchair sports.

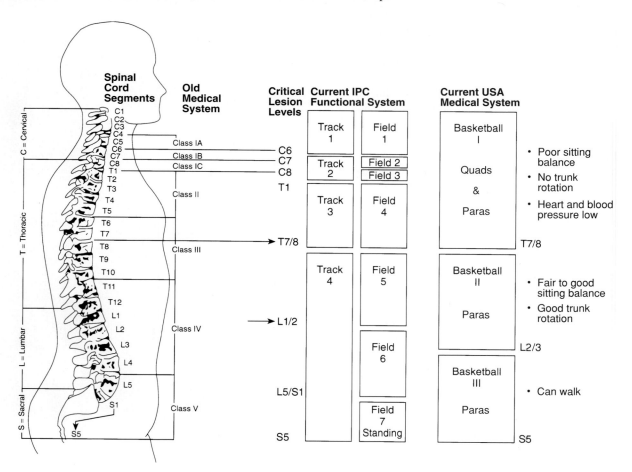

sport class. Classification practices are changing rapidly because it is difficult to establish a system that everyone considers fair. Following are definitions:

Medical classification is an anatomically based, muscle-testing system that assigns classifications on the basis of complete or incomplete spinal lesions and level of lesion (see Figure 2.10) or, in the case of amputations, on the amount of a body part that is present. Anatomical terminology is *C1–8* for the eight cervical spinal cord segments, *T1–12* for the thoracic segments, and *L1–5* for the lumbar segments. Athletes are commonly called by their classification (e.g., T7s or L2s). In a **complete lesion,** the spinal cord is completely severed, and all sensation and movement controlled at that segment and above are lost. In an **incomplete lesion,** any combination of residual abilities may be present.

Traditionally, medical classification has been associated with wheelchair sport. In 1983, Dr. Horst Strohkendl of Germany recommended changing from the medical system to a functional or player system for wheelchair basketball (Strohkendl, 1986). Subsequently the functional system was accepted worldwide for wheelchair basketball, except in the United States, which continues to use the three-class medical system (see Figure 2.10). Track, field, swimming, table tennis, and many other sports shifted to the functional system in the late 1980s and early 1990s (DePauw & Gavron, 1995).

Functional classification is an observation-based system in which expert classifiers analyze functional ability in specific sport skills or settings and assign classes that are standardized by written profiles (see Table 2.1). When supplementary information is needed, muscle tests similar to those in the medical system are used. Functional classifications were first used in the late 1970s by the newly organized CP sport organization. The trend is toward functional classification.

General classification is a global class believed to be appropriate for participation in two or more sports. This system is associated with medical classification.

Sport-specific classification is a class believed to be appropriate only for one sport (i.e., an athlete has a different class for every sport). This system is associated with functional classification.

Integrated classification is a system that combines or integrates athletes with different physical disabilities (e.g., CP, spinal paralysis, muscular dystrophy) into the same event or heat. Professionals often use this system in schools and local settings because there are insufficient numbers of individuals with the same disability and the same classification to allow disability-specific competition. This system, which was used in the Paralympics in 1992, evoked much controversy. In particular, athletes with CP did not feel that events were fair when they had to swim, run, and throw against athletes without CP.

Disability-specific classification is the opposite of the integrated system. It is guided by the philosophy that fairness occurs only when individuals with the same disability and the same

T a b l e 2 . 1   Sport classification profiles for cerebral palsy.

Class	Description
1	Uses motorized wheelchair. Severe involvement in all four limbs, limited trunk control, and unable to grasp softball.
2	Propels chair with feet and/or very slowly with arms. Severe to moderate involvement in all four limbs. Uneven profile necessitating subclassifications as 2 Upper (2U) or 2 Lower (2L), with adjective denoting limbs having greater ability. Severe control problems in accuracy tasks.
3	Propels chair with short, choppy arm pushes but generates fairly good speed. Moderate involvement in three or four limbs and trunk. Can take a few steps with assistive devices, but is not functionally ambulatory.
4	Propels chair with forceful, continuous arm pushes, demonstrating excellent functional ability for wheelchair sports. Involvement primarily in lower limbs. Good strength in trunk and upper extremities. Minimal control problems.
5	Typically uses assistive devices (crutches, canes, walkers). Moderate to severe spasticity of either (a) arm and leg on same side (hemiplegia) or (b) both lower limbs (paraplegia).
6	Ambulates without assistive devices, but has balance and coordination difficulties. Moderate to severe involvement of three or four limbs.
7	Ambulates well, but with slight limp. Moderate to mild spasticity in arm and leg on same side (i.e., hemiplegic).
8	Runs and jumps freely without noticeable limp. Demonstrates good balance and symmetric form but has obvious (although minimal) coordination problems. Has normal range of motion.

classification compete against each other. If there is no other athlete with the same disability and the same classification, then competition focuses on surpassing one's personal best. Historically, classification has been disability-specific in countries where different disability sport organizations (DSOs) autonomously control sport rather than cooperate through a central DSO governing body. This has been the case in the United States, where seven DSOs have separate philosophies and practices.

Issues in sport classification dominate disability sport gatherings and research. The best resource for detailed information is a conference proceedings called *Vista '93: The Outlook,* edited by Robert Steadward, Ewen Nelson, and Garry Wheeler, available through the Rick Hansen Centre, W1-67, Van Vliet Complex, University of Alberta, Edmonton, Alberta, Canada T6G 2H9. Steadward, president of the International Paralympic Committee (IPC), and his staff members Nelson and Wheeler can also be reached through the Rick Hansen Centre.

Trends in sport classification primarily affect athletes with physical disabilities in individual sports like swimming and track and field, as experts continue to experiment with the ranges of ability that can be clustered together and still offer fair competition. The trend in world competition seems to be toward a combination of functional, sport-specific, and integrated classification. DSO experts are exerting their personal bests in trying to evolve a system that is fair for everyone.

Athletes with blindness and mental retardation are not much affected by the sport classification issues because thus far they compete in separate heats or events. Blind sport uses three visual acuity classes, in what might be called a medical, general, and disability-specific system (see Table 2.2). MR or MH sport requires that physicians or appropriate authorities substantiate eligibility by documenting that individuals have low adaptive behaviors and IQs.

Sport classification in school physical education requires that adapted physical activity personnel complete training in classification theory and procedures and/or use the resources of DSOs as volunteer or salaried consultants. Each DSO con-

T a b l e 2 . 2   Sport classifications for blindness.

B1	Totally blind
B2	Partially blind, about 40% of normal vision
B3	Legally blind, about 80% of normal vision

ducts training schools or workshops to certify participants as classifiers in various sports. Addresses of DSOs appear in Appendix C. This text has provided basic information for communicating with athletes with disabilities about their sport classes and for introducing children and youth to this body of knowledge. More information about sport classification and related programming for each disability is provided in Part 3 of this text.

Other Approaches to Fairness

Open competition refers to freedom to enter an event in which one meets eligibility requirements with respect to times and distances, with no consideration given to functional or medical classification. The best athletes, with the highest levels of functional ability, often choose open competition. Additionally, INAS-FMH (the IPC-based MR sport organization) uses open competition to advance athletes through national and regional competition to world-level events, thereby permitting only the most elite to compete in international events (Atha, 1994).

Divisioning or banded competition refers to the Special Olympics practice of classifying individuals with MR into divisions based on times and distances submitted before competition. The goal is to allow every individual a chance to compete against others within approximately a 10% ability range. Specifically, the top and bottom scores of a division may not exceed each other by more than 10%. This does not allow every athlete to be a winner, a popular misconception, but does allow every athlete a fair chance at winning. Special Olympics specifies that each division must have no less than three or more than eight competitors. Only the top three performers in a division win

FIGURE 2.11 Teams in wheelchair basketball are equalized by a point system based on player classifications.

medals. Divisioning permits individuals with a wide range of abilities to experience and grow from competition at varied levels.

Age equity refers to the practice of grouping athletes by age to maximize fairness. The different DSOs define age categories in different ways, but the trend is to make definitions as close as possible to those of AB sports. In general, **youth sports** refers to ages 8 to 11; **junior sports** to ages 12 to 15; and **senior or adult sports** to ages 16 upward. **Masters sports** are for older athletes, with "older" defined differently by each DSO.

Gender equity refers to the practice of grouping athletes by gender to maximize fairness. The principle underlying this practice emphasizes that most females are socialized into sport in different ways than males are and that average females are significantly different from average males in height, weight, and physiological capacity. These differences favor females in some sports and males in some sports.

Point systems are numerical ways of establishing team balance so that each team has an equitable chance of winning (see Figure 2.11). For example, the National Wheelchair Basketball Association (NWBA) of the United States assigns 1, 2, or 3 points to each player, depending on his or her medical classification. Coaches then must decide what combination of players to use. Rules indicate that players on the floor cannot total more than 12 points. Combinations most frequently used are (a) three 3-point players, two 2-point players and one 1-point player and (b) two 3-point players and three 2-point players. Obviously 3-point players have the highest performance capacity, but rules require that others have a chance to play.

Inclusion requirement systems involve rules-governed team balances that call for a certain number of lower-functioning players to be on the floor at all times. Team handball, a wheelchair sport for athletes with CP, for example, has nine players on a team. Rules state that four persons from Sport Classes 1, 2, 3, or 6 (the lowest-functioning classes) must be on the floor. A similar system is used in seven-a-side ambulatory soccer, also a CP sport. At least one Class 6 (lowest-functioning ambulatory athlete) must play at all times, and at most four Class 8 (highest-functioning) athletes may play at one time.

Adaptation theory, which is explained in more detail in Chapter 3, is closely related to classification practices. The foregoing sections indicate that classification and other equity systems are the major adaptations that separate disability sport from AB sport. Understanding these is the key to being a good spectator and teaching individuals (both AB and disabled) about sport. Mainstream physical education can be much improved by teachers' creating classification and other equity systems, based on the models in this chapter. Fairness in learning, playing, and competing does not happen spontaneously, even in predominantly AB settings. Classification promotes the principle of zero reject or zero exclusion; no one sits on the bench.

Finding and Using DSOs as Resources

To achieve the goal of *transition,* professionals must form partnerships with DSOs and community sport clubs that support the Sport for All philosophy. Most local clubs are linked with national and international governing bodies. Table 2.3 presents the names of international organizations that govern two or more Olympic sports, their equivalents in the United States, and the population served by each.

Sports for Deaf Persons

Table 2.3 shows that the deaf population was the first to organize an international sport movement. Since the 1920s, deaf athletes have regularly held competitions. Because of the importance of sign language, deaf athletes hold their events separately from those of other DSOs. International games are conducted quadrennially in the year after the regular Olympics. Videotapes of these games can be obtained from Gallaudet University, 7th & Florida NE, Washington, DC 20002.

Sports for Persons With Mental Disabilities

Table 2.3 shows that two organizations govern sports for persons with mental disabilities. Special Olympics International (SOI), founded in 1968 by Eunice Kennedy Shriver (a sister of President John F. Kennedy), has branches in over 130 countries and holds international summer and winter competitions every 4 years in the year prior to the regular Olympics. These international meets are usually held in the United States. The International Sports Federation for Persons with Mental Handicap (INAS-FMH) was founded in the Netherlands in 1986. It began conducting international competitions in 1989.

Eligibility requirements for Special Olympics competition, published in 1994, indicate that persons must be at least 8 years old and must have been identified by an agency or a professional as having mental retardation *or* must have a cognitive delay as determined by standardized measures *or* must have significant learning or vocational problems due to cognitive delays that require or have required specially designed instruction. Children 5 to 7 years old may participate in Special Olympics training but may not compete. Thus, Special Olympics does not serve individuals with physical impairments unless their primary disability is mental.

Special Olympics programs are operative in almost every community. State offices offer opportunities for training to become certified as coaches in various Special Olympics sports, and volunteers are welcomed in all program areas. Certification

T a b l e   2 . 3   International sport organizations and U.S. equivalents with dates of founding.

International	United States	Population Served
Comite International des Sports des Sourds (CISS), 1924	American Athletic Association for the Deaf (AAAD), 1945	Sports for deaf athletes (i.e., hearing loss of 55 decibels or greater in the better ear)
International Stoke Mandeville Wheelchair Sports Federation (ISMWSF), 1957	Wheelchair Sports, USA (WS, USA)	Wheelchair sports for spinally impaired
International Sports Organization for the Disabled (ISOD), 1963	No equivalent. The United States has three separate organizations: Disabled Sports/USA (DS/USA) has governed amputee sports since 1989 U.S. Les Autres Sports Association (USLASA), 1986 Dwarf Athletic Association of America (DAAA), 1986	Wheelchair and ambulatory sports for amputees (nine classes) and les autres (six classes)
Cerebral Palsy International Sports and Recreation Association (CP-ISRA), 1978	U.S. Cerebral Palsy Athletic Association (USCPAA), 1978	Wheelchair and ambulatory sports for eight cerebral palsy classes
International Blind Sports Association (IBSA), 1981	U.S Association for Blind Athletes (USABA), 1976	Sports for three classes of visual impairment
Special Olympics International (SOI), 1968	Special Olympics International (SOI), 1968	Sports for athletes with mental retardation
International Sports Federation for Persons with Mental Handicap (INAS-FMH), 1986	No U.S. equivalent	Sports for athletes with mental handicaps, also called learning difficulties

Note: Disabled Sports/USA, called National Handicapped Sports (NHS) until 1995, is a powerful U.S. sport organization that governs winter sports and other events for several disability groups. Wheelchair Sports, USA, was called the National Wheelchair Athletic Association (NWAA) until 1994. CISS (French) translates to "International Committee of Sports of Silence."

training is a good activity to coordinate with adapted physical education course work.

Sports for Persons With Physical Disabilities

Table 2.3 shows that four international organizations govern Paralympic sports for athletes with physical disabilities:

- ISMWSF
- ISOD
- CP-ISRA
- IBSA

Visual impairments are included under the umbrella term *physical disability*. Prior to 1996, those organizations provided all of the athletes for the Paralympics. In 1996, athletes with mental disabilities, representing INAS-FMH, participated in full medal events at the Summer Paralympics in Atlanta. Thus the original meaning of Paralympics (sport only for persons with spinal paralysis, then for persons with other physical disabilities) is gradually changing.

The term *les autres* (French, meaning "the others") has evolved to describe locomotor disabilities not served by ISMWSF, CP-ISRA, and IBSA. *Les autres* includes such diverse conditions as dwarfism, muscular dystrophy, polio, and many kinds of muscular-skeletal-nervous disorders. In most countries, one organization governs all les autres athletes. In the United States, however, separate organizations have evolved to meet the needs of individuals with amputations, dwarfism, and les autres conditions (see Table 2.3).

As shown in Table 2.3, six national U.S. organizations sponsor two or more sports for athletes with physical disabilities:

- WS, USA formerly NWAA
- DS/USA, formerly NHS
- USLASA
- DAAA
- USCPAA
- USABA

Learning these and the international abbreviations is important because the sports world communicates almost entirely through abbreviations. In the United States, each of these organizations is separately incorporated and historically has functioned independently from the others. The desire of athletes to participate in the Paralympic movement, however, is leading to increased cooperation among organizations. This trend is promoted by the Committee on Sports for the Disabled (COSD), formed in 1979, by the United States Olympic Committee (USOC), which has its headquarters in Colorado Springs (DePauw & Gavron, 1995; Sherrill, 1986).

Introduction to Wheelchairs and Cycles

Establishing equal-status relationships with individuals with physical disabilities and appreciating disability sport requires a knowledge of wheelchairs. Much sport conversation and interaction pertains to wheelchairs and hand-crank cycles. Figure 2.12 shows that chair styles vary by sport. **Sport chairs** are chairs manufactured specifically for basketball, tennis, and other activities that require maximal maneuverability. **Track and racing chairs** are chairs with three wheels, lowered seat positions, longer wheelbases, and much camber. **Wheelbase** is the distance from front to back wheels. **Camber** is the vertical angle or degree of slant of the big wheels. Knowledge about camber, wheelbase, and other characteristics of chairs enhances communication and inclusion of ABs in the wheelchair community.

Note that chairs used for sports have low backs with no push handles because the athletes do not need anyone to push them. Sport chairs have rigid frames and do not fold, so a first skill to learn is how to remove the wheels, thereby enabling the chair to be transported by car. Athletes drive, make transfers independently from chair to car, and typically throw their chairs into the back seat. AB persons are needed, however, when chairs are to be transported in the car trunk. Athletes can, of course, remove their own wheels from chair frames, but it is thoughtful for ABs to offer help.

Chairs and cycles for individuals with spinal paralysis, les autres, and CP conditions are individualized, based on personal measurements and sport needs. DSOs for athletes with spinal paralysis do not permit motorized chairs, but these are used by athletes with CP and les autres conditions in Classes 1 and 2. Chair styles change frequently as technology improves. *Sports 'N Spokes* is an excellent journal for staying abreast of wheelchair changes.

Physical Disability Terminology

Following are terms used in disability sport and similar contexts.

Quadriplegia/tetraplegia refers to involvement of all four limbs, the trunk, and many organ functions, like blood pressure, maximal heart response to exercise, temperature regulation, and respiration. Involvement is caused by damage to the brain (CP) or to cervical segments of the spine (spinal paralysis). Athletes with this condition call themselves **quads.**

Paraplegia refers to involvement of the lower limbs and, depending on the level of damage, involvement of the trunk and alterations of organ function as in quadriplegia (see Figure 2.10). Involvement is caused by damage to the thoracic or lumbar spine. Individuals with paraplegia demonstrate a wide range of abilities, depending on whether muscles are paralyzed or merely weakened. Athletes with spinal paralysis call themselves **paras.** CP sport prefers *diplegia* or *triplegia* because damage originates in the brain.

Diplegia and **triplegia** refer, respectively, to conditions in which two (*di-*) or three (*tri-*) limbs are more involved than the others. Usually the legs are more involved than the arms. The condition is of cerebral origin rather than spinal origin.

Hemiplegia refers to loss of sensation and/or movement on either the right or the left side of the body. Athletes with this condition call themselves **hemis.** The origin of this condition may be either cerebral or spinal, so the term is used by all disability sport groups.

Functional ambulation refers to ability to walk with assistive devices. Ability to walk is generally divided into **community ambulators** (can walk 1,000 yards nonstop and ascend and descend stairs) and **household ambulators** (can walk only a few steps). To meet the community ambulator criterion, damage to the spine is at L2/3 or below. Note that this is the criterion for placement in Wheelchair Basketball Class 3. Individuals with CP with Sport Class 5 are community ambulators.

Prosthesis (singular) refers to an external artificial body part (e.g., limb or eye). The plural is **prostheses.**

Orthosis refers to a brace. The plural is **orthoses.** (See Figure 2.13.)

Time-of-Onset Concerns in Sport

Time of onset of disability is typically categorized as congenital or acquired. This variable is extremely important in that it reflects sport socialization and life experiences that influence self-esteem and self-actualization. **Sport socialization** is the process of becoming actively involved in sport and learning how to perform sport roles. This process is facilitated by family, teachers, caretakers, and service providers, but differences in attitudes toward disability often create barriers.

Congenital refers to a condition present at birth. The most common congenital conditions are mental retardation, cerebral palsy, and spina bifida. The more severe a congenital condition is, the less likely it is that the individual will be socialized into sport and become aware of his or her sports potential.

Acquired refers to conditions that occur after birth. These are specified by life stage to indicate the amount of sport socialization that occurred before disability. Youth who acquire a disability during or after puberty have the same sport beliefs, interests, and values as AB people.

Achieving Inclusion in Sport

The first half of this chapter emphasized that the personal meaning of sport varies widely. Sport can be developmental, rehabilitative, recreational, or competitive. Thus far, this chapter has emphasized competition because many individuals in the past have been denied access to competition. Professionals need to know that individuals with disabilities, even very severe conditions, can be elite athletes in the same sense as AB athletes can.

Some individuals with disabilities have the functional capacity to compete in the regular Olympics (Lindstrom, 1992). Illustrative of these are **Paolo Fantato,** Italian wheelchair archer in the 1996 Olympics; **Neroly Fairhall,** New Zealand wheelchair archer in the 1984 Olympics; **Wilma Rudolph,** U.S. athlete who overcame polio and birth defects to become a triple gold medalist in track events at the 1960 Olympics; **Liz Hartel,** Danish horseback rider with polio who won silver medals in the 1952 and 1956 Olympics; and **Oliver Halazy,** Hungarian below-knee amputee water polo player who won gold medals in the 1932 and 1936 Olympics.

Many athletes without the functional capacity to compete in the regular Olympics have achieved recognition as the best in the world compared to others with similar functional capacity. These are the gold medalists at the Paralympics, the Special Olympics, and the Deaf World Games. They also include

FIGURE 2.12 Chairs and cycles must be designed for sports. Read *Sports 'N Spokes* to keep up with rapidly changing chair styles. (Photos courtesy of Mary Carol Peterson, Action Top End, Invacare Corporation.)

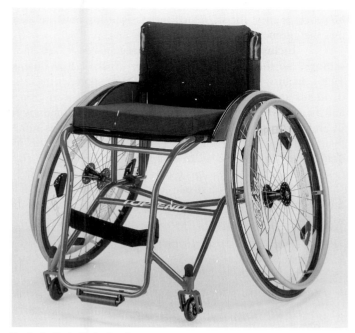

Basketball chair, 4 wheels
Terminator style

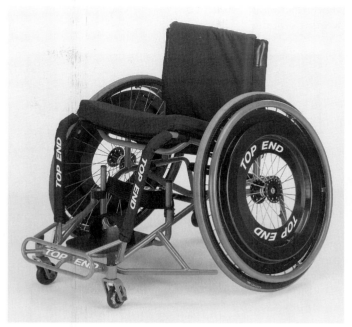

Quad rugby chair, 4 wheels
Offensive play, Terminator style

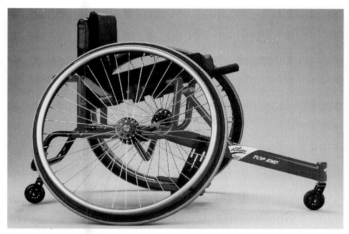

Tennis chair, 3 wheels, with antitop swivel caster option

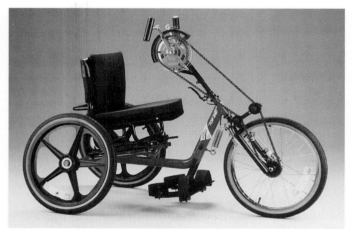

Hand-crank cycle, one of many models

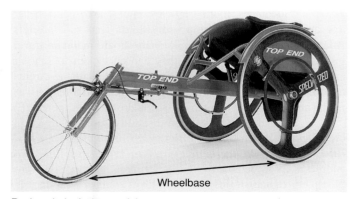

Racing chair, Action model
Note long wheelbase

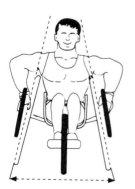

Camber
Racing chair showing wheel
camber and diagonal force
applied to handrims

FIGURE 2.13 Recreational wheelchair sports at Cal State Bernadino are conducted jointly by university students of Dr. Terry Rizzo and adult athletes from Casa Colina Wheelchair Sports. Note that many of these athletes are wearing *ortheses.*

gold medalists in wheelchair divisions of races like the Boston Marathon. Some persons, however, aspire only to the fun and challenge of competition at the local level.

Others prefer recreational sport. An excellent resource manual by Paciorek and Jones (1994) describes 53 summer and winter sports in which people with disabilities participate. These sports are available in many settings. Choices include the following:

1. Predominantly AB, also known as mainstream, like regular physical education, sport, and recreation

2. Predominantly disability sport conducted by a local DSO

3. Parallel involvement in organized events, in which athletes with and without disabilities compete in separate divisions conducted at the same time and place, like running and cycling events and marathons

4. Adaptations that purposively bring individuals with and without disabilities together in interactive training, recreation, and competition:
   (a) **Integrated wheelchair basketball,** which is particularly popular in Canada, and **integrated doubles wheelchair tennis**
   (b) **Unified Sport in Special Olympics,** which specifies that 50% of the players on the floor or field must have MR while the other 50% are matched as closely as possible in age and ability
   (c) **Challenger Division Baseball,** sponsored by Little League baseball, which uses AB buddies (parents, siblings, coaches, friends, or peer tutors) on the field to assist youth with mental or physical disabilities to enjoy the full benefit of Little League participation in an environment structured to their abilities.

Many individuals with disabilities crave as much sport as possible and want help in achieving inclusion. Others prefer one or two sports. Others dislike sport or feel neutral about inclusion. A major goal of adapted physical activity, however, is sport for all, which means focusing on competencies that promote inclusion.

Inclusion is associated with acceptance in AB sport settings, but the issue is much broader (Sherrill & Williams, 1996). Inclusion is a concern in all kinds of sport settings. Individuals are not automatically accepted in new social groups and facilities. Professionals must empower individuals with disabilities to take the initiative to include themselves rather than wait passively for someone else to include them. This requires learning specific social competencies, overcoming shyness, and coping with various forms of rejection.

Individuals with disabilities must typically overcome more barriers than AB peers. Among the main barriers are the following:

1. No companion or friend with whom to share sport experiences

2. A lack of money to pay club memberships, buy equipment, etc.

3. A lack of transportation, especially for individuals with blindness

4. Inadequate exposure to sport and lack of socialization into sport

5. A lack of role models

A goal of this chapter is to motivate university students and others to create equal-status relationships with individuals with disabilities that will help overcome these barriers. As university students become professionals, it is hoped that they will continue such relationships and thereby become role models for others. Individuals with disabilities must also be recruited and trained as role models.

Finding Role Models in Disability Sport

Individuals with and without disabilities can all benefit from role models who have overcome barriers to achieve success. All students, not just those with disabilities, should be introduced to disability sport and taught how to be spectators, participants, and advocates. Athletes with disabilities, when brought into schools as teachers, coaches, and consultants, should be given the widest visibility possible.

Videotapes, journal articles, books, and media coverage are resources that help individuals find role models. Adapted physical activity professionals should maintain traveling libraries of resources that they can check out to schools, agencies, and individuals. Such resources are available through national and international sport organizations and a few private media and publishing companies (see addresses in Appendix E).

Journals that give good disability sport coverage include *Sports 'N Spokes* and *Palaestra: Forum of Sport, Physical Education, and Recreation for Those With Disabilities* (see addresses in Appendix E). These journals, in particular, provide pictures and stories about top-level athletes with disabilities who can serve as role models. Their articles also provide performance standards (times and distances) for eligibility in various disability sport events and enable aspiring athletes to judge their abilities and potential. Because of the relative newness of disability sport, many athletes with excellent promise have not yet been discovered. Seeing and hearing about role models sensitizes everyone in the ecosystem to the importance of socializing individuals with disabilities into sport at the same age as their AB peers.

Taking Pride in the Paralympic Movement

Individuals with and without disabilities need to understand and feel pride in the Paralympic movement. Helping to develop this pride is an important advocacy role of the adapted physical activity professional. Three facts should be emphasized:

1. The Paralympic Games are the highest-level multisport competition for athletes with disabilities.
2. The Paralympic Games have high eligibility standards that permit only the most elite athletes to participate.
3. The Paralympic Games are governed by criteria similar to those used in the Olympic Games.

Many films and videos show the approximately 4,500 athletes from over 120 countries participating in the 1996 Paralympic Games. These athletes competed in 17 Paralympic and two exhibition sports (see Table 2.4). Over the 10-day competition period, these sports were broken down into over 500 events and conducted at many different venues, mostly the same as those of the Olympic Games. Having the 1996 Paralympics in Atlanta helped to increase the awareness of U.S. citizens that athletes with disabilities progress through local, regional, and national competition to the World Games and then to the Paralympics in the same way that AB athletes advance to the Olympics. The next Summer Paralympics will be held in Australia in 2000.

Previous Summer Paralympics were held in Spain (1992), South Korea (1988), New York and the United Kingdom (1984), the Netherlands (1980), Canada (1976), Germany (1972), Israel (1968), Japan (1964), and Italy (1960). From 1960 to 1976, only wheelchair athletes with spinal paralysis competed in the Paralympics. Canada, in 1976, changed this tradition by inviting athletes with amputations and blindness to compete in their Paralympics. Subsequently, the Netherlands invited ambulatory athletes with CP, and New York broadened eligibility requirements to include wheelchair athletes with CP and competitors with various les autres conditions.

The Winter Paralympics were held in Norway (1994), France (1992), Austria (1988 and 1984), Norway (1980), and Sweden (1976). Whereas Summer and Winter Paralympics originally were conducted in the same year, the practice of alternating them began in 1992. The next Winter Paralympics will be held in Nagano, Japan, in 1998.

Summer Paralympic Sports

Following is a brief description of sports to enable intelligent spectatorism and to guide professionals in prioritizing what sports should be taught to individuals with disabilities. The Paralympic movement has established proof that these sports, with very few minor adaptations, are suitable for one or more types of disabilities. Although these sports are adapted, athletes

T a b l e 2 . 4   The seventeen medal sports and two exhibition sports at the 1996 Paralympics in Atlanta.

Medal Sports	Exhibition Sports
Archery	Rugby (quad rugby)
Athletics	Yachting (sailing)
Boccia	
Cycling	
Equestrian	
Fencing	
Goalball	
Judo	
Lawn bowling	
Power lifting	
Shooting	
Swimming	
Table tennis	
Soccer (football)	
Volleyball (sitting and standing)	
Wheelchair basketball	
Wheelchair tennis	

with disabilities typically dislike the term *adapted sport.* They prefer that emphasis be placed on the sport (i.e., *sport for athletes with disabilities* or *disability sport*), not on the adaptation.

The basic sport skills underlying success are the same as those in AB sports; therefore individuals with and without disabilities can be taught many of these sports in an integrated instructional setting. An integrated setting is also excellent for recreation, but individuals with disabilities who desire serious competition must generally engage in disability sports that employ classification systems.

Archery

Archery competition distances and rules are the same as for the Olympics except for adaptations in equipment for various disabilities. Competition begins with a qualification round (36 arrows each at 90, 70, 50, and 30 m for men; the same for women except 60 m substituted for 70 m) after which athletes shoot from 70 m only and are eliminated by pairs.

Athletics

In international terminology, athletics means track, field, and marathon (26.2 miles). Distances are generally the same as in AB sport. Prior to 1992, only athletes belonging to the same disability category competed against each other. Now a functional classification system is used to try to cluster athletes by abilities so that individuals in wheelchairs compete against each other regardless of disability category. Likewise, athletes who are ambulatory compete against each other, regardless of disability category. The exceptions to this trend are events for athletes with blindness and a few events designated specifically for athletes with CP.

Boccia

Boccia originally was for wheelchair athletes with severe CP, but now athletes with other disabilities compete in it. Similar to Italian lawn bowling, the purpose is to throw, kick, roll, push, or strike baseball-size leather balls of color toward a white target ball (see Figure 2.14). Any body part or a head-pointing device can be used to give momentum to the ball.

Cycling

Many cycling events are held: tandem biking with sighted guides on a 50/60-m course for athletes with blindness; 5,000-m bicycle and 1,500-m tricycle races for individuals with mild and severe CP, respectively; and road races of various distances (e.g., 65–75 km, 55–65 km, 45–55 km) for athletes with various lower limb capabilities. Road races for tandem bikes are 60/70 km and 110/120 km.

Equestrian

Horseback riding competitions for numerous disability conditions are conducted in many countries, but thus far only CP-ISRA and ISOD have advanced equestrian competition at the Paralympic level. Events are offered in dressage, handy rider (obstacle course), and equitation in five CP and five non-CP classes. National competitions offer both assisted (use of a sidewalker or leader) and unassisted events, but international competition includes only unassisted events.

Fencing

Fencing is a wheelchair sport, organized by type of sword used: foil (flexible blade targeting opponent's torso), eppe (stiff blade targeting any part of the body), and saber (heavier, stiff blade, targeting any body part above the waist). Electronic scoring is used.

Goalball

Goalball is a team sport, three players on each team, played by athletes with blindness who wear eyeshades to equalize the amount of sight (i.e., make everyone totally blind). The goal is to throw a basketball-size bell ball across the opponents' court and into a goal cage to score points while the other team defends. The court is 9 × 18 m, and the goal cage is 9 m long and 1.3 m high.

Judo

Judo competition is limited to athletes with blindness; it replaced wrestling at the 1988 Paralympics and has become very popular. After the ritual bow, the two opponents walk toward each other and touch (this is the only rule difference between Paralympic and Olympic judo); then they put their arms at their sides to indicate readiness. After the umpire's signal to start, approximately 40 basic techniques, plus hold-downs, chokes, and arm bars, are used. Pinning the opponent on his or her back for 30 seconds or several other achievements end the match.

Lawn Bowling

Lawn bowling is conducted by ISMWSF (in wheelchairs) and ISOD (with prostheses, for athletes with amputations). The purpose is to throw wooden balls at a small target ball called a jack. Points are awarded after each round. Rules of AB lawn bowls, a very popular sport in the British Commonwealth countries, are followed.

FIGURE 2.14 Recreational boccia, in which students with disabilities and students without disabilities keep each other company. The challenge is "Who can roll the balls closest to the small white target ball?"

Power Lifting

Power lifting includes the bench press, squat, and dead lift for individuals in 10 weight classes. All Paralympic sport organizations offer the bench press, but only IBSA provides competition in the squat and dead lift. Lifters are allowed three trials at each weight. Power lifting is different from weight lifting, which includes the clean and jerk and the snatch. Somewhat confusing is the fact that the bench-press event for athletes with spinal paralysis has traditionally been called *wheelchair weight lifting*. In the future this event will be called *power lifting* even though it uses a different style and bench than those used in other Paralympic bench presses.

Shooting

Shooting includes rifle and pistol competition with stationary targets. Four classifications help equalize opportunity:

> Class 1—Standing competitors who require no assistance
>
> Class 2—Sitting competitors at paraplegic functional level
>
> Class 3—Sitting competitors at quadriplegic function level
>
> Class 4—Used for rifle only; for standing competitors who cannot support the weight of a rifle and therefore require a shooting stand

Swimming

Swimming competitions use the same distances as AB competition but are complicated organizationally by the need to classify swimmers with physical disabilities into 10 functional classifications in order to match as closely as possible competitors of the same functional abilities (see Figure 2.15). Three stroke categories are used for classification: (a) freestyle, backstroke, and butterfly, (b) breaststroke, and (c) individual medley. USABA athletes (blind) are not integrated with other swimmers.

FIGURE 2.15 Swimming competition requires many functional classifications to accommodate individual differences.

Table Tennis

Table tennis competition uses the same rules as AB table tennis but permits a few adaptations, like strapping the paddle to the hand for athletes who lack grip strength. A classification system is used that first divides athletes into wheelchair and ambulatory divisions and then separates athletes into more specific competition classes based on functional ability. All Paralympic DSOs except IBSA promote this sport.

Soccer (Seven-a-Side)

Soccer competition is only for athletes with CP, stroke, and traumatic brain injury who are ambulatory (i.e., Classes 5, 6, 7, 8). In most of the world, soccer is called football. International rules require that at least one Class 5 or 6 athlete (those with lowest functional ability) be on the field at all times; these individuals usually serve as goalies. Class 7 players have hemiplegia, whereas Class 8 players have coordination problems but no noticeable limp. The field is 75×55 m with goal cages slightly smaller than regulation size. This is because motor dysfunction of cerebral origin makes defending a standard-size goal very difficult. With these exceptions, the rules are mostly the same as regulation soccer.

Volleyball

Volleyball competition is organized into standing and sitting divisions. Standing volleyball is sponsored by ISOD (mainly for athletes with amputations, no rules adaptations). However, a classification system is used to equalize team abilities, especially the number of upper and lower limb disabilities on the court. In the United States, volleyball is an official dwarf sport

with only one rule change, a lower net. Sitting volleyball, also sponsored by ISOD, has six players on a team and uses a smaller court (16×12 m) and lower net (1.15 m). The major rule adaptations are these: (a) Position on the court is determined by location of buttocks; (b) a player hitting or blocking the ball at the net must maintain contact between floor and buttocks; and (c) a player may block an opponent's serve at the net.

Wheelchair Basketball

Although wheelchair basketball is an ISMWSF sport, since 1982 this competition has been open to anyone with a permanent lower limb disability. Team composition is structured by a sophisticated classification system that assigns each player a certain number of points, based on functional ability, and then permits any combination of points on the floor that adds up to 14 points in international competition and 12 points in U.S. competition. Since 1992, international classification has used an eight-class system, in which players are assigned points as follows: 1, 1.5, 2, 2.5, 3, 3.5, 4, 4.5 points. The lower the points, the more severe the disability. In contrast, the United States continues to use a three-class system with players assigned only 1, 2, or 3 points.

Wheelchair basketball is identical to AB basketball with a few exceptions:

1. The number of seconds allowed in the lane is 5 rather than 3.
2. The player in possession of the ball can take only two wheel thrusts, after which she or he must dribble, shoot, or pass.
3. No double-dribble rule is enforced.
4. Raising the buttocks off of the chair, a physical advantage some players have, is treated as a technical foul.

Wheelchair Tennis

Although wheelchair tennis is an ISOD sport, this competition is open to anyone with a permanent lower limb disability. Instead of a classification system, division play is used to ensure fairness. Men play in five divisions and women in three. Divisions are designated as Open (for the best players), then A, B, C, and D (from high skill to low). Players start in the lowest division and move up by winning regional and then national tournaments. Each knows his or her rank or standing within a division.

Wheelchair tennis is identical to AB tennis with a few exceptions:

1. Two bounces instead of one are permitted.
2. A bounce-drop serve can be used if the overarm serve is not functionally possible. Regardless of type of serve, the back wheels of the chair must remain behind the service line until the ball is contacted.
3. Elastic, tape, or special orthotic devices can be used to bind the racquet to the hand to adapt for weak grip strength.

Rugby

Rugby (also called quad rugby or wheelchair rugby) is a team sport in which points are scored by carrying the ball over the opponent's goal line (Yilla & Sherrill, 1994). Played on a regulation basketball court with a four-person team and a volleyball, the sport combines elements of football, basketball, and ice hockey. Ball

FIGURE 2.16   Adaptations for skiing.

Four-track skiing

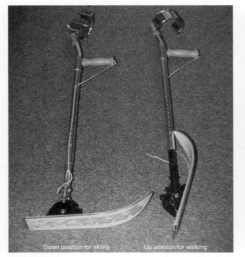

Outriggers

handlers may take any number of wheel thrusts but must bounce or pass the ball every 10 sec. The ball is passed from player to player by whatever movement patterns individual abilities allow. Rugby was developed specifically for persons who do not have the arm and shoulder strength to participate in wheelchair basketball. A classification system is used that assigns points on the basis of hand, arm, and trunk functions. The combined classification score of the four players on the court may not exceed 8 points.

Yachting

Yachting is a race of sailboats, which is conducted by rules as close as possible to those of AB competition. At the 1996 Paralympics, a 2-square-mile course was used with 23-ft keel boats with open cockpits. Three sailors managed each yacht, and athletes with all disabilities were eligible. Points were accumulated over 5 days of racing to determine the winning crew.

Winter Paralympic Sports

Following is a brief description of sports performed on snow or ice in the quadrennial Winter Paralympics. Few adaptations are needed for athletes with mental disabilities or deafness. This section therefore emphasizes the adaptations associated with physical disabilities and blindness.

Alpine Skiing

Also called downhill skiing, the alpine skiing competition is similar to AB skiing except that specialized, adapted equipment and classification systems are used. *Outriggers* are special ski crutches attached by hinges to mini-skis that enable balance and steering maneuverability in ambulatory skiing. The use of two outriggers and two skis is called *four-track skiing* (see Figure 2.16), an adaptation for individuals with severe balance problems as in CP or with disability of both legs. The use of one outrigger and two skis is called *three-track skiing,* an adaptation typically used by individuals with single leg amputations or hemiplegia.

Twelve classifications are used to equalize competitive opportunity for individuals with physical disabilities in Alpine skiing:

Class 1—Four-track skiers

Class 2—Three-track skiers

Class 3—Two skis and poles; both legs disabled

Class 4—Two skis and poles; one leg disabled

Class 5/7—Two skis and no poles; both arms or hands disabled

Class 6/9—Two skis and one pole; one arm or hand disabled

Class 10/12—Use of sit ski, pulk, mono-ski, or bi-ski for individuals who are nonambulatory.

FIGURE 2.17 Sledge speed racing at Beitostølen, an internationally known center near Oslo, Norway.

Poles, picks (special short poles for pushing), or short outriggers are used with sitting ski apparatus. Good balance and trunk control are needed for success. The sit ski, essentially a sled with a bucket seat affixed, was invented first (1970s) and is still used for learning basic skills and engaging in sports like sledge or ice hockey. The pulk is similar to the sit ski except that the pulk has a solid bottom instead of runners. The mono-ski, introduced in the 1980s, is a seat (10 to 18 inches high) connected to a single ski by means of a complex suspension system that enables speeds approaching 70 mph. Bi-skis are similar except that the seat is attached to two skis. For pictures and more information about sit skis, see Chapter 23.

Individuals with blindness also compete in Alpine skiing. Three classifications are used in recognition of different levels of visual acuity (B1–B3; see Table 2.2). The main adaptation is the use of a buddy or sighted guide to verbally assist individuals down the slope.

Nordic Skiing

Also called cross-country, Nordic skiing includes races, relays, and a biathlon. The biathlon is a combination event of shooting and racing. Classifications are similar to those for Alpine skiing. Race distances for athletes with physical disabilities are usually 5, 10, 15, 20, and 30 km. Race distances for athletes with blindness are usually 5, 10, and 25 km.

Sledge or Ice Hockey

For nonambulatory athletes, ice hockey uses sledges (like pulks, but with very thin metal runners adapted for hockey), a regulation-size ice rink, a puck, and picks for propulsion and maneuvering the puck. Six players on each team play offense and defense, as in stand-up hockey, except that two picks are substituted for the hockey stick. Gloves and picks can be adapted to accommodate weak hand grips.

Sledge Speed Racing

Sledge speed racing, which is most advanced in the Scandinavian countries, involves racing on sledges that are either self-propelled by picks or drawn by animals (see Figure 2.17).

References

Atha, B. P. (1994). Issues in classification in sport for the mentally handicapped. In R. D. Steadward, E. R. Nelson, & G. D. Wheeler (Eds.), *Vista '93: The outlook* (pp. 302–309). Edmonton, Alberta, Canada: Rick Hansen Centre.

Brasile, F. M. (1990). Wheelchair sports: A new perspective on integration. *Adapted Physical Activity Quarterly, 7*(1), 3–11.

Buscaglia, L. (1975). *The disabled and their parents: A counseling challenge.* Thorofare, NJ: Charles B. Slack.

Davis, W. E., & Rizzo, T. L. (1991). Issues in the classification of motor disorders. *Adapted Physical Activity Quarterly, 8*(4), 280–304.

DePauw, K. P., & Gavron, S. (1995). *Disability and sport.* Champaign, IL: Human Kinetics.

Eichstaedt, C., & Kalakian, L. (1987). *Developmental/adapted physical education* (2nd ed.). New York: Macmillan.

Federal Register, September 29, 1992, Vol. 57, No. 189, The Individuals with Disabilities Education Act.

Hansen, R., & Taylor, J. (1987). *Rick Hansen: Man in motion.* Vancouver: Douglas & McIntyre.

Henderson, S. E. (1994). Editorial: Developmental coordination disorder issue. *Adapted Physical Activity Quarterly, 11*(2), 111–114.

Lindstrom, H. (1992). Integration of sport for athletes with disabilities into sport programs for able-bodied athletes. *Palaestra, 8*(3), 28–32, 58–59.

Paciorek, M. J., & Jones, J. A. (1994). *Sports and recreation for the disabled* (2nd ed.). Carmel, IN: Cooper.

Research and Training Center on Independent Living. (1990). *Guidelines for reporting and writing about people with disabilities.* Lawrence: University of Kansas.

Richter, K. (1994). Integrated classification: An analysis. In R. D. Steadward, E. R. Nelson, & G. D. Wheeler (Eds.), *Vista '93: The outlook* (pp. 255–259). Edmonton, Alberta, Canada: Rick Hansen Centre.

Riding, M. (1994). Functional classification: A revolution and evolution. In R. D. Steadward, E. R. Nelson, & G. D. Wheeler (Eds.), *Vista '93: The outlook* (pp. 289–293). Edmonton, Alberta, Canada: Rick Hansen Centre.

Sherrill, C. (Ed.). (1986). *Sport and disabled athletes.* Champaign, IL: Human Kinetics.

Sherrill, C., Heikinaro-Johansson, P., & Slininger, D. (1994). Equal-status relationships in the gym. *Journal of Physical Education, Recreation and Dance, 65*(1), 27–31, 56.

Sherrill, C., & Williams, T. (1996). Disability and sport: Psychosocial perspectives on inclusion, integration, and participation. *Sport Science Review, 4*(1), 42–64.

Steadward, R. D., Nelson, E. R., & Wheeler, G. D. (Eds.). (1994). *Vista '93: The outlook.* Edmonton, Alberta, Canada: Rick Hansen Centre.

Stewart, D. A. (1991). *Deaf sport: The impact of sports within the deaf community.* Washington, DC: Gallaudet University Press.

Strohkendl, H. (1986). The new classification system for wheelchair basketball. In C. Sherrill (Ed.), *Sport and disabled athletes* (pp. 101–112). Champaign, IL: Human Kinetics.

Wall, A. (1982). Physically awkward children: A motor development perspective. In J. Das, R. Mulcahy, & A. Wall (Eds.), *Theory and research in learning disabilities* (pp. 253–268). New York: Plenum.

World Health Organization. (1980). *International classification of disabilities and handicaps: A manual of classification relating to the consequences of disease.* Geneva, Switzerland: Author.

Wright, B. (1983). *Physical disability: A psychosocial approach* (2nd ed.). Philadelphia: Harper & Row.

Yilla, A., & Sherrill, C. (1994). Quad rugby illustrated. *Palaestra, 10*(4), 25–31.

CHAPTER

3

Teamwork, Communication, Adaptation, and Creativity

FIGURE 3.1   A model to guide home-school-community teamwork.

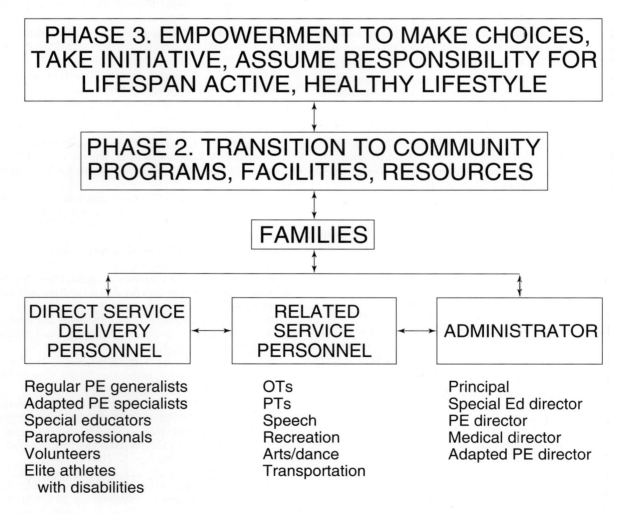

PHASE 3. EMPOWERMENT TO MAKE CHOICES, TAKE INITIATIVE, ASSUME RESPONSIBILITY FOR LIFESPAN ACTIVE, HEALTHY LIFESTYLE

PHASE 2. TRANSITION TO COMMUNITY PROGRAMS, FACILITIES, RESOURCES

FAMILIES

DIRECT SERVICE DELIVERY PERSONNEL	RELATED SERVICE PERSONNEL	ADMINISTRATOR
Regular PE generalists	OTs	Principal
Adapted PE specialists	PTs	Special Ed director
Special educators	Speech	PE director
Paraprofessionals	Recreation	Medical director
Volunteers	Arts/dance	Adapted PE director
Elite athletes with disabilities	Transportation	

PHASE 1. SCHOOL-BASED REGULAR AND ADAPTED PHYSICAL EDUCATION TEAMWORK WITH FAMILIES AND ALL POSSIBLE RESOURCES

After you have studied this chapter, you should be able to do the following:

1. Discuss how families, schools, and communities can work together toward achievement of lifespan active, healthy lifestyles for all.

2. Discuss roles and responsibilities of direct and related service delivery personnel, family members, and other human resources. Develop a semester plan for getting acquainted with resources from many disciplines and for many kinds of family structures.

3. Explain different kinds of teamwork in adapted physical activity service delivery, and develop a semester plan for observing various kinds of teams in action.

4. Understand and apply major communication theories in achieving such goals as persuasion, consensus, equal-status sharing, and attitude change.

5. Understand and apply adaptation theory in (a) managing program variables that contribute to success and (b) performing service delivery roles.

6. Understand and apply creativity theory in problem solving related to adapted physical activity concerns.

7. Critically think about the processes of teamwork, communication, adaptation, and creativity in relation to all aspects of home-school-community programming.

8. Know how to use the Appendixes of this text to find information about organizations, journals, and other nonhuman resources. Make a semester plan for getting acquainted with professional journals representing various disciplines.

The achievement of lifespan active, healthy lifestyles for all is dependent upon families, schools, and communities sharing a common vision and working together to assure that many physical activity options (both integrated and special) are available. The purpose of this chapter is to encourage critical thinking about teamwork, communication, adaptation, and creativity and to develop basic competencies in these processes. Among the topics covered are human and nonhuman resources in service delivery and empowerment; team approaches and differences between multidisciplinary, interdisciplinary, and crossdisciplinary teamwork; and communication, adaptation, and creativity theories that drive good practices.

A Home-School-Community Teamwork Model

Figure 3.1 presents a model to guide physical educators in helping to shape a community vision. Central to meeting the diverse needs of citizens in any community is teamwork between family members and school and community professionals (Fiorini, Stanton, & Reid, 1996). The model features three developmental phases.

The first phase emphasizes cooperation between regular and adapted physical educators and families in identifying and using as many resources as possible in teaching children and youth the beliefs, attitudes, and skills that will make physical activity enjoyable. Although instruction is primarily school-based during this phase, field trips are taken to both integrated and special community physical activity programs. The primary goal is to enable students to see adults with disabilities participating in a wide range of recreational, competitive, and exercise settings (e.g., integrated swimming, fitness, and tennis clubs; highly competitive wheelchair basketball; Special Olympics). During this phase, families are also helped to create physical education homework plans, utilize school and community resources as a family unit, and understand their role in shaping lifespan physical activity attitudes and practices.

The second phase of the model focuses on transition from predominantly school resources to community programs and facilities. This phase can begin at any age, but law re-

quires that transition instruction occur by age 16. The term **transition services** refers to assistance in shifting from traditional school-based instruction to use of community resources in achieving independent living; active, healthy lifestyle; rich, satisfying leisure; and competitive employment. Much teamwork among families and professionals is needed to assure that students have transportation several times a week to a variety of community programs, that they have the social competence skills to promote inclusion, and that the individuals who own or manage the facilities are friendly and welcoming (Dattilo, 1994; Krebs & Block, 1992).

The third phase, empowerment, represents formal exit from adapted physical activity service delivery and personal assumption of responsibility for meeting one's exercise and leisure needs. Involvement may be in integrated programs or in disability sport, since both are funded by public taxes or private enterprise and thus can be considered community options. Adults who function at this level do not like their sports to be called adapted; they associate the term *adapted* with *service delivery* and emphasize that, once competencies in sport are mastered and individuals assume responsibility for their own activity, philosophy and terminology should change.

Empowerment can be process or outcome. In Phase 3, empowerment is conceptualized as the outcome of high-quality, team-oriented physical education service delivery, both adapted and regular. Empowerment thus is closely associated with self-actualization (see Chapter 1). However, many individuals with and without disabilities either do not progress to this phase or lack resources to remain in it. For these individuals, communities should continue to make available transition and adapted physical activity services, including fitness and leisure counseling, regardless of age. This is why the arrows in Figure 3.1 are bidirectional.

Figure 3.1 is futuristic in that many communities do not yet have professionals trained in school-community-family teamwork who can provide the leadership for implementation of such models. The trend, however, is toward serving wider and wider ranges of individual differences in inclusive settings. This calls for the involvement of many professionals and team approaches. Of particular importance is the concept of employing regular and adapted physical activity professionals as partners in service delivery in many settings.

Some of these settings are schools; recreation, sport, and camp facilities; hospitals and rehabilitation centers; fitness clubs; infant and early childhood intervention programs; senior citizen centers; and agencies that provide social, psychological, vocational, and advocacy services. These settings may be either integrated or special. The law prohibits settings that exclude individuals with disabilities (Block, 1995).

A first step in teamwork is to learn about the types of human resources who share concerns about lifespan active, healthy lifestyles. It is hoped that readers will visit as many employment settings as possible and view firsthand the interactions of various professionals, volunteers, and family members. When appropriate, ask individuals for interviews or engage them in small-group discussions about their work, beliefs, and concerns. This will strengthen your communication skills as well as your knowledge base.

Human Resources in Service Delivery and Empowerment

Professionals, paraprofessionals, volunteers, and family members constitute major categories of adult human resources. Additionally, students may contribute in various ways as peer teachers, tutors, buddies, and partners. Following are descriptions of adult human resources.

Regular Physical Educators or Generalists

Regular physical educators teach both regular and special education students in the integrated setting, adapting pedagogy, equipment, and environment as needed. They also may be assigned classes of adapted physical education for students with severe psychomotor problems. Involvement in Special Olympics, cerebral palsy sports, wheelchair sports, and other special events is common.

If the school system does not have an adapted physical education specialist, regular physical educators perform all of the tasks normally expected of a specialist. To fulfill these responsibilities, teachers must often request specific **support services** (i.e., supplementary human and nonhuman resources and aids). Illustrative of these are an adapted physical activity specialist as a dual or team teacher and specially trained paraprofessionals and volunteers. Regular physical educators may also ask their principals to employ an adapted physical activity consultant to come once or twice weekly and/or to fund participation in workshops, conferences, and courses. When a school district has 30 or 40 students with severe disabilities, regular physical educators may band together and ask their administration to employ a full-time adapted physical activity specialist.

With regard to meeting the needs of students with disabilities or below-average performance, regular physical educators are involved in all of the PAP-TE-CA services (i.e., planning, assessment, prescription, teaching, evaluation, coordination of resources, and advocacy). They are limited only by the breadth and depth of their competencies. When adapted physical activity specialists are available, generalists work in close cooperation with them. If such specialists cannot be obtained, physical educators may turn to parents, the principal, special educators, therapists, or resources in the community (e.g., organizations, agencies, disability sport groups). In the latter case, physical educators must act as strong advocates in helping non-physical-education people to understand the need to give attention to physical activity, fitness, and leisure concerns.

Of particular importance is the generalist's role in screening and referral, two components of the PAP-TE-CA assessment process. **Screening** is the process (formal or informal) by which students are identified who need help beyond what the generalist can offer. **Referral** is the process of reporting the results of screening to the parents and/or the administration and making sure that further action is taken by the appropriate persons. If the identified student appears to have one of the disabilities recognized by federal law (see Appendix A), the special education individualized education program (IEP) process is initiated (see Chapter 4). If not, the physical educator works with the principal and parents to create a plan and find resources for help.

Adapted Physical Activity Specialists

Adapted physical activity specialists usually have a bachelor's degree in regular physical education and a master's degree in adapted physical education. Specialists employed as administrators in large or affluent school districts often have a doctoral degree. Specialists work primarily in four roles: (a) direct service delivery, (b) consulting and resource room functions, (c) in-service training, and (d) administration and research. Specialists typically work as partners with generalists or as members of multidisciplinary, interdisciplinary, or crossdisciplinary teams in performing PAP-TE-CA services.

Specifically, direct service adapted physical activity specialists are responsible for the following:

1. **Planning**—Helping school districts and schools create overall plans, curricula, and programs that maximize the success of all students; finding or developing resources; purchasing equipment; communicating with power figures about needs; writing and directing grants

2. **Assessment**—In-depth testing after a student has been referred for the IEP process or an alternative process if eligibility for special education services cannot be established; writing and presenting comprehensive reports pertaining to different kinds of assessment; assisting regular physical educators and others with screening and other kinds of testing; coordinating community-based assessment initiatives

3. **Prescription**—Serving on IEP committees and interacting with parents and professionals at IEP meetings; sharing in decision making about placement; interacting with physical education generalists, principal, parents, and others in prescribing services, activities, and programs for nonspecial education students who need help

4. **Teaching, counseling, and coaching**—Working with students with disabilities who are assigned full- or part-time to separate adapted physical education or individual tutoring; serving as a resource room dual or team teacher in gymnasium with a regular physical educator or in a nearby resource room or station; assisting with crisis management and special problems in large physical education classes; interacting with parents in establishing backyard homework programs; conducting integrated home-school-community fitness and sport programs; initiating and managing sport programs for students not accommodated in regular settings; mentoring students with disabilities who are entering integrated programs for the first time

5. **Evaluation**—Evaluating all aspects of adapted physical activity service delivery in both regular and special settings; interacting with others on committees and teams responsible for evaluation of architectural, aspirational, and attitudinal barriers and other constraints to inclusive programs

6. **Consulting and coordinating resources**—Helping generalists, families, and others obtain support services and create support networks; fundraising and grant writing; consulting day-by-day as needed; making individuals aware of needs and rights

7. **Advocacy**—Working in many ways at many levels (local, state, national, international) to change beliefs, attitudes, and behaviors

School systems sometimes assign specific names to overall job roles or positions. The following are commonly used synonyms for direct service adapted physical activity personnel:

1. **Resource teacher** (a teacher who serves a single school, team-teaches with regular physical educators, and provides instruction for individuals not in regular physical education)

2. **Itinerant teacher** (a teacher who works in several schools, but performs essentially the same job functions as a resource teacher)

3. **Consulting teacher** (a teacher who travels from school to school and does some direct service delivery but mostly provides support services to regular physical educators and helps them learn how to adapt instruction)

In-service training and administration are roles that specialists perform in addition to direct service delivery (Tymeson, 1988). **In-service training** refers to planning and conducting workshops and learning experiences for school district personnel. Administration involves many tasks, most of which center on planning, consulting, conducting in-service training, supervising, evaluating, and conducting research for the entire community. Many adapted physical activity specialists, when employed in administrative capacities, are called consulting teachers although their work includes many functions in addition to consultation.

Special Education Personnel

This category of professionals includes administrators, teachers, and paraprofessionals funded with special education money to provide services that benefit students in diagnostic categories defined by federal law (see Appendix A). These services may be direct (PAP-TE-CA) or indirect (e.g., support to regular educators and other team and administrative roles). Typically, a school district employs one or more special education administrators and several special education teachers and paraprofessionals. Specific job functions vary with the school district philosophy. Some teachers work full-time in self-contained classrooms, whereas others work as resource teachers or support personnel. Some teachers serve as educational diagnosticians or full-time in various assessment and IEP roles.

Paraprofessionals may be assigned to a classroom or to a particular student. Paraprofessionals who assist physical educators are typically designated as special education or regular education, depending on which budget pays their salaries. Often, students with severe disabilities or special needs, such as wheelchair adaptations, are assigned their own paraprofessional who stays with them all day, accompanying them to mainstream classes. An important competency of both regular and adapted physical educators is knowing how to obtain, train, and use paraprofessionals.

Some school districts use special education money to employ adapted physical activity personnel. Such individuals are considered special educators rather than physical educators and typically must have special education certification in addition to adapted physical education training. The training and work of such professionals is thus crossdisciplinary.

Athletes With Disabilities: Many Roles

Elite athletes with disabilities can make significant contributions as teachers, coaches, paraprofessionals, and consultants. Specific employment roles vary, of course, with university background and expertise. A growing number of athletes with disabilities are earning graduate degrees in adapted physical activity and/or completing teacher certification requirements. As direct service providers, such individuals are powerful models. As consultants, they can assist regular and adapted personnel to make contact with sport organizations and utilize the rich resources that organizations offer. They can also provide information on wheelchair technology, assistive devices, and adapted equipment (see Figure 3.2). Because the rules and strategies of disability sport are continuously changing, athletes with disabilities are more likely to have up-to-date information than published sources are.

Athletes with disabilities also offer a pool from which to draw volunteers. They frequently give speeches and provide demonstration sport events for elementary and secondary schools, serve on committees, and help with resource identification and usage. Of particular value, they are often willing to serve as tutor, coach, or "big sister" or "big brother" to students with and without disabilities.

Parents and Family Members

In the ecological approach to service delivery, educators not only serve students with disabilities but also work with parents, siblings, and significant others (Hanson & Carta, 1995). The only way to teach the whole person is to understand the

FIGURE 3.2 Athletes with disabilities are excellent resources and should be used in university and public school team teaching.

 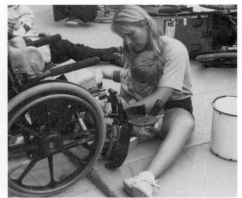

total social environment in which she or he lives. Such desired social outcomes of physical education as self-worth, acceptance by others, and life satisfaction depend more on family and neighborhood interactions than on school training. Thus, the teaching and learning process must be a partnership between school and family.

In planning home-school-community activities, it is important to consider such variables as family composition and size, parent and sibling employment patterns, parental age, socioeconomic level, ethnic group, and cultural background. The two-parent family no longer is the dominant pattern. Depending upon the ethnic group, between 50% and 80% of all children will live in a single-parent home at some time in their lives (Hernandez, 1994). In most instances, these are mother-only families with male adults absent or frequently changing. This variable and the fact that most mothers now work outside the home strongly affect sport socialization both as a spectator and as an active participant. Physical educators must be sensitive to including all kinds of parents (never-married, remarried, gay and lesbian, rich and poor, employed and nonemployed) in after-school programs and in maintaining equity in choice of volunteer helpers.

Both congenital and acquired disabilities affect family life, although in different ways. The incidence of divorce, substance abuse, and health problems (both physical and mental) is greater in families trying to cope with disability concerns than in families without such concerns. Physical educators often have more contact with family members than other

school personnel do, because of after-school and weekend sport programs. This contact increases the likelihood that physical educators will be asked to help with family problems in addition to their traditional school responsibilities.

Sports involvement and transition programming typically require additional money, which presumably comes from families. Physical educators should know that approximately 1 out of every 7 Americans is living in poverty, and these are the individuals most likely to be coping with disabilities and other developmental risk factors. Families often feel they must make choices about whether to support extraclass activities of siblings with or without disabilities. Siblings are affected in many ways by older and younger family members with disabilities. In summary, many factors must be considered when physical educators seek to form partnerships with families.

Related Services Personnel

Related services personnel, broadly, are all school employees (except special educators and physical educators) who assist with education, including therapy, of students with disabilities. Federal legislation explains **related services** as

transportation and such developmental, corrective, and other supportive services . . . as may be required to assist a child with a disability to benefit from special education (Individuals with Disabilities Education Act of 1990, Sec. 1401)

Among the related services most relevant to helping students benefit from adapted physical education are therapeutic recreation, occupational therapy, physical therapy, corrective therapy, and the arts. These professions historically have been associated with the medical model, but many changes are occurring. Inviting related services personnel to lecture and observing these professionals in the field are ways of remaining current.

Therapeutic Recreation Specialists

Therapeutic recreation (TR) is a specialization within the broad discipline of recreation. Most therapeutic recreators (TRs) belong to their parent organization, the National Recreation and Park Association (NRPA), and consider themselves recreation and leisure specialists. NRPA began as the Playground Association of America in 1906 and thus has a rich history of resources. The official journal of NRPA is *Parks and Recreation.*

Early terms for TR were *hospital recreation, medical recreation,* and *recreation therapy.* Since 1967, the date of the founding of the National Therapeutic Recreation Society (NTRS), the official name of the profession has been *therapeutic recreation.* There is no one definition that professionals universally embrace. O'Morrow and Reynolds (1989) explain:

Therapeutic recreation is multifaceted and multidimensional. We cannot help but feel that maybe there is no one definition or purpose of therapeutic recreation because of the many variables operating: persons, needs, settings. (p. 114)

TRs belong to two organizations: (a) NTRS, which is an official structure within the NRPA, and (b) the American Therapeutic Recreation Association (ATRA), which was founded in 1984. NTRS publishes *Therapeutic Recreation Journal;* thus far, ATRA has published only newsletters. The two organizations offer slightly different definitions of TR. NTRS uses the following definition:

Therapeutic recreation—is service delivery that facilitates the development, maintenance, and expression of an appropriate leisure lifestyle for individuals with physical, mental, emotional, or social limitations . . . Three specific areas of professional services are employed to provide this comprehensive leisure ability approach toward enabling appropriate leisure lifestyles: therapy, leisure education, and recreation participation. (National Therapeutic Recreation Society, 1982, p. 1)

This NTRS definition is broad, encompassing service delivery in accordance with both medical and educational models, and is particularly favored by community recreation proponents. Such specialists are typically employed by facilities financed by taxes (residential and day-care centers run by government agencies, schools, and parks and recreation departments) and are not directly concerned with generating revenues to pay bills or their salaries.

In contrast, many TRs are employed by private hospitals and rehabilitation centers or work in private practice. These individuals prefer a definition acceptable to health in-surance companies that pay fees for treatment and therapy. Key concepts in a definition that meets these needs are intervention, health, and well-being. ATRA thus adopted the following definition:

Therapeutic recreation—is the application, by qualified professionals, of appropriate intervention strategies, using recreation services to promote independent functioning and to enhance optimal health and well-being of individuals with illnesses and/or disabling conditions. Therapeutic recreation places a special emphasis on the development of an appropriate leisure lifestyle as an integral part of that independent functioning. (American Therapeutic Recreation Association, 1984, p. 2)

Central to both definitions is the promotion of positive leisure lifestyles. Leisure encompasses thoughts, feelings, attitudes, and behaviors. Traditionally, leisure was defined as discretionary or nonwork time. Contemporary theorists point out that leisure can be a state of mind that influences perception during both work and nonwork time. TRs focus, therefore, on helping persons to (a) assess life satisfaction; (b) set goals for learning and participating in activities that are healthy, pleasurable, satisfying, and self-actualizing; and (c) achieve these goals. Several professions share TR's interest in leisure: occupational therapy, education, and physical education.

TRs are competent in widely diversified program areas, such as music, dance, art, drama, horticulture, camping, and sports. They are also skilled in leisure education and counseling and assist persons in making the transition from institutions or schools to community recreation. TRs utilize all possible community resources (both human and physical) to make leisure rich, varied, satisfying, and self-actualizing.

The greatest difference between adapted physical educators and TRs lies in the scope of the program each is qualified to conduct. Adapted physical educators are responsible only for physical activities and the state of mind related to such activities. TRs are responsible for 10 or more widely diversified program areas. Both professions emphasize carryover values and use of community resources. Leisure-time education and counseling are performed by both types of specialist.

Occupational Therapists

The related service that is broadest in scope and most likely to overlap physical education services, particularly in infancy and early childhood programs, is *occupational therapy* (OT). In its early years, OT focused mainly on activities of daily living (ADL), particularly on the rehabilitation of arm and hand skills relevant to self-care, work, and leisure. Often, arts and crafts activities were the medium through which goals were achieved. OT, however, has changed tremendously. This is the official definition of OT:

Occupational therapy—is the therapeutic use of self-care, work, and play activities to increase independent function, enhance development, and prevent disability. (Hopkins & Smith, 1993, p. 4)

Whereas, in the past, OT was prescribed and directed by a physician, the American Occupation Therapy Association (AOTA) no longer requires this practice. Occupational therapists (OTs) now can determine treatment on the basis of their own assessments.

Traditionally, OTs worked in hospitals and rehabilitation centers. Today, over one third of the OTs in the United States work in school settings. Much of their focus in on infants, toddlers, and young children who need assistance in learning self-care activities to benefit from special education instruction (see Figure 3.3). OT has embraced a broad and holistic philosophy that enables its practitioners to do almost anything. Concurrently, the profession has developed high-quality training programs and certification standards.

Two levels of OTs work in schools and other settings: (a) registered occupational therapists (OTRs) and (b) certified occupational therapy assistants (COTAs). In addition to meeting other requirements, both must pass stiff national examinations (mostly multiple choice) to be eligible for employment. States that require licensure currently accept the professional organization's quality-control system. The major textbook used in OT training is *Willard and Spackman's Occupational Therapy* (Hopkins & Smith, 1993). The journal published by the professional organization is the *American Journal of Occupational Therapy*.

Physical Therapists

Traditionally, *physical therapy* (PT) has been defined as treatment that uses heat, cold, light, water, electricity, massage, ultrasound, exercise, and functional training. Physical therapists (PTs) devote much of their time to gait training and wheelchair use. Many work in sports medicine and orthopedic rehabilitation. They use therapeutic exercise to relieve pain, prevent deformity and further disability, develop or improve muscle strength or motor skills, and restore or maintain maximal functional capacities. *Functional training* refers to teaching the patient to use crutches, prostheses, and braces.

Most PTs work within a medical model. This means that they carry out an exercise prescription written by a physician. They also work with very sophisticated equipment, like that used in functional electrical stimulation (FES) which enables individuals with paralyzed legs to walk or use limbs, actions previously deemed impossible. State and national certification requirements are changing, however. Some states permit PTs to work without a physician prescription.

PTs belong to the American Physical Therapy Association (APTA), which publishes the journal *Physical Therapy*. Like OTs, they must pass a national certification examination administered by their national organization; there is also a system for certifying PT aides.

Corrective Therapists

Corrective therapy is an alternative certification area for persons who are especially interested in therapeutic exercise. Its definition is this:

Corrective therapy—is the applied science of medically prescribed therapeutic exercise, education, and adapted physical activities to improve the quality of life and health of adults and children by developing

physical fitness, increasing functional mobility and independence, and improving psychosocial behavior. The corrective therapist evaluates, develops, implements, and modifies adapted exercise programs for disease, injury, congenital defects, and other functional disabilities. (Purvis, 1985, p. 5)

Persons especially interested in corrective therapy affiliate with an organization called the American Kinesiotherapy Association, Inc. (new name in 1988), which publishes *Clinical Kinesiology*. Previously known as the *American Corrective Therapy Journal* (1967–1987) and the *Journal of the Association for Physical and Mental Rehabilitation* (1946–1966), this resource was the first periodical to evolve for adapted physical activity.

Arts Educators and Therapists

The arts are extremely helpful in assisting persons with disabilities to benefit from special education instruction and to live rich, full lives (Boswell, 1989; Sherrill, 1979). The National Dance Association (NDA) of AAHPERD is an extremely supportive resource on dance for special populations. Periodically, articles on this topic appear in the *Journal of Physical Education, Recreation and Dance* (see the November/December 1989 issue), and conference programs are offered.

Dance, although now recognized as a discipline separate from physical education, has traditionally been part of the training of the well-rounded physical educator. Chapter 16 focuses on the use of dance.

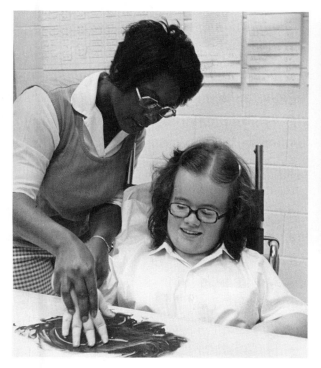

Many educators believe that the arts (appropriately adapted) are particularly valuable in teaching self-help skills, language, and socialization. An arts-oriented approach to adapted physical activity blends music, dance, drama, and the visual/graphic arts with the teaching of movement. The resulting emphasis on movement exploration to a variety of sounds and tempos (music); colors, shapes, and textures (art); and thematic ideas (drama) stimulates creative behaviors and builds self-confidence.

Also acting as proponents of the arts are several professions, each of which has its own organization: *music therapy* (founded in 1950), *dance therapy* (1966), and *art therapy* (1969). By utilizing the expertise of arts educators and therapists, adapted physical educators can enrich learnings about the body and its capacity for creative movement and artistic expression (see Figure 3.4).

Professional Organizations, Journals, and Other Resources

Both regular and adapted physical activity professionals maintain membership in the American Alliance for Health, Physical Education, Recreation and Dance (AAHPERD), which has its headquarters in Reston, Virginia, just outside of Washington, DC. AAHPERD comprises seven independent organizations, and members select two of these when joining. The organization within AAHPERD of most interest to adapted physical activity people is the American Association for Active Lifestyles and Fitness (AAALF), which houses the Adapted Physical Activity Council (APAC). This council, alone and in conjunction with other AAHPERD structures, offers many educational ses-

sions at annual national conferences, develops recommendations for policy, and provides advocacy services that help keep the profession strong. AAHPERD members can choose to receive several journals. Among these are the *Journal of Physical Education, Recreation and Dance (JOPERD),* the *Research Quarterly for Exercise and Sport,* and *Strategies.*

Physical educators also affiliate with regional, state, and local branches of AAHPERD, with the National Consortium for Physical Education and Recreation for Individuals with Disabilities (NCPERID), and with the International Federation of Adapted Physical Activity (IFAPA) and its regional affiliates. Addresses for these organizations appear in Appendix D. Information about these organizations appears in Chapter 1.

Adapted physical educators subscribe to specialized journals like the *Adapted Physical Activity Quarterly (APAQ), Palaestra: The Forum of Sport and Physical Education for the Disabled,* and *Clinical Kinesiology,* formerly the *American Corrective Therapy Journal.* The year 1984 marked the beginning of both *APAQ* and *Palaestra,* strong recognition that adapted physical activity was becoming increasingly scholarly and versatile (see Figure 3.5). Addresses for these journals appear in Appendix E.

Many adapted physical educators are also active in the Council for Exceptional Children (CEC), read its journals, and rely on its excellent Department of Governmental Relations for leadership in legislation and advocacy. The CEC has its national headquarters in Reston, Virginia.

The CEC publishes the excellent resource journals *Exceptional Children* and *Teaching Exceptional Children.* The CEC has 14 divisions, each with its own officers, conference programs, and journals. Illustrative of these separate structures

FIGURE 3.5 Dr. Claudine Sherrill (*right*) and Dr. Wanda Rainbolt survey resources for learning.

Send: majordomo@indiana.edu
Subject: skip this line, go directly to message
Message: subscribe ulrich_adapted your user name

The Need for Teamwork

The helping professions, including adapted physical activity, have changed tremendously in recent years. As the knowledge explosion continues and the economy of the nation ebbs and flows, professionals must become increasingly adept at coping with transience. Persons who work in the psychomotor domain, regardless of disciplinary affiliation, have much to gain through unification and cooperation. New models of person-centered service delivery systems are replacing traditional unidisciplinary systems.

Interactions with other professions should begin in the undergraduate years. Consider the commonalities among the helping professions: (a) each has its earliest roots in medicine; (b) each is extending its scope in response to new legislation; and (c) each is dedicated to the self-actualization of persons with disabilities.

Professional boundaries among disciplines are becoming more and more ambiguous (Blumenkopf, Levangie, & Nelson, 1985). The following are some common ambiguities and misconceptions:

1. Therapists often see themselves as responsible for *individualized* exercise and physical educators for *group* exercise. This is not a valid perception, because adapted physical educators, like special educators, work on a one-to-one basis when needed.

2. Cane- and crutch-walking procedures and wheelchair transfers were once believed to belong to the therapies, but now many public school physical educators teach them.

3. Recreation specialists often believe that theirs is the major discipline concerned with play, but OTs also consider play a major goal.

4. Sensory integration therapy is conducted by many professionals. Its originator, Jean Ayres, stated that it "may be carried out by educators, psychologists, or health-related professionals" (Ayres, 1972, p. ix).

5. Adapted physical educators sometimes naively assume that physical and occupational therapy curricula do not include content on legislation and writing individualized education programs (IEPs). Therapists change their curricula in accordance with new legislation, just as educators do.

These commonalities emphasize the importance of every professional's developing as many skills as possible. During economic crises, when job markets narrow, the major criteria for employing adapted physical educators will be breadth and depth of competence, excellence in work performance, high energy level, and good personality (i.e., the demonstrated ability to get along well with others).

Team Approaches

Numerous combinations of individuals function as teams to implement the goal of active, healthy lifestyles. Adapted physical

are the Division for Early Childhood, the Division for Learning Disabilities, the Council for Educational Diagnostic Services, and the Teacher Education Division. Like AAHPERD, the CEC has state organizations and student memberships. At the university level, there are often student CEC clubs. A good crossdisciplinary activity is for physical education majors to attend CEC campus meetings and offer to conduct a program on adapted physical education.

Physical educators may also belong to organizations that focus on one condition. One of the oldest and most influential of these is the American Association on Mental Retardation (AAMR), founded in 1876. AAMR publishes two research-oriented journals: *Mental Retardation* and the *American Journal of Mental Retardation.* AAMR also establishes the official terminology and definitions used in mental retardation.

Another excellent resource is the *Journal of Special Education* and other journals published by the Pro•Ed Company (see Appendix E). The special education profession offers many rich resources, and many physical education majors elect courses in this area. In some states, adapted physical educators are required to earn special education certification.

Computer networks are also a valuable resource. Information on these is given in Appendixes C, D, and E for organizations that offer computer services. Of particular significance is a listserv specifically on adapted physical activity made possible through the North American Federation of Adapted Physical Activity (NAFAPA) and Dale Ulrich, a professor at Indiana University. To subscribe to this listserv, use these e-mail commands:

activity specialists often assume leadership in suggesting team approaches, promoting day-to-day cooperation, and coordinating human resources. Teams are typically categorized by purpose (e.g., teaching, IEP, CAPE) or by structure and type of cooperation (e.g., multidisciplinary, interdisciplinary, crossdisciplinary).

Team Teaching

Team teaching utilizes the resources of two or more individuals in achieving instructional goals. Team members share the same space, time, and students in creative ways that permit optimal individualization. Usually one person is designated as lead teacher and the others as assistants. Assistants often assume responsibility for teaching stations and resource areas for students with special needs. Whether classes are large or small, the inclusion of an adapted physical educator as a team member increases the probability of meeting individual needs and achieving inclusion goals.

The homework concept uses parents, grandparents, siblings, and significant others in the neighborhood as members of home-school-community teams that strive to reinforce classroom instruction. Parents may guide physical education homework or employ a high school or university student to serve as teacher. This latter pattern can provide male role models for children in single-parent families. Adult athletes with disabilities may also be employed as school homework team members.

IEP, IFSP, CAPE, and RPEI Teams

Several types of placement teams are used to reach consensus about the most desirable type of physical activity programming. Federal law mandates individualized education program (IEP) and individualized family service plan (IFSP) teams to share decision making about placement, goals, objectives, and services for students with disabilities (see Chapters 4 and 18). IEP teams are for students ages 3 to 21, whereas IFSP teams are for infants and toddlers. For both types of teams, law requires that individuals be present who represent parental, administrative, instructional, and diagnostic roles. Physical educators may be asked to submit assessment data and recommendations to teams or to attend meetings and interact directly with team members.

Personal ethics and moral beliefs about equal opportunity lead physical educators to establish similar teams for students who do not qualify for special education services but nevertheless require assistance to achieve physical education goals. Committee on Adapted Physical Education (CAPE) and Regular Physical Education Initiative (RPEI) teams are two approaches to program decisions for nondisabled students.

School districts should establish a CAPE that addresses needs of students not covered by law. The CAPE should include at least three members (e.g., an adapted physical educator, the school nurse, and the director of physical education or a designee). Procedures to be followed by CAPEs are similar to those of IEP teams, and the outcome is an individualized physical education program (IPEP) to guide services (Short, 1995).

Frequently, it is easier to make programming decisions by using the resources of the student's school and immediate neighborhood rather than the whole school district. In this case, a regular physical education initiative (RPEI) committee

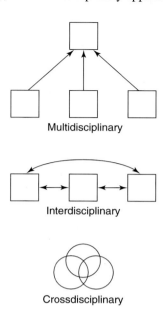

FIGURE 3.6   Models depicting multidisciplinary, interdisciplinary, and crossdisciplinary approaches.

or team can be established. This team is chaired by the regular physical educator or designee and is composed of family members and other resources who can provide support services to the regular physical educator. The RPEI team is similar to mainstream assistance or teacher assistance teams currently in use in academic areas to promote solution of learning problems in the regular classroom (Fuchs, Fuchs, & Bahr, 1990).

ADA and 504 Committees

Other groups that frequently include physical activity professionals have advisory or due-process functions that relate to laws or sections of laws, such as the Americans with Disabilities Act (ADA) (Block, 1995) and Section 504 of the Rehabilitation Act (French, Kinnison, Sherrill, & Henderson, in press). **Due process** refers to the right of an individual to fair treatment as guaranteed by the Fifth and Fourteenth Amendments to the U.S. Constitution. In particular, physical educators are responsible for ascertaining that sport, dance, and exercise programs are accessible to individuals with disabilities (see Chapter 4) and for advocating the importance of lifespan physical activity for all.

Multidisciplinary, Interdisciplinary, Crossdisciplinary

Figure 3.6 depicts the multi-, inter-, and crossdisciplinary approaches. Professionals need to understand each approach and think critically about how to move from multidisciplinary to inter- and crossdisciplinary teamwork.

Multi- means "many." **Multidisciplinary** refers to involvement of many disciplines in the service delivery process. Federal law, since 1975, has required that many professionals provide input into the evaluation (assessment) of individuals with disabilities and the IEP process. This mandate is implemented in most school systems by having several professionals independently assess a student. Each professional then writes a report of findings and submits it to the chair of the IEP meeting. Sometimes professionals are invited to attend the IEP meeting and present their report, but this is often not the case. The work of each professional tends to parallel that of other team members. According to Klein (1990, p. 56), the multidisciplinary approach is "additive, not integrative." It provides different perspectives, but synthesis and interpretation are left to a responsible individual or committee.

Inter- means "between." **Interdisciplinary** refers to cooperation between two or more persons from different disciplines in a joint project (e.g., conducting assessment, providing service, writing a report, working for consensus on a placement decision). Interdisciplinary teams work together closely, sharing the same space and time, but members are careful to respect disciplinary boundaries. Service delivery is mostly integrated but sometimes constrained by disciplinary defensiveness.

Cross- or *trans-* means "across." **Crossdisciplinary** refers to holistic, multigoal, multilevel sharing in which disciplinary boundaries are crossed, and the coordination of efforts is maximized by team members' helping each other to gain and use the combined, integrated knowledge of all the disciplines. Traditional names of disciplines are seldom used, because emphasis is on the whole rather than the parts. This type of teamwork is far more comprehensive in scope and vision than the others and requires many years to develop. It often evolves from intensive interdisciplinary sharing in which members begin to learn and use knowledge not traditionally associated with their field. They "cross over" more and more in job performance and eventually become crossdisciplinary as cooperative teaching/learning among members leads to a common knowledge base.

Applications to Adapted Physical Activity

A central theme of this textbook is that adapted physical activity has a crossdisciplinary knowledge base. Many types of teamwork are used in translating this knowledge into practice. This chapter emphasizes that regular physical educators are often expected to provide adapted physical activity in inclusive settings. They need not feel alone, however, if they understand team approaches. Moreover, an important part of their teaching success is knowing when and how to ask for help from an adapted physical activity specialist.

Communication Competencies

Effective communication underlies all of the PAP-TE-CA competencies but is especially important in teamwork interactions, the coordination of resources, consulting, advocacy, and attitude change (see the discussion of PAP-TE-CA competencies, pages 17–19). Professionals must have good skills in listening, observing, speaking, discussing, writing, and reading, and be able to adapt their communication styles to individuals of different ages, educational levels, socioeconomic backgrounds, genders, ethnic groups, native languages, and cultural backgrounds. This means flexibility in choice of vocabulary, careful selection of words and phrases that are nonbiased, and staying abreast of current events so as to be able to converse on a number of topics. This latter ability is essential to establishing rapport (i.e., finding areas of mutual interest) and assessing beliefs and attitudes that may impact on future interactions.

Facilitating Interpersonal Comfort

Books and articles on interviewing and conducting qualitative research are helpful in improving communication skills (Bogdan & Biklen, 1992). Individuals must feel at ease before open and honest sharing can occur. Conversation about mutual interests and concerns therefore serves as a warm-up. Eye contact, dress, postures, position and distance in relation to each other, gestures, and facial expressions all contribute to feeling at ease, but these variables have different meanings in different cultures. For example, white people of middle-class background typically appreciate good eye contact, but people of other cultures may find this disrespectful or threatening. Formal training in communication and group dynamics theory is helpful in understanding differences, but skill in observation offers insight into how others are relating to you.

Using Specific Communication Strategies

In individual and small-group settings, people tend to communicate best with people they like and respect. Engaging in cooperative activities promotes these feelings, particularly if you are perceived as a good listener. Skills related to listening include appropriate eye contact, head nods, and encouraging verbal cues (e.g., "Uh-huh," "I understand," "Really?"). Also important is **reflective listening,** the spontaneous restatement in summary form of ideas presented by the speaker. Such restatement assures the speaker that his or her message is heard and is viewed as important (Seaman & Heilbuth, 1988). Reflective listening also is a technique for encouraging speakers to continue, thereby giving more depth and substance to the shared meaning. **Asking questions** is the joint art of wording and timing so as to obtain the most comprehensive answer possible. This means avoiding questions that elicit yes-or-no answers. Good listening also involves openness, acceptance, and careful avoidance of facial expressions, words, or gestures that might imply bias or discomfort.

Coordination of resources often involves calling and conducting meetings. The purpose of these meetings may be consensus as in IEP meetings or open sharing as in focus group meetings. The purpose of a meeting should be clearly stated at the time of invitation and again as the meeting is opened. In **consensus groups,** leadership centers on allowing team members equal opportunity to express their views and on promoting reflective listening by other team members to maximize understanding. When all possible solutions appear to have been listed, the leader guides team members in prioritizing the solutions and reaching a majority agreement. In **focus groups,** leaders engage team members in open sharing of perceptions and concerns on a particular topic in a permissive, accepting environment in which no voting occurs. Reflective listening is used, and the chair avoids expressing her or his views. Focus groups are excellent sources of information to guide decision makers who want to be sure they have heard all sides (Schleien, Meyer, Heyne, & Brandt, 1995).

Communication skills differ for individual, small-, and large-group settings. In general, the ideal size for a focus group

FIGURE 3.7   A model depicting persuasive communication theory.

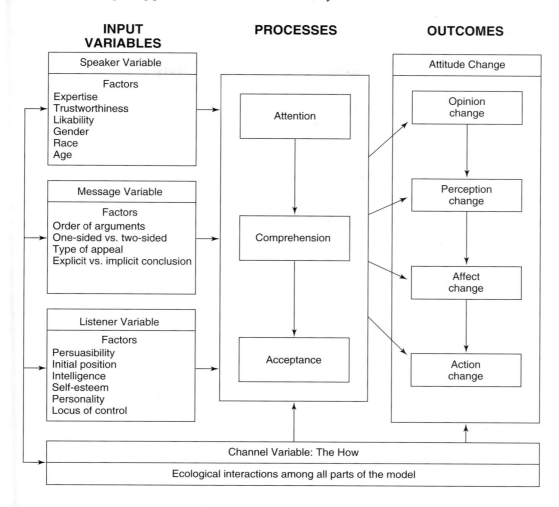

is seven (Schleien et al., 1995). Little control can be exerted over the size of consensus meetings for IEP committees, but the average number attending is five. Seating arrangements are important. First, individuals with visual and auditory impairments must be accommodated (i.e., placed where they can see the most faces or hear the best; where lighting is best). Second, individuals new to the group or shy should be placed opposite the moderator, where eye contact is readily established. Strong leaders or domineering people should be convinced to sit in corner positions at a table (the weak positions) because they will persevere regardless of seating. The moderator should sit at the head of the table.

Major Communication Theories

Many theories underlie strategies used in individual and group communication. Some of these are explained in Chapters 7 and 9 in relation to consulting and attitude-change competencies. Two theories, however, are so important to teamwork and advocacy that they are introduced now. The first, persuasive communication theory, is particularly applicable to consensus meetings, advocacy initiatives, and other settings where your goal is to change opinions or attitudes so that everyone will vote or act in a particular way. The second, social cognitive communication theory, helps you to understand how contact

affects cognition and decision making. Following are terms basic to critical thinking about theories.

Variables, Factors, Levels

Both of the theories just mentioned indicate input variables that professionals should understand and skillfully manage. A **variable** is a dimension of a human being, relationship, task, or environment that can be changed. Variables typically are broken down into **factors,** which are analyzed into **levels.** For example, speaker, message, audience, and channels are input variables that affect process and outcome. Speaker is then subdivided into factors like expertise, gender, and occupation. Each of these in turn is analyzed into levels (e.g., high and low expertise, female and male gender, teaching and nonteaching occupations). These theories are presented to encourage critical thinking about how to manage variables so as to make communication more effective.

Persuasive Communication Theory

Persuasive communication theory focuses on attitude change as the desired outcome of effective communication (see Figure 3.7). Attitudes are conceptualized as multidimensional and hierarchical. Figure 3.7 shows that opinions, perceptions, emotions, and actions can all be changed (see the outcomes column). If opinions (cognition) can be changed, it follows that the other dimensions of attitude will adapt and realign themselves to be consistent with the new opinions. Information is considered the primary method for changing attitudes, and all variables pertaining to information are carefully managed: (a) speaker factors (*who* presents the information), (b) message or content factors (*what* is presented), (c) listener factors (*who* receives the information), and (d) channel factors (*how* the message is delivered, everything within the listening, receiving environment).

Many speaker factors influence opinion change. Chief among these is the extent to which listeners perceive the speaker to be knowledgeable (e.g., have actual experience and thus expertise), trustworthy (e.g., have no hidden motives and thus tell it as it is), and likable. If the speaker is perceived to hold high status and/or to be valued by one's significant others, then the content is likely to receive more attention than if status is perceived as average or low. Persons with disabilities who are successful athletes or professionals are among the most powerful sources.

Demographic variables like race, religion, gender, age, and occupation are more important to some persons than to others. Matching characteristics of a speaker with those of the audience is often strategic. Adolescents, for example, may be more influenced by peers than by adults. One secret to attitude change is knowing the speaker variables most significant to a particular group.

Message factors that influence attention, comprehension, and acceptance are listed in Figure 3.7. Illustrative questions that should be asked about message factors are these:

1. **In planning the order of arguments, should the strongest come first or last?**

   Answer: First, in most cases.

2. **Should the argument be one-sided or two-sided?**

   Answer: Generally, two-sided (i.e., both pros and cons) is best, especially when (a) students are opposed to the desired position and/or (b) students will be exposed later to counterarguments.

3. **What type of appeal (emotional vs. factual) is more effective?**

   Answer: Depends on the audience and the topic under discussion.

4. **Which type of conclusion (explicit or implicit) is better?**

   Answer: Explicit; explain clearly the attitudes and behaviors desired and the recommendations for achieving them. Use implicit conclusions (e.g., make up your own mind) only with a very intelligent, mature audience.

Figure 3.7 also indicates that several listener variables are related to opinion change: (a) persuasibility, (b) initial position, (c) intelligence, (d) self-esteem, and (e) personality. How these relate, however, depends on the nature of the information, the intensity of the initial position, the function the attitude plays in one's life, and the perceived consequences of change.

Space does not permit further elaboration on persuasive communication theory. However, attempting to modify attitudes by means of persuasion techniques is both an art and a science based on research literature that continues to grow and change. Carl Hovland, director of the Yale University Communication Research Program, is acknowledged as the father of this theory, which is also called the Yale approach and was first posited in the early 1950s. Consider how persuasion can be through direct methods (lectures, one-to-one talks, small-group discussions, films, presentations by persons who are disabled) or indirect methods (personal contact, role playing, or simulating activities of persons who are different).

Social Cognitive Communication Theory

Social cognitive communication theory focuses on the importance of situational or environmental variables, especially those affecting social contact. Theorists posit that team work and communication are affected at least as much by social context as by information processing as emphasized in persuasive communication theory (Bandura, 1986; Bem, 1972; Lewin, 1951). Figure 3.8 presents a model that synthesizes several theories that relate to communication. The model is called dynamic because it is nonlinear, multilevel, and continuous. Arrows are multidirectional to indicate the dynamic interactiveness of all components.

Input Considerations

Figure 3.8 indicates that social contact variables provide the input that stimulates cognition and feeling (affect). These processes merge to cause cognitive comfort or discomfort, which in turn results in social action change and new or modified feelings. This model is especially helpful in planning and evaluating teamwork. Professionals should skillfully manage contact variables when they desire (a) effective partnerships, (b) team cohesiveness and productivity, or (c) acceptance or inclusion of a new or different group member. The model in Figure 3.8, while directed toward adult teamwork and communication, is applicable also to classroom settings.

Look at the input column. Goal, status, time, intensity, and control variables have been broken down into factors that, in turn, can be analyzed into levels. Goal, for example, can be broken down into amount of focus (lots, little), type of sharing (mutual, unidirectional), and meaningfulness (equal to all members, unequal; high, low). Status can be broken down into factors that represent equal, greater, or lesser status between a new member and group members. Levels of each type of status might relate to competence, race, gender, dress, income, and so on, depending on how a particular group forms opinions about status. Each variable in the input column should be given careful thought, especially when convening a new group or changing the goal of an established group. Skill in this kind of analysis enables the team leader or teacher to adapt the social contact climate within the ecosystem so that the desired results are produced.

In regard to the input column, most research supports the management of variables so that the following occurs: high focus on a specific, well-understood goal; goal-related activity that maximizes sharing, interacting, and meaning; equal-status relationships; high frequency of interactions; long duration of interactions; short intervals between interactions; high-intensity

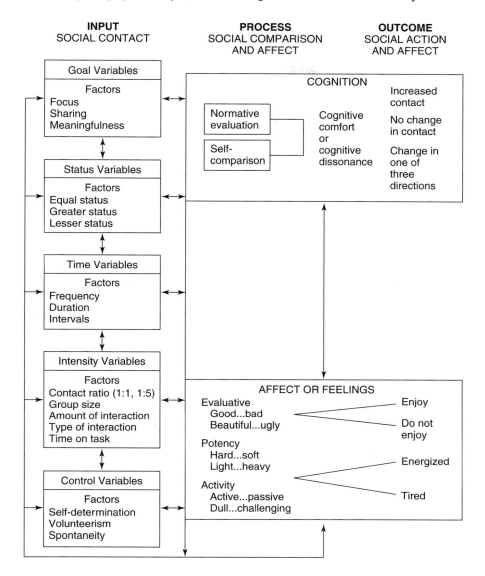

involvement characterized by low ratios, small groups, and emphasis on time on task; and internal locus of control, with lots of options and choices within the meeting or activity structure (Allport, 1954; Tripp, French, & Sherrill, 1995). Much research is needed on these input variables, however, because their viability is affected by ecosystem, situational, and other variables that change from day to day and from group to group.

Process Considerations

Process, although complex, centers on social comparison and affect. In this model, social comparison theory (Festinger, 1954) provides the framework for understanding how the mind processes input. The social comparison process encompasses two central ideas: (a) normative evaluation and (b) self-comparison. The first concerns perceptions about how significant others believe and act; this represents "the norm" in psychosocial theories. The second involves the comparison of all aspects of self (e.g., opinions, beliefs, behaviors) with those of significant others.

The two-part social comparison process results in either psychological consonance (comfort) or dissonance (discomfort), because most individuals believe and act like others in their immediate social groups (i.e., family, friends, church, work). For example, if we are part of the norm or the majority, we feel comfortable and tend to identify strongly with what is happening. If we perceive that we are a minority of one or two, we experience **cognitive dissonance,** psychological discomfort that results from a realization of lack of congruence or consistency between self and significant others. This cognitive dissonance motivates individuals to act in ways that reduce the discomfort: (a) to change self in the direction of the norm, (b) to try to change the group norm, or (c) to reject the group norm as wrong or irrelevant. Professionals who understand social comparison processes can direct their skills toward supporting either majority or minority beliefs and actions and helping people change in desired ways.

Desired outcomes are often influenced by enjoyment and other feelings that interact in various ways with cognition (Scanlan & Simons, 1992; Scanlan, Carpenter, Schmidt, Simons, & Keeler, 1993). Figure 3.8 therefore depicts an affect or feelings variable with three factors (evaluative, potency, and activity) that link personal meaning of input to such feelings as enjoyment and energy. The three factors come from semantic differential theory (Osgood, Suci, & Tannenbaum, 1957), which uses polar adjectives and 7-point scales to assess personal meaning of something. This part of the model challenges professionals to consider feelings that stem from social contact and how these feelings are linked to personal meaning and accompanying feelings. Research indicates that enjoyment is strongly related to commitment and continued involvement in an activity or a project (Scanlan et al., 1993).

Outcome Considerations

Professionals seek many outcomes when they interact with other team members in service delivery. Dynamic systems social cognitive communication theory, like persuasive communication theory, gives attention to both affect and action change. Study of the two models in this section has familiarized the reader with the importance of critical thinking about variables, factors, and levels. Study has also promoted the development of **concepts,** a synonym for variables that have been carefully analyzed into factors and levels and woven into theories or models. **Concepts** can also be defined as basic ideas. Stop now, and try to summarize the many concepts presented in the two communication models.

Note that the teaching-and-learning process is largely a matter of communication. Both models can be adapted to guide aspects of physical education pedagogy. Communication can, in fact, be considered one part of the grand theory, adaptation, that underlies adapted physical activity service delivery.

Adaptation Theory

Adapted physical activity takes its name from the process of adapting. It seems fitting, therefore, to call this body of knowledge *adaptation theory.* Ernst Kiphard of Germany was the first to suggest that a theory of motor adaptation should be evolved to describe the work of adapted physical educators. Kiphard (1983) stressed individual and environmental interactions as a means of maintaining homeostasis (a state of dynamic equilibrium). Persons not only adapt to the environment but alter and change the environment each time they respond to it (i.e., adaptation is a reciprocal process).

Adapted physical activity, as a profession and emerging discipline, potentially has many theories, but adaptation seems an appropriate central theme to guide **theorizing,** the process of critically thinking about relationships among concepts (variables) and systematically constructing theories. Experts define theories in many ways (Fawcett & Downs, 1992). A simple definition follows: A **theory** is a cluster of interrelated concepts that enhances understanding of a phenomenon. Theories may be used to describe, explain, or predict.

Following are some interrelated concepts about the adaptation phenomenon.

1. Adaptation is the fundamental process of change that underlies survival, health, wellness, and self-actualization.

2. Adaptation is an interactive, dynamic, bidirectional process involving the individual and the environment (i.e., ecosystem) in facilitating desired change. Thus adaptation focuses on complex, multidimensional relationships, not on the individual apart from the environment.

3. Adaptation can be either spontaneous (part of the natural self-organizing and self-actualizing process) or purposively initiated by self or others (reasoned, planned, focused) to achieve a specific goal.

4. Adaptation, whether spontaneous or purposive, entails modifying, adjusting, or accommodating relationships within the ecosystem (person, environment, task) in accordance with assessed needs. This assessment may be formal or informal, conscious or unconscious.

5. Adaptation, within the adapted physical activity context, is the unifying theme in creating and using knowledge about four variables: (a) physical activity, (b) individual and ecosystem differences, (c) service delivery, and (d) empowerment.

6. Adaptation requires skillful use of family, school, and community resources in promoting lifespan active, healthy lifestyles for all.

7. Adaptation occurs at many levels, ranging from micro to macro. At the micro level, the emphasis is on variables and task analysis. At the macro level, the focus is on service delivery and empowerment.

Adaptation and Analysis of Variables

To address psychomotor problems, physical educators must carefully assess all of the interacting variables in the teaching-and-learning process (see Figure 3.9). Consider, for instance, the individual differences in needs pertaining to physical environment for individuals with visual, auditory, cognitive, and mobility impairments. After assessing both the environment and the learner, the professional carefully plans and structures all aspects of the physical and social environment and then specifies instructional and task variables that will maximize success.

The joint process of assessing and decision making about all the variables that affect learning is called **ecological task analysis.** It is a complex, time-consuming activity but well worth the effort. Other types of task analysis are used also. For example, a task like throwing can be analyzed into developmental progressions that indicate easy to difficult challenges for most individuals. These progressions can be quantitative (e.g., throw 2 feet, now 5 feet, now 10 feet) or qualitative (e.g., meet criteria for various age-appropriate throws like trunk rotation, weight transfer, and follow-through). Assumptions about the ease of a task, however, should never be made. A motor development progression based on norms for the nondisabled population might not be applicable to an individual with a disability. The only way to maximize performance success is to

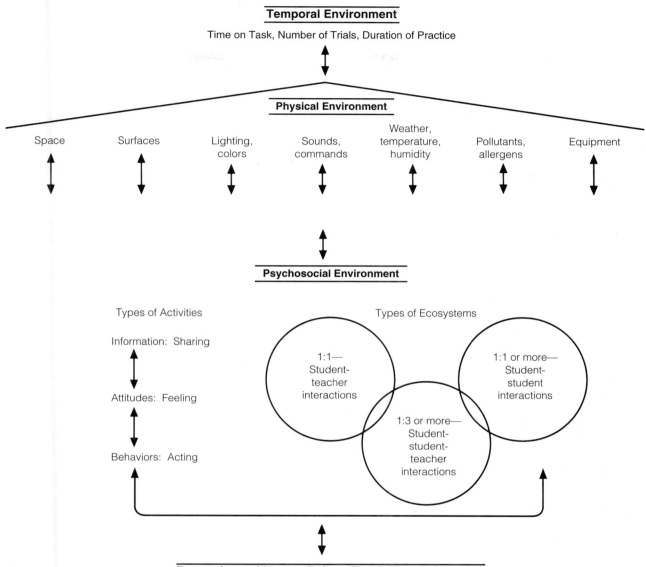

Temporal Environment

Time on Task, Number of Trials, Duration of Practice

Physical Environment

| Space | Surfaces | Lighting, colors | Sounds, commands | Weather, temperature, humidity | Pollutants, allergens | Equipment |

Psychosocial Environment

Types of Activities

Information: Sharing

Attitudes: Feeling

Behaviors: Acting

Types of Ecosystems

1:1— Student-teacher interactions

1:3 or more— Student-student-teacher interactions

1:1 or more— Student-student interactions

Perceptions of Human Beings That Influence Learning

What We See	**What We Hear**	**What We Smell**	**What We Feel**
Model or demonstration	Verbal instructions	Perfumes	Physical touch
Facial expression	Voice	Soap/water	Close/distant
Gestures	Footsteps	Bad breath	Light/heavy touch
Postures	Breathing	Perspiration	Firm/weak grasp
Clothing/style	Gum chewing	Tobacco	Short/long contact
Height/weight	Gestures	Alcohol	Friendly/unfriendly
Body proportions	Clothing	Garlic	Hot/cold
Eye contact, how much	Background		Rough/smooth skin
Locomotion, how much	Distracting		
	Facilitating		

assess and then adapt variables as needed for each individual within her or his ecosystem.

Interacting Variables

The science and art of adapting physical activity are inextricably linked with decision making about variables. In adapted physical activity, thousands of variables are operative. Figure 3.9, for example, shows several categories of input variables that interact in the teaching-and-learning process. Time or trials is featured as a major instructional variable because research shows that *time on task* determines amount of learning. Teachers make many decisions about use of time that students either honor or sabotage.

The seven variables with bidirectional arrows beneath them emphasize that adaptation of these variables is continuous, dynamic, and bidirectional. For example, space factors determine the kinds of movements and games that can be taught. Human beings interact with space, however, to change it in many ways. Adapted physical activity specialists take time to analyze these factors and determine conditions under which students learn best. They recognize that information, actions, and attitudes/feelings influence each other.

The interlocking circles show how interpersonal relations affect teaching and learning. Each represents a different kind of relationship. Beneath the circles are lists of human variables that teachers and students perceive in different ways. Most of these can be altered to enhance learning, but some, like height and body proportions, are relatively stable. Teachers give careful attention to these variables, altering self and environment in accordance with students' assessed needs.

Consider, for example, how what you wear may affect approach/avoidance behaviors. What do students see, hear, smell, and feel while you are teaching? How does this vary from student to student?

The following variables can be altered to promote success:

1. **Temporal environment variables.** These include how you structure use of time and determine appropriate speed of instructions and activities.
   a. Planned time, unplanned time.
   b. Time on task, number of trials within time period.
   c. Duration of time for each set of instructions and other parts of lesson.
   d. Time intervals between cues, performance, correction, reinforcement.

2. **Physical environment variables.** These include
   a. Space—open, closed; blank or structured by lines, ropes, or barriers; large or small; moving like a swing or escalator, or stationary.
   b. Support, wall, and ceiling surfaces—their stability and colors; their influence on sound, lighting, and movement. The support surface, for example, can be moving or stationary when the goal is to enhance balance. Or the walls and ceilings can be made to move.
   c. Lighting—bright, dull; direct, indirect; positioning to avoid looking into the sun.

   d. Sound—loud, average, soft; clear, muffled; use of music and various kinds of accompaniment to guide or structure movement.
   e. Temperature and humidity.
   f. Allergens, pollens, molds, dust.
   g. Equipment for play, sport, exercise, mobility, communication. Which equipment is brought by student (e.g., wheelchair, communication device) and which is supplied by teacher.

3. **Object or equipment variables.** Balls, for example, can be described in terms of the following categories:
   a. Size—small, medium, large, or 8-inch, 10-inch, 13-inch.
   b. Weight—light, medium, heavy, or 5 oz, 1 lb, or 6 lb.
   c. Color—blue ball against white background, yellow or orange ball against a black background.
   d. Surface—*smooth* like a balloon or leather ball; *rough* with tiny indentations like a basketball; *cushy* with many soft, rubber, hairlike projections; consistent or changing.
   e. Texture—soft, firm, or hard; consistent or inconsistent.
   f. Sound—silent, beeping loud or soft, jingling with bells, or rattling with noisemakers.
   g. Shape—round, oblong, or irregular.
   h. Movement—stationary or moving.

4. **Psychosocial environmental variables.** This refers to attitudes/feelings about self and others. It encompasses the nature and number of persons sharing the space, how they are perceived by the teacher and the learner, and how they affect learning. Is only one person recognized as the teacher, or are several individuals helping and sometimes giving conflicting directions? Are peers viewed as supportive, indifferent, neutral, or hostile? What are expectations, reactions, and actions? Are partners and peer tutors used?

5. **Learner variables.** These include interest, previous experience, level of sport socialization, personal meaning of a new skill or activity, modality preferences, learning style, self-concept, strengths and weaknesses, and demographics like age, gender, race, and socioeconomic class. Strengths and weaknesses can be categorized by domains (cognitive, affective, psychomotor) or by specific fitness and movement abilities.

6. **General instructional or informational variables.** These include teaching style, type of feedback, method of presenting new material, level of assistance during practice, structured use of time, and physical distance between learner and teacher. Of particular importance is model type. The model may be the teacher or a student who is similar or dissimilar to the learner. Models may be silent or verbal.

7. **Task variables.** These include specific instructions about the task to be learned or practiced. These vary, of course, for locomotor, object propulsion, and object reception tasks. If the task is to throw a ball, the following factors should be considered:
   a. Speed—fast, medium, slow; constant or changing.
   b. Pathway—horizontal, vertical, arc.

c. Direction—constant, changing; to midline, preferred side, or nonpreferred side; forward, backward; to a target or unspecified.

d. Height—way above head, eye level, chest or waist level, ground level.

e. Accuracy—no error, some error, lots of error.

f. Force—hard, medium, soft.

Adaptation theory posits that professionals who are knowledgeable about variables are able to match abilities with content and teaching style to create optimal learning opportunities. **To adapt** means to make suitable, to adjust, or to modify in accordance with individual needs. *Adaptation involves individualization.* For some persons, *adapt* may mean to make a task easier, but for others, the challenge is to make it harder or more interesting. For most, *adapt* simply means to find another way: to experiment, discover, create!

Adaptation and Service Delivery

Adapting is important in all aspects of service delivery. Each of the seven services constituting the PAP-TE-CA model in Chapter 1 (planning, assessment, prescription/placement, teaching/counseling/coaching, evaluation, coordination of resources, and advocacy) are made more viable by appropriate adaptation. Although these services are described in considerable detail later in the text, an overview of adapting in relation to each is presented here to assist in planning practicum experiences.

Planning

Most university students have little control over the people they are assigned for practicum work. Planning thus requires getting ready for anything. Visiting ahead of time, getting acquainted with staff and facilities, and acquiring general information about the neighborhood and such variables as ethnic group, socioeconomic status, and leisure-time practices are helpful.

Whenever possible, obtain photograph and videotape clearance for your practicum student. Access to files is also essential. Discussing these needs with supervisory personnel and sharing ideas about responsibilities and benefits creates the structure for an optimal practicum experience.

Planning, after the initial meeting, involves getting acquainted, establishing rapport, and cooperatively agreeing on goals. For example, assume that you are assigned an 8-year-old named Bob who is receiving physical education in an integrated setting. A unit on catching and throwing is underway, and Bob's catching proficiency is far below that of his classmates.

Planning involves gathering information about relevant variables so that time and space can be used wisely. Instructional planning is often enhanced by asking Who? What? Where? When? and How? Let's consider each of these in relation to Bob:

Who? The *who* is obviously Bob, but this question also involves thinking through yours and Bob's relationship to the other students in the class. Should lessons be confined to interactions only between Bob and you (i.e., a pull-out type of instructional arrangement), or should

part of each class period be spent with other students? If the answer is other students, then which ones, how many, and in what roles?

What? The *what* is primarily the motor skill of catching because a multidisciplinary diagnostic team has already indicated that this is a major goal for the year. Specifics about catching, however, will be determined cooperatively by you and Bob as part of instructional assessment.

Where? The *where* is the location you select or are assigned for your one-to-one interactions with Bob. Negotiate for a private space with as few distractors as possible. Make a list of other important variables. What kind of equipment is needed? Do you want the same location for each lesson, or is it desirable to schedule different learning stations?

When? The *when* is the number of minutes allocated to physical education instruction each day. For example, if your time allotment is 30 min, how much of this time each day should be devoted to catching? Your decisions will depend largely on assessment data. The *when* variable can also involve your motivating Bob to spend after-school and weekend time on catching.

How? The *how* (pedagogy) should be related to assessment data and determined cooperatively by you and Bob. Find out what kinds of balls, gloves, backboards, and related equipment are available and the procedures to be used in reserving them. Often, you must create or purchase your own equipment. The practicum experience is a good time to begin your personal suitcase (preferably one with wheels) with homemade balls and other novel objects that enhance goal attainment (see Figure 3.10). *How* also involves planning to ascertain that Bob has balls at home for practice and that parents and significant others are motivated to help him.

In summary, planning is extremely complex because it relates to every aspect of service delivery. There is daily, weekly, and semester planning. Some of this is done by the teacher alone, but much of it is cooperative.

Assessment

Assessment involves examination of both the environment and the individual to determine what needs to be changed and what can remain the same. Environment is total lifespace (physical, social, and psychological) and can be broken down into hundreds of variables, each of which may affect behavior. Consider, for instance, how light and noise factors influence test results of persons with different disabilities.

In Bob's case, the goal is to learn to catch. Goals must be operationalized by breaking them down into behavioral objectives. Prior to establishing objectives, however, explore personal meaning. Does Bob care about learning to catch? Do his friends know how to catch? Does he have opportunities to play catching games? What kind of instruction has he already had? Where? By whom? Has he had previous

FIGURE 3.10 Physical educators need suitcases on wheels to transport their homemade equipment.

experiences that cause fear, anxiety, or doubt? Through question-and-answer interactions, teacher and student together cooperatively agree on the goal, verbalize it, and perhaps write it or sign a contract indicating intent to teach and learn.

Assessment is individualized to focus on strengths as well as weaknesses. What kinds of objects can the student catch? What movement variables must be addressed? The best way to find out is usually to ask the student and/or engage in cooperative problem solving. Together, teacher and student identify present level of performance, determine learning style, and work out details concerning pedagogy. This process should be activity oriented, fun, and free from anxiety. Encourage the student to discuss what task requirements he or she wants and/or needs. If Bob says, "Hey, I think I can catch that big yellow ball," then you may say, "Good, where do you want me to stand when I throw it?" Then a few tosses may be exchanged before other variables are brainstormed.

The level of task difficulty appropriate for Bob is established by experimenting with balls with varying object dimensions (size, weight, shape, color, texture, sound) and movement dimensions (speed, force, direction, pathway, height at moment of contact). Environmental and instructional variables also are considered. **Environmental variables** include (a) postures (sitting, standing, running), (b) use of glove/nature of glove, (c) lighting, (d) noise control and/or choice of verbal cues, (e) assistive devices to help with balance, and (f) floor or ground surface. **Instructional variables** that relate to task difficulty include amount of assistance needed, nature of assistance, length and wording of verbal instructions, and use of demonstrations. Thus, assessment focuses not only on what the student can do but also on environmental and instructional variables to be manipulated.

Prescription/Placement

Prescription/placement in the instructional setting refers to prescribing the objectives to be met and the activities needed for learning to occur. Specific behavioral objectives are cooperatively set by teacher and student, and amount of practice time and effort are agreed on. A **behavioral objective** is a specific statement that includes (a) condition, (b) observable behavior, and (c) criterion level. For example,

Condition: Given a ball of a certain size, weight, color, texture, and sound, thrown in a certain way from a set distance,

Observable behavior: Bob will perform a two-hand mature catch

Criterion level: in 7 out of 10 trials.

To achieve this objective, Bob may sign a contract in which he agrees to do 50 catches, with various balls under a variety of conditions, every class period for 6 weeks. Or he may agree to go to the catching station and practice a certain number of minutes three times a week. An important part of individualization is the student's understanding of both objective and process.

Teaching/Counseling/Coaching

Adaptation in teaching/counseling/coaching requires individualization. This is easy in a one-to-one practicum setting, but individualization does not necessarily mean teaching one-to-one. Learning to individualize in group settings is important, since teachers are often responsible for 20 or more students.

For example, while working with Bob on catching, you could consider pedagogies that might be used in assisting 30 students to meet personalized objectives with regard to catching. One approach is creative utilization of gymnasium space so that many different stations, each offering a progressively more difficult level of challenge, are operative. Another is to encourage students to assume partial responsibility for their learning by using contracts, task cards, and videotape technology. Partner and small-group feedback permits students to help one another.

Movement education is an approach that permits many students to work simultaneously on the same skill but at their own level of difficulty. In movement education, the teacher asks questions that guide students in discovering the ways their bodies can move and how they can use movement elements (time, space, force, and flow) in new and different ways. For example, a movement education session on catching could involve every person having one or more balls and the teacher asking questions about the following:

Time (fast, slow concepts; rhythms). Can you throw your ball into the air somewhere in front of you and then very swiftly run and catch it? Can you do this same thing but change the toss so you can move very slowly and still catch it? Can you do this same thing except toss the ball against a wall and catch the rebound?

Space (concepts of level—high, low). How high can you throw your ball into the air and make a successful catch? Try some different-sized balls. What difference does this make? Find a partner and see how low you

FIGURE 3.11 Barbara Wood of Homer, New York, challenges her first-graders to find how many ways they can toss objects in the air and catch them with a cup.

can toss the ball to him or her and still have a successful catch. How far away do you need to stand from each other? Can you toss a ball so it arrives at exactly waist height for your partner?

Force (concepts of hard, soft; heavy, light). What makes it hurt when you catch a hard ball? How can you change a toss so that it does not hurt? Can you toss and catch a ball with different body parts? How about just your wrist and fingers? Now how about a toss and catch that uses shoulders, elbows, wrists, and fingers? Which way results in a soft throw? a hard throw?

Flow (concepts of graceful vs. jerky; free vs. floor-bound). Can you follow through in the direction of your toss—let your whole body flow with the movement? Can you relax when you catch and pull the ball in toward you? Try jumping up as you catch a fly ball. Now try catching the same kind of ball but play like your feet are glued to the floor. What is the difference in the feeling?

In movement education, there is no right or wrong answer, so the teacher does not make corrections or give demonstrations. The secret is to generate questions that motivate each student to discover all he or she can about catching. Often, novel tasks, such as catching objects thrown into the air with a large cup, are helpful (see Figure 3.11). Such a task promotes hand-eye coordination as well as creativity in thinking up items that can be tossed and caught. Movement exploration involves few discipline problems because there is no set formation and only two rules: (a) stay on task, and (b) respect other persons' space and objects.

Games analysis is another approach to individualizing learning. The goal is to create games in which several students can participate fully while functioning with different levels of skill. An illustrative game for practicing catching skills is *Dodge or Catch*. This is a variation of dodgeball and can be played as either an individual or team game. The formation is free, with students allowed to move wherever they want except when a ball is in their hands, during which time one foot is "frozen" to the floor. The goal of the game, like in dodgeball, is to throw the ball and hit someone below the chest. In *Dodge or Catch,* however, the student can either dodge or reach out and catch the throw. There can be several balls of different sizes and shapes in motion, and point systems can be created. Numerous variations are possible.

Counseling goes hand in hand with teaching, a recognition that students with movement or fitness problems need someone to talk to. Counseling in adapted physical education uses the knowledge base of sport psychology. Students are helped with relaxing, focusing, imaging, and the like.

Coaching, properly planned and conducted, follows the same principles as teaching and counseling. Adaptation is the key to success as each athlete is helped to achieve a personal best. Coaches are sensitive to individual differences in participation incentives and other psychosocial parameters, as well as improvement in skill and fitness.

Evaluation

Evaluation is individualized by permitting students to help decide what criteria must be met for each letter grade. Various schemes can be agreed upon, with different percentages for effort, improvement, and achievement. Here, as in sport competition, the emphasis should be on achieving one's personal best (PB) rather than comparison with classmates and/or norms. Given a student like Bob, for example, what percentage of his grade should be based on effort, improvement, and achievement? What other criteria should be used in grading? Evaluation should also be directed toward teachers. What criteria should be established for you as the teacher?

Coordination of Resources, Consulting, and Advocacy

Coordination of resources, consulting, and advocacy also are individualized in accordance with each student's needs. In regard to catching, for instance, the child may be referred to a vision specialist or optometrist. Parents may be encouraged to set up home training programs and to build innovative equipment. The teacher advocates both for the student and for high-quality physical education and recreation experiences.

Considerations in Adapting

The preceding section does not mention Bob's disability because such information often is not relevant to the adaptation process. Adapting should be based on assessment, with no preconceived ideas about what persons can or cannot do. A philosophy of adapting for individual differences and the evolution of successful service delivery practices should be based on principles or guidelines that apply across several areas. The following are ideas to consider.

Affordances and Constraints

Adaptation requires thinking about the strengths and weaknesses of persons in environmental or functional terms. To do this, you must strive to increase your awareness of variables that serve as constraints and affordances to performance and learning. **Constraints** are interactions between persons and environments that serve as limitations; constraints must be accepted or overcome. **Affordances** are interactions that facilitate goal achievement; affordances must be maximized. Each student must be afforded the combination of variables that best facilitates goal attainment. This is achieved through ecological task analysis.

Affordances and *constraints* are relatively new educational terms that help capture the idea of simultaneously working with human and environmental variables rather than stressing one or the other. Begin using these terms, and practice thinking about affordances and constraints.

Adapting in Different Domains

When a student is placed in a group setting, the adaptation process may need to be directed toward goals in the affective and cognitive domains instead of, or in addition to, the psychomotor domain. For example, to participate in games, a student must have cognitive skills, such as understanding game formations and such play concepts as chase, flee, safe, you're out. Adapting instruction to teach the mental operations for mastering rules and strategies is much harder than focusing exclusively on skills or fitness. Success in a gymnasium is often perceived as feeling good about oneself. This attribute is related to game performance and to social interactions with peers as well as to perceived efficacy in motor skills. Sometimes, the structure of a class needs to be temporarily changed or adapted to permit work toward goals of social competency and acceptance.

Cooperative, Reciprocal Process

Adapting, regardless of the setting and goals, is a cooperative, reciprocal process shared by teacher and student(s). When students have a role in assessing and planning, they are more likely to support and advance instructional activities. While collaborative decision making is more time consuming than authoritarian patterns, the potential outcomes are richer and lead more directly to self-actualizing individuals who care about each other and know how to work together.

Normalization

Adapting should also be related to the goal of **normalization.** This term, widely used in special education and rehabilitation, means to make available to differently abled individuals conditions as close as possible to that of the group norm (average). It does not mean to make a person normal or like everyone else. The changes involved in activity adaptation should be minimal so that games resemble those played by the able-bodied (AB) as much as possible. Wheelchair basketball, tennis, and handball are examples of adapted sports with minimal changes.

Normalization requires that adapting be a process applied to all students in the class, not just those with disabilities. Part of creating a warm, positive classroom climate is teaching students that adapting is fun, good, and beneficial to all. Thus, the teacher may involve students in the adapting process by challenging, "How can we change this game (or drill) so that everyone has fun?" or "Is there a way to adapt our gymnasium environment (e.g., lighting, temperature, smell, placement of objects) so that it is more pleasant and/or makes learning easier?" or "This is the way I usually give this test. Are there some ways we can adapt the testing procedures so everyone has a better chance at success?"

Use of Social Criteria

Adapting, in relation to normalization, also supports the use of social criteria when making decisions about appropriate conditions, apparatus, dress, games, sports, and toys. Care should be taken that students will not be teased or ridiculed because of adaptations. For example, a group of teenagers with severe retardation might enjoy *Ring Around the Rosy* because it is appropriate to their mental ages (2 to 7 years). If such persons, however, go home or to their sheltered work environments and say, "I had a good time at the club meeting last night when we played *Ring Around the Rosy,*" this will likely cause smiles. Appropriate adaptation would be selection of a simple square or social dance activity.

Sport Classification Systems

Adaptation involves using functional classification systems to structure activity so that everyone has an equal opportunity to participate in sports and learn about cooperation and competition. Fairness in team sports depends on the balance of abilities among teams. There are many ways to achieve this balance. One way is to assign points to different ability levels and then require that the combination of players in the game at any given time must not surpass a set sum (e.g., 12 points). Wheelchair basketball is a game governed by this type of classification system. Rules followed in the United States require that every player be classified as a 1, 2, or 3, depending upon his or her functional abilities. Players on the floor cannot total more than 12 points. This system allows teams to use their members as they wish, with various combinations of classifications on the floor.

Another approach is to require that one player with low functional ability be in the game at all times. Regardless of approach, the key is to eliminate the practice of having persons sit on the bench or serve as scorekeepers and managers. Classes (as opposed to after-school sport structures) must afford all students an equal opportunity to participate. This demands adaptations. Students must be helped to understand that the purpose of team sports in the instructional setting is different from that in the recreational or competitive setting.

Principles of Adapting

In summary, several principles guide the process of adapting:

1. Adapting should be based on assessment of affordances and constraints and include examination of the person, the environment, and interactions between the two.

2. Adapting is achieved through ecological task analysis. This is skillful management of variables, task requirements, and environmental conditions so that each person can succeed.

3. Adapting requires prioritizing goals and attending to needs in the cognitive and affective domains that affect success in physical activity.

4. Adapting, regardless of environmental setting and goals, is a cooperative, reciprocal process shared by teacher and student(s).

5. Adapting should advance the goal of normalization. This means that adapting is used to make available opportunities as close as possible to the group norm (average). For example, adapting should entail minimal change in the structure, rules, equipment, and strategies of sports for persons with disabilities so that the opportunities afforded are as similar as possible to those of regular sport.

6. Adapting should be based on social criteria so that individuals are treated with dignity and respect. Adapting should never result in ridicule or teasing.

7. Adapting should use functional sport classification systems to provide equitable opportunities in competition.

Creativity Theory

Adaptation and creativity are the essential ingredients of adapted physical education. What is the meaning of creativity and the specific behaviors we must strive to develop in order to be creative? The following are two definitions:

Creativity—is "the ability to transcend traditional ideas, rules, patterns, relationships, or the like, and to create meaningful new ideas, forms, methods, interpretations, etc.; originality, progressiveness, or imagination." (*Random House Dictionary,* 1987, p. 473)

Creativity—is "a process of being sensitive to problems, deficiencies, gaps in knowledge, missing elements, disharmonies, and so on; identifying the difficulty; searching for solutions, making guesses, or formulating hypotheses about the deficiencies; testing and retesting them; and finally communicating the results." (Torrance, 1974, p. 8)

The definition by Paul Torrance, retired professor from the University of Georgia, was selected to supplement the dictionary explanation because Dr. Torrance is an acknowledged pioneer in the development and assessment of creativity in teachers and schoolchildren (Torrance, 1962, 1974, 1981). Torrance's definition encompasses both affective and cognitive domains and is behavioral in its approach. Note that the dictionary defined creativity as an ability, whereas Torrance defined it as a process.

Creativity can be analyzed into specific, observable, measurable behaviors in each domain (cognitive, affective, and psychomotor). Table 3.1 presents cognitive and affective behaviors that are important in adapted physical education. The table's four cognitive creative behaviors have a well-established knowledge base (Guilford, 1952; Torrance, 1962; Williams, 1972). Less attention has been given to affective domain components (Williams, 1972). The five affective behaviors in Table 3.1 reflect the author's beliefs about the attitudinal-behavioral composites that are essential in working with individual differences.

As we shall see in the next sections, adapting, as an approach to service delivery, is largely dependent upon the behaviors of fluency, flexibility, originality, and elaboration (cognitive domain) and acceptance, imagination, curiosity, caring, and courage (affective domain). The body of knowledge being developed on creative behaviors is called *creativity theory*. Much research is needed in this area.

Cognitive Creative Behaviors

Cognitive creative behaviors are *f*luency, *f*lexibility, *o*riginality, and *e*laboration (FFOE). These four behaviors act as a "foe" to boredom and burnout and are important for professionals to develop.

The illustrations of fluency, flexibility, originality, and elaboration that you are about to read may seem far-out, by adult standards, but they work with children—not just those with problems, but all children. Most students need many more repetitions to learn skills than their interest and concentration can sustain. Part of adapting is trying enough different ways, with abundant enthusiasm, to maintain student interest.

Fluency

Fluency is the generation of a large number of relevant, workable ideas and was illustrated in the earlier discussion on adaptation and teaching Bob to catch. A large number of variables was generated in specified categories: (a) student, (b) object or equipment, (c) movement, (d) physical environment, (e) psychosocial, and (f) task, activity, and event dimensions. Consider each of these categories and others relevant to service delivery. Can you add to the list of variables? The larger the number of relevant variables, the more fluent

Table 3.1   Behaviors in the creative process.

Behavior	Meaning
Cognitive	
1. Fluent thinking: To think of the *most*	Generation of a quantity, flow of thought, number of relevant responses
2. Flexible thinking: To take *different* approaches	A variety of kinds of ideas, ability to shift categories, detours in direction of thought
3. Original thinking: To think in *novel* or unique ways	Unusual responses, clever ideas, production away from the obvious
4. Elaborate thinking: To *add on* to	Embellishing upon an idea, embroidering upon a simple idea or response to make it more elegant, stretching or expanding upon things or ideas
Affective	
1. Acceptance: To reach out and embrace	To feel a sense of identity and empathy with others, accept self and others in spite of weaknesses, generally feel good about life and human beings, perceive differences among people as inevitable and normal
2. Imagination: To have power to envision	To see each human being as unique, different from all others; visualize what this person can become, dream about things that have never happened; feel intuitively that this person can grow, develop, and succeed; have a mind that reaches beyond barriers and boundaries
3. Curiosity: To have a problem-solving mind	To be inquisitive and wonder, toy with ideas, be open to alternatives; seek new and different ways; ponder the mystery of things
4. Caring: To be driven to action	To become involved; find the inner resources to endure and persist until solutions are found; have faith in ability to bring order out of chaos, find missing pieces, derive solutions
5. Courage: To be willing to take risks	To devise and try new strategies; expose oneself to failure and criticism; support and defend persons, ideas, or things that are different or unpopular

the teacher. Fluency is also seen in the number of different games, drills, and movement education challenges that you can devise for practicing a particular skill, and in the many different ways you can word a question, give instructions, and explain a problem. The more synonyms known, the more fluent you are. Persons who know sign language are more fluent than those who rely entirely on verbal communication. The essence of fluency is *find another way.*

Flexibility

Flexibility is making change with ease, especially about different categories and kinds of ideas. It is adaptability to changing situations and stimuli, freedom from inertia or blockage of thought, and spontaneous shifting of mind-set. Flexibility in teaching Bob was illustrated by the ability to shift categories during assessment and brainstorming processes. In getting acquainted with Bob, the teacher can switch from the category of interests (does Bob want to learn to catch?) to relevance (do Bob's friends play catch?) to sport socialization (what kind of lessons has Bob already had in catching?). The teacher also shifts easily among the following categories of variables in discovering the kinds of balls Bob could catch: (a) size, (b) weight, (c) color, (d) direction, (e) path, (f) postures, and (g) lighting.

Flexible persons do not usually list all possibilities in one category and then move in orderly fashion to another category; instead, they move back and forth among categories with ease. This helps them to plan and teach in a **holistic** man-

ner (i.e., see the whole, synthesize parts from many categories, combine them to make a new whole).

Originality

Originality pertains to unusual, new, and clever ideas, such as different kinds of balls and gloves during the individualized skill assessment or goal/objective-setting phase. The teacher wants to motivate the student and/or maintain his or her interest. The balls and gloves might have velcro strips on them to make catching easier, or they might have bells embedded in them and painted faces to enhance interest and motivation. Balls might smell and taste good, like an orange or marshmallow, and be offered as a reward for effort and/or success.

Unique starting and stopping signals, lighting conditions, and background music also can enhance interest. Putting game elements together in new and different ways to create adapted sports and new recreational play activities is also originality. Consider, for instance, how an egg-tossing game might be devised to reinforce and motivate catching skills. Originality might playfully be thought of as the crazy things a teacher does to keep from going crazy when skill mastery requires lots of repetition.

Elaboration

Elaboration refers to the richness of interesting details or extras supplied. Think about the last lecture you attended. Did the speaker just state facts, or did he or she supplement points with anecdotes, illustrations, examples, poems, or problem-solving exercises? During catching practice, for example, elaboration might be evidenced by the use of imagery and metaphors: "Run to meet the ball . . . play like it's a bolt of lightning . . . if you don't stop it, the forest will catch on fire"; "Reach out for the ball . . . think of it as a puppy or child falling out of a window . . . don't wait for it to come to you . . . go after it, gently, gently, now draw it in toward your chest."

The idea of catching might be embellished by coordinating skill practice with a story, music, drama, costumes, or puppets (see Figure 3.12). After each successful catch, various reinforcers might make the experience more elegant. Catching practice with a wind machine or electric fan on at one station and flickering lights at another station are embellishments, particularly when interwoven with a story.

Affective Creative Behaviors

The five affective domain creative behaviors are acceptance, imagination, curiosity, caring, and courage (see Table 3.1). These behaviors stem from feelings and emotions, rather than ideas and thoughts, and highlight sensitivity to human needs and situational problems. Sensitivity varies among individuals, but good self-concept and confidence in your abilities are related to creative behaviors. Teachers have to believe in themselves and expect success.

Acceptance

Acceptance is favorable reception. Teacher acceptance can be defined as behaviors showing that a student is perceived and treated as capable, worthy, agreeable, and welcome. Acceptance is often measured in terms of approach and avoidance behaviors. Certainly, you must approach, and be relatively close to, a student to assess her or his abilities and plan how to adapt instruction. You can be close to a student in many ways: (a) physically (hug, touch), (b) visually (smile, eye contact), (c) auditorially (warm, pleasant voice), and (d) mentally (an affinity for each other's ideas, thoughts, beliefs; a similar learning or problem-solving style, and so on). List the things that teachers say and do that help you to feel capable, worthy, agreeable, and welcome and prioritize them in terms of importance. How does your ranking of items compare with those of classmates? The specific behaviors of acceptance probably have different meanings for different individuals.

The state of acceptance between two persons provides the environmental readiness for other creative behaviors. Some teachers, however, find it easy to accept persons (and things) that are different in appearance, sound, smell, and touch, whereas others find it hard. Which are you? This pertains partly to flexibility, the ability to shift back and forth between categories of similarity and dissimilarity in people, foods, cars, beds, and the like. Some persons prefer sameness, whereas others like to liven up their existence with new and different things, people, and experiences. Which are you?

Acceptance is also closely related to empathy, an innate quality that varies from person to person and is not well understood. **Empathy** is identification with or vicarious experiencing of the feelings, thoughts, and attitudes of another.

FIGURE 3.12 A child who is fearful or doesn't want to play needs a teacher with creative behaviors. Here, the puppet says, "Please let me play with you . . . I want to roll you a pretty ball."

Empathy is often explained as the ability to walk in another's shoes, to see and feel the world as another does. Thus, it encompasses both sensitivity and responsivity. "Awareness Days" to enhance understanding of individual differences often include challenges to able-bodied (AB) persons to spend a day in a wheelchair or to play a game while blindfolded or wearing earplugs. Such simulated activities promote empathy and, thus, acceptance.

Imagination

Imagination is the power to envision things and people as different from what they are. Within the adapted physical activity context, imagination is the ability to visualize all that a person can become. Although imagination can dwell on the negative, the emphasis in teaching is on positive thinking. Are you an optimist or a pessimist?

Consider the effect of teacher expectations. If a teacher imagines that a student can do something, does this make it easier? What behaviors convey that the teacher imagines the student to be a leader, an athlete, or a scholar in the future? For instruction to be adapted, the process must be imagined. You must intuitively feel good about the capacity of students to change and have a clear view of the direction to lead.

Curiosity

Curious behaviors are inquisitive and searching. Some persons seem to be fascinated by the unknown; they spend a lot of time analyzing how and why things work. Others can solve problems, if challenged to do so, but typically are not curious enough to ask questions. Which are you? Some persons are interested in how the human mind works and spend a lot of time thinking about behaviors. Others are more fascinated by machines or laboratory apparatus. Which is more like you? Within the adapted physical activity context, curiosity is spontaneous involvement in problem-solving behaviors in order to answer self-generated questions.

Caring

Caring has many definitions, each of which connotes the ability to feel deeply and intensely. For our purposes, **caring** is operationally defined as having feelings and beliefs so strong that you get involved in positive action directed toward making things better for an individual or group. As used in this model of creative behaviors, caring is a complex emotion. It is intertwined with faith in your ability to create, in the probability that people and things will change in the desired direction, and in the meaning of life. Caring also is linked with the inner resources to endure and persist until solutions are found (i.e., caring enough usually evokes the stamina to keep going).

Courage

Courage is the quality that enables you to try something new, to delve into the unknown, and to expose self to failure or criticisms. Because the essence of creativity is finding new, different, and original ways to assure success for people with problems, the probability is high that at least several of the attempts will fail or receive criticism. Courage enables you to work alone, if need be, in the generation of new ideas and solutions.

Courage is needed also in adapted physical activity specialists who act as advocates for persons with disabilities and who fight for removal of attitudinal, aspirational, and architectural barriers. Proposals to change the environment, even when changes clearly benefit the lives of persons with disabilities, are often met with criticism because of the expense and inconvenience involved. To create and adapt, you must be able to withstand pressures from those who prefer traditional ways. Likewise, to become a close friend of someone different in appearance and abilities requires the courage to withstand peer pressures and the advice of significant others. To create is to dare to take risks.

References

Allport, G. W. (1954). *The nature of prejudice.* Cambridge, MA: Addison-Wesley.

American Therapeutic Recreation Association. (1984). *ATRA Newsletter, 1*(2).

Ayres, A. J. (1972). *Sensory integration and learning disorders.* Los Angeles: Western Psychological Services.

Bandura, A. (1986). *Social foundations of thought and action: A social cognitive theory.* Englewood Cliffs, NJ: Prentice Hall.

Bem, D. J. (1972). Self-perception theory. In L. Berkowitz (Ed.), *Advances in experimental social psychology* (Vol. 6, pp. 2–62). New York: Academic Press.

Block, M. E. (1995). Americans with Disabilities Act: Its impact on youth sports. *Journal of Physical Education, Recreation and Dance, 66*(1), 28–32.

Blumenkopf, M., Levangie, P., & Nelson, D. (1985). Perceived role responsibilities of physical therapists and adapted physical educators in the public school setting. *Physical Therapy, 65*(7), 1046–1051.

Bogdan, R. C., & Biklen, S. K. (1992). *Qualitative research for education.* Boston: Allyn & Bacon.

Boswell, B. (1989). Dance as creative expression for the disabled. *Palaestra, 6*(1), 28–30.

Dattilo, J. (1994). *Inclusive leisure services.* State College, PA: Venture.

Fawcett, J., & Downs, F. S. (1992). *The relationship of theory and research* (2nd ed.). Philadelphia: F. A. Davis.

Festinger, L. (1954). *A theory of cognitive dissonance.* Stanford, CA: Stanford University Press.

Fiorini, J., Stanton, K., & Reid, G. (1996). Understanding of parents and families of children with disabilities. *Palaestra, 12*(2), 16–23, 51.

French, R., Kinnison, L., Sherrill, C., & Henderson, H. (in press). Relationship of Section 504 to physical education and sport: Revisited. *Journal of Physical Education, Recreation and Dance.*

Fuchs, D., Fuchs, L. S., & Bahr, M. W. (1990). Mainstream assistance teams: A scientific basis for the art of consultation. *Exceptional Children, 57,* 128–139.

Guilford, J. (1952). *A factor analytic study of creative thinking.* Report from the psychological laboratory. No. 8, University of Southern California.

Hanson, M., & Carta, J. (1995). Addressing the challenges of families with multiple risks. *Exceptional Children, 62*(3), 201–212.

Hernandez, D. J. (1994). Children's changing access to resources: A historical perspective. *Society for Research in Child Development Social Policy Report, 8*(1), 1–23.

Hopkins, H., & Smith, H. (Eds.). (1993). *Willard and Spackman's occupational therapy* (8th ed.). Philadelphia: Lippincott.

Kiphard, E. (1983). Adapted physical education in Germany. In R. Eason, T. Smith, & F. Caron (Eds.), *Adapted physical activity: From theory to application* (pp. 25–32). Champaign, IL: Human Kinetics.

Klein, J. T. (1990). *Interdisciplinarity: History, theory, and practice.* Detroit, MI: Wayne State University.

Krebs, P. L., & Block, M. E. (1992). Transition of students with disabilities into community recreation: The role of the adapted physical educator. *Adapted Physical Activity Quarterly, 9*(4), 305–315.

National Therapeutic Recreation Society. (1982). *Philosophical position statement.* Alexandria, VA: Author.

O'Morrow, G., & Reynolds, R. (1989). *Therapeutic recreation: A helping profession* (3rd ed.). Englewood Cliffs, NJ: Prentice Hall.

Osgood, C. E., Suci, G. J., & Tannenbaum, P. H. (1957). *The measurement of meaning.* Urbana, IL: University of Illinois Press.

Purvis, J. (1985). A new description of corrective therapy. *American Corrective Therapy Journal, 39*(1), 4–5.

Scanlan, T. K., Carpenter, P. J., Schmidt, G. W., Simons, J. P., & Keeler, B. (1993). An introduction to the Sport Commitment Model. *Journal of Sport and Exercise Psychology, 15,* 1–15.

Scanlan, T. K., & Simons, J. P. (1992). The construct of sport enjoyment. In G. C. Roberts (Ed.), *Motivation in sport and exercise* (pp. 199–215). Champaign, IL: Human Kinetics.

Schleien, S. J., Meyer, L. H., Heyne, L. A., & Brandt, B. B. (1995). *Lifelong leisure skills and lifestyles for persons with developmental disabilities.* Baltimore: Paul H. Brookes.

Seaman, J. A., & Heilbuth, L. (1988). Competencies needed to function in the interdisciplinary arena. In C. Sherrill (Ed.), *Leadership training in adapted physical education* (pp. 161–168). Champaign, IL: Human Kinetics.

Sherrill, C. (Ed.). (1979). *Creative arts for the severely handicapped.* Springfield, IL: Charles C Thomas.

Short, F. X. (1995). Individualized education programs. In J. P. Winnick (Ed.), *Adapted physical education and sport* (pp. 33–44). Champaign, IL: Human Kinetics.

Torrance, E. P. (1962). *Guiding creative talent.* Englewood Cliffs, NJ: Prentice Hall.

Torrance, E. P. (1974). *Torrance tests of creative thinking.* Bensenville, IL: Scholastic Test Service.

Torrance, E. P. (1981). *Thinking creatively in action and movement.* Bensenville, IL: Scholastic Test Service.

Tripp, A., French, R., & Sherrill, C. (1995). Contact theory and attitudes of children in physical education programs toward peers with disabilities. *Adapted Physical Activity Quarterly, 12*(4), 323–332.

Tymeson, G. (1988). In-service teacher education: A review of general practices and suggested guidelines for adapted physical education teacher trainers. In C. Sherrill (Ed.), *Leadership training in adapted physical education* (pp. 401–410). Champaign, IL: Human Kinetics.

Williams, F. (1972). *Total creativity program.* Englewood Cliffs, NJ: Educational Technology Publications. Now available through Pro•Ed (see Appendix E).

CHAPTER

4

Advocacy, the Law, and the IEP

FIGURE 4.1   Advocacy requires knowledge of laws that mandate rights. (DD = Developmental Disabilities; PE-R = Physical Education and Recreation; MR = Mental Retardation; MR-MH = Mental Retardation-Mental Health.)

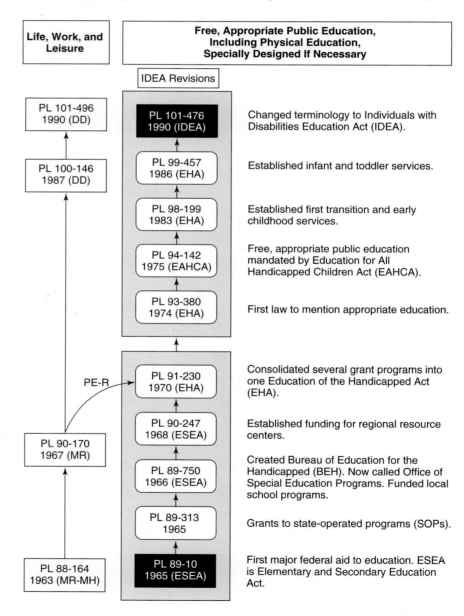

Life, Work, and Leisure	Free, Appropriate Public Education, Including Physical Education, Specially Designed If Necessary	

IDEA Revisions

PL 101-496 1990 (DD)	PL 101-476 1990 (IDEA)	Changed terminology to Individuals with Disabilities Education Act (IDEA).
	PL 99-457 1986 (EHA)	Established infant and toddler services.
PL 100-146 1987 (DD)	PL 98-199 1983 (EHA)	Established first transition and early childhood services.
	PL 94-142 1975 (EAHCA)	Free, appropriate public education mandated by Education for All Handicapped Children Act (EAHCA).
	PL 93-380 1974 (EHA)	First law to mention appropriate education.

PE-R

	PL 91-230 1970 (EHA)	Consolidated several grant programs into one Education of the Handicapped Act (EHA).
	PL 90-247 1968 (ESEA)	Established funding for regional resource centers.
PL 90-170 1967 (MR)	PL 89-750 1966 (ESEA)	Created Bureau of Education for the Handicapped (BEH). Now called Office of Special Education Programs. Funded local school programs.
	PL 89-313 1965	Grants to state-operated programs (SOPs).
PL 88-164 1963 (MR-MH)	PL 89-10 1965 (ESEA)	First major federal aid to education. ESEA is Elementary and Secondary Education Act.

After you have studied this chapter, you should be able to do the following:

1. Define advocacy, identify advocacy causes, and discuss five advocacy behaviors. Summarize your experiences in advocacy and make a personal plan for growth in this area.

2. Find out about the physical education requirement in your state and contrast it with recommendations by organizations and authorities. Suggest improvements.

3. Discuss how various minority groups have striven for equal opportunity and consider the role of adapted physical education in this struggle.

4. Discuss landmark laws of the 1970s and describe how each influenced change.

5. Summarize basic concepts underlying legislative advocacy and describe resources. Know where to find resources, both written and human.

6. Explain current RA, ADA, DDA, and IDEA legislation. Give examples of how each of these is changing lives.

7. Discuss the legislative basis of practices in adapted physical education.

8. Differentiate between the IEP and the IEP process. Identify and explain the parts of each. Create an original story or play to illustrate them.

9. Discuss different kinds of placement and the legislative basis of each.

10. Discuss the state plan in relation to IDEA and funding of adapted physical education. State strategies for improving local education agency (LEA) delivery of services.

Much of the adapted physical activity professional's time and energy is spent in advocacy for individual dignity and equality. **Advocacy** is action aimed at promoting, maintaining, or defending a cause. Adapted physical activity specialists typically are advocates for two causes: (a) the right to high-quality physical education instruction and (b) the elimination of attitudinal, aspirational, and architectural barriers that limit opportunity, especially in regard to sport, dance, aquatics, fitness, and leisure.

Figure 4.1 summarizes some of the laws discussed in this chapter. Effective advocates know laws and use them to assure equal opportunity (Block, 1995, 1996; Dougherty, Auxter, Goldberger, & Heinzmann, 1994). History shows that children and youth with disabilities do not receive good physical education unless someone fights for them. Likewise, adults with disabilities need advocates for their right to independence, productivity, and integration into community life, work, and leisure.

The knowledge base underlying advocacy is fraught with numbers and abbreviations. Because laws' numbering changes approximately every 3 years, it is better to focus on abbreviations: *MR-MH* (Mental Retardation–Mental Health), *DDA* (Developmental Disabilities Act), and *ESEA, EHA, EAHCA,* and *IDEA* (each explained in Figure 4.1). Not shown but also important are *RA* (Rehabilitation Act) and *ADA* (Americans with Disabilities Act).

Law forms the basis for good service delivery. Many practices in adapted physical education have their roots in law. Planning, assessment, and placement are particularly affected by law, and these are emphasized in this chapter. Implementation depends on money, and this chapter aims to increase awareness of how taxes, grants, and fundraising are linked to desirable school practices. When money is tight, for example, school districts reduce services. Advocacy skills are needed to assure compliance with law in relation to physical education and to help with fundraising.

Education is primarily the responsibility of local and state governments and rests on their ability to generate money.

Laws and policies thus vary widely. Only a small percentage of school funding comes from the federal government, and this must be justified as necessary for the general welfare (health and education) of a particular group, such as individuals with disabilities or economic disadvantage. Both special education and adapted physical education are funded mainly by local money, and services are influenced by attitudes and aspirations.

Advocacy for Physical Education

Adapted physical educators are advocates for both regular and adapted physical education. Advocacy begins with learning about the state physical education requirement and examining its implementation in local schools. Principals who value physical education in the regular program and who champion services needed by students with disabilities should be identified and used as models. Persons not aware of the importance of adapted physical education need to be provided with guidelines from professional organizations and authorities.

The American Alliance for Health, Physical Education, Recreation and Dance (AAHPERD) recommends the following minimum instructional requirements:

> Elementary schoolchildren should have a *daily* physical education program of 30 minutes a day, five times a week—or a total of 150 minutes a week. The size of the class should be consistent with that of other classes in the school.

> Secondary school students should have *daily* physical education programs which are equal in length and class size to other classes. (AAHPERD, 1980, v-3)

The Canadian Association for Health, Physical Education, and Recreation (CAHPER) and the International Council for Health, Physical Education, Recreation, Sport and Dance (ICHPER•SD) also endorse the policies of daily physical education instruction and 150 to 300 minutes per week of physical education activities. Increasingly, physical educators are learning to be advocates for these recommendations and for better methods of enforcing state laws at the local level.

Federal Intervention: General Welfare Concerns

Advocates must know and use both state and federal law. Federal law can be enacted to intervene with state policy and practices only when the courts rule that the general welfare of citizens is inequitable or endangered. **General welfare,** which refers to health and education, has its constitutional basis in Article I, Section 8, of the U.S. Constitution. This is often called the **General Welfare Clause.** Abbreviated, Section 8 states:

> The Congress shall have the power To . . . provide for the common Defense and general Welfare of the United States . . . To make all laws which shall be necessary and proper for carrying into Execution the foregoing Powers.

The General Welfare Clause, interpreted differently by Republicans and Democrats, generates much controversy in regard to issues concerning states' rights and federal control. However, the General Welfare Clause is one basis of legislation that assures students with disabilities free, appropriate education, including, if necessary, physical education services that are specially designed. This legislation, referred to throughout the book, is called the Individuals with Disabilities Education Act (IDEA).

Class Placement and Advocacy

A major controversy that advocates must address is the best class placement for students with disabilities (Sherrill, 1994; Stein, 1994). Some advocates believe that a wide variety of educational settings (e.g., regular, resource, separate) should be made available so that a student's abilities can be matched to a particular learning environment. Other advocates believe that all students should be educated together in the regular instructional program. These two belief systems are called **least restrictive environment (LRE)** and **inclusive placement** philosophy, respectively.

LRE placement, which is supported by the law (IDEA), requires that multidisciplinary assessment and the combined judgment of parents and school personnel be used to select a placement for each school subject that meets two criteria: (a) individual abilities are matched with appropriate services and (b) individual freedom is preserved to the greatest extent possible. Freedom, in this context, refers to the student's right to be in the regular classroom unless assessment data indicate that prescribed goals cannot be met in that setting, even with support services. In regard to physical education, a student might be assigned to

1. regular physical education with no support services,
2. regular physical education with support services,
3. specially designed integrated physical education (e.g., a buddy for every student with a disability; a community recreation setting to learn transition skills),

4. a resource room, separate setting, or one-to-one tutoring, or
5. combinations and variations of these.

Central to LRE placement philosophy is the school district's compliance with the law that there be available many different placement options.

Inclusive placement, in contrast, requires the same placement (regular physical education) for everyone, with the assumption that appropriate support services will be made available in the mainstream. Advocates of inclusive placement believe that the Fifth and Fourteenth amendments (see the next section) are violated when students are removed from the regular classroom. However, the courts do not agree that IDEA, when properly implemented, violates constitutional law. Advocates for inclusive placement encourage lawsuits to clarify ambiguous parts of the law and promote critical thinking. For an excellent review of recent court cases, see Block (1996).

Inclusive placement philosophy is not the same as **inclusion philosophy,** which refers to attitudes and beliefs of acceptance that promote positive, meaningful integration. Both LRE and inclusive placement belief systems support inclusion philosophy. The law (IDEA) clearly states that the LRE for most students with disabilities is the regular education classroom and that no student can be removed from the regular setting unless the IEP process documents a failure to achieve prescribed goals, even with the help of support services.

Essentially, the conflict between advocates for LRE and inclusive placement advocates centers on a very small percentage of students with disabilities, less than 5%. These are students with severe and profound disabilities (see Chapter 10) and/or with special mobility, vision, or cognition needs that require specific transition training for community sports involvement. LRE advocates believe that these students require services beyond what is possible in a regular classroom. This removal of students from the regular classroom for special services is serious business because legal experts consider removal as unequal treatment that violates the Fifth and Fourteenth amendments unless due process is followed.

Due Process and Advocacy

Due process is the constitutional guarantee that fair and impartial treatment procedures will be followed whenever life, liberty, or property rights are challenged or removed. IDEA specifies many due process requirements for removing a student from regular education, but many individuals (especially parents) need help in understanding the legal process. Advocates play an important role in assuring that due process is followed. Following is basic information that advocates must know.

Due process comes from two constitutional amendments. The **Fifth Amendment,** which applies only to the federal government, states, "No person . . . shall be deprived of life, liberty, or property without due process of law." The **Fourteenth Amendment** extends this concept to state government operations, stating, "nor shall any State deprive any person of life, liberty, or property without due process of law."

Due process, within the educational context, pertains to fair treatment in the removal of students from regular education classes and/or subjecting them to assessment or other procedures different from those for their peers. In general, law distinguishes between two types of due process: substantive and procedural. **Substantive due process** pertains to whether the rule that was violated was fair and reasonable (Dougherty et al., 1994). For example, is the rule that all students be educated in regular classrooms reasonable? Is the rule that all students must have vaccinations before attending school reasonable? Both of these rules pertain to life, liberty, or property rights. **Procedural due process** guarantees a person the right and a meaningful opportunity to be heard and to protest before action can be taken in regard to his or her life, liberty, or property. *Assignment to special education is considered action in regard to basic constitutional rights.*

IDEA-Part B makes many references to procedural due process. Proper procedures in regard to assessment/evaluation, the parents' role in the IEP process, and the right to an impartial due process hearing are described in detail. Of particular importance to physical educators is the requirement that schools must give parents written notice that their child has been referred for assessment and that parents must give written consent before such assessment can be undertaken. The written notice to parents should include reasons for the referral, information about who will administer tests, names and descriptions of tests or data collection protocols, and a statement of parents' rights. In most school systems, this paperwork is under the jurisdiction of the director of special education. School administrators have the responsibility of ensuring that teachers understand due process.

Advocacy Behaviors—the Five Ls

Advocacy can be broken down into several tasks or behaviors known as the five Ls: (a) look at me, (b) leverage, (c) literature, (d) legislation, and (e) litigation.

Look at Me—Individual Action: Modeling

First and foremost, advocacy involves setting a good example, modeling a positive attitude toward both physical activity and persons with disabilities. Each time adapted physical activity professionals are seen in a friendship relationship with persons who are disabled, this is advocacy. Each time professionals support a candidate running for public office and become actively involved in promoting education and human rights as campaign issues, they are demonstrating advocacy.

Leverage—Group Action

Leverage refers to group action as a means of gaining advantage in the fight for human rights. Whereas one individual can make a small difference, a professional organization can create pressures that make elected officials vote in desired ways. Adapted physical activity professionals therefore belong to organizations like AAHPERD and the Council for Exceptional Children (CEC) and expect part of their membership dues to be applied toward advocacy activities. They are also active in organizations run jointly by parents and professionals, such as the Parent Teachers Association (PTA), ARC, formerly the Association for Retarded Citizens, and the Learning Disability Association of America (LDA). Only by joining together with persons who have similar concerns can sufficient leverage be created to make a difference.

Leverage also can be wielded by supporting or boycotting businesses and industries. For example, buying products from stores that employ persons with disabilities is an advocacy activity. Knowing the companies that financially support sport organizations for athletes with disabilities guides advocates in their choice of what brands to buy.

Literature

Literature refers to assertiveness in writing advocacy articles for newspapers and journals, in conducting research, and in using the written word to promote, maintain, or defend a cause. Letters to the editor of a newspaper and to elected officials are particularly powerful forms of advocacy. Chain letters can be initiated to further a cause. Research concerning the efficacy of physical education and recreation programs and/or attitudes toward persons who are different can lead to the publication of findings that advance specific advocacy goals.

Legislation

Legislation is the preparation and enactment of laws at the local, state, and national levels. Advocates must know the laws at each level of government that pertain to education and human rights and must monitor school and agency administrators to be sure that these laws are enforced. Advocacy also involves acquainting others (especially parents) with laws and encouraging them to become involved in the legislative process.

Legislation is closely related to finance because laws cannot be implemented without money. Sometimes, laws contain passages about the amount of money needed to make them viable. IDEA, for example, specifies the amount of money that should be made available to implement each of its sections. Raising the money, however, is achieved through enactment of laws that pertain to taxation and other sources of revenue (e.g., state lotteries, parking meters, highway toll fees, and special service charges). Most state and local government money comes from taxes; therefore, most advocates for high-quality education are also advocates for tax laws.

Advocates must be involved in the politics of taxing and spending. Although raising taxes is unpopular, the money to run schools and social services is largely dependent upon such government revenue. Legislation thus not only encompasses the making of laws about education and human rights but also the enactment of laws that generate money. Advocates need to be assertive in deciding how federal (as well as state and local) money is spent, must monitor appropriations carefully, and must ascertain that education (especially physical education) gets its fair share.

Litigation

Litigation is the use of the judicial process (i.e., due process hearings, lawsuits, court action) to force the creation of new laws or compliance with existing laws. Advocates encourage parents and persons with disabilities to use due process procedures when rights are violated. These procedures, which are described in IDEA and other laws, include a hierarchy of activities that begin with an impartial due process hearing and end with court action in response to a lawsuit filed by an attorney. Usually, problems are resolved in the early stages of formal negotiation, and lawsuits are not necessary. Sometimes, however, governmental agencies, schools, and business and industry do not obey laws unless forced to do so.

Advocacy, a Way of Life

Advocacy is a way of life. It governs the way we teach, influences the friends we select, and affects the products we buy. To be a good advocate, we must believe in ourselves, in the democratic process, and in the power of individuals to create change. We must *care* enough to learn about legislation and litigation and to use these processes to improve quality of life.

The five Ls also are important in the human rights movement. Concern for life, liberty, and the pursuit of happiness extends beyond people with disabilities to other minority groups who share similar problems of inequality. To be an effective advocate, it is helpful to have a sense of history and to understand how events relate to one another. There is a definite trend toward minority groups working together at the grass roots level.

Classic Lawsuits

Two classic lawsuits are particularly important. **The principle of school integration** is derived from the 1954 case of *Brown v. Board of Education of Topeka, Kansas.* In this litigation, the U.S. Supreme Court ruled that the doctrine "separate but equal" in the field of public education was unconstitutional and deprived the segregated group (Blacks) of rights guaranteed by the Fourteenth Amendment.

The principle of zero reject, or free appropriate public education for all children, has its roots in the 1972 class-action suit *Pennsylvania Association for Retarded Citizens (PARC) v. Commonwealth of Pennsylvania.* The court ruling that no child can be excluded from public school programs led directly to enactment of PL 94-142 in 1975. This case continues to serve as the basis for challenging the constitutionality of excluding children with severe disabilities from public school programs.

Other especially important lawsuits are reviewed in a 1986 issue of *Exceptional Children* (vol. 52, no. 4) and in an article by Block (1996). Of particular note is the *Rowley* case that clarified the meaning of *appropriate education* (Turnbull, 1986) and the *Daniel R. R.* case that clarified LRE doctrine (Block, 1996). The *Daniel R. R.* case resulted in standards to determine when separate class placement may be more appropriate than regular class placement, with support services.

The Human Rights Movement

History shows that equality of opportunity does not come easily. The Civil War (1860s) was fought to achieve the right of all males, regardless of race or color, to vote. Approximately 50 years later, in 1920, women won the right to vote. Persons of color, women, individuals with disabilities, and other minorities

are all related in the sense that their rights are often violated. One way or another, they are denied citizenship privileges, including equal opportunities for education and physical activity. Why does this happen? What can you, as a professional, do?

Advocacy for equal and/or appropriate physical education is but one link in the chain of events whereby minority groups have fought discrimination. From 1950 to 1980, several groups sequentially achieved access to equal education. Figure 4.2 shows the relationship between the U.S. Constitution and early laws.

Blacks

The human rights movement intensified after World War II, with the battle against school segregation culminating in the already mentioned 1954 federal Supreme Court case *Brown v. Board of Education of Topeka, Kansas.* This litigation resulted in the ruling that the doctrine of "separate but equal" schooling for Black students was unconstitutional in that it violated the Fourteenth Amendment. According to the Fourteenth Amendment:

> No state shall make or enforce any law which shall abridge the privileges or immunities of citizens of the United States, nor shall any State deprive any person of life, liberty, or property, without due process of law; nor deny to any person within its jurisdiction the equal protection of the laws.

In spite of the Supreme Court's ruling that segregated education was unconstitutional, most local school districts did not change their policies and practices. Thus, the 1960s brought the demonstrations, boycotts, and violence now known as the civil rights movement. President John F. Kennedy urged the enactment of federal legislation to end the widespread discontent, and shortly after his assassination, the Civil Rights Act of 1964 (PL 88-352) was passed by the 88th Congress.

Women

In the 1960s, the groundwork was also laid for legislation to prevent sex discrimination in education. These efforts resulted in Title IX of the Educational Amendments Act of 1972 (PL 92-318). Thus, the doctrine of separate but equal found unconstitutional for Blacks in 1964 was also declared illegal for women. The Fourteenth Amendment was cited as the basis for making school physical education programs coeducational and for upgrading girls' and women's athletic programs.

Persons With Disabilities

The 1960s were also a time of beginning awareness of mental retardation (MR). President John F. Kennedy was particularly interested in MR because his oldest sister (Rose) had this condition. In 1961, he created the first President's Panel on Mental Retardation. Most persons with MR were served by residential facilities in the 1960s, and this panel worked to upgrade conditions and increase awareness of alternative living arrangements. Acting on the panel's recommendations, President Kennedy encouraged enactment in 1963 of the first

FIGURE 4.2 The human rights movement is rooted in the Constitution and based on two concepts: (a) that federal aid is a necessary intervention, and (b) that separate but equal is not constitutional. (MR-MH = Mental Retardation-Mental Health; ESEA = Elementary and Secondary Education Act.)

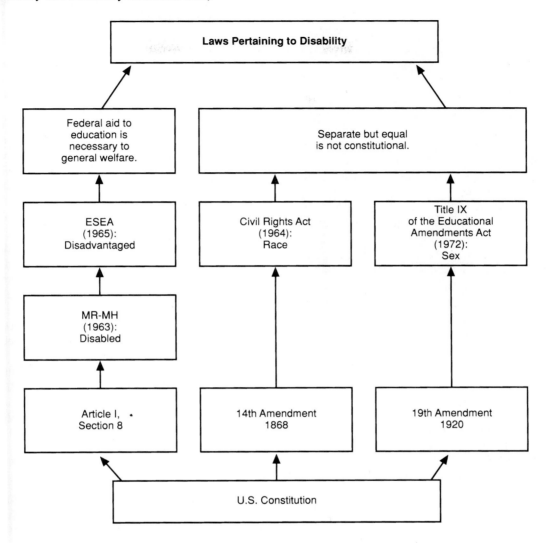

major MR legislation, the Mental Retardation Facilities and Community Mental Health Centers Construction Act.

Amendments to this law in 1967 initiated the advocacy movement for physical education and recreation (PE-R) for persons with disabilities. Specifically, the Mental Retardation Amendments of 1967 (PL 90-170) provided funds for university training programs to teach physical educators and recreators how to work with individuals with MR. In 1970, funding of PE-R training was switched to EHA (see Figure 4.1), and authorization of grants for graduate programs and research in PE-R continues today under IDEA. The legislation introduced by Kennedy was periodically reauthorized and is now known as the Developmental Disabilities Act (DDA). Figure 4.1 shows that two tracks were established early, one to improve living conditions and one to improve education.

Through the example set by the Kennedy family, professionals began to take an active interest in MR. Many physical educators became involved in **Special Olympics,** the sport movement for persons with MR, founded in 1968 by Eunice Kennedy Shriver, a sister of President Kennedy. Senator Edward Kennedy of Massachusetts has led the battle in Congress for legislation to protect the rights of persons with disabilities and to improve education (see Figure 4.3).

The Disadvantaged or Poor

The 1960s also brought concern about disparities in education provided by rich and poor school districts. Local and state governments either could not or would not do anything about the welfare of many disadvantaged students. Therefore, the federal government began to intervene, using legislation as a means of enhancing the education and health of disadvantaged and/or minority group children. The Democratic party spearheaded this movement, citing the General Welfare Clause of the U.S. Constitution as its basis for action.

The first federal law to provide substantial aid to education was the Elementary and Secondary Education Act (ESEA) of 1965. This legislation provided funds for *compensatory education* for disadvantaged students. It also made

FIGURE 4.3   Eunice Kennedy Shriver and Edward Kennedy in the 1960s were among the first advocates for physical education and recreation for people with disabilities.

available money for innovative and/or exemplary local school district physical education programs like Project ACTIVE and Project PEOPEL (Sherrill & Hillman, 1988), which were designed for students with disabilities.

Landmark Laws of the 1970s

In the 1970s, a new era for adapted physical activity and sport for athletes with disabilities evolved because of the advocacy movement and resulting legislation and litigation. Three landmark laws were enacted that all adapted physical activity professionals should know well. The constitutional basis for important parts of each of these laws was the Fourteenth Amendment.

PL 93-112: The Rehabilitation Amendments, Section 504

PL 93-112, enacted in 1973 but not implemented until its rules were printed in the *Federal Register* in 1977, includes many mandates but is best known for Section 504, often called the "Nondiscrimination Clause" (*Federal Register,* May 4, 1977). Section 504 states:

> No otherwise qualified handicapped individual . . . shall, solely by reason of his handicap, be excluded from participation in, be denied the benefits of, or be subjected to discrimination under any program or activity receiving Federal financial assistance.

This means that schools conducting interscholastic athletics and extraclass activities must provide qualified students with disabilities an equal opportunity with nondisabled peers for participation. Such opportunities must be given in the least restrictive environment, which is generally the regular program. Persons with artificial limbs or one eye or kidney cannot be barred from sport competition. Likewise, athletic events in public places receiving federal funds (almost all do) must be accessible to all spectators, including those in wheelchairs. All facilities do not have to be accessible as long as programs are accessible. Students with disabilities must have access to at least one playing field, gymnasium, and swimming pool if able-bodied (AB) students are provided opportunities for sports, dance, and aquatics programs.

Accessibility refers to communication (the ability to understand) as well as architecture; hence, interpreters for persons who are deaf must be available as well as braille or tape-recorded signs/directions for persons who are blind. This type of accessibility should be kept in mind when planning workshops, tournaments, and meets.

The Office of Civil Rights (OCR) is responsible for administering the Rehabilitation Act (RA), which undergoes a number change each time it is amended. OCR does not, however, take action until a specific complaint for noncompliance is registered. Most schools, agencies, and universities prefer to handle Section 504 problems rather than have to cope with legal action. Therefore, institutions that receive federal funds designate one of their staff as a **504 compliance officer**. This person is contacted regarding problems related to physical, learning, living, and work environments.

Institutions also establish 504 committees or councils, which serve as advisory and advocacy bodies. Such committees often conduct awareness programs and assess barriers. Membership on the 504 committee is a good volunteer activity for students who want to learn advocacy skills.

PL 94-142: The Education for All Handicapped Children Act

PL 94-142, the Education for All Handicapped Children Act (EAHCA), later called Part B or Chapter II of the Education of the Handicapped Act (EHA), was enacted in 1975. It was not implemented, however, until its rules were printed in the *Federal Register* in 1977 (*Federal Register,* August 23, 1977). This law provided the first legal basis for adapted physical education. It required that physical education services, specially designed if necessary, be made available to students declared eligible by the IEP process and that these be free, appropriate, and in the least restrictive environment. PL 94-142 separated **direct services** (i.e., required special education) from **related services** (not required unless proven needed as a *prerequisite* to benefiting from special education). By including physical education as a part of the special education definition, PL 94-142 specified physical education as a direct and, therefore, required service.

In terms of its contributions to special education as a whole, PL 94-142 mandated five rights that changed the nature of public schooling for children and youth with disabilities:

1. Right to a *free* education
2. Right to an *appropriate* education

FIGURE 4.4 Athletes with cerebral palsy participate actively in the governance of the U.S. Cerebral Palsy Athletic Association, which is affiliated with the U.S. Olympic Committee (USOC). Pictured from left to right are Dick Hosty, Ken Wells, Wendy Shugal, and Sal Ficara.

3. Right to *nondiscriminatory* testing, evaluation, and placement procedures
4. Right to be educated in the *least restrictive environment*
5. Right to *procedural due process* of the law

PL 94-142 was a momentous achievement. By the early 1980s, official government documents called it EHA-B, since it was an amendment to EHA. Since 1990, it has been called IDEA-Part B or Subchapter II. It is reauthorized about every 3 years and assigned a new number.

PL 95-606: The Amateur Sports Act

When the U.S. Olympic Committee (USOC) was reorganized in the 1970s and plans made for better promotion and coordination of amateur athletics, sports for athletes with disabilities were included in the master plan. Specifically, PL 95-606, the Amateur Sports Act of 1978, charged the USOC

> to encourage and provide assistance to amateur athletic programs and competition for handicapped individuals, including, where feasible, the expansion of opportunities for meaningful participation by handicapped individuals in programs of athletic competition for able-bodied individuals. (Article II, 13, p. 2)

Today, athletes with disabilities use the U.S. Olympic Training Center at Colorado Springs (see Figure 4.4), and their sport organizations are assisted by USOC. New role models are emerging from within the ranks of persons with disabilities. Contemporary adapted physical education exposes students to these role models and uses them as resources.

Within the USOC, the Committee on Sports for the Disabled (COSD) is responsible for policy development in relation to disability sports. Organizations that sponsor two or more sports of Olympic caliber for citizens with disabilities are governed by this committee. Names and addresses of these organizations appear in Appendix C.

The COSD meets semiannually. Its goals are to (a) enlist increasing support from and involvement by the national governing bodies of able-bodied sports, (b) promote more aggressively the concept of sports for persons with disabilities, (c) exert more influence internationally on sports and disability, (d) foster more and better research on sports for individuals with disabilities, (e) enhance the status of athletes within the USOC, and (f) obtain a fair share of USOC funds.

Basic Concepts in Federal Law Advocacy

Effective advocacy requires an understanding of (a) how laws are numbered, (b) the difference between authorization and appropriation, (c) the procedures by which a bill becomes a law, (d) the protocol followed in determining rules and regulations for implementation of a law, (e) how copies of laws can be obtained, (f) enforcement of laws, (g) ways to find your congresspersons, and (h) the importance of the *Annual Report to Congress.* An understanding of basic concepts pertaining to federal laws will generalize to state-level legislative action since all states but one (Nebraska) are organized like the federal government with a Senate and House of Representatives.

The Numbering of Laws and Bills

How does a law like PL 94-142 derive its number? The first number indicates the Congress that enacted it. The second number states the law's rank or order. For example, PL 94-142 was the 142nd bill passed by the 94th Congress.

A Congress keeps the same number for a 2-year period. The number changes at the beginning of each odd-numbered year. The first Congress was 1789–1790, reminding us that George Washington was inaugurated in 1789. We celebrated the U.S. Constitution's 200th birthday in 1987; this was the Bicentennial, and the 100th Congress (1987–1988) was in progress. Can you use this information to determine the number that bills passed this year will have?

The Structure of Congress

Congress changes its number every 2 years because the entire membership of the House of Representatives ($N = 435$) is elected every 2 years. Members of the Senate hold 6-year terms, and one third of the Senate's 100 members are elected every 2 years.

Before enactment, bills have separate Senate and House of Representatives numbers. This is because the two structures of Congress consider and pass bills independently. For example, the influential Americans with Disabilities Act, enacted in 1990, was Senate (S) 933 and House of Representatives (HR) 2273. After both Houses passed the bill and it was signed by the president, the Americans with Disabilities Act became PL 101-336. Knowing HR and S numbers is important in advocacy activities pertaining to getting a law passed. When you write a letter to a congressperson, for example, urging him or her to vote for a law, it is essential to cite the law's number. Advocacy organizations can generally supply these numbers.

Authorization and Appropriation

Almost all laws involve the granting of money to carry out particular programs or initiatives. Two terms are used to designate decision making about money: authorization and appropriation. **Authorization** is the authoring of a mandate that empowers Congress to grant money, up to a specified ceiling level, to carry out the intent of a law. **Appropriation** is decision making about the actual amount to be given each year to particular programs or initiatives. Authorization is like promising an ice-cream cone contingent upon whether or not there is money to pay for it. In contrast, appropriation is like handing someone a dollar and saying, "Buy your ice-cream cone." Authorizations always involve greater sums of money than appropriations.

Authorization comes from specific laws like IDEA and may be formula-based (permanent) or discretionary (usually established for 3-year periods). In contrast, appropriation is determined year by year in conjunction with the preparation of the overall government budget. Only the president can initiate the annual appropriations bill, but both Houses must agree on expenditures. Once decisions are made, the money appropriated for a particular program is given to the federal agency responsible for overseeing that program. If advocates want federal money to be spent on programs for persons with disabilities, they must be assertive in conveying this wish to their congresspersons.

Enactment of Laws

Except for the annual appropriations bill, which is the president's responsibility, members of Congress are responsible for writing bills and introducing them to the Senate and House of Representatives. Much of this work is done by legislative aides, and input from individuals and professional organizations is welcomed. Committees and subcommittees from both branches of Congress study proposed bills, conduct hearings, gather testimony, and make numerous revisions. Over 95% of the 10,000 to 15,000 new bills introduced every 2 years die at the subcommittee level because of lack of support. The other 5% advance to the floor, are voted upon, and (if approved by both the House and the Senate) are signed by the president and become laws. Advocates can monitor how their legislator votes and who speaks for and against bills by reading the *Congressional Record,* a daily periodical found in most university libraries.

Many bills are reauthorizations of earlier legislation. IDEA legislation is typically reauthorized (i.e., updated or amended) every 3 to 5 years. Various advocacy groups monitor the rewording of laws and typically keep educators informed through organizations like AAHPERD and CEC. Occasionally, adapted physical activity professionals are requested to participate in letter-writing campaigns or telephone action.

Permanent or Discretionary Status

The separate parts of a law are designated as either permanent or discretionary. The parts of IDEA that are permanent continue without reauthorization. These are Subchapter II (PL 94-142, Assistance for Education of All Handicapped Individuals) and Subchapter VIII (Infants and Toddlers with Disabilities). These parts (also known as B and H) are permanent because their funding and authorization are formula-based rather than a set sum agreed upon at the discretion of Congress. For example, IDEA-Part B states that special education funding for each state shall be a maximum of 40% of the national average per pupil expenditure in public elementary and secondary schools.

The discretionary parts of IDEA can be revised, deleted, or expanded every 3 to 5 years at the discretion of Congress. **Discretionary status** also means that the amount of money to be authorized for implementation of programs can be raised, lowered, or left the same. For example, grants to universities to fund personnel training in special education, physical education, and related services are discretionary. The amount authorized is usually around $2 million. Far less than this is actually appropriated.

Rules and Regulations

After a bill is signed into law by the president, a period of several months is required for the federal agency responsible for implementation to write the official rules and regulations. Until these are published, a law cannot be enforced. Laws are usually relatively brief. The complete text of PL 94-142 was only 17 pages long (see Weintraub, Abeson, Ballard, & LaVor, 1976). The rules and regulations for implementation, published in the *Federal Register* almost 2 years after enactment, required 45 pages.

The *Federal Register* is the official government publication for disseminating (a) the rules and regulations that govern implementation of laws, (b) notices pertaining to grant applications, (c) presidential proclamations and executive orders, and (d) information about other government business. Published daily (except weekends), the *Federal Register* is an 8½-by-11-inch newspaper-like periodical that is available in most university libraries. Copies of a particular *Federal Register* can be obtained from your congressperson. Many university teachers own a copy of the August 23, 1977, *Federal Register,* which serves as the primary source for PL 94-142 theory and practice.

Hearings must be held throughout the nation so that all interested persons can offer suggestions and recommendations for implementing a new law. Written and oral testimony presented at hearings is used in formulating proposed rules. After these proposed rules are published in the *Federal Register,* more hearings are held and experts are brought to Washington, DC, to help with decision making. The final official rules and regulations are then published in the *Federal Register.* An important advocacy role is presence at public hearings and the submission of both oral and written testimony. Encouraging parents to participate in hearings is essential also.

Obtaining Copies of Laws and Bills

Advocates obtain copies of laws and bills so that they know firsthand what is going on. They share these with parents and others who may be less assertive in obtaining copies. A powerful strategy is carrying a copy of the law or its rules and regulations (the *Federal Register*) to meetings where policy and/or compliance are to be discussed. Monitoring bills when they are in draft stage and assisting professional organizations in providing input are also important.

Copies of IDEA legislation, soon after enactment, can be purchased from CRR Publishing Company, P.O. Box 1905, Alexandria, VA 22313-1905, or from the National Association of State Directors of Special Education, (703) 519-3800. Copies can also be obtained through your legislator. Copies of established laws appear in legal reference books like the *Code of Federal Regulations (CFR)* and the *United States Code (U.S.C.).* These multivolume sets of books can be found in most university libraries.

The *CFR* and *U.S.C.* **codify** (i.e., systematize and classify) everything on a particular topic into the same bound volume. The *CFR,* which is published annually, codifies the

FIGURE 4.5 Formats used in writing and recording law. Can you describe each source? Do you know where each source can be found?

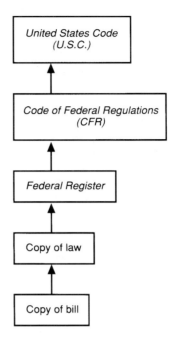

laws from the previous 12 months. EHA and IDEA information is codified in Volume 34 of the *CFR.* The *U.S.C.,* which is published every 6 years, codifies legislation over a longer time period. EHA and IDEA information is codified in Volume 20 of the *U.S.C.*

Knowledge of the *CFR* and *U.S.C.* helps in understanding the referencing system used in finding laws and citing particular passages. For example, the definition of physical education in EHA is referenced as 34 *CFR,* 300.14 or 20 *U.S.C.* 1401 [16]. Figure 4.5 summarizes the formats in which law is written.

Single copies of all House bills and committee reports can be obtained by calling the U.S. House of Representatives Document Room at (202) 225-3456. Additional copies may be obtained by writing the House Document Room, U.S. House of Representatives, Washington, DC 20515. Include a self-addressed mailing label. Copies of Senate bills and reports may be obtained by writing the U.S. Senate Document Room at Hart Office Building, B-04, Washington, DC 20510, and including a self-addressed mailing label.

Up-to-date information on pending federal legislation can be obtained by calling the U.S. Legislative Status Office at (202) 225-1772. You must know the bill's number and title.

Enforcement of Laws

Once a law is enacted, many years are required for 100% compliance. Often, if no one points out that rights are being violated, no attempt is made to enforce the law. The parts of IDEA that pertain to physical education are not being enforced in many school districts. One reason is that parents have not forced compliance. Perhaps they do not understand the law, or they may not appreciate the importance of physical education in the health, fitness, and happiness of their children.

Teachers, if they want to keep their jobs, often cannot challenge school administrators directly. There are many ethical dilemmas (Churton, 1987; Loovis, 1986; Minner, Prater, & Beane, 1984). A viable approach to improved law enforcement is to work through parents, acquainting them with publications that describe the success of other parents (Kennedy, French, & Henderson, 1989) and getting them involved in sport and recreation activities that heighten their awareness of the values of physical education.

Parent Power

IDEA legislation gives parents tremendous power. Procedures are outlined whereby parents can present complaints with respect to any matter relating to the educational placement or to the provision of a free, appropriate public education (20 *U.S.C.* 1415). If problems are not resolved, parents can request that a formal due process hearing be conducted by the local education agency (LEA). If the outcome at this level is not satisfactory, parents may then request the state education agency (SEA) to conduct a due process hearing. If parents dislike SEA decisions, they then have the right to initiate litigation (i.e., file a civil action suit in the courts).

Advocates help parents to understand and use their power. They provide support for resolving differences without formal due process hearings and civil court action if possible. The following is a list of hierarchical steps that parents should follow when they are unhappy with service delivery (Kennedy et al., 1989):

1. Talk to your child's teacher to see if adjustments or changes can be made.
2. Talk to other school personnel who are aware of your child's needs (e.g., counselor, nurse, psychologist, educational diagnostician, principal, special education director) to discuss alternatives and solutions.
3. Discuss concerns with professionals outside the school who know your child (e.g., psychologist, neurologist, family physician). These individuals may have ideas to solve the problem or may document support for your position.
4. Request that a child study team meeting (IEP meeting) be convened to discuss alternatives.
5. Write a letter to the school principal or special education director, requesting a meeting.
6. Write a similar letter to the superintendent of schools. Include with this letter a copy of all previous correspondence with school personnel and document your efforts to solve the problem.
7. Notify the school board of the problem.
8. Contact state and local chapters of parent and advocacy organizations for advice and assistance.
9. Contact the SEA for information and advice.

If these steps do not produce satisfactory enforcement of the law in parents' minds, then the due process hearing and litigation options should be taken. This may be the only way that some students will receive appropriate physical education and thus have their rights to health, fitness, and leisure skills upheld.

Finding Your Congresspersons

Citizens in every state elect two senators and several representatives who shape the legislation of this country. These persons maintain offices in Washington, DC, and in various cities throughout their state. Everyone is welcome to visit these offices, and advocates use this approach to get acquainted with legislative aides and advance the IDEA cause. While a face-to-face meeting with congresspersons is preferable, their legislative aides usually represent the first level of access.

If you know the names of your congresspersons, you can reach them in Washington, DC, by telephoning the Capitol Operator at (202) 224-3121. Or you can contact them by writing to the following addresses: U.S. Senate, Washington, DC 20510, or U.S. House of Representatives, Washington, DC 20515.

To obtain names of congresspersons, as well as information about other government officials, books like the *United States Government Manual* and the *Official Directory of the Congress* can be ordered from the Superintendent of Documents, U.S. Government Printing Office, P.O. Box 371954, Pittsburgh, PA 15250-7954. The telephone number for ordering documents by mail is (202) 512-1800. Libraries and local offices of political parties have these and other directories.

Annual Report to Congress

The U.S. Department of Education is required each year to publish the *Annual Report to Congress,* which describes (a) progress made in implementation of IDEA legislation, (b) national and state statistics pertaining to service delivery, and (c) needs (met and unmet). This report, published since 1979, typically is about 300 pages long and is the best primary source available for staying abreast of IDEA.

The *Annual Report to Congress* can be obtained at no cost by writing or telephoning the Division of Innovation and Development, Office of Special Education Programs, Switzer Building, Washington, DC 20202, telephone (202) 205-9864. Copies of these reports are also available at many university libraries through the computer-based information network of the Education Resources Information Center (ERIC).

The *Annual Report to Congress* summarizes what each state is doing with respect to IDEA implementation and thus enables advocates to compare their state with other states. It also provides statistics on the number of children and youth served by age, condition, and educational setting for each state. *This resource is a must for advocates.*

Current RA, ADA, and DDA Legislation

Figure 4.6 summarizes four tracks of legislation that are important in the 1990s. Each has a different number every 3 to 5 years. These laws, unlike IDEA, do not identify specific disability categories. Instead, **disability** is conceptualized as an impairment that substantially limits one or more of the major life activities (e.g., walking, breathing, seeing, hearing, learning, working).

FIGURE 4.6 Follow the yellow brick road to somewhere over the rainbow: A model summarizing laws, outcomes, and advocacy behaviors. (MR-MH = Mental Retardation-Mental Health; ESEA = Elementary and Secondary Education Act; EHA = Education of the Handicapped Act; EAHCA = Education for All Handicapped Children Act; IEP = Individualized Education Program; IFSP = Individualized Family Service Plan.)

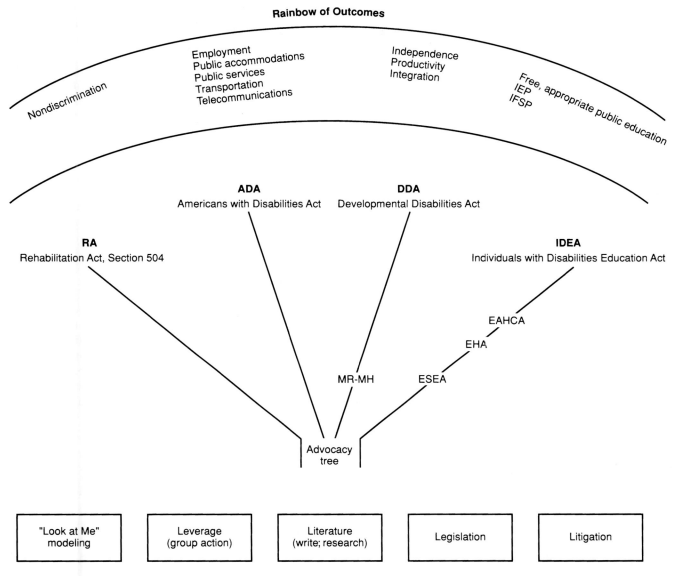

The Rehabilitation Act, Section 504

The Rehabilitation Act (RA), described earlier, continues to address discrimination against persons with disabilities. It is helpful, however, only when the offending agency or facility receives federal funds. In such cases, proven discrimination may result in withdrawal of federal funds. Most schools and universities have 504 committees (French, Kinnison, Sherrill, & Henderson, in press).

Americans With Disabilities Act

The Americans with Disabilities Act (ADA) (PL 101-336), passed in 1990, applies to all discrimination, regardless of

funding source. The purpose of this law is to end discrimination against persons with disabilities and to bring them into the economic and social mainstream of American life. The law addresses five areas in which discrimination was rampant in the 1980s: (a) employment in the private sector, (b) public accommodations, (c) public services, (d) transportation, and (e) telecommunications.

Some examples follow. All facilities, whether or not they receive federal funding, must provide equal access and equal services to persons with disabilities. This includes playgrounds, swimming pools, health spas, bowling alleys, golf courses, gymnasiums, and the like. Separate but equal will not be tolerated. Under ADA, persons with disabilities can no longer be denied insurance or be subject to different conditions based on disability alone. The nation's telephone services are being remodeled so that persons with hearing and/or speech impairments have services functionally equivalent to individuals without impairments.

The ADA is heralded as a landmark law that will do for persons with disabilities what the Civil Rights Act did for persons of color (Block, 1995). For additional information, contact the U.S. Department of Justice, Civil Rights Division, Coordination and Review Section, P.O. Box 66118, Washington, DC 20035-6118.

Developmental Disabilities Assistance and Bill of Rights Act

The Developmental Disabilities Assistance and Bill of Rights Act (DDA) of 1990 (PL 101-496) emphasized three goals (independence, productivity, and integration into the community) and mandated that state-level Developmental Disabilities Councils direct their efforts toward achievement of these goals. DDA activities are regulated and funded by the U.S. Department of Health and Human Services. Goals are achieved through (a) individual and family support, including federal funds for child welfare and older Americans; (b) education; (c) employment; (d) income, including the Supplemental Security Income and the Social Security Disability Insurance programs; (e) housing; and (f) health, including Medicaid programs.

Unlike IDEA, which defines disabilities categorically (e.g., mental retardation, severe emotional disturbance), the DDA uses the following definition:

Developmental disability is a severe, chronic disability which:

(1) is attributable to a mental or physical impairment or combination of mental and physical impairments;
(2) is manifested before the person attains age twenty-two;
(3) is likely to continue indefinitely;
(4) results in substantial functional limitations in three or more of the following areas of major life activity: (a) self-care, (b) receptive and expressive language, (c) learning, (d) mobility, (e) self-direction, (f) capacity for independent living, and (g) economic self-sufficiency; and
(5) reflects the person's need for a combination and sequence of special, interdisciplinary, or generic care, treatment, or other services which are of lifelong or extended duration and are individually planned and coordinated. (Section 102(5) of PL 100-146)

Community programs that can show success in helping persons with developmental disabilities achieve independence, productivity, and integration may apply for grants. Physical activity and recreation programs, if properly conducted, can promote these goals.

IDEA Legislation: Basic Concepts

The Individuals with Disabilities Education Act (IDEA) is the legislation that guides policies and practices in educating stu-

dents with disabilities. This legislation, first passed in 1970, has been updated and/or amended every 3 to 5 years. The most recent reauthorization is 1997 (Arnhold & Auxter, 1995).

Age Range Covered by IDEA

The age range covered by IDEA is from birth to 21 years of age. IDEA-Part B provides for ages 3 to 21 years, and IDEA-Part H provides for infants and toddlers, defined as individuals from birth to age 2.

IDEA-Part C emphasizes the importance of secondary and postsecondary education and transitional services for youth with disabilities. The law defines **youth with disabilities** as persons who are 12 years of age or older or who are enrolled in the seventh or higher grade in school.

Special Education Definition

IDEA, Sec. 1401 (16), states:

(16) The term *special education* means specially designed instruction, at no cost to parents or guardians, to meet the unique needs of a child with a disability, including—
(A) instruction conducted in the classroom, in the home, in hospitals and institutions, and in other settings; and
(B) instruction in physical education.

Physical education is the only school subject mentioned in this definition. Essentially, this definition makes specially designed physical education a component of special education. This is why adapted physical educators hired to teach separate classes, usually of children with severe disabilities, are often salaried by IDEA-Part B monies and considered members of the special education staff.

Definitions of Disabilities

IDEA, Sec. 1401a (1), states:

(1) The term *children with disabilities* means children—
(A) with mental retardation, hearing impairments including deafness, speech or language impairments, visual impairments including blindness, serious emotional disturbance, orthopedic impairments, autism, traumatic brain injury, other health impairments, or specific learning disabilities; and
(B) who, by reason thereof, need special education and related services.

Definitions of disabilities recognized under IDEA appear in Appendix A.

IEP Definition

The individualized education program (IEP) is one of the most important concepts of IDEA legislation. Key words in the definition are in bold print.

(20) The term *individualized education program* means **a written statement** for each child with a disability developed in any meeting by a **representative of the local educational agency** or

an intermediate educational unit who shall be qualified to provide, or supervise the provision of, specially designed instruction to meet the unique needs of children with disabilities, the **teacher,** the **parents or guardian** of such child, and whenever appropriate, such **child,** which statement shall include

(A) a statement of the present levels of educational **performance** of such child,

(B) a statement of **annual goals,** including short-term instructional objectives,

(C) a statement of the specific educational **services** to be provided to such child, and the extent to which such child will be able to participate in regular education programs,

(D) a statement of the needed **transition** services for students beginning no later than age 16 and annually thereafter (and, when determined appropriate for the individual, beginning at age 14 or younger), including, when appropriate, a statement of the interagency responsibilities or linkages (or both) before the student leaves the school setting,

(E) the projected **date** for initiation and anticipated duration of such services, and

(F) appropriate objective criteria and **evaluation** procedures and schedules for determining, on at least an annual basis, whether instructional objectives are being achieved. (PL 101-475, Sec. 1401 [20])

This definition includes *what* the IEP is (a written statement developed in a meeting), *who* must be present at the meeting (four types of persons), and the *required contents* of the IEP. The sections can be remembered by the acronym **PAST-DE,** conceptualized as follows:

P—Performance, present level

A—Annual goals, including short-term objectives

S—Services to be provided

T—Transition services for ages 16 and over

D—Dates and duration

E—Evaluation to determine whether objectives are achieved

To remember PAST-DE, think about how the age of ignorance about educating students with disabilities is past history or dead (DE).

IEP Purpose

The IEP is an official special education document. Its main purpose is to document the placement decision. This decision has two parts. First, evidence must be presented to show that the student meets entry-level criteria to be classified as having a disability in the subject matter under consideration. Second, evidence must be presented to support the specific services designated (regular class, resource room, separate class, etc.) as the least restrictive placement. By law, the IEP must encompass physical education. This inclusion is generally a

mention of the type of physical education placement (regular, adapted, or some combination) and a description of psychomotor performance.

The physical education section must be brief because all subject matter areas are included in the IEP. Each school district uses a different form, but most special education IEPs are about three to four pages long.

In many school districts, the three-to-four-page special education IEP represents a summary of IEPs written by specialists in different areas. The adapted physical educator, for instance, may be expected to write a physical education IEP.

Free Appropriate Public Education Definition

Free appropriate public education is defined in IDEA Part A as follows:

(18) The term *free appropriate public education* means special education and related services that
(A) have been provided at public expense, under public supervision and direction, and without charge,
(B) meet the standards of the State educational agency,
(C) include an appropriate preschool, elementary, or secondary school education in the state involved, and
(D) are provided in conformity with the individualized education program required under section 1414(a)(5) of this title. (PL 101-475, Sec 1401 [18])

The term *appropriate* has caused considerable debate, resulting in several lawsuits. In one of these (*Board of Education of Hendrick Hudson Central Schools District v. Rowley,* 458 US. 176, 1982), the U.S. Supreme Court declared that *appropriate education was personalized instruction with sufficient support services to permit the student to benefit educationally from instruction.* Now called the **Rowley standard,** this decision clarifies that a school is not required to maximize a student's potential for learning. Rather, the IDEA sets forth a "basic floor opportunity" for students with disabilities. **Appropriate** depends on standards established by state education agencies. One characteristic of appropriate instruction is congruency with what is written on the IEP.

Least Restrictive Environment

Least restrictive environment (LRE) philosophy, according to the Individuals with Disabilities Education Act (IDEA) of 1990, is built on two fundamental beliefs:

To the maximum extent appropriate, children with disabilities, including those in public or private institutions or other care facilities, are educated with children who do not have disabilities; and . . . special classes, separate schooling, or other removal of children with disabilities from the regular educational environment occurs only when the nature and severity of the disability is such that education in regular classes cannot be achieved satisfactorily. (U.S. Department of Education, 1992, p. 135, citing 34 CFR 300.550 [a] and [b])

Transition Services

IDEA, Section 401(19), states:

(19) The term 'transition services' means a coordinated set of activities for a student, designed within an outcome-oriented process, which promotes movement from school to post-school activities, including post-secondary education, vocational training, integrated employment (including supported employment), continuing and adult education, adult services, independent living, or community participation. The coordinated set of activities shall be based upon the individual student's needs, taking into account the student's preferences and interests, and shall include instruction, community experiences, the development of employment and other post-school adult living objectives and, when appropriate, acquisition of daily living skills and functional vocational evaluation.

Physical Education Mentions in IDEA

The following mentions of physical education in IDEA form the basis for public school practices. Advocates must be ever vigilant that school personnel are complying with the law.

Physical Education Definition

Page 42480 of the August 23, 1977, *Federal Register* states:

(2) *Physical education* is defined as follows:
  (i) The term means the development of:
      (A) physical and motor fitness;
      (B) fundamental motor skills and patterns; and
      (C) skills in aquatics, dance, and individual and group games and sports (including intramural and lifetime sports).
  (ii) The term includes special physical education, adapted physical education, movement education, and motor development.

This definition differentiates physical education from such related services as occupational and physical therapy. The term *skills,* as used in IDEA, encompasses mental and social (as well as physical) skills needed to learn rules and strategies. Nowhere in IDEA is there a definition specifically for adapted physical education.

Physical Education Requirement

Page 42489 of the August 23, 1977, *Federal Register* states:

121a.307 Physical Education
(a) *General.* Physical education services, specially designed if necessary, must be made available to every handicapped child receiving a free appropriate public education.

This passage, together with the mention of physical education in the special education definition, comprises the legal basis for adapted physical education service delivery for students with disabilities. Whether a specially designed pro-

gram is needed is determined by IDEA-Part B eligibility procedures, which are described later in the chapter.

Integration in Regular Physical Education

Page 42489 of the August 23, 1977, *Federal Register* states:

(b) *Regular physical education.* Each handicapped child must be afforded the opportunity to participate in the regular physical education program available to nonhandicapped children unless:
  (1) the child is enrolled full-time in a separate facility; or
  (2) the child needs specially designed physical education, as prescribed in the child's individualized education program.

The intent is to place each student in his or her *least restrictive environment* based on individual assessment data and multidisciplinary deliberation. To justify segregation, the IEP process must document that the present level of performance, goals, and objectives are such that needs cannot be met in the regular physical education setting.

Special Physical Education

Page 42489 of the August 23, 1977, *Federal Register* states:

(c) *Special physical education.* If specially designed physical education is prescribed in a child's individualized education program, the public agency responsible for the education of that child shall provide the service directly, or make arrangements for it to be provided through other public or private programs.

Specially designed physical education, as defined, does not have to be full-time placement in a separate class. It can refer to specific conditions imposed upon regular class placement, like limited class size, the presence of an assistant for one-to-one instruction, and the availability of wheelchairs and other special or adapted equipment. Just as special education is taught by a certified special education teacher, specially designed physical education should be planned and, when possible, implemented by an adapted physical activity specialist.

Evaluation Procedures in IDEA

IDEA has also contributed to the improvement of evaluation (sometimes called assessment) procedures, particularly as they pertain to placement. Physical educators, because of their potential role in placement decision making, should know the legal bases for evaluation. The August 23, 1977, *Federal Register,* pages 42496–42497, states:

121a532 **Evaluation procedures.**
State and local education agencies shall ensure, at a minimum, that:
(a) Tests and other evaluation materials
  (1) are provided and administered in the child's native language or other mode of communication, unless it is clearly not feasible to do so;
  (2) have been validated for the specific purpose for which they are used; and

(3) are administered by trained personnel in conformance with the instructions provided by their producer;

(b) Tests and other evaluation materials include those tailored to assess specific areas of educational need and not merely those which are designed to provide a single general intelligence quotient;

(c) Tests are selected and administered so as best to ensure that when a test is administered to a child with impaired sensory, manual, or speaking skills, the test results accurately reflect the child's aptitude or achievement level or whatever other factors the test purports to measure, rather than reflecting the child's impaired sensory, manual, or speaking skills (except where those skills are the factors which the test purports to measure);

(d) No single procedure is used as the sole criterion for determining an appropriate educational program for a child;

(e) The evaluation is made by a multidisciplinary team or group of persons, including at least one teacher or other specialist with knowledge in the area of suspected disability; and

(f) The child is assessed in all areas related to the suspected disability, including, where appropriate, health, vision, hearing, social and emotional status, general intelligence, academic performance, communicative status, and motor abilities. (20 U.S.C. 1412[5]0)

The U.S. Department of Education reports that parents lodge more official complaints about placement than any other area. Many of these complaints are related to the evaluation procedures used in decision making. Of particular concern to physical educators is the general lack of physical education tests validated for the specific purpose of placement.

Services for Infants and Toddlers

The EHA of 1986 (PL 99-457) was the first federal legislation to mandate early intervention services for infants and toddlers with disabilities, defined as individuals from birth to age 2 years. Rules and regulations for this law were published in the *Federal Register,* June 22, 1989. Today this legislation is incorporated into IDEA and constitutes Part H (see Chapter 18).

Instead of an IEP, early intervention services for infants and toddlers with disabilities are guided by an **individualized family service plan** (IFSP). This plan is described in Chapter 18.

The IFSP, like the IEP, must be based on multidisciplinary assessment and developed by a multidisciplinary team, including the parent or guardian. IDEA-Part H does not specifically mention adapted physical education, but these services may be provided under special education since IDEA-Part A includes physical education as a part of special education.

Especially significant in the regulations are the role of the family in the decision-making process and the strong preference shown for services in integrated settings. On the issue of integration, the *Federal Register* (June 29, 1989) states:

(b) *Location of Services.* To the extent appropriate, early intervention programs must be provided in the types of settings in which infants and toddlers without disabilities will participate . . . it is important that efforts be made to provide early intervention services in settings and facilities that do not remove the children from natural environments (e.g., the home, day-care centers, or other community settings). Thus, it is recommended that services be community-based, and not isolate an eligible child or the child's family from settings or activities in which children without disabilities would participate. (Sec. 303.12)

Funding of Adapted Physical Education

Whether a school district initiates and maintains a high-quality adapted physical education program is often dependent upon funding. Therefore, physical educators must understand methods of public school funding and problems involved in the equalization of educational opportunity for all children.

The cost of educating students with disabilities is about 2.3 times more than that of educating the nondisabled. In recognition of this fact, IDEA-Part B provides that federal grants be awarded to state education agencies (SEAs). These federal monies must be spent only for the **excess cost** of special education (including adapted physical education) over the average per-pupil expenditure in regular education. These are called flow-through monies because the SEA keeps about 25% of them and distributes the other 75% to local education agencies (LEAs).

Adapted physical educators employed to serve only students with disabilities are often salaried by IDEA-Part B flow-through monies. There are, however, many other ways of funding adapted physical educators. A philosophically sound approach is for regular education to contribute toward the salary of adapted physical educators the monies that would be spent on regular physical education if the student had not been placed in a separate setting. Then, special education monies are applied only toward the excess cost.

Regardless of where the monies come from, if adapted physical education is written into the student's IEP, the school administration must find a way of providing the needed services. The law is clear that related services (physical and occupational therapy) cannot substitute for physical education instruction. *The regular physical educator is responsible for teaching students with disabilities if no adapted physical education specialist is available.* This explains why so many regular physical educators are undertaking graduate work in adapted physical education; they might not wish to become specialists, but they do graduate work because they need additional knowledge to fulfill the expectations of their school systems.

The IEP Process

The IEP process—sometimes called the child study or ARD (Admission, Review, Dismissal) process—is a series of public school procedures that culminates in the written IEP. These procedures are directed toward finding unserved children with disabilities, *admitting* them to the school district's special education program, providing them with special services, *reviewing* their progress at least annually, and subsequently *dismissing*

T a b l e 4 . 1   The IEP process as required by IDEA, adapted to show roles of regular and adapted physical education instructors.

Phase 1 *Child Find*	**District-wide screening process** for all children in all school subjects. (1) Usually done by regular physical education instructor or classroom teacher.	(2) Usually conducted at beginning of school year but can occur anytime. (3) Often informal, resulting from observation and/or conference with parent.	(4) Parent can initiate process instead of teacher.
Phase 2 *Initial Data Collection and Pre-IEP Meeting*	**Referral for further testing** begins the process to determine if adapted physical education/special education services are needed. (1) Special education director is asked to determine pupil's eligibility for special services.	(2) Parents are contacted for consent to test and/or collect eligibility data. (3) Data collection usually done by regular physical education instructor.	(4) Pre-IEP meeting to determine need for more extensive testing. (5) Written report of findings.

Phase 3 *Admission to Special Education, Including Adapted Physical Education*	**Comprehensive Individual Assessment** Initiated by written report signed by referral committee—see Phase 2.
	(1) Special education director assigns persons to do assessment.
	(2) Notification of rights is sent to parents.
	(3) Parent consent is obtained for comprehensive assessment by multidisciplinary team.
	(4) Comprehensive individual assessment with psychomotor part is done by adapted physical education specialist.
		IEP Meeting
		(1) Procedural due process safeguards must be observed in planning meeting. Consider:
		  (a) who must be present,
		  (b) time and place, and
		  (c) native language.
		(2) Presentation and analysis of assessment data by different team members.
		(3) Agreement on present level of functioning.
			(4) Decision making concerning:
			  (a) goals and objectives,
			  (b) services,
			    (i) educational placement,
			    (ii) interventions,
			    (iii) transition,
			    (iv) et cetera,
			  (c) dates/timeline,
			  (d) evaluation plan.
			(5) Write IEP.
			(6) Sign IEP.

Phase 4 *Program Implementation With Annual Program Review*			
Phase 5 *Dismissal From Special Education Into Full-Time Regular Education*			

them from special education. The precise roles of regular and adapted physical educators are not discussed in IDEA and thus vary by school district. In most instances, however, the physical educator is expected to contribute expertise in the identification and solution of problems in the psychomotor domain.

Five Phases of the IEP Process

Table 4.1 depicts five phases of the IEP process: (a) child find (identification of students who may be eligible for special education services, including adapted physical education); (b) initial data collection and pre-IEP meeting; (c) formal admission to special education, including *comprehensive individual assessment* and the official *IEP meeting;* (d) program implementation with annual program review, for the purpose of evaluat-

ing the effectiveness of the learning activities in achieving goals and objectives; and (e) dismissal from the special education program into regular education. This last phase may seem idealistic, but it demonstrates IDEA philosophy that students should, if possible, be integrated into regular education.

Regulations Relating to Dates

IDEA requires that an IEP must be in effect *before* students with disabilities can receive special education. This is because the IEP process is the means by which eligibility for services is determined and educational placement is assigned.

Parental consent is required before comprehensive individual assessment for special education (including adapted physical education) placement can begin. Once this consent is obtained, most states require that the IEP process be completed in 30 to 60 days.

IDEA also requires that the written IEP be officially reviewed once each year. Many states require more frequent reviews. The purpose of these reviews is to analyze the student's educational progress and to make revisions in the IEP.

IEP Meeting Participants

In general, participants in IEP meetings represent four types of roles: (a) parental, (b) administrative, (c) instructional, and (d) diagnostic. Most adapted physical activity authorities believe that a physical educator should be present at the IEP meeting to provide input concerning performance and needs in the psychomotor domain. If, however, a physical educator cannot be released from teaching responsibilities to attend, he or she should submit written recommendations to the special education director and, when possible, confer with the parents before the meeting and ask them to serve as advocates for physical education.

IEP Principles and Practices

The IEP and the IEP process are praiseworthy concepts that have shaped and changed practices in the field. Most of the principles that guide school district practices in relation to assessment, evaluation, and placement have their roots in the IEP process and thus come from IDEA-Part B. Among the most important of these principles are the following:

1. A student shall be considered nondisabled (i.e., normal) until sufficient evidence is presented that he or she meets criteria to be labeled disabled. This principle is similar to that followed in a court of law: All persons are considered innocent until proven guilty. Educational classification is a legal procedure with due process requirements.

2. The regular education placement (i.e., integration) shall be considered the most appropriate placement for each student until evidence is presented, through the IEP process, that special services are required and that these services cannot be provided in the regular classroom.

3. A student may be declared disabled in one curricular area but not another. The placement decision for each subject matter area must therefore be made separately and independently from all others.

4. Placement decisions shall be based on comprehensive assessment data generated by instruments that are *valid* for the purpose for which they are being used.

5. The evaluation procedures used in making placement decisions must meet the six criteria stated in IDEA (see pages 86–87).

6. Placement decisions must be based on multidisciplinary data and made by teams of experts rather than one person.

7. School districts should make available a continuum of placements and services so that students in separate education settings can be moved into progressively more integrated environments.

8. Placement decisions must be reviewed at least once each year to determine whether the student is ready yet for a more integrated environment and to update goals and objectives.

9. Every student shall be placed in his or her least restrictive environment.

10. Due process procedures to protect the rights of every student shall be clearly delineated.

More extensive coverage of these principles is provided in Chapters 5 to 7 on service delivery.

The State Plan and Adapted Physical Education

IDEA requires every SEA to develop a *state plan* that describes specifically how IDEA will be implemented in that state. This state plan is then submitted to the U.S. Department of Education every 3 years; this official document enables the state government to receive federal funds to supplement the cost of quality education for students with disabilities.

Ideally, the state plan should include all of the mentions of physical education that appear in IDEA regulations. If, however, SEA personnel are not knowledgeable and/or supportive of physical education, they may neglect writing out procedures for implementing physical education mandates. If the state plan does not include these procedures, then IDEA cannot be enforced in regard to physical education. It is, therefore, imperative that university classes teach physical educators about the state plan and that a copy of it be available for study. A copy can be obtained from a local special education administrator or by writing the state education agency.

Before a state plan is filed with the federal government, it must be made available to all interested persons, and public hearings must be held to allow individuals and special interest groups to offer input. Input may involve agreement or disagreement with changes or the pointing out of inconsistencies between the state plan and IDEA. The dates of these public hearings, by law, are announced in newspapers of the large cities in which they are held. The SEA decides which cities these shall be, but everyone is free to attend and speak. In addition to attending public hearings, physical educators and parents should submit written testimony to the SEA concerning the state plan. Deadlines for receiving these letters are also published.

The process for becoming involved in the state plan is outlined in Figure 4.7. It is appropriate for university classes to attend public hearings and write individual letters. Ideally, physical educators take parents of children with disabilities to these hearings to speak in favor of physical education mandates and the values their children have derived from physical education instruction. Only by caring and acting at the state level can IDEA be translated into action.

The Need for State Laws

IDEA forms the legal basis for adapted physical education only for students declared disabled by IEP eligibility procedures. Many, many other students have psychomotor problems serious enough to merit adapted physical education intervention. Federal law cannot be passed to improve the general education system for nondisabled students since education is not a power given to the U.S. government by the Constitution.

FIGURE 4.7 The legislative process for influencing the rules and regulations of the state plan. This series of steps occurs once every 3 years. The resulting 3-year plan governs all aspects of state education agency (SEA) and local education agency (LEA) compliance with the Individuals with Disabilities Education Act.

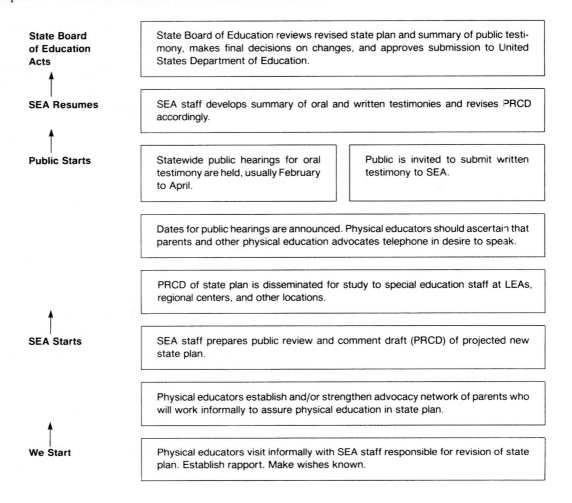

State Board of Education Acts — State Board of Education reviews revised state plan and summary of public testimony, makes final decisions on changes, and approves submission to United States Department of Education.

SEA Resumes — SEA staff develops summary of oral and written testimonies and revises PRCD accordingly.

Public Starts — Statewide public hearings for oral testimony are held, usually February to April.

Public is invited to submit written testimony to SEA.

Dates for public hearings are announced. Physical educators should ascertain that parents and other physical education advocates telephone in desire to speak.

PRCD of state plan is disseminated for study to special education staff at LEAs, regional centers, and other locations.

SEA Starts — SEA staff prepares public review and comment draft (PRCD) of projected new state plan.

Physical educators establish and/or strengthen advocacy network of parents who will work informally to assure physical education in state plan.

We Start — Physical educators visit informally with SEA staff responsible for revision of state plan. Establish rapport. Make wishes known.

The only way to ensure high-quality physical education, including adapted physical education when needed, for all students is through state legislation. Many states have or are working on legislation that parallels IDEA. Physical educators should work actively with state legislators to ensure that the physical education passages in IDEA are included and expanded to encompass nondisabled students in state law.

Advocacy for Needed Legislation

This chapter has emphasized the importance of federal and state laws in shaping adapted physical education. These laws are not static because implementation depends on funding, which may change annually. New laws are needed year by year to actually appropriate the money for use.

The following is a list of strategies that physical educators can use in advocating for needed legislation:

1. Get to know your state and federal legislators. Let them know you vote for them specifically because they support legislation favorable to education and/or equal opportunity for persons with disabilities.

2. Visit your legislator in his or her office in the Capitol. Get to know the legislator's staff by name and personality; usually, they are the ones responsible for compiling materials, reading and answering letters sent to the legislator, and keeping him or her informed.

3. Make frequent contacts with legislators. The best communication is face-to-face, but telephone calls, telegrams, and letters are crucial when bills are ready for a vote.

4. Do not mail form letters; make contents brief and personal. Be sure to mention the law by name and number, and state specifically which passage you wish to retain or change.

5. Develop parent advocacy corps for physical education. Take different kinds of stationery to Special Olympics and other sport practices and ask parents who are waiting to jot letters to their legislators. Offer to speak at meetings of parent groups, inform them about IDEA, and ask them to visit, telephone, and write legislators specifically on behalf of physical education.

6. Become a member of parent and other advocacy groups for persons with disabilities and encourage them to invite

legislators to speak at their meetings. Volunteering to be program chairperson will guarantee that the invitations are extended. Legislators, as well as candidates running for office, are particularly willing to speak during election years.

7. Become personal friends with people who are disabled and encourage them to advocate for physical education.

8. When you write to a legislator, be sure to ask for an answer in which he or she states intent to support or not to support your request. When you speak to a legislator, do the same.

9. Invite legislators, with the approval of your administration, to visit your adapted physical education program and/or to be a dignitary in the opening or closing ceremonies of Special Olympics, Cerebral Palsy Sports, or other events.

10. Keep abreast of funding issues, especially which parties and which persons support federal and state funding favorable to education. Find out how your legislator votes on critical issues by reading newspapers or the *Congressional Record* or by telephoning his or her office. Let your legislator know when you approve, as well as when you disapprove.

11. Get to know the state directors of physical education and special education and their staff, all of whom are part of the SEA, and encourage them to communicate with legislators.

12. Be sure local and state meetings of physical educators include legislative updates concerning action that may affect adapted physical education. Exhibit bulletin boards showing progress made in implementation of laws. Encourage officers of local and state physical education organizations, as well as members, to maintain close contact with their legislators.

References

American Alliance for Health, Physical Education, Recreation and Dance. (1980). *Shaping the body politic: Legislative training for the physical educator.* Reston, VA: Author.

Arnhold, R. W., & Auxter, D. (1995). The reauthorization of IDEA. *Palaestra, 11*(3), 37–44.

Block, M. E. (1995). Americans with Disabilities Act: Its impact on youth sports. *Journal of Physical Education, Recreation and Dance, 66*(1), 28–32.

Block, M. E. (1996). Implications of U.S. federal law and court cases for physical education placement of students with disabilities. *Adapted Physical Activity Quarterly, 13*(2), 127–152.

Churton, M. (1987). Impact of the Education of the Handicapped Act on adapted physical education: A 10-year overview. *Adapted Physical Activity Quarterly, 4*(1), 1–8.

Dougherty, N. J., Auxter, D., Goldberger, A. S., & Heinzmann, G. S. (1994). *Sport, physical activity, and the law.* Champaign, IL: Human Kinetics.

Federal Register, May 4, 1977, PL 93-112, the Rehabilitation Act of 1973, Section 504.

Federal Register, August 23, 1977, PL 94-142, the Education for All Handicapped Children Act.

Federal Register, June 22, 1989, PL 99-457, the Education of the Handicapped Act.

French, R., Kinnison, L., Sherrill, C., & Henderson, H. (in press). Relationship of Section 504 to physical education and sport: Revisited. *Journal of Physical Education, Recreation and Dance.*

Kennedy, S. O., French, R., & Henderson, H. L. (1989). The due-able process could happen to you! Physical educators, handicapped students, and the law. *Journal of Physical Education, Recreation and Dance, 60*(8), 86–93.

Loovis, E. M. (1986). Placement of handicapped students: The perpetual dilemma. *Adapted Physical Activity Quarterly, 3*(3), 193–198.

Minner, S., Prater, G., & Beane, A. (1984). Provision of adapted physical education: A dilemma for special educators. *Adapted Physical Activity Quarterly, 1*(4), 282–286.

Sherrill, C. (1994). Least restrictive environment and total inclusion philosophies: Critical analysis. *Palaestra, 10*(3), 25–28, 31, 34–35, 52–54.

Sherrill, C., & Hillman, W. (1988). Legislation, funding, and adapted physical education teacher training. In C. Sherrill (Ed.), *Leadership training in adapted physical education* (pp. 85–103). Champaign, IL: Human Kinetics.

Stein, J. (1994). Total inclusion or least restrictive environment. *Journal of Physical Education, Recreation and Dance, 65*(9), 21–25.

Turnbull, H. R. (1986). Appropriate education and Rowley. *Exceptional Children, 52*(4), 347–352.

U.S. Department of Education. (1992). *To assure the free appropriate public education of all children with disabilities: Fourteenth annual report to Congress on the implementation of the Individuals with Disabilities Education Act.* Washington, DC: Author.

Weintraub, F. J., Abeson, A., Ballard, J., & LaVor, M. (1976). *Public policy and the education of exceptional children.* Reston, VA: Council for Exceptional Children.

C H A P T E R

5

Philosophy, Planning, and Curriculum Design

FIGURE 5.1 A life situation for consideration: *(A)* Bob (on crutches) and Joe (in the wheelchair) are 10-year-olds with normal intelligence. Both are average or better students in their fourth-grade classroom but have had little opportunity to learn sports, dance, and aquatics. *(B)* Jim is 5 years old and obviously small for his age; he learns slowly but tries hard to please. *(C)* Dick has a brace on one leg and lots of problems with asthma. How will you and your school district plan for these students? What philosophy will guide your planning?

A

B

C

After you have studied this chapter, you should be able to do the following:

1. Explain the PAP-TE-CA service delivery model and discuss how planning is affected by philosophy.

2. Discuss humanistic philosophy and theories helpful in planning curricular and instructional programs.

3. Develop purposes, goals, and objectives for students, when assessment data are available.

4. Understand that organizing centers (i.e., frames of references, themes, or emphases) guide planning and curriculum design. Apply this concept to goal areas, top-down and bottom-up approaches, and different kinds of placement.

5. Contrast least restrictive environment (LRE), regular education initiative (REI), and inclusive placement philosophies.

6. Identify and discuss eight variables that should be considered when making placement decisions. Add other variables to the ones in this chapter.

7. Critically think about curriculum models used in physical education; describe some and evaluate their strengths and weaknesses.

8. Explain these four steps in planning instruction for a semester or year: (a) calculating instructional time, (b) planning use of time, (c) developing instructional units, and (d) making decisions about space, equipment, and resources.

9. Discuss how number of minutes of instructional time is used to determine number of objectives. Give examples.

Chapters 5, 6, and 7 pertain to PAP-TE-CA service delivery. This chapter concerns philosophy, planning, and curriculum design, because these are the first part of the model and fundamental to decision making in all other parts. Chapter 6 focuses on assessment, and Chapter 7 describes teaching, evaluating, and consulting.

Differences Between Regular and Adapted Physical Activity

Adapted physical activity extends the humanistic qualities of prizing, caring, trusting, and respecting to all individuals, with emphasis on those who are clumsy and/or have disabilities (see Figure 5.1). Adapted physical activity professionals must be outstanding service providers who empower themselves and others to become the best they can be. This is possible only when philosophy evolves from carefully considered theories.

Regular and adapted physical activity have the same purpose and goals. Goals are, however, prioritized differently. In regular education, many assumptions are made. First, students are assumed to have sufficient self-concept, social competency, and mental health to benefit from instruction that employs traditional methodology and provides direct corrective feedback. A second assumption is that students have the play and game behaviors needed to get into a game formation, to follow basic rules, and to derive expected outcomes (fun, enjoyment, satisfaction). A third assumption is that sensory input and perceptual processes are intact and that students can handle a vast amount of stimuli at one time. Finally, it is assumed that students can generalize skills and fitness developed in school to lifespan behaviors supportive of good health and leisure.

In adapted physical activity, no assumptions are made. Goals are individualized and based on assessment data. Differently abled students have many more needs than regular students. These may be developmental or acquired because of gradual demoralization experiences in physical education (Robinson, 1990). Perceived failure in activities that seem easy to others may result in low self-esteem and learned helplessness that must be remediated before traditional instruction can be effective.

The scope of responsibility of regular and adapted physical activity, as dynamic delivery systems, varies considerably, especially for school-age individuals. Regular physical education is concerned primarily with curriculum, instruction, and pedagogy in school facilities. In contrast, adapted physical education is concerned with overall coordinated service delivery in home-school-community contexts and involves considerable travel and teamwork.

Regular and adapted physical activity professionals have different knowledge bases also. The former are trained primarily in the exercise and movement sciences, and the latter are trained in all aspects of adaptation theory. Regular physical education is guided by a traditional teacher-training curriculum, whereas adapted physical activity is a relatively new profession that is just beginning to generate and test theory.

These many differences between regular and adapted physical activity are most manifest in the area of planning, the first part of the PAP-TE-CA model. Planning, both for the total school district and the individuals served, is dependent upon philosophy. This chapter therefore focuses first on philosophy and then on planning.

How Philosophy and Knowledge Interact

Figure 5.2 shows that philosophy evolves from knowledge but also interacts with and changes knowledge. This table expands on adaptation theory, which was introduced in Chapter 3. Because adaptation is theorized as the unifying theme for creating and using knowledge about four variables (physical activity, individual and ecosystem differences, service delivery, and empowerment), adaptation is specified as the grand theory. A **grand theory** is a conceptual framework that drives the generation of theories, philosophy, and practices.

The philosophy that guides adaptation is influenced by both evolving and time-tested, accepted theories. The time-tested

FIGURE 5.2 Philosophy evolves from knowledge but also interacts with and changes knowledge.

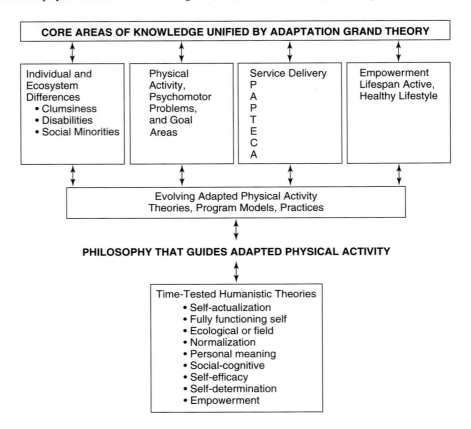

theories listed in Figure 5.2 fall within the humanistic school of thought. Each of these theories is discussed in this chapter. Some specific theories, like social cognitive and self-efficacy theories, are associated also with other schools of thought, but this does not detract from their importance in a humanistic philosophy.

Humanistic Philosophy

Humanism, as the term is used in this text, is a service delivery philosophy that pertains to helping people become fully human, thereby actualizing their potentials for making our world the best possible place for all forms of life. In particular, humanism emphasizes goals pertaining to self-concept, relationships with others, intrinsic motivation, and personal responsibility. The central tenet of humanism is **holism,** the careful planning of each learning experience to meet the needs of the whole person. In physical education, this means that movement and fitness activities are taught and conducted in ways that promote and preserve self-esteem. Self-concept is not conceptualized as a concomitant or incidental goal but as a primary concern.

Humanistic philosophy is the hallmark of adapted physical activity because of the nature of the individuals served. Persons with low motor skills and fitness typically have little faith in their ability to overcome these problems. They tend to be self-conscious, poorly motivated, and strongly influenced by past failures and disappointments. Many perceive physical activity as having few benefits; for them, it is

not easy, fun, relaxing, or satisfying. They are unlikely to develop active lifestyles unless the service delivery approach helps them to feel good about themselves and their capacity for change.

Humanism and Religion

Humanism, as the term is used in educational philosophy, has no connection with religious beliefs. It does not mean believing in human beings instead of God (Reilly & Lewis, 1983). Humanism is a specific approach to service delivery that has its roots in the humanistic psychology movement of the 1950s. Most adapted physical educators with this orientation believe deeply in God.

Theories Helpful in Planning

Although many theories provide the knowledge base for humanistic service delivery, the self-actualization theory of Abraham Maslow (1908–1970) and the fully functioning self theory of Carl Rogers (1902–1987) are the pioneer works that gave humanistic psychology its initial impetus. These and related theories are called **organismic** in that they focus on the whole organism as a unified system (i.e., they are **holistic**). Also important to contemporary humanism are theories that stress interactions between the environment and people: (a) field or ecological, (b) normalization, (c) personal meaning, (d) social cognitive, (e) self-efficacy, (f) self-determination, and (g) empowerment. Figure 5.2 lists the theories discussed in this chapter.

Self-Actualization Theory

Self-actualization is an individual's self-fulfillment of her or his potentialities, the inner drive to become all that one can be. Self-actualization theory evolved out of Maslow's hierarchy of human needs, first formulated as motivation theory in Maslow's text *Motivation and Personality* (1954). This hierarchy of needs looked like a pyramid, with physiological needs like hunger and thirst at the bottom and aesthetic and creative needs at the top (see Figure 5.3). The needs are arranged in a hierarchy to illustrate Maslow's contention that motivation is concentrated primarily on one level at a time. According to Maslow, individuals cannot move to a higher level until at least a minimal degree of satisfaction is derived at the lower level.

Maslow hypothesized two sets of needs: (a) deficiency needs and (b) growth or "being" needs. Distinctly different processes are required to meet these needs. *Deficiency needs* require external help. Parents, teachers, and significant others should provide as much gratification of these needs as possible, according to Maslow. *"Being" needs* are intrinsically motivated once a person achieves self-esteem. These "being" needs drive the great thinkers to enlighten the world (see the enlightenment level of the hierarchy) and likewise impel artists and creators to use their talents. Maslow posited, however, that only a small percentage of the adult population ever achieves self-actualization, which explains why the really great thinkers, artists, and creators in the history of the world number so few.

Maslow's hierarchy has implications for physical activity service delivery. One is that deficiency needs should be addressed in a particular order. Professionals should ascertain that (a) nutritional and fluid needs are being met, (b) prescribed medications have been taken, and (c) temperature, lighting, and other environmental conditions are conducive to physiological well-being.

Concern about safety needs includes psychological security as well as physical safety. Freedom from fear, anxiety, and confusion is a prerequisite for attending to and learning subject matter. Students must not be afraid of teachers or of failure. The safety mandate of Maslow's hierarchy thus guides educators to select assessment and learning tasks that build trust, faith, and confidence. Students must be helped to perceive the teacher as a partner in learning and classmates as a support group.

The love and belonging step has been interpreted as emphasizing the social basis of learning. Students need to be loved, appreciated, and accepted for who they are rather than what they can or cannot do. If love is unconditional, then persons can become intrinsically motivated to do their best because they are not worried about pleasing the teacher and being liked. Maslow's writing emphasizes the fragility of the inner being. Self-actualization theory suggests that the whole person (the self) must feel safe, loved, and accepted before the ego can survive objective, corrective feedback directed at specific behaviors. Only when love and belonging needs are met is the student able to benefit from formal motor skill and fitness instruction that enhances competence, mastery, achievement, and other outcomes related to esteem.

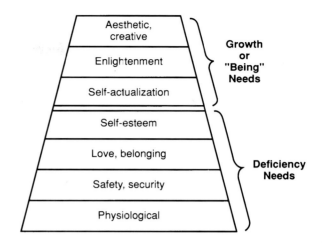

FIGURE 5.3 Self-actualization theory evolved out of Maslow's hierarchy of human needs.

According to Maslow (1970, p. 45), "satisfaction of the self-esteem need leads to feelings of self-confidence, worth, strength, capability, and adequacy, of being useful and necessary in the world." Once this need is met, individuals are internally motivated to become all that they can be. Concurrently, they feel responsible for making the world a better place to live. Good teaching, according to Maslow's theory, is not changing the person but rather manipulating the environment so that needs are met.

Maslow's second contribution to humanistic psychology is not as well known as his hierarchy of human needs but is tremendously important. This is his qualitative research on the nature of psychological health and how it can be achieved. After an intensive study of self-actualizing people, Maslow proposed criteria that distinguish between self-actualizers and non-self-actualizers. His findings offer a composite model to help us each become the best we can be. Some of these markers are:

1. Positive self-acceptance
2. Positive acceptance of others in general
3. Capacity for intimate relationships
4. Sense of identity with all humanity
5. Spontaneity of thought, feeling, and action
6. Thought processes that are independent, creative, ethical, and democratic
7. Realistic orientation to life

Self-actualizing is thus largely concerned with relationships. It is not an egotistical process but an ecological one. The self can be actualized only to the extent that we feel at home in the world, identify with all humanity, and care for the ecosystem. In humanistic physical education, the teacher uses movement experiences to develop desired behaviors.

Regular education is based on the belief that nondisabled students can develop these behaviors and become self-actualizing without concrete, specific help from teachers. This may be the case when development is normal and no illness or disability intensifies deficiency needs. Adapted physical activity, however, is concerned with people who have psychomotor problems. A different philosophy is needed when the process of becoming entails conquering problems (clumsiness, environmental barriers, perceptual-motor deficits, health impairments) rather than the self evolving naturally. Maslow's theory thus has been extended and refined by many leaders in the search for ways to help teachers, students, and athletes become self-actualizing (Sherrill, Silliman, Gench, & Hinson, 1990).

Fully Functioning Self Theory

Carl Rogers, recognized worldwide as the father of humanistic counseling, systematically applied self-actualization theory to teaching, counseling, and rehabilitation. Of his many contributions, the one most relevant to adapted physical activity is the idea of the fully functioning self. Rogers posited that *self-concept is the central concept in psychology and provides the best perspective for understanding an individual's behavior.*

Rogers hypothesized that all of us have an **ideal self** and a **real or actual self.** The more congruent these two selves are, the more fully functioning and self-actualizing we are. According to this theory, teachers must spend time talking to students and helping them clarify the self they really want to be. Personal goal setting is an important part of this theory. Teachers must know how to ask the right questions to motivate students to assess themselves, set goals, and follow through.

Rogers posited that people come to know themselves through experiences, including verbal feedback from others. To maintain or enhance congruence between ideal self and real self, people tend to seek out experiences that confirm the self they want to be and avoid experiences that cause discrepancy. The clumsy child who wants to become a good athlete may avoid practice and block out corrective feedback because these experiences are painful. They heighten realization of how separate the ideal and the real selves are. Creating a make-believe world and daydreaming about the self are easier. Knowledge of this phenomenon helps teachers to understand why the behaviors of so many students seem counterproductive to the logical approach to acquiring motor competence.

Defense Mechanisms

When persons cannot cope with discrepancies between experiential feedback (kinesthetic, visual, verbal) and the ideal self, they develop *defense mechanisms* of distortion and denial. **Distortion** alters the meaning of the experience (i.e., the individual begins to perceive self and world as he or she wants to see it rather than how it really is). **Denial** removes or blocks from consciousness things that are hurtful. Illustrative of distortion and denial are findings that self-concept scores of youth with physical disabilities on a physical appearance scale are higher than the norm for able-bodied youth (Sherrill, Hinson, Gench, Kennedy, & Low, 1990).

When disability causes the body to look different and/or limits motor prowess, distortion and denial may be mechanisms for trying to keep the self integrated and psychologically healthy. According to Rogers, these mechanisms lead to conceptual rigidity and maladjustment. They are like putting bandaids on a wound rather than treating it. Sooner or later, the wound festers. Rogers therefore developed a system of counseling techniques to help persons modify the way they conceptualize themselves. This system, described in his most famous book (Rogers, 1951), was first called *client-centered therapy* and later referred to as *person-centered therapy.* The approach is also called Rogerian counseling or teaching.

Rogers applied his theory directly to teaching in his book *Freedom to Learn* (1969). In it, he described teachers as facilitators and stressed that the warmth, empathy, and genuineness of teachers make students free to learn (see Figure 5.4). He emphasized that students learn to use freedom and to become internally motivated only when they are given freedom. From Rogers comes many of the indicators of good teaching that are taught in education courses (Reilly & Lewis, 1983) and also the belief that teaching and counseling should be inseparable.

Principles

Implications of the fully functioning self theory (also called person-centered theory) for adapted physical activity are many. Threads of this theory run throughout the text. First and foremost, however, is *the principle that self-concept should be the central concern in planning and implementing service delivery.* Second is the principle that physical educators should have the counseling skills to help students resolve problems in the psychomotor domain. Sport psychology courses are increasingly becoming the source of training in this area. Techniques for enhancing the performance of athletes need to be generalized to persons with disabilities and, perhaps even more important, to clumsy children.

Ecological or Field Theory

Ecological theory pertains to interactions between an individual and everything in his or her ecosystem. An interactionist approach blends strategies for changing both the individual and the environment. Kurt Lewin's field theory is acknowledged as the forerunner of ecological theory. Lewin's (1951) work was the first to blend the tenets of individual and social psychology and thus is considered by many to be the theoretical basis of contemporary rehabilitation psychology (Cook, 1987; Golden, 1984). It also has played a meaningful role in adapted physical activity.

Lewin's work was consistent with Gestalt theory in that he believed the total pattern, or **field,** of events determines behavior. Lewin coined the term **lifespace** to refer to all of the external and internal forces acting on an individual. Lifespace consists of the total psychological world (i.e., everything seen, heard, sensed, or inferred). Field theory then emphasizes analysis of the individual, the environment, and interactions between the two. Change is promoted by altering person-by-situation interactions.

Ecological Task Analysis

Ecological task analysis (ETA) is one of the first offshoots of ecological theory to directly impact adapted physical activity practice (Davis & Burton, 1991; Davis & van Emmerik, 1995). ETA refers to analyzing relationships among task goal, learner, and ecosystem in holistic functional terms (e.g., how a throw toward a target is performed by a particular child with a

given body build, anthropometric measures, fitness level, and motivation under specific environmental conditions) rather than focusing solely on the biomechanics of separate movement parts (e.g., backswing, forward swing, release). Walter Davis and Allen Burton, ETA theorizers, emphasize that both assessment and instruction should center on critical thinking about relationships rather than the use of traditional developmental task analysis procedures that assume orderly, sequential learning progressions and that use part-whole approaches. Of particular importance is individualization, with special attention to modifying relationships between learner-ecosystem affordances and barriers rather than routinely changing characteristics of the task goal in traditional easy-to-difficult learning progressions (e.g., lengthen distance, increase size of ball and/or target).

ETA is discussed further in Chapters 6 and 7. ETA is totally revolutionizing assessment, because it has created a trend away from assessing only an individual and toward assessing and problem solving about person/ecosystem relationships. The primary sources for ETA are Lewin's field theory, James Gibson's ecological theory of affordances (Gibson, 1977) and visual perception (Gibson, 1979), and recent motor control theory.

Other Ecological Theories

Two of Lewin's followers have been particularly influential in stressing the importance of natural settings (i.e., ecologically valid settings) and home-school-community ecosystems in assessment and instruction. These are Roger Barker, who wrote *Ecological Psychology* (1968), and Urie Bronfenbrenner, who wrote *The Ecology of Human Development* (1979).

Ecological theory also provides the framework for families and professionals working together and for collaborative models in which many disciplines cooperate. Perhaps, however, the greatest impact of ecological theory is its implications for integration and normalization.

Normalization or Social Role Valorization Theory

Normalization refers to making available to persons with disabilities living, learning, and working conditions as close as possible to the norms of able-bodied society. Normalization theory does not mean making such individuals normal, as it has sometimes been incorrectly conceptualized, but rather affording them access to the same environment and opportunities as their able-bodied peers.

Success in sports competition, especially in events like the Boston Marathon, in which elite athletes with disabilities compete side by side with those who are nondisabled, is believed to be normalizing in the sense that it changes perceptions. It alters the way we see persons with disabilities as well as the way they see themselves. Fred McBee, coauthor of *The Continental Quest* (McBee & Ballinger, 1984) and a wheelchair user, described how the 1978 Boston Marathon changed his life. He conveys his feelings as George Murray (Figure 5.5) finished first in this race—before any of the able-bodied runners:

> For his friend, Fred McBee, that day would change his life. . . . He'd seen the gimps come from wheezing through the 40-yd dash in shaking, quaking, rattletrap wheelchairs, to winning the greatest 26.2-m race in the world. From a bunch of convalescing cripples out for a little recreation, they'd become muscled, highly fit gimps out for blood. (McBee & Ballinger, 1984, p. 2)

McBee earlier explained that only persons in wheelchairs can use such words as *gimps* and *cripples;* they are part of the "in-language" of the wheelchair athlete community but are never appropriate for an outsider.

Normalization theory was introduced to the United States from Sweden by Bengt Nirje in the late 1960s and is recognized as a major factor in the deinstitutionalization of persons with mental retardation and their subsequent social integration into the community (Nirje, 1969, 1980). Wolf Wolfensberger, who began the citizen advocacy movement within ARC (formerly called the Association for Retarded Citizens), has devoted a lifetime to expanding and operationalizing normalization theory, now often called **social role valorization theory**. *Valorization* refers to improving or defending the social roles of people at risk of social devaluation. (Wolfensberger, 1972, 1991, 1995).

Although initially applied only to mental retardation issues, normalization theory is now widely used in relation to all disabilities in which persons are perceived as looking or behaving differently. Wolfensberger (1972) stated that three principles underlie normalization theory:

FIGURE 5.5 George Murray, of Florida, is one of the best-known pioneer wheelchair marathoners in the world. (Photo courtesy of Top End Wheelchair Sports, Inc.)

1. Behavioral and appearance deviancy can be reduced by minimizing the degree to which persons with disabilities are treated differently from able-bodied persons.
2. Conversely, deviancy is enhanced by treating persons as if they were deviant.
3. To the degree that they are grouped together and segregated from the mainstream of society, individuals will be perceived as different from others and will tend to behave differently.

Today Wolfensberger's work focuses on the social devaluation of people who are different and the negative roles that society assigns them. He stresses that we must use culturally valued means to enable people to live culturally valued lives. There are seven core themes of social role valorization:

1. Social role valorization is concerned with identification of unconscious dynamics that contribute to the devaluation and oppression of certain groups.
2. Social role valorization focuses on the creation of valued social roles and the elimination of negative role expectancies.
3. It is not enough to use approaches that are normal or neutral; we must select means and tools that enhance the image of persons who are devalued.

4. The developmental model, properly implemented, can lead to tremendous client growth because of its positive presumptions about human potential, its high demands and expectancies, and its requirement of effective pedagogies.

5. Social role valorization recognizes that imitation is one of the most powerful learning mechanisms known and provides models that will help people function in appropriate and valued ways.

6. Social imagery strongly influences role expectancies; therefore, the social image of devalued people must be enhanced.

7. A number of supports are needed for *personal,* valued, social integration of a devalued person to be successful. Integration must be personal and social rather than physical. (paraphrased from Wolfensberger & Thomas, 1983, pp. 24–27)

Clearly, many humanistic practices have their roots in normalization or social role valorization theory. This theory particularly supports integration; the use of person-first terminology; careful, systematic selection of models; and concentrated work on attitude change.

Personal Meaning Theory

Personal meaning theory, attributed to Beatrice Wright, stresses that it is the personal meaning of a disability that is important rather than the disability itself. This personal meaning is derived from a host of psychosocial factors "that underlie the way *disability as a value loss* is perceived and reacted to by other people, as well as the self" (Wright, 1983, p. 6). Author of *Physical Disability: A Psychological Approach* (1960) and a second edition with a modified title, *Physical Disability: A Psychosocial Approach* (1983), Wright acknowledges that Kurt Lewin and Carl Rogers most influenced her thinking. Wright is considered the leading theorist in contemporary rehabilitation psychology. The implications of personal meaning theory in disability are discussed in Chapter 2, which describes how physical education and sport have different meanings for each individual. The teacher must be especially aware of the social environment in learning.

The application of personal meaning theory to adapted physical education leads to formal and informal assessment of personal meaning in relation to the activities to be taught. Students should be actively involved in planning their instructional program, encouraged to set goals, and taught how to monitor their progress.

Research shows that fun is the reason most children give for participation in youth sports (Wankel & Sefton, 1989). To facilitate the development of an active lifestyle, teachers need to explore with students the personal meaning of fun. For some individuals, this seems to have a social basis, whereas for others, it seems to be challenge or mastery oriented.

One approach to assessing personal meaning is the use of instruments that measure the importance of sports and physical appearance (Fox & Corbin, 1989). For example, students may be given pairs of items like those that follow and asked to circle the one of each pair that better describes how important something is to them:

| Some teenagers don't think that being athletic is that important. | BUT | Other teenagers think that being athletic is important. |
| Some teenagers think that how they look is important. | BUT | Other teenagers don't care that much about how they look. |

Harter (1988)

Only by caring about personal meaning can you personalize instruction. Know and accept that physical activity and competence are not the central constructs in everyone's lives. For some persons, finding a job, acquiring a close friend or lover, or gaining access to a social group may be foremost. Take the time to listen and to show the link between physical activity and other goals.

Personal meaning is extremely important in self-concept theory (discussed in Chapter 8) because it provides insight into the ideal or desired self. Asking students to state their level of aspiration or to rate importance of a particular domain or activity enables you to examine the discrepancy between actual and ideal self.

Social Cognitive Theory

Social cognitive theory, proposed by Albert Bandura, supports the humanistic perspective. Bandura (1986) emphasizes that human functioning can best be explained in terms of "a model of triadic reciprocality in which behavior, cognitive and other personal factors, and environmental events all operate as interacting determinants of each other" (p. 18). He states that *social cognitive* is a replacement label for his earlier theory of social learning.

Social cognitive theory is the conceptual framework for many theories that sometimes are classified as behaviorism and associated with behavior management. Preference for the term *social cognitive* is based on the role that cognition and the total social environment play in stimulus-response teaching and learning. There is always some kind of cognition between the stimulus (cue or command) and the response (verbal or physical performance). The one-to-one relationship between the teacher and the student in behavior management makes the context social rather than exclusively instructional. Even individuals with severe mental retardation respond differently to cuegivers they like and those they dislike.

An illustration of social cognitive theory was presented in Chapter 3. The application was to communication, with attention to input, process, and outcome. Embedded in the social cognitive communication model in Chapter 3 were several separate theories (e.g., contact, social comparison, cognitive dissonance, and enjoyment theories). See the index for more references to these theories. Following is the most famous social cognitive theory. Because of its widespread use,

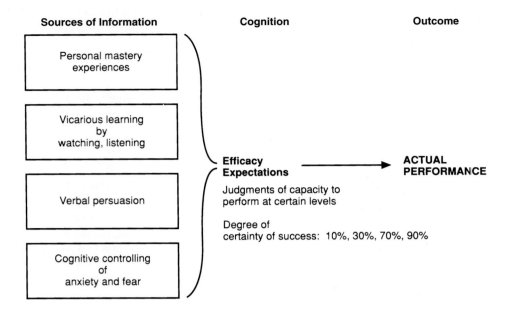

it is presented as a separate theory rather than as a component of social cognitive theory.

Self-Efficacy Theory

Bandura (1977) proposed self-efficacy theory as a conceptual framework for changing fearful and avoidant behaviors. As such, it has considerable relevance for low-skilled individuals. According to Bandura (1986), **perceived self-efficacy** is "a judgment of one's capacity to accomplish a certain level of performance" (p. 391). It is concerned, not with skills, but with what we think we can do with these skills. Self-efficacy is also defined as a situation-specific form of self-confidence.

Self-efficacy is typically measured with a yes/no response scale in relation to specific questions (e.g., "Can you jump over a 3-ft height?" "Can you run a 12-min mile?" "Can you score 7 out of 10 on a volleyball serve test?"). Another approach is to ask individuals their degree of certainty that they can do something: 0%, 20%, 40%, 60%, 80%, 100%. An **efficacy expectation** is a good predictor of actual performance. If an individual expresses a negative efficacy expectation, the humanistic professional does not force him or her to try the task. Instead, the reasons for the belief are explored, and four antecedent events are used to change the belief (see Figure 5.6). Partner- or team-teaching practices are helpful when implementing self-efficacy theory because they allow giving students with negative expectancies a choice. The students can either go to the resource teacher station for help or stay and watch the successful performances of others. A time limit, however, is placed on the watching option (also called symbolic modeling or vicarious learning by Bandura).

Figure 5.6 shows the four sources of information posited by Bandura as determinants of an efficacy expectation. Of these, Bandura believed that personal mastery experiences were the most important. He stressed that success raises expectations of further success and discussed structuring the en-

vironment to ensure efficacy. Students should be taught to visualize themselves and others coping successfully with the phobia or fear. Performance accomplishments thus can be direct or indirect. As a pioneer in social learning theory, Bandura believed strongly in partner follow-the-leader type activities called **participant modeling.** He also supported cognitive training to control anxiety and to cope with stress.

Self-efficacy theory seems similar to the self-concept theories described in Chapter 8, but Bandura (1986) pointed out several differences. Mainly, self-efficacy is more cognitively oriented. It is a *judgment* that one can do something, regardless of whether the consequences are pleasant. A skilled combat soldier might judge himself to be efficacious but derive neither pleasure nor self-esteem from his work. In contrast, according to Bandura, most self-concept theories emphasize feelings. This is not entirely true in that new approaches treat self-concept as an attitude with cognitive, affective, and behavioral dimensions.

Self-Determination Theory

Self-determination theory posits that a high degree of perceived personal control over life's events contributes to intrinsic motivation, goal achievement, and psychological well-being (Deci & Ryan, 1985; Wehmeyer, Kelchner, & Richards, 1996). Physical educators thus need to understand personal control (perceived and actual) and consider ways it can be enhanced. Vallerand and Reid (1990) provide an excellent review of various self-determination theories.

Perceived Control or Locus of Control

Perceived control, also called **locus of control** (LOC), is the perception of the connection or lack of connection between one's actions and their consequences. Julian Rotter (1966) posited that persons vary in LOC along an internal to external continuum. Some persons are in the middle, but others tend to be either internally or externally controlled. **Internal LOC** is belief and/or perception that events in one's life are dependent upon ability and effort. **External LOC** is the feeling that events in life are not based on one's actions but are a result of chance, fate, luck, or controls imposed by others, like task difficulty. **Confused LOC** is lack of understanding or inability to decide what causes events.

Child development theory emphasizes that LOC shifts from external to internal as students mature. The degree of this shift depends, however, on child rearing and classroom teaching practices and on such variables as health and disabilities that may prevent independent thought and action. Some persons remain more externally than internally controlled throughout life. This includes many persons with severe mental retardation or emotional disturbance.

Persons with disabilities want to control their own lives, just as do able-bodied persons. Humanistic teachers are careful not to do for such persons without first asking for permission or direction. When feeding persons with a disability, for instance, ask them to indicate what they want from the plate and in what order. Before assisting mobility-impaired persons, ask first if they want help and how help can best be given. The movie *Whose Life Is It Anyhow?* is an excellent resource for learning about LOC.

Because of the tendency of parents and society to overprotect persons with disabilities and deny them control of their own lives, physical educators need to stress independence, personal control, and responsibility. Remember expectancy theory. Expect persons to assume control over the situational factors in their lives, and gradually, they will assume that control.

Learned Helplessness

Learned helplessness is a composite of beliefs and behaviors that characterize many persons with external LOC (Dweck, 1980; Seligman, 1975). It is a particular problem in a person with a severe disability or chronic illness when nothing the person does seems to ameliorate the condition. Likewise, learned helplessness has been associated with demoralization because of repeated failure in motor activities despite best efforts. When, over a period of time, persons come to believe that there is no relationship between effort and outcome, the result is reduced motivation, low self-esteem, and generalized depression. Physical educators must recognize the learned helplessness syndrome and work to prevent it.

Types of Motivation

Motivation refers to all of the forces (internal and external) that focus behaviors, start and stop them, and determine their frequency and duration. Deci and Ryan (1985) distinguish between three types of motivation: (a) intrinsic, (b) extrinsic, and (c) amotivation. **Intrinsic motivation** refers to forces that are 100% self-determined; these come directly from voluntary activity and are experienced as fun, pleasurable, and satisfying. **Extrinsic motivation** may be self- or other-determined, depending on who sets the goals and establishes rewards and sanctions; these forces are focused on either obtaining rewards or avoiding sanctions. **Amotivation** refers to absence of forces because no cognitive link is established between behavior and outcomes. This may occur because mental function is frozen

at or below the level of a 7- or 8-month-old infant or because life experiences are so confusing and overpowering that persons no longer try to make sense of cause-effect relationships.

Goal Achievement

Goal achievement is enhanced when individuals have partial to full control over setting their own goals, according to self-determination theory. This means that professionals should systematically teach individuals with disabilities how to make choices between activities and to set goals. A trend in the 1990s is teaching students to help write their IEPs.

Psychological Well-Being and Rewards

Humanistic professionals strive to make activities intrinsically rewarding through adaptations that assure success, fun, and satisfaction. They provide abundant choices in order to promote feelings of self-determination, and much of their verbal feedback requires problem solving (e.g., "That was great! Why is your performance so good today? How many times have you practiced that? Have you shown your mother that you can do this? What part of that skill is the easiest for you? What part is the hardest?").

Humanistic professionals deemphasize tangible rewards like tokens, ribbons, and trophies because research shows that such reinforcement eventually leads to dependence on others for motivation. Feedback is used to praise effort as well as success (e.g., "I can tell you worked really hard on that." "I can see you are concentrating." "You remembered all the instructions."). Feedback also frequently mentions fun (e.g., "What was the most fun about that?" "Isn't this fun?").

Empowerment Theory

Empowerment theory posits that professionals should systematically enable individuals in social minorities or marginal groups to become more self-determined, especially in relation to goals pertaining to control, power, governance, and responsibility. A relatively new expansion of self-determination theory, empowerment encompasses both processes and products (Fetterman, Kaftarian, & Wandersman, 1996). **Empowerment processes** pertain to helping others to (a) achieve control over their life events; (b) obtain needed resources; (c) develop teamwork skills; (d) assume responsibility for self, others, and the environment; and (e) attain equitable power with others in the ecosystem. **Empowerment outcomes** include organizational and community involvement, shared governance and leadership, responsible decision making, accessible programs and resources, effective networking, the perception that rights are not being violated, and a general feeling of well-being and life satisfaction.

Empowerment is also a process of teaching individuals to become self-advocates (see Figure 5.7). This can be achieved through the 5L model (Look at me, Leverage, Literature, Legislation, Litigation) discussed in Chapter 4. When people know how to use these advocacy processes, they generally feel empowered. Central to all of these processes is attainment of such personal attributes as self-esteem, self-efficacy, internal locus of control, and commitment to self-actualization. If professionals believe in empowerment, they must plan

FIGURE 5.7 Dr. Ron French *(standing)* of Texas Woman's University works with a joint committee of parents, teachers, and athletes with disabilities on 5L advocacy concerns.

FIGURE 5.8 Students with severe mental retardation can be taught skiing when skills are task analyzed and objectives are carefully written.

carefully for development of these attributes and the realization of empowerment and self-advocacy outcomes.

As you read the section on planning that follows, consider how you can use these theories in shaping your own and others' philosophy.

Planning: The First PAP-TE-CA Service

Planning may be a school district, school, classroom, or individual function. However, because many adapted physical activity specialists are employed to plan and implement service delivery for an entire school district, we begin planning at this level. The United States has approximately 16,000 school districts, each governed by a local education agency (LEA), which is recognized by and responsible to the state education agency (SEA). A **school district** thus can be defined as a city, community, or other designated local structure that is responsible for the governance and funding of public schools. In accordance with the philosophy of this text, a school district is conceptualized as a combined home-school-community entity that shares resources.

School district planning refers to shared decision making about the philosophy, principles, policies, and practices that guide the day-to-day operation of schools and the development and use of resources to meet educational needs. Administrators and consultants often do most of the planning for school districts, but ideally everyone is involved. Because adapted physical activity service delivery is still not well understood in many communities, both regular and adapted physical educators are needed to advocate for services and explain benefits. The remainder of this chapter is designed to help develop competencies that will enhance planning at the school district, school, and classroom levels. Philosophy developed for a school district usually generalizes to schools and classrooms within the system.

School systems have different visions of what physical education programs can and should accomplish. Visions are typically operationalized by statements of purpose and goals. In Chapter 1, purpose and goals were introduced (see Figure 1.1). The following section provides detail concerning each and also clarifies the difference between goals and objectives.

Purpose, Goals, and Objectives

In adapted physical activity, the terms *purpose, goal,* and *objectives* are used in very specific ways. A **purpose** is the overall aim or intention. The purpose of adapted physical activity is the same as that of regular activity: to change psychomotor behaviors, thereby facilitating self-actualization.

Goals are broad, global statements that are long range in nature, whereas **objectives** are short term and often written in behavioral format. These definitions come from federal legislation that guides the development of individualized education programs (IEPs). Long range refers to annual, semiannual, or quarterly statements that guide instruction. Table 5.1 presents nine goal areas. Usually, time permits work on only three or four goals. Therefore, teachers must use assessment data to select the goals most appropriate for each individual.

Each goal then is broken down into specific, short-term objectives that require 3 to 5 hours for achievement. Often, lesson plans allocate only 5 or 10 minutes per session to an objective, so work continues over several weeks. For example, consider the goal of developing a good self-concept in the athletic domain. An objective might be: *Given opportunity to engage in a leisure activity like skiing for 30 minutes and to evaluate success after the activity, student will say at least one good thing about self* (see Figure 5.8). If the goal were to develop fitness, then the objectives might be: *Given instructions to do as many curl-ups as possible in 30 seconds, student will*

T a b l e   5 . 1   Goal areas as organizing centers. Goals A through I are the themes of Chapters 8 through 17.

A. Positive Self-Concept

To develop a positive self-concept and body image through activity involvement; to increase understanding and appreciation of the body and its capacity for movement; to accept limitations that cannot be changed; to learn to adapt environment so as to make the most of strengths (i.e., to work toward self-actualization).

B. Social Competence

To learn social behaviors that promote inclusion (i.e., how to interact with others—sharing, taking turns, following, and leading); to develop beliefs and attitudes about self and others that facilitate equal-status relationships; to reduce social isolation; to learn how to develop and maintain friendships; to demonstrate good sportsmanship and self-discipline in winning and losing; to develop other skills necessary for acceptance by peers in the mainstream.

C. Sensorimotor Integration

To remediate serious, multiple problems that stem primarily from central nervous system (CNS) dysfunctions (e.g., cerebral palsy, stroke, traumatic brain injury) and interfere with body control, upright postures, and locomotion. Some of these problems are muscle or postural tone abnormalities, pathological reflexes, postural reaction delays, associated movements or overflow, stereotypies, spasticity, ataxia, and tactile-kinesthetic-vestibular-visual (TKVV) disorders that interfere with initiating and sustaining exploratory movement.

D. Perceptual-Motor Learning

To remediate clumsiness or developmental coordination disorders (DCDs) associated with perceptual-motor, cognitive, attention, and memory problems; to develop and/or reinforce specific underlying movement abilities (e.g., static and dynamic balancing; hand-eye, head and trunk rotatory, and foot-eye coordinations; imitating models; following auditory instructions; motor planning and sequencing; rhythm and reaction time abilities).

E. Motor Skills and Patterns

To learn fundamental motor skills and patterns; to master the motor skills indigenous to games, sports, dance, and aquatics participation; to improve fine and gross motor coordination for self-care, school, work, and play activities.

F. Fitness and Healthy Lifestyle

To meet health-related standards for cardiorespiratory endurance, body composition, muscular strength and endurance, and flexibility; and to develop beliefs and attitudes that lead to fitness and a healthy lifestyle.

G. Postures and Appearance

To remediate posture problems (e.g., round shoulders, kyphosis, scoliosis) and accommodate structural deviations that cannot be changed except by surgery (e.g., hip and knee joint problems); to improve appearance and body mechanics; to decrease muscular imbalance and prevent injury.

H. Play and Game Competence, Active Leisure, and Relaxation

To have fun and learn to enjoy physical activity; to develop positive beliefs and attitudes toward exercise and sport that lead to lifespan active, healthy lifestyles; to learn physical activity approaches to relaxation and tension release; to learn play, game, and sport rules and strategies to enhance leisure time choices and habits; to develop the knowledge and commitment to use community resources and to seek help when needed.

I. Dance and Aquatic Skills

To learn dance and aquatic activities that can be used throughout the lifespan to achieve numerous goals.

J. Sport Skills and Competition.

To learn sport activities that can be used throughout the lifespan. This goal is emphasized in Chapters 19 through 27.

complete 25; or *Given the opportunity to ski on slopes for 3 hours, student will be able to engage in ski activities continuously with no more than three refreshment and toilet breaks, not to exceed 15 minutes each.*

Objectives have three parts:

1. Conditions, referring to the *given statement* that usually starts the objective
2. One specific, observable behavior that is denoted by an action verb (e.g., *say, do, perform, demonstrate, show, run*)
3. A criterion level for success, such as "at least one good thing" *or* "25 curl-ups" *or* "continuously with no more than three breaks of 15 minutes each"

Purpose and goals are integral parts of a philosophy. They determine the kind of assessment administered and thus establish the framework of opportunity. Objectives are not part of a philosophy; they are tools or vehicles for accomplishing goals.

Each of the goal areas in Table 5.1 contributes to self-actualization in one of three domains (affective, psychomotor, or cognitive). Try writing objectives for each goal area. Remember that an objective should require only 3 to 5 hours for achievement.

Goal Area Organizing Centers

Goals serve as organizing centers or themes for school district planning and curriculum design. They may also serve as themes for programs offered by community agencies and organizations for all age groups. Each of the goal areas in Table 5.1 contributes to self-actualization in one or more domains (affective, psychomotor, or cognitive). These goals are the basis for the organization of Part 2 (Chapters 8–17). Each chapter presents specific assessment and pedagogy strategies to accomplish a goal.

An important part of school district planning is to determine whether home-school-community team members value all of these goals and to resolve differences concerning which goals are most important. Often parents see self-concept and social competency as the critical needs to be met, whereas physical educators are likely to rank motor skills and fitness highest. Community and therapeutic recreation personnel, in contrast, emphasize the values of fun and training in lifelong leisure skills and lifestyles. These leisure skills may be associated with intense competition (e.g., wheelchair basketball, Paralympics, Special Olympics, Deaf sport) or with recreational activities. Professionals who work with individuals with severe multiple disabilities typically identify with sensorimotor integration, perceptual-motor learning, and adapted dance and aquatics. These goals are particularly effective in meeting needs of individuals who are nonambulatory.

School districts with sufficient resources should seek to make all goals available to professionals who plan assessment, curricula, and after-school programs. The essence of individualization is choice, and the more choices district programming offers teachers, the better they can meet the needs of students and operationalize the concept of reasonable accommodation. When resources are not available within school facilities, planning teams need to consider home and community facilities and determine how transportation can be arranged and financed (see Figure 5.9).

Each of the goals in Table 5.1 can be achieved in regular physical education classes, if support services are available. Physical educators must understand how educational trends such as inclusive education and outcome-based instruction influence the implementation of goals at school district and classroom levels.

Most of the goals in Table 5.1 can be matched with commercially available curriculum models like I CAN (Wessel, 1977) and Body Skills (Werder & Bruininks, 1988) or operationalized in models created by professionals that are based on their original thinking, ideas from the literature, or participation in workshops. These curriculum models are described in Chapters 8 through 17. In some cases, where curriculum models are associated with a specific disability, the models are presented in Chapters 18 through 27.

Functional, Developmental, and Interactive Organizing Centers

Planning also involves selecting organizing centers or frames of reference that can help facilitate teamwork and organize efforts. A **frame of reference** is an approach to education or treatment that is based on your philosophy and theoretical knowledge base (Hopkins, 1988). Synonyms for *frame of reference* are *approach, perspective,* and *value orientation.* This section highlights three frames of reference: (a) functional, (b) developmental, and (c) interactional. Each represents a different body of knowledge. While a delivery system could be based on one perspective, good professionals utilize information from each frame of reference to individualize and adapt instruction.

Professionals must have a good understanding of both function and development. **Function,** derived from the Latin *functio* (meaning "activity," "performance"), refers to the acts, tasks, or activities that a person can perform. **Development,** derived from the Old French *desveloper* (meaning "to unwrap"), refers to changes that occur throughout the lifespan (i.e., the unwrapping or evolving of the human being).

Functional Frame of Reference (Top Down)

The functional frame of reference focuses on the roles and functions needed for success in a specific activity. Assessment determines whether or not the person can perform these functions. Then education and treatment are directed toward mastery of task or activity components that comprise the function.

The pedagogy used is typically **behavior management** (i.e., a precisely planned, systematic application of cues and consequences to guide the student through a series of tasks or activities that are ordered from easy to hard). Behavior management begins with analysis of an age-appropriate function. This may be either an ecological task analysis like that discussed earlier in this chapter or a traditional analysis that breaks a task into smaller, teachable steps (see Table 5.2). Next, the teacher determines the cues and consequences to be used. A **cue** is a command or instruction telling the student what to do. A **consequence** is immediate feedback designed to either increase or decrease a behavior.

For example, in teaching a target throw, using the functional approach and behavior management, the teacher models (demonstrates) the task and gives a simple cue like, "Jim, pick up the ball." If the student imitates correctly, the consequence is an immediate **reward** (i.e., verbal praise, "Good boy!" or a reinforcer known to be especially effective with that student). If the student does not make the desired response within 5 seconds, a **correction procedure** is initiated (e.g., "No, watch me pick up the ball. I pick up the ball with my fingers. Jim, pick up the ball."). Learning is primarily by repetition. These same cues and corrective strategies are used until the student is successful in a set number of trials. Then, the instruction proceeds to the next task in the easy-to-hard sequence (e.g., "Watch how I face the target. See my forward leg. Jim, face the target with your leg forward.").

In the functional approach, little or no attention is given to the student's chronological age or to whether he or she has progressed through the normal developmental levels or stages associated with the function to be taught. The functional approach, in its pure form, is generally used in adolescent or adult programs that serve individuals with severe disabilities. Underlying the functional frame of reference is the philosophy that tasks, activities, and pedagogy should be age-appropriate.

Developmental Frame of Reference (Bottom Up)

The developmental frame of reference focuses on the abilities that society expects individuals to have at certain chronological ages and on developmental sequences. This approach has its roots in the traditional body of knowledge taught in such courses as developmental psychology, human development, and motor development. In this approach, standardized assessment instruments with norms are used to determine whether or not a

Table 5.2   Traditional task analysis of target throw for person with severe mental retardation.

Short, Easy Chain	Longer, Harder Chain		Hardest Chain	
	10.	Praise self; say "Good, I threw the ball."	10.	Same
	9.	Look where ball goes.	9.	Same
	8.	Follow through.	8.	Same
	7.	Release ball.	7.	Same
	6.	Swing throwing arm forward.	6.	Add trunk rotation.
	5.	Swing throwing arm backward.	5.	Add trunk rotation.
4. Look where ball goes.	4.	Assume shoulder-to-target stance.	4.	Same
3. Release ball.	3.	Look at target.	3.	Same
2. Pick up ball.	2.	Pick up ball	2.	Same
1. Look at ball.	1.	Look at ball.	1.	Same

Note. Steps are taught separately and linked together by forward or backward chaining.

person is performing at or near the level of others the same age. Then, education and treatment are directed toward learning age-related skills, knowledge, and strategies. Any pedagogy, including behavior management, may be used. The same developmental sequence is followed, however, for all students, with the entry level into the sequence individualized. A **developmental sequence** is a list of tasks or activities in which items are ordered according to the mean chronological age that each is achieved by normal infants and children (see Table 5.3).

Central to developmental theory is the assumption that learning proceeds in a spiral, upward direction, with performance at each level dependent on knowledge and skill acquired at earlier levels. For example, persons are taught a long jump only after they have mastered jumping down from a 1-ft height and demonstrated that they can perform stand-to-squat and squat-to-stand position changes without losing balance. This is because these tasks are developmentally easier than the long jump. Likewise, persons are taught tosses at floor targets before wall targets because downward tosses, aided by gravity, require less strength and thus are developmentally easier than horizontal tosses.

The developmental frame of reference is particularly applicable to infants, toddlers, and young children. A knowledge of the developmental milestones normally achieved at each age enables professionals to plan and deliver appropriate assessment, teaching, and evaluation services.

Interactional Frame of Reference (Ecological)

The interactional frame of reference is a combination of functional and developmental perspectives based on critical thinking

Table 5.3 Developmental sequence for teaching/testing throwing.

Task	Criterion to Pass	Average Age (in Months)
1. First voluntary grasp	Grasps objects, holds 5 sec	4–5
2. First voluntary release	Releases object on command	10–11
3. Throw (hurl) playground ball	Travels 5 ft forward	24–29
4. Throw (hurl) tennis ball	Travels 7 ft forward	24–29
5. Throw tennis ball	Shows trunk rotation, follow-through; ball travels 10 ft	42–47
6. Use underarm toss to hit wall target from 5 ft	Hits target two of three trials with tennis ball	42–47

Note. Distance objectives (e.g., "Throw hard!") are worked on before accuracy objectives.

about individuals and their ecosystems. During the school years (i.e., from birth until age 21, according to federal law), development and function are inseparable. This is because regular education is organized by grades, with each grade level representing a mixture of chronological age and function. Although some special education students are placed in nongraded, self-contained classrooms that serve several age groups, develop-

ment remains an important consideration. The goal is to move as many special education children into integrated settings as possible. To do this, the teacher must be ever mindful of whether students are functioning at levels comparable to regular education students of more or less the same age. Adherence to the principle of normalization also requires that teachers know what is normal or average for chronological age groups. Students must be afforded the same opportunities to learn, develop, and function as others within the same life stage.

Thus, development and function are two sides of the same coin. Development is a vertical or longitudinal perspective. The developmental frame of reference focuses on how far up the age-related continuum of motor skills a person can progress. In contrast, function is a horizontal perspective. The functional frame of reference focuses on environmental demands and the functions required to perform at adequate levels. Good teachers move back and forth between these two frames of reference, utilizing both in their daily service delivery. *The combination of these two approaches is an interactional or ecological perspective.*

Placement Organizing Centers

Available placements for students is another organizing center that affects curriculum design. Figure 5.10 shows that the planning of adapted physical education depends on whether the school district follows the regular education initiative (REI) approach, the least restrictive environment (LRE), or the inclusive placement approach. The REI and inclusive approaches are very similar. In REI, *most students* are placed in the regular classroom; in inclusive placement, *all students* are in the regular classroom.

FIGURE 5.10 Planning, assessment, and prescription depend on whether the school system follows the regular education initiative (REI), the least restrictive environment (LRE) approach, or inclusive placement.

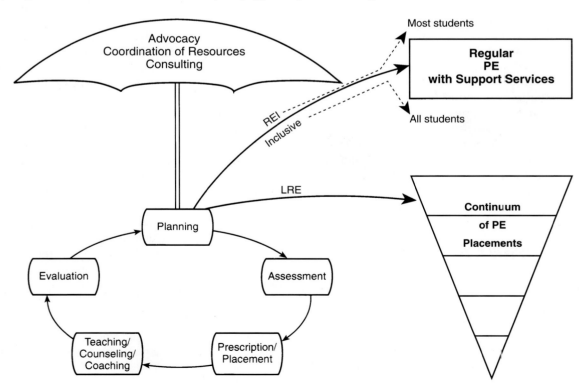

REI was a popular approach in the early 1990s, but now many of its proponents are advocating full inclusion for everyone. Readers will remember from Chapter 4 that the law supports LRE and REI but not inclusive placement philosophy; therefore this section of the chapter emphasizes LRE and REI philosophy. To clarify philosophy, the philosophies are briefly reviewed.

Least Restrictive Environment Approach

LRE philosophy is essentially the use of the individualized education program (IEP) or child study process to place students in their least restrictive environment for each content area. An environment is considered least restrictive when it (a) matches individual abilities with appropriate services and (b) preserves as much freedom as possible. For this philosophy to work, there must be a continuum of available placements for each subject matter area, and the LRE assignment must be based on comprehensive assessment and collaborative parent-professional decision making. The LRE philosophy was created by special educators in the 1970s and operationalized by federal law, which described the IEP and procedures for making LRE placements.

A weakness in LRE conceptualization is that many school systems never created a continuum of placements for physical education. They placed all students either in separate adapted physical education or in integrated regular physical education. This, of course, was an improvement over the earlier practice of ignoring students with disabilities and providing them with no physical education. But a two-category system does not provide enough options for matching individual abilities with appropriate services.

Another weakness is that eligibility criteria for justifying LRE placement and/or services have typically been designed to identify cognitive or behavioral problems that interfere with academic achievement. Motor and health problems, unless associated with cognitive or behavioral deficits, have often been ignored. Many students, both special and regular education, who cannot succeed in a traditional physical education curriculum are assigned to regular education environments with the mistaken belief that such environments are least restrictive (i.e., abilities match the content to be taught). Historically, good physical educators have tried to accommodate such students and adapted instruction accordingly. Often, however, large class sizes, inadequate training, and lack of support services have defeated good intentions.

In summary, the LRE philosophy and IEP process are great ideas. Both are supported by law, but a double standard seems to exist in the interpretation of these constructs in relation to planning academic versus physical education services. Physical educators need to understand LRE and IEP concepts and to advocate that special educators extend their beliefs to assessment, placement, and instruction in the psychomotor domain. Concurrently, physical educators must take the initiative in making regular physical education the best it can be for all of the students assigned this placement.

Regular Education Initiative and Inclusive Approaches

The regular education initiative (REI) philosophy is the belief that most students should be placed in the regular classroom setting. The inclusive philosophy insists that all students be in the regular classroom. Some proponents assert that any other placement is discriminatory. Others take the stance that removal from the regular classroom is justifiable only if instruction with the use of supplementary aids and services is documented as not successful. REI is a special education and parent movement that began to have an impact in the 1980s.

Both philosophies are currently the subject of much debate among special educators. In contrast, the practice of assigning almost everyone to regular physical education and assuming that teachers will take the initiative in adapting instruction is widespread.

One Adapted Physical Educator in Every School District

Regardless of which approach is operative in a particular community, regular physical educators should advocate and negotiate for at least one full-time adapted physical educator in their school district. This is because *support services* are an integral part of all approaches. Ideally, this specialist should be funded from both the special education and regular education budgets and should assist all students with special psychomotor needs, not just those declared eligible by the IEP process.

Support Services

The term **support services** refers to supplementary aids and services (the definition used in IDEA legislation, 20 *U.S.C.,* 143). This is usually the presence of extra personnel in the regular classroom (e.g., adapted physical education specialist, special educator, specially trained adult aides, peer or crossage tutors). Extra personnel may also be available in a nearby adapted physical activity resource room, learning center, or counseling office. In the REI mode, students are not assigned to these separate areas but float in and out as needed.

Support services may include things as well as people. The availability of video cameras and monitors for students to observe and analyze their movement patterns is an aid to instruction. Likewise, the availability of machines that pitch balls provides clumsy students with the thousands of practice trials needed. To individualize instruction, there must be much adapted equipment and sufficient space to set up different stations for varying the time and space attributes that determine degree of difficulty of motor skills. Likewise, computer and electronic technology can be used in many creative ways to reinforce students' effort and ease teacher load.

Support services are often not automatically provided. Regular physical educators must learn to ask, to negotiate, and to create. Success breeds success. The better a teacher is, the more likely he or she can convince the principal of the need for support services. Remember, support services cost extra money. Your requests will be weighed against others and sometimes be deferred. A positive and persistent attitude, coupled with a strong knowledge base of negotiation techniques, will eventually yield results. Warm, positive relationships with parents are also helpful. Parents often can find the time and energy to raise money, negotiate with the principal, and pose innovative alternatives.

The basic question to be posed to administrators is "Where is our school district adapted physical educator? Can

FIGURE 5.11   A continuum of placements and services for schools that implement least restrictive environment philosophy. The most imagination is needed at the "Part-time in Adapted PE" level.

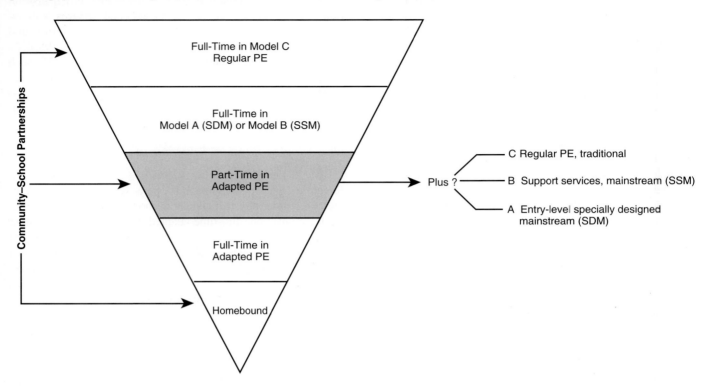

you arrange for him or her to visit and help me?" Once this specialist is identified, he or she can act as a mediator in obtaining support services. If no specialists are employed by the school district, then regular educators can be advocates for the creation of such a position. Another basic question is "What in-service training can you provide for me in order to learn more about adapting instruction?"

A Continuum of Placements and Services

For schools and school systems to plan services, decision makers must be aware of placement options. Figure 5.11 shows the different placements that might be used. Within the LRE philosophy, each step of this continuum is least restrictive for some students. Home- or hospital-bound instruction might be the only option immediately after surgery and in long-term illnesses in which much time is spent in bed. Often, the physical education of persons in such situations is neglected, but play or recreational activities and a system for maintaining or building fitness should be provided. Terminally ill and medically fragile children, whether at home or in a hospital, need to sustain relationships with peers and physical education teachers, and creative school systems can make this possible.

The second step, full-time adapted physical education in a separate class, also depends on the philosophy and creativeness of the school system. Such programs usually follow a curriculum model like I CAN (Wessel, 1977) or the database gymnasium (Dunn, Morehouse, & Fredericks, 1986). These models are explained later in this chapter.

Progressing up the continuum in Figure 5.11, the third step—part-time adapted physical education—is the beginning of the transition from separate to integrated placement. This critical step is analogous to the resource room concept in special education. Placement at this level demands two decisions: (a) How shall time be distributed between adapted and regular physical education? and (b) What shall be the nature of the regular physical education?

Figure 5.11 suggests that the answer to the second question should be Model A, B, or C. LRE philosophy requires having options, an area in many school systems in which imagination is nonexistent. However, it takes only one person to understand and advocate for a system like that in Figure 5.11.

Model A, an entry-level specially designed mainstream program, is usually implemented by an adapted physical activity specialist. This is a system specially designed to integrate students with disabilities for the first time. Regular education students volunteer to help, receive special training, and are carefully selected for exemplary attitudes and peer teaching abilities. Among the variations of Model A that have been successful are (a) partners or peer tutors and (b) reverse mainstream strategies. In these variations, the ratio of students with and without disabilities is about equal.

Models B and C are conducted by regular physical educators. In these, the ratio of students with and without disabilities is about 1:10, the same as in society in general. Model B is a support services mainstream class. Teaching style, content, and orientation are purposely designed to meet individual needs and assure success. This intent is much harder to implement than it sounds and requires training and experience. Model C is a class in which mastery of regulation sports or a designated fitness criterion is the main goal.

Mainstream Variables Affecting Placement

Planning service delivery begins with evaluation of regular physical education. Before making recommendations about placement, you need to know about class size, teaching style, skill performance level of students, and many other variables. Only by systematically examining such variables can you plan intelligently for differently abled students. Evaluation may result in placement in existing programs and/or the creation of new curriculum models.

Regular Class Size

When physical education classes contain over 30 students, it is difficult and perhaps impossible for one person to individualize and adapt. This is not only because of pupil-teacher ratio limitations but because space in the average gymnasium does not permit more than about five learning stations. *The optimal size for small-group interaction and skill practice is two to six students at a station.* There must be ample space between stations, particularly when balls are involved, to assure safety. Individualization implies personalization, and there should be the possibility within every class session of calling every student by name at least once, praising him or her for something, and engaging in personal talk. Class sizes larger than 30 build in defeat, contribute to teacher burnout, and intensify discipline problems.

Class size should be negotiated. For students with attention deficit disorders, hyperactivity, and behavior problems, the maximum class size may be 10 or 12. For students with severe disabilities, the class size specification may also entail provision of a permanently assigned partner or aide. Class size should be matched with assessment data on social competence and learning style. Class size can be manipulated by decreasing the number of students or by increasing the number of teachers.

Teaching Styles: Regular and Inclusive

Muska Mosston in 1966 introduced the idea of a spectrum of teaching styles in which students are given increasing freedom and responsibility for their own learning. Over the years, 11 teaching styles have evolved (Mosston, 1992; Mosston & Ashworth, 1986, 1990). These styles are loosely combined into two categories: regular and inclusive.

Regular Style

Method of judging student success is the major factor that distinguishes between regular and inclusive styles in Table 5.4. In the regular style (also called command, practice, reciprocal, or self-check), all students must achieve a uniform standard or minimal competency level. The correct or efficient movement pattern is modeled and explained, and students are expected to approximate this pattern through on-task practice of specific, assigned activities. Feedback is largely corrective to enable

Table 5.4   Two teaching styles used in regular physical education.

Regular (Traditional)	Inclusive (Nontraditional)
1. Regulation rules	Flexible rules
2. Do as I say	Find your own way
3. Focus on average	Focus on individual
4. Minimal competency expectancy for all	Individual personal-best expectancy

students to meet age-appropriate minimum standards. Ultimately, each student passes or fails each task or step.

In the regular style, all students usually practice the same activity or participate in the same game. Sports and games are played by regulation rules to enhance generalization to leisure activities. Minimum health-related fitness standards are identical for everyone. Most traditional classes teach motor skills, fitness activities, and leisure competencies this way. The placement question then is, "Does the differently abled student, given his or her present level of performance, have a chance at achieving the required minimum competency set for each class objective?" If so, what kind of support services will this student need when placed in the regular class?

Inclusive Style

The inclusive teaching style, according to Mosston (1992), is characterized by use of multiple performance standards or the criterion of everyone doing his or her best. Sports and games are not played by regulation rules; hence, the emphasis is not on mastering traditional sports. Instead, the major goal is getting to know and care about oneself and others through movement. Emphasis is on finding many ways of doing one skill, activity, or game, rather than one correct or efficient way. Feedback is facilitative rather than corrective, with students encouraged to explore their personal best and/or a collaborative best with a partner or small group.

In the inclusive style, students are given a choice about degree of difficulty. This means that every activity is task-analyzed from easy to difficult. Within the class, students are all performing at different levels. Traditional games are adapted so that there is no elimination and every student is maximally active.

With the inclusive style, differently abled students can be accommodated in regular physical education. Many regular physical educators, however, have never been taught how to adapt and include all students. Others find it difficult or impossible to apply this style because class size is too large or space is inadequate for parallel group activities of different difficulty levels. Finally, this style is inappropriate when the class goal is to learn regulation sports.

In conclusion, persons who make placement decisions should check on the teaching styles used in regular physical education. Ideally, every school has some classes representative of each style. Then the placement can be regular physical education with an inclusive teaching style and support services. If no such classes exist, then regular physical education is probably not an appropriate assignment.

T a b l e 5 . 5   **50-yd dash times (in seconds) for grades 1 to 6 (SD = standard deviation).**

	Boys						Girls					
Grade	1	2	3	4	5	6	1	2	3	4	5	6
Age	6	7	8	9	10	11	6	7	8	9	10	11
Mean	9.9	9.3	8.8	8.5	8.2	8.1	10.3	9.5	9.2	8.7	8.6	8.3
SD	1.0	.9	.7	.7	.7	.7	1.0	.9	.9	.7	.6	.7
	Percentiles											
95	8.4	8.1	7.8	7.5	7.4	7.1	8.9	8.2	8.0	7.6	7.7	7.2
75	9.2	8.7	8.3	8.1	7.8	7.7	9.5	8.9	8.7	8.3	8.2	7.8
50	9.9	9.2	8.8	8.6	8.2	8.0	10.2	9.3	9.2	8.7	8.6	8.3
30	10.4	9.6	9.0	8.9	8.6	8.4	10.9	9.7	9.5	9.0	9.0	8.7
25	10.6	9.9	9.1	9.0	8.6	8.5	11.0	9.9	9.6	9.1	9.1	8.8
15	11.0	10.2	9.4	9.3	8.9	8.8	11.3	10.4	9.9	9.5	9.4	9.1
5	11.6	11.0	9.9	9.6	9.5	9.3	12.0	11.1	10.8	10.1	9.8	9.5

Note. From Margie Hanson, *Motor Performance Testing of Elementary School Age Children,* p. 265, unpublished doctoral dissertation, University of Washington, Seattle.

Competence Level of Regular Education Students

Whether or not students can succeed in a regular class taught in a traditional style depends on how close their performance is to the class mean (numerical average) on the skills, knowledges, strategies, and behaviors being taught. Persons who make placement decisions should have access to regular class statistics. These may be for a class, school, school district, or some larger conglomerate like several school districts from different parts of the country.

If running speed, for example, is important to success in the activities to be taught (e.g., low organized games), then a student's speed should be compared to that of the regular class student. Table 5.5 shows that, in the school system represented, the average 6-year-old boy runs the 50-yd dash in 9.9 sec. The standard deviation (SD) is included in the table to allow determination of whether a score meets the criterion of being no more than 1 standard deviation from the mean. This is a good criterion for deciding whether or not a student needs special help.

Means and norms are essential guides when making placement decisions involving regular classes governed by regulation teaching styles. A knowledge of the average student's skills, rules, strategies, and behaviors in the regular class lends insight into the probability of success for students with disabilities.

The ability to use rules and strategies in a game setting and/or to exhibit appropriate behaviors is difficult to assess by standardized tests that yield norms. In this area, videotapes are recommended. Experts can then view videotapes of the differently abled student in several game settings and determine whether or not he or she can fit into and benefit from instruction in these settings.

Content Orientation: Competition, Cooperation, or Individualistic

Orientation refers to whether the content in a particular class emphasizes competition, cooperation, or individual achievement. Two brothers, David and Roger Johnson (1975; John-

T a b l e 5 . 6   **A comparison of cooperative and traditional learning groups.**

Cooperative Learning Groups	Traditional Learning Groups
Positive interdependence	No interdependence
Individual accountability	No individual accountability
Heterogeneous	Homogeneous
Shared leadership	One appointed leader
Shared responsibility for each other	Responsibility only for self
Task and maintenance emphasized	Only task emphasized
Social skills directly taught	Social skills assumed
Teacher observes and intervenes	Teacher ignores group functioning
Groups process their effectiveness	No group processing

Note. From *Circles of Learning: Cooperation in the Classroom* (p. 10) by D. W. Johnson, R. T. Johnson, E. J. Holubec, & P. Roy, 1984, Alexandria, VA: Association for Supervision and Curriculum Development.

son, Johnson, Holubec, & Roy, 1984), both professors at the University of Minnesota, have spearheaded a comprehensive research movement that shows that classroom orientation significantly affects the differently abled person's social acceptance, performance level, and rate of learning. Their findings indicate that a cooperative goal structure is more appropriate for differently abled persons than the other two orientations.

Table 5.6 shows the desired characteristics of the cooperative learning structure. The recommended small-group size is 2 to 6, depending on the students' social skills and the amount of time available to work on a particular task. The shorter the time, the smaller the group should be. Positive interdependence, the most important characteristic of the cooperative learning structure, is often promoted by joint reward systems, such as partner or group grades or points. The goal is to create a system whereby everyone helps everyone else, and success (task completion, winning, praise) is dependent upon everyone's contributions.

Many physical activities can be taught and practiced using a cooperative group structure. For example, throwing, catching, and volleying practice can be structured around the challenge of which group can keep the ball in the air the longest while giving everyone an equal number of trials. Traditional team games can be changed so that a certain number of people must touch the ball (e.g., three or five passes) before it goes over the net or is used to make a basket or goal. Team bowling or shooting scores can be highlighted instead of individual ones.

Our society, however, expects most students to learn the rules, strategies, and skills of regulation team and individual sports before graduation. These activities are essentially competitive, even though cooperation with teammates is stressed. If the class goal is to teach mastery of regulation sports, then placement of a differently abled student in the class is inappropriate unless the ability to participate fully and to succeed can be documented in the assessment process.

Content to Be Taught

Like any other subject matter, the nature of physical education content varies by grade. Elementary school physical education is easier to adapt than secondary because the emphasis is on teaching basic skills, rules, and strategies and on developing minimum fitness. This content can be taught using traditional or nontraditional styles within competitive, cooperative, or individualistic orientations. In middle and secondary school, increasingly more time is spent teaching regulation sports that will generalize into lifelong leisure and fitness practices. Curriculum at this level assumes that basic skills, rules, and strategies have been mastered, so accommodation of students without these abilities requires team-teaching and the running of parallel programs.

At the secondary school level, most good physical education programs use a multiactivity curriculum approach that covers several units over the school year. Ideally, some units teach regulation team sports, but others focus on fitness, movement education, dance, gymnastics, swimming, individual sports, and recreational games. The student with a disability may have potential for success in some of these but not others. Therefore, the IEP team should not assign secondary school students to generic regular physical education but rather to specific instructional units that are appropriate.

Use of Community Resources

When full participation is not possible in regulation sport units, arrangements should be made for students to receive parallel instruction in sports specific to their disability (e.g., wheelchair basketball or handball) or to learn an individual sport not usually taught in regular physical education. An excellent approach is for school systems to employ athletes with disabilities to provide such instruction. The student not only benefits from new content but is introduced to role models and community resources. A growing number of athletes with disabilities are earning physical education degrees and qualify su-

perbly for employment. If available athletes have not had teacher training, then special arrangements for in-service and supervision may be needed.

Disability-specific instruction often involves transportation to locations where special sports equipment and facilities are available. Budgeting for this is as important as transportation for the school's football team, but resources often are obtained only through advocacy and negotiation. Some school systems collaborate with community recreation programs, which make available transportation, facilities, and staff. This is an excellent way to facilitate transition from school to community resources, and many experimental mainstream programs can be devised.

The normalization principle must guide the planning of content. Differently abled students must be afforded the same opportunities as peers to learn lifetime leisure skills and to develop fitness and positive attitudes toward physical activity. This requires careful planning. Does the regular physical education program afford these opportunities?

Teacher Attitudes and Training

The attitudes and training of the regular physical education teacher ultimately determine success for the differently abled student. The availability of support services influences how teachers feel and their assessment of personal competency. Generally, we feel good about things we think we do well. Preservice and in-service training in adapted physical education enhances competence and contributes to good attitudes. A personality that is warm, friendly, and open to new people, ideas, and strategies creates a regular education climate that promotes humanistic learning for students with disabilities.

Overall Program Quality: Summary

In summary, the overall quality of the regular physical education program affects planning, assessment, and placement. One role of the adapted physical education specialist is to serve as a liaison between regular physical education and special education and ascertain that students with disabilities are properly assessed and placed. At IEP meetings, information should be available, not only about the student, but about the regular education environment: (a) class sizes; (b) teaching styles; (c) skill level of regular education students; (d) competition, cooperation, or individualistic orientation; (e) content; (f) use of community resources; (g) teacher attitudes and training; and (h) overall program quality.

Service Delivery for Regular Education Students

Many regular education students also need adapted physical activity services, but they are not eligible for help under the IEP-based special education model. Many school districts, however, want to serve students who are overweight, unfit, or clumsy, even though the law does not protect them. When a continuum of placements is available, there is no rule that only students with disabilities can have adapted physical activity. Upon the recommendation of the physical educator, principals or school counselors can initiate an assessment-placement process for regular education students similar to that used for students with disabilities.

Many regular education students need help as much or more than special education students. Families also need help. The 1990s offer opportunities for new, creative models for applying the content of this chapter to all persons, not just those with disabilities recognized by law. For students with psychomotor problems not covered by law, two approaches to assessment and goal setting are commonly used: a committee on adapted physical education (CAPE) or the regular physical education initiative (RPEI) advisory committee (see Chapter 3). CAPE is a school district approach, whereas RPEI is a classroom or single-school approach. The resulting assessment procedures, called diagnostic, are described in Chapter 6.

Selecting Goals and Writing Objectives

Usually within the traditional goal areas, a school curriculum guide lists objectives that are age appropriate for certain grades that a teacher can use. Table 5.7 presents some illustrative objectives. Each of these objectives should be achievable after 3 to 5 hours of instruction. Remember, however, that instruction pertaining to a specific objective is typically spread out over several weeks. Think of objectives not only as guides to curriculum and lesson plans, but also as statements of tests to be passed at the end of instruction.

Remember that objectives have three parts: (a) condition, (b) one specific, observable behavior, and (c) criterion level for success. The objectives in Table 5.7, as in many curriculum guides, do not include conditions. This is because conditions are highly individual, depending on resources and many other factors. Teachers must add the conditions when they choose to use a specific objective. Examples for some conditions for objectives in Table 5.7 follow:

For Objective A1: Given the Harter Self-Perception Scale in accordance with instructions in the manual,

For Objective A4: Given a notebook to use as an activity journal, daily reminders to write in the journal, and a deadline for submitting it,

For Objective B3: Given 5 min in a 10-ft-by-10-ft room with five pieces of play apparatus (tricycle, wagon, long rope, life-size rag doll, cloth tunnel) in designated places and three children (A, B, and C) present,

For Objective C2: Given a regulation softball, a wall target (60 by 40 inches in size) set at a designated distance and height, the command, "Throw as hard as you can," and three trials,

Now that you can identify the parts of an objective, select some goals for the children in Figure 5.12 and try writing some objectives for them. Use the format in Table 5.7 so that the relationship of objectives to goals is clear. State whether the objectives are for Child A, B, or C. Table 5.8 presents a checklist of criteria to determine whether or not your objectives are correctly written.

Selecting Curricular Models

Packaged curricular models often include goals and objectives, thereby minimizing teacher work in this area. Curricular models for use throughout a school system are often selected by teams of teachers from different schools who serve on curriculum committees. Choices reflect philosophy, prioritization of physical education goals, breadth of knowledge about possible options, and resources.

Curricular models vary widely. Some are developed by individuals or school systems with minimal financial support, whereas others come from well-funded research grants that permit program ideas to be tested over a period of years. In particular, the Department of Education's National Diffusion Network (NDN) has funded many models that meet the following criteria: valid, exemplary, and exportable. Often models are popular for a while, and then interest wanes as key developers retire or switch to other projects or grant money is no longer available. Some curricular models are packaged for sale by commercial companies, while others are described in articles, books, videotapes, and other sources. Still others are made available by organizations like Special Olympics International.

Most curricular models include both assessment and instructional components. See Appendix E for addresses of companies that make available curricular models. It is not necessary, however, to purchase ready-made models. Many professionals can create their own models by combining ideas from existing models with original ideas from their personal experience. Following are some models that have been popular in adapted physical activity and are still in use. Most of these models are described in more detail in later chapters that focus on either the model's major goal or on the population for which the model was designed.

I CAN and ABC Models

Developed by Janet Wessel of Michigan State University, these two NDN curricular models are applicable to regular and adapted physical education. *I CAN* (Wessel, 1977) is an acronym for four principles believed to underlie successful teaching:

I	Individualize instruction
C	Create social leisure competence
A	Associate all learnings
N	Narrow the gap between theory and practice

The Achievement-Based Curriculum (ABC) model is a 1980s refinement of the I CAN model (Wessel & Kelly, 1986). Wessel is now retired, and work concerning these models is guided by Luke Kelly at the University of Virginia. The PAP-TE-CA model followed in this text is an adaptation and expansion of the curriculum components (plan, assess, prescribe, teach, evaluate, and modify) used in the I CAN and ABC models.

T a b l e   5 . 7   **Illustrative objectives for selected goals as they might appear in a curriculum guide or an IEP.**

Goal	Objectives
A. To Demonstrate Positive Self-Concept in Relation to Fitness, Motor, and Leisure Performance	1. To improve score on sport section of a standardized self-concept test by a set amount 2. To demonstrate understanding and appreciation of self by stating accurately one's personal best time, distance, or score on selected tasks like mile run, 50-yd dash, overarm throw 3. To demonstrate belief in ability to improve through hard work by stating high (but realistic) levels of aspiration on selected tasks 4. To demonstrate pride by stating five concrete physical activity achievements 5. To demonstrate commitment to change by showing chart kept over several weeks and/or diary that describes time spent in exercise, games, sports, and dance and/or a diet plan

B. To Demonstrate Functional Competence in Selected Play and Game Behaviors	1. To participate successfully in five selected games by
	  a. Remaining on task for the entire game without verbal prompting from teacher or peers
	  b. Following all rules without prompts
	  c. Not being tagged, made "it," or sent to prison more often than other players
	2. To demonstrate ability to get into the following formations with nine other students within a count of 10 sec: single circle, file, line, double circle
	3. To demonstrate appropriate use of the following play objects and apparatus by playing for 3 min in response to "Show me how you play with this:" tricycle, wagon, life-size doll, cloth tunnel
	4. To show a diary that records at least 1 hour of participation in at least three different sport activities at community facilities each week

C. To Demonstrate Functional Competence in Selected Motor Skills and Patterns	1. To perform three of four components of a mature run, throw, and jump 2. To increase overarm throw distance by 10 ft 3. To decrease 50-m dash speed by 0.5 sec 4. To demonstrate the first five steps or focal points in a task analysis or learning progression
D. To Demonstrate Functional Fitness and a Healthy Lifestyle	1. To demonstrate sufficient arm and shoulder strength to engage in a ball activity for 30 minutes or to shoot a basket 50 times 2. To demonstrate sufficient cardiorespiratory endurance to engage in a vigorous team sport for 15 minutes 3. To demonstrate sufficient arm and shoulder flexibility to fully extend both arms in 8 out of 10 basketball shots

Note. "To demonstrate functional competence" means to perform within an average range for one's age and gender.

FIGURE 5.12   Three students with distinctly different needs. Which goals would you set for each? Write objectives for each of these students and use criteria in Table 5.8 to evaluate your objectives.

Child A is age 6, is partially sighted, has minor learning problems, expresses lots of fear about new experiences, and is an only child of parents who tend to be overprotective.

Child B is age 10, has three brothers and athletic parents, has been adopted as mascot of the local wheelchair basketball team, talks about basketball all the time, but refuses to try other sports and to recreate with able-bodied peers.

Child C is age 9, has severe mental retardation, does not play spontaneously, has a mild congenital heart defect, and lives with a mother and older sister who are not athletic.

Table 5.8   Checklist for evaluating objectives that you write for class practice.

		Objectives			
Criteria		**1**	**2**	**3**	**4**
1.	Describes learner behavior, not teacher behavior				
2.	Describes product, not process (i.e., the terminal behavior, not the learning activity)				
3.	Includes a verb that specifies a definite, observable behavior				
4.	Contains a single learning outcome, not several				
5.	Contains three parts: condition, observable behavior, and criterion level				
6.	Matches assessment data to specified behavior				
7.	Focuses on functions that are usable and relevant in everyday life				
8.	Selects product that is achievable through 4 to 5 hours of instruction and practice				

In addition to excellent information about curriculum development (Wessel, 1977), I CAN included a criterion-referenced assessment system in which hundreds of motor skills were broken down into observable tasks that could be assessed pass/fail; these tasks were presented developmentally, making the system particularly applicable to individuals with cognitive and motor delays. The system was described as diagnostic-prescriptive, in that numerous learning activities were prescribed to help achieve various motor, fitness, and leisure goals. I CAN was packaged in boxes that held 9- × 12-inch cardboard sheets and is still available through the Pro•Ed Company.

Project ACTIVE

Developed by Thomas Vodola (1976) of the Oakhurst, New Jersey, public schools, ACTIVE was also marketed as an NDN-funded, diagnostic-prescriptive model. ACTIVE was an acronym for **A**ll **C**hildren **T**otally **I**nvolved **E**xercising. The curriculum, designed to meet the needs of both regular and adapted physical education, was marketed as seven paperback curriculum manuals, five competency-based in-service training manuals, and various other training materials. Specifically, curriculum manuals were available for the following disabilities: low motor ability, low physical vitality, nutritional deficiencies, posture abnormalities, motor disabilities or limitations, communication disorders, and breathing problems.

The organization of each curriculum manual was guided by the **T**est-**A**ssess-**P**rescribe-**E**valuate (TAPE) model. Each manual included the same norm-referenced tests (Motor Ability Tests, Levels 1 and 2; and Physical Fitness Tests, Levels 1 and 2) as well as specialized tests specific to the disability addressed. The motor ability tests measured five factors: gross body coordination, balance/postural orientation, eye-hand coordination, eye-hand accuracy, and foot-eye accuracy. Activities were prescribed in relation to assessment data.

Vodola is now deceased, and Project ACTIVE has been directed since 1986 by Joe Karp, a public school teacher in Washington State. Materials are available at this address: Joe Karp, 20214 103rd Place, NE, Bothell, WA 98011-2455.

The Data-Based Gymnasium

Developed by John Dunn of Oregon State University and several associates in the late 1970s and later refined, the data-based gymnasium (DBG) model is "a prescriptive physical activity program for students whereby decisions are based upon the student performance data" (Dunn et al., 1986, p. 170). This model is marketed as a book (Dunn et al., 1986), which has served as the major primary source for behavior management and task analysis in adapted physical education. Assessment is criterion-referenced, based on lengthy task analyses that break skills into phases and steps. Many forms are provided for recording multiple trials, preferred cues and reinforcers, and information about baseline, review, revision, and maintenance of individual programs. These forms have led to DBG often being called a "clipboard approach."

Originally DBG was developed specifically for individuals with severe disabilities, but now its principles are recognized as appropriate to anyone who can benefit from behavior management. Embedded within DBG is a component called the Game, Exercise, and Leisure Sport Curriculum; this section presents task analyses for many motor skills. Forward chaining (adding parts to the task in the order in which they naturally occur) and backward chaining (starting with the whole and adding parts in reverse) are emphasized. DBG is available from Pro•Ed.

Project PEOPEL

Developed by Ed Long and associates in Arizona in the 1970s, this NDN model stressed social competence as well as sport skills. *PEOPEL* is an acronym for Physical Education Opportunity for Exceptional Learners, and the curriculum was directed toward students in Grades 9 to 12 (Long, Irmer, Burkett, Glasenapp, & Odenkirk, 1980). This was the first physical education model to gain widespread attention for a peer tutors or partners-type class orientation. Small-size classes were specially constructed so that students with and without disabilities were matched and spent the semester together; the recommended ratio was 12:12.

Able-bodied students received intensive in-service training to qualify as student aides, and many materials (film and written) were available to individuals who wished to adopt the PEOPEL model. The curriculum was sports-centered, with task-analyzed objectives. Funding for PEOPEL was available from 1974 to 1986. Since then, many teachers, like Linda Barnes in the Richardson, Texas, school district, have kept the PEOPEL concept alive, often calling their programs PARTNERS models. Today, information about PEOPEL can be obtained from Dr. Lee Burkett, Physical Education Department, Arizona State University, Tempe, AZ 85287.

Body Skills: A Motor Development Curriculum for Children

Developed by Judy Werder and Robert Bruininks (1988) of Minnesota, this curriculum was developed in the 1980s to complement the Bruininks-Oseretsky Test of Motor Proficiency (BOTMP) (Bruininks, 1978), a major diagnostic test used by adapted physical educators. The curriculum is based on data from a criterion-referenced measure called the Motor Skills Inventory (MSI) as well as the BOTMP, a norm-referenced instrument.

Body Skills encompasses 31 motor skills important to children ages 2 to 12 years. Developmental sequences leading to mature skill are presented pictorially. Instructional units are provided on body management, locomotion, body fitness, object movement, and fine motor development. This curriculum is available through the American Guidance Service (see Appendix E).

Special Olympics Sports Skills Program

Developed in the 1980s by the staff at the Special Olympics International (SOI) headquarters, the SOI Sports Skills Program offers separate sports skills guides for numerous summer and winter sports. Although developed by an agency for people with mental retardation, this curriculum is applicable to both regular and adapted physical education and to all age groups for whom regulation sports training is appropriate.

Each guide includes long-term goals, short-term objectives, criterion-referenced assessment checklists, and detailed task analyses with excellent illustrations. Goals and objectives encompass skills, social behavior, and functional knowledge of rules. These excellent guides are available through state Special Olympics offices, or SOI, 1350 New York Avenue, NW, Suite 500, Washington, DC 20005.

Moving to Inclusion

The Moving to Inclusion model developed by the Active Living Alliance for Canadians with a Disability (1994) and Fitness Canada, in cooperation with 11 national organizations, provincial education departments, and other expert sources, is available in both English and French. Nine excellent, well-illustrated books, all entitled *Active Living Through Physical Education: Maximizing Opportunities,* are available on these subjects: introduction, multiple disabilities, amputation, skiing, cerebral palsy, visual impairment, deaf or hard of hearing, intellectual disability, and wheelchair.

Moving to Inclusion is referred to as a national initiative, and readers of the manuals are encouraged to mail in a personal data form and become part of the Moving to Inclusion Network. By their definition, **inclusive physical education**

is a step-by-step process;

includes all students;

has a range of activities and supports; and

is based on the needs and interest of students.

Each book emphasizes and elaborates on four principles:

1. Activities are modified and individualized as necessary.
2. Expectations are realistic yet challenging.
3. Assistance is provided only to the degree required.
4. Dignity of risk and availability of choices are respected and fostered.

Assessment instruments include Transport Skills Checklist, Object Control Skills Checklist, and Basic Movement Skills Observation Profile. The latter, which uses *satisfactory, developing,* or *not observed* responses, includes 15 tasks and assesses the development of manipulative and transport skills, balance ability, and body/space awareness. The impact of Moving to Inclusion is being felt worldwide (see Figure 5.13). This model is available through Moving to Inclusion, 707A-1600 James Naismith Drive, Gloucester, Ontario, Canada K1B 5N4.

You Stay Active

You Stay Active, a model developed jointly by AAHPERD and the Cooper Institute for Aerobics Research (CIAR) in 1995, is a comprehensive recognition program built around the AAHPERD's Physical Best fitness materials and CIAR's FITNESSGRAM (see Chapter 13). The purpose is to provide teachers with materials to help teach and reinforce the message of lifetime physical activity. The model emphasizes providing recognition for regular participation in physical activity rather than awards or bribes for specific physical fitness achievements. This strategy marks a shift from the traditional

FIGURE 5.13 Dr. Lisa Silliman-French, Adapted PE Coordinator of Denton Public Schools, makes sure that special education children are included in regular classes.

school practice of focusing primarily on fitness tests and physical best criteria.

The You Stay Active book includes an activity promotion program called *It's Your Move,* Fit for Life Activity Logs for monitoring activities over an 8- to 10-week period, a Get Fit 6-week general conditioning exercise tracking program, and many other materials. It also stresses the inclusion of students with physical disabilities and recommends the recent work of Seaman (1995). The You Stay Active model is available from the Cooper Institute for Aerobics Research, 12330 Preston Road, Dallas, TX 75230.

Using, Creating, and Evaluating Curricular Models

Evaluate these models and determine whether to use the whole model or parts. In particular, use these models to stimulate your personal creativity and initiative. For example, several of these models include descriptions of how to involve parents and other volunteers in programming (e.g., Dunn et al., 1986; Wessel, 1977). How can you incorporate this idea into your curriculum planning? In general, models that are collaboratively developed by the people who use them work better than models exported from other sources. Regardless of whether models are adopted or personally created, much planning is needed.

Planning Instruction for the Year

Procedures involved in planning instruction include (a) calculating instructional time, (b) planning use of time, (c) developing instructional units, and (d) making decisions about space, equipment, and resources.

T a b l e 5 . 9   Calculating available instructional time for the year.

1. *Total number* of instructional weeks available: __36__ weeks
   180-day school year = 36 instructional weeks
   230-day school year = 46 instructional weeks
   (Christmas, spring, summer vacations already excluded.)

2. Subtract 2 weeks of the total time available to allow for *cancelled physical*   __2__ weeks
   education classes resulting from conference time, psychological testing,
   swimming schedule, snow days, field trips, voting days (gym in use),
   holiday assemblies, beginning and end of school, and others.

3. Subtract 2 weeks of the total time available to allow for **flex time**   __2__ weeks
   (unplanned adjustments that need to be made to allow for additional
   instructional needs).

4. Total weeks available (#1 minus #2 and #3) =   __32__ weeks (16 each semester)

5. Total days available:
   a. Multiply #4 by the number of physcial education classes per week.   × __5__ days gym/week
                                                                                                                      = __160__ days gym/year

   b. Multiply total number of days by the length (minutes) of your
      physical education class (instructional time—not dressing or set-up time).   × __30__ min gym/day
                                                                                                                          = __4,800__ min gym/year

---

Calculating Instructional Time

Before determining number of objectives, calculate available instructional time for a specific class and/or student. Table 5.9, based on Wessel's (1977) I CAN system and the ABC curriculum (Wessel & Kelly, 1986), shows how the school calendar is used to do this for the academic year. Table 5.9 shows that the average student assigned to physical education 5 days a week (30 min a day) has 4,800 min (80 hr) of instructional time. This is 2,400 min (40 hr) a semester, a phenomenally short amount of time for the changing of behaviors.

Planning Use of Time

The next step is to decide how many objectives can be achieved in 2,400 min. Remember that students who are disabled or clumsy typically learn more slowly than their normal peers and that young students learn more slowly than older ones. Approximately 270 min (4.5 hr) are required for a preschool child with developmental delay to master one objective (Wessel & Kelly, 1986). Low-skilled students in elementary school and secondary school require about 210 min (3.5 hr) and 180 min (3 hr), respectively, per objective. To calculate number of objectives per semester, divide time needed to master one objective into total instructional time. For example, for elementary school:

$$\frac{2,400 \text{ min per semester}}{210 \text{ min per objective}} = 11.43 \text{ objectives per semester}$$

The next decision involves how many objectives should be selected from each goal area. Most IEPs include three or four goals, each broken down into three or four objectives. Time estimates often relate only to teaching motor and fitness skills; much research is needed on amount of time required to teach rules, strategies, and games. Research is also needed on amount of time required to increase cooperative behaviors and peer interactions and to decrease the many negative behaviors that constitute discipline problems.

Developing Instructional Units

The last step in group planning of time usage is to arrange objectives into instructional units and to specify the beginning and ending date of instruction for each unit. The IEP form, remember, requires a projected date for beginning service delivery. Legislation requires that progress on achievement of objectives must be reviewed for students with disabilities every 12 months. Many states require more frequent reviews. This should be considered in determining number of instructional units and duration of each unit. For convenience, assume that the periodic IEP review falls at the same time as the end of a semester (i.e., after about 2,400 min of instructional time).

Table 5.10 presents a sample semester plan for a student who requires approximately 270 min to achieve an objective (i.e., a preschool child who is slow or a student of any age with a severe disability). In 16 weeks, students on this plan are expected to complete four full objectives and make progress toward six others. Develop some lists of objectives for hypothetical students and then show your competence in prioritizing and organizing these objectives into semester plans. *Remember that planning should always be done in units of minutes.*

The amount of time required for a student to achieve an objective varies widely. The estimates of 270, 210, and 180 min for preschool, elementary, and secondary students are based on averages. Difficult objectives naturally require more time than easy ones. The art of writing objectives is enhanced by keeping in mind the number of minutes. *Flexible time* is needed for review and reinforcement of skills, knowledge, rules, and strategies learned in previous units. The planning of instruction is directed primarily toward new learning.

Table 5.10   Sample semester plan to guide service delivery.

Instructional Unit		Time in Minutes	Time Spent Each Week, in Minutes	Number of Weeks
1. Running games				
a. Motor skill—running		1,050	105	
b. Self-concept		450	45	
c. Social interactions		Embedded	Embedded	
d. Play and game concepts		Embedded	Embedded	
	Total	1,500	150	10
2. Aquatics				
a. Water entry and locomotion		270	67.5	
b. Breathing		270	67.5	
c. Self-concept and body image		60	15	
	Total	600	150	4
3. Creative movement/dance				
a. Portraying animals		100	50	
b. Moving to accompaniment		100	50	
c. Abdominal strength		100	50	
	Total	300	150	2

Note. a, b, c, and *d* refer to specific objectives. If 540 min are allocated, two objectives can be achieved. If 270 min are allocated, one objective can be achieved. If fewer than 270 min are allocated, there is not time for completion of one objective.

Other Decision Making

Planning also entails decision making about space, equipment, and resources. Size of class is tremendously important, since every student should have maximum on-task time. This means that, in a ball-handling unit, every student should have a ball and not be standing in line, waiting for a turn. It also means that every student has a chance to learn sports by practicing as a member of a regulation-size team, not by being one of 15 players scattered over the softball field. If too many students are assigned to a class in proportion to available space and equipment, selection of objectives and time planning are obviously affected.

In summary, planning reflects the philosophy of teacher, school, and community. Some of the processes involved in group planning are the same processes used for the IEP as required by legislation.

References

Active Living Alliance for Canadians with a Disability (1994). *Moving to inclusion.* Gloucester, Ontario: Author.

American Alliance for Health, Physical Education, Recreation and Dance, and Cooper Institute for Aerobics Research. (1995). *You stay active.* Dallas: Cooper Institute for Aerobics Research.

Bandura, A. (1977). Self-efficacy: Toward a unifying theory of behavioral change. *Psychological Review, 84*(7), 191–215.

Bandura, A. (1986). *Social foundations of thought and action: A social cognitive theory.* Englewood Cliffs, NJ: Prentice Hall.

Barker, R. (1968). *Ecological pscyhology.* Stanford, CA: Stanford University Press.

Bronfenbrenner, U. (1979). *The ecology of human development.* Cambridge, MA: Harvard University.

Cook, D. (1987). Psychological impact of disability. In R. Parker (Ed.), *Rehabilitation counseling: Basics & beyond* (pp. 97–120). Austin, TX: Pro•Ed.

Davis, W. E., & Burton, A. W. (1991). Ecological task analysis: Transforming movement behavior theory into practice. *Adapted Physical Activity Quarterly, 8*(2), 154–177.

Davis, W. E., & van Emmerik, R. E. A. (1995). An ecological task analysis approach for understanding motor development in mental retardation: Research questions and strategies. In A. Vermeer & W. E. Davis (Eds.), *Physical and motor development in mental retardation* (pp. 33–66). Basel, Switzerland: Karger.

Deci, E. L., & Ryan, R. M. (1985). *Intrinsic motivation and self-determination in human behavior.* New York: Plenum.

Dunn, J. M., Morehouse, J., & Fredericks, H. (1986). *Physical education for the severely handicapped: A systematic approach to a data-based gymnasium.* Austin, TX: Pro•Ed.

Dweck, C. S. (1980). Learned helplessness in sport. In C. H. Nadeau, W. R. Halliwell, K. M. Newell, & G. C. Roberts (Eds.), *Psychology of motor behavior and sport—1979* (pp. 1–11). Champaign, IL: Human Kinetics.

Fetterman, D., Kaftarian, S., & Wancersman, A. (Eds.). (1996). *Empowerment evaluation.* Thousand Oaks, CA: Sage.

Fox, K. R., & Corbin, C. B. (1989). The physical self-perception profile: Development and preliminary validation. *Journal of Sport and Exercise Psychology, 11,* 408–430.

Gibson, J. J. (1977). The theory of affordances. In R. Shaw & J. Bransford (Eds.), *Perceiving, acting, and knowing: Toward an ecological psychology* (pp. 67–82). Hillsdale, NJ: Erlbaum.

Gibson, J. J. (1979). *The ecological approach to visual perception.* Boston: Houghton Mifflin.

Golden, C. (Ed.). (1984). *Current topics in rehabilitation psychology.* New York: Grune & Stratton.

Hopkins, H. (1988). Current basis for theory and philosophy of occupational therapy. In H. Hopkins and H. Smith (Eds.), *Willard and Spackman's Occupational Therapy* (7th ed., pp. 38–42). Philadelphia: Lippincott.

Johnson, D. W., & Johnson, R. (1975). *Learning together and alone: Cooperation, competition, and individualization.* Englewood Cliffs, NJ: Prentice Hall.

Johnson, D. W., Johnson, R., Holubec, E., & Roy, P. (1984). *Circles of learning: Cooperation in the classroom.* Alexandria, VA: Association for Supervision and Curriculum Development.

Lewin, K. (1951). *Field theory in the social sciences.* New York: Harper & Row.

Long, E., Irmer, L., Burkett, L., Glasenapp, G., & Odenkirk, B. (1980). PEOPEL. *Journal of Physical Education and Recreation, 51,* 28–29.

Maslow, A. (1954). *Motivation and personality.* New York: Harper & Row.

Maslow, A. (1970). *Motivation and personality* (2nd ed.). New York: Harper & Row.

McBee, F., & Ballinger, J. (1984). *The continental quest.* Tampa, FL: Overland Press.

Mosston, M. (1992). Tug-O-War, No more: Meeting teaching-learning objectives using the spectrum of teaching styles. *Journal of Physical Education, Recreation and Dance, 63*(1), 27–31, 56.

Mosston, M., & Ashworth, S. (1986). *Teaching physical education* (3rd ed.). Columbus, OH: Merrill.

Mosston, M., & Ashworth, S. (1990). *The spectrum of teaching styles: From command to discovery.* White Plains, NY: Longman.

Nirje, B. (1969). The normalization principle and its human management implications. In R. Kugel & W. Wolfensberger (Eds.), *Changing patterns in residential services for the mentally retarded* (pp. 179–195). Washington, DC: President's Committee on Mental Retardation.

Nirje, B. (1980). The normalization principle. In R. J. Flynn & K. E. Nitsch (Eds.), *Normalization, social integration, and community services* (pp. 31–49). Baltimore: University Park Press.

Reilly, R., & Lewis, E. (1983). *Educational psychology.* New York: Macmillan.

Robinson, D. W. (1990). An attributional analysis of student demoralization in physical education settings. *Quest, 42*(1), 27–39.

Rogers, C. R. (1951). *Client-centered therapy.* Boston: Houghton Mifflin.

Rogers, C. R. (1969). *Freedom to learn.* Columbus, OH: Merrill.

Rotter, J. B. (1966). Generalized expectancies for internal versus external control of reinforcement. *Psychological Monographs: General and Applied, 80*(1), 1–28.

Seaman, J. A. (Ed.). (1995). *Physical best and individuals with disabilities: A handbook for inclusion in fitness programs.* Reston, VA: American Alliance for Health, Physical Education, Recreation and Dance.

Seligman, M. (1975). *Helplessness: On depression, development, and death.* San Francisco: W. H. Freeman.

Sherrill, C., Hinson, M., Gench, B., Kennedy, S., & Low, L. (1990). Self-concepts of disabled youth athletes. *Perceptual and Motor Skills, 70,* 1093–1098.

Sherrill, C., Silliman, L., Gench, B., & Hinson, M. (1990). Self-actualization of elite wheelchair athletes. *Paraplegia, 28,* 252–260.

Special Olympics International. (1980s, dates vary). *Sports skills program guides.* Washington, DC: Author.

Vallerand, R. J., & Reid, G. (1990). Motivation and special populations: Theory, research, and implications regarding motor behaviour. In G. Reid (Ed.), *Problems in movement control* (pp. 159–197). Amsterdam: North Holland.

Vodola, T. (1976). *Project ACTIVE maxi-model: Nine training manuals.* Oakhurst, NJ: Project ACTIVE.

Wankel, L., & Sefton, J. (1989). A season-long investigation of fun in youth sports. *Journal of Sport and Exercise Psychology, 11,* 355–366.

Wehmeyer, M. L., Kelchner, K., & Richards, S. (1996). Essential characteristics of self-determined behavior of individuals with mental retardation. *American Journal of Mental Retardation, 100*(6), 632–642.

Werder, J. K., & Bruininks, R. H. (1988). *Body skills: A motor development curriculum for children.* Circle Pines, MN: American Guidance Service.

Wessel, J. (1977). *Planning individualized education programs in special education with examples from I CAN physical education.* Northbrook, IL: H. Hubbard. (Now available from Pro•Ed, Austin, TX.)

Wessel, J., & Kelly, L. (1986). *Achievement-based curriculum development in physical education.* Philadephia: Lea & Febiger.

Wolfensberger, W. (1972). *Normalization.* Toronto: National Institute on Mental Retardation.

Wolfensberger, W. (1991). Reflections on a lifetime in human services and mental retardation. *Mental Retardation, 29*(1), 1–15.

Wolfensberger, W. (1995). An "if this, then that" formulation of decisions related to social role valorization as a better way of interpreting it to people. *Mental Retardation, 33*(3), 163–169.

Wolfensberger, W., & Thomas, S. (1983). *PASSING: Program analysis of service systems' implementation of normalization goals.* Ontario, Canada: National Institute on Mental Retardation.

Wright, B. (1960). *Physical disability: A psychological approach.* New York: Harper & Row.

Wright, B. (1983). *Physical disability: A psychosocial approach* (2nd ed.). New York: Harper & Row.

C H A P T E R
6

Assessing, Prescribing, and
Writing the IEP

FIGURE 6.1 Assessment of dynamic balance is a good way to start the year.

After you have studied this chapter, you should be able to do the following:

1. Identify and discuss four purposes of assessment.

2. Contrast the following types of assessment:
   (a) formal/informal, (b) product/process, (c) norm/criterion, (d) standardized/content-referenced, (e) tests/instruments, and (f) self/other.

3. List and discuss seven planning procedures for assessment. Explain three criteria that good instruments meet.

4. Identify at least one test specifically designed for screening, one test for placement, and one test for student progress in the psychomotor domain. Discuss and be able to administer each.

5. Discuss instruments associated with various goal areas.

6. Identify and discuss three assessment theories. Discuss which is most meaningful to you and why.

7. Explain mean, median, mode, and standard deviation. Discuss application in relation to placement and the structuring of balanced class teams.

8. Explain the conversion of raw data to z scores. When are conversions necessary?

9. Identify and discuss three types of norms. Give examples of use in placement, grading, and awards.

10. Explain special considerations in assessment of persons with severe disabilities.

Some physical educators walk into the gymnasium in September, greet the students, and immediately begin teaching. They assume that all students have more or less the same needs and possess age-appropriate skills, fitness, and knowledge. Other physical educators begin each school year with 1 or 2 weeks of assessment activities (see Figure 6.1). They screen to determine which students are above and below the group average and arrange time for more comprehensive assessment of these individuals. These teachers explain the goals of physical education and the purposes of assessment. They encourage students to identify their own strengths and weaknesses and to set goals. The central theme of this beginning-of-the-year assessment unit is getting to know and care about oneself and others. This is the essence of individualized physical education.

Assessment refers to data collection, interpretation, and decision making. Federal law, however, uses the term *evaluation* to encompass these functions. *Assessment* and *evaluation* can thus be considered synonyms, although experts specify that assessment is the broader term (Burton, 1997; King-Thomas & Hacker, 1987; Salvia & Ysseldyke, 1995).

Four Purposes of Assessment

Assessment should be directed toward a specific purpose. Four purposes that entail different decision-making processes are (a) screening and referral, (b) diagnosis and placement, (c) instruction and student progress, and (d) sport classification.

Screening and Referral

Screening is the process used by regular educators to determine who needs referrals for further testing. It is typically done at the beginning of each school year. Screening in physical education is usually a group process but may be individual if a second teacher is available to cover the class. *Screening tests should never be called diagnostic.* In assessment theory, these terms have different meanings.

Screening is typically a pass/fail or yes/no protocol that requires only a few minutes per student. Consider, for instance, how long it would require to screen 100 students if each one took 15 minutes. To minimize the time needed, stations are often set up, with students rotating to a new area as soon as they complete designated tasks. The choice of tasks is dictated by the goals and objectives of the regular physical education curriculum. Usually, however, stations are used to screen (a) balance; (b) ball skills, both hand-eye and foot-eye; (c) bilateral coordination and rhythm (mainly jumping, hopping, and imitation of movement skills); (d) visual motor control (pencil-and-paper and scissors tasks); (e) skills on a tricycle or bicycle and playground apparatus; and (f) understanding of game and sport concepts. Many school systems also screen vision, height, weight, posture, and cardiovascular fitness.

Screening can also be conducted during a group follow-the-leader activity or game. Of central importance to physical activity personnel is whether individuals can perform the gross motor skills expected of their age level and have the language, cognition, and personal-social skills to benefit from instruction in the mainstream setting.

Diagnosis and Placement

Diagnosis is comprehensive, individual assessment by a specialist or group of specialists to determine placement and special services needs. Two assessment models guide diagnosis: (a) the individualized education program (IEP) model, which is structured by law and uses diagnosis to obtain information for writing an IEP, and (b) the regular education initiative (REI) or inclusion model, which uses a variety of data-gathering approaches to identify students who need assistance or supplemental programming. The latter is often used to establish home and community programs for students with health, weight, or perceptual-motor problems. Diagnostic testing typically requires at least 1 hour per person. Table 6.1 lists tests that are frequently used for diagnosis. Most of these tests are discussed in Chapters 8 through 17, which describe goal-oriented assessment and pedagogy.

When educators decide to place a student in a separate rather than a regular class, the assessment data must clearly show performance below the norms of chronological age-mates and/or inability to learn in a regular setting. This chapter explains norms and the simple statistics necessary for making placement decisions.

T a b l e 6 . 1   The diagnostic tests most frequently used in 1985 and in 1993 in adapted physical education in the United States, based on research by Dr. Dale Ulrich at Indiana University.

Year	Measure	Type of Measure
1985	1. Bruininks-Oseretsky Test of Motor Proficiency (Bruininks, 1978)	Norm-referenced
	2. Brigance Diagnostic Inventory for Early Development (Brigance, 1978)	Norm-referenced
	3. Hughes Basic Gross Motor Assessment (Hughes, 1979)	Norm-referenced
	4. Purdue Perceptual Motor Survey (Roach & Kephart, 1966)	Norm-referenced
	5. I CAN Curriculum Assessment (Wessel, 1976)	Criterion-referenced
1993	1. Test of Gross Motor Development (Ulrich, 1985)	Norm- and criterion-referenced
	2. Bruininks-Oseretsky Test of Motor Proficiency (Bruininks, 1978)	Norm-referenced
	3. Peabody Developmental Motor Scales (Folio & Fewell, 1983)	Norm-referenced
	4. Motor Skills Inventory (Werder & Bruininks, 1988)	Criterion-referenced
	5. Assessment, Evaluation and Programming System (Bricker, 1993)	Criterion-referenced

Note. The Movement Assessment Battery for Children (Henderson & Sugden, 1992), formerly named the Test of Motor Impairment (TOMI), ranks among the top five instruments used in Canada and Europe. See the description of Movement ABC in Chapter 12.

Instruction and Student Progress

Assessment of instruction and student progress occurs after placement, is done cooperatively by the teacher and student, and is guided by specific goals and objectives. It identifies strengths and weaknesses to guide lesson planning and day-to-day instruction.

Some teachers administer only two or three tests a semester, but the best practice is continuous assessment, using line or bar graphs, to show day-to-day or week-to-week progress toward objectives. Students should share in record keeping.

Data-based teaching is a specific type of assessment that is frequently used in adapted physical education. In this approach, teaching is directed by a task or ecological analysis. The teacher uses developmental sequences that list skills to be taught and records pass or fail for each trial. This process totally integrates teaching and assessment.

Sport Classification

Sport classification is used to assign ability (or disability) classifications based on medical condition and/or functional capacity. First applied by sport organizations, sport classification is now widely used in adapted physical activity as a quick, efficient method of communicating general ability level and prescribing ecologically valid activities. One of the main purposes of classification is to promote equity in competition through balanced teams.

Authorities in all major sport areas except mental retardation, deafness, and learning disabilities have agreed on criteria and tests for assigning sport classifications. Further-more, they have determined distances and times appropriate for each classification and ways of combining classifications to create balanced teams for sports like basketball, soccer, and handball. The resulting body of knowledge, known as **sport classification theory,** is important for adapted physical educators to master. Sport classification assessment is discussed in Chapters 19 through 27.

Six Types of Assessment

Types of assessment are so diverse that they are best described by several sets of bipolar terms: (a) formal versus informal, (b) product versus process, (c) norm versus criterion tests, (d) standardized versus content-referenced tests, (e) tests versus instruments, and (f) self versus other. The best assessment systems use combinations of all of these.

Formal Versus Informal

Formal assessment is data collection in which students are aware that they are being tested and /or observed. Typically, they are told the purpose and encouraged to do their best. Many individuals, however, experience anxiety in such situations and fail to give a true picture of what they can do. Formal assessment thus should be supplemented with informal data gathering within a game or play context as explained later in this chapter.

When assessment is conducted as part of the IEP process, the protocol must be formal and adhere to legislative requirements. Written parental permission must be obtained. Legal specifications include these: (a) The tests must be validated for the specific purpose for which they are used. (b) the

T a b l e 6 . 2   **Illustrative percentile ranks: 50-yd dash norms. Percentile scores based on age test scores in seconds and tenths.**

	Boys									Girls							
Percentile	Age								Percentile	Age							
	9–10	11	12	13	14	15	16	17+		9–10	11	12	13	14	15	16	17+
100th	7.0	6.3	6.3	5.8	5.9	5.5	5.5	5.4	100th	7.0	6.9	6.0	6.0	6.0	6.0	5.6	6.4
95th	7.3	7.1	6.8	6.5	6.2	6.0	6.0	5.9	95th	7.4	7.3	7.0	6.9	6.8	6.9	7.0	6.8
90th	7.5	7.2	7.0	6.7	6.4	6.2	6.2	6.0	90th	7.5	7.5	7.2	7.0	7.0	7.0	7.1	7.0
85th	7.7	7.4	7.1	6.9	6.5	6.3	6.3	6.1	85th	7.8	7.5	7.4	7.2	7.1	7.1	7.3	7.1
80th	7.8	7.5	7.3	7.0	6.6	6.4	6.4	6.3	80th	8.0	7.8	7.5	7.3	7.2	7.2	7.4	7.3
75th	7.8	7.6	7.4	7.0	6.8	6.5	6.5	6.3	75th	8.0	7.9	7.6	7.4	7.3	7.4	7.5	7.4
70th	7.9	7.7	7.5	7.1	6.9	6.6	6.5	6.4	70th	8.1	7.9	7.7	7.5	7.4	7.5	7.5	7.5
65th	8.0	7.9	7.5	7.2	7.0	6.6	6.6	6.5	65th	8.3	8.0	7.9	7.6	7.5	7.5	7.6	7.5
60th	8.0	7.9	7.6	7.3	7.0	6.8	6.6	6.5	60th	8.4	8.1	8.0	7.7	7.6	7.6	7.7	7.6
55th	8.1	8.0	7.7	7.4	7.1	6.8	6.7	6.6	55th	8.5	8.2	8.0	7.9	7.6	7.7	7.8	7.7
50th	8.2	8.0	7.8	7.5	7.2	6.9	6.7	6.6	50th	8.6	8.3	8.1	8.0	7.8	7.8	7.9	7.9
45th	8.4	8.2	7.9	7.5	7.3	6.9	6.8	6.7	45th	8.8	8.4	8.2	8.0	7.9	7.9	8.0	8.0
40th	8.6	8.3	8.0	7.6	7.4	7.0	6.8	6.8	40th	8.9	8.5	8.3	8.1	8.0	8.0	8.0	8.0
35th	8.7	8.4	8.1	7.7	7.5	7.1	6.9	6.9	35th	9.0	8.6	8.4	8.2	8.0	8.0	8.1	8.1
30th	8.8	8.5	8.2	7.9	7.6	7.2	7.0	7.0	30th	9.0	8.8	8.5	8.3	8.2	8.1	8.2	8.2
25th	8.9	8.6	8.3	8.0	7.7	7.3	7.0	7.0	25th	9.1	9.0	8.7	8.5	8.3	8.2	8.3	8.4
20th	9.0	8.7	8.5	8.1	7.9	7.4	7.1	7.1	20th	9.4	9.1	8.9	8.7	8.5	8.4	8.5	8.5
15th	9.2	9.0	8.6	8.3	8.0	7.5	7.2	7.3	15th	9.6	9.3	9.1	8.9	8.8	8.6	8.5	8.8
10th	9.5	9.1	9.0	8.7	8.2	7.6	7.4	7.5	10th	9.9	9.6	9.4	9.2	9.0	8.8	8.8	9.0
5th	9.9	9.5	9.5	9.0	8.8	8.0	7.7	7.9	5th	10.3	10.0	10.0	10.0	9.6	9.2	9.3	9.5
0	11.0	11.5	11.3	15.0	11.1	11.0	9.9	12.0	0	13.5	12.9	14.9	14.2	11.0	15.6	15.6	15.0

From *AAHPER Youth Fitness Test Manual* (American Alliance for Health, Physical Education, and Recreation, 1976a).

test administrator must be able to document training and skill in the protocol used, and (c) the tests must be administered in the student's native language or in sign if this is the preferred modality. No one procedure can be used as the sole criterion for placement, and decision making must reflect the consensus of a multidisciplinary team, the parents, and, when possible, the student. Chapter 4 provides direct quotes from the law in relation to these requirements.

Formal assessment for placement purposes requires that test directions be followed precisely. This means that students may fail some items. The teacher must develop skill in helping students to handle such failures and to remain optimally motivated. When testing is for purposes other than placement, the humanistic teacher adapts the items and the environment so as to assure success.

Product Versus Process

Assessment should involve both product and process. **Product** is the end result of performance—traditionally, a numerical measure (like distance or speed), the number performed (as in curl-up or push-up tests), or a numerical rating. In contrast, **process** refers to quality, form, or experience and generally relates to whether a movement pattern is mature or immature. Several checklists and pictorial instruments are included in Chapter 12 to encourage process evaluation. Other examples of process measures are journals, diaries, anecdotes, pictures, and film. Synonyms for product and process measures are, respectively, *quantitative* and *qualitative*.

Norm Versus Criterion Tests

Both norm and criterion standards should be used in assessment. Norm-referenced instruments permit comparison of the individual's performance with a statistical standard. Criterion-referenced instruments enable comparison with a mastery standard.

Norm-Referenced Tests

A **norm,** an abbreviated form of the word *normal,* is a statistic that describes group performance and enables comparisons. **Norm-referenced** means that an instrument has been administered to several hundred persons and that statistics are available on the performance of chronological age groups and perhaps genders.

There are many kinds of norms, such as (a) percentile ranks, (b) standard scores, and (c) age equivalents. Best known of these are percentile ranks published by the American Alliance for Health, Physical Education, Recreation and Dance (AAHPERD) (see Table 6.2). Percentile ranks extend from 0 to 100. A score at the 50th percentile means that 50% of those who have taken the test scored higher and 50% scored lower than that score. Any student who consistently scores below the 50th percentile should receive special help. But when is performance low enough to warrant placement in a separate setting? Some states set the standard at the 30th percentile; others suggest the 15th percentile. Performance at the 15th percentile means that 85% of the individual's chronological peers score above him or her. Tables of percentile ranks can be found in most test manuals and in assessment textbooks.

Norm-referenced tests can be classified according to the population on which they are based: (a) regular education students or (b) students with disabilities. For placement decisions, regular education norms should be used, even though the student may be mentally retarded, blind, or physically disabled. When a student is placed in a regular class, the assumption is that she or he is not disabled in that particular school subject, regardless of medical condition. This means that performance must be equivalent to that of regular class members.

Several norm-referenced tests have been developed specifically for disabled populations, including the Project UNIQUE Physical Fitness Test (Winnick & Short, 1985) and fitness batteries for persons with various levels of mental retardation (AAHPER, 1976b, 1976c; Seaman, 1995) and blindness (Buell, 1973). These instruments permit comparison with others of similar disabilities. Such information is useful when instruction is conducted in separate settings and/or awards specifically for persons with disabilities are available.

Ideally, local school districts develop their own tables of percentile ranks for regular and separate education placements. Any test that yields numerical data can become a norm-referenced instrument if administered to enough persons. A rule of thumb when developing norms is that there must be at least 50 males and 50 females for every age or grade group represented. Once norms are developed and related statistics are computed, a test is considered standardized.

Criterion-Referenced Tests

Criterion-referenced tests are designed to measure mastery learning and/or assess achievement of developmental milestones, mature movement patterns, and minimal fitness levels. Usually, the format is a checklist, task analysis, or set of behavioral objectives. Data yielded are pass/fail rather than numbers.

Illustrative of a criterion-referenced approach is the Prudential FITNESSGRAM (Cooper Institute for Aerobics Research, 1994) (see Table 6.3). In this test, one mastery standard is set in each fitness domain for every age group. The mastery standard is presented as a range of scores (low to high) that indicates the healthy fitness zone. These standards are, of course, subject to change. In some criterion-referenced tests, there is controversy about how high to set the standard. In others, as in the performance criteria that characterize a mature movement pattern, the standard is well accepted. For example, there is general agreement that four performance criteria must be met for a run to be judged mature. Thus, Ulrich (1985) developed the criterion-referenced test for the run shown in Table 6.4. Other criteria could be added to these, like "Eyes focused straight ahead (not on feet)," but research shows that most observers can assess only three or four things at one time. The key in this kind of criterion-referenced test is to identify the most important criteria. Ulrich's (1985) Test of Gross Motor Development (TGMD) includes excellent criteria for seven locomotor skills and five object control skills (see Chapter 12).

Criterion-referenced instruments related to motor skills typically emphasize process rather than product. They enable teachers to analyze the components of a skill and write objectives that focus on ameliorating weakness or immaturity of arm, leg, trunk, or head action. Activities can then be di-

rected toward a particular criterion (e.g., "Demonstrate improving running form by bending elbows" or "Pass Criterion #2 on the run").

Criteria can also be written in task analysis format. Systems like I CAN (Wessel, 1976), the Data-Based Gymnasium (Dunn, Morehouse, & Fredericks, 1986), and the Brigance Diagnostic Inventory (Brigance, 1978) all use lists of progressively more difficult tasks like that shown in Table 6.5. Such lists are particularly helpful in teaching students with severe disabilities. Instructional objectives can be worded like this: "Pass four of six items on the ball-rolling task analysis." If the test includes information on the age at which a student should be able to perform each task or item, the instrument is considered standardized.

Standardized Versus Content-Referenced Tests

Standardized tests are commercially published instruments with manuals that describe the performance of a standardization sample of several hundred persons. Statistics present information on both averages and individual differences. A norm-referenced test is always standardized. **Criterion-referenced tests** can be either standardized or teacher-made to assess the specific content or skills being taught.

Content-referenced tests are teacher-made tests that are designed to measure what is being taught. Such tests permit the teacher to assess where a student falls in relation to the continuum of possible scores or behaviors. A content-referenced test becomes criterion-referenced when the teacher designates the scores required to pass or to earn particular letter grades.

Tests Versus Instruments

Test, correctly defined, refers only to instruments for which there are right and wrong answers or mature and immature responses. A test is something that can be passed or failed. Many kinds of data are collected that do not fit this description (e.g., data about self-concept, attitudes, social behaviors, friendship choices, movement creativity). **Instrument** is a broader term than *test* and refers to inventories, rating scales, interview schedules, questionnaires, and other forms of data collection that do not yield right and wrong answers.

Self Versus Other

Teacher-directed assessment is the traditional approach to data collection. In humanistic teaching, however, assessment responsibility is gradually shifted to the student. The simplest and best method of screening is often simply asking the student, "Can you do thus and so? What are your greatest strengths and weaknesses? What are you interested in learning? How can I (the teacher) best help you?"

Requiring students to grade or in some way evaluate their performance provides insight into their self-concept and motivation. Whenever possible, assessment should be a shared responsibility.

Holistic, Ecological Assessment

Professionals should assess both development and function rather than choose one perspective over the other. Function is important in terms of ability to achieve goals and objectives.

T a b l e   6 . 3   Illustrative criterion-referenced standards: The Prudential FITNESSGRAM standards for lower (L) and upper (U) ends of the healthy fitness zone.

			BOYS												
Age	One Mile (min:sec)		Body Mass Index		Curl-up (# completed)		Push-up (# completed)		Modified Pull-up (# completed)		Pull-up (# completed)		Flexed Arm Hang (seconds)	
			L	U	L	U	L	U	L	U	L	U	L	U
5	Completion of		20	14.7	2	10	3	8	2	7	1	2	2	8
6	distance. Time		20	14.7	2	10	3	8	2	7	1	2	2	8
7	standards not		20	14.9	4	14	4	10	3	9	1	2	3	8
8	recommended.		20	15.1	6	20	5	13	4	11	1	2	3	10
9			20	15.2	9	24	6	15	5	11	1	2	4	10
10	11:30	9:00	21	15.3	12	24	7	20	5	15	1	2	4	10
11	11:00	8:30	21	15.8	15	28	8	20	6	17	1	3	6	13
12	10:30	8:00	22	16.0	18	36	10	20	7	20	1	3	10	15
13	10:00	7:30	23	16.6	21	40	12	25	8	22	1	4	12	17
14	9:30	7:00	24.5	17.5	24	45	14	30	9	25	2	5	15	20
15	9:00	7:00	25	18.1	24	47	16	35	10	27	3	7	15	20
16	8:30	7:00	26.5	18.5	24	47	18	35	12	30	5	8	15	20
17	8:30	7:00	27	18.8	24	47	18	35	14	30	5	8	15	20
17+	8:30	7:00	27.8	19.0	24	47	18	35	14	30	5	8	15	20
			GIRLS											
5	Completion of		21	16.2	2	10	3	8	2	7	1	2	2	8
6	distance. Time		21	16.2	2	10	3	8	2	7	1	2	2	8
7	standards not		22	16.2	4	14	4	10	3	9	1	2	3	8
8	recommended.		22	16.2	6	20	5	13	4	11	1	2	3	10
9			23	16.2	9	22	6	15	4	11	1	2	4	10
10	12:30	9:30	23.5	16.6	12	26	7	15	4	13	1	2	4	10
11	12:00	9:00	24	16.9	15	29	7	15	4	13	1	2	6	12
12	12:00	9:00	24.5	16.9	18	32	7	15	4	13	1	2	7	12
13	11:30	9:00	24.5	17.5	18	32	7	15	4	13	1	2	8	12
14	11:00	8:30	25	17.5	18	32	7	15	4	13	1	2	8	12
15	10:30	8:00	25	17.5	18	35	7	15	4	13	1	2	8	12
16	10:00	8:00	25	17.5	18	35	7	15	4	13	1	2	8	12
17	10:00	8:00	26	17.5	18	35	7	15	4	13	1	2	8	12
17+	10:00	8:00	27.3	18.0	18	35	7	15	4	13	1	2	8	12

© The Cooper Institute for Aerobics Research, Dallas, Texas.
Note. The trunk lift standards are the same for boys and girls: L = 6 inches, U = 12 inches. The backsaver sit-and-reach for boys is 8 inches at all ages; for girls, varies from 9 to 12 inches.

T a b l e   6 . 4   Criterion-referenced test for a run from the Test of Gross Motor Development (TGMD).

Performance Criteria	Trials	
	1	2
1. Brief period where both feet are off the ground	1	1
2. Arms in opposition to legs, elbows bent	0	1
3. Foot placement near or on a line (not flat-footed)	1	1
4. Nonsupport leg bent approximately 90° (close to buttocks)	0	0

Note. Under "Trials," 1 denotes pass, 0 denotes fail.

T a b l e   6 . 5   Task-analysis test for rolling a ball.

Task	Standard or Criterion
1. Sit and roll or push a ball	Ball travels 1 ft
2. Sit or stand and roll or push a ball	Ball travels 2 ft
3. Same	Ball travels 5 ft
4. Same except direct the ball toward a specific target 10 ft away	Ball travels 8 ft in direction of target
5. Same	Ball travels 10 ft and touches target
6. Same	Same except ball touches designated area on target

However, professionals must know whether a targeted task goal is appropriate for a student's chronological age.

Many teachers, for instance, try to teach games like tag before students are ready for them. Tag games require reversal of chasing and fleeing roles and memory of several rules, and learning these games requires cognitive abilities that typically appear at about age 7. Some individuals with severe mental retardation may never possess the readiness to learn tag games. The functional ability to use motor skills in games and sports and to generalize knowledge to different environments is linked closely to cognitive, moral, and play development.

Observation in Natural Environments

The best way to learn about development and function is to observe persons in natural environments. Identify some physical activity settings in which you can observe and assess individuals of different ages. Your presence will always have some effect on behaviors: Some persons like to be watched and perform at their best in front of an audience; others hate it. Sometimes it is best to enter into the activity; in such cases, you are called a **participant-observer.**

The best natural environments for observation of adolescents and adults are sport events and activities at recreation and fitness centers. To plan observations, obtain schedules of wheelchair basketball and tennis games, Special Olympics training sessions, and the like.

For children and youth, a room or outdoor area full of apparatus and play equipment makes an excellent initial assessment environment (see Figure 6.2). There should be ladders and ropes to climb, ramps or slides for moving up and down, bars to hang and swing from, balance beams and interesting surfaces to navigate, tunnels, and a variety of movement challenges like swinging bridges, structures that rock, and walls made of tires or heavy cargo nets. The apparatus should provide access for wheelchairs and be appropriate for all kinds of individual differences.

This kind of setting allows observation of whether or not persons know how to play, like to play, or have the language and motor skills to play. Most persons, given this environment, will demonstrate the full repertoire of their locomotor movement patterns. They will run, jump, leap, hop, climb, swing, roll, slide, and the like. Moreover, you can observe the personal meaning of each movement pattern, determine which movements are favorites and why, and develop a list of movement strengths and weaknesses. To assess object play (including the use of balls, striking implements, targets, and hoops), place additional equipment around the room.

To assess social interactions, introduce two persons to a play or sport environment, then three, then four, and so on. Observe who initiates interactions, listen to what they say to each other, and note the kind of partner and small-group activities that evolve.

When possible, videotape observations. Videotapes provide study aids for beginning teachers and are especially helpful in university classes to focus attention on real persons and environments instead of imagined ones. Videotapes also provide permanent records of locomotor, object control, and social abilities. As such, they can be used to justify placement decisions and guide programming.

FIGURE 6.2 Play apparatus can be used to assess many different kinds of abilities. Here, Dr. Ellen Lubin Curtis-Pierce, an authority in early childhood adapted physical activity, uses the London trestle tree apparatus test environment.

Sherrill Assessment and Programming Model

Figure 6.3 depicts the Sherrill Assessment and Programming Model, which is used to guide the study of school-age children. To use this model, make a copy of Figure 6.3 for each child. When you have completed your observations, circle the descriptor in each column that best represents the child's present level of performance. Be able to cite anecdotes that support your decisions.

Figure 6.3 shows that development is a vertical, bottom-up process. Each age (see the left-hand column of the figure) is associated with specific milestones, tasks, or functions that are societal expectations.

Developmental theory posits that the sequence of milestones/tasks is uniform but that the rate of development varies. For example, adults with severe mental retardation may function at a cognitive level of 2 to 3 years of age. Their progress is very slow and may even appear frozen.

To interpret what this means for programming, find ages 2 to 3 on the assessment and programming model in Figure 6.3 and read horizontally across. The figure shows that persons with a mental age or cognitive level of 2 to 3 years are primarily in the perceptual-motor stage of reasoning, unlikely to understand rules beyond "yes" and "no," seldom able to initiate and sustain meaningful play interactions, and likely to have a repertoire of locomotor motor skills that includes only roll, crawl, creep, walk, and run. There are, of course, many individual differences within this range of abilities and some exceptions. But assessment of function must be grounded in this developmental framework.

Some persons progress faster up some channels than others because of a combination of genetic and environmental factors. Few children in our society actualize their potential, partly because they do not have the internal motivation and partly because teachers and parents do not know how to help.

FIGURE 6.3   Sherrill Assessment and Programming Model: Cognitive-moral-social-motor developmental channels.

Average Age	Piaget's Stages of Cognitive Development	Kohlberg's Levels of Moral Development	Levels of Social Play Development	Levels of Motor Development
Adult		Universal ethical principles		Increasingly advanced sport skills
16				
15				
14				
13				
12	Formal mental operations; abstract thought		Individualized leisure preferences	
11				
10		Flexible rule adherence, common sense	Team sports	
9				
8	Concrete mental operations; cause-effect linkages; relationships		Individual/dual sports, relays, and lead-up games	Beginning sport skills
7				
6			Low organized games and movement education	Skill combinations
5		Rules are regarded as sacred and absolute— rigid adherence	Cooperative play	Skip
4	Preoperational mental operations and perceptual-motor thought; language links		Associative play	Hop
3		No comprehension of rules		Jump
2			Parallel play	Run
1		Responds to "no"		Walk
8 months			Peek-a-boo games	Creep, Crawl, Roll, Righting reactions
6 months			Solitary play	Beginning limb control
4 months				Head, neck control, Eye control
Birth	Sensorimotor mental operations	No comprehension of language	Eyes and mouth responsive to sensory input	Reflexes

Children with disabilities are more likely than their peers to have **uneven development across channels.** Therefore, assess each channel separately and identify strengths to build on.

The assessment and programming model in Figure 6.3 is based on the developmental theories of Jean Piaget (1932; 1952), Lawrence Kohlberg (1984), Mildred Parten (1932), and many physical education researchers. Although parts of these theories have been challenged, the data about average ages at which individuals exhibit abilities remain valid. Following is information to guide the use of Figure 6.3.

Screening Cognition in Relation to Play Concepts

Cognition in this model refers to thought, perception, memory, and attention, because these processes are closely interwoven. **Moral development** refers to progressive understanding of rules and standards. This is also a part of cognition but is presented separately in the table because of the importance of mastering sport and game rules and assimilating societal and cultural standards of sportsmanship, fitness, and wellness.

Sensorimotor Performance (Ages 0 to 2)

Sensorimotor mental operations are the brain's translation of sensory input (e.g., visual, auditory, tactile) into initial meanings that form the basis of later cognitive, affective, and psychomotor function. The input can come from self or others. Infants first act on their environment during these years and begin to acquire **inner language** (meanings that relate to experience rather than words).

The horizontal line at about the 4-month period in the model indicates that the major barrier to be crossed for infants is integration of primitive reflexes so that voluntary, purposive movement can occur. Once this barrier is crossed, only about 4 months are required for independent sitting, rolling, crawling, and creeping patterns to emerge. Each additional pattern brings new sensory information for the brain to process and assign meaning.

The first 2 years of life are thus primarily a time of sensorimotor integration, the development of beginning locomotor and object control patterns, and the emergence of thought and social play behaviors. The ability to imitate is acquired during these years, and children learn appropriate responses to yes/no and short commands like "Come here," "Sit down," and "Throw me the ball."

Preoperational Performance (Ages 2 to 7)

Preoperational mental operations involve thought that is tied to perception rather than logic and is limited by language, memory, and attention capabilities. The years from age 2 to 7 are clustered together because they are the time when children first acquire receptive and expressive language. **Receptive language** refers to the understanding of specific words and signs. **Expressive language** refers to talking or using signs.

At age 2 children can use about 300 words, and at age 7 they can use several thousand. Play tends to be parallel until children have sufficient language and mobility skills to interact with each other. **Parallel play** means that children establish play space near each other, do similar activities, and sometimes even imitate each other but do not directly interact without help.

In many disabilities, delayed or different language development affects progression up the social play channel. **Associative play** is the term given to early interactive activities in which children talk to each other as they explore the environment (locomotor, playground apparatus, wheeled toys) or engage in "make-believe" (doll play, cowboys and Indians, monsters, gangsters). Nonambulatory children, even if they have language, typically cannot initiate associations with others until they are fitted with wheelchairs. Thus, passivity and external locus of control (LOC) are reinforced by life events for these children, while their able-bodied peers are beginning the transition from external to internal LOC and self-determination.

Cooperative play is the term for participation in simple, low-organized games that have only one or two rules, like ring-around-the-rosy, follow-the-leader, and "Run to a pretend home when given a cue indicating make-believe danger like 'The wolf is coming.'" Cooperative play is associated with kindergarten, or age 5, although it is often taught earlier to children attending nursery schools. Cooperation assumes that

FIGURE 6.4   Games like "Run to the wall, get the red valentine, and bring it to me" reinforce preoperational matching skills.

the mental operations of attending to short game directions, sharing a group activity, and taking turns being *it* are developing. These operations must be carefully taught, because children are naturally **egocentric,** or I-centered, until concrete mental operations emerge at age 7 or 8.

Preoperational performance is essentially perceptual or perceptual-motor, in that, for children at this developmental level, early thought processes center on similarities and differences (i.e., matching, classifying) and ways to please adults or the powerful others in their lives. Rules and concepts are synonymous in early play. Imitation games are matching activities that demand perception of similarity or difference in relation to a leader's movements. Stop-and-start games like musical chairs demand perception of same/opposite or reversal concepts. Retrieval games (fetch the ball; bring me a valentine) require here/there concepts (see Figure 6.4). As children begin to acquire an understanding of these and other rules, their need to please adults is so great that they adhere rigidly to rules and tattle on peers who seem to deviate. Prior to age 7 (concrete mental operations), failure to follow a rule usually means that the child lacks the cognition or memory to grasp or apply the rule.

Attention and memory capabilities are limited to two or three chunks until about age 7. Assessment should ascertain

FIGURE 6.5 Level of cognition is an indicator of how much help will be needed in problem-solving activities. Here, Barbara Wood of the Homer, New York, school system teaches balancing, throwing, and spelling.

FIGURE 6.6 Ideally, team competition should be introduced at about the third-grade level, when children are socially and cognitively mature enough to handle complex interactions with teammates and opponents.

the length of sentences and the number of sentences in instructional sequences that an individual can process. Before about age 7, most children learn movement skills primarily by trial and error (kinesthetic input) and visual input. Thereafter auditory input becomes increasingly useful to most individuals.

Preferred sensory modalities for input and the number of modalities that can be accommodated should be assessed also. Obviously, blindness, deafness, and mobility impairments change the ways in which individuals attend to, comprehend, and remember instructions. Such psychomotor problems also affect self-determination in terms of spontaneous exploration of the social and physical environment. The extent to which children act on the environment without adult or peer prompting should be assessed.

Concrete Mental Operations (Ages 7 to 11)

Concrete mental operations are thought processes that involve problem solving, cause-effect linkages, and generalizing to identical situations and things of a tangible nature (see Figure 6.5). Concrete things can be seen, heard, touched, smelled, or tasted. With regard to social play or game skills, this means that children begin to assimilate role reversal and cause-effect rules like "I flee until I am tagged; then I am *it* and I chase"; "I am *in* the center of the circle dodging until the ball hits me; then I am *out* and throw the ball at others"; and "I am at bat until I hit the ball; then I must run to the base on my right."

Careful assessment of each of these game concepts is essential to goal setting and teaching the whole person. These

concrete mental operations are closely associated with social competence and inclusion by peers. The horizontal line between ages 7 and 8 in the model is the barrier that must be crossed before persons are mentally, socially, and emotionally ready to function as team members in both cooperative games and competitive sport activities. This is also approximately when children change from being *egocentric* (I-centered) to *empathetic* (able to understand the view or role of another) and when they begin to make social comparisons ("Am I as good as others, better, or worse?"). (See Figure 6.6.) Most persons with moderate mental retardation (IQs of about 35 to 55) never cross this barrier. Persons with mild mental retardation, in contrast, are usually able to participate successfully in team competition but at older ages than most peers.

Moral development is interwoven with cognitive and social development. From age 7 on, children increasingly identify with their peers and begin to test their authority against that of adults by exploring the limits of rules. Cause-effect mental operations enable children to consider relationships like these: "If I break this rule, the adult might punish me, or my peers might get angry with me"; "If I break this rule and no one notices, I or my team might benefit." The ability to perform cause-effect thinking in relation to game rules and strategies should be assessed.

Moral development entails comprehension of standards like personal best, active living, and optimal wellness as well as rules. Standards like these are more abstract than game rules, and abstractions are not easily handled by most children until age 11. Nevertheless, because of the tremendous variability among children, conventional wisdom suggests an assessment of "what if" mental operations regarding personal best,

T a b l e   6 . 6   Game checklist for screening cognitive readiness for games.

Sensorimotor	Concrete Operations (3 to 7 concepts)
Peak-a-boo type games	Tag
Imitating movements of another	Relays
Retrieving objects someone else throws	Role-reversal running games
Coactive moving with another	Hide-and-seek
Rolling a ball back and forth to adult	I'm Going to Grandmother's House, movement version
	Simon Says
Preoperational (1 to 2 concepts)	Dodgeball
Follow-the-leader	Kickball
Find the hidden object or person	Keep the cageball up
Musical chairs	Lead-up games to sports
Red light, green light; Mother, may I	Regulation sports
Action song games	
Run-on-cue games, everyone does same thing	**Formal Operations**
T-ball, with no strategy, one rule[a]	Complex sport competition strategy
Soccer, with no strategy, one rule[a]	Creating or choreographing
Basketball, with no strategy, one rule[a]	

[a]Many children aged 3 to 7 are wearing uniforms and are believed to be playing T-ball, soccer, basketball, and the like. Observation reveals, however, that typically only one or two rules are being enforced (e.g., get the ball and make a goal; get the ball and run; inbounds and out-of-bounds).

winning and losing, succeeding and failing, and health and sickness. As children realize that rules are not absolute and that personal ability is not identical with effort, they begin to make conscious lifestyle choices that relate to physical education goals. Assessment should encompass examination of these choices and the reasons for these choices.

Assessment should also determine the number of choices or alternatives that the individual's cognitive ability permits: Can the individual intelligently make choices between two things, or three, or four? This is essential to teaching for self-determination and self-actualization.

Memory for sequences increases during the concrete operations years, from about 3 to 7, as does the ability to attend to several things simultaneously and block out irrelevant information.

Seriation, usually called **sequencing** in physical education, is the ability to remember sequences, as in *I'm Going to Grandmother's House.* **I'm Going to Grandmother's House** (GH) is a game in which each child repeats in correct order what other children have said and then adds something new. For example, Child 1 says, "I'm going to Grandmother's house and I'm taking my toothbrush." Child 2 says, "I'm going to Grandmother's house and I'm taking my toothbrush and my dog." Child 3 says, "I'm going to Grandmother's house and I'm taking my toothbrush, my dog, and my pajamas."

The traditional GH game assesses only auditory memory for things. Physical educators often alter the memory assessment to focus on movement. For example, Child 1 takes three hops; Child 2 does three hops and one twirling umbrella step; and Child 3 does three hops, one twirling umbrella step, and five jumping jacks. This approach can be used with or without words, depending on what kinds of memory are to be assessed. Until children acquire the mental operation of sequencing, they cannot remember game rules and act appropriately, as in what to do in softball when a fly ball happens, a batter hits a foul ball, or runners are on first and third bases.

Table 6.6 presents an illustrative game checklist for screening cognitive readiness for games. Readiness depends both on cognition (the number of concepts that can be handled at one time) and motor skill (speed, coordination).

Cognition is also affected at every age by body composition, height and weight, motor skills, and fitness. This is because cognition is primarily based on concrete perceptions, and it is difficult to consider abstractions that have never been experienced. Thus, directions to grasp the ball in a certain way, rotate the trunk, or release the ball at a specific angle are perceived differently and produce learning styles that are different from what may be considered average or normal for a certain age. Children with disabilities often have shorter than average heights and limbs and thus experience the world in a different way. The same is true of individuals in wheelchairs, whose eye level is different from that of peers, and of people with coordination problems whose kinesthetic input may be different from that experienced by peers.

Table 6.7 presents an instrument to guide your observations of individuals who are primarily in the preoperational or concrete mental operations stage. This instrument also serves as a summary of the most important things to look for during observation in natural settings. Remember to look for strengths as well as weaknesses! Duplicate several copies of this instrument and use them to screen the present level of performance of individuals of different ages with and without disabilities. Find a partner who will assess the same individuals and plan a time to discuss the similarities and differences in your findings.

Formal Mental Operations (Ages 11 and Up)

Formal mental operations involve the use of inductive and deductive logic, the ability to critically and creatively think about abstractions, and skill in simultaneously processing many cause-effect and relationship ideas. Formal mental operations involve the understanding, application, and creation of

T a b l e 6 . 7 Instrument to guide observation.

SCREENING OBSERVATION FORM BY _____

1. Name of Person Observed _____
2. Gender _____   3. Chronological age _____
4. Dates of observation, setting, number of children present, available equipment, and other conditions.
   _____
   _____

5. Circle motor skills and patterns student used.

Log roll	**Walk**	**Ascend stairs**	**Strike**	**Serve**
Crawl	**Run**	**Descend stairs**	**Bat**	**Catch**
Creep	**Jump down**	**Hang from bar**	**Bounce**	**Kick**
Scoot	**Jump over**	**Climb**	**Dribble**	**Trap**
Rise-to-stand	**Leap**	**Dodge**	**Pivot**	**Dribble, feet**
Stand-to-lie	**Hop**	**Throw**	**Volley**	**Tag**

   Others _____

6. In general, compared to peers of same age, how would you rank motor skills and patterns?

Superior	**High**	**Average**	**Low**	**Inferior**
Top 10%		**Middle 50%**		**Bottom 10%**

7. Which hand was preferred in throwing/striking?   **R**   **L**
8. Which foot was preferred in kicking?   **R**   **L**
9. Which motor skills and patterns were used most?
   _____

10. What is major method of ambulation?

Independent	**Braces, prostheses**	**Crutches, canes**	**Wheelchair**

11. In general, compared to peers of same age, how would you rank activity level?

Hyperactive	**High**	**Average**	**Low**	**Hypoactive**

12. What problems, interactions, or other variables seemed to be contributing to high or low energy level?
   _____

13. Which stage best describes mental operations?

Sensorimotor	**Preoperational**	**Concrete**	**Formal**

14. What level best describes rules understanding and compliance?

No comprehension	**Rigid adherence**	**Inconsistent adherence**	**Flexible adherence**

15. What best describes language and communication ability?

Highly verbal	**High average**	**Average**	**Low average**	**Nonverbal**

16. What best describes social play level?

Solitary	**Parallel**	**Associative**	**Cooperative**

17. What best describes readiness level on cooperation-competition continuum?

Egocentric	**Cooperation with 2–5 others**	**Personal best self-testing**	**Individual or dual competition**	**Team competition**

18. Circle the one phrase that seems to best describe initiative, understanding of instructions, and mental flexibility.

Initiative	**Understanding of instructions**	**Mental flexibility**
A self-starter	Grasps instructions	Leads in generating new ideas
Has considerable initiative	Understands after asking questions	Gets excited about new ideas
Average	Average	Prefers the old and familiar
Responds to prodding	Confused, but tries	Resents change
Relies entirely on others	Confused and helpless	Appears unable to change

19. Who did the person interact with the most? One person or several?
   _____

20. In programming for this person, what three physical education goal areas (see #22) seem to be his or her major strengths? Why?
   _____

21. What three physical education goal areas (see #22) seem to be his or her major weaknesses? Why?
   _____

22. Rank this student's goal areas that need work from 1 (most important) to 9 (least important)
    _____ 1. Self-concept
    _____ 2. Social competence, inclusion
    _____ 3. Sensorimotor integration
    _____ 4. Perceptual-motor learning
    _____ 5. Motor skills and patterns
    _____ 6. Physical fitness and healthy lifestyle
    _____ 7. Postures, appearance
    _____ 8. Fun, leisure, relaxation
    _____ 9. Dance, aquatics, and movement creativity

formal thought structures like theories, models, and strategic game plans. Participation in most sports and games does not require this level of cognition, but following the complex game strategy of coaches or engaging in group decision making about complex game strategy is a formal mental operation.

The best way to assess formal mental operations is by talking to persons about abstractions or by observing them talking to others. Abstractions often require problem solving about feelings and the variables that affect feelings, your own as well as those of others. Some paper-pencil instruments allow insight into formal mental operations.

Of particular importance to developing a lifespan active healthy lifestyle is **attributions analysis,** the ability to examine cause-effect relationships among ability, effort, fate, luck, and task difficulty in maintaining desired levels of fitness, wellness, and satisfying leisure. Specifically, **attribution** means a cause or a reason for why something happens. Children engage in simple attributions analysis of concrete behaviors and outcomes from about age 7 on, but serious attributions analysis about such abstractions as life, death, and health requires formal mental operations. Assessment of adolescents should focus on their understanding of relationships among inputs, processes, and outcomes. This is the key to setting goals that will promote understanding of the relationship between quality of life and health behaviors like exercising, not smoking, and practicing safe sex.

Assessment of Responsivity

Another area important to observe is responsivity to stimuli. Four descriptors are used: (a) **hyper** (over, above, too much), (b) **average,** (c) **hypo** (under, too little), and (d) **fluctuating,** inconsistent, or labile. Persons who are hyperactive or hypoactive need special environmental adaptations, and teachers should ask questions about (a) energy levels and similar states of parents and siblings; (b) side effects of drugs, prescribed and nonprescribed; (c) presence of headache or illness; and (d) other variables (personal and environmental) that might affect responsivity.

Inattention, impulsivity, and hyperactivity are considered separate responsivity disorders. They often occur together but may appear independently of each other. Because these often contribute to learning disabilities, they are described in detail in Chapter 20. Age affects each of these, and assessment should determine the amount of time a person can concentrate and remain on task.

Assessment of Limb Preferences

Individuals who use a preferred limb in throwing, striking, and kicking activities typically perform better than those who show no preference or strong side. On the screening observation form in Table 6.7, make tally marks to record each time the individual uses the right or left side. Try to obtain at least 10 observations of hand and foot preferences in a natural play setting.

Using Observations

Table 6.7 is illustrative of the kinds of instruments that can be used to summarize observations in natural settings. This type of assessment can help determine the need for more formal assessment and the use of goal-specific instruments that are known to be valid and reliable.

Table 6.7 can be used to guide either live or videotaped assessments. When videotapes are used, a strong case can be made for the validity of this assessment protocol. Several experts independently viewing a videotape and then sharing decision making about a student's needs is a good way to meet the criterion of reliability (i.e., do experts perceive the needs in the same way?).

Planning Formal Testing Procedures

Each time assessment is planned, you should adhere to the following procedures:

1. Establish the specific purpose of the assessment.
2. Decide on the specific variables to be assessed.
3. Establish criteria for the selection of instruments or data collection protocols.
4. Review all available instruments and protocols that purport to assess the variables you selected.
5. Select the instruments or protocols to be used and state the rationale for selection (i.e., discuss how each meets every criterion).
6. Select the setting for the assessment.
7. Determine environmental factors to be considered and/or adapted.

Establishing Specific Purpose

Remember there are four purposes of assessment: (a) screening and referral, (b) diagnosis and placement, (c) instruction and student progress, and (d) sport classification. Select procedures that achieve your main purpose.

Relating Assessment to Goals and Variables

Assessment should relate to the goals of the school system and/or teacher. If self-concept is an important goal, then dimensions of this variable should be assessed. If social competence or play and game behaviors are expected outcomes of instruction, then these variables should be broken into assessable components. If motor skills and patterns is the goal, then locomotor and object control skills should be examined.

Using Criteria to Select Instruments

The universally accepted criteria are validity, reliability, and objectivity. Other criteria may be added, depending upon special needs. All criteria are important, but federal law mentions only validity and states that instruments must be validated for the specific purpose for which they are used.

Validity comes from the Latin word for "strong." It means founded on truth or fact and capable of being justified, supported, or defended. In regard to a test, validity refers to the extent to which a test measures what it is supposed to measure. Think of the last exam you took. Did it measure what the teacher taught? If so, it was valid. Sometimes there is a discrepancy between what teacher and students think has been taught.

Broadly generalizing, there are three kinds of validity. **Content validity** is the extent to which test items match the information or skills that were taught. Often, a panel of experts is used to verify a test's content validity. **Criterion validity** is the extent to which an instrument derives the same score/rank as another instrument or protocol believed to assess the same thing. **Construct validity** is the extent to which statistics support three constructs: (a) the instrument discriminates between two groups known to be high and low in the attributes being measured; (b) the test items, when subjected to factor analysis, fall into logical clusters; and (c) the instrument is sensitive enough to show changes caused by instruction.

Reliability is also a statistical concept. There are two types: (a) stability and (b) internal consistency. Test-retest measures indicate stability of performance over several trials, also called **repeated measures reliability.** Alpha coefficients and other special formulae indicate internal consistency for a single administration. High internal consistency is evidenced when all items assessing a particular topic or skill elicit the same or consistent responses. The highest possible reliability coefficient is 1.00; thus, .80 or .90 is considered high.

Objectivity, sometimes called interrater reliability, refers to several scorers or raters each perceiving a performance in the same way and giving the student the same rating or grade. This is especially important in observational assessment.

Reviewing Available Instruments

Every physical education professional should maintain a file of instruments with information about purpose, age range, validity, reliability, and objectivity. Some textbooks include copies of instruments. Most, however, do not because of copyright laws. In such cases, you must write to commercial companies and pay a small charge for sample copies. See Appendix E for addresses.

The classic reference book for use in reviewing and evaluating instruments is the *Mental Measurements Yearbook,* edited by Buros (1938 to 1978 editions), Mitchell (1985), Conoley and Kramer (1989), and Impara (1995). In spite of its title, the book includes reviews of many physical and motor measures and indicates where they can be ordered. It also includes a list of research studies related to each instrument. Zittel (1994) and Cowden and Torrey (1995) provide excellent examples of ways to review instruments.

Selecting Instruments

Many instruments measure the same things. Therefore, you must be able to show that your selected tools have higher validity and /or reliability than other possible choices. Moreover, to satisfy federal legislation, written documentation must show that the instrument is valid.

Do not make up diagnostic instruments by pulling items from several different sources. Doing so changes validity and reliability. Teachers who wish to create a new instrument may do so by enrolling in graduate studies and making this their thesis or dissertation. Properly done, this task requires thousands of hours.

Determining the Setting

Once the purpose of assessment is clarified and instruments are selected, you must decide which setting will elicit the best performance.

1. Should data be gathered in an individual or a group setting?
2. If a group, how large? Does everyone take the instrument at the same time, or do some students watch or assist while others perform?
3. Should the setting be formal or informal? Should the students know they are being assessed?

Setting depends largely on the purpose of the assessment. Because testing in relation to placement is a legal process, it must be done in a formal context. Settings for other purposes should be individualized because students respond to assessment with different degrees of anxiety, frustration, and coping.

An informal setting, whenever possible, seems best. The Yellow Brick Road, a screening instrument to assess perceptual-motor strengths and weaknesses, illustrates a setting that maximizes abilities and minimizes anxiety (Kallstrom, 1975). The setting is based on the movie *The Wizard of Oz.* Four stations are established for doing tricks that Oz characters request. In full costume, the Cowardly Lion gives instructions at one station, the Scarecrow at another, the Tin Man at another, and Munchkins at another. A yellow brick road made of contact paper stepping stones provides the structure for getting from one station to another. Periodically, music is played from the movie. Each child carries a ticket for admission to the stations on the way to finding the wizard. Reinforcement is provided by punching the ticket when each task is performed. When the ticket shows four punches, the reward is admission to a play area that is supervised by the Wizard, who is also in costume.

This gamelike setting can be varied in as many ways as themes exist. What a wonderful way to be tested! For older students, a carnival or field day often achieves the same purpose.

Determining Environmental Factors

Students cannot be assessed within a vacuum. How they perform is influenced by hundreds of factors: weather, room temperature, allergens, gender and mood of the test administrator, and presence or absence of spectators. Test administrators are likewise influenced by environmental factors, particularly when the assessment is primarily observational. In such cases, test administrators must place themselves where they can see best, where sun is not in their eyes, and where the angle of observation is most favorable.

In regular physical education, the tradition has been to keep all environmental factors constant (i.e., all students use the same equipment and follow uniform procedures). For some students, this practice inevitably results in failure.

Instructional assessment, like learning, should be success oriented. Equipment should be altered in accordance with individual needs. In a test of striking, throwing, or

FIGURE 6.7 Test condition variables and profile sheets. Dates in grids are dates of first satisfactory performance. (Adapted from G. S. D. Morris, *How to change the games children play* (Minneapolis: Burgess, 1976), pp. 62–67.)

Striking implement	Trajectory of object being struck	Size of object being struck	Object direction in fight	Weight of object being struck	Color of object being struck	Anticipation location	Speed object is traveling
Hand ↓ Paddle ↓ Bat	Horizontal ↓ Vertical ↓ Arc	Large ↓ Small	Right ↓ Left ↓ Center	Light ↓ Heavy	Blue ↓ Yellow ↓ White	How far must the performer move before striking the object	Slow ↓ Fast

A. Test-condition variables that can be altered to attain success-oriented assessment.

Easy ⟶ Difficult

		Color		
	Size	C_1	C_2	C_3
Easy ↓ Difficult	S_1	3/15		
	S_2		3/21	
	S_3		3/22	
	S_4		3/29	4/22

Key for object size

S_1 = Largest ball (18" diameter)
S_2 = Large ball (14" diameter)
S_3 = Small ball (12" diameter)
S_4 = Smallest ball (8" diameter)

Key for object color

C_1 = Blue
C_2 = Yellow
C_3 = White

B. Striking profile sheet for individual student.

Easy ⟶ Difficult

		Angle of trajection		
	Texture	A_1	A_2	A_3
Easy ↓ Difficult	T_1	3/15		
	T_2		3/21	
	T_3		3/22	
	T_4			4/22

Key for texture

T_1 = Balloon
T_2 = Nerf ball
T_3 = Rubber ball
T_4 = Softball

Key for angle of trajection

A_1 = Horizontal plane
A_2 = Vertical plane
A_3 = Ball travels in arc

C. Catching profile sheet for individual students.

catching ability, for instance, the characteristics of the striking implement and/or object are varied along a continuum from easy to difficult (see Figure 6.7). Motor performance over several days or weeks is recorded on a profile sheet that describes assessment conditions. The charts in Figure 6.7B and 6.7C are examples of profile sheets. The date recorded in each box in these profile sheets indicates when there was success in 7 of 10 trials, the criterion established in the instructional objectives and written on the physical education IEP. Can you think of other ways to make assessment success oriented?

Formal Test Administration Procedures

Both common sense and federal law dictate humanistic testing procedures. The following are required.

1. Professionals who administer instruments should be able to document that they have formal training and competence in the protocols used. This means that most adapted physical activity professionals must complete graduate courses in assessment and remain up-to-date by attending workshops on specific instruments.

2. A team approach should be used to determine underlying abilities that need to be assessed (e.g., vision, hearing, social and emotional status, motor and cognitive abilities, communication status) in order to problem-solve about findings on goal-related testing.

3. Tests should be administered in the student's native language and in the most appropriate communication mode (e.g., sign language, large-print written directions, words enunciated clearly against a quiet background). Professionals are responsible for finding, training, and supervising test administrators with language abilities that meet students' needs.

4. Multidisciplinary assessment teams should include parents or solicit input from parents on what children can and cannot do to ascertain that performance at school is consistent with performance at home and in other settings.

1. **Positive Self-Concept**
     Harter Self-Perception Instruments (all ages)
     Martinek-Zaichkowsky Self-Concept Scale (pictorial)
     Piers-Harris Children's Self-Concept Scale
     Tennessee Self-Concept Scale, Revised (adults)

2. **Social Competence, Inclusion, and Attitudes**
     Behavior Rating Profile–2
     AAMR Adaptive Behavior Scales
     Assessment of Social Competence (ASC) Scale
     Sherrill Social Play Behaviors Inventory

3. **Sensorimotor Integration**
     Milani-Comparetti Motor Development Screening Test
     Fiorentino Reflex Test
     Sherrill Reflexes Affecting Physical Education Test

4. **Perceptual-Motor Learning**
     Bruininks-Oseretsky Tests of Motor Proficiency
     Movement Assessment Battery for Children
     Purdue Perceptual-Motor Survey
     Sherrill Perceptual-Motor Tasks for Physical Education

5. **Motor Skills and Patterns**
     Ulrich Test of Gross Motor Development (TGMD)
     Peabody Developmental Motor Scales
     Motor Skills Inventory
     I CAN Skills Test

6. **Fitness and Healthy Lifestyle**
     Prudential FITNESSGRAM
     AAHPERD Physical Best
     Fit for Life Activity Log
     Project UNIQUE Physical Fitness Test

7. **Postures and Appearance**
     New York Posture Test
     Scoliosis Keynote Positions

8. **Play and Game Competence, Active Leisure, Relaxation**
     Lifelong Leisure Skills and Lifestyles Forms
     Leisure Satisfaction Scale (LSS)
     Sport Enjoyment Scale

9. **Dance and Aquatics Skills**
     Red Cross Swimming Tests
     Sherrill Water Fun and Success Tests

Note. These instruments are discussed in Chapters 8–17.

5. No single test should be used as the sole criterion for placement or for determining instructional needs. Several valid tests or protocols that purport to measure the same thing should be administered.

6. When the purpose of testing is diagnosis and placement, parental written permission must be obtained, and due process procedures must be followed (see Chapter 4).

Additional considerations in test administration that are not required by law but are important in increasing the likelihood of personal best performance by students and the overall usefulness of the data include the following.

1. Assessment should be focused on **functional competence** (i.e., proficiency in life functions like locomotion, play, work, and self-care). The ability to throw a ball or do curl-ups only in response to cues in a test situation might suggest that these skills are not **ecologically valid** (meaningful) for a particular individual. Alternative test items should be considered.

2. Assessment should cover motor skills, fitness, game and sport concepts, and social competence in several contexts: (a) informal play, (b) structured game or sport settings, and (c) formal drills or tests. Check for generalization to different environments and settings.

3. Tests should be administered frequently. Individuals with disabilities show more variability than nondisabled peers.

4. Test performance should be videotaped when possible. Show the videotape to parents, and discuss what different viewers see and why.

5. Records should be kept of information that will help with interpretation, such as whether test behavior was typical, whether compliance or attention span problems were present, and whether the child seemed fearful or anxious.

6. Cultural, gender, and other kinds of bias should be avoided in selecting, administering, and interpreting tests.

7. Before the day of the testing, the student should meet the outside experts brought in specifically to do the testing. Consider ways to promote rapport between the student and the outside experts.

8. Test anxiety should be minimized. Remember that different things cause anxiety in different people, and these things may vary day by day for the same person.

Instruments for Different Goal Areas

Table 6.8 presents a list of frequently used instruments classified according to goal areas. For more information on these instruments, refer to Chapters 8 through 17. Each of these

T a b l e 6 . 9   Test of gross motor development (TGMD).

Purpose

To identify children ages 3 to 10 years who are significantly behind their peers in the execution of 12 gross motor skill patterns.

Description

Two subtests are designed to assess different aspects of gross motor development: locomotion and object control. The examiner is required to judge the presence or absence of 3 or 4 motor behaviors in each of 12 gross motor skills: run, gallop, hop, leap, horizontal jump, skip, slide, two-hand strike, stationary bounce, catch, kick, and overhand throw. Each skill is illustrated in the test manual.

Validity

Content validity was established by having three content experts judge whether the specific gross motor skills selected represented skills that are frequently taught to young children. *Construct validity* was established by testing the hypothesis that gross motor development would improve significantly across age levels. It was also supported by testing the hypothesis that children with MR would score significantly lower than peers of similar age. The test was also validated for instructional sensitivity. The results indicate that the test is sensitive to formal instruction in gross motor development.

Reliability

Test-retest reliability coefficients for the 12 gross motor skills ranged for .84 to .99. Interscorer reliability estimates for the skills ranged from .79 to .98 for 10 raters. Reliability of mastery decisions was reported also for samples using the total test score.

Primary Sources

Ulrich, D. A. (1984). The reliability of classification decisions made with the objectives-based motor skill assessment instrument. *Adapted Physical Activity Quarterly, 1,* 52–60.

Ulrich D. A. (1985). *The Test of Gross Motor Development.* Austin, TX: PRO•ED.

Ulrich, D. A., & Ulrich, B. D. (1984). The objectives-based motor skill assessment instrument: Validation of instructional sensitivity. *Perceptual and Motor Skills, 59,* 175–179.

Ulrich, D. A., & Wise, S. L. (1984). The reliability of scores obtained with the objectives-based motor skill assessment instrument. *Adapted Physical Activity Quarterly, 1,* 230–239.

Address for Ordering

PRO•ED Publishing Co., 8700 Shoal Creek Blvd., Austin, TX 78757.

---

chapters focuses on a different goal area, thereby offering professionals considerable detail about how to assess, teach, and evaluate in each area.

So far, this chapter has acquainted you with the Sherrill Assessment and Programming Model, which is recommended for screening, planning instruction, and measuring day-to-day progress. This section introduces two instruments that are widely used for diagnosis and placement: (a) the Test of Gross Motor Development (TGMD) and (b) the Bruininks-Oseretsky Test of Motor Proficiency (BOTMP). The TGMD can be used for instruction as well as diagnosis and placement. The TGMD and BOTMP represent different philosophical approaches to diagnosis and placement. The TGMD assesses qualitative performance of 12 gross motor skills believed to be fundamental to sport and game success. In contrast, the BOTMP purports to measure underlying abilities that are predictive of motor skills performance and physical education success. These underlying abilities are grouped into eight areas (e.g., running speed and agility, balance, bilateral coordination), each of which is given a score.

The controversy about whether to assess motor skills or underlying motor abilities is long-standing and affects instructional approaches as well as assessment. In this text, underlying motor abilities for individuals who are ambulatory are covered in Chapter 12 (Perceptual-Motor Learning) and Chapter 13 (Fitness and Healthy Lifestyle). The underlying motor abilities approach can be traced back to the 1930s, when researchers believed that general motor ability existed and could be measured. Today, this belief is considered outdated, and no one seeks to obtain one general motor ability or fitness score. Instead, BOTMP is considered **multidimensional,** meaning

that a separate score is obtained and interpreted for each area or dimension measured. TGMD is also multidimensional.

A statistical technique called **factor analysis** is used in the test development phase to determine which test items cluster together and comprise a factor or an area. Factor analysis is one way of demonstrating construct validity. The TGMD, like almost all good instruments, also has been validated through factor analysis techniques. This means that both the TGMD and the BOTMP are true measures of what their test manuals promise they will test. If you decide to use either the TGMD or the BOTMP for diagnosis in relation to the IEP process, it is essential to purchase the test manual and study the details with regard to administration and interpretation. Often these test manuals serve as textbooks in graduate courses in assessment. See Appendix E for addresses for purchasing these and other test manuals.

Following are brief discussions of both the TGMD and the BOTMP, because both require considerable practice for building assessment skill. It is recommended that readers plan to administer some test items from each instrument to individuals of various ages, with different disabilities, every week. Presenting these tests early in the course encourages planning practicum experiences specifically on assessment. Another reason for presenting the TGMD and the BOTMP is to enable better understanding of the section later in this chapter that pertains to the interpretation of data and statistics.

Test of Gross Motor Development (TGMD)

The TGMD, validated for ages 3 through 10, involves the administration of 12 test items (see Table 6.9). Criteria for assessing the quality of performance for each item appear in Chapter 11, so these will not be repeated here. Refer to Table

6.4, however, for a quick reminder of how the criteria are stated. Note that TGMD does not require that times, distances, or accuracy measures be recorded; the emphasis is completely on determining whether the student exhibits mature form on the major components of each skill.

Locomotor Skills

The locomotor skills tested in the TGMD are these:

1. Run 50 feet. (Instruct the student to "run fast" from one line to another.)
2. Gallop back and forth between two lines set 30 feet apart. (The student should go the 30-foot distance three times.)
3. Hop three times, first on one foot and then on the other.
4. Leap. (Instruct the student to take large steps, leaping from one foot to the other.)
5. Horizontal jump. (Instruct the student to "jump far.")
6. Skip back and forth between two lines set 30 feet apart. (The student should cover the 30-foot distance three times.)
7. Slide back and forth between two lines set 30 feet apart, always facing the same direction. (The student should cover the 30-foot distance three times.)

Object Control Skills

The TGMD tests the following object control skills:

1. Two-hand strike with plastic bat. (Toss a 4- to 6-inch lightweight ball to the student at about waist level; tell the student, "Hit the ball hard.")
2. Stationary bounce (dribble) of an 8- to 10-inch playground ball with one hand. (Tell the student, "Bounce the ball three times with one hand.")
3. Catch with both hands a 6- to 8-inch sponge ball. (Toss the ball underhand from 15 feet away so that it arrives at a height between the student's shoulders and waist; tell the student, "Catch it with your hands.")
4. Kick a stationary 8- to 10-inch plastic or slightly deflated playground ball by running 10 feet to contact the ball and aiming it at a wall that is 20 feet from where ball rests. (Tell the student, "Kick the ball hard at the wall.")
5. Overhand throw of three tennis balls at a wall that is 25 feet away. (Tell the student, "Throw the ball hard at the wall.")

Discussion of the TGMD

A value of this test is the very clear and short directions given to the student. Two trials are allowed for each item, and each performance criterion is scored as 0 (fail) or 1 (pass). The test manual gives information about the average age at which most children pass each criterion. The criteria tell teachers exactly what to look for when analyzing skills and also provide guidance for writing lesson plans that specify work on a particular component of a motor skill. Videotaping performance of these items on a regular basis is ideal in that it creates a permanent record and permits both parents and student to see improvements that occur as a result of school instruction and homework practice of skills.

Practice of skills should not be specific to the test. Instead, these basic skills should be performed in many different environments. For locomotor skills, the floor or ground surface should be varied (grass, concrete, sand, wooden floor), the inclination should be changed, and bumpy, uneven ground, as is found in the real world, should sometimes be substituted for smooth surfaces. Mirrors on the wall are helpful to many students. For object control skills, practice should introduce objects of different sizes, shapes, weights, and colors. Distances and targets should be altered.

Bruininks-Oseretsky Test of Motor Proficiency

The Bruininks-Oseretsky Test of Motor Proficiency (BOTMP) is widely used as a diagnostic instrument for making placement decisions (see Table 6.10). This instrument purports to measure the specific abilities that underlie success in motor skills. **Motor proficiency** is not a synonym for motor performance; rather, it refers to the specific abilities on which performance is built. *The best definition of motor proficiency is the specific abilities measured by tests of running speed and agility, balance, bilateral coordination, strength, upper-limb coordination, response speed, visual-motor control, and upper-limb speed and dexterity.* This method of defining a constellation of abilities is called an operational definition and is frequently used in research.

A copy of the test manual is needed to administer the BOTMP. The item descriptions in the test manual give an operational definition of each factor—for example, bilateral coordination is what is measured by (a) jumps, (b) rhythmic tapping, and (c) index finger touching of body parts (i.e., a kinesthetic measure).

You need special training to score and convert BOTMP raw data to point scores and subsequently to standard scores. Figure 6.8 shows scoring for the long form. Norms are available for composite scores, but not for the individual factors. For the short form, norms are given in the test manual only for the total battery score. Broadhead and Bruininks (1982) have published means and standard deviations for short-form items.

The major decision with regard to the BOTMP is whether to use the long or short form. The long form requires about 1 hr to administer, whereas the short form takes about 20 min. In general, the short form is recommended as a screening instrument. The long form is used for diagnosis and placement because it is a better discriminator of students who need help (Verdeber & Payne, 1987).

Interpreting Data and Recommending Placement

Once data are collected, time must be spent on interpretation and on writing the results. Some school systems employ adapted physical educators and other specialists full-time to collect and interpret data. There is widespread agreement that adapted physical educators should have statistics and computer competencies. Of particular importance in making placement recommendations is an understanding of normal curve theory.

Table 6.10   Bruininks-Oseretsky Test of Motor Proficiency (BOTMP)—Placement.

Purpose

To assess motor performance of children from 4.6 to 14.6 years of age. Validated specifically for use in placement of students.

Description

Two forms are available: short and long.

Short Form

Norm-referenced, with 14 items assessing eight factors: (a) running speed and agility, (b) balance, (c) bilateral coordination, (d) strength, (e) upper-limb coordination, (f) response speed, (g) visual-motor control, and (h) upper-limb speed and dexterity.

Long Form of BOTMP

Same as short form, except with 46 items.

Scoring

Total test scores, subtest scores, and gross motor and fine motor composite scores can be derived. (See Figure 6.7.)

Validity

BOTMP is a revision of the well-known Lincoln-Oseretsky Test of Motor Proficiency. Content validity and construct validity are confirmed by similarity between factor analysis studies of BOTMP and works of Cratty (1967), Fleishman (1964), Guilford (1958), Harrow (1972), and Rarick, Dobbins, and Broadhead (1976).

Reliability

For short form: Test-retest rs ranging from .81 to .89 for 126 children. For long form: Test-retest rs ranging from .80 to .94. For the separate subtests, rs ranging from .15 to .89.

Primary Sources

Beitel, P. A., & Mead, B. (1980). Bruininks-Oseretsky test of motor proficiency: A viable measure for 3–5 year old children. *Perceptual and Motor Skills, 51,* 919–923.

Broadhead, G., & Bruininks, R. (1982). Childhood motor performance traits on the short form Bruininks-Oseretsky Test. *Physical Educator, 39,* 149–155.

Bruininks, R. H. (1978). *Bruininks-Oseretsky Test of Motor Proficiency manual.* Circle Pines, MN: American Guidance Service.

Bruininks, V., & Bruininks, R. (1977). Motor proficiency of learning disabled and nondisabled students. *Perceptual and Motor Skills, 44,* 1131–1137.

Address for Ordering

American Guidance Service, Circle Pines, MN 55014

Bruininks-Oseretsky Test Items
(*Denotes items on short form)

Factor: Running Speed and Agility Subtests: 1 on both long and short forms
*30-yard shuttle run

Factor: Balance
Subtests: 8 on long form, 2 on short form
 1. Standing on preferred leg on floor for 10 seconds
*2. Standing on preferred leg on balance beam for 10 seconds
 3. Standing on preferred leg on balance beam—eyes closed—for 10 seconds
 4. Walking forward on line on floor, 6 steps
 5. Walking forward on balance beam, 6 steps
 6. Walking forward heel-to-toe on line on floor, 6 steps
*7. Walking forward heel-to-toe on balance beam, 6 steps
 8. Stepping over response speed stick on balance beam

Factor: Bilateral Coordination
Subtests: 8 on long form, 2 on short form
*1. Tapping feet alternately while making circles with fingers, 90 seconds
 2. Tapping—foot and index finger on same side synchronized, 90 seconds
 3. Tapping—foot and index finger on opposite side synchronized, 90 seconds maximum
 4. Jumping in place—leg and arm on same side synchronized, 90 seconds
*5. Jumping in place—leg and arm on opposite sides synchronized, 90 seconds
*6. Jumping up and clapping hands
 7. Jumping up and touching heels with hands
 8. Drawing lines and crosses simultaneously, 15 seconds

Factor: Strength
Subtests: 3 on long form, 1 on short form
*1. Standing long jump
 2. Sit-ups, 20 seconds
 3. Knee push-ups, 20 seconds—for all girls and boys under age 8
 4. Full push-ups—for boys age 8 and over

Factor: Upper-Limb Coordination
Subtests: 9 on long form, 2 on short form
 1. Bouncing a tennis ball 5 times and catching it with both hands
 2. Bouncing a tennis ball 5 times and catching it with preferred hand
*3. Catching a tennis ball 5 times with both hands tossed from 10 feet
 4. Catching a tennis ball 5 times with preferred hand tossed from 10 feet
*5. Throwing a tennis ball overhand at an eye-height target 5 feet away (1 practice and 5 trials)
 6. Touching a swinging ball with preferred hand, 5 trials
 7. Touching nose with index fingers—eyes closed, 90 seconds
 8. Touching thumb to index fingers—eyes closed, 90 seconds
 9. Pivoting thumb and index finger, 90 seconds

Factor: Response Speed
Subtest: 1 on both long and short forms
Stopping a falling stick with preferred thumb. The teacher holds the response speed stick against the wall and then drops it.

Factor: Visual-Motor Control
Subtests: 8 on long form, 3 on short form
 1. Cutting out a circle with preferred hand
 2. Drawing a line through a crooked path with preferred hand
*3. Drawing a line through a straight path with preferred hand
 4. Drawing a line through a curved path with preferred hand
*5. Copying a circle with preferred hand
 6. Copying a triangle with preferred hand

 7. Copying a horizontal diamond with preferred hand
*8. Copying overlapping pencils with preferred hand

Factor: Upper-Limb Speed and Dexterity
Subtests: 8 on long form, 2 on short form
 1. Placing pennies in a box with preferred hand, 15 seconds
 2. Placing pennies in two boxes with both hands
*3. Sorting shape cards with preferred hand
 4. Stringing beads with preferred hand
 5. Displacing pegs with preferred hand
 6. Drawing vertical lines with preferred hand
*7. Making dots in circles with preferred hand
 8. Making dots with preferred hand

Normal Curve Theory

The **normal curve** is a theoretical model derived by mathematicians that shows statistically how persons will place when tested. The model is based on the laws of chance and shows that scores, when graphed, depict a bell-shaped distribution (see Figure 6.9). This phenomenon occurs because, when large groups are tested, most persons (roughly 68%) score in the middle of the distribution. On Figure 6.9, the markers –1 SD to +1 SD indicate the middle 68% of the distribution, –2 SD to +2 SD indicate the middle 95% of the distribution, and –3 SD to +3 SD indicate the middle 99.7%. It can be seen that 68% of the population have IQs between 85 and 115 and can do between 19 and 39 sit-ups. These persons are considered statistically normal or average.

The laws of chance dictate that an equal number of persons score in the areas above and below the center point designated as 0 on the baseline of the normal curve model. Adapted physical educators are mainly concerned with people who score on the left-hand side of the curve.

Originally, normal curve theory was applied mainly to interpretation of intelligence tests because school placement was made solely on the basis of mental functioning. Persons scoring in the middle 68% of the distribution were placed in regular education. Those scoring in the upper 16% were assigned to advanced or faster-paced classes, whereas those scoring in the lower 16% were assigned to special education. Today, placement is typically based on achievement tests, but the concept is the same. The laws of chance and the resulting normal distribution of data can be applied to many human attributes. Thus, everyone involved in assessment and placement must understand normal curve theory.

Some states, for instance, have set **placement criteria** for assignment to adapted physical education. These are illustrative of such criteria:

 1. Score 1 standard deviation below the mean
 2. Score 1.5 standard deviations below the mean
 3. Score below the 30th percentile

What does all of this mean? Do you agree with these standards? In states where no universal placement criteria have been agreed on, school districts often set their own cutoff points. If asked to do this, how would you respond? Moreover, should placement decisions be based only on normal curve theory, or are there other considerations? The following sections should help you to develop the knowledge base needed to make and/or understand placement decisions.

The information also will enable you to interpret test results and use them to develop instructional objectives and to plan lessons. For every test administered, teachers are especially interested in two things: (a) average performance and (b) individual differences. Normal curve theory relates to both of these.

The normal curve is a model to aid with interpretation of real scores. To achieve this, the baseline (horizontal line) of the normal curve depicts only *standard scores* (–3, –2, –1, 0, +1, +2, +3), also called z scores. A **standard score** is a number that is used in *conversion, transformation,* and *interpretation.* During test interpretation, real scores are substituted for standard scores. For example, when sit-up data are being interpreted, the 0 and 1 might be replaced with 29 (an average sit-up score) and 10 (a measure of individual differences called a standard deviation). On a z-score scale, the mean is always 0, and the standard deviation is always 1.

Mean, Median, and Mode

Normal curve models always have a vertical line in the middle that is labeled 0. This 0 represents the mean, median, and mode. The **mean** is the average score on a test. The **median** is the midpoint of the scores, the point above and below which 50% of the group score. The **mode** is the one score made most frequently. When real data are graphed, the mean, median, and mode may not fall at precisely the same spot. With real data, especially when a test has only a few items, there may be more than one mode.

FIGURE 6.8 Bruininks-Oseretsky Test of Motor Proficiency test score summary. (*A*) Example of how BOTMP raw scores are converted to point scores. (*B*) Example of conversion of a student's point scores to norms. (Reproduced with the permission of American Guidance Service, Inc. *Bruininks-Oseretsky Test of Motor Proficiency* by Robert N. Bruininks. Copyright 1978. All rights reserved.)

SUBTEST 1: Running Speed and Agility Guide for Converting Raw Scores.

1. Running Speed and Agility ^{SF*}

   TRIAL 1: _8.7_ seconds   TRIAL 2: _7.5_ seconds

Raw Score	Above 11.0	10.9-11.0	10.5-10.8	9.9-10.4	9.5-9.8	8.9-9.4	8.5-8.8	7.9-8.4	7.5-7.8	6.9-7.4	6.7-6.8	6.3-6.6	6.1-6.2	5.7-6.0	5.5-5.6	Below 5.5
Point Score	0	1	2	3	4	5	6	7	8	9	10	11	12	13	14	15

RECORD POINT SCORES FOR COMPLETE BATTERY ▼

RECORD POINT SCORES FOR SHORT FORM ▼

⑧ POINT SCORE SUBTEST 1 (Max: 16)

A

SAMPLE OF TEST SCORE SUMMARY FOR CHILD AGE 5 YEARS, 9 MONTHS

SUBTEST	POINT SCORE Maximum	POINT SCORE Subject's	STANDARD SCORE Test (Table 23)	STANDARD SCORE Composite (Table 24)	PERCENTILE RANK (Table 25)	STANINE (Table 25)	OTHER Age (Equiv.)
GROSS MOTOR SUBTESTS:							
1. Running Speed and Agility	15	8	21				7-8
2. Balance	32	16	13				5-2
3. Bilateral Coordination	20	9	23				7-11
4. Strength	42	5	11				4-11
GROSS MOTOR COMPOSITE			*68 SUM	56	72	6	6-5
5. Upper-Limb Coordination	21	13	*21				6-11
FINE MOTOR SUBTESTS:							
6. Response Speed	17	5	16				6-2
7. Visual-Motor Control	24	18	23				8-5
8. Upper-Limb Speed and Dexterity	72	27	20				6-8
FINE MOTOR COMPOSITE			*59 SUM	64	92	8	6-8
BATTERY COMPOSITE			*148 SUM	63	90	8	6-9

*To obtain Battery Composite: Add Gross Motor Composite, Subtest 5 Standard Score, and Fine Motor Composite. Check result by adding Standard Scores on Subtests 1–8.

Short Form

	POINT SCORE Maximum	POINT SCORE Subject's	STANDARD SCORE (Table 27)	PERCENTILE RANK (Table 27)	STANINE (Table 27)
SHORT FORM	98				

B

FIGURE 6.9 This normal curve is the theoretical model that guides test interpretation and educational placement. The percentages inside the curve have been rounded off to facilitate memory. In realty, the 3% is 2.27%, the 13% is 13.59%, and the 34% is 34.13%. In reality, the shapes of the curves for the IQ and sit-up data also would be different. (SD = Standard deviation.)

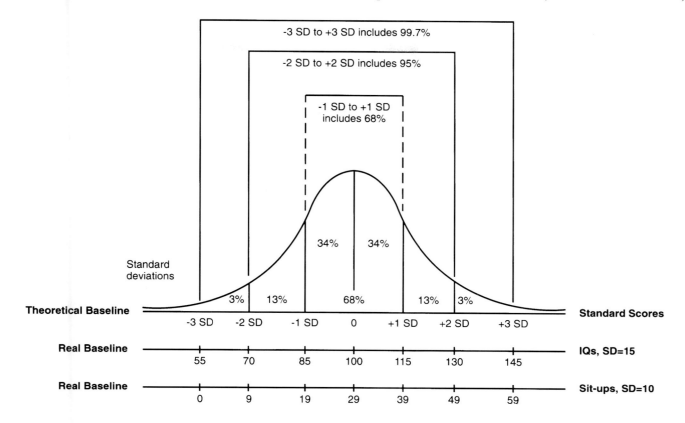

Thus, the theoretical model may or may not be a good fit for real data. The goodness of fit depends on whether the real data were collected from over 100 persons and are representative of the full range of individual differences in the population. Tests that are marketed for use in making placement decisions are administered to large groups so that the resulting data will fit the normal curve model.

The mean, median, and mode are called **measures of central tendency** because they describe the center, or middle, of the score distribution. Once teachers know the class average, they are interested in whether their students mostly scored close to the mean or were spread out along the baseline. Note how the baselines of the normal curves in Figure 6.8 are divided by markers into equal spaces. Some baselines have 10 equal spaces, while others have 8, 6, 4, or 2. The number of spaces depends on the individual differences (i.e., spread of scores) and the number of persons tested. The normal curve model uses six equal spaces, but real data may result in any number.

Standard Deviations

Standard deviation (SD) is the term for a marker on the baseline that indicates the degree that scores deviate from the mean. A standard deviation is a **measure of variability** or individual differences. Standard deviations are written as −1, −2, and −3 to show how far scores deviate to the left and as +1, +2, and +3 to show how far scores deviate to the right. When

real data are involved, the standard units (1, 2, 3) are transformed to actual values.

Figure 6.10 shows some real standard deviations and how they are used in calculations. To determine how far a real score deviates from its mean, the standard deviation is multiplied by 1, 2, or 3 and subtracted from or added to the mean. Overarm throw data in Figure 6.10 illustrate this. The average throw for a Grade 6 boy is 115 ft. The standard deviation is 22. Thus, the calculations are 115 − 22 = 93 and 115 + 22 = 137. If the data are normally distributed, then the interpretation is that about 68% of Grade 6 boys throw between 93 and 137 ft. Any Grade 6 boy unable to throw 93 feet is performing below 1 standard deviation. To find out who is throwing below 1.5 standard deviations, subtract 33 (22 + 11) from the mean and get 82 ft. To find out who is throwing below 2 standard deviations, subtract 44 (2 × 22) from the mean and get 71 ft.

Applications

This information is useful in many ways. One application is the structuring of teams and practice groups. To equalize chances of winning, class teams should be balanced in terms of ability. If throwing is an important skill in the game being played, then an equal number of students scoring −1 or −1.5 standard deviations below the mean should be on every team. This is true also of persons scoring +1 or +1.5 standard deviations above the mean. In the old days, students scoring below

FIGURE 6.10 Transformation of z scores to real data for placement and teaching. The math calculations involve subtracting and adding the standard deviation (SD) to the mean (M), starting in the center of the curve and working outward. Also shown in this figure is the relationship between percentiles and standard deviations. (TGMD = Test of Gross Motor Development; BOTMP = Bruininks-Oseretsky Test of Motor Proficiency.)

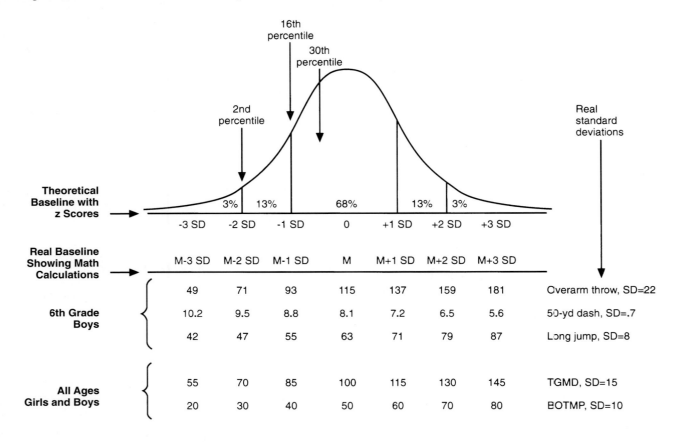

1 standard deviation would have been grouped together and taught separately. Today, the trend is to integrate them in carefully balanced teams or practice groups.

Another application pertains to decision making about special help and/or placement. Standard deviations are sometimes used as cutoff points for deciding when a student needs adapted physical education placement. Figure 6.10 shows what the −1 and −2 standard deviations cutoff points for Grade 6 boys on the overarm throw, 50-yd dash, and long jump would be. Most school systems, however, use standardized test batteries like the BOTMP and the TGMD for making placement decisions.

To aid in placement, the raw scores yielded by these batteries have been converted to **normalized standard scores** or quotients that have the same mean and standard deviation for each age group. To obtain a normalized standard score or quotient, simply use tables in the test manual. No math is involved.

For example, on the BOTMP, there are tables for converting (a) raw scores to point scores, (b) point scores to standard scores, and (c) battery composite standard scores to normalized standard scores. These normalized standard scores range from 20 and below to 80 and above. The mean is 50 and the standard deviation is 10 (Bruininks, 1978, p. 135). Figure 6.10 shows that the 1 standard deviation cutoff mark is 40 (M − 1 SD).

Use of a cutoff for the BOTMP has more meaning if standard deviations are equated with percentile ranks. The 1

standard deviation mark is the 16th percentile. This means that 16% of the test manual standardization sample scored below 40 and 84% scored above. If a cutoff of 1 standard deviation is used for placement, only a few students will receive the benefits of separate placement (i.e., about 16 out of every 100). This is perhaps an acceptable criterion if the regular physical educator who serves the other 84 students is assisted by an adapted physical education consultant and/or specially trained aides and peer tutors.

The TGMD conversions are less complicated than those of BOTMP. First, look up the standard scores for the locomotor and object control subtests and add them together for a summed standard score. Then, turn to the test manual page that converts summed standard scores to quotients. These motor quotients range from 46 to 154, similar to the system used in IQ test scoring. The mean is 100, and the standard deviation is 15 (Ulrich, 1985, p. 26). Figure 6.10 shows that the 1 standard deviation cutoff mark is 85, derived by subtracting 15 from 100.

These examples show that adapted physical education specialists who attend IEP meetings and assist with placement decisions need special training, not only in administering tests, but also in using test manuals to interpret data. Separate courses in assessment should be provided to teach about BOTMP, TMGD, and similar standardized tests. Criterion- and content-referenced tests are fine for teaching, but norm-referenced standardized tests should be used for placement decisions.

Standard Scores (z and T conversions)

The preceding section introduced the idea of standard scores. These are conversions or transformations of raw scores into equivalent units that permit adding different items or subscales. Whenever composite battery scores are needed, raw scores must be converted to standard scores because adding data yielded in different units, like seconds, feet, and counts of sit-ups or push-ups, is impossible.

There are many kinds of standard scores: z scores, stanines, and T scores, to name a few. Of these, z scores are most common because they are a part of normal curve theory. The −3, −2, −1, 0, +1, +2, +3 baseline of the normal curve shows standard scores, also called the standard scale of measurement. This scale always has a mean of 0 and a standard deviation of 1.

To convert raw scores to z scores so that they can be added, the following formula is used:

$$z \text{ score} = \frac{\text{Student's score} - \text{Mean score}}{\text{Standard deviation}}$$

In Figure 6.10, for example, if an 11-year-old boy long-jumped a distance of 48 inches and the mean and standard deviation were 63 and 8, respectively, the calculation would be:

$$z = \frac{48 - 63}{8} \text{ or } \frac{-15}{8} = -1.88$$

In Figure 6.10, for a softball throw of 40, the age group mean and standard deviation are 115 and 22, respectively. Thus,

$$z = \frac{40 - 115}{22} \text{ or } \frac{-75}{22} = -3.41$$

For a 50-yd dash time of 9.8, the age group mean and standard deviation are 8.1 and .7, respectively. Thus,

$$z = \frac{9.8 - 8.1}{0.7} \text{ or } \frac{+1.7}{0.7} = 2.43, \text{ reversed to } -2.43$$

Note that in calculations that involve speed, a low score is considered better than a high score. Thus, the sign of the z score is always reversed.

Once the conversions are completed, the z scores can be added:

Long jump		−1.88
Overarm throw		−3.41
50-yd dash		−2.43
	Sum	−7.72
	Average	**−2.57 or 2.6**

On the normal curve baseline, this average z score will fall:

−2.6

```
 −3    −2    −1    0    +1    +2    +3
```

This student's composite score falls about 2.6 standard deviations below the mean, which indicates that the individual definitely qualifies for adapted physical education placement in a separate class with a specialist.

After z scores, the second most frequently used type of standard score in adapted physical education assessment is the stanine. **Stanine** is a contraction of the words *standard nine* and refers to a system of standard scores with a range of 1 to 9, a mean of 5, and a standard deviation of 1.96, which is typically rounded to 2. Figure 6.11 shows that the nine stanines equal the plus and minus 2 standard deviations of the mean area in a normal curve. Stanines of 4, 5, and 6 are interpreted as average. Stanines below 4 are low, and stanines above 6 are high. Stanines permit generalizations about which students fall within the middle 20%, 54%, 78%, and 92% of the mean (see stanine percentages line in Figure 6.11). They are more precise than z scores in describing placement but less precise than percentile ranks. Both BOTMP and TGMD provide the option of reporting data in stanines.

T scores are standard scores that range between 20 and 80 with a mean of 50 and a standard deviation of 10. To transform a z score to a T score, this formula is used:

$$T = (10)z + 50$$

Norms

As mentioned earlier in the chapter, the three types of norms are (a) standard scores (e.g., z scores and stanines), (b) percentile ranks, and (c) age equivalents. Suppose, for example, that on the first subtest of BOTMP—running speed and agility—a child aged 5 years, 9 months made the following scores:

Raw score	Percentile	Stanine	Age equivalent
7.5 sec	72%	6	7.8

The raw score has little meaning until it is converted to one of the norms. A *percentile* of 72 means that the child scored higher than 72% of his or her agemates. The *stanine* of 6 means that the child scored in the high average range. The *age equivalent* of 7.8 indicates that the raw score was the midpoint score for all children 7 years, 8 months old. School records often state only one norm for each raw score. Regardless of whether the percentile, stanine, or age equivalent is reported, teachers are expected to be competent at interpretation.

Age equivalents are often given for subscales and test items but seldom for whole batteries. Criterion-referenced tests often use age equivalents. For example, the Denver Developmental Screening Test (DDST) of Frankenburg, Dodds, and Archer (1990) states the ages at which 25%, 50%, 75%, and 90% of the population pass each item. To illustrate, the age equivalents for the last 7 of the 31 DDST items are presented in Table 6.11.

Often, the 75% column is used as the criterion for placement. For example, a 3-year-old who cannot perform a broad jump is functioning below 75% of agemates (i.e., he or she is scoring at the 25th percentile).

The TGMD gives the ages at which 60% and 80% of the standardization sample achieved the performance criteria for each of its seven locomotor and five object control skills.

FIGURE 6.11 Relationships between kinds of norms, the normal curve, and the stanine bar graph with examples from the Bruininks-Oseretsky Test of Motor Proficiency (BOTMP) and Ulrich's Test of Gross Motor Development (TGMD).

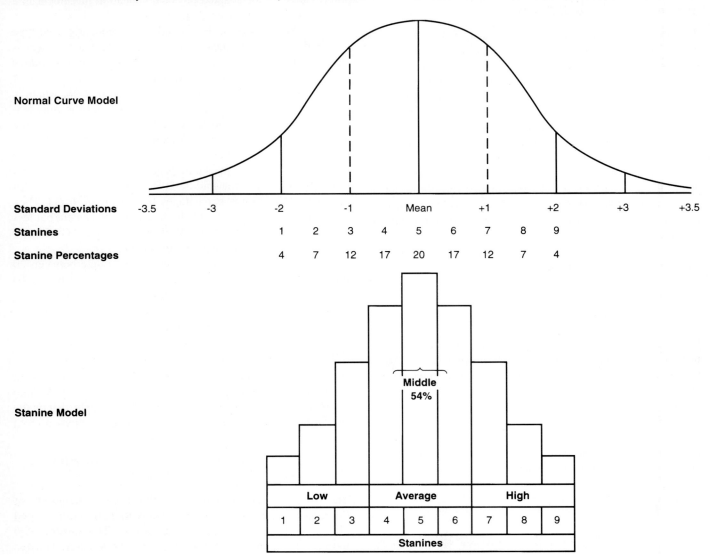

Table 6.11 Age equivalents for sample items on the Denver Developmental Screening Test (DDST).

DDST Item	Ages			
	25%	*50%*	*75%*	*90%*
Broad jump, 8.5 inches	2.0	2.8	3.0	3.2
5-sec balance, 1 foot	2.6	3.2	3.9	4.3
10-sec balance, 1 foot	3.0	4.5	5.0	5.9
Hops on one foot two times	3.0	3.4	4.0	4.9
Catches bounced ball two of three times	3.5	3.9	4.9	5.5
Heel-toe walk, four or more steps	3.3	3.6	4.2	5.0
Backward heel-toe walk, four or more steps	3.9	4.7	5.6	6.3

For example, 80% of the 3-year-olds met the first criterion for a run (a brief period where both feet are off the ground). Not until age 5, however, did 80% of children run with arms in opposition to legs, elbow bent. The BOTMP also provides a table for converting subscale scores into age equivalents.

In summary, most major placement instruments provide several kinds of norms: standard scores like stanines and z scores, percentiles, and age equivalents. Percentiles are the most common.

Assessing Students With Severe Disabilities

Severe disability is defined as an IQ under 35 (i.e., a mental age between 0 and 3 years), serious emotional disturbance or autism, and/or multiple disabilities like deaf-blindness and cerebral palsy/mental retardation combinations. These persons are often nonverbal, nonambulatory, and dominated by primitive reflexes. Sometimes they are ambulatory but cannot or will not stay in one place and attend to instructions. Obviously, assessment is a challenge. Standardized instruments often are not appropriate.

When assessing such individuals, first establish rapport. Even though they may appear oblivious of you, take the time to get acquainted. Talk to them like you would to anyone else; try to initiate some kind of play, like peek-a-boo or copycat. If they make a movement, mirror them and see if they notice. **Mirroring** or reflecting another's movement shows acceptance and is especially recommended for persons who are autistic or emotionally disturbed.

Obtain background information from other persons and the files. Often, such students are on behavior management programs and respond to certain signs/words and reinforcers. Remember, no student is too severely disabled to receive physical education services. Assess play and game behaviors as well as motor skill, fitness, perceptual-motor function, and sensory integration.

Questions to guide assessment include these:

1. Does the person attend to what you say or demonstrate? If not, does he or she respond to loud noises, light flashes, or other unusual stimuli (i.e., give evidence of seeing or hearing)? Keep trying until you find something.
2. What words/signs/gestures are understood? Often, these are on the individual's language board.
3. Does the person have some kind of expressive language (signs, words, pointing, eye blinks, facial expression)?
4. Can the person imitate? What kind of instructions will he or she follow?
5. What reinforcers (food, tokens, verbal praise, hug, touch) obtain the best responses?
6. What is the primary means of ambulation: (a) feet, (b) regular wheelchair, (c) motorized wheelchair? If regular wheelchair, is it propelled by hands or by feet?
7. How can muscle tone be described (normal, fluctuating, hypotonic, hypertonic)?
8. What primitive reflexes dominate or affect movement? Do head movements elicit associated movements? How can these reflexes be minimized or controlled?
9. If in a wheelchair, what is the disability? In most instances, it will be cerebral palsy, spina bifida, or muscular dystrophy.
10. If cerebral palsy, assign sport classification to obtain general idea of movement function. This primarily involves noting the type of ambulation, the hand-grasp function, and the range of motion (i.e., ability to independently move body parts). See Figure 6.12 and Chapter 25 on cerebral palsy.
11. Are there any contractures and/or abnormal postures or pain that need immediate attention?
12. Does the wheelchair and/or braces and assistive devices fit correctly? Is the person correctly positioned for physical education activities? Are body parts properly strapped?

These questions show that assessment competencies for students with severe disabilities are different from those of others. In general, criterion-referenced instruments (particularly the task-analysis types) work better than norm-referenced. Usually, the emphasis is on range of motion and postures, rather than strength and skills.

Instruments especially appropriate for certain kinds of severe conditions are described in Chapter 25 on cerebral palsy, Chapter 22 on emotional disturbance and autism, and Chapter 21 on mental retardation. For students who appear to be functioning motorically at the 0- to 5-year level, developmental inventories are useful.

Prescribing/Placing

Now that you have studied statistics and ways to interpret diagnostic test data, it is appropriate to consider the PAP-TE-CA function of prescribing. The term *prescribing* was borrowed from the medical model in the 1960s and became associated with the individualized education program (IEP) process mandated by law in the 1970s. **Prescription** is the process of officially or formally recommending placement, services, or activities. Prescription can be long-term, as in the annual IEP document that governs service delivery for students with disabilities, or for a 16-week exercise program or a semester academic plan. Prescription can also be short-term, as in daily or weekly lessons plans.

Prescription in the IEP/IPEP

This section expands on information presented in Chapters 3 and 4. It also describes the **individualized physical education program (IPEP),** a written document that parallels the IEP in form and content but is specific to physical education. The IEP is a legal document that covers all academic areas, including physical education. The IPEP is not a legal document, but rather a summary of assessment data, needs, and recommendations for placement, services, and teaching and learning conditions.

FIGURE 6.12   Classification determines the type of projectile used with persons with cerebral palsy.

Class 2 lower athlete with no functional arm movements performing a distance kick with a 13-inch playground ball.

Class 3 athlete performing a club throw for distance.

Class 2 upper athlete almost making a bull's-eye with a 5-oz soft shot.

IEP/IPEP Teamwork

Chapter 3 introduced the idea of several types of placement teams or committees that work to reach consensus about students' needs. The teams were these:

> IEP, Individualized Education Program committee for ages 3 to 21
>
> IFSP, Individualized Family Service Plan committee for ages 0 to 2
>
> CAPE, Committee for Adapted Physical Education for school district action on students not covered by the law
>
> RPEI, Regular Physical Education Initiative committee set up by an individual teacher for his or her students not covered by the law

These committees meet to analyze assessment data and agree on the contents of a written program, including placement, that will guide instruction for a year. Some states require review and revision of programs more frequently than once a year, and these state requirements influence the definition of long-term goals (3, 6, 9, or 12 months).

IEP Meeting Participants

The law requires five types of participants in IEP meetings: (a) parents or guardians, (b) an administrator, (c) a teacher, (d) an educational diagnostician or assessment specialist, and (e) the student, if appropriate. Since 1990, the law requires that students age 16 and over be present at their IEP meeting. Younger students should be present if they can benefit from observation and participation. More team members may be involved, but usually the smallest possible group is convened unless parents request attendance by particular professionals. Physical educators should discuss psychomotor needs with parents and indicate their willingness to help. The structure of CAPE and RPEI committees should include the resources most helpful in making physical activity decisions.

Parts of the IEP/IPEP

Chapter 4 introduced the six parts of the written IEP and the team process that must be followed in making prescriptions. These parts are

> P—Performance, present level
>
> A—Annual goals, including short-term objectives
>
> S—Services to be provided
>
> T—Transition services, recommended at all ages but required from age 16 on
>
> D—Dates and duration
>
> E—Evaluation to determine whether objectives are achieved

The acronym *PAST-DE* was recommended for remembering these parts, based on the idea that the age of ignorance about disability is *past* and/or *dead*. Figure 6.13 is an example of an individualized physical education program (IPEP). The IPEP is submitted to the IEP team members for their consideration. Some school systems include this kind of detail about physical education in their IEPs, but most include only a few sentences.

If a student is placed in regular physical education, no information except the assignment "regular physical education" is required on the IEP. However, if support services are needed, parents should be taught to insist that these be written into the IEP. Likewise, conditions believed necessary for learning to occur, like limited class size, specific teaching style, and formal adapted physical activity training for teachers and aides, should be written into the IEP. The IEP is a legal document that determines services. Both professionals and parents must sign the IEP for it to meet requirements of the law; this gives parents considerable negotiation power. An important role of the physical educator is to teach parents what to negotiate for.

The IPEP in Figure 6.13 was written by an adapted physical activity specialist with special training in BOTMP, TGMD, and other kinds of assessment. Classroom teachers and regular physical educators should be given copies of the IPEP as well as IEP team members. The IPEP, although not required by law, is an excellent help in programming for all students with special needs. It is therefore recommended as the document that is used for CAPE and RPEI committee meetings as well as for IEP meetings. Regular physical educators should ask their administrators to supply consultant help to assess students with problems and to write IPEPs. If class sizes and free time permit, regular physical educators may assume responsibility for writing their own IPEPs.

Helping Students Develop IEPs/IPEPs

With the increasing emphasis given to participation of students in IEP meetings, new curricular materials are appearing to help teachers prepare students for this involvement (NICHCY, 1995; Van Reusen & Box, 1994). It is recommended that students be taught to read, study, and recommend changes in their IEPs several weeks before the formal meeting. Work on the IEP should be woven into classes over the entire year using a combination of class discussions, seatwork, one-on-one meetings with various teachers who contribute to their IEP, and homework done either individually or with parents. Some of the benefits students derive are these:

> Learning how to speak for themselves
>
> Developing some of the skills necessary for self-determination and independent decision making
>
> Understanding assessment, engaging in self-testing, and performing at their personal best in tests administered by others
>
> Learning more about their strengths and weaknesses and how these relate to goals, objectives, and prescribed activities

FIGURE 6.13   Sample IPEP.

Alief Independent School District—IPEP

Parent Signature of Approval _____   Date _____

Name _____Amy S._____   Date _8-1-97___   School _Washington Elem._____

D.O. B. _7-3-92_____   Age _5_____   Grade _Early Childhood____   Classification _OI_____

APA Specialist _C. Pope_____   Projected Starting Date of Services _9-1997_____

Physical Abilities/Disabilities _Mild Cerebral Palsy — L. side, hemiplegic spastic, ambulatory_____

_____   Related Services _OT, PT_____

PRESENT LEVEL OF PSYCHOMOTOR PERFORMANCE
1. On BOTMP Long Form, Amy received overall percentile rank of 6 and stanine placement of 2. Her age equivalent score was below her actual age (5–9) on all 8 BOTMP subcomponents, but greatest weaknesses were in balance and strength components because she has not yet learned to compensate for L side spasticity on jump and land in balance skills.
2. On TGMD, Amy failed to meet criteria for mature performance on all 7 locomotor skills and 2 of 5 object control skills (2-hand strike, catch with both hands). Performed well on items requiring only one hand.
3. On social play skills, Amy is just entering associative play level and appears to have had little experience interacting with other children; plays no group games. She attends well, seems eager to please, but timid.

ANNUAL GOALS
1. Develop functional competence in locomotor and object control skills.
2. Improve social interaction skills to cooperative play level.
3. Play 10 low organized games, with success, with nondisabled peers.
4. Improve static and dynamic balance by learning to adapt to spasticity.

ILLUSTRATIVE SHORT-TERM OBJECTIVES
1. Perform various jumps without falling (pass, fail criterion).
2. Pass TGMD criteria for mature catch with two hands.
3. Interact with 3 or more classmates, when play is videotaped for 30 min.
4. Demonstrate success in 10 games on videotape: Pass specific criteria for success in each game.

SERVICES AND PLACEMENT FOR 12-MONTH PERIOD, BEGINNING SEPTEMBER 1
1. Regular PE 5 times a week, Model A, specially designed mainstream (SDM), with same age or slightly older buddy assigned fulltime to her.
2. Class size limited to 16, 8 with disabilities and 8 without.
3. Regular PE teacher with one adult aide, both of whom have documented adapted PE training within the last 3 years.
4. Adapted physical activity specialist-consultant available as needed.
5. School district curriculum guide available that lists appropriate games for age group and includes task analyses.

TRANSITION
1. Parent-guided homework plan agreed on that involves neighborhood children at least 3 times a week, 50 min each time.
2. Contact made with local branch of USCPAA, with weekly visits to observe and interact with others with cerebral palsy.

References

American Alliance for Health, Physical Education and Recreation. (1976a). *AAHPER youth fitness test manual.* Washington, DC: Author.

American Alliance for Health, Physical Education and Recreation. (1976b). *Motor fitness testing manual for the moderately mentally retarded.* Washington, DC: Author.

American Alliance for Health, Physical Education and Recreation. (1976c). *Special fitness test manual for the mildly mentally retarded* (2nd ed.). Washington, DC: Author. (First edition, 1968).

American Alliance for Health, Physical Education, Recreation and Dance. (1988). *Physical best: A physical fitness education and assessment program.* Reston, VA: Author.

Bricker, D. (1993). *Assessment, evaluation, and programming system.* Baltimore: Paul H. Brookes.

Brigance, A. (1978). *The Brigance Diagnostic Inventory of early development.* Woburn, MA: Curriculum Associates.

Broadhead, G., & Bruininks, R. (1982). Childhood motor performance traits on the short form Bruininks-Oseretsky Test. *Physical Educator, 39,* 149–155.

Bruininks, R. H. (1978). *Bruininks-Oseretsky Test of Motor Proficiency: Examiner's manual.* Circle Pines, MN: American Guidance Service.

Buell, C. (1973). AAHPER youth fitness test adaptation for the blind. In *Physical education and recreation for the visually handicapped.* Washington, DC: American Alliance for Health, Physical Education and Recreation.

Buros, O. (1978). *The eighth mental measurements yearbook.* Lincoln: University of Nebraska Press.

Burton, A. W. (1997). *Movement skill assessment.* Champaign, IL: Human Kinetics.

Conoley, J. C., & Kramer, J. J. (Eds.). (1989). *The tenth mental measurements yearbook.* Lincoln: University of Nebraska Press.

Cooper Institute for Aerobics Research. (1994). *The Prudential FITNESSGRAM test adiministration manual.* Dallas: Author.

Cowden, J. E., & Torrey, C. C. (1995). A ROADMAP for assessing infants, toddlers, and preschoolers: The role of the adapted motor developmentalist. *Adapted Physical Activity Quarterly, 12*(1), 1–11.

Dunn, J., Morehouse, J., & Fredericks, H. (1986). *Physical education for the severely handicapped: A systematic approach to a data-based gymnasium* (2nd ed.). Austin, TX: Pro•Ed.

Folio, M. R., & Fewell, R. R. (1983). *Peabody Developmental Motor Scales.* Hingham, MA: Teaching Resources.

Frankenburg, W. K., Dodds, J., & Archer, P. (1990). *Denver II technical manual.* Denver, CO: Denver Developmental Materials.

Henderson, S. E., & Sugden, D. A. (1992). *Movement Assessment Battery for Children.* San Antonio, TX: Psychological Corporation.

Hughes, J. (1979). *Hughes basic gross motor assessment manual.* Yonkers, NY: G. E. Miller.

Impara, J. (Ed.). (1995). *The twelfth mental measurements yearbook.* Lincoln, NE: Buros Institute of Mental Measurements.

Kallstrom, C. (1975). *Yellow brick road manual.* Garland, TX: R & K. (Address for ordering is R & K, Inc., P.O. Box 461262, Garland, TX 75046)

King-Thomas, L., & Hacker, B. (Eds.). (1987). *A therapist's guide to pediatric assessment.* Boston: Little, Brown.

Kohlberg, L. (1984). *The psychology of moral development: The nature and validity of moral stages.* San Francisco: Harper & Row.

Mitchell, J. (Ed.). (1985). *The ninth mental measurements yearbook.* Lincoln: University of Nebraska Press.

NICHCY. (1995, December). *Helping students develop their IEPs: Technical assistance guide.* Washington, DC: Author. (Address is NICHCY, P.O. Box 1492, Washington, DC 20013)

Parten, M. (1932). Social participation among preschool children. *Journal of Abnormal and Social Psychology, 27,* 243–269.

Piaget, J. (1932). *The moral judgment of the child.* New York: Harcourt, Brace & World.

Piaget, J. (1952). *The origins of intelligence in children.* New York: International Universities Press.

Roach, E. F., & Kephart, N. (1966). *Purdue perceptual-motor survey.* Columbus, OH: Charles E. Merrill.

Salvia, J., & Ysseldyke, J. (1995). *Assessment* (6th ed.). Princeton, NJ: Houghton Mifflin.

Ulrich, D. A. (1985). *Test of gross motor development.* Austin, TX: Pro•Ed.

Van Reusen, A. K., & Box, C. S. (1994). Facilitating student participation in individualized education programs through motivation strategy instruction. *Exceptional Children, 60*(5), 466–475.

Verderber, J., & Payne, V. G. (1987). A comparison of the long and short forms of the Bruininks-Oseretsky Test of Motor Proficiency. *Adapted Physical Activity Quarterly, 4*(1), 51–59.

Werder, J., & Bruininks, R. H. (1988). *Body Skills: A motor development curriculum for children.* Circle Pines, MN: American Guidance Service.

Wessel, J. A. (1976). *I CAN—Primary Skills.* Northbrook, IL: Hubbard. (Now available through Pro•Ed)

Wessel, J. A. (1977). *Planning individualized education programs in special education.* Northbrook, IL: Hubbard. (Now available through Pro•Ed)

Winnick, J., & Short, F. (1985). *Physical fitness testing of the disabled: Project UNIQUE.* Champaign, IL: Human Kinetics.

Zittel, L. L. (1994). Gross motor assessment of preschool children with special needs: Instrument selection considerations. *Adapted Physical Activity Quarterly, 11*(3), 245–260.

C H A P T E R

7

Teaching, Evaluating, and Consulting

FIGURE 7.1   Peer teacher demonstrates hitting a piñata for a classmate with Down syndrome.

After you have studied this chapter, you should be able to do the following:

1. Identify indicators of effective teaching, and discuss how input, process, and outcomes are used to guide decision making that leads to effective teaching.

2. Identify and discuss at least 10 instructional principles. Cite examples of how you or others have applied these principles in practicum or salaried teaching experiences.

3. Differentiate among traditional task analysis, ecological task analysis, and activity analysis and demonstrate competence in each.

4. Analyze four teaching styles, from most to least restrictive, and describe each in relation to (a) learning environment, (b) starting routine, (c) presentation of new activities, and (d) execution. Relate teaching styles to behaviors that students with various disabilities might exhibit.

5. Discuss behavior management concepts in relation to teaching, and describe some specific techniques.

6. Give examples of some adaptations for problems of (a) strength and endurance, (b) balance and agility, and (c) coordination and accuracy.

7. Identify characteristics of a healthy counseling relationship and discuss them in relation to teaching.

8. Discuss program evaluation and document practice in using the Checklist for Evaluating School District Adapted Physical Education.

9. Given some case studies of families, schools, and communities, discuss how to obtain and use consultant services in those cases. Or make up some case studies demonstrating your understanding of consultant services.

This chapter pertains to three components of the PAP-TE-CA model: teaching/counseling/coaching, evaluation, and consulting/coordination of resources. Although these functions can be treated as six independent entities, they are clustered together in this chapter because of their close interrelatedness. Four concepts underlie the decision to group these functions together.

1. All six functions are processes of facilitating permanent change (i.e., learning) while building and/or preserving ego strength so as to evoke personal bests in performance (see Figure 7.1).

2. **Counseling,** in this text, is defined as a helping relationship based on good interpersonal communication skills rather than as functions performed by a salaried professional called a counselor. For students and teachers to become better listeners and helpers, completion of courses in counseling is highly recommended. Adapted physical activity professionals are often asked to listen and help with individual and family problems. Teaching sometimes cannot progress until these problems are addressed.

3. **Consulting,** in this text, is defined as providing (a) support services to parents, teachers, and other professionals; (b) adult education, which may include various forms of in-service education, parent training, and collaborative teamwork; and (c) expert advice and contract services, such as assessment or evaluation for a school district. The function of identifying and coordinating resources is central to all parts of consulting as well as to teaching. All teachers are asked to serve as consultants in their area of expertise at one time or another. In particular, physical educators often serve as consultants for parents and regular classroom teachers who instruct children in motor skills and game concepts.

Adapted physical activity specialists who are employed as consultants are first and foremost teachers.

4. Coaching and evaluation are specialized teaching functions that require particular competencies. **Coaching,** in this text, refers to responsibility for after-school sport training and competition in a home, school, or community context. **Evaluation** is the process of examining program outcomes (e.g., Are students achieving goals?), analyzing the reasons for the findings, and making recommendations for the future.

This chapter therefore focuses on teaching as a generic function that can encompass counseling, coaching, consulting, and evaluating. The emphasis, however, is on **teaching** as service delivery within the classroom that is directed toward setting and achieving physical education goals. **Pedagogy,** the art and science of teaching, is synonymous with content taught in methods courses.

Indicators of Effective Teaching

Curricular models (e.g., ABC, I CAN, and ACTIVE) and service organizations capture the essence of effective teaching in their acronyms and mottos (see Table 7.1). As you read this chapter, relate the ideas in Table 7.1 to principles and processes of good teaching. In Chapter 1, it was emphasized that good teaching is adapting. Adaptation should result in the following indicators of effective teaching, which are based on research (Siedentop, 1983):

1. The development of a warm, positive climate

2. An appropriate matching of content to student abilities (ensuring success-oriented activity)

3. A high percentage of time devoted to lesson objectives

4. High rates of on-task behaviors

5. The use of strategies that contribute to on-task behavior but are not incompatible with a warm, positive climate

T a b l e 7.1 Acronyms and mottos associated with good teaching.

1. **I CAN:** Individualize, Create social leisure competence, Associate all learnings, Narrow the gap between theory and practice (Wessel, 1977).
2. **ABC:** Achievement-Based Curriculum (Wessel & Kelly, 1986).
3. **PAP-TE-CA:** Plan, Assess, Prescribe, Teach, Evaluate, Consult/Coordinate, Advocate. This is an expansion of the ABC model.
4. **ACTIVE:** All Children Totally Involved in Exercising (Vodola, 1976). This means no waiting in lines, a ball or rope for every student.
5. **Every Child a Winner** (Owens, 1974): Recognition for personal bests, emphasis on a warm, positive classroom climate.
6. **Find Another Way** (Gold, 1980): This motto refers to the teacher's creativity in finding a way each student can succeed on every task.
7. **Catch 'Em Being Good** (O'Leary & Schneider, 1980): This is a behavior management principle that emphasizes giving five praises before each correction.
8. **Moving to Inclusion** (Active Living Alliance for Canadians With a Disability, 1994): This refers to the teacher's creativity in finding ways to include students in the regular instructional setting and in obtaining support services.
9. **Data-Based Gymnasium** (Dunn, Morehouse, & Fredericks, 1986): This refers to basing all decisions in the gymnasium on student performance data.
10. **PEOPEL:** Physical Education Opportunity for Exceptional Learners (Long, Irmer, Burkett, Glasenapp, & Odenkirk, 1980). *Opportunity* here refers to every student having a partner to enable learning and success.
11. **Special Olympics motto:** "Let me win. But if I cannot win, let me be brave in the attempt."
12. **United States Cerebral Palsy Athletic Association (USCPAA) motto:** "Sports by ability, not disability."
13. **Disability Sports/USA motto:** "If I can do this [sports], I can do anything."
14. **Alcoholics Anonymous motto:** "God, Grant me the *serenity* to accept the things I cannot change; the *courage* to change the things I can; and the *wisdom* to know the difference."

Instructional Model to Guide Thinking

Teaching is a chain of decision making (Mosston & Ashworth, 1986, p. 4). To guide these decisions, Table 7.2 presents an instructional model with three basic parts (input, process, and outcomes). **Input** refers to information about all of the variables that affect teaching and learning. Decision making about planning, assessing, and prescribing determines the quality and quantity of input. **Process** refers to the actual interactions that lead to behavior change. Decision making about these interactions is typically guided by principles. **Outcomes** refers to the desired results; these are usually stated as goals.

Theories Underlying the Model

Systems theory, dynamical systems theory, and ecological theory (Boss, Doherty, LaRossa, Schumm, & Steinmetz, 1993) all contribute to instructional models. The I CAN, ABC, and ACTIVE curricular models are examples of systems theory. PAP-TE-CA illustrates dynamical systems theory and ecological theory.

Systems theory, which evolved in the 1940s in conjunction with computer technology and information processing, is a linear approach to input, process, and output systems that enhances understanding of the whole. Systems theory starts with input (all the information that comes from planning, assessing, and prescribing), then moves to process (teaching, counseling, coaching, and consulting), and then focuses on outcomes that provide feedback for revising the process and starting the cycle again.

Dynamical systems theory, which is popular in the 1990s, is a modification of traditional systems theory, based on a recognition of the increasing complexity, multidimensionality, and interactiveness of the many chaotic systems in life (Devaney, 1989; Gleick, 1987; Smith & Thelen, 1993). For example, variables within the PAP-TE-CA model are conceptualized as continuously interacting in all directions (i.e., the systems are dynamic and sometimes described as chaotic). This is consistent with the trend away from linear thinking and toward interactional or dynamic thinking.

Ecological theory, also increasingly popular in the 1990s, is an approach to analyzing the interactions and interdependence between humans and all aspects of their environment, both physical and social. The PAP-TE-CA model, like the philosophy of this text, is ecological.

Interactiveness of Model Components

The evolving PAP-TE-CA model, consistent with trends of the 1990s, uses input, process, and outcome instructional components but emphasizes the dynamic, multidirectional, chaotic complexity of what occurs in the classroom. This complexity has long perplexed researchers and serves as one explanation of why so little research has been conducted on effective teaching in physical education. The model in Table 7.2 is based on reviews of research (Sherrill, Heikinaro-Johansson, & Slininger, 1994; Vogler, DePaepe, & Martinek, 1990; Webster, 1993) but also presents ideas and principles based on experience. This model is used to guide the organization of content about teaching on the following pages.

T a b l e 7 . 2   **Instructional model to guide thinking.**

Inputs	Processes	Outcomes

Assessment of people (presage variables)
  Student
  Teacher
  Peers
  Family
  Significant others
Assessment of environment (context)
  Barriers
  Resources
  Class size
  Facilities
  Equipment
  Space
  Lighting, color
  Sound, distractions
  Etc.
Assessment of time
  PE time
  Recess
  Other class time
  After-school time
Assessment of opportunity
  Philosophy
  Cultural factors
  Economic factors
  Possibility of change
  Probability of change
	1. Maintain a warm, positive climate.
	2. Individualize instruction by making adaptations.
	3. Promote a data-based gymnasium.
	4. Use ecologically valid activities and settings.
	5. Devote a high percentage of time to class objectives.
	6. Maximize time-on-task with success.
	7. Emphasize variability of practice and contextual interference.
	8. Try a wide variety of strategies and techniques.
	9. Adapt teaching styles to individual needs.
	10. Apply behavior management strategies.
	11. Weave counseling into teaching.
		1. Students achieve IEP, IPEP, and other objectives.
		2. Teachers achieve objectives.
		3. Significant others achieve objectives.
		4. Laws and school policy are followed.
		5. Lawsuits are avoided.
		6. Family pride, school pride, and community pride are enhanced.
		7. Collaboration by home, school, and community is increased.

Inputs That Influence Teaching

Inputs have traditionally been classified as (a) **presage,** which means human predictor variables like age, gender, and perceived competence, and (b) **context,** which means nonhuman predictor variables like class size, facilities, and equipment (Dunkin & Biddle, 1974; Vogler, van der Mars, Cusimano, & Darst, 1992). Research indicates that context variables like class size are better predictors of student achievement than presage variables are (Vogler et al., 1992). Neither experience nor expertise seems to affect teacher time usage in mainstream physical education (Vogler et al., 1992). However, experience does positively influence adapted physical activity planning behaviors (Solomon & Lee, 1991).

Research findings, of course, depend on which human variables are examined and the measures of teacher effectiveness selected. Teacher expectancy about student ability is an important variable in the teaching process (Karper & Martinek, 1985). Attitude research (Rizzo & Kirkendall, 1995; Rizzo & Vispoel, 1992) indicates that academic preparation in adapted physical activity and perceived competence of teachers (as opposed to age, gender, and experience) are significant predictors of attitudes toward teaching children with disabilities. This finding helps school systems justify in-service training for teachers.

Input About People

Concerning people (both students and teachers), some of the variables related to input are age, gender, ethnicity, socioeconomic class, culture or subculture, self-concept, attitudes, knowledge, actual and perceived competence, creativity, interests, concerns, motivations, expectations, perceptions, body build, emotions, personality, fears, health, fitness, teaching styles, preferred sensory modalities, abilities and disabilities, past history of opportunities and barriers, and beliefs, attitudes, and practices of significant others. Many of these variables are situational or contextual, meaning that they change with the situation, are positive when the person feels comfortable, and otherwise are negative.

Some personal variables affect physical education learning more directly than others. The use of cooperative or collaborative approaches to planning, assessing, and prescribing increases the likelihood of identifying and addressing the best set of personal variable inputs. In particular, the student variables of interest, motivation, and perceived usefulness of physical activities interact with process to affect goal achievement. These variables are strongly influenced by family and neighborhood leisure practices, facilities, and values; therefore PAP functions should be based on concern for ecosystems rather than for individuals. Effective teachers make home visits and/or devise sport events that families attend, thereby creating opportunities for getting acquainted.

Input About Environment

Concerning physical environment, some of the variables are class size, facilities (indoor/outdoor), equipment, and school, home, and community resources. When students have sensory or mobility impairments, it is important to analyze these categories into such components as space and surfaces, lighting and color, sounds, smells, weather and temperature conditions, pollutions and allergens, barriers, distance to bathrooms and water fountains, and optimal location of equipment. Skillful management of these variables and their relationships with people is extremely important in effective teaching.

Input About Time

Careful planning, assessing, and prescribing of physical education time is critical to effective teaching. Of course, lesson plans are important in all kinds of teaching, but their use is essential in structuring goal-specific instruction for students with disabilities.

Developing Lesson Plans

Lesson plans should include three parts: introductory activity, lesson body, and summary. Table 7.3 outlines a 30-min elementary school lesson plan designed to achieve goals in running skills, self-concept, social interactions, and play and game concepts.

The introductory activity (about 5 min) is usually an obstacle course, game, or dance activity in which everyone is involved. Physiologically, this is warm-up time, but instruction should be directed toward self-concept and social interactions by stressing that warm-ups are the way we show respect and appreciation for our bodies and prevent injury. Also during this time, we get in touch with our body and establish a mental attitude favorable to learning. The first 5 min are also a time for partner interactions, particularly in class structures guided by social competence and inclusion goals.

The lesson body (21 min) is specific to the individual. It is divided between self-testing and game activities for achieving functional competence. Note that a group game usually requires at least 8 min (2 min of teacher talk, 1 min to get into formation, and 5 min of actual activity). Every minute must be carefully used. Waste during transitions from one activity to another can be eliminated by the rule that everyone must be in place within 60 sec. The transition time is structured by counting, a timer that buzzes, or tape-recorded music.

Self-testing is usually done in stations and guided by task cards. These state what skill is to be practiced, under what conditions (e.g., size, weight, and color of ball; distance from target; type of target), and number of trials. Task cards are kept at stations, stored in individual mailboxes or in files containing clipboards. Or they may be made of heavy cardboard with string attached for wearing around the neck.

The summary (4 min) can be activity or talk time or both. Physiologically, this is cool-down and relaxation time. In terms of self-concept, this is evaluation and cooperative goal-

Table 7.3 Thirty-minute lesson plan for running skills.

I. Introductory Activities	**5 min**
a. A 1-min or less attendance-taking protocol	
b. Obstacle or challenge course *or*	
c. Group aerobics with music	
II. Body of Lesson	**21 min**
a. Self-testing (state number of trials)	5 min
b. Two games (8 min each)	16 min
2 min—instructions	
1 min—get into formation	
5 min—actual activity	
III. Summary/Evaluation/Cool-Down	**4 min**
a. Group or partner discussion *or*	
b. Individual counseling	
Total	**30 min**

setting time. Emphasis should be on (a) "How are we going to use what we learned today?" (b) "When can we show our parents?" (c) "How much can we practice this at home?" and (d) "Who can we practice with?" Students need this kind of reinforcement to internalize that they have learned something, met their goals, and so on.

Linking Lessons With Objectives

Each part of the lesson plan should be directly linked to terminal objectives. Some of these require time of their own, whereas others are embedded in activities that teach motor skills and practice. There are not enough minutes of instructional time in a semester to permit free play. When free time is awarded as part of a behavior management approach, the freedom should be to choose from among established activities that reinforce learning of objectives, not the freedom to engage in social dance, card games, and other activities that are unrelated to physical education objectives.

Table 7.4 shows specifically how class activities contribute to four objectives for running games. Motor skills and patterns are broken down into two terminal objectives, and most of class time is spent on these. Skill time, however, is task analyzed into listening, getting into formation, and actual learning or practice. Self-concept is broken down into two terminal objectives and allotted 10 min, the parts of the lesson designated as introduction and summary. Social interactions and play and game behaviors are broken down into two and three objectives, respectively, and allocated no time because their achievement is embedded in other activities.

Using Out-of-School Time

When working toward the goals of self-actualization and lifespan active, healthy lifestyle, teachers must involve students and parents in structuring out-of-school time to include physical education and recreation experiences. All should cooperatively agree upon homework that requires students to submit activity logs or diaries recording the number of minutes spent in vigorous physical activity each day and time spent in

Table 7.4   Daily plan showing how terminal objectives direct the use of time.

Goal	Terminal Objectives	Minutes per Day

Motor skills and patterns	1. To run 50-m dash in 9.9 sec or less
	  Activity—Self-testing: Race against best time
	  a. Listen to instructions
	  b. Get into formations
	  c. Stay on task
	2. To demonstrate functional competence in 10 running games
	  Activity—Running games
	  a. Listen to instructions
	  b. Get into formations
	  c. Stay on task
		20

Self-concept	1. To feel good about self in running activities
	  Activity—Embedded
	  Activity—Discussions
	  a. Pregame visual imagery: "I am good at running"
	  b. Prompts and praise
	  c. Postgame evaluation: Tell things you did well
	  d. Ask others what you did well
	2. To respect self and body
	  Activity—Embedded
	  Activity—Warm-up and cool-down
	  a. Listen to instructions
	  b. Stay on task
	  c. Discuss why this is good for body
	  d. Praise and prompts
		10

Social interactions	1. To say hello and goodbye to relevant persons 2. To praise at least one person during every 5 min of game time Activity—Embedded, but may need prompts	0
Play and game behaviors	1. To listen to 2 min of teacher talk (game instructions) without interruption 2. To stay on-task during a 5-min game 3. To get into designated formations within 60-sec count Activity—Embedded, but may need prompts	0

Note. Social interactions and play and game behaviors are not assigned minutes of their own because their achievement is embedded in other activities.

various roles (spectator as well as participant) in community facilities. Family trips should be planned to include disability sport events like wheelchair basketball and tennis, Special Olympics, and Deaf sport. Likewise, families should participate together in mainstream sport events.

These uses of time may be considered transition activities in the IEP and IPEP, but essentially family and community sport and fitness activities are the primary means for socializing children into sport. The earlier these activities begin, the more likely it is that individuals with disabilities will develop beliefs, attitudes, and practices necessary to achieve active, healthy lifestyles. Families in which neither parent has an interest in or time for sport should be encouraged to employ a "big brother" or "big sister" or find resources for transporting the children to community recreation programs. Adapted physical activity professionals are key people in promoting the wise use of leisure time.

Input About Opportunity

The last input in Table 7.2 to be assessed, planned, and prescribed is opportunity, which can be broken down into family, school, and community positives and negatives in relation to individual students. Opportunity is largely determined by cultural, economic, and moral variables: for instance, how power structures choose to allocate resources, and whether minority groups challenge choices that they perceive as unfair. Assessment should focus on philosophy, the identification of what needs to be changed, and the planning of strategies to promote change. Under philosophy, topics of particular concern include architectural, attitudinal, and aspirational barriers; placement practices and contexts; criteria used to evaluate teachers and programs; expectations and traditions; required curricular elements or content by outside agencies; and the support of significant and/or powerful others.

The Teaching Process and Outcomes

Effective teaching is defined in many ways. At the beginning of this chapter we said that teaching is effective when certain indicators are present. These indicators can be converted to instructional principles (see the Processes column of Table 7.2), and evaluation can focus on the extent to which these principles are followed. Effective teaching can also be defined in terms of product or outcomes—specifically, whether the process results in optimal goal achievement (see the Outcomes column of Table 7.2).

The next section presents instructional principles. In implementing these principles, teachers must constantly be aware of the four types of inputs (people, physical setting, time, opportunity) and skillfully manage input, process, and outcome interrelationships so as to promote optimal goal achievement.

Maintain a Warm, Positive Learning Climate

Warm, positive environments involve personalization; nurturing; high rates of positive interactions; high but realistic expectations; cooperative relationships and activities; mutual respect; availability of many choices; treatment with dignity, fairness, and inclusiveness; seeing every child as a winner; and focusing on abilities, not disabilities. Teachers need to establish criteria for determining whether their classrooms have warm, positive climates.

One criterion might be the number of times that students are called by their first names and the number of times they receive personal attention, assuming that these episodes are positive in nature (Heikinaro-Johansson, Sherrill, French, & Huuhka, 1995). The use of a videotape protocol or a small tape recorder attached to the body enables teachers to check themselves on the number and types of personalizations. For example, when a 9-year-old boy in a wheelchair was integrated into a class of 20, Heikinaro-Johansson et al. (1995) reported that personal attention was given to this student an average of five times, each episode varying from 0.5 to 1.8 min in duration, during 45-min sessions.

Others have defined a positive climate as one in which teacher-student interactions are (a) more positive than negative or corrective, (b) more skill than behavior oriented, and (c) more specific than general in nature (Vogler, van der Mars, Darst, & Cusimano, 1990). For example, an analysis of 30 mainstreamed elementary classes indicated 70% positive feedback, 10% negative feedback, and 20% corrective feedback; 72% motor skill feedback and 28% behavior feedback; and 63% general and 37% specific feedback (Vogler, van der Mars, et al., 1990). Thus, two out of three of the criteria for a positive climate were met. The last criterion, giving specific rather than general feedback, is one that teachers often fail to meet (Heikinaro-Johansson et al., 1995), indicating that more attention should be given to this in teacher training.

Research thus far has focused on teachers' feedback to students, but also important is students' feedback to teachers and to other students. **Feedback,** broadly defined, includes all interactions (verbal and nonverbal). Who initiates these interactions and under what conditions is important, especially when inclusiveness is a criterion for a warm, positive climate. Students must be systematically taught to praise each other and to give other kinds of positive feedback (see Chapters 8 and 9).

FIGURE 7.2 Students with cerebral palsy and other conditions of low muscle strength need a lowered basket for optimal success.

Individualize Instruction by Making Adaptations

A warm, positive learning climate is also enhanced by teacher flexibility in assessing and implementing adaptations that might help individual students be more successful. Equipment, facilities, body position, time and space requirements, and other variables can be easily adapted by creative teachers and students working together to achieve personal bests. Following are some principles to guide adaptations for students with problems of strength, endurance, balance, agility, coordination, or accuracy.

Problems of Strength and Endurance

1. Lower the net or basketball goal (Figure 7.2).
2. Reduce the distance the ball must be thrown or served (a) between bases, (b) between serving line and net, (c) between partners.
3. Reduce the weight and/or the size of the ball or projectile. Balloons are probably lightest, whereas medicine balls are heaviest (Figure 7.3).
4. Reduce the weight of the bat or striking implement. Shorten the length of the striking implement or choke up on the bat.
5. Lower the center of gravity. Games played in a lying or sitting position demand less fitness than those in a standing/running position.

FIGURE 7.3 In a task analysis, the manipulation of light balls (like balloons) comes before heavy balls. This teenager has so little arm and shoulder strength that shaking a balloon on a string is the first ball-handling activity he is able to master.

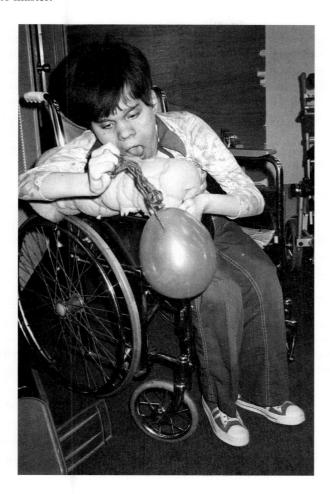

6. Deflate air from the ball or select one that will not get away so fast in case the student misses a catch and has to chase the ball.
7. Decrease activity time. Reduce the number of points needed to win.
8. Increase the number of rest periods during the activity.
9. Utilize frequent rotation in and out of the game or a system for substitution when needed.
10. Reduce the speed of the game. Walk rather than run through movements.
11. Consider ambulation alternatives—for example, one inning on scooterboards, one inning on feet.

Problems of Balance and Agility

1. Lower the center of gravity. On a trampoline, for instance, practice logrolls, creeping, and four-point bounces before trying activities in a standing position. Stress bending the knees (or landing low) when jumping or coming to quick stops.
2. Keep as much of the body as possible in contact with the surface. Flat-footed ambulation is more stable than on tiptoe. Balancing on four or five body parts is more stable than balancing on one.
3. Widen the base of support (distance between the feet).
4. Increase the width of lines, rails, or beams to be walked on. Note that straight lines are easier to walk than curved ones.
5. Extend arms for balance. Holding a fishing pole horizontally in front of the torso while walking the beam facilitates balance.
6. Use carpeted rather than slick surfaces. Modify surfaces to increase friction. Select footwear (rubber soles) to reduce falls.
7. Learn to fall; practice different kinds of falls; make falls into games and creative dramatics.
8. Provide a barre to assist with stability during exercises or have a table or chair to hold on to.
9. Understand the role of visual perception in balance; learn to use eyes optimally.
10. Determine whether balance problems are related to prescribed medications. If there appears to be a relationship, confer with the physician.

Problems of Coordination and Accuracy

1. For catching and striking activities, use larger, lighter, softer balls. Balls thrown to midline are easier to catch and strike than those thrown to the right or left. Decrease the distance the ball is thrown and reduce speed.
2. For throwing activities, use smaller balls (e.g., tennis balls). If grasp and release is a problem, try yarn or Nerf balls and beanbags.
3. Distance throwing is an easier progression than throwing for accuracy.
4. In striking and kicking activities, succeed with a stationary ball before trying a moving one. Increase the surface of the striking implement; choke up on the bat for greater control.
5. Reduce frustration when balls are missed by using backdrops, backstops, nets, and rebounder frame sets. Or attach a string to the ball for ease of recovery (Figure 7.4).
6. Increase the size of the target or goal cage to be hit, the circumference of the basket to be made. Give points for nearness (like hitting backboard) to avoid feeling failure until basket is actually made.
7. In bowling-type games, use lighter, less stable pins. Milk cartons are good.
8. Optimize safety by more attention than normal to glasses protectors, shin guards, helmets, and face masks. Do not remove the child's glasses!

FIGURE 7.4 Adapting equipment (like attaching a string to the ball) and using backstops increase easy recovery of ball and maximize time devoted to practicing a skill.

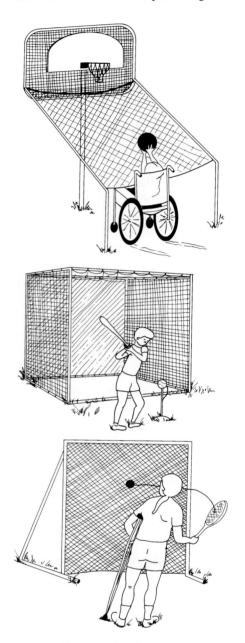

Promote a Data-Based Gymnasium

The data-based gymnasium (DBG) concept is usually associated with a behavior management curriculum model developed by John Dunn and associates at Oregon State University (Dunn, Morehouse, & Fredericks, 1986). In this text, however, the concept refers to **individualization of instruction,** which means basing classroom decisions on student performance data. The use of an IEP or IPEP individualizes goals, objectives, and overall instructional services for a set number of weeks, but the DBG concept emphasizes minute-by-minute individualization within a specific lesson. This requires continuous assessment and record keeping in conjunction with instruction. The number of trials is prescribed for practice of each part of a motor skill or game, and a pass or fail is recorded for each trial. Hence, DBG is often called the clipboard system.

Part Method Versus Whole Method

DBG was developed originally for students with severe mental retardation, whom research shows to learn better by the part method than by the whole method (Weld & Evans, 1990). The **whole method** (total task presentation through demonstration and/or verbal instructions) is typically used (a) with students who have no cognitive or attention problems and (b) when the task to be learned is relatively easy. When a student has difficulty learning through the whole method, various whole-part-whole combinations are generally introduced. It is important to demonstrate the whole, however, so students can conceptualize where their practice of parts is leading.

Two types of part methods are common. In the **pure part method,** each part is practiced separately many times before all are combined or chained. Beginning swimming illustrates this, in that a float is practiced many, many times before arms, legs, and breathing are added. In the **progressive part method,** parts of a skill are chained together in a particular order, generally in either a forward or a backward order.

Traditional Task Analysis by Parts and Steps

The use of part methods of teaching depends on skill in **task analysis,** the breaking down of a task into its parts and the ordering of these parts from easy to hard. For example, for persons with mild to moderate mental retardation, bowling might be broken down into four parts:

A. Raise the ball chest high and step forward on the right foot

B. Step forward on the left foot and push the ball forward

C. Step forward on the right foot and swing the ball backward

D. Step forward on the left foot, swing the ball forward, and release the ball in the direction of the pins

Typically, either forward or backward chaining is prescribed as the strategy for practicing a task analysis and encoding a motor skill into short-term memory. **Forward chaining** refers to practicing the first part in the chain until a specific criterion is reached, then learning the second part and combining it with the first, then learning the third part and combining it with the first and second parts, and so on. Using the bowling task analysis, a forward chain might be A; A and B; A, B, and C; A, B, C, and D. **Backward chaining** is the reverse (e.g., D; C and D; B, C, and D; A, B, C, and D). Backward chaining is particularly effective in movement patterns like bowling, throwing, and kicking, in which the last step is dramatic and constitutes a reward within itself (e.g., the noise of a ball hitting a target or striking a ball). Research particularly supports backward chaining for teaching bowling (Hsu & Dunn, 1984).

The number and size of parts in a task analysis must be consistent with the student's ability level. For persons with severe mental retardation, Phase 1 of a task analysis might be this:

A. Sit facing the pins and holding an adapted ball by the handle

B. Swing the arm forward with assistance and release the handle

Phase 1 would be repeated until a criterion is met, like Knocks down at least one pin in 8 out of 10 trials. Then Phase 2, in which B is altered to include a backward and a forward swing, with assistance, is introduced. In Phase 3 the adaptation might be no assistance. Phase 4 might involve doing the movement from a standing position.

After practice of parts enables a student to perform a motor skill that is fairly functional, the teacher develops checklists of easy to difficult steps to guide further learning of the skill. **Steps** are learning increments or additional breakdowns in task phases that gradually increase task difficulty. Examples of some checklists of steps follow.

A first checklist or learning progression might read:

1. Jump down from an 8-inch step.
2. Jump down from a 12-inch step.
3. Jump down from an 18-inch bench.
4. Jump down from a 24-inch bench.
5. Perform a challenge course that requires jumping down from varying heights.

A second learning progression might read:

1. Jump forward 6 inches.
2. Jump forward 12 inches.
3. Jump forward 18 inches.
4. Play a game with others called "Jumping the stream" or "Crossing the brook."

A third learning progression might read:

1. Jump over a rope 3 inches high.
2. Jump over a rope 6 inches high.
3. Jump over a rope 12 inches high.
4. Play a game with others that involves jumping over a rope or bar.

Note that task analysis teaching should end with the ability to perform the task in a game, sport, or fitness setting. This ability is called **functional competence.**

Levels of Assistance

In performing a task or sequence of tasks, students require different levels of assistance: physical, visual, verbal, or a combination of these (Figure 7.5). Evaluation and record keeping entail writing next to the task the type of assistance needed. A student might progress, for instance, through the following levels of assistance:

1. **P**—Performs overarm throw with *physical* and verbal assistance.
2. **D**—Performs overarm throw with visual and verbal assistance (i.e., a *demonstration* accompanied by explanation).
3. **C5**—Performs overarm throw with much verbal assistance (i.e., *cues* throughout the sequence).
4. **C1**—Performs overarm throw with minimal verbal assistance (i.e., one or two *cues* only).
5. **I**—Performs overarm throw with no assistance (i.e., *independently*).

FIGURE 7.5 Physical and verbal assistance are almost always needed in teaching children with severe disabilities to bat. Note that the target is waist high to make the skill easier. A ball on top of a coffee can is an excellent target because noise is reinforcing.

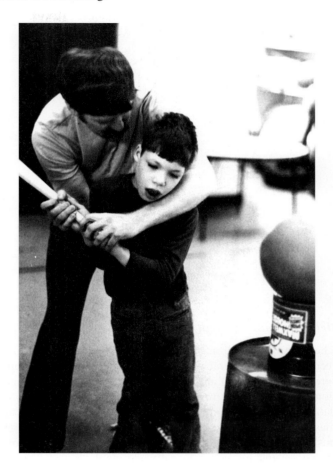

These five levels of assistance can be applied to a single step within a task analysis or to a movement pattern or a sequence of movement patterns (i.e., folk dance). Use of initials to represent levels facilitates ease of record keeping and lesson writing.

Physical assistance should always be accompanied by verbal cues. These cues can be spoken, chanted, or sung. Physical assistance should never be called "physical manipulation" (a medical term often used in therapy and orthopedics). Several learning theorists have created good synonyms for physical assistance. The term **coactive movement,** taken from the Van Dijk (1966) approach from Holland, is now widely used throughout the world in working with individuals who are deaf-blind (Leuw, 1972). In coactive movement, the bodies of the teacher and student move as one, closely touching, in activities like rolling, seat scooting, creeping, knee walking, and upright walking. As the student gets the feel of the task, the distance between the two bodies is gradually increased. The emphasis is then on **mirroring** (i.e., imitating the teacher's movements).

FIGURE 7.6 The adaptation process. Note that a task is analyzed into *variables*. Variables are analyzed into *factors*. Factors are analyzed into levels that are designated when writing goals.

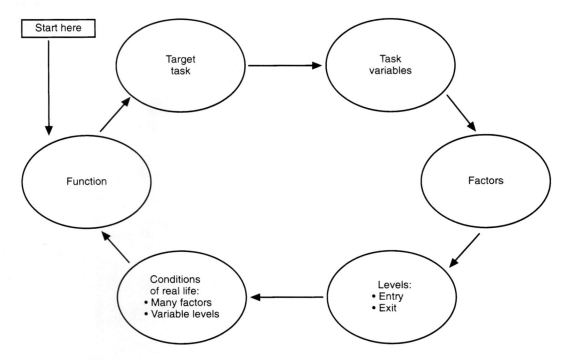

Behavior Management

The data-based gymnasium (DBG) concept also requires record keeping on which kind of instructions (cues) and reinforcements (rewards) are best for each student. This information is often specific to a particular task analysis, so lots of data are maintained on each student, with dates that indicate mastery of phases and steps of the task analysis. DBG obviously requires a very low teacher–student ratio, preferably one to one, so students are totally active during the lesson. This requires the training and supervision of volunteers. Additional information about behavior management is provided later in the chapter because behavior management can be used in conjunction with any instructional principle or program.

Use Ecologically Valid Activities and Settings

The instructional principle of using ecologically valid activities and settings emphasizes selecting content that enables the student to function better in her or his ecosystem (i.e., the real world). In the I CAN instructional model, the *A* for "Associate all learnings" refers to strategies that increase ecological validity. This is variously called the principle of social validity, ecological validity, or functionality. Each term captures the idea that the activity is practical, useful, meaningful, age appropriate, developmentally appropriate, and generalizable to real-life situations. Because traditional task analyses often do not meet these criteria, ecological task analysis has been proposed as an alternative approach (Balan & Davis, 1993; Davis & Burton, 1991).

Ecological Task Analysis

Ecological task analysis (ETA) is an adaptation process that starts with the selection of a real-life function, focuses on relationships between the learner and the environment, and analyzes variables into factors and levels that relate to real-life conditions. **Function** refers to the ability to perform the tasks of daily living, work, or play. Depending upon its complexity, function can be specified as *tasks* (locomotor, nonlocomotor, and object manipulation), *problem-solving processes* (skills, strategies, rules, interpersonal relations), or *lead-up activities* (games, drills, relays, races, or routines). Figure 7.6 shows the process of (a) specifying a function; (b) selecting a target task; (c) analyzing the task into variables, factors, and levels; and (d) determining the conditions requisite to success.

Ecological task analysis can be applied to planning, assessment, or instruction. These are often interwoven and occur simultaneously rather than sequentially. Whenever possible, the student is involved in each step.

In explaining the theory underlying task analysis, Davis and Burton (1991) emphasized that ETA focuses on relationships between the learner and the ecosystem, not on parts. Thus, ETA creates new relationships as variables, factors, and levels are altered to enhance success.

Table 7.5 shows that, ultimately, many factors and levels compose the conditions requisite to performing self-care, play, or work functions. **Condition** is defined as the combination of relationships that students must handle to be successful in real life. For example, to play simple ball games, they must cope with changing speeds and directions of the other players as well as the ball. If outdoors, they must also cope with variable ground, lighting, and sound relationships.

Instructional objectives, to be effective, must specify conditions. If the *function* is to play a tennis lead-up game and the *task* is to strike a ball, then the *objective* might be *"Given*

T a b l e 7 . 5 Illustrative ecological task analysis.

Variables	Factors	Levels
1. Ball	Size	Large, medium, small
	Momentum	None, slow, fast
	Height	Waist, higher, lower
2. Model or demonstration	Type	Live, videotaped
	Age	Same age, older, younger
	Pattern	Forehand, backhand
3. Verbal instructions	Duration	Short, medium, long
	Timing	Concurrent, before
4. Reinforcers	Type	Verbal, smile, touch
	Timing	Immediate, delayed
	Frequency	Every trial, every three trials

certain conditions, the student will strike a tennis ball over the net so that it lands inside the boundary lines." The conditions might be (a) a regulation racquet, (b) an outdoor court with good surface, (c) 15 trials not facing the sun and 15 trials facing it, (d) wind factor not more than 10 mph, and (e) balls directed at slow and medium speeds so that they land in front of the student into three areas designated as midline, left, and right. Conditions in a terminal objective should be as close as possible to the normal game setting.

Assessment and ecological task analysis are interwoven in the adaptation process of moving the student from entry to exit level. For most beginners in racquet sports, for example, the easiest ball-size level is large. The easiest momentum level may be none, so practice consists of running three steps forward and striking a suspended motionless ball. Waist high is the easiest height level for most persons. Teachers involve students in helping to select the easiest levels and then summarize findings into a prescription that describes the entry-level condition and specifies number of practice trials. For some variables, there is general agreement about a complexity continuum from easy to difficult. However, what is easy for one person may not be easy for another. Therefore, assessment encompasses cooperative teacher-student problem solving to determine the order in which tasks are taught.

Generalization

Classroom learning is meaningless if generalization does not occur. **Generalization** refers to the transfer of learning from one piece of equipment to another and from one setting to another. In students with intact intelligence, generalization usually occurs without specific training. When teaching students with MR, however, generalization should be built into task sequences. For example, a learning progression might read

1. Roll 10-inch rubber ball toward milk cartons.
2. Roll 10-inch rubber ball toward bowling pins.
3. Roll bowling ball toward bowling pins.
4. Roll bocce ball toward target ball.
5. Roll 10-inch rubber ball toward persons inside a circle (as in dodgeball).

Such tasks should be practiced on different surfaces (grass, dirt, floor) and in different environments (gymnasium, outdoors, bowling alley). Use generalization training to develop creativity in students. Repeatedly ask, "How many things can we make roll? How many places can we go to roll things? At how many targets can we roll things?"

Activity Analysis

Activity analysis is the process of breaking down an activity into the behavioral components requisite for success. In physical education and recreation, the activity to be analyzed is usually a game, sport, or exercise. The process can, however, be directed toward activities of daily living, leisure, or work. Whereas special educators and physical educators commonly use the terms *task analysis* and *activity analysis* interchangeably, therapeutic recreation specialists and occupational therapists prefer *activity analysis.* This is because they are concerned with the total activity, not just the motor skill and fitness requisites.

Activity analysis typically entails consideration of the three educational domains: cognitive, psychomotor, and affective. Table 7.6 presents an activity analysis for a simple tag game. This type of detailed analysis is needed in teaching games to students with severe disabilities. Note the use of a beanbag, squeaky toy, orange, or make-believe tail; a prop is usually necessary with children deficient in pretending skills; otherwise, they simply cannot understand the point of chasing and fleeing.

Prior to being taught the simple tag game described in Table 7.6, children should have learned games involving only one or two concepts: *stop-start,* as in "red light, green light," musical chairs, and follow-the-leader, and *safety–not safety,* as in "Flying Dutchman" and "huntsman" (see Chapter 15). In developmental progressions for teaching games, tag is relatively difficult. Tag involves eight concepts: start-stop, safety–not safety, chasing, tagging, fleeing, dodging, penalty, and changing roles. When mental retardation is severe, each concept must be taught and practiced separately; then, chains of concepts must be practiced. Task and activity analyses are essential processes in the assessment and instruction of students with disabilities.

T a b l e 7 . 6   Behavioral requirements of a simple tag game: An activity analysis showing teaching progression.

Cognitive

1. Responds to name
2. Follows simple directions:
   a. "Sit down."
   b. "Stay."
   c. "Stand up."
   d. "Run."
3. Responds appropriately to cues:
   a. "Stop," "Start"
   b. "Good," "Bad"
4. Attends to teacher long enough to grasp game structure and rules:
   a. Visually
   b. Auditorially
5. Understands fleeing role:
   a. "You (Amy) have a beanbag, squeaky toy, orange, or make-believe tail."
   b. "Someone (Bob) wants it."
   c. "You (Amy) do not want Bob to have object."
   d. "You (Amy) run away from Bob when I give cue."
6. Understands chasing role:
   a. "Bob chases you when I give cue."
   b. "Bob chases you until
      (1) you touch safety base or
      (2) he tags you."
7. Understands concept of safety base
8. Understands concepts of tagging, penalty, and changing roles
   a. "When tagged, the penalty is you must give Bob the object."
   b. "You change roles because you want the object (i.e., you chase Bob or someone else who has object)."

Affective

1. Has fun
   a. Is not frightened by being chased
   b. Is sufficiently involved that attention does not wander
   c. Smiles and/or makes joyous sounds
2. Shows awareness of others
3. Displays competitive spirit
4. Tags other person gently

Psychomotor

1. Performs motor skills
   a. Runs
   b. Dodges/ducks
   c. Tags
2. Demonstrates sufficient fitness
   a. Does not become breathless
   b. Does not develop muscle cramps

Devote a High Percentage of Time to Class Objectives

The principle of devoting a high percentage of time to class objectives emphasizes that every class activity should pertain to a particular objective on the student's IEP and IPEP. The average time allocated to elementary and secondary physical education is 30 and 50 minutes, respectively. This means that no time can be wasted. There should be no free time. If free time is promised as a behavior management strategy for being good, the free time should be structured as two or three choices of activity, each of which relates to instructional objectives.

Since the early 1980s, effective teaching in physical education has been assessed by examining teacher behaviors. Research indicates that teachers spend too much time on managerial tasks (about 25 to 30%) and on instruction (defined as demonstrating and explaining, about 30%), which leaves only

40 to 45% of class time for students to be actively involved in movement related to class or individual objectives (Siedentop, 1983). Following are categories of teacher behaviors used in analyzing use of time. Videotape yourself or have a friend observe and analyze how you spend your time by putting tally marks next to each observed behavior.

Teacher Behaviors

Teacher behaviors include the following:

1. **Managing:** Taking roll; making general announcements; giving directions about getting into formations, using equipment, or following safety rules; organizing activities and transitions; record keeping; attending to recording equipment, aides, or volunteers
2. **Instructing:** Demonstrating and explaining activities related to instructional objectives; conducting closure episodes related to objectives
3. **Monitoring:** Observing students but giving no feedback
4. **Feedback:** Responding to student words or actions that relate to instructional objectives (i.e., teacher responses to students who are engaged in assigned motor activity)
5. **Controlling:** Using disciplinary techniques directed toward off-task behaviors of students

Concerns About Teacher Behaviors

Most research shows that teachers talk too much and too long when giving initial instructions and that they spend too much time getting students into game formations, stations, or floor spots. Another common weakness, once students begin to practice or play, is to observe but not offer specific feedback. Effective teaching takes lots of energy because the teacher should be moving constantly from student to student, using their names, and giving specific praise and correctional feedback. Teacher movement around the room, location at specific intervals, and proximity to students are additional variables to assess. A good rule of thumb is to always be standing within a giant step of one or more students, close enough that they can hear feedback and establish eye contact. Another guideline is to blow the whistle or interrupt the whole class as little as possible, because such actions cause transitions in student attention and decrease on-task time (Vogler, van der Mars, et al., 1990).

Maximize Time-on-Task With Success

Time-on-task is defined as the actual number of minutes that a student is engaged motorically in activities related to his or her individual objectives. This variable is often called **Academic Learning Time–Physical Education (ALT-PE)** because the curriculum and instruction subdiscipline uses this abbreviation (DePaepe, 1985; Vogler, van der Mars, et al., 1990; Webster, 1987). Success is defined in various ways but usually refers to (a) the student and teacher feeling good about the learning process, (b) mastery or observable improvement, and (c) agreement between the student and the teacher that a personal best is occurring or has been exerted. Following are categories of student behaviors that can be used in assessing how students use class time.

Student Behaviors

Student behaviors include the following:

1. **Management responses:** Following teacher instructions pertaining to class routines and activities that do not provide practice of motor skills, fitness, games, or other objectives (e.g., listening for roll call, getting out or putting away equipment, moving to stations or getting into formations)
2. **Knowledge assimilation:** Receiving information or instructions pertaining to objectives
3. **Time-on-task:** Engaging in tasks related to objectives (a) with success (implying appropriate), and (b) without success (implying inappropriate)
4. **Waiting:** Unoccupied or inappropriately occupied time between turns or beginning of new activity
5. **Time-off-task:** Time spent not engaged in the activity in which student should be engaged

Concerns About Student Behaviors

Research indicates that time-on-task is low compared to other categories (Vogler, van der Mars, et al., 1990), largely because of teaching behaviors. The principle of maximizing student time-on-task should be given high priority. Support for this principle is the central theme of several curricular models (e.g., ACTIVE, Every Child A Winner, You Stay Active).

Research has documented that several strategies do increase time-on-task; these should be used as much as possible. Individualized instruction within a mainstream setting, for instance, increases time-on-task (Aufderheide, 1983). The use of peer tutors (DePaepe, 1985; Webster, 1987) and of specific feedback and reinforcers (Webster, 1993) also increases time-on-task.

Of particular concern is how integration of students with severe disabilities into regular classrooms affects the time-on-task of students with and without disabilities. Physical education research concerning this issue indicates that students with severe disabilities need extensive support services when taught in mainstream settings (DePaepe, 1985; Vogler et al., 1992). For example, Vogler et al. (1992) reported that behaviors of students with severe disabilities were significantly less motor-appropriate and more off-task than those of nondisabled peers and that the experience level and expertise of teachers seemed to make no difference in this finding. Special education research tends to find comparable levels of engaged time for students with and without severe disabilities (e.g., Hollowood, Salisbury, Rainforth, & Palombaro, 1994), but high levels of support services are present in such studies.

Although time-on-task is important, be aware that the underlying assumption that students learn by repetition deserves consideration. The amount of practice and the type of practice (massed vs. distributed; blocked vs. random) is specific to individual students and tasks. **Massed practice** is continuous (with very little rest, less than 5 sec between trials), until a criterion is reached, and is associated with pure part and progressive part instruction (Weld & Evans, 1990).

FIGURE 7.7 Dr. Laurie Zittell of Northern Illinois University teaches early childhood students movement creativity. The challenge is "How many things can you do with scarves?"

Distributed practice is intermittent or episodic, with breaks for rest or different content.

When whole or whole-part-whole pedagogy is used to teach a new skill to students without disabilities, *distributed* practice is considered better than massed; *short* practices are better than long; and *frequent* practices are better than infrequent. Little is known, however, about how students with disabilities respond to different kinds of practice, although some research has focused on blocked versus random order of tasks and indicates that random order of presentation is better (Painter, Inman, & Vincent, 1994; Porretta & O'Brien, 1991).

Emphasize Variability of Practice and Contextual Interference

The essence of teaching students who are clumsy or have disabilities is captured in the motto *Try another way* (Gold, 1980). Success-oriented physical education depends on the collaborative creativity of the teacher and students in practicing skills in as many ways as possible and trying alternative pedagogies and adaptations until the best way for a particular individual or group is found (see Figure 7.7).

Research indicates that having students practice at many levels (e.g., large, medium, small balls; short, medium, long distances) and under variable conditions leads to success

(Eidson & Stadulis, 1991; Weber & Thorpe, 1989). This is called the **variability of practice principle.**

Closely associated with the variability of practice principle is **contextual interference,** a motor learning term for testing memory by involving persons in an unrelated activity between skill practice time and retention testing time. The unrelated activity is the contextual interference. An example is when you come to class ready to take a test, but your professor gives a lecture the first half of the period and the test the second half. The lecture, filled with new material, interrupts your concentration on the old facts; it serves as contextual interference.

Blocked Versus Random Trials

To understand the difference between blocked and random trials, suppose you wish to teach beanbag or soft shot throwing at a floor target. When a regulation soft shot and target are used, this task is an official cerebral palsy sport for individuals with severe disabilities (see Chapter 25). You need to prescribe the types of throws (underarm, overarm, and side or hook), the number of trials, and the order of the trials. A good decision might be 15 trials of each type of throw every day for 6 weeks. In a **blocked condition,** students would perform all trials of one type of throw before practicing the next type of

Table 7.7   How creative are you?

Regulation Round Balls That Vary in Size, Weight, Texture	Homemade Projectiles	Projectiles of Varying Shapes
Baseballs	Beanbags: 3 × 3 inches, small;	Airplanes (paper, cloth)
Basketballs	5 × 5 inches jumbo	Arrows
Boccia balls	Clay	Balloons
Bowling balls	Cork	Beanbags (soft shots)
Cage balls: 18, 24, 30, 36, 48, 60 and	Felt	Beans
72 inches	Foam	Clubs
Croquet balls	Leather	Coffee can lids (plastic)
Golf balls	Nerf ball	Coins
Field hockey balls	Nylon sock, stuffed	Darts
Lacrosse balls	Paper crumpled into ball	Discs
Marbles	Plastic: Ping-Pong balls, scoop balls,	Footballs
Medicine balls: 4–5 lb, 6–7 lb, 8–9 lb,	whiffle balls	Frisbees
11–12 lb, 14–15 lb	Rubber	Hoops
Playground balls: 5, 6, 7, 8 1/2, 10,	Snowballs	Horseshoes
13, and 16 inches	Sponge	Javelins
Racket balls	Velcro-covered yarnballs	Lemmi sticks
Rhythm balls: 3¼-inch		Paper plate Frisbees
Soccer balls		Peas
Softballs: 9, 10, and 12 inches		Pucks: shuffleboard, ice hockey
Table tennis (Ping-Pong)		Rings (quoits): plastic game rings,
Tennis ball		embroidery hoops, canning rubbers
Tetherball		Rocks (pebbles)
Volleyball		Shots: iron or plastic
Water polo ball		Shuttlecocks
		Yardsticks

throw. In a **random condition,** students would practice each type of throw in a random order, with no type performed more than two times consecutively. Research indicates that students in a random practice condition tend to develop accuracy in the target toss more quickly than students in a blocked condition do (Painter et al., 1994).

Contextual Interference, Retention, and Transfer

After skill practice each day, a good strategy is to provide a **contextual interference activity** for about 10 minutes during which students play a game that does not necessarily use the skills just practiced. Then a **retention test** is given (e.g., two trials of each type of throw at the target) in either random or blocked order. This allows the teacher to check whether the skill level achieved during practice is retained. Usually random order is prescribed in retention tests because most game situations call for random responses. A **transfer test** is also often administered; this is a test that uses the new skill in performing a novel task. In this example, a novel task might require transfer of learning from beanbags and a floor target to the use of balls to knock down a bowling ball.

Ecological Task Analysis, Movement Education, and Creativity Theory

Ecological task analysis (ETA), movement education, and creativity theory all offer pedagogy that supports variability of practice. Each of these approaches emphasizes exploring the many different ways a task can be performed and encouraging students to make choices with respect to the use of their body parts, objects, and equipment.

Two traits of creativity—fluency and flexibility—are important in variability of practice. Conceptualize a movement education session in which you want every student to have a ball or projectile of some kind. They do not all have to have the same kind. How many different kinds can you think of? **Fluency** is your ability to generate a large number of relevant responses. When you thought of different kinds, did you vary your ideas with respect to size, weight, shape, color, texture, and composition? **Flexibility** is your ability to shift categories and think of different kinds. Table 7.7 gives a sampling of the fluent and flexible responses you might have made.

Having thought of numerous alternatives, the next step is to match balls and projectiles with the students' abilities. A student who has coordination problems needs something big and soft. One with grasp and release problems (cerebral palsy) might do best with a yarn or Nerf (sponge rubber) ball. A student who is blind needs an object with a bell or noisemaker in it, whereas a student who is visually impaired simply needs a bright color like yellow. Someone in a wheelchair can profit from a string attached to the ball to facilitate recovery, whereas a hyperactive or high-energy student can enjoy a "crazy ball" with unpredictable bounces and great distance capacity.

Next, pretend that you have a class of 10 students, each with a different disability, but all needing to work on objectives pertaining to throwing. Your assessment records reveal that the students represent all the different stages of throwing ability. Specific objectives to be worked on have been circled on each student's assessment form. In this kind of setting, the more projectiles the students experiment with, the more likely it is that their skills will generalize from one game or sport to another. The important thing is that the students do not get bored, that each has a maximum number of trials to practice, and that each experiences some success.

Developing throwing skills often takes 5 or 10 min of every class period for several weeks. How many different targets can you think of, and how will you organize your space for the different kinds of projectiles and targets? Appropriate degree of difficulty is essential to both success and motivation. How can you change projectiles and/or targets to organize stations for students needing easy, medium, or difficult learning progressions? The number of different kinds of targets you conceptualize is a measure of fluency. If your targets are of different colors, sizes, shapes, heights, widths, and materials, you have demonstrated good flexibility (the ability to think of different categories). If some of your targets make noise or fall down when they are hit, you are more likely to maximize on-task practice time. Have you devised moving as well as stationary targets? Targets that integrate story, television, or movie themes are a measure of originality. If these have a lot of detail, lending themselves to different scoring systems, you have demonstrated elaboration.

So now you have targets! How many different kinds of games can you devise for teaching and practicing throwing? How many different scoring systems can you think of? How many ways can a student experience success? Try applying this process to teaching other motor skills. Will it work in the development of specific play and/or social skills?

Individualization and Variability

Instruction can be individualized through creative teaching and/or adapting pedagogy, content, and environment to specific needs of students. The individualized education program (IEP) required by law is based on the belief that teachers are creative. Individualization does not mean teaching one-to-one, but changing classroom organization and pedagogical approaches to meet the needs of individuals.

Integration of students with disabilities into regular physical education tends to make classes more *heterogeneous* (encompassing wide individual differences). Integration does not necessarily increase heterogeneity with regard to psychomotor abilities, however, since students in regular classes have always displayed a wide range of motor abilities. Some students with disabilities are better in motor ability than their nondisabled peers. Mental retardation (MR), learning disabilities (LD), and emotional disturbances (ED) primarily affect heterogeneity in cognitive and affective behaviors (i.e., actual game behaviors like rules, strategies, sportsmanship). Sensory impairments primarily affect mode of presentation and enhancement of environmental stimuli.

All in all, integration within the gymnasium setting affects group dynamics and interpersonal relationships more than actual motor teaching and learning. Individual differences generally intensify problems of classroom management, motivation, and discipline. *Teachers of mainstream physical education must be excellent— more competent in every respect than regular physical educators with students of the same or similar ability levels.*

No longer is good physical education a teacher standing in front of the entire class and instructing all students simultaneously on the same skill. With the trend away from ability grouping in all educational settings (not just physical education), the role of teaching is changing from information giver to learning facilitator. Most mainstream physical education seems to function best in classes organized as *learning stations* with an adult teacher aide, a peer tutor, or a cross-age tutor responsible for each station (Jenkins & Jenkins, 1981).

The mainstream physical educator then moves from station to station, giving attention and assistance as needed. Much of the mainstream teacher's work must be completed before class: reviewing assessment data; developing *task cards* for individuals, pairs, and triads and *learning plans* for stations; and teaching (in-servicing) aides and student leaders. Unless teachers are allowed planning periods for such management tasks, mainstreaming is apt to function less than smoothly.

Try a Wide Variety of Strategies and Techniques

Many strategies and techniques can be used to individualize and personalize instruction to achieve desired outcomes. Among these are learning stations; task cards, videotapes, and computer technology; peer teachers; and teachers who are athletes with disabilities.

Learning Stations

Learning stations may vary according to the number of students assigned, permanency of assignment, nature of learning tasks, and type of teaching style. In an elementary school unit on games, for instance, the largest station may be the playing area for the game itself. Additionally, there should be two or three smaller learning stations (two to six persons in each) with different instructional objectives being implemented at each. A student who experiences a problem pertaining to a skill, rule, strategy, or interpersonal relationship (sportsmanship) during the game goes to the appropriate learning station for help (Figure 7.8). One station may be for motorically gifted students who do not need the game for skill practice as do their peers. Such athletes should have the opportunity for *new learning* of alternative skills/sports. Physical education should be primarily a time of *learning for everyone*, with practice (repetition) and competition occurring mainly after school and during weekends.

In an alternative gymnasium/playing field arrangement, the student might elect (or be assigned) to the same station for several days or weeks. A different sport, dance, or movement education activity is taught at each station. Peers and cross-age tutors can serve as teachers at the stations.

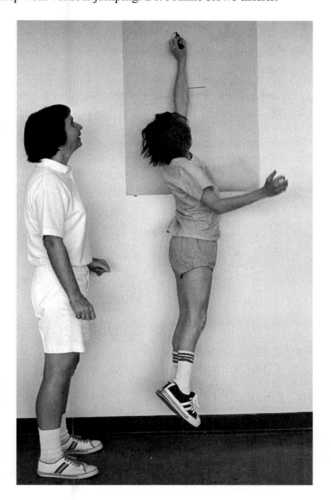

FIGURE 7.8 A student who exhibits jumping difficulties during a basketball game has rotated out of the game to a *learning station,* where he receives individualized help with vertical jumping. Dr. Joanne Rowe assists.

Occasionally, an adult athlete with a disability from the community can be recruited to teach a unit at a particular station, thereby serving as a model for students and facilitating positive attitude change.

Still another classroom arrangement is rotation of students from station to station for learning different skills during the same period. Not all students have to rotate around all stations. The *direction* of rotation (counterclockwise), however, should be the same for everyone, to avoid confusion. The *time* for changing stations can be the same for everyone (on a set signal) or can vary according to individual differences in learning and completing task cards. For students for whom changing stations may be confusing or impossible without help, *buddies* can volunteer (or be assigned) as partners for the day or the unit.

Task Cards, Videotapes, and Computer Technology

Predeveloped learning materials are necessary for individualized and personalized physical education. These may be task cards that the student picks up as he or she enters class, audio-visuals as individualized learning packages or modules that the student can carry along, or an infinite variety of other materials. Computers are already within the price range of some school districts and increasingly will be used to record IEPs, behavioral objectives, and progressive, day-by-day achievements of students. Videotapes can capture trial-by-trial performance and provide immediate, personalized feedback for the student as well as assessment data that can be used later by teachers.

Peer Teachers

Peer teaching may be unidirectional or reciprocal. In the **unidirectional or traditional approach,** the teacher selects and trains students without disabilities to help peers with disabilities. Selection is an honor, and students must meet criteria and complete intensive training to qualify for the peer teacher role. In models like PEOPEL (Long et al., 1980) and Challenger Baseball (Castaneda, 1997), every student with a disability has a peer teacher, partner, or buddy. In regular physical education, only one or two students typically need peer tutors; these may come from inside or outside the class but should be required to complete training before assuming responsibility. In the **reciprocal or newer equal-status approach,** students take turns in the tutor and tutee roles (Mosston & Ashworth, 1986; Sherrill, Heikinaro-Johansson, & Slininger, 1994).

Students who have been peer tutors praise and encourage each other more, express more empathy, provide and ask for more feedback, and show evidence of more meaningful, interactive contacts than do students without such experience (Sherrill et al., 1994). The reciprocal peer teaching approach is based on the belief that students with disabilities should not be denied these benefits. Also, students without disabilities are more likely to perceive peers with disabilities as equal in status if they are exposed to reciprocal sharing of tutor responsibilities.

Special education research indicates that students with disabilities can be successful in reciprocal peer tutor roles in academic settings (Byrd, 1990), but no physical education research on this topic has been reported. Mosston and Ashworth (1986), however, fully describe reciprocal teaching for regular physical education and provide many examples of criteria sheets to guide peer interactions. Criteria sheets include the task broken down into sequential parts, specific points to check during performance, illustrations of the task, samples of verbal feedback, and reminders of the peer tutor's responsibilities. Central to the effectiveness of this style is good teacher monitoring and continuous refinement of peer tutors' verbal feedback skills.

Peer teaching is helpful in achieving many physical education goals, but it is especially associated with the goal of social competence and inclusion. See Chapter 9 for additional coverage.

Teachers Who Are Athletes With Disabilities

To be able to conceptualize themselves as self-determined adults, it is important that students with disabilities have opportunities to see individuals with similar disabilities in salaried positions of status. According to Bandura's (1977) self-efficacy theory, self-confidence can be facilitated by direct association with people who serve as models or by videotapes, books, pictures, posters, and other sources that feature models. This textbook emphasizes the employment of athletes with disabilities in as many roles as possible. Such individuals can teach motor skills, fitness, and other content to students with and without disabilities (see Figure 7.9).

Adapt Teaching Styles to Individual Needs

Teaching style is important to the learning success of all students. Muska Mosston, in 1966, revolutionized physical education pedagogy by describing a spectrum of 7 teaching styles and suggesting that teachers master all styles. Today, there are 11 teaching styles, and spectrum theory guides pedagogy (Goldberger, 1992). Mosston emphasizes that teaching style should match the needs of students and, thus, vary from group to group. The ultimate goal, however, is to progressively increase the student's responsibility for his or her learning by moving from the command and practice styles to learner-initiated and self-teaching styles. Mosston's concept provided the stimulus for Figure 7.10, which presents a simplified spectrum of teaching styles appropriate for adapted physical activity.

The command teaching style is usually prescribed for students with severe mental retardation, severe learning disabilities, severe emotional disturbance, autism, severe hyperactivity or distractibility, and inner or receptive language deficits. Four basic principles guide the creation of a learning environment for the command teaching style:

1. Use optimal structure.
2. Reduce space.
3. Eliminate irrelevant stimuli.
4. Enhance the stimulus value of specific equipment or materials.

Table 7.8 describes in detail the optimal teaching procedures within each style. Particular attention is given to the learning environment itself and to starting and stopping protocols. In the mainstream setting, different teaching styles may be in operation at the various learning stations. The same teaching style the child experiences in other subject areas should be used in physical education. Especially for students with severe disabilities, such *consistency* is imperative.

Teaching styles to a large extent determine educational environment (Mosston & Ashworth, 1986, 1990). The IEP should prescribe the teaching style for which the student is ready. The guiding principle is to facilitate progress from the teaching style and environment that are most restrictive (command style) to the one that is least restrictive (motor creativity). Some children who need *optimal structure* and lack the ability to cope with freedom (manage their own behaviors) may remain at the command or traditional skills level throughout their schooling. Others, who have no cognitive, perceptual, or behavior problems, may enter the spectrum at the guided discovery level.

FIGURE 7.9 Dr. Abu Yilla, of the University of Texas at Arlington, challenges a child to take the ball away from him in a modified keep-away game.

FIGURE 7.10 Sherrill's spectrum of teaching styles, based on concepts of Mosston & Ashworth (1986). The variables that the teacher manipulates to create different teaching styles are learning environment, starting and stopping routine, presentation mode, and practice of execution mode. See Table 7.8 for suggestions.

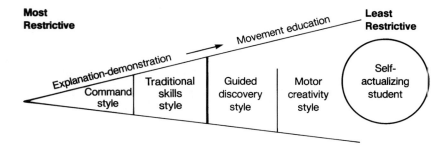

T a b l e 7 . 8   **Four teaching styles, reflecting increasing freedom for learners.**

Situation	Least Freedom		Most Freedom	
	Command Style	*Traditional Skills Style*	*Guided Discovery Style*	*Motor Creativity Style*
Learning environment	Small space/ Clearly defined boundaries/ Floor spots/ Circles and lines painted on floor/ Equipment always set up in same location/ Cubicles available	Normal play space/ Clearly defined boundaries/ No floor spots/ Regulation sport markings painted on floor/ Equipment at different stations	Space varies/ Boundaries clearly defined, but space changes with each problem/ Imaginary floor markings/ Equipment moved freely	Determined by student within the limits imposed by school rules and regulations about use of space and equipment
Starting routine	Student goes to assigned floor spot or station and sits/ Waits for teacher to give *start* cue	Student goes to space of own choice and warms up/Warm-ups may be prescribed as a set routine for each piece of equipment *or* Warm-ups may be created or chosen freely by student	Same as traditional skills approach except that student assumes responsibility for own warm-ups, explores alternative ways of warming up, discovers best warm-ups for self	Determined by student within the limits imposed by school rules and regulations about use of time
Presentation of new learning activities	Teacher states objectives/ Teacher designates student leaders/ Teacher puts students into formation/ Teacher gives directions: One task presented at a time, accompanied by demonstrations	Teacher states objectives/ Students choose own leaders/ Teacher puts students into formation/ Teacher gives directions: Several tasks presented at a time, accompanied by demonstrations	Teacher states objectives/ Teacher establishes structure in form of questions designed to elicit movement/ Teacher offers *no* demonstration; stresses that there is no one correct answer, and reassures pupils that no one can fail	Student states objectives/ Student establishes own structure, poses original movement or game questions
Execution	**Student** Practices in formation prescribed by teacher/ Starts on signal/ Moves in unison with peers to verbal cues, drum, or music/ Stops on signal/ Rotates or changes activity on signal; in same direction (CCW)	**Student** Chooses own space or formation for practice/ Chooses own time to start/ Moves in own rhythm/ Chooses own time to stop/ Rotates or changes activity when chooses; in same direction (CCW)	**Student** Finds own space/ Chooses own time to start and stop/ Moves in own rhythm/ Finds movement responses to teacher's questions/ Considers movement alternatives/ Discovers movement patterns most efficient for self	**Student** Finds own space/ Chooses own time to start and stop/ Moves in own rhythm/ Finds movement responses to own questions through creative processes
Feedback	**Teacher** Moves about room/ Offers individual praise/ Identifies and corrects movement errors by verbal *cues* and modeling	**Teacher** Moves about room/ Offers individual praise/ Identifies and corrects movement errors by *questions* that evoke answers from students	**Teacher** Moves about room/ Offers words and phrases of acceptance/ Poses additional questions to individuals/ Acquaints students with names of their movement discoveries	**Teacher** Moves about room/ Offers words and phrases of acceptance/ Mostly observes and shows interest/ Reinforces initiative

Note. CCW = counterclockwise; teacher may be an adult or a peer.

Table 7.9	Characteristics of teaching styles.
Least Freedom	**Most Freedom**
Teacher Dominated	**Student Dominated**
Assisted Movement	**Independent Movement**
Coactive/enactive	Self-initiated
Shaping/chaining	Exploring/creating
Homogeneous Grouping	**Heterogeneous Grouping**
Much structure	Little structure
Assigned floor spots	Free choice
Move on cue	Free choice
Drum or musical accompaniment	Own rhythm
Sameness	Role differentiation
Reduced Space	**Increased Space**
Decreased Stimuli	**Increased Stimuli**
One instruction	Several instructions
No equipment	Lots of balls/props
One "it"	Several "its"
One base	Several bases
Indoors	Outdoors
Enhanced Stimulus Intensity	**Weakened Stimulus Intensity**
Bright lights	Normal lighting
Loud signals	Soft, quiet signals
Colorful equipment	Regulation colors
Increased size balls, bases	Regulation size
Memorable texture	Regulation texture
Exaggerated teacher gestures and facial expressions	Normal teacher gestures and facial expressions
External Motivation	**Intrinsic Motivation**
Rewards/awards	No external rewards
Praise	Facilitating/accepting
Consistency of teacher	Flexibility of teacher

Table 7.9 summarizes the characteristics of most and least restrictive teaching styles for normal students. Remember that what is most restrictive for the normal student may be least restrictive for students with disabilities.

Behavior management is a pedagogy specific to the command teaching style. Because of its effectiveness in working with students with severe MR and ED problems, it is presented separately.

Apply Behavior Management Strategies

Behavior management is a precisely planned, systematic application of cues and consequences to guide students through tasks or activities that are ordered from easy to difficult. It is used in the functional teaching approach and comes from a philosophy and body of knowledge called **behaviorism.**

All humanistic teachers are, to some extent, behaviorists. This is because contemporary teacher education stresses such practices as (a) breaking goals down into behavioral objectives, (b) assessing students on observable behaviors, (c) task-analyzing activities to be taught and ordering them into easy-to-hard sequences, (d) matching instruction to spe-

cific assessed needs, and (e) carefully managing the learning environment to maximize desired behavior changes. These practices are important in humanistic teaching.

There are many forms of behaviorism. Followers of B. F. Skinner, who created operant reinforcement theory in the 1940s, today are called radical behaviorists (Bandura, 1986). These theorists believe that behavior is cued by the stimuli that precede it and shaped and controlled by the reinforcing stimuli that follow it. Originally, behaviorism did not recognize thought or cognition as a mediating variable. Neither did it consider self-concept or the affective domain. The theory had only three components: (a) a stimulus or situational cue, (b) a response or behavior, and (c) a consequence. Behavior management, based only on these three components, was mechanistic and presumably wholly dependent upon managing the environment.

In the 1950s, cognitive psychology or cognitivism began to replace stimulus-response psychology (Bell-Gredler, 1986; Hoover & Wade, 1985). As its name indicates, cognitivism centers on the mental processes involved in learning new skills and demonstrating appropriate behavior. The predominant cognitive model since the early 1970s has been information processing and the development of strategies to improve attention, memory, perception, and cognition. Most behaviorists today are cognitive behaviorists in that they recognize the role of thought in interpreting a stimulus and deciding on a response. A continuum thus exists between educators who focus on cues, consequences, and observable behaviors and those who concentrate on cognitive and/or affective processes.

Whereas cognitivism emphasizes attention, memory, perception, and cognition, behaviorism is concerned with the development and application of learning theories to weaken, strengthen, or maintain a specific behavior. In the real world of teaching, there is considerable overlap between use of instructional strategies to improve information processing and the application of behavior management principles to weaken, strengthen, or maintain specific strategies.

General Procedures

General behavior management procedures include (a) specify the desired behavior, (b) establish baseline performance by graphing the number of times the behavior normally occurs, (c) apply the intervention, and (d) continue graphing the number of times the behavior occurs to see if the intervention is effective—that is, the desired behavior increases in frequency.

Figure 7.11 illustrates the kind of graphing procedure used to record changes in play behaviors with toys and social interactions as the result of an **educational intervention.** The intervention in such programs is generally social reinforcement, attention, and praise for showing the desired behavior and no attention otherwise. While such graphing and recording of frequency of behavior is time consuming, the technique is used in many settings (Tawney & Gast, 1984; Watkinson & Wasson, 1984).

In Figure 7.11, one person was observed for 10 sessions to determine baseline interactions with peers and toys. On the IEP, this student's present level of performance,

FIGURE 7.11   Frequency of social interactions with peers and appropriate play behaviors with toys for a child over a 6-week period (30 sessions).

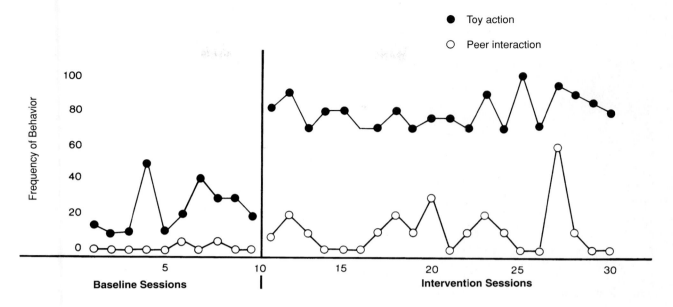

T a b l e   7 . 1 0   **Illustrative short-term objectives derived from baseline observations.**

Condition	Behavior	Criterion Level
While playing in a room with five to seven other children,	Joe will interact positively by initiating conversation, sharing a toy, or coactively using toys in episodes of at least 3 sec duration	for an average of 6 episodes per 5-min observation over 20 sessions.
While playing in a room with tricycle, jungle gym, slide, drums, balls, dolls, and toy cars and trucks,	Joe will interact with toys in appropriate ways for 3-sec episodes	for an average of 80 episodes per 5-min observation session over 20 sessions.

derived from the graph's baseline, was written as follows: (a) "Joe usually has no interactions with peers during play sessions (i.e., he is in the parallel play stage)," and (b) "Joe interacts with toys for about 20 sec out of every 5-min play period; the remainder of the time he stares into space, rocks, or watches others."

Using this baseline information, the teacher described Joe's desired behaviors in the form of short-term objectives, as depicted in Table 7.10. Then, during 20 sessions of intervention, Joe was given 10-min, specific lessons on how to interact with peers and toys, followed by 5 min of free play. Behaviors tallied and graphed during the free-play period (see Figure 7.11) show that Joe's peer interactions varied from 0 to 50, with an average of 7.75; Joe, therefore, achieved the first objective. With regard to the second objective, Joe's toy interactions improved tremendously, but not quite enough to meet the criterion level.

Cues and Consequences

Behavior management is based on the concepts of **cues** and **consequences,** the actions used by a teacher to change student behavior. Behavior management, in its strictest and most effective sense, demands a one-to-one relationship so that virtually every response of the student can have an immediate consequence. Nothing the student says or does goes unnoticed.

Cue is the behavior management term for a command or instruction telling a student what to do. Three rules should be followed in giving cues:

1. Make the cue as brief as possible in the beginning (i.e., "Sit" or "Stay" or "Ready, run").

2. Use the same cue each time.

3. Never repeat a cue until the student makes some kind of response. If correct response is made, reinforce. If no response or wrong one is made, use a correction procedure.

The correction procedure is to say, "No, that is not correct; do it this way," and then demonstrate again and/or take the student through the task coactively.

A **consequence** is the immediate feedback to a behavior that increases or decreases its occurrence (see Figure 7.12).

FIGURE 7.12 A basic principle of behavior management is *Catch 'em being good!* Authorities recommend a 5:1 praise/criticism ratio. When teachers issue a criticism or correct a motor skill, they should offer at least five praises around the class before criticizing anyone again.

For instance, for aggressive behavior (hitting, kicking, biting, and the like), the consequence should be punishment. For noncompliant behavior ("I don't want to"; "I can't"; "I don't have to"), the consequences should be ignoring the student's words or actions and, if appropriate, coactively taking him or her through the activity.

A consequence can be **reinforcement** (causing a behavior to increase), **punishment** (causing a behavior to decrease), or a **time-out** (ignoring inappropriate behavior, removal from a reinforcing environment, or withholding of reinforcers). Rules to be followed in enacting consequences are these:

1. Give immediate feedback to every response the student makes.
2. Accompany nonverbal reinforcement (food, tokens, hugs) with words or, for deaf students, signs.
3. Reinforce within 2 sec after a student responds correctly.
4. Ignore inappropriate behavior that affects only the student.
5. Punish inappropriate behavior that hurts others.

The use of consequences to teach or manage behavior is also called **contingency management**. A **contingency** is the relationship between a behavior and the events following the behavior. Giving **tokens** (or points) for correct responses or good behavior is a method of contingency management, providing the tokens are meaningful to the students and can be traded in on things or privileges of real value.

To encourage practice of motor skills, tokens are sometimes given for a set number of minutes or practice trials in which an individual, a team, or an entire class exhibits on-task behavior. **Response cost** is another method of contingency management. In it, points, tokens, or privileges are taken away when students fail to show appropriate behaviors.

In summary, behavior management pedagogy is based on four general concepts: **cues, consequences, task analysis,** and a **data-based gymnasium.** Most authorities consider behavior management the best pedagogical approach for instructing students with severe mental retardation, autism, and emotional disturbance. In the continuum of most to least restrictive teaching styles and environments, behavior management is least restrictive for students with severe problems, but, strictly applied in its entirety, is most restrictive for most students.

Specific Behavior Management Techniques

Although few physical educators have the student-teacher ratio necessary for using behavior management in its entirety, all good teachers use some behavior management techniques. Teaching a complex motor skill to normal students, for instance, requires the techniques of shaping, chaining, and fading. Reinforcement and punishment are integral parts of the structure of every classroom. Table 7.11 presents specific behavior management techniques commonly used in physical education.

Weave Counseling Into Teaching

Counseling is any teacher communication about a student's personal problem that is helpful rather than neutral or hurtful. Most counseling is based on cognitive psychology and incorporates tenets of attitude, self-concept, and motivation theory. This section is short because counseling techniques are woven throughout this text.

Characteristics of a healthy counseling relationship are active listening, understanding the other's point of view, acceptance, willingness to become committed and involved, and genuineness (Adams & Younger, 1988). There is a difference between hearing what is being said and understanding what is being felt. You need both skills. Taking the time to **actively listen** is a challenge that many busy teachers find difficult, but persons with disabilities need to be able to talk through problems related to movement and fitness, use of leisure time, and barriers that limit self-actualization through sport.

Techniques associated with active listening are (a) establishing and maintaining eye contact, (b) squarely facing the person who is talking, (c) maintaining an open posture (i.e., not crossing the arms or legs because these gestures suggest disagreement or closing out the speaker), (d) leaning slightly forward to show interest and involvement, and (e) appearing

T a b l e   7 . 1 1   **Specific behavior management techniques.**

Technique	Description
Shaping	Reinforcing small steps or approximations of a desired behavior; an analogy might be the praise "You're getting warmer" in the old game of finding a hidden object. Inappropriate or undesired behaviors are ignored.
Chaining	Leading a person through a sequence of responses, as is done in a task-analyzed progression of skills from easy to hard. The sequential mastery of a folk dance with many parts might also be considered chaining.
Backward chaining	Starting with the last step in the chain. For instance, in an overarm throw, the backward chain would begin with the release of the ball; then the forward swing of arm and release are practiced; and then the backswing, the foreswing, and the release are practiced. Usually, manual guidance is used in backward chaining.
Prompting	The cue or stimulus that makes a behavior occur. It can be physical, verbal, visual, or some combination of sensory stimuli. In physical education, prompting is usually the behavior management term for physical guidance of the body or limb through a skill.
Fading	The gradual removal of the physical guidance as the person gains the ability to perform the skill unassisted. It can be gradual reduction in any reinforcement that is designed to help the student become increasingly independent.
Modeling	The behavior management term for demonstrating.
Positive reinforcement	An increase in the frequency of a behavior when followed by an event or stimulus the student finds pleasurable. This term should not be confused with *reward*. Although a reward is pleasurable, it does not necessarily increase behavior.
Negative reinforcement	An increase in the frequency of a behavior as a result of removing or terminating something the student perceives as unpleasant, such as being ignored, scolded, or punished by teachers or peers or hearing a loud buzz every time a postural slouch occurs. Negative reinforcement is when students exhibit good behavior because they are intimidated or frightened by the consequence. In contrast, positive reinforcement is when students exhibit good behavior because they look forward to the consequence.
Punishment	The opposite of both positive and negative reinforcement. Punishment is anything that decreases the frequency of a behavior. A spanking, in the behavioral management context, is not punishment unless it decreases undesired behavior.
Extinction	Failure to reinforce (i.e., ignoring a response or behavior). It is a method of decreasing the frequency of a behavior. It can occur unintentionally, as when teachers are too busy or too insensitive to reinforce, or it may be done purposely to eliminate a previously reinforced response to make way for the teaching of a new behavior.
Premack technique	A method of reinforcement that involves pairing something a student likes with something the teacher wants him or her to learn or do. The promise of free play when work is done illustrates this technique.
Contract teaching	A method of ensuring understanding and agreement between student and teacher concerning what is to be learned. A contract is a written document signed by all parties concerned. It lists what is to be learned and the possible consequences of learning and not learning.
Time-out	Withholding of reinforcers, ignoring inappropriate behaviors, or removal from a reinforcing environment. When a game or activity becomes so stimulating to a student that he or she cannot control negative behaviors, there should be a quiet place to go. Time-out can be either required by a teacher or opted by a student.
Good behavior game	Refers to use of a group contingency approach in which all students are affected by the behaviors of each individual. Rules governing good behavior are in writing. The goal of the game is to accumulate points that can be used in buying a pleasant consequence (like free time or a field trip) agreed upon by majority vote. Points are gained by adhering to rules and are subtracted for breaking rules.

relaxed and comfortable. In counseling, the person being helped (the helpee) does most of the talking.

The following are three roles associated with active listening:

1. **Encourager.** During pauses, the listener says "Uh-huh," "Go on," "Yes," and "Then what happened?" This enables the student who is upset to calm down and gain perspective as he or she hears self and considers reasons and alternatives.

2. **Interpreter.** In this role, the teacher attempts to clarify and objectify the student's feelings by restating the student's words in a different way, more clearly and objectively. For example:

   Student: I know that everyone is always laughing at me because I am so clumsy and awkward. No one wants me on the team. I don't have many friends.

   Teacher: You resent the fact that your classmates seem to judge you on the basis of your athletic ability and not for who you are.

3. **Reflector.** The teacher responds with reflective statements that convey an understanding and acceptance. The role moves beyond paraphrasing into reflecting the feelings of the student and indicating that it is OK or normal to have such feelings. The teacher asks questions to help guide the student into positive thinking and problem solving. For example:

   Student: I hate being fat. I hate myself because I can't take control and do something about it.

   Teacher: Yes, lots of people feel that way. Have you considered asking a friend to help you? Who are some people who might tackle this problem with you?

During a counseling session, the teacher's attitude and responses should make it easier for a student to listen to himself or herself. When the student perceives that the teacher thinks that she or he is worth listening to, the student's self-respect is heightened. When another self (the teacher) can look upon the student's obesity, awkwardness, or lack of fitness without shame or emotion, the student's capacity to look at himself or herself grows. Realization that whatever attitude the student expresses is understood and accepted leads to a feeling of safety and the subsequent courage to test new ideas and try different methods of improving self.

Conferences with students should be held in a quiet setting where the teacher is free from interruption. Students should be assured that information will be kept in confidence. Two feelings are most important for optimal growth and positive change: (a) "I exist; therefore, I am lovable" and (b) "I am competent." Early conferences may be devoted to getting acquainted, finding common interests and values, and sharing ideas. An invitation to go fishing, take a walk, or eat out may contribute to the establishment of rapport more readily than formal interviews or conferences. Only when the student feels lovable and competent is he or she ready for preplanned regular counseling sessions.

Every word spoken by a teacher carries some meaning to the student. Likewise, shifts in postures, hand gestures, slight changes in tone, pauses, and silences convey acceptance or nonacceptance. Over 50% of the teacher's responses in a counseling session should fall into the reflection category. The teacher sets the limits on how long a session may last, but the student determines how short it can be. In other words, a student should feel free to terminate a session whenever he or she wishes.

Successes and failures in the gymnasium are accepted with equanimity. Neither praise nor blame is offered. The teacher uses words primarily to reflect what the student is feeling in a manner similar to that employed in the counseling session. On some occasions, the teacher may imitate the movement of the student, using this technique to reflect how the student looks to another and to reinforce the belief that others can accept the student and his or her movement as the best of which he or she is capable at the moment. Imitation of movements, performed without words, shows willingness to suffer what the student is suffering, to feel as he or she feels, to perform through his or her body, and to walk in his or her shoes.

Success in counseling is dependent upon the skill of the teacher in the following functions: (a) seeing the student as a coworker on a common problem, (b) treating the student as an equal, (c) understanding the student's feelings, (d) following the student's line of thought, (e) commenting in line with what the student is trying to convey, and (f) participating completely in the student's communication. The teacher's tone of voice is extremely important in conveying willingness and ability to share a student's feelings.

As counseling proceeds, the student should grow in self-acceptance. The following criteria may serve as one basis for evaluation: (a) the student perceives self as a person of worth, worthy of respect rather than criticism; (b) the student perceives his or her abilities with more objectivity and greater comfort; (c) the student perceives self as more independent and more able to cope with problems; (d) the student perceives self as more able to be spontaneous and genuine; and (e) the student perceives self as more integrated, less divided.

Leisure counseling is particularly important in helping persons with disabilities generalize skills learned at school to the community setting (Schleien, Meyer, Heyne, & Brandt, 1995; Taylor, 1987). This involves asking persons what they want to do during free time and helping them overcome environmental and personal constraints. Often, it is necessary to provide information about opportunities and resources; this can be done through field trips written into the IEP under transitional services and conducted as part of school physical education.

Counseling is very time consuming. Teachers need to know when and how to refer students for additional help. **Support or empowerment groups** are often as facilitative as one-to-one counseling (Chesler & Chesney, 1988).

The Evaluation Process

Evaluation consists of formative and summative processes that enable judgments about the effectiveness, efficiency, and affectiveness of service delivery. *Formative* and *summative* are terms that indicate *when* evaluation occurs. **Formative evaluation** is continuous examination that provides immediate input to decision makers and enables revision or reformulation on a day-to-day basis. **Summative evaluation** is systematic examination of a program during its final days or at its conclusion; it contributes to decision making about which program

FIGURE 7.13 Services included in the adapted physical activity delivery system.

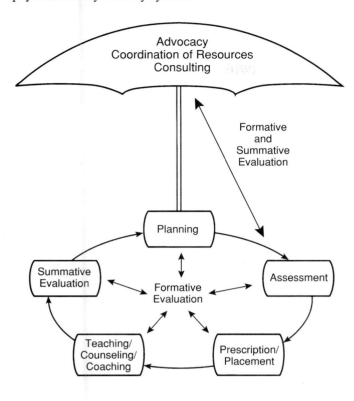

For the instructional model that guides this chapter, broad standards might be as follows:

1. **Inputs**
   a. People, environment, time, and opportunity inputs were considered in planning, assessing, and prescribing.
   b. Team approaches were used in the input process, and law and school policy were followed.
   c. Professionals involved in input decisions met high standards of professional preparation and performance.

2. **Processes**
   a. Teachers, students, and significant others collaborated in the implementation of major instructional principles.
   b. Resources and support services were sufficient for instruction to meet the criteria of effectiveness, efficiency, and affectiveness.

3. **Outcomes**
   a. Desired outcomes were achieved.
   b. Team approaches were used in evaluation.

A checklist for evaluating school district adapted physical education practice appears in Table 7.12.

Consulting/Coordination of Resources

Adapted physical activity consulting is a specialist role incorporating such multiple functions as (a) support services and team teaching to enable goal achievement; (b) adult education, including various forms of in-service education, parent training, and collaborative teamwork; (c) expert advice and specific administrative responsibilities, such as assessment or evaluation for a school district; and (d) identifying and coordinating resources for home-school-community and interdisciplinary cooperation.

Creating the Consultant Position

With the current trend toward interpreting the least restrictive environment (LRE) in physical education as the regular classroom, every school district needs one or more adapted physical activity consultants to assist regular physical education teachers. This is especially urgent at the elementary school level, where most instruction is conducted by classroom teachers rather than physical education specialists. Because adapted physical activity is a relatively new profession, strong advocacy is needed to increase the awareness of administrators, school board members, and parents of the benefits of building an adapted physical activity (APA) consultant-administrator into their budget. Following are three approaches to achieving this goal.

The 5L Model

Remember the 5L model of advocacy described in Chapter 4:

1. *Look At Me*—Providing examples and models
2. *Leverage*—Group action, such as recommendations from the parent-teachers association (PTA) and/or various teacher organizations or unions
3. *Literature*—Letters to the newspaper, articles in journals that administrators and parents read, awareness flyers, and so on

variables to keep the same and which to change. As a dynamical systems model, PAP-TE-CA includes both formative and summative evaluation (see Figure 7.13).

Effectiveness, efficiency, and affectiveness are criteria to guide evaluation (Idol, Nevin, & Paolucci-Whitcomb, 1994). **Effectiveness** refers to achievement of objectives. **Efficiency** refers to achievement of objectives in accordance with preestablished timelines, resource utilization, and cost. **Affectiveness** refers to whether service providers, receivers, and significant others enjoyed being involved in the program (this is assessed by self-reports).

Several models are available to guide program evaluation. See Sherrill and Oakley (1988) for a description of the four most popular models, and the new book *Empowerment Evaluation* (Fetterman, Kaftarian, & Wandersman, 1996) for futuristic ideas. The most popular model in adapted physical activity is the **discrepancy evaluation model (DEM)** of Provus (1971), and this is recommended for use in PAP-TE-CA service delivery. DEM calls for formative and summative evaluation of inputs, processes, and outcomes. This is why the instructional model (Table 7.2) that guides this chapter is organized by inputs, processes, and outcomes.

In DEM, evaluation involves

1. Agreeing on program standards or criteria
2. Determining whether a discrepancy exists between some aspect of the actual program and its standard(s)
3. Using this discrepancy information to identify and correct weaknesses in service delivery

T a b l e 7 . 1 2   Checklist for evaluating school district adapted physical education needs.

Instructions: First, check yes or no to indicate whether the item is a school district practice. Then rate the item in order of its importance to you. *The highest rating is 5.* Do not give all items an equal rating. Use the rating procedure to help you decide on the relative importance of each item.

Section 1: Assessment, Placement, and IEP Process

Yes	No	Importance		
___	___	5 4 3 2 1	1.	The school district has an effective screening program for the identification of students with motor and physical problems that need attention.
___	___	5 4 3 2 1	2.	The school district has specific eligibility standards for placement of students in adapted PE.
___	___	5 4 3 2 1	3.	Adapted physical education services are made available for all students with medical excuses that exempt them from *regular* physical education.
___	___	5 4 3 2 1	4.	The school district provides for a continuum of placements, including separate adapted physical education, partial integration in mainstream physical education, and full integration.
___	___	5 4 3 2 1	5.	Motor and physical ability assessment in the IEP process is done by a physical educator specially trained in motor evaluation who utilizes appropriate assessment tools.
___	___	5 4 3 2 1	6.	Specially trained physical education personnel participate in the IEP process and/or other interdisciplinary planning sessions concerning the education of students with disabilities.
___	___	5 4 3 2 1	7.	Appropriate physical education placement is agreed upon by school personnel and parents at the initial IEP meeting and at each program review thereafter.
___	___	5 4 3 2 1	8.	Medical excuses that exempt students from regular physical education classes are reevaluated/ renewed annually.
___	___	5 4 3 2 1	9.	IEPs include the present level of motor and physical performance, physical education goals and short-term objectives, and specific physical education services to be provided.

Section 2: Instruction and Programming

Yes	No	Importance		
___	___	5 4 3 2 1	1.	The school district provides evaluative criteria to guide administrators in monitoring the quality of adapted physical education service delivery.
___	___	5 4 3 2 1	2.	A curriculum manual describing physical education instruction and services for students with disabilities is available.
___	___	5 4 3 2 1	3.	When students with disabilities are integrated into regular physical education classes, the student–staff ratio is 30-to-1 or less.
___	___	5 4 3 2 1	4.	Adapted physical education classes designed specially for students with severe disabilities have a student–staff ratio of 5-to-1 or less.
___	___	5 4 3 2 1	5.	The content of adapted physical education classes is diversified and includes opportunities to learn movement patterns, games, sports, dance, and aquatics adapted to individual abilities.
___	___	5 4 3 2 1	6.	Physical education programming is based on IEPs that include present levels of motor performance, long-range goals, and short-term objectives.
___	___	5 4 3 2 1	7.	Students with disabilities in regular physical education classes receive attention and instruction comparable to what their peers receive.
___	___	5 4 3 2 1	8.	Students with disabilities are adequately prepared for optimal leisure and lifetime sports through school physical education programs.
___	___	5 4 3 2 1	9.	An education goal of physical education teachers is strengthening the self-concept of students with disabilities.
___	___	5 4 3 2 1	10.	The physical education curriculum for grades K–12 creates positive attitudes toward people who "differ" from the norm.

Section 3: Personnel

Yes	No	Importance	
___	___	5 4 3 2 1	1. The local school district employs at least one adapted physical education specialist *full-time* to provide assessment, IEP, and instructional services for students with disabilities and/or to assist regular educators in these tasks.
___	___	5 4 3 2 1	2. The number of qualified personnel available in the school district is sufficient to meet the physical education requirements in federal legislation.
___	___	5 4 3 2 1	3. Certified physical education teachers and/or adapted physical education specialists deliver physical education instruction and services to students with disabilities.
___	___	5 4 3 2 1	4. Administrators understand the competencies that adapted physical education specialists should possess and know who to contact for additional consultant and/or in-service training assistance.
___	___	5 4 3 2 1	5. Teachers of students with disabilities possess the necessary adapted physical education competencies and knowledges.
___	___	5 4 3 2 1	6. Regular physical education personnel are provided at least one in-service training session each year on adapted physical education by specialists in this area.
___	___	5 4 3 2 1	7. Teacher's aides are provided at least one session of in-service training each year by an adapted physical education specialist on instructional techniques.
___	___	5 4 3 2 1	8. Peer and cross-age tutors are used to *supplement* service delivery by regular and adapted physical education teachers.
___	___	5 4 3 2 1	9. Administrators encourage persons who teach physical education to attend professional meetings, workshops, and seminars in order to strengthen their adapted physical education competencies.
___	___	5 4 3 2 1	10. Persons with disabilities who have achieved success in sports, dance, or aquatics are employed as consultants, teachers, or aides and serve as role models for students with disabilities.
___	___	5 4 3 2 1	11. Persons who teach physical education are knowledgeable about federal and state legislation, policies, and guidelines regarding physical education for students with disabilities.

Section 4: Time Allocation, Equipment, and Facilities

Yes	No	Importance	
___	___	5 4 3 2 1	1. Secondary school students with disabilities receive at least 200 minutes of physical education instruction each week.
___	___	5 4 3 2 1	2. Elementary school students with disabilities receive at least 150 minutes of physical education instruction each week.
___	___	5 4 3 2 1	3. Kindergarten students with disabilities receive at least 100 minutes of physical education/motor development instruction each week.
___	___	5 4 3 2 1	4. Early childhood students with disabilities receive at least 100 minutes of physical education/motor development instruction each week.
___	___	5 4 3 2 1	5. Students with disabilities receive the same number of minutes of physical education/motor development instruction each week as students without disabilities receive.
___	___	5 4 3 2 1	6. Program resources (instructional materials, equipment, and media) are available for effective physical education instruction of students with disabilities.
___	___	5 4 3 2 1	7. Facilities used in physical education for students with disabilities are architecturally accessible.
___	___	5 4 3 2 1	8. Comparable facilities and equipment are allocated for instruction in physical education for students with and without disabilities.
___	___	5 4 3 2 1	9. School districts with an enrollment of 500 or more students have at least two sport wheelchairs as part of their permanent physical education equipment.
___	___	5 4 3 2 1	10. Community sport and recreation facilities and resources are used in joint school-community programs to promote transition goals.
___	___	5 4 3 2 1	11. Home sport and recreation facilities and resources are used in joint home-school programs to reinforce skills and fitness.

			Section 5: Ecological and Administrative Perspectives

Yes	No	Importance	
___	___	5 4 3 2 1	1. Administrators are knowledgeable about federal and state legislation, policies, and guidelines regarding physical education for students with disabilities.
___	___	5 4 3 2 1	2. Administrative personnel understand that adapted physical education services are separate and different from those provided by a physical, occupational, or recreational therapist.
___	___	5 4 3 2 1	3. Administrators are utilizing funding alternatives for hiring adapted physical education specialists.
___	___	5 4 3 2 1	4. Administrators in physical education and special education work together effectively in the promotion of physical education for students with disabilities.
___	___	5 4 3 2 1	5. Special educators and physical educators work together to develop optimal physical education programs for students with disabilities.
___	___	5 4 3 2 1	6. Physical education teachers of students with disabilities seek cooperation from and maintain communication with parents.
___	___	5 4 3 2 1	7. Parents of students with disabilities are made aware of adapted physical education services through a variety of techniques, including special meetings.
___	___	5 4 3 2 1	8. Physical educators provide special counseling on fitness, weight control, and the use of leisure time for students and their families to facilitate increased involvement in home and community activities.
___	___	5 4 3 2 1	9. Students with disabilities who can succeed in regular interscholastic athletics are given the opportunity to do so.
___	___	5 4 3 2 1	10. The school district works with parents and other groups in promoting Special Olympics and/or other special athletic programs.
___	___	5 4 3 2 1	11. Students with disabilities take field trips to recreation and health/fitness facilities in the community as part of their school physical education instruction.

4. *Legislation*—Involvement in bills and policies regarding taxation and how taxes and other resources are used

5. *Litigation*—Registering formal complaints and initiating due process hearings when students with disabilities are found sitting on the sidelines instead of receiving physical education instruction comparable to what their peers receive

The 5L advocacy model, properly implemented, is a team or partnership between parents and teachers to convince the power structure to allocate resources for the employment of an APA consultant-administrator as well as direct service delivery APA personnel. The strongest of the 5Ls is litigation, an action that only parents can initiate. Typically parent complaints and requests for hearings are resolved in the parents' favor without initiation of a lawsuit, but parents need knowledge about their children's rights, the characteristics of good physical education instruction, and the due process procedures to be used when these rights are violated.

Cowden Administrator In-Service Model

Another approach to convincing administrators to employ an APA consultant-administrator is to design action research directed toward changing attitudes and practices. Illustrative of this is a doctoral dissertation by Jo Cowden (1980), now a professor at the University of New Orleans, based on involvement of 25 administrators in the Fort Bend Independent School Dis-

trict (ISD) of Texas in 9 hours of in-service training (three half-day workshops) spaced over 3 weeks. Some pretest-posttest significant differences occurred in the 36-item administrator opinion survey (Cowden & Megginson, 1988), but the more important outcome was the decision by school district administrators to employ its first full-time adapted physical activity specialist.

Collaborative University/Public School Model

Another approach is for school districts in cities with universities to employ a full-time APA consultant-administrator to initiate and sustain collaborative planning on how resources of the public school and university can best be used to provide excellent school-based instruction for students with disabilities while concurrently meeting the need for high-quality, supervised, structured practicum experiences for university students. Denton ISD, in conjunction with Texas Woman's University, is pioneering in the development of this model, which is implemented by Ron French and Lisa Silliman-French, both of whom have doctorates in adapted physical education. This model is an outstanding example of the Look At Me strategy of the 5L advocacy model.

Performing Consultant Work

Consultants, of course, may be employed either part-time or full-time. Job descriptions vary considerably. Chapter 1 lists

FIGURE 7.14 Illustrative school district consultant model. (From P. Heikinaro-Johansson, C. Sherrill, R. French, & H. Huuhka (1995). Adapted physical education consultant model to facilitate integration. *Adapted Physical Activity Quarterly, 12*(1), 12–33.)

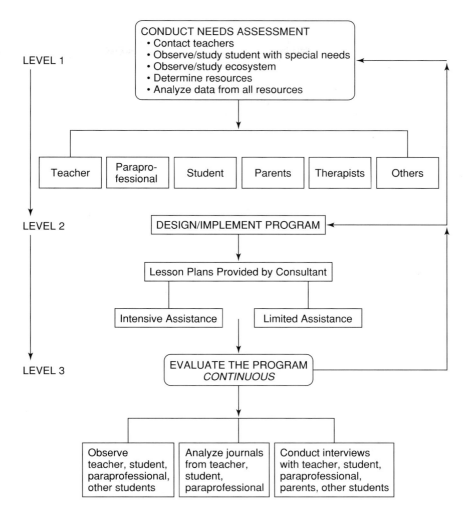

competencies that school districts should expect specialists to have. Figure 7.14 presents a consultant model, designed specifically to facilitate integration, that has been validated by research (Heikinaro-Johansson et al., 1995).

School district work typically begins with some kind of **needs assessment,** a special type of program evaluation based on ratings of program or school district conditions that exist and should exist. Following the collection of these "exist and should exist" data from teachers, paraprofessionals, students, parents, therapists, and others, a team of experts performs a discrepancy analysis, decides on the conditions that most need attention, and sets school district goals for change (Cowden, 1980; Heikinaro-Johanssen & Sherrill, 1994; Sherrill & Megginson, 1984).

Table 7.13 indicates the format of a needs assessment instrument. Illustrated are some items from an instrument called the Survey of Adapted Physical Education Needs (SAPEN), which was validated by five national experts and has alpha reliability coefficients of .73 to .91 on its various

scales (Sherrill & Megginson, 1984). The items composing a revision of SAPEN appeared in Table 7.12, which presented a simplified response format.

The SAPEN needs-assessment approach, which has been used in both the United States and Finland, is helpful in several ways. First, the discrepancy analysis data often convince school district administrators to employ additional adapted physical activity personnel. Second, if an APA consultant-administrator is already part of the school district team, the data provide direction for making needed changes and initiating some kind of intensive or limited assistance to regular physical educators.

In the **intensive assistance program** specified in Figure 7.14, every Monday a consultant delivered to a regular classroom teacher lesson plans that guided the integration of a 9-year-old boy in a wheelchair into regular physical education. On Tuesday, when the lesson plan was taught by the classroom teacher, the consultant observed her and the paraprofessional, collected videotape data to document the effectiveness of the

T a b l e 7 . 1 3   **Format of a needs assessment instrument.**

Survey of Adapted Physical Education Needs (SAPEN)

Give Your Opinion Now Exist							Give Your Opinion Should Exist					
6-Completely Agree	5-Mostly Agree	4-Slightly Agree	3-Slightly Disagree	2-Mostly Disagree	1-Completely Disagree	Please circle in the left-hand column the number that you feel best represents the services that *now exist* in your school district. Circle in the right-hand column the number that best represents your opinion about what *should exist*. IT IS CRITICAL THAT YOU CIRCLE A NUMBER FOR EACH ITEM IN EACH COLUMN. Once you are completed, double check to see if you have responded to every item using both columns.	6-Completely Agree	5-Mostly Agree	4-Slightly Agree	3-Slightly Disagree	2-Mostly Disagree	1-Completely Disagree
6	5	4	3	2	1	1. A curriculum manual describing physical education instruction/services for students with disabilities is available.	6	5	4	3	2	1
6	5	4	3	2	1	2. Elementary school students with disabilities receive at least 150 minutes of physical education instruction each week.	6	5	4	3	2	1
6	5	4	3	2	1	3. Administrative personnel understand that adapted physical education services are separate and different from those provided by a physical, occupational, or recreational therapist.	6	5	4	3	2	1

lesson and provided feedback to the teacher for improvement. On Thursday, the teacher and the paraprofessional taught the lesson a second time so that they had an opportunity to use the feedback. This procedure was followed for 2 months before the regular classroom teacher felt secure enough to agree to only monthly visits from the consultant.

In the **limited assistance program,** the consultant visited the regular classroom teacher only once a month. Lesson plans were supplied as in the intensive assistance plan, and the classroom teacher assumed responsibility for videotaping lessons for the consultant to see and evaluate. Frequent telephone contact was substituted for direct contact, but this approach was not nearly as effective as the intensive assistance plan.

Little research has been published on the use of consultants in physical education, although the literature is full of recommendations concerning the need for such specialists. Each consultant must experiment with approaches that fit her or his school district's resources. Continuous evaluation will supply feedback for refining service delivery.

References

Active Living Alliance for Canadians With a Disability. (1994). *Moving to inclusion.* Gloucester, Ontario: Author.

Aufderheide, S. (1983). ALT-PE in mainstreamed physical education classes. *Journal of Teaching in Physical Education, 1,* 22–26.

Balan, C., & Davis, W. (1993). Ecological task analysis: An approach to teaching physical education. *Journal of Physical Education, Recreation and Dance, 64*(9), 54–61.

Bandura, A. (1977). Self-efficacy: Toward a unifying theory of behavioral change. *Psychological Review, 84*(7), 191–215.

Bandura, A. (1986). *Social foundations of thought and action: A social cognitive theory.* Englewood Cliffs, NJ: Prentice Hall.

Bell-Gredler, M. (1986). *Learning and instruction: Theory into practice.* New York: Macmillan.

Boss, P. G., Doherty, W. J., LaRossa, R., Schumm, W. R., & Steinmetz, S. K. (1993). *Sourcebook of family theories and methods.* New York: Plenum Press.

Byrd, D. E. (1990). Peer tutoring with the learning disabled: A critical review. *Journal of Educational Research, 84*(2), 115–118.

Castañeda, L. D. (1997). *Perceived outcomes of participation in Challenger Baseball.* Unpublished thesis, Texas Woman's University, Denton.

Chesler, M., & Chesney, B. (1988). Self-help groups: Empowerment attitudes and behaviors of disabled or chronically ill persons. In H. E. Yuker (Ed.), *Attitudes toward persons with disabilities* (pp. 230–245). New York: Springer.

Cowden, J. E. (1980). *Administrator inservice training for program implementation in adapted and developmental physical education.* Unpublished doctoral dissertation, Texas Woman's University (ERIC #ED204-29B).

Cowden, J. E., & Megginson, N. (1988). Opinion and attitude assessment: The first step in changing public school service delivery. In C. Sherrill (Ed.), *Leadership training in adapted physical activity* (pp. 227–256). Champaign, IL: Human Kinetics.

Davis, W. E., & Burton, A. W. (1991). Ecological task analysis: Translating movement behavior theory into practice. *Adapted Physical Activity Quarterly, 8*(2), 154–177.

DePaepe, J. L. (1985). The influence of three least restrictive environments on the content motor-ALT and performance of moderately mentally retarded students. *Journal of Teaching in Physical Education, 5,* 34–41.

Devaney, R. L. (1989). *An introduction to chaotic dynamical systems.* Redwood City, CA: Addison-Wesley.

Dunkin, M. J., & Biddle, B. J. (1974). *The study of teaching.* New York: Holt, Rinehart & Winston.

Dunn, J., Morehouse, J., & Fredericks, H. (1986). *Physical education for the severely handicapped: A systematic approach to a data-based gymnasium* (2nd ed.). Austin, TX: Pro•Ed.

Eidson, T. A., & Stadulis, R. E. (1991). Effects of variability of practice on the transfer and performance of open and closed motor skills. *Adapted Physical Activity Quarterly, 8*, 342–356.

Fetterman, D. M., Kaftarian, S. J., & Wandersman, A. (Eds.). (1996). *Empowerment evaluation.* Thousand Oaks, CA: Sage.

Gleick, J. (1987). *Chaos: Making a new science.* New York: Viking.

Gold, M. W. (1980). *Try Another Way training manual.* Champaign, IL: Research Press.

Goldberger, M. (1992). The spectrum of teaching styles: A perspective for research on teaching physical education. *Journal of Physical Education, Recreation and Dance, 63*(1), 42–46.

Heikinaro-Johansson, P., & Sherrill, C. (1994). Integrating children with special needs in physical education: A school district assessment model from Finland. *Adapted Physical Activity Quarterly, 11*(1), 44–56.

Heikinaro-Johansson, P., Sherrill, C., French, R., & Huuhka, H. (1995). Adapted physical education consultant service model to facilitate integration. *Adapted Physical Activity Quarterly, 12*(1), 12–33.

Hollowood, T., Salisbury, C., Rainforth, B., & Palombaro, M. (1994). Use of instructional time in classrooms serving students with and without severe disabilities. *Exceptional Children, 61*(3), 242–252.

Hoover, J., & Wade, M. (1985). Motor learning theory and mentally retarded individuals: A historical review. *Adapted Physical Activity Quarterly, 2*, 228–252.

Hsu, P., & Dunn, J. M. (1984). Comparing reverse and forward chaining instructional methods on a motor task with moderately mentally retarded individuals. *Adapted Physical Activity Quarterly, 1*(3), 240–246.

Idol, L., Nevin, A., & Paolucci-Whitcomb, P. (1994). *Collaborative consultation* (2nd ed.). Austin, TX: Pro•Ed.

Jenkins, J., & Jenkins, L. (1981). *Cross-age and peer tutoring: Help for children with learning problems.* Reston, VA: Council for Exceptional Children.

Karper, W. B., & Martinek, T. J. (1985). The integration of handicapped and nonhandicapped children in elementary physical education. *Adapted Physical Activity Quarterly, 2*(4), 314–319.

Leuw, L. (1972). *Co-active movement with deaf-blind children: The Van Dijk model.* Videotape made at the Michigan School for Blind. (Available through many regional centers for the deaf-blind.)

Long, E., Irmer, L., Burkett, L., Glasenapp, G., & Odenkirk, B. (1980). PEOPEL. *Journal of Physical Education and Recreation, 51,* 28–29.

Mosston, M. (1966). *Teaching physical education.* Columbus, OH: Charles E. Merrill.

Mosston, M. (1992). Tug-o-war, no more: Meeting teaching-learning objectives using the spectrum of teaching styles. *Journal of Physical Education, Recreation and Dance, 63*(1), 27–31, 56.

Mosston, M., & Ashworth, S. (1986). *Teaching physical education* (3rd ed.). Columbus, OH: Charles E. Merrill.

Mosston, M., & Ashworth, S. (1990). *The spectrum of teaching styles: From command to discovery.* White Plains, NY: Longman.

O'Leary, K. D., & Schneider, M. R. (1980). *Catch 'em being good: Approaches to motivation and discipline* [film]. Champaign, IL: Research Press.

Owens, M. F. (1974). *Every child a winner.* Ocilla, GA: Irwin County Schools.

Painter, M. A., Inman, K. B., & Vincent, W. J. (1994). Contextual interference effects in the acquisition and retention of motor tasks by individuals with mild mental handicaps. *Adapted Physical Activity Quarterly, 11*(4), 383–395.

Porretta, D. L., & O'Brien, K. (1991). The use of contextual interference trials by mildly mentally retarded children. *Research Quarterly for Exercise and Sport, 62*, 244–248.

Provus, M. (1971). *The discrepancy evaluation model.* Berkeley, CA: McCutchan.

Rizzo, T. L., & Kirkendall, D. R. (1995). Teaching students with mild disabilities: What affects attitudes of future physical educators? *Adapted Physical Activity Quarterly, 12*(3), 205–216.

Rizzo, T. L., & Vispoel, W. P. (1992). Changing attitudes about teaching students with handicaps. *Adapted Physical Activity Quarterly, 9*(7), 54–63.

Schleien, S. J., Meyer, L. H., Heyne, L. A., & Brandt, B. B. (1995). *Lifelong leisure skills and lifestyles for persons with developmental disabilities.* Baltimore: Paul H. Brookes.

Sherrill, C., Heikinaro-Johansson, P., & Slininger, D. (1994). Equal status relationships in the gym. *Journal of Physical Education, Recreation and Dance, 65*(1), 27–30, 56.

Sherrill, C., & Megginson, N. (1984). A needs assessment instrument for local school district use in adapted physical education. *Adapted Physical Activity Quarterly, 1*, 147–157.

Sherrill, C., & Oakley, T. (1988). Evaluation and curriculum processes in adapted physical education: Understanding and creating theory. In C. Sherrill (Ed.), *Leadership training in adapted physical education* (pp. 123–138). Champaign, IL: Human Kinetics.

Siedentop, D. (1983). *Developing teaching skills in physical education.* Palo Alto, CA: Mayfield.

Smith, L. B., & Thelen, E. (Eds.). (1993). *A dynamic systems approach to development: Applications.* Cambridge, MA: MIT Press.

Solmon, M. A., & Lee, A. M. (1991). A contrast of the planning behaviors between expert and novice adapted physical education teachers. *Adapted Physical Activity Quarterly, 8*(2), 115–127.

Tawney, J. W., & Gast, D. L. (1984). *Single subject research in special education.* Columbus, OH: Merrill.

Taylor, M. J. (1987). Leisure counseling as an integral part of program development. *Canadian Association for Health, Physical Education, and Recreation Journal, 53*, 21–25.

Van Dijk, J. (1966). The first steps of the deaf-blind child towards language. *International Journal for the Education of the Blind, 15*(1), 112–115.

Vodola, T. (1976). *Project ACTIVE maxi-model: Nine training manuals.* Oakhurst, NJ: Project ACTIVE.

Vogler, E. W., DePaepe, J., & Martinek, T. (1990). Effective teaching in adapted physical education. In G. Doll-Tepper, C. Dahms, B. Doll, & H. V. Selzam (Eds.), *Adapted physical activity: An interdisciplinary approach* (pp. 246–250). Berlin: Springer-Verlag.

Vogler, E. W., van der Mars, H., Cusimano, B., & Darst, P. (1992). Experience, expertise, and teaching effectiveness with mainstreamed and nondisabled children in physical education. *Adapted Physical Activity Quarterly, 9*, 316–329.

Vogler, E. W., van der Mars, H., Darst, P., & Cusimano, B. (1990). Relationship of presage, context, and process variables to ALT-PE of elementary level mainstreamed students. *Adapted Physical Activity Quarterly, 7*, 298–313.

Watkinson, E. J., & Wasson, D. L. (1984). The use of single-subject time-series designs in adapted physical activity. *Adapted Physical Activity Quarterly, 1*(1), 19–29.

Weber, R. C., & Thorpe, J. (1989). Comparison of task variation and constant task methods for severely disabled in physical education. *Adapted Physical Activity Quarterly, 6*, 338–353.

Webster, G. E. (1987). Influence of peer tutors upon academic learning time-physical education of mentally handicapped students. *Journal of Teaching in Physical Education, 6*, 393–403.

Webster, G. E. (1993). Effective teaching in adapted physical education: A review. *Palaestra, 9*(3), 25–31.

Weld, E. M., & Evans, I. M. (1990). Effects of part vs. whole instructional strategies. *American Journal of Mental Deficiency, 94*(4), 377–386.

Wessel, J. A. (Ed.). (1977). *Planning individualized education programs in special education.* Chicago: Hubbard Scientific.

Wessel, J. A., & Kelly, L. (1986). *Achievement-based curriculum development in physical education.* Philadelphia: Lea & Febiger.

PART

II

Assessment and Pedagogy for Specific Goals

C H A P T E R

8

Self-Concept, Motivation, and Well-Being

FIGURE 8.1 Warm, subjective, human encounters with persons with disabilities in a variety of settings are essential to good self-concept. There must be quiet times to talk together, to listen, and to feel. *(A)* Dance instruction in a leotard is a part of normalization. *(B)* Risk recreation activities are as important for persons with disabilities as they are for the able-bodied. *(C)* Teachers cheer an athlete who is mentally retarded and has cerebral palsy on to victory.

A

B

C

After you have studied this chapter, you should be able to do the following:

1. Explain why and how self-concept should be included as a physical education goal in lesson plans and/or the IEP.

2. Discuss self-concept terminology, and explain how terminology is linked to assessment trends.

3. Discuss ways to assess the cognitive, affective, and behavioral dimensions of the self. Show your ability to write objectives related to assessment data.

4. Identify and discuss some standardized instruments that measure self-concept and related variables. Administer the sample instruments in this chapter, and discuss findings and implications for physical education.

5. Discuss self-concept strengths and weaknesses of individuals with disabilities (athletes and nonathletes) and individuals with movement difficulties, identify variables that affect self-concept, and explain principles you would apply in working with these individuals.

6. Describe the development of self-concept and changes that occur with age. Discuss the application of self-concept principles to various age groups.

7. Discuss the relationship between perceived failure in the physical activity setting, self-perceptions, and motivation (see Figure 8.10).

8. Explain implications of competence motivation, teacher expectancy, and attribution theories for teaching. Give particular attention to feedback.

The development of positive self-concept in relation to an active, healthy lifestyle is an important goal in adapted physical activity service delivery. Physical self-perceptions are clearly linked to mental well-being, motivational states, and goal achievement in exercise and sport (Fox, 1990, 1997; Robinson, 1990; Whitehead, 1995). Students with low motor skills and fitness particularly need physical education goals directly related to self-concept (see Figure 8.1). This goal area was delineated in Chapter 5:

> **Positive self-concept:** To develop positive feelings about the physical self; to increase understanding and appreciation of the body and its capacity for movement; to accept limitations that cannot be changed; to develop motivation to achieve personal bests; to adapt tasks and the environment to make the most of strengths (i.e., to work toward self-actualization).

The purpose of this chapter is to increase awareness of the importance of self-concept variables in lifelong physical activity success and participation; to develop competencies in assessment and writing goals and objectives; and to introduce principles, practices, and models that contribute to self-concept. It is hoped that this knowledge will encourage physical educators to assess and attend to self-concept needs.

Dynamical Systems Self-Concept Theory

Dynamical systems self-concept theory posits that cognitive, affective, and behavioral self-concept domains constantly interact with each other. Thus, knowledge about self influences attitudes and feelings, which in turn affect motivation and actions. The reverse is true also. Actual and perceived competence and appearance affect the way people set goals, feel about themselves, and cognitively construct their identities. Self-concept is thus multidimensional, dynamical, interactional, and nonlinear. Figure 8.2, which depicts this theory and basic self-concept terms, has multidirectional arrows.

Carl Rogers, the father of self-concept theory, did not use the term *dynamical systems*. However, he captured its essence by stating that self-concept is the central construct in teaching and provides the best perspective for helping persons to understand and change their behaviors (see Chapter 5).

Terminology and Assessment Approaches

Definitions of terms related to the self-concept goal area have changed considerably since the 1980s. New assessment approaches have switched the emphasis from global self-concept, which is difficult to measure, to specific self-concept domains like the physical self, social self, and scholastic self. Each of these can be further broken down into cognitive, affective, and behavioral dimensions as indicated in Figure 8.2. *Cognitive* refers to knowledge about self that is nonjudgmental. *Affective* refers to attitudes, feelings, and emotions that are associated with evaluation by self or others. *Behavioral* refers to thought and action that reflect motivation.

Today self-concept terminology is driven by assessment instruments and their underlying theories. When writing goals and objectives for students, be sure that your terminology matches that used in the instruments you are administering. Older instruments tend to use the terms *self-concept, self-esteem,* and *self-worth* as synonyms, but newer sources make sharp distinctions between these terms. Examples of many kinds of assessment instruments are included in this chapter.

Cognitive Dimensions of the Self

Cognitive dimensions of the self include self-concept, identity, level of aspiration, self-efficacy, and movement confidence. Individuals with cognitive limitations and/or movement difficulties have special needs in this area.

Self-Concept

Self-concept has two meanings, both of which are included in Figure 8.2. Traditionally, *self-concept* has been an umbrella term for all of the beliefs, feelings, and intentions that a person holds in regard to the self. The newer meaning of **self-concept** is observable or measurable knowledge that a person holds about the self. This includes awareness of the many identities,

FIGURE 8.2 Two definitions of self-concept: *(A) Self-concept* as an umbrella term that encompasses the cognitive, affective, and behavioral domains. *(B) Self-concept* delimited to mean only the cognitive or knowledge aspects of self within a dynamical systems model.

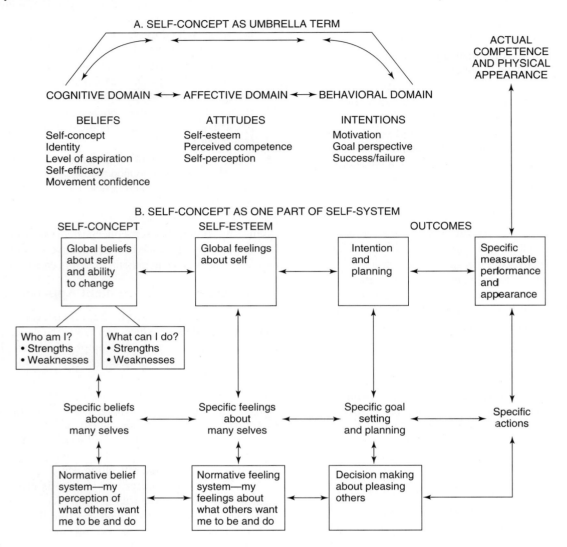

A. SELF-CONCEPT AS UMBRELLA TERM

COGNITIVE DOMAIN ⟷ AFFECTIVE DOMAIN ⟷ BEHAVIORAL DOMAIN

BELIEFS	ATTITUDES	INTENTIONS
Self-concept	Self-esteem	Motivation
Identity	Perceived competence	Goal perspective
Level of aspiration	Self-perception	Success/failure
Self-efficacy		
Movement confidence		

ACTUAL COMPETENCE AND PHYSICAL APPEARANCE

B. SELF-CONCEPT AS ONE PART OF SELF-SYSTEM

SELF-CONCEPT — SELF-ESTEEM — OUTCOMES

Global beliefs about self and ability to change ⟷ Global feelings about self ⟷ Intention and planning ⟷ Specific measurable performance and appearance

Who am I?
• Strengths
• Weaknesses

What can I do?
• Strengths
• Weaknesses

Specific beliefs about many selves ⟷ Specific feelings about many selves ⟷ Specific goal setting and planning ⟷ Specific actions

Normative belief system—my perception of what others want me to be and do ⟷ Normative feeling system—my feelings about what others want me to be and do ⟷ Decision making about pleasing others

roles, and competencies that contribute to personal uniqueness. This newer meaning encompasses everything in the cognitive domain, but particular attention has been given to identity, level of aspiration, self-efficacy, and movement competence.

Identity

Identity is self-knowledge about who one is, what one can do, and the selves, roles, and tasks most central in one's everyday decision making. For example, a woman might view herself as a professional, a spouse or partner, a daughter, a mother, a Catholic, a Democrat, a soccer player, a physically attractive person, a healthy individual, and an able-bodied (AB) self with average vision and hearing. Each of these selves implies different competencies and responsibilities. These many selves have unequal salience (prominence), depending on specific situations, demands, and expectations. To illustrate, make a list of all of your selves and then reorder the list into a hierar-

chy reflecting the five selves that are most central in your everyday use of time and energy. Try this activity with friends and students.

Unless they are taught to make health and physical activity central in their lives, many individuals give little attention to these dimensions of their identity. A major goal of physical education is therefore to teach understanding and appreciation of the physical self and specific behaviors for managing challenges, barriers, and losses that threaten to diminish the self. Especially important is helping persons to clarify the things they can and cannot change, to motivate them to change what they can, and to support them in learning to accept what they cannot change.

Individuals with disabilities have more complex identities than their AB peers because of the numerous ways disability interacts with other dimensions of the self (Levy-Shiff, Kedem, & Sevillia, 1990; Sherrill, 1997). Identity in the early years evolves largely in response to social feedback from family, caregivers, and teachers. The attitudes and behaviors of these persons determine whether children think of themselves in predominantly categorical ways (e.g., as disabled or nondisabled) or as multidimensional selves with many strengths and weaknesses. Societal ambivalence in feelings and actions toward people who are different complicates the formation of an integrated identity.

In identity theory, the opposite of integration is diffusion. Research indicates that individuals with disabilities have more **diffused identities** than their AB peers have. This is particularly true of females. Areas in which diffused identity is greatest are (a) feelings that life is uninteresting, empty, and meaningless; (b) mastery; and (c) physical self (Levy-Shiff et al., 1990). Identity theory is based on the works of Erik Erikson (1950, 1968). Ideally, as individuals progress through different life stages, their identity becomes increasingly integrated. This means that they become more confident in their knowledge of self, who they are, who they want to be, and how to reduce discrepancies between actual and ideal selves.

Physical education is most concerned with physical and social selves. Assessment should answer questions like these:

1. Do you see yourself as a couch potato, a recreational athlete, or an elite athlete? Why?
2. Do you see yourself as a daily exerciser, a 1-day-a-week exerciser, or as someone too inconsistent to have a clear exercise identity? Why?
3. Do you see yourself as a friend of people who exercise and engage in sports, or is your social identity primarily linked with nonactive people?
4. Do you have social supports for constructing an active, healthy lifestyle? Give examples.

Identity is linked also with competence, enjoyment, and cognitions concerning what one can and cannot do and what is fun and not fun. This can be assessed in many ways. Pairs of pictures depicting success and nonsuccess in movement activities can be presented to students, who point to the picture most like themselves. Pictures can also be used for a yes/no survey of activities a child can do or would like to learn and as a means of evaluating activities as fun or not fun. Individuals can also be challenged to tell or write all of the physical education things they can do or would like to do.

Teaching students to think about their physical education identity leads to an end product called **metacognition** (self-knowledge especially in regard to learning or mastery). Students with good metacognition can judge the level of their knowledge and skills and make wise decisions about ways to improve their learning and ensure their retention of facts and skills. Teachers can help by requiring problem solving through questions like these:

1. How many practice trials do you need on this particular task?
2. Do you want to stop practice on this task now or have one more trial?

3. How long do you plan to practice ball throwing tonight?
4. Who will you ask to practice this skill with you tonight?

Questions like these contribute to self-determination and empowerment and enhance metacognition.

Level of Aspiration

Level of aspiration is a self-stated, specific, numerical goal (like 8 out of 10 free throws or 30 sit-ups in 30 sec) that is set after a first performance of a task (Magill, 1993). Asking individuals to state their level of aspiration to a partner or to write it down typically improves performance. Individuals with cognitive limitations and/or movement difficulties, however, tend to overestimate or underestimate their abilities. Level of aspiration should therefore be considered a measure of both self-understanding and self-confidence. Students should be helped to understand and remediate discrepancies between level of aspiration and actual performance scores.

Level of aspiration can also be assessed by asking an individual to show you where he or she wants to stand when performing a throwing, striking, or kicking task at a target or asking the student to indicate what size target or ball she or he wants to use. This should be done in a one-to-one setting in which the student cannot be influenced by choices made by others. The "show me" approach is particularly useful with young children and individuals with limited verbal ability. Although level of aspiration, like other kinds of goal setting, is a cognitive ability, it can be used in making inferences about the self.

Level of aspiration is sometimes called **goal setting,** but level of aspiration denotes a specific goal for a specific task and thus is more like a daily teaching objective, except that it is set by the student immediately before performing a designated task. Level of aspiration promotes reciprocal communication between the student and the teacher or partner and helps keep communication focused on goals.

Self-Efficacy

Self-efficacy is "a judgment of one's capability to accomplish a certain level of performance" (Bandura, 1986, p. 391) or a situation-specific expression of self-confidence. This judgment is made after a goal or level of aspiration has been stated. After the student states a level of aspiration on a task, the teacher asks for an estimate of the student's degree of certainty of success on that task. Responses may be percentages (e.g., 30%, 70%, 90%) or categories (e.g., very sure, sort of sure, not very sure). For example, before a test, the teacher asks, "How confident are you that you can run a mile today in less than 12 minutes?"

The self-efficacy theory of Bandura (1986) was discussed in Chapter 5. Efficacy cognitions and expectations can be increased by providing models who have overcome similar problems and barriers, by structuring activities to assure mastery, by verbal persuasion, and by instruction aimed specifically at controlling anxiety and fear. Assessment should examine which of these approaches seems to work best for a particular person. Research indicates that self-efficacy

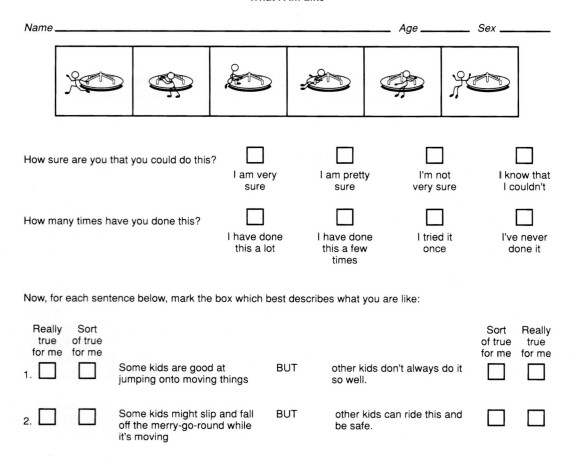

What I Am Like

Name _____ Age _____ Sex _____

How sure are you that you could do this?

☐ I am very sure   ☐ I am pretty sure   ☐ I'm not very sure   ☐ I know that I couldn't

How many times have you done this?

☐ I have done this a lot   ☐ I have done this a few times   ☐ I tried it once   ☐ I've never done it

Now, for each sentence below, mark the box which best describes what you are like:

Really true for me	Sort of true for me				Sort of true for me	Really true for me
1. ☐	☐	Some kids are good at jumping onto moving things	BUT	other kids don't always do it so well.	☐	☐
2. ☐	☐	Some kids might slip and fall off the merry-go-round while it's moving	BUT	other kids can ride this and be safe.	☐	☐

measures are good predictors of physical activity and sport behavior (Roberts, 1992).

Movement Confidence

Movement confidence is a combination of perceived competence, enjoyment, and risk that can be assessed by pictorial instruments like that depicted in Figure 8.3. Norma Griffin and Jack Keogh (1982) offer a movement confidence model that is of particular interest to adapted physical activity because it focuses on the assessment and remediation of fears and phobias often seen in gymnasium and play settings. Pictorial instruments are available for assessing children's self-confidence about performing on playground apparatus (Crawford & Griffin, 1986) and engaging in various stunt-type activities like rope climbing, skateboarding, and stilt walking (Griffin & Crawford, 1989). In the gymnasium and swimming pool settings, fears and phobias often arise.

This model indicates that, in coping with lack of self-confidence, three kinds of perception must be considered: (a) competence or adequacy, (b) enjoyment of moving sensations, and (c) harm or risk. There are two categories of the latter: (a) perceptions related to risk of personal injury and (b) perceptions related to the mental health factor of having to cope with unpleasant movement sensations. In helping students understand and work through fears of height, falling, dizziness, and other perceived risks, be aware of the separateness of these factors. The following formula summarizes the movement confidence model:

$$MC = (C - H1) + (E - H2)$$

where MC represents movement confidence, $C - H1$ represents perceived competence minus harm/personal injury factor, and $E - H2$ represents enjoyment minus harm/unpleasant movement sensation factor.

Movement confidence instruments can be obtained from Dr. Michael Crawford, Department of Parks, Recreation, and Tourism, University of Missouri, Columbia, MO 65211, or Dr. Norma S. Griffin, School of HPER, University of Nebraska, Lincoln, NE 68588.

Affective Dimensions of the Self

Affective dimensions of the self include self-esteem, perceived competence, and self-perceptions. Self-esteem is a global entity, whereas other terms are associated with instruments that yield separate scores for physical, social, scholastic, and other selves.

T a b l e 8 . 1   **The subscales comprising several inventories.**

Piers-Harris (CSCS): The Way I Feel About Myself	Martinek-Zaichkowsky Self-Concept Scale (MZSC)	Harter Self-Perception Profile: What Am I Like	Marsh Self-Description Questionnaire (SDQ)

1. Behavior
2. Intellectual and school
   status
	1. Behavioral, personal,
	   and social characteristics
		1. Behavioral conduct
		2. Scholastic
			Academic
			Math
			Reading
			General-school

3. Physical appearance
   and attributes
4. Anxiety
	2. Ability in games,
	   recreation, and sports
	3. Personality traits and
	   emotional tendency
		3. Physical appearance
		4. Athletic competence
			Nonacademic
			Physical abilities
			Physical appearance
			Peer relations
			Parent relations

5. Popularity
6. Happiness and satisfaction
	4. Home and family
	   relationships and
	   circumstances
	5. Satisfaction and happiness
		5. Social acceptance
		6. Close friendship
		7. Romantic appeal
		8. Job competence
		9. *Global self-worth*
			Global
			Total academic
			Total nonacademic
			Total self
			General-self

Note. See also Figure 8.4. The Harter profile is the only inventory of this group that *never* uses a total score; it thus reflects belief that global self-worth (the last item) is not the sum of the parts. Harter and Marsh use the term *global* in different ways.

Self-Esteem

Self-esteem is positive self-regard, self-worth, or overall good feelings about the self. Self-esteem is often called the evaluative component of the umbrella self-concept. Individuals with good self-esteem are believed to be free of depression, loneliness, state and trait mood disorders, and other generalized bad feelings. Some theorists distinguish between the terms **global self** (measured by a scale specifically designed to examine overall feelings) and **total self** (determined by adding together scores of all the specific self-perception subscales of an instrument).

Perceived Competence

Perceived competence is domain-specific self-esteem that relates to ability or skill to perform specific tasks. This relatively new term was popularized by Susan Harter (1985) of the University of Denver, who demonstrated that perceived competence can be measured and profiled in many different domains (e.g., scholastic, athletic, job, close friendships, social acceptance, romantic appeal, physical appearance, and behavioral conduct). Harter's first instrument, called the Perceived Competence Scale for Children, in 1985 was renamed the Self-Perception Profile for Children. Subsequently all of her other instruments, with the exception of a pictorial scale for ages 3 to 7, bear the term *self-perception* in the title rather than *perceived competence*.

Many researchers who use Harter's instruments, or who have developed new instruments based on Harter's protocol, continue to use the term *perceived competence*. Illustrative of these are the Perceived Competence in Soccer Skills Scale (Feltz & Brown, 1984) and the Ulrich Pictorial Perceived Physical Competence Scale (Ulrich & Collier, 1990). Use of the term *perceived competence* typically means that the individual subscribes to Harter's competence motivation theory, described later in this chapter. Briefly, the essence of this theory is that perceived competence (also called mastery) is the most important of the many social and psychological factors that influence the motivation to try new things and to persist in skill improvement activities.

Self-Perception

Self-perception denotes all kinds of self-referent evaluative statements, from global to situation-specific. Whereas Harter has developed one physical-domain self-perception scale (for athletic competence), Kenneth Fox in England and colleague Chuck Corbin in America (1989) have developed an entire instrument for the measurement of various aspects of the physical self (physical self-worth, sports competence, physical attractiveness, physical strength, and physical condition). This instrument, described later in this chapter, is called the Physical Self-Perception Profile (PSPP). It has been modified for use with British adolescents (Biddle et al., 1993) and for American adolescents (Whitehead, 1995). Fox (1997) increasingly is recognized as the father of contemporary physical self theory.

Behavioral Domain and Achievement

A discussion of self-concept terminology would not be complete without a definition of the behavioral domain, because all theories seek to link cognitive and affective aspects of self to motivation and/or achievement behaviors. For example, as we will see in a moment, Table 8.1 places the behavioral domain between the affective domain and an outcome column called actual competence and physical appearance. **Behavioral domain** is the broad term for the cluster of behaviors that relate to initiating and sustaining skill practice and fitness activity. These behaviors can be assessed directly by observation or inferred from various scales. When using observation, the teacher records incidents that document that "participants try harder, concentrate more, persist longer, pay more attention, perform better, choose to practice longer, and join or drop out of sporting activities" (Roberts, 1992, p. 6).

Achievement Goal Perspectives

Goal perspectives are personality orientations that motivate individuals to demonstrate competence and effort in specific contexts. Assessment can place most individuals into one of two goal perspectives: task orientation or ego orientation. These goal perspectives interact with self-concept dimensions in the lifelong construction of the self.

Task orientation means defining success in terms of achieving a personal best and the feeling of having invested all of one's personal resources in meeting a challenge or mastering a goal. Individuals with task orientation do not compare themselves with others. Their attention is completely focused on trying hard, practicing as much as possible, and making their best better.

Ego orientation means defining success by verifying that one is as good as or better than others. This process is called social comparison and is associated with competition. Persons with ego orientation are often insecure or have deep-seated feelings of inferiority. They might strive for a personal best, but feelings of task mastery are not enough to make them feel good about themselves. Feeling good is linked with being like others or achieving recognition as being better than others.

Success and Failure

The terms *success* and *failure,* often used in assessment and evaluation, denote psychological states based upon individualized interpretations of outcomes in relation to effort, personal investment, and enjoyment. Success is closely associated with feeling good about oneself, one's team, one's supports, or specific products and processes. **Products** can be task or ego oriented (I met my performance goal; I achieved a personal best; I came in second in the race; I won the free-throw contest). Likewise, **processes** can center on feeling good about mastering a task or demonstrating that one is as good as or better than one's peers.

In assessing and teaching for high self-esteem, teachers must carefully examine each student's definitions of success and failure. Always ask a student to explain her or his understanding of success and failure.

Assessment Issues

There are many standardized instruments with good validity and reliability for assessing self-concept and self-esteem. Most of these instruments have been normed, however, for use with individuals without a disability. A tremendous need exists for examination of the validity and reliability of instruments in relation to specific disabilities, age groups, and genders. This need, however, is probably no greater in the affective domain than in skill and fitness tests. Teachers should use their common sense in determining the validity of instruments and

should cross-check data yielded by the instruments with other kinds of observations, including interviews and diaries or journals. To assess reliability, teachers should administer instruments frequently and chart individual scores.

Authorities disagree on the age when self-concept can be measured. Some believe that an accurate estimate of feelings about concrete aspects of the self can be obtained at about age 4 or 5 years (Harter & Pike, 1984). Pictorial inventories in which the child chooses between two drawings ("Which one is more like you?") are typically used until about age 8 (i.e., the emergence of third-grade thinking and evaluation capacity). Thereafter, standardized written inventories are typically used unless disability makes pictorial measures preferable.

Other issues pertain to the nature of self-perceptions (whether they are unidimensional, multidimensional, or hierarchical). Older instruments are unidimensional, but the current trend favors multidimensional or hierarchical formats.

In **unidimensional self-concept theory,** the self is the sum of all of its parts. Items measure both being and doing selves, and every item contributes equally to the total score, which is considered an estimate of the general, total self. In Table 8.1, the Piers-Harris Children's Self-Concept Scale (CSCS) and the Martinek-Zaichkowsky Self-Concept Scale (MZSC) are illustrative of the unidimensional stance. Separate subscale scores can be calculated to guide goal setting, but the total score is always examined.

In **multidimensional self-concept theory,** the self is *not* the sum of all of its parts but rather a multifaceted structure that becomes increasingly complex. By about age 4, children have the ability to evaluate only *concrete aspects* of the self: physical competence, cognitive competence, peer acceptance, and parental acceptance. At about age 8, a separate, global self-concept can be measured. **Global self** is defined as *abstract feelings* of overall happiness and life satisfaction. In Table 8.1, the Harter scale is illustrative of a multidimensional philosophy.

In **hierarchical self-concept theory,** the idea of multidimensionality is extended by breaking the total self into major parts (e.g., academic and nonacademic) and then further analyzing each part into subcomponents. In Table 8.1, the Marsh Self-Description Questionnaire (SDQ) is illustrative of a hierarchical philosophy.

Examples of hierarchical self-perception instruments that are most relevant to physical education, however, are the Physical Self-Perception Profile of Fox and Corbin (1989); adaptations of this instrument for younger ages (Biddle et al., 1993; Whitehead, 1995); and an instrument used in Australia (Marsh, Richards, Johnson, Roche, & Tremayne, 1994). Figure 8.4 shows how Fox (1990) conceptualizes the hierarchy of global self-esteem, physical self-worth (PSW), and components of PSW.

Another self-concept issue is determining the major domains (dimensions, clusters, factors) of self-concept. Table 8.1, which lists the subscales included in four well-known

FIGURE 8.4 The hierarchical physical self-esteem model that guided the development of the Physical Self-Perception Profile.

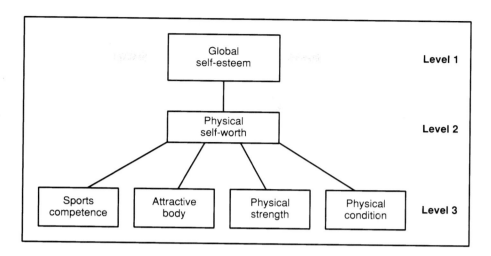

inventories, shows that there is general agreement about most (but not all) of the components. Physical educators must study both scales and items to decide which instruments are most appropriate for their needs. Most libraries have copies of the major self-concept manuals. Otherwise, they can be ordered from publishing companies (see Appendix E).

Assessment Protocol

Self-concept assessment early in the school year provides a way of getting acquainted with the whole student. Generally, students' estimates of their physical appearance, athletic competence, and social acceptance are good predictors of physical education interest and performance, so these measures are helpful in screening to find students who need special help.

Audiotapes, Videotapes, and Journals

Self-concept information should be used in personalized goal setting. Periodically, ask students to make audio or videotapes or develop journals or scrapbooks about who they are and what they can do at present, what they want for the future, and how physical education can help them become the self they want to be. This serves as the basis for setting goals, breaking goals into objectives, deciding on activities, and agreeing on evaluation methodology.

Another approach is to ask students to identify problems that physical education can help resolve and then check to see if the problems match self-concept data. Problems that students often list include these: (a) "My asthma [or other condition] makes me miss a lot of school and I feel left out," (b) "I don't have the energy to do what everyone wants me to do," (c) "I feel depressed or blah a lot of the time," (d) "I have a lot of friends but no really close friend—I want someone to like me better than anyone else," and (e) "I feel scared (high-strung, nervous) so much of the time." Many students need help in making the connection between physical activity and mental health, tension release, friendships, and energy.

Asking students to keep physical activity journals or diaries is a good technique. Such self-reports should include duration and intensity of activity, whether it was done alone or with people, what goals the activity was directed toward (e.g., fun, relaxation, losing weight), and whether the goals were achieved.

Standardized Instruments

Self-concept instruments should never be called *tests,* because this word traditionally infers right and wrong answers. Self-concept measures are called scales, inventories, or questionnaires. Students must understand that there are no right and wrong answers, only individual differences, and that these differences are what make us unique, wonderful, and interesting humans. Students also need to know that their responses will be held in confidence. If you feel that a student needs the services of a professional counselor, then the goal is to convince the student to go to a counselor and share. Never do the sharing for the student.

Profiling

The construction of individual profiles enables the teacher to sit down with a student, discuss strengths and weaknesses, and set physical education goals. Scores of average, same-age students help in the interpretation of profiles. Inventory manuals typically give this information. Average scores (means) on self-concept tend to run high. On a 4-point scale, the means tend to fluctuate around 2.9. On an 80-item instrument, the average usually ranges between 45 and 55. On a 25-item instrument, the average falls between 19 and 21.

Figure 8.5 shows how self-concept scores are profiled. The scores for an individual student are here compared with the average scores presented in the inventory manual for 14-year-olds (Harter, 1988). Consider what the dialogue between the teacher and this student might be. How can physical education help strengthen areas of weakness?

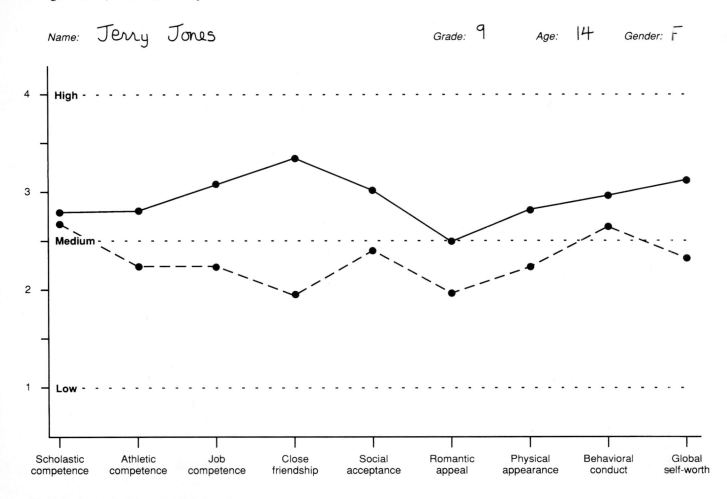

Name: Jerry Jones *Grade:* 9 *Age:* 14 *Gender:* F

Scholastic competence · Athletic competence · Job competence · Close friendship · Social acceptance · Romantic appeal · Physical appearance · Behavioral conduct · Global self-worth

Descriptions of Major Instruments

Familiarity with several instruments allows wise choices to be made in planning the physical education assessment model. Descriptions of several instruments that have good validity and reliability follow.

Piers-Harris Children's Self-Concept Scale

The Piers-Harris Children's Self-Concept Scale (CSCS), revised by Ellen Piers in 1984, is a widely used measure of self-concept in Grades 3 to 12. It includes 80 items written at a third-grade reading level and yields separate scores for six areas (see Table 8.1). The revised manual emphasizes, however: "The single most reliable measure for the *Piers-Harris,* and the one with the best research support, is the total score" (Piers, 1984, p. 37).

Illustrative items are "I have a pleasant face" and "I am among the last to be chosen for games." Respondents circle either *yes* or *no* for each item. The test manual for this inventory (Piers, 1984) is available from Western Psychological Services, 12031 Wilshire Blvd., Los Angeles, CA 90025. An advantage of the CSCS is availability of computerized scoring and interpretation, which generates profiles of strengths and weaknesses in six areas.

Cratty Self-Concept Scale

Bryant Cratty, a physical educator at UCLA, developed the Cratty Self-Concept Scale specifically to measure dimensions of self-concept that discriminate between clumsy and well-skilled children in kindergarten through Grade 6. Most of the 20 questions comprising this scale are rewordings of Piers-Harris items. Because this scale is especially recommended for use in movement settings, it appears in its entirety in Table 8.2

Scoring of the inventory is directed by common sense, with 1 point given for each *yes* answer that reflects a good self-concept. Cratty defined *high self-concept* as a score of 16 or over and *low self-concept* as a score of 14 or under. Average scores ranged between 14.1 and 15.7 for kindergarten through Grade 6, with no significant differences between grades or genders. This instrument is highly recommended for screening purposes.

Martinek-Zaichkowsky Self-Concept Scale

The Martinek-Zaichkowsky Self-Concept Scale (MZSC) was developed in 1977 by two physical educators, Thomas Martinek and Leonard Zaichkowsky, and has been used extensively in physical education research (Gruber, 1985). This pictorial

Table 8.2   Cratty Self-Concept Scale.

1. Are you good at making things with your hands?   Yes/No
2. Can you draw well?   Yes/No
3. Are you strong?   Yes/No
4. Do you like the way you look?   Yes/No
5. Do your friends make fun of you?   Yes/No
6. Are you handsome/pretty?   Yes/No
7. Do you have trouble making friends?   Yes/No
8. Do you like school?   Yes/No
9. Do you wish you were different?   Yes/No
10. Are you sad most of the time?   Yes/No
11. Are you the last to be chosen in games?   Yes/No
12. Do girls like you?   Yes/No
13. Are you a good leader in games and sports?   Yes/No
14. Are you clumsy?   Yes/No
15. In games, do you watch instead of play?   Yes/No
16. Do boys like you?   Yes/No
17. Are you happy most of the time?   Yes/No
18. Do you have nice hair?   Yes/No
19. Do you play with younger children a lot?   Yes/No
20. Is reading easy to you?   Yes/No

From B. Cratty, N. Ikedo, M. Martin, C. Jennett, & M. Morris, *Movement activities, motor ability, and the education of children.* (Springfield, IL: Charles C Thomas, 1970).

FIGURE 8.6   Sample item from the Martinek-Zaichkowsky Self-Concept Scale.

scale consists of 25 pairs of drawings (see sample item in Figure 8.6). Males and females are equally represented in the drawings. Six of the 25 items depict physical activities.

The MZSC is recommended for children in Grades 1 to 8 as a nonverbal, culture-free measure (Martinek & Zaichkowsky, 1977). Its pictorial format makes the MZSC especially valuable in assessing self-concepts of children who cannot read. Although the MZSC is designed as a nonverbal measure, explaining the items in individual and small-group administrations may be helpful. In regard to the sample item in Figure 8.6, for instance, you could say: "We see two children trying to do a push-up exercise. The child in the top picture has trouble doing the push-up. The child in the bottom picture is doing the push-up with ease. Which child is most like you?" Furthermore, when the inventory is administered individually, ask the child "Why?" or "How do you know that?" This is an excellent way to get acquainted with children and to cooperatively set goals for the year.

The MZSC is available from Psychologists and Educators, Inc., P.O. Box 513, Chesterfield, MO 63006. So far, most research has reported only total scores, but separate scores for five areas can be calculated (see Table 8.1).

Harter Self-Perception Instruments

Susan Harter and colleagues at the University of Denver have developed instruments for several different age groups (see Table 8.3). Additionally, there is an inventory specifically for students with learning disabilities in Grades 3 to 8 (Renick & Harter, 1988) that is appropriate also for normally achieving students. The items for athletic competence on this and the Self-Perception Profile for Children (Harter, 1985) are the

Table 8.3   Harter self-perception instruments.

Age Group	Self-Perception Instrument
4–7	Pictorial Scale for Perceived Competence and Social Acceptance for Young Children (Harter & Pike, 1984)—There are two versions of this instrument: (a) preschool/kindergarten and (b) first-/second-graders. For each, there are separate booklets for boys and girls.
8–13	Self-Perception Profile for Children (Harter, 1985)—This is a revision of the Perceived Competence Scale for Children, published in 1979.
Adolescents	Self-Perception Profile for Adolescents (Harter, 1988)
College students	Self-Perception Profile for College Students (Neemann & Harter, 1986)
Adults	Self-Perception Profile for Adults (Messer & Harter, 1986)
Ages 9–19 with learning disabilities (LD)	Self-Perception Profile for LD Students (Renick & Harter, 1988)—This is an adaptation of Harter (1985).

T a b l e 8 . 4 **Items that measure global self-worth from the Harter (1988) Self-Perception Profile for Adolescents.**

Really True for Me	Sort of True for Me		Items			Sort of True for Me	Really True for Me
1	2	9.	Some teenagers are often disappointed with themselves	BUT	other teenagers are pretty pleased with themselves.	3	4
1	2	18.	Some teenagers don't like the way they are leading their life	BUT	other teenagers do like the way they are leading their life.	3	4
4	3	27.	Some teenagers are happy with themselves most of the time	BUT	other teenagers are often not happy with themselves.	2	1
4	3	36.	Some teenagers like the kind of person they are	BUT	other teenagers often wish they were someone else.	2	1
4	3	45.	Some teenagers are very happy being the way they are	BUT	other teenagers wish they were different.	2	1

Note. Numbers show scoring system and should not be used on inventory given to students.

same except for simplification of wording on one item and deletion of one item.

Harter's instruments are all characterized by a **structured alternative-response format** (see Table 8.4). Only one box is checked. Students first indicate which of the two descriptions they are most like. Then, within this category, they check "Really True for Me" or "Sort of True for Me." This format reduces the chance that persons will give what they think are desirable responses rather than the truth.

Harter's instruments are different from most others in another way. From age 8 and up, one scale is designed to measure global self-worth. The global self-worth score is derived only from the five items in Table 8.4, and this score is considered separate from the domain-specific self-perception scores. Items on Harter's inventories are never added together to make a total self-concept score.

The number of domains measured increases for each age group. The pictorial scale for young children yields four scores: cognitive competence, physical competence, peer acceptance, and maternal acceptance. The childhood scale yields a global self-worth score and five domain scores: scholastic competence, social acceptance, athletic competence, physical appearance, and behavioral conduct. The adolescent scale measures the same things as the childhood scale, plus close friendship, romantic appeal, and job competence. The college and adult scales measure all of these areas plus more.

Harter uses the five items in Table 8.5 to measure perceived competence in sports and games. The numerical value of each box is included in these examples to help you understand how items are scored. On the forms administered to students, however, the boxes do not have numbers in them.

For young children and/or those who have difficulty reading, the pictorial format can be used to determine feelings about physical competence and to set goals. Harter uses six pairs of pictures for this purpose.

Harter's self-perception instruments, as well as other inventories related to her theory of competence motivation, can be obtained from Dr. Susan Harter, Psychology Department, University of Denver, 2040 S. York St., Denver, CO 80208.

Ulrich Pictorial Perceived Physical Competence Scale

Beverly and Dale Ulrich, physical educators at Indiana University, have extended Harter's pictorial scales to include 21 pairs of pictures in the Ulrich Pictorial Perceived Physical Competence Scale (see Figure 8.7 and Table 8.6). Like Harter, they have developed separate test booklets for boys and girls (Ulrich & Ulrich, 1990). This extended scale holds tremendous promise for learning more, not only about young children, but also about students who are mentally retarded and learning disabled (Ulrich & Collier, 1990).

Unlike the Martinek-Zaichkowsky pictorial instrument, which is described in the test manual as a nonverbal measure, the Harter-Ulrich approach requires that the pairs of pictures be explained to the student. Illustrative directions for Figure 8.7 are "This boy isn't very good at running." (Tester points to picture on the right.) "This boy is pretty good at running." (Tester points to picture on the left.) "Please point to the picture which is most like you." After the child points, the tester continues: "Are you a lot like this boy?" (Tester points to a big circle.) "Or are you a little like this boy?" (Tester points to a little circle.) "Which one?" The tester must be sure

Table 8.5 Items that measure athletic competence from the Harter (1988) Self-Perception Profile for Adolescents.

Really True for Me	Sort of True for Me	Items			Sort of True for Me	Really True for Me
4	3	3. Some teenagers do very well at all kinds of sports	BUT	other teenagers don't feel that they are very good when it comes to sports.	2	1
4	3	12. Some teenagers think they could do well at just about any new athletic activity	BUT	other teenagers are afraid they might not do well at a new athletic activity.	2	1
4	3	21. Some teenagers feel that they are better than others their age at sports	BUT	other teenagers don't feel they can play as well.	2	1
1	2	30. Some teenagers don't do well at new outdoor games	BUT	other teenagers are good at games right away.	3	4
1	2	39. Some teenagers do not feel that they are very athletic	BUT	other teenagers feel that they are very athletic.	3	4

Note. Numbers show scoring system and should not be used on inventory given to students.

FIGURE 8.7 Sample item from the Ulrich Pictorial Perceived Physical Competence Scale.

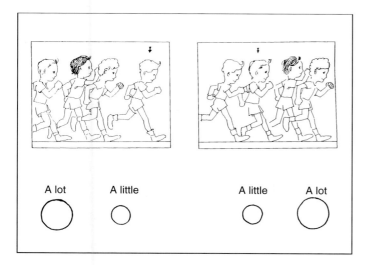

that the item is understood and should find out what kinds of experience prompt the response. Students should be asked: "Have you ever done this skill? When? A lot or a little? Who taught you? Do you like doing this skill? Is it fun?"

The Ulrich pictorial scale can be obtained from Dr. Beverly Ulrich or Dr. Dale Ulrich, Kinesiology Department, Indiana University, Bloomington, IN 47405.

Table 8.6 A list of the items included on the Ulrich Pictorial Perceived Physical Competence Scale.

Grade K	Grades 1 and 2
Harter's Original Six Pictorial Items	
1. Swinging	1. Swinging
2. Climbing on jungle gym	2. Climbing on jungle gym
3. Skipping	3. Skipping
4. Running	4. Running
5. Tying shoes	5. Bouncing a ball
6. Hopping	6. Jumping rope
Ulrichs' Additional Fundamental Motor Skill Pictorial Items	
7. Jumping	7. Jumping
8. Kicking	8. Kicking
9. Throwing	9. Throwing
10. Catching	10. Catching
11. Am strong	11. Am strong
12. Bouncing a ball	12. Batting a ball
Ulrichs' Additional Sport-Specific Skill Pictorial Items (Same for Grades K, 1, and 2)	
Baseball:	13. Batting a baseball
	14. Throwing a baseball
	15. Catching a baseball
Basketball:	16. Dribbling a basketball
	17. Shooting a basketball
	18. Passing a basketball
Soccer:	19. Dribbling a soccer ball
	20. Kicking a soccer ball
	21. Soccer throw-in

Self-Description Questionnaires

Herbert Marsh of Australia, with colleagues, has developed the Physical Self-Description Questionnaire (PSDQ) for individuals ages 12 and over as well as general self-concept instruments—the Self-Description Questionnaires I, II, and III (SDQ I, II, and III)—that include separate scales for the measurement of physical and appearance selves. These instruments all use a hierarchical model, following Marsh, who was a founder of this approach (Marsh & Shavelson, 1985).

The PSDQ measures 11 components: strength, body fat, physical activity, endurance/fitness, sport competence, coordination, health, appearance, flexibility, general physical self-concept, and self-esteem (Marsh et al., 1994). Of the 70 items, these are illustrative:

3. Several times a week I exercise or play hard enough to breathe hard (to huff and puff).
4. I am too fat.
5. Other people think I am good at sports.
6. I am satisfied with the kind of person I am physically.
7. I am attractive for my age.

Both the PSDQ and the SDQ instruments use a 6-point **Likert response format** varying from 1 (false) to 6 (true). Possible responses are these: false, mostly false, more false than true, more true than false, mostly true, and true. Although this response system seems complicated for individuals with cognitive disabilities, the SDQ-II has been shown to work with adolescents whose disabilities are mild (Widaman, MacMillan, Hemsley, Little, & Balow, 1992). Marsh has probably published more research on self-measurements than anyone else, and his instruments are widely used around the world.

The PSDQ and SDQ manuals and instruments are available from Dr. Herbert Marsh, University of Western Sydney, Macarthur, P.O. Box 555, Campbelltown, NSW 2560, Australia, fax (046) 28 5353. Marsh includes all the questionnaire items in many of his published articles (e.g., Marsh et al., 1994), but manuals are needed to know which items measure which components and to learn how to score.

Physical Self-Perception Profile (PSPP)

The PSPP, developed by Kenneth Fox and Chuck Corbin in 1989, is widely used in North America and England. The theoretical model underlying this instrument appeared in Figure 8.4, showing that four domains (sports competence, attractive body, strength, and physical condition/stamina) contribute to global physical self-worth (PSW), which in turn contributes to global self-esteem.

The PSPP consists of 30 items, 6 each for its four subscales and one global physical self-worth scale. Originally validated for high school students (Fox, 1990), the PSPP is now reported as valid for adults (Sonstroem, Speliotis, & Fava, 1992) and for children in Grades 7 and 8 (Whitehead, 1995). A slightly revised format called the Children's Physical Self-Perception Profile (C-PSPP) is recommended for Grades 7 and 8, and the actual profile items are included in the article by Whitehead (1995).

Scoring is by Harter's four-choice, structured, alternative-response scales, which are believed to reduce the **social desirability effect,** a term given the test-taking behavior of individuals who give answers they think the teacher wants rather than what they really believe about themselves. Table 8.7 provides a reminder of what the structured, alternative response format looks like as well as insight into how to measure the attractive body domain. The attractive body domain was chosen for illustration because it is the PSPP scale that best predicts, and thus contributes most to, global feelings of physical self-worth. Physical educators should use this scale early in the year and help students understand the relationship between class activities and development of an attractive body.

The PSPP can be ordered from the Office for Health Promotion, Northern Illinois University, DeKalb, IL 60115, or from Dr. Kenneth Fox, School of Education, University of Exeter, Heavitree Road, Exeter, England, EX1 2LU; fax (011) 44 392 264 706. A book edited by Fox (1997) and entitled *The Physical Self: From Motivation to Well-Being* is the most comprehensive source of information available on physical self-perception; this book includes a chapter on disability.

Disability, Self-Concept, and Self-Esteem

Before using the knowledge you have just acquired about assessment to write goals and objectives, it is important to consider what research tells us about disability, self-concept, and self-esteem. Disability, in this section, will include developmental coordination disorder, clumsiness, and awkwardness as well as traditional categories. Space does not permit discussion of individual studies, so two reviews of the research literature (Hutzler & Bar-Eli, 1993; Sherrill, 1997) serve as the primary sources for the information that follows.

Athletes With Disabilities

Almost all research on athletes with disabilities reports self-measures equal to or higher than those of individuals without disabilities. Research also indicates that athletes with disabilities have higher self-concepts than nonathletes with disabilities. Thus, the relationship between sport participation and self-esteem is clear, although statistics do not indicate whether sport caused the self-esteem or whether it existed already and was the prime motivator for becoming involved in sports. According to the dynamical systems or interactionist perspective, the relationship between sport participation and self-esteem is supported both by gains that occur during participation and by the motivation that prompts participation.

Basing their review of research on studies of general self-concept and self-worth, Hutzler and Bar-Eli (1993) concluded:

> In general, the studies reviewed reveal significant positive changes varying in intensity and duration in the self-concept of disabled populations after sports participation sessions. In addition, significantly higher values of self-concept were observed among

Really True for Me	Sort of True for Me	Items			Sort of True for Me	Really True for Me
4	3	3. Some people feel that, compared to most, they have an attractive body	BUT	others feels that, compared to most, their body is not quite so attractive.	2	1
1	2	8. Some people feel that they have difficulty maintaining an attractive body	BUT	others feel that they are easily able to keep their body looking attractive.	3	4
1	2	13. Some people feel embarrassed by their bodies when it comes to wearing few clothes	BUT	others do not feel embarrassed by their bodies when it comes to wearing few clothes.	3	4
4	3	18. Some people feel that they are often admired because their physique or figure is considered attractive	BUT	others rarely feel that they receive admiration for the way their body looks.	2	1
1	2	23. Some people feel that, compared to most, their bodies do not look in the best of shape	BUT	others feel that, compared to most, their bodies always look in excellent physical shape.	3	4
4	3	28. Some people are extremely confident about the appearance of their body	BUT	others are a little self-conscious about the appearance of their body.	2	1

Note. Numbers show scoring system and should not be used on inventory given to students.

disabled people regularly participating in sports compared with sedentary, inactive individuals. (p. 221)

From 1989 onward, researchers began to use Harter's various instruments (see Table 8.3). Findings reviewed by Sherrill (1997) included these:

1. Special Olympians in a 1½-day track meet showed higher gain scores than nonparticipants in perceived physical competence and social acceptance.

2. Special Olympians in unified sports developed increased abilities in social perception, which remained unchanged in the athletes in segregated sports. Neither group had an increase in physical self-perception or general self-worth.

3. Athletes ages 9 to 18 years old who participated in the first Pan American Victory Games for Physically Disabled Youth, in 1989, had mean scores for each of the Harter subscales within or very close to those reported for the able-bodied population.

Also reviewed by Sherrill (1997) was her extensive research on self-actualization of elite adult athletes with physical disabilities or visual impairments. Subscales of the self-actualization instrument specifically measured self-regard and self-acceptance. Findings revealed that all disability groups except females with cerebral palsy (CP) and males with visual impairments scored significantly higher on self-regard than norms for able-bodied (AB) individuals. In contrast, and causing surprise, all disability groups except females in wheelchairs scored significantly lower on self-acceptance than AB norms.

The findings support the idea that general self-esteem probably consists of two or more components. **Self-acceptance** was defined as affirmation or acceptance of self in spite of one's weaknesses or deficiencies; it relates to identity or the "I am" component of self. **Self-regard** was defined as affirmation of self because of worth or strength; it relates more to competence or the "I can do" self. Teachers and coaches should consciously work toward developing both types of self-esteem.

So far, only one researcher, Mary Flintoff (1994) of Ireland, has applied Fox's PSPP to athletes. Flintoff reported that both Paralympic and recreational athletes with cerebral palsy had high PSPP scores and positive attitudes toward their disability. Additionally, interview data indicated that all athletes perceived themselves as successful, regardless of whether they had been selected for international teams. In summary, considerable evidence indicates that athletes with disabilities have high self-perceptions. This finding can be used in advocacy for greater involvement of individuals with disabilities of all ages in home-school-community sport and activity programs.

Nonathletes (Ordinary People) With Disabilities

Findings about nonathletes' self-perceptions vary considerably depending on type of disability, age at onset of disability, severity of disability, number of years since onset of disability, gender, support systems, and attitudes and expectancies of significant others (see Figure 8.8). Factors exerting the most influence seem to be age at onset and severity of disability.

Congenital Disabilities

In general, research indicates that individuals with learning disabilities, cerebral palsy, or mental retardation have lower self-esteem than nondisabled peers. It is noteworthy that all of these conditions are congenital, and researchers comparing congenital and acquired types of disability consistently report lower self-concepts when the disability is congenital.

   The birth of a visibly different child affects all aspects of parenting and family relations. The more severe the disability is perceived to be, the more it tends to lower expectancies and to reduce the likelihood that the child will be treated like other children. Parents of such children tend to be overprotective, ambivalent in attitudes and child-rearing practices, and uncertain about how to access support systems. From age 4 onward, unless planned intervention promotes their acceptance, children who are different begin to experience social rejection and avoidance by peers. Patterns of sport socialization tend to be different from those for AB peers.

These and many other factors affect self-esteem and help to explain why individuals with congenital disabilities need special help with self-esteem.

Acquired Disabilities

Most physical disabilities are acquired through vehicular and other accidents, violence, disease, famine, and/or poor health and fitness practices. The older individuals are at the onset of disability, the more likely it is that their self-perceptions will be stable and resistant to permanent change. Because spinal cord injury typically occurs after age 16, most research on physical disability focuses on young adults. A person who experiences a spinal cord injury requires about 4 years for psychological adjustment. Comparisons of individuals who have had injuries for 4 or more years with AB peers indicate no significant difference in self-perception.

   In some research, persons with disabilities have higher self-perceptions than their AB peers do. This has been explained by the **growth through adversity phenomenon.** Successful coping empowers the development of an exceptionally strong, integrated sense of identity and competence. Coping is discussed later in this chapter because of its obvious importance in self-esteem.

   Variability in self-esteem among persons with physical disabilities parallels that of AB peers. The life experiences of persons before disability shape their self-perceptions, so no generalizations can be made about all or most people.

Acquired disability, by itself, does not permanently change global self-worth. Little is known, however, about physical self-perceptions of individuals of different ages with physical disabilities. When the onset of disability is during adolescence or other stressful times in life, help with self-esteem is an essential need (Levy-Shiff et al., 1990; Rosenberg, 1965).

Movement Difficulties in Able-Bodied Individuals

Many individuals considered to be able-bodied (AB) have movement difficulties severe enough to affect their self-perceptions, social interactions, and involvement in physical activity. Their conditions are variously called motor awkwardness, clumsiness, or developmental coordination disorder (DCD), but recent sources recommend the term *movement difficulties* as more supportive of self-esteem goals and practices (Bouffard, Watkinson, Thompson, Dunn, & Romanow, 1996).

Research concerning children and adolescents with movement difficulties indicates the following:

1. At ages 6 to 9, these children are more introverted than children without movement difficulties, are significantly more anxious, and have lower perceived physical competence and social acceptance than peers (Schoemaker & Kalverboer, 1994).

2. At ages 6 to 9, these children demonstrate different behaviors during recess than peers. Specifically, children with movement difficulties spend less time in positive social interactions, are vigorously active less often, and play less often on large playground equipment (Bouffard et al., 1996). This avoidance of activity contributes to lifestyles that give low priority to health and fitness, social supports, and skill development.

3. Gender, the importance attached to physical competence, and the interaction between awkwardness and grade are significant predictors of physical self-perceptions in Grades 3 to 6 (Dunn & Watkinson, 1994). Females have lower physical self-perceptions than males. Children who think physical competence is important tend to perceive themselves as good in this area. Severity of awkwardness leads to more self-perception problems in Grade 3 than in other grades, presumably because older children tend to discount evaluative input that is damaging to their self-esteem.

4. Almost 50% of children diagnosed as motor delayed at age 5 remain clumsy in adolescence. These adolescents differ significantly from peers in their perception of their athletic and scholastic competence but not in their self-perceptions regarding Harter's other competence domains (Cantell, Smyth, & Ahonen, 1994).

The findings of these and many other studies indicate that individuals with movement difficulties need pedagogy that specifically addresses their self-esteem. The strong relationship between physical self-perceptions, motivation in physical activity settings, social initiative, and mental well-being justifies adapted physical activity service delivery for these individuals.

Development of Self-Concept

Regardless of the age of individuals receiving adapted physical activity services, improving their self-concept should be a major goal. In infancy and early childhood, self-concept is difficult to separate from body image, because early feelings about the body and its capacity for movement form the basis for self-concept. Chapter 18 discusses body image goals and pedagogy for infants and toddlers.

Initially, self-concept is formed at home and includes only factors relating to home and family. By the second grade, however, the school and other interactions outside the home have begun to exert a major influence on self-concept formation. By this age, also, children with visible disabilities have come to realize that their appearance is different from that of their peers; this naturally affects their self-concept. Thus, with increasing age and experience, the ego identity of individuals expands to include more and more domains or dimensions.

The concept of the self also becomes more stable and resistant to change as persons grow older. With young children, day-to-day (and sometimes moment-to-moment) variability is a problem in self-concept measurement. It is easy to change the young child's mind about self or almost anything. Every experience causes fluctuations because the self is not yet integrated by a formal system of thought. Understanding of these facts guides teachers to assess self-concept several times rather than once. Then an average is recorded as the estimate of real self.

The issue of stability must also be considered in evaluating self-concept change. Before age 8 (or the equivalent mental functioning), significant change scores may be obtained as a result of special programs of short duration. To ascertain that such self-concept changes are permanent, it is necessary to assess again about 1 month later. After age 8, self-concept becomes increasingly difficult to change. Long-term, intensive programs in which family and school work together are most effective in causing change.

Age and sex differences in self-concept seem to depend on the assessment instrument. Many assessment manuals report that self-concept is highest in the first grade and then begins to decline, at least until the third or fourth grade, when it stabilizes. The high early childhood self-concept probably relates to immaturity of evaluation processes; the child has not yet begun to compare self to others. Old global self-concept instruments show no gender differences or only very small ones that are not interpreted as meaningful. Newer physical self-perception instruments indicate definite gender differences.

Progress from one life stage to another affects self-concept, because persons must meet new societal expectations and adjust to changes in body (e.g., puberty, old age) and abilities. The transition into adolescence, with its challenge to succeed in romantic and job realms, may cause fluctuations in self-concept. Likewise, changing one's comparison group, as in the shift from high school to college or from one job to another, affects self-concept.

The longitudinal development of self-concept in persons with disabilities and/or health problems has received little study. Much depends on coping skills, social support, and the intensity and duration of stress. The comparison group that a person uses in evaluating self also makes a big difference. A clumsy child in a class of good athletes may have lower physical self-esteem than a clumsy child in a class with peers of similar ability. On the other hand, placement outside the mainstream may cause feelings of inferiority.

General Principles of Self-Concept Enhancement

Five principles serve as guides to enhancing self-concept. Which of the following principles would you rely on the most as you teach differently abled students?

1. **Principle of Reflected Appraisals.** This principle emphasizes that children grow up seeing themselves as they *think* others see them. This has been called the looking-glass or mirror phenomenon. Every facial expression, gesture, and word of another is interpreted as having meaning for oneself. The more perceived significance of the other, the more influential the reflected appraisal. Because many persons do not interpret the feelings and actions of others accurately, you must work to assure real rather than distorted or denied perceptions.

   Reflected appraisal is feedback, and you must be aware of individual differences in sensitivity. Clarification is important: "I like you but I do not like this particular behavior." "You are a good person, but this behavior is not acceptable." Equally important is the principle "Catch'em being good" (O'Leary & Schneider, 1980). The more frequently you can see students doing something well or behaving in a thoughtful, caring, responsible way, the more often the reflected appraisal (both conscious and subconscious) will be positive.

2. **Principle of Self-Attribution.** This principle, derived from behavioral theory, states that past behavior (i.e., through feelings of efficacy or competency) affects the formation of self-concept. We make attributions about ourselves on the basis of our observations of a particular behavior. After eating a large meal, for instance, we think, "I was hungrier than I thought." After achieving a success, we infer, "Hey, I'm pretty good." Self-concept is thus based on analysis of overt behaviors and the circumstances under which they occurred. Implications for teaching are reminding students of past successes, encouraging analysis of reasons for success, and structuring situations so that the same conditions are present as when the remembered success occurred.

3. **Principle of Mastery Challenge or Perceived Competence.** This principle, derived from humanistic psychology, is future oriented, whereas the self-attribution principle is past oriented. *Mastery challenge* is the principle of making students feel safe, loved, and appropriately challenged so that they see themselves as competent before trying the task. If Maslow's hierarchy of needs is met by creating a warm, success-oriented environment, then persons are intrinsically motivated to reduce the discrepancy between what they can do and what they wish they could do. This is called the innate mastery challenge. Positive self-concept develops when

persons set goals (consciously or unconsciously), expect to be successful, and then validate their expectancies.

Shaping the environment so that Maslow's deficiency needs are met and persons perceive that they will be successful is a shared responsibility of everyone in the ecosystem; this is a holistic approach with everyone agreeing to provide social support. It also respects the freedom of a student to say, "I'm not ready yet. I want to do it but I can't by myself." This opens the way for teacher-student and peer partnerships based on the idea: "Trust me. I'll lead you through it. Together we can be successful. Then, when you are ready, you can try it alone."

4. **Principle of Social Comparison.** This principle, based on the social comparison theory of Leon Festinger (1954), states that self-concept is formed through the lifelong process of comparing oneself to others (see Figure 8.9). Between the ages of 5 and 7, children begin to make peer comparisons (I'm better, the same, or worse than others"). This information source becomes increasingly important, peaking at about ages 10 to 11. Thereafter, persons tend to develop predominantly either a task or an ego orientation. *Task-oriented* persons judge themselves in terms of effort ("I did the best I could"), whereas *ego-oriented* persons judge their self-worth by means of social comparison.

   Humanistic teaching tries to deemphasize social comparison and help persons feel good about their own ability and effort. Students are taught to monitor their learning progress by charting scores and behaviors. Questions emphasized are "Did you achieve your goal?" and "Did you make a personal best?" Nevertheless, everyone uses social comparison from time to time. When this is the case, ask questions to encourage students to think about whether they have selected a similar or appropriate other to use for comparison. Social comparison should involve more than outcomes; it should also include attributions (reasons) like effort, ability, and chance.

5. **Principle of Personal Meaning.** This principle emphasizes that self-concept is a structure with many dimensions that have unequal salience (prominence). There is a hierarchy of salience, and pedagogy must address what is central to personal goals and/or needs. These may be stable or vary by situation and/or task. A particularly important aspect of personal meaning is whether events and behaviors are internally or externally controlled. For most persons, internal control is linked with greater personal meaning.

Writing Goals and Objectives for the IEP

When assessment indicates that a student has low self-concept, this problem should be addressed in writing on the IEP. The goal in this regard might be *to demonstrate average or better self-concept in the physical education or sport setting.* For observation and measurement purposes, 10 indicators of average or better self-concept follow. They can be written as specific objectives for the IEP or for class lessons.

1. Voluntary, enthusiastic participation (without prompts) in class activity
2. Body language (smiles, noises, gestures, body postures) that reflects general well-being and enjoyment of class activities

FIGURE 8.9 Social comparison theory states that self-concept is formed through the lifetime process of comparing self to others.

3. Movement confidence (i.e., absence of crying, whining, complaining, hiding, and other fear or anxiety indicators)

4. A high level of energy or effort directed toward goal achievement

5. Problem-solving behaviors in adapting tasks or the environment to cope with challenges; trying many different ways

6. Asking for help when it is needed

7. Cheerful, attentive responsiveness to corrective and praise feedback

8. Persistence in sustaining practice and obtaining help

9. Accuracy and realism in judging when a task is mastered and it is time to switch to something else

10. Independence in judgments about success/nonsuccess; using feedback from one's own body rather than comparing oneself to others or waiting for external feedback

Use of a yes/no checklist including these indicators easily identifies individuals with low self-concept. Therefore, these are the behaviors that specific objectives should target. If documentation is needed for the IEP process, videotapes should be made of several randomly selected class sessions. These indicators can guide the writing of specific objectives, in that they describe the classroom behaviors that are conducive to learning.

In addition to observation-based objectives, many other objectives can be written, based on the content in this chapter. The following are some examples:

1. Given a standardized instrument that measures physical self-perception, sport-specific competitive anxiety, physical activity enjoyment, or related variables, the student will score within one standard deviation of the mean for her or his age group and gender.

2. Asked to respond to "Who am I?" and "What can I do?" and similar questions, the student will mention some aspect of the physical self in at least 20% of responses.

3. Given the opportunity to discuss or write about his or her physical self for 30 min, the student will state five good things about the self for every bad thing mentioned.

4. Shown pictures of 25 physical activities engaged in by most children in her or his school, the student will indicate *can do* to 20; *like to do* to 20; and *have friends to do with* to 20. Responses will be consistent with the teacher's and/or parent's observations.

Mastery of movement tasks and social acceptance and inclusion in games are other indicators of average or better self-concept. This is because perceived success is strongly linked with good self-concept.

A Self-Perception Model to Guide Pedagogy

Perceived success and perceived failure are linked with different self-concept profiles. Figure 8.10 presents a model that shows differences between people who fail and those who succeed in the physical education setting. The purpose of this model is to help professionals write objectives and plan pedagogy that addresses problems that arise in conjunction with

FIGURE 8.10 Self-perception model depicting success and failure patterns in physical activity.

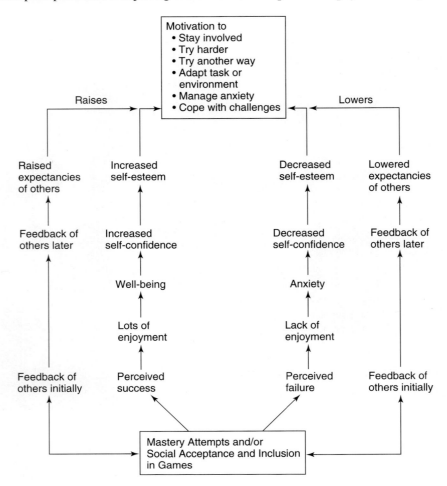

failure. To read Figure 8.10, start with the box that says *Mastery Attempts and/or Social Acceptance/Inclusion in Games.* These are the heart of most physical education lessons: to provide as many attempts as possible to master movement tasks and to promote social acceptance/inclusion. Move up the right side of the page and note that repeated failure has an effect on many variables. The end result, at the top of the table, is the influence of failure and lowered physical self-perceptions on classroom motivation.

Following is a discussion of variables that need special teacher attention when a student perceives his or her mastery attempts or inclusion initiatives as mostly failures. Much research is needed on each of these variables in relation to people with disabilities and movement difficulties.

Enjoyment

Enjoyment is a positive emotional response that is indicated by overt manifestations of fun, pleasure, and liking. Enjoyment is typically assessed by ratings of self or others in response to questions like these:

1. Do you *enjoy* playing in Little League this season?
2. Are you *happy* playing in Little League this season?
3. Do you have *fun* playing in Little League this season?
4. Do you *like* playing in Little League this season?

Self-ratings of enjoyment using such questions with a 5-point scale *(not at all, a little, sort of, pretty much, very much)* is the strongest predictor of **sport commitment,** which is defined as the "psychological state representing the desire or resolve to continue sport participation" (Scanlan, Carpenter, Schmidt, Simons, & Keeler, 1993). Self-ratings of enjoyment of specific activities in a class setting likewise offer insight into motivation and feelings about the self.

With low-skilled students, enjoyment seems to be tremendously important. This enjoyment must come from sources other than kinesthetic feedback and the good feeling that comes from mastering a task. Enjoyment is needed to keep students persevering in practice long after their peers have stopped. Often this enjoyment comes primarily from feelings of acceptance and inclusion in classes carefully structured to achieve a warm, positive social climate.

Personal Investment

Personal investment refers to focusing energy and other resources on the achievement of physical activity goals (Scanlan et al., 1993). Most individuals respond to failure by investing a little less of themselves in the next effort. This seems to be a protective defense mechanism, in that failing does not hurt as much when the effort to succeed is not an all-out personal best. Often people convince themselves that the task is not really important and use this line of reasoning to support their decreased investment. In self-concept terminology, this behavior is called **discounting.**

High personal investment is closely associated with internal locus of control (LOC) and voluntary behaviors that would enhance the possibility of task mastery. A decrease in voluntary involvement leads to teacher feedback that is different from the feedback successful students receive. Teachers typically offer more prompts and encouragement immediately after a failure. If the feedback seems ineffectual, however, teachers tend to give up and gradually lessen feedback. Often they also lower their expectancies, and students recognize and internalize this.

Anxiety

Anxiety is a "heightened level of *psychological* arousal that produces feelings of discomfort, both psychologically and physically" (Magill, 1993, p. 199). As such, anxiety is linked with self-esteem, motivation, and performance outcomes. Two types of anxiety must be addressed. **Trait anxiety** is a personality characteristic or an enduring predisposition to worry. Persons high in trait anxiety tend to worry about almost everything and to perceive many situations as threatening. **State anxiety** is an emotional or mood state specific to a threat, challenge, or desire to do well in a situation deemed important, like a test or a sport competition. State anxiety thus is situational, in that it varies from one situation to another. State anxiety is high in situations where the individual expects to fail.

Some instruments purport to measure general trait and state anxiety, but the trend since the 1970s has been to assess sport-specific anxiety. Illustrative instruments are the Sport Competition Anxiety Test (SCAT) of Martens (1977), a measure of trait anxiety, and the Competitive State Anxiety Inventory-II (CSAI-II) of Martens, Burton, Vealey, Bump, and Smith (1990). These instruments are all available through Human Kinetics Publishers (see Appendix E).

The CSAI-II is based on multidimensional anxiety theory that posits that two types of state anxiety and situational self-confidence interact to affect sports performance. The two types of state anxiety are cognitive and somatic. *Cognitive* refers to mental worries, and *somatic* refers to body tensions like rapid heartbeat, dry throat, and excessive sweating.

Recently instruments have been developed that measure worry about social approval in exercise settings. Illustrative of these is the Social Physique Anxiety Scale (SPAS) of Hart, Leary, and Rejeski (1989). This instrument is particularly useful in determining the amount of discomfort that persons who are overweight or have physical disabilities experience in mainstream exercise classes. Research indicates that the type of uniform required influences social physique anxiety (Crawford & Eklund, 1994). Loose-fitting shorts and shirts cause less psychological discomfort than tights and leotards.

Anxiety thus far has received little attention in adapted physical activity and disability sport (Mastro & French, 1986; Porretta, Moore, & Sappenfield, 1992; Schoemaker & Kalverboer, 1994). Recent research indicates that anxiety should be addressed. Specifically, for the 6- to 9-year-old group, approximately one-third of those identified as clumsy "feel uncomfortable, are not sure of themselves, and feel terrified and troubled prior to assessment of motor skills compared to controls" (Schoemaker & Kalverboer, 1994, p. 134).

Self-Confidence and Self-Esteem

The combination of perceived failure, lack of enjoyment, diminished personal investment, and anxiety contributes to lowered self-confidence and poor self-esteem. As shown in Figure 8.10, these influence motivation and external feedback. It is especially important in adapted physical activity to give specific praise and corrective feedback and offer incentives for such observable behaviors as staying involved in the activity, trying hard, testing alternative ways, seeking help, managing anxiety, and coping with challenges. The physical activity experiences of students with movement difficulties are far different from those of average, ordinary people. This should be reflected in goals, objectives, and pedagogy.

Pedagogy in Relation to Low Self-Concept

Teaching practices that enhance self-concept generally also contribute to improvement of attitude toward movement and/or physical education. Ideally, the practices that follow would be used with all students. Large class sizes and various other factors, however, often make the practices impractical for regular physical education, which is why they are described here as critical to effective teaching in adapted physical education.

1. **Conceptualize individual and small-group counseling as an integral part of physical education instruction.** Remember, the characteristics of a healthy counseling relationship are active listening, empathy, acceptance, willingness to become involved in another person's problems, and commitment to helping a person change in the way he or she chooses, which may or may not be the way you would choose. Listening to a student, asking questions to draw him or her out, and taking the initiative in following up when the student seems to withdraw are ways of showing that you genuinely care.

2. **Teach students to care about each other and to show that they care.** This is sometimes called *social reciprocity* and begins with the facilitation of one-to-one relationships, followed by increasingly complex social structures. *Reciprocity* is an interaction in which persons positively reinforce each other at an equitable rate, thereby increasing the probability of continuing interactions. Reinforcement can be facial and gestural expressions, verbal praise, or cheering for one another. Students typically model the teacher's behavior toward people who are different or disabled. Therefore, you must model encouragement, positive expectation, faith that the student really is exerting his or her best effort, and day-by-day acceptance of motor and social outcomes.

3. **Emphasize cooperation and social interaction rather than individual performance.** Plan lots of partner and small-group work (see Figure 8.11). When necessary, assign partners who will bring out the best in one another rather than allowing chance to determine class twosomes. Match students with the same care used by computerized dating services. Remember, the creation of a friendship is often more valuable than any other factor in enhancing self-concept. Show awareness of emerging friendships

FIGURE 8.11 Alex Spitzer, in the wheelchair, makes friends through small-group movement exploration activities. (Photo by Deborah Buswell.)

and praise students for behaviors that help and support each other.

4. **Stress the importance of genuineness and honesty in praise.** Accept, but do not praise, motor attempts that are obviously unsuccessful. Instead, provide such input as: "Hey, this isn't like you. Tomorrow will be better." or "What's wrong? Let's try another way of throwing the ball!" or "I can tell you are upset by your performance today. You seem to be trying very hard and still not reaching your goal. How can I help?" Apply the same kind of sports psychology strategies to students with disabilities as you do to the able-bodied. In the real world of sport and competition, it is not effort that counts, but success. Therefore, structure lessons so as to build in success.

5. **Build in success through the use of task and activity analysis.** Also important is identifying the student's unique learning style. Does she or he learn best through visual or auditory input, or a combination of the two? Or must the student learn kinesthetically through trial and error, trying alternative ways until one works? Motor planning and subsequent performance is enhanced in most students if the students talk aloud as they perform, giving themselves step-by-step directions. Remember, in many clumsy students, the mind grasps what is to be done motorically, but the body simply does not do what the mind wills. Therefore, do not repeatedly tell students what they are doing wrong. Ask questions and let them tell you. When possible, videotape or film and provide opportunities for students to watch and analyze their motor performance. Expect students to set their own goals but provide counseling in terms of realistic aspirations.

6. **Increase perceived competence in relation to motor skill and fitness.** There is no substitute for success.

Perceived competence enhances intrinsic motivation to persevere. Competence, however, is typically perceived in terms of a **reference group.** Help students to compare their efforts, successes, and failures against others of similar abilities and disabilities, rather than the population as a whole. This is often more difficult than it sounds because many students with disabilities have not yet learned to accept their limitations and still model average performers. Yearning to be normal and, thus, to perform motorically as normal people leads to anger and depression, which ultimately must be worked through.

7. **Convey that you like and respect students as human beings, for themselves as whole persons, not just for their motor skills and fitness.** The bottom line is that many clumsy students will remain clumsy in spite of best efforts of self, teacher, and peers. This is the rationale for separate instructional settings and sport organizations like the U.S. Cerebral Palsy Athletic Association and Special Olympics. Students need realistic **reference groups** for forming opinions about themselves and for setting leisure-time use goals. Clumsiness and low skill do not have to be reasons for disliking and avoiding physical education. Too often, physical educators have equated skill with fun. The emphasis, instead, should be on using sport classifications to equalize abilities and on counseling to find and accept a realistic reference group. Movement is intrinsically fun and satisfying when one does not feel different from everyone else and embarrassed by that difference.

8. **Stress movement education and motor creativity rather than sports competition in the early stages of learning.** Many clumsy students can excel in fluency, flexibility, originality, and elaboration, largely because *try another way* is an intrinsic part of their lifestyles. Such students can find much satisfaction in choreographing original aerobic exercise, dance, gymnastics, and synchronized swimming routines. Likewise, clumsy students may be adept at creating new games and/or changing rules, strategies, and skills in existing ones. The teacher who truly values individual differences conveys this to students who, in turn, learn to value themselves as the "different drummers in the physical education world." In this regard, the words of Henry David Thoreau remain timely:

> If a man does not keep pace with his companions, perhaps it is because he hears a different drummer. Let him step to the music which he hears, however measured or far away.

9. **Enhance self-concept by leisure counseling directed toward achieving desired leisure lifestyle.** Help students to see the relationship between physical education instruction and present, as well as future, use of leisure time. Activities to be learned and practiced during class time ideally should be selected by the student rather than the teacher. Because many adults with disabilities are unable to find full-time employment, it is especially important that they learn early that leisure can be meaningful. Wholesome attitudes toward leisure contribute to good self-concept in persons who have an abundance of leisure time.

204

10. **Help students to feel that they are in control of many aspects of their lives.** They can change many of the things they do not like, providing they are willing to put forth enough effort. Other things they must accept and learn to manage. Teach coping strategies, assertiveness, and initiative.

11. **Apply theories that link the cognitive, affective, and behavioral dimensions of self-concept to motivation.** The self-efficacy theory of Bandura, for example, provides cognitive pedagogical approaches. The competence motivation theory that follows focuses on the affective domain.

Motivation Theories and Pedagogy

Motivation refers to either the forces that cause behaviors or the internal state that focuses behaviors toward goal achievement. Theories of particular importance in adapted physical activity are discussed in the following sections.

Competence Motivation Theory

Competence motivation is the urge to engage in achievement-oriented activity as a means of feeling good and satisfying self-actualization needs. Competence motivation theory posits that persons engage in activity because certain behaviors (orientations) make them feel good. The more competent persons feel, the more they will sustain interest and persist in the activity. This, in turn, leads to high physical achievement.

Of the several competence motivation theories, the one best known in physical education is by Susan Harter (Weiss, 1987). This is perhaps because she not only has developed theory but also has validated instruments for testing the theory. The competence motivation process can be explained mainly by four variables: (a) perceived competence, (b) perceived control, (c) motivation orientations, and (d) actual physical performance (see Figure 8.12).

Perceived competence (high or low physical self-esteem) is interrelated with perceived control (internal, external, or unknown). These factors both influence motivation orientations and actual physical achievement. Harter recommends measurement of five motivation orientations (see Figure 8.12). Preliminary research shows that the score on the challenge scale is most predictive of actual physical achievement, but this may vary with task and ability levels.

Individuals act in ways that are consistent with their (a) perceived competence, (b) perceived control, and

FIGURE 8.12 Competence motivation theory.

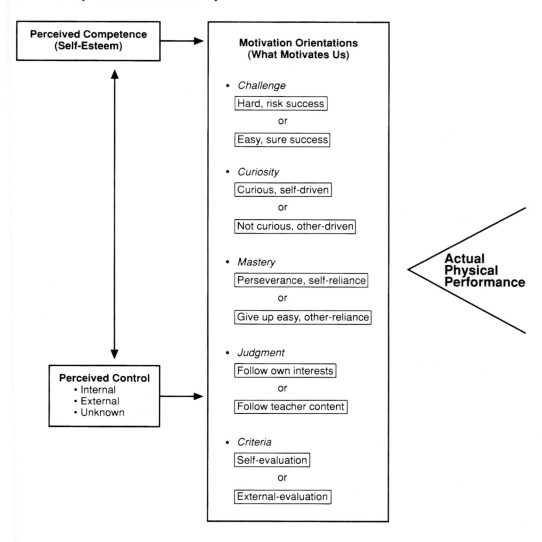

205

(c) motivation orientations. Therefore, plan strategies that make students feel that they are competent and that they have at least partial control over task variables and outcomes. **Ecological task analysis,** when student and teacher jointly analyze variables and set goals, is a way of enhancing perceived internal control. With regard to the five motivation orientations, find ways to reinforce orientations that keep students intrinsically motivated and actively involved. Competence motivation theory essentially is a rationale for giving self-esteem equal attention with motor skill instruction.

Teacher Expectancy Theory

Expectancy theory embodies two basic assumptions: (a) Persons will perform as they think others expect them to perform and (b) persons will expect of themselves what others expect of them. This theory, also called Pygmalion theory, takes its name from George Bernard Shaw's play *Pygmalion,* which was made into a famous Broadway play and later became the movie *My Fair Lady.* In *Pygmalion,* an English professor boasts that he can change an ignorant, unkempt young woman from the London slums into a beautiful, polished lady with perfect manners and flawless speech. Professor Higgins succeeds in achieving this with Eliza Doolittle, changing her from a person who makes a living by selling flowers on the street to a much-sought-after woman of high society. He does not, however, change the way he perceives and treats her, as indicated in Eliza's comments to one of her suitors:

> You see, really and truly, apart from the things
> anyone can pick up (the dressing and the proper way
> of speaking, and so on), the difference between a lady
> and a flower girl is not how she behaves, but how
> she's treated. I shall always be a flower girl to
> Professor Higgins, because he always treats me as a
> flower girl, and always will; but I know I can be a
> lady to you, because you always treat me as a lady,
> and always will.
>
> —George Bernard Shaw, *Pygmalion*

This passage clearly illustrates the importance of positive thinking, believing, and acting. Just as coaches convey to their athletes the expectation that they will win, so must physical educators demonstrate belief in persons with disabilities. How perception of oneself influences motivation and success is called the *self-fulfilling prophecy;* persons unconsciously fulfill expectancies held by themselves and others.

Rosenthal and followers (Rosenthal & Jacobsen, 1968) have conducted so much research on Pygmalion theory that it is also called *Rosenthal theory.* The *Rosenthal effect* (i.e., the outcome of expectancy theory) is said to be operative in classes in which teachers communicate positive expectations to students. In physical education, Thomas Martinek, professor at the University of North Carolina at Greensboro, has spearheaded most of the research (Martinek, Crowe, & Rejeski, 1982). Among the most relevant of his studies is research on the effects of teacher expectation on self-concept.

Martinek and Johnson (1979) emphasize that physical educators typically expect more from and appear to care more about their good performers than others:

Within a physical education setting, high achievers have all the advantages—more attention, more praise, more acceptance, more intellectual stimulation, and better self-concept. It follows, then, that the physical education teacher should become sensitized to those behavior mechanisms that mediate expectation which perpetuates success and failure in children. (p. 69)

Physical attractiveness, as well as mental, physical, and social performance, has been shown to affect teacher and, later, employer expectations. Persons whose physical disability makes their appearance visibly different from that of peers often are exposed to low expectations and special treatment that sets them still further apart.

Attribution Theory and Training

Attributions are causal inferences or perceptions of why things happen. Attribution theory focuses on the relationships between event outcomes (success vs. failure; winning vs. losing), beliefs about causes, and subsequent emotions and behaviors. Attribution theory, as begun by Bernard Weiner (1972), is an umbrella motivation theory subscribed to by most cognitive psychologists. It posits that the need to understand self, others, and the world in general is a major phenomenon in personal fulfillment and self-actualization.

Weiner identified four major causes that persons use to explain success and failure outcomes: (a) ability, (b) effort, (c) task difficulty, and (d) luck. Attribution theory is so complex that it is helpful to define each term by giving examples. Figure 8.13 presents the items used by Gail Dummer and associates (1987) to study the attributions of athletes with cerebral palsy. This model shows only the stability and locus of causality aspects of attribution. Immediately after their events, athletes used a 9-point response scale to rate each of the attributions in Figure 8.13. Additionally, they rated one item on affect ("I enjoy competition"), which was not in Weiner's model.

Persons with severe disability and/or low skills use different attributions than able-bodied peers and thus need different motivational approaches. Persons with severe disabilities tend to explain their successes and failures more by luck and task difficulty than by ability and effort. This is an indication of external locus of causality or control. Task difficulty is closely related to feelings about the person who required the task or determined its difficulty (e.g., "The teacher doesn't like me. Otherwise, he [or she] wouldn't make the task so hard." or "The teacher doesn't give me the help I need.").

Low-skilled children often attribute poor performance to a lack of innate ability (e.g., "I'm just not good enough"). This may be because of feelings of inferiority or the inability to differentiate between ability and effort. Children progress through several developmental levels in the acquisition of attributional skills. Until age 5 or 6, children believe that effort and ability are the same; they evaluate themselves in terms of simple task mastery (e.g., "I did it" or "I didn't do it"). Between ages 7 and 9, children begin to understand effort. This leads to the misconception that effort is the sole determinant of outcome (e.g., if persons put forth the same effort, they will achieve equal outcomes). Around age 9, children can finally handle abstract thought and thus begin to accurately distinguish between effort and ability. At about age 12, this

Stability Factor

	Stable	Unstable
Internal	**Ability** I perform well because of my ability. I have special skills for this task.	**Effort** I tried hard. I was physically ready. I was mentally ready. I perform well in these situations. I used the right strategy.
External	**Task Difficulty** I spent a lot of time working on my skills.	**Luck** I was lucky. I was able to meet the challenge.

Locus of Causality Factor

understanding matures, and children can analyze relationships between event outcomes and multiple causative factors.

Among students with cognitive disabilities, the ability to understand and use attributions to improve their performance may be delayed or frozen. Special educators recommend the use of attributional training or retraining to ameliorate this problem (Borkowski, Weyhing, & Turner, 1986). Procedures include (a) discussion of beliefs regarding the causes of failure and success; (b) instruction on the meaning of ability, effort, chance, and task difficulty; and (c) use of self-talk as a metacognitive and control strategy when doing tasks. Self-talk might resemble this:

> Why did I goof or make a mistake last time? Maybe it was chance, but probably not. Maybe it was because the task was too hard. Probably not, because the teacher thinks I can do it. Maybe I just don't have the ability. This is silly. I have control over my ability. I can improve my ability. I can do this by effort. OK, now I am going to do this task again and try harder.

Attributional training requires that students talk through tasks with passages like this one. It also provides stories, poems, and mottos about effort and self-control and encourages visualization of the self expending effort and succeeding.

Judgments that teachers and significant others make about attributions are as important as self-judgments because they influence the way students are subsequently treated. For example, a teacher who believes that a student has low ability will reduce the level of difficulty for that student. On the other hand, a teacher who believes that the student is not trying hard enough will enact various motivational strategies. Obviously,

all classroom interactions are dependent upon attributional analysis, and perceptions may be accurate or inaccurate. Emotional responses to attributions may be logical and valid or the opposite.

Stress and Coping Theory

Stress, which is closely akin to anxiety, has many meanings but usually is associated with major life events that complicate or interfere with effective functioning. Illustrative of such events are the onset of a disability, the loss of a close friend or a family member, chronic illness, and a change of jobs, schools, or communities. **Stress** refers to negative responses to harm, threat, or challenge that occur when perceived demands exceed perceived resources. Stress responses can be physical (like hives, listlessness, and weight gain or loss) or emotional (like temper outbursts, bouts of crying, and generalized numbness or irritability).

Disability and illness complicate life in a myriad of ways, causing everyone's roles to change and heightening stress. A person might be unable to attend school or work, enjoy sex, or meet interpersonal demands for long periods of time. Often there is **role ambiguity,** conflict, and confusion because persons do not know what to expect of each other and/or do not like the new roles forced on them by their own or a significant other's disability or illness. Students bring this generalized stress to school, and teachers must seek to understand home and community conditions that intensify problems. Adapted physical activity service delivery must include close contact with parents and a partnership approach to learning coping strategies.

Coping is the cognitive appraisal of demands and resources, decision making about needed changes, and assertiveness in making these changes. The **transactional stress model,** on the basis of which many coping strategies have been developed, is presented by Lazarus and Folkman (1984). Of particular importance is the mental flexibility to think of and try many different ways to solve problems. Mental flexibility, a component of creativity, can be taught through ecological task analysis (ETA), movement education, and other specially designed gymnasium activities (see Chapters 7 and 9). This is an important part of the self-concept goal area (i.e., learning to understand and appreciate the self, to accept what cannot be changed, and to change what can be changed). Meeting challenges through coping strategies contributes to good self-esteem and positive affect (Crocker, 1993).

References

Bandura, A. (1986). *Social foundations of thought and action: A social cognitive theory.* Englewood Cliffs, NJ: Prentice Hall.

Biddle, S., Page, A., Ashford, B., Jennings, D., Brooke, R., & Fox, K. (1993). Assessment of children's physical self-perceptions. *International Journal of Adolescence and Youth, 4,* 93–109.

Borkowski, J., Weyhing, R., & Turner, L. (1986). Attributional retraining and teaching of strategies. *Exceptional Children, 53*(2), 130–137.

Bouffard, M., Watkinson, E. J., Thompson, L. P., Dunn, J. L., & Romanow, S. (1996). A test of the activity deficit hypothesis with children with movement difficulties. *Adapted Physical Activity Quarterly, 13*(1), 61–73.

Cantell, M. H., Smyth, M. M., & Ahonen, T. P. (1994). Clumsiness in adolescence: Education, motor, and social outcomes. *Adapted Physical Activity Quarterly, 11*(2), 115–129.

Crawford, M., & Griffin, N. S. (1986). Testing the validity of the Griffin/Keogh model for movement confidence by analyzing self-report playground involvement decisions of elementary school children. *Research Quarterly for Exercise and Sport, 57,* 67–78.

Crawford, S., & Eklund, R. C. (1994). Social physique anxiety, reasons for exercise, and attitudes toward exercise setting. *Journal of Sport and Exercise Psychology, 16,* 70–82.

Crocker, P. R. E. (1993). Sport and exercise psychology and research with individuals with physical disabilities: Using theory to advance knowledge. *Adapted Physical Activity Quarterly, 10*(4), 324–335.

Dummer, G., Ewing, M., Habeck, R., & Overton, S. (1987). Attributions of athletes with cerebral palsy. *Adapted Physical Activity Quarterly, 4*(4), 278–292.

Dunn, J. L., & Watkinson, E. J. (1994). A study of the relationship between physical awkwardness and children's perceptions of physical competence. *Adapted Physical Activity Quarterly, 11*(3), 275–283.

Erikson, E. H. (1950). *Childhood and society.* New York: W. W. Norton.

Erikson, E. H. (1968). *Identity: Youth and crisis.* New York: W. W. Norton.

Feltz, D. L., & Brown, E. W. (1984). Perceived competence in soccer skills among young soccer players. *Journal of Sport Psychology, 6,* 385–394.

Festinger, L. (1954). A theory of social comparison processes. *Human Relations, 7,* 117–140.

Flintoff, M. (1994). *An investigation into the relationship between the self-esteem and sport of persons with cerebral palsy.* Unpublished thesis, University College, Dublin, Ireland.

Fox, K. R. (1990). *The Physical Self-Perception Profile manual.* DeKalb, IL: Northern Illinois University, Office for Health Promotion.

Fox, K. R. (Ed). (1997). *The physical self: From motivation to well-being.* Champaign, IL: Human Kinetics.

Fox, K. R., & Corbin, C. B. (1989). The physical self-perception profile: Development and preliminary validation. *Journal of Sport and Exercise Psychology, 11,* 408–430.

Griffin, N. S., & Crawford, M. (1989). Measurement of movement confidence with a stunt movement confidence inventory. *Journal of Sport and Exercise Psychology, 11,* 26–40.

Griffin, N. S., & Keogh, J. F. (1982). A model for movement competence. In J. Kelso & J. E. Clark (Eds.), *The development of movement control and coordination* (pp. 213–236). New York: Wiley.

Gruber, J. J. (1985). Physical activity and self-esteem development in children: A meta-analysis. In G. A. Stull & H. Eckert (Eds.), *Effects of physical activity on children: American Academy of Physical Education Papers No. 19* (pp. 30–48. Champaign, IL: Human Kinetics.

Hart, E. A., Leary, M. R., & Rejeski, W. J. (1989). The measurement of social physique anxiety. *Journal of Sport and Exercise Psychology, 11,* 94–104.

Harter, S. (1985). *Manual for the Self-Perception Profile for Children.* Denver: Author.

Harter, S. (1988). *Manual for the Self-Perception Profile for Adolescents.* Denver: Author.

Harter, S., & Pike, R. (1984). The pictorial scale of perceived competence and social acceptance for young children. *Child Development, 55,* 1969–1982.

Hutzler, Y., & Bar-Eli, M. (1993). Psychological benefits of sports for disabled people: A review. *Scandinavian Journal of Medical Science and Sports, 3,* 217–228.

Lazarus, R. S., & Folkman, S. (1984). *Stress, appraisal, and coping.* New York: Springer.

Levy-Shiff, R., Kedem, P., & Sevillia, Z. (1990). Ego identity in mentally retarded adolescents. *American Journal on Mental Retardation, 96*(4), 387–404.

Magill, R. A. (1993). *Motor learning: Concepts and applications* (4th ed.). Dubuque, IA: Brown & Benchmark.

Marsh, H. W., Richards, G. E., Johnson, S., Roche, L., & Tremayne, P. (1994). Physical self-description questionnaire: Psychometric properties and a multitrait-multimethod analysis of relations to existing instruments. *Journal of Sport and Exercise Psychology, 16,* 270–305.

Marsh, H. W., & Shavelson, R. (1985). Self-concept: Its multifaceted, hierarchical structure. *Educational Psychologist, 20,* 107–125.

Martens, R. (1977). *The sport competition anxiety test.* Champaign, IL: Human Kinetics.

Martens, R., Burton, D., Vealey, R. S., Bump, L. A., & Smith, D. E. (1990). The competitive state anxiety–2 (CSAI-2). In R. Martens, R. S. Vealey, & D. Burton, *Competitive anxiety in sport* (pp. 117–190). Champaign, IL: Human Kinetics.

Martinek, T. J., Crowe, P., & Rejeski, W. (1982). *Pygmalion in the gymnasium.* West Point, NY: Leisure Press.

Martinek, T. J., & Johnson, S. (1979). Teacher expectations: Effects on dyadic interactions and self-concept in elementary age children. *Research Quarterly, 50,* 60–70.

Martinek, T. J., & Zaichkowsky, L. D. (1977). *Manual for the Martinek-Zaichkowsky Self-Concept Scale for Children.* Chesterfield, MO: Psychologists and Educators, Inc.

Mastro, J., & French, R. (1986). Sport anxiety and elite blind athletes. In C. Sherrill (Ed.), *Sport and disabled athletes* (pp. 203–208). Champaign, IL: Human Kinetics.

Messer, B., & Harter, S. (1986). *Manual for the Self-Perception Profile for Adults.* Denver: Authors.

Neemann, J., & Harter, S. (1986). *Manual for the Self-Perception Profile for College Students.* Denver: Authors.

O'Leary, K. D., & Schneider, M. R. (1980). *Catch 'em being good: Approaches to motivation and discipline* [film]. Champaign, IL: Research Press.

Piers, E. V. (1984). *Piers-Harris Children's Self-Concept Scale* (rev. ed.). Los Angeles: Western Psychological Services.

Porretta, D. L., Moore, W., & Sappenfield, C. (1992). Situational anxiety in Special Olympics athletes. *Palaestra, 8*(3), 46–50.

Renick, M. J., & Harter, S. (1988). *Manual for the Self-Perception Profile for Learning Disabled Students.* Denver: Authors.

Roberts, G. C. (Ed.). (1992). *Motivation in sport and exercise.* Champaign, IL: Human Kinetics.

Robinson, D. W. (1990). An attributional analysis of student demoralization in physical education settings. *Quest, 42*(1), 27–39.

Rosenberg, M. (1965). *Society and the adolescent self-image.* Princeton, NJ: Princeton University Press.

Rosenthal, R., & Jacobsen, L. (1968). *Pygmalion in the classroom.* New York: Holt, Rinehart & Winston.

Scanlan, T. K., Carpenter, P. J., Schmidt, G. W., Simons, J. P., & Keeler, B. (1993). An introduction to the sport commitment model. *Journal of Sport and Exercise Psychology, 15,* 1–15.

Schoemaker, M. M., & Kalverboer, A. F. (1994). Social and affective problems of children who are clumsy: How early do they begin? *Adapted Physical Activity Quarterly, 11*(2), 130–140.

Sherrill, C. (1997). Disability, identity, and involvement in sport and exercise. In K. R. Fox (Ed.), *The physical self: From motivation to well-being.* Champaign, IL: Human Kinetics.

Sonstroem, R. J., Speliotis, E. D., & Fava, J. L. (1992). Perceived physical competence in adults: An examination of the Physical Self-Perception Profile. *Journal of Sport and Exercise Psychology, 14,* 207–221.

Ulrich, B. D., & Ulrich, D. A. (1990). *An expanded pictorial scale of perceived physical competence for young children.* Unpublished manuscript, Indiana University, Bloomington.

Ulrich, D. A., & Collier, D. H. (1990). Perceived physical competence in children with mental retardation: Modification of a pictorial scale. *Adapted Physical Activity Quarterly, 7*(4), 338–354.

Weiner, B. (1972). *Theories of motivation from mechanism to cognition.* Chicago: Markham.

Weiss, M. R. (1987). Self-esteem and achievement in children's sport and physical activity. In D. Gould & M. R. Weiss (Eds.), *Advances in pediatric sport sciences* (Vol. 2, pp. 87–119). Champaign, IL: Human Kinetics.

Whitehead, J. R. (1995). A study of children's physical self-perceptions using an adapted physical self-perception profile questionnaire. *Pediatric Exercise Science, 7*(2), 132–151.

Widaman, K. F., MacMillan, D. L., Hemsley, R. E., Little, T. D., & Balow, I. H. (1992). Differences in adolescents' self-concept as a function of academic level, ethnicity, and gender. *American Journal on Mental Retardation, 96*(4), 387–404.

C H A P T E R
9

Inclusion, Social Competence, and Attitude Change

FIGURE 9.1   Inclusion has many meanings, depending on age, context, and physical activity goals. Dr. Marty Block and Dr. Abu Yilla demonstrate different kinds of inclusion.

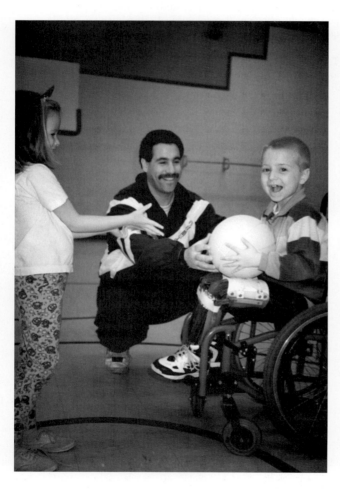

After you have studied this chapter, you should be able to do the following:

1. Define social competence and discuss its relationship to inclusion in physical activities with peers with and without disabilities.

2. Discuss physical education placement, the law, and the *AAHPERD Position Statement on Inclusion.*

3. Give examples of different types of inclusion, and discuss each.

4. Contrast curriculum models that have been designed to enhance inclusion, and find more information on them. Given case studies of students, discuss which curriculum you would recommend and why.

5. Given case studies or videotapes of various students with social competence problems, write goals and objectives for IEPs and for unit lesson plans for these students.

6. Discuss problems in being different and associated attitudes and behaviors. Give examples you have observed and role-play some situations that illustrate these.

7. Explain five theories that can be applied to guide attitude change and discuss strategies associated with each.

8. Administer some attitude assessment instruments to yourself and to other persons of various ages, and discuss the experience and findings.

9. Engage in debates about various issues: (a) Should social competence be a main goal of regular physical education? (b) Should a student in a wheelchair be placed full-time in regular physical education? (c) Should a student be assigned a personal paraprofessional? (d) Should children without disabilities be allowed to substitute peer tutoring for their regular physical education class?

Social competence has many meanings, but typically it is linked to quality of life in least restrictive environment (LRE) and inclusive settings. This, in turn, is linked with attitudes of individuals with and without disabilities. This chapter therefore addresses goals, objectives, and behavioral changes for everyone. As you read the following definition of the social competence goal area, think of how it applies to individuals of all ages, with and without disabilities, and the meaning of each component in a physical activity setting. Remember that inclusion is a reciprocal relationship that requires effort on the part of everyone involved.

The **social competence goal area** encompasses the following: to learn social behaviors that promote inclusion (i.e., how to interact with others—sharing, taking turns, following, and leading); to develop beliefs and attitudes about self and others that facilitate equal-status social relationships; to reduce social isolation; to learn how to initiate and maintain friendships; to develop other skills necessary for acceptance by peers with and without disabilities in exercise and sport settings.

Figure 9.1 shows two types of inclusion: in a regular physical education class, and on a wheelchair basketball team. The photo features leading advocates of inclusion: Dr. Marty Block of the University of Virginia, and Dr. Abu Yilla of the University of Texas at Arlington. Yilla (1994, p. 18) stresses the importance of both kinds of inclusion in the following statement:

> One primary function of education is to equip students with lifetime skills. It is logical to extend this to adapted physical education and to ask the question, "What do fully ENabled, disABLED adults do for their physical activity? and then equip students with disabilities to emulate their adult peers. I, like a number of ENabled, disABLED adults, employ a continuum of LRE placements in my life. I work and study in a fully integrated environment. When I compete I am in the realistically segregated environment of wheelchair basketball. When I recreate, I can be at almost any point in the LRE continuum.

The purpose of this chapter is to increase awareness that social competence is an ecosystem problem; to develop beliefs, attitudes, and behaviors that promote acceptance and inclusion; to develop competencies in assessment and writing goals and objectives; and to encourage critical thinking about principles, practices, and models. Physical educators often are reluctant to establish social competence as one of their two or three major instructional goals, but research emphasizes the importance of social competence in lifespan physical activity involvement. The ability to develop friends who support and encourage physical activity is essential in exercise adherence (Dishman, 1988), sport self-efficacy (Martin & Mushett, 1996), and inclusion (Sherrill, Heikinaro-Johansson, & Slininger, 1994).

Physical Education Placement and the Law

Social competence is important because federal law states that separate class placement is justifiable only when "the nature or severity of the disability is such that education in regular classes *with the use of supplementary aids and services* cannot be achieved satisfactorily." This means that teachers and students must have the social competence to accept and include students with disabilities in regular classes. It also means that individuals with disabilities and their families must want inclusion and have the social competence to help change the attitudes and behaviors of others.

Illustrative court cases challenging educational placements indicate that school systems must apply three standards in removing students from regular classrooms (Block, 1996):

1. The school system must document that supplementary aids and supports were tried for a reasonable amount of time and that these steps did not enable satisfactory education.

2. The school system must document that the student did not benefit from mainstream placement (i.e., did not make reasonable progress toward IEP goals).

3. The school system must document that the presence of the student with a disability, even with supplementary aids and supports present, was so disruptive to the class that the safety and/or learning of other students was seriously impaired.

As yet, no related court case has centered specifically on physical education. It is clear, however, that school systems that have been placing students with special needs in separate physical education classes will soon be rethinking their procedures. Professionals must be prepared for school system shifts in philosophy and practices and must know the kinds of supplementary aids and supports to request in order to maximize the likelihood that students will benefit from regular physical education instruction.

AAHPERD Position Statement on Inclusion

AAHPERD (1995) has developed a position statement on inclusion and physical education. This statement reviews the law and then elaborates on the following points:

1. All students, including those with disabilities, should start in regular physical education. It then becomes the school's responsibility to justify why a particular student should be removed from regular physical education.

2. Most unique learning and motor needs can be met within regular physical education.

3. Many students with disabilities need support services to be successful in regular physical education. Exact supports should be written in the IEP/IFSP.

4. Many physical education teachers need support, and every effort should be made to provide supports like team teaching with an adapted physical activity specialist, formal training, and regular consultation.

5. Regular physical education might not be an appropriate placement. If this seems to be the case, the nature and amount of support the student and teacher are receiving should be reviewed and modified.

6. If regular physical education placement is documented as providing no benefit to the student and/or posing a severe safety threat or learning problem for other students, part-time alternative placement should be explored.

7. The major IEP/IFSP goal in physical education should never be social development. Educational benefits from physical education instruction should be judged on progress toward becoming active, efficient, and healthy movers.

Types of Inclusion

Inclusion is a broad term with many meanings. **Physical inclusion,** or the assignment of all students to regular physical education, is a standard practice in the United States (Decker & Jansma, 1995; Sherrill, 1994). Exceptions to this practice occur primarily with the 3 to 5% of the population with disabilities who have severe to profound retardation and/or multi-ple disabilities that make success in the regular classroom unlikely. Exceptions also occur when parents insist on adapted physical education services part- or full-time in separate settings that afford opportunity for instruction individualized to meet special needs.

Instructional inclusion refers to the extent of involvement in learning activities with regular class students. This depends, of course, on the extent to which the learning objectives of a student with a disability are similar to those of peers and the extent to which resources are available to enhance inclusion. If the severity of the condition makes objectives different, then the student can engage in activities with a paraprofessional or a peer tutor in the same physical setting, but probably with few interactions with classmates who do not have a disability. Teachers can plan some activities like warm-up exercises that everyone does together, but these will not necessarily lead to social interactions.

Social inclusion refers to the nature and number of personal interactions with classmates. Typically it is assumed that these interactions are positive and contribute to feelings of accepting and liking each other. Of particular importance is whether these interactions are **unidirectional,** with nondisabled persons taking most of the initiative and seeing themselves as helpers, or **equal status,** with both parties reaching out to include each other (Sherrill et al., 1994). Equal-status relationships lead to shared initiative in social inclusion.

Whereas physical inclusion is achieved easily by administrative mandate, instructional and social inclusion are problems that require considerable commitment and hard work. These are not problems specific to individuals with disabilities, because many students in physical education are isolates for many reasons. Indeed, society is comprised of ingroups and out-groups, and everyone experiences exclusionary behaviors at one time or another.

Exclusion, real or perceived, strongly influences self-concept, well-being, and motivation. Individuals with disabilities, when asked, provide many examples of exclusion, rejection, and discrimination that hurt and demoralize. Physical inclusion is stressful when individuals are repeatedly ignored, hear derogatory remarks about themselves, or feel disliked or irrelevant. Pedagogy must therefore address self-esteem. An important goal is to help every student develop at least one "best" friend of approximately the same age (see Figure 9.2). This friend then helps to provide the emotional support for preserving ego while coping with environments or situations that are neutral or uncaring.

Scheduling Alternatives: Fixed and Flexible

Scheduling affects the development of social competency as well as progress toward other objectives. The advantages of fixed versus flexible scheduling should be weighed carefully in determining the best use of resources. Split schedules are particularly recommended and can be either fixed or flexible.

Most school systems use fixed placements with assignment to a physical education class that meets at the same place and time for an entire semester. A recommended alternative for individuals with special needs is a split schedule, with regular physical education and adapted physical activity variations assigned in 4:1, 3:2, 2:3, or 1:4 ratios as needed. In the

FIGURE 9.2   Partner activities help to promote friendships.

4:1 ratio, for instance, the student would go 4 days a week to regular class and 1 day a week to resource room. This 1 day a week can be used for troubleshooting and individualized help to enable satisfactory progress in the regular class, or it can be a time to provide disability-specific sport instruction that is not possible in the regular class. For example, an adult athlete with the same disability might come once a week to teach or provide practice in wheelchair, blind, or cerebral palsy sports.

Another type of split scheduling is by instructional unit. For example, a student with a disability might be assigned to regular class for units that permit equal-status participation (e.g., swimming, fitness, individual and recreational games), but assigned to a different class during team sport instruction and competition. This different class can be a mainstream or separate setting. However, the availability of open time like this is ideal for disability-specific sport instruction, including trips to community recreation settings where such sports are conducted and there are opportunities to meet with and practice with others having the same disability. This is especially important for students with mental retardation, who need special help in generalizing the knowledge and skills they have gained at school to community settings and to Special Olympics events.

Flexible scheduling is possible when regular and adapted teachers work as a team, making available a resource room or station where students can receive individualized motor skill instruction or behavior management help as soon as these are needed. The station can also serve as a special kind of time-out for getting control of oneself as well as for social and leisure counseling. The provision of a resource adapted physical activity room also serves as an alternative for regular class students with temporary disabilities or health conditions that prevent full participation in regular classes.

Curriculum Models to Enhance Inclusion

Numerous mainstream physical education models have been created to help students with special needs gain the social competence and other skills to function independently in regular physical education. Students can be assigned full-time or part-time to programs based on these models. The following logical progression meets requirements of the law:

1. Start in regular physical education.
2. If progress is not satisfactory, move part-time to a specially designed mainstream model.
3. If necessary, move full-time to a specially designed mainstream model or to a combination of part-time mainstream model and part-time separate class or tutoring.

Reverse Mainstreaming

Reverse mainstreaming refers to the integration of nondisabled students into the facilities for students with disabilities (i.e., a separate school or class). Rarick and Beuter (1985) described the success of reverse mainstreaming in improving the motor skills of students with mental retardation, ages 11 to 13 and 13 to 16, when nondisabled students (Grades 3 and 6) were brought to their facility. The ratio of disabled to nondisabled was approximately 1 to 3, and the teacher-pupil ratio was 1 to 8. The program was conducted by two experienced adapted physical educators and one aide, using a station approach.

Titus and Watkinson (1987) also reported use of reverse mainstreaming. Their research focused on children, ages 5 to 10, with moderate mental retardation and minimal language ability integrated with nondisabled 5-year-olds from a local day-care center. The playroom had a variety of large and small apparatuses as well as 10 vehicles (tricycles, wagons, and scooters). Lessons featured small-group instruction (teacher–pupil ratio of 1 to 4) for 15 min, followed by 7.5 min of free play. Findings indicated that exposure to the integrated program did not increase activity participation and social interaction.

Peer and Cross-Age Tutors

One of the best-known models of peer teaching is the PEOPEL (Physical Education Opportunity Program for Exceptional Learners) Project, which originated in Arizona and was disseminated through the National Diffusion Network and the Office of Special Education (Long, Irmer, Burkett, Glasenapp, & Odenkirk, 1980). In the PEOPEL model, nondisabled high school students complete a one-semester physical education careers class that trains them to work with peers who have disabilities. They are then assigned to PEOPEL classes, where they serve as peer tutors to provide individualized instruction based upon task-analyzed objectives. Generally, PEOPEL classes are comprised of 12 students with disabilities and 12 peer tutors under the supervision of an adult instructor. Statistical research (pretest-posttest design) shows that PEOPEL significantly improves the physical fitness of students with disabilities, as well as their attitudes toward physical education. It also facilitates mainstreaming and encourages peer tutors with special promise to choose physical education as their university major.

Project PEOPEL is no longer receiving federal funds, but the idea lives on. Many teachers throughout the country were trained to become PEOPEL facilitators and still conduct programs. Others simply use the idea of PEOPEL to innovate various kinds of "partners" curricula. One of the best resources for information on PEOPEL is Dr. Lee Burkett, Physical Education Dept., Arizona State University, Tempe, AZ 85287.

PARTNERS clubs, used by Special Olympics International, are a variation of the peer tutor idea. They bring nondisabled students together with persons who are mentally retarded to practice skills and game strategies and encourage after-school and weekend activities using community resources. This idea can be extended to all kinds of partnership relationships.

Many books and articles have been written on peer tutor models (Jenkins & Jenkins, 1981; Sherrill et al., 1994), but little research has been published in physical education. One excellent study (DePaepe, 1985) reported that peer teaching was the best of three models for youth with mental retardation. Research has also documented the positive effect of peer tutors on the academic learning time (ALT-PE) of students with mental retardation (Lieberman, Newcomer, & McCubbin, 1996; Webster, 1987).

Cross-age tutor programs are effective in many communities (see Figure 9.3). Older students, designated as members of the "Honor PE Corps," are released from their classes one or two periods a day to work in elementary schools as physical education teacher aides. Such students generally are required to meet certain criteria and to complete after-school or weekend training programs. The honors corps often functions as a club (sometimes a subdivision of Future Teachers of America) and meets periodically for in-service training.

Reciprocal Peer Tutoring and Teaching

Special education literature reports that children with learning disabilities, mild mental retardation, autism, and behavior disorders can function effectively as peer tutors and should be given opportunities to learn through reciprocal tutoring and teaching with nondisabled partners. Two types of peer tutoring, both applicable to physical education, are described in special education literature: classwide peer tutoring (CWPT) and classwide tutoring teams (CWTT). In both, the partners switch roles about every 7 minutes. Also in both, the twosomes are randomly divided into two teams and there are daily or weekly tests to generate points and determine winning teams.

The difference between CWPT and CWTT is how often partners change and winning teams are declared. In CWPT, partners are changed every week after announcement of the winning team. In CWTT, partners and teams remain the same for 4 to 8 weeks, after which a winning team is declared. Research indicates that children with and without disabilities who have been peer tutors praise and encourage each other more, express more empathy, provide and ask for more feed-

FIGURE 9.3 Research shows that children can often teach other children more effectively than adults can. In mainstream physical education, well-skilled children are often given special training to qualify as *peer teachers.*

back, and show evidence of more meaningful, interactive contact time than children in control groups (Sherrill et al., 1994).

Both CWPT and CWTT are similar to the reciprocal teaching style described by Mosston and Ashworth (1986), who note that even third-grade children are capable of observing and correcting one another's movement errors. Research shows that children *learn* through teaching. Students with disabilities need the opportunity to teach. Success in reciprocal teaching depends largely on preclass organization—the development of task cards or tangible instructions for pairs to follow with regard to learning objectives, principles of good performance, and the like.

Reciprocal and peer teaching generally involve **modeling** (learning through observing and imitating others). Modeling occurs incidentally in mainstream physical education, even without reciprocal teaching. A growing body of special education research substantiates that modeling modifies inappropriate behaviors and facilitates interactions among students with and without disabilities. Children are reinforced by being imitated, and they subsequently value the imitator more highly. The reverse may also be true. Modeling appears to be most effective when there is age and sex similarity.

Table 9.1 An analysis of a traditional game (softball) into six components.

Players	Equipment	Movements	Organization Pattern	Limitations (Rules)	Purpose
9 per team	Ball Bats Four bases Gloves Backstop	Throw Catch Field Pitch Bat Tag Run Slide	Offense at bat, defense in field, each covering designated areas	Diamond, run bases counterclockwise, defense pitches ball, three strikes equals out, three outs per team each inning, seven innings, out- of-bounds rules, fly ball rule, etc.	Win, or practice skills, or have fun! Which is priority?

Challenger Baseball

Challenger baseball, developed in 1989 by Little League baseball for children with mental or physical disabilities, is a mainstream model that features the use of buddies and community facilities. Players are encouraged to play as independently as possible, but buddies are provided for all children who need help with skills, rules, or game concepts. Games are held on the same fields as those used for other divisions in Little League baseball, and players wear the same uniforms.

Major and minor divisions of Challenger baseball permit ability grouping. Score is kept, but not emphasized, in major division play. Score is not kept in minor division play. In major division play, the regular rules of base running, including the possibility of being tagged or thrown out, are applied. In contrast, players in the minor division are allowed to remain on base whether or not they are thrown out or tagged.

Both major and minor divisions play by roster turns rather than number of outs. The side is retired when half of the players on the roster have batted. Players in both divisions also have the choice of using a batting tee or having their coach pitch. Players attempting to hit a pitched ball are allowed three swings. If the ball is not hit, the batter is then required to use the batting tee until the ball is hit into fair territory. Strikeouts and walks are not permitted.

Over 30,000 children, ages 5 to 21, compete in Challenger baseball in five countries (Canada, Czechoslovakia, Puerto Rico, Poland, United States). This mainstream model has much to offer physical education teachers who are thinking up ways to improve both social and motor competency.

Games Design Model

The games design model is a systematic approach to changing established games and developing new games that (a) are inclusive in nature, (b) meet individual needs, and (c) promote cooperative problem solving and creativity among students and teacher. G. S. Don Morris of California State Polytechnic University in Pomona first described games design pedagogy in 1976; his classic book (Morris & Stiehl, 1989) has undergone several revisions and it is recommended as a supplementary text for adapted physical education courses.

Although many elementary school physical education textbooks discuss ways of changing games, Morris was the first to suggest a model. According to his model, three steps are required in designing games:

1. Understanding the basic structure underlying all games
2. Modifying the basic game structure
3. Managing the game's degree of difficulty

If a regulation game is to be changed, the first procedure is to analyze the game's components and develop a chart like that in Table 9.1. All games can be broken down into six components: (a) the number and function of players, (b) equipment and space requirements, (c) movements (what, who, when, where, how), (d) organization (game formation), (e) limitations or rules, and (f) purpose(s). Games design begins with reviewing these components with students on a chalkboard or poster board.

The next procedure, when working with students who are beginners at games design, is to select one category in which to make a change. In kickball and softball, for example, two bases might be used instead of four. Under limitations, the out-of-bounds rule might be eliminated so there are no foul balls—the batter runs on everything. Or the method of putting the ball in play might be changed, with each batter choosing her or his own way. It is important that students choose the change, not the teacher. Much of the value in the games design model is practice in problem solving and creative thinking.

Once the majority agree on a change, students try it out. As they become increasingly adept at implementing change, several components can be altered simultaneously. An important role of the teacher is to provide guidance about degree of difficulty. Tell students that they can change anything as long as (a) all students get to play all the time (i.e., there is no elimination) and (b) all students have an equal opportunity of success.

The games design model is an excellent way to enhance students' understanding of the many purposes of physical education, the need to use class time wisely and get as much physical activity as possible, and the importance of caring about and including everyone. A common criticism of many games like softball and kickball is that half the students are sitting and watching all the time. Students offer great solutions when posed a problem like this.

One variation that my students devised was *Everyone-in-Action Softball*. Each time the ball was put into play (batted, thrown, kicked), everyone on the batting team had to do one of the three things (sit-ups, rope jump, stair stepping) until the batter rounded all the bases. The defensive team had to run to whoever fielded the ball, form a file behind that player, and pass the ball backward and then forward so everyone touched the ball two times before the original fielder could yell "Fisheye!" This call permitted the batter to cease running and the batting team members to quit their respective fitness activities. The score was the number of bases run. The students changed this game hundreds of ways and never seemed to tire of it.

Two research studies have been published on the games design model. Marlowe, Algozzine, Lerch, and Welch (1978) reported the success of the model in decreasing "sissy" games choices of emotionally disturbed boys whose play interests were too "feminine" for social acceptance. Marlowe (1980) reported a second study in which the games design model was effective in increasing peer acceptance of socially isolated children.

Cooperative or New Games

The cooperative or new games model has been explained and promoted by Terry Orlick (1978) of Canada and colleagues (Mender, Kerr, & Orlick, 1982), who report that this approach significantly improves the motor skills of children with learning disabilities. Orlick points out that games are played cooperatively in many cultures (e.g., Eskimos, Chinese, New Guineans) but that in North America, few games are designed specifically so that everyone works toward one common, mutually desirable goal. Alternatives to the competitive games and sports that currently dominate physical education are needed. Cooperation, according to Orlick (1978),

> is directly related to communication, cohesiveness, trust, and the development of positive social-interaction skills. Through cooperative ventures, children learn to share, to empathize with others, to be concerned with others' feelings, and to work to get along better. (pp. 6–7)

Four criteria must be met for an activity to be considered cooperative: (a) All players help each other to achieve a common goal, (b) everyone's efforts are accepted, (c) everyone is involved, and (d) everyone has fun. Orlick's books describe many such games and offer suggestions for creating others.

Illustrative of a cooperative game is devising as many ways as possible for a small group (three to six people) to keep a beach ball in the air (see Figure 9.4). One way, of course, is volleying, but another way is to permit the use of any body parts. Try everyone assuming a sitting or shoulder-lying position and the rule that only feet or legs can touch the ball. Or try a blanket, parachute, or tablecloth series of tosses with everyone holding on. Each group tries to better its best time in the air. Groups never compete with one another to see who can keep the ball in the air the longest.

Another example is nonelimination musical chairs (or hoops or towels). In the beginning, each student has one chair. The object is to keep everyone in the game, even though a chair is removed every time the music stops. As more and more chairs are removed, persons must share. Orlick reports

that 20 children can perch on one chair and/or sit on top of each other so that at least one body part of each child touches some part of the chair.

Numerous partner activities and stunts can be devised, such as three-legged runs and three-armed target tosses. Sometimes, the variation is one person blindfolded and one sighted. Carrying stunts also are fun: How many ways can three people cooperate to carry another person or some object like a tumbling mat or chair?

Unified Sports

Unified Sports is a mainstream model introduced by Special Olympics International (SOI) in the 1980s. Although developed by SOI specifically to promote integration of persons with and without mental retardation, the idea can be applied in many ways. At present, SOI has applied the Unified Sports concept to 14 sports: aquatics, athletics, basketball, boccia, bowling, cycling, golf, roller skating, sailing, soccer, softball, table tennis, tennis, and volleyball.

Two principles guide Unified Sports: (a) age grouping and (b) ability grouping. Team members are matched as closely as possible on chronological age, and teams compete with other teams composed of members of the same age. Within a team, the sport abilities of players with and without mental retardation are matched so that the nonretarded peers do not dominate or assume peer tutor relationships. Persons with disabilities other than mental retardation can be members of Unified Sports teams, but they must be counted as nonretarded. At all times, 50% of the players on the floor or field must be mentally retarded.

The Unified Sports program has been tried in public schools in several states. Although Unified Sports teams primarily play other Unified Sports teams, innovators envision competition with groups of varied composition as long as general ability level is matched. In fairness, the term *Unified Sports* should be used only in relation to Special Olympics and mental retardation.

Integrated Cooperative Sports

Illustrative of integrated cooperative sports is a study of 13- to 15-year-olds in bowling (Rynders, Johnson, Johnson, & Schmidt, 1980). Each bowling group was constituted by four students with Down syndrome and six without disabilities. Group members were told that they would be bowling together for 8 weeks (1 hr a week) and would be rewarded with prizes for improvement in performance.

In the **cooperative condition,** the students were instructed to increase their group bowling score by over 50 points from the previous week and to offer each other verbal encouragement, reinforcement, and help in ball handling. In the **competitive condition,** the students were instructed to outperform the other students in their group by maximizing their own scores. In the **individualistic condition,** the students were told to increase their own score by 10 points compared to the previous week.

The findings favored the cooperative condition, showing it produced significantly more positive interactions than the other conditions. The implication, of course, is that physical education conducted to promote mainstreaming and

FIGURE 9.4 Cooperative games.

Ladder Travel

Miniparachute Keep-It-Up

Big Snake

Turtle Keep-It-Up

Partner Balance

FIGURE 9.5   Adventure activities to overcome fears.

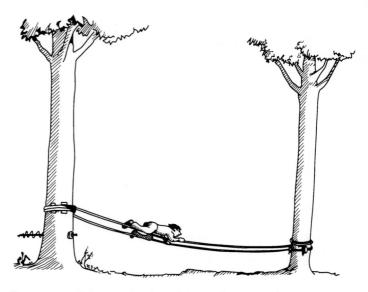

Jump forward from various distances to grab horizontal bar.

Traverse parallel ropes at various distances from ground.

Move from swing to swing at various distances from ground.

peer acceptance must utilize a cooperative class structure rather than the traditional games that encourage individual skill development and competition.

Numerous partner activities and stunts can be devised, such as three-legged runs and three-armed target tosses. Sometimes, the variation is one person blindfolded and one sighted. Carrying stunts also are fun: How many ways can three people cooperate to carry another person or some object like a tumbling mat or chair?

Adventure Activities

Adventure activities are challenges that involve ropes courses, jumps, climbs, and swings, with several persons helping one another (see Figure 9.5). Sometimes called risk recreation, the idea is to successfully cope with fears and anxieties and/or to

develop trust and other social behaviors. The ropes to be traversed can be any distance from the ground. This is true also of various kinds of beams to be walked and jumped from. There are also walls to be climbed, rope ladders to be mastered, and map and compass orienteering activities.

Teachers need special training about safety aspects, and a budget is needed to underwrite ropes courses and other equipment. The adventure concept and activities have been particularly successful with students with behavior disorders, low self-esteem, or relationships problems (Rohnke, 1977). Information can be obtained from Project ADVENTURE, P.O. Box 100, Hamilton, MA 01936.

Movement Education

Movement education was described in Chapter 3 as an approach that permits many students to work simultaneously on the same skill but at their own level of difficulty. In movement education, the teacher does not demonstrate or ask students to do so. Instead, lessons are built around problems that are solved through movement and have no right or wrong answers. Often, a series of questions is used to guide discovery of the body, effort, space, and relationships. Mosston and Ashworth (1986) designated this general approach a "guided discovery teaching style."

The idea of movement education was first proposed by Rudolph Laban, a Hungarian who spent most of his adult life in England and greatly influenced the teaching of dance and movement both there and abroad. His two classic books, *Modern Educational Dance* (1975) and *The Mastery of Movement* (1960), are the primary sources for movement education pedagogy.

Both regular and adapted physical educators should learn to use the movement education model. This model is described in many elementary school physical education methods texts, often under the headings of educational gymnastics, dance, and games.

Creative dance, educational gymnastics, and developmental movement are other terms used for teaching styles that stress fluency, originality, and imagination (components of motor creativity). This approach not only guides exploration of what the body can do but teaches students how to relate to each other in partner and small-group problem solving and choreography.

Other Models

Classes that center on individual and dual activities also offer success for differently abled students. Among the units that work especially well are recreational games (e.g., darts, horseshoes, shuffleboard, croquet, table tennis), dance, individual sports (archery, bowling, rifle shooting), and swimming.

Writing Goals and Objectives

Each of the instructional models we have just described was developed to promote inclusion. Table 9.2 provides a summary to guide the consideration of alternatives and to remind us that supplemental human supports, existing human resources, and specific intervention plans might also be needed. The IEP should specifically prescribe the models and strategies to be used in physical education, the class size, the ratio of students with and without disabilities, the ratio of students and teachers and/or paraprofessionals, and the minimal acceptable competency level of the regular physical educator in charge.

For inclusion to occur, specific goals and objectives must be written and agreed upon for everyone in the inclusion setting: (a) students with and without disabilities, (b) the teacher in charge, and (c) consultants, paraprofessionals, volunteers, and others brought to the class as supplemental human supports. The inclusion goal can be broken down into many observable behaviors that comprise objectives. Some inclusion settings favor particular objectives more than others. For example, the **specially created instructional groups models** especially promote the following objective: *Demonstrate ability to interact positively with a same-age partner while working on specific motor skill or fitness objectives for progressively longer periods of time.* Illustrative specific behaviors to be assessed and timed are these:

Table 9.2 Inclusion models and strategies.

1. **Specially Created Instructional Groups**
   Reverse mainstreaming
   Peer and cross-age tutors
   PEOPEL model
   Reciprocal peer tutoring and teaching
   Unified Sports
   Challenger baseball
   Structured cooperative goal groups

2. **Specially Selected Instructional Content**
   Games Design model
   Cooperative or New Games
   Adventure Activities
   Movement education
   Individual sports and dance

3. **Supplemental Human Supports**
   Paraprofessional designated for student
   Paraprofessional assigned to teacher
   Consultant assigned to teacher
   Adult athlete with disability volunteer
   Dual and team teacher collaborations
   Video and data collection personnel

4. **Existing Human Resources**
   Formal
   a. New partner assigned each class
   b. New partner assigned each week
   Less Formal
   a. Helper designated as activity changes
   b. Helper designated as needed

5. **Written Plans Specifically for Inclusion**
   Goals and objectives
   Behavior management plans
   Curriculum plans
   Social skills intervention and direct instruction

6. **Facility, Equipment, and Transportation**
   Accessible
   Close proximity
   Success-oriented

7. **Attitude Change Interventions**

a. Maintain eye contact with your partner

b. Maintain physical proximity to your partner (e.g., within an arm's length)

c. Initiate talk with your partner

d. Engage in response talk with your partner

e. Model or demonstrate for your partner

f. Ask your partner to model or demonstrate for you

g. Praise your partner for effort

h. Praise your partner for achievement

i. Use your partner's first name

j. Give appropriate corrective feedback (one chunk at a time)

k. Ask for "hands-on" help

l. Give "hands-on" help

This list could go on forever! It illustrates, however, specific behaviors that students with and without disabilities must demonstrate to achieve social competence as partners. Students must receive constant reminders to work on these objectives and regular feedback concerning how well they are doing. Videotape feedback is perhaps best, and videotape equipment and assistants should be written into IEPs when social competence is an objective. A list of these objectives should be posted at each station, and the teacher should rotate around the stations, pointing to the lists and asking such things as, "Are you remembering Item C?" Self-evaluation and examples of success in class discussions and in journals further reinforce the need to attend to objectives.

A frequent problem in specially created instructional groups models is that students without a disability often interact too much with other students without a disability in class and not enough with their assigned partners. This is natural, because peers who do not have a disability have many mutual interests, and the life experiences of the partner with a disability might have produced different interests, so that it would take more effort to discover mutual interests with that person. Talking with nondisabled peers, however, should be considered off-task partner behavior and discouraged unless the partner with a disability can be drawn into the conversation. This requires real skill and deserves a specific goal, such as *Demonstrate ability to interact socially in a group of three while practicing a motor or fitness task.* This can be broken down into the same measurable observable behaviors as when working with partners, with duration of time and number of threesome sharing incidents recorded. Attention must be given particularly to the skill of taking turns and providing equal opportunity for each person to talk and be listened to and to demonstrate and be followed. Working in a threesome is the beginning of leadership and followership skills.

Partnership and small-group social competence should probably be acquired before true inclusion can be expected in any of the specially selected instructional content models, such as Games Design, New Games, or Adventure Activities. Outcomes of specially created instructional groups models include friendship, mentoring, and support that carries over into other settings. A student with a disability who enters an already established mainstream class should have at least one same-age friend in that class who acts as a friend and models social acceptance.

Social competence in a class or free-play setting when students are on their own is much different from the partnership and small-group demands of the specially created instructional groups models. IEP teams must decide whether the student needs supplemental human supports to benefit from instruction or can make do with existing human resources in the class (see Table 9.2). Decisions should also be made about the best way to prepare students with and without disabilities for the inclusion experience.

Virtually all motor and fitness activities in a gymnasium require social interactions, because space must be shared with others. Students must be aware of safety as they move through space and/or propel objects. Listening to class instructions, watching and imitating a motor skill, and getting into

game formations are all social skills. In elementary school, many games involve holding hands in circles or lines, changing places, taking turns, and sharing equipment. As games become more complex and require an understanding of offense and defense, much social competence is needed. This social competence is typically taken for granted, but consider how the ecosystem changes when a student with visual or hearing impairments is integrated into the class. Consider how a person with cognitive limitations or a different kind of mobility might change ways of communicating or using space.

When a student with a severe disability is in mainstream physical education, his or her special needs should be acknowledged by an IEP or curriculum goal, such as the following: *Demonstrate ability to perform necessary social interactions in a class of 25 [specify class size] while working on physical education skills and playing games.* Specific objectives related to this goal might be these:

1. Demonstrate insight into when help is needed and request help in an appropriate way.
   a. Hold up a hand and ask for help from the teacher.
   b. Call the name of a student within a 5-foot radius and request help.
   c. Go across the room or the needed distance to ask someone for help.
2. Say thank you and/or give praise to the individual who helps.
3. Give corrective feedback in an appropriate way to the individual who tries to help but does not know how.
4. Greet three or more individuals upon arrival to class and on the way to an assigned station.
5. Initiate positive social interactions of at least 3-min duration with at least one same-age peer.
6. Sustain social interactions an average of ___ minutes.
7. Do "high fives" with class members at appropriate times.
8. Yell, scream, cheer, or express excitement about the game and show support for your teammates in the same ways that others do.
9. Request a turn or ask to be included, if you have been excluded from an activity.

These objectives should be individualized by adding the number of times within set time periods, stating the duration of time an interaction should be sustained, or indicating the number of social interactions with different people in a specific class period. Note that each objective is interactive and requires the cooperation of others. Failure to achieve an objective should be analyzed ecologically, with consideration given to all human and environmental factors. When a major goal for the student is social competence or inclusion, support personnel for collecting data as to whether or not the goal is being achieved should be planned and included in the school budget (see Figure 9.6).

Another approach to goal setting is to emphasize the development of friendships that will promote involvement in physical activity during leisure time. These may be "best friend" relationships, romantic or spouse relationships, or friendships

FIGURE 9.6 Deborah Buswell and Kerrie Berends of Texas Woman's University analyze videotapes showing social behavior in the gymnasium.

for specific activities. Objectives should clearly state the type of friendship. Many adults with disabilities report that, growing up, they felt they had lots of friends but no "best friend" close to their own age who liked them better than anyone else. As they watched others with "best friends," they felt cheated out of an important part of childhood and adolescence.

As individuals grow older, they tend to have a larger number of friends but see and interact with each friend less often. This is because many friendships evolve out of specific activities (e.g., work, exercise, child rearing, church, volunteer services, golf, fishing, travel) and time is limited for each activity. Research indicates that the most frequently reported barrier to physical activity involvement is lack of a friend, companion, or advocate with whom to share the experiences (Ittenbach, Abery, Larson, Spiegel, & Prouty, 1994; Sherrill & Williams, 1996). It is important therefore to teach social competence for overcoming this barrier. The following are illustrative goals and objectives for students:

Demonstrate an Understanding of the Factors That Enable People to Initiate Relationships.

1. Identify potential friends with similar recreational interests.
2. Identify potential friends who live close enough to one's home to make after-school visiting realistic (or problem-solve ways to enhance getting together in after-school hours).
3. Identify one or two students in class who are likely to say yes to an after-school invitation.

Demonstrate an Ability to Initiate and Respond to Invitations for After-School Exercise and Play, and Keep a Journal or Photo Album to Document Evidence of Achieving Each Objective.

1. Keep a journal describing how you invited one or more students to join you to exercise or play during nonschool hours.
2. Keep a journal of invitations you have received from others to play or exercise together.
3. Respond appropriately to an invitation and take initiative in getting to the play or exercise site [this involves many steps, like asking parents' permission, finding transportation, and reading the clock to leave at the right time].
4. Respond gracefully to a rejection, saying something like "That's OK, maybe next time!"
5. Ask an adult or a peer for help when you are unsure of how to handle an invitation, rejection, or other social interaction.

Social competence objectives might also address discipline problems or specific behaviors that make students unacceptable to peers and/or other age groups. The following are illustrative goals and objectives for students. Typically the teacher assumes responsibility for recording behaviors to document the student's achievement of these objectives.

Demonstrate Social Behaviors That Are Acceptable to Peers and Teachers in the Physical Activity Setting.

1. Decrease the number of your violations of physical education class rules.
2. Increase the duration of time between warnings from the teacher for inappropriate behaviors.
3. Decrease the number of your incidents of crying, temper outbursts, etc. (specify one behavior in each objective) during class.

Demonstrate Dress, Grooming, and Postures Similar to Those of Peers.

1. Increase the number of days that you come to school with clean fingernails (hair, body odor, or whatever grooming problem needs to be corrected).
2. Increase the number of days that you wear clothes, shoes, caps, makeup similar to those of your peers.

Problems of Social Acceptance

The goals and objectives stated in the preceding section address many reasons why students with disabilities experience problems with social acceptance in mainstream physical education. Many nondisabled peers have the same problems. In general, social acceptance is related to one's (a) repertoire of social skills, (b) physical attractiveness, and (c) competence in areas deemed important by peers (Strain, 1982; Walker et al., 1988). For boys, athletic competence is the area most likely to determine acceptance and popularity (Chase & Dummer, 1992).

Many physical educators therefore emphasize increasing physical attractiveness, motor skills, and fitness as a means of improving social acceptance. This approach works with some students but almost always requires supplementary instruction focusing on increasing the student's repertoire of social skills and physical attractiveness. Many students who need adapted physical activity services, moreover, have underlying ability deficits or health problems that preclude their physical attractiveness, motor skills, and fitness from ever approximating those of their peers. Teachers must find ways for these individuals to be socially accepted despite their differences.

Research indicates that students with disabilities who are placed in mainstream settings seldom interact with nondisabled peers unless instructional activities promote interaction and schools provide support services (Gresham, 1982; Strain, 1982). Peer acceptance is not easily achieved when people are perceived as different (Fishbein, 1996). Many students with disabilities in mainstream physical education report that no one wants them as partners (Heikinaro-Johansson & Vogler, 1996).

Peer perceptions of disruptive behaviors are significantly related to social acceptance in children with and without disabilities (Roberts & Zubrick, 1993). Research also indicates that children with and without disabilities exhibit about the same amount of aggressive and disruptive behaviors in regular classrooms and behaviors (Roberts, Pratt, & Leach, 1991).

Specially Designed Social Skills Curriculums

Specially designed curriculums have been developed for students who need systematic instruction in social skills (e.g., Hellison, 1978, 1984; Waksman, Messmer, & Waksman, 1988; Walker et al., 1988). These curriculums use various combinations of cognitive training, behavior management, self-esteem, and empowerment techniques. Typically, also, the physical environment is carefully planned, and staff–student ratios permit much individual and small-group instruction and counseling. Following are descriptions of two such curriculums.

ACCEPTS: The Walker Social Skills Curriculum

ACCEPTS is an acronym for A Curriculum for Children's Effective Peer and Teacher Skills. The goal of this curriculum is to teach social competence requisite to successful adjustment in regular classes in Grades K through 6 (Walker et al., 1988). The program can be purchased from Pro·Ed (see Appendix E), or this description can help you create your own original social skills curriculum.

ACCEPTS includes assessment procedures for selecting children who can benefit from this program, teaching guidelines for effective instruction, role-playing scripts and formats for teaching 28 social skills, and behavior management techniques. Table 9.3 lists the 28 social skills. Each of these is taught through this nine-step procedure:

1. **Definition.** The teacher defines a specific behavior, then guides student discussion of examples and applications.
2. **Positive example.** A videotape of correct behavior is shown, and/or the teacher models the right way to behave.
3. **Negative example.** A second videotape is shown, but this one shows the wrong way to behave.

Table 9.3   Content of ACCEPTS curriculum: 28 social skills.

Area I.   Classroom Skills
    Skills 1. Listening to the teacher
       2. Responding appropriately when the teacher asks you to do something
       3. Doing your best work
       4. Following classroom rules
Area II. Basic Interaction Skills
    Skills 1. Eye contact
       2. Using the right voice
       3. Starting
       4. Listening
       5. Answering
       6. Making sense
       7. Taking turns talking
       8. Asking a question
       9. Continuing practice of these skills
Area III. Getting Along
    Skills 1. Using polite words
       2. Sharing
       3. Following rules
       4. Assisting others
       5. Touching the right way
Area IV. Making Friends
    Skills 1. Good grooming
       2. Smiling
       3. Complimenting
       4. Making friends
Area V.   Coping Skills
    Skills 1. Responding appropriately when someone says "No"
       2. Responding appropriately when you express anger
       3. Responding appropriately when someone teases
       4. Responding appropriately when someone tries to hurt you
       5. Responding appropriately when someone asks you to do something you can't do
       6. Responding appropriately when things don't go right

4. **Review.** The teacher reviews, restates the definition, and guides more student discussion.
5. **Positive example.** A third video scene is shown; this one shows an applied behavioral application.
6. **Role-playing activity.** The teacher models a correct behavior and then involves the students in a role-playing situation to practice the behavior.
7. **Positive example.** A final video scene of correct behavior is shown, and/or the teacher models to give closure to the instruction.
8. **Criterion role-playing.** Students play assigned roles and are evaluated in accordance with criteria or standards. If

their performance is successful, they move on to the next step. If not, they must go through the previous steps again.

9. **Informal contracting.** The teacher presents the students with natural situations that will occur outside of class, and the students respond with verbal commitments to behave correctly. These are considered contracts.

Many of the modeling and role-playing activities in ACCEPTS relate to physical education and playground behaviors. The role-playing scripts are very short and involve only the teacher and one child. Many scripts focus on **coping,** a complex behavioral set that requires cognitive appraisal of demands and resources, decision making about needed changes, and assertiveness in making these changes. This program is based on the assumption that some children do not learn proper social skills spontaneously. They misbehave because they do not know how to act or are confused by the complexity of a social situation.

The skills in Table 9.3 look very simple, but many students with severe disabilities who are being assigned to regular physical education lack experience in interacting with others. Often these students are accompanied by a personal paraprofessional and interact only with this adult rather than with peers. Involvement in a social skills curriculum should be written into the IEP of these students so that they can benefit socially from the mainstream setting. Benefits often do not occur without special training.

Social Development Curriculum: The Don Hellison Approach

The best-known physical education model for social training is based on a six-level hierarchy designed to help the student grow from irresponsibility to self-control (Hellison, 1978, 1984). Originally developed for juvenile delinquents, this model effectively empowers students to take charge of their lives and assume increased responsibility for others and the total ecosystem. The model involves direct instruction regarding six levels of social responsibility:

Level 0: Irresponsibility. Discipline problems are analyzed as incidents of irresponsibility caused by fear or reluctance to change the things that cause one to feel bad. Individual and small-group counseling focus on understanding the why of behaviors and on increasing self-esteem and self-confidence so that students begin to believe that they can change themselves and others.

Level 1: Self-Control. Students are taught to monitor their own behavior, to set specific goals, and to keep track of the number of minutes they are able to maintain control of themselves. Goals might be for 10, 20, or 30 minutes or for the whole class period. Illustrative goals are "I will not call others bad names," "I will not get into a fight," and "I will not interrupt the teacher." Students who feel a loss of control coming on can give themselves a "time-out" by asking permission to go to the sitting bench for a few minutes.

Level 2: Involvement. Students at this level are helped to focus on the positive benefits of involvement, like having fun, getting fit, and making friends. They see that freedom from behavior problems enables them to think about other kinds of self-control, like choosing how many sit-ups to do, what exercise station to start at, or which partners to link with. The pedagogy emphasizes frequent changes in activity, space, and partners so that students have many opportunities to make choices and to feel in control. The class climate is essentially recreational in order to teach and reinforce the meaning of fun.

Level 3: Self-Responsibility. Students at this level begin to systematically assess their physical education strengths and weaknesses, set personal goals for class and out-of-school time, and assume responsibility for engaging in activities that will achieve goals. The pedagogy continues to emphasize choices but now links choices to specific goal achievement. Students are taught how to use community resources and to build support networks of people working on similar physical education goals.

Level 4: Caring. Students at this level can think and act beyond meeting personal goals. They begin to assess the needs of others and to assume responsibility for helping others. Whereas activities for Levels 0 to 3 tend to be individual or partner, Level 4 concentrates on cooperative activities of all kinds. Students must typically be at the caring level to possess the ability to assist with the integration and inclusion of a classmate with a disability.

Level 5: Going Beyond. Students at this level enjoy working with teachers in planning, conducting, and evaluating units of instruction. They begin to assume leadership in many roles and practice switching between leadership and followership.

Hellison's social development model can be accommodated within many different curriculum designs, but some time must be allocated for direct instruction and individual counseling in social competence. This might be whole classes (perhaps one out of five each week) or a designated number of minutes of every class. Overall, individual and dual activities are stressed more than traditional competitive team games. The major outcome is self-responsibility and self-determination.

Problems Associated With Being Different

The major social problem of many students with disabilities seems to be society's attitudes toward people and things that are different. In this regard, individuals with disabilities are like other minority groups. The following poem captures the feelings of many persons who are different:

ON BEING DIFFERENT

Watching without sight,
Running without legs,
Conversing without voice,
Loving without prejudice,

Ofttimes it is belief that makes it happen . . .

> What's the difference in being different?
> Acts which are naive, those deemed grand,
> Small, tall, some with, some without,
> Some who can, some who can't . . .

> What's the difference in being different?
> Thinking, feeling, acting, sharing,
> moving, gaming, loving, romping,
> You and I, not the same but
> yet the same because we are by fate just people . . .

> What's the difference in being different?
> Oh for the chance to share my dreams,
> to hold hands, to join in happiness,
> to play your games, to taste the differences in life,
> and not be scorned and turned away . . .

> What's the difference in being different?
>
> —Dave Compton
> *Leisurability, 2* (July 1975), 27

One thing that persons with disabilities have in common is that they are different on some observable physical, mental, or emotional parameter. Difference theory posits that, if someone is different from the norm, even on a dimension that is generally evaluated positively, he or she will have problems with being socially accepted (Katz, 1981). Difference theory also applies to discrepancies between expected and perceived attributes of objects, like taste, color, temperature, and sound. Judgments about something's acceptability depend on the size of the differences. Small discrepancies might be considered pleasant surprises (i.e., "a nice change"), but large differences typically result in negative feelings. Small wonder then that persons with disabilities sometimes want to be like everyone else! But is it good to want to be like everyone else! Is it possible?

An often-used approach to differentness is emphasizing the many ways that persons are similar and promoting the development of further similarity. This pedagogy tends to support the idea that being different is bad, whereas being like everyone else is good. The philosophy of this text celebrates individual differences and the importance of understanding and accepting ourselves as we are: a unique and wonderful combination of strengths and weaknesses.

Unfortunately, many persons are not logical in the ways they think, feel, and act toward persons who are different. Among the problems confronting persons with disabilities are prejudice, discrimination, stigmatization, and stereotyping (Sherrill, 1986; Wright, 1983). These problems affect every aspect of adapted physical activity service delivery. Some problems are caused by attitudes; others by behaviors. Often, in real life, it is difficult to separate attitudes from behaviors.

Prejudice

Prejudice refers to an unfavorable opinion or feeling formed beforehand and without knowledge, thought, or reason. The word is derived from Latin (*pre+ judicium*), meaning, literally, "judgment before." Prejudice is an attitude that predisposes

persons to avoid situations that may involve contact with persons with disabilities. All kinds of reasons might be offered ("I'm too busy"; "I don't have the skills"), but the underlying problem may be fear and/or unwillingness to take risks. Prejudice is also associated with an authoritarian personality. Prejudiced persons tend to be conceptually rigid, preoccupied with power and morality, and rejecting of individuals and groups who represent different abilities, races, religions, socioeconomic classes, and value systems.

The first authority to write extensively about prejudice was Gordon Allport (1897–1967), an American psychologist with special interest in individuality, motivation, and the process of becoming. His many works include *The Nature of Prejudice,* published in 1954, the year the U.S. Supreme Court ruled in favor of integrated public schooling for students of different racial origins. Allport was one of the first to propose that prejudice could be reduced and attitudes changed by meaningful contact among persons who are different.

Persons with disabilities are sometimes prejudiced against others with dissimilar disabilities. Thus, some athletes with physical disabilities express considerable prejudice toward Special Olympians. They feel that persons with mental retardation cannot be athletes in the same sense as individuals with other disabilities; moreover, they strongly oppose their games being held at the same time and place as the Special Olympics. Their reasons are complex. Many, however, are reacting to deep hurts caused by persons mistakenly thinking they are mentally retarded because they have other disabilities.

The Spread Phenomenon

The generalization of mental retardation prejudice to other disabilities by the general public is called the **spread phenomenon.** This phenomenon can be curtailed by teaching parents and children about individual differences within disabilities. For example, Special Olympics is only for persons with mental retardation. Separate sport organizations exist for other disabilities. Most persons, however, also want acceptance in integrated recreation and sport. They want to be known by name and judged on a personal basis. Generalization causes hurt and anger.

The term *spread* also refers to "the power of single characteristics to evoke inferences about a person" (Wright, 1983, p. 32). In assessment theory, this is called the halo or pitchfork effect. Make an *A* on the first test a teacher administers, and the teacher is likely to invest you with a halo symbolic of all kinds of positive attributes and abilities. Make a *D,* and your pitchfork (i.e., that one weakness) may influence how you are viewed and treated all year long.

Persons not knowledgeable about individual differences theory often generalize from one disability a vast array of expectations about personality and behavior. Chief among these is the belief that disability implies incompetence in all or several areas of life.

Preference Hierarchies That Show Prejudice

Personal attitudes about disabilities (one's own and those of others) are influenced by societal practices. Research indicates

FIGURE 9.7 Will these children be stereotyped as physically disabled? as Special Olympians? as Asians? Adapted physical activity emphasizes the elimination of stereotypes.

that societal attitudinal or preference hierarchies exist in the ways people feel about different kinds of disabilities. Persons with physical disabilities are near the top of the preference hierarchy, whereas persons with mental retardation and cerebral palsy are invariably at the bottom of the preference hierarchy. Preference for some disabilities, like visual and hearing impairments, depends on context and thus is variable. The prejudice and discrimination that accompany these attitudinal hierarchies influence coping needs, styles, and effectiveness.

Stereotyping

Stereotyping refers to conceptualizing persons as being the same without regard for their individuality. Stereotypes are assigned primarily to persons and groups about whom the person doing the stereotyping knows little. Stereotypes may be good or bad—the problem is that they depersonalize. Generally, stereotypes are learned from authority figures (parents, journalists, textbook writers) and tend to be more rigid than beliefs developed on our own. The broader the categories used in stereotyping, the less likely the stereotypes are to be accurate (see Figure 9.7).

Discrimination

Discrimination refers to actions that treat individuals in unequal and unfair ways. Causes of discrimination are prejudice, the spread phenomenon, stereotyping, and ignorance.

Stigmatization

Stigmatization refers to discriminatory or unjust treatment directed toward persons perceived as different. First conceptualized by Goffman (1963), stigma theory defines **stigma** as an undesired differentness, an attribute perceived as discrediting, a failing, a shortcoming, or a handicap. Underlying stigma theory are fear of individuals who are different from oneself, the equating of differentness with inferiority and/or danger, and the belief that persons with stigmata (plural of *stigma*) are not quite human and, thus, need not be accorded the same acceptance, respect, and regard given others.

The word *stigma* is Greek and means, literally, "tatoo mark." It can be traced back to such practices as branding slaves and criminals and forcing persons believed to be inferior or bad to wear distinguishing clothes or symbols (e.g., Nazis' requiring Jews to wear a star; swimming teachers' requiring students who are seizure-prone to wear red caps). Today, the concept of stigma has been broadened to include any physical, mental, or social attribute or assistive device that results in unfair or bad treatment (e.g., color of skin, eyeglasses, crutches, obesity, speech impairment, mental retardation).

Attitude Change

The key to changing behaviors toward people who are different is attitudes. This is the essence of adapted physical activity, integration, and inclusion. **Attitude** is derived from the Latin word *aptitude* (meaning "fitness," "faculty"), which, in turn, comes from the word *aptus* (meaning "fit," apt," "suited"). This derivation suggests that attitudes and behaviors are reciprocally related. **Attitudes** indicate one's fitness or predisposition to either approach or avoid something. Approaching or avoiding behaviors, in turn, evoke new attitudes about self and environment. The attitude-behavior relationship can be conceptualized as a continuous circle with change occurring in both directions.

Attitudes may be directed toward many kinds of psychological objects: self, other persons, a racial or ethnic group, religion, a disability, an undesired difference, exercise, physical activity, an idea, a behavior, or a situation. The more global a psychological object is, the more difficult it is to measure attitude toward it and plan change. When we feel uncomfortable about something or dislike it, we should pinpoint the specific variables causing the unfavorable affect. Logically, for example, disliking a whole person is rather silly, although we sometimes say, "I hate myself" or "I dislike so-and-so." We should determine the specific behaviors causing our attitudes and then take steps to change these behaviors. An often-used motto in education is "Accept people, change behaviors!"

Physical educators need to understand the major theories that guide attitude change and apply these theories in everyday teaching (Tripp & Sherrill, 1991; Rizzo & Vispoel, 1991). Five approaches to attitude change—(a) contact theory,

FIGURE 9.8   A model for attitude change based on contact theory.

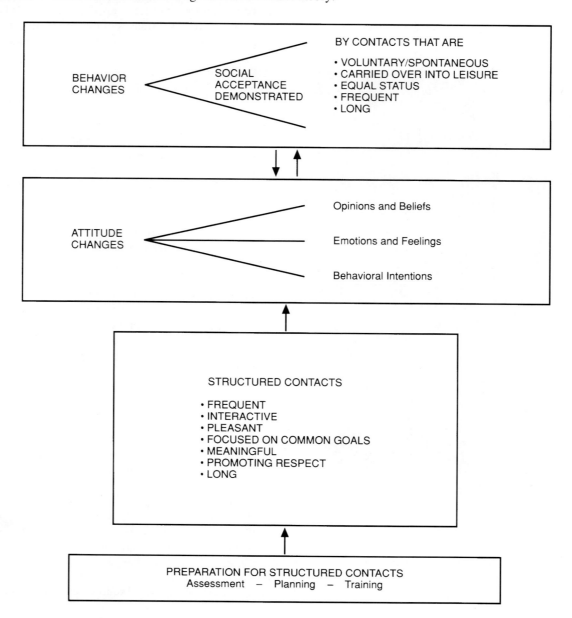

(b) persuasive communication theory, (c) social cognitive theory, (d) reasoned action theory, and (e) planned behavior—are described in the sections that follow. These theories can be applied to attitude change in relation to any psychological object. The emphasis in this chapter, however, is on attitudes toward persons with disabilities.

Contact Theory

Contact theory posits that contact between individuals with differences produces positive attitudes when the interactions are frequent, pleasant, and meaningful. Gordon Allport (1954) is acknowledged as the pioneer who created the structural framework for this theory, which serves as the basis of integration practices in schools and communities. Early theorists focused only on getting persons together in the same physical setting. Today, contact at the observational and casual interac-

tion levels is known to be not enough to create positive attitudes (Archie & Sherrill, 1989; Jones, 1984; Tripp, French, & Sherrill, 1995).

Research indicates that integration does not promote positive attitudes unless specific interaction experiences are planned and the environment is carefully structured (Horne, 1985; Jones, 1984). Favorable conditions that tend to promote the development of positive attitudes are (a) equal-status relationships, (b) a social and instructional climate that requires frequent contacts, (c) cooperative rather than competitive or individual activities, (d) contacts that are pleasant and rewarding, (e) modeling of positive attitudes by teacher and significant others, and (f) scientifically planned and applied persuasion.

Figure 9.8 presents a model based on contact theory to guide attitude and behavior change. The model begins with teacher preparation through assessment, planning, and training strategies that help teachers feel competent. Two factors are especially important in teacher preparation: (a) the promise of support services, if needed, and (b) an equal-status relationship with an adult who has some kind of disability. *Equal status* infers a mutually satisfying association in which both individuals contribute in equal amounts, building on each other's strengths. Teachers, in turn, prepare students to interact with each other.

The model next shows that classroom activities must be designed to afford structured contacts. Contacts must be frequent, interactive, pleasant, and focused on common, meaningful goals that promote respect. In the beginning, these contacts may be brief, but programming should gradually increase the duration of interaction. Partner activities typically are first, followed by small-group cooperative games. The equal-status criterion dictates that partners should be matched as much as possible on common interests and goals.

Partnerships in which one person gives and the other receives assistance do not have the same impact as partnerships in which giving and taking are reciprocal. In addition, opportunities for following and for leading should be equal. Regardless of the degree of equal status possible, teachers must reinforce positive contacts in every way possible. *Interactive* means that time must be planned for listening or making sense of signs and gestures.

Social acceptance is facilitated by cooperative rather than competitive or individual activities. When integration is practiced in a competitive game structure, social acceptance increases only in those teams that win and are rewarded (Lott & Lott, 1960). This is sometimes called **mediated generalization** (Tripp & Sherrill, 1991). In other words, players who feel good about a game outcome tend to generalize this feeling to everyone and everything associated with the game.

Ultimately, structured contacts in the instructional setting should result in attitude and behavior changes. Social acceptance implies that contacts become voluntary, spontaneous, equal status, and generalized. For example, social acceptance would be indicated by the person with a disability being included in after-school activities with increasing frequency and duration.

Persuasive Communication Theory

The use of persuasion to change attitudes is a common approach. Persuasion can be through direct methods (lectures, one-to-one talks, small-group discussions, films, presentations by persons with disabilities) or indirect methods (personal contact, role playing, or simulating activities of persons who are different). Thus, a body of knowledge has emerged called persuasive communication theory. Carl Hovland, Director of the Yale University Communication Research Program, is acknowledged as the father of this theory, also called the Yale approach, which was first posited in the early 1950s.

Proponents of persuasive communication theory define attitudes as multidimensional. Attitude change is posited to progress through four stages: (a) opinion change, (b) perception change, (c) affect or emotional change, and (d) action

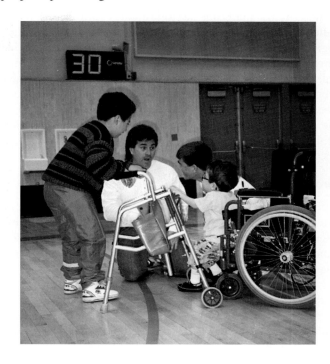

FIGURE 9.9 Dr. Terry Rizzo talks to children about attitudes and emphasizes the importance of contact between people representing all kinds of individual differences.

change. Information is carefully designed to (a) catch attention, (b) increase comprehension, and (c) promote acceptance.

Sales, marketing, and advocacy workers use persuasion communication and serve as good models for people who want to change attitudes. Most in-service training and many university classes also rely on persuasive talk by experts or creditable authorities. In public schools, creating opportunities for students with disabilities to talk about themselves and ways people can help them is a way of combining persuasive communication with contact theory. See Chapter 3 for a model on persuasive theory.

Social Cognitive Theory

Social cognitive theories focus on the importance of situational or environmental factors, especially those of a social nature. They posit that attitudes are formed primarily from total life experiences rather than from the passive cognition emphasized in persuasive communication theory (see Figure 9.9).

Field or Ecological Theory

Kurt Lewin, whose work is associated with the Massachusetts Institute of Technology and the University of Michigan, is acknowledged as the major pioneer in the early evolution of social cognitive attitude theories. Lewin's field theory evolved from the Gestalt psychology of the 1930s, which posited that behavior is determined, not by stimulus-response methodology or passive cognition, but by the total environmental field or life space. This field consists of an organized system of psychosocial stresses or forces, analogous to a gravitational or electromagnetic field, which must be kept in balance.

According to Lewin (1951), behavior can be understood only by analyzing the total field, or life space, today called the ecosystem. Life space consists of the total psychological world (i.e., everything that is seen, heard, sensed, or inferred). **Field theory,** then, emphasizes analysis of the individual, the environment, and the interactions between the two and working for change by altering person-by-situation interactions. Lewin's field theory has been particularly influential in the evolution of rehabilitation counseling and in the creation of theories pertaining to interpersonal relations, group dynamics, and social learning.

Group Dynamics Theory

Attitudes are strongly influenced by the norms and goals of groups to which people belong or aspire to belong. This is especially true in adolescence, when the need for group affiliation is very strong. Within most groups, various pressures cause members to behave, think, feel, and dress alike.

Complex reward and punishment systems exist within group structures. People often are unaware of these. They simply know that they feel good when in compliance with group expectations and bad otherwise. Areas particularly dominated by group mores are friendships and treatment of minorities. Some groups are open, whereas others are closed. Teachers need to understand the group dynamics of their classrooms and know which leaders and groups are most open to including new members. These, then, are generally the best people to select as partners for students with disabilities. When class leaders model social acceptance behaviors, others follow. Therefore, try to get leaders involved!

Cognitive Dissonance Theory

This theory, developed by Leon Festinger (1957), states that dissonance (discomfort) occurs when an individual holds two cognitions that are inconsistent with each other. For example, assume that a student has been taught *similarity theory* (e.g., "Birds of a feather flock together" or "One should stick to his or her own kind"). The student meets, likes, and begins to associate with someone of a different race, religion, or ability level. The new cognitions that oppose existing cognitions cause much turmoil and critical thinking. In particular, if the new cognition conflicts with cognitions of one's social group, a decision must be made.

To reduce cognitive dissonance, an individual chooses from three alternatives: (a) change one's position in the direction of the norm, (b) try to influence the group norm, or (c) reject the group as irrelevant. **Values clarification** in individual and small groups often helps students to cope with group dynamics processes. For instance, how might you guide group discussion in a physical education class that contains some students who are social isolates? Chapter 3 presents information on focus groups and other ways to help individuals clarify values and change beliefs. Often values clarification is helpful for parent and community groups.

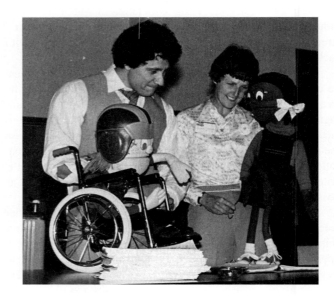

FIGURE 9.10   Puppets and dolls with disabilities can be used to facilitate understanding of wheelchairs and architectural barriers in the integrated setting.

Interpersonal Relations Theory

Interpersonal relations theory focuses on observing other individuals and learning to understand why they think, feel, and act as they do (Selman, 1980). Various forms of **sensitivity training** come from this theory. Specific activities are used to help individuals become better observers of body language and more sensitive to tone of voice and meaning of words. Popular techniques are (a) repeating in your own words what you think someone said before giving a response and (b) mirroring or shadowing the movements of a partner in follow-the-leader type games. Chapter 16 on dance therapy offers other ideas for sensitivity training. The goal is to reinforce the understanding that how we *perceive* others to feel and act toward us influences our attitudes and behaviors toward them, and vice versa.

Training of professionals, peer tutors, paraprofessionals, and volunteers should include activities to increase awareness, perception, and empathy. One of the best activities is **role-playing** situations that are likely to occur when service begins. In such activities, persons are assigned the roles they least understand and most fear or dislike. Role-playing can be spontaneous sociodrama, or it can be structured as a group assignment to write and present a play, dialogue, or monologue.

Puppet shows accomplish the same purpose. Puppets, dolls, or stuffed animals can be designed so that they are different in appearance or abilities. These promote analysis as well as the sharing of ideas and feelings. Kids on the Block is a set of commercial puppets with published scripts that has been widely used to promote attitude change about persons with disabilities (see Figure 9.10) (Aiello, 1988).

FIGURE 9.11 The theory of reasoned action approach to attitude assessment and behavior change. Note that beliefs, attitudes, intentions, and behaviors are separate components. (Based on concepts of Icek Ajzen/Martin Fishbein, *Understanding Attitudes and Predicting Social Behavior,* © 1980.)

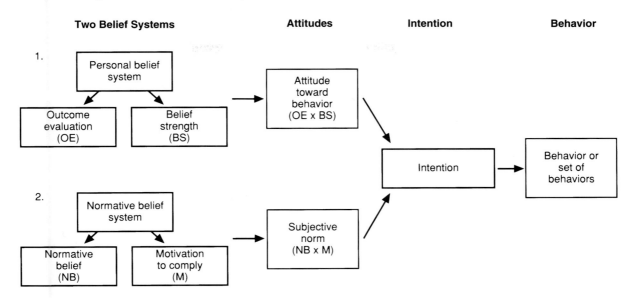

Experiential and Observational Theory

In the early 1900s, John Dewey at Columbia University created the motto *We learn to do by doing.* Albert Bandura of Stanford University has expanded this motto: *We learn to do by observing a model and then imitating the model.* Teachers should create structured direct experiences that enable students to learn how it feels to have a disability. Students can first observe individuals with mobility or sensory disabilities (live or filmed). Then students are given opportunities for *simulations* (pretend situations). Simulating disabilities (e.g., spending a day in a wheelchair or on crutches, wearing a blindfold or earplugs to create seeing and hearing impairments) sensitizes persons to how varying situational demands affect attitudes and behaviors. A good strategy is to have people try their simulated disabilities in different settings with varied goals (e.g., participate in a team sport, an individual sport, a recreational partner activity, a cooperative game, a competition). This helps them to analyze the effects of different situations on interpersonal relations.

Social Learning and Social Cognitive Theory

Albert Bandura, today's leader in social cognitive theorizing, first became known for his social learning and self-efficacy theories (see Chapter 5, Table 5.3). These theories stressed that behaviors can best be changed through a combination of activities that include (a) vicarious learning by watching and listening to *models,* (b) structured direct experiences that provide cognitive self-confidence, called *self-efficacy,* and (c) cognitive training that teaches analytical, self-reflective, and self-regulatory thought through such techniques as imagery and mental rehearsal.

Bandura (1986) is credited with today's widespread use of the term *social cognitive theory* because it was part of

the title of his famous book that summarized all of the ways that behavior, cognition, personal factors, and the environment can be used to achieve specific learning goals. The title of this book was *Social Foundations of Thought and Action: A Social Cognitive Theory.*

Bandura's focus as a social-learning theorist is primarily in the cognitive rather than the affective domain. He does, however, discuss attitude, noting that the assumption that attitudes determine behavior is only partially true. Bandura emphasizes that experiences accompanying changes in behavior also alter attitudes:

> Both attitudinal and behavioral changes are best accomplished by creating conditions that foster the desired behavior. After people behave in new ways, their attitudes accommodate to their actions. . . . If the new practices are advantageous, adopters either alter their attitudes to coincide with their new behavior or they construe their behavior in a manner consistent with their traditional beliefs. (Bandura, 1986, p. 160)

Bandura's primary contribution to attitude theory is thus the interactionist perspective that helps us dismiss unproductive arguments about which occurs first (attitudes or behaviors) and encourages new theorizing about bidirectionality and reciprocality.

Theory of Reasoned Action

The theory of reasoned action has been popularized in adapted physical education by Dr. Terry Rizzo of California State University at San Bernardino, who developed an attitude inventory based on this theory. The term *reasoned action* indicates that behaviors originate in people's belief systems (see Figure 9.11).

T a b l e   9 . 4   A teacher's personal beliefs about adapting instruction for a student with a disability.

My Adapting Instruction for Joe Will Result in These Outcomes/Consequences:	Outcome Evaluation (OE)			Belief Strength (BS) That Outcome Will Occur			Attitude (A) OE × BS = A
	Good		*Bad*	*Certain*		*Uncertain*	
1. Joe will achieve goals.	③	2	1	3	②	1	6
2. Other students will achieve their goals (i.e., Joe's presence will not interfere with learning of nondisabled students).	③	2	1	③	2	1	9
3. Adaptations needed will increase pressures on me so I'm more tired at night, maybe grouchy.	3	2	①	3	②	1	2
4. I'll have to give up some of my recreation to find the extra time needed for planning and individualizing.	3	2	①	3	②	1	2
5. The principal will be pleased and give me a merit raise.	③	2	1	3	2	①	3
Total Attitude Toward Behavior Score							22

Note: Highest possible total attitude score is 45.

Thus, people can be taught to reason about the right way to act. However, many factors must be considered in this training.

The theory of reasoned action, proposed in the 1970s by Martin Fishbein, University of Illinois, and Icek Ajzen, University of Massachusetts, emphasizes the link between (a) two belief systems, (b) intentions, and (c) actual behaviors (Ajzen & Fishbein, 1980). This approach is vastly different from others and merits careful study. The two belief systems are (a) personal beliefs and (b) normative beliefs. These are examined in relation to some desired behavior (e.g., adapting physical education instruction, losing weight, changing jobs).

Personal beliefs pertain to probable outcomes/consequences of a behavior and are broken down into two components. Component 1 is an evaluation of whether the outcome is likely to be good or bad. Component 2 is a prediction about whether the outcome will really occur (certain or uncertain). The numerical scores for Component 1 (outcome evaluation) and Component 2 (belief strength) are multiplied to obtain a score for attitude toward behavior.

Normative beliefs pertain to perceptions about what significant others think you should do and your motivation to comply with their beliefs. The numerical scores for these two components are multiplied to obtain a score called the subjective norm.

The links between beliefs and intention are designated as the **attitude toward behavior** and the **subjective norm** and are expressed as numerical scores that can be used to predict intention level (e.g., 20%, 40%, 60%). From this predicted level, the probability of behavior is inferred.

Let's apply the theory of reasoned action to a typical physical education setting in which we want to predict probable behaviors of a physical education teacher who has been assigned a 14-year-old boy with cerebral palsy. The boy has normal intelligence, good speech, and Class 4 functional motor ability (i.e., no involvement of the upper extremities, but needs a wheelchair for ambulation; see Chapter 25 on cerebral palsy). There are 27 other 14-year-olds in the class, all of whom are able-bodied (AB) and represent the usual wide range of sport skills. The teacher has no assistant. The boy, Joe, arrives on the first day of the spring term, accompanied by an individualized education program (IEP), written by a multidisciplinary team in accordance with federal law and school district policy. This IEP briefly states Joe's annual physical education goals, including short-term instructional objectives. The teacher notes that these are compatible with those of the regular education students. For Joe to achieve these goals, however, the teacher will have to adapt instruction. The question is, will he or she do this? How can classroom behavior be predicted?

According to the theory of reasoned action, two inventories should be administered to the teacher: (a) one to determine the teacher's personal beliefs about adapting instruction and (b) one to determine the teacher's normative beliefs about adapting instruction. Each inventory would include 5 to 7 items, each of which would be rated on two 3-point scales. From these scores, an attitude toward behavior and a subjective norm would be derived, which, in turn, could be used to predict strength of intention to adapt instruction and probable actual behavior.

Table 9.4 presents an example of how personal beliefs about adapting instruction might be measured. Each of the five items represents an outcome or consequence of adapting instruction. Note that there are separate items in relation to the consequences for (a) Joe, (b) regular education students, and (c) the teacher. Note also that both positive and negative consequences are included. In the first response column of the

T a b l e 9 . 5   **A teacher's normative beliefs about adapting instruction for a student with a disability.**

My Significant Others Believe I Should Adapt Instruction for Joe:	Normative Belief (NB)			My Motivation to Comply (M)			Subjective Norm (N) NB × M = N
	Yes		No	Strong		Weak	
1. My spouse or housemate	3	2	①	3	②	1	2
2. My mother	3	②	1	3	②	1	4
3. My principal	③	2	1	3	②	1	6
4. My best friend	3	2	①	3	②	1	2
5. Other teachers in my school	3	②	1	3	②	1	4
Subjective Norm Score							18

Note: Highest possible score, when there are five significant others, is 45.

inventory (Outcome Evaluation), the teacher circles the numbers to express her or his overall feeling about each outcome. In the second response column (Belief Strength), numbers are circled to indicate degree of certainty that the outcome will occur. The third column (Attitude) would not appear on the actual inventory. It is included here simply to illustrate how the attitude score is derived.

Table 9.5 presents an example of how normative beliefs about adapting instruction might be measured. Each of the five items represents a significant other. In the first response column (Normative Belief), numbers are circled to indicate the degree of probability that significant others will support the behavior. In the second response column (Motivation to Comply), the teacher circles numbers to indicate degree of motivation. The third column (Subjective Norm) would not appear on the actual inventory but is included to show how this score is derived.

The attitude score of 22 out of 45 (48.9%) from the first inventory and the subjective norm score of 18 out of 45 (40%) from the second inventory are then examined in terms of the relative importance of these two variables. This provides insight into the relationship between attitude, subjective norm, and intention. In this example, the teacher's commitment to adapting instruction, as expressed by intention, ranges somewhere between 40 and 49%. With such a low intention level, the teacher probably will not do much adapting in relation to the boy's special needs. This kind of information is valuable in that it helps (a) teacher trainers assess where more work on belief and attitude change are needed, (b) principals assess which teachers are likely to do the best job and which teachers need more in-service training, and (c) prospective teachers assess themselves and set personal change goals.

Theory of Planned Behavior

The theory of planned behavior is an extension of reasoned action theory. Ajzen (1985, 1991) proposed the theory of planned behavior to correct a weakness in the belief systems aspect of reasoned action theory. This weakness was the assumption that the behavior to be changed was totally under the control of the person doing the reasoning. In actuality, many factors (e.g., health, time, money, skills, cooperation of others,

administrative mandates) affect the amount of ability persons have to carry out their intentions.

The theory of planned behavior adds a third belief system to the model. This belief system is called **perceived behavioral control** and is defined as beliefs concerning how easy or difficult it will be to perform the desired behavior. Ajzen (1991) stated that the additional belief system is comparable to Bandura's perceived concept of self-efficacy (i.e., judgments about how well one can execute courses of action in specific situations). It supports the idea that situation-specific self-confidence correlates highly with success.

Perceived behavioral control is typically assessed by responses on 7-point scales (Gatch & Kendzierski, 1990; Theodorakis, Bagiatis, & Goudas, 1995). The following items are illustrative:

1. If I wanted to, I could teach students with disabilities during this year.
   Respond: Likely 7 6 5 4 3 2 1 Unlikely
2. For me to teach students with disabilities during this year is _____.
   Respond: Easy 7 6 5 4 3 2 1 Difficult
3. How much control do you exert over the decision to teach students with disabilities during this year?
   Respond: Complete Control 7 6 5 4 3 2 1 Very Little Control
4. I believe I have the resources required to teach students with disabilities this year.
   Respond: True 7 6 5 4 3 2 1 False

Implementation of planned behavior theory entails direct instruction and counseling on how to reason about all of the components in Figure 9.11 plus the additional perceived behavioral control component. Much of the instruction on reasoning pertaining to control relates to learning how to manage time and resources as well as how to negotiate for more time and resources. These are tremendously important skills for regular physical educators who are accommodating students with severe disabilities in their classes. Attention should also be given to self-concept and role identity in relation to control matters, because these variables influence behavioral intentions (Theodorakis et al., 1995).

T a b l e 9 . 6   Illustrative PEATID questions.

Teachers who take the PEATID are instructed to respond to questions like the following according to their understanding of PEATID definitions of disability conditions.

SD = strongly disagree
D = disagree
U = undecided
A = agree
SA = strongly disagree

Students labeled _____ will learn more rapidly if they are taught in my regular physical education class with nondisabled students.

Emotional/behavioral disorder	SD	D	U	A	SA
Specific learning disability	SD	D	U	A	SA
Mild–moderate mentally impaired	SD	D	U	A	SA
Moderate–severe mentally impaired	SD	D	U	A	SA

Students labeled _____ will develop a more favorable self-concept as a result of learning motor skills in my regular physical education class with nondisabled peers.

Emotional/behavioral disorder	SD	D	U	A	SA
Specific learning disability	SD	D	U	A	SA
Mild–moderate mentally impaired	SD	D	U	A	SA
Moderate–severe mentally impaired	SD	D	U	A	SA

As a physical education teacher, I need more course work and training before I will feel comfortable teaching physical education classes with students labeled _____ with nondisabled students.

Emotional/behavioral disorder	SD	D	U	A	SA
Specific learning disability	SD	D	U	A	SA
Mild–moderate mentally impaired	SD	D	U	A	SA
Moderate–severe mentally impaired	SD	D	U	A	SA

Using Attitude Theories

Five groups of attitude theories have been described: (a) contact theory, (b) persuasive communication, (c) social cognitive theories, (d) reasoned action, and (e) planned behavior. Use of these theories will help you plan all aspects of service delivery, and they will be particularly helpful in advocacy activities. It is important for you to feel comfortable with theories and theorizing. Feel free to criticize these theories, test them, play with them, and propose changes. Consider each theory a brick in our wall of knowledge about individual differences, attitudes, and behaviors. Each generation of teachers and researchers leaves its mark on this wall. Are you ready to begin? Try it; you'll like it!

Assessment of Attitudes and Intentions

Attitude change begins with an assessment of attitude components and related behaviors. Then objectives can be written and instructional time and activities planned. Attitude instruments are typically called surveys, adjective checklists, opinionnaires, inventories, rating scales, and sociometric measures. Attitude measures are never called *tests,* a term properly used only when there are right and wrong answers and the domain examined is cognitive. Responses to attitude inventories are not considered right or wrong, good or bad, but only a reflection of feelings or beliefs at a given time. This fact is important to convey to subjects before conducting an attitude assessment; otherwise, persons may tend to give socially desirable ("right") answers rather than the truth, a phenomenon called *response bias.*

Following are descriptions of some attitude instruments that relate specifically to students with disabilities in regular physical education.

PEATID-III

The Physical Educators' Attitude Toward Teaching Individuals with Disabilities–III (PEATID-III by Terry Rizzo (1995) is a revision (terminology only) of the much used PEATH II (Rizzo & Kirkendall, 1995) and PEATH I (Rizzo, 1984), which are based on reasoned action theory. *PEATH* is the acronym for Physical Educators' Attitudes toward Teaching the Handicapped questionnaire, a title now changed to PEATID.

PEATID requires that teachers read definitions of disability conditions from the PEATID instruction sheet and then answer 12 statements, based on their understanding of the definitions. A Likert-type 5-point scale is used to score their responses. Illustrative questions are shown in Table 9.6.

CAIPE-R

The Children's Attitudes Toward Integrated Physical Education–Revised (CAIPE-R) inventory, by Martin Block (1995), consists of a description of a student with a disability, then 12 to 14 statements, depending on the sport featured in Part 2 of the inventory (see Table 9.7). Thus far the inventory has been validated only with sixth-graders (Block & Zeman, 1996), but

T a b l e   9 . 7   Examples from the Children's Attitudes Toward Integrated Physical Education–Revised (Block, 1995).

Insert here a description of a child who might be coming to class

Part 1

1. It would be OK having Mike in PE class.
   Yes   Probably Yes   Probably No   No
2. Because Mike cannot play sports very well, he would slow the game down for everyone.
   Yes   Probably Yes   Probably No   No
3. If we were playing a team sport such as basketball, it would be OK having Mike on my team.
   Yes   Probably Yes   Probably No   No
4. PE would be fun if Mike were in my PE class.
   Yes   Probably Yes   Probably No   No
5. If Mike were in my PE class, I would talk to him and be his friend.
   Yes   Probably Yes   Probably No   No
6. If Mike were in my PE class, I would like to help him practice and play the games.
   Yes   Probably Yes   Probably No   No
7. During practice, it would be OK to allow Mike to use special equipment such as a lower basket in basketball or a batting tee in softball.
   Yes   Probably Yes   Probably No   No

Part 2

What rule changes during PE do you think would be OK if a kid like Mike were playing?

8. Mike could hit a ball placed on a batting tee.
   Yes   Probably Yes   Probably No   No
9. Someone could tell Mike where to run when he hits the ball.
   Yes   Probably Yes   Probably No   No
10. The distance between home and first base could be shorter for Mike.
    Yes   Probably Yes   Probably No   No
11. Someone could help Mike when he plays in the field.
    Yes   Probably Yes   Probably No   No
12. If the ball were hit to Mike, the batter could only run as far as second base.
    Yes   Probably Yes   Probably No   No

Note: For permission to use this instrument for research, contact Dr. Martin E. Block, Curry School of Education, University of Virginia, Charlottesville, VA 22903.

it seems appropriate for other middle school grades. Following are two illustrative descriptions of target children. Only *one* description is presented to students, usually with a picture. Then students mark their responses according to the 4-point scale. The example in Table 9.7 assumes that the students have been given a description of "Mike" (Target Child 1).

Target Child 1

Mike is the same age as you are. However, he has mental retardation, so he doesn't learn as quickly as you can. Because of his mental retardation, he also doesn't talk very well, so sometimes it is hard to understand what he is saying. Michael likes playing the same games as you do, but he does not do very well in the games. Even though he can run, he is slower than you and tires easily. He can throw and catch and hit a softball, but not very well. He likes soccer, but he cannot kick a ball very far. He also likes basketball, but he is not very good at shooting or dribbling, and he doesn't really know the rules of the game.

Target Child 2

Bart is the same age as you are. However, he cannot walk, so he uses a wheelchair to get around. Bart likes playing the same games as you do, but he does not do very well in the games. Even though he can push his wheelchair, he is slower than you and tires easily. He can throw a ball, but not very far. He can catch balls that are tossed straight to him, and he can hit a baseball off a tee, but he cannot shoot a basketball high enough to make a basket. Because his legs do not work, he cannot kick a ball.

Sociograms

Sociograms (see Figure 9.12) are visual records of students' responses to questions like these:

1. What two people in this class do you *most* like to play with in PE class and after-school sports?
2. When I assign you to exercise stations (or sport teams), what two persons do you *most* want to be with?

FIGURE 9.12   Two types of sociograms for examining peer attitudes.

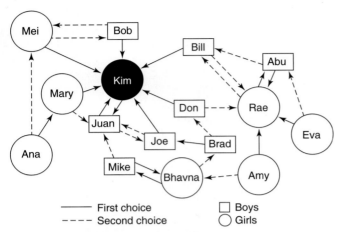

——— First choice   ☐ Boys
- - - - Second choice   ○ Girls

Arrows show first and second choices of best friends in a class of 16 students.

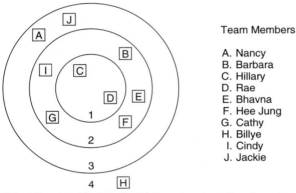

Team Members

A. Nancy
B. Barbara
C. Hillary
D. Rae
E. Bhavna
F. Hee Jung
G. Cathy
H. Billye
I. Cindy
J. Jackie

Boxes in center show leaders, whereas succeeding rings show persons considered less relevant to group goals.

These are excellent measures of attitudes. Questions can also ask whom students would *least* like to be with, because peer acceptance and peer rejection are independent dimensions of interpersonal attractiveness. Sociograms give teachers good information about *stars* (the most popular individuals) and *isolates* (the least popular individuals). Also valuable is information about whether choices are *reciprocal* (if Kim chooses Juan, does Juan choose Kim?). Cliques can also be identified in sociograms.

In Figure 9.12, it is clear that Kim and Rae are stars, or the class leaders. They also are the centers of cliques and seldom interact with each other, although Bill and Don are *peacemakers* who maintain links with both cliques. Most important in adapted physical activity service is the need to help Amy, Ana, and Eva find some close friends.

Sociograms can be as simple or complex as teachers wish. Color coding the arrows helps when more than two responses are recorded. If the goal is simply to identify leaders

Table 9.8   Siperstein adjective checklist for describing classmates.

If you had to describe _____ to your classmates, what kinds of words would you use? Below is a list of words to help you. CIRCLE the words you would use. You can use as many or as few words as you want. Here is the list:

healthy	honest	bored	dishonest
slow	ashamed	helpful	smart
sloppy	neat	dumb	unhappy
clever	lonely	friendly	mean
alert	pretty	sad	ugly
alright	cruel	careful	happy
crazy	proud	glad	kind
greedy	weak	stupid	
cheerful	bright	careless	

and isolates, then the circle sociogram (see Figure 9.12) can be used. Following are directions for this method.

Classify each team member as nearly as possible to how you view her influence on the behavior of the other team members as it relates to the overall team goals. Place the player's name within the numbered circle as you view the strength of her influence on the other team members.

1—Players with great influence

2—Players with influence sometimes

3—Players who never influence others; they are primarily followers

4—Players who are not even followers; they merely "occupy space"

Adjective Checklists

The adjective checklist is based on the assumption that adjective choice reveals opinions and feelings. Many such checklists are available for attitude measurement, but the Siperstein (1980) checklist in Table 9.8 was developed specifically for use with schoolchildren and has provided data for several published studies. Either the name of a particular child or a category (e.g., mental retardation) can be placed in the blank to elicit responses. After using this checklist, students should be helped to understand the fallacy of generalizations. For example, a term like *slow* is relative. Does it mean slow in running, slow in learning, or slow in giving affection? Also, because a person is slow on one dimension does not mean that he or she should automatically be judged slow on other dimensions.

Sources of Attitude Instruments

Table 9.9 lists attitude instruments and states sources in journals that have articles about these instruments. Some addresses are stated. These instruments can be used as worksheet activities as well as for assessment and goal writing.

T a b l e   9 . 9   Types of attitude inventories with references and some addresses.

Social Distance Measures

1. *Cowell Personal Distance Scale*—Uses a 7-point scale to indicate acceptance (e.g., into my family, as a next-door neighbor, into my school).	Cowell, C. (1958). Validating an index of social adjustment for high school use. *Research Quarterly, 29,* 7–18. (Appears in Barrow, McGee, & Tritschler, 1989, p. 261.)
2. *Siperstein Friendship Activity Scale*—Uses a 4-point Likert scale to measure behavioral intentions in regard to 15 activities.	Siperstein, G., Bak, J., & O'Keefe, P. (1988). Relationship between children's attitudes toward and their social acceptance of mentally retarded peers. *American Journal of Mental Retardation, 93*(1), 24–27.
3. *Aufsesser Ranking of Disabilities Protocol*—Requests *ranking* of 10 disabilities from high to low to express friendship and self-affliction preferences and provides *checking* criteria that explain rankings.	Aufsesser, P. M. (1982). Comparison of the attitudes of physical education, recreation, and special education majors toward the disabled. *American Corrective Therapy Journal, 36,* 35–41.
4. *Bagley and Greene PATHS (Peer Attitudes Toward the Handicapped Scale)*—Uses a 5-point social distance scale (in my home, in another group, in no group, outside of class, at home) to rate descriptions of 30 students.	Bagley, M., & Green, J. (1981). *Peer attitude toward the handicapped scale.* Austin, TX: PRO•ED.

Teacher Attitude Measures—Likert-Type Scales

1. *Rizzo Physical Educators' Attitude Toward Teaching Individuals With Disabilities (PEATID-III) Inventory*—Uses a 5-point Likert scale (strongly disagree, disagree, undecided, agree, strongly agree) to respond to 12 statements with embedded blanks, such as "Teaching students labeled as _____ in my regular PE classes with nonhandicapped students will disrupt the harmony of the class."	Note the Rizzo sources in the "References" at the end of this chapter or contact him at California State University at San Bernardino, 5500 University Parkway, San Bernardino, CA 92407-2397. Jansma, P., & Schultz, B. (1982). Validation and use of a mainstreaming attitude inventory with physical educators. *American Corrective Therapy Journal, 36,* 150–157.
2. *Jansma & Schultz Mainstreaming Attitude Inventory for Physical Educators*—Uses a +3 to –3 point scale (strongly disagree, disagree, slightly disagree, slightly agree, agree, strongly agree) to respond to 20 items about a 10-year-old boy.	

Agree/Disagree Opinion Scale

1. *Attitudes Toward Disabled Persons Scale (ATDP)*—Uses a +3 to –3 point scale (I agree very much to I disagree very much) to respond to 30 items. This scale has generated more publications than any other.	Yuker, H., & Block, J. (1986). *Research with the ATDP Scales, 1960–1985.* Order from Hofstra University Bookstore, Hempstead, NY 11550.

Adjective and Phrase Checklists

1. *Siperstein Adjective Checklist for Describing Classmates*—Asks students to circle as many adjectives as they wish to describe a peer. List includes 16 positive and 18 negative adjectives.	Same source as Siperstein Friendship Activity Scale. These can be ordered from Dr. Gary Siperstein, Center for the Study of Social Acceptance, University of Massachusetts, Boston, MA 02125.
2. *Children's Attitudes Toward Handicapped Scale (CAHS)*—Asks students to respond to 20 descriptors of a peer by circling one of three phrases for each (e.g., are lots of fun, are fun, are not any fun).	Rapier, J., Adelson, R., Carey, R., & Croke, K. (1972). Changes in children's attitudes toward the physically handicapped. *Exceptional Children, 39,* 219–223.

Children's Attitude Measures—Likert-Type Scales

1. *Children's Attitudes Toward Integrated Physical Education-Revised (CAIPE-R)*—Uses a 4-point Likert scale (yes, probably yes, probably no, no) to respond to 12–14 feeling and intention statements.	Block, M. E. (1995). Development and validation of the Children's Attitudes Toward Physical Education-Revised Inventory. *Adapted Physical Activity Quarterly, 12*(1), 60–77.

References

Aiello, B. (1988). The Kids on the Block and attitude change. In H. E. Yuker (Ed.), *Attitudes toward persons with disabilities* (pp. 223–229). New York: Springer.

Ajzen, I. (1985). From intentions to actions: A theory of planned behavior. In J. Kuhl & J. Beckmann (Eds.), *Action-control from cognition to behavior* (pp. 11–39). Heidelberg: Springer.

Ajzen, I. (1991). The theory of planned behavior. *Organizational Behavior and Human Decision Processes, 50,* 179–211.

Ajzen, I., & Fishbein, M. (1980). *Understanding attitudes and predicting social behavior.* Englewood Cliffs, NJ: Prentice Hall.

Allport, G. W. (1954). *The nature of prejudice.* Cambridge, MA: Addison-Wesley.

American Alliance for Health, Physical Education, Recreation and Dance (1995). *AAHPERD position statement on inclusion.* Reston, VA: Author.

Archie, V., & Sherrill, C. (1989). Attitudes toward handicapped peers of mainstreamed and nonmainstreamed children in physical education. *Perceptual and Motor Skills, 69,* 319–322.

Bandura, A. (1986). *Social foundations of thought and action: A social cognitive theory.* Englewood Cliffs, NJ: Prentice Hall.

Block, M. E. (1995). Development and validation of the Children's Attitudes Toward Integrated Physical Education–Revised (CAIPE-R) Inventory. *Adapted Physical Activity Quarterly, 12,* 60–77.

Block, M. E. (1996). Implications of U.S. federal law and court cases for physical education placement of students with disabilities. *Adapted Physical Activity Quarterly, 13*(2), 127–152.

Block, M. E., & Zeman, R. (1996). Including students with disabilities in regular physical education: Effects on nondisabled children. *Adapted Physical Activity Quarterly, 13*(1), 38–49.

Chase, M. A., & Dummer, G. (1992). The role of sports as a social determinant for children. *Research Quarterly for Exercise and Sport, 63,* 418–424.

Decker, J., & Jansma, P. (1995). Physical education least restrictive continua used in the United States. *Adapted Physical Activity Quarterly, 12*(2), 124–138.

DePaepe, J. L. (1985). The influence of three least restrictive environments on the content motor ALT and performance of moderately mentally retarded students. *Journal of Teaching in Physical Education, 3,* 34–41.

Dishman, R. (Ed.). (1988). *Exercise adherence: Its impact on public health.* Champaign, IL: Human Kinetics.

Festinger, L. (1957). *A theory of cognitive dissonance.* Stanford, CA: Stanford University Press.

Fishbein, H. D. (1996). *Peer prejudice and discrimination.* Boulder, CO: Westview Press.

Gatch, C. L., & Kendzierski, D. (1990). Predicting exercise intentions: The theory of planned behavior. *Research Quarterly for Exercise and Sport, 61*(1), 100–102.

Goffman, E. (1963). *Stigma: Notes on the management of a spoiled identity.* Englewood Cliffs, NJ: Prentice Hall.

Gresham, F. (1982). Misguided mainstreaming: The case for social skills training with handicapped children. *Exceptional Children, 48,* 422–433.

Heikinaro-Johansson, P., & Vogler, E. W. (1996). Physical education including individuals with disabilities in school settings. *Sport Science Review, 5*(1), 12–25.

Hellison, D. (1978). *Beyond balls and bats: Alienated youth in the gym.* Washington, DC: American Alliance for Health, Physical Education, and Recreation.

Hellison, D. (1984). *Goals and strategies for teaching physical education.* Champaign, IL: Human Kinetics.

Horne, M. (1985). *Attitudes toward handicapped students: Professional, peer, and parent reactions.* Hillsdale, NJ: Erlbaum.

Ittenbach, R., Abery, B., Larson, S., Spiegel, A., & Prouty, R. (1994). Community adjustment of young adults with mental retardation: Overcoming barriers to inclusion. *Palaestra, 10*(2), 32–42.

Jones, R. L. (Ed.). (1984). *Attitudes and attitude change in special education: Theory and practices.* Reston, VA: Council for Exceptional Children.

Katz, I. (1981). *Stigma: A social psychological analysis.* Hillsdale, NJ: Erlbaum.

Laban, R. (1960). *The mastery of movement* (2nd ed.). London: MacDonald & Evans.

Laban, R. (1975). *Modern educational dance.* London: MacDonald & Evans.

Lewin, K. (1951). *Field theory in the social sciences.* New York: Harper.

Lieberman, L. J., Newcomer, J., & McCubbin, J. (1996). *The effects of cross aged peer tutors on the academic learning time in physical education of students with disabilities in inclusive elementary physical education.* Research presentation, AAHPERD conference, Atlanta.

Long, E., Irmer, L., Burkett, L., Glasenapp, G., & Odenkirk, B. (1980). PEOPEL. *Journal of Physical Education and Recreation, 51,* 28–29.

Lott, B. E., & Lott, A. J. (1960). The formation of positive attitude toward group members. *Journal of Abnormal and Social Psychology, 61,* 297–300.

Marlowe, M. (1980). Games analysis intervention: A procedure to increase peer acceptance of socially isolated children. *Research Quarterly for Exercise and Sport, 51,* 422–426.

Marlowe, M., Algozzine, G., Lerch, H. A., & Welch, F. D. (1978). Games analysis intervention: A procedure to decrease the feminine play patterns of emotionally disturbed boys, *Research Quarterly, 49,* 484–490.

Martin, J. J., & Mushett, C. A. (1996). Social support mechanisms among athletes with disabilities. *Adapted Physical Activity Quarterly, 13*(1), 74–83.

Mender, J., Kerr, R., & Orlick, T. (1982). A cooperative games program for learning disabled children. *International Journal of Sports Psychology, 13,* 222–233.

Morris, G. S. D., & Stiehl, J. (1989). *Changing kids' games.* Champaign, IL: Human Kinetics.

Mosston, M., & Ashworth, S. (1986). *Teaching physical education* (3d ed.). Columbus, OH: Merrill.

Orlick, T. (1978). *The cooperative sports and games book.* New York: Pantheon.

Rarick, G. L., & Beuter, A. (1985). The effect of mainstreaming on the motor performance of mentally retarded and nonhandicapped students. *Adapted Physical Activity Quarterly, 2,* 277–282.

Rizzo, T. L. (1984). Attitudes of physical educators toward teaching handicapped pupils. *Adapted Physical Activity Quarterly, 1,* 267–274.

Rizzo, T. L. (1995). *The Physical Educators' Attitude Toward Teaching Individuals with Disabilities–III.* Unpublished instrument. Available from Dr. Terry Rizzo, California State University at San Bernardino, 5500 University Parkway, San Bernardino, CA 92407-2397.

Rizzo, T. L., & Kirkendall, D. R. (1995). Teaching students with mild disabilities: What affects attitudes of future physical educators? *Adapted Physical Activity Quarterly, 12*(3), 205–216.

Rizzo, T. L., & Vispoel, W. P. (1991). Physical educators' attributes and attitudes toward teaching students with handicaps. *Adapted Physical Activity Quarterly, 8*(1), 4–11.

Roberts, C., Pratt, C., & Leach, D. (1991). Classroom and playground interaction of students with and without disabilities. *Exceptional Children, 57*, 212–225.

Roberts, C., & Zubrick, S. (1993). Factors influencing the social status of children with mild academic disabilities in regular classrooms. *Exceptional Children, 59*(3), 192–202.

Rohnke, K. (1977). *Cowstails and cobras: A guide to ropes courses, initiative games, and other adventure activities.* Hamilton, MA: Project Adventure.

Rynders, J., Johnson, R., Johnson, D. W., & Schmidt, R. (1980). Producing positive interaction among Down syndrome and nonhandicapped teenagers through cooperative goal structuring. *American Journal of Mental Deficiency, 85,* 268–273.

Selman, R. L. (1980). *The growth of interpersonal understanding.* New York: Academic Press.

Sherrill, C. (1986). Social and psychological dimensions of sports for disabled athletes. In C. Sherrill (Ed.), *Sports and disabled athletes* (pp. 21–33). Champaign, IL: Human Kinetics.

Sherrill, C. (1994). Least restrictive environments and total inclusion philosophies: Critical analysis. *Palaestra, 10*(3), 25–35.

Sherrill, C., Heikinaro-Johansson, P., & Slininger, D. (1994). Equal-status relationships in the gym. *Journal of Physical Education, Recreation and Dance, 65*(1), 27–31, 56.

Sherrill, C., & Williams, T. (1996). Disability and sport: Psychosocial perspectives on inclusion, integration, and participation. *Sport Science Review, 5*(1), 42–64.

Strain, P. S. (1982). *Social development of exceptional children.* Rockville, MD: Aspen.

Theodorakis, Y., Bagiatis, K., & Goudas, M. (1995). Attitudes toward teaching individuals with disabilities: Application of planned behavior theory. *Adapted Physical Activity Quarterly,12*(2), 151–160.

Titus, J. A., & Watkinson, E. J. (1987). Effects of segregated and integrated programs on the participation and social interaction of moderately mentally handicapped children in play. *Adapted Physical Activity Quarterly, 4,* 204–319.

Tripp, A., French, R., & Sherrill, C. (1995). Contact theory and attitudes of children in physical education programs toward peers with disabilities. *Adapted Physical Activity Quarterly, 12*(4), 323–332.

Tripp, A., & Sherrill, C. (1991). Attitude theories of relevance to adapted physical education. *Adapted Physical Activity Quarterly, 8*(1), 112–127.

Waksman, S., Messmer, C. L., & Waksman, D. D. (1988). *The Waksman social skills program.* Austin: Pro·Ed.

Walker, H. M., McConnell, S., Holmes, D., Todis, B., Walker, J., & Golden, N. (1988). *The Walker Social Skills Curriculum: The ACCEPTS Program.* Austin: Pro•Ed.

Webster, G. E. (1987). Influence of peer tutors upon academic learning time—Physical education of mentally handicapped students. *Journal of Teaching in Physical Education, 6,* 393–403.

Wright, B. (1983). *Physical disability—A psychosocial approach* (2nd ed.). Philadelphia: Harper & Row.

Yilla, A. (1994). Full inclusion—A philosophical statement. *Palaestra, 10*(4), 18.

CHAPTER

10

Sensorimotor Integration and Severe Disability

FIGURE 10.1 Children with developmental delays, including cerebral palsy, need teachers who understand all of the systems of the body, as well as environmental interactions and constraints. Of particular importance is knowledge of *(A)* postural and balance reactions and *(B)* reflexes that interfere with body control.

A   B

After you have studied this chapter, you should be able to do the following:

1. Contrast sensorimotor integration with perceptual-motor learning.

2. Identify 10 sense modalities and discuss four sensory systems that are especially important in motor learning. Explain common developmental problems in each and techniques used for remediation.

3. Describe 10 reflex patterns of most importance to physical educators and discuss problems caused by abnormal retention.

4. Discuss pedagogy in working with persons whose reflexes are interfering with motor learning and performance. Identify four principles that guide pedagogy.

5. Identify and discuss these reactions: (a) righting, (b) parachute, and (c) equilibrium. Discuss how these relate to balance and how they can be strengthened and reinforced.

6. Use the Milani-Comparetti system to assess 9 motor milestones, 5 primitive reflexes, and 13 postural reactions.

7. Demonstrate understanding of the neurological bases of motor development. Know how each part of the central nervous system (CNS) develops. Be able to (a) identify parts of the nerve cell and the CNS; (b) describe their structure, location, and function; and (c) discuss how delayed and abnormal development affect motor learning and control.

8. Discuss the neurological bases of clumsiness. Include in your discussion the seven characteristics of a mature, intact CNS.

9. Identify some theories that guide teaching practices in this chapter. Go to the library and read more about these theories.

Consider an individual who is clumsy and/or unable to perform locomotor and object control activities that are easy for peers. This individual might be in a regular or an alternative physical activity setting but obviously has severe, complex motor problems that interfere with learning and performance and affect social acceptance, inclusion, and self-esteem. Many of these individuals have **cerebral palsy** (damage to parts of the brain controlling movement and posture), the most common physical disability in the public schools (see Figure 10.1). Others have movement difficulties or clumsiness of undetermined origin. In addition to motor skill instruction, these individuals need work on underlying problems. This work is typically called **sensorimotor integration.**

Chapter 10 and 12 focus on sensorimotor and perceptual-motor difficulties, respectively. Chapter 10 specifically addresses muscle and postural tone; tactile, kinesthetic, vestibular, and visual integration; reflex and postural reaction problems; and fundamentals of neurology necessary to understanding clumsiness. Chapter 12 specifically addresses clumsiness associated with perceptual-motor problems. Perception is inseparable from cognition; thus, these problems require pedagogical strategies different from those described in this chapter.

The Organization of Sensory Input

Sensorimotor integration and *sensory integration* are synonyms. Both are defined as *the organization of sensory information for use* (Ayres, 1972, 1980). This organization occurs within the brain and spinal cord (the central nervous system, CNS) and is often called **central processing.** The content of this chapter is guided by both neuromaturational/hierarchical models and dynamic systems theory. These are described in the final section of this chapter.

Intrasensory and intersensory integration are outcomes of both sensorimotor and perceptual-motor training. **Intrasensory integration** refers to improved function within *(intra-)* one sensory system. Visual training, for example, promotes intrasensory integration of the visual system. **Intersensory integration** refers to improved function between *(inter-)* several sensory systems.

Many factors affect intrasensory and intersensory integration. Among these are normalcy of CNS development; damage to the CNS by injury, disease, or activity deprivation; normalcy of function of other body systems; environmental affordances and constraints; motivation, and aspects of psychosocial functioning that influence effort and persistence.

Definitions, Goals, and Objectives

Table 10.1 presents brief definitions of the major psychomotor problems of concern in sensorimotor integration. Use of the terms in Table 10.1 facilitates writing goals and objectives. The following are illustrative goals:

1. To integrate or normalize abnormal muscle and postural tone

2. To reduce hypertonus or hypotonus in a particular body part

3. To enable independent, purposeful movement of body parts

4. To reduce tactile integration disorders

5. To reduce abnormal reflex activity and/or to learn to cope with reflexes or use them to advantage in movement tasks

6. To demonstrate protective extension or propping reactions

7. To demonstrate body control in physical education activities done from lying positions (prone, supine, side)

8. To increase the number of seconds of head control or sitting balance or other tasks of importance to nonambulatory individuals

9. To demonstrate sufficient visual-motor control for 60% success in tetherball striking activities from a wheelchair for 3 minutes

T a b l e   1 0 . 1   Major psychomotor problems related to the nervous system: Definitions.

1. **Muscle or postural tone irregularities.** An abnormal amount of tension within a muscle or muscle group. *Hypertonus* is too much tension, a stiff appearance, and reduced range of motion. *Hypotonus* is too little tension, a flaccid or floppy appearance, weakness, or paralysis. *Fluctuating tonus* is involuntary shifting between hypertonic and hypotonic states.

2. **Sensory input system problems.** Problems of structure or function of sensory organs or nerve fibers that carry impulses to the brain. These are generally manifested as impaired acuity (accurateness of seeing, hearing, touching) or sensitivity (too much, *hypersensitive;* or too little, *hyposensitive*).

3. **Sensory and perceptual central processing problems.** Organizational problems within the brain. Difficulty translating input into desired or appropriate output.

4. **Reflex integration problems.** Reflexes are involuntary, predictable changes in muscle or postural tone in response to sensory input. *Reflexes* are normal in newborn infants, but these reflexes are *pathological* when they persist beyond infancy.

5. **Postural reaction problems.** Reactions are automatic responses to sensory input that keep body parts in alignment, enable control, maintain balance, and prevent falls.

6. **Associated movements or overflow.** The inability to move one body part without associated movements of other parts. Sometimes called *differentiation problems.*

7. **Stereotypies.** Purposeless, rhythmical, patterned movements of body parts (such as leg kicking) that are normal in infants but pathological when they persist as rocking, waving, wriggling, or banging mannerisms.

8. **Ataxia.** Generalized motor clumsiness related to balance and coordination difficulties. Largely related to a lack of movement and position sense (kinesthesis), but influenced by all the movement sensory systems (tactile, kinesthetic, vestibular, visual).

9. **Spasticity.** Multidimensional impairment of voluntary movement that can be of either cerebral or spinal cord origin. **Spasticity caused by cerebral damage** (the most common) is *hypertonus* complicated by overly active reflex activity so that movement is restricted, stiff, and clumsy. **Spasticity caused by spinal cord injury** is the occasional occurrence of spasms or jerks in muscles below the injury level.

These goals are illustrative of the needs of individuals with severe disabilities. To benefit from instruction, some of these individuals need one-to-one help. Physical educators should request paraprofessionals or peer tutors for each person. Knowledge gained in this chapter will help you train helpers as well as do "hands-on" work yourself. Other individuals with severe disabilities have enough body control to move their limbs without help and to follow class instructions. Regardless of the highest level of motor performance possible, these individuals should be helped to see movement as fun and to visualize themselves as athletes, dancers, or swimmers working toward personal bests.

Before studying specific sensory integration problems, it is helpful to think about the nervous system and gain insight into its complexity. Knowledge about nervous system function facilitates teamwork with therapists and rehabilitation personnel and aids in communication with parents.

The Organization of the Nervous System

The nervous system is organized as a **central nervous system** (brain and spinal cord) and a **peripheral nervous system** (12 pairs of cranial nerves, 12 pairs of spinal nerves, and the autonomic nervous system). The central nervous system (CNS) is of primary interest in working with persons who are clumsy or have developmental coordination disorder (DCD). Sensory integration problems often occur while neural impulses are traveling up and down the spinal cord or inside the brain. Imagine thousands of neural impulses (some sensory, some motor, some interpretive, some cognitive) traveling at various speeds inside the CNS. Impulses like those that enable cognition can originate in the brain without sensory input, but cognition

about movement usually starts when sensory input arrives via the spinal cord and various tracts within the brain. Figure 10.2 shows the parts of the CNS that perform major functions.

Tracts for Sensory and Motor Impulses

The spinal cord is comprised of **tracts** (pathways) containing nerve fibers that carry impulses to and from the brain. Impulses that originate in sensory receptors in the skin, muscles, tendons, and joints travel up the spinal cord in **dorsal ascending sensory tracts** (see Figure 10.2). The names of these tracts, like *spinocerebellar* and *spinothalamic,* indicate the starting and end points of the tract. For example, the **spinocerebellar tract** starts in the spinal cord and ends in the cerebellum. Each tract carries only one kind of sensory information (e.g., touch, pain, heat, movement) and has a specific destination. Sensory information is sometimes called **afferent,** meaning "to or toward the brain."

Motor commands that cause movement originate inside the brain and are called **efferent,** meaning "out of the brain." Motor impulses travel down the spinal cord in **ventral descending motor tracts.** Inside the brain, these tracts have special names (*cortical* or *noncortical; pyramidal* and *extrapyramidal*), but outside they are simply called motor tracts. Sensorimotor problems typically occur inside the brain, not in the spinal cord.

Parts and Functions of the Brain

The major parts of the brain toward which sensory integration remediation is directed are the brain stem, midbrain, cerebellum, cerebral cortex, and internal capsule of the cerebrum (see Figure 10.2). Each of these has specific functions in preventing clumsiness and motor pathology.

FIGURE 10.2   Areas of the cerebral cortex that perform specific functions, noncortical structures (specified at left) that affect these functions, and spinal cord tracts that carry neural impulses to activate functions.

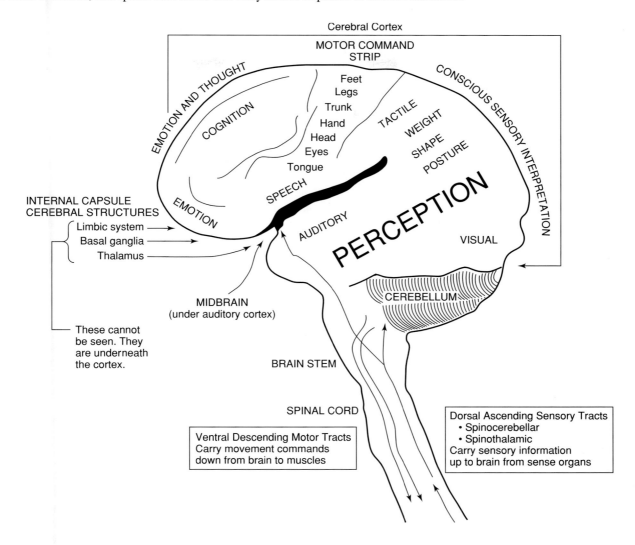

The Brain Stem

The **brain stem** regulates muscle and postural tone and reflexes (see Table 10.1 for definitions of these). In normal development, reflexes are associated with infants. However, in adapted physical activity, reflexes are associated with clumsiness and/or pathology in individuals of all ages. The brain stem receives sensory information from all of the **sensory modalities,** except vision and smell, and thus performs a lot of organizational activity.

Pathological muscle tone and reflexes are caused when the brain stem receives sensory information about touch, pressure, or movement experienced by body parts and does not permit this sensory input to travel to higher levels of the brain. Instead the brain stem immediately converts the sensory information into motor commands that are sent down the spinal cord to excite muscle fibers to change length. This results in a shifting of muscle tone or a movement of a body part.

The brain stem also contains the structures that regulate attention, arousal, wakefulness, and general activity level. These processes involve filtering incoming sensory information and selectively transferring some sensory impulses to higher levels of the brain while inhibiting others. Damage to

the brain stem can result in attention and activity excesses in either direction—too much *(hyper-)* or too little *(hypo-).*

The Midbrain

The **midbrain,** located at about ear level deep inside the brain, regulates postural reactions. These include all of the **automatic patterns** that enable stability and mobility in activities of daily living (ADL). The midbrain also receives all of the sensory information from the eyes, which helps to explain why vision is so important to balance.

The Cerebellum

The **cerebellum** has many functions but is particularly important in the automatic performance of skilled movement so that conscious thought is not needed. The cerebellum is also essential to good balance and the timing of fast movements.

The Cerebrum

The **cerebrum** is divided into the cerebral cortex (the six-layer outer covering of the brain) and the internal capsule.

The **cerebral cortex** performs all of the higher-level mental functions that enable thought, emotion, perception, memory, language, and voluntary, spontaneous movement (see Figure 10.2). The **internal capsule** contains clusters of cell bodies that perform specific functions. Greatly simplified, these include the **limbic system,** which regulates emotion; the **basal ganglia,** which enable steady postures and movement without tremors; and the **thalamus,** which acts as a major relay station for sensory impulses.

Sensory information is processed, integrated, or organized in the cerebral cortex. Simplified, the **occipital** (rear) lobe governs vision and visual perception. The **temporal** area (above the ears, the temples) governs audition and provides memory for both auditory and visual experiences. The **parietal** (side) area is responsible for the interpretation of skin and muscular sensations and speech. The **frontal** area includes the motor strip, where motor impulses for voluntary movement originate, and the sites of cognitive function and personality. In reality, there is much overlapping of function. This information, however, gives insight into the amount of organizational activity that occurs within the cortex.

Almost all of the cerebral cortex is involved in organizational activity that affects voluntary movement. Remember that voluntary movement is functionally inseparable from attention, perception, cognition, and memory. Much of everyday movement, however, is involuntary or automatic and under the control of lower levels of the brain. In severe disability, problems at lower levels of the brain are typically addressed before problems at higher levels. **Involuntary** refers to reflex or brain stem activity, whereas **automatic** refers to postural reactions (midbrain activity) and skilled movement patterns that are performed without conscious thought (cerebellar activity).

Cortical and Subcortical Disorders

For assessment and remediation purposes, movement disorders are classified as cortical and subcortical. **Cortical disorders** can be improved by conscious thought, practice, and determination and thus are responsive to ordinary teaching methods. **Subcortical disorders** typically do not respond to ordinary teaching methods and thus constitute a particular challenge. Remediation directed toward cortical disorders is called **perceptual-motor** because perception (interpretation) is a cognitive activity. Remediation directed toward subcortical disorders is called **sensorimotor** because sensation, neurologically defined, occurs without cognition. Many individuals who are clumsy have both cortical and subcortical disorders, so teachers need to decide specifically which problems must be addressed first.

Cortical Functions

Cortical refers to functions of the cerebral cortex (the outer covering of the cerebrum) and the cortical tracts that carry neural impulses. The **cerebral cortex** performs all of the higher-level functions, including the planning and execution of conscious movement, and helps to regulate excitation and inhibition processes that determine muscle and postural tone.

The **cortical tracts** carry impulses from one part of the brain to another, thereby enabling the integration and association of different kinds of data.

Subcortical Functions

Subcortical refers to functions of all the CNS structures except the cerebral cortex and cortical tracts. Subcortical functions include (a) skilled movements that no longer require conscious attention and (b) automatic movements like postural reactions and basic movement patterns that enable activities of daily living (ADL). Common problems include early reflexes that have not been integrated, overflow movement, stereotypies, inefficient protective mechanisms like the postural reactions, integration deficits that interfere with smooth, accurate movements performed at the desired force and speed, and arousal/attention deficits.

Clearly, clumsiness pertains to a breakdown between cortical and subcortical functions. Consider persons who bend their elbow or do not keep their eyes on the ball in tennis. These persons generally cognitively understand what to do, but they cannot make their body do what their mind wants. Identifying specific problems for remediation is difficult because all of the neural functions interact in complex ways. Usually something is wrong with **central processing** (the generation, organization, or relaying of neural impulses inside the CNS).

Following are sections on several factors that affect sensorimotor function. The first factor to be assessed and attended to is muscle and postural tone.

Muscle and Postural Tone

Muscle tone refers to contractile tension or firmness within a muscle or group of muscles, whereas **postural tone** refers to the mobility and stability functional capacity of the total body, especially the tone of the postural muscles that hold the body upright against the pull of gravity. The **postural muscles** (also called antigravity muscles) are the extensors of the head, neck, trunk, and lower extremities and the flexors of the upper extremities.

Muscle Families and Actions

Muscle families is a simplified way of referring to prime mover groups on the same surface that perform the same actions. The **extensor families** are on the posterior surface and the **flexor families** are on the anterior surface, with one exception—the muscle groups that work on the knee joint are the opposite of the rest of the body, with the extensors (quadriceps) on the anterior thigh and the flexors (hamstrings) on the posterior thigh. The **adductor families** are on the medial or inside surface and pull body parts toward or across midline. The **abductor families** are on the lateral or outside surface and pull body parts away from midline. The prefixes *ad-* ("to, toward") and *ab-* ("away from") help us remember direction of movement.

Rotator muscle groups are more complex in location. Most inward rotators are on the anteromedial surface, and most outward rotators are on the posterolateral surface. Thus, inward rotators tend to work with adductors, and outward rotators tend to work with extensors. This is particularly evident in spastic gaits of cerebral origin, which are called **scissors gaits,** because the inward rotators, flexors, and adductors of the hip joint are tighter than their antagonistic or opposite muscle groups and therefore cause a pigeon-toed walk. This tightness has nothing to do with strength and is caused by an imbalance in excitation and inhibition impulses that come from the brain.

Reciprocal Innervation or Inhibition

Reciprocal innervation (also called inhibition) is the neural process that regulates muscle and postural tone. Simply explained, reciprocal innervation is the act of muscles on one surface *contracting* (the prime movers or agonists) while muscles on the opposite surface (the antagonists) are *relaxing.* For smooth, graceful, and effective movement to occur, this continuous shifting of muscle tone must be perfectly timed and balanced. This shifting of muscle tone is complex, with upper motor neurons (those in the brain) responsible for generating **excitation** (facilitation) and **inhibition** (suppression) impulses. Excitation increases muscle tone, and inhibition decreases muscle tone.

Muscle Tone Disorders

The muscle tone disorders are **hypotonia** (floppiness), **hypertonia** (stiffness, spasticity), and **fluctuating tone** (mixed cerebral palsy). These are associated with both congenital and acquired conditions that cause damage to the motor part of the brain (see Figure 10.3). Illustrative *congenital* conditions are Down syndrome, severe mental retardation, and cerebral palsy. Illustrative *acquired* conditions are stroke, brain disease, and traumatic brain injury.

Some muscle tone disorders can be remediated, and some cannot. For example, persons with spastic cerebral palsy tend to have hypertonia problems throughout their lifespan. Their upper extremities are dominated by flexor tone, and their lower extremities are dominated by extensor tone. Some persons with Down syndrome seem to grow out of the generalized hypotonia at birth, but others do not.

Assessment of Muscle Tone Disorders

Muscle tone is assessed through either observation and palpation (examination by touch) or electromyography (EMG). It is easy to discern muscle tone disorders, and this task is typically conducted as a fast screening procedure. Muscle tone of different body parts varies according to the area of the brain that is damaged. Each part of the body should therefore be screened separately. A 3-point scale is often used:

1 point—Hypotonia: Floppiness, inability to resist gravity, inability to grasp or hold an object. An abnormally large range of motion, with no control, that results in froglike lying and sitting postures.

2 points—Normal muscle tone: Balance between excitation and inhibition and prime mover and antagonist muscle groups; ability to use muscles in groups or to isolate a given muscle if necessary. A distinction is made between normal relaxed tone and innervated, moving tone.

FIGURE 10.3 Children with severe muscle tone disorders need one-to-one instruction.

3 points—Hypertonia: Spasticity, a feeling of tightness or resistance to passive stretch, limited range of movement. In severe cases, joint contractures (permanent fixations) might be present.

Fatigue, anxiety and environmental variables (e.g., temperature, noise, demands) influence muscle tone, so the examiner should note such conditions. Also, several observations over different days should be used.

Hypotonia Remediation Activities

Many infants with severe disability exhibit low tone and consequently are delayed in achieving motor milestones like lifts head, sits, and rolls. These individuals (often throughout their lifespan) initiate little spontaneous, purposeful activity and must therefore be massaged, bounced, rocked, rolled, swung, tilted, or carried by another to obtain sensory input that will help normalize muscle tone. Motivation devices like mirrors, noisemaking objects, and electronic devices that create music or activate vibration should be used to encourage and reinforce spontaneous movement. The remediation goal, overall, is facilitation of active movement in every possible way; passive movement is used only to supplement and stimulate self-movement, not as a substitute.

By age 5 or 6 years, individuals with severe hypotonia will probably be fitted with wheelchairs to help with correct positioning and mobility. Physical education instruction should include developmentally appropriate sport, dance, and exercise wheelchair activities as well as total body movement

FIGURE 10.4 Sensory receptors. Each sensory input system has distinctly different receptors.

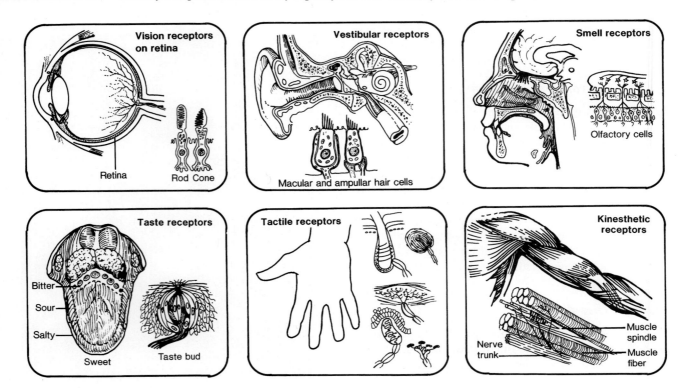

Sensory Input Systems

Ten modalities provide sensory input that must be organized and processed. These are (a) touch and pressure, (b) kinesthesis, (c) the vestibular system, (d) temperature, (e) pain, (f) smell, (g) taste, (h) vision, (i) audition, and (j) the common chemical sense. With the exception of the last one, these senses are familiar to all of us. The common chemical sense controls the complex reaction to such activities as peeling an onion (eyes burning, nose sneezing) or eating a hot pepper. Each modality has a special type of end organ (sensory receptor) that is sensitive only to certain stimuli, and each has a separate pathway from the sensory receptor up the spinal cord to the brain. Figure 10.4 depicts some of these sensory receptors.

Sensory systems especially important to motor learning are tactile and deep pressure, kinesthetic, vestibular, and visual. When these systems exhibit delayed or abnormal functioning, motor development and/or learning is affected.

Tactile Integration

The tactile system is probably the most fully developed resource at birth, as evidenced by the infant's cries signifying discomfort with wet diapers. Therefore, many authorities recommend targeting this system when working with individuals with severe learning problems who are nonambulatory and compromised in many aspects of movement. The brain organizes tactile system input in many ways and has different locations for processing light touch, deep pressure (massage or weight taken on body parts, such as the soles of the feet), cold, heat, and different kinds of pain that originate in skin receptor organs.

executed by others on mats and apparatus and in the water. Many individuals with *hypotonia* (individuals with brain injury and stroke at all ages as well as infants) experience extreme muscle tone shifts after a few months and thereafter have *hypertonia* (spasticity).

Hypertonia (Spasticity) Remediation Activities

Inhibition or relaxation techniques (slow, rhythmic, repetitive actions) are recommended to decrease spasticity. These should be done in warm water (90 to 98 degrees F) and on every possible land surface. A major strategy for decreasing overall spasticity is rotation of the trunk by the teacher, assisted by a mobile surface like a large beachball or therapy ball, tiltboard, hammock, or other apparatus that enables rolling and rotation.

Spasticity compromises righting, protective extension, and equilibrium postural reactions, so activities that address these goals are important. This calls for many kinds of static and dynamic balances on all kinds of surfaces in all kinds of positions (lying, sitting, four-point, standing, etc.).

Stretching exercises are important also, because spasticity limits range of motion and eventually causes joint contractures (permanent fixation) if frequent, appropriate stretching is not done. *Exercises should use patterns opposite the spastic postures.* For example, slow elevation of the extended, outwardly rotated arm over the head inhibits the fixed spastic flexor position of the arm. For more information on stretching, see the chapters on cerebral palsy and relaxation. The chapters on dance and aquatics also describe appropriate total body activities. The goal is to independently perform stretches in good alignment. If the individual cannot do so, then stretching should be provided by an outside source.

Tactile integration disorders of most interest to physical educators include these:

1. Tactile defensiveness: Touch (one's own and that of others) causes generalized discomfort, irritability, or temper outbursts.
2. Tactile craving or aggressiveness: A greater than average need to touch and be touched.
3. Body image and object awareness problems related to body boundaries, feeling the difference between self and not-self, and processing information that comes from touch.

Assessment of Tactile Integration Problems

Observation in natural settings is probably the best approach. Self-reporting works well with older individuals. Assess yourself and others.

Tactile Defensiveness

Look for the following tactile defensive behaviors:

1. Stiffening when tactile praise like a shoulder touch or pat on the back is given; ducking or moving aside to avoid a hug or tactile praise
2. Complaining more than peers about feeling dirty or sweaty or hot or cold, or showing distaste through gesture and facial expression
3. Avoiding tight clothes, shoes, gloves, automobile seat belts, elevators full of people, and other variables that increase tactile input
4. Disliking certain food textures, unusual sensitivity to these
5. Complaining that peers tag too hard in games or push too much in lines; inability to cope with normal roughhousing among peers

Note that these behaviors might be specific to certain body parts or might occur in response to touch anywhere on the body.

Tactile Craving

Look for the opposite extremes in identifying tactile craving behaviors. Remember, however, that response to touch is cultural and also specific to families. Check whether the individual is responding as other family members do or is showing excessive extremes.

Body Image and Object Awareness

In regard to these problems, check for tactile awareness through informal observation and formal testing. Problems include these:

1. **Stereoagnosia**—inability to identify shapes, textures, and other characteristics of three-dimensional objects by touch alone
2. **Finger or body part agnosia**—inability, when eyes are closed, to recognize which body part has been touched; also called one-point discrimination or localization problems; called **tag agnosia** when individuals do not realize they have been tagged as part of a game
3. **Multiple-point discrimination agnosia**—inability to identify two or more body parts touched simultaneously

4. Affective domain concerns pertaining to body and object touch, feelings, or attitudes that interfere with wellness or learning

Activities for Remediation of Tactile Integration Problems

Write IEP objectives for both strengths and weaknesses. Remember to use rewards specific to each individual's assessed preferences. In general, remediate tactile defensiveness by pairing touch activities with reward and gradually increasing the amount of touch that can be tolerated (specify seconds or minutes of tolerance on the objective). For tactile craving, pair reward with not touching. For improved awareness, also give reward. Manipulate different environmental variables for generalization; use both land and water settings.

1. Use massage, either by hand or vibrator, to activate deep pressure receptors. Massage can be by another or by self. Encourage stroking or rubbing of own body parts. The back of the hands and the forearms are the least defensive and thus constitute the first progression activity when severe tactile defensiveness is present.
2. Stroke or brush body parts with fabrics and brushes of different textures. Coarse or rough textures are more easily tolerated than smooth textures, so build the teaching progression from coarse to smooth. Use a washcloth to rub the skin in a tub, spa, or pool.
3. Introduce weights of different textures as part of touch-feel-lift progressions in weight-lifting units. Stuffed animals are good with young children; use hug-and-release movements as well as touch-and-lift.
4. Conduct activities with a reach-in grab bag or box that require guessing the object one is touching without use of sight. Have children run from one station to another where different touch-and-guess activities are done.
5. Conduct "blind person's bluff" type games in which blindfolded persons try to catch and identify others. Do this on land and in water.

Kinesthetic Integration

The kinesthetic or muscle sense system enables organizational activity in both the noncortical and the cortical areas of the brain that contributes to movement awareness (time, space, force, flow) and coordination of body parts. Problems include these:

1. *Time*—inability to feel whether body parts are moving or stationary; if moving, inability to feel the speed of the motion
2. *Space*—inability to feel where body parts are in space, the direction in which they are moving, and whether body parts are bent or straight, aligned or not aligned, upright or inverted
3. *Force*—inability to feel the amount of force being exerted or the amount of weight being pushed, pulled, lifted, or lowered
4. *Flow*—inability to feel the smoothness or jerkiness of movement, especially in transitions from one speed to another, one direction to another, one shape to another, etc.

Receptors in every muscle, tendon, and joint contribute to kinesthesis, and this sensory system matures with movement experience. Kinesthetic integration is specific to muscle groups and thus difficult to assess, because the isolation of muscle groups—so that only one acts at a time—is impossible to achieve in a nonlaboratory setting. Noncortical kinesthetic integration (i.e, without thought) occurs during reflex integration, postural reaction emergence, and achievement of basic motor milestones or body control tasks. As soon as infants (or persons who have had a stroke) become consciously aware of a movement, cortical kinesthetic integration merges with noncortical. Thereafter, the degree of kinesthetic integration determines the ease of learning and automatizing all movement patterns.

Assessment of Kinesthetic Integration Problems

Assessment strategies vary according to whether the individual can understand and use language (i.e, whether the process is noncortical or combined noncortical and cortical). *Before language,* observe the following:

1. Reflex integration
2. Postural reaction emergence
3. Motor milestone achievement
4. Unsolicited, spontaneous imitations of movement

After language, observe the following:

1. Ability to imitate body movements on command (assess separately the time, space, force, and flow aspects of movement)
2. Ability to do a movement (independently or assisted), feel it kinesthetically, and then repeat it exactly after increasingly longer periods of time have elapsed

Activities for Remediation of Kinesthetic Integration Problems

Write IEP goals for both strengths and weaknesses. Use rewards specific to each individual's assessed preferences. Use the following activities:

1. Movement drills that emphasize exact repetition of a movement.
2. Games that require movement targeted toward a stationary point, like "pin the tail on the donkey," "hit a ball off a tee," or "jump exactly to a designated point."
3. Games that require movement targeted toward a moving object, like intercepting or striking a ball directed toward specific locations on the body (e.g., chest level, waist level).
4. Assisted and coactive movement. In **assisted movement,** the teacher guides body parts of the student through desired movement. In **coactive movement,** the student and teacher are in full-body contact, and the two move in unison.
5. Extension activities. The kinesthetic receptors are activated by changing the tension within muscle, tendon, and joint fibers. Therefore, any movement involving prolonged contraction of extensor muscles against gravity is especially facilitative. Scooterboard activities done in a prone position with the head up heightens kinesthetic awareness of midline. Applying pressure to the sites where muscles attach to bones normalizes muscle tone, relaxes muscles, and increases kinesthetic awareness. This practice is based on the same theory that underlies neck and back rubs as a means of reducing tension.
6. Movement exploration approaches.

Note that activities for kinesthetic integration invariably encompass tactile, vestibular, and visual input. Use blindfolds after individuals are 6 or 7 years old or can tolerate occlusion of vision. Minimize other input system actions as much as possible.

Vestibular Integration

The vestibular system originates in the inner ear area of the temporal lobe, where hair cell receptors take in information about the position of the head and all of its movements, however subtle (see Figure 10.5). This information, when interpreted and acted upon by other parts of the brain, helps to maintain static and dynamic balance. The vestibular system is the most important structure in the regulation of body postures. It prevents falling, keeps body parts properly aligned, and contributes to graceful, coordinated movement.

Equilibrium and balance, once used as synonyms, are now defined separately. **Equilibrium** is a biomechanical term denoting equal forces acting upon an object. In the human body, the forces exerted by muscles must equal external forces like gravity to keep the body upright. **Balance** is a more global term, referring to the control processes that maintain body parts in the specific alignments necessary to achieve different kinds of mobility and stability. Most persons with psychomotor problems have difficulty with balance. Four sensory systems (vestibular, kinesthetic, tactile, and visual) interact with environmental variables to enable balance. These, especially the vestibular system, are of considerable interest in adapted physical activity.

The vestibular apparatus, the part of the vestibular system that provides sensory information, is named for the hollow, bony *vestibule* (chamber) within the inner ear. This vestibule contains a *labyrinth* (maze) of interconnecting membranous tubes and sacs filled with fluid. The tubes are three *semicircular* canals arranged at right angles to each other. Two are vertical, and one is horizontal (see Figure 10.6). They are named superior, inferior, and horizontal (or anterior, posterior, and lateral). The sacs are the utricle and saccule. When the head is upright, the utricle is in a more superior position.

The two types of structures (canals and sacs) take in different kinds of sensory information about head movement. The semicircular canals are responsive to *angular movements,* especially rotation of the head to the left or right and diagonal movements forward and backward toward the floor. The sacs are responsive to *linear* or straight plane movements, like side to side, up and down, or forward and backward in the same plan (Crutchfield & Barnes, 1995).

The sensory receptors of the canals and sacs have different names. The hair cells of the canals are called *ampullae,*

FIGURE 10.5   The vestibular system. The *sensory component* consists of the semicircular canals (rotatory input) and sacs (linear input). The *motor component* consists of the four vestibular nuclei and the vestibulo-spinal tract. The vestibular nuclei relay information about the position of the head to many parts of the brain.

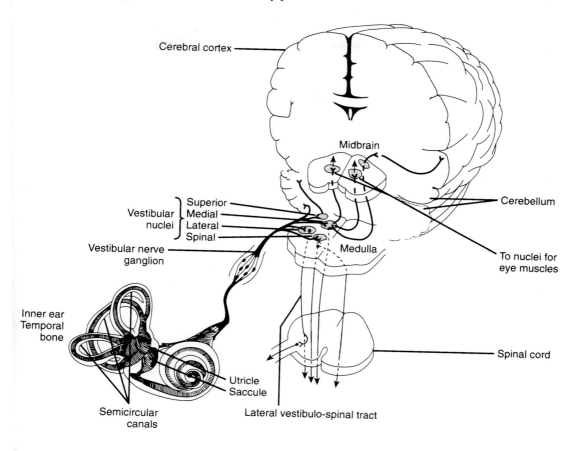

FIGURE 10.6   Semicircular canals and sacs (utricle and saccule).

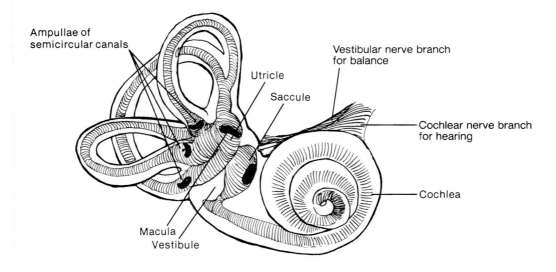

cristae, or *ampullary cristae* and are located in the bulbous enlargements of the canals at the point where they join the utricle. The hair cells of the sacs are called *maculae* or *otoliths.* To help remember, visualize Big Macs from McDonalds in sacs. Thinking of the sacs in straight lines on the counter correctly associates the maculae with linear movements of the head.

The maintenance of balance involves both sensory input and motor output. Vestibular impulses are carried via the vestibular nerve (eighth cranial) to four vestibular nuclei (clumps of gray matter) in the medulla (brain stem) (see Figure 10.5). Here, many motor impulses are generated to control balance. Some go directly to muscles that activate reflexes and/or reactions, some go to the cerebellum, and some go to midbrain nuclei or cranial nerves that innervate the eye muscles.

This process is very complicated because vestibular impulses are modified, reorganized, and integrated by tactile, kinesthetic, and visual input. Balance in young children is heavily influenced by vision, whereas adults rely more on tactile and kinesthetic input (Crutchfield & Barnes, 1995; Woollacott & Shumway-Cook, 1989). This explains why children and persons with developmental delays should be encouraged to focus their eyes on a designated point during balance activities. It also explains why blindfolds are often used in testing and remediating balance.

Assessment of Vestibular Integration

Vestibular function is activated by changes of head position. Assessment thus requires that challenges be made that cause momentary losses of balance (perturbations) that change head position. Many of these can be observed in natural playground settings in conjunction with the use of swings, seesaws, merry-go-rounds, and other apparatuses that owe their popularity to children's natural craving for vestibular stimulation. Assessment activities can be divided into natural activities and vestibular spinning.

Natural Activities That Change Head Position

1. For individuals with severe, nonambulatory conditions, use rocking motions in arms, rocking chair, tilt board, or therapy ball.
2. For others, use natural play environments with as many pieces of apparatus as possible (playground equipment, balance beams, swinging bridges, and changing-consistency locomotor surfaces like moon walks, mattresses, water beds, and trampolines).

Note whether head change causes pathological reflexes. If not, record the ease with which body parts adapt to head changes.

Vestibular Spinning Activities and Nystagmus

Vestibular testing is done by rapid spinning of individuals sitting on a stool; 20 seconds of spinning normally results in 9 to 11 seconds of **nystagmus** (rapid eye movements), an automatic midbrain response. A longer or shorter duration of nystagmus indicates a lack of vestibular integration. No dizziness or discomfort, or the opposite, including nausea, signal vestibular problems also. Vestibular spinning should be used only by individuals with special training (Ayres, 1972). Spinning is contraindicated when individuals are seizure-prone or have inner-ear or upper-respiratory infections. This test is extremely unpleasant for some and fun for others.

Activities for Remediation of Vestibular Integration Problems

Write IEP objectives based on strengths and weaknesses. Use rewards specific to each individual's assessed preferences. Note that vestibular remediation cannot be isolated from kinesthetic integration. The use of blindfolds can negate effects of visual in-

FIGURE 10.7 The use of unstable surfaces in early childhood play promotes development of the vestibular system.

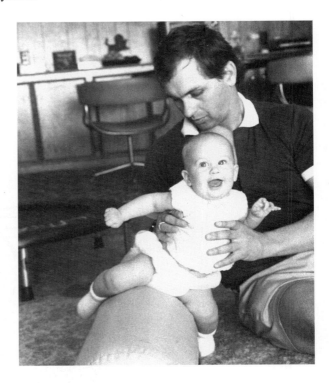

tegration, but typically the goal is TKVV (tactile, kinesthetic, vestibular, visual) integration, not work with a single system.

1. Use activities listed in the assessment section.
2. Use movement exploration activities and games that incorporate spinning and rolling.
3. Create numerous static and dynamic balance challenges in all positions. Use vestibular (balance) boards, hammocks, large balls, and equipment that can be used to cause momentary losses of balance (see Figure 10.7).

Visual Integration

The visual system is comprised of many subsystems, some reflexive and some voluntary. All are important in postural control and motor performance. The many subsystems can be organized into two types of vision: (a) refractive and (b) orthoptic.

Refractive Vision (Acuity)

Refractive vision refers to visual acuity, the product of light rays bending and reaching the receptor cells (rods and cones) of the retina. Visual impulses are transmitted via the optic nerve (second cranial) to many parts of the brain for interpretation. Refractive problems include **myopia** (nearsightedness), **hyperopia** (farsightedness), and **astigmatism** (blurring and distortion). Refraction is influenced by the size and shape of the eyeball, which changes with age. At birth, the eyeball is short (about three-fourths of adult length), which explains why young children tend to focus more easily on middle-distance items than on near ones.

Orthoptic Vision (Coordination)

Orthoptic vision refers to activity of the six external muscles of the eyeball, which are innervated by cranial nerves 3, 4, and 6. These muscles move the eyeballs up, down, in, out, and in diagonal directions. Of particular importance is **binocular coordination,** the ability of the two eyes to work in unison. Physiologically, because of their separate locations, each eye receives slightly different sensory stimuli and thus forms a different image. The two eyes must work together to fuse these separate images into one which, when interpreted by the brain, is seen as a solid with height, width, and depth dimensions and interpreted in relation to distance. The closer something is to the eyes, the greater the disparity between the images and the harder it is to fuse them into one. Likewise, the farther away the two eyes are set from one another, the more difficult the fusion (see Figure 10.8).

Binocular coordination is closely linked with balance and postural reactions. We take for granted the subcortical processing of three dimensions of space and the automatic adjustment of body parts to avoid bumping into things, falling, and other inappropriate movements.

Depth perception is often used as a synonym for *binocular coordination,* but this oversimplification is inaccurate (Guyton, 1981). **Depth perception** is the mental process of deriving meaning from visual space-time relationships, as in judging the distance of a balance beam from the ground or the speed/distance of a moving object. It is dependent upon three complex mechanisms, one of which is binocular coordination. Simplified, depth perception is problem-solving about near/far relationships. Abilities can be classified as static (near/far judgments about stationary things) and dynamic (near/far judgments about moving things). Developmentally, we refine static perception abilities first. By age 12, depth perception is usually mature.

Eye muscle coordination problems are common among persons with disabilities. These include (a) developmental delays in binocular coordination and depth perception, (b) **strabismus** (squint or crossed eyes), and (c) pathological **nystagmus** (constant, involuntary movement of the eyeballs). Strabismus is associated with cerebral palsy, Down syndrome, and fetal alcohol syndrome (see Figure 10.8). Nystagmus has a high prevalence among visually impaired persons with albinism (blond, blue eyes, pale skin).

Assessment of Visual Integration

Most screening tests used by teachers relate to vision for reading rather than for body control. Findings regarding binocular control in near-vision tasks (30 inches or closer) do not generalize to the depth perception demands in dodgeball, catching, and striking activities. Vision problems related to hand-eye and foot-eye coordination should be assessed by observing students performing striking, kicking, dodging, tagging, and catching skills. Note differences when the ball is stationary and when it is moving toward the person at midline, to the right, and to the left.

When vision problems are suspected, an **ophthalmologist** (eye specialist) should be consulted. Refractive problems are treated by prescriptive glasses or surgery. Some orthoptic problems like strabismus can also be treated with surgery.

FIGURE 10.8 Eye problems affect vision and sensorimotor function. *(A)* Eyes set abnormally far apart interfere with binocular coordination. *(B)* Strabismus in Down syndrome interferes with depth perception.

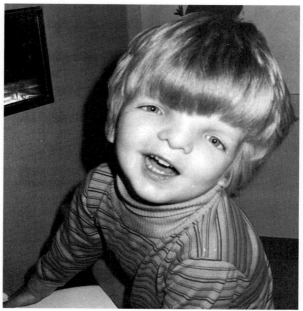

A

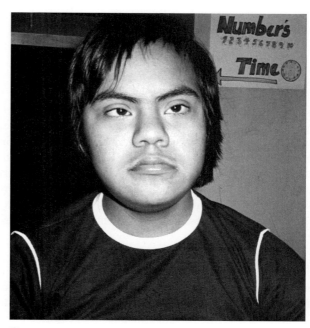

B

Ophthalmic problems of individuals with developmental disabilities are usually very complex. The best description of ophthalmic testing in adapted physical activity literature is offered by Mon-Williams, Pascal, and Wann (1994). After testing 500 children, aged 5 to 7 years, these researchers concluded that many children with developmental coordination disorder (DCD) do not have ophthalmic problems. It was suggested therefore that assessment should focus on the higher levels of visual processing that relate to cognition.

Activities for Remediation of Visual Integration Problems

The best way to enhance vision for body control is to provide lots of practice in many and varied movement tasks. The breakdown in vision typically is not exclusively a problem of the eyes but rather the complex process of integrating inputs from several sensory modalities and translating them into appropriate motor outputs.

1. Use suspended-ball activities in which the height of the ball is periodically changed so the head and eyes must practice accommodations.

2. Do lying and locomotor activities on tables of different heights so the eyes look down and accommodate. When appropriate, switch from tables to wide balance beams.

3. Lift the child into the air and do various airplane activities so the child sees the world from different perspectives.

4. Practice object handling from many positions: midline and looking up, down, and sideways. This includes prone-, supine-, and side-lying on mats as well as on apparatus of different heights and tilts to give looking downward new perspectives.

5. Practice with (a) the body stationary, (b) the body in locomotion, and (c) the body moved by external forces like swings, balance boards, scooterboards, merry-go-rounds, escalators, treadmills, and the like. Only the creativity of the professional limits the ways vision can be practiced and enhanced.

Infant and Pathological Reflexes

Whereas motor development books describe infant reflexes, adapted physical activity texts emphasize pathological reflex-activity that interferes with motor performance. The following section briefly reviews infant reflexes and stereotypies because nonambulatory individuals with severe cerebral palsy and traumatic brain injury exhibit many postures and patterns similar to those of infants. Failure to totally integrate reflexes is a problem in clumsiness or developmental coordination disorder at all ages.

Infant Reflexes and Stereotypies

Infant reflexes are involuntary, predictable muscle and postural tone shifts that are age-specific and important to normal development between birth and 9 months of age. These movement pattern shifts can be spontaneous or elicited by external stimuli (Crutchfield & Barnes, 1995). In this text, reflexes that appear to be spontaneous are called *stereotypies.* This is to avoid confusion, because reflexes traditionally have been linked to specific sensory input (e.g., head turning).

In infancy, all reflexes are good and serve a definite purpose. Reflexes are the building blocks on which the developing sensorimotor system rests. Each reflex contributes to either the achievement of spontaneous, voluntary movement abilities (e.g., head lifting, unilateral reaching, sitting) or the emergence of lifelong, automatic, postural reactions that serve righting, protection, and equilibrium functions. This is important because infants are born without the capacity to think about a movement and then plan and execute it.

Different Kinds of Reflexes

Infant reflexes vary in nature. Some cause total-body postural tone shifts, others cause body parts to flex (as in the hand and foot grasps), and others link body parts to the head so that muscle tone shifts occur in the limbs in response to certain head movements. The word *tonic* appears in the name of many reflexes because of this shifting muscle tone. Some of these shifts are **bilateral and symmetrical,** meaning that two body parts work in unison and perform the same movements. Other shifts involve only one limb and hence are **unilateral and asymmetrical.**

Muscle tone in newborn infants shifts involuntarily with body position, presumably because of tactile response to the external environment and kinesthetic and vestibular feedback responses to length changes in muscles and tendons. At birth, the muscle tone of anterior groups (flexors, adductors, inward rotators) is better developed than that of posterior groups. This is evident in the curled postures of infants during their first weeks. Each time that infants are placed on their backs, however, the tone shifts to strengthen the extensor muscle responses. Gradually, the flexor and extensor postural tones mature so body parts can act independently.

Body parts achieve independent, spontaneous, cognitively initiated movements in predictable sequences. The head can move first, in a lift from prone, at about 2 months of age. Most infants can voluntarily bring their arms to midline at about 4 months of age. This indicates that bilateral coordinations tend to evolve first. The first cognitively initiated reach-and-grasp unilateral sequences occur at about 5 or 6 months. At 8 months of age, most infants can wave bye-bye, but voluntary release of objects seldom is seen before 10 to 11 months.

The achievement of infant motor milestones like these results from CNS maturation helped by both reflexes and stereotypies. Both of these are involuntary but have different origins and roles. **Stereotypies** are rhythmical, presumably pleasant, movements of body parts that are performed over and over for no apparent reason. Kicking stereotypies are among the first to appear, usually at about 4 weeks of age. Stereotypies tend to appear just before infants display voluntary control of body parts and seem to provide needed input for maturation of the CNS. Most reflexes are integrated by about 9 months, and most stereotypies are integrated by about 12 months.

Integration of Reflexes and Stereotypies

When reflexes and stereotypies do not disappear in infancy, they are classified as pathological and targeted for remediation. **Integration** refers to the neural process of layering over, inhibiting, or suppressing reflexes and stereotypies.

Integration, however, occurs in various degrees. Under fatigue and stress conditions, integration sometimes breaks down. This is especially true when trying new motor skills or responding to a surprise motor demand, as when someone tosses you the house keys. Integration is never total or complete. Abnormal reflex activity is recognizable in clumsy movement at all ages. Although new cortically initiated movements continuously layer over reflex patterns, the layering or integration varies greatly from individual to individual.

Pathological Reflexes

Reflexes that are not integrated at the developmentally appropriate times become pathological, in that involuntary shifts of muscle tone, however subtle, interfere with smooth, coordinated movement (see Figure 10.9). Consider what makes a movement look clumsy. Often the underlying causes are imbalances in force, timing, and rhythm and/or tenseness. Individual differences in reflex integration help to explain the many degrees of clumsiness seen in the so-called normal population. Adapted physical activity personnel have only recently begun to think of abnormal reflex activity as a source of clumsiness, but occupational therapists have advanced this idea for years (Ayers, 1972).

FIGURE 10.9 Reflex problems make movements look clumsy.

Abnormal retention of reflexes contributes to the clumsiness associated with cerebral palsy, the most common orthopedic impairment in the public schools, and many other disabilities. Both regular physical educators and APA specialists need to understand the reflexes that interfere with skilled sport, dance, and aquatics performance.

Reflexes Important in Physical Education

Approximately 30 primitive reflexes dominate infants' motor behavior. Some assessment approaches include all of these reflexes (Barnes et al., 1990; Fiorentino, 1963). In extensive observation of clumsy students, Sherrill has found that only about 10 reflexes affect physical education performance (see Table 10.2). Only these reflexes are covered in this text, and they are presented in a special format so that you can copy the information on each one and paste it on a 5-inch-by-7-inch study card.

Table 10.2 shows the average age range during which each reflex dominates in normal development and indicates that most reflexes are integrated by 4 months of age, and all are integrated by 9 months of age. *Integration, however, is never total or complete.*

Table 10.2 shows the muscle tone that becomes dominant in each pattern, thereby interrupting the balance between opposing muscle groups. When the predominant tone is flexion, more tension is seen on the anterior surface of the body than the posterior. Usually, the affected body parts are bent. When the predominant tone is extension, the opposite is true. The posterior surface shows tenseness, and the body parts are straightened and sometimes stiff. The exception to this generalization is knee joint actions.

Table 10.2 also summarizes the body parts affected by the reflexes and the nature of the muscle tone distribution (total, symmetrical, or asymmetrical). The two reflexes affecting the total body are the most serious. Reflexes affecting the legs interfere with locomotor activities, while those affecting the arms and hands make ball-handling patterns look awkward.

The following explanations of each reflex include three parts: (a) description, (b) contributions during the time the reflex is normal, and (c) problems caused by abnormal retention of the reflexes.

T a b l e 1 0 . 2   **Reflexes of most importance to physical educators.**

Reflex	Average Age of Dominance	Dominant Muscle Tone	Body Part to Watch	Distribution
1. Tonic labyrinthine–prone	0–4 months	Flexion	Total body	Total
2. Tonic labyrinthine–supine	0–4 months	Extension	Total body	Total
3. Asymmetrical tonic neck	0–4 months	Flexion-extension	Arms	Asymmetrical
4. Symmetrical tonic neck	6–8 months	Flexion-extension	Arms-legs	Symmetrical
5. Moro	0–4 months	Extension	Arms-hands	Symmetrical
6. Hand grasp	0–4 months	Flexion	Hands-arms	Symmetrical
7. Foot grasp	0–9 months	Flexion	Toes, feet	Symmetrical
8. Extensor thrust	0–3 months	Extension	Legs	Symmetrical
9. Crossed extension	0–3 months	Flexion-extension	Legs	Symmetrical
10. Positive supporting-legs	3–8 months	Extension	Legs-trunk	Symmetrical

Note. Content for table was taken from Fiorentino (1981) and the *Milani-Comparetti Motor Development Screening Test Manual* (1987). Age range in which reflex is considered normal varies considerably, with some sources adding 1 to 2 months to those cited above.

Description
Increased flexor tone in response to any change in the position of head. Figure 10.10A shows an infant in prone; the TLR is responsible for this position. Figure 10.10B shows an older child who is severely delayed.

Contributions
Stimulate flexor tone of total body.

Problems
Results in abnormal distribution of muscle tone and inability of body segments to move independently of one another. Prevents raising head, which, in turn, prevents development of symmetrical tonic neck reflex, righting reactions, and Landau extensor reaction. Shoulder **protraction** (abduction) results in inability to move arms from under body (see Figure 10.10B). Infant or person with severe disabilities dominated by TLR is virtually helpless. Compromises any activity done against gravity from a prone position.

FIGURE 10.10   Two examples of tonic labyrinthine reflex—prone.

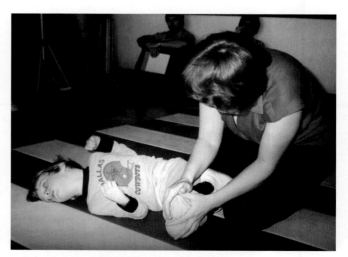

A   Normal infant dominated by flexor tone

B   Child with severe brain damage

Description
Increased extensor tone in response to any change in position of head.

Contributions
Helps create a balance between extensor and flexor muscles.

Problems
Domination by extensor tone, which holds shoulders in retraction (adduction) and prevents or compromises head raising, bringing limbs to midline, and rotation (turning) of body. In persons with severe disability, may contribute to windswept (opisthotonic) position (see Figure 10.11A).

FIGURE 10.11   Two examples of tonic labyrinthine reflex–supine.

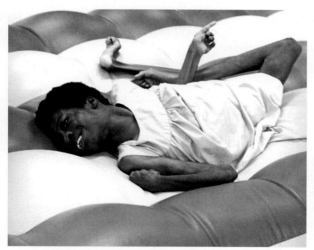

A Older adult showing opisthotonic or windswept position, spasticity in which head and heels are bent backward

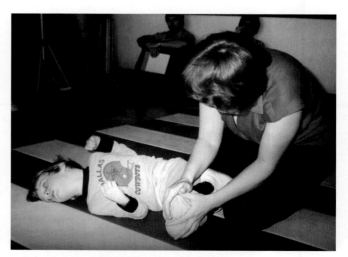

B Six-year-old with severe cerebral palsy

Description

On-guard, fencing position activated by rotation or lateral flexion (tilt) of head. Increased extensor tonus of limbs on chin side and increased flexor tonus in limbs on head side.

Contributions

Helps break up flexor and extensor pattern dominance so that each side of body can function separately.

Problems

1. Prevents learning to roll from supine to prone and vice versa since extended arm gets in the way.

2. Interferes with limb movement, which, in turn, impairs normal hand-eye coordination development. Associated problem is loss of visual fixation.

3. Prevents independent flexing of limb to bring it toward midline, as in playing with object or feeding self. Helps explain why persons bend their elbow in tennis forehand drive; as head rotates to left to see ball, right elbow flexes.

4. Causes one arm to bend or collapse in the beginning forward roll position if head tilts or rotates even slightly.

5. In sport positions that involve a rotated head, such as softball batting or tennis stance, prevents or compromises the bat or racquet crossing midline and, thus, properly following through.

6. In severe conditions, may contribute to scoliosis, subluxed or dislocated hips, or windswept lying position.

Failure of the reflex to become integrated explains much of the clumsiness physical educators observe, especially in relation to ball

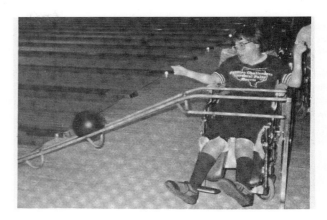

FIGURE 10.12   Adolescent with cerebral palsy exhibiting asymmetrical tonic neck reflex.

activities (see Figure 10.12). Many of the verbal cues that physical educators give ("Keep your eye on the ball"; "Don't bend your elbow"; "Remember to follow through") are not commands that can be entirely consciously implemented. Thus, bright, but clumsy, students often think and sometimes respond, "I know what I'm doing wrong, but my body won't do what my mind tells it."

Description

Flexion and extension movements of the head influence muscle tone distribution in relation to upper and lower body. Head flexion increases flexor tone of upper body and extensor tone of lower body; head extension does the opposite (see Figure 10.13). Predominant upper-body muscle tone is always that of the head and neck.

Contributions

Contributes to such important motor milestones as lifting and supporting upper body on arms and rising to four-point creeping position.

Problems

1. Prevents reciprocal flexion and extension movement of legs needed in creeping (i.e., with head up, child is frozen in bunny-hop position).

2. Compromises ability to do certain stunts, exercises, and animal walks with head up. Makes holding legs extended difficult in regulation push-up position, in prone scooterboard activities, and in wheelbarrow races.

3. Compromises ability to do exercises, stunts, gymnastics, and synchronized swimming that require head held down in tucked position with knees simultaneously tucked to chest. Explains why "tuck position" is difficult to maintain as head changes position from flexion to extension (i.e., why persons come out of their tuck too soon).

4. Compromises sitting position. Head down activates extensor thrust in lower extremities; increases high-guard position of arms. Head up contributes to good sitting posture but increases difficulty of hand and arm activities that entail flexion, like lifting arm for overarm throw.

5. Looking down at ground or balance beam when walking compromises distribution of muscle tone; helps to explain gait of toddler with arms in high guard and abnormally stiff leg action and/or tendency to toe walk.

FIGURE 10.13   Two symmetrical tonic neck reflexes (STNR).

Flexion STNR: Head flexion causes legs to extend

Extension STNR: Head extension causes creeping or bunny-hop position

Description

Flexion of toes (clawing motion) in response to deep pressure stimulation of soles of feet, as in standing or when object is pressed against toes (see Figure 10.14).

Contributions

Tactile stimulation enhances body awareness. The reflex also strengthens foot muscles.

Problems

Interferes with balance in walking and standing. Often seen in conjunction with **positive supporting reflex** (increased extensor tone that results in toe walking).

FIGURE 10.14   Foot grasp reflex.

Description

Increased extensor tone throughout the body evoked by stimulus of sudden pressure to soles of feet. Most often mentioned in conjunction with sitting postures, a common problem in nonambulatory persons with cerebral palsy (see Figure 10.15). In first 2 months, sometimes mistaken for early standing ability.

Contributions

Strengthens extensors, thereby promoting balance between flexor and extensor postural tone.

Problems

Inability to maintain proper sitting position; entire body stiffens so that person slides out of wheelchair unless strapped into one that is specially made. Usually occurs in conjunction with positive supporting reflex of legs and/or tonic labyrinthine supine reflex or symmetrical tonic neck reflex. Often, the abnormal movement produced by one or both of these is called an *extensor thrust pattern* (i.e., the term is not limited to action of the extensor thrust reflex alone).

FIGURE 10.15   Extensor thrust reflex or pattern.

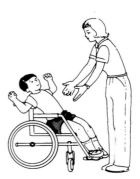

Description
Elicited by flexing or tapping medial surface of one leg. One leg reflexly affects the other (see Figure 10.16A). Evidenced when one leg cannot flex (as in kicking a ball) without associated extension of the other leg. Also evidenced when medial surface of upper legs touches or rubs against one another; this stimulus contributes to scissoring. Correct positioning in a wheelchair, with bolster between thighs, prevents this.

Contributions
Helps to break up dominant symmetrical flexion and extension patterns. Facilitates development of extensor tone to stand on one leg while the other leg flexes (i.e., permits reciprocal leg movements needed for creeping and walking).

Problems
1. Prevents coordinated leg movements needed to crawl, creep, and walk.
2. Causes scissoring of legs (see Figure 10.16B).
3. Sometimes serves as substitute for absent positive support reflex in athetosis and ataxia. Child can stand only on stiffly extended legs and raises legs too high in walking.

Problems Combined With Positive Supporting Reflex
1. Affects kicking in a standing position. When leg is lifted to kick ball, a strong extensor spasm affects support leg and causes loss of balance. Child loses balance because he or she pushes reflexly against ground with ball of support foot (positive supporting reflex thereby reinforcing extensor spasm); this is accompanied by knee hyperextension and clawing of toes. To prevent falling backward, reflex activates flexion of trunk at hips and brings kicking leg down and forward, leaving weight-bearing foot, leg, hip, and shoulder behind. This rotary movement prevents straight follow-through in the kick.
2. Affects walking pattern. Results in hyperextended knees, clawing of toes, and hip flexion in support leg to prevent falling. This is typically compensated for by forward flexion of head and lordosis.

FIGURE 10.16 Two examples of crossed extension reflex.

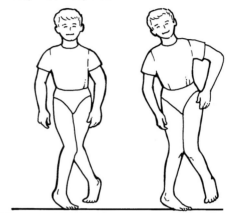

A Test position response

B Scissors gait response

Description
Increased extensor tone (plantar flexion at ankle joint) caused by soles of feet touching floor or footrests of wheelchair.

Contributions
Strengthens hip and leg extensors needed for straight-back sitting and standing.

Problems
1. When fully present, prevents independent standing and walking; creates difficulty (along with extensor thrust reflex) in wheelchair posture adjustments and/or wheelchair transfers because sensory input from foot plates stimulates soles of feet, which, in turn, increases extensor tone.
2. When partially present, affects walking gait by causing toe walking (prevents placing heel on floor), contributing (with crossed extension reflex) to scissoring, narrowing base of support, and producing backward thrust of trunk with compensatory lordosis and arm out to assist with balance (see Figure 10.17)
3. Also interferes with kicking a ball (see crossed extensor reflex).

FIGURE 10.17 Two examples of positive supporting reflex.

Toes point and feet stiffen on landing in assisted jumping

Toe walk pattern, usually unstable

Description
The body stiffens and arms and legs involuntarily spread and close in response to unstable lying/sitting surface or falling movement (see Figure 10.18).

Contributions
Contributes to development of extensor and abductor strength of upper extremities, including fingers; serves as precursor to propping and parachute reactions.

Problems
Interferes with learning to sit and using the arms for balance. Prevents using one arm at a time.

Caution
Do not confuse with startle reflex.

FIGURE 10.18   Two phases of the Moro reflex.

Spread phase

Close phase

Description
Flexion of fingers in response to object being drawn across palm or hypertension of wrist (see Figure 10.19).

Contributions
Tactile stimulation by object in hand is the beginning of eye-hand coordination and visual body awareness.

Problems
Interferes with development of voluntary grasp and release mechanism; compromises tactile sensory input.

FIGURE 10.19   Hand grasp reflex.

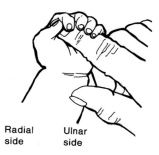

Radial   Ulnar
side   side

Assessment Criteria for Physical Education Reflexes

The following criteria help determine the presence of pathological reflexes.

Tonic Labyrinthine–Prone

1. Total body dominated by flexor tone.
2. Difficulty in moving one body part independently from others.
3. Head lift from prone difficult.
4. Arm movement to rear limited by shoulder protraction (abduction).
5. Pivot prone, swan, and front rocker stunts difficult.
6. Arm movement upward and outward limited.
7. Slouched walking posture.

Tonic Labyrinthine–Supine

1. Total body (except hips) dominated by extensor tone.
2. Difficulty in moving one body part independently from others.
3. Head lift from supine difficult.
4. Tuck position in supine difficult.
5. Arm movements to midline difficult.
6. Trunk rotation movements difficult.

Asymmetrical Tonic Neck Reflexes

1. Head turn causes limb tension or movement.
2. Extensor dominance on face side of body and flexor dominance on nonface side.
3. Difficulty with log roll; arm gets in the way.
4. If the head turns, the limbs cannot continue midline movement.
5. Head and trunk rotation to right in softball or tennis backswing makes bending right arm difficult.
6. Head and trunk rotation to left for contact and follow-through makes straightening right arm difficult.

Symmetrical Tonic Neck Reflex

A. Head-down position
   1. Stiff leg action in walking.
   2. Tendency to toe walk.
   3. Tucking legs to chest difficult.
   4. Lifting leg difficult in kick follow-through.
   5. Crouch starting position compromised.
   6. Arms and upper body more flexed than desired.

B. Head-up position
   1. Excessive knee and ankle flexion.
   2. Tendency to shuffle or walk flat-footed.
   3. Inability to keep legs straight in wheelbarrow walk stunt.
   4. Legs cannot move reciprocally in animal walks.
   5. Arms and upper body more extended than desired.

Moro Reflex

1. Sitting balance problems.
2. Use of arms in balance impaired.
3. Bilateral movement response to loss of balance.

Hand Grasp Reflex

1. Release activities in ball handling difficult.
2. Letting go of pool edge for swim race difficult.
3. Flat hands in contact with floor difficult.

Foot Grasp Reflex

1. Balance problem.
2. Difficulty doing flat-footed or heel walk.

Extensor Thrust Reflex

1. Slides out of chair unless strapped in.
2. Total body dominated by extensor tone.

Reflex Integration in Teaching

If not integrated, the primitive reflexes discussed in the preceding section affect physical education instruction. First, they explain why some students continue to make movement errors in spite of corrective feedback. Good examples are students who continue bending the elbow in tennis strokes, who fail to follow through across midline in throwing, and who cannot get the total body to work together smoothly in a forward roll or jump. Such students often say, "I know what I'm supposed to do. I can visualize every part. I just can't make my body do what my mind says." In essence, these students are saying that they do not have the cortical control to override reflex patterns. Visual and auditory instructions (their own self-talk or the teacher's input) are not effective when used alone because they are directed toward the thinking parts of the brain when the problem is at the lower levels.

Four Principles of Reflex Integration

In working with students with reflex problems, remember these four principles:

1. Maximize tactile, kinesthetic, and vestibular (TKV) input.
2. Use total body movement patterns and games that inhibit reflexes (i.e., emphasize opposite patterns).
3. Increase practice time and time-on-task for correctly executed patterns.
4. Intensify individual assistance so that patterns are performed correctly. Pay particular attention to head position.

Strategies of Reflex Integration

TKV input is maximized mainly by five strategies. *Coactive movement* is the professional term for teacher and student moving together, bodies touching, so that the student receives input from all three modalities (TKV) concurrently. *Passive assistance* refers to the teacher's moving only one body part of the student. *Tactile cueing* refers to tapping or rubbing a body part to reinforce memory. *Balancing activities* (both static and dynamic) give the CNS practice in processing input from TKV modalities as well as vision. Balancing should be interpreted as achieving and maintaining stability in all kinds of positions. *Reward* emphasizes frequent praise and correctional feedback. Use rewards specific to individual preferences.

The Four Most Troublesome Reflexes

Of the 10 reflexes, the four initiated by head movements are generally the most troublesome. These are the tonic labyrinthine reflex-prone (TLR-prone), tonic labyrinthine reflex-supine (TLR-supine), asymmetrical tonic neck reflex (ATNR), and symmetrical tonic neck reflex (STNR). In these four reflexes, the student cannot move the head without initiating associated movements or subtle muscle tone tensions of other body parts.

Remediation is thus directed toward practice in moving the head and (a) keeping everything else stationary or (b) simultaneously performing body part movements that are the opposites of what the reflex mechanisms enact. This is essentially the same as repeatedly performing a skill the *right way* as called for in the principle of specificity (i.e., practice the specific pattern in which you want skill). Achieving the *right way*, however, is often impossible without special focus on the head.

The tonic labyrinthine reflexes help explain coordination and control problems in exercises done from lying positions like, for example, sit-ups from supine, trunk lifts from prone, rolling over, and moving rapidly from lying to standing positions, as in recoveries from falls and dives in such sports as volleyball. The tonic labyrinthine reflexes also help to explain the abnormal standing, walking, and jumping postures seen in many persons with severe disability. When gravity acts to pull the head downward and the total body responds by assuming a flexion posture, the reflex responsible is the TLR-prone. When the head, for any reason, is thrown backward and the total body responds in an extension posture, the reflex responsible is the TLR-supine.

The ATNR and STNR are operative when only part of the body responds reflexively to head movements. The ATNR explains clumsiness in activities involving head and trunk rotation. Head turning causes obligatory extension patterns of limbs on the face side and simultaneous obligatory flexion patterns on the nonface side. Think how many sport patterns require turning the head to the right and left and how obligatory arm responses or subtle muscle tone shifts make movements look and feel awkward. In contrast, the STNR explains clumsiness in activities that involve the top and bottom parts of the body working together. When the STNR is operative, up and down head movements cause obligatory bilateral arm and leg responses.

Sometimes, several reflexes, rather than one, contribute to lack of coordination and control. This is often the case in the jump. In addition to the STNR, the jump may be affected by the four reflexes that act on the feet and legs: foot grasp, extensor thrust, crossed extension, and positive supporting-legs. Except for the foot grasp, these reflexes all cause extension of the lower extremities and interfere with the flexion needed to land smoothly and comfortably. These four reflexes also affect locomotion. Extreme pigeon-toed walking (hip adduction and inward rotation patterns) called *scissoring* is elicited by crossed extension and positive supporting reflexes.

TLR-Prone Remediation Activities—Emphasize Extension

1. Stunts in prone on mats that involve lifting the head (easiest progression), or head and shoulders, or trunk with arms outstretched forward over the head or sideways. These stunts have many names: *pivot prone, swan, wing lifts, airplane.*
2. Stunts in prone in water while supported or moving independently: various floats, glides, and transitions between tucked and straight positions.
3. Prone lie in full extension or net hammock or blanket that is pulled along the floor by another or suspended in the air and gently rocked or swung.
4. Prone lie in full extension on a therapy ball, slant board, or other surfaces of various textures that can be rocked; practice in controlled transition from full extension to full tuck to full extension.
5. Prone lie in full extension on scooterboard. Holding onto a rope when being pulled by another, or pulling a rope that is attached to wall to move self. Create scooterboard games and challenge tasks.
6. Rise-to-stand games from prone lie and stand-to-prone-lie transitions on mats, trampolines, floors, and surfaces of various consistencies. Start running games and relays from prone lie instead of crouch.
7. Use the fully extended prone lie as a safety position in tag games.
8. Push-ups and other fitness activities from prone.
9. Walking activities at various speeds, while performing novelty tasks like carrying objects on the head. Check that the students do not look at their feet, because this is an indication that the TLR-prone is not integrated.

TLR-Supine Remediation Activities—Emphasize Flexion

1. Stunts in supine on various surfaces that involve tucking the head and making the body into a ball. Often novelty rolls are done in tucked position and given names like *egg roll, human ball.* Avoid forward and backward rolls until this reflex disappears.
2. Stunts in supine in water while supported or moving independently; practice transitions between tuck-and-extend sequences in supine.
3. Partial and bent-knee sit-ups and curl-ups.
4. Supine tuck position games and exercises with unilateral, bilateral, and crosslateral arm or leg movements or timed holds.
5. Use the supine tuck in drills from standing position or as a safety position in tag games; this is called turtle tag—you look like a turtle upside down.

ATNR Remediation Activities—Emphasize Head Turn

1. Rotations of the head to the left (L) or right (R) while keeping other body parts motionless. *Simon Says* games with surprise commands to turn the head and penalty for moving other body parts.
2. Creeping forward or backward, with head turned to one side.

3. Animal walks and stunts with eyes straight forward. Students must respond appropriately when leader calls out surprise commands: "Look to left" and "Look to right." Have the students do the same thing on a balance beam or while performing other locomotor challenges.

4. Head exercises like turn head to side, touch chin to shoulder, and hold (an excellent exercise for forward head posture problem); check that students move only the head; have them view videotapes of their movements to see if they moved other body parts.

5. Sideward rolling that is initiated by the head while other body parts are kept motionless.

6. Racket games that require keeping the side to the net. Check that when students rotate head and trunk, they maintain the elbow in correct position.

7. Corrective postures, like hand on hip or right hand holding right ear, that will tend to prevent a body part from moving in response to head movement.

STNR Remediation Activities—Emphasize Head Up or Down

1. Activities in which the upper and lower body can do the same or opposite things, like bend the head and legs in a supine body tuck and lift the head and neck from a prone lie.

2. Belly crawling and four-point creeping in which limbs move reciprocally (i.e, bend and straighten). Practice with head up and head down.

3. Jumping and diving activities with progressively more difficult coordinations.

4. Partner stunts like walking on hands with the head up while the legs are held extended (wheelbarrow), or dumping sand (the same activity, but with an up-and-down motion instead of a forward walk).

5. Horseback and bicycle riding in which the upper body is straight and the lower limbs straighten and bend.

6. Scooterboard and other wheel apparatuses in which the arms and legs work reciprocally.

7. Rope and tree climbing.

Overflow (Associated Movements)

A common indicator of clumsiness is associated movements, also called overflow. These are undesired reflex responses of body parts that should remain stationary. Examples are (a) facial grimaces when concentrating on a hand-eye or hand-foot motor task, (b) an increase in muscle tone or a mirroring action on the noninvolved side when trying to perform one-arm or one-leg acts, and (c) unnecessary, uncoordinated, or funny-looking movements of the arms during locomotion. Associated movements are caused by poorly integrated reflexes. They are remnants of the mass flexor and extensor patterns present at birth, when body parts cannot move independently of one another. As such, associated movements are normal in early childhood, diminish by ages 6 to 8 years, and generally disappear by adolescence.

FIGURE 10.20 "Angels in the Snow" assessment test to diagnose overflow.

Together   Spread   Return

Simply telling a student to stop an associated movement does not work because reflex mechanisms can be overridden only by many, many repetitions of the correct movement pattern. Programming should therefore include many activities like "Angels in the Snow" and "Simon Says" that provide practice in moving one body part at a time. Such activities, which help the nervous system to organize sensorimotor processes and facilitate subcortical motor planning, are discussed further in Chapters 12, 16, and 17.

Figure 10.20 shows the "Angels in the Snow" task. In the traditional activity, performed in supine, all limbs move simultaneously outward and inward in a bilateral pattern. To use "Angels in the Snow" as an assessment test, adapt the instructions so that students move only limbs that are touched or limbs that are modeled by another who challenges, "Can you do this?" Try various combinations: arms only, legs only, right arm and right leg only, and so on.

Postural Reactions

Reactions are automatic responses to sensory input that act to keep body parts in alignment, maintain equilibrium, and prevent injury. Some reactions replace reflexes, but others emerge to perform unique functions. In normal development, reactions appear between the ages of 2 and 18 months. With a few exceptions (e.g, the Landau and body derotative), these reactions persist throughout life. Some authorities believe that delays in the appearance of postural reactions are more detrimental to motor success than reflex disorders, especially in severe mental retardation (Molnar, 1978). Many persons, of course, have both reflex and reaction problems.

This text uses the terminology of the Milani-Comparetti Assessment System (see page 266) and such leading authorities as Crutchfield and Barnes (1995) and Levitt (1995). Reactions are primarily important for their role in balance and help to explain why so many clumsy individuals have balance problems.

Assessment of Postural Reactions

There are basically three categories of reactions: (a) righting, (b) parachute, and (c) equilibrium. *Righting reactions* are adjustments of the head or trunk. *Parachute reactions* are protective extension movements of the limbs. *Equilibrium reactions* are total body responses. To assess the presence of these reactions,

FIGURE 10.21 Four types of righting reactions. Optical righting reactions constitute the fifth type.

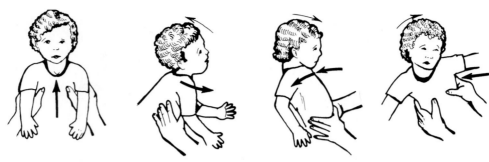

Head-in-space and optical righting reactions when held upright and tilted forward, backward, and sideward. *Bottom arrow* shows movement created by teacher's positioning or testing. *Top arrow* shows head movement that results if child has normal response.

Body righting in sagittal plane (Landau): Head and trunk lift

Body derotative (segmental rolling)

Body rotative (rise to sit or stand)

teachers must hold, tilt, or position the children in specific ways (e.g., see Figure 10.21).

Five Righting Reactions

Righting reactions are the automatic postural responses elicited by sensory input that signals that the head or trunk is not in midline. The first three righting reactions (head-in-space, optical righting, and Landau) are up, down, and sideways compensatory actions, whereas the last two reactions (body derotative and body rotative) are rotational movements. Figure 10.21 illustrates the righting reactions.

Head-in-Space or Labyrinthine

The head-in-space righting reactions emerge at about 2 months of age and persist throughout life. They are elicited by holding the child vertically upright in the air and then slowly

tilting him or her forward, backward, and sideward (see Figure 10.21). In each tilt, the head automatically moves in the direction opposite the tilt. Of course, the entire body follows the head, so this mechanism helps a person to return to an upright, midline position. **Midline** is defined as the position in which the nose is vertical and the mouth and eyes are horizontal. The head-in-space righting reactions are elicited by vestibular input. Hence, the head-in-space righting reactions are also called labyrinthine or vestibular patterns.

Optical or Visual

The optical righting reactions are precisely the same as the head-in-space reactions except that the responses are elicited by visual input instead of vestibular input. Optical righting develops soon after the head-in-space reactions appear and remains active throughout the lifespan. The optical righting reactions are dependent upon the integrity of the head-in-space reactions and the integration of the primitive reflexes that act on the head. Persons with abnormal muscle tone distribution, like those with cerebral palsy, can use vision to know the head is not properly aligned. However, this knowledge cannot enable correction of the head alignment problem. In young children and/or those with severe disability, no attempt should be made to assess or work with head-in-space and optical righting separately. With older individuals, however, a blindfold may be used in head-in-space work to eliminate visual input.

In summary, the vestibular and visual systems work together to always return the head to midline. Body parts follow the head, and balance is preserved. These reactions must be overridden by higher CNS centers in activities requiring purposeful loss of balance (e.g., falls for fun, various activities in dance, gymnastics, and aquatics, and diving).

Landau Reaction or Body-in-Sagittal Plane Righting

The **Landau reaction,** also called body-in-sagittal plane righting, is an extension response of the trunk, hips, knees, and ankles that occurs in prone position when the head is lifted (see Figure 10.21). As the term *sagittal* indicates, the righting is in the up-and-down or flexion-extension plane. The Landau develops shortly after the head-in-space reactions are established. In essence, the Landau is a spreading of the extensor tone of the lifted head down the muscles of the back and legs.

The Landau is assessed from a prone position in the air or water, called *ventral suspension*. The Landau is one of the few reactions that is integrated instead of persisting throughout life. It serves a specific developmental function not needed after about 3 years of age. Specifically, the Landau facilitates the change from the flexion posture of infancy to the fully extended prone position with head up and back arched, called the *pivot prone, swan, wing lift,* or *front rocker.* The Landau overrides the STNR pattern (head extended, arms extended, legs flexed) so that the legs can be fully extended at the same time the head and arms are extended. The ability to maintain a pivot prone position is one of the first milestones in mastering the one-handed reach and grasp from a prone position. Without the Landau, the pivot prone pattern cannot emerge.

Body Derotative (Segmental Rolling)

The body derotative is an automatic segmental rolling response that occurs when the examiner rotates a body part. Until the age of 4 months, the infant does not have this reaction, and the body plops over as a rigid unit, called a logroll pattern. From age 4 months until about 5 years, the normally functioning individual responds to external body part rotation by rolling over one segment at a time (head, then shoulders, then trunk, then hips, or vice versa). Abnormal retention of the ATNR delays segmental rolling, because the extended arm is stiff and will not get out of the way.

Body Rotative (Rise to Stand)

The body rotative or rise-to-sit/rise-to-stand reaction is elicited by placing a wide-awake child in a supine lie. The body rotative is the ability to move segment by segment from a supine lie to some other position: a four-point, a sit, or a stand, depending on developmental level. If children have the coordination to rotate up to a more functional position, doing so is a normal response.

Rise-to-stand or **scramble up,** a widely used screening activity for all age groups, is derived from the body rotative reaction. Beginning in a supine lie, the person is challenged to rise to a stand as fast as he or she can. Observation of the efficiency of this action provides insight into overall coordination. The speed of rise-to-stand (body rotative) is the righting reaction most often examined in school-age children (see Figure 10.21).

Parachute or Propping Reactions

The parachute or propping reactions are protective extension movements of the limbs used to break or prevent a fall. There are four such reactions, named for the direction in which the body is falling (downward, sideward, forward, and backward) (see Figure 10.22). The **downward parachute,** which refers to being dropped or falling feet first, is the only one that involves the legs. The other three reactions are the natural propping responses of both arms (falling forward or backward) or one arm (falling sideward).

The parachute reactions, like the reflexes that cause arm movements, are elicited by vestibular input, which signals a change in the movement of the head. The arm-propping reactions are generally tested from a sitting position, with the examiner gently pushing the child off balance. Developmentally, the **downward parachute** develops first (about 4 months); in it, the child extends and spreads the legs, thereby automatically preparing for a wide-based and therefore safe landing. The **sideward parachute** develops next, at 6 to 8 months, then the **forward parachute** at 7 to 8 months, and the **backward parachute** at 9 to 10 months. All of the parachute reactions remain throughout the lifespan. These reactions are often delayed or absent in persons with severe disability and thus constitute adapted physical education goals.

Equilibrium or Tilting Reactions

The equilibrium (or tilting) reactions are total body responses that, when mature, prevent falls. They appear between the ages of 5 and 18 months and remain the entire life. These reactions, initiated primarily by vestibular input, can be elicited in any position the body assumes, but testing is usually limited to five positions (see Figure 10.23). These are presented in the correct assessment order, from easiest to hardest. Ages in Figure 10.23 indicate the average age at completion or mature response.

To assess these reactions, the teacher must have or be able to create an unstable surface that can be tipped about 15° in any direction. A mat or cushion can be moved from side to side, or a tilt board or large ball can be maneuvered to cause loss of equilibrium. These reactions can also be observed in trampoline work or in locomotor activities on unstable surfaces.

The equilibrium responses are all rotatory and can perhaps best be observed by focusing on the spinal curvature needed to maintain balance. Curves are described as convex (rounded like the back of a *C*) or concave (hollow like the front of a *C*). In mature equilibrium responses, the concavity of the spinal curve is always uphill. *The face and trunk are rotated toward the uphill side.* In some sources, the uphill side is called the stressed side (Ramm, 1988). In forward-backward

FIGURE 10.22   Four types of parachute or propping reactions (protective extensions). All responses are limb movements.

Downward. Normal response to downward thrust: abduction, wide base, 4 months on.

Sideward. Normal response to sideward thrust, 6 to 8 months.

Forward. Normal response to forward thrust, 7 to 8 months.

Backward. Normal response to backward thrust, 9 to 10 months.

tilts, the face and trunk bend or curve toward uphill. In side-to-side tilts, the face and trunk rotate toward the up side.

The position of the limbs also should be noted. Limbs on the uphill side are abducted (raised or held away from midline) and extended. Limbs on the downhill side tend to be adducted (drawn in toward the body) and flexed. Forward-backward tilts elicit bilateral arm movements (i.e., both arms do the same thing). Sideward tilts cause the arms to do opposite things.

In normal development, this rhythmical shifting of the arm and leg positions with the up-and-down movement of the tilting surface is automatic and graceful. Absence or immaturity of these reactions results in balance problems. If the student's balance is disrupted to the extent that the reactions are not effective in recovering an upright posture, the arms will automatically move into the protective extension patterns of the parachute reactions to break the fall.

Standing equilibrium may involve steps as well as shifts in alignment of body parts. **Stepping reactions** (also called hopping, shifting, or staggering reactions) are the steps a person automatically takes to keep his or her balance in a standing posture. Stepping reactions also occur as the last component of a mature kick (see Chapter 11). Stepping reactions often are seen when children try to maintain a one-foot balance.

Postural Reactions Summary

Postural reactions must be present for individuals to adjust to changing environmental conditions during locomotion. Changes in the slope and texture of a surface, the uneven height of grass,

or a hole in the ground are likely to cause clumsy-looking responses or falls when reactions are not mature. Likewise, immature reactions compromise the agility and gracefulness of activities involving the shifting of weight and the moving of body parts against gravity, as in jumping and hopping.

It is noteworthy that postural reactions normally are functioning by age 18 months, the time when most children perform their first jumps, using two-foot takeoffs. The distance achieved is 4 inches on a long jump and 2 inches off the floor in a vertical jump. Walking sideward for 10 ft, which also occurs at 18 months, also requires postural reactions. Harder activities, like walking tiptoe and taking three steps on a low balance beam, occur at 24 months, when the postural reactions are more mature.

Remediation of Postural Reaction Problems

Remediation entails thousands of trials in which the individual performs the same righting, parachute, and equilibrium tasks over and over again. The positions used for testing are the same as those used for remediation.

To promote generalization of practice, many different environments and pieces of equipment are used (i.e, indoors/outdoors, noise/no noise; light/dark; soft/hard surfaces; level/slanted surfaces; water/air; windy with air current caused by electric fan/nonwindy). Different clothes and shoes are worn also because these influence postural reactions to the environment. Velcro is used to strap various kinds of weights to body parts, and back- and chestpacks are worn to give the nervous system practice in adapting to change.

FIGURE 10.23 Five types of equilibrium reactions when board is tilted 15°. Note the concavity of the spinal curve is always uphill in the mature response. Also, the face and trunk are rotated toward the uphill side.

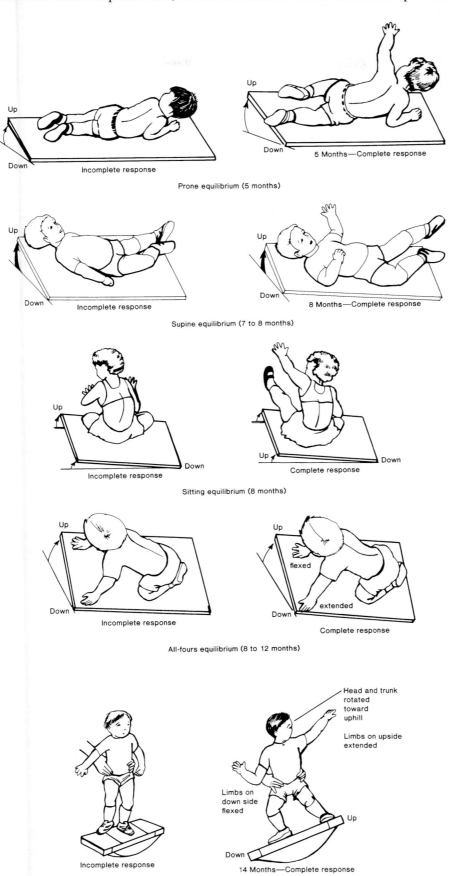

Overall Assessment Approach: Milani-Comparetti

Before writing goals for the IEP and determining appropriate pedagogy, it is important to plan an overall assessment approach that is applicable to individuals with either nonambulatory or ambulatory clumsy conditions. Of the many assessment systems, the Milani-Comparetti (MC) protocol is perhaps the easiest and most appropriate for physical educators. This screening system, which requires only about 5 min to administer, was originally developed for ages birth to 2 years (Milani-Comparetti & Gidoni, 1967), but now it is frequently used with individuals of all age groups with severe body control problems. The address for the test manual is in the reference list for this chapter, and a training film can be obtained from the same source.

Figure 10.24 shows that the MC scoring system is divided into two sections: **spontaneous behavior** (motor strengths) and **evoked responses** (reflexes and postural reactions). Months listed horizontally across the top of the chart indicate the ages at which responses are normal, to aid in the estimation of motor delays. Although function on the MC can be scored numerically (Ellison, Browning, Larson, & Denny, 1983), most teachers use letters to note absence *(A)* or presence *(P)* of spontaneous behavior, reflexes, and reactions. Figure 10.24 shows the MC scoring protocol for a 9-year-old girl with severe cerebral palsy.

Spontaneous Behaviors

Spontaneous behavior encompasses motor tasks in nine broad areas: four head positions, three body postures, and two active movement sequences. Following are brief descriptions of each.

Head Control

Assess head control in four positions. As early as 1 month of age, infants can hold the head upright when they are held vertically in the air or against someone's chest. The angular lines on the MC chart next to "Body held vertical" denote growing control from a few seconds at 1 month of age to several minutes at 4 months of age. In contrast, many adults with cerebral palsy have difficulty with this task.

In "Body lying prone," infants exhibit three distinct developmental stages:

1.5 months Lifts head momentarily

3.0 months Holds head up 45° to 90° with chest up

4.0 months Holds head up; props self up on extended arms

In "Body lying supine," the infant lifts the head at about 5 months (note the location of the word *lifts* on MC chart). This head lifting is observed in conjunction with playing with feet.

In "Body pulled up from supine," the stick figures on the MC chart indicate the amount of head lag normal at each age when the body is pulled upward by the arms.

Body Control

Assess body control in three positions. Stick figures on the MC chart indicate normal performances. Five developmental stages are depicted for "Sitting." These are based on the amount of spinal curve and the ability to fully extend legs. Independent sitting is achieved between 6 and 8 months. The *L3* next to the second figure on the MC chart indicates that the progressive head-to-foot uncurving of the vertebral column has extended downward to the level of the third lumbar segment by the age of 4 months.

"All-fours" refers to three developmental stages. *Forearms/hands* denotes a propping position, with head and chest up and weight taken on the forearms. This propping behavior begins between the ages of 3.5 and 6 months. The *creeping position* is listed as 4-feet kneeling; it begins between the ages of 7 and 9 months. *Plantigrade* refers to a bear-walk position (4-foot walking with straight arms and legs).

"Standing" also develops through several stages, the first of which is controlled subcortically by supporting reflexes. When the infant loses this reflex, *astasia* occurs. This is a condition in which weight is taken momentarily, after which the body collapses. When infants take weight on their feet at about age 5 months, this is a more mature movement under cortical control. Independent standing does not occur until about 10 months.

Active Movement

"Standing up from a supine (lying) position" is evaluated in terms of amount of trunk rotation and arm assistance. Note four levels on the MC chart, extending from 9 months of age until 5 years. The mature rise-to-stand requires no trunk rotation and no arm assistance. "Locomotion" emphasizes rolling over between 4 and 6 months of age, creeping at around 7 months of age, and walking at about 12 months of age. The terms *high, medium, no guard* refer to the position of the arms.

Evoked Responses

Evoked responses encompass five early reflexes and three types of postural reactions (righting, parachute, and tilting or equilibrium). Reflexes and postural reactions are associated with subcortical function and sensorimotor integration. The purpose of this section is to develop awareness and reinforce understanding of the need for both adapted and regular physical educators to understand reflexes and reactions.

Application to a 9-Year-Old

Let's now apply our knowledge about motor milestones, reflexes, and reactions to Kay, a 9-year-old born with cerebral palsy (CP) affecting all four limbs (see Figure 10.24). Kay's intelligence quotient is about 90 (i.e., low average). She is in the fourth grade of a public school in which she is mainstreamed into first-grade spelling and mathematics classes. The rest of the school day, she is in a self-contained class for multidisabled students. Kay receives adapted physical education on a one-to-one basis three times a week, 30 min a day. She also receives physical, occupational, speech, and music therapy in 30-min sessions.

Kay needs special equipment to help her function independently. She lacks the arm strength and control to maneuver a manual wheelchair, so a motorized chair is required. Kay is nonverbal, so a head pointer is essential so that she can point out words on a Bliss symbol board, type, and do artwork.

FIGURE 10.24 Milani-Comparetti evaluation for Kay, a 9-year-old girl with athetoid cerebral palsy affecting control of head and all four limbs. An *A* on the chart indicates absence of a response, and a *P* indicates presence of a response. Note that absence is interpreted as bad under spontaneous behaviors and under righting, parachute, and tilting reactions, but as good in relation to primitive reflexes. The circled areas indicate the body positions that were attained. To interpret, the "Spontaneous Behavior" section indicates the actions Kay could perform independently. The "Evoked Responses" section indicates that all five reflexes were still present and that all reactions except *body derotative* were absent (i.e., Kay could do mature segmental rolling but otherwise totally lacked head and neck control and body equilibrium).

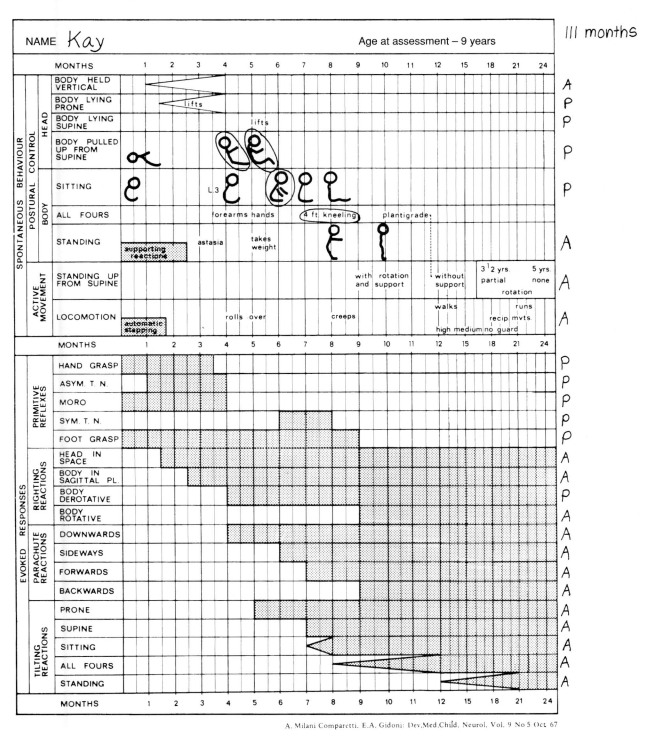

A. Milani Comparetti. E.A. Gidoni: Dev.Med.Child. Neurol. Vol. 9 No 5 Oct 67

A. Kay has no arm/hand control, so she uses a head pointer to touch symbols on a communication board. This photo also shows absent head control in body held vertical, the first MC item. Kay's teacher, who also has CP, shows poor head control.

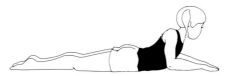

C. Under "all fours" on the MC chart, Kay can maintain the prone-on-elbows position and can do 4-ft kneeling (the creep position) but cannot hold this position long or creep. She also cannot do *plantigrade* (the all-fours stunt with straight arms and legs called the *bear walk*) because of pathological reflexes.

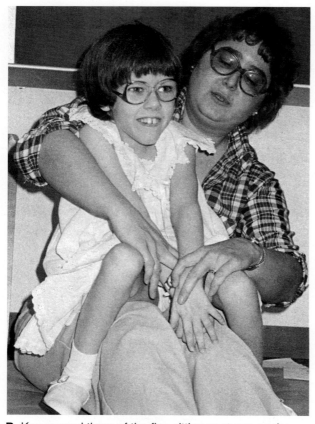

B. Kay passed three of the five sitting postures on the MC. She can sit in good alignment only with help because of the presence of reflexes and the absence of reactions.

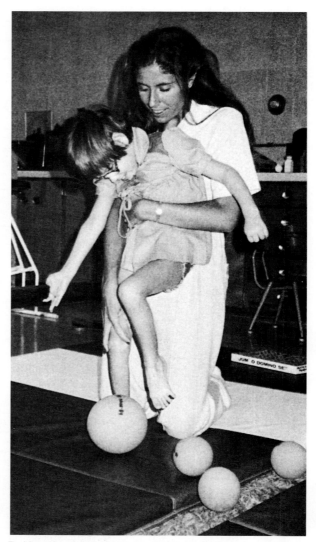

D. Kay should do kicking activities only from a seated position. The crossed extensor reflex interferes with kicking in a standing position.

Figure 10.25 shows that all five early reflexes are present: hand grasp, ATNR, Moro, STNR, and foot grasp. This knowledge guides the physical educator in selecting which throwing, striking, and kicking patterns to teach Kay.

Also present is the crossed extensor reflex (not covered by the MC chart). This reflex adversely affects kicking a ball from a standing position and other reciprocal leg movements. When one leg is lifted to kick the ball, a strong extensor spasm affects the support leg and causes loss of balance. The crossed extensor reflex explains much of the awkwardness in young children learning to kick, as well as problems of students with CP.

FIGURE 10.26   Tilting activities to reinforce equilibrium reactions. Activities like these should be prescribed for Kay and children like her. Also recommended are other balance activities in a sitting position like horseback riding, riding three- or four-wheel cycles, and riding in a wagon or on a scooter board pulled by another.

Backward tilt

Level

Forward tilt

Forward tilt should result in extension/hyperextension of head, neck, and trunk and in adduction of scapulae. *Backward tilt* should result in flexion of head, neck, and trunk and abduction of scapulae.

Backward tilt

Level

Forward tilt

Sideward tilt should result in rotation of the head and trunk toward the uptilting side. There is also flexion and abduction of the limbs on the uptilting side; the opposite characterizes limbs on the downtilting side.

Backward tilt

Level

Forward tilt

Forward tilt on all-fours results in symmetrical extension tonic neck reflex posture.

Pedagogy in Relation to Reflexes and Reactions

Physical education for young students with abnormal reflexes and balance problems is guided by the neurophysiological treatment approach of Bobath (1980), which is supported by Levitt (1995) and others who specialize in cerebral palsy and related disorders. This approach rests on two principles:

1. Inhibition or suppression of abnormal reflex activity
2. Facilitation of righting, parachute, and equilibrium reactions in their proper developmental sequence

The first principle is achieved primarily through correct positioning and the proper selection of activities. With students who are severely disabled, correct positioning is achieved through specially designed wheelchairs and strapping of body parts. Maintaining the head in midline is especially important, since head rotation and flexion/extension elicit the ATNR and STNR, respectively. Velcro ties are often used to prevent undesirable head movement. Targets and/or balls to be hit off tees should be placed at eye level or, in the case of floor targets, far enough away so that the student does not drop the head to look downward. As long as therapists are striving to inhibit or suppress abnormal reflex activity, physical educators should cooperate. Often, however, this goal is reevaluated at age 7 or 8 years, if it becomes evident that it may not be achievable. In this situation, the emphasis may change to finding ways the student can utilize reflex activity to his or her advantage. For instance, a side position to the target, with the head rotated to the right, thereby eliciting the ATNR, may make it easier to release objects with the right arm.

The second principle is achieved primarily through exercises, stunts, and games that follow the natural developmental sequence whereby students gain the strength and coordination needed to attain a proper balance between mobility and stability (i.e., voluntary control over purposeful movement as well as maintenance of a set posture against the pull of gravity). To understand students like Kay, we must know the neurological bases of movement.

Neurological Bases of Motor Development

Adapted physical activity specialists need to understand the neurological bases of motor development (Cowden & Eason, 1991; Sherrill, 1988). Regular educators also need to understand the neurological basis of clumsiness and some of the theories that guide teaching practices. The sections that follow introduce or review fundamentals.

Nerve Cells and Synapses

The normal adult has approximately 100 billion nerve cells, called **neurons.** Each neuron has a cell body, one axon, and several dendrites. Figure 10.27 shows how the appearance of these cells changes from birth until about 15 months. During this time, in normal development, the **dendrites** rapidly form many treelike branches that receive impulses from other neurons. Through this **dendritization,** each neuron becomes interconnected with approximately 10,000 other neurons.

The **axon** conducts impulses away from the cell body (the executive part of the neuron). The speed and efficiency

FIGURE 10.27 Growth of nerve cells (neurons) during infancy. Each nerve cell has three parts: cell body, dendrites, and axon. Cell bodies are located in the brain and spinal cord. Dendrites and axons are the nerve fibers that comprise nerves throughout the body and neural pathways (tracts) inside the spinal cord and brain.

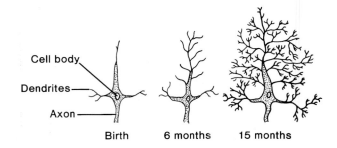

with which neurons transmit impulses determine, to a large extent, motor control. The junction between two neurons is a **synapse.** From the time that sensory input is received until a mental or motor response occurs, hundreds (and sometimes millions) of neurons are involved via synaptic linkups throughout the body.

There are many kinds of neurons. In general, their functions are described as (a) motor, (b) sensory, or (c) associative or internuncial. The location of the cell body and the pathway of its fibers (dendrites and axon) determine function. Motor and associative neurons have their cell bodies in the gray matter of the spinal cord or brain (see Figure 10.28). *They receive information via a dendrites-to-cell body pathway.* The cell body then sends an action impulse to another part of the spinal cord or brain or to an effector organ (muscle) via its axon.

Sensory neurons, in contrast, have their cell bodies in the dorsal root ganglia of spinal nerves, close to where these nerves issue from the spinal cord (see Figure 10.28). *Their cell bodies receive sensory information also via a dendrites-to-cell body pathway.* The cell body then directs the axon to carry the sensory message to the dendrites of a motor or associative neuron.

Billions of different kinds of neurons are thus interacting or synapsing all of the time. Think, for instance, about movement when you have been sitting and decide to get up. The impulse to move originates in the thinking part of the brain (cerebral cortex), which generates thousands of action impulses that are transmitted from neuron to neuron down through the various parts of the brain to the spinal cord. Since getting up from a chair requires almost all of the body parts to move, motor neuron axons carrying the command to move must simultaneously exit at each level of the spinal cord via the 31 pairs of spinal nerves. The exit is always via the anterior or ventral root of the spinal nerve.

Thousands of individual nerve fibers are grouped together into bundles to make a nerve (see Figure 10.28). Note how the dorsal and ventral roots join together in the spinal nerve. Thus, inside every spinal nerve are (a) sensory fibers carrying messages from receptor organs in the skin, muscles, tendons, ligaments, and bones back to the spinal cord and (b) motor fibers carrying messages from the brain and spinal cord out to the muscles and other effector organs.

FIGURE 10.28   The peripheral nervous system. *(A)* Each of the 31 spinal nerves emerges from the spinal cord by a dorsal (posterior) root and a ventral (anterior) root. The dorsal root transmits sensory messages, whereas the ventral root transmits motor messages. *(B)* The roots merge after leaving the vertebral area to form a nerve. Nerves are made up of nerve fibers called dendrites and axons.

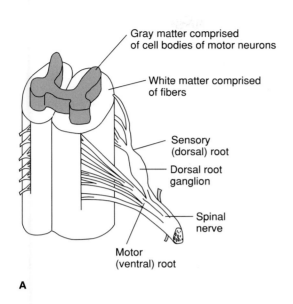

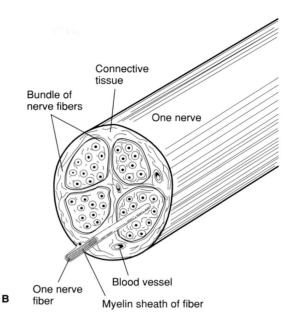

A

B

Myelination

Approximately 5 months before birth, **myelination** begins. This is the development of the fatlike protein and lipid substance that forms the covering of axons and influences their ability to conduct impulses. At birth, some parts of the nervous system (optic tract, motor and sensory roots of the 31 pairs of spinal nerves) have a moderate amount of myelination, but others have none.

Myelination continues rapidly from birth until 3 or 4 years of age, when it is mostly complete except for the association areas of the brain—in these areas, myelination is finished between ages 20 and 30 years. Sensorimotor and cognitive function can occur before completion of myelination in related nerves and CNS parts. However, efficiency of movement and thought patterns is believed to relate to degree of myelination. Specifically, myelination is associated with improved speed, precision, steadiness, and strength.

A characteristic of nerve cell injury and/or disease is *demyelination* (the disintegration of the myelin covering of the nerve's fibers) and subsequent loss of motor coordination. Demyelination is the cause of **multiple sclerosis,** a CNS condition that mainly occurs in adults (see the Index).

The Human Brain

The human brain, much simplified, can be thought of as composed of white and gray matter. The **white matter** is comprised of all the nerve fibers. These are grouped together as tracts and given names (e.g., pyramidal and extrapyramidal). In the cerebrum, these tracts collectively are called the internal capsule. The **gray matter,** made up of concentrations of cell bodies, is (a) the cortex or outer covering of the cerebrum and cerebellum and (b) nuclei with specific names like thalamus, hypothalamus, and basal ganglia. The cerebral cortex performs

all of the higher level mental functions (voluntary movement, perception, cognition, and memory). The cerebellar cortex is less well understood but plays an important part in regulating both voluntary and involuntary movements, especially during rapid changes in body position and equilibrium. The nuclei located within the white matter of the cerebrum perform or govern reflex or regulatory functions.

The cerebral cortex, which is smooth before birth, rapidly develops numerous **convolutions** (folds, hills, gyri) and **depressions** (grooves, sulci, fissures). Some of these, like the central sulcus that separates the frontal lobe from the parietal lobe, have names. The cerebral cortex is divided into right and left hemispheres. In right-handed persons, the **right hemisphere** governs spatial, artistic, and creative abilities. The **left hemisphere** governs analytical and verbal skills, like mathematics, reading, and writing.

Figure 10.29 shows that each hemisphere is divided into four lobes: frontal, parietal, occipital, and temporal. Each lobe performs different functions. *Simplified,* the **occipital lobe** governs vision and visual perception. The **temporal lobe** governs audition and provides memory storage for both auditory and visual experiences. The **parietal lobe** is responsible for the interpretation of skin and muscular sensations and for speech. The **frontal lobe** is the site of processes pertaining to cognition, personality, and voluntary movement. In reality, there is much overlapping of function.

Figure 10.29 also shows the brain stem, the cerebellum, and the midbrain, a small, distinct area between the brain stem and the cerebrum. Theorists on reflexes and postural reactions posit that the evolution of voluntary movement is related to the structure and function of (a) the *brain stem,* which governs reflexes; (b) the *midbrain,* which governs postural

FIGURE 10.29 Lobes of the right cerebral hemisphere, separated by dotted lines.

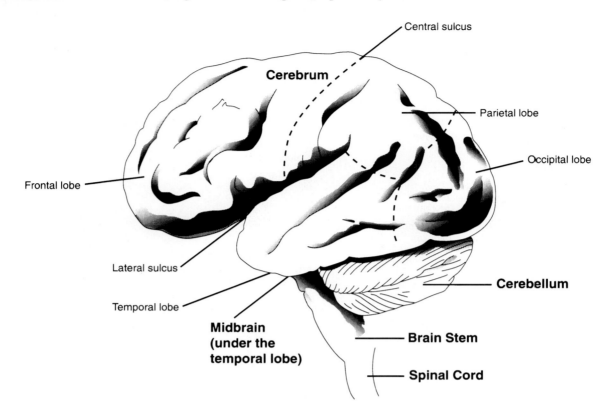

reactions; and (c) the *cortex of the cerebrum and cerebellum,* which governs equilibrium and voluntary movement.

Brain growth follows a specific pattern. The brain stem becomes functional first, then the midbrain, and last the cortical areas controlling voluntary movement. This explains why infants are born with reflexes, righting reactions begin at about 1.5 months of age, and voluntary movement is evident at about 4 months of age. In normal growth and development, this happens so fast we hardly notice. In delayed or abnormal development, teachers must devote much time and energy to reflexes and reactions.

Development of the Central Nervous System

Just as the body progresses through stages of development (embryo to fetus to infant), so also does the CNS. Beginning as cells called the *ectoderm* (see age 23 days in Figure 10.30), the CNS evolves into the neural tube that, 28 days after conception, has subdivided into four distinct parts: fore-brain, midbrain, hindbrain, and neural tube (spinal cord). Long before birth, these structures evolve into the parts of the CNS with which we are familiar. The hindbrain separates into medulla and pons (the brain stem); the cerebellum de-velops later, in the ninth week. The midbrain expands in size, but its name does not change. The forebrain evolves into a cerebrum with several interdependent structures. The inner-most of these are the thalamus, hypothalamus, basal ganglia (clumps of cell bodies), and limbic system. The outermost part is the cerebral cortex.

Parts of the Central Nervous System

Knowing the function of each part of the CNS is essential to understanding individual differences in motor functioning. The following is a simplified explanation of each.

1. **Spinal cord.** A cord composed of numerous tracts (pathways), each of which contains nerve fibers carrying impulses to and from the brain. Each tract has a distinct name and function. The name typically indicates the direction in which impulses are carried and the two parts of the CNS connected by the pathway. Illustrative *ascending pathways* are spinocerebellar and spinothalamic. Illustrative *descending pathways* are corticospinal and vestibulospinal. The speed and efficiency with which impulses are carried up and down these tracts are major determinants of motor coordination and control. Spinal cord damage results in muscle weakness or paralysis and lack of sensation.

2. **Medulla.** The upper part of the spinal cord that regulates such vital functions as respiration, heart rate, and blood pressure. Contains nuclei (cell bodies) from which cranial nerves 9 to 12 emerge. These nerves pertain to swallowing, chewing, salivating, moving the tongue, and speaking.

3. **Pons ("bridge").** Mainly, fibers forming a bridge between the medulla and the cerebellum. Contains nuclei from which cranial nerves 5 to 8 emerge. The *eighth cranial nerve* is the vestibulocochlear nerve. The vestibular branch is important in the reflex control of head, neck, and eyes and helps regulate coordination and posture. The cochlear branch is important in audition.

FIGURE 10.30   The rapid growth of the body and brain before birth.

Age	Length	Appearance
4 days		
23 days	2 mm	Ectoderm / Mesoderm / Endoderm
28 days	4 mm	
45 days	17 mm	
7 weeks	2.8 cm	
12 weeks	8.8 cm	
28 weeks	38.5 cm	
First postnatal year+		

Embryo at 28 Days
Forebrain — Midbrain — Hindbrain — Neural tube

Embryo at 45 Days
Thalamus/Hypothalamus — Midbrain — Cerebellum — Medulla — Cerebrum — Limb bud

Infant at Birth
Limbic system with thalamus and hypothalamus — Cerebrum — Midbrain — Cerebellum — Medulla — Spinal cord

4. **Brain stem.** The bundle of nerve tissue that extends upward from the spinal cord to the base of the cerebrum. The brain stem regulates reflexes. It contains all of the centers for the 10 sense modalities except vision and smell. Some authorities say that it includes the medulla, pons, and midbrain. Others say that it includes only the medulla and that the pons and midbrain are independent structures. The primary reason for considering these three structures together is the presence in all of them of the *reticular formation,* also called the reticular activating system (see Figure 10.31).

5. **Reticular activating system (RAF).** A complex network of nerve fibers with tiny clumps of cell bodies that connects the brain stem with virtually all other parts of the brain. Its main functions pertain to reciprocal innervation, activation, wakefulness, and arousal; thus, it is important in attention, learning, and behavior deficits involving hyperactivity versus hypoactivity. The RAF filters incoming sensory impulses and prevents sensory bombardment of the cortex by selectively transferring some sensory impulses upward and inhibiting others. This permits the cortex to process significant stimuli, rather than coping with all neural impulses.

6. **Midbrain.** A short portion between the pons and the cerebral hemispheres or upper part of the brain stem.

FIGURE 10.31   Side view of brain stem, midbrain, and lower cerebrum. This level of the brain governs the primitive reflexes and righting reactions.

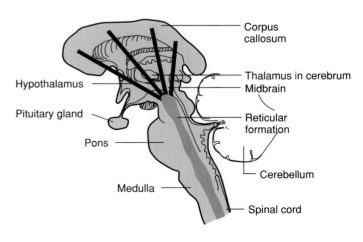

Hypothalamus — Pituitary gland — Pons — Medulla — Corpus callosum — Thalamus in cerebrum — Midbrain — Reticular formation — Cerebellum — Spinal cord

Contains nuclei for nerves pertaining to vision. These are in the red (rubro) nucleus. The midbrain is essentially a servomechanism (relay center) for transmitting impulses related to righting and postural reactions. The rubrospinal tract starts here.

7. **Cerebellum ("little brain").** Essentially, a servomechanism (relay center) for transmitting nerve impulses from kinesthetic and vestibular input and for regulating postures and automatic movement. The cerebellum is important in excitation (activation) and inhibition of muscles, a major determinant in smooth versus jerky movements. It is especially important in the control of fast movements. It is also believed to be the structure that, after training and practice of a new motor skill, assumes responsibility for automatic rather than conscious control of motor performance. A major goal of physical education is to motivate students to practice a new skill until it no longer requires motor planning (i.e., conscious thought). At that point, performance becomes subcortical, or automatic, meaning that it can be executed at the cerebellar level.

8. **Thalamus ("little chamber or anteroom").** A football-shaped cluster of nerve cells deep within the cerebrum, located immediately above the midbrain. One part acts as a servomechanism for relaying sensory impulses, and the other helps to regulate arousal in relation to activity. Except for smell, each of the senses relays its impulses through the thalamus.

9. **Hypothalamus.** A group of small nuclei underneath the thalamus and close to the pituitary gland that integrate autonomic nervous system responses, thereby playing a key role in *homeostasis* (the regulation of balance in internal bodily functions). Among these are regulation of physical growth, heart rate, body temperature, sleep and wakefulness, hunger, dehydration, emotion, and control of stress. This regulation occurs primarily through stimulation of glands that release hormones.

10. **Basal ganglia.** Masses of subcortical gray matter (cell bodies) in the interior of the cerebrum, mainly in the corpus callosum area near the junction of right and left cerebral hemispheres. Some of the basal ganglia have specific names: globus pallidus, putamen, caudate nucleus, subthalamic nucleus, and substantia nigra. In general, the basal ganglia help to regulate posture and movement, particularly slow movement. Damage to basal ganglia results in such conditions as athetosis (involuntary, purposeless, slow, repeated motions), tremors of face and hands, and Huntington's chorea.

11. **Limbic system.** A ring of interconnecting pathways and centers in the cerebrum that includes the hypothalamus, thalamus, basal ganglia, and other subcortical nuclei that are important in control of emotional responses and activity levels (i.e., hyperactivity vs. hypoactivity). *Limbus* is Latin for "rim" or "border"; the limbic system forms the inner rim of structures that comprise the evolutionarily old cortex. It is closely connected to the sense of smell in that the olfactory bulbs and tracts are nearby. Evolutionally, the cerebrum is believed to have begun as a center for smell.

12. **Cerebral cortex ("bark of tree").** Six layers of gray matter (cell bodies) that comprise the outer part of the cerebrum. The cortex performs the higher level functions: voluntary movement, perception, thought, memory, and creativity. Cortical areas are named according to function: sensory, association, and motor. *Sensory areas* interpret impulses from 10 kinds of sensory receptors. *Association areas* link sensory and motor input and create associations essential to verbalization, memory, reasoning, judgment, and creativity. *Motor areas* control voluntary movement; damage to the motor cortex and/or its descending tracts results in spasticity.

13. **Corpus callosum.** A bridge of nerve fibers that connects right and left cerebral hemispheres, thus allowing them to keep in touch with one another. An important function is transfer of learning from one hemisphere to another.

Pyramidal and Extrapyramidal Systems

Pyramidal and *extrapyramidal* are terms used to describe the higher-level motor control systems of the brain. The systems are named after large, pyramid-shaped cells of the cerebral cortex. The pyramidal system includes motor neurons that form the corticospinal or pyramidal tracts. The extrapyramidal system includes motor neurons not in the pyramidal system (i.e., those that are extra). Names of some of the extrapyramidal tracts are vestibulospinal, rubrospinal, and reticulospinal.

The pyramidal tracts are mostly concerned with the voluntary initiation of controlled movements. The extrapyramidal tracts are mainly responsible for automatic reactions and postural control.

Upper and Lower Motor Neuron Disorders

Figure 10.32 indicates disorders caused by damage to motor neurons in the brain. These conditions are often called upper motor neuron syndromes to distinguish them from motor problems that have their origin in the spinal cord (i.e., lower motor neuron syndromes). Most lower motor neuron problems are the result of spinal cord lesions that cause weakness or paralysis. The main upper motor neuron problems are spasticity and athetosis. **Spasticity,** caused by pyramidal system malfunction, is primarily a problem of overexcitation or too much tightness in muscles. **Athetosis,** caused by extrapyramidal breakdown, is a problem of excessive movement (i.e., inhibition is impaired). **Ataxia,** or general incoordination, may be either an upper motor neuron disorder (cerebellum) or a lower motor neuron problem. In the latter, degeneration of cell bodies in the posterior spinal cord interferes with kinesthesis.

Neurological Bases of Clumsiness

Clumsiness, the inability to perform culturally normative motor activities with acceptable proficiency, is caused by delayed or abnormal CNS development, musculoskeletal limitations, and other constraints. The severity of the CNS condition(s) typically determines whether the person is called clumsy or cerebral palsied. Without sophisticated laboratory equipment, determining the CNS site and other contributing factors is difficult. Always, the problem is complex; certainly,

FIGURE 10.32   Areas of the central nervous system where most developmental motor problems occur.

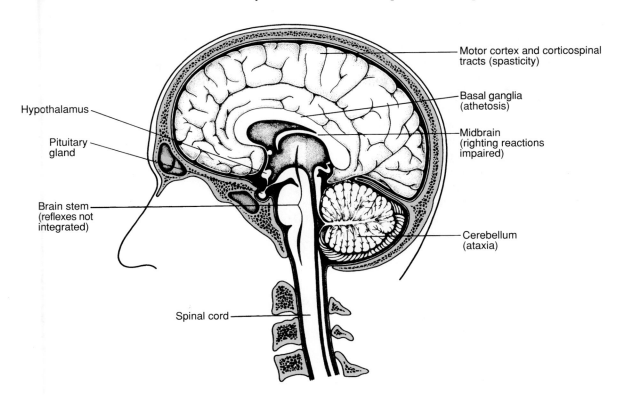

sound motor functioning cannot occur without intact sensory and central processing systems.

The following questions typically are used in searching for neurological reasons for clumsiness:

1. Is something wrong with the sense organs?
2. Is something wrong with the nerve fibers that carry sensory input?
3. Is something wrong with central processing (i.e., the servomechanisms that relay impulses, the reticular activating system that controls arousal, or the association areas of the cerebral cortex that translate impulses into meaning)?
4. Is something wrong with motor output (i.e., the motor areas of the CNS that activate movement; the nerve fibers that carry motor input to muscles, tendons, and joints; or the motor effectors [endings] within these structures)?

This approach, while interesting, seldom results in specific answers that help physical education programming.

Systems or Distributed Motor Control Models

An alternative approach to explaining clumsiness, used in the therapies and in adapted physical activity, entails assessing characteristics of a mature, intact CNS (see Table 10.3) and directing remediation at specific problems. Instead of concern with specific parts of the brain, *systems or distributed motor control models* recognize that sensorimotor integration is shared by several parts or is broadly distributed (Crutchfield & Barnes, 1995; Thelen & Smith, 1994). Proponents of these models assert that there is no strict hierarchy of control from one part of the brain to another. Instead, requirements of the task and environmental conditions determine brain function. Biomechanics is also important in these models, with attention given to musculoskeletal constraints like overall shortness, limb lengths, and postural deviations.

Systems models emphasize that remediation should be directed toward several CNS parts simultaneously, and practice should be variable, utilizing all resources. *Teaching the whole child, not the separate systems, means working simultaneously on reflexes, reactions, voluntary movement, and environmental constraints.*

Theories That Guide Practices

In the past, therapists and educators have tended to rely on different theories to explain and guide practices. Today, however, sources are synthesizing information from several disciplines and professions (Crutchfield & Barnes, 1995; Burton, 1990a, 1990b; Hoover & Wade, 1985; Reid, 1990). The following are brief descriptions of theories that are pertinent to adapted physical activity.

Maturation or Neuromaturation Theory

Arnold Gesell, a physician and director of the Yale University Clinic of Child Development from 1911 to 1948, is generally accredited with evolution of maturation theory (Clark & Whitall, 1989; Salkind, 1985). Maturation theory posits the orderly, sequential appearance of developmental milestones in accordance with an inborn biological timetable. Gesell recognized environment as important also but not capable of

Table 10.3 Characteristics of a mature, intact central nervous system.

1. **Reflex integration.** Reflexes are involuntary muscle and postural tone shifts that normally are integrated during infancy. Reflexes must be integrated before coordinated, graceful, voluntary movement can occur.
2. **Optimal functioning of reactions.** Reactions are generalized involuntary responses that pertain to static and dynamic balance. Developmentally, reactions replace early reflexes.
3. **Freedom from ataxia.** Ataxia is incoordination characterized primarily by irregularity and lack of precision in voluntary motor acts. Ataxic behaviors include overshooting or undershooting the object when reaching for something or going through an obstacle course; problems include spilling, bumping into things, knocking things over, or stumbling for no apparent reason. In stepping over an object or climbing stairs, persons with ataxia tend to lift their feet too high. An ataxic gait is characterized by irregular steps.
4. **Freedom from athetosis.** Athetosis is involuntary, purposeless, relatively slow, repeated movement that interferes with steadiness, accuracy, and control of one or more body parts.
5. **Freedom from spasticity.** Spasticity is hypertonus (too much muscle tone) that results in reduced range of movement, overly active tonic reflex activity, and stiff, awkward-looking movements. Spasticity occurs only in relation to voluntary movement.
6. **Freedom from associated movements.** The ability to move one body part without associated movements of other parts. This problem is sometimes called *overflow*.
7. **Freedom from sensory input problems.** Visual and auditory problems affect the teaching/learning process in mastering new motor skills and patterns.
8. **Freedom from other constraints.** These constraints might be in the body (e.g., orthopedic, health), in the environment, or in interactions of the body and the environment.

Note. The terms *ataxia, athetosis,* and *spasticity,* although used to specify types of cerebral palsy, are not limited to this group of conditions. They also describe clumsy movements and gaits with an infinite variety of etiologies (causes), including brain damage from vehicular accidents, drugs, alcohol, and disease. A person intoxicated with alcohol, for instance, is said to have an ataxic gait; likewise, the toddler just learning to walk evidences developmental ataxia, which disappears with neuromuscular maturation.

Table 10.4 Normal reflex/reaction development.

Level of Development	Level of CNS Maturation	Motor Behaviors
Primitive reflexes	Spinal cord and/ or brain stem	Prone-lying
		Supine-lying
Righting reactions	Midbrain	Right self, turn over, sit, crawl, creep
Equilibrium reactions	Cortical	Stand, walk

changing essential genetic potential. Today's principles of motor development (see Chapter 18 on infant, toddler, and early childhood programming) are based on Gesell's *Infancy and Human Growth* (1928) and subsequent publications.

Gesell, like others of his time, did not use the term *theory.* His principles and developmental sequences, however, were tested and refined by followers, who subsequently organized them into maturation theory. Today, some of his principles are being challenged (Crutchfield & Barnes, 1995), but his developmental sequences continue to guide developmental di-

agnosis and norm-based tests for children from birth to age 6 (Gesell & Amatruda, 1941; Knobloch & Pasamanick, 1974).

Theories Based on Hierarchical Levels of Function

Several developmental theories are based on hierarchical levels of CNS functioning. Among these are the neurophysiological theory of the Bobaths, the reflex-testing theory of Fiorentino, the sensorimotor theory of Rood, and the sensory integration theory of Jean Ayres. The three levels of reflex/reaction development that form the basis of these theories are presented in Table 10.4.

Neurodevelopmental/Neurophysiological Theory

The origin of neurodevelopmental/neurophysiological theories is generally accredited to Karel Bobath, a physician, and his wife, Berta Bobath, a physical therapist (Huss, 1988). Their work began in England in the 1940s and is now known worldwide. Physical therapists, occupational therapists, and adapted physical educators all use the Bobath treatment approaches, especially with persons severely disabled by cerebral palsy or brain injury. The Bobaths (B. Bobath, 1985; K. Bobath, 1980) posited that (a) delayed or abnormal motor development is the result of interference with normal brain maturation, (b) this interference is manifested as an impairment of the postural reflex mechanism, (c) abnormal reflex activity produces abnormal degree and distribution of postural and muscle tone, and (d) righting and equilibrium reactions should be used to inhibit abnormal movements while simultaneously stimulating and facilitating normal postural responses.

The *normal postural reflex mechanism,* according to the Bobaths, is the product of interactions among three factors: (a) normal postural tone, (b) reciprocal innervation, and (c) the proper emergence of developmental sequences of postural reactions and voluntary movement. Interference with any of these factors requires treatment or therapy. The Bobaths thus stressed that all movement behavior is postural (we assume thousands of postures each day) and that the integration of reflexes and the emergence of righting and equilibrium reactions form the basis of normal movement.

Mary Fiorentino, an occupational therapist from Connecticut, built upon the ideas of the Bobaths and other developmentalists and synthesized existing knowledge about reflexes and reactions into reflex testing theory in the 1960s. Fiorentino (1963) described and illustrated 37 distinct reflexes and reactions, organized according to the scheme presented in

Body tuck. Helps normalize tonic labyrinthine reflexes.

Rollover with limbs on one side flexed. Helps normalize asymmetrical tonic neck reflex.

Pivot prone, swan, or wing lift. Helps normalize tonic labyrinthine and symmetrical tonic neck reflexes.

Head lift and hold neck co-contraction. Promotes strength.

Prone-on-elbows or belly crawl. Helps normalize symmetrical tonic neck reflex.

Four-point or creeping. Promotes strength.

Standing. With practice on stand-to-squat, stand-to-sit, stand-to-lie, and vice versa.

Walking. Arm opposition and trunk rotation begin at age 4 to 5 years.

Table 10.4. Later Fiorentino (1981) wrote a comprehensive text on the influence of reflexes and reactions on normal and abnormal motor development.

Sensorimotor/Sensory Integration Theory

Margaret Rood, who was certified in both occupational and physical therapy, evolved a sensorimotor theoretical approach to treatment in the 1950s based on three principles: (a) motor output is dependent on sensory input, (b) activation of motor responses should follow the normal developmental sequence, and (c) stimuli used to remediate one sensory function will influence other functions (Huss, 1988). Rood posited that an eight-step developmental mobility-stability model (total flexion pattern, rolling, prone-lying with hyperextension of the entire spine, prone lying with contraction of neck muscles, prone-lying with weight on elbows, hands and knees kneeling, standing, and walking) should be used in conjunction with sensory stimulation (icing, heating, brushing, exerting deep muscle pressure, and the like) (see Figure 10.33). Rood's work was the basis for much of Ayres' (1972) sensory integration theory.

The body tuck, rollover, and pivot prone shown in Figure 10.33 are universally accepted as tasks that promote neurological integration (Pyfer, 1988; Stockmeyer, 1978). Rood's model emphasizes many exercises and positions common to physical educators, such as the supine tuck and hold, modified logroll, swan, and creeping. Whereas regular physical educators have used these exercises primarily to develop abdominal and back extensor strength, therapists believe the exercises facilitate sensory integration and neurological maturation. Whatever the rationale, the tasks have stood the test of time and should be incorporated into programming for awkward students.

Jean Ayres, an occupational therapist with a doctoral degree in neuropsychology, outlined sensory integration theory in the 1970s. A professor at the University of Southern California, Ayres focused most of her research on learning disabilities. Her ideas, however, have been widely applied, especially in infant and early childhood programs. Ayres' theory emphasizes that the nervous system must be integrated at the lower levels before cognitive approaches like watching demonstrations and listening to directions can be successful. Development is spiral, with the integrity of each system built on sound functioning of the level immediately below it.

Ayres continued to refine sensory integration theory and practice throughout her lifetime, and colleagues continue this work (e.g., Fisher, Murray, & Bundy, 1991). Ayres' (1989) final definition of sensory integration, published shortly after her death, was

> [s]ensory integration is the neurological process that organizes sensation from one's own body and from the environment and makes it possible to use the body effectively within the environment. The spatial

and temporal aspects of inputs from different sensory modalities are interpreted, associated, and unified. Sensory integration is information processing. . . . The brain must select, enhance, inhibit, compare, and associate the sensory information in a flexible, constantly changing pattern; in other words, the brain must integrate it (p. 11).

Ayres believes that movement therapy should be directed at six levels: spinal cord, brain stem with emphasis on reticular formation, cerebellum, basal ganglia, old cortex and/or limbic system, and neocortex. She cautions, however, that, in reality, several CNS levels function simultaneously in human motor behavior.

Therapy is based on several principles:

1. Because the brain stem is developmentally the lowest level of the brain, it receives the greatest focus of therapeutic attention. The brain stem regulates reflexes. Therefore, reflex inhibition and integration are important parts of therapy.

2. Tactile stimulation contributes to generalized neurological integration and enhances perception of other sensory modalities.

3. One approach to normalization of vestibular mechanisms is swinging and spinning activities. These can be initiated by the child or therapist, but extreme care should be taken to avoid overstimulation (nausea, dizziness).

4. Activities involving extensor muscles should be emphasized. Prone-lying on a scooterboard with head held high is an illustrative extensor muscle activity. Among the many scooterboard tasks recommended are 30 ways to descend a ramp that is elevated at one end about 2 ft.

5. Body control activities should be emphasized. Some of these are (a) moving on all-fours through tunnels or obstacle courses, (b) jumping games, and (c) balancing tasks.

Parts of sensory integration theory have been challenged (Arendt, MacLean, & Baumeister, 1988) and defended (Cermak, 1988; Ottenbacher, 1988). Most of the activities recommended by Ayres, however, have been used in elementary physical education and in therapeutic settings for many years. The activities appear sound, but researchers are still trying to explain neurologically how and why they work.

Information-Processing Theory

Information-processing theory, popular from the 1950s through the 1980s, posits that the central nervous system works in a linear fashion like a computer. Motor behavior, according to this theory, occurs in a chainlike fashion (sensory input, central processing, motor output) and can be modified by feedback. In contrast to neuromaturational theory, which emphasizes heredity and biology, information-processing theory mainly focuses on environment, stimulus-response mechanisms, and the role of cognition in altering behavior. The reflex-hierarchical theories explained in the previous section contain many elements of information-processing theory.

Motor Behavior and Theory Pertaining to Disability

Motor behavior, recognized as one of the basic subdisciplines of exercise and sport science (also known as physical education or kinesiology), is generally defined as including motor control, development, and learning. A recent history of the evolution of knowledge in these three areas indicates that motor development has generated the least research and remains relatively atheoretical (Thomas, 1997). Motor development textbooks used in physical education teacher training typically present information only on normal development.

Adapted physical activity, as a crossdisciplinary knowledge area concerned with delayed and abnormal motor behavior, thus relies heavily on textbooks used by therapists. Particularly recommended is *Motor Control and Motor Learning in Rehabilitation* by Carolyn Crutchfield and Marylou Barnes (1995), professors in the Department of Physical Therapy at Georgia State University.

Contemporary Reflex Theory

Crutchfield and Barnes (1995) state that the prevalent model of motor control used in working with individuals with disabilities is probably the reflex-hierarchical perspective. They believe that a problem exists in the semantics relative to reflexes and reactions because these words convey outdated concepts to some people. For example, reflexes traditionally have been defined as stimulus-response reactions to external stimuli. Now neuroscience reveals that some reflexive movements (called stereotypies in this chapter) do not require external stimuli. Reflexes, in the past, have always been associated with hierarchical models. These now are controversial, and many individuals prefer systems approaches that are interactive and multidirectional.

Crutchfield and Barnes (1995) recommend a redefinition of reflexes and reactions as "coordinated patterns of movement that may be demonstrated spontaneously by the infant, child, or adult and that may also be elicited by external stimuli" (p. 141). Furthermore, they state that movement patterns that are apparent in fetal life and in early infancy should be called *early reflexes* (not "primitive") and those that are more mature and appear later in life should be called *reactions*. Sherrill's text treats reflexes and reactions as patterns or synergies that generally occur in response to sensory input; unlike many texts, it does not state that this sensory input must be from an external source. Clearly, something within the nervous system stimulates self-initiated action, because many movements cannot be linked with external stimuli.

Crutchfield and Barnes (1995) state that "it is not possible to dispense with the concept of hierarchy in modern theories of motor control" (p. 6). Brain growth is hierarchical, and modern neuroscience confirms that certain parts of the brain perform specific functions. The brain, however, functions holistically so that the total effect of damage to certain parts cannot be predicted. Recognition of the complexity of brain function has altered the traditional belief that retention of specific reflexes directly prevents neural maturation of higher levels of the brain. Today, we know that many systems of the body dynamically interact with each other and the environment and influence neural function. There are many ways to

FIGURE 10.34   Rhythmical stereotypies of the legs and arms.

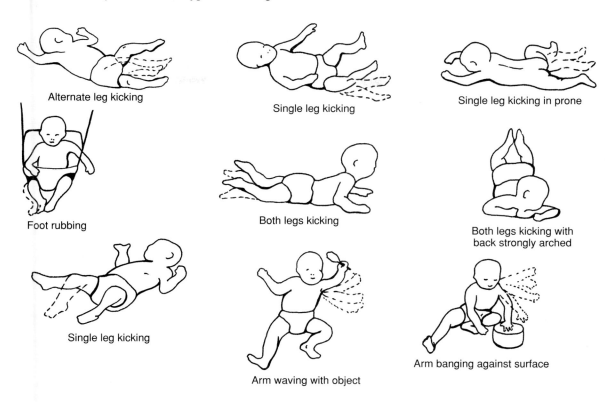

Alternate leg kicking

Single leg kicking

Single leg kicking in prone

Foot rubbing

Both legs kicking

Both legs kicking with back strongly arched

Single leg kicking

Arm waving with object

Arm banging against surface

promote reflex integration, and intervention should be ecological as well as hierarchical.

Dynamic Systems Theory

In marked contrast to older theories, dynamic or dynamical systems theory is an approach that adapted physical activity, as a scholarly discipline, can use to explain ecological change processes. Dynamic systems theory, which is based on the principles of modern biology and physics, is extremely complex (Kelso, 1996; Kugler, Kelso, & Turvey, 1982; Smith & Thelen, 1993; Thelen & Smith, 1994). Simplified, dynamic systems theory is the opposite of information-processing theory and hierarchical approaches to intervention. Common synonyms for *dynamic systems theory* are *ecological theory* and *action theory*. However, the use of these terms often indicates that only selected aspects (i.e., usually a modified or simple version) of dynamic systems theory is being discussed.

Some of the key principles of dynamic systems theory are the following:

1. Function, rather than an inborn genetic timetable or a generalized motor program (schema) within the brain, drives movement behavior.
2. Multilevel subsystems (e.g., reflexes, genes, joint structure, muscle strength, percent body fat, visual perception) dynamically interact with the supports (affordances) and constraints (limitations) of the ever-changing environment to produce movement.
3. The central nervous system, like all of the other systems and subsystems, works in a holistic, plastic, and self-organizing fashion.

Dynamic systems theory guides research and practice in many scientific fields. Esther Thelen, a developmental psychologist at Indiana University, is acknowledged as the leader in applying this theory to help explain infant motor development. Thelen's first major work (1979) is the basis of the concept of rhythmical stereotypies in infants, which was explained earlier in this chapter. Thelen (1979) described 47 rhythmical stereotypies that emerged at specific times, persisted for weeks, peaked, and then declined. These included various kicking and arm patterns, as well as shaking and pounding object manipulations (see Figure 10.34). Since 1979, Thelen has conducted numerous studies of the emergence of locomotor patterns in infants, first noting that their emergence is not dependent on sensory input and later using her findings to explain dynamic systems theory (e.g., Smith & Thelen, 1993; Thelen & Smith, 1994).

The first adapted physical activity leader to investigate dynamic systems theory is Dale Ulrich, professor at Indiana University, who has conducted several studies with his wife, Beverly (e.g., Ulrich & Ulrich, 1995). The Ulrichs have studied both rhythmical stereotypies and the emergence of locomotor patterns in infants with Down syndrome.

Eclectic Theory

In this chapter, an attempt has been made to incorporate parts of several theories. This is called *eclecticism*. Given the complex movement behavior of individuals with severe cerebral palsy and other forms of developmental disability, it may be plausible that different theories are needed to explain intra- and interindividual differences. In particular, individuals with severe brain damage might lack the capacity for the self-organizing behavior that is central to dynamic systems theory.

References

Arendt, R. E., MacLean, W., & Baumeister, A. (1988). Critique of sensory integration therapy and its application in mental retardation. *Mental Retardation, 92*(5), 401–411.

Ayres, A. J. (1972). *Sensory integration and learning disorders.* Los Angeles: Western Psychological Services.

Ayres, A. J. (1980). *Sensory integration and the child.* Los Angeles: Western Psychological Services.

Ayres, A. J. (1989). *Sensory integration and praxis tests.* Los Angeles: Western Psychological Services.

Barnes, M. R., Crutchfield, C., Heriza, C., & Herdman, S. (1990). *Reflex and vestibular aspects of motor control, motor development, and motor learning.* Atlanta: Stokesville.

Bobath, B. (1985). *Abnormal postural reflex activity caused by brain lesions* (3rd ed.). Rockville, MD: Aspen Systems.

Bobath, K. (1980). *A neurophysiological basis for the treatment of cerebral palsy.* Philadelphia: J. B. Lippincott.

Burton, A. W. (1990a). Applying principles of coordination in adapted physical education. *Adapted Physical Activity Quarterly, 7*(2), 126–142.

Burton, A. W. (1990b). Assessing the perceptual-motor interaction in developmentally disabled and nonhandicapped children. *Adapted Physical Activity Quarterly, 7*(4), 325–337.

Burton, A. W., & Davis, W. E. (1992). Assessing balance in adapted physical education: Fundamental concepts and applications. *Adapted Physical Activity Quarterly, 9*(1), 14–46.

Cermak, S. A. (1988). Sensible integration. *Mental Retardation, 92*(5), 413–414.

Clark, J. E., & Whitall, J. (1989). What is motor development? The lessons of history. *Quest, 41*(3), 183–202.

Cowden, J. E., & Eason, B. L. (1991). Pediatric adapted physical education for infants, toddlers, and preschoolers: Meeting IDEA-H and IDEA-B challenges. *Adapted Physical Activity Quarterly, 8*(4), 263–279.

Crutchfield, C. A., & Barnes, M. R. (1995). *Motor control and motor learning in rehabilitation* (2nd ed.). Atlanta: Stokesville.

Ellison, P., Browning, C., Larson, B., & Denny, J. (1983). Development of a scoring system for the Milani-Comparetti and Gidoni methods of assessing neurological abnormality in infancy. *Physical Therapy, 63*(9), 1414–1423.

Fiorentino, M. (1963). *Reflex testing methods for evaluating C.N.S. development.* Springfield, IL: Charles C Thomas.

Fiorentino, M. (1981). *A basis for sensorimotor development—Normal and abnormal.* Springfield, IL: Charles C Thomas.

Fisher, A. G., Murray, E. A., & Bundy, A. C. (1991). *Sensory integration: Theory and practice.* Philadelphia: F. A. Davis.

Gesell, A. (1928). *Infancy and human growth.* New York: Macmillan.

Gesell, A., & Amatruda, C. S. (1941). *Developmental diagnosis: The evaluation and management of normal and abnormal neuropsychologic development in infant and early childhood.* New York: Hoeber.

Guyton, A. (1981). *Basic human neurophysiology* (3rd ed.). Philadelphia: W. B. Saunders.

Herman, E., & Retish, P. (1989). Vision therapy—Hoax, hope, or homilies? A physical education perspective. *Adapted Physical Activity Quarterly, 6*(4), 299–306.

Hoover, J. H. & Wade, M. G. (1985). Motor learning theory and mentally retarded individuals: A historical review. *Adapted Physical Activity Quarterly, 2*(3), 228–252.

Huss, A. J. (1988). Sensorimotor and neurodevelopmental frames of reference. In H. Hopkins & H. Smith (Eds.), *Willard and Spackman's occupational therapy* (7th ed.) (pp. 114–127). Philadelphia: J. B. Lippincott.

Kelso, J. A. S. (1996). *Dynamic patterns: The organization of brain and behavior.* Cambridge, MA: MIT Press.

Knobloch, H., & Pasamanick, B. (Eds.). (1974). *Gesell and Amatruda's developmental diagnosis.* New York: Harper & Row.

Kugler, P. N., Kelso, J. A. S., & Turvey, M. T. (1982). On coordination and control in naturally developing systems. In J. A. S. Kelso & J. E. Clark (Eds.), *The development of movement control and coordination* (pp. 5–78). New York: Wiley.

Levitt, S. (1995). *Treatment of cerebral palsy and motor delay* (3rd ed.). Cambridge, MA: Blackwell Scientific.

Milani-Comparetti, A. (1981). The neurophysiologic and clinical implications of studies on fetal motor behavior. *Seminars in Perinatology, 5,* 183–189.

Milani-Camparetti Motor Development Screening Test manual (1987). Available from Meyer Children's Rehabilitation Institute, University of Nebraska Medical Center, 444 South 44th Street, Omaha, Nebraska 68131-3795.

Milani-Comparetti, A., & Gidoni, E. (1967). Pattern analysis of motor development and its disorders. *Developmental Medicine and Child Neurology, 9,* 625–630.

Molnar, G. (1978). Analysis of motor disorder in retarded infants and young children. *American Journal of Mental Deficiency, 83,* 213–221.

Mon-Williams, M. A., Pascal, E., & Wann, J. P. (1994). Opthalmic factors in developmental coordination disorder. *Adapted Physical Activity Quarterly, 11*(2), 170–178.

Ottenbacher, K. J. (1988). Sensory integration—Myth, method, imperative. *Mental Retardation, 92*(5), 425–426.

Pyfer, J. (1988). Teachers, don't let your students grow up to be clumsy adults. *Journal of Physical Education, Recreation and Dance, 59*(1), 38–42.

Ramm, P. (1988). Pediatric occupational therapy. In H. Hopkins & H. Smith (Eds.), *Willard and Spackman's occupational therapy* (7th ed.) (pp. 601–627). Philadelphia: J. B. Lippincott.

Reid, G. (Ed.). (1990). *Problems in movement control.* Amsterdam: North-Holland.

Salkind, J. T. (1985). *Theories of human development* (2nd ed.). New York: John Wiley.

Sherrill, C. (Ed.). (1988). *Leadership training in adapted physical education.* Champaign, IL: Human Kinetics.

Smith, L. B., & Thelen, E. (Eds.). (1993). *A dynamic systems approach to development: Applications.* Cambridge, MA: MIT Press.

Stockmeyer, S. A. (1978). A sensorimotor approach to treatment. In P. H. Pearson & C. E. Williams (Ed.), *Physical therapy services in the developmental disabilities* (pp. 186–217). Springfield: IL: Charles C Thomas.

Thelen, E. (1979). Rhythmical stereotypies in normal human infants. *Animal Behavior, 27,* 699–715.

Thelen, E., Kelso, J. A. S., & Fogel, A. (1987). Self-organizing systems and infant motor development. *Developmental Review, 7,* 39–65.

Thelen, E., & Smith, L. B. (1994). *A dynamic systems approach to the development of cognition and action.* Cambridge, MA: MIT Press.

Thelen, E., Ulrich, B. D., & Jensen, J. (1989). The developmental origins of locomotion. In M. H. Woollacott & A. Shumway-Cook (Eds.), *Development of posture and gait across the lifespan* (pp. 25–47). Columbia: University of South Carolina Press.

Thomas, J. R. (1997). Motor behavior. In J. D. Massengale & R. A. Swanson (Eds.), *The history of exercise and sport science* (pp. 203–292). Champaign, IL: Human Kinetics.

Ulrich, B. D., & Ulrich, D. A. (1995). Spontaneous leg movements of infants with Down syndrome and nondisabled infants. *Child Development, 66,* 1844–1855.

Woollacott, M. H., & Shumway-Cook, A. (Eds.). (1989). *Development of posture and gait across the lifespan.* Columbia: University of South Carolina Press.

11

Motor Performance: Assessment and Instruction

FIGURE 11.1   Practice of skills in a game setting leads to functional competence.

After you have studied this chapter, you should be able to do the following:

1. Identify basic locomotor and object control skills.

2. Discuss five basic questions in assessing and teaching motor skills: (a) performance, (b) functional competence, (c) performance standards, (d) constraints, and (e) developmental level.

3. Develop task sheets for use in clipboard assessment and teaching.

4. Identify different kinds of gaits used with and without crutches. Given a picture or videotape of a gait, discuss assessment and programming. State which motor skills are appropriate goals and discuss pedagogy.

5. Demonstrate understanding of biomechanical analysis. Given a motor skill, be able to analyze it into major parts or phases.

6. Discuss qualitative and quantitative assessment of each locomotor and object control skill. State evaluative criteria for mature form and be able to apply this knowledge in assessing several children (live or videotaped).

7. List in correct developmental sequence locomotor skills and the approximate age when each should be mastered. Do the same for object control skills.

8. Identify problems associated with performance of selected locomotor and object control skills and suggest adaptations and strategies.

9. Assuming that motor skills and patterns is the priority goal, write an IEP for a selected child.

A primary goal of adapted physical education is **functional competence** in motor skills and patterns (see Figure 11.1). This chapter discusses assessment of and instruction in motor performance. Knowledge in these areas must extend beyond that of the regular physical educator to include all kinds of individual differences, including motor development delays, abnormal muscle tone (spasticity, athetosis, paralysis, and paresis), structural deviations, and learning problems caused by perceptual-motor deficits.

Motor skills and patterns is the term used in the federal definition of physical education. **Skills,** as defined in motor learning literature, are acts or tasks that must be *learned* in order to be correctly executed. **Patterns** is a broader term. It refers to acts or tasks that have a similar appearance. A pattern may be learned, or it may emerge naturally as the result of normal motor development.

Some theorists say that acts like walking and running are not skills, but patterns that occur without instruction. To qualify for adapted physical education, however, students typically do not evidence normal development. They have delays and/or abnormal structure and function that require careful instruction. In this text, the terms *skills* and *patterns* are therefore used interchangeably.

Basic Questions in Assessing and Teaching Motor Skills

Table 11.1 lists basic locomotor and object control skills covered in this chapter. Instruction should begin by assessing present level of performance and setting goals and objectives that match assessment information. The five basic questions that guide assessment and instruction also appear in Table 11.1. The sections that follow show that assessment and instruction proceed together. Hundreds of trials are required to learn a motor skill. Task sheets that guide instruction should provide space for recording success or failure on each trial.

Table 11.1 Basic locomotor and object control skills and the five basic questions that guide assessment.

Locomotor Skills	Object Control Skills
1. Walk or use wheelchair	Roll/bowl
2. Run	Throw
3. Ascend/descend	Catch
4. Jump	Bounce/dribble
5. Hop	Strike
6. Leap	Kick
7. Gallop	Stop/trap
8. Skip	
9. Slide	

Basic Assessment Questions

1. Performance—Does student perform skill?
2. Functional competence—Does student use skill in activities for fun and/or fitness?
3. Performance standards—Does student meet form, distance, accuracy, speed, and function standards for age group?
4. Constraints—Does student have muscle tone, bone, or joint abnormalities that limit success and/or contraindications to be remembered?
5. Developmental level or form—Is form immature, mature, or adapted to accommodate pathology?

Performance

Assessment at the first level addresses whether the student can perform a skill (yes or no) in a particular context under designated conditions (see Figure 11.2). Three *contexts* that are very different are (a) informal play, (b) structured games, and (c) formal command-response situations. Students may, for example, perform a skill in an informal play setting but be unable to do so in the other settings because of comprehension or

FIGURE 11.2 Clipboard sheet indicating objective, context, and task conditions and providing space to record performance on 60 trials.

Task _____ Overarm throw _____   Date _____ 9/12 _____

Student name _____ J. Garza _____   Partner/aide name _____ CS _____

Objective _____ To throw 30 ft. using correct form _____

Context: C1 Informal play   (C2 Structured game)   C3 Formal drill or test

DIRECTIONS:

Go to station _____ #2 _____ . Work on objective under the circled task
conditions. Record number of trials attempted and succeeded in boxes at bottom.

SIX TASK CONDITIONS

Object Size

(O1) Tennis ball

O2 Small softball

O3 Regular softball

Texture/Weight

T1 Nerf or sponge

T2 Rubber

(T3) Regular

Assistance

A1 Maximal

(A2) Many cues

A3 Three or fewer cues

A4 None

Instructions

(I1) Short, two to three words

I2 Medium, four to seven words

I3 Long, eight or more words

Modeling/Teacher Talk

M1 Coactive

M2 Verbal, then visual

M3 Visual, then verbal

(M4) Concurrent visual-verbal

M5 Verbal only

Reinforcers

R1 Maximal: Token, hug/pat,(praise)(smile)

(R2) Two or three of above

R3 Same as nondisabled

R4 Self-praise

Other _____

Trials (Tr)—Record Performance Here

1	2	3	4	5	6	7	8	9	10	11	12	13	14	15

motivation problems. Therefore, informal play (preferably in a small group) should be observed first.

If the student does not play spontaneously and/or try to imitate classmates, then one-to-one testing is initiated to determine the conditions needed for successful performance. The first condition to be considered is language comprehension, including what language (English, Spanish, sign) is being used and how many words are in the instructions (two to three, four to seven, eight or more). Often, the problem is simply communicating what needs to be done and how!

Some students do not comprehend and/or pay attention to words. For them, the next condition is assistance, including how much assistance is needed (maximal, many cues, three or fewer cues, no cues) and what kind of modeling/teacher talk (physical, verbal, visual, or a combination) should be used. *No assistance* means that the student understands and responds to verbal instructions. If this is not the case, then demonstrations and words are used in various combinations to find the type of modeling/teacher talk condition that works best (verbal, then visual; visual, then verbal;

concurrent visual and verbal). On occasion, physical (kinesthetic) assistance may be needed. This is called **coactive** to emphasize that it is more than physical manipulation. Under this maximal input condition, the teacher uses both verbal and physical prompts. The student says or sings the key words in unison with the teacher. Levels of assistance then range from none to maximal, which means a combination of physical-verbal-visual input.

In addition to these instructional conditions, environmental variables also influence success. Among these are size, weight, and texture of an object, as well as surface, slope, and stability of the movement area. Also important is number of persons at each station and whether or not the student can work independently or needs a helper. Footprints and floor markings can assure that every person at a station is in the right place and in his or her own space. The direction a student faces should also be controlled to block out irrelevant stimuli or to systematically teach coping skills in relation to multiple environmental input.

Conditions are important in both testing and practice. Figure 11.2 shows how conditions are prescribed. A common practice in adapted physical activity skill development is a clipboard for each student containing task sheets like Figure 11.2. During a 30-min class, for example, a student might work on different skills at three stations, each of which provides a rich choice of equipment so that level of difficulty can be matched with prescription on the task card. A separate task sheet for each station is on the clipboard. The order of the sheets on the clipboard indicates the order in which the student should progress from station to station.

The task card provides spaces to indicate performance on 60 trials. After each set of 15 trials, an alternate activity may be used to break monotony and/or provide work on another objective, such as abdominal strength (curl-ups), cardiovascular endurance (bench stepping), or tension release (slow stretches). Sometimes, this alternative activity should be in one of the student's areas of strength so that it can serve as a reward. In general, however, the focus should be on completion of as many trials as possible before the signal to rotate to the next station. The greater the student's time on task, the better the learning outcome.

Reinforcers are not left to chance. Their inclusion on the task sheet signals their importance. *Other* under "Reinforcers" on Figure 11.2 recognizes what works best for each student. *Self-praise* is included as a reinforcer because students need to learn to tell themselves that they are good and to gradually rely on their own self-reinforcement more than that of an external source. The *same as nondisabled* reinforcer category implies use of informational and questioning feedback that requires problem solving. Reinforcement obviously can take many forms. The key is for the teacher or partner to respond in some way, thereby showing interest and support.

The *objective* that guides the task sheet can focus on quantitative or qualitative performance or both. Assessment and instruction should attend to each (Burton, 1997; Kelly, Reuschlein, & Haubenstricker, 1989; Ulrich, 1988).

Functional Competence

Functional competence refers to proficiency in performing life functions like locomotion, play, work, and self-care. It is not enough, for example, to run or throw a ball in response to demonstrations and prompts in the instructional setting. Students must be able to spontaneously use runs and throws in a variety of settings to achieve a number of purposes (e.g., safety, joy, fitness).

Functional competence also implies performance similar to that of others within the same chronological age range. This second part of the definition is important when the placement goal is integration because the student must have the skills to participate fully, safely, and successfully. For example, to benefit from the numerous third- and fourth-grade lead-up games that teach and reinforce softball skills, students must be able to stop a ball on the ground or in the air and to throw it accurately and quickly to a base or teammate. Functional competence thus involves chaining together several motor skills and decision making about where to throw the ball.

Performance Standards

Instruction in motor skills is directed toward meeting **performance standards** with respect to form, distance, speed, accuracy, and function. These task variables are not equally important for all skills, and time limitations usually force teachers to select two or three rather than all five. When an integrated setting is the placement goal or the student is already integrated, assessment should focus on the skill levels expected of the grade or chronological age level.

Much of adapted physical education is devoted to initial-level skills teaching. Students with motor delays and/or pathology often do not have time to master all of the motor skills of normal children, ages 2 to 7 years. In this case, the walk, run, jump, throw, strike, and kick are usually emphasized.

To help plan the order in which basic skills should be taught, three teaching/testing progressions (TTPs) are included in this chapter: walk and run, jump and hop, and object control skills. Each TTP breaks skills into observable, measurable tasks that are ordered from easy to hard. By stating a criterion level and the average age at which normal children pass, the TTPs permit the teacher to determine the number of months of developmental delay. This information is often helpful in making placement decisions.

Constraints

Constraints, within an assessment context, refer to abnormalities of body structure and function that limit functional ability. These include short stature, obesity, posture problems, deviant sizes and shapes of body parts, amputations, and abnormalities of muscle tone. Little is known about good form, mechanical efficiency, and developmental levels when such constraints are present. Indicating pathology in assessment reports is therefore important.

Describing present level of performance for a person with spasticity, athetosis, or paralysis takes many, many

Present Level of Performance
Form: Mostly Level 3 (homolateral throw) with the following appearance. No muscle tone or reflex pathology.

Distance: Throws softball 70 ft, best of 3 trials (15th percentile).
Accuracy: Scores 3 on target overarm throw at distance of 50 ft, 10 trials (below school district average).
Function: Cannot use throw in game setting.
Long-Term Goal—Functional competence for placement with nondisabled 8- and 9-year-olds.

Short-Term Objectives
Form: 1. Pass TGMD #2, full trunk rotation.
         2. Pass TGMD #4, opposition of limbs.
Distance: 3. Throw softball 79 ft, best of 3 trials.
Accuracy: 4. Score 5 on accuracy test at 50 ft, 10 trials.
Function: 5. Perform throw-and-run and field ball-and-throw sequences in softball lead-up games.

words. Therefore, professionals describe abnormal patterns in terms of muscle tone.

Abnormalities of muscle tone are these:

1. **Spasticity or hypertonus.** Muscle tone is too tight; may be evidenced by contractures or spasms. Usually associated with cerebral palsy but can be caused by many conditions.

2. **Athetosis or fluctuating muscle tone.** Body parts in constant, purposeless motion. A type of cerebral palsy.

3. **Paralysis or atonus.** Common in spina bifida.

4. **Paresis or hypotonus.** Weakness caused by partial paralysis or muscle deterioration. Common in muscular dystrophy.

Problems like round shoulders, swayback, and pigeon toes (see Chapter 14) should be taken into consideration in assessment and instruction of basic movement patterns. Also important are neurological constraints like deficits of balance, coordination, and motor planning. Identification of constraints forces attention on adaptation, especially in regard to ideas about good form and procedures of qualitative analysis.

Developmental Level

Qualitative analysis of form sometimes focuses on **developmental level.** Normal children progress fairly rapidly from immature to mature patterns (McClenaghan & Gallahue, 1978; Wickstrom, 1983). Immature patterns, often broken down into initial and elementary levels, are called developmental in that they are normal for a particular chronological age. Children with disabilities and/or clumsiness typically display initial and elementary performance levels far longer than normal peers. This not only results in inefficient and energy-exhausting movement but often affects social acceptance and self-esteem. The sissy throw, seen in both girls and boys of elementary age,

is an example of an immature movement. This movement pattern, however, is totally acceptable in early childhood, when it would be called developmental.

Mature movement patterns are mechanically efficient, a quality called good form. Although there are many individual differences in mature form, certain performance criteria must be met. Ulrich's (1985) Test of Gross Motor Development (TGMD) is recommended to assess form.

To assist teachers in visualizing different developmental levels and planning remediation for progress toward mature form, this chapter includes pictorial and checklist assessment instruments based on the concept of developmental levels. Use of these instruments simplifies writing the individualized education program (IEP) and other reports that require a description of present level of performance.

Figure 11.3 is a sample IEP format that illustrates how developmental level is described under form. When movement patterns are immature, the major goal is to assist students in progressing to the next developmental level. This is done by specifying objectives that pertain to form (e.g., demonstrate opposition of limbs).

Writing Goals and Objectives

Because of heavy workloads, teachers devise many shortcuts to writing goals and objectives. For students whose assessment data indicate that work is needed on basic motor skills, the goal is almost always this: *To achieve functional competence in locomotor and object control skills.* Sometimes, particular skills, such as running or jumping, are specified. Functional competence for each age or grade level is explained in school district curriculum guides. These explanations include performance standards that must be met and/or a minimal percentile (e.g., the 30th percentile) to be achieved on district norms. Also in curriculum guides are lists of games and sport activities that a student of a certain age or grade should be able to play in order to be in an integrated classroom.

Short-term objectives are often computerized or printed in list form in curriculum guides so that the teacher can use numbers or abbreviations when making out IEPs for large numbers of students. Objectives, remember, have three parts: (a) condition, (b) observable behavior, and (c) criterion level. The part of the objective that requires the most words is the condition, which typically includes many parts. Consider, for example, an objective pertaining to throwing:

1. Given these conditions,
   - A specified object (size, weight, texture)
   - A set number of trials
   - In a designated context (informal play, structured game, formal test)
   - With appropriate instructions (short, medium, long)
   - With needed assistance (physical, verbal, visual)
   - With necessary reinforcers (token, hug/pat, praise, smile)
2. the student will throw
3. at a designated criterion level (e.g., form, distance, accuracy, function).

Writing out all of these conditions for every objective takes too much time, so most teachers use an abbreviation system (see Figure 11.2). The objective might therefore look like this:

1. Given these conditions, O2, T2, Tr10, C3, I2, A3, R2
2. the student will throw
3. at a designated criterion level (state what it is).

Individualizing instruction requires considerable record keeping so that the teacher can remember the task conditions under which a student is most likely to succeed. This is often facilitated by creating a clipboard with printed sheets like that in Figure 11.2 for each student. The clipboard system permits an aide, peer tutor, or partner to understand and work toward a designated objective.

As you progress through this chapter, consider the task conditions that can be altered in teaching and/or testing each skill. In locomotor skills, for instance, the surface slope (even, uphill, downhill, variable), surface texture (floor, short grass, long grass, sand), and surface stability (rigid, yielding, variable) might be altered. Likewise, tasks might be executed under a blindfold or a rhythm condition. Try developing your own sheets to show your understanding of task analysis.

Biomechanical Analysis of a Movement Pattern

An ability to break skills into their respective phases or parts aids observation, identification, and description of problems. Terms used for phases of locomotor skills are *heel strike, foot plant, midstance, swing, recovery, pushoff, takeoff, flight* and *landing*. Terms used for most object control skills are *starting position* or *preparation, backswing, forward swing, release* or *contact,* and *follow-through.*

For each phase, the teacher must look carefully at the actions of individual body segments: head, trunk, arms/hands, legs/feet. In analysis of normal movement, criteria like those in Ulrich's (1985) Test of Gross Motor Development (TGMD) are used. When movement is abnormal or structural deviations are present, phases and segmental actions are analyzed in more detail.

Good teaching requires providing informational feedback. Since most students can attend only to one or two correctional cues at a time, prioritizing which body part should be worked on first is important. Often, head control is selected as the focus, and students are told to keep their eyes on a designated target. For informational feedback to be helpful, students must be taught a vocabulary of body parts and actions. Movement exploration helps them to match words with feedback from other sources (vestibular, kinesthetic, mirrors, sounds). Taps on shoes and noise-making equivalents in gloves are especially useful in reinforcing correct foot/ankle and hand/wrist positions. For example, children, especially those with mental retardation or learning disabilities, often do not know the meaning of such cues as "Land on the *balls* of your feet."

With average performers, detailed biomechanical analysis is not necessary. Adapted physical activity specialists, however, must become skilled observers to give useful feedback. Most important, they must know how much feedback to give, when, and how. Some students learn best by seeing wholes, others by seeing parts. Learning style determines the nature of both demonstration and verbal input.

Walking: The Foundation Skill

Walking is the first locomotor pattern to be performed in the upright position. In normal children, the onset of walking is between 9 and 18 months of age. In children with disabilities, this skill may be delayed for only a few months or up to 6 or 7 years. The average age of independent walking ranges from 20 to 36 months for children who are blind and from 12 to 65 months for youngsters with Down syndrome. Children with cerebral palsy on one side of the body (hemiplegia) usually walk before age 2, but those with all four limbs involved (quadriplegia) often do not walk until age 6 or 7. Many children with mental retardation have confounding neurological deficits that delay walking by several years.

Typically, children who are slow to walk are provided physical therapy until age 7 or 8. If functional locomotion is not achieved by this time, experts agree that mobility goals should switch to wheelchair ambulation. Bleck (1982) states: "Physical therapy to improve a child's walking once he or she has reached 7 or 8 years is unlikely to be worth the time and effort expended, and other areas of function (like play and sports) should take precedence" (p. 79).

Adapted physical education typically focuses on the walk as an activity for improving dynamic balance, enhancing physical attractiveness via good postures, and increasing fitness. Beam walking is an important skill in perceptual-motor training and gymnastics. Walking in time to a drumbeat or music is a way of learning rhythm and relaxation. Walking across the swimming pool provides confidence for trying to float. Many persons with health impairments (e.g., obesity, asthma, heart conditions) walk for exercise, at least in the beginning sessions of a fitness or rehabilitation program. Walking can also be a competitive sport; race walking is a popular event among able-bodied persons and is an official track event for Special Olympians.

FIGURE 11.4 Abnormal gaits associated with spasticity and ataxia.

Scissors gait. Associated with quadriplegic spastic cerebral palsy. The legs are flexed, inwardly rotated, and adducted at the hip joint, causing them to cross alternately in front of each other. There is excessive knee flexion. Toe walking causes a narrow base. Scissoring and toe walking may be caused also by the *positive supporting reflex*. The positive supporting reflex is an extension (plantar flexion) response of the feet to tactile stimuli.

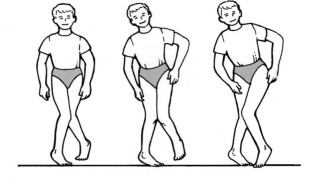

Hemiplegic gait. Associated with hemiplegic spastic cerebral palsy and stroke. Arm and leg on the same side are involved. Tends to occur with any disorder producing an immobile hip or knee. Individual leans to the affected side, and arm on that side is held in a rigid, semiflexed position.

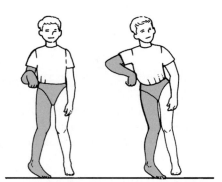

Ataxic or cerebellar gait. Associated with ataxic cerebral palsy, Friedreich's ataxia, and similar *les autres* conditions. Individual walks with a wide base, and there is irregularity of steps, unsteadiness, tendency to reel to one side. Individual seems to experience difficulty in judging how high to lift legs when climbing stairs. Problems are increased when the ground is uneven. Note the similarity between this and the immature walk of early childhood before the central nervous system has matured.

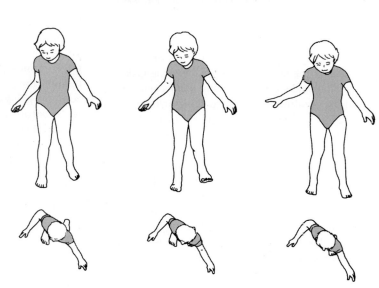

Among adults, walking is the most popular leisure-time physical activity. Walking or wheeling (the wheelchair equivalent) is something that everyone can do. Thus, physical educators strive to help persons of all ages to make their walking patterns efficient and fun.

Individual Differences in Gaits

One of the first assessment challenges in getting acquainted with a new student is determining whether the walk is normal or pathological and why. Physical educators should be able to recognize abnormal gaits and associate them with common conditions. Figures 11.4 to 11.6 present three groups of gaits categorized loosely by appearance. For each gait, there are many individual differences depending, in part, on whether the impairment is mild or severe. Persons with these gaits are often in mainstream physical education.

In studying these figures, remember that cerebral palsy, spina bifida, and muscular dystrophy are the three most common physical disabilities among school-age persons. These conditions are covered in Part 3 of this text, but the first knowledge acquired about each should be basic walking pattern.

Shuffling or slouch gait. Associated with central nervous system immaturity (probably retention of tonic labyrinthine reflex-prone and symmetrical tonic neck reflex). Inability of lower body to move independently of upper body. Seen in severe mental retardation. Excessive flexion at hip, knee, and ankle joints, and the trunk is usually inclined forward. Contact with floor is flatfooted. Usually, there is no opposition of arms and legs.

Propulsion or festination gait. Associated with Parkinson's disease, also called *paralysis agitans.* Individual walks with a forward leaning posture and short, shuffling steps that begin slowly and become progressively more rapid. This gait is seen also in very old persons with low fitness.

Steppage gait. Also called foot-drop gait and is associated with flopping of the foot on the floor. Knee action is higher than normal, but toes still tend to drag on floor. Caused by paralysis or weakness of the ankle dorsiflexors. Results in excessive hip and knee flexor work.

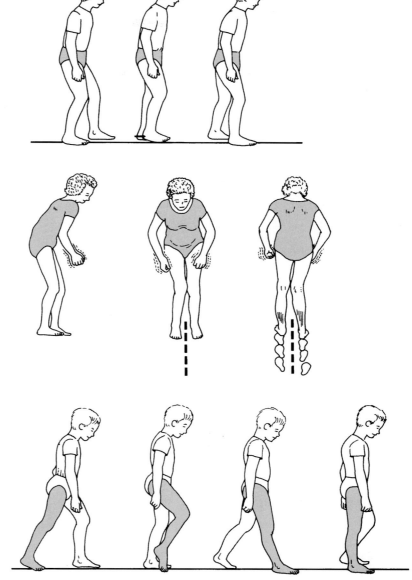

The shuffling gait is associated with developmental delays often seen in adapted physical education. Abnormal retention of several reflexes—tonic labyrinthine-prone, symmetrical tonic neck, positive support, and toe grasp—contributes to shuffling. With the tonic labyrinthine-prone reflex, flexor tone dominates, explaining why the person seems always to be looking at the feet. Flexion of the head is also nature's way of facilitating leg extension via the symmetrical tonic neck reflex. With the positive support and toe grasp reflexes, contact with the floor heightens extensor activity, making flexion to lift the leg difficult. Remediation of the shuffling gait should begin with activities in Chapter 10.

Also helpful are games that require reciprocal lifting of feet, as in stepping over bamboo poles, rungs of a ladder, tires, and other obstacles. Tap-dance games, in which the goal is to make noises with different parts of the foot (heel-toe, heel-toe, toe-toe-toe), also help. These can be done in a sitting position or while holding onto a bar for support. Hundreds of walking games, particularly when songs and creative dramatics are woven in, are helpful. Marching, for instance, is fun when children play that they are members of a band or participants in a parade. Walking, combined with carrying loads of different sizes and weights, generalizes to activities of daily living, such as carrying in the groceries and taking out the garbage.

FIGURE 11.6   Gaits characterized by waddling, lurching, or abnormal lateral movement.

Waddling gait. Main deviation from normal is rolling movement from side to side. This is usually caused by structural problems like bowlegs (genu varum), hip problems and dislocations (coxa vara), knock-knees, or one leg longer than the other.

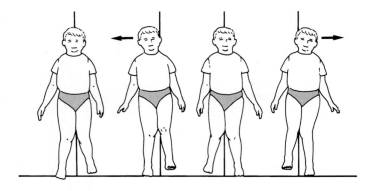

Muscular dystrophy gait. This is an awkward, side to side waddle, swayback (lordosis), arms held in backward position, and frequent falling. Shoulder girdle muscles are often badly atrophied. Calf muscles may be hypertrophied but weak because fat has replaced the muscle tissue.

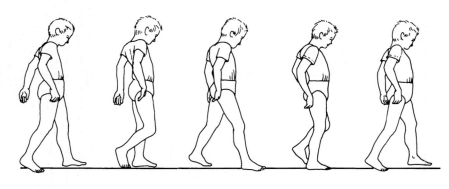

Gluteus maximus lurch. Associated with polio and other spinal paralysis conditions in which the paralyzed limb cannot shift the body weight forward onto the normal limb. To compensate, the trunk is thrust forward. The gait is thus associated with alternate sticking out of chest (salutation) and pulling back of shoulders.

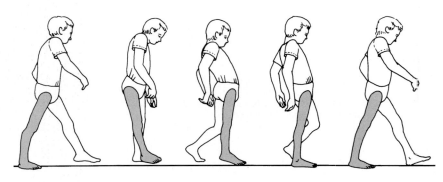

Trendelenburg gait. Limp caused by paralysis or weakness of gluteus medius. Pelvis is lower on nonaffected side. In walking, each time the weight is transferred, the body leans slightly in the direction of the weight transfer. Shifting the weight compensates for weak abductors.

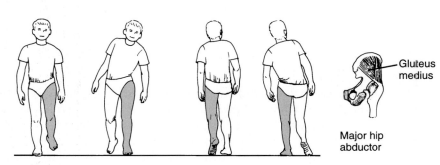

Developmental Levels in Walking

Normal walking gait varies with age. Walking matures as the central nervous system (CNS) develops and myelination is completed. If maturation is delayed or frozen or brain damage occurs, a person may exhibit a gait similar to the pattern of a young child. Figure 11.7 depicts normal gaits at different ages.

Major changes in the transition from immature to mature walking pertain to (a) carriage of arms, (b) trunk rotation, (c) opposition of limbs, (d) hip and knee action, and (e) type of foot plant and pushoff. Especially important in the mature walk is the heel-toe transfer of weight.

FIGURE 11.7 Normal gaits at different ages. Focus on the shaded leg.

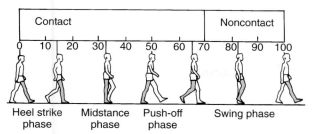

Heel strike phase · Midstance phase · Push-off phase · Swing phase

Normal, mature walking gait of children from ages 4 to 5 years and older. A gait cycle begins with the heel strike and ends when the heel of the same leg strikes again. Step and stride length relate to height.

Initial-Toddler

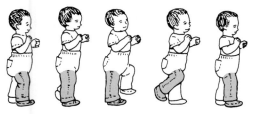

First walking pattern, showing **high guard position** of arms, rigid torso, excessive flexion of hip and knee joints, and flat-footed or toe-walking steps.

Early Childhood

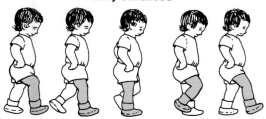

Walking pattern of children until age 4 or 5. There is still no trunk rotation and, hence, no opposition of arm and leg movements. Hip and knee action is still excessive, but heel-toe transfer of weight is beginning to appear.

Figure 11.8 shows illustrative children with walking problems and strategies that help. The girl with Down syndrome, who is still wobbly because of hypotonus, can push a cart filled with weights more easily than walking without something to hang onto. The use of creative dramatics helps to motivate time on task. For example, the teacher can make up a story about a little girl taking her doll for a walk and what she sees on the way. The boy with spina bifida needs lots of practice to gain arm and shoulder strength. Puppets are useful motivational devices in keeping a child moving back and forth across the room.

FIGURE 11.8 Illustrative walking activities and motivational devices.

Down syndrome with hypotonus

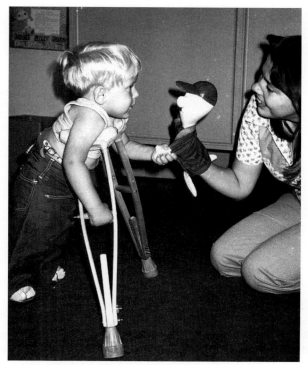

Spina bifida, necessitating swing-to gait

Three-point gait. In this gait, both crutches move forward in unison as in the step-to and swing-through gaits, but the feet move separately. Unlike most gaits, the involved, or weaker, leg takes the first step up to and even with the crutches, so it bears only partial body weight as the good leg then steps out in front of the crutches. The pattern is (1) advance both crutches, (2) advance weak leg, and (3) advance strong leg.

Two-point gait. This gait is most like normal walking and running. It is the fastest of the gaits but requires the most balance because there are only two points of contact with the ground at any time. Whenever a crutch moves, the opposite leg moves in unison. The pattern is (1) advance left crutch and right leg simultaneously and (2) advance right crutch and left leg simultaneously.

Hemiplegic gait. This gait is similar to the three-point except that one cane is used instead of two crutches. The cane moves first, then the weak leg opposite the cane, then the strong leg. The steps taken with each leg should be equal in length, with emphasis placed on establishing a rhythmic gait. Although used by persons of all ages, this gait is most common in older persons who have had strokes.

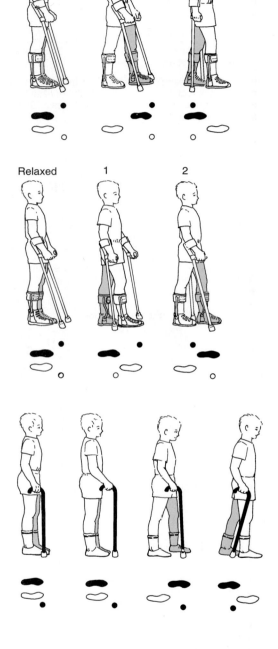

Many students ambulate with crutches or canes. To assess and describe present level of psychomotor performance, crutch gaits must be referred to by name (see Figures 11.9–11.11). Students who use crutches and canes can compete in track-and-field events like able-bodied peers. They are limited only by your ability to teach and coach.

Table 11.2 provides a checklist for evaluating immature and mature walking. The 11 criteria under the mature pattern can be used as objectives.

Table 11.3 shows a developmentally sequenced teaching/test progression (TTP) to show walking and running activities. These should be done on many surfaces, with different degrees of incline and stability, with and without blindfolds. How many ways can you vary each activity?

FIGURE 11.10 Crutch gaits used by persons with severe disabilities.

Step to, swing to, or drag to gait. This is used by persons with severe disability who have little or no control of legs. In public schools, the young child with spina bifida in long leg braces is the best example. In rehabilitation settings, this is the first gait taught to persons with lesions above T10. It is a staccato gait with no follow-through in front of the crutches. All the weight is taken by the arms, while the legs are lifted and swung or dragged forward. The pattern is lift and drop, lift and drop. The crutches shown are axillary crutches. Axillary refers to armpit area, and axillary crutches are those that fit under the arms. These should never be used for running because of possible damage to the brachial plexus (a network of nerves under the arm).

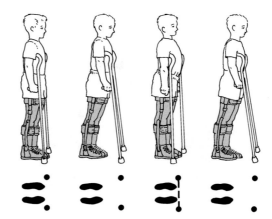

Four-point gait. This gait is used by persons with severe disability who can move each leg independently. The pattern is (1) advance left crutch, (2) advance right foot, (3) advance right crutch, and (4) advance left foot. The weaker leg is shaded. The crutches shown are Lofstrand (also called Canadian or forearm) crutches.

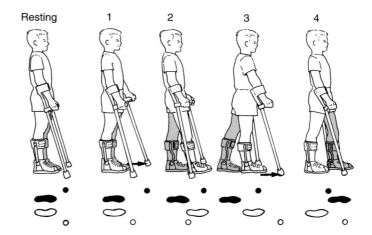

FIGURE 11.11 Crutch gait used with temporary disabilities or amputation.

Swing-through gait. The person leans into the crutches, lifting the body off the ground by extending the elbows. The body is swung through the crutches so that the good foot lands in *front* of the crutches. Then the crutches are brought forward, and the sequence is repeated.

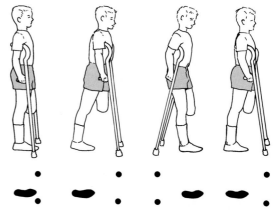

DO NOT CONFUSE SWING-THROUGH WITH SWING-TO.

Table 11.2   Checklist for the evaluation of walking in persons of different ages.

Directions: Observe the student walking on several different terrains or surfaces (even or uneven), uphill, downhill, and on a level surface. Consider the 11 sets of alternate descriptions and check the one of each set that represents the student's level of performance. Until the child is about age 4 years, most checks will be in the left-hand column. After age 4, the average child exhibits mature walking. Use findings to write specific behavioral objectives.

Check One	Developmental or Immature Walking	Check One	Mature Walking

	1. Forward lean
	   a. From ground
	   b. From waist and hips
			1. Good body alignment
			   a. Head up
			   b. Good extension of spine

	2. Wide base of support, with heels 5–8 inches from line of progression		2. Narrower base of support with heels 2–3 inches from line of progression
	3. Toes and knees pointed outward		3. Toes and knees pointed straight ahead
	4. Flat-footed gait		4. Heel-ball-toe transfer of weight
	5. Excessive flexion at knee and hip; no double knee lock		5. Strong pushoff from toes; double knee lock present
	6. Uneven, jerky steps[a]		6. Smooth and rhythmical shift of weight, with minimal up-and-down movement
	7. Little or no pelvic rotation until second or third year. Body sways from side to side.		7. Minimal rotatory action of pelvis (short persons will have more than tall ones)
	8. Rigidity of upper torso		8. Compensatory shoulder rotation inversely related to pelvic rotation
	9. Outstretched arms, also called high guard position		9. Arms swing freely and in opposition with legs
	10. Relatively short stride. In preschool children, the distance from heel to heel is 11–18 inches		10. Greater length of stride dependent upon length of leg
	11. Rate of walking stabilizes at about 170 steps per minute		11. Rate of walking decreases to about 115 to 145 steps per minute

[a]Jerkiness may be caused by a flat-footed or shuffle gait or by excessive stride length.

Teaching the Run

Ability to analyze a walk carries over into the teaching of other locomotor skills. Many of the items for evaluation of walking are applicable to running (see Figure 11.12). The run is a locomotor pattern comprised of four phases: foot plant, recovery, pushoff, and flight. Unlike the walk, the run has no period of double support. Children pass through three distinct developmental levels in running. Normal children demonstrate Levels 1, 2, and 3 at about ages 2, 3, and 5, respectively. All of the components of a mature run, however, are not typically present until age 7 or 8. In adapted physical activity, you will see many developmental delays. Let's consider what to emphasize in teaching the run.

Leg Action

Foot plant, similar to the heel strike in the walk, marks the end of the forward leg swing. The foot plant in the sprint is on the metatarsals; the teacher stresses "Run on the balls of your feet." In the mature run (Level 3), the support foot contacts the floor approximately under the body's center of gravity (CG). In immature runs, the support foot lands in front of the CG. The body lean (line between support foot and CG) in the mature run is at 1 o'clock, whereas it is too far forward or backward in the immature pattern.

    Recovery, similar to the midstance in the walk, is the best time to check the presence of a high heel kick. This mechanism readies the knee to spring forward with maximal propulsive thrust in the pushoff phase. In the immature run, the hip and knee may be outwardly rotated and cause a toe-out gait, but this problem ameliorates itself in normal development. Unless there are muscle imbalances, 6-year-olds can run straight, placing their feet on or near a designated line.

    Pushoff, the same term as in the walk, demands excellent bilateral coordination inasmuch as the support leg pushes backward and downward while the swing leg lifts forward and upward. Focal points to be checked are the amount of extension in the pushoff leg and the height of the knee lift of the swing leg. At the end of the knee lift, the thigh is more or less horizontal to the ground.

    Flight is the period of nonsupport, the time when both legs are in the air. As children mature, an increasing

Table 11.3   Walk and run skills listed from easy to hard: a developmentally sequenced teaching/testing progression.

Task	Criterion to Pass	Average Age (Months)
1. Walk, Level 1 pattern (see Figure 11.9)	4–5 steps	12–14
2. Walk, Level 2 pattern	10-ft distance	15–17
3. Walk backward	5 steps	15–17
4. Walk sideward	10-ft distance	15–17
5. Run, Level 1 pattern (see Figure 11.11)	10-ft distance	18–23
6. Walk on tiptoes	5 steps, hands on hips	24–29
7. Walk backward	10-ft distance	24–29
8. Walk 4-inch beam	3 steps forward	24–29
9. Walk 4-ft circular pattern	Fewer than 5 stepoffs	24–29
10. Walk line on tiptoes	8-ft distance	30–35
11. Walk backward, 4-ft circular pattern	Fewer than 2 stepoffs	42–47
12. Walk 4-inch beam	4 steps forward	48–53
13. Heel-toe walk backward, 4-inch beam	5 steps, toes touching heels	54–59
14. Walk 4-inch beam, hands on hips	8-ft distance	54–59
15. Walk on tiptoes, hands on hips	15-ft distance	60–71
16. Walk 4-inch beam, sideward	8-ft distance	60–71
17. Run/walk 1 mile as fast as possible	13 min for boys; 14 min for girls	60–71
18. Run/walk 1 mile as fast as possible	12 min for boys; 13 min for girls	72–83
19. Run 50 yd for speed	9.9 sec for boys; 10.2 for girls	72–83
20. Shuttle run for speed, 12 ft apart, 2 cans	Complete cycle of 2 cans in 12 sec	72–83

Note. Information for Items 1–16 and 20 was abstracted from the Peabody Developmental Motor Scales (Folio & Fewell, 1983). Items 17–19 come from AAHPERD (1988) and Hanson (1965).

proportion of time is spent in flight. In addition, the elevation of the flight decreases, an indication that force is being properly directed forward and not upward.

Arm Movements

The coordination of proper arm movements with the leg actions is the hardest part of the run and the last to appear. Level 3 of Figure 11.12 shows the opposition of limbs and the use of a pumping action of the arms to increase forward momentum. The elbows are kept bent at about 90°. The hand swings as high as the chin in the forward swing; the elbow reaches as high as the shoulder in the backswing. In the less mature runs, the arms' range of motion is very limited.

Assessment Ideas

Assessment of the run can be complex or simple, depending on the number of performance criteria. Ulrich (1985) in the Test of Gross Motor Development (TGMD) indicated that the four most important criteria are

1. Brief period where both feet are off the ground
2. Arms moving in opposition to legs, elbows bent
3. Foot placement near or on a line (not flat-footed)
4. Nonsupport leg bent approximately 90° (close to buttocks)

Runners should be observed at their fastest speed over a minimum distance of 50 ft in two or more trials. Devise game settings for examining the run. Challenges might be "How fast can you run around the baseball diamond?" "How fast can you run to a designated goal line?" Low organized games, in which students chase and tag one another or run from place to place on cue, also can be used for assessment purposes.

Use both process and product assessment. When measuring speed, plan adaptations for poor reaction time and the problem of slowing down before reaching the finish line. Typically, both problems are resolved by having the student run further than the timed distance (see Figure 11.13). Regardless of the activity, teach students not to slow down until after they have crossed the finish line.

Teach runners start signals ("On your mark, get set, go") that are the same as those used in track meets. Conduct assessment and practice in a class setting in such a way that skills learned can be generalized to Special Olympics or other competitive events. The running task, the finish line, and the concept of personal best should all be clearly understood.

Pedagogy

Children who lack the concept of running should be introduced to it by walks down hills steep enough to quicken the pace to a run. In early stages of learning, they may have a rope around the waist and be pulled into a running gait. Patient teaching is required also to convey the concepts of starting, stopping, and staying in a lane.

Less involved children need special instruction related to running on the balls of the feet, lifting the knees, and swinging the arms. To facilitate running on the balls of the feet, practice can be up steep hills or steps. Jumping and hopping activities also tend to emphasize staying on the balls of the feet. Possible solutions to inadequate knee lift include riding a bicycle, particularly uphill; running up steep hills or steps; and running in place with knee action exaggerated to

FIGURE 11.12   Pictorial checklist for assessing running.

Directions: Observe several 50-ft runs. Circle the level that best depicts the pattern you observe and underline the descriptors that can be used on the IEP to indicate present level of performance.

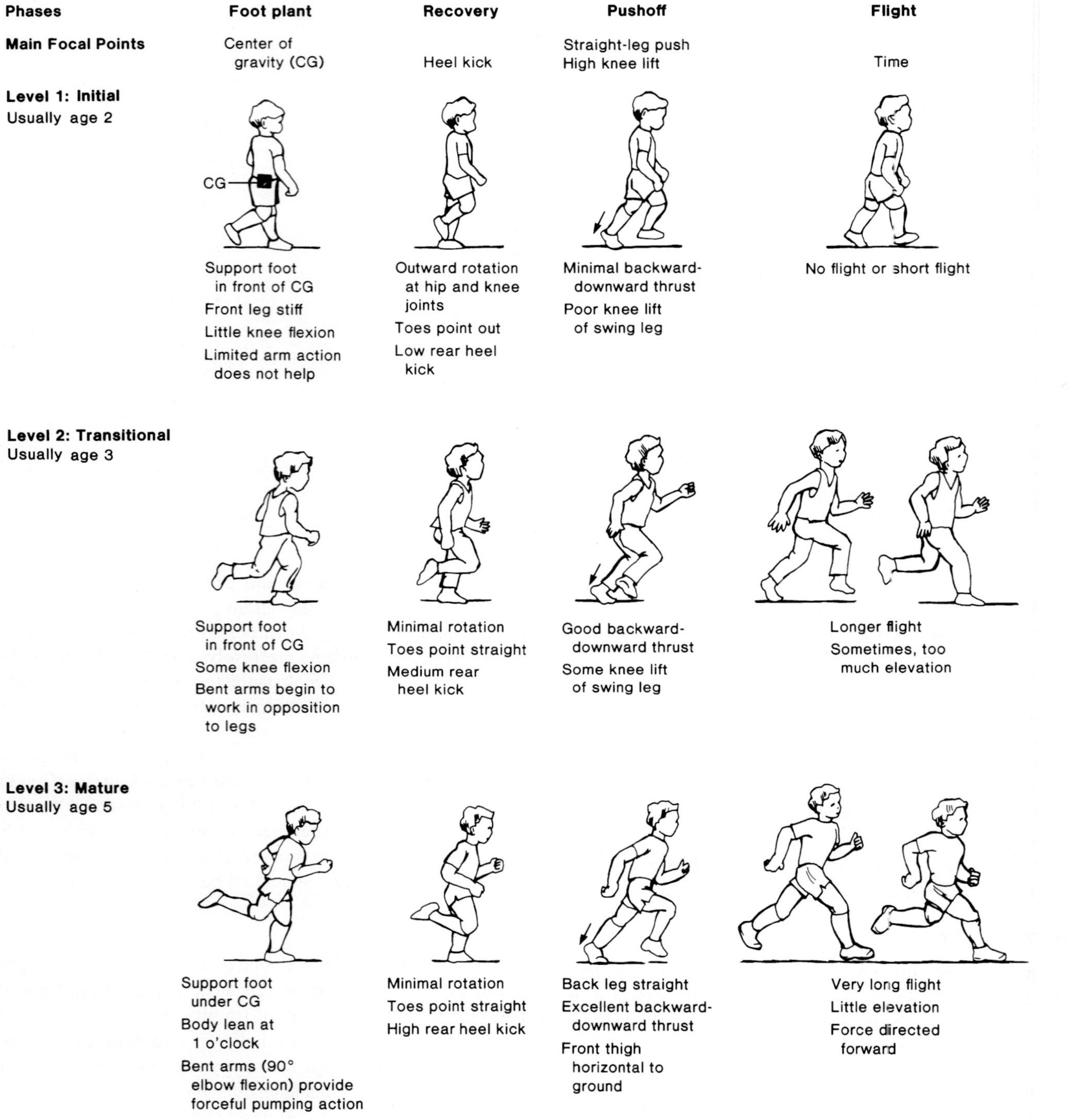

Phases	Foot plant	Recovery	Pushoff	Flight
Main Focal Points	Center of gravity (CG)	Heel kick	Straight-leg push High knee lift	Time

Level 1: Initial
Usually age 2

CG —

| Support foot in front of CG
Front leg stiff
Little knee flexion
Limited arm action does not help | Outward rotation at hip and knee joints
Toes point out
Low rear heel kick | Minimal backward-downward thrust
Poor knee lift of swing leg | No flight or short flight |

Level 2: Transitional
Usually age 3

| Support foot in front of CG
Some knee flexion
Bent arms begin to work in opposition to legs | Minimal rotation
Toes point straight
Medium rear heel kick | Good backward-downward thrust
Some knee lift of swing leg | Longer flight
Sometimes, too much elevation |

Level 3: Mature
Usually age 5

| Support foot under CG
Body lean at 1 o'clock
Bent arms (90° elbow flexion) provide forceful pumping action | Minimal rotation
Toes point straight
High rear heel kick | Back leg straight
Excellent backward-downward thrust
Front thigh horizontal to ground | Very long flight
Little elevation
Force directed forward |

touch the outstretched palms of hands. Corrections for swinging arms across the body or without vigor include practice in front of a mirror and running with a baton or small weight bar.

To understand the mechanics of running, children should be taught the meanings of such words as *forward lean, driving leg, recovery leg, center of gravity,* and *striding.* **Forward lean** is the line between foot contact and center of gravity. Forward lean is greatest early in the spring, when the runner is accelerating rapidly, and levels off after the point of maximum speed is reached. The **driving leg** is the one that extends and pushes against the ground. The **recovery leg** is the one in which the high knee lift is important. The **center of gravity** is the point in the pelvis below which the recovery foot should try to land.

The rate of striding depends upon four factors: (a) speed of extension of driving leg, (b) speed with which

FIGURE 11.13 Adaptation when timing a 50-yd-dash for persons with developmental delay.

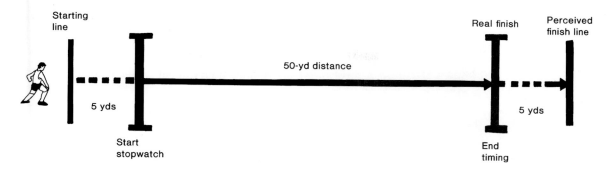

recovery leg is brought through, (c) length of time body is in air, and (d) landing position of the recovery foot in relation to the center of gravity. Speed, of course, is dependent on range of motion.

Children may need help to understand the concept of speed. Any child with number concepts up to 15 can understand running a 50-yd dash in 9 versus 13 sec. In track meets, emphasis can be placed on self-competition by pinning cards with the children's best times on their backs. As they finish a dash, they are told whether or not they beat their own time. Ribbons can be awarded to children who beat their own times rather than (or in addition to) children who beat others. An alternative technique is recording the child's expressed level of aspiration and making awards for meeting or surpassing this estimate.

Types of Runs

The physical educator should be able to evaluate different kinds of runs: (a) sprinting; (b) middle-distance runs—880 yd and up; and (c) long-distance runs—mile and over for children. The 440-yd dash can be classified as either a sprint or a middle-distance run, depending upon cardiorespiratory endurance. Jogging can be either a middle- or long-distance run. Table 11.4 shows that each type of run varies with respect to foot plant, knee action, forward body lean, and arm action.

These four components are generally the ones on which students need the most practice.

The **shuttle run** is traditionally used as a test of running speed and agility and should be practiced frequently. In this type of run, the goal is to shuttle back and forth between two end lines. On a signal, the student runs to a designated line and picks up an object (wooden block, eraser, sponge); then he or she returns to the starting line and deposits the object on the ground. The distance between lines and the number of objects vary. The American Alliance for Health, Physical Education, Recreation, and Dance (AAHPERD) uses a 30-ft distance and two blocks. The Bruininks-Oseretsky Test of Motor Proficiency (BOTMP) uses a 15-ft distance and one block.

Teaching Stair Skills

Functional locomotion in the community requires that children with developmental delays be given instruction and practice in the use of various kinds of stairsteps and ladders. Every school should have playground apparatus that motivates children to want to climb and affords opportunities for seeing the world at different heights (see Figure 11.14).

Ascending is much easier than descending and should be taught first. Slides are particularly good because they eliminate the problem of how to get the child down. Slides do not

T a b l e 1 1 . 4 **Comparison of three types of runs.**

Phases	Sprint	Middle-Distance Run	Long-Distance Run
Foot plant	Land high on ball of foot; heel does not touch	Land lower on ball of foot than in sprint; heel does not touch	Land low on ball of foot, drop to heel
Knee action	Less rear kick than in other kinds of runs	More rear kick than in sprint	More rear kick than other runs
	Lift knee high and straight forward	Lift knee less high than in sprint	Lift knee slightly as compared to other runs
	Thigh should be more or less horizontal to ground at end of knee lift	Thigh should be less horizontal, about 70° to 80° at end of knee lift	Thigh is less horizontal at end of knee lift than in other runs
Forward body lean	Lean between 25° and 30°— about 1 o'clock	Lean between 15° and 18°— about halfway between 12 and 1 o'clock	Lean about 10°—about one-third of way between 12 and 1 o'clock
Arm action	Pump arms vigorously, with hands reaching chin level or higher	Use slightly less vigorous arm action	Swing arms naturally at about shoulder level

FIGURE 11.14 Play apparatus should be designed so that children practice progressively more difficult kinds of climbing, balancing, and jumping.

Table 11.5   **Average ages (in months) for stair skills.**

Developmental Patterns	Ascending	Descending
1. Marking time using handrail	18–23 months	18–23 months
2. Marking time without support	24–29 months	24–34 months
3. Alternate feet using handrail	29–31 months	30–50 months
4. Alternate feet without support	31–41 months	49–55 months

Note. These patterns should be assessed on staircases of variable height (2, 4, 6, 8 inches) and width.

FIGURE 11.15   Thirteen-year-old child with Down syndrome descends stairs in immature fashion, leading with the same foot and marking time on each rung. This pattern is exhibited in the normal child at about 23 months of age.

have to be slick. They can also be carpeted and made with a gentle slope that can be scooted or rolled down. Some apparatus should have only two or three steps, while others should offer more challenge.

    Marking time and *alternate feet* are the terms used to assess developmental levels in ascending and descending. **Marking time** is a pattern in which the same foot always leads. The name is derived from the lead foot marking time while the other foot steps up to create a period of double support on the one step. **Alternate feet** (also called a foot-over-foot pattern) is the mature pattern, in which left and right feet take turns leading, and only one foot is on a step at a time.

    Table 11.5 shows four developmental levels of stair skills. Height and width of steps affect success, so assessment and goal setting should be specific to each piece of apparatus. Marking time skills occur at about the same age for ascending and descending, but the balance demands of the alternate feet pattern make descending more difficult. Typically, children cannot use the mature pattern in descending until about 15 months after it has been mastered in ascending. Thus, most children do not exhibit alternate-step ascending and descending until age 4. Persons with disabilities show considerable

delay (see Figure 11.15) and thus are often denied the opportunities for motor and social development afforded by playground apparatus.

    The mature pattern of stair climbing is an excellent cardiovascular fitness activity. The task can be made more demanding by adding weights (e.g., backpacks, books, stuffed animals).

Jump, Hop, Leap

Teachers must use the terms *jump, hop,* and *leap* correctly to communicate movement challenges to students. Table 11.6 clarifies the meaning of these words. These patterns are similar in that they have three phases: a takeoff, flight, and landing.

The jump for distance or height has an additional phase (the preliminary crouch) at the beginning of the sequence.

Average children learn to jump at about the same time they master the marking-time/ascending-stairs skills. Once a position of height has been attained, it makes sense to want to jump down. The earliest jumps, therefore, are usually step-downs in which one foot leads.

The ages at which children master jump, hop, and leap skills are of interest in planning assessment and designing instruction. Table 11.7 presents information about the jump and the hop, and also a teaching progression, with tasks listed from easiest to hardest. In general, children begin to learn jumping skills at about 18 months, hopping at about 30 months, and leaping after they are in kindergarten or first grade.

In the jump, hop, and leap, students must know kinesthetically what the flight phase feels like. Figure 11.16 presents one approach to facilitating a kinesthetic awareness of up and down. The trampoline is another way. Manually lifting the student into the air while saying *"up"* may be necessary. Think of how many ways this can be done, alone and with a partner.

Teaching the Jump

Jumping is an extremely difficult skill for persons with neurological deficits because of its demand for good balance and bilateral integration. Many persons with severe mental retardation (MR) never learn to jump. Persons with mild MR conditions usually learn to jump, but their movement patterns may be immature compared to those of peers (DiRocco, Clark, & Phillips, 1987; Ersing, Loovis, & Ryan, 1982; Hemmert, 1978). Likewise, distance jumped lags 2 to 3 years behind nondisabled peers.

Jumping is a popular field event, however, in meets for athletes with disabilities. Attending these meets enables prospective teachers to see persons with amputations, blindness, cerebral palsy, and other conditions excelling in jump events. There is widespread agreement that persons can learn to jump if physical educators make this a major goal.

Table 11.6   **Comparison of jump, hop, and leap.**

	Jump	Hop	Leap
Takeoff	May be either two-foot or one-foot takeoff	Always a one-foot takeoff	Always a one-foot takeoff
Flight	Weight always transferred to two feet	Weight never transferred	Weight always transferred from one foot to the other
Landing	Always a two-foot landing	Always a one-foot landing on same foot	Always a one-foot landing

Table 11.7   **Jumping and hopping tasks listed from easy to hard: A developmentally sequenced teaching/testing progression.**

Task	Criterion to Pass	Average Age (Months)
1. Step down from 8- to 10-inch height	One foot leads	18–23
2. Jump forward, two-foot takeoff	4 inches without falling	18–23
3. Jump up, two-foot takeoff	2 inches, both feet together	18–23
4. Jump down from 16- to 20-inch height	One foot leads	24–29
5. Jump over 2-inch high rope	Two-foot takeoff	30–35
6. Jump down from 18- to 24-inch height	Two-foot takeoff, land	30–35
7. Jump forward, two-foot takeoff	24 inches	30–35
8. Hop in place on one foot	3 times	30–35
9. Jump down from 24- to 30-inch height	Two-foot takeoff, land	36–41
10. Hop forward, one foot	5 times on one foot, then 3 times on other	36–41
11. Jump forward, two-foot takeoff	26 to 30 inches	36–41
12. Hop for distance	6 inches	42–47
13. Hop forward, one foot	8 times on one foot, then 8 times on other	42–47
14. Vertical jump for height	3 inches beyond normal reach	48–53
15. Jump down from 32-inch height	One foot leads	48–53
16. Hop for distance, preferred foot	16 inches	48–53
17. Hop for distance, nonpreferred foot	16 inches	48–53
18. Jump and turn 180°	Feet together, hands on hips	54–59
19. Jump sideways back and forth across line	3 times without stopping	54–59
20. Jump forward, two-foot takeoff	36 inches	54–59
21. Jump over 10-inch-high rope	Two-foot takeoff, land	60–71
22. Hop for speed, 20-ft distance	6 sec	60–71
23. Vertical jump for height	8 inches beyond normal reach	72–83

Note. The information in this table has been abstracted from the Peabody Developmental Motor Scales (Folio & Fewell, 1983).

Once you have ascertained the task or step that should be the focus, the next protocol is assessment to determine how to improve the quality of the jump. For the long jump, Ulrich (1985) suggested the following performance criteria:

1. Preparatory movement, including flexion of both knees with arms extended behind the body

2. Arms extended forcefully forward and upward, reaching full extension above head

3. Takeoff and landing on both feet simultaneously

4. Arms brought downward during landing

Of these criteria, the arm movements are the most difficult to master. Ulrich (1985) reported that 60% of nondisabled children do not master Criterion 2 until age 9. DiRocco et al. (1987) reported that arm actions were more of a problem than leg actions in children with mild MR.

Because many children with disabilities exhibit delays in jumping, different developmental levels must be recognized (see Figure 11.17). Persons exhibiting a Level 1 pattern probably have not yet sufficiently integrated the symmetrical tonic neck reflex; they obviously have deficits in bilateral coordination (see Chapter 10). Table 11.8 provides a checklist for evaluation.

Developmental Sport Training

A developmental gymnastics or track-and-field program is recommended to provide practice in jumping. This approach supports the normalization principle and gives older students who still need work on basic skills the self-esteem of having a sport and of training to be an athlete. By using terms like *dismount, vault,* and *mount,* you can lend dignity to basic skill practice.

Jump Used as a Dismount

The gymnastics term **dismount** is a jump from a piece of apparatus down to the floor. Dismounts are used to end routines on the balance beam, the even parallel bars, the uneven parallel bars, the horse, and the buck. Judged for their aesthetic appearance and mechanical efficiency, dismounts may involve difficult movements, such as handsprings and cartwheels, or simple jumps downward using a two-foot takeoff and land.

Children need to know how to get off a piece of gymnastic apparatus or play equipment safely. The first skill that should be taught on a balance beam is the **jump-off dismount.** Children who feel secure about their jumping ability will no longer fear falling. Only then should locomotor movements (walks, runs, skips) on the balance beam be introduced.

Vault

Jumping becomes a sport skill when it is used in gymnastics as a means of getting over a piece of apparatus. Students can *vault* over many different kinds of apparatus: (a) a low beam about thigh or hip height, (b) a tumbling bench, (c) a vaulting box, (d) a horse, or (e) a buck.

Instead of demonstrating standard vaults and expecting the student to imitate, observe the different movement approaches explored by the student in attempts to get over the apparatus. Which of the following movement patterns offer the student the most success?

1. **Squat vault.** Weight taken equally on both arms, knees are pulled upward, tucked to chest, and then continue forward. Body passes over box in a squat position.

2. **Straddle vault.** Weight taken equally on both arms, and legs are abducted in wide-stride semi-sitting position. Hands are on inside and legs on the outside. Body passes over box in this straddle position.

3. **Flank vault.** Initially done with both arms on the box. Standard flank vault is performed with one arm. While arms support weight of body, both legs are lifted simultaneously over the box. The side of the body passes over the box. Sometimes called a side vault.

4. **Front vault.** Same as flank vault except that the front of the body passes over the box.

The beginning vault is often a combined side-front vault with both hands on the box and the knees bent as the legs pass over. Most elementary school textbooks recommend that the squat vault be taught first. The law of individual differences rules that children should not all be introduced to the same progression of vaults nor tested on a single movement pattern selected by the teacher. When allowed to discover their own ways of getting over, first-grade children can succeed at vaulting. A beatboard or springboard is necessary to attain the height necessary for propulsion of the body over the box.

FIGURE 11.17 Pictorial checklist for assessing standing long jump.

Directions. Circle the level that best depicts the pattern you observe and underline the descriptors that can be used on the IEP to indicate present level of performance.

Level 1: Initial

Incomplete crouch

Difficulty in using both feet and arms simultaneously

Arms used for balance during flight but not contributing to forward momentum

Feet leading in flight and landing phases rather than arms

Level 2: Transitional

Forward body lean

Arms initiating takeoff

Body not fully straightening out during flight

Insufficient trunk flexion during flight downward

Unsteady landing

Level 3: Mature

Trunk parallel to ground in preliminary crouch

Angle of takeoff about 45°

Body fully extended during upward flight with arms stretched upward

Full trunk flexion during flight downward

Steady landing with arms forward

Movement Patterns for Jumping on a Springboard or Beatboard

The movement patterns used on the springboard, beatboard, minitramp, and diving board are similar. For better transfer of learning, the child should have experience on all four pieces of apparatus. If the budget allows the purchase of only one, the beatboard is recommended.

The following questions serve as guides for observation and evaluation of the child's natural movement pattern when challenged to run up the board, jump once on the end of the board, and then land on the mat:

1. Does the child run slowly, with hesitancy, or at an appropriate speed?

2. How long is the child's approach—that is, how many steps does he or she take prior to reaching the beatboard?

3. Does the child run flat-footed or on the balls of the feet?

4. Does the child slow down or stop before executing the jump on the end of the board?

5. Does the child use a two-foot takeoff from the board?

6. Which foot is the last to push off before the two-foot takeoff is initiated?

7. Does the child gain maximum height in his or her jump?

8. Is the amount of forward lean mechanically efficient so that the child falls neither forward nor backward?

9. Does the child bend at hip, knee, and ankle joints upon landing in order to absorb the shock?

10. Does the child have trouble maintaining balance upon landing?

Directions: Observe the student performing several jumps. Consider the 18 sets of alternate descriptions and check the one of each set that represents the student's present level of performance. Average children exhibit mature jumps by ages 7 or 8 years. Use findings to write specific behavioral objectives.

	Check One	Developmental or Immature	Check One	Mature
Preliminary Crouch		1. Little or no crouch		1. Assume preparatory crouch with hips, knees, and ankles in deep flexion.
		2. Trunk not parallel to ground		2. Trunk is almost parallel to ground.
		3. No backward-upward swing of arms		3. Weight moves forward as arms swing backward-upward.
		4. No return movement of arms; no weight shift forward		4. Weight continues to move forward as arms swing forward-downward.
		5. Insufficient shoulder joint flexion—arms not lifted high enough		5. Crouch phase ends when arms are in line with trunk.
Takeoff		6. Takeoff begins with *simultaneous* extension at hip, knee, and ankle joints.		6. Takeoff begins with *successive* initiation of extension at hip, knee, and ankle joints.
		7. Takeoff angle is more than 45°.		7. Takeoff is approximately 45°.
		8. Arm swing not coordinated with leg movements		8. Arms swing forward-upward as heels are lifted.
Flight Upward		9. Incomplete body extension at takeoff		9. Body is in full extension at beginning of flight.
		10. Arms never fully flexed overhead to form single, long lever with trunk		10. Arms are flexed at shoulder joint and elbows extended. Arms are in line with trunk to form single, long lever.
		11. Knee and hip flexion occur simultaneously.		11. Lower legs flex first during flight.
Flight Downward		12. Incomplete hip flexion during flight		12. Hip joint flexion begins when knee flexion reaches 90°.
		13. Forward arm action not coordinated well with knee and hip extension		13. As knees come forward and knee joint extends, arms and trunk reach forward.
		14. Incomplete knee extension at end of flight		14. Knees are fully extended at end of flight.
Landing		15. Toes contact ground first.		15. Heels touch ground before toes.
		16. Incomplete spinal and hip flexion at moment of contact		16. Trunk and thighs are almost touching at moment of contact.
		17. Center of gravity too far backward at moment of contact, resulting in unsteady landing		17. Instantaneous flexion of knees when heels contact ground
		18. Hands touch the floor.		18. Arms reach forward-upward to help maintain balance.

Specific tasks that the child can be asked to perform while jumping are these:

1. Clap hands overhead, behind back, in front of body.
2. Land beyond a certain line or marker on the mat.
3. Assume a tuck position in the air.
4. Assume a pike position in the air.
5. Assume a straddle position in the air.
6. Assume a hurdle position in the air.
7. Assume a laterally flexed position in the air.
8. Make a turn in the air.
9. Land with feet together, feet apart, one foot in front of the other.
10. Land with arms in various positions.
11. Land and immediately perform a forward roll.

Jump Used as a Mount

In gymnastics, a **mount** is a jump from a beatboard, springboard, or minitramp onto a piece of apparatus. Mounts are used to begin routines on the balance beam, the even parallel bars, the uneven parallel bars, the horse, and the buck.

Children need practice jumping up onto things as well as jumping down. If no apparatus can be improvised, they may jump (two-foot takeoff) *up* the stairs, *up* on automobile tires, *up* on street curbs, *up* on rocks, and so on.

Jumping on a Trampoline

The trampoline is an excellent vehicle for improving balance. This objective is best achieved if the student is afforded many opportunities for movement exploration.

Emphasis should not be on the learning of such traditional skills as the seat drop during early lessons, but rather upon motor fluency and originality. The child may attempt rolls, animal walks, rope jumping, turns in the air, and other stunts. The teacher who is capable of maintaining silence, accepting a child as he or she is, and observing closely will find the trampoline an extremely valuable diagnostic aid. The problems that a child exhibits on the trampoline are the same as those the child has overcome and/or learned to compensate for when on the ground.

Teaching the Hop

Taking off and landing on the same foot requires both static and dynamic balance. To determine whether children are ready for hopping instruction, ask them to imitate you in a single-foot standing balance, free leg bent backward, and hands at hips. Given two trials, most normal children can hold this stance for 3 sec by age 30 to 35 months. Shortly thereafter, they can hop in place on one foot three times without losing balance (Folio & Fewell, 1983). Approximately 6 months later, they can hop forward on the preferred foot five times and the nonpreferred foot three times.

Some insist that hopping forward is an easier developmental progression than hopping in place, but no research seems to have addressed this. Individual differences in balance, strength, body weight, and limb positioning may explain why some children find it easier to hop moving forward. Hopscotch and other games using floor patterns require forward locomotion, so this skill may be practiced more.

Little research has been conducted on hopping and disability. Cratty (1967) reported that children with mild MR seem to improve significantly in their ability to balance between the ages of 8 and 14 years. Using a test that required hopping in circular and square patterns, Cratty reported that few children with Down syndrome (25%) and moderate MR (5%) were successful. The performance of children with mild MR approached that of normal peers, although games like hopscotch were decidedly difficult for about half of them. Hemmert (1978) reported that students with moderate MR did not exhibit mature hopping patterns until a mean age of 15 years.

Process evaluation of hopping can be guided by the four criteria that follow (Ulrich, 1985). The student should be asked to hop three times on the preferred and then on the nonpreferred foot.

1. Foot of nonsupport leg bent and carried in back of the body
2. Nonsupport leg swinging in pendular fashion to produce force
3. Arms bent at elbows and swinging forward on takeoff
4. Able to hop on the right and left foot.

Testing and games of hopping can also involve speed, distance, floor patterns, and rhythmic sequences. Cratty (1986) reported that most 5-year-olds can hop 50 ft in about 10 sec. The Purdue Perceptual Motor Survey (Roach & Kephart, 1966) emphasized the following bilateral coordinations:

Hop 1/1. The person is asked to stand with feet together, then to hop on the right foot, lifting the left, and next to alternate, hopping first on the right and then on the left.

Hop 2/2. This task is the same as the foregoing except that the person hops twice on the right foot, twice on the left, and so on.

Hop 2/1. The person is asked to hop twice on the right foot, once on the left, twice on the right, and so on.

Hop 1/2. The person is asked to hop once on the right foot, twice on the left, and so on.

Performance on these tasks is evaluated in accordance with the following 4-point scale:

4—Performs all tasks easily

3—Can alter sides symmetrically

2—Can hop on either foot at will; can alternate, but cannot maintain a rhythm

1—Can perform only symmetrically

Teaching the Leap

A **leap** is a special kind of run in which the upward and forward direction of the flight is increased as much as possible. Consequently, the period of nonsupport is greater than the run. Children usually describe the leap as "going way up in the air, stretching out from one leg to the other—like going over a big puddle." The leap is used mostly in crossing-the-brook type games (leap over an obstacle), gymnastics (stride leap on floor and beam), and creative dance.

The leap is not included in most tests of motor development; thus, little information is available on its emergence. When shown a leap across a pretend brook (narrow sheet of paper or cloth), many children as young as 3 years old can follow the leader. However, the leap is usually considered an elementary school skill.

For several leaps in succession, Ulrich (1985) recommended the following evaluation criteria:

1. Takeoff on one foot and landing on the opposite foot
2. A period when both feet are off the ground (longer than running)
3. Forward reach with arm opposite the lead foot

These criteria are similar to those used for the run. The main difference is the long flight period. Other criteria, usually emphasized with older children, are full extension of the back leg and pointed toes. The front leg may be fully extended during the entire leap, or bent and held high (deer leap) during the flight and then quickly extended for the landing. In general, the leap in the air is similar to splits on the ground by cheerleaders. Practicing the splits seems to have carryover value in improving leaps.

Teaching Rhythmic, Two-Part Motion

The gallop, skip, and slide are rhythmic two-part patterns derived from combinations of the walk, hop, and leap. They are called rhythmic patterns because the major challenge is to capture the long-short rhythm of each two-part combination. Each pattern has a short period when both feet are off the floor, so considerable balance is required for execution.

The order in which these patterns are learned is the gallop, skip, and slide (Clark & Whitall, 1989; Murray, 1963). This order is based on the criterion of consistency over several trials in performing 8 to 10 steps with the correct rhythmic pattern. Ordering of these rhythmic patterns according to time of first occurrence is difficult because of different criteria used.

Gallop

The **gallop** is a walk-and-leap pattern, with the same foot always leading, done in a forward or backward direction in a long-short rhythm. This is the first asymmetrical gait learned by the young child (Clark & Whithall, 1989). The front foot takes a step (walk), which is long in duration, while the back foot tries to catch up with a leap that is short in duration.

Performance criteria for judging the gallop (Ulrich, 1985) are as follows:

1. A step forward with the lead foot followed by a step with the trailing foot to a position adjacent to or behind the lead foot
2. Brief period when both feet are off the ground
3. Arms bent and lifted to waist level
4. Able to lead with the right and left foot

A fifth criterion might be consistency of the long-short rhythm. Children may demonstrate a primitive form of the gallop as early as age 3, but the correct rhythmic leg action does not generally appear until about age 5. Between 60 and 71 months, most children can gallop 8 to 10 steps with the same foot leading (Folio & Fewell, 1983).

Rhythmic accompaniment (voice, hand clapping, drum, music) helps in learning to gallop. The idea of moving like a horse or playing cowboys and Indians, together with a demonstration, elicits a gallop. You can then cue children to gallop higher and higher and to push with the arms to achieve height.

Skip

The **skip** is a walk and a hop, with alternate feet leading, in a long-short rhythm. The pattern is smooth and symmetrical, with each foot taking a long-in-duration walk step followed by a short-in-duration hop.

The following are performance criteria for judging the skip (Ulrich, 1985):

1. A rhythmical repetition of the step-hop on alternate feet
2. Foot of nonsupport leg carried near surface during hop phase
3. Arms alternately moving in opposition to legs at about waist level

Criterion 1 might be clearer if "rhythmical repetition" was changed to "a long-short rhythm" because approximately twice as much time must be spent on the step as on the hop.

The skip is difficult for many children. To assist with assessment, three levels can be identified:

Level 1—Shuffling or one-foot skipping
Level 2—Jerky and/or inconsistent skipping
Level 3—Mature, smooth, symmetrical, long-short foot action

At Level 1, children alternate a step-hop with a walk; usually, the preferred foot does the step-hop. These children simply lack the bilateral coordination to enable both sides of the body to perform the same way. At Level 2, children can do alternate step-hops, but they are not yet consistent in the long-short rhythm. Level 1 and 2 skipping characterizes most 3- and 4-year-olds. Level 3 emerges at about age 5.

Between 60 and 71 months, most children can skip 8 to 10 steps with mature foot action (Folio & Fewell, 1983). Coordination of the arms to move in opposition to the legs often does not appear until ages 8 or 9. Instruction in skipping, like galloping, is facilitated by rhythmic accompaniment. When students seem frozen at the one-footed skip level, skip with them in partner position, holding hands on the problem side.

Slide

The **slide** (a walk and a leap) is identical to the gallop except that it is performed sideward rather than forward and, hence, requires better balance. The importance of moving sideward as a means of improving laterality was emphasized by Kephart (1971), who noted that this is one of the few skills that teach lateral body control.

The following are performance criteria for judging the slide (Ulrich, 1985):

1. Body turned sideways to desired direction of travel
2. A step sideways, followed by a slide of the trailing foot to a point next to the lead foot
3. A short period where both feet are off the floor
4. Able to slide to the right and to the left side

In Criterion 2, the foot action must reflect a long-short rhythm. Ability to slide equally well on both sides is seldom seen, and most children perform a mature pattern to their preferred side before their nonpreferred side.

The slide is used in gymnastics (floor exercise and balance beam) and in all forms of dance. Often, the arms are extended sideward at shoulder height, and children should practice with different arm positions. In dances that use a single circle formation, the slide is one of the easiest and most popular steps. The pattern traditionally used is seven slides to the right with a transfer of weight to the opposite foot on the eighth count, followed by seven slides to the left and a transfer of weight. This sequence should be practiced early.

Teaching Object Control Skills

Object control skills may be gross or fine motor. **Gross motor** refers to use of large muscles (i.e., moving the hands, feet, or larger body parts), as in ball handling. **Fine motor** refers to use of small muscles (i.e., fingers) as in paper-pencil-scissors-blocks-shoelace activities. This chapter is delimited to gross motor object control.

Mastery of object control skills is dependent upon development of normal muscle tone, integration of primitive reflexes, maturation of perceptual-motor abilities, and CNS organizational and sequencing abilities. Research shows that perception and action are coordinated from birth (Bard, Fleury, & Hay, 1990); one does not precede the other, as some early theorists posited. Effective interaction with the environment, however, is not possible until voluntary grasping and holding behaviors appear at about 4 to 5 months of age.

Normal infants thus begin exhibiting pounding, shaking, striking, pushing, and pulling play behaviors during their first year. Many children with disabilities, however, need help in learning these initial object control skills. The ability to grasp is often absent or weak in persons with cerebral palsy, muscular dystrophy, and conditions that cause hypotonus, paresis, or paralysis.

Adaptations When Grasp Is Absent or Weak

When grasp is impaired, object control focuses on pushing or striking a light object with the hand or a head pointer. Games like wheelchair boccia, bowling, and shuffleboard typically permit use of ramps so that gravity can assist in moving the object (Jones, 1988). The games can be played on the floor or adapted to a tabletop with sideboards. Balloon tetherball is another game option (see Figure 11.18).

Two-handled paddles and other implements that can be held with two hands offer another alternative. These work well in balloon tetherball and tabletop games like shuffleboard and table tennis. If grasp is too weak, one or both hands can be strapped to the implement or special gloves worn with a Velcro surface that sticks to Velcro strips on the handles.

Use of Velcro or other kinds of straps to attach a paddle, racquet, mallet, or stick to one hand opens opportunities for many types of games for practicing striking skills. Creating oilcloth or plastic tablecloth shuffleboard or target patterns that can be moved easily from floor to tabletop increases game options.

Adaptations When Release Is Difficult

The ability to throw is dependent upon the emergence of voluntary release abilities at about 10 to 11 months. Although the hand grasp reflex is integrated at 3.5 to 4 months, the CNS does not permit voluntary object release until much later. In persons with brain injury that causes hypertonus (namely, cerebral palsy), voluntary grasp and release are impaired throughout the lifespan.

In such cases, the normal teaching progression must be altered and emphasis placed on striking activities rather than those requiring a release. Striking can be directed at objects in the air, on a table with sideboards, or on a ramp. Either the hand or an implement can be used. When success in striking games is achieved, instruction can begin to alternate between striking and throwing. A major adaptation for persons with grasp and release problems is use of yarn, sponge, or Nerf balls, a soft discus, or beanbags ("soft puts") when throwing. Floor targets are typically used. Experiment with wheelchair placement in relation to the target or partner. Determine which position is best for each student and record this information on the IEP.

Adaptations for Slow Learners

Most children in adapted physical education are simply delayed in the emergence of grasp and release abilities and follow the developmental sequence of normal children, with skills mastered 1 to 3 years later than normal peers. Table 11.9 presents the order in which object control skills are learned by most students.

Adaptations for Throws While Seated

Many conditions prevent persons from throwing in a standing position. Roper (1988) is an excellent source for teaching the throw from a wheelchair. Particularly recommended is extensive practice in trunk rotation, with the ball held in a position just behind the head. The chair should be placed at an oblique angle to the direction of intended throw. The sides and back of the chair should be as low as possible.

Teaching Rolling or Bowling

The first ball-handling activity is usually rolling an 8- to 10-inch playground ball while sitting widestride on the floor. For children whose orthopedic impairment prohibits floor sitting, a long table can be used, with partners sitting in chairs at either end. This adaptation allows a pushing rather than rolling pattern.

From rolling in the sitting position, children progress to rolling in the standing position. They also begin rolling balls toward wall targets, bowling pins, and similar targets. For persons with severe disability, a long cord on the ball facilitates recovery. Through rolling, children have their first visual tracking activities. Stress to the children that they should *watch the ball move*.

Teaching Throwing

Throws should be practiced with objects of many sizes, shapes, textures, and colors. Each lesson should involve hundreds of practice trials, with variety provided at different stations. Use lots of different objects and interesting targets set at varied heights (see Figure 11.19).

In teaching throwing, the first objective is an efficient throwing pattern. The cue used to obtain a good pattern is "Throw hard." The pedagogy is demonstration of the overarm throw. No verbal corrective feedback is given, other than "Nice try. Let's do it again. Throw hard." Table 11.9 shows

FIGURE 11.18   Object control activities when grasp is weak.

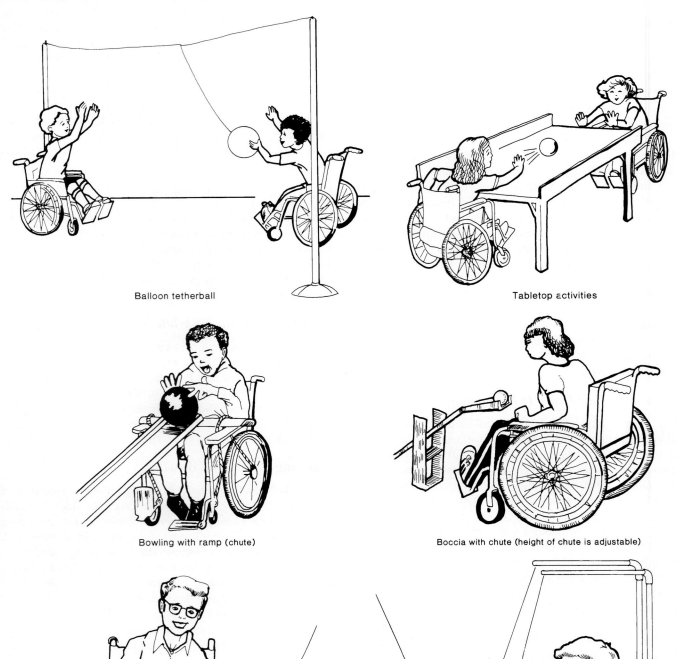

Balloon tetherball

Tabletop activities

Bowling with ramp (chute)

Boccia with chute (height of chute is adjustable)

Two-handed racket for tetherball

Table tennis with double-handle paddle suspended from frame

Task	Criterion to Pass	Average Age (Months)
1. First voluntary grasp	Grasps rattle	4–5
2. First voluntary release	Releases cube on command	10–11
3. Roll ball from sitting position	Moves ball 3 ft	12–14
4. Throw (cast) tennis ball	Level 1 pattern (see Figure 11.20)	12–14
5. Kick ball	Steps on or kicks into ball	15–17
6. Throw (hurl) tennis ball	Level 2 pattern (see Figure 11.20)	15–17
7. Throw (hurl) tennis ball	Travels 3 ft forward	18–23
8. Kick ball	Travels 3 ft forward	18–23
9. Throw (hurl) playground ball	Travels 5 ft forward	24–29
10. Throw (hurl) tennis ball	Travels 7 ft forward	24–29
11. Kick ball	Travels 6 ft forward	30–35
12. Catch large ball from 5-ft distance	2 of 3 trials; Level 1 (see Figure 11.21)	30–35
13. Bounce-throw tennis ball against wall 5 ft away	Ball hits floor once before wall contact	36–41
14. Catch large ball from 5-ft distance	1 of 2 trials; Level 2	36–41
15. Throw tennis ball	10 ft with trunk rotation and follow-through	42–47
16. Use underarm toss to hit wall target from 5 ft	Hits target 2 of 3 trials with tennis ball	42–47
17. Catch tennis ball from 5-ft distance	2 of 3 trials; Level 2	42–47
18. Use overarm throw to hit wall target from 5 ft	Hits target 2 of 3 trials with large ball	42–47
19. Throw playground ball	10 ft, 1 of 2 trials	48–53
20. Use overarm throw to hit wall target from 12 ft	Hits target 2 of 3 trials with tennis ball	54–59
21. Bounce and catch tennis ball two times	Two hands, successful 2 of 3 trials	60–71
22. Kick stationary ball into air	Travels 12 ft in air	60–71
23. Run and kick moving ball	Travels 8 ft	72–83
24. Drop-kick ball	Travels 5 ft, 2 of 3 trials	72–83
25. Wall pass and catch at 5-ft distance	Catches large ball on rebound after first bounce	72–83

Note. Large ball is 8 to 10 inches. Wall target is 2-ft-square and 2 ft above floor. A wall pass is like a basketball pass except that you throw at a wall and catch the rebound. The information in this table was abstracted from the Peabody Developmental Motor Scales (Folio & Fewell, 1983).

that early throws are assessed in terms of distance achieved and developmental level.

Throwing is comprised of several phases: (a) starting position, (b) preparatory or backward swing, (c) forward swing, (d) release, and (e) follow-through. In relation to each of these, specific body parts should be observed: (a) feet, (b) trunk, and (c) arm (shoulder, elbow, wrist, fingers).

Figure 11.20 presents the four developmental levels through which average children, ages 1 to 7, progress. Use of names for each level (casting, hurling, homolateral, crosslateral) saves time when describing performance on the IEP. Many adults with severe/profound mental retardation use the casting pattern. Hurling and the homolateral patterns typically characterize clumsy persons of all ages.

Some persons, however, demonstrate components characteristic of more than one level. The performance descriptors in Figure 11.20 permit the teacher to check the movement components that best describe present performance level. Then, specific components that need work are listed when writing instructional objectives (e.g., Demonstrate Components 3, 4, and 6 of crosslateral pattern).

This assessment process can be simplified by using four performance criteria (Ulrich, 1985):

1. A downward arc of the throwing arm initiating the windup

2. Rotation of hip and shoulder to a point where the nondominant side faces an imaginary target

3. Weight transfer by stepping with the foot opposite the throwing hand

4. Follow-through beyond ball release diagonally across body toward side opposite throwing arm

In addition to task analysis and process assessment, the throw should be examined in terms of product. The usual measures are distance and accuracy. Throws from base to base on a softball diamond permit good assessment of distance and accuracy.

Teaching Catching

Catching entails a *reach, bend, pull* movement pattern. It also presupposes integrity of the visual tracking system. It is a more difficult task to master than throwing, and early learning of throwing and catching should probably occur separately at different stations.

The principle of specificity should guide the teaching of catching in that large balls demand movement patterns different from small balls. Catching lessons should involve practice with all sizes of balls coming in different flight patterns

FIGURE 11.19 Targets recommended for accuracy throwing and kicking.

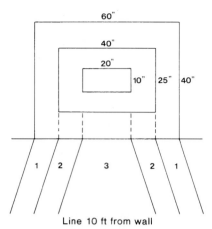

Project ACTIVE target for throwing and kicking assessment.

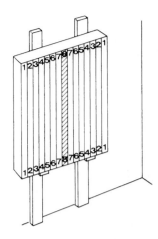

Rarick tennis ball toss target. May be used vertically or horizontally. Parallel divisions are 4.8 inches each.

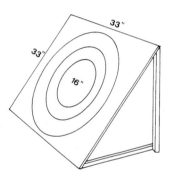

Rarick soccer ball accuracy toss from distances of 9, 12, 15, and 18 ft.

High-toss target for overarm throw.

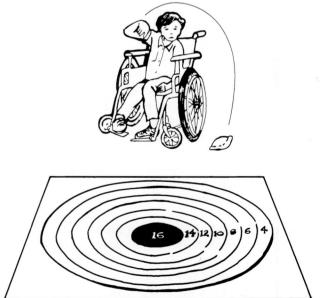

Precision throw with seven scoring areas.

FIGURE 11.20   Pictorial checklist for assessing overarm throw.

Level 1: Casting

| Feet stationary; no weight shift | No trunk rotation | Elbow extension supplies force | No follow thru; no involvement of nondominant side |

Level 2: Hurling

| Feet stationary; no weight shift | Slight trunk rotation on backswing | Shoulder supplies force | Slight forward rotation; angle of release 80–100° | No follow thru; no involvement of nondominant side |

Level 3: Homolateral Throwing

| Dominant foot steps forward; slight weight shift | Slight trunk rotation on backswing | Dominant side supplies force; angle of release 80–50° | Some follow thru; no involvement of nondominant side |

Level 4: Crosslateral Throwing

| Feet move in opposition to arms; good weight transfer | Full backswing trunk rotation | Total body supplies force; good coordination | Angle of release 45° | Good follow thru; coordinated involvement of nondominant arm |

(horizontal vs. vertical) at different speeds. Little transfer of learning from one kind of catch to another occurs.

Visual acuity, which is poor in infants and improves up to age 8 or 9 years, affects catching. Many children with Down syndrome, for instance, are nearsighted (myopic). **Astigmatism** causes blurring of the ball. Poor binocular fusion **(integration)** is manifested in double vision **(diplopia)** and functional blindness in one eye **(amblyopia).** Many persons with cerebral palsy and mental retardation have **strabismus** (cross-eyes), which also affects visual acuity and tracking.

Practice in visual tracking of a suspended ball is a good lead-up activity for catching as well as for striking and kicking skills. A tetherball apparatus or a homemade system of balls of different sizes, shapes, and colors suspended at different heights works well. Simply tracking a moving object is boring, so the activity should entail touching, striking, kicking, or catching the object being tracked. Developmentally, **horizontal tracking** occurs before vertical tracking, and near-to-far tracking is successful before far-to-near.

Visual tracking should be practiced with (a) *ground balls;* (b) *straight trajectory balls* coming to knee, waist, shoulder, and head; and (c) *fly balls* with curved trajectories. Research shows that, in far-to-near tracking for catching, young children attend to the thrower rather than to the flight of the ball. Developmentally, children next are able to attend both to the source of the flight and to their own motor response. Only with much practice do children achieve the ability to visually monitor the entire flight and make discriminatory judgments with respect to velocity.

Figure 11.21 presents levels in catching that can be used in describing present level of performance and writing objectives for the IEP. Remember that catching problems are *visuomotor,* and work with other team members in the development of comprehensive visual programs.

Performance criteria for evaluating a catch follow (Ulrich, 1985):

1. Preparation phase where elbows are flexed and hands are in front of body
2. Arms extended in preparation for ball contact
3. Ball caught and controlled by hands only
4. Elbows bent to absorb force

These criteria are for a 6- to 8-inch sponge ball tossed underhand with a slight arc from a 15-ft distance. The ball should arrive at a point between shoulders and waist, the easiest zone for catching.

Teaching Stationary Bounce/Dribble

Ability to dribble is an important factor in basketball success. Beginners can be assessed on this skill by the following performance criteria (Ulrich, 1985):

1. Ball contacted with one hand at about hip height
2. Ball pushed with fingers (not a slap)
3. Ball contacting floor in front of (or to the outside of) foot on the side of the hand being used

Once children can dribble the ball in place, they add a walk or run. This should be practiced in all directions.

Other bouncing/dribbling skills to be learned are (a) two-hand bounce and catch to self, (b) one-hand bounce and catch to self, and (c) propelling ball by means of a bounce throw or pass. This last activity is typically practiced against a wall and concurrently provides experience with rebounds. When this is the case, the task is called a **wall pass.** It can also be practiced with floor patterns and/or a partner.

Teaching Striking

Striking is any arm and hand movement pattern (sidearm, overarm, underarm) used to hit an object. Examples are skills used in tetherball, volleyball, handball, hockey, golf, shuffleboard, croquet, paddle and racquet sports, and activities involving batting (teeball, softball, cricket). In general, these movement patterns are analyzed like the throw. The phases are (a) starting position, (b) preparatory or backward swing, (c) forward swing, (d) contact, and (e) follow-through. In each, judgments are made about action of the (a) feet, (b) trunk, and (c) arm (shoulder, elbow, wrist, and fingers).

Provide opportunities for striking objects of different sizes, weights, and colors with all kinds of implements. Lighting conditions should be optimal, with the student never facing the sun. Carefully regulate the degree of difficulty, keeping in mind the variables in Figure 11.22.

Batting is probably the striking activity most popular in our culture, with children exhibiting skill directly proportional to their parents' interest and willingness to toss them balls. Often, 3-year-olds use implements with large heads (racquets, paddles, special bats) quite successfully. Almost universally, the first striking pattern is a downward, chopping action. As bilateral coordination and strength increase, the swing becomes increasingly horizontal. The following are performance criteria for evaluating batting (Ulrich, 1985):

1. Dominant hand gripping bat above nondominant hand
2. Nondominant side of body facing the tosser (feet parallel)
3. Hip and spine rotation
4. Weight transfer by stepping with front foot

A ball-tossing apparatus that can be regulated for speed is probably more important in adapted physical activity than for the tennis or softball team. If a sharing arrangement cannot be worked out, purchase is of high priority. Homemade systems of pulleys with suspended balls moving horizontally or vertically at different speeds also can be created. Learning to control the direction balls are sent is important. See Chapter 12 for ideas regarding timing and body positioning in relation to the arriving ball.

The principle of leverage *(the shorter the lever, the easier it is to achieve accuracy and control)* should be applied in selecting bats, rackets, and other striking implements. Hitting a balloon or yarn ball with the hand creates a shorter lever for beginners than use of an implement. Thus, balloon volleyball and movement exploration activities comprise an excellent first teaching progression.

Adapted games using field or ice hockey, croquet, and golf concepts, in which a ball or puck on the floor is given impetus, are sometimes easier for clumsy persons to master

FIGURE 11.21 Pictorial checklist for assessing catching skills.

Directions. Circle the level that best depicts the pattern you observe and underline the descriptors that can be used on the IEP to indicate present level of performance.

Level 1: Passive Arm Cradle

Level 2: Stiff-Arm Clapping

Descriptors: (1) making arm cradle, often with adult help, before ball is tossed; (2) rigid stationary position of feet and body; (3) no response until after ball has landed in cradle; (4) pulling toward chest.

Descriptors: (1) extending arms and spreading fingers, (2) rigid stationary position of feet and body, (3) clapping response when ball touches either hand, (4) gaining control by forearm pull toward chest.

Level 3: Initial Eye-Hand Control

Descriptors: (1) eyes tracking ball from far to near, with most attention given to the source of flight and own motor responses; (2) body moving to position self in line with trajectory of ball; (3) arms outstretched while running to meet the ball; (4) hands only contacting the ball; (5) ball pulled toward chest.

Level 4: Mature Basketball Catch

Descriptors: (1) eyes tracking ball continuously through entire flight; (2) body moving to position self in line with trajectory of ball; (3) arms, hands, and fingers relaxed until time to catch ball; (4) catch accomplished by simultaneously stepping toward ball, partially extending arms, and spreading fingers; (5) following through by a slight flexion at shoulder and elbow joints.

FIGURE 11.22   Variables to be altered in teaching striking skills.

Striking Implement	Trajectory of Object Being Struck	Size of Object Being Struck	Object Direction in Flight	Weight of Object Being Struck	Color of Object Being Struck	Anticipation Location	Speed Object Is Traveling
Hand ↓	Horizontal ↓	Large ↓	Right ↓	Light ↓	Blue ↓	How far must the performer move before striking the object	Slow ↓
Paddle ↓	Vertical ↓	Small	Left ↓	Heavy	Yellow ↓		Fast
Bat	High arc		Center		White		

Hand   Paddle

Bat

than throwing, catching, and striking games. This is particularly true of persons with grasp and release problems.

Teaching Kicking

Kicking is a striking activity using the feet and legs. The popularity of soccer and football give this skill prime importance. Kicking is analyzed in the same way as striking, using the same phases and body parts to guide observation. Likewise,

the variables to be considered in planning teaching progressions are similar.

Table 11.9 indicates that children begin kicking balls between the ages of 15 and 17 months, shortly after they achieve stability in walking. Developmentally, they first kick a stationary ball forward along the ground and later propel it 12 ft in the air (see Figure 11.23). Next, they learn to judge direction and speed and become successful at running and kicking a moving ball.

FIGURE 11.23 Dr. Dale Ulrich of Indiana University administers his Test of Gross Motor Development (TGMD) to a student.

The following are performance criteria for kicking an 8- to 10-inch stationary playground ball (Ulrich, 1985):

1. Rapid, continuous approach to the ball
2. The trunk inclined backward during ball contact
3. Forward swing of the arm opposite kicking leg
4. Follow-through by hopping on nonkicking foot

Verbal instructions are "Kick the ball *hard* toward the wall." Many persons who are clumsy in hand-eye coordination activities seem to do well in kicking games. Try experimenting with kicking at various targets. Children also profit from kicking rocks, cans, and other objects as they walk or run. Soccer is the preferred sport in many private schools for students with learning disabilities.

References

American Alliance for Health, Physical Education, Recreation, and Dance (1988). *Physical best: A physical fitness education and assessment program.* Reston, VA: Author.

Bard, C., Fleury, M., & Hay, L. (1990). *Eye-hand coordination across the life span.* Columbia: University of South Carolina Press.

Burton, A. W. (1997). *Movement skill assessment.* Champaign, IL: Human Kinetics.

Clark, J. E., & Whithall, J. (1989). Changing patterns of locomotion: From walking to skipping. In M. H. Woollacott & A. Shumway-Cook (Eds.). *Development of posture and gait across the lifespan.* Columbia: University of South Carolina Press.

Cratty, B. J. (1967). *Developmental sequences of perceptual motor tasks.* Long Island, NY: Educational Activities.

Cratty, B. J. (1986). *Perceptual and motor development in infants and children* (3rd ed.). Englewood Cliffs, NJ: Prentice Hall.

DiRocco, P., Clark, J., & Phillips, S. (1987). Jumping coordination patterns of mentally retarded children. *Adapted Physical Activity Quarterly, 4*(3), 178–191.

Ersing, W., Loovis, E. M., & Ryan, T. (1982). On the nature of motor development in special populations. *Exceptional Education Quarterly, 3*(1), 64–72.

Folio, M. R., & Fewell, R. (1983). *Peabody developmental motor scales.* Allen, TX: DLM Teaching Resources.

Hanson, M. (1965). *Motor performance testing of elementary schoolchildren.* Unpublished doctoral dissertation, University of Washington, Pullman.

Hemmert, T. J. (1978). *An investigation of basic gross motor skill development of moderately retarded children and youth.* Unpublished doctoral dissertation, Ohio State University.

Jones, J. A. (Ed.). (1988). *Training guide to cerebral palsy sports* (3rd ed.). Champaign, IL: Human Kinetics.

Kelly, L., Reuschlein, P., & Haubenstricker, J. (1989). Qualitative analysis of overhand throwing and catching skills: Implications for assessing and teaching. *Journal of the International Council for Health, Physical Education, and Recreation, 25,* 14–17.

Kephart, N. (1971). *Slow learner in the classroom* (2nd ed.). Columbus, OH: Charles E. Merrill.

McClenaghan, B., & Gallahue, D. (1978). *Fundamental movement patterns: A developmental and remedial approach.* Philadelphia: Saunders.

Murray, R. L. (1963). *Dance in elementary education* (2nd ed.). New York: Harper & Row.

Roach, E., & Kephart, N. (1966). *The Purdue perceptual-motor survey.* Columbus, OH: Charles E. Merrill.

Roper, P. (1988). Throwing patterns of individuals with cerebral palsy. *Palaestra, 4*(4), 9–11, 51.

Ulrich, D. A. (1985). *The test of gross motor development.* Austin, TX: Pro•Ed.

Ulrich, D. A. (1988). Children with special needs—Assessing the quality of movement competence. *Journal of Physical Education, Recreation and Dance, 59*(91), 43–47.

Wickstrom, R. (1983). *Fundamental motor patterns* (3rd ed.). Philadelphia: Lea & Febiger.

CHAPTER

12

Perceptual-Motor Learning:
An Ecological Approach

FIGURE 12.1   Movement exploration uses kinesthetic, vestibular, and visual sensory input to increase body awareness.

After you have studied this chapter, you should be able to do the following:

1. Discuss perceptual-motor learning and explain the ecological theory and model that guide learning.

2. Explain the perceptual-motor models in this chapter and/or create your own. Include all of the basic abilities requisite to learning and refining motor skills and patterns.

3. Discuss common breakdowns under (a) sensorimotor integration disorders, (b) perceptual disorders, and (c) perceptual-motor disorders. Recommend activities for remediation of each.

4. Explain ataxia, apraxia, and aphasia.

5. Discuss the evolution of perceptual-motor theory and implications for practice. Contrast the approaches of special educators and physical educators.

6. Identify and discuss perceptual-motor tests that can be used for comprehensive testing.

7. Use concepts in Table 12.5 to plan task cards and lessons. Apply ecological task analysis to expand learning opportunities.

8. Explain how practice in basic game and dance formations contributes to perceptual-motor abilities.

9. Describe how perceptual-motor learning occurs in sports and everyday game and play activities.

Perceptual-motor learning is acquiring knowledge about the self and the environment through the integrated processes of sensation, perception, and action that occur during spontaneous or teacher-guided movement exploration (see Figure 12.1). Knowledge, according to Wall (1990), may be declarative (factual), procedural (skill execution, body action), affective (feelings and emotions), or metacognitive (understanding of and executive control of one's personal learning). **Sensation** is input to the brain from sensory receptors in all parts of the body. **Perception** is central or cortical processing of sensory input that results in awareness or consciousness of self and environment. Perception is also defined as **decoding,** or giving meaning to, sensory input. **Action** is output that begins as executive planning and organization inside the brain and ends as observable cognition, language, memory, attention, and movement.

Perceptual-motor learning is an appropriate physical education goal for children 2 to 7 years old without disabilities and for individuals capable of cognition at the 2-year-old level or higher who cannot perform culturally normative motor activities with acceptable proficiency. Individuals who meet this latter criterion are often diagnosed as having *clumsy child syndrome, developmental dyspraxia,* or **developmental coordination disorder.** Developmental coordination disorder (DCD) is a relatively new diagnostic category. It was first described in the 1987 edition of the *Diagnostic and Statistical Manual of the American Psychiatric Association* and subsequently was the theme of the April 1994 issue of the *Adapted Physical Activity Quarterly.* DCD is a complex condition, with two subtypes already described (coordination and praxic) and many other subtypes proposed (Henderson, 1994; Hoare, 1994).

In the perceptual-motor approach, we try to identify the underlying abilities that are acting as constraints to movement success. Concurrently, we analyze the environment to determine variables that affect these abilities. Perceptual-motor learning is similar to *motor fitness* in that both are concerned with balance, coordination, and basic abilities. Health-related fitness also relies on a similar underlying abilities approach.

Perceptual-motor training in physical education refers to the systematic use of person-environment relationships in *large muscle activities* to improve knowledge and un-

derlying movement abilities such as balance, coordination, motor planning/sequencing, imitation, following directions, and metacognition. The pedagogy that guides perceptual-motor training is largely ecological task analysis (see Chapter 7). Remember that **ecological task analysis** is systematic altering of task and environmental variables so that large muscle activities are practiced in many different ways, each of which requires a different kind of problem solving.

The theories underlying perceptual-motor learning and training in contemporary adapted physical activity are different from those used by special educators in the 1960s and 1970s. Today's practices are heavily influenced by Jean Piaget (1952), Harriet Williams (1983), and proponents of ecological theory and ecological task analysis (Burton, 1990; Davis, 1983; Davis & Burton, 1991).

Perceptual-Motor Learning in Early Childhood

Perceptual-motor learning is the primary means of acquiring knowledge from ages 2 to 7 years, according to Piaget (1952), who designated this time period as the stage of *preoperational mental functions.* From age 2 onward, children are increasingly able to use language and movement in exploring the environment and acquiring knowledge. This stage is called *preoperational* because mental functions are governed by perception rather than problem solving or reasoning, the operations associated with cognition from about age 7 on.

Perception, the process of decoding or obtaining meaning from sensory input, is a lead-up activity to problem solving. Consider, for instance, what children learn from such games as *I see something you don't see* or *I hear something you don't hear.* The environment is a room or outside area rich with either visual or auditory stimuli. The leader picks out some object or sound (the degree of obviousness dependent upon players' abilities) and tells players whether they are hot (close) or cold (distant) as they guess the right answer. This game can also be played with a picture that has lots of hidden or embedded objects or a piece of music like "Peter and the Wolf," in which the challenge is to identify different sounds or instruments. Hide-and-seek games and scavenger hunts also call on perceptual abilities; they can involve objects, people, or sounds. Seeking usually involves moving around a large area so that big muscle exercise is assured as well as practice in perception. How many games like this do you remember? What did you learn by playing them?

Games like *I See* and *I Hear* provide clues about visual and hearing impairments and whether or not persons are decoding and learning to name things at age-appropriate developmental levels. One measure of perception is the amount of time needed to process a sensation and derive meaning. Another is the amount of sensory information that can be simultaneously converted into meaning. To study problems of duration and capacity, teachers break perception into several subprocesses: (a) awareness, (b) discrimination, and (c) organization.

Awareness, typically the first level of perception assessed, is consciousness at the *there* or *not there* levels. There is light or no light, sound or no sound, smell or no smell, touch sensation or no feeling. Awareness is closely associated with **localization,** knowing where something is. Lack of awareness can be caused by a breakdown at the sensory receptor area (e.g., injury to the eye), during the information transmission process (nerve fibers), at the sensory integration level (noncortical area of brain), or at the perceptual level (cortical areas). Obviously, determining the site of breakdown is important for planning remediation.

Discrimination is multilevel, higher order awareness or the ability to differentiate between many levels of some variable (e.g., colors, sizes, shapes, identities, similarities, movements, weights, speeds). For example, children first learn to distinguish between colors (red, blue, green) and then hues or shades of the same color. They first learn to imitate up-and-down movements, as in bye-bye and pounding and shaking tasks, and then learn to discriminate between qualities and can be taught to vary up-and-down movements by making them big and little, fast and slow, straight and curved. Discrimination is dependent on **acuity** (good vision, hearing, or kinesthesis), and sometimes *discrimination* and *acuity* are used as synonyms. Discrimination obviously follows a developmental sequence, with ability to discriminate between two things coming before three things and so on. Discrimination is typically measured by matching, classification, and imitation games and tasks (e.g., *Can you do what I do?* and *Follow-the-leader*).

Organization is the ability to synthesize stimuli into meaningful, conceptual wholes (e.g., trees into a forest or body parts into a person) and to disassemble the parts of a whole (e.g., the separate trees that make up the forest). Organization, for assessment and remediation purposes, is broken down into such subabilities as these:

1. **Whole/part/whole relationships.** "Can you identify this figure even though some parts are missing?" "Can you assemble parts of a puzzle to make a whole?"
2. **Figure/background relationships.** "Can you find hidden or embedded figures?"
3. **Object constancy.** "Can you find all of the balls and bats in this room regardless of color, size, background, and tilt?"
4. **Object position.** "Can you identify which object is rotated or reversed, near or far?"
5. **Sequences.** "Can you put several things in correct sequence or recognize when sequences are faulty?"

Attention, or cue selection, was once considered a subcomponent of perception. Today, attention is acknowledged as a separate entity that influences all aspects of information processing, not just perception.

Functional Interrelationships With Cognition

The higher levels of perception, discrimination, and organization are often considered aspects of cognition. After age 7, in normally developing children, perception and cognition are functionally inseparable. Memory and attention limit perception, cognition, and all aspects of perceptual-motor learning. These, in turn, are dependent on language and movement for expression. Theories that guide contemporary perceptual-motor practices tend therefore to be broad and to emphasize the interrelatedness of sensation, perception, attention, memory, language, cognition, and perceptual-motor abilities. For simplicity, this chapter blends cognition and language together. Each of the other components of learning is addressed.

Ecological Perceptual-Motor Theory

Perceptual-motor training is guided by ecological theory (see Figure 12.2). Both assessment and remediation begin with consideration of environmental conditions. Theorists divide these into **affordances** (opportunities) and **constraints** (limitations). During assessment, the environment is changed in various ways to determine which set of conditions affords the most success. When the student is consistently successful across several trials, the environmental conditions that contributed to success are noted and considered the baseline condition. From this point, training consists of manipulating one or two variables at a time, so practice is in many environments.

The arrows circling around the model in Figure 12.2 emphasize that the networking between sensation, perception, and action is multilevel and multidirectional, rather than linear. Each process affects every other process, and all systems are activated. Brief definitions of terms follow.

Intersensory Integration and Perceptual-Motor Learning

Intersensory integration, the ability to synthesize and use multiple sources of sensory information, is an important factor in perceptual-motor learning. Consider, for instance, the last time that you tried to learn a new motor skill or game strategy. You probably received visual input from a demonstration, auditory input from verbal instructions, and combined tactile, kinesthetic, and vestibular (TKV) input from different parts of your body.

Did you use these multiple sources of information equally, or were some sensory inputs more valuable than others? Did you consciously block out some information in order to concentrate on other input? Did extraneous visual, auditory, or other sensory inputs (e.g., temperature, wind, the constraints of clothing) annoy or distract you? The answers to these questions lend insight into your cognitive or perceptual-motor style. Whereas most adults are mixed-modality learners, you might be a visual preference learner, an auditory preference learner, or a TKV preference learner.

FIGURE 12.2 A model of ecological perceptual-motor theory.

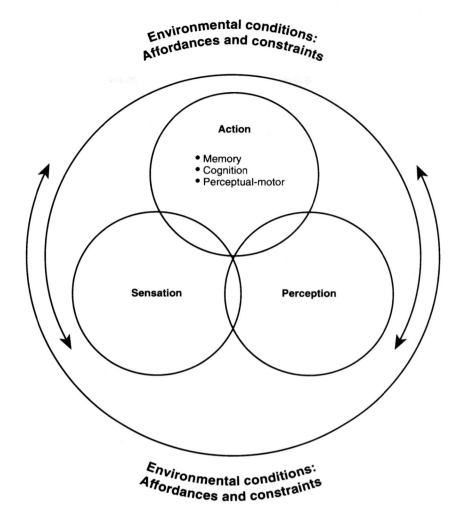

Environmental conditions:
Affordances and constraints

Action
- Memory
- Cognition
- Perceptual-motor

Sensation

Perception

Environmental conditions:
Affordances and constraints

Personal understanding of one's cognitive or perceptual-motor learning styles is called **metacognition.** Learning styles often vary with the nature of the motor or cognitive task and environmental variables. Effective integration of multiple sources of sensory information and/or structuring the environment to provide the kinds of sensory input that are most useful are skills that distinguish adults with good motor coordination from those with coordination disorders. One purpose of perceptual-motor learning is to improve metacognition so that individuals can purposively adapt environments and sensory inputs to meet their personal learning needs.

Intersensory integration is age-related (Williams, 1983) and affected by the richness or poverty of the environment. In most children, visual-TKV integration abilities are relatively mature by age 5, although some aspects continue to improve until ages 11 or 12. Poorly developed auditory integration abilities explain why most children are not good listeners in early childhood physical education and prefer to find their own best ways of moving through trial and error or imitation rather than follow verbal instructions.

Auditory-visual and auditory-visual-TKV integration abilities are mature enough in most children by age 7 for them to benefit from the predominantly verbal instruction used by many teachers. Auditory-visual integration continues to im-

prove substantially until age 11 or 12 and then plateaus. The slow maturation of auditory-visual integration explains why teachers should carefully plan the number and length of verbal instructions used to introduce physical activities.

In conclusion, most individuals are visual-TKV learners until about age 7, at which time they become mixed-modality learners. Some individuals (about 20% of students with learning disabilities), however, remain predominantly visual learners. Others (about 10% of students with learning disabilities) become predominantly auditory learners. Individuals with visual or auditory learning preferences tend to experience learning difficulties more than mixed-modality peers do. Difficulties typically relate to attention and memory aspects of learning, and often are manifested by behavior problems.

Illustrative Perceptual-Motor Learning Goals and Objectives

Impairments in perceptual-motor learning are difficult to identify and treat because of the interrelatedness of the many underlying abilities that enable movement. Assessment should result in prioritization of specific abilities and tasks. These should be **ecologically valid,** meaning that they relate to fitness, sport, dance, and aquatic activities that the student wants to master.

Goals can be written broadly, like the following: *to demonstrate functional competence in static and dynamic balances related to basketball skills; to demonstrate functional competence in motor planning and sequencing related to decision-making in age-related games; to correctly follow sets of auditory instructions related to class activities.*

Broad goals, in turn, must be broken down into specific objectives that clearly describe required behaviors and indicate evaluation protocol. Illustrative objectives are the following:

1. To maintain various static and dynamic balances [list them] for a set number of seconds
2. To demonstrate hand-eye, foot-eye, and total body coordinations by performing correctly (pass or fail) selected stunts, tasks, or movement routines [list these]
3. To correctly imitate total body movements or specific body part movements [list these] demonstrated by a model after a 15-, 30-, or 60-sec delay [specify]
4. To perform sequences of seven body positions or locomotor tasks after hearing this sequence one time, given a 60-sec delay between hearing the sequence and the start signal, and given two trials to achieve success
5. To demonstrate efficient motor planning in fielding balls rolled at random to the right, center, and left (12 balls, must touch or stop 9)
6. To respond correctly, within 10 sec, to each of 10 verbal one-word instructions for getting into various game formations [list these]
7. To demonstrate space perception by staying in the correct lane for 10 min of a soccer game
8. To demonstrate dynamic visual perception by kicking or throwing the ball to a teammate who is "open" at least 3 out of 5 times that such openings arise while the student has the ball
9. To rotate correctly from position to position in volleyball, with no errors or obvious confusion, for three consecutive games
10. After batting a ball, to run toward the correct base, without helper cues, in three consecutive Challenger baseball games.

Perceptual-Motor Learning Model

Figure 12.3 presents a model to guide understanding of the many components of perceptual-motor learning. In this model, skilled movement is the outcome of a process that is pictured as a five-dip ice-cream cone. The cone or foundation represents attention processes because formal learning cannot occur without attention. Each dip of ice cream is analogous to a set of processes requisite to motor learning and performance. Perceptual-motor abilities, although represented by only one circle, are not viable without the other abilities. Hence, perceptual-motor training begins with consideration of each set of abilities and the environmental conditions that influence them.

Attention Processes

Individual differences in attention affect both performance and learning. There are many kinds of attention, each of which may be specific to a sense modality. Let us consider (a) selective attention, (b) attention span or duration, and (c) limited attention capacity.

Selective attention is the process of blocking non-pertinent information from entering short-term memory. Because what is pertinent varies from second to second, this is an adaptive mechanism that switches attention from one input to another. This process is related to **cue selection** (knowing what cues to attend to).

Attention span or duration refers to the amount of time an individual can attend to the same task. This varies by sense modality, interest level, motivation, meaningfulness of the material, and many other factors (Krupski, 1987; Samuels, 1987).

Attention capacity refers to the number of items or chunks that can be assimilated at one time. For most adults, this is between five and nine. An *item* is a letter, musical note, fact, or movement. A *chunk* is a word, phrase, or series of facts or movements. Attention capacity also denotes number of sense modalities that can be attended to simultaneously. Some persons, for example, can read a book and listen to music at the same time. When motor skills are taught by providing a visual demonstration concurrent with a verbal explanation, the teacher assumes that students can attend to simultaneous input from both sense modalities or successfully block out one. When this is not the case, **contextual interference** is said to be occurring.

See Chapter 20 for information on attention deficits and the diagnostic criteria used to identify attention deficit disorder with hyperactivity (ADDH). Chapter 21 also includes information on attention problems and describes specific interventions.

Memory Processes

Motor learning specialists are more likely than therapists to conceptualize disorders as problems of memory rather than perception. This is probably because learning is defined as a permanent change in behavior, and permanency is measured by retention or memory. *In actuality, memory and perception are linked because meaning cannot occur without memory.* Both processes (a) depend upon the integrity of input systems, (b) result in output, and (c) have duration and capacity deficiencies.

There are two kinds of memory: (a) short-term and (b) long-term. The **short-term memory** is a perceptual mechanism in that it is associated with central processing. It is also the source of cognitive, affective, and motor outputs. According to Schmidt (1988), data can be held in the short-term memory store only about 60 sec before decay or loss occurs. Thus, when trying to learn something new, we must immediately use an effective rehearsal (practice) strategy. We have only about 1 min to get the new information or motor pattern into long-term memory. **Long-term memory** is essentially a storage mechanism; schemas and representations of past actions are organized so that they can be retrieved and linked with new ideas and experiences.

FIGURE 12.3 Perceptual-motor model: The five-dip ice-cream cone. Central processing includes everything that happens inside the brain. Like a five-dip ice-cream cone, the overlapping areas melt and blend together to constitute central processing. Everything is influenced by environmental conditions.

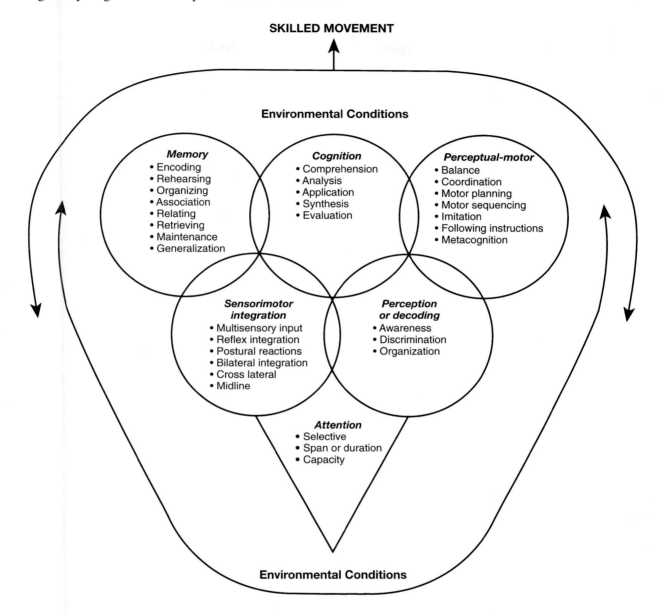

Memory subprocesses have names to help teachers and researchers (see Figure 12.3). Assessment is directed toward determining which processes need specific help. **Encoding** is screening and assimilating new data into short-term memory, a task that requires both attention and memory. Encoding success is evaluated by asking people to immediately imitate a pattern that they have just seen or been coactively moved through. The discrepancy between the model and the imitation reveals the extent of encoding problems. Timing is very important when assessing encoding. Check what a learner can do 15 sec after a demonstration, 30 sec after, and so on. Consider also whether there is *contextual interference* between the time instructions are given and the task is performed. This is the term given to irrelevant stimuli, detractors, or interpolated activity.

Rehearsal refers to practice strategies, whereas **organization** describes planning strategies. Associating, relating, and retrieving can be considered either rehearsal or organization. All of these emphasize the importance of *active learning*. Thus, students are taught (a) self-cueing by talking aloud, (b) repeating aloud cues or labels stated by others, (c) associating or relating with something already known, and (d) imagery (Gallagher & Thomas, 1984; Hoover & Horgan, 1990; Kowalski & Sherrill, 1992; Rose, Cundick, & Higbee, 1983; Surburg, 1989; Weiss & Klint, 1987). Holding the endpoint of a movement for about 10 sec and concentrating on its feel before beginning another repetition is also emphasized (Reid, 1980; Hoover & Horgan, 1990). **Associating** or **relating** with something already known involves *retrieval,* pulling things from long-term memory and organizing them in new and different ways. **Maintenance** refers to periodically pulling something out of long-term memory and using it so the ability is not lost. **Generalization** refers to ability to apply newly learned tasks to many and varied situations.

Memory does not necessarily imply understanding. Memorizing a list or paragraph is easier than trying to understand it. Dustin Hoffman, in the Oscar winning movie **Rainman,** portrayed a person with phenomenal memory abilities who could not care for himself and live independently. Persons who have impaired mental processes but show genius in recalling dates, performing mathematical calculations, or playing musical instruments by ear are called **savants.**

Memory function (as well as attention, perception, and cognition) is directly related to age. The memory system operates much more slowly in children than adults. *This is probably because children do not yet know efficient rehearsal strategies.* When watching demonstrations and hearing instructions, they do not know what cues to attend to unless carefully taught. Thus, cue selection is often a breakdown targeted for remediation in perceptual-motor training. Children also do not use error information unless taught to do so. The younger they are, the more impulsive and less reflective. While still in the preoperative mental stage, children are motivated to have fun simply by doing. They do not try to analyze and improve performance unless systematically taught how to do so. Persons with developmental delays obviously need much help with higher order cortical functions like analysis.

There appear to be no standardized tests or protocols for assessment of memory functions and processes related to learning large muscle physical education activities. You can, however, identify duration and capability deficiencies by experimenting with the number of words you use in giving instructions. You can also probe periodically by asking students to recall and perform a task that has not been practiced for several days. Later, you should repeatedly ask, "How do you remember? What strategies do you use?"

Cognition

Perceptual-motor learning cannot occur without cognitive processing. **Cognition,** according to Bloom (1956), includes six measurable processes: comprehension, analysis, application, synthesis, and evaluation. **Comprehension** refers to understanding of instructions. **Analysis** is ability to break a task down into parts and relationships, to consider variables and conditions, and to plan new combinations or orders. Think, for example, of the body parts and time-space-force-flow elements being assembled and ordered each time a new balance, coordination, or motor-sequencing task is learned. **Application** is analogous to generalization; persons apply new learning when task and environmental demands are varied. **Synthesis** and **evaluation** are higher order cortical tasks that entail the development of products (movement sequence, choreographed dance or aquatics composition, sport performance demonstrating game strategies) and the ability to judge these products according to standards or criteria. These processes are associated with **metacognition.**

The acronym *CAASE* is a memory device standing for comprehension-analysis-application-synthesis-evaluation. To remember this, think that we need to make a case (CAASE) for cognition as one basis for physical education success. Assessment involves creating tasks that require different types and levels of cognition. These should relate specifically to physical education.

Cognitive processes can also be broken down into types of knowledge: declarative, procedural, affective, and metacognitive (Wall, 1990). Illustrative of this assessment approach are a ball-catching test by Kourtessis and Reid (1997) and a table tennis protocol by Bouffard and Wall (1991).

See Chapter 21 for the **knowledge-based model** of Ted Wall and colleagues in Canada, which is recommended for remediating cognitive problems related to movement. In all physical education lessons, increased attention should be given to cognition.

Other Components of the Perceptual-Motor Model

Perception, sensorimotor integration, and perceptual-motor learning are areas of special concern to adapted physical educators. Writing objectives to guide instruction requires identifying **specific areas of breakdown,** a term used to emphasize the fact that organizational processes within the brain have broken down. A special model has been developed, therefore, to help understand and remediate CNS breakdowns (see Figure 12.4).

The 4A Assessment/Remediation Model

Figure 12.4 synthesizes the information to be presented on the following pages. Although much information is included, the model is named *4A* to emphasize four new terms that are widely used among professionals: *agnosias, ataxias, apraxias,* and *aphasias.*

Start your study of this model by noting the three columns: Inputs, Central Processing, and Outputs. Consider the complexity of the learning process, and remember dynamic systems theory. All of the systems in the body influence the CNS, and vice versa. The process depicted in the 4A model is not linear; it is multidirectional and chaotic.

Inputs and central processing cannot be directly measured, except in laboratories. Teachers therefore focus on **outputs,** the observable behaviors of a student. Specific outputs are called by the same names in the CNS and Output columns, because the processes are inseparable. The 4A model, however, highlights names for general output problems (e.g., agnosias, ataxias).

Agnosias, Ataxias, Apraxias, and Aphasias

Agnosia, ataxia, apraxia, and aphasia are output problems that can be traced to perceptual-motor origins. Each denotes deficits in central processing caused by brain damage. The etiology is often unknown and undifferentiated.

Agnosia, a diagnostic term for perceptual deficits, is inability to recognize sensory stimuli when there is no known structural or physiological damage. The word *agnosia* is derived from a- ("without") and *gnosis* (meaning "knowledge"). A way to remember agnosia and to distinguish it from all of

FIGURE 12.4 The 4A assessment/remediation model for identifying specific areas of CNS breakdown.

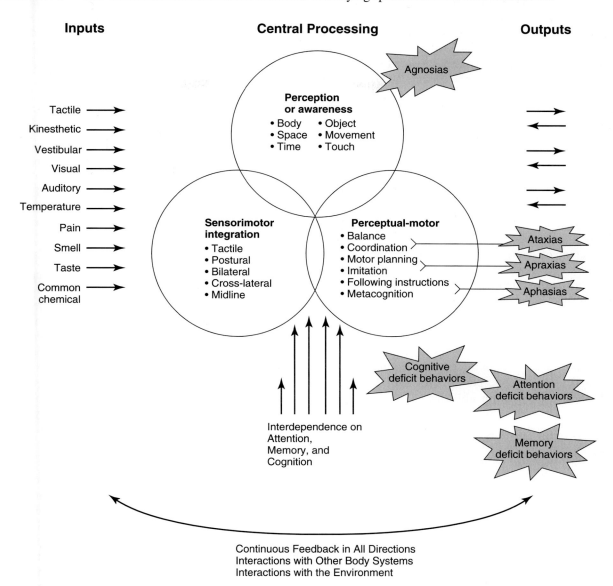

the conditions beginning with *a* is to associate the pronunciation (ag-nō-zē-a) with *knows (noze),* a word that sounds the same while reminding us of its derivation. Agnosias can affect any part of the body or a particular sense (e.g., visual and auditory agnosias). Agnosias for sounds and music are commonly called tone and melody deafness. Agnosias are particularly common after strokes.

Ataxia, from the Greek word meaning "lack of order," is defective muscular coordination, especially in relation to reaching and walking. There are many kinds of ataxia. Different parts of the CNS cause the condition (cerebellar damage in cerebral palsy; degeneration of ascending spinal cord tracts in alcoholism, syphilis, and Friedreich's ataxia). In each of these, the vestibular-kinesthetic-tactile sensations are impaired. Both balance and coordination are affected. Reaching problems are manifested primarily in overshooting or undershooting objects. Walking problems are evidenced by balance deficits and a peculiar reeling or wide-based staggering

gait. To help you remember, think about a*tax*ia as very energy-*tax*ing.

Apraxia, essentially the same as dyspraxia, is discussed under motor planning as a thought-organization disorder that is particularly observable in movements that require correct sequencing and timing. Three words (*apraxia, dyspraxia,* motor *planning*) each include a *p,* the key for keeping apraxia (the *p* word) separate from ataxia (the *t* word) in your mind.

Aphasia, derived from *a-* ("not") and *phasis,* ("speaking"), can be sensory or motor or both. It refers to all kinds of language and communication deficits caused by brain injury, not just speaking problems. The brain injury can be developmental or acquired, as in the case of a stroke or trauma.

Common aphasias are **dyslexia** or **alexia** (reading disorders), **dysgraphia** or **agraphia** (writing disorders), and word-finding problems in speech, like the inability to name an object or action even though we know what it is. Aphasias can encompass any kind of language system, concrete or abstract.

In educational diagnoses, aphasias are often grouped together as language and learning disorders. They have no relationship to intelligence and are not caused by sensory deficits. Diagnosis of an aphasia first requires ruling out mental retardation, inability to see and hear, and lack of learning opportunity or motivation. Aphasia relates only to central processing in the association parts of the cerebral cortex. It is possible, of course, to have both aphasias and sensory input deficits, especially in persons with widespread CNS damage who are severely disabled.

Perceptual Disorders

The ability to derive meaning from what we see, hear, and feel is perception, linked, of course, with cognition. Abilities begin to develop shortly after birth, but assessment often is not accurate until language is acquired. Perception builds schema about the body, movement, space, objects, and time. Major breakdown areas of interest to physical educators are visual and auditory perception, body awareness, directional awareness, spatial awareness, and temporal awareness. Breakdowns in these areas (perceptual deficits) are called *agnosias*.

Visual and Auditory Perception

Visual and auditory perception includes the use of vision and audition to make sense of both the external and internal environment. Static and dynamic perception should be assessed separately. **Static perception abilities** can be assessed by (a) guessing games ("What do you see? What do you hear?"), (b) hide-and-seek games ("Can you find a hidden object? Can you locate the hidden source of a sound?"). **Dynamic perception abilities** are harder to assess but more relevant to physical education, where moving balls, as well as moving teammates and opponents, must be perceived and judged. Dynamic visual perception is especially important to sport success. In order to aid assessment, children should be taught to talk aloud about what they perceive, including estimates of speed and landing location, when told to visually track balls of various sizes, shapes, and colors moving at various speeds in different directions and kinds of arcs.

The process of perceiving and making judgments about object interception is called **coincidence-anticipation.** Dynamic visual perception is age related; most children are unable to track and catch balls that travel in an arc until age 8 or 9. Games should be devised that require visual tracking of all kinds of sport objects at distances commonly used in motor skill practice and games. Lots of time should be devoted to passing balls (throwing and kicking) to partners moving at varying speeds.

Body Awareness

Body awareness is the ability to derive meaning from the body. Illustrative assessment questions are (a) What body parts is the student aware of? (b) What body surfaces is the student aware of? (c) What body positions (upside down vs. erect; leans in various directions; tucked vs. straight) is the student aware of? and (d) What movements is the student aware of? For each of these, determine whether problems are primarily tactile, kinesthetic, and vestibular (TKV); visual; or auditory.

Body awareness relates to the elements of space and time. These, in turn, are perceived differently under various environmental conditions (light, dark; loud, quiet; soft, hard; stable, unstable; hot, cold) and in various states of motion (externally imposed, self-initiated; fast, slow; airborne, one-, two-, or three-part contact with a surface; linear, rotatory; in balance, out of balance).

Directional Awareness

Directional awareness denotes consciousness of up-down, north-south, in-out, forward-backward, right-left, and other descriptors of location or movement. Directional awareness becomes progressively keener between ages 2 and 8 years, with up-down typically the first direction learned and right-left the last. Sometimes, these abilities are called *discriminations* to indicate a more advanced level than general awareness.

Spatial Awareness

Spatial awareness, which develops after directional awareness, is perception of space and the objects or forms that occupy space. The child understands space first as it relates to her or his own body, then as it relates to other persons and objects. Early awareness focuses on *large* and *small* and on making objects (including the body) fit into spaces. Awareness also expands from stationary to moving objects. In the well-integrated child, spatial awareness is both cognitive and somatic. In some children, however, there is a split. The mind knows what is happening in space but the body does not, or vice versa.

Temporal Awareness

Temporal or time awareness is the ability to derive meaning in relation to such qualities as fast and slow, now and later, long and short, continuous and intermittent, even and uneven, and set variations in rhythm like 4/4, 3/4, or 6/8. This kind of awareness is needed to succeed in reaction-time tasks and ball-handling activities that require judgments about how fast a ball is moving. Temporal awareness intersensory, primarily visual-auditory, and very complex. Matching of visual and auditory input, as in judging speeds and distances, usually occurs by chance rather than ability until about age 7. Thereafter, temporal awareness slowly matures, progressing from discrimination to perceptual organization and cognition.

Activities for Remediation of Perceptual Disorders

Within the physical education context, perception should be combined with big muscle action for remediation. Games, movement exploration, and drills in a variety of environments should emphasize *awareness* (there, not there), *discrimination* (different intensities, qualities, and sources), and *organization* (parts/wholes, assembly/disassembly, similarities/differences, correct/incorrect, sequencing).

1. Use follow-the-leader games in moving (visual perception) and in making noises or rhythm patterns (auditory perception).
2. Emphasize follow-the-leader games that entail space and time judgments, like squeezing through narrow openings,

climbing over and under barriers, jumping over moving ropes or poles, and navigating surfaces that respond in unpredictable ways.

3. Use blindfolds for locomotor, ball-handling, and object manipulation games. Hitting a piñata or paper sack filled with goodies is fun. *Blindperson's Bluff* is an age-old favorite.

4. Use discover-and-gather games in which cardboard cutouts of different colors, sizes, and shapes are taped to a distant wall or floor. Challenge, "How many times can you run to the wall and bring back something red? Bring back only one thing each time."

5. Scatter parts of broken dolls all over the room and challenge, "Who can find a head, trunk, two arms, and two legs and build a doll?" Repeat with other three-dimensional objects.

6. Scatter letters all over the room and challenge children to run about finding the letters to match the word you are showing or to form words and sentences of their own choice.

7. Cut pictures or greeting cards into several pieces and scatter all but one piece of each. Give students the one piece and challenge them to find the others to make a whole.

8. Sound different notes on musical instruments and have students respond with a preestablished stunt for each sound.

9. Bring pets to class and have students imitate animals while learning names for stunts like the dog walk (see Figure 12.5). Animals can also be used to increase awareness of others and how they use time and space.

10. Keep creating. There are hundreds of activities. Be sure that each uses the entire body and thus reinforces motor skills and patterns and builds fitness.

Sensorimotor Integration Disorders

Major breakdown areas of interest to physical educators are (1) intersensory integration; (b) postural or bilateral integration; (c) laterality, verticality, and directionality; and (d) crossing the midline. Sensorimotor integration disorders coexist with and are often indistinguishable from perceptual-motor problems. When clumsiness or developmental coordination disorder (DCD) of children without other disabilities is analyzed, **sensorimotor integration disorders** refers to generalized breakdown of all or most of the underlying abilities needed to perform complex basic movement skills such as moving through obstacle courses, jumping, hopping, and game-related ball- and object-handling skills.

Intersensory Integration

Intersensory integration, the ability to synthesize and use multiple sources of sensory information, should be observed in several environments that afford opportunities to interact with different combinations of sensory input. Obstacle courses in natural environments permit the assessment of many kinds of perceptual judgments. Likewise, use one-sentence movement

FIGURE 12.5 Imitating animals while learning names of stunts like the dog walk enhances perception.

exploration challenges ("Can you do this?" or "Can you jump?"). The child's motor response provides input into the quality of intersensory integration.

Next, evaluate the child in formal learning settings in which the goal is imitation of a model, following instructions with no visual demonstration, or simultaneous processing of a demonstration with verbal instructions. Pay particular attention to the *cues* that the child selects and the *rehearsal strategies* employed. Also try different kinds of *models* to see if this factor affects intersensory integration.

If intersensory integration is a major area of weakness, then check the use of each sense modality individually (i.e., intrasensory integration). In particular, *check tactile integration,* because this set of underlying abilities is strongly related to body awareness in various changing environments.

Activities for remediation include the following:

1. Use exercise, stunts, and games in water (see Chapter 17). Stress the feel of *in* and *out* of the water; jump in and climb out again and again.

2. Use lots of rolling activities on different kinds of surfaces. Also use crawling and similar activities that keep most of the body in contact with a surface.

3. Use coactive activities in which two bodies or body parts touch and move in unison.

4. Use rolling activities on unstable surfaces, such as balls, that elicit protective arm extension.

5. Use barefoot activities on sand, carpet, grass, and interesting textures. Create obstacle courses that require moving across different textures.

6. Use games and relays that require putting on, taking off, and playing in clothes, blankets, or sacks of various textures. Tubular jersey is good for this purpose (see Figure 12.6).

7. Let children body-paint or sponge each other, wrestle in mud, or run in and out of showers from a garden hose. Activities that alternate getting dirty and getting clean are helpful in some kinds of tactile defensiveness.

FIGURE 12.6 Activities inside stretchable, tubular jersey help remediate tactile integration disorders in relation to intersensory integration.

Postural or Bilateral Integration

Postural or bilateral integration refers to the smooth assembly of body parts to perform total body actions (postural integration) or the smooth working together of both sides of the body or of the top and bottom halves (bilateral integration). Some authorities prefer the term *postural integration,* but others prefer *bilateral integration.* Also included in this broad diagnostic category is **unilateral integration,** the ability to move one body part independently without unwanted **overflow** (extraneous movement of other body parts).

The postural or bilateral integration diagnosis is closely related to body awareness, specifically vestibular-kinesthetic awareness of where the body and/or specific body parts are in relation to space. Specifically, movement that shows laterality, verticality, and directionality should be assessed.

Laterality is internal or vestibular-kinesthetic awareness of the two sides of the body, a dimension of body image that evolves through experimenting with the two sides of the body and their relationship to each other. According to Kephart (1971, p. 87), "The primary pattern out of which this differentiation develops is that of balance." Laterality is well established by age 3 in most children. Kephart (1971, p. 88) clarifies that *laterality is not handedness or the ability to name right and left.* Laterality is a subcortical and nonverbal ability.

Verticality is internal or vestibular-kinesthetic awareness of up and down that evolves as the infant gains the body control to move from horizontal to upright positions. Some children do not seem aware of forward and backward alignments in postures. Others, when asked to raise or lower limbs a certain distance, do not have the kinesthetic feel to enable success. Problems in rise-to-stand positions and jumping relate to verticality because top and bottom halves of the body must work together. Problems with these kinds of activities often indicate inadequate integration of the symmetrical tonic neck reflex.

Directionality is internal or vestibular-kinesthetic awareness of all of the different directions that the body and/or body parts can move. *Directionality* is a broad term that encompasses laterality and verticality. Remember that these abilities are primarily perceptual-motor; they should be assessed by observing movement, particularly balance, under many environmental conditions that challenge balance.

Game sense, the ability of good athletes to be in the right place at the right time, is an outcome of good postural and bilateral integration. Game sense comes from within, reflecting integration of mind and body and total awareness of the body-in-space phenomenon.

Activities for remediation include the following:

1. Use activities that activate and promote tactile, kinesthetic, vestibular, and visual systems working together—tiltboards and balance boards, barrels, and balls controlled by you because integration deficits are characterized by inadequate balance for independent control of such apparatus (see Figure 12.7).
2. Use hammock activities (see Chapter 16 on dance therapy).
3. Use traditional playground swings for sitting and standing or specially constructed ones for lying and four-point.
4. Use slides, seesaws, merry-go-rounds, and other playground apparatus that can accommodate nonambulatory children.
5. Use surfaces that respond in unpredictable ways to locomotor movements (rolling, crawling, creeping, walking). These include moon walks, mattresses, trampolines, and changing-consistency balance boards and beams.
6. Lift children into the air and play airplane in various directions.
7. Use wheel toys and vehicles to move children across variable surfaces and inclinations.
8. Passively or coactively move children through several trials of up-and-down and side-to-side patterns. (This activity is used when the children cannot move themselves through these patterns.)
9. Create reach-and-grasp and reach-and-strike activities that can be done from all positions (prone, supine, sit, four-point, stand) while stationary or moving.
10. With good personal flotation devices (PFDs) and individual monitoring, use water activities. Bilateral arm patterns usually happen spontaneously.
11. Use therapeutic horseback riding conducted by persons certified in this area (Biery & Kauffman, 1989).

Crosslateral and Midline Problems

Crosslateral integration, the most mature limb pattern, refers to right arm and left leg (contralateral limbs) working

FIGURE 12.7 The teacher moves the barrel in unexpected ways to help students with bilateral integration.

in opposition to each other as in a mature locomotor, throwing, or kicking pattern. Age 6 or 7 is when failure to exhibit crosslateral patterns is diagnosed as a problem. Crosslateral integration cannot really be distinguished from coordination because crosslateral patterns emerge long after children acquire imitation and modeling abilities.

The ability to move a limb across the body's midline is a special kind of crosslateral integration. Problems in this area are evidenced in ball-handling activities, such as failure to follow-through in the direction of a throw or a racquet swing and difficulty in reaching across the body to field balls coming to the left or right. Standing at a chalkboard and reaching the right hand across the board to the far left to draw a long horizontal line is also a good test. Individuals with problems will walk or take steps as they draw to avoid crossing midline. The mature chalkboard pattern requires keeping the feet stationary. Many midline problems reflect inadequate integration of the asymmetrical tonic neck reflex.

Activities for remediation include the following:

1. Use the previously mentioned activities that reinforce bilateral and unilateral integration. Many authorities believe that these build the foundation on which crosslateral efficiency is built.

2. Use agility locomotor activities that require moving as fast as possible around curves and obstacles.

3. Use exercises and games (supine, four-point, sitting, standing) that require the right hand to touch the left leg or body parts and vice versa. Sit-ups and toe touches with trunk twists are good. Integrate these into Simon Says games.

4. Use games that require crossing midline to pick up stationary and moving objects of all sizes and shapes.

5. Use games that require crossing midline to block or trap objects rolled or tossed. This can be done with hands, broom, hockey stick, or other implement.

6. Use a variety of objects in games that require crossing midline when throwing and striking.

7. Use games that require crossing midline, such as catch the snake (a rope carried by a runner), catch the stick (a broomstick released from vertical), catch the hoop, and catch the soft discus, beanbag, or ball.

8. Use games that require students to leap brooks or barriers.

Perceptual-Motor Disorders

Perceptual-motor processing varies with respect to amount of time that elapses between perceiving and moving. Task difficulty and novelty obviously affect delays. Much depends on whether the movement impulse or idea occurs within the student (i.e., spontaneous movement exploration) or is externally prompted by a visual demonstration and/or verbal input.

Balance

Balance is to body control what information processing is to cognition. As such, *balance* is the process of integrating sensory input from multiple sources (vestibular, kinesthetic, tactile, and visual) so as to plan and execute static and dynamic postures. Balance is a conscious state and thus capable of some regulation by the cerebral cortex. It is largely determined, however, by various automatic righting and equilibrium reactions. Dynamic balance has a very low correlation with static balance and should be assessed and remediated separately. Balance is extremely task specific, so success on one balancing task cannot be generalized to other tasks, even those of the same type.

Activities for remediation include the following:

1. Use the activities described under sensorimotor integration disorders.

2. Use activities in which the student, rather than the teacher, controls apparatus like tiltboards and balance boards and beams.

3. Challenge students to discover how many ways they can perform static balances. For example, (a) use one, two, or three body parts; (b) use different surfaces; (c) alter positions of body parts at different speeds while balancing.

4. Ask students to imitate various static balances (see Figure 12.8). The best known of these is the stork or single-leg stand with sole of nonsupport leg on the inner surface of the support knee; arms are folded across the chest, or hands are placed on hips. Two others are (a) tip-toe balance stand, with heels lifted and hands on hips, and (b) tandem stand on beam (also called heel-to-toe stance).

5. Perform static balances under various visual conditions: eyes open, eyes closed, and eyes focused on targets set at various heights and distances. Try looking at moving targets while balancing.

FIGURE 12.8 Tiltboards, like the homemade one pictured, are used to improve dynamic balance and thereby enhance vestibular functioning.

6. Try static balances while holding different weights in one or both arms or on the head. Use Velcro to attach weights to legs or other body parts.

7. Try holding static balances while raising and lowering the center of gravity.

8. Try dynamic balances under various conditions.

9. Combine creative dramatics with beam walking so that students portray characters as a story is read. Have these characters move at different speeds and levels and do lots of turns.

10. Teach gymnastics routines that combine various kinds of balances.

Coordination

Coordination is the CNS processing needed to assemble body parts into a skilled movement. For coordination to occur, there must already be body, object, space, time, and movement schemes stored in long-term memory from past experience. Of particular importance are postural, bilateral, and crosslateral integration and freedom from midline problems. Coordination is thus the cortical activity of short- and long-term memory interacting to refine schema pertaining to the body parts working together.

Coordination, like balance, is specific to the task. Thus, fine motor coordination (use of fingers or toes in manipulative activities) is not much related to gross or large muscle motor coordination (locomotor and object control patterns). This is recognized in standardized motor proficiency tests that have separate batteries or subtests to measure (a) *bilateral coordination* (tapping feet alternately while making circles with fingers, jumping up and clapping hands); (b) *upper limb coordination* (catching a ball tossed from 10 ft, throwing a ball at a target); (c) *visual-motor control* (paper-pencil and scissors activities); and (d) *upper limb speed and dexterity* (sorting shape cards, displacing pegs, making dots in a small circle).

Coordination is often assessed by speed, accuracy, and distance measures. Each of these is a task-specific coordination and calls for a different kind of CNS processing. Much research is needed in this area.

Coordination is interwoven with body composition and fitness attributes like body weight, strength, and range of motion. These can act as constraints or affordances. It is also dependent upon static and dynamic balances in the many postures the task demands.

Burton (1990) suggested two basic principles to guide remediation of coordination problems. The *first principle is that movement coordination must be developed before movement control.* This principle applies to persons with disabilities who perform a coordination in a stereotypical pattern. For example, they can do the jumping jacks exercise only under certain conditions. If environmental variables are changed, they cannot adapt or generalize. Coordination is developed best by ameliorating this problem. The teacher therefore changes the jumping jacks task in many ways: (a) altering the surface by tilting it or making it soft or slick, (b) changing from land to chest-high water, (c) adding a drumbeat or music to guide the speed or rhythm, and (d) adding weights to limbs or having the person hold streamers.

The *second principle* is that *movement coordination and control should be developed in hierarchial sequences.* This principle emphasizes task-analyzing the body part assembly. The easiest assembly is movement of arms or legs only in a bilateral pattern. Next might be movements of limbs on right side only and left side only (a lateral pattern). Then come combinations: (a) right and left sides together or (b) top and bottom parts together. Practice at each hierarchical level should include different body positions, speeds, rhythms, ranges of motion, and visual conditions.

Activities for remediation include the following:

1. Teach various coordinations in prone- and supine-lying to eliminate balance constraints of working against gravity.

2. Teach students to say verbal cues aloud as they move (e.g., "in-out" or "apart-together" for jumping jacks). Use words as cues rather than numbers.

3. Teach students to use visual imagery before attempting new coordinations.

4. Teach students to hold the endpoint of a coordination 7 to 10 sec and to concentrate on remembering its feel.

5. Alter practice conditions in many ways.

6. For standing and locomotion coordinations, supply bars or apparatus to hold on to if balance is a constraint.

7. Supply videotaped and other kinds of feedback.

8. Make available time-out environments where students can go to practice in private or with a peer tutor.

9. Reward lots of trials and self-initiated efforts.

Motor Planning (Praxis)

Motor planning and **motor programming** are global terms used in physical education to denote the organizational activity of the neural systems that command coordinated movement patterns. Sports and games, for example, do not require individual coordinations but many kinds linked together in appropriate sequences.

There are many kinds of motor-planning problems. In one kind, persons can see a sequence of body actions and state correctly what they have seen (e.g., "Run to red line, duck under bar, climb up ladder, and then jump down"), but they cannot execute the sequence. The inability to imitate or follow visual and verbal directions in executing a series of actions is called **apraxia** or **dyspraxia.** The ability to sequence develops with age, and inability to sequence should not be considered a dyspraxia until age 6 or 7. **Motor sequencing** is sometimes used as a synonym for *motor planning* because both abilities denote cortical command systems that activate patterns or chunk responses, rather than initiate single actions like running, jumping, and throwing.

Of concern in motor planning is whether skills are closed or open. **Closed skills** are repetitive activities in a predictable environment. Examples are bowling, archery, and similar activities in which the target does not change. **Open skills** are those in a multiplayer game setting in which movements of the ball are unpredictable. Obviously, open skills re-

quire quick motor planning for success. Planning errors in such cases can be selective or executive. **Selection errors** are mismatches between the expected condition and what really happens. Examples are readiness for a straight ball when a curved one arrives or readiness for a smooth running surface when a hole suddenly appears. **Executive errors** occur when the CNS program is correct but the muscles do not do what they are told because of fatigue or other constraints.

Little is known about remediating apraxia (Croce, 1993; Sugden & Keogh, 1990). This term is just beginning to be used in adapted physical activity, although it has been part of the vocabulary of occupational therapists since the 1970s (Ayres, 1972).

Activities for remediation include the following:

1. Practice increasingly longer sequences. Start with combining two things and then gradually add more. For example,
   a. *Run* to meet the ball, *catch* or field it
   b. Add to sequence, "*Look* around you"
   c. Add to sequence, *throw* ball to proper place

2. Play I'm Going to Grandmother's House games. The traditional game involves repeating words that others have said and then adding something new. For example,
   Lisa says, "I'm going to Grandmother's House [IGGH] and I'm going to take my pajamas."
   Abu says, "IGGH and I'm going to take my pajamas and my dog."
   Juan says, "IGGH and I'm going to take my pajamas, my dog, and my toothbrush."
   And so on.

For the physical education setting, this game is changed to movement. The lead-in theme can be changed also. For example,
   Heejung says, "I'm going to a soccer game and I'm going to do three jumps on the way"—(she jumps)
   Bob says, "I'm going to do three jumps and five push ups"—(he does 3 jumps, 5 pushups)

And so on. The movement sequences can be done with or without words.

3. Play **Copy Cat** sequence games in which the teacher or leader challenges the children to remember and imitate, after delays of various lengths, various locomotor or body part sequences. Delays between the demonstration and the start signal might be 10, 20, 30 sec and longer, encouraging children to visually rehearse the sequence during the delay.

4. Find out the conditions under which persons best learn sequences: (a) visual demonstration only, (b) verbal instructions only, (c) simultaneous visual demonstration and verbal instructions, (d) visual first followed by verbal, or (e) verbal first followed by visual.

5. Find out if background music helps with motor planning. Experiment with different kinds of music.

6. Provide lots of practice in game settings that require *open skill proficiency.* Vary these settings to match perceptual-motor decision making with greater and lesser demands.

Imitation

Imitation (also called modeling) of a motor act, depending on how many parts are involved, is a complex perceptual-motor ability. Imitation of single hand movements (bye-bye) begins around 10 months of age. As children become aware of other body parts, imitation becomes increasingly sophisticated visual reproduction. Breakdowns in imitation are hard to trace. The origin can be input, sensory integration, one of the perceptual processes (awareness, discrimination, organization), or one of the perceptual-motor processes (balance, coordination, motor planning, and the like). The problem can also be attention or memory.

Following Instructions

Assuming that there is no behavioral disorder, following instructions is a perceptual-motor ability. Breakdown sites for this ability are the same as for imitation except that audition is the modality used. The breakdown is often in the complexity of the command. *At age 5 or 6 years, most normal children can follow only three or four commands in sequence.* The more words in a command, the harder to follow. Auditory processing improves rapidly from ages 5 to 8. The ceiling most persons eventually reach for remembering sequences is seven *commands or tasks plus or minus two.*

Comprehensive Perceptual-Motor Testing

When the goal is to teach or improve motor skills and patterns, professionals must decide whether to focus objectives on skills or on the abilities underlying the skills. The profession is divided about half and half on which approach to take. Chapter 11 described the skill approach. This chapter explains the abilities approach.

Perceptual-Motor Screening

The adapted physical educator must assume initiative in preparing materials to help colleagues identify children who may benefit from perceptual-motor training. The Sherrill Perceptual-Motor Screening Checklist, developed specifically for use by classroom teachers, lists behaviors commonly exhibited by children with learning disabilities and/or mild neurological damage and has proven successful as a screening device for identifying perceptual-motor awkwardness (see Table 12.1). This checklist should be filled out for each child early in the year. The Purdue Perceptual Motor Survey is also a helpful screening instrument (see Table 12.2 and Figure 12.9).

Perceptual-Motor Diagnostic and Placement Tests

Perceptual-motor screening is followed by comprehensive testing to identify areas of breakdown. Table 12.3 presents perceptual-motor abilities measured by some of the better-known tests. The Bruininks-Oseretsky Test of Motor Proficiency (BOTMP) (Bruininks, 1978) was discussed extensively in Chapter 6 on assessment because it is widely used in making placement decisions. It generates data for writing objectives and selecting remediation activities in six gross motor areas and two fine motor areas. The tests created by Roach

and Kephart (1966) and Ayres (1965) include similar areas and items but are no longer widely used by physical educators. The Ayres test, however, remains popular with occupational therapists.

The newest test in Table 12.3 is the Movement Assessment Battery for Children (Movement ABC) by Sheila Henderson and Dave Sugden of England. This test (Henderson & Sugden, 1992) has evolved from the popular Test of Motor Impairment (TOMI) by Stott, Moyes, and Henderson (1972), later referred to as the TOMI-Henderson revision (Riggen, Ulrich, & Ozmun, 1990). The 1972 edition of TOMI had 45 items, 5 at each of nine age levels, and proved to be impractical for use in the field. In contrast, the Movement ABC has 32 items organized by four age levels so that the general movement competence of a child can be assessed with 8 items (see Table 12.4).

Worldwide, Movement ABC appears to be the most frequently used diagnostic test to identify children who are clumsy (see the April 1994 issue of the *Adapted Physical Activity Quarterly,* edited by Sheila Henderson). An address for ordering Movement ABC appears in Appendix E. Movement ABC includes the ABC Checklist (48 questions to be answered by teachers or parents, based on observation over 1 to 2 weeks) as well as the ABC Test described in Table 12.4. The Movement ABC manual (Henderson & Sugden, 1992) is an excellent resource that teaches use of the instruments and provides strong coverage on the cognitive-motor approach to intervention.

The official recognition of the condition called developmental coordination disorder (American Psychiatric Association, 1987) challenges physical educators to learn diagnostic approaches that can help children receive services. The World Health Organization has also officially recognized developmental coordination disorder (Henderson, 1994), and this means that insurance companies in some countries will pay for intervention and treatment. The recognition of DCD is an important milestone in the history of the controversial perceptual-motor training movement. Because this history is intertwined with beliefs about testing and the specific underlying abilities to be examined, the next section focuses on perceptual-motor history and early perceptual-motor theorists. The chapter then ends with a section on pedagogy and intervention.

Perceptual-Motor Training: Past and Present

The beginning of perceptual-motor training is often traced back to 1800, when **Jean-Marc Itard,** a physician in France, created a system for educating a nonverbal child, now called the Wild Boy of Aveyron, who was found wandering the forest. Itard's student, **Edouard Seguin,** brought Itard's ideas to America in the 1860s, where they were applied in residential schools for persons with mental retardation.

Another innovator of perceptual-motor training was **Maria Montessori,** a physician in Italy, who wrote classic books about the education of the senses in 1912 and 1917. Her works, however, did not stimulate much interest in America until the 1940s and 1950s. Then her ideas were used more in early childhood than in special education.

Hallahan and Cruickshank (1973) point out that, between 1936 and 1970, perceptual-motor training was the most

T a b l e 1 2 . 1   Sherrill Perceptual-Motor Screening Checklist.

_____ 1. Fails to show opposition of limbs in walking, sitting, throwing.
_____ 2. Sits or stands with poor posture.
_____ 3. Does not transfer weight from one foot to the other when throwing.
_____ 4. Cannot name body parts or move them on command.
_____ 5. Has poor muscle tone (tense or flaccid).
_____ 6. Uses one extremity much more often than the other.
_____ 7. Cannot use arm without "overflow" movements from other body parts.
_____ 8. Cannot jump rope.
_____ 9. Cannot clap out a rhythm with both hands or stamp rhythm with feet.
_____ 10. Has trouble crossing the midline of the body.
_____ 11. Often confuses right and left sides.
_____ 12. Confuses vertical, horizontal, up, down directions.
_____ 13. Cannot hop or maintain balance in squatting.
_____ 14. Has trouble getting in and out of seat.
_____ 15. Approaches new tasks with excessive clumsiness.
_____ 16. Fails to plan movements before initiating task.
_____ 17. Walks or runs with awkward gait.
_____ 18. Cannot tie shoes, use scissors, manipulate small objects.
_____ 19. Cannot identify fingers as they are touched without vision.
_____ 20. Has messy handwriting.
_____ 21. Has difficulty tracing over line or staying between lines.
_____ 22. Cannot discriminate tactually between different coins or fabrics.
_____ 23. Cannot imitate body postures and movements.
_____ 24. Demonstrates poor ocular control; unable to maintain eye contact with moving objects; loses place while reading.
_____ 25. Lacks body awareness; bumps into things; spills and drops objects.
_____ 26. Appears tense and anxious; cries or angers easily.
_____ 27. Responds negatively to physical contact; avoids touch.
_____ 28. Craves to be touched or held.
_____ 29. Overreacts to high-frequency noise, bright lights, odors.
_____ 30. Exhibits difficulty in concentrating.
_____ 31. Shows tendency to fight when standing in line or in crowds.
_____ 32. Avoids group games; spends most of time alone.
_____ 33. Complains of clothes irritating skin; avoids wearing coat.
_____ 34. Does not stay in assigned place; moves about excessively.
_____ 35. Uses either hand in motor activities.
_____ 36. Avoids using the nondominant side of body.
_____ 37. Cannot walk sideways on balance beam.
_____ 38. Holds one shoulder lower than the other.
_____ 39. Cannot hold a paper in place with one hand while writing with the other.
_____ 40. Avoids turning to the nondominant side whenever possible.
_____ 41. Cannot assemble puzzles that offer no difficulty to peers.
_____ 42. Cannot match basic geometric shapes to each other.
_____ 43. Cannot recognize letters and numbers.
_____ 44. Cannot differentiate background from foreground in a picture.
_____ 45. Cannot identify hidden figures in a picture.
_____ 46. Cannot catch balls.

Note. Students with 10 or more items checked should be referred for comprehensive examination.

popular method of education of children with learning disabilities (LD). It was also used widely in teaching persons with mental retardation (MR). Hallahan and Cruickshank trace the origins of perceptual-motor theory in America to **Alfred A. Strauss** and **Heinz Werner,** German psychologists who migrated to the United States in the 1930s to escape Hitler. Both eventually settled in Michigan, where they conducted the pioneer research on children with brain injury and/or MR that formed the basis for almost all early LD practices.

Some of the people influenced by Strauss and Werner were **William Cruickshank,** a special educator who applied their research specifically to persons with cerebral palsy (CP)

Table 12.2 Roach-Kephart Purdue Perceptual-Motor Survey.

Purpose

To identify children, ages 6 to 10 years, who do not possess perceptual-motor abilities necessary for acquiring academic skills by the usual instructional methods (i.e., this was designed to be a screening instrument, not a test).

Description

Thirty items organized under five headings: balance and postural flexibility, body image and differentiation, perceptual-motor match, ocular control, and form perception. Of these, only the first two sections include physical education type movements.

Balance and Postural Flexibility

1. Walking board forward.
2. Walking board backward.
3. Walking board sideward.
4. Jumping (including jump, hop forward, skip, hop in place 1/1, 2/2, 2/1, and 1/2).

Body Image and Differentiation

1. Identification of nine body parts: shoulders, hips, head, ankles, ears, feet, eyes, elbows, mouth.
2. Imitation of 17 arm movements categorized as unilateral, bilateral, and crosslateral (see Figure 12.9).
3. Obstacle course (chairs and 3-ft broomstick) entailing three tasks: going over, going under, and going between.
4. Strength tests in prone position from Kraus-Weber: (a) raise chest and hold 10 sec and (b) raise legs and hold 10 sec.
5. Angels-in-the-snow sequence including 10 tasks (R arm only, R leg only, L arm only, L leg only, both arms, both legs, L arm and L leg, R arm and R leg, R arm and L leg, L arm and R leg).

Scoring

See test manual. Different system used for each of 30 items, but score ranges from 1 to 4 on each.

Validity

Criterion-related against teachers' ratings of 297 children; coefficient was .65.

Reliability

Test-retest *r* of .95 on 30 children (Seaman & DePauw, 1982). For 88 children with mild mental retardation, ages 8 to 10 years, test-retest coefficients for specific items were identification of body parts, .75; imitation of movement, .51; obstacle course, .64; and angels-in-the-snow, .35 (Sherrill, 1985).

Primary Sources

Roach, E., & Kephart, N. (1966). *The Purdue perceptual-motor survey.* Columbus, OH: Charles C. Merrill.
Seaman, J., & DePauw, K. (1982). *The new adapted physical education.* Palo Alto, CA: Mayfield Publishing Co.
Sherrill, C. (1985). *Reliability coefficients for selected body image items performed by mentally retarded children.* Unpublished manuscript, Texas Woman's University, Denton.

Address for Ordering

Charles E. Merrill Publishing Co., 1300 Alum Creek Drive, Columbus, OH 43216.

and traumatic brain injury; **Newell C. Kephart,** an educational psychologist, whose 1960 classic *The Slow Learner in the Classroom* (2nd ed., 1971) still serves as the guide for some perceptual-motor practitioners; and **Gerald Getman,** an optometrist, who popularized the importance of vision in learning. **Marianne Frostig,** a developmental psychologist in Los Angeles, whose *Test of Developmental Vision* and prolific writing/speaking on perceptual-motor remediation dominated the 1950s and 1960s, also regards the works of Strauss and Werner as important to her orientation.

Individually, these perceptual-motor theorists who all believed that perceptual-motor activities led to improved reading skills and cognition might not have made a great impact on education. In 1964, however, they all (with the exception of Getman) became part of the Professional Advisory Board of the newly formed Association for Children with Learning Disabilities. Collectively, they exerted tremendous influence on teaching practices. Parents especially came to believe in their theories. This enthusiasm attracted the attention of many physical educators, who were supportive of movement and games as strategies for enhancing academic learning. Chief among these was **Bryant J. Cratty.**

FIGURE 12.9 Arm positions that children should be able to imitate. The top seven positions are used in the Purdue Perceptual-Motor Survey. These positions should be incorporated into follow-the-leader activities with dramatic themes like imitating airplanes or robots.

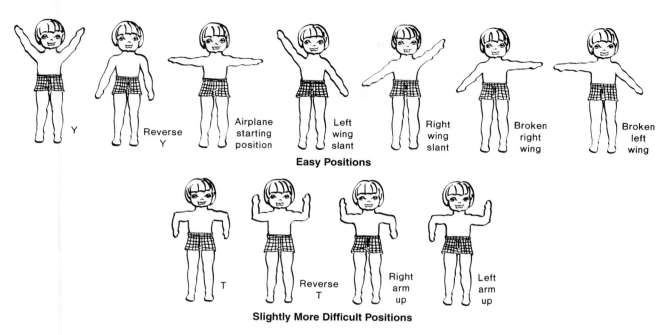

Easy Positions

Slightly More Difficult Positions

Table 12.3 Perceptual-motor factors that widely used tests purport to measure.

Roach-Kephart Purdue Perceptual-Motor Survey (1966)	Ayres Southern California Perceptual-Motor Tests (1965–69)	Bruininks-Oseretsky Test of Motor Proficiency (1978) (Ages 4.6 to 14.6)	Henderson-Sugden Movement ABC (1992) (Ages 4–12)

1. Balance and posture
  a. Walking board
  b. Hopping and jumping
2. Body image and right-left discrimination
  a. Identification of body parts
  b. Imitation of movement
  c. Obstacle course
  d. Kraus-Weber
  e. Angels-in-the-snow
3. Perceptual-motor match
  a. Chalkboard activities
  b. Rhythmic writing
4. Ocular control; ocular pursuits
5. Form reproduction; drawing simple geometric figures on blank paper
	1. Imitation of postures; reproduction of 12 arm and hand movements
	2. Crossing midline of body; using right or left hand to touch designated ear or eye
	3. Bilateral motor coordination; rhythmic tapping, using palms of hands on thighs
	4. Right-left discrimination; identification of right and left dimensions of various objects
	5. Standing balance, eyes open
	6. Standing balance, eyes closed
		1. Running speed and agility—a 30-yd shuttle run
		2. Balance, static and dynamic
		3. Bilateral coordination—tapping and jumping tasks
		4. Strength—long jump, sit-ups, push-ups
		5. Upper-limb coordination, mostly ball handling
		6. Response speed
		7. Visual-motor control—hand-eye activities like cutting, drawing, and copying
		8. Upper-limb speed and dexterity—hand-eye activities like sorting shape cards and making dots
			1. Manual dexterity
			2. Ball skills
			3. Static balance
			4. Dynamic balance

Note. Ayres's most recent test is *Sensory Integration and Praxis Tests* (SIPT). This test measures four factors: (a) form and space perception, (b) somatic and vestibular processing, (c) praxis, and (d) bilateral integration and sequencing (Ayres, 1989).

Table 12.4 **Test items for Movement ABC, formerly TOMI-H.**

Age Band 1 Ages 4–6	Age Band 2 Ages 7–8	Age Band 3 Ages 9–10	Age Band 4 Ages 11–12
Manual Dexterity			
Put 12 coins in bank. Test each hand.	Place 12 pegs in holes. Test each hand.	Shift 12 pegs into new rows. Test each hand.	Turn 12 pegs so opposite side is down.
Thread cube-shaped beads onto shoelace.	Thread lace in and out of holes in board. Test preferred hand.	Thread three nuts onto bolt. Test preferred hand.	Use scissors to cut out elephant.
Stay inside bicycle trail on paper with pen.	Trace flower on paper with pen.	Trace flower on paper with pen.	Trace flower on paper with pen.
Ball Skills			
Catch beanbag thrown from 6 feet with two hands.	Bounce tennis ball on floor and catch with one hand. Test each hand.	Throw tennis ball at wall 6 feet away and catch with two hands.	Throw tennis ball at wall 6 feet away and catch with one hand. Test each hand.
Roll tennis ball into 16-inch goal from 6 feet.	Throw beanbag into box on floor from 6 feet.	Throw beanbag into box on floor from 8 feet.	Throw tennis ball at small circle on wall from 8 feet.
Static Balance			
Stand on one leg for 20 sec. Test each leg.	Do stork stand for 20 sec. Test each leg.	Do one-foot balance on balance board for 20 sec.	Do heel-to-toe balance on broomstick affixed to board for 30 sec.
Dynamic Balance			
Jump over cord set at knee height.	Jump into 6 squares on floor, 18 × 18 inches.	Hop into 6 squares on floor, 18 × 18 inches.	Jump and clap while going over cord at knee height.
Walk line with heels raised, 15 steps.	Walk line, heel to toe, 15 steps.	Balance tennis ball on board in palm of hand while walking.	Walk backward heel to toe on line for 15 feet.

Note: Administration requires 20 to 40 minutes.

In the 1970s, the occupational therapy profession became involved in perceptual-motor training, largely through the leadership of **A. Jean Ayres,** who had published a factor analysis research study that established the components of perceptual-motor dysfunction (Ayres, 1965). Subsequently, Ayres chose to call her theory *sensory integration* (see Chapter 10) and wrote the classic *Sensory Integration and Learning Disorders* (Ayres, 1972), which all physical educators should read. The content of this book has guided many physical educators in developing perceptual-motor programs. Ayres also developed the Southern California Perceptual-Motor Tests (see Table 12.3), based on her 1965 factor analysis. The revision of this test is called *Sensory Integration and Praxis Tests* (Ayres, 1989). Ayres popularized the term *developmental dyspraxia* and focused attention on CNS processing, especially the construct of *motor planning.*

In the early 1980s, special educators rejected perceptual-motor training because research showed that it did not significantly change academic performance (Kavale & Mattson, 1983). This stance had little influence on physical educators, who primarily used perceptual-motor training to improve motor abilities rather than reading and math. The activities associated with perceptual-motor training have always been part of elementary school physical education. The special education stance also had little influence on the occupational therapy profession, which has substituted the term *sensory integration* for *perceptual-motor training.*

Of the many perceptual-motor theorists, let's consider the contributions of one special educator—Newell Kephart—and one physical educator—Bryant Cratty. Each wrote classic books that are well worth reading.

Contributions of Kephart (1911–1973)

Newell C. Kephart's theory is presented in *The Slow Learner in the Classroom,* published in 1960 and revised in 1971. Kephart, like Piaget, is a developmentalist. Whereas Piaget established the sensorimotor stage as 0 to 2 years of age, Kephart emphasized that movement is the basis of the intellect, without clarifying an age span for which the assumption is most true. Under the motor bases of achievement, Kephart (1971) discussed infant motor explorations, reflex and postural adjustments, laterality, directionality, body image, motor generalization, and motor learning. The terms *laterality* (internal awareness of two sides of the body) and *directionality* (understanding of directional concepts in relation to self and

FIGURE 12.10 Balance beam work was popularized by Kephart as an integral part of perceptual-motor training.

space) were coined by Kephart and continue to influence theory and practice.

Kephart taught at Purdue University in Indiana during most of his career. There, he and a colleague developed the well-known screening instrument called the Purdue Perceptual-Motor Survey (Roach & Kephart, 1966). Most of the items contained in the Purdue Perceptual-Motor Survey are presented in *The Slow Learner in the Classroom* as training activities. Kephart used the term *slow learner* to denote clumsy children, not individuals with mental retardation. Kephart's recommendations of physical activities are still timely and deserve careful study.

Kephart's greatest emphasis in perceptual-motor training was on balance. To improve balance, Kephart emphasized that students must be exposed to many and varied activities that make them lose balance. Only by struggling to regain balance does a child improve. Hence, Kephart recommended locomotor activities and stunts on walking boards (i.e., low balance beam) (see Figure 12.10), balance boards, trampolines, and bedsprings and mattresses. Kephart believed that laterality was largely a matter of balance (i.e., without internal awareness of the two sides of the body, one can hardly balance), so these activities are now widely accepted as contributing to the development of laterality.

In regard to body image and the ability to move one or more body parts without overflow (i.e., differentiation), Kephart recommended use of an angels-in-the-snow sequence, including unilateral, bilateral, and crosslateral movements. He also stressed the importance of follow-the-leader activities in which the teacher performed an arm movement and then the students imitated it from memory. In such imitations, students were taught *not to mirror activities,* but to use the same body parts (right and left) as the demonstrator. Kephart's idea of an obstacle course was two chairs and a broomstick; with these, he created problem-solving situations that required squeezing through, stepping over, and ducking under.

Kephart believed that stunts and games entailing forward, backward, and sideward movements also were important to body image development. Specifically, he recommended the duck walk, rabbit hop, crab walk, inchworm walk, and elephant walk (see Figure 12.11). Today, physical educators continue to emphasize all of these except the duck walk, which is believed injurious to knee joints.

Kephart stressed the practice of rhythmic patterns as important in remediating kinesthetic and tactual problems. In this regard, he recommended the use of bongo drums and the child learning to imitate even and uneven rhythms, first using one side of the body and then alternating right and left sides. Theorists later named this *bilateral motor coordination* because it combines ability to make right-left discriminations with ability to imitate rhythmic patterns and gestures.

In regard to hand-eye coordination, Kephart focused most of his attention on perceptual-motor match, ocular control, and form perception. This part of his theory was primarily visual motor. It emphasized use of chalkboard activities like drawing circles simultaneously with both arms and drawing lines to connect dots. Also important were tasks that required that the student fixate eyes on a small object and then follow its movement. Most of today's striking activities that use a ball suspended on a string come from Kephart's marsden ball tasks.

The *marsden ball,* named after the optometrist who conceived the idea in the 1950s, is a soft object about the size of a tennis ball, suspended by a string from overhead. The child stands about an arm's length from the ball and tries to touch it as the teacher swings it from side to side and forward and backward. Physical educators tend to conceptualize this activity as individual, dual, or team **tetherball** and to vary the size of the balls in accordance with students' skill levels.

Work on form perception was primarily tracing and copying crosses, circles, rectangles, diamonds, and other shapes. Whereas Kephart conceived this as a paper-pencil activity, physical educators have generalized it to large shapes and patterns on the floor that form paths to be followed in practicing locomotor activities. Likewise, various shapes are used on walls so that form perception is taught concurrently with target throwing. The copying tasks on the Purdue Perceptual-Motor Test come directly from the Bender-Gestalt Test (Bender, 1938).

Contributions of Cratty

Although many physical educators have subscribed to perceptual-motor training at one time or another, few have contributed to theory and practice through writing or research. Bryant J. Cratty, a physical education professor at the University of California at Los Angeles, thus stands out as the major contributor. Throughout the 1960s and 1970s, Cratty published about 30 books on this topic (Cratty, 1969a, 1969b, 1971). He also developed a test (the Six-Category Gross Motor Test; Cratty, 1969) to measure body image and perceptual-motor function (Knapczyk & Liemohn, 1976).

FIGURE 12.11 Stunts recommended by Kephart and still used to teach body awareness and other perceptual-motor abilities.

A. Rabbit hop   B. Crab walk   C. Elephant walk

Push-up position   Bear walk   Push-up position

D. Inch worm walk (consists of push-up starting position, walking on feet up to bear walk position, and then walking on hands to push-up position)

FIGURE 12.12 Perceptual-motor training, as advocated by Cratty, emphasized the integration of problem solving with movement tasks. Here, Dr. Gail Webster challenges a child to find New Mexico and do a forward roll on top of it.

In his books, Cratty described games that incorporated concepts of perceptual-motor match, ocular control, and form perception. He stressed that academic learning would not improve as the result of Kephart-like activities unless numbers, letters of the alphabet, and words were woven into floor and wall grids (patterns) and emphasized. Thus, Cratty called attention to the **principle of specificity.** He emphasized that movement is not the sole basis of the intellect. If properly planned and conducted, however, movement can contribute to problem-solving skills and academic learning (see Figure 12.12).

The New Perceptual-Motor Emphasis

In the 1980s, physical educators continued to affirm their belief in perceptual-motor learning as a means of enhancing motor performance. Walter Davis of Kent State University in Ohio applied the *ecological approach* of James J. Gibson (1979) to perceptual-motor learning (Davis, 1983) and worked with Allen Burton of the University of Minnesota to establish *ecological task analysis* as important pedagogy (Davis & Burton, 1991). Burton (1990) showed how perceptual-motor interactions can be assessed in children and recommended that future research be directed toward ways that motor behavior is limited by perceptual problems.

Also in the 1980s, many physical educators became serious scholars of perception and perceptual development. In most instances, their primary sources were the works of Eleanor and James Gibson (husband and wife) of Cornell University, who independently have published much research (E. J. Gibson, 1969, 1987; J. J. Gibson, 1969, 1979; Pick, 1979).

New books on the development of eye-hand coordination (Bard, Fleury, & Hay, 1990), postural control and balance (Woollacott & Shumway-Cook, 1989), and movement skill development (Burton, 1997; Sugden & Keogh, 1990) cite the Gibsons and many researchers who have followed their lead.

Most experts agree that understanding and teaching movement is impossible without a strong background in perception and neurology. This belief particularly relates to the remediation of balance deficits (Shumway-Cook, 1989; Woollacott, Shumway-Cook, & Williams, 1989).

Task-Specific Perceptual-Motor Pedagogy

Task-specific intervention is more effective than general training. This principle of specificity applies to underlying abilities as well as to motor skills and patterns. Task-specific intervention means that lesson plans are directed toward remediating perceptual-motor weaknesses in specific physical education tasks that are meaningful to the student. The procedures in task-specific intervention are these:

1. Determine a perceptual-motor weakness that compromises physical education performance.

2. Identify a particular game or sport in which the student would like to be more successful.

3. Ask the student to help analyze all the ways that the identified weakness (e.g., dynamic vision tracking, dynamic balance) interferes with success in the selected game or sport.

4. Collaborate with the student in determining specific perceptual-motor tasks that need practice and various activities that will provide practice.

5. Help the student to write a contract in which she or he agrees to practice a specific task a set number of minutes or to do a set number of trials during each class and/or at home as physical education homework.

Usually several weaknesses concurrently compromise movement efficiency, but teachers should focus on one at a time. Individual tutoring or small-group instruction is necessary to remediate perceptual-motor learning problems, because such problems are complex and not easily eliminated. In addition, teachers should realize that participation in games and sports can enhance perceptual-motor learning if instruction and coaching includes references to seeing and hearing, attending to kinesthetic cues, and thinking about one's learning style.

Illustrative Sport-Related Perceptual-Motor Tasks

The Sherrill Perceptual-Motor Tasks Checklist (SPMTC) was developed to help teachers understand how perceptual-motor

training can be integrated with sports instruction (see Table 12.5). The checklist can be used for either testing or teaching, but Sherrill recommends teaching through repeated testing and challenging, "Can you do this?" The SPMTC includes 10 perceptual-motor areas important to movement success. The tasks in the 10 areas can be reproduced on task cards to guide practice at stations. The tasks in each area are illustrative, and both children and teachers can add to the tasks and cover sports not included in the SPMTC. For example, children need to know the names of body parts to benefit from corrective feedback that refers to correct positioning of parts. Teachers use phrases such as *cock your wrist, run on the balls of your feet,* and *tuck your chin;* children often understand these verbally but lack the mind-body unity to make their body parts comply.

The last task on the SPMTC, lateral dominance, has not been discussed yet in this chapter. Lateral dominance (or preference) refers to the ability to use one side of the body more efficiently than the other. In sport this is desirable, but the other side should be capable of coordinated skills also. Usually the concern is with handedness. The relationship between handedness and motor proficiency is not well understood, but left-handedness is more prevalent among children with learning difficulties than among normal children (Henderson & Sugden, 1992). Likewise, mixed dominance (e.g., being left-handed, right-eyed, and left-footed) is more common. Contemporary theorists do not recommend remediation of left-handedness or mixed dominance. They do recommend working with children who seem to have no preference in handedness and children who are especially awkward with the nonpreferred hand.

Teaching Game Formations

Getting students into game formations is a difficult task. This is because persons with disabilities often cannot visually image what they are supposed to do when the teacher says, "Form a circle" or "Everyone stand in two-deep formation on the line." Getting into various game formations is thus important perceptual-motor learning. Likewise, responding correctly to instructions like "Move to the left" and "Go counterclockwise" requires careful teaching.

Design lessons that teach students the names of formations and provide practice for getting into formations with increasingly larger numbers. This practice results not only in perceptual-motor learning but also in improved social awareness and cooperation. Begin with groups of three or four. Give the same verbal cues each time, followed by a count from 1 to 10. Teach students that they must be in the new formation by the count of 10 and that they should help anyone having trouble.

Circles and lines on the floor help beginners, but eventually, form or shape perception should be good enough to enable success without floor cues. Table 12.6 presents the basic game and dance formations that students should learn. The drills or movement exploration column contains the verbal cues that initiate movement.

Table 12.5 Sherrill Perceptual-Motor Tasks Checklist.

Checklist for Teaching-Testing Perceptual-Motor Tasks

Name _____ Date _____

I. Major Task: Identification of Body Parts.
Other tasks: Auditory discrimination, memory, and sequencing.
A. Given cues to touch body parts, the student can:
_____ 1. Touch body parts one by one in response to one-word directions:

_____ Mouth	_____ Ankles
_____ Elbow	_____ Head
_____ Eyes	_____ Hips
_____ Feet	_____ Shoulders
_____ Ears	_____ Chin
_____ Wrist	_____ Waist

_____ 2. Touch two body parts simultaneously.
_____ 3. Touch five body parts in the same sequence as they are named by the teacher.
_____ 4. Do all of the above with eyes closed.

II. Major Task: Right-Left Discriminations with Body Parts.
Other tasks: Auditory discrimination, memory, and sequencing.
A. Given cues to touch body parts, the student can:
_____ 1. Use the right hand to touch parts named on right side.
_____ 2. Use the right hand to touch parts named on left side (this involves crossing the midline and is more difficult than item 1).
_____ 3. Use the left hand to touch parts named on the left side.
_____ 4. Use the left hand to touch parts named on the right side.
B. Given opportunities to play Simon Says, the student can follow commands at least 90% of game.
C. Given cues, the student can:
_____ 1. Use the right hand to touch body parts on the right side of partner.
_____ 2. Use the right hand to touch body parts on the left side of partner.

III. Major Task: Changing Positions in Space.
Other tasks: Auditory discrimination, memory, and sequencing.
A. Given instructions, the student can:
_____ 1. Stand in front of, in back of, to the right of, and to the left of a chair or a softball base.
_____ 2. Run to first base on a softball diamond.
_____ 3. Demonstrate where the right fielder, the left fielder, and the center fielder stand on a softball diamond.
_____ 4. Play a running game with 20 other students for 5 min without bumping into another student.
_____ 5. Climb over a rope or horizontal bar and duck under it in an obstacle course.

B. Given verbal directions in warm-ups without the benefit of demonstration, the student can:
_____ 1. Assume the following basic exercise positions: supine lying, hook lying, prone lying, long sitting, hook sitting, cross-legged sitting, kneel, half-kneel, squat, half-squat.
_____ 2. Demonstrate the following different foot positions in response to commands: wide base, narrow base, forward-backward stance, square stance, closed stance, open stance.
_____ 3. Perform a specific exercise seven times, use the eighth count to return to starting position, and stop precisely on the stop signal. For example,
_____ Seven walks and stop
_____ Seven stretches and stop
_____ Seven jumps and stop

IV. Major Task: Crossing the Midline.
Other tasks: Auditory discrimination, memory, and sequencing.
A. Given verbal instructions with no demonstration, the student can:
_____ 1. Throw a ball diagonally to a target on the far left.
_____ 2. Field a ball on the ground that is approaching the left foot.
_____ 3. Perform a backhand drive in tennis.
_____ 4. Catch a ball that rebounds off the wall to the left.
_____ 5. Toss a tennis ball vertically upward in front of left shoulder.

V. Major Task: Imitation of Movements; Motor Planning.
Other tasks: Visual discrimination, memory, and sequencing.
A. Given opportunities to imitate the teacher in an **Angel-in-the-Snow** sequence, the student can:
1. Imitate **bilateral** movements.
_____ a. Move both arms apart and together while legs remain stationary.
_____ b. Move both legs apart and together while arms remain stationary.
_____ c. Move all four limbs apart and together simultaneously.
_____ d. Move any three limbs apart and together simultaneously while the fourth limb remains stationary.
2. Imitate **unilateral** movements.
_____ a. Move the right arm and right leg apart and together simultaneously while the left limbs remain stationary.
_____ b. Move the left arm and left leg apart and together simultaneously while the right limbs remain stationary.
3. Imitate **cross-lateral** movements.
_____ a. Move the right arm and left leg apart and together simultaneously while the other limbs remain stationary.

_____ b. Move the left arm and right leg apart and together simultaneously while the other limbs remain stationary.

B. Given opportunities to imitate the arm movements in Figure 12.9, without verbal instructions, the student can:

_____ 1. Start and stop both arms simultaneously.

_____ 2. Correctly imitate six of nine arm movements.

C. Given opportunities to imitate the arm movements of the teacher who is holding a racquet, the student can correctly imitate, while holding a racquet, 6 out of 11 arm movements in Figure 12.9.

D. Given instructions to play the **Copy Cat Game,** student will watch teacher perform a sequence of stunts, wait 30 sec, and then perform the sequence in correct order.

_____ a. Three stunts (tiptoe walk, dog walk, sit-up)

_____ b. Four stunts

_____ c. Five stunts

VI. Major Task: Imitation of Sport Movements.

Other tasks: Visual discrimination, memory, and sequencing.

A. Given opportunities to imitate the movements of the teacher, without verbal instructions, the student with a tennis ball can:

_____ 1. Imitate the teacher's movements precisely, using the right arm when the teacher does.

_____ 2. Toss the ball into the air to exactly the same height as the teacher tosses the ball. Stand under a rope to help assess height.

_____ 3. Bounce the ball so it lands on the floor in precisely the same place as does the teacher's (in front of right foot, to the left side of left foot, and so on).

_____ 4. Bounce the ball so that it rises to the same height as the teacher's before it is caught.

_____ 5. Throw the ball so that it touches a wall target in a designated place.

VII. Major Task: Visual Tracking in Sports.

Other tasks: Visual discrimination, memory, and sequencing.

A. Told to track beanbags (easier than flying balls) thrown by teacher or partner, the student can:

_____ 1. Run or move the body so that the beanbag hits some part of him or her as it falls.

_____ 2. Run or move the body so that he or she catches 7 of 10 beanbags before they fall.

_____ 3. Run or move the body so that he or she strikes the beanbag with some kind of a racquet, paddle, or bat before it falls.

B. Given opportunities to track 30 ground balls being rolled toward him or her from a 15-ft distance, the student can

_____ 1. Stop 8 of 10 balls coming to the right.

_____ 2. Stop 8 of 10 balls coming to the midline.

_____ 3. Stop 8 of 10 balls coming to the left.

VIII. Major Task: Static Balances.

Other tasks: Visual or auditory.

A. Given opportunities to explore static balances, the student can:

_____ 1. Balance on one foot with eyes open for 10 sec.

_____ 2. Balance on tiptoes with eyes open for 10 sec.

_____ 3. Balance on a stick, a rock, or a log with one foot.

_____ 4. Perform a knee scale.

_____ 5. Balance while maintaining a squatting position.

_____ 6. Assume a tripod balance or head stand.

_____ 7. Repeat each of the above with eyes closed.

IX. Major Task: Dynamic Balances.

Other tasks: Visual or auditory.

A. Given opportunities to explore dynamic balances, the student can:

_____ 1. Walk a straight line in heel-to-toe fashion for six steps.

_____ 2. Jump backward five times and stop without losing balance.

_____ 3. Walk six steps on a balance beam while holding a 10-lb weight in one arm.

_____ 4. Alternate walking and squatting on a balance beam. Use a step-step-step-squat sequence and repeat three times.

_____ 5. Turn completely around three times while walking a beam.

_____ 6. Play a game that requires fast starts and stops (e.g., _Red Light, Green Light_) for 3 min without falling.

_____ 7. Maintain balance on a tiltboard or stabilometer for 20 sec.

X. Major Tasks: Lateral Dominance in Sports.

Other tasks: Visual or auditory.

A. Given opportunities to explore movement possibilities with beanbags, balls, ropes, bats, pencils, and other implements, the student can:

_____ 1. Demonstrate more skill with the preferred hand than the nonpreferred hand.

_____ 10 balls tossed from 10 ft
Record whether caught by R or L hand

_____ 5 kinds of striking apparatus
Record whether held by R or L hand

_____ 10 target throws, beanbags on floor
Record whether thrown with R or L hand

_____ 2. Exhibit a consistent preference for one hand over the other.

T a b l e 1 2 . 6   **Basic game and dance formations.**

Formation	Drills or Movement Exploration	Games	Dances
Single circle X X X X X X X X	Facing in Facing out Facing counterclockwise (CCW) Facing clockwise (CW) With "It" in the middle With "It" as part of the circle	Parachute activities Hot Potato Cat and Rat Duck, Duck, Goose Mickey Mouse (Spaceman) With "It" in middle, Circle Call-Ball, Catch the Cane	Farmer in the Dell Hokey-Pokey Loopty Loo Did You Ever See a Lassie? Go In and Out the Windows Captain Jinks Cshebogar

Double circle or two-deep
X
✢   X   ✢
✢   ✢
✢   ✢
✢   X   ✢
X
	Both facing in (also called
	   two-deep)
	Both facing out
	Facing partner
	Facing in, side by side
	Facing out, side by side
	Facing CCW, side by side
	Facing CW, side by side
	Boy rotates CCW, girl
	   remains stationary
	Girl rotates CCW, boy
	   remains stationary
	Grand right and left, girl
	   rotates CCW while boy
	   rotates CW
		Two-Deep
		Caboose Dodgeball
		Run for Your Supper
			How D'Ye Do, My Partner
			Seven Steps
			Hot Cross Buns
			Pop Goes the Weasel
			Skip to My Lou
			Bleking
			American Schottische
			Patticake Polka

Single line or row XXXXX X	Side by side Straight versus crooked Curved Staggered With teacher in front	Mother, May I? Red Light, Green Light Fire Engine (Beef Steak) Midnight	Technique classes in modern dance, ballet, tap dance
Double line or two-deep XXXXX XXXXX	Side by side Two-deep, all facing front Two-deep, all facing back Two-deep, facing partner Two-deep, back to back With net between lines	Brownies and Fairies Crows and Cranes Steal the Bacon Line Dodgeball Volleyball Newcomb	Crested Hen (three pupils) I See You (any number) Troika (three pupils)
Single file or column X X X	Each child behind the other Straight versus crooked "It" in front of file Everyone in file facing forward	Follow the leader Huntsman Relays Basketball shooting games	Marching to rhythm
Double file or longways set XX XX XX	Each child and a partner behind lead couple Girl traditionally on the right	Three-legged relay Partner relay Tandem relays	A Hunting We Will Go London Bridge Paw Paw Patch

Shuttle formation
drill and relays:
XXXXX   XXXXX
	Two files, facing one another	Throw object and shuttle to
		   end of own file *or* to end of
		   the other file
			Good use of space in
			   continuous practice of
			   locomotor skills

Target shooting
O
X X
X X
X X
	Two files, diagonally facing
	   same goal, like a basket or
	   wall target
		Throw and shuttle to end of
		   other file	

Children enjoy fast-paced drills to these cues, and various routines can be developed. For example:

Single circle 1–2–3–4–5–6–7–8–9–10
Facing in
Facing out
Facing in, walk forward
Facing out, jump to place
Facing in, clap-clap-clap-clap
Single line 1–2–3–4–5–6–7–8–9–10
Run to the wall
Single circle 1–2–3–4–5–6–7–8–9–10

Easy to Hard Formations

The scattered or random formation is the easiest because it permits persons to stand wherever they wish as long as they do not touch anyone else. This structure avoids discipline problems and teaches respect for each other's space. The verbal cue is "Find your own space. Good, now stretch in all directions to show that you cannot touch anyone. Great, you each have your own space."

To play games, however, structured formations must be learned. Circles and lines are easiest, and most primary school games use these. Files, shuttles, and target-shooting and square dance formations are progressively harder. When girls and boys are partners, the girls traditionally stand on the right.

Two-Deep: Beginning Partner Work

The "two-deep" verbal cue is especially useful and can be used with a circle or line. It comes from the game *Two-Deep*, in which a circle is formed by twosomes, standing one behind the other and facing in. On the outside of the circle is an "It" (person who is chasing) and a target person who is fleeing. To avoid being tagged, the target person can duck inside the circle and stand in front of any twosome. Since there can only be two people in two-deep, the one on the outside becomes the new runner who is chased. The game can also be played as three- or four-deep. It is fun, but the value lies in being able to use the cue "two-deep" whenever you want to structure a partner activity. This also serves as a lead-up to teaching the file or column formation.

Counterclockwise Direction Dominates

Telling children to move right and left often results in bedlam, particularly in activities in which partners are facing. Most experienced teachers therefore use clockwise (CW) and counterclockwise (CCW) terminology. This avoids right-left discrimination problems and also reinforces clock-reading skills.

The counterclockwise direction should be emphasized because this is the traditional direction for running laps around a field, performing partner folk dances, and moving around bases in softball. CCW rotation from station to station helps students to internalize and generalize this. Students typically need lots of practice and structure in moving from one place to another because this skill requires much perceptual-motor processing.

Novel Floor Patterns

Adhesive-paper shapes (circles, triangles, squares) on the floor reinforce form perception and permit lots of games that teach CW, CCW, right-left, and north-south-east-west directions. Maps of states and countries on the floor create similar opportunities. Some gymnasiums have the alphabet in cursive writing on the floor, with all letters 5 to 8 ft high. Various games entail running the letters of the alphabet with the same self-talk used as when learning to write at a desk (e.g., *up, down, up,* and *horizontal* for a cursive *b*).

Teaching Perception Through Volleyball

The lead-up games to volleyball, which are begun at about the third-grade level, can be used to reinforce right-left discriminations and to provide practice in visual pursuit and/or tracking. For most children, these-lead-up games represent their initial experience in tracking large objects that move through a predictable low-high-low arc and in catching and/or striking balls that *descend* rather than ascend (like a bouncing ball) or approach horizontally (like a thrown ball).

Newcomb, the best-known lead-up game to volleyball, substitutes throwing and catching various objects over a net for volleying. It is based on the assumption that tracking and catching a descending ball are prerequisites to tracking and striking (volleying). Certainly, catching and throwing are more familiar skills than volleying and serving. *Visual tracking* is an important contribution of volleyball at the elementary grade level. Children should not be rushed into mastery of the relatively difficult skills of volleying and serving. Nor should individual differences be ignored and all children forced to use the same skills in a game setting. When a volleyball approaches, each child should have options: to catch the ball and return it across the net with a throw or to volley it across. Likewise, the child whose turn it is to serve may choose to put the ball into play with a throw from behind the baseline or a serve from any place on the right-hand side of the court. Thus, in the early stages of learning the serve, some children may be only three giant steps behind the net, while others may have the coordination and arm and shoulder strength to achieve success from behind the baseline. *Balloons* can be substituted for volleyballs with the very young or very weak.

Team games teach spatial awareness through **position play.** Playing a particular position on the court and rotating from position to position reinforces the concepts of right, center, and left and of front and back. Starting with a small number of children on a team and gradually increasing the number of team members is educationally sound.

Rotation in volleyball depends upon the child's ability to make right-left discriminations; ability to a walk or move sideward, backward, and forward; and *comprehension of clockwise as a direction.* Teachers who care about transfer of learning and wish to save children with directional deficits embarrassment on the playground use the concept of rotation in the classroom. They have the child sitting in the *RB* (right back) chair stand, recite, and then allow everyone to rotate in a clockwise position so that a new child is *RB* and preparing to recite.

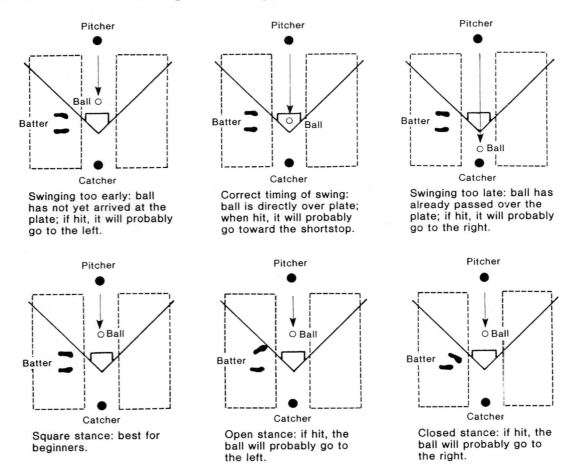

Swinging too early: ball has not yet arrived at the plate; if hit, it will probably go to the left.

Correct timing of swing: ball is directly over plate; when hit, it will probably go toward the shortstop.

Swinging too late: ball has already passed over the plate; if hit, it will probably go to the right.

Square stance: best for beginners.

Open stance: if hit, the ball will probably go to the left.

Closed stance: if hit, the ball will probably go to the right.

Teaching Perception Through Softball

A child's success or lack of success in softball, kickball, and baseball may be an excellent indicator of perceptual-motor efficiency, especially with respect to right-left discriminations, crossing the midline, and visual pursuits. No other physical activity offers richer opportunities for perceptual-motor training.

First, the understanding of the diamond and the positions of the players on the field requires the ability to make right-left discriminations. The concept of infield versus outfield offers a new dimension of spatial awareness. The expectation that each player *cover* a particular area of the field and *back up* other players is based upon spatial awareness. Bases are run in a *counterclockwise* direction. Pitches are described as inside, outside, high, low, and curved to the right or left. Decision making by a fielder as to where to throw the ball is based upon visual memory of sequences. Is there a player on third base? On first and third? On all the bases? Where should the ball be thrown first? The batter must make decisions with respect to directions also. If there is a runner on third base, where should the batter hit the ball? If there are runners on first and second base, where should the ball be hit? And so on, *ad infinitum.*

Batting depends not only on visual perception but also on knowledge of timing and stance (see Figure 12.13). A batter who misses the ball is told that she or he swung too early or too late. Batters are taught to purposely swing early or late to control the direction of the ball. Square, open, and closed stances also affect the direction of the ball and thus must be carefully taught. Knowledge gained in games with bats can be generalized to other sports. For instance, when the ball goes to the right instead of over the net in a tennis game, can the child reason why? When the golf ball goes to the left into a sand trap instead of straight down the fairway, does the student know what caused the directional deviation?

References

American Psychiatric Association. (1987). *Diagnostic and statistical manual of mental disorders* (3rd ed., rev.). Washington, DC: Author.

Ayres, A. J. (1965). Patterns of perceptual-motor dysfunction in children: A factor analytic study. *Perceptual and Motor Skills, 20,* 335–368.

Ayres, A. J. (1972). *Sensory integration and learning disorders.* Los Angeles: Western Psychological Services.

Ayres, A. J. (1989). *Sensory integration and praxis tests.* Los Angeles: Western Psychological Services.

Bard, C., Fleury, M., & Hay, L. (Eds). (1990). *Development of eye-hand coordination across the life span.* Columbia: University of South Carolina Press.

Bender, L. (1938). *Bender gestalt test.* New York: American Orthopsychiatric Association.

Biery, M. J., & Kauffman, N. (1989). The effects of therapeutic horseback riding on balance. *Adapted Physical Activity Quarterly, 6*(3), 221–229.

Bloom, B. (Ed.). (1956). *Taxonomy of educational objectives. Handbook I: Cognitive domain.* New York: David McKay.

Bouffard, M., & Wall, A. E. (1991). Knowledge, decision making, and performance in table tennis by educable mentally handicapped adolescents. *Adapted Physical Activity Quarterly, 8*(1), 57–90.

Bruininks, R. H. (1978). *Bruininks-Oseretsky Test of Motor Proficiency: Examiner's manual.* Circle Pines, MN: American Guidance Service.

Burton, A. W. (1990). Assessing the perceptual-motor interaction in developmentally disabled and nonhandicapped children. *Adapted Physical Activity Quarterly, 7,* 325–337.

Burton, A. W. (1997). *Movement skill assessment.* Champaign, IL: Human Kinetics.

Cratty, B. J. (1969a). Cratty six-category gross motor test. In B. J. Cratty, *Perceptual-motor behavior and educational processes* (pp. 220–241). Springfield, IL: Charles C Thomas.

Cratty, B. J. (1969b). *Motor activity and the education of retardates.* Philadelphia: Lea & Febiger.

Cratty, B. J. (1971). *Active learning.* Englewood Cliffs, NJ: Prentice Hall.

Croce, R. (1993). A review of the neural basis of apractic disorders with implications for remediation. *Adapted Physical Activity Quarterly, 10*(3), 173–215.

Davis, W. E. (1983). An ecological approach to perceptual-motor learning. In R. L. Eason, T. L. Smith, & F. Caron (Eds.), *Adapted physical activity: From theory to application.* Champaign, IL: Human Kinetics.

Davis, W. E., & Burton, A. W. (1991). Ecological task analysis: Translating movement behavior theory into practice. *Adapted Physical Activity Quarterly, 8,* 154–177.

Gallagher, J., & Thomas, J. (1984). Rehearsal strategy effects on developmental differences for recall of a movement series. *Research Quarterly for Exercise and Sport, 55*(2), 123–128.

Gibson, E. J. (1969). *Principles of perceptual learning and development.* Englewood Cliffs, NJ: Prentice Hall.

Gibson, E. J. (1987). What does infant perception tell us about theories of perception? *Journal of Experimental Psychology: Human Perception and Performance, 13,* 515–523.

Gibson, J. J. (1966). *The senses considered as perceptual systems.* Boston: Houghton Mifflin.

Gibson, J. J. (1979). *The ecological approach to visual perception.* Boston: Houghton, Mifflin.

Hallahan, D., & Cruickshank, W. (1973). *Psychoeducational foundations of learning disabilities.* Englewood Cliffs, NJ: Prentice Hall.

Henderson, S. E. (1994). Editorial [on developmental coordination disorder]. *Adapted Physical Activity Quarterly, 11*(2), 111–114.

Henderson, S. E., & Sugden, D. A. (1992). *Movement assessment battery (ABC) for children.* London: Psychological Corporation.

Hoare, D. (1994). Subtypes of developmental coordination disorder. *Adapted Physical Activity Quarterly, 11*(2), 158–169.

Hoover, J. H., & Horgan, J. S. (1990). Short-term memory for motor skills in mentally retarded persons: Training and research issues. In G. Reid (Ed.), *Problems in movement control* (pp. 217–239). Amsterdam: North-Holland.

Kavale, K., & Mattson, P. D. (1983). One jumped off the balance beam: Meta-analysis of perceptual-motor training. *Journal of Learning Disabilities, 16,* 165–173.

Kephart, N. C. (1971). *The slow learner in the classroom* (2nd ed.). Columbus, OH: Charles E. Merrill.

Knapczyk, D., & Liemohn, W. (1976). A factor study of Cratty's body perception test. *Research Quarterly, 47,* 678–682.

Kourtessis, T., & Reid, G. (1997). Knowledge and skill of ball catching in children with cerebral palsy and other physical disabilities. *Adapted Physical Activity Quarterly, 14.*

Kowalski, E., & Sherrill, C. (1992). Motor sequencing of learning disabled boys: Modeling and verbal rehearsal strategies. *Adapted Physical Activity Quarterly, 9*(3), 261–272.

Krupski, A. (1987). Attention: The verbal phantom strikes again in response to Samuels. *Exceptional Children, 54*(1), 62–65.

Piaget, J. (1952). *The origins of intelligence in children.* New York: International Universities Press.

Pick, A. D. (1979). *Perception and its development: A tribute to Eleanor J. Gibson.* Hillsdale, NJ: Lawrence Erlbaum.

Reid, G. (1980). The effects of memory strategy instruction in the short-term memory of the mentally retarded. *Journal of Motor Behavior, 12,* 221–227.

Riggen, K. J., Ulrich, D. A., & Ozmun, J. C. (1990). Reliability and concurrent validity of the Test of Motor Impairment–Henderson Revision. *Adapted Physical Activity Quarterly, 7,* 249–258.

Roach, E., & Kephart, N. (1966). *The Purdue Perceptual-Motor Survey.* Columbus, OH: Charles E. Merrill.

Rose, M., Cundick, B., & Higbee, K. (1983). Verbal rehearsal and verbal imagery: Mnemonic aids for learning disabled children. *Journal of Learning Disabilities, 16*(6), 352–354.

Samuels, S. J. (1987). Why is it difficult to characterize the underlying cognitive deficits in special education populations? *Exceptional Children, 54,* 60–62.

Shumway-Cook, A. (1989). Equilibrium defects in children. In M. H. Woollacott & A. Shumway-Cook (Eds.), *Development of posture and gait across the life span* (pp. 230–252). Columbia: University of South Carolina Press.

Stott, D. H., Moyes, F. A., & Hendersen, S. E. (1972). *The Test of Motor Impairment.* San Antonio: Psychological Corporation.

Sugden, D. A., & Keogh, J. F. (1990). *Problems in movement skill development.* Columbia: University of South Carolina Press.

Surburg, P. R. (1989). Application of imagery techniques to special populations. *Adapted Physical Activity Quarterly, 6*(4), 328–337.

Wall, A. E. (1990). Skill acquisition research with persons with developmental disabilities: Research design considerations. In G. Reid (Ed.), *Problems in movement control* (pp. 31–63). Amsterdam: North-Holland.

Weiss, M., & Klint, K. (1987). "Show and tell" in the gymnasium: An investigation of developmental differences in modeling and verbal rehearsal of motor skills. *Research Quarterly for Exercise and Sport, 58*(2), 234–241.

Williams, H. (1983). *Perceptual and motor development.* Englewood Cliffs, NJ: Prentice Hall.

Woollacott, M. H., Shumway-Cook, A., & Williams, H. G. (1989). The development of posture and balance control in children. In M. H. Woollacott & A. Shumway-Cook (Eds.), *Development of posture and gait across the life span* (pp. 77–96). Columbia: University of South Carolina Press.

CHAPTER

13

Fitness and Healthy Lifestyle

FIGURE 13.1   Jim Mastro, internationally known athlete who is blind, serves as role model for university students. Jim can do over 3,000 push-ups in a row.

After you have studied this chapter, you should be able to do the following:

1. Discuss trends and issues in relation to such concepts as physical fitness, physical activity, rehabilitation, exercise, health, and lifestyle.

2. Contrast the current American College of Sports Medicine (ACSM) recommendations for exercise prescription with those of other organizations. Discuss applications and implications for individuals with disabilities.

3. Identify five components of health-related fitness, discuss assessment of each for individuals with average and health-impaired fitness status, and demonstrate ability to administer selected fitness test items.

4. Identify and explain the five components of an exercise prescription.

5. Discuss basic exercise prescription and training concepts such as ratings of perceived exertion (RPE), metabolic equivalents (METS), the Karvonen formula, and proprioceptive neuromuscular facilitation (PNF).

6. Explain adaptations and exercise contraindications that are especially important for (a) severe developmental disabilities, (b) spinal paralysis, (c) other health impairments, (d) limited mental function, and (e) limited sensory function. Relate this to exercise prescription guidelines and fitness components.

7. Discuss weather, temperature, space, and equipment in assessment and programming for fitness.

8. Select and describe a disability, and develop several lesson plans that focus on fitness. What five parts should a fitness lesson include?

9. Critique the 16 principles recommended to guide fitness teaching. Which are most and least important? Discuss applications and cite anecdotes from your experience.

10. Explain and discuss exercise conditioning methods: (a) interval, (b) circuits, (c) continuous, and (d) combinations.

Fitness and healthy lifestyle is a major goal in adapted physical activity. This chapter focuses on individuals who lack the knowledge, self-determination, self-confidence, and self-esteem to achieve personal fitness goals. Such individuals need role models, support groups, and excellent teachers and counselors.

Many individuals with disabilities can serve as role models. For instance, Jim Mastro, a Paralympic judo and field athlete who is blind, can perform over 3,000 push-ups in a row (see Figure 13.1). Jean Driscoll, born with spina bifida, and many individuals in wheelchairs because of spinal cord injuries routinely compete in marathons (26.2 miles). Tom Becke and Jaronnie Smith are among the many Paralympians with cerebral palsy (CP) who excel at power lifting as a result of many years of disciplined weight training. Many athletes in both the Paralympics and the Olympics cope with chronic asthma. Similarly, athletes with mental disabilities in international competition demonstrate the high levels of fitness associated with disciplined training.

In contrast, many individuals with and without disabilities lack the ability to perform routine daily activity with vigor and have enough energy left over to enjoy leisure and meet emergency demands. Such individuals tend to be overweight and to have sedentary lifestyles. The most frequently used criteria for identifying people with severe fitness problems are the following:

1. If ambulatory, inability to walk a mile (1,609.34 meters) in 12 minutes.

2. If nonambulatory, inability to propel a manual wheelchair ¾ mile (1,207 meters) in 12 minutes.

Individuals who cannot meet these criteria are the focus of this chapter, although information is provided also for helping others to meet personal fitness goals.

Recent Changes in the Knowledge Base

The knowledge base related to helping individuals achieve personal fitness goals undergoes constant revision. Among the changes incorporated into this chapter are the following:

1. The Prudential FITNESSGRAM has replaced the AAHPERD Health-Related Fitness Test as the recommended assessment tool for school-age children and youth (Cooper Institute for Aerobics Research, 1994b; Seaman, 1995). The FITNESSGRAM requires testing in three areas: (a) aerobic capacity, (b) body composition, and (c) muscle strength, endurance, and flexibility. Some of the test items are the same as on the AAHPERD test. A major change is the substitution of curl-ups for sit-ups to assess abdominal strength.

2. The American College of Sports Medicine (ACSM) has modified several training standards related to exercise prescription in the fifth edition (1995) of *ACSM's Guidelines for Exercise Testing and Prescription*. This book, traditionally considered the most authoritative reference in the fitness area, stresses high levels of exercise intensity as a protection against heart disease and other conditions that can shorten life or decrease general health and well-being. Individuals with low fitness often require many weeks to acquire the exercise capacity to perform at ACSM recommended levels: *exercise 3 to 5 times a week at 60 to 90% of maximal heart rate or 50 to 85% of VO₂max, performing continuous aerobic activity for 20 to 60 min each session.*

3. Fitness authorities have agreed on a minimal physical activity standard for health benefits: *Every adult should accumulate 30 min or more of moderate-intensity physical activity on most, preferably all, days of the week* (Pate et al., 1995). **Moderate intensity** is defined as 3 to 6 METS (work metabolic rate/resting metabolic rate),

which is equivalent to the effort expended in walking a mile in 15 to 20 min. For most individuals, meeting this standard calls for walking 2 miles a day at a brisk pace or engaging in equivalent activity. In general, there is agreement that children should also meet this minimal standard.

4. The American Heart Association has issued a minimal physical activity standard that pertains to calories expended during activity: *Activity, for minimal conditioning and health benefits, should consume a minimum total of 700 calories a week spread over three or four sessions a week. For maximal health benefits, activity should consume 2,000 calories a week* (Fletcher et al., 1995). Use of 2,000 calories is the equivalent of walking 20 miles a week.

5. Several new books (e.g., Lockette & Keyes, 1994; Miller, 1995; Rimmer, 1994; Seaman, 1995) and research articles (see the *Adapted Physical Activity Quarterly*) for the first time are providing specific, easy-to-understand information about conditioning and training people with disabilities.

6. Project TARGET, a national research initiative to create criterion-based fitness standards for school-age individuals with disabilities (Winnick, 1995) is supplementing the knowledge base established by Project UNIQUE, a national research study that provided norm-based fitness standards for individuals with physical and sensory impairments (Winnick & Short, 1985).

7. The National Consortium for Physical Education and Recreation for Individuals with Disabilities (NCPERID, 1995) has published specific standards to guide the mastery of exercise science knowledge related to adapted physical activity and disability sport. These standards are high and might necessitate the addition of courses specifically on fitness and disability to teacher-training curricula. Most of the NCPERID standards are addressed in this chapter and in chapters on specific individual differences in Part 3 of this book. Information on metabolic, cardiac, and respiratory disorders is mostly in Chapter 19, and information on spinal cord injuries, progressive neuromuscular conditions, and cerebral palsy is in Chapters 23, 24, and 25, respectively.

8. The year 1996 will be remembered for the publication of *The Surgeon General's Report on Physical Activity and Health* (U.S. Department of Health and Human Services, 1996), which marked the strongest support ever given to the role of physical activity in the maintenance of health by the federal government. This report emphasized that 30 min or more of daily moderate-intensity physical activity is essential to health. Furthermore, the report stated that enough research has been accumulated to confirm that physical activity reduces the risk of death in general and in coronary heart disease, hypertension, colon cancer, and diabetes in particular.

Definitions of Fitness, Activity, and Related Terms

Following are definitions that appear in the recent literature. **Physical fitness** is "a set of attributes that people have or achieve that relates to the ability to perform physical activity" (Pate et al., 1995, p. 402). According to Winnick (1995), "AAHPERD describes physical fitness as a physical state of well-being that allows people to perform daily activities with vigor, reduce their risk of health problems related to lack of exercise, and establish a fitness base for participation in a variety of physical activities" (p. 21). The trend is toward conceptualizing physical fitness as a personalized profile that reflects individual beliefs, attitudes, and practices in relation to activity and exercise.

Physical activity is "any bodily activity produced by skeletal muscles that results in energy expenditure" (Pate et al., 1995, p. 402). The amount of energy expenditure, designated in METS or calories, is dependent upon body mass and metabolic efficiency. There appears to be a trend toward prescribing general activity rather than specific exercises.

Exercise is "a subset of physical activity defined as planned, structured, and repetitive bodily movement done to improve or maintain one or more components of physical fitness" (Pate et al., 1995, p. 402). The term *exercise* is used more carefully than in the past. Exercise must be planned, whereas activity may be spontaneous and occur in conjunction with either work or play.

Functional ability or capacity typically is a term used to explain limitations. When an individual lacks the functional capacity to sustain activity at a prescribed level of intensity, the goal is generally *to improve exercise capacity tolerance* rather than to improve fitness.

Health, according to the World Health Organization (WHO, 1947), is a state of complete physical, mental, and social well-being and not merely absence of disease or infirmity. This definition is *holistic,* meaning that it focuses on the whole person. The trend in the 1990s is toward holistic testing and programming. That is one reason this textbook includes a strong chapter on self-concept, motivation, and well-being (Chapter 8). Self-concept and physical fitness testing and programming should be coordinated (see Figure 13.2).

Wellness is the integration of all parts of health (physical, mental, social, emotional, and spiritual) that results in a healthy lifestyle and feeling good about oneself. Central to wellness is the ability to assess one's personal resources and to set realistic goals with specific time lines for their achievement.

Rehabilitation Versus Fitness Programming

Rehabilitation is "the restoration and/or maintenance of physical function, which allows an individual to perform activities of daily living (ADL) without incurring high levels of stress or fatigue" (Rimmer, 1994, p. 2). Rehabilitation typically occurs in hospitals and centers that provide services for persons temporarily disabled by surgery, disease, or sedentary lifestyle or permanently disabled by trauma, disease, disuse, or other factors. Therefore, rehabilitation follows a medical model. The cost of rehabilitation is typically reimbursed by insurance.

In contrast, fitness testing and training is conducted in many settings and follows many models (e.g., educational, sport, weight loss). Fitness training is associated with goals over and beyond activities of daily living (ADL). These goals are highly personal and might focus on fitness components, time spent in physical activity, or healthy, active lifestyle.

FIGURE 13.2   Personalized attention should focus equally on self-esteem and fitness goals.

Of particular concern at all ages is prevention of *hypokinetic conditions* like obesity, heart disease, high blood pressure low back pain, adult-onset diabetes, stress, and bone degeneration (osteoporosis). **Hypokinetic** means insufficient movement or exercise. Although often not manifested until middle age, hypokinetic disease begins in childhood and is aggravated by bed rest and/or activity restrictions imposed by injury, illness, or environmental barriers.

Lifestyle Problems of Americans

Lifestyle problems include everything that interferes with health and negatively affects lifespan. Numerous factors such as diet, stress, smoking, drug abuse, and physical inactivity are risk factors. This chapter, however, focuses on the physical inactivity that characterizes modern life. Recent research describes the physical activity levels of U.S. adults as follows (Pate et al., 1995):

1. Only 22% are active at the level recommended for health benefits (i.e., light to moderate activity at least 30 min every day).
2. About 54% are somewhat active but fail to meet minimum standards.
3. About 24% are completely sedentary.

Women are less likely to meet activity standards than men, and ethnic minority populations are less active than white Americans.

A recent survey of 11,631 high school students in the United States indicated that only 50% of the males and 25% of the females reported being vigorously active three or more times a week (Heath, Pratt, Warren, & Kann, 1995). *Vigorously active* was defined as engaging in 20 min or more of activity "that made you breathe heavily and made your heart beat fast." At all ages, white students reported more vigorous activities than black and Hispanic students. Approximately 51% of males and 35% of females reported participation in one or more varsity sports during the 12 months preceding the survey.

Less than half of all students in Grades 9 to 12 reported that they were enrolled in physical education classes. The number enrolled declined steadily by grade: 34% of ninth-graders and 11% of twelfth-graders. Still more disconcerting was the fact that almost one fourth of the students in physical education did not exercise 20 min or more during any of their classes. Female students were significantly more likely than males not to exercise during physical education classes.

About half of those who set exercise goals fail to follow through (Dishman, 1994). Even in supervised programs established for persons at medical risk, about 50% drop out within 6 months to a year. The best dropout predictors for adults are body weight, percent body fat, and self-motivation. For children and youth, the best predictors are fun, enjoyment, and the desire to please significant others. In general, exercise dropouts tend to be those who need exercise the most. *An important goal of adapted physical activity is to persuade persons with low fitness that regular exercise increases the richness of life and prevents health problems.*

Lifestyle Concerns Pertaining to Disability

Persons with disabilities and health impairments obviously have to work harder at fitness than able-bodied (AB) peers. Because this process often takes far longer than average and demands considerable perseverance, the benefits of fitness training must be clear.

Fitness is a special concern in adapted physical activity for many reasons:

1. Poor body alignment and inefficient movement patterns increase energy expenditure beyond normal ranges and result in fatigue that reduces job efficiency, leisure-time activities, and overall quality of life (Shephard, 1990).
2. Mechanical efficiency, and thus energy level, is negatively affected by (a) reduced or altered sensory input, as in blindness, deafness, and perceptual deficits (Kobberling, Jankowski, & Leger, 1989); (b) spasticity and abnormal reflex activity (Skrotsky, 1983); (c) use of crutches and prostheses (Fisher & Gullickson, 1978); and (d) loss of functional muscle mass, as in paresis/paralysis (Wells & Hooker, 1990). These and other problems place heavy burdens on the cardiorespiratory and neuromuscular systems.
3. Coping with architectural, attitudinal, and aspirational barriers requires extra energy. Architectural barriers alone increase the energy expenditure of persons with physical disabilities 15-fold over that of able-bodied peers (Miller, Merritt, Merkel, & Westbrook, 1984).
4. Persons with cognitive and/or language disabilities are more likely to be employed in manual labor than desk jobs and thus need high levels of fitness. Fitness training promotes on-the-job success for persons with mental retardation (Beasley, 1982).
5. Persons with disabilities need the best possible physiques and exemplary fitness to overcome discrimination and obtain social acceptance. Physical appearance is an important factor in finding employment.

Table 13.1 Responses of persons with disabilities concerning active lifestyles.

Reasons for Being Active		Changes That Would Encourage More Activity	
To feel better	59%	More leisure time	29%
To improve flexibility	43	Better or closer facilities	22
To control weight	39	People with whom to participate	22
To relax, reduce stress	38	Common interest of family	19
For pleasure and fun	37	Less expensive facilities	18
Doctor's advice	35	Common interest of friends	15
For companionship	26	Organized fitness classes	11
Fitness leader's advice	21	A fitness test and program	11
To challenge abilities	18	Information on benefits	7
To learn new things	17		

From *Physical Activity Among Activity-Limited and Disabled Adults in Canada* by permission of the Canadian Fitness and Lifestyle Research Institute, Ontario, Canada.
Note: Forty-seven percent responded that nothing would make them increase their activity. Percentages do not add up to 100% because persons could check any number of items.

6. Chronic depression and other mental health problems that plague some persons with disabilities can be ameliorated by fitness programs (ACSM, 1995). Persons with disabilities who are active typically rate their emotional well-being and total health higher than do sedentary persons (Canada Fitness Survey, 1986).

7. Many persons with disabilities have never been socialized into sport and/or physically active lifestyles and thus have weight problems and other health concerns associated with sedentary living.

8. Clumsy persons whose body image and self-concept have been negatively affected by balance-coordination-timing problems often find success in walking, jogging, cycling, swimming, and weight lifting. This success can be the springboard for better attitudes toward self.

9. An *activity deficit hypothesis* has been asserted and supported (Bouffard, Watkinson, Thompson, Dunn, & Romanow, 1996). Children with movement difficulties are vigorously active less often than their peers, engage in fewer social interactions, and play less on playground equipment. Movement difficulties are linked directly with physical inactivity.

10. Obesity is statistically associated with movement problems in children (Marshall & Bouffard, 1994), but problems can be lessened by quality physical education instruction.

Canada in the 1980s surveyed both its able-bodied and disabled populations (Canada Fitness Survey, 1986), applying a holistic model to determine patterns of physical activity and related beliefs and attitudes (see Table 13.1). Responses of persons with disabilities were similar to those of able-bodied Canadians except that the able-bodied ranked "for pleasure and fun" as the second most important reason. Perhaps persons with disabilities are not socialized early in life to perceive physical activity as fun; often, their first regular exercise is physical therapy. Clearly, more emphasis needs to be placed on enjoyment. Note in Table 13.1 that 47% indicated that nothing would make them exercise more. Counseling is needed on time management, assertiveness in locating facilities and friends, and ways to increase family support and involvement.

Components of Health-Related Fitness

Fitness, like self-concept, is multidimensional. Individuals can be high in some components of fitness and low in others. According to the American College of Sports Medicine (ACSM, 1995, p. 50), "**Health-related physical fitness** is typically defined as including cardiorespiratory endurance, body composition, muscular strength and endurance, and flexibility." This four-component definition guides most fitness testing and programming. A fifth component, often forgotten, is the composite of beliefs, attitudes, and intentions that give persons the self-determination, self-confidence, and self-esteem to achieve and maintain fitness goals.

The Cooper Institute for Aerobics Research (CIAR) in Dallas was designated in December 1993 as the authority in fitness testing for school-age youth. The CIAR was founded in the 1960s by Dr. Kenneth H. Cooper, a physician and a major in the U.S. Air Force Medical Corps (Cooper, 1968). Cooper popularized **aerobic training,** a progressive physical conditioning program that uses continuous, long-duration, big-muscle exercise to develop cardiorespiratory endurance and related health benefits. The CIAR uses slightly different terminology than the ACSM in specifying three major components of physical fitness: (a) aerobic capacity, (b) body composition, and (c) muscle strength, endurance, and flexibility.

An easy way to define fitness components is by the tests used to measure them and the associated health-related standards, which indicate the levels of performance necessary to achieve health benefits. Because the CIAR-recommended fitness test is the Prudential FITNESSGRAM, the items for this test appear in Figure 13.3. More-detailed explanations of the fitness components appear later in this chapter.

The Prudential FITNESSGRAM

Directions for administering the FITNESSGRAM tests appear in many sources (e.g., Cooper Institute for Aerobics Research, 1994b; Seaman, 1995). A detailed explanation of the validity and reliability of the tests and other information can be found in the *Technical Reference Manual* (Cooper Institute for Aerobics Research, 1994a). This test is recommended for all school-age individuals with the functional capacity to perform the test items; this includes most students with disabilities. To

The Pacer

Age	Girls		Boys	
5				
6				
7	*Participate in run. Lap count standards not recommended.*			
8				
9				
	Good	Better	Good	Better
10	7	35	17	55
11	9	37	23	61
12	13	40	29	68
13	15	42	35	74
14	18	44	41	80
15	23	50	46	85
16	28	56	52	90
17	34	61	57	94
17+	34	61	57	94

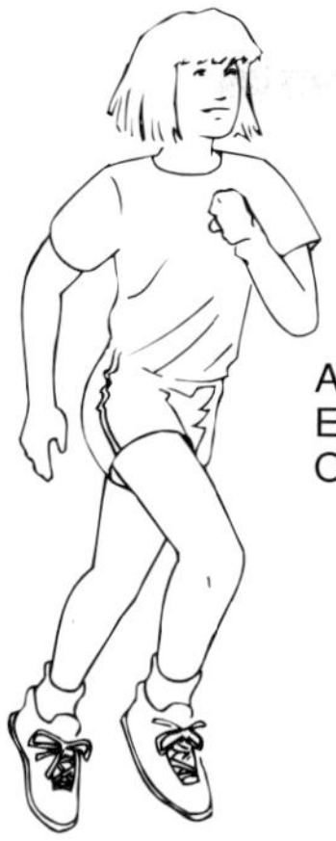

Alternate Exercise: One Mile-Walk/Run

MEASURES AEROBIC CAPACITY

Skinfold Tests With Calipers

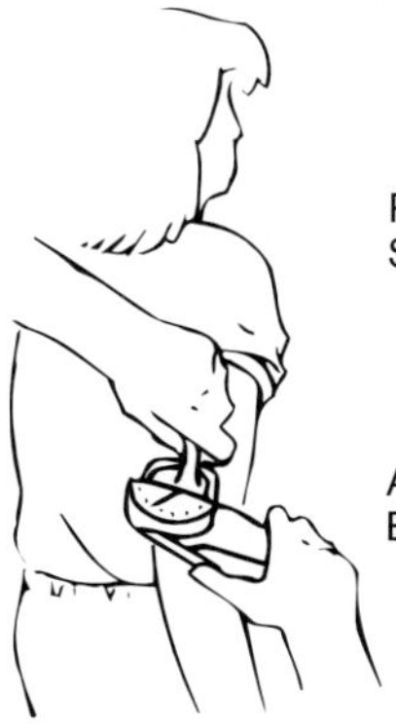

Age	Girls Body Mass Index		Boys Body Mass Index	
	Good	Better	Good	Better
5	21	16.2	20	14.7
6	21	16.2	20	14.7
7	22	16.2	20	14.9
8	22	16.2	20	15.1
9	23	16.2	20	15.2
10	23.5	16.6	21	15.3
11	24	16.9	21	15.8
12	24.5	16.9	22	16.0
13	24.5	17.5	23	16.6
14	25	17.5	24.5	17.5
15	25	17.5	25	18.1
16	25	17.5	26.5	18.5
17	26	17.5	27	18.8
17+	27.3	18.0	27.8	19.0

Percent Fat
Sum of
    triceps and
    calf skinfolds

Alternate:
Body Mass Index
$$\frac{\text{Body weight (kg)}}{\text{Height}^2 \text{ (m}^2)}$$

MEASURES BODY COMPOSITION
Girls, all ages, 32% to 17% body fat
Boys, all ages, 25% to 10% body fat

enable individualization, alternative items are specified for students who cannot perform the prescribed six tests. Additionally, a chapter on modification for special populations is included in the test manual.

The FITNESSGRAM is a criterion-referenced test, in that standards, called healthy fitness zones (HFZs), are established to indicate goals that represent good and better protection against health and injury risks in activities of daily living. The lower HFZ level corresponds closely to the 20th percentile of the population, and the upper HFZ level is comparable to the 60th percentile (Winnick, 1995). These levels might seem low, but research indicates that they are adequate for the average person to be considered healthy.

The FITNESSGRAM, now recommended, and the AAHPERD health-related fitness tests, used from 1980 through 1993, have some similarities. Both tests include the one-mile walk/run, the summed triceps and calf skinfold measures, and the sit-and-reach test. The body position for performing the sit-and-reach test is different, however. The standards are different also, indicating different philosophies about the level of performance necessary for health protection.

The FITNESSGRAM is different from the AAHPERD tests in the following ways: (a) the use of curl-ups instead of bent-knee sit-ups; (b) the addition of push-ups and alternative tests to measure upper body strength; (c) the addition of the trunk lift to measure trunk extensor strength and flexibility; (d) the addition of a PACER test as an alternative to the walk/run; and (e) the emphasis on the use of audiotaped cadences. Following is an explanation of some unique aspects of the FITNESSGRAM.

The PACER

The PACER (Progressive Aerobic Cardiovascular Endurance Run), a test that starts easy and gets progressively harder, requires running back and forth across a 20-m distance (20 yd, 32 inches) at a pace specified by an audiotape that gets faster each minute. The test requires 21 min of running, with the pace increasing by one-half second at the end of each minute. Beeps on the audiotape tell the runners when to reverse directions; the goal is to reach the opposite side before the beep

FIGURE 13.3 Continued.

Curl-Up Test

Age	Girls		Boys	
	Good	Better	Good	Better
5	2	10	2	10
6	2	10	2	10
7	4	14	4	14
8	6	20	6	20
9	9	22	9	24
10	12	26	12	24
11	15	29	15	28
12	18	32	18	36
13	18	32	21	40
14	18	32	24	45
15	18	35	24	47
16	18	35	24	47
17	18	35	24	47
17+	18	35	24	47

3 or 4¹⁄₂ inch
measuring strip

MEASURES ABDOMINAL STRENGTH
Complete 75 or as many as
    possible at specified pace.

Start with arms straight, palms down
Knees bent at 140° angle
Feet flat on floor

Curl up until fingers slide to end of
    measuring strip (3 inches for ages
    5–9; 4¹⁄₂ inches for ages 10–17+)
Keep heels in contact with mat

Push-Up

Age	Girls		Boys	
	Good	Better	Good	Better
5	3	8	3	8
6	3	8	3	8
7	4	10	4	10
8	5	13	5	13
9	6	15	6	15
10	7	15	7	20
11	7	15	8	20
12	7	15	10	20
13	7	15	12	25
14	7	15	14	30
15	7	15	16	35
16	7	15	18	35
17	7	15	18	35
17+	7	15	18	35

Alternate Exercises:
Pull-Up
Flexed Arm Hang
Modified Pull-Up

MEASURES UPPER BODY STRENGTH
Complete as many as possible at
    specified pace.
Start with elbows bent at 90°
    angle, upper arms parallel
    to floor
Push up until arms are straight
Keep legs and back straight

One Trunk Lift (Two trials)

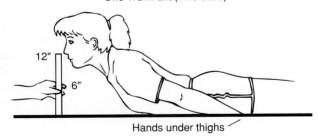

MEASURES TRUNK AND BACK STRENGTH AND FLEXIBILITY
No gender differences
Ages 5–9, 6 to 12 inches
Ages 10–17+, 9 to 12 inches

One Back-Saver Sit-and-Reach on Left and Right Sides

Alternate Exercise:
Shoulder Stretch

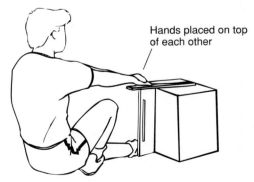

Hands placed on top
of each other

MEASURES FLEXIBILITY
Girls, ages 5–10, 9 inches
        ages 11–14, 10 inches
        ages 15–17+, 12 inches
Boys, all ages, 8 inches

sounds. A student who arrives early at a line must wait for the beep to sound before starting to run again. The beginning speeds are very slow (9 sec for 20 m) in order to build in success. If, as the pace gets faster, students cannot reach the line by the time the beep sounds, they are given two more beeps to attempt to regain the pace before being withdrawn from the test. The score is the number of laps completed by the student. The PACER is particularly recommended for Grades 1 to 3 and for individuals with mental retardation.

The Use of Audiotape With Curl-ups and Push-ups

The PACER audiotape, which can be purchased through CIAR, is also used with curl-ups and push-ups. For curl-ups, the cadence is about 20 curl-ups per minute (one curl every 3 sec). Students must continue curls without pausing until they can no longer adhere to the pace or they have completed the test maximum of 75 curl-ups. For push-ups, the correct cadence is 20 push-ups per minute (one every 3 sec). The push-up test is ended if the student cannot maintain the correct cadence, stops to rest, or fails to use correct technique despite corrections; three corrections are allowed.

Alternative Tests for Upper Body Strength

Tests recommended as alternatives to the push-up are the pull-up, the flexed-arm hang, and the modified pull-up. These are all performed with the overarm grasp (palms facing away from the body). The starting position for both the pull-up and the flexed-arm hang is hanging from a bar with arms extended. In the pull-up, the chin must be above the bar on the up position. Most persons with low strength, however, will need to do the modified pull-up test, which starts by lying on the back with the shoulders directly under a bar that is set about 1 or 2 inches above normal reach. An elastic band is placed 7 or 8 inches below and parallel to the bar, and the goal is to pull up until the chin is above this elastic band.

Other Fitness Tests

Many other fitness tests are available, of course. Each country has its own test (Government of Canada, 1987), norms, and minimal standards. The President's Council on Physical Fitness and Sports (1987) includes five items: 1-mi run/walk, curl-ups, V-sit reach, shuttle run, and pull-ups. The 30-ft shuttle run is used to evaluate leg strength/endurance/power/ agility, and skinfold measures are not taken. The President's Council supports the use of norms and offers awards to individuals who score at the 85th percentile on all five of its items. The YMCA has its own test battery (one of the few with norms for adults) and is used worldwide (Golding, Myers, & Sinning, 1989). In addition to these batteries, many tests have been validated as measures of a single fitness component. These are fully described in tests and measurements texts. In selecting tests, pay attention to the date that the test was first published and to dates of follow-up validity and reliability research.

Personalized Fitness Testing

Some individuals with disabilities, for various reasons, cannot perform the FITNESSGRAM items and other tests traditionally used to measure fitness. The trend toward personalized fitness testing requires that common sense be used in deter-mining what individuals can do with their bodies. For individuals who are overweight, the goal of reducing body fat through combined diet and exercise should take precedence over other goals. Work often focuses on increasing exercise capacity tolerance and convincing persons to try a new lifestyle. Start fitness testing with a personal interview to determine activity interests and lifestyle; then cooperatively plan goals and select appropriate tests.

Little research exists to indicate health-related standards that individuals with disabilities should reach to attain protection from health and injury risks. Joseph Winnick of the State University of New York (SUNY) at Brockport is considered the father of the current personalized approach to fitness testing for individuals with disabilities. Winnick's Project TARGET, now in progress, aims to provide information about modified tests, test items, and standards for adolescents with disabilities.

The knowledge base concerning fitness of individuals with disabilities is changing so fast that professionals need to form partnerships with exercise scientists with special expertise in disability. Many fitness tests and training approaches are outdated.

School Fitness Testing: History, Issues, Trends

Knowledge of early fitness tests helps teachers to evaluate current tests. Much controversy has always surrounded the school fitness movement. Each decade, the issue of which tests are best to use has been addressed and temporarily resolved. Likewise, the issue of how high to set fitness standards is argued repeatedly. Other issues are how much time to give fitness testing and training, and whether fitness should be given precedence over sports and motor skills training. A current trend is away from maximum fitness, with everyone urged to make the highest score possible, toward performance within healthy fitness zones (HFZs) believed to provide adequate protection against health and fitness risks. Another trend is to personalize fitness goals and tests, with individuals who aspire to become or remain elite athletes setting higher goals than individuals who prefer recreational activity.

Types of Fitness: Physical and Motor

Two types of fitness historically have been recognized: (a) physical and (b) motor. **Physical fitness** is health-related and includes several components: cardiorespiratory endurance, body composition, muscular strength and endurance, and flexibility. **Motor fitness** is skill-related and includes agility, balance, coordination, speed, power, and reaction time. Since 1980, regular physical educators have given little attention to motor fitness. In adapted physical education, however, motor fitness components are helpful in diagnosing problem areas. *In this text, motor fitness is associated with perceptual-motor function* (see Chapters 10 and 12). The Individuals with Disabilities Education Act includes the term *physical and motor fitness* in its definition of physical education.

The 1950s: Early Beginnings

Fitness as a physical education goal gained recognition in the 1950s, when Dwight Eisenhower was president and the world was impressed by Russia's shooting of Sputnik into space. The 1950s is the decade of the Kraus-Weber research findings (Kraus & Hirschland, 1954), the founding of the American College of Sports Medicine (ACSM), the establishment of the President's Council on Youth and Fitness (now called the President's Council on Physical Fitness and Sports), and the creation of the first AAHPER Youth Physical Fitness Test.

Kraus-Weber Tests, 1950s

The first fitness test to gain widespread recognition was the six-item Kraus-Weber battery, which included straight- and bent-knee sit-ups, double-leg lift-and-hold from supine and prone, trunk lift from prone, and toe touch from stand. The Kraus-Weber research indicated that American children were less fit than those in several European countries. This finding provided impetus for fitness testing and training in the schools.

First AAHPER Fitness Test, 1950s

The AAHPER fitness test battery originally included seven items, four to measure *motor fitness* (standing broad jump, 50-yd dash, 30-ft shuttle run, and overarm throw for distance) and three to measure *physical fitness* (a distance run, bent-knee sit-ups, and pull-ups or flexed arm hang). The overarm throw was eliminated in the first revision because improper warm-up was causing injuries. The distance run also was subject to much debate. Some authorities accepted the 600-yd walk-run as a measure of cardiorespiratory function, but most supported the 9- or 12-min runs.

Rarick's Contributions on Mental Retardation

G. Lawrence Rarick of the University of California at Berkeley was the first to conduct research on issues related to fitness testing of school-age persons with mental retardation. Rarick's finding that students with MR performed 2 to 4 years behind peers was a major factor in the enactment of federal laws pertaining to physical education and recreation for this population. His work began in the 1950s (Francis & Rarick, 1959) and continued until his retirement in the late 1970s. About 50 test items were administered to hundreds of subjects to determine the factor structure of fitness for educable and trainable MR (Rarick, 1980). *Rarick concluded that persons with MR should be tested with the same items as peers but that separate sets of norms were needed.* His work created the foundation for other researchers.

The 1960s to the 1980s

During the 1960s and 1970s, testing encompassed both physical and motor fitness. In 1980, AAHPERD tests were changed to focus exclusively on health-related fitness. Test batteries and sets of norms for individuals with disabilities were created.

Early Tests for Persons With Mental Retardation

Early tests mirrored the philosophy of the times and contained items similar to, but less demanding than, items for able-bodied peers.

In the 1960s, Frank Hayden of Canada and Julian Stein of AAHPER were pioneers in the adaptation of fitness tests for youth with mental retardation (see Figure 13.4). The AAHPER fitness tests for individuals with mild mental retardation (AAHPER, 1976) and for moderate mental retardation (Johnson & Londeree, 1976) are no longer in print because of the AAHPERD and CIAR philosophy that the minimal standards for health-related fitness are applicable to everyone. Norms for tests published in the 1960s and 1970s are no longer valid.

Tests for Persons With Blindness

Charles Buell (1973), who was legally blind, developed fitness norms and recommendations for youth who were blind or visually impaired. Almost 10 years later, however, Buell (1982) indicated that the regular norms for the AAHPERD health-related fitness tests were applicable to the blind population, with one exception—the distance run. Running requires holding the elbow of a sighted partner, and this slows the speed, leaving the impression that cardiorespiratory endurance is lower than it actually is.

The 1980s Onward: Health-Related Fitness

The 1980 and 1988 revisions of the AAHPERD test included only health-related items. The 1980 battery included (a) a 1- or 1.5-mi run, (b) skin caliper measures of body fat, (c) bent-knee sit-ups, and (d) a sit-and-reach flexibility item. This test was normative, with norms published for each gender by age. The 1988 revision included the same items, except for changes in body fat measurement sites and the addition of pull-ups. The major change in 1988 was philosophical: AAHPERD's 1988 Physical Best Test was recommended for use by all populations, including those with disabilities. Instead of norms, the criterion level necessary for good health was stated for each item. AAHPERD philosophy was that the same minimal health standards should apply to everyone and that fitness pedagogy should be individualized, with each student striving for a physical best. This philosophy promoted least restrictive environment and inclusion concepts.

In 1993, as indicated earlier, the AAHPERD Physical Best test was replaced by CIAR's Prudential FITNESS-GRAM. Several exercise scientists with expertise in adapted physical activity are currently providing leadership in the development of an accurate knowledge base about fitness and individuals with disabilities (see Figure 13.4). See, for instance, the books by Shephard (1990), Rimmer (1994), Seaman (1995), and Winnick and Short (1985).

The U.S. government has also funded major research grants to investigate the fitness of various populations. Of these, two have been particularly outstanding in the area of severe mental retardation:

1. Data-Based Gymnasium (Dunn, Morehouse, & Fredericks, 1986) at Oregon State University
2. Project TRANSITION (Jansma, Decker, Ersing, McCubbin, & Combs, 1988) at Ohio State University

Two other projects, directed by Winnick and Short of the State University of New York (SUNY) at Brockport, have contributed to knowledge about multiple disabilities:

1. Project UNIQUE (Winnick & Short, 1985), which established norms and test adaptations for adolescents with blindness, deafness, and various orthopedic impairments

Pioneers in Physical and Motor Fitness

G. Lawrence Rarick

Julian Stein

Frank Hayden

Leaders in Health-Related Fitness

Joseph Winnick

Roy Shephard

James Rimmer

Kenneth Pitetti

2. Project TARGET (in progress, report not yet published), which is establishing criterion-based health standards for adolescents with blindness, mental retardation, and various orthopedic impairments

Fitness Classifications Requiring Special Help

Figure 13.5 shows methods of classifying fitness and identifying individuals who require special help. The emphasis in this table is on aerobic capacity, because this is the fitness component that experts believe is most important in preventing heart disease and other hypokinetic conditions.

Adapted physical activity is primarily concerned with individuals classified as having **symptomatic clinical status**. This includes adults unable to walk a mile in 12 minutes, a minimal criterion for relative freedom from health risks, and youth unable to meet FITNESSGRAM minimal standards (a mile in 8.5 to 12.5 minutes, depending on age and sex). Many school-age children who fail to meet this criterion are eligible to be categorized as other health impaired (OHI) and thus receive federal funding for special services. Conditions commonly associated with symptomatic or OHI clinical status are obesity, asthma, high blood pressure, heart disease, and poorly managed diabetes (see Chapter 19).

Individuals with OHI conditions are often referred to specialists who give laboratory exercise tests and write exercise prescriptions. Adapted physical activity personnel should have knowledge about VO_2max and METS in order to collaborate with exercise specialists. Knowledge about these laboratory values is also crucial to understanding principles and theories related to fitness and lifestyle.

VO_2max

VO_2max refers to the maximum amount of oxygen consumed by cells in the final seconds of exercise prior to total exhaustion. VO_2max values are reported in weight-relative units (milliliters of oxygen consumed times body weight in kilograms times number of minutes exercised, or ml·kg·min). Values typically range from 3.5 ml·kg·min at rest to 56 ml·kg·min during exercise. When best speed is 9 mph or a 6.5-min mile, the amount of oxygen consumed is 56 ml·kg·min.

Age and gender affect VO_2max. Compared to adults, children have high values. VO_2max ranges from 40 to 60 ml·kg·min for boys and 35 to 50 ml·kg·min for girls. VO_2max peaks between ages 17 and 25 and then declines approximately

FIGURE 13.5 Methods of classifying fitness (METS = metabolic equivalents).

Functional Class	Clinical Status			VO$_2$ max ml • kg • min	METS	Walk/Run Profile	
						Miles per hour	Minutes per mile
Normal and I	Healthy, dependent on age, activity			56.0	16	9	6.5
				52.5	15		
				49.0	14	8	7.5
				45.5	13		
				42.0	12	7	8.5
				38.5	11		
		Sedentary healthy		35.0	10	6	10
				31.5	9		
				28.0	8	5	12
				24.5	7		
II			Limited	21.0	6	4	15
				17.5	5		
III			Symptomatic	14.0	4	3	20
				10.5	3		
				7.0	2	2	30
IV				3.5	1	Bed rest	

Moderate intensity 3–6 METS

9% per decade. Average values for males are 10 to 20% higher than for females, probably because men have less body fat, higher hemoglobin concentrations, and more active lifestyles. **Hemoglobin concentration** refers to the amount of oxygen in the red blood cells. Sex differences in VO$_2$max are not generally significant and meaningful until puberty.

Many factors affect estimates of VO$_2$max of individuals with disabilities, including active muscle mass and understanding of test instructions. Individuals with paralyzed or missing limbs, because of their decreased muscle mass, have lower values than normal. Individuals with mental retardation who do not understand the concept of all-out effort also generate low values.

METS

METS refers to metabolic equivalents and represents an alternative way of indicating the amount of aerobic capacity. The range of METS is typically 1 to 16, as indicated on Figure 13.5. Bed rest requires 1 MET, or 3.5·kg·min. Individuals who function within the 1 to 6 METS range have severe fitness problems that interfere with activities of daily living. For example, 5 METs is the criterion level associated with walking up hills and stairs, carrying groceries, and having sexual intercourse. From 3 to 5 MET capacity is needed to take a quick shower, make a bed, scrub the floor, push a power mower, and garden.

Exercise Prescription: Five Components

Exercise prescription is a process of recommending activity for health, fitness, or wellness in an individualized and sys-

tematic manner. It is analogous to the individualized education program (IEP) process in that implementation requires (a) assessment, (b) goal setting, (c) decision making about training, (d) establishment of dates and program duration, and (e) evaluation to determine if goals are being achieved.

Components of an exercise prescription are frequency, intensity, time, modality, and rate of progression. These can be remembered by the acronym **FIT-MR.** Guidelines for *aerobic fitness* for able-bodied persons (ACSM, 1995) are:

F *Frequency*—3–5 times a week

I *Intensity*—60 to 90% of maximal heart rate

T *Time*—20 to 60 min

M *Modality*—A rhythmic, large muscle activity like walking, jogging, cycling, aerobic dance, swimming

R *Rate of progression*—Gradual increase in intensity

This prescription and most fitness guidelines are based on the assumption that individuals are functioning at the 6 METS level or higher. Table 13.2 shows how exercise prescription guidelines must be adapted for persons with very low fitness. The prescription often reads *whatever is possible,* and the major challenge is to motivate individuals to "better their best," once baseline performance is determined.

Frequency refers to the number of exercise sessions per week. The less fit a person is, the more sessions are needed, because individuals can sustain all-out effort for only very short periods.

Intensity (how hard) refers to amount of exertion. For *muscle strength/endurance,* intensity refers to the number of pounds (the weight or resistance) to be lifted, pushed, pulled, or propelled. For *flexibility,* intensity refers to the distance a

T a b l e   1 3 . 2   **Comparison of exercise prescription guidelines for people with average and health-impaired fitness status.**

Fitness Component	Frequency	Intensity	Time
Cardiorespiratory endurance			
Average	3–5 times a week	60 to 90% of maximal heart rate; or 50–85% of VO₂max	20–60 min
Health-impaired	Several times daily	40 to 70% of maximal heart rate or whatever is possible	3–15 min or whatever is possible
Body composition			
Average	Usual	Calorie expenditure *equals* calorie intake	Usual
Health-impaired	Daily or several times daily	Calorie expenditure *greater than* calorie intake in low-intensity/low-impact exercise	Long duration
Flexibility			
Average	3 times a week	Slow, static stretch held 10–30 sec	3–5 repetitions
Health-impaired	Daily or several times daily	Slow, static stretch held 5–10 sec	3–5 repetitions
Muscle strength and endurance			
Average	2–3 times a week	Maximum weight that can be moved 8–12 times at moderate to slow speed and not interfere with normal breathing	3 sets, 8–12 repetitions per set
Health-impaired	Daily	Exercises or calisthenics like curl-ups and pull-ups at moderate to slow speed; *isometrics*	As many as possible until able to meet FITNESSGRAM standards

Note: Average refers to the typical person wanting to improve or maintain fitness. *Health-impaired* refers to persons who are functioning at the 1 to 6 MET level (i.e., unable to walk a 12-min mile and/or to meet healthy fitness standards for their age).

muscle group is stretched beyond normal length. For *body composition,* intensity refers to caloric expenditure in relation to caloric intake. For *cardiorespiratory fitness,* intensity refers to distance and speed.

Time refers to the number of minutes spent in exercise during each session. Some prescriptions indicate warm-up time, all-out effort time, and cool-down time. Persons who function in the 1 to 6 METS level often become exhausted during time periods that others consider warm-up.

Modality refers to the type of exercise. For *muscle strength/endurance,* modality refers to isotonic, isometric, or isokinetic. For *flexibility,* modality refers to a specific slow, static stretch and whether it is independent (active) or assisted (passive). For *body composition,* modality refers to combinations of diet, aerobic exercise, and counseling. For *cardiorespiratory endurance,* modality refers to type of rhythmic, large muscle activity and whether it is continuous or discontinuous (intermittent).

Rate of progression is analogous to dates and program duration on the IEP. Exercise prescription theory recognizes three stages of progression: (a) initial conditioning (usually 4 to 6 weeks), (b) improvement conditioning (the next 5 or 6 months), and (c) maintenance.

For most persons with poor fitness, change is slow during the first few weeks. This is the critical time in regard to attitude formation, injury prevention, and weight loss. ACSM (1995) recommended that exercise intensity during this stage be at a step lower than functional ability. For example, if a person's best effort is a mile in 18 min, then the targeted goal for the first week might be a 20-min mile done daily. Table 13.3 presents an illustrative walking program for a person classified as having poor fitness (i.e., unable to perform a 20-min mile). Awarding points is a good incentive, especially when everyone understands that the goal is to work up to the maintenance level of 30 points a week.

Improvement should be targeted mostly for the 5 to 6 months after the initial conditioning stage and will occur only if intensity and time are progressively increased. The rate of this progression depends on the physical and mental state. Whenever there are performance plateaus and/or persons indicate a desire to slow down, the maintenance phase begins. At this point, a decision must be made about the minimum frequency, intensity, and time (FIT) required to maintain the training effect. If regular exercise is stopped or decreased too much, *detraining* occurs. **Detraining** refers to the gradual loss of all that was gained.

T a b l e 1 3 . 3   A 14-week aerobics program illustrating progression.

Week	Distance in Miles	Time Goal in Minutes	Points
1	1	20:00	3
2	1	18:00	5
3	1	16:00	5
4	1	15:00	5
5	1½	27:00	7½
6	1½	26:00	7½
7	1½	25:00	7½
8	1	14:25	10
9	2	33:00	10
10	2	32:00	10
11	1½	21:40	15
12	2	28:50	20
13	2	28:30	20
14	2½	36:00	25

Note: The goal is 30 points a week. This point system is used only for conditioning, not maintenance.

Exercise prescription theory constitutes a large body of knowledge. It is not attributed to one person, as are many theories, but is often associated with ACSM, the organization that publishes *Guidelines for Exercise Testing and Prescription* (1995) and offers certification for various levels of fitness expertise. Exercise prescription theory can be broken down into specific theories and/or practices associated with pioneers like Cooper (1968) (aerobic fitness), Lange (1919) and Hellebrandt and Houtz (1956) (the overload principle), DeLorme and Watkins (1948) (progressive resistance exercise), and Hettinger and Müller (1953) (isometric exercise). There is much to be learned. This chapter presents only beginning level essentials.

Personalizing Goals for Various Conditions

The meaning of fitness varies with the nature and severity of disability. Let's consider the needs of some of the populations served and the prioritization of goals to guide training.

Severe Developmental Disabilities

In nonambulatory persons with severe developmental disabilities like cerebral palsy, physical fitness is dependent upon adequacy of the postural reflex mechanism and muscle tone to perform basic movements like lift head, roll over, sit, and crawl/creep. These persons are extremely limited in both mental and physical capacities. They do not play spontaneously and do not initiate movement. Their muscle tone is hypertonic (spastic) or hypotonic (flaccid). A major concern is **contractures,** the permanent shortening and distortion of muscle groups caused by hypertonicity. Problems are not strength and endurance but rather related to basic central nervous system (CNS) function, especially sensorimotor integration.

Major goals for such persons are (a) range of motion (ROM) to prevent contractures and stimulate CNS integration, (b) functional ability to perform movement patterns used in

fitness tasks, and (c) exercise capacity tolerance. These goals, strictly speaking, are prerequisites to fitness training (see Figure 13.6). Emphasis is on increasing the time dimension of prescription (i.e., the number of minutes or trials the person will persist or tolerate).

Many individuals with severe disability, however, have limited physical capacities but good intelligence. They are able to use motorized wheelchairs at an early age and to independently exercise. ROM to prevent contractures is their primary fitness goal. *As slow, static stretches increase ROM on one surface, the opposite surface is automatically strengthened.* Thus, ROM and strength are developed concurrently, and muscle imbalances caused by pathology are corrected. Chapter 14 on postures and muscle imbalances is particularly applicable to this group. The breathing exercises described under asthma in Chapter 19 on other health impaired conditions are also important.

When persons are not at risk for contractures and muscle imbalances, equal attention is given to ROM and strength goals. Free weights, pulleys, and Nautilus- or Universal-type machines are used in ways similar to those in able-bodied programs, but more emphasis is placed on concurrent ROM exercises (Holland & Steadward, 1990; Lockette & Keyes, 1994). Weight control and cardiorespiratory endurance goals depend upon mobility options and aspirations to be athletes and/or maintain active, healthy lifestyles.

Spinal Paralysis and Injury Rehabilitation

Strength is a special concern of persons with paralysis, paresis (muscle weakness), or injury that has required surgery. Physical therapy and physical medicine are professions particularly known for work in strength rehabilitation. In paralysis, strength is associated with ROM (i.e., is there enough strength to move the body part?). Residual strength is tested manually (Daniels & Worthingham, 1986) and graded on a 5 (normal) to 0 (complete paralysis) scale as follows:

Grade 5   Normal strength. Full ROM against gravity and full resistance applied by the examiner.

Grade 4   Good strength. Full ROM against gravity with only moderate resistance applied by the examiner.

Grade 3   Fair strength. Full ROM against gravity only.

Grade 2   Poor strength. Full ROM only if the part is positioned so that the force of gravity is negated.

Grade 1   Trace strength. Muscle contraction can be seen or palpated, but strength is insufficient to produce motion even with gravity eliminated.

Grade 0 Zero strength. Complete paralysis. No visible or palpable contraction.

This system of strength testing is used in sport classification of athletes with spinal cord injury, polio, and related disabilities (see Chapter 23). Volunteer work with a wheelchair team and/or persons in a rehabilitation center is perhaps the best way to learn about strength from a paralysis/paresis perspective.

Strength and flexibility in adapted physical activity are often approached as components of *postural fitness.* Imbalances in strength and flexibility, whether developmental or acquired, cause postural deviations, low mechanical efficiency, and problems of coordination, control, and balance. Chapter

FIGURE 13.6 Fitness training. *(A)* For individuals with severe developmental disabilities, the emphasis should be on functional ability to perform movement patterns. *(B)* Nonambulatory persons need to develop strength to move their bodies from place to place.

A

B

14 on postures presents exercises for developing strength and flexibility in specific muscle groups.

Other Health Impairments

Persons with other health impairments (OHI) are typically more interested in weight loss and aerobic endurance than strength and flexibility. Sedentary lifestyle may have contributed to their disability or vice versa. Often, these persons are coping concurrently with several conditions: heart disease, hypertension, obesity, asthma, diabetes, cancer, and the like. These may have been present since birth or a young age, distorting their perceptions of what feeling good is like. More than likely, however, the onset has been slow and insidious. They do not realize how poor their condition is until challenged to take a fitness test or advised to exercise by their physicians.

Limited Mental Function

Persons with mental retardation (MR) typically have the same fitness needs and capacities as the general population. In the hierarchy of possible goals, weight loss and cardiorespiratory endurance usually rank highest. Of major concern in assessment and programming is the individual's ability to understand speed and distance (i.e., "Run as fast as you can for a mile"). Adaptations like a partner or role model to set the pace are often required (Reid, Seidl, & Montgomery, 1989). Additionally, more care is needed in programming because 20 to 60% of infants born with chromosomal defects like Down syndrome have congenital heart disease. When MR is severe or profound, the autonomic nervous system that regulates heartbeat may be affected. In such cases, the heart rate response to strenuous exercise is not normal, and traditional methods of monitoring exertion are not valid.

A consideration in severe retardation is whether goals like play and game behaviors, social competency/acceptance, and perceptual-motor function should take precedence over fitness. These persons have so many needs that deciding which are most important is difficult. In most cases, however, play and game behaviors are necessary to make fitness training ecologically valid.

Limited Sensory Function

Persons with visual and hearing impairments also have the same fitness needs and capabilities as the general population. Many senior citizens fall into this category and need help with cardiorespiratory fitness.

Aerobic Capacity or Cardiorespiratory Endurance

Aerobic capacity, or cardiorespiratory endurance, is the most important component of health-related fitness. To improve aerobic capacity, individuals must perform vigorous activities that elevate the heart rate over prolonged periods of time. The definition of *prolonged* varies, but the minimal target time is 3 minutes. Individuals who cannot sustain vigorous activity for 3 minutes may need to begin training with **interval conditioning,** a system in which bouts of 1 minute of exercise are interspersed with 1 or 2 minutes of rest. The goal is to gradually increase the time spent in vigorous exercise until 20 to 60 minutes can be sustained with relative ease. Stationary bicycles are often used to achieve this goal in school and exercise settings, especially when weather is extremely hot or cold (see Figure 13.7).

Assessment of Aerobic Capacity

While laboratory measurement is common in university, hospital, and rehabilitation settings, most adapted physical activity specialists use field tests to estimate aerobic capacity: (a) step tests, (b) distance runs, and (c) walking tests. Distance runs (12-min or 1 to 1.5 mi) at the fastest possible speeds are popular, but fast walking may be maximal effort for many unfit persons. ACSM recognizes the **Rockport Fitness Walking Test** (Rippe & Ward, 1989) as a valid aerobic fitness measure. The goal of this test is to walk 1 mi as fast as possible.

Roy Shephard, a Canadian physician, is a leader in applying fitness concepts to special populations. In an excellent text (Shephard, 1990), he describes a 12-min wheelchair distance field test. VO_2max on this test ranged from below 12 to above 36, showing that the decreased muscle mass of persons

FIGURE 13.7 Work on the bicycle ergometer is one of the best ways to increase aerobic fitness. Here, Dr. Lane Goodwin of the University of Wisconsin at LaCrosse works with an adolescent with Down syndrome.

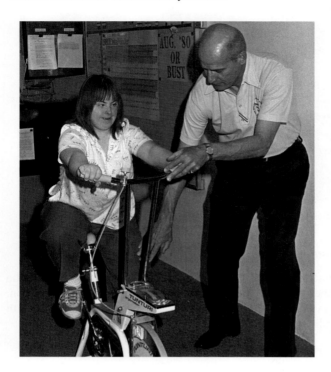

with paralysis lowers their endurance. Individual differences in height, weight, usable body parts, and coordination-control parameters make accurate measurement of VO_2max a challenge. *Field test results are only estimates of ability.*

Common laboratory tests are done on treadmills, bicycle ergometers, wheelchair ergometers, and arm-cranking devices. VO_2max values are obtained by protocols in which work load is progressively increased until exhaustion sets in.

Regardless of whether field or laboratory tests are used, it is important to be knowledgeable about resting and exercise recovery rates. Watch students for signs of distress, and know when to stop testing.

Cardiac Resting and Exercise Recovery Rates

Resting heart rate is a good indicator of fitness. The following ranges are considered normal for each age group (Bates, 1983):

Newborns	110–200
1–24 months	100–200
2–12 years	80–150
13 years and older	60–100

Highly trained adult athletes may have rates as low as 40 beats a minute. In general, however, resting rates outside these ranges indicate serious problems. Slow rates are associated with an active lifestyle and fast rates with sedentary habits.

Recovery time after aerobic exercise helps determine whether exercise demands are appropriate or excessive. Heart rate should decrease to below 120 after 5 min of rest and to below 100 after 10 min of rest (Cooper, 1982). The faster this

recovery, of course, the better. The pulse rates of most persons decrease to under 100 during the first minute of rest. Generally, the heart rate decreases during the first 2 to 3 min after exercise at about the same rate that it increased during activity.

Recovery rates determine the amount of time needed for cool-down. For healthy young persons, cool-down should last until the heart rate is about 120. For middle-aged and older adults, respectively, rates for ending cool-down are 110 and 100.

Respiratory Resting and Exercise Recovery Rates

Recovery breathing rate is also a concern. At rest, normal respiration is 12 to 16 breaths a minute. Recovery to this rate should require less than 10 min.

Prescribing Aerobic Exercise

Continuous, low-impact exercise is recommended for persons with low fitness. *Continuous* means that the activity lasts more than 3 min. This marks the approximate point at which contracting skeletal muscle shifts to aerobic metabolism to produce energy.

Principles to Guide Work With Low-Fit People

Four principles guide cardiorespiratory or aerobic endurance work with low-fit people: (a) use low-impact activities; (b) match frequency, intensity, and time to ability; (c) pay attention to self-concept and motivation; and (d) teach acceptance that rate of progression will be slower than for average people. Low- and high-impact activities refer to modality choices. *Low-impact* includes (a) non-weight-bearing activities like swimming, cycling, and rowing and (b) exercises that put minimal stress on joints, like walking, cross-country skiing, and slow stair climbing. *High-impact* includes any activity with a running or jumping component.

The most challenging principle is matching frequency, intensity, and time to ability. Many experts agree that frequency should be daily, when working with low-fit people. Time is typically as many minutes as can be tolerated and/or woven into a person's overall schedule. Intensity can be prescribed by several methods: (a) VO_2max, METS, or calories; (b) maximal heart rate; and (c) rating of perceived effort (RPE), pain, and breathlessness.

Intensity Prescribed by VO₂max, METS, or Calories

The ACSM (1995) recommends a 40 to 70% VO_2max exercise intensity for various conditions in its chapter on special populations. Tables of METS and calories can be used to make sense of this ACSM principle (see Table 13.4, and look at the METS and calories required to walk a 20-min mile). *Moderate intensity* is defined as 3 to 6 METS, which is equivalent to walking a mile in 15 to 20 minutes. Experts agree that everyone should try to accumulate 30 minutes or more of moderate-intensity activity every day.

Several sources make recommendations about the minimal total of calories that should be used per week and in individual exercise sessions. The ACSM (1995) recommends that at least 300 calories be spent each exercise session. The American Heart Association endorses a minimum of 700 calories a week spread over three or four sessions.

Energy requirements of activities depend on weight. The information in Table 13.4 should be adjusted for body

Table 13.4   Energy requirements of various activities for persons weighing 154 lb.

Activity or Exercise	METs[a]	Cal Per Hr[b]	Activity or Exercise	METs[a]	Cal Per Hr[b]
Archery	2–3	150–250	Karate/Judo	6–10+	450–800+
Backpacking	3–8	250–600	Kayaking (see canoeing)		
Badminton			Mountain climbing	6–8	450–800
Social doubles	3–4	250–300	Mowing		
Social singles	6	450	Pushing mower	3–4	250–300
Competitive singles	8–10	600–750	Pushing hand	6–8	450–600
Baseball or softball			Paddleball/Platform tennis	4–8	300–600
Except pitcher	2–3	150–250	Ping-Pong (table tennis)	4–6	300–450
Pitcher	6	450	Racquetball	6–10	450–750
Basketball	4–10	300–750	Raking leaves	3–5	250–400
Bicycling (on level)			Rope skipping	8–12	600–900
5 mph or 8 km	3	250	Rowing	3–12	250–900
10 mph or 16.1 km	6	450	Rugby	6–8	450–600
13 mph or 20.9 km	9	650	Running and jogging		
Boardsailing	3–8	250–600	5 mph	7–8	500–600
Bowling	1½–3	100–225	7 mph	12	800
Calisthenics	2–8	150–600	9 mph	15	1,100
Canoeing			Sailing		
Flat water	2–8	150–600	Crew	2–4	150–300
White water	5–10	400–750	Skipper	1–3	75–200
Dancing			Scuba diving	6–10	450–750
Ballet and modern	4–9+	300–700+	Sexual intercourse	5–8	400–600
Vigorous ballroom	3–8+	250–600	Shoveling	5–9	400–700
Folk and square	3–8+	250–600+	Skating	4–10+	300–800+
"Aerobic"	5–9	300–700	Skiing		
Driving car	2	170–200	Cross-country	5–12+	400–900+
Fencing	6–9	450–700	Downhill	4–10+	300–800+
Fishing			Soccer	8–10+	600–750+
Casting	2–3	150–250	Squash	8–10+	600–750
Walking with waders	4–6	300–500	Surfing	4–7	300–500
Football (while active)	6–9	450–700	Swimming	4–10+	300–750
Gardening	2–8	150–600	Tennis	4–10	300–750
Golf	2–4	150–300	Volleyball	4–7	300–500
Gymnastics	3–5	250–400	Walking (on level)		
Handball	6–10	450–750	2 mph/3 kph	2	150
Hockey			3 mph/5 kph (20-min mile)	3+	250
Field	8–10	600–750	4 mph/6.5 kph	5–6	400–500
Ice	8–10	600–750	Walking stairs/hills	7–12+	500–900
Horseback riding	6–8	480–600	Waterskiing	4–8	300–600
Isometrics	2–5	150–400	Weight lifting	3–6	250–450
Isotonics	2–10+	150–800	Woodsplitting	2–6+	150–500
Jogging (see running)			Yoga	1–4	75–300

Note: Adapted from H. A. deVries, *Physiology of exercise for physical education and athletics,* 4th ed. (Dubuque, IA: Wm. C. Brown, 1986), p. 350.
[a]METs. The range reflects the varying intensity, from the leisurely or recreational pace to the competitive or frenetic.
[b]Calories per hour—based on a weight of 70 kg (154 lbs). A 10% increase or decrease should be applied for each 7 kg (15 lb) over or under 70 kg, respectively.

weight by calculating a 10% increase or decrease for each 15 lb over or under a body weight of 154 lb.

Checking the Appropriateness of Intensity

During aerobic training, persons should be taught to take pulse rate frequently. For hearts that respond normally to exercise, there is a rapid increase during the first 3 to 5 min, after which a steady state or plateau occurs. In children, the steady state occurs earlier, after about 2 min. A good way to check whether intensity is appropriate is to exercise moderately (as hard as possible while maintaining a conversation) for 3 to 5 min, take an immediate 10-sec pulse, and multiply by 6. The result should be within the heart rate target zone.

Intensity Prescribed by Maximal Heart Rate

Maximal heart rate (MHR) is the fastest speed (beats per minute) a heart can attain during exhaustive exercise without

Ratings of Perceived Effort (RPE) Scales

Original Category	*Revised Category-Ratio*
6	0 Nothing at all
7 Very, very light	0.5 Very, very weak
8	1 Very weak
9 Very light	2 Weak
10	3 Moderate
11 Fairly light	4 Somewhat strong
12	5 Strong
13 Somewhat hard	6
14	7 Very strong
15 Hard	8
16	9
17 Very hard	10 Very, very strong
18	+ Maximal
19 Very, very hard	
20	

Ratings of Pain and Dyspnea Scales

Pain Scale

1+	Light, barely noticeable
2+	Moderate, bothersome
3+	Severe, very uncomfortable
4+	Most severe pain ever experienced

Dyspnea Scale for Breathing Comfort

1+	Mild, noticeable to exerciser but not observer
2+	Mild, some difficulty, noticeable to observer
3+	Moderate difficulty, but can continue
4+	Severe difficulty, cannot continue

Note: The RPE scales are from *Medicine and Science in Sports and Exercise,* vol. 14, p. 377–387h, "Rating of Perceived Effort (RPE) Scales." © The American College of Sports Medicine.

compromising or endangering life. Figure 13.8 shows estimated MHRs (150 when over 65; 200 when under 20) and recommended target zones to guide exercise intensity (i.e., 70 to 90% of MHR). For average persons, the 70% level allows conversation during exercise and is considered a moderate energy expenditure.

Laboratory protocols can be used to determine MHR, but usually it is estimated by an age-adjusted maximal heart rate formula: 220 – age in years. Thus, a 40-year-old has a MHR of about 180, and a 10-year-old has a MHR of about 210. This formula has a prediction error of about ±15 beats a minute (e.g., the MHR of 10-year-olds ranges between 195 and 225). There is little or no difference in MHR between sexes.

For persons of low fitness, the lower level of the MHR threshold range is adapted. ACSM (1995) indicated that a 40 to 70% threshold level is appropriate for persons with health impairments; 40% of a MHR of 200 is 80. This is an appropriate target heart rate for starting the initial 4- to 6-week conditioning stage. Starting too low is better than starting too

high. The goal is to gradually increase intensity until the 60 to 90% range can be tolerated.

Several formulas are recommended, but the age-adjusted maximal heart rate seems best for adapted physical activity settings. The well-known **Karvonen formula** (max heart rate – resting heart rate) is a more aggressive method that is often used with elite athletes without disabilities.

Cautions About Using Maximal Heart Rate

The information in Figure 13.8 is not applicable to all persons. When active muscle mass is limited by paralysis, amputations, and muscular dystrophies/atrophies, persons have lower MHRs. Several heart conditions are characterized by lower than normal MHR. Brain stem and autonomic nervous system damage can cause low MHRs. Medications like the beta blockers used to manage high blood pressure and heart conditions suppress both MHR and exercise response. Diabetes can also make MHR an inaccurate value. In cases like this, intensity is generally prescribed by **rating of perceived exertion** (RPE) or METs rather than by heart rate.

Many factors affect heart rate response and must be taken into account. Among these are hot temperatures, high humidity, emotional stress, and medications. Overweight conditions cause hearts to beat faster than average. Infections with fever increase heart rate response so much that elevated body temperature is an exercise contraindication.

Intensity Prescribed by Perceived Exertion, Pain, and Dyspnea

Creating a regimen light enough for persons with low fitness requires much experimentation. It is important to provide instruction on intensity and to help exercisers get in touch with their bodies and develop a vocabulary for describing perceived exertion, pain/discomfort, and breathlessness. Table 13.5 presents scales commonly used in exercise assessment, prescription, and communication (ACSM, 1995; Borg, 1982). The rating of perceived exertion (RPE) scale is best known.

The original RPE scale (6 to 20) is preferred in the field setting because adding a 0 to each number provides a rough estimate of heart rate per minute. *Somewhat hard,* for example, corresponds with a heart rate of 130. *Hard* and *very hard,* respectively, are comparable to heart rates of 150 and 170. The typical intensity range for training is 11 to 16. RPEs of 18 and over describe fatigue so great that exercise must be stopped. In general, warm-ups and cool-downs range between 7 and 11.

Children from age 7 onward give RPEs that correlate highly with heart rate (Bar-Or, 1983). Overweight persons tend to overestimate RPE (Ward & Bar-Or, 1990) but can be taught accurate perceptions. RPEs eliminate the nuisance of counting pulse rate during aerobic activities. The RPE is also recommended for people whose hearts do not respond properly to exercise. Charts with RPE adjectives in large print are hung on walls to teach about intensity and increase awareness of its importance.

For persons who are unable to sustain large muscle exercise at 55 to 90% of maximal heart rate for 15 min, the goal should be exercise tolerance or functional capacity rather than cardiorespiratory endurance. Tolerance is influenced mainly by (a) cognition/motivation; (b) muscle pain caused by lactic acid accumulation, oxygen deprivation, or tissue

FIGURE 13.8 Maximal heart rate and target zone for use in aerobic exercise training programs. Caution: This figure is not applicable to all persons.

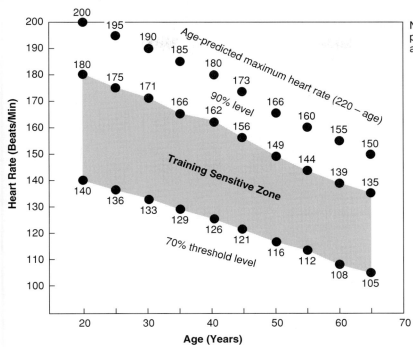

Note: Maximal heart rate for people with quadriplegia is about 20 to 40 beats lower.

swelling; (c) chest pain or stitch in side caused by insufficient oxygen supply; and (d) breathing discomfort, called **dyspnea.**

Everyone experiences some discomfort as intensity of exercise increases, but persons with low fitness often perceive real pain. Asthma and obesity particularly challenge pain threshold. Persons who cannot get enough oxygen into the blood may experience sever hip, leg, or foot pain called **claudication.** The calf is most commonly affected, and the intense pain occurs after only a short distance (half a block to quarter mile) has been covered. Claudication should not be confused with ordinary muscle cramps. It is rare in the general population but relatively common in persons with oxygen deficiency conditions.

The challenge in adapted physical activity is to increase intensity so gradually that discomfort is minimal. Otherwise, persons tend to drop out. Also, coping with or ignoring discomfort may need to be taught. Athletes and physical education majors take "No pain, no gain" for granted. In contrast, sedentary persons have no experience in judging exercise-induced discomfort.

Numerical scales are used to objectify ratings of pain and dyspnea (see Table 13.5). An objective for a person with asthma, for example, might be to reduce dyspnea from 3 to 2 during a 1-mi walk for speed. The scales in Table 13.5 should be incorporated into assessment systems that urge all-out effort. Fitness training for health should be adapted (slower, lighter than training for sports) so that activity is associated with pleasure, not pain and dyspnea.

Body Composition (Also See Chapter 19)

Body composition refers to the individual components that constitute the total body mass. The relative percentages are

Table 13.6 Relative percentages of components of total body mass.

Component	Average Male	Average Female
Muscle	45%	36%
Bone	15%	12%
Fat	15%	27%
Remainder	25%	25%

shown in Table 13.6. Females have more fat, and males have more muscle tissue. Differences between genders are minimal until puberty, when sex hormones become active and promote development of male and female characteristics. In general, children have less body fat than adults (10 to 15% compared to 15 to 27%). Body composition is largely genetically determined, as evidenced by similarities in fat distribution and body shapes/sizes/builds within families. Genetic predisposition, however, can be tempered by exercise and nutrition. Some disabilities affect body composition. Spinal cord injuries, for example, increase body fat percentage and decrease lean body mass. These changes are more pronounced in quadriplegia than paraplegia.

Body fat percentages, rather than body weight, are the major fitness concern. Healthy body fat standards depend on whether or not an individual wants to excel in sports. For nonathletes, desirable percentages of fat are 18 to 30% for women and 10 to 25% for men. For athletes, less fat is desirable: 12 to 22% for women and 5 to 13% for men. Fat reduction goals thus depend on leisure interests.

Assessment of Body Fat

Percentage of body fat can be determined by laboratory protocols and formulae or estimated by skinfold caliper measures. Calipers provide a measure of the amount of fat that can be pinched away from a body part at a particular landmark (see Figures 13.9 and 13.10).

When time is so limited that only one measure can be taken, the triceps skinfold is recommended. To assure accuracy, measurements are taken three times, and the middle value is recorded. Care must be taken to pinch the skin at precisely the point indicated in test directions. Measurements are usually taken on the right side only.

When possible, several skinfold measures are used. The best combination of skinfold measures is controversial. The Prudential FITNESSGRAM recommends a triceps and calf skinfolds combination. The 1987 Canadian Standardized Test of Fitness recommends the sum of triceps, biceps, subscapular, and suprailiac skinfolds. Figure 13.10 presents various skinfold measures.

Body Mass Index: Substitute Measure

Body mass index (BMI) refers to weight divided by height and is accepted as a substitute for body fat measures when skinfold calipers are not available. The BMI (also called the Quetelet index) is the ratio of body weight to the square of body height:

$$BMI = \frac{Body\ weight\ (kg)}{Height^2\ (meters)}$$

where 1 kg = 2.2 lb and 1 m = 39.37 inches. Health fitness standards for BMI vary with age and gender.

Physical and motor fitness scores should be interpreted in relation to height, weight, and skinfolds. The classic research of Dobbins, Garron, and Rarick (1981) showed that many statistically significant differences between persons with and without MR disappear when adjustments are made for differences in body size.

Height-weight tables heighten motivation for lifestyle changes because they are easily understood. However, the correlation between weight and percent body fat is about .67. Thus, weight is not a reliable predictor of body fat. Nevertheless, height and weight are important indicators of normal growth. Most youth reach the final 2% of their height by age 18 (females) and age 20 (males). After about age 45, height begins to decrease, probably because of loss of bone mass and related degeneration of the spinal column. Bone loss (**osteoporosis**) in old age proceeds faster in women than men.

Prescribing Exercise for Fat Loss

Body fat can best be reduced by assuring that large muscle activity uses more calories than daily intake. This is achieved through change of lifestyle (both exercise and nutrition) and generally requires counseling as well as participation in a support group. Exercise should be aerobic at whatever intensity is possible. Table 13.4 shows the calories expended per hour in various activities for a person weighing 154 lb. *The heavier a person, the more calories are expended.* Tables like this must

FIGURE 13.9 Triceps skinfold. *(A)* The midpoint of the back upper arm is the standard place to make the measurement. *(B)* Minimum triceps skinfold thickness indicating obesity (in millimeters).

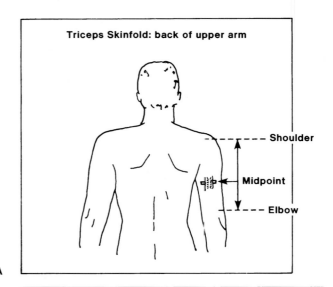

Age (Years)	Males	Females
5	12	14
6	12	15
7	13	16
8	14	17
9	15	18
10	16	20
11	17	21
12	18	22
13	18	23
14	17	23
15	16	24
16	15	25
17	14	26
18	15	27
19	15	27
20	16	28
21	17	28
22	18	28
23	18	28
24	19	28
25	20	29
26	20	29
27	21	29
28	22	29
29	23	29
30	23	30

therefore be adjusted for individual differences. A good formula for this purpose is to increase or decrease the calories by 10% for each 15 lb (7 kg) over or under 154 lb (70 kg).

One pound of fat equals 3,500 calories. No more than 2.2 lb (1 kg) should be lost each week (ACSM, 1995). To achieve this goal, exercise should be increased by at least 300 calories a day. For a 154-lb person whose highest intensity

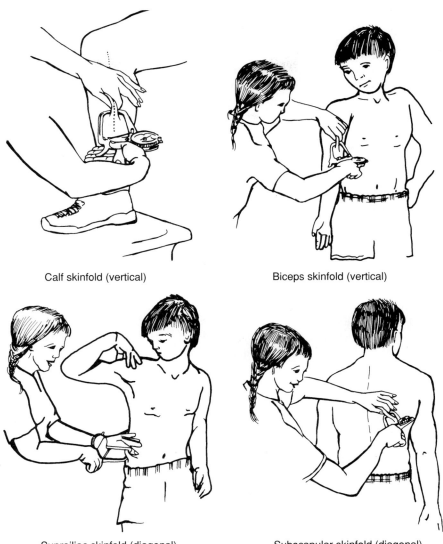

Calf skinfold (vertical)

Biceps skinfold (vertical)

Suprailiac skinfold (diagonal)

Subscapular skinfold (diagonal)

level is 2 mph (one 30-min mi), 2 hr a day must be spent walking to expend 300 calories. Obviously, the more fit a person is, the less time per day is needed to expend calories.

Obesity is addressed in Chapter 19 (other health impairments) because it is a medical problem as serious as asthma, diabetes, and the like. Obese persons need to be assured that long-duration activity at low intensity is as effective as short-duration/high-intensity activity. Time management counseling is a high-priority need because most persons have a difficult time finding an extra 1 to 2 hr a day in their schedules to use for exercise. Counseling and support group involvement should continue after weight loss to assure maintenance of target weight.

Muscle Strength/Endurance

Muscle strength and endurance are developed concurrently in childhood through vigorous activities of daily living. *Strength* is developed every time that muscle exertion is near maximum, as in lifting, pushing, pulling, holding, or carrying a heavy object. Jumping as far as possible, for example, requires a maximal lift of body weight. Pull-ups and rope climbing also demand lifting body weight. *Endurance* is developed when-

ever a muscular activity continues for several seconds, as in curl-ups, push-ups, running in place, continuous jumps, or short-distance sprints.

Age and gender differences in strength parallel changes in muscle mass. Females tend to show a steady increase in strength until about age 30. Males likewise increase steadily but demonstrate a sudden, rapid increase at puberty (ages 13 to 14), which is associated with testosterone, the sex hormone that stimulates muscle growth. At all ages, the average male is stronger than the average female. After adolescence, muscle bulk (the result of muscle fiber hypertrophy) characterizes males who engage in strength training. Women in equivalent programs increase in strength but do not develop comparable bulk because of their lack of testosterone. After age 30, strength plateaus and then begins to gradually decline. The rate of this decline is largely dependent on amount of physical activity.

Assessment of Muscle Strength/Endurance

The **principle of specificity** states that the benefits of exercises done in one position will not transfer when the muscle is used in other positions. There is no such thing as total body strength/endurance, so choices must be made about which muscle groups are the most important to test. Generally, the groups selected are abdominal (curl-ups), upper arm and shoulder (pull-ups, push-ups), hip and thigh (distance jump or sprint), and back (trunk lifts from prone).

Assessment focuses on the number of times an exercise can be done in the prescribed posture or position. Body alignment is very important in both calisthenic-type exercises and weight lifting, because injury can occur when body parts are improperly placed or used. The cadence of exercise is also important, in that *slow* movements indicate control against gravity's force.

When physical disability results in paralysis or paresis, assessment is more comprehensive. In such cases, movement capacity graded on a 0-to-5 scale (see page 352).

Prescribing Exercise for Muscle Strength/Endurance

Sedentary persons should take all their major muscle groups through both strength and endurance exercises at least 2 days a week (ACSM, 1995). Adapted physical activity for young people uses animal walks, stunts, games, self-testing activities, and movement education to achieve this purpose (see Figure 13.11). For example, *arm and shoulder strength/endurance* can be increased by crab walk, dog walk, lame-dog walk, inchworm, and coffee grinder. Any activity in which the arms support, propel, or lift body weight develops muscles. Hanging, rope or apparatus climbing, and overarm travel on a horizontal ladder are especially good. *Abdominal strength/endurance* is developed by hands and knees creeping and by lifting body parts (trunk or legs) from a supine position. *Back strength* is developed by lifting body parts from a prone position. Swimming is often considered the best all-round muscle developer, and exercises/games can be devised that use arm and leg movements from the various strokes.

Central to the development of muscles is the **principle of overload,** which refers to progressively increasing the demands made on a muscle group. When planning progressions, first increase the number of repetitions, then increase the resistance. Strength/endurance can be developed by three types of activity: (a) isotonic, (b) isometric, and (c) isokinetic (see Figure 13.12).

Isotonic Exercise (Dynamic or Moving)

Isotonic exercise is categorized according to equipment needed: (a) no equipment, as in animal walks, push-ups, and curl-ups; (b) stationary bars for pull-ups; (c) wall, floor, or ceiling pulleys; (d) free weights; and (e) variable resistance machines like the Universal and Nautilus. Free weights are divided into *dumbbells* for one-hand lifts, *barbells* for two-hand lifts, and *cuff weights* that are attached to body parts via Velcro. Machines offer multiple stations for pushing, pulling, and lifting and provide either constant or variable resistance.

Creative teachers devise all kinds of free weights and color-code or mark them to indicate number of pounds. Examples are

1. Stuffed animals filled with 7, 10, and 15 lb of sand
2. Fireplace logs, bricks, or rocks
3. Sacks of potatoes and other grocery store purchases
4. Plastic bottles filled with sand
5. Backpacks filled with weights
6. Buckets, chairs, and other daily living objects
7. Weights made from tin cans, cement, and broomsticks

Adolescents and adults benefit tremendously from weight training. Prescriptions are stated in terms of sets and the repetition maximum (RM). One set is the number of repetitions done consecutively without resting. RM is the maximal weight that can be lifted in one set. Strength is best developed when the resistance (weight) allows no more than 8–12 repetitions and three sets are performed two or three times a week (ACSM, 1995). This guideline varies, however, with disability and purpose of training. In general, training for muscle endurance requires use of lighter weights (one half or three fourths of maximum), with greater number of repetitions. In contrast, training for strength uses heavier weights with fewer repetitions.

Progressive resistance exercise (PRE) is a popular rehabilitation technique used to ameliorate weakness and atrophy after surgery. Often called the DeLorme method after one of its founders (DeLorme & Watkins, 1948), PRE is based on maximal resistance that pain tolerance permits to be lifted 10 times (10RM) and a lifting program of 30 repetitions executed several times each week as follows:

1 set of 10 repetitions at one-half 10RM
1 set of 10 repetitions at three-fourths 10RM
1 set of 10 repetitions at full 10RM

Much research indicates that fewer repetitions (four to eight) may be effective.

Safety is a concern when using free weights. Persons should not lift alone for obvious reasons. Lifts should be slow, smooth, and continuous to avoid injury, and breathing should be natural. Strength training should be coordinated with a good flexibility routine.

Isometric Exercise (Static)

Isometric exercise is a maximum or near-maximum muscle contraction that is held for 6 sec and repeated several times during the day. This exercise is highly specific, strengthening muscles only for work at the same angle as the training. Squeezing a **dynamometer** or tennis ball to develop hand grip strength is an example; the isometric part of the exercise begins after movement has ceased. Persons with low back pain use the gluteal pinch and pelvic tilt. Almost everyone occasionally pulls inward on abdominal muscles and holds to improve appearance. Straining during bowel movements is another example of isometric exercise. Arm and leg exercises entail pressing against doorways and walls and pulling against towels, ropes, or tire strips that permit no movement and hence no change in muscle length.

Isometric exercise is the only form of strength training that is not based on the overload principle. Founded by Hettinger and Müller (1953) of Germany, isometrics are especially recommended for persons bedridden or limited in movement for reasons other than cardiorespiratory disease. Because of associated breath holding, isometrics is the worst form of strength training for individuals with heart disease and high blood pressure.

FIGURE 13.11   Fun activities for developing arm and shoulder strength.

1. Can you do a dog walk? Note that knees are bent.

2. Can you lift one leg and do a lame-dog walk?

3. Can you do a bear walk? Note that legs are straight.

4. Can you do the inchworm walk? Start in push-up position, then inch forward using only your feet to the bear walk position, then inch forward, using only your hands, to the push-up position again.

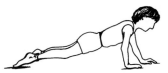

5. Can you do a seal (walrus) crawl? Only your arms can move.

6. Can you touch your chin to the mat and come back up? This is called *dumping sand*. Can you do the wheelbarrow walk?

7. Can you do the crab walk?

8. Can you hold a bridge?

9. Can you hold a one-arm side stretch?

10. Can you do the coffee grinder?

11. Can you do a rabbit jump? Knees stay bent.

12. Can you do a mule kick? Knees straighten out.

13. Can you do an elephant walk with a partner?

14. Can you do a centipede walk with one or two partners?

FIGURE 13.12 Three types of strength training.

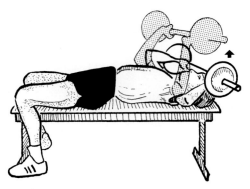

A. Isotonic

B. Isometric

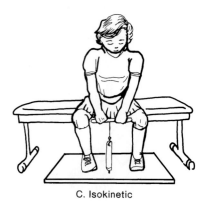

C. Isokinetic

Isokinetic Exercise (Machine-generated)

Isokinetic exercise is associated with constant resistance machines. These keep velocity of a movement constant and match the resistance to the effort of the exerciser. This allows maximal tension to be exerted throughout the range of motion. Illustrative machines of this type are Cybex II, Apollo, Exer-Genie, MERAC, and Hydra-Fitness. Isokinetics is the newest type of weight training and, theoretically, should lead to the greatest improvement.

Valsalva Effect and Contraindications

The **Valsalva effect** is an increase in intraabdominal and intrathoracic pressure that results when breath is held, as in straining to lift a heavy object or to exert maximal force. Increased pressure causes slowing of heart rate, decreased return

of blood to the heart, and elevated blood pressure. *Heavy strength training is generally contraindicated in high blood pressure conditions and heart disease.* Breath holding during exercise can also rupture tissues, especially in the abdominal region (**hernias**) and in the eyes when pathology already is present, such as increased internal pressure (**glaucoma**) and torn or detached retina.

Range of Motion and Flexibility

The range of motion and flexibility component refers to ability to move body segments through the actions and planes designated as normal for each joint. For example, movements in three planes are possible at the shoulder and hip joints: (a) sagittal plane—flexion and extension; (b) frontal plane—abduction, adduction; and (c) horizontal plane—rotation. In contrast, the elbow and ankle joints permit movement in only one plane.

Range of motion (ROM) is the term used when the movement capacity at a joint is measured in degrees through use of a **goniometer** (a protractor-type device) or a **flexometer** (a 360° dial with pointer that is strapped to the body part). These devices can be purchased through equipment companies like J. A. Preston (see Appendix E). A knowledge of goniometry is necessary when the goal is increased ROM at designated joints (see Figure 13.13). In pathological conditions that require therapeutic exercise to prevent contractures or to rehabilitate a body part after surgery, ROM is the accepted term. Conditions like cerebral palsy, muscular dystrophy, arthritis, spina bifida, and paralysis require daily ROM exercises. These are typically prescribed by physicians and therapists and carried out by parents, teachers, and aides (Kottke, 1990; Surburg, 1986).

Flexibility is the term used in physical education and sport settings to specify functional stretching ability (i.e., ability to stretch well enough to perform activities of daily living and to achieve personal sport and dance goals without injury). Flexibility tests measure simultaneous function of several joints in performing a function like reaching. When movement is limited by illness, disability, or sedentary lifestyle, flexibility is the first fitness parameter to suffer. Thus, activity programs for convalescing or sedentary persons often focus on gentle stretching exercises during the first weeks.

Gender, age, occupation, and musculoskeletal differences affect flexibility. At all ages and most joints, females demonstrate more flexibility than males. This difference widens with age. Flexibility seems to improve from childhood through adolescence. Thereafter, it declines steadily. Persons in occupations demanding much physical activity are more flexible than those in sedentary jobs. Flexibility is affected by bony structure or configuration of joints, muscles, tendons, ligaments, and skin. Arthritis, dwarfism, muscular dystrophy, paralysis, cerebral palsy, and burns are examples of conditions that limit flexibility. In contrast, some disabilities like Down syndrome are associated with excessive flexibility.

Assessment of ROM/Flexibility

Flexibility is specific to each muscle group. Since testing all muscle groups is not feasible in large-scale fitness tests, AAHPERD and its Canadian counterpart include the sit-and-reach test as a combined estimate of hamstring, hip, and spine flexibility. These muscle groups, when tight, contribute to injury

FIGURE 13.13   Two types of goniometers with their respective measurement systems. The movable bar indicates the number of degrees a body part can be moved.

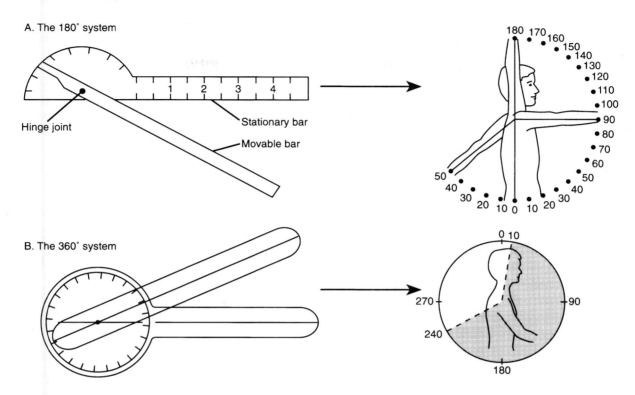

A. The 180° system

Hinge joint

Stationary bar

Movable bar

B. The 360° system

and/or chronic lower back problems. Tightness is associated with excessive sitting, and the sit-and-reach test is a good predictor of sedentary lifestyle.

Measurement of ROM begins with the body part in anatomical position, which is designated as 0 in the 180° system (see Figure 13.13). The hinge joint of the goniometer is placed over the joint so that both bars point to 0. The movable bar moves with the body part, and its pointer marks the angle of motion achieved. Two or three measures of each movement are taken to assure reliability. Either the maximum or the average is recorded. Measurements are often taken from a supine position to eliminate balance and gravity problems.

Prescribing Stretching Exercises

The nature of stretching depends on its purpose: (a) to maintain elasticity, (b) to warm-up and cool-down, or (c) to correct pathological tightness. Stretches that take body parts to their movement extremes should be done after warm-ups, not before. If done incorrectly, stretches can cause injury or worsen disability. Chapter 14 on postures and muscle imbalance covers stretches for specific body parts and contraindications. Overall body stretching for maintenance is described in Chapter 15 on relaxation, where Yoga and Tai Chi are emphasized. These are particularly good for older populations.

Regardless of nature, stretches should be only slow and static. **Ballistic movements** (i.e., bobbing and bounces) are no longer considered as stretching exercises and are, in fact, contraindicated when the purpose is flexibility. Modalities used in stretching are (a) active, (b) passive, and (c) combinations. When stretches are directed toward correcting specific tight-

ness, they should slowly move the body part to the extreme of its range of motion, where it remains for several seconds. Sport references recommend 10 to 30 sec (ACSM, 1995; Alter, 1996; Curtis, 1981), whereas therapeutic exercise references suggest 5 to 10 sec (Basmajian & Wolf, 1990; Surburg, 1986). Each stretch should be repeated three to five times.

Using Proprioceptive Neuromuscular Facilitation (PNF)

Proprioceptive neuromuscular facilitation (PNF) is a system of stretching that requires the help of an assistant to perform either a contract-relax or a hold-relax exercise sequence that stimulates the **proprioceptors** (sensory receptors in tendons and joints) to enhance functional flexibility. PNF is based on the physiological principle of **reciprocal innervation** (i.e., when an agonist or prime mover muscle contracts, the antagonist on the opposite surface relaxes). Relaxation of the antagonist facilitates subsequent stretching of the agonist. In athletic training, PNF is called *superstretching*. In adapted physical activity, PNF is particularly recommended for individuals with cerebral palsy and arthritis.

In the **contract-relax type** of PNF, the individual isotonically contracts a muscle group for 5 to 10 sec while the assistant resists this contraction as strongly as possible; then the individual relaxes the muscle group, after which the assistant moves the body part slowly through its complete ROM to the *limitation point,* where the muscle group cannot safely be stretched further. This three-part sequence is repeated, each time from a new point of greater elongation.

In the **hold-relax type** of PNF, the assistant moves the body part passively through its complete ROM, stopping at

363

the limitation point. At the limitation point, the individual does an isometric or holding type of contraction for 5 to 10 sec, followed by complete relaxation. The assistant supports the body part during the relaxation phase. The hold-relax sequence is repeated several times. The hold-relax type is the method of choice when pain is an issue, as in arthritis.

Beliefs, Attitudes, and Practices

Several theories can be applied to help persons develop fitness and change lifestyle. Statements of goals and objectives should always include targeted beliefs, attitudes, and practices.

According to **reasoned action attitude theory** (see Chapter 9), persons will change their lifestyles to include regular exercise if they are helped to reason out the probable outcomes/consequences and perceive the support of significant others. They are asked to write a personal exercise goal, list the possible good and bad consequences, and then predict the likelihood of these consequences coming true. This becomes their attitude toward behavior score. Next, they identify four or five significant others and what these people think they should do. A subjective norm score is derived by multiplying this with a rating of personal motivation to comply. Together, attitude toward behavior and subjective norm determine intention to implement the exercise goal and exercise behaviors.

According to **self-efficacy** or **social cognitive theory** (see Chapter 5), one must perceive self as capable of carrying out a desired behavior and expect to succeed. Efficacy expectations result when certain antecedents are planned and implemented: (a) reminders of past mastery, (b) role models to provide vicarious learning opportunities, (c) verbal persuasion by self and others, and (d) cognitive control of anxiety, fear, and related negative emotions. These four antecedents represent the most important variables that shape social cognitive behaviors. This comprehensive model works well if the person has been fit in the past and has memories to pull from.

According to **perceived competence theory** (see Chapter 8), three variables affect achievement: (a) perceived competence, (b) perceived control (self, others, unknown), and (c) motivation orientation (challenge, curiosity, mastery, judgment, criteria). Attention to these variables will enhance fitness programming, especially if the person has had little fitness success in the past.

New assessment approaches include self-reports of motivation, food intake, physical activity, and attitudes about the body and exercise. Illustrative is the Self-Motivation Inventory (Dishman, Ickes, & Morgan, 1980). This 40-item instrument includes items like the following that are rated on a 5-point scale ("very unlike me" to "very much like me"):

1. I get discouraged easily.
2. Sometimes, I push myself harder than I should.
3. I can persevere at stressful tasks, even when they are physically tiring or painful.

Research indicates that the self-motivation score combined with body weight and percent fat is an excellent predictor of exercise adherence. Information yielded by instruments like the Self-Motivation Inventory helps in counseling and individualized teaching.

Diaries or logs of food intake (Block et al., 1986) and physical activity (Baranowski, 1988) help structure goal setting.

They focus attention on goals and provide concrete facts; 24-hr recalls tend to be more accurate than 3- or 7-day recalls. Illustrative of an interview format to assess activity is the following:

Teacher: In order to set goals for after-school and weekend physical activity for the next month, let's think about what you did this past week. Let's start with yesterday, and you list everything you did that was of moderate, hard, or very hard intensity. *Moderate* things are activities that make you feel like you are taking a brisk walk. *Very hard* activities make you feel like you are running. *Hard* activities are those that fall between brisk walking and running. Ready? Let's start.

Client/Student: OK, yesterday was Sunday. I got up about 7 A.M., messed around, took a shower, and went to church.

Teacher: What kind of transportation did you take to church? It is important that you tell me about transportation so that we can determine how much energy you spent. Did you walk, and was the pace slow, medium, or fast? Or did you cycle or take a car?

Client/Student: Dad drove the car, but after church, I went with my friends, and we walked about 12 blocks to Bill's house. We messed around a while and then took the bus to a movie.

Teacher: Then what did you do in the evening?

Client/Student: Shot baskets for about an hour with some friends, watched TV a couple of hours, and studied an hour or so. Went to bed about 11 P.M.

Teacher: So your main exercise for the day was basketball shooting. Can you think of any other activities?

Client/Student: No, it rained most of the day.

Teacher: Then let's go back to Saturday. Tell me about your day. You don't need to tell me everything, just the activities that you consider moderate, hard, or very hard.

The interview continues until the past 7 days are covered.

Weather and Temperature Concerns

Weather and temperature are important in all aspects of fitness testing and training. Persons with disabilities tend to be more vulnerable to extremes of hot and cold than able-bodied peers. This is particularly true in spinal paralysis, cerebral palsy, and the widespread nervous system damage associated with severe MR. The hypothalamus in the brain (temperature regulation center) and the autonomic nervous system must be intact for sweat glands, skeletal muscles, and blood vessels to function properly in temperature regulation. *Nervous system damage above T8 (the eighth thoracic segment of the spinal cord) renders the body incapable of maintaining normal temperature (98.6° F or 37° C).*

Anyone with damage above T8 should be closely watched for **poikilothermy,** a condition in which the body assumes the same temperature as the surrounding environment. Such persons are entirely dependent upon clothing, external heating and cooling systems, and ingestion of warm or cool fluids. Temperature regulation problems do not contraindicate heavy exercise; they simply require appropriate adaptations.

Regardless of whether temperature regulation problems are present, persons should not be expected to exert all-out

FIGURE 13.14   Weather guide for prevention of heat illness. Zone 1 is safe; for Zone 2, use caution; for Zone 3, use extreme caution.

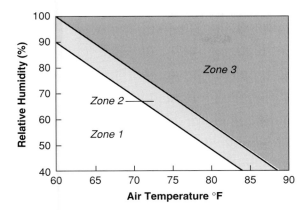

effort when temperatures are above 90° or below 50° or when temperature plus humidity exceed 175°. Figure 13.14 presents a simple system for determining when caution and extreme caution are essential. Whereas humidity is the greatest problem in hot weather, wind-chill factor should be considered in cold weather.

Generic terms for body temperature responses are hypothermia (absence of heat) and hyperthermia (excessive heat). **Hypothermia** is associated with frostbite, frozen parts, progressive loss of consciousness, and death. **Hyperthermia** results in heat cramps, heat exhaustion (headache, sweating, dizziness, awkwardness, goose bumps with cold sensation, paleness of face and lips), and heat stroke (diminished sweating, loss of consciousness, life threatening when oral temperature reaches 105° F or about 40° C). Obesity and fluid depletion increase the risk of heat-related disorders.

Dehydration, a normal exercise response, is intensified in persons with autonomic nervous system dysfunction. Several prescribed medications also increase thirst. Water and other fluids should be taken at regular intervals during exercise, whether or not the person is thirsty.

Space and Equipment

Schools should have several exercise areas to supplement gymnasium and sport field space. The more equipment available, the more likely people are to use it. Figure 13.15 shows some homemade, inexpensive equipment appropriate for indoor or outdoor use in schools, homes, and community centers. Selection of equipment is typically based on muscle groups weakest in the individuals served. For most children and youth, these are the abdominal and arm and shoulder muscles. Persons in wheelchairs or on crutches also have a special need for strong arm and shoulder muscles. Therefore, equipment for sit-ups, pull-ups, push-ups, and arm hangs/travel is of first priority. Equally important is equipment for aerobic endurance. When space is limited, the equipment of choice is stationary cycles, jump ropes and/or obstacles, stairs for climbing, and benches or steps for continuous stepping. Tracks and jog/walk/cycle paths with distances clearly marked should be available in schools, parks, and neighborhoods. These require no equipment other than signs.

Lifestyle change requires that schools, homes, and other facilities budget for equipment, plan for space, and provide incentives for use. Equipment should be available in self-contained classrooms, hallways, restrooms, and the like, as well as special exercise stations. Schools should also provide instruction and experience in use of community health and exercise centers to assure carryover when school facilities are not available.

Equipment design should take into account easy, medium, and hard progressions so that individual differences can be met. Inclined boards, for example, can be used to make sit-ups easier or harder. Persons with low abdominal strength should have head higher than feet; many persons in wheelchairs need this adaptation. A bar to tuck feet under provides needed stability and frees partners to do their own exercise. Different heights of pull-up bars, stair steps, ladders, and rails/ropes allow concurrent work by persons of various heights, weights, and abilities.

Organization of the Lesson: Five Parts

Ideally, each fitness session includes five parts: (a) warm-up, (b) endurance conditioning, (c) flexibility exercises for each major muscle group, (d) muscle strength/endurance exercises, and (e) cool-down. For the average person, sessions last 30 to 45 min because the endurance component requires only 15 to 30 min. For persons with low fitness, however, considerably more time is needed. Often, exercise tolerance is so poor that exercise time must be distributed throughout the day.

Regardless of the fitness components chosen for emphasis, every session should include a 5- to 10-min warm-up and cool-down. During this time, the same muscles and movements should be used as in the regular workout, except at a lower intensity. Typically, 2 or 3 min are spent in walking or slow running, and the remaining time is devoted to slow, static stretches, rhythmical circling of body parts, and gentle calisthenics. Obstacle courses and follow-the-leader activities work well with children. In persons with very low fitness, the warm-up may be all the exercise that can be endured.

Teaching for Fitness: A Review of Principles

A common misconception is that physical activities automatically develop fitness. Two laps around the field or 3 min of calisthenics seldom have the effect desired. The same amount of exercise executed faithfully each day contributes to the maintenance of whatever level fitness already exists, but it *does not improve* fitness.

Fitness lessons should include scientifically planned warm-up, training, and cool-down activities conducted in accordance with the following principles of fitness training:

1. **Individual differences.** Every exercise prescription and/or IEP should be different, based on specific assessment of data, motivation level, and activity preferences. Remember the acronym FIT when making exercise prescriptions:

   F   Frequency

   I   Intensity or resistance

   T   Time or duration

   Let individuals choose their own modality!

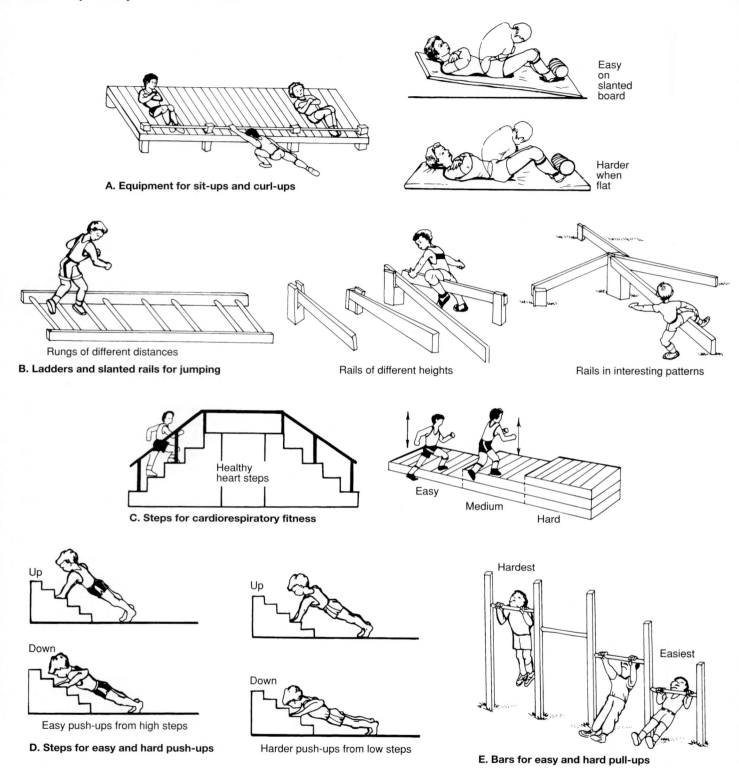

A. Equipment for sit-ups and curl-ups

Easy on slanted board

Harder when flat

Rungs of different distances

B. Ladders and slanted rails for jumping

Rails of different heights

Rails in interesting patterns

Healthy heart steps

C. Steps for cardiorespiratory fitness

Easy

Medium

Hard

Up

Down

Easy push-ups from high steps

D. Steps for easy and hard push-ups

Up

Down

Harder push-ups from low steps

Hardest

Easiest

E. Bars for easy and hard pull-ups

2. **Overload/intensity.** Increases in fitness result when the *work load* is greater than usual. Overload is associated with muscle strength/endurance. Intensity relates more to cardiorespiratory endurance. *Progressive resistance* refers to increasing overload gradually but consistently over time. Overload/intensity can be achieved in the following ways:

a. Increase the number of pounds being lifted, pushed, or pulled. This results in progressive resistance exercises.
b. Increase the number of repetitions, sets, or types of exercise performed.
c. Increase the distance covered.
d. Increase the speed.

e. Increase the number of minutes of continuous all-out effort.

f. Decrease the rest interval between active sessions.

g. Increase the intensity/type of activity during rest/relaxation phases.

h. Use any combination of the above.

3. **Frequency.** Training sessions (particularly those of all-out effort) should be scientifically spaced so that there is time for **physiological homeostasis** to occur (i.e., for muscles to rest). Too frequent practices tend to result in chronic fatigue, muscle stress, and motivation problems.

4. **Specificity/transfer.** Values gained from exercises done in one position or at one speed will not transfer or benefit the person in other positions or at alternative speeds. Exercises are highly specific; thus, strength exercises particularly need to be done at many joint angles and many intensities. Warm-ups should use the same movements and positions that will be used later in the game or training exercise.

5. **Active/voluntary movement.** Outcome is most effective when the exercise is *active* (done by the student) rather than passive (done by a therapist or teacher). In the case of persons with severe disability with little or no movement capacity of a particular body part, encourage an all-out effort to initiate the movement, which then can be assisted by the teacher. The student should be actively concentrating and assisting in coactive movement.

6. **Correct breathing.** Breath holding should be avoided because of the Valsalva effect.

7. **Recovery/cool-down.** Persons should not lie or sit down immediately after high-intensity exercise. This tends to subvert the return of blood to the heart and causes dizziness. *Cool-down* should entail continued slow walking or mild activity.

8. **Warm-up.** Warm-ups using movements specific to the game or training to follow should precede high-intensity activity. Warm-up is particularly important for persons with chronic respiratory or cardiorespiratory conditions.

9. **Static stretch.** Slow, static stretches are effective in increasing range of motion and flexibility. Note that ballistic exercises are contraindicated when the goal is to stretch. In spastic cerebral palsy, ballistic exercise elicits an exaggerated stretch reflex.

10. **Contraindication.** If correct postural alignment cannot be maintained during execution of an exercise, it is usually too difficult a progression and is therefore contraindicated.

11. **Adaptation.** Exercises should be analyzed into easy, medium, and difficult progressions so that each person is doing the adaptation best for him or her. A biomechanical principle often used in adapting exercises is *leverage;* the shorter the lever, the easier the exercise. For instance, straight-leg lifts from a supine position to develop or assess abdominal strength are very difficult since the body (as a lever) is in its longest position. By doing bent-knee leg lifts, the body lever is shortened and the exercise is made easier.

12. **Motivation.** Persons who wish to be physically fit must be willing to pay the price. They must be motivated to tolerate boredom, fatigue, and discomfort. Fitness does not come easily.

13. **Maintenance.** Lifespan fitness requires lifespan activity. Instruction should emphasize maintenance.

14. **Nutrition.** Food and liquid intake should be balanced with activity. Instruction on eating and exercise should be integrated.

15. **Environmental factors.** Activity should be safe and pleasurable. Give particular attention to temperature, humidity, windchill, and pollution.

16. **Ecological or social validity.** Fitness activity should make sense and have carryover value. For example, to persons with severe MR, lifting chairs or sacks of groceries may make more sense than lifting bars and dumbbells.

Exercise Conditioning Methods

This chapter concludes with methods that can be applied to more than one fitness component: (a) interval or intermittent, (b) circuits, (c) continuous, and (d) combinations. For adults, these methods are often built around one modality (weight lifting, running, cycling, swimming). With children, animal walks, stunts, calisthenics, and locomotor activities that are known to develop specific muscle groups are fun. Any large muscle activity done long enough at the right intensity develops cardiorespiratory endurance.

Interval or Intermittent Training

Developed originally to condition long-distance runners and swimmers, interval training can be adapted to any physical activity. It is especially beneficial for persons with asthma, muscular dystrophy, multiple sclerosis, and other neuromuscular conditions. The basic objective is to exercise for short periods of time with rest intervals between.

The interval training prescription (ITP) should be planned for each person individually or for small, homogeneous groups, rather than for the class as a whole (see Table 13.7). After the first 2 weeks, training only twice weekly will result in significant gains in cardiorespiratory endurance.

ITPs require an understanding of the following terms:

1. **Set.** Term that encompasses both the work interval and the rest interval. An ITP may have any number of sets.

2. **Work interval.** Also called a bout. A prescribed number of repetitions of the same activity under identical conditions. Traditionally, the work has been walking, running, or swimming a prescribed number of yards at optimum or near-optimum speed *in an effort to raise the heart rate to a prescribed level.* For variety, work intervals may entail performing an optimum number of squat thrusts, curl-ups, or push-ups within a prescribed number of seconds.

3. **Rest interval.** The number of seconds or minutes between work intervals. During rest, persons should walk rather that sit, lie, or stand. A light activity like walking, arm circles, or toe touches may be psychologically beneficial in that it keeps the mind off exhaustion. The number of seconds comprising the rest interval depends

Table 13.7 Sample ITP card for pupils of similar ability.

Day 5	Repetitions (reps)	Activity	Rest Interval	Self-Evaluation		
				Easy	*Medium*	*Hard*
Set 1	4 reps	Runs 220 yd	Walk for 60 sec between sprints			
Set 2	6 reps	Squat thrusts for 10 sec	Arm circling for 20 sec between bouts			
Set 3	4 reps	Crab walk for 10 sec	Movement of choice for 20 sec between bouts			
Set 4	8 reps	Run 100 yd	Walk for 30 sec between sprints			

on individual heart recovery rate. *The next repetition should not begin until the heart rate drops to 120 beats per minute or lower, depending on age and fitness status.* If taking the pulse rate is not feasible, the time of the rest interval initially should be approximately twice the amount of time consumed by the work interval.

4. **Repetitions.** The number of times the work is repeated under identical conditions. The amount of effort exerted in each repetition should be more or less constant.

5. **Target time.** The best score that a person can make on the prescribed activity. Target times are generally not set until after the first 2 weeks and are then used as a motivational device to encourage all-out performance.

6. **Level of aspiration.** A statement made by the exerciser indicating expected score or level. This is also a motivational device.

All-out effort is often motivated after the first few weeks by prescribing the speed of the sprint as follows:

One repetition of 660 yd in 2:03
Six repetitions of 220 yd in 0:33
Six repetitions of 110 yd in 0:15

Persons may be guided in developing individualized exercise sessions comprised of sets that reflect their own levels of aspiration. Presumably, this is more motivating than trying to accomplish goals set by others.

In keeping with the overload/intensity principle, the exercise sessions become increasingly more demanding each week. As training progresses, the long, slow runs are gradually replaced with shorter, faster sprints. *For healthy adolescents and adults, a total workout distance of over 1.5 mi must eventually be achieved for maximum benefits.*

Circuit Training

Circuit training is a method that involves moving from station to station. Ideally, the task performed at each station uses different groups of muscles. For adolescents and adults, from 6 to 10 stations are recommended, depending upon available space and

equipment. For elementary school children and persons with mental limitations, from two to six stations may be attempted.

The amount of time at each station varies, but initially is relatively brief. Thirty seconds at each station, with 10 sec for rotation, is satisfactory. Thus, a four-station circuit can be completed in approximately 2.5 min. As training progresses, the amount of time at each station can be extended or the number of circuits increased. The intensity of the work demanded should be increased gradually in keeping with the overload principle.

Procedures to be followed are these:

1. Ascertain that everyone knows how to perform the fitness tasks.

2. Divide the group into squads of two to six persons, and assign each squad to a different starting point on the circuit.

3. Practice rotating in a counterclockwise direction from station to station.

4. Develop an individualized circuit-training plan for each student:
   a. Determine the best score on each task during a set time limit like 30 sec. Base future work at each station on one half to three fourths of the student's best score.
   b. Determine the best time in completing the circuit and challenge the person to better this time on the next test, which is scheduled after several days of practice.

An alternative or adapted method for young children and persons with mental limitations who cannot work independently is to have a leader at each station who keeps people exercising until the whistle blows. Persons then join hands or form a file and follow the leader to the next station. This procedure works best if someone calls out, "Rotate, 1–2–3–4–5–6–7–8–9–10," and everyone knows that he or she must be at a new station by the count of 10. To implement the overload/intensity principle, time at each station is periodically increased and/or number of circuits is increased. For this adapted method to work, squads must be homogeneous in fitness level.

Table 13.8   Twelve-minute walking/running test (distance [miles] covered in 12 min).

Fitness Category	Sex	Age (Years)					
		13–19	*20–29*	*30–39*	*40–49*	*50–59*	*60+*
I. Very poor	M	<1.30	<1.22	<1.18	<1.14	<1.03	<.87
	F	<1.0	<.96	<.94	<.88	<.84	<.78
II. Poor	M	1.30–1.37	1.22–1.31	1.18–1.30	1.14–1.24	1.03–1.16	.87–1.02
	F	1.00–1.18	.96–1.11	.95–1.05	.88–.98	.84–.93	.78–.86
III. Fair	M	1.38–1.56	1.32–1.49	1.31–1.45	1.25–1.39	1.17–1.30	1.03–1.20
	F	1.19–1.29	1.12–1.22	1.06–1.18	.99–1.11	.94–1.05	.87–.98
IV. Good	M	1.57–1.72	1.50–1.64	1.46–1.56	1.40–1.53	1.31–1.44	1.21–1.32
	F	1.30–1.43	1.23–1.34	1.19–1.29	1.12–1.24	1.06–1.18	.99–1.09
V. Excellent	M	1.73–1.86	1.65–1.76	1.57–1.69	1.54–1.65	1.45–1.58	1.33–1.55
	F	1.44–1.51	1.35–1.45	1.30–1.39	1.25–1.34	1.19–1.30	1.10–1.18
VI. Superior	M	>1.87	>1.77	>1.70	>1.66	>1.59	>1.56
	F	>1.52	>1.46	>1.40	>1.35	>1.31	>1.19

From *The Aerobics Program for Total Well-Being* by Kenneth H. Cooper M.D., M.P.H. Copyright © 1982 by Kenneth H. Cooper. Used by permission of Bantam Books, a division of Bantam Doubleday Dell Publishing Group, Inc.

Continuous Conditioning

Continuous conditioning refers to exercise that imposes a consistent submaximal energy requirement throughout the training session. Examples are aerobics and rope jumping.

Aerobics

The aerobics exercise program can be divided into three phases: (a) evaluation or cardiorespiratory fitness, (b) a period of progressive conditioning that extends over several weeks, and (c) maintenance of optimal fitness by earning a specific number of points for exercise each week.

Prior to undertaking an aerobics program, individuals are assessed on distance covered in 12 min in the modality of their choice (walking, running, swimming, cycling). They are then assigned to one of six fitness categories based on gender and age. For males under age 50, a good classification hovers around 1.5 mi in 12 min (see Table 13.8). For females, it is slightly less. Aerobic fitness peaks at ages 20 to 29 and then slowly drops.

The fitness classification determines the number of weeks of conditioning required to work up to the maintenance phase of 30 points per week. Use the following guidelines: (a) very poor category—16 weeks, (b) poor category—13 weeks, and (c) fair category—10 weeks. Points are awarded to determine the frequency of walks per week. Persons who score in the "good," "excellent," or "superior" fitness categories do not participate in the program of progressive conditioning. They go directly to the maintenance phase, earning 30 points each week.

The most efficient way to earn 30 points is to jog 1.5 mi in 12 min (for which, 7.5 points are awarded) four times a week. The following activities, each worth 5 points, create a basis for developing an individualized maintenance program:

Bicycling 5 mi in less than 20 min

Running 1 mi in less than 8 min

Swimming 600 yd in less than 15 min

Handball played for a total of 35 min

Stationary running for a total of 12.5 min

For individual sports enthusiasts, one set of singles tennis earns 1.5 points, nine holes of golf earn 1.5 points, waterskiing or snow skiing for 30 min earns 3 points, and ice or roller skating for 15 min earns 1 point. For the bicycle rider who enjoys leisurely pedaling, at least 30 min of cycling is required to earn 1 point.

Aerobic dancing and water exercises, called **hydro-aerobics** or **hydrorobics,** are popular applications of aerobic theory. Many persons with lower limb disabilities can walk or run laps in chest-high water even though they cannot walk on land. Continuous calisthenics produce lower heart rates in water than on land and are particularly recommended for low fitness, obesity, and heart disease.

Rope Jumping, Continuous

Individual rope jumping and long-rope jumping done to chants or music of different speeds and duration provide excellent exercise, especially for maintenance. The usual cadence of 60 to 80 jumps a minute requires 9 METs, about the equivalent of running an 11-min mile. This high metabolic demand may make rope jumping inappropriate for sedentary persons, especially those who are obese or have heart disease. Rope jumping is a high-impact exercise and particularly stresses joints in obesity, so weight loss is a prerequisite.

Individual rope jumping has been promoted by AAH-PERD and the American Heart Association, and an adapted physical education goal may be developing fitness to participate in school "jump for heart" programs. Ropes of different lengths should be available. Ropes should be long enough so that the ends reach the armpits or slightly higher when the jumper stands on the rope's center. Wrists should supply the force to turn the rope so that energy is not wasted with unnecessary arm motions.

Combination Conditioning

Combination methods use both continuous and intermittent activity. Rope jumping, for example, can use the protocol in

T a b l e   1 3 . 9   Illustrative rope-jumping sequences individualized to meet capabilities.

Easy Sequence	Medium Sequence	Difficult Sequence
1. Rope jump 1 min	1. Rope jump 3 min	1. Rope jump 4 min
2. Rest 60 sec	2. Rest 30 sec	2. Rest 20 sec
3. Rope jump 30 sec	3. Rope jump 1½ min	3. Rope jump 2 min

Table 13.9 until students build up the fitness for aerobic-level jumping. The goal is to be able to jump 60 to 80 times a minute. During the rest, students should walk or do stretches.

Astronaut or Football Drills

Astronaut or *football drills* are continuous exercise routines done in response to one-word cues that require changes of body position. The correct response to each cue follows:

1. **Go.** Run in place with vigorous high-knee action. Maintain top speed.
2. **Front.** Drop to prone lying position and assume a ready position to ensure quick response to the next cue.
3. **Back.** Drop to supine position and assume a ready position to ensure quick response to the next cue.

These cues are given in various orders, challenging the student to persist in continuous motion. The principle of overload is applied by progressively increasing the duration of time spent in the "go" position. After students have mastered these cues, others might be added: right side lie, left side lie, squat, long sit, and so on. Astronaut drills teach and reinforce concepts and vocabulary concerning body parts and body positions.

Jogging, Hiking, and Cycling

Long walks are called hikes and can be combined with map reading, nature study, scavenger hunts, and other themes. Hiking, jogging, and cycling are particularly successful when correlated with social studies and/or related to a trip across the state, North America, or another continent. Students can update individual mileage sheets, superimposed upon maps. Merit badges or achievement certificates may be awarded for the completion of every 50-mile distance.

The **scout's pace** can be used in early stages of training as follows: jog 110 yd, walk 55 yd, jog 110 yd, walk 55 yd, ad infinitum. The scout's pace can also be interpreted as meaning run as far as you can, then walk until breath is restored, after which running is resumed. Wheelchair activities are conducted like walks and jogs.

Cycling can be done on two- or three-wheeled vehicles and be stationary or moving. Persons with cerebral palsy or other balance impairments may use special adult-size tricycles available through Sears and similar stores. Cycles must be adjustable to body size. Seat height should permit the knee to be slightly bent when toes are on the lower pedal. Handlebar height should encourage good posture, with slight body lean.

Obstacle or Challenge Courses

Perhaps no activity is as popular with elementary school students as following a leader through an obstacle course. Apparatus for these courses can be purchased commercially or constructed by teachers and parents. Homemade obstacle courses are often built around a theme. Assigning pieces of equipment novel names creates the mood for activity built around space travel, a jungle trek, a western outpost, or an Indian village.

Seldom is a class small enough that all students can move through an obstacle course simultaneously. Congestion and confusion are prevented by assigning not more than two students to each piece of apparatus and by having them stand at their assigned apparatus while awaiting the signal "go," rather than all standing in a file behind the leader. Thus, only 14 students can move efficiently through a seven-piece obstacle course at any given time. Flexible teachers post time schedules listing each student's name and stating the time at which he or she is excused from regular class activities to go through the obstacle course.

References

Alter, M. J. (1996). *Science of flexibility and stretching* (2nd ed.). Champaign, IL: Human Kinetics.

American Alliance for Health, Physical Education and Recreation. (1976). *Special fitness test manual for the mildly mentally retarded.* Washington, DC: Author. (First edition, 1968).

American Alliance for Health, Physical Education, Recreation and Dance. (1988). *Physical best.* Reston, VA: Author.

American College of Sports Medicine. (1995). *Guidelines for exercise testing and prescription* (5th ed.). Philadelphia: Lea & Febiger.

Baranowski, T. (1988). Validity and reliability of self-report measures of physical activity: An information processing perspective. *Research Quarterly for Exercise and Sport, 59*(4), 314–327.

Bar-Or, O. (1983). *Pediatric sports medicine for the practitioner.* New York: Springer-Verlag.

Basmajian, J., & Wolf, S. (Eds.). (1990). *Therapeutic exercise* (5th ed.). Baltimore: Williams & Wilkins.

Bates, B. (1983). *A guide to physical examination* (3rd ed.). Philadelphia: J. B. Lippincott.

Beasley, C. R. (1982). Effects of a jogging program on cardiovascular fitness and work performance of mentally retarded persons. *American Journal of Mental Deficiency, 6,* 609–613.

Block, G., Hartman, A., Dresser, C., Carroll, M., Gannon, J., & Gardner, L. (1986). A data-based approach to diet questionnaire design and testing. *American Journal of Epidemiology, 124*(3), 453–469.

Borg, G. A. (1982). Psychophysical bases of perceived exertion. *Medicine and Science in Sports and Exercise, 14,* 377–381.

Bouffard, M., Watkinson, E. J., Thompson, L. P., Dunn, J. L., & Romanow, K. E. (1996). A test of the activity deficit hypothesis with children with movement difficulties. *Adapted Physical Activity Quarterly, 13*(1), 61–73.

Buell, C. (1973). *Physical education and recreation for the visually handicapped.* Washington, DC: American Alliance for Health, Physical Education and Recreation.

Buell, C. (1982). *Physical education and recreation for the visually handicapped* (2nd ed). Reston VA: American Alliance for Health, Physical Education, Recreation and Dance.

Canada Fitness Survey. (1986). *Physical activity among activity-limited and disabled adults in Canada.* Montreal: Author.

Cooper Institute for Aerobics Research. (1994a). *The Prudential FITNESSGRAM technical reference manual.* Dallas: Author.

Cooper Institute for Aerobics Research. (1994b). *The Prudential FITNESSGRAM test administration manual.* Dallas: Author.

Cooper, K. H. (1968). *Aerobics.* New York: M. Evans.

Cooper, K. H. (1982). *The aerobics program for total well-being.* New York: Bantam Books.

Curtis, K. (1981). Stretching routines. *Sports 'N Spokes, 7*(3), 16–18.

Daniels, L., & Worthingham, C. (1986). *Muscle testing: Techniques of manual examination* (5th ed.). Philadelphia: Saunders.

DeLorme, T., & Watkins, A. (1948). Techniques of progressive resistance exercise. *Archives of Physical and Medical Rehabilitation, 29,* 263–273.

Dishman, R. K. (Ed.). (1994). *Advances in exercise adherence.* Champaign, IL: Human Kinetics.

Dishman, R. K., Ickes, W., & Morgan, W. (1980). Self-motivation and adherence to habitual physical activity. *Journal of Applied Social Psychology, 10,* 115–132.

Dobbins, D., Garron, R., & Rarick, G. S. (1981). The motor performance of EMR and intellectually normal boys after covariate control for differences in body size. *Research Quarterly for Exercise and Sport, 52*(1), 1–8.

Dunn, J., Morehouse, J., & Fredericks, H. (1986). *Physical education for the severely handicapped: A systematic approach to a data-based gymnasium.* Austin, TX: Pro•Ed.

Fisher, S. V., & Gullickson, G. (1978). Energy cost of ambulation in health and disability: A literature view. *Archives of Physical Medicine and Rehabilitation, 59,* 124–132.

Fletcher, G. F., Balady, G., Froelicher, V. F., Hartely, L. H., Haskell, W. L., & Pollock, M. L. (1995). Exercise standards: A statement for healthcare professionals for the American Heart Association. *Circulation, 91,* 580–615.

Francis, R. J., & Rarick, G. L. (1959). Motor characteristics of the mentally retarded. *American Journal of Mental Deficiency, 63,* 792–811.

Golding, L. A., Myers, C. R., & Sinning, W. (1989). *Y's way to physical fitness.* Champaign, IL: Human Kinetics.

Government of Canada. (1987). *Canadian standardized test of fitness, interpretation, and counseling manual.* Ottawa: Fitness Canada.

Hayden, F. J. (1964). *Physical fitness for the mentally retarded.* Toronto: Toronto Association for Retarded Children.

Heath, G. W., Pratt, M., Warren, C. W., & Kann, L. (1995, fall). Physical activity patterns in American high school students. *Canadian Journal of Health, Physical Education, Recreation, and Dance,* 35–39.

Hellebrandt, F., & Houtz, S. (1956). Mechanisms of muscle training in man: Experimental demonstration of the overload principle. *Physical Therapy Review, 36,* 371–383.

Hettinger, T., & Müller, E. (1953). Muskelleistung und muskeltraining. *Arbeitphysiologie, 15,* 111–126.

Holland, L., & Steadward, D. (1990). Effects of resistance and flexibility training on strength, spasticity/muscle tone, and range of motion of elite athletes with cerebral palsy. *Palaestra, 6*(4), 27–31.

Jansma, J., Decker, J., Ersing, W., McCubbin, H., & Combs, S. (1988). A fitness assessment system for individuals with severe mental retardation. *Adapted Physical Activity Quarterly, 5*(3), 223–232.

Johnson, L., & Londeree, B. (1976). *Motor fitness testing manual for the moderately mentally retarded.* Washington, DC: American Alliance for Health, Physical Education and Recreation.

Kobberling, G., Jankowski, L., & Leger, L. (1989). Energy cost of locomotion in blind adolescents. *Adapted Physical Activity Quarterly, 6*(1), 58–67.

Kottke, F. (1990). Therapeutic exercise to maintain mobility. In F. Kottke & J. Lehmann (Eds.), *Krusen's handbook of physical medicine and rehabilitation* (4th ed., pp. 436–451). Philadelphia: W. B. Saunders.

Kraus, H., & Hirschland, R. (1954). Minimum muscular fitness tests in schoolchildren. *Research Quarterly, 25*(2), 177–188.

Lange, L. (1919). *Uber funktionelle anpassurig.* Berlin: Springer-Verlag.

Lockette, K. F., & Keyes, A. M. (1994). *Conditioning with physical disabilities.* Champaign, IL: Human Kinetics.

Marshall, J. D., & Bouffard, M. (1994). Obesity and movement competency in children. *Adapted Physical Activity Quarterly, 11*(3), 297–365.

Miller, N., Merritt, J., Merkel, K., & Westbrook, P. (1984). Paraplegic energy expenditure during negotiation of architectural barriers. *Archives of Physical Medicine and Rehabilitation, 65,* 778–779.

Miller, P. D. (Ed.). (1995). *Fitness programming for physical disabilities: A publication for Disabled Sports USA.* Champaign, IL: Human Kinetics.

National Consortium for Physical Education and Recreation for Individuals with Disabilities. (1995). *Adapted physical education national standards.* Champaign, IL: Human Kinetics.

Pate, R. R., Pratt, M., Blair, S. N., Haskell, W. L., Macera, C. A., Bouchard, C., et al. (1995). Physical activity and public health: A recommendation from the Centers for Disease Control and Prevention and the American College of Sports Medicine. *Journal of the American Medical Association, 273,* 402–407.

President's Council on Physical Fitness and Sports. (1987). *Get fit: A handbook for youth ages 6–17.* Washington, DC: Author.

Rarick, G. L. (1980). Cognitive-motor relationships in the growing years. *Research Quarterly for Exercise and Sport, 51*(1), 174–192.

Reid, G., Seidl, C., & Montgomery, D. (1989). Fitness tests for retarded adults: Tips for test selection, subject familiarization, administration, and interpretation. *Journal of Physical Education, Recreation and Dance, 60*(6), 76–78.

Rimmer, J. H. (1994). *Fitness and rehabilitation programs for special populations.* Dubuque, IA: Brown & Benchmark.

Rippe, J. M., & Ward, A. (1989). *The Rockport walking program.* New York: Prentice Hall.

Seaman, J. A. (Ed.). (1995). *Physical Best and individuals with disabilities: A handbook for inclusion in fitness programs.* Reston, VA: AAHPERD, American Association for Active Lifestyles and Fitness.

Shephard, R. (1990). *Fitness in special populations.* Champaign, IL: Human Kinetics.

Skrotsky, K. (1983). Gait analysis in cerebral palsied and nonhandicapped children. *Archives of Physical Medicine and Rehabilitation, 64,* 291–295.

Surburg, P. R. (1986). New perspectives for developing range of motion and flexibility for special populations. *Adapted Physical Activity Quarterly, 3*(3), 227–235.

U.S. Department of Health and Human Services. (1996). *The surgeon general's report on physical activity and health.* Washington, DC: Author.

Ward, D. S., & Bar-Or, O. (1990). Use of the Borg scale in exercise prescription for overweight youth. *Canadian Journal of Sport Science, 15*(2), 120–125.

Wells, C., & Hooker, S. (1990). The spinal injured athlete. *Adapted Physical Activity Quarterly, 7*(3), 265–285.

Winnick, J. (1995). Personalizing measurement and evaluation for individuals with disabilities. In J. A. Seaman (Ed.), *Physical Best for individuals with disabilities: A handbook for inclusion in fitness programs* (pp. 21–31). Reston, VA: American Alliance for Health, Physical Education, Recreation and Dance.

Winnick, J., & Short, F. (1985). *Physical fitness testing of the disabled: Project UNIQUE.* Champaign, IL: Human Kinetics.

World Health Organization. (1947). Constitution of the World Health Organization. *Chronicle of WHO, 1,* 1–2.

C H A P T E R
14

Postures, Appearance, and Muscle Imbalance

FIGURE 14.1   Mirror work to increase body awareness.

After you have studied this chapter, you should be able to do the following:

1. Discuss assessment techniques for postures.

2. Explain normal postural development with implications for strength and flexibility training at different ages.

3. State posture training guidelines and contrast old and new approaches to ameliorating posture problems.

4. Identify the most common postural problems and explain which muscle groups (extensors, flexors, abductors, and adductors) are abnormally weak or tight in relation to each. Apply this to activity selection.

5. Discuss kyphosis and scoliosis as orthopedic problems that require cooperative program planning by physician, teacher, and family. State the procedures for initiating and/or facilitating this cooperation.

Improvement of postures and overall physical appearance is an important objective within the fitness/wellness goal domain. Physical attractiveness is strongly related to global self-esteem (Harter, 1988) and socialization (Zakahi & Duran, 1988). Many persons are not in tune with their bodies and lack awareness of how they look. Yet we often form lasting first impressions on the basis of appearance.

Normalization philosophy challenges physical educators to make persons aware of movement patterns and to give them opportunities for developing the postures most likely to help them make friends, win social acceptance, and obtain jobs (Sherrill, 1980). This includes living, learning, and working in environments where significant others model good postures.

Persons with disabilities and/or clumsiness particularly need help with postures (see Figure 14.1). Whenever strength and flexibility are targeted as fitness goals, postures must be given special attention.

Many Postures: Plural

Each person possesses not one but many postures. Any position is a posture, and we assume thousands of static and dynamic postures each day—standing, walking, running, sitting, sleeping, stooping, climbing, and on ad infinitum. Josephine Rathbone, a pioneer in postures education and physical disabilities, emphasized that postures is a plural concept (Rathbone & Hunt, 1965). Head postures cannot be considered without shoulder postures; shoulder postures cannot be taught without back postures; and so on. Reference is thus made to *postures* training; the word is not used in the singular.

Good Postures: Strength and Flexibility

Good postures are mechanically efficient body positions and movement patterns. Mechanical efficiency is possible only when muscles on all the body surfaces are in perfect balance with just the right amount of strength and flexibility. Muscles on the anterior surface (flexors) must be in balance with muscles on the posterior surface (extensors). Muscles on the lateral surface (abductors) must be in balance with muscles on the medial surface (adductors). In general the names of muscle groups (flexors, extensors, abductors, adductors, inward and outward rotators) are used when instructing persons about their bodies.

The powerful force of gravity tends to pull body parts downward, thereby tightening and strengthening the flexors. This causes an imbalance between flexors and extensors that underlies the major principle of postures training: *Strengthen the extensors!* The extensors of the neck and back, called the *antigravity muscles,* are the target of most postures training.

Assessment of Postures

Figure 14.2 shows the assessment form most frequently used in the examination of postures. This form shows the major body parts that should be checked for alignment. Alignment is primarily a matter of muscle balance. Muscles on the right and left sides of the spine, for example, must be of equal strength, or the spine will be pulled out of alignment by the stronger group. Unequal muscle pulls, in time, distort the shape of bones, as well as their position.

Persons with paralysis and spasticity are particularly vulnerable to severe alignment problems. Muscle imbalance is minimized by strapping, bracing, casting, and surgery. Proper positioning when sitting or lying for long periods is obviously important because muscle groups adapt their size and shape to the position in which they spend the most time.

Spinal Column Curves

The development of spinal column curves is mature in most children by ages 7 or 8. Viewed from the side, these are the curves:

1. **Concave.** Cervical spine, composed of 7 vertebrae.
2. **Convex.** Thoracic spine, composed of 12 vertebrae.
3. **Concave.** Lumbar spine, composed of 5 vertebrae.
4. **Convex.** Sacral spine, composed of 5 sacral vertebrae fused in adulthood and called the sacrum.

Erect, extended carriage results when the thoracic and sacral flexion curves are in balance with the cervical and lumbar hyperextension curves. Whenever one curve increases, the other curves also tend to increase to compensate for the imbalance.

Analysis of Muscle Imbalance

When a posture problem is evident, analyze the imbalance of the muscle groups by considering these questions:

1. Muscles on which surface are too tight—that is, stronger than their antagonists? Which **stretching exercises** are indicated?
2. Muscles on which surface are too loose—that is, weaker than their antagonists? Which **strengthening exercises** are indicated?
3. What role is gravity playing in the muscle imbalance?

FIGURE 14.2 Posture score sheet associated with the New York Posture Test.

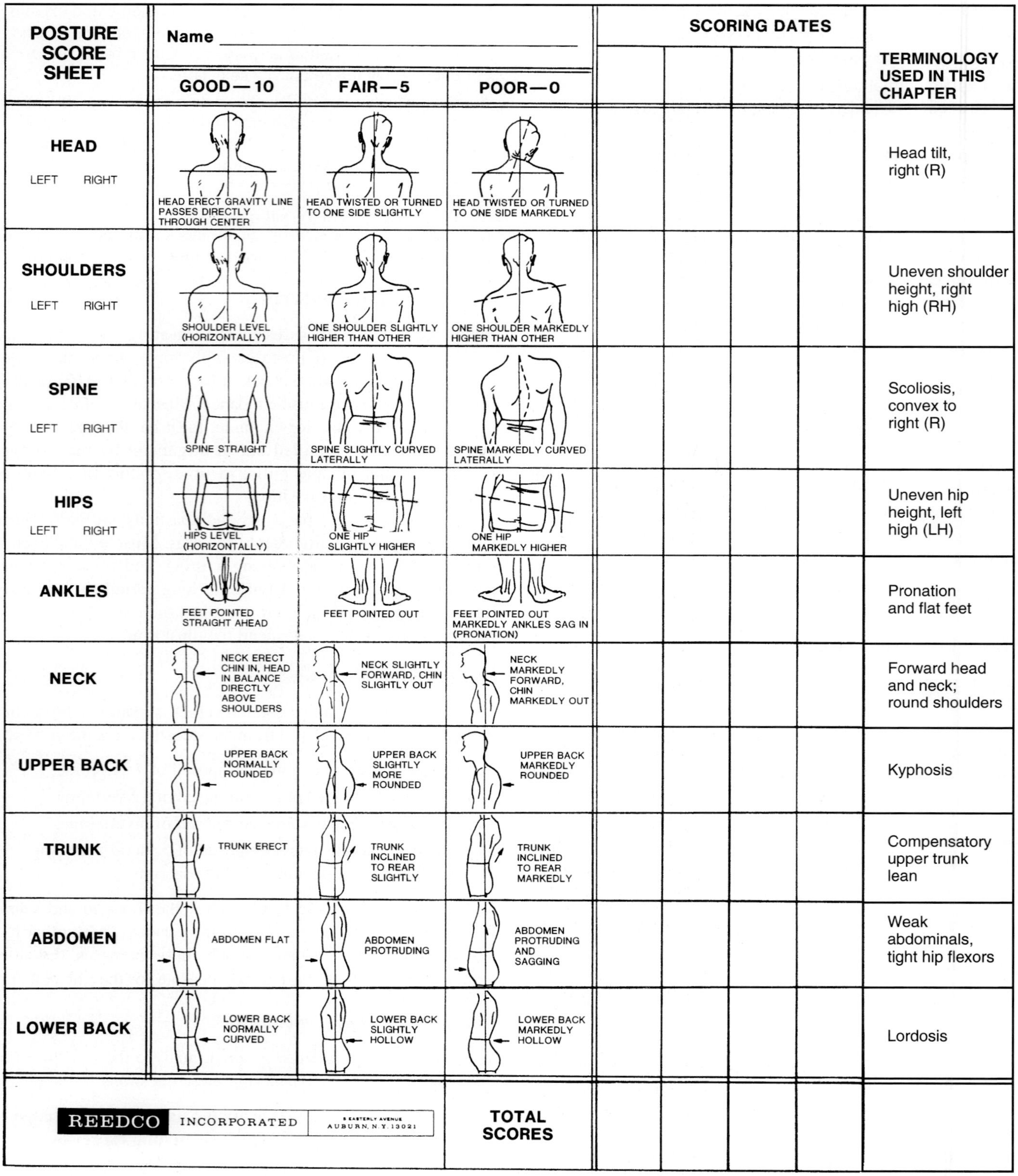

POSTURE SCORE SHEET	Name _____			SCORING DATES				TERMINOLOGY USED IN THIS CHAPTER
	GOOD — 10	FAIR — 5	POOR — 0					
HEAD LEFT RIGHT	HEAD ERECT GRAVITY LINE PASSES DIRECTLY THROUGH CENTER	HEAD TWISTED OR TURNED TO ONE SIDE SLIGHTLY	HEAD TWISTED OR TURNED TO ONE SIDE MARKEDLY					Head tilt, right (R)
SHOULDERS LEFT RIGHT	SHOULDER LEVEL (HORIZONTALLY)	ONE SHOULDER SLIGHTLY HIGHER THAN OTHER	ONE SHOULDER MARKEDLY HIGHER THAN OTHER					Uneven shoulder height, right high (RH)
SPINE LEFT RIGHT	SPINE STRAIGHT	SPINE SLIGHTLY CURVED LATERALLY	SPINE MARKEDLY CURVED LATERALLY					Scoliosis, convex to right (R)
HIPS LEFT RIGHT	HIPS LEVEL (HORIZONTALLY)	ONE HIP SLIGHTLY HIGHER	ONE HIP MARKEDLY HIGHER					Uneven hip height, left high (LH)
ANKLES	FEET POINTED STRAIGHT AHEAD	FEET POINTED OUT	FEET POINTED OUT MARKEDLY ANKLES SAG IN (PRONATION)					Pronation and flat feet
NECK	NECK ERECT CHIN IN, HEAD IN BALANCE DIRECTLY ABOVE SHOULDERS	NECK SLIGHTLY FORWARD, CHIN SLIGHTLY OUT	NECK MARKEDLY FORWARD, CHIN MARKEDLY OUT					Forward head and neck; round shoulders
UPPER BACK	UPPER BACK NORMALLY ROUNDED	UPPER BACK SLIGHTLY MORE ROUNDED	UPPER BACK MARKEDLY ROUNDED					Kyphosis
TRUNK	TRUNK ERECT	TRUNK INCLINED TO REAR SLIGHTLY	TRUNK INCLINED TO REAR MARKEDLY					Compensatory upper trunk lean
ABDOMEN	ABDOMEN FLAT	ABDOMEN PROTRUDING	ABDOMEN PROTRUDING AND SAGGING					Weak abdominals, tight hip flexors
LOWER BACK	LOWER BACK NORMALLY CURVED	LOWER BACK SLIGHTLY HOLLOW	LOWER BACK MARKEDLY HOLLOW					Lordosis
REEDCO INCORPORATED 8 EASTERLY AVENUE AUBURN, N.Y. 13021		**TOTAL SCORES**						

FIGURE 14.3 Normal postures in *(A)* a two-year-old and *(B)* a preadolescent.

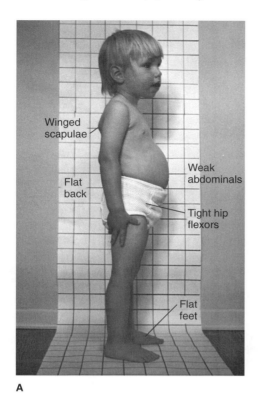

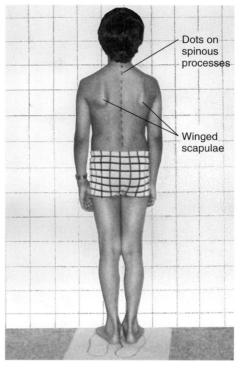

A

B

Usually, strength exercises are chosen for amelioration of posture problems. Remember the principle of **reciprocal innervation:** When muscles on one surface are being strengthened, muscles on the antagonistic surface are being stretched simultaneously. Regardless of the type of exercise selected, both surfaces are affected (Lowman & Young, 1960).

Normal Postural Development

Infant and toddler postural development depends largely upon vigorous movement. At birth, the entire spinal column of the infant is flexed in a single C curve. Only when the extensor muscles of the neck and back are sufficiently strengthened by random kicking and wiggling do the cervical and lumbar curves begin to appear. The cervical curve develops at about 4 to 5 months of age, while the lumbar curve begins to develop sometime after the child learns to walk. Children with severe disabilities that prevent walking tend to have **flat back,** a condition denoting the absence of spinal column curves, unless spasticity causes pathological curves. Flat back is normal in all children until age 3 or 4, when they begin to exhibit the opposite condition, **lordosis,** or sway back. This condition is caused by the imbalance in the strength of the abdominal muscles and the hip flexors. The abdominal musculature of the preschool child normally is too weak to maintain the pelvis in a neutral position (see Figure 14.3A). Lordosis, therefore, is normal in a young child and should not be labeled as a postural deviation until adolescence. The degree of lumbar curvature should, however, lessen from year to year.

Winged scapulae, prominence or protrusion of the scapulae, is normal until adolescence (see Figure 14.3B). Winged scapulae is caused by an imbalance in the muscle groups that cause abduction/upward rotation and adduction/downward rotation.

Posture Training Guidelines

Once the present level of postural fitness is assessed and annual goals written to include posture training, short-term objectives are developed. These objectives can be broken down into behaviors. Illustrative target behaviors for improving walking postures are (a) keeps head and trunk erect with eyes generally focused straight ahead; (b) swings arms in opposition with normal range of motion; (c) uses regular, rhythmic, heel-ball-toe transfer of weight; and (d) maintains normal support base—that is, heels, 2 to 3 inches from line of progression.

For many years, individualized, prescribed exercises were the accepted practice in posture training and body mechanics activities. These exercises were often boring and, if not rigidly adhered to, ineffective. Moreover, if performed incorrectly, such exercises could actually injure the child. The trend now is away from isolated exercises and toward gamelike activities that utilize muscle groups in therapeutically sound ways. This chapter, therefore, includes only a few exercises for each condition.

General physical education programming designed to achieve posture training objectives emphasizes use of the kinesthetic, vestibular, and visual sense modalities in such activities as body awareness or proprioceptive training, body

FIGURE 14.4 Exercises that are contraindicated when certain posture problems are present.

A. Straight leg lift and hold should not be used when persons have weak abdominal muscles and/or lordosis.

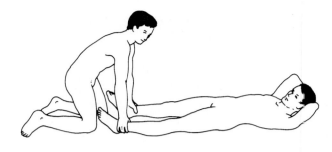

B. Straight leg sit-ups should not be used when persons have weak abdominal muscles or low back problems.

C. Push-ups should not be used when persons have round shoulders.

D. The swan or cobra should not be used when persons have lordosis.

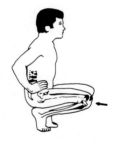

E. Deep knee bends and the duck walk are contraindicated for most students because of the strain put on the knee joints.

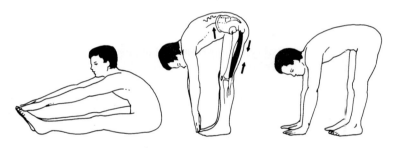

F. Straight leg toe touch and bear walk should not be used when persons have hyperextended knees or low back weakness.

image work, static and dynamic balance tasks, and body alignment activities in front of mirrors. Whenever possible, videotape feedback is provided. Sports, dance, and aquatics activities that demand full extension of the trunk, head, neck, and limbs—that is, reaching toward the sky, lifting the chest, stretching upward—are emphasized. Dance, gymnastics (free exercise and balance beam routines), trampolining, and swimming typically reinforce extension, correct body alignment, and good balance. Relaxation training is used to teach and/or reinforce understanding of tightness/tension in muscle groups versus looseness/nontension.

Contraindicated Exercises

Strength and flexibility exercises can cause severe body damage when posture problems are present. Figure 14.4 depicts exercises that are *contraindicated* by certain types of problems. **Contraindicated** is a medical term meaning that there is an indication against *(contra)* prescription of such exercises. The exercises shown may make tight muscles even tighter, as

in push-ups and the swan, or they may lead to stretching and tearing of a tight muscle group, as in straight-leg toe touches.

Behavior Management and Postures

Posture problems can be corrected by behavior management techniques. The types of behavior management apparatus used for correcting postures include these:

1. A portable apparatus worn on the back at about the level of the second thoracic vertebra that emits a 550-cps (cycles per second) tone at an intensity of 55 decibels whenever the wearer slouches (Rubin, O'Brien, Ayllon, & Roll, 1968). Twenty-five adults, ages 18 to 49 years, showed a mean 86% reduction in slouching.

2. A vibrotactile posture harness designed to detect slouching and energize a vibrotactile stimulator on the shoulder whenever slouching occurs. There is no auditory signal, just tactile; the harness is not detectable by others (O'Brien & Azrin, 1970). Eight adults showed a mean 35% reduction in slouching.

FIGURE 14.5 Severe degree of forward head and neck causes compensatory dorsal and lumbar curves.

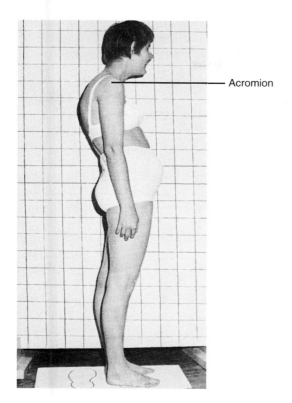

Acromion

3. A foam helmet training device with a mercury switch and buzzer that emits noise whenever the head deviates from the upright position, used in conjunction with a vest containing a buzzer system that makes noise whenever the torso inclines abnormally (Tiller, Stygar, Hess, & Reimer, 1982). Used with one female, age 20 years, in 4 months of training (200 steps each session).

4. Music played during the duration of appropriate posture for 9-year-old boy with cerebral palsy and mental retardation who needed physical support of orthopedic chair and straps for good posture. Johnson, Catherman, and Spiro (1981) reported that response-contingent music is more effective than physical support alone in teaching a child with multiple disabilities good posture.

Forward Head and Neck

Normally, the head is balanced above the cervical vertebrae in such a way that minimal muscle effort is required to resist the pull of gravity. When the earlobe is no longer in alignment with the tip of the shoulder (**acromion**), forward head and neck is diagnosed.

In its *mildest form,* the head tends to droop forward. The cervical spine curve increases so slowly that most persons are unaware that forward head and neck is developing. In the mild stage, the best exercise is mirror work to increase awareness of good head postures.

In more *severe cases,* usually accompanied by round back, the cervical spine hyperextends to compensate for the forward droop of the head and the increasing dorsal convexity of

FIGURE 14.6 Cervical extensors adaptively shorten and tighten as forward head and neck becomes severe. (A) Splenius capitis and cervicis. (B) Trapezius.

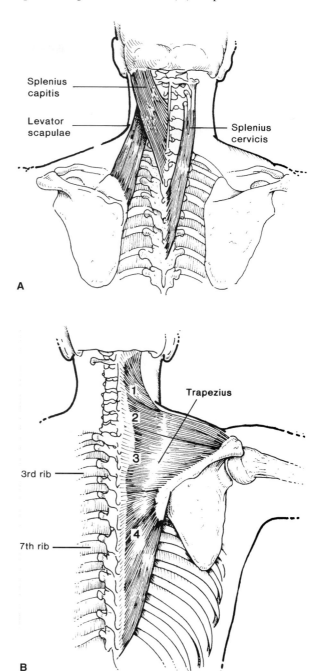

Splenius capitis

Levator scapulae

Splenius cervicis

A

Trapezius

3rd rib

7th rib

B

the thoracic spine (Figure 14.5). This results in adaptive shortening and tightening of the cervical extensors, mainly the upper trapezius and splenius capitis and cervicis (Figure 14.6). This tightness is accentuated in the area of the seventh cervical vertebra, where a layer of fat tends to accumulate. The combined prominence of the seventh cervical vertebra and excess adipose tissue is called a **dowager's hump.** The neck flexors tend to stretch, sag, and become functionally worthless. This hyperextension of the neck is sometimes called cervical lordosis.

In mild forward head and neck, the extensors primarily need strengthening exercises. Flexibility is not a problem. As the condition becomes progressively severe, the muscles may feel stiff, tense, and sore. The emphasis in exercise shifts to flexibility, particularly stretching the cervical extensors.

Ameliorative Exercises

1. **Chin-to-shoulder touch stretch.** Attempt to align the head and neck with other segments of the body. Rotate slowly to the left until the chin touches the shoulder. Repeat to the opposite side.
2. **Lateral flex stretch with ear touch.** Attempt to align the head and neck with other segments of the body. Laterally flex to the left until the ear touches the shoulder. Repeat to the opposite side.
3. **Halo push.** Stand or sit with fingers interlaced above the head. Extend the head upward toward the "halo."
4. **Object-on-head walk.** Walk, race, or play games with different objects on the head. Experiment with different head and trunk positions.

Contraindicated Exercises

1. Circling the head
2. Neck hyperextension
3. Activities related to atlantoaxial instability when working with individuals with Down syndrome (see Chapter 21 on mental retardation)

Excessive Head Tilt

The top of the head tilting toward the right is called a right tilt (RT). The symbol LT is used for the opposite condition. A head habitually held in a tilted position is often symptomatic of vision or hearing impairments. Almost always, the individual is unaware of the tilt and needs exercises for improving proprioception.

Over a long time, head tilt causes an adaptive shortening and tightening of the neck muscles on the side of the tilt. Tight muscles on the right side may be stretched by lateral flexion exercises to the left, and vice versa. A slow, static stretch and hold is more effective than rhythmic exercises.

Kyphosis

Translated literally, *kyphos* means a sharp angulation. Increasing backward convexity in the thoracic region results in the condition commonly known as humpback, hunchback, Pott's curvature, or round upper back. The condition is rare among normal children in the public school setting.

True kyphosis is associated with disease of the intervertebral disks or of the epiphyseal area of the vertebrae. The **intervertebral disk** is the fibrocartilage padding between vertebral bodies (see Figure 14.7). The disk is composed of two parts: the outer annulus fibrosus, known for its strength and elasticity, and the inner nucleus pulposus, which contains fluid that absorbs shock in locomotor movements and maintains the separation of the vertebral bodies. The nucleus pulposus has all the characteristics of a hydraulic system.

FIGURE 14.7 The intervertebral disk. *(A)* Flexion of the spine permitted by shift of fluid. *(B)* Compression of the disk occurs when noncompressible fluid of nucleus expands the elastic annulus. *(C)* Normal extended position with annulus fibers held taut; internal pressure is indicated by arrows. *(D)* Section of vertebrae. *(E)* Cross section of intervertebral disk.

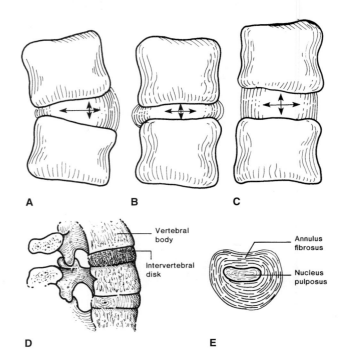

Any degenerative disease of the intervertebral disk is characterized by changes in pressure that cause pain. **Scheuermann's disease,** described in Chapter 24 on les autres, is a kyphosis condition affecting adolescents. **Osteoporosis** is a common cause of kyphosis in older adults, especially women. In old age, the fluid content of the nucleus pulposus decreases, and the annulus fibrosus becomes progressively less elastic. These changes limit motion of the back. Any prolonged inactivity seems to contribute to degeneration of the intervertebral disks. Individuals with severe or profound mental retardation whose mobility is limited often exhibit kyphosis at a young age.

Lordosis

Lordosis, also called swayback or hollow back, is an exaggeration of the normal posterior concave curve in the lumbar region. It not only affects the five lumbar vertebrae but also throws the pelvis out of correct alignment (see Figure 14.8).

Lordosis has many possible causes: genetic predisposition; weak abdominal muscles, which allow the pelvis to tilt downward anteriorly; weak gluteal muscles and hamstrings, which cannot counteract this anterior tilt; overly tight lumbar extensors, which contribute to an anterior tilt; overdeveloped hip flexors, which cause anterior tilt; and, on rare occasions, occupations like professional dance.

FIGURE 14.8 Pelvic tilts. (*A*) Normal pelvic tilt (neutral position). The buttocks are tucked in. Anterior and posterior muscles are equal in strength. (*B*) Anterior pelvic tilt causes lordosis and protruding abdomen.

FIGURE 14.9 Good posture for a normal preschooler includes a protruding abdomen and lordosis.

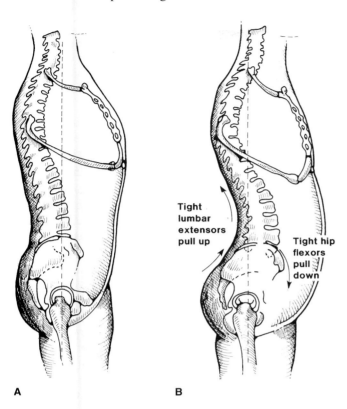

Tight lumbar extensors pull up

Tight hip flexors pull down

A   B

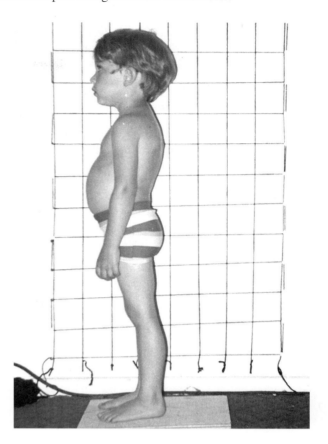

True lordosis usually has the following characteristics:

1. Anterior tilt of the pelvis.
2. Tight lower back muscles, tight lumbodorsal fascia, tight hip flexors, tight iliofemoral (Y) ligaments, weak abdominals, weak hamstrings, and weak gluteals.
3. Knees may be hyperextended.
4. Compensatory kyphosis may develop to balance the increased concavity; if so, the pectorals and anterior intercostals may be tight also.
5. Upper body tends to shift backward as a compensatory measure.
6. Lower back pain.
7. Faulty functioning of internal organs, including those of digestion, elimination, and reproduction.
8. Predisposition toward **dysmenorrhea** (menstrual pain).
9. Increased incidence of back strain and back injuries.

Correction of lordosis, at least in the early stages, is largely a matter of increasing proprioceptive awareness so that the student can feel the difference between an anterior and a posterior tilt. Alternate anterior and posterior pelvic tilts should be practiced while lying supine, kneeling, sitting, standing, and performing various locomotor activities. Helpful exercise cues are "Tuck your buttocks in" and "Pinch the gluteals together." Activities like the backbend, which emphasize hyperextension of the lumbar spine, are contraindicated.

Weak abdominals almost universally accompany lordosis. For this reason, strength exercises for the abdominals should be undertaken along with stretching exercises for the tight lumbar extensors. This dual purpose is accomplished to some extent without special effort in accordance with the principle of reciprocal innervation.

Abdominal Weakness

Abdominal weakness is classified as mild, moderate, or severe or as first, second, and third degree. Abdominal protrusion is normal in the young child and usually accompanied by lordosis (see Figure 14.9). This posture defect is almost always present in adolescents and adults who lead sedentary lifestyles, especially if they are overweight. The protruding abdomen also characterizes paralysis or muscle weakness that results from spinal cord injuries.

When a lifestyle changes from active to sedentary, regardless of the reason, abdominal exercises should become a part of the daily routine. In middle and old age, the upper abdominal wall may become slightly rounded, but the musculature below the umbilicus should remain flat and taut.

The *lower part of the abdomen* contracts reflexly whenever the body is in complete extension, as in most locomotor activities. The emphasis upon extension in modern dance contributes particularly to abdominal strength, as does swimming the front crawl and other strokes executed from an extended position. The *upper part of the abdomen* works in conjunction with the diaphragm, gaining strength each time breathlessness in endurance-type activities forces the diaphragm to contract vigorously in inhalation.

Visceroptosis is the term used when an abdominal protrusion is severe and the **viscera** (internal organs) drop down into a new position. The stomach, liver, spleen, kidneys, and intestines may all be displaced, resulting in adverse effects upon their various functions. This condition occurs mainly in adults.

Exercise Principles for Abdomen and Lower Back

1. Teach abdominal exercises that will simultaneously stretch the tight lumbar extensors and hip flexors (psoas and iliacus).
2. Use the curl-up bent-knee sit-up position rather than the straight-leg lying position to eliminate the action of the strong hip flexors.
3. Avoid hyperextension of the spine. For most persons, this means avoid the double-leg lift and hold.
4. Avoid prone-lying exercises like the swan and the rocking chair.
5. Eliminate breath holding during exercise by requesting the students to count, sing, whistle, hum, or exhale. Incorrect breathing tends to build up intraabdominal pressure, which may result in a hernia. This is called the *Valsalva effect*.
6. Include lots of twisting movements of the trunk to strengthen oblique abdominal muscles.
7. Gradually build tolerance for endurance-type exercises that cause vigorous breathing, which in turn, strengthens the upper abdominal wall.
8. Use locomotor activities that emphasize extension of the spine. Skipping and swimming are especially good.
9. Take advantage of the extensor reflex elicited in the creeping position.
10. Use the upside-down positions in yoga for training the extensor muscles. The neck stand is preferred to the head stand.
11. If there is a history of back problems, avoid sit-ups and exercises using trunk lift from supine.

Exercises in the Creeping Position

For these exercises, always wear knee pads or move across mats. Make these into games. Also use music and create routines.

1. Crosslateral creeping. As the right arm moves forward, the left knee should move forward.
2. Crosslateral creeping combined with blowing a Ping-Pong ball across the floor.
3. Crosslateral creeping combined with pushing an object like a bottle cap or toy automobile with the nose.
4. Angry cat. Alternate (a) humping the back and letting the head hang down with (b) extending the spine with the head held high.
5. In static creeping position, move the hips from side to side. For fun, pin tail on and play wag the tail.

Exercises in Supine or Bent-Knee Sit-Up Position

1. Abdominal pumping (Mosher exercise). Arms in reverse T to prevent arching the back. **Reverse T** means arms outstretched above head. Put book or weight on abdomen. Forcefully push abdomen up and down and feel the weight move.
2. Curl down or reverse trunk curl. Knees and hips are flexed, and knees are drawn toward chest, so curl commences at the lower spinal levels. Obliques are more active in reverse curls than in regular trunk curls. First third of curl is most valuable.
3. Sit-up with trunk twist for maximal activity of oblique abdominals. Feet should not be held down because holding them activates the unwanted hip flexors.
4. Double-knee raise and patticake. Keep the knees bent.
5. Alternate ballet legs. From bent-knee position, raise knees to chest and then lift legs alternately, as done in the synchronized swimming stunt by the same name. To make this more difficult, legs can be adducted and abducted in this position.
6. Double knee circling. Keep heels close to thighs, arms in reverse T. Flex the hips until the thighs are vertical. Keeping the shoulders flat, make circles with the knees. *More difficult variation:* Flex knees toward the chest, straighten legs to vertical, and make circles with both feet. Keep the shoulders flat and the heels together.
7. Alternate leg circling. Retract the abdominal wall and flex both knees to chest. Extend one leg and then the other in reciprocal leg circling or bicycle motion. Return the flexed legs to the chest and then lower to the floor.
8. Leg circling games. Vary the difficulty by changing the size of the circles, the number completed before resting, and the speed of the performance. The most difficult is making small circles at slow speed just above the floor. The right foot makes clockwise circles, while the left foot makes counterclockwise circles. Both legs make clockwise circles. Both legs make counterclockwise circles. Describe a figure eight with one foot or both together.
9. Drumming. Feet are used like drumsticks, alternately beating the floor.
10. Alternate knee and elbow touch in opposition. Hands behind neck. Each time, try to reach farther with the elbow and less far with the opposite knee.
11. Supine bent-knee lower trunk twist. Arms in reverse T. Raise both knees until the thighs are vertical. Keep the shoulders flat, and lower the knees toward the mat on one side; return to a vertical position. Repeat to the other side and return. Legs should not be allowed to fall; must be controlled throughout the movement.

Values of Abdominal Exercises

Abdominal exercises do the following:

1. Relieve congestion in the abdominal or pelvic cavities; this includes expelling gas and improving local circulation.

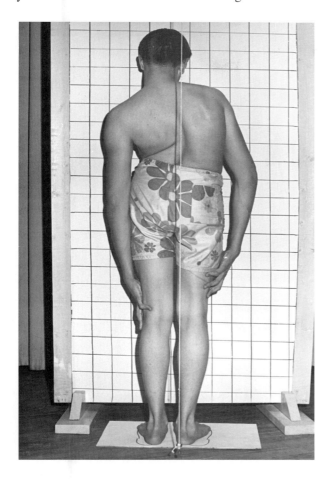

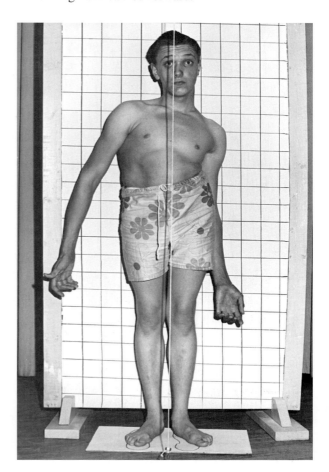

2. Relieve menstrual pain.
3. Strengthen muscles needed for coughing in asthma and respiratory diseases.
4. Strengthen muscles to improve appearance and function.

Flat Back

Flat back is a decrease or absence of the normal anteroposterior curves. It is the opposite condition from lordosis. The posterior concavity of the lumbar curve is decreased—that is, the normal posterior concavity is gradually changing toward convexity.

Characteristics of flat back include these:

1. The pelvic inclination is less than normal, with the pelvis held in posterior tilt.
2. The back appears too flat, with little or no protrusion of the buttocks.
3. Lower back muscles are weak.
4. Hip flexors, especially the psoas major, are weak and elongated.
5. Hamstrings are abnormally tight.

Flat back is associated with the debutante slouch, seen so often in fashion magazines, in which young women pose lan-

guidly with hips thrust forward and upper back rounded. Such models are usually flat chested and so thin that the abdomen cannot protrude. It is sad that the fashion world sometimes chooses to present this image to the American public, rather than one of good body alignment with normal busts, hips, and buttocks in gracefully curved balance. Flat back is also characteristic of the body build of young toddlers who have not been walking long enough to develop the lumbar curve.

Ameliorative exercises include these:

1. Alternate anterior and posterior pelvic tilts from a hook lying position to increase proprioceptive awareness.
2. Hyperextension of the lumbar spine to strengthen back muscles.
3. Most exercises in supine or bent-knee sit-up position from the previous section.

Scoliosis

Scoliosis is a lateral curvature of the spine (see Figures 14.10–14.13). Although the condition begins with a single curve, it usually consists of a primary curve and a compensatory curve in the opposite direction.

FIGURE 14.12 Right (convex) side of right total scoliosis shows back hump and bulging rib cage. Muscles on this side require strengthening.

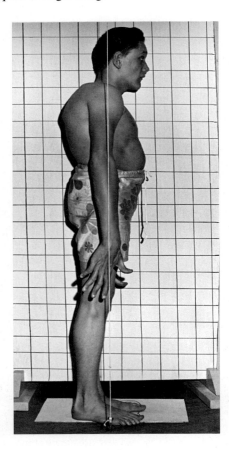

FIGURE 14.13 Left (concave) side of right total scoliosis reveals muscles that need stretching.

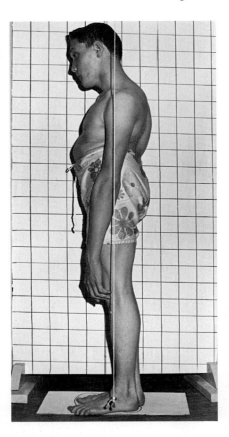

Keynote Positions

Keynote positions are diagnostic devices or corrective exercises specifically for scoliosis (see Figure 14.14). Among the most common keynote positions are the following:

1. Adam's position—relaxed forward bending held for several seconds from a standing posture. The knees are straight so that the flexion occurs from the hips and spinal column.
2. Hanging with both arms from a horizontal bar.
3. Symmetrical arm raise from a standing position. The individual with a total left curve flexes the right arm at the shoulder joint to whatever height is necessary to straighten the spine. The other arm is maintained in a position of abduction. In some cases, raising both arms and/or raising one leg sideways may help the curve to disappear.

If the lateral curve is not temporarily obliterated by any of these positions, it can be assumed that scoliosis is in a transitional or structural stage. In such instances, the physical educator should insist that the child be examined by a physician. No corrective exercises should be undertaken without a permission slip from the parents and a medical clearance from the physician. Ideally, the physician will prescribe specific exercises to be practiced under the supervision of adapted physical education personnel.

Lateral curves are named in terms of the direction of their convexity. Among right-handed persons, the most common type of scoliosis is the *total left curve*.

Characteristics of Left Curve

In the total left lumbar curve to the convex side, the following characteristics may be observed:

1. Spinous processes deviate from midline, rotating toward the concavity of the curve.
2. The left shoulder is higher than the other shoulder and may also be carried forward.
3. The head may be tilted to one side.
4. The trunk is displaced toward the side of convexity. This can limit breathing.
5. Posteriorly, the ribs usually bulge out on the convex side of the curve; the rib cage tends to lose its flexibility.
6. The right hip is usually higher than the other and the right iliac crest more prominent. Said in another way, when there is a lateral pelvic tilt, the convexity of the spine is toward the lower hip.
7. The contour of the waistline is affected, with the notch on the concave side greater than that on the convex.
8. The right leg may be longer than the left. In other words, a long leg will push the hip to a higher level and contribute to curvature on the opposite side.

382   Assessment and Pedagogy for Specific Goals

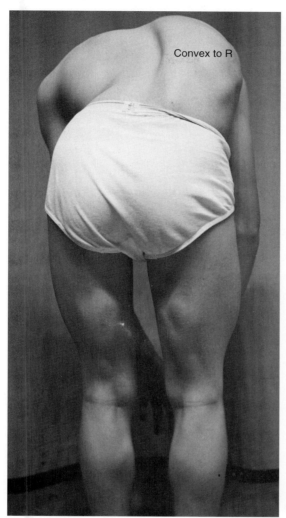

A. Start Position

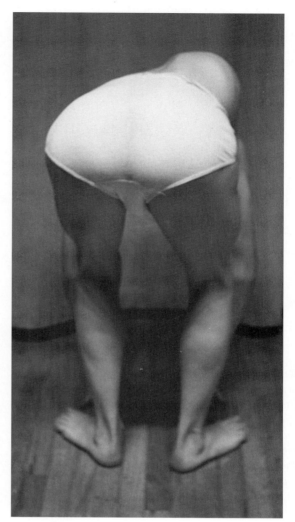

B. End Position

9. Side bending tends to be freer to the right (concave side) than to the left.

10. Forward flexibility of the spine may be limited as a natural protective mechanism of the body against further deformity.

11. Muscles on the concave side become increasingly tight, while those on the convex side are stretched and weakened.

Ameliorative Exercises

Principles for planning ameliorative exercises for a child with functional scoliosis include the following:

1. Work on improvement of body alignment in front of a mirror before undertaking specific exercises for scoliosis.

2. Use keynote positions (with exception of Adam's position) as corrective exercises. When a position is identified in which the curve is temporarily obliterated, spend as many seconds as comfortable in it; rest and repeat.

3. Emphasize swimming and other activities that encourage development of the trunk without placing weight-bearing strain on the spine.

4. Avoid forward flexibility of spine unless prescribed by a physician.

5. Use breathing and chest expansion exercises to maintain flexibility of chest and prevent further distortion of thorax.

6. If you tend to be conservative and wish to avoid controversial practices, use only symmetrical exercises that develop left and right sides equally. Exercises for strengthening the back extensors are recommended.

7. If you are willing to use activities that authorities are about equally divided on, try such *asymmetrical* exercises as
   a. Hang facing outward from stall bars and swing legs in.
   b. Hang from stall bars with right hand only (for left total curve). Right side is to the stall bars, and left hand is used whenever needed for balance.

FIGURE 14.15
Milwaukee brace fitted to a right thoracic, left lumbar scoliotic curve. It is generally worn 23 hours a day over a long undershirt, and children can run and play in it with few restrictions.

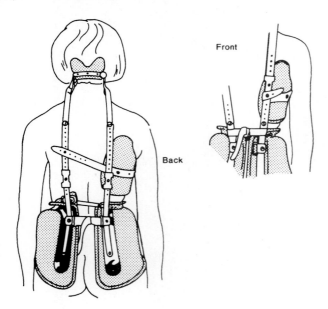

FIGURE 14.16
Right dorsal scoliosis with 65° curve. This 18-year-old has worn a Milwaukee brace and had Harrington instrumentation and spinal fusion. Further correction is not feasible.

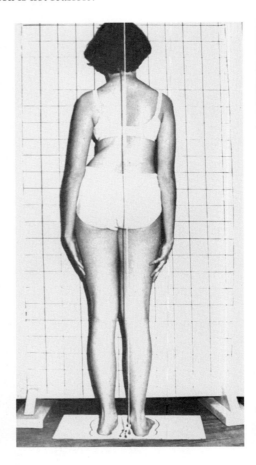

c. Kneel on right knee, with leg extended to side, right arm curved above head. Laterally flex trunk several times to the left. *The purpose of most asymmetrical exercises is to stretch muscles on the concave side and/or to strengthen muscles on the convex side.* Generally, exercises prescribed by physicians are asymmetrical in nature.

8. Encourage the student with scoliosis to participate in regular physical education classes and athletic competition.

Scoliosis is more prevalent in girls and among ectomorphic body types, but it is not confined to either. About 75% of the known cases are idiopathic, about 12.5% are congenital anomalies, and the other 12.5% result from paralysis or paresis of muscles on one side of the spinal column. Many persons with poliomyelitis have scoliosis.

Among the kinds of treatments used are the Milwaukee brace, Harrington instrumentation and spinal fusion, and various kinds of body casts (see Figures 14.15 and 14.16). Students with severe scoliosis or kyphosis in the Milwaukee brace should have a well-rounded physical activity program rather than exercise alone. Cailliet (1975) stated in this regard:

> Just as exercises alone are of limited value in either correcting or controlling scoliosis, applying a Milwaukee brace without exercises is of limited value. . . . The brace permits almost unlimited activities, excluding only contact sports for the safety of other children and very active sports, such as tumbling on a trampoline, horseback riding, and strenuous gymnastics. (pp. 72, 75)

Uneven Shoulder Height

When the two shoulders are of unequal height, the higher one is recorded as LH (left high) or RH (right high). Shoulder unevenness is best ascertained by using a horizontal line on the wall behind the student. Other techniques include

1. If the head is not tilted, comparing the distance between the shoulders and earlobes on the right and left side.
2. Comparing the level of the inferior angles of the scapulae. The inferior angles are at about the level of the seventh thoracic spinous process.
3. Comparing the level of the two clavicles.

Whenever a high shoulder is recorded, a lateral spinal curve convex on the same side should be suspected (see Figures 14.16 and 14.17). If scoliosis is not found, shoulder asymmetries are not a problem. *In normal development, the dominant side of the body has a slightly depressed shoulder and slightly higher hip.* This should not be confused with scoliosis.

Uneven Hip Height

When two hips are of unequal height, the higher one is recorded as LH or RH. Traditionally, the anterior superior iliac

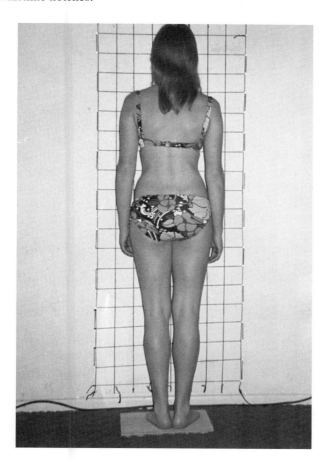

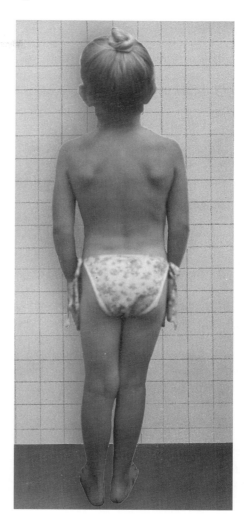

spines serve as the anatomical landmarks for judging asymmetry. A string may be stretched between these two points.

Differences in hip height may be caused by scoliosis, uneven leg length, or the habit of standing on one leg for long periods of time. To determine leg lengths, the student lies in a supine position. The length of each leg is recorded as the distance from the anterior superior iliac spine to the medial ankle bone.

Winged Scapulae

Also called projected scapulae, the term **winged scapulae** refers to a prominence of the inferior angles of the scapulae. The scapulae are pulled away from the rib cage, and the vertebral borders are lifted. The serratus anterior, the muscle that normally holds the inferior angle of the scapula close to the rib cage, is believed to be weak when winging occurs.

Winged scapulae are normal in preschool and elementary school children since the serratus is slower in developing than its antagonists (see Figure 14.18). Since the serratus anterior is a prime mover for upward rotation and abduction, it is strengthened by hanging, climbing, and other activities executed above the head. Many girls in our society do not outgrow winged scapulae as do boys. This postural deviation is often a part of the debutante slouch described earlier.

Winged scapulae often accompany round shoulders. They are associated also with congenital anomalies and postural conditions in which the ribs protrude.

Round Shoulders

Round shoulders is a forward deviation of the shoulder girdle that brings the acromion processes (shoulder tips) in front of the normal gravitational line. Round shoulders should not be confused with round back (kyphosis). They are distinctly different problems.

Synonyms for round shoulders are abducted scapulae, forward deviation of the shoulder girdle, protraction of scapulae, and separation of scapulae. Round shoulders results when the strength of the shoulder girdle abductors (pectoralis minor and serratus anterior) becomes greater than that of the adductors (rhomboids and trapezius III). To determine the extent of the forward deviation, the distance between the vertebral borders of the scapulae is measured. In the adult, the normal spread is 4 to 5 inches, depending on the breadth of the shoulders.

The incidence of round shoulders is high among persons who work at desk jobs and, hence, spend much of their time with shoulders abducted. Athletes often exhibit round shoulders because of overdevelopment of the anterior arm, shoulder, and chest muscles resulting from sports and aquatics activities, which stress forward movements of the arms. This tendency may be counteracted by engaging in an exercise program designed specifically to keep the posterior muscles equal in strength to their antagonists. Perhaps the easiest way to do this is to swim a few laps of the back crawl each day. Certainly, the well-rounded athlete who enjoys many different activities is less likely to develop round shoulders than is one who specializes almost exclusively in tennis, basketball, or volleyball.

Changes in Body Alignment from Round Shoulders

The following segmental analysis demonstrates the compensatory changes in alignment of body parts that result from round shoulders:

1. **Head and neck.** Out of alignment and displaced forward.
2. **Thoracic spine.** Increasing convexity that tends to negate the upward pull of the muscles that normally maintain the upper ribs and sternum in a high position. The weak back muscles are elongated by the increased convexity of the spine.
3. **Chest.** Lowered position. The failure of the anterior muscles to exert their usual effect on the sternum and ribs results in a lowered position of the diaphragm, which, in turn, affects breathing.
4. **Shoulder girdle.** Scapulae abducted. Anterior muscles need to be stretched, and posterior muscles need to be strengthened.
5. **Shoulder joint.** Increased inward rotation of the humeral head.
6. **Arms.** Arms are carried more forward than usual, with palms facing toward the rear, whereas normally, only the little finger of the hand can be seen from the rear (see Figure 14.19). The elbows may be held out close to the body.
7. **Lumbar spine.** Lordosis may develop to compensate for increased convexity of thoracic spine.
8. **Knees.** Knees may hyperextend to compensate for the change in the lumbar curve.

With the alignment of almost all the body segments altered, the entire body slumps, creating the impression of general fatigue. This posture is assumed temporarily in times of extreme mental depression or bereavement, revealing the unity of mind and body. Persons with mental illness often assume the round-shouldered postures of defeat.

Ameliorative Exercises

Exercises for round shoulders are directed toward the shoulder girdle (scapular) abductors and adductors. *They should simultaneously stretch the tightened anterior muscles and*

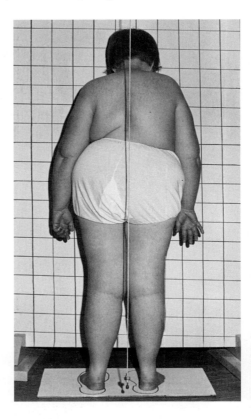

FIGURE 14.19   Round shoulders can be detected from a rear view by the palms of the hands. This child also has mild scoliosis, knock-knees, and pronated feet.

strengthen the trapezius III and the rhomboids. So many exercises for round shoulders are recommended in textbooks that it is difficult to evaluate their respective effectiveness in accomplishing these goals. The four that appear to be most effective, in rank order from best to good, are these:

1. **Pull resistance.** Sit on a chair facing the wall with pulleys, with the arms extended sideward at shoulder height and the hands grasping the handles. Slowly move the arms backward, keeping them at shoulder height.
2. **Prone lateral raise of weights.** Assume a prone position on a bench. The hands grasp dumbbells on the floor to each side of the body. The weights are lifted toward the ceiling as far as possible, keeping the arms straight. Hold. (Chin should remain on the bench.)
3. **Push against wall.** Sit cross-legged with the head and back flat against the wall. The arms are bent at shoulder height with the palms facing the chest, fingertips touching, and elbows against the wall. Keeping the head and spine against the wall, press the elbows back with as much force as possible.
4. **Head resistance.** Lie on back, arms out to side, palms down, knees flexed, and feet spread. Raise hips and arch back so that shoulders are off mat, supporting weight on feet, hands, and back of head in a modified wrestler's bridge.

Deviations of the Chest

Asthma, other chronic upper respiratory disorders, and rickets may cause changes in the rib cage with resulting limitations in chest flexibility and improper breathing practices. These changes are designated as functional, transitional, and structural, depending upon their degree of severity. Congenital anomalies, of course, do account for some chest deviations.

Hollow Chest

The most common of the chest deviations, **hollow chest** denotes the depression of the anterior thorax that normally accompanies round shoulders and/or kyphosis. Specific characteristics of hollow chest are concave or flattened appearance of anterior thoracic wall, depressed (lowered) ribs, low sternum, tight intercostal and pectoral muscles, limited chest flexibility, and habitually lowered diaphragm that limits breathing.

Hollow chest can be traced to the failure of the neck and pectoral muscles to exert their usual lifting effect on the ribs and sternum. The neck muscles are elongated and weak. The pectoral muscles are excessively tight.

Barrel Chest

Barrel chest occurs in persons with severe, chronic asthma who become permanently hyperventilated because of their inability to exhale properly. Over a period of years, the excess air retained in the lungs tends to expand the anteroposterior dimensions of the thorax so that it takes on a rounded appearance similar to that of full inspiration.

Barrel chest is normal for infants and preschool children. The lateral widening of the thorax from side to side so that it no longer resembles a barrel occurs normally as a result of the vigorous play activities of young children. Individuals with severe disabilities who cannot engage in physical activities often have chests that remain infantile and underdeveloped.

Funnel Chest

The opposite of barrel chest, **funnel chest** is an abnormal increase in the lateral diameter of the chest with a marked depression of the sternum and anterior thorax. The sternum and adjacent costal cartilages appear to have been sucked inward.

Funnel chest, also called *pectus excavatum,* is usually a congenital anomaly. It appears in many persons with severe mental retardation. It also may be caused by rickets or severe nasal obstruction—that is, enlarged adenoids—and characterizes syndromes like Turner and Noonan caused by sex chromosome aberrations.

Pigeon Chest

Also called chicken breast, or *pectus carinatum,* **pigeon chest** takes its name from the abnormal prominence of the sternum. The anteroposterior diameter of the thorax is increased as a result of the forward displacement of the sternum. The deviation is rare, caused by rickets during the early growth period. It may also be congenital or caused by les autres conditions like osteogenesis imperfecta.

FIGURE 14.20 Mild to moderate bowlegs is normal in infancy and corrects itself, usually by 2 years of age. Children then tend to develop knock-knees, which is most obvious at ages 3 to 4. This condition also corrects itself.

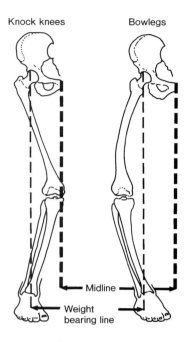

Alignment of Lower Extremities

A quick screening device to judge the overall alignment of the legs is the game known as *Four Coins.* The challenge is, "Can you put a coin between your thighs, your knees, your calves, and your ankles and simultaneously hold all the coins in place?" If the body parts are well proportioned and correctly aligned, this task should present no problem. When the student stands with feet together and parallel, the medial aspects of the knees and ankles should be touching their opposites. Figure 14.20 depicts developmental changes in hip and leg alignment. It is normal for infants and toddlers to have bowlegs and for preschool children to have knock-knees. These conditions generally correct themselves.

Individual differences in leg alignment and in locomotor patterns are largely dependent upon the hip joint. Students who toe inward or outward in their normal walking gait, for instance, usually have nothing wrong with their feet. The problem's origin usually can be traced to a strength imbalance in the muscles that rotate the femur at the hip joint.

Hip Joint Problems

The hip joint is formed by the articulation between the head of the femur and the acetabulum of the pelvis. Figure 14.21 depicts its anatomy. How the head fits into the acetabulum determines function and stability. Important to the understanding of several problems is the angulation of the neck of the femur, depicted in Figure 14.22. Hip joint problems affect leg alignment and gait. Several of these are discussed in Chapter 24 on les autres conditions.

FIGURE 14.21 Anatomy of the hip joint. The acetabulum is a cup-shaped hollow socket that is formed medially by the pubis, above the ilium, and laterally and behind by the ischium.

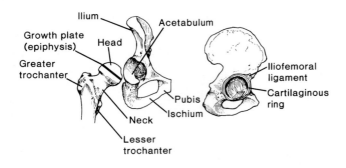

FIGURE 14.22 Angulation of the neck of the femur helps to explain coxa valga and vara. *(A)* Decreased neck-shaft angle shortens leg. *(B)* Normal for adolescents and adults. *(C)* Increased neck-shaft angle lengthens leg. Normal for infants.

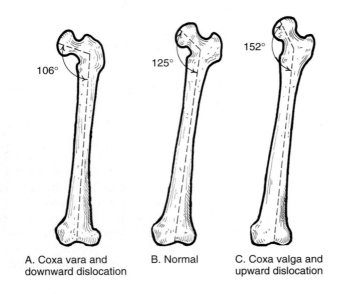

A. Coxa vara and downward dislocation

B. Normal

C. Coxa valga and upward dislocation

Abnormal positioning of the femoral head within the acetabulum is called **coxa vara** (decreased angulation) or **coxa valga** (increased angulation). Both cause waddling gaits. Neither condition can be corrected by exercise. Casting, bracing, and surgery are used.

Coxa Vara

The decreased angulation in *coxa vara* may result in the affected leg becoming shorter. Inward rotation and abduction are limited. Bowlegs in early childhood is associated with *coxa vara* (see Figure 14.23). *Coxa vara* also often appears in adolescence. It may be called either **slipped femoral epiphysis** or *adolescent coxa vara* and is more common in males than females. The epiphysis (growth center) of the femoral head slips down and backward, making the angulation of the femoral neck more horizontal.

FIGURE 14.23 Bowlegs in early childhood are almost always accompanied by coxa vara. *(A)* The horizontalization of the femoral neck limits the action of the gluteus medius. *(B)* The result is a waddling gait in which the shoulders incline toward the weight-bearing foot.

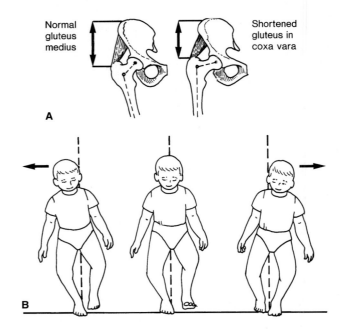

Coxa Valga

In contrast, *coxa valga* malpositions in normal children are associated with upward, anterior dislocations of the hip. The condition is almost always congenital and is often called **congenital dislocation of the hip** (CDH), rather than *coxa valga*. This is the fourth most common orthopedic birth defect. The affected leg is longer, and both inward and outward rotation are limited. Adductors are very tight. Many nonambulatory persons with severe disability develop *coxa valga* between ages 2 and 10; in this condition, the head of the femur is usually displaced upward (like CDH) and posteriorly (unlike CDH).

Knee Joint Problems

Knee joint problems include (a) bowlegs, (b) knock-knees, (c) hyperextended knees, and (d) tibial torsion. These problems may be congenital or acquired through injury. Malalignment increases the risk of **osteoarthritis** in middle and old age. Obesity, over time, injures the knee joint. This is why weight-bearing exercises are often contraindicated for obese persons.

Bowlegs (Genu Varum)

Although the Latin term *genu,* meaning "knee," emphasizes the capacity for knees and ankles to touch simultaneously, bowing can occur in the shaft of the femur as well as the tibia. **Varum** refers to inward bowing. One or both legs may be affected.

The legs of infants often bow during the first few months of walking because of imbalance of strength between the peroneal and tibial muscle groups. By age 2, this problem resolves itself in most children.

Persistent or late-appearing bowlegs may be caused by disorders that affect the epiphyseal plates. Illustrative of these is

Blount's disease, or **tibia vara,** an outward bowing of the tibia caused by retardation of growth of the medial epiphyseal plate at the top of the tibia. Blount's disease usually occurs between 1 and 3 years of age and is corrected by surgery. Pathological conditions that are often complicated by bowed legs include *arthrogryposis, dwarfism,* and *osteogenesis imperfecta* (check the index at the back of the book for specific discussions).

Many individuals with mild to moderate bowing conditions have strong muscles and are not impaired noticeably by this deviation. Bowlegs tends to shift the weight toward the lateral border of the foot and to maintain the foot in a supinated position. Exercises are not recommended.

Knock-Knees (Genu Valga)

The Latin word **valgum** can mean either knock-knees or bowlegs but is used in most adapted physical education references as knock-knees, referring specifically to the *bending outward of the lower legs* so that the knees touch, but the ankles do not.

Knock-knees occurs almost universally in obese persons. In the standing position, the gravitational line passes lateral to the center of the knee rather than directly through the patella, as is normal. This deviation in the weight-bearing line predisposes the knee joint to injury. Knock-knees is usually accompanied by weakness in the longitudinal arch and pronation of the feet (see Figure 14.24).

No treatment or exercises are recommended for knock-knees in children younger than age 7 because, developmentally, this is a normal condition. In severe knock-knees, physicians often prescribe a 1/8-inch heel-raise on the medial border and/or use of a night splint. Severe cases that persist are treated with surgery **(osteotomy).**

Ameliorative exercises include these:

1. Stretch the muscles on the lateral aspect of the leg (peroneal group) by doing supination exercises (inversion and adduction of the foot).
2. Strengthen the tibials by doing supination exercises; this also helps to strengthen longitudinal arch.
3. Strengthen the outward rotators of the hip joint by doing activities that stress outward rotation.

Hyperextended Knees

Also called *back knees* or *genu recurvatum,* hyperextended knees is a deviation in which the knees are pulled backward beyond their normal position. This posture problem can be identified best from a side view (see Figure 14.25). Hyperextension of the knees tends to tilt the pelvis forward and contributes to lordosis, thereby throwing all of the body segments out of alignment.

This condition can be caused by knee extensor weakness, tight calf muscles, Achilles tendon contractures, and bony abnormalities. In cerebral palsy, back knees often result from surgical overcorrection of knee flexion deformities. In spinal cord injuries and polio, the knees are sometimes surgically placed in recurvatum to permit independent walking as an alternative to wheelchair locomotion (see the information on gaits in Chapter 11).

Severe cases of back knees are usually treated by prescription of a knee-ankle brace that holds the foot in slight dorsiflexion and the knee in flexion. Specific exercise should not be done in physical education unless medically prescribed. *Contraindicated activities include touching the toes from a standing position, deep-knee squats, and duck and bear walks.* Standing with knees in hyperextension should always be discouraged by telling people to relax or bend at the knees.

Tibial Torsion

With tibial torsion, the tibia is twisted and the weight-bearing line is shifted to the medial aspect of the foot. The deviation is often more marked in one leg than in the other, with the affected foot toeing inward and pronating. Tibial torsion often accompanies knock-knees, flat feet, and pronated feet (see Figure 14.26). Congenital anomalies of the foot may be accompanied by twisting of the lower end of the tibia. Congenital tibial torsion is usually corrected in infancy by plaster casts, braces, splints, and/or surgery.

Deviations of the Feet

Poor alignment in any part of the body affects the weight-bearing function of the feet. Obesity increases the stress on the joints. Abnormal formation of bones, as in clubfoot (see foot in Figure 14.26), also affects alignment, as does weak or paralyzed leg and foot muscles resulting from spinal cord injury or neuromuscular conditions like cerebral palsy.

Toeing Inward

Toeing inward (pigeon toes) is usually caused by a strength imbalance in the hip joint muscles. When the inward rotators— *gluteus minimis* and *gluteus medius*—are stronger than the outward rotators, the student toes inward. This problem is also associated with the scissors gait in cerebral palsy.

Ameliorative exercises include these:

1. Develop proprioceptive awareness of the different foot positions through movement exploration on all kinds of surfaces.
2. Stretch the tight inward rotators by doing activities that emphasize outward rotation. Ballet techniques are especially effective.
3. Strengthen the weak outward rotators by doing activities that emphasize outward rotation.
4. Avoid inward rotation movements.

Toeing Outward

Toeing outward occurs when the posterior group of muscles on the sacrum, called "the six outward rotators," is stronger than the prime movers for inward rotation (see Figure 14.24). Since toeing outward is a way of widening the stance and improving the balance, it may be observed in toddlers just learning to walk, the aged, persons who are blind, and others who are unsure of their footing. *Ameliorative exercises are the opposite of those done for toeing inward.*

Supination and Pronation

The two joints of the foot where most of the movements occur—and subsequently, the deviations—are the *talonavicular* and *talocalcaneal* joints (see Figure 14.27). In the former,

FIGURE 14.24 Knock-knees elongates tendons on the medial side and tightens tendons on the lateral side. Lateral muscles of the lower leg tighten, pulling the outer border of the foot upward and forcing weight onto the inner border.

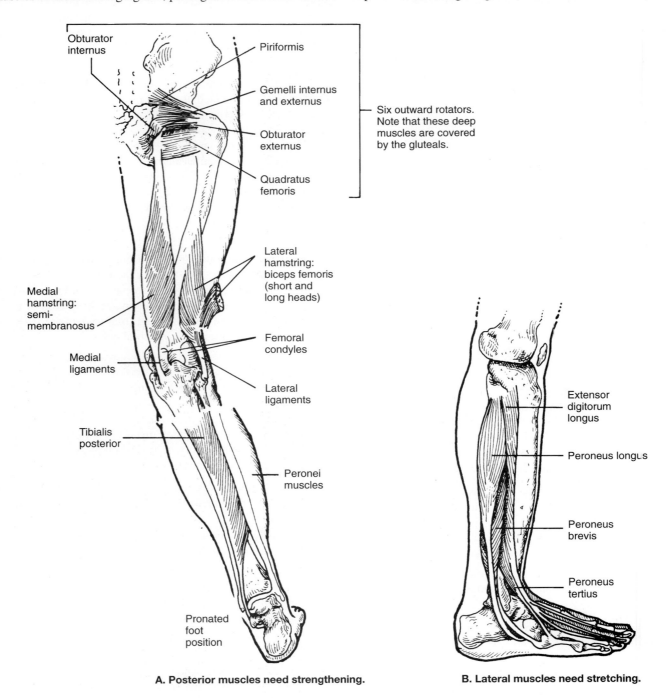

A. Posterior muscles need strengthening.   **B. Lateral muscles need stretching.**

the talus is transferring the weight of the body to the forward part of the foot, and in the latter, it is transferring the weight to the back part of the foot. How this weight is transferred determines the presence or absence of foot problems.

Normally, the weight of the body in locomotor activities is taken on the outer border of the foot and then transferred via the metatarsal area to the big toe, which provides the push-off force for forward movement. During this sequence, the foot is maintained in **slight supination,** which is considered the foot's "strong position." All locomotor activi-

ties should be performed in this slightly supinated position, which forces the weight of the body to be taken on the foot's outer border.

Pronation, the most common and the most debilitating of foot problems, is defined variously as taking the weight of the body on the inner border of the foot, rolling inward on the ankles, and combined eversion and abduction. *Eversion,* or turning the sole of the foot outward, occurs when the lateral muscles of the lower leg (peroneals) are tighter than the tibials. This deviation occurs mainly in the talonavicular and talocalcaneal joints.

FIGURE 14.25 Right knee in hyperextension after knee surgery following an automobile accident. Malalignment of legs contributes to lordosis.

FIGURE 14.26 Medial torsion of left tibia in a young adolescent with surgically corrected clubfoot.

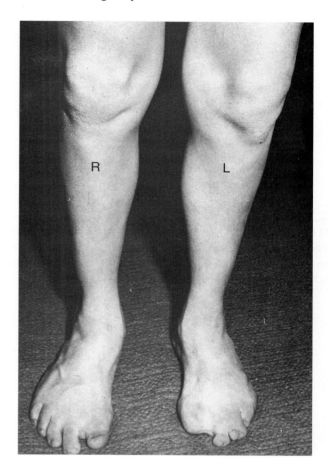

Flat foot is a related disorder. The Feiss line and the Helbing's sign (described under flat foot) are also used for diagnosis of pronation.

Pronation may occur in early childhood as well as other growth periods. In affluent areas, well over 10 to 20% of the children may wear corrective shoes designed to ameliorate pronation (see Figure 14.28). In these shoes, the medial border is built up in such a way as to force the weight of the body to be taken on the foot's outer border. The shoes are prescribed by physicians. Children who wear corrective shoes should not change to tennis shoes for physical education activity; nor should they go barefooted without the permission of their orthopedist.

Ameliorative exercises include these:

1. Begin with non-weight-bearing exercises and do not add weight-bearing exercises until indicated by orthopedist.
2. Emphasize toe-curling exercises to strengthen the flexors of the toes.
3. Emphasize plantar flexion and inversion.
4. Avoid dorsiflexion exercises and maintenance of foot in dorsiflexion for long periods of time.

FIGURE 14.27 Joints are named for the two bones that touch. Thus, the ankle joint is the talotibial joint. The talocalcaneal and talonavicular joints are the sites of *varus* (inward) and *valgus* (outward) foot deformities.

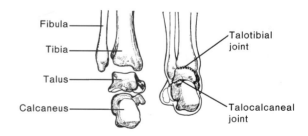

5. Avoid eversion movements.
6. In picking up marbles and other objects with the toes, stress a position of inversion, as in this sequence:
   a. Pick up marbles with toes.
   b. Deposit into box across the midline, which forces the foot into inversion.
7. In relay activities for correction of pronation, make sure objects held by toes of right foot are passed to the left to ensure inversion.

FIGURE 14.28 Thomas heel shoes used to correct flat foot and other alignment problems. The medial border of the shoe is extended forward and raised.

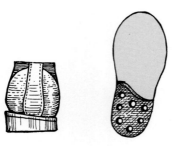

FIGURE 14.30 Medial view of foot illustrating pain centers and structures that support the longitudinal arch. Pain centers are *(A)* under metatarsophalangeal joints, *(B)* where the plantar ligaments are attached to the calcaneus, *(C)* under navicular, and *(D)* middorsum, where shoelaces tie.

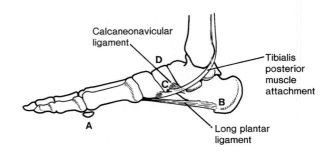

FIGURE 14.29 Assessment of severity of flat foot and pronation. *(A)* Feiss line method, arrows point to location of the navicular. *(B)* Helbing sign method, arrows show whether Achilles tendon is straight or flared inward.

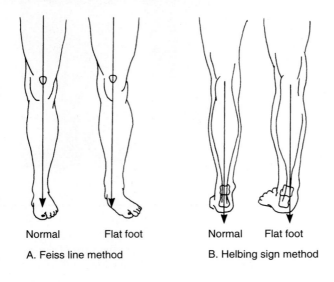

agnosed as first, second, or third degree, depending on whether the navicular is 1, 2, or 3 inches from its correct position. The **Helbing sign method,** associated with the rear of the leg, uses a string to determine whether the **Achilles tendon** is straight (correct) or flared inward (flat foot).

Ameliorative exercises include these:

1. Strengthen the tibials by supination exercises like patticake, with feet together, apart.
2. Strengthen and tighten other muscles, ligaments, and tendons on the medial aspect of the foot by inversion exercises.
3. Stretch the tight muscles, ligaments, and tendons on the lateral aspect of the foot.

Pain Centers

Examinations of the feet should include questions concerning pain or discomfort in the following five "pain centers" of the foot:

1. sole of the foot under the metatarsophalangeal joints;
2. sole of the foot close to the heel where the plantar ligaments attach to the calcaneus;
3. under the surface of the navicular;
4. middorsum, where shoelaces tie;
5. outer surface of the sole of the foot, where most of the weight is borne (see Figure 14.30).

These areas should be inspected closely for thickness and other abnormalities.

Syndactylism

Extra toes, the absence of toes, or the webbing of toes all affect mechanical efficiency in locomotor activities (see Figure 14.31), but a child with good coordination can learn to compensate well enough to achieve recognition as an outstanding athlete. An example is Tom Dempsey, stellar kicker for the Philadelphia Eagles of the National Football Conference, who has part of his kicking foot missing.

Webbing of toes is usually corrected surgically, and extra toes may be removed to facilitate purchase of shoes. The

Flat Foot (Pes Planus)

Flat foot may be congenital or postural. If the muscles of the legs and feet are strong and flexible and the body is in good alignment, congenital flat foot is not considered a postural deviation.

Infants are born with varying degrees of flat foot. Strong arches develop as the natural consequence of vigorous kicking and strenuous locomotor activities. Sedentary children do not develop strong arches and tend to be at risk for sprains. Faulty body mechanics, especially pronation, contributes to flat foot. This condition is worsened by obesity.

Two diagnostic tests are used to determine the severity of combined flat foot and pronation disorders (see Figure 14.29). The **Feiss line method**, associated with the front of the leg, requires stretching a string from the kneecap to the big toe and checking how distant the navicular is from the string. The **navicular** (a tarsal bone) should be directly under the string on the top of the foot, where shoelaces are tied. Flat foot is di-

FIGURE 14.31 Absence of big toe affects balance and locomotor efficiency.

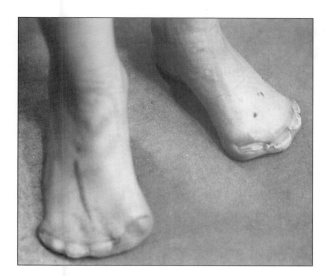

FIGURE 14.32 Bunion limits flexion of big toe.

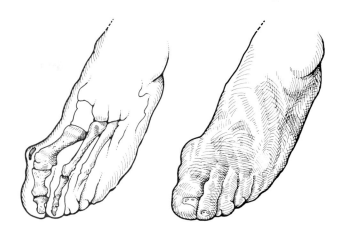

most debilitating defect is absence of the big toe, which plays a major role in static balance and in the push-off phase of locomotor activities.

Hallux Valgus (Bunion)

Hallux is the Latin word for "big toe" and *valgus* is a descriptive adjective meaning "bent outward." Hence, **hallux valgus** is a marked deviation of the big toe toward the four lesser toes. This adduction at the first metatarsophalangeal joint causes shoes to exert undue pressure against the medial aspect of the head of the first metatarsal, where a bursa (sac of synovial fluid) is present in the joint. This bursa may change as a result of the pressure exerted by the shoe. If the bursa enlarges, it is called a *bunion,* the Greek word for "turnip" (see Figure 14.32). This phenomenon happens so often that the terms **bunion** and *hallux valgus* are used as synonyms. If the bursa becomes inflamed, it is called *bursitis.* If the irritation results in a deposit of additional calcium on the first metatarsal head, this new growth is called an *exostosis.*

References

Harter, S. (1988). *Manual for the Self-Perception Profile for Adolescents.* Denver: Author.

Johnson, C. M., Catherman, G. D., & Spiro, S. H. (1981). Improving posture in a cerebral palsied child with response-contingent music. *Education and Treatment of Children, 4*(3), 243–251.

Lowman, C. L., & Young, C. H. (1960). *Postural fitness.* Philadelphia: Lea & Febiger.

O'Brien, F., & Azrin, N. H. (1970). Behavioral engineering: Control of posture by informational feedback. *Journal of Applied Behavior Analysis, 3,* 235–240.

Rathbone, J., & Hunt, V. V. (1965). *Corrective physical education* (7th ed.). Philadelphia: W. B. Saunders.

Rubin, H., O'Brien, T., Ayllon, T., & Roll, D. (1968). Behavioral engineering: Postural control by a portable operant apparatus. *Journal of Applied Behavior Analysis, 1,* 99–108.

Sherrill, C. (1980). Posture training as a means of normalization. *Mental Retardation, 18,* 135–138.

Tiller, J., Stygar, M. K., Hess, C., & Reimer, L. (1982). Treatment of functional chronic stooped posture using a training device and behavior therapy. *Physical Therapy, 11,* 1597–1600.

Zakahi, W., & Duran, R. (1988). Physical attractiveness as a contributing factor to loneliness. *Psychological Reports, 63,* 747–751.

CHAPTER

15

Play and Game Competence, Active Leisure, and Relaxation

FIGURE 15.1 Play and game competence requires attention to social and emotional skills as well as environmental factors and technology.

After you have studied this chapter, you should be able to do the following:

1. Discuss the legal and moral basis for school-based instruction in play and game competence, and suggest ways this instruction should be implemented.

2. Identify barriers to active leisure at various ages, and discuss ways of overcoming these barriers.

3. Discuss the importance of fun and enjoyment in physical activity, identify factors that contribute to fun, and specify ways teachers, parents, and students can work together to assure that fun occurs.

4. Discuss the assessment of sport socialization, play deficits, motor creativity, play and game competence, and hypertension. Apply your knowledge by assessing individuals of various ages with and without disabilities and putting your findings in IEP format.

5. Write goals and objectives for IEPs and lesson plans to guide instruction in play and game competence and related areas.

6. Describe ways to teach motor creativity, play and game competence, and the use of community resources. Demonstrate your ability to teach games and other appropriate activities to individuals with different levels of cognitive and physical abilities.

7. Explain ways that physical educators should work with parents. What should be the outcome of partnerships between teachers and parents?

8. Demonstrate your ability to use the following approaches to teaching relaxation: imagery, deep body awareness, Jacobson techniques, static stretching exercises, yoga, and Tai Chi.

IDEA, the Individuals with Disabilities Education Act, emphasizes that physical education instruction includes three areas: physical and motor fitness; fundamental motor skills and patterns; and skills in games, sports, dance, and aquatics. The third area is sometimes called *play and game competence, active leisure,* or *functional competence in the psychomotor domain.* It is the ability to initiate and sustain involvement in physical activities that are fun, meaningful, and satisfying. **Functional competence** is linked with the wise use of leisure time and the development of lifelong active leisure skills. Functional competence is the focus of Chapters 15, 16, and 17, which address games and sports, dance, and aquatics, respectively.

This chapter consolidates several goals that were treated independently in previous editions: play and game skills, leisure-time skills, fun/tension release, and creative expression. Research indicates that these goals are generally given lower priority than motor skills, fitness, self-concept, and perceptual-motor function/sensory integration (Sherrill & Montelione, 1990). This finding might help to explain why the leisure of so many individuals with disabilities is impoverished.

The philosophy of this text is that play and game competence should be developed concurrently with fitness and motor skills. This holistic approach, in turn, leads to active leisure during nonschool hours and adult years (see Figure 15.1). **Play and game competence** is the term chosen to encompass play and game skills, leisure-time skills, fun/tension release, and motor creativity (called "creative expression" in previous editions of this text).

The Transition Services Mandate in the Law

The legal basis for school-based instruction in play and game competence is not only in the law's definition of physical education but also in the transition services mandate in IDEA. The term **transition services** means a coordinated set of activities written into the IEP that promotes movement from school to postschool activities, including postsecondary education, vocational training, integrated employment, continuing and adult education, adult services, independent living, and community participation (Public Law 101-476, 1990). The law requires a statement of the needed transition services in the IEP for each student from age 16 onward and earlier, if appropriate.

Independent living and community participation, as specified in the transition services mandate, require skills for leisure as well as for work. To develop leisure skills, students must be provided with functional, community-based, lifetime sport and fitness skills training that is based on individual needs and preferences (Dattilo, 1994; Krebs & Block, 1992). **Functional** means that the activities taught in physical education are age-appropriate and usable in recreation settings with family and friends. **Community-based** means that, whenever possible, instruction and practice occur in the neighborhood settings that students will use after graduation. **Lifetime** means that activities are taught that can be meaningful and satisfying throughout the adult years.

Achievement of the outcomes targeted in the transition services mandate of the law requires attention to each of the components of play and game competence: active leisure, play skills, fun and relaxation, and motor creativity. Central to each of these components is the development of self-esteem, self-confidence, and initiative, which enable individuals to voluntarily involve themselves in physical activities afforded by the community.

Leisure, Play, and Sport for All

Active leisure, as a physical education goal, is defined as voluntary engagement in daily large-muscle physical activity that is fun, meaningful, and satisfying during free or discretionary time. Leisure and play are closely associated concepts, which are explained by many diverse theories (Hopkins & Smith, 1988; Levy, 1978). **Leisure** can be a state of mind, free time, or activity engaged in during free time when school and work obligations are fulfilled. What people choose to do in their leisure is a major concern of many professions (e.g., occupational therapy, physical education, recreation).

Barriers to Active Leisure

The adapted physical activity profession is particularly concerned with barriers to active leisure (see Figure 15.2).

FIGURE 15.2 Consider the barriers that individuals with disabilities must overcome in order to use community swimming pools.

Disproportionate numbers of individuals with and without disabilities participate in sport, dance, and aquatics. The most frequently reported barrier to active leisure is not having a companion, friend, or advocate to share the experience with (Sherrill & Williams, 1996). Other barriers include a lack of money, a lack of transportation, inadequate equipment or facilities, the desired activity not being available, a lack of time, a lack of specific skills, insufficient support groups, and inappropriate behaviors that diminish peer acceptance in an activity setting (Ferrara, Dattilo, & Dattilo, 1994; Ittenbach, Abery, Larson, Spiegel, & Prouty, 1994). Physical education instruction must extend beyond fitness and motor skills to address each of these barriers.

Overabundance of Free Time

Instruction leading to play and game competence and active leisure is particularly important for individuals who have an overabundance of free time. Only about one-third of the working-age population with disabilities hold full-time jobs, as opposed to about 80% of able-bodied (AB) peers (Bowe, 1990; Levine & Edgar, 1994). Overall, the mean earnings of individuals with disabilities continue to be about 35% less than those of AB peers. Problems of employment and salary are far greater for females than for males, warranting particular attention to helping girls and women develop play and game competence and active leisure (Sherrill, 1993).

Play: Important at All Ages

Play is any activity that is voluntary, fun, pleasurable, enjoyable, intrinsically rewarding, and self-actualizing. As such, play can be synonymous with active leisure. Recreation and leisure theorists emphasize that play is important at all ages, and occupational therapists specify play/leisure as an occupation equally important to work. Play, however, is also linked with infancy and childhood and is considered an important medium for learning. There are many kinds of play (e.g., toy play, childhood games, sports competition, creative dramatics, arts and crafts, computer games). When play is linked with games, as in the title of this chapter, the intent is to emphasize the affective dimensions of participation as well as the actual physical activity.

Fun and Relaxation

Fun and relaxation (tension release) are characteristics of both play and active leisure. These phenomena mean different things to different people, vary from day to day, and change with the situation. Some persons find fun in the challenge of competition or cooperation, whereas others find fun in the tension release and social interactions afforded by physical activity. Professionals must carefully assess facial expressions, postures, vocal utterances, language, breathing ease, and other indicators of fun and relaxation. Remember that fun is the major factor in choosing to become involved and stay involved in an activity.

The challenge to increase the number of individuals who commit a portion of every day to active leisure has motivated considerable research on sport commitment and sport enjoyment (Scanlan & Simons, 1992). **Sport commitment** is defined as "a psychological construct representing the desire and resolve to continue sport participation" (Scanlan & Simons, 1992, p. 201). **Sport enjoyment** is defined as "a positive affective response to the sport experience that reflects generalized feelings such as pleasure, liking, and fun" (Scanlan & Simons, 1992, p. 201).

Research indicates that sport enjoyment is the major predictor of sport commitment (Scanlan, Carpenter, Schmidt, Simons, & Keeler, 1993). Physical educators often link enjoyment with improved skill and higher levels of achievement, but enjoyment can also come from nonachievement sources (e.g., being with friends, the sensation of movement, beauty or the aesthetics of the environment). This fact is particularly important to remember when working with individuals whose achievement potential is limited by clumsiness or health impairments. For such persons, strive to identify and optimize sources of enjoyment that do not involve a motor skill focus!

Sport for All

Internationally, active leisure and play are associated with the "Sport for All" motto and movement. In many parts of the world, the term *sport* encompasses all kinds of large-muscle physical activity (DePauw & Doll-Tepper, 1989). The Sport for All movement recognizes four types of sport that individuals may choose during nonschool or nonwork hours: (a) top-level or elite sport, (b) organized or club sport, (c) recreational sport, and (d) health or fitness sport. Adapted physical activity aims to get individuals involved in as many of these types of sport as possible (see Figure 15.3).

Sport Socialization

Sport socialization is the process of becoming involved in sport, learning sport roles and values, and acquiring a sporting identity. Persons who are socialized into sport think of themselves as athletes with specialized skills and responsibilities. The process, of course, is different for people with and without disabilities, as it is for people with congenital conditions and those with acquired conditions (Sherrill, Rainbolt, Montelione, & Pope, 1986; Williams, 1994). Children without disabilities are

FIGURE 15.3 What barriers must be overcome to bring children in wheelchairs together for after-school or weekend club sport? Make a list and share it with classmates.

often enrolled in community sport at an early age, thus learning sport roles and acquiring a sporting identity as part of the natural process of growing up and striving to please significant others. When one or both parents are or have been athletes, their children typically are socialized into sport by age 8.

In contrast, the sport socialization of individuals with congenital disabilities is constrained by parents' and teachers' lack of knowledge about sport in relation to disability. There might be considerable debate over whether to involve the child in disability sport (e.g., Special Olympics, Deaf Sport, or Cerebral Palsy Sport), in nondisability sport, or both. Overprotection, fluctuating parental expectations, and a lack of role models of athletes with similar conditions delay and complicate serious involvement in sport. As a result, individuals with congenital disabilities tend to play a more active role in socializing themselves into sport than AB peers do.

Individuals with acquired disabilities experience discontinuous sport socialization. Time of onset of disability is very important; the older the child, the more likely it is that his or her sport socialization will continue along its original path. Injury or disease is an interruption, which calls for reevaluation and consideration of new sport options.

Table 15.1 presents questions that can be used to assess the ongoing sport socialization of children during different sport seasons. The use of these questions as a paper-and-pencil instrument should be supplemented with interviews that explore why the child gives particular responses and how the child defines sport. This instrument can be varied by inserting the child's favorite sport (e.g., basketball, soccer) into each question. Both individual item scores and total scores should be recorded, analyzed, and used to set physical education goals. The questions in Table 15.1 are part of a 40-item inventory called the Sport Interest Inventory (Greendorfer & Lewko, 1978). The other items explore the contributions of father, mother, siblings, teachers, and friends to the sport socialization process.

Play Deficits in Children With Disabilities

In most infants, play is inborn and instinctive. Give them a rattle, and they will shake, mouth, and pound it. Put a toy in front of them and they will reach for it. Put them on the floor, and once they have learned to crawl and creep, they will spontaneously move from place to place, exploring their environment. Physical play provides the activity through which most initial learning occurs. Social and imitative play, which is largely dependent on vision, develops concurrently with physical play. Peek-a-boo and waving bye-bye, for instance, are widely recognized as the first games that infants play. The development of speech, which requires intact hearing, enriches both physical and social play because it affords increased opportunity for feedback and interaction.

Congenital and early childhood disabilities are associated with play deficits (Linder, 1993; Wehman, 1977). Severe disability often negates the ability to play spontaneously.

T a b l e   1 5 . 1   Questions about interest and involvement in sports from an instrument developed by Susan Greendorfer and John Lewko (1978).

1. How much do you play sports after school and on weekends?				
5	4	3	2	1
Very much	A lot	Some	Not much	Not at all
2. How important is it to you that you participate in sports?				
1	2	3	4	5
Not important	Not too	In between	Somewhat	Very important
3. How much do you like playing sports?				
5	4	3	2	1
Very much	A lot	Some	Not much	Not at all
4. In general, how good are you at sports?				
1	2	3	4	5
Not good at all	Not good	In between	Good	Very good
5. How easy is it for you to learn new sports skills?				
5	4	3	2	1
Very easy	Somewhat easy	Average	Not very easy	Not easy at all

T a b l e   1 5 . 2   Developmental stages in social play.

Stages	Level
Preplay	1. **Autistic or unoccupied.** Manipulates body parts or objects, without apparent purpose. Lies, sits, or wanders about aimlessly. Exhibits stereotyped or repetitive behaviors.
Practice Play	2. **Exploratory or sensorimotor play.** Plays alone with definite goal/purpose. Seems unaware of others in close proximity. Reactions to toys/stimuli can be classified as approach or avoidance.
Symbolic Play	3. **Parallel play.** Plays independently, but shows awareness and occasional interest in others. Brings toys and/or establishes play space near others.
	4. **Associative play (interactive).** Initiates contacts with other children. Interacts on playground apparatus and in "playing house" or other make-believe games. Interactions can be classified as positive or negative and as dyads, triads, and the like.
Rules Play	5. **Cooperative play.** Shares toys and apparatus. Participates in simple organized games; understands game formation and base or safety line; knows game goal and can switch roles (chase/flee, tag/dodge, roll/catch). Optimal group size seems to be three to six.
	6. **Increasingly complex games play.** Engages in progressively more complex, organized games to lead-up games to regulation team sports. Concurrently engages in progression of movement activities demanding self-competition (self-testing), partner competition, and group competition. Individual preferences emerge for team vs. individual vs. no competition.

Adapted from Parten (1932) and Piaget (1962). See the checklist for assessing social play in Chapter 18.

Children with severe developmental disabilities, when left alone without the stimulation of a partner or assistant, are likely to be sitting, lying, rocking back and forth, staring into space, or repetitively manipulating an object (i.e., demonstrating autistic-like behaviors). The play behavior of such children is described as *autistic* or *unoccupied* (see Table 15.2). A primary goal is to teach purposeful, spontaneous response to as many play stimuli as possible, thereby enabling the individual to advance to the next play stage.

Individuals with less severe disabilities play spontaneously but to a lesser extent than AB peers. Upper extremity disabilities can make the manipulation of play objects, toys, and table games (cards, checkers, and monopoly, for example) difficult or impossible. Lower extremity disabilities limit play to that which can be done from wheelchairs, scooter boards, crutches, or walkers. Speech problems, such as occur in congenital deafness and severe cerebral palsy, affect the development of social play skills. Mental retardation and learning disabilities prevent engaging in game play that requires fully matured mental operations and intact perceptual abilities. A goal of adapted physical education is to find games and sports that utilize the abilities that such students have and then help them to fully develop their play potential.

Failure to progress through the developmental stages of social play at the same age as peers affects many aspects of life. Play is the major medium through which children learn about human relationships, and high priority should be given to helping children advance from one social play stage to another (see Table 15.2). If, however, this goal is not reached by adolescence, play stages should be forgotten and attention should be focused on the specific social functions needed to perform selected sport skills.

Motor Creativity

Motor creativity is problem solving concerning ways that the body, space, and play objects can be used for fun and enjoy-

ment in large-muscle play. The following four distinct components of motor creativity can be assessed and taught.

Fluency is the ability to generate many different responses. Given a play space, a play object, a piece of playground apparatus, or an environment full of play objects and props, the child shows many different ways of exploring and having fun (see Figure 15.4). The tester might use a verbal prompt like "Show me all the things you can do!" or might simply suggest, "Here is a good place to play," or "Why don't you play here while I rest a moment or while I do my paperwork?"

Flexibility is the ability to generate categorically different responses, spontaneity in changing from one category of activities to another, and evidence of fully exploring all possibilities rather than "getting hung up" in a particular category of responses. For example, in the *time category,* responses would use various speeds and even and uneven rhythms. In the *space category,* responses might be close to the floor, at tiptoe level, or in the air; movements might use different amounts and directions of space. In the *force category,* responses might be heavy or light, direct or indirect, aggressive or passive. In the *flow category,* responses might be sustained or staccato.

Originality is the ability to generate imaginative, novel, relevant responses that few other individuals have demonstrated. Originality is associated with uniqueness that is admired and appreciated.

Elaboration is the ability to embellish, add detail, integrate things into meaningful or entertaining themes, and/or initiate drama or choreography. Children who elaborate often add vocalization (e.g., animal or machine sounds) or words to their movement.

Assessment of Motor Creativity

Several measures of motor creativity exist (Sherrill, 1986). The most popular of these is the Test of Thinking Creatively in Action and Movement (TCAM) by E. Paul Torrance (1981), a renowned authority on all kinds of creativity. The TCAM has norms for children ages 3 to 8, but the items can be used with

older age groups. This test requires about 20 min and no equipment except a wastebasket and lots of paper cups.

The TCAM includes four items. Item 1 focuses on how many different ways a student can move across a room. Torrance does not specify distance, but Sherrill uses 6 feet. A short distance avoids fatigue and puts the emphasis on new ways. This item and two others (3 and 4) are scored for both fluency (the frequency of responses) and originality (a 0 to 3 rating scale keyed to responses in the test manual that reflect whether the movement is common or infrequent). For example, hopping, skipping, and jumping receive 0 points because almost all students think of these. Frog, kangaroo, and various animal walks receive 1 point. Tumbling and spinning receive 2 points. Walking on knees backwards and running in circles receive 3 points.

Items 3 and 4 both pertain to possible uses of paper cups. Item 3 asks how many ways the student can put a paper cup in a wastebasket. Item 4 asks how many different things the student can do with a paper cup (i.e., imagine it is something else and show its use). Both fluency and originality scores are recorded. The following examples illustrate how 0, 1, 2, or 3 points are awarded:

0 points for hat, pencil, or jumping cup (response made by 10% or more of normative group)

1 point for spider, worm, and pop game (response made by 5 to 9% of normative group)

2 points for telescope, shoe cover, and nose cover (response made by 2 to 4% of normative group)

3 points for baseball bat, cow's milk, and dog's bowl (response made by 2% or less of normative group)

The imagination item (Item 2) requires children to pretend that they are six different things: a tree in the wind, a rabbit, a fish, a snake, a person driving a car, and a person trying to push an elephant. The child's response to each "Can you move like?" is scored on a 5-point scale as follows:

1 point—Child does not move.

2 points—Action is inadequate.

3 points—Action is adequate but without interpretation.

4 points—Action shows imagination.

5 points—Action tells a story beyond the assigned role.

Obviously, the TCAM, especially Item 1, can elicit a lot of information about movement abilities. Torrance allows students to either tell or show responses. Sherrill has adapted the TCAM to permit only showing. The TCAM can be ordered from the Scholastic Testing Service, 480 Meyer Rd., Bensenville, IL 60106.

Other motor creativity protocols entail videotaping students on a multipurpose playground apparatus (rope, slide, ladder, balance beam, etc.) or in a room with various props (hoops, balls, ropes, scarves, broomsticks). The instructions are *"Show me all the different things you can do."* The prompt *"Show me something new"* is given every 60 sec. Videotapes of 3 to 5 minutes in length provide a permanent record of children's movement vocabulary. Fluency and originality scores are derived by counting and rating responses using a Torrance protocol or by using a criterion-based motor creativity rating scale.

Videotapes can also be used to record children's responses to toys, play vehicles, and sports equipment. Adults need to allow children time to figure out play objects for themselves. Exploratory activity is recognized as a form of play that should be reinforced, even though inappropriate play responses sometimes occur. Initiative and self-determination, generally expressed first in play, are behaviors important in learning how to cope with an overabundance of leisure time.

Teaching Motor Creativity

Several approaches to teaching motor creativity have been discussed in this text. Movement education, explained in Chapter 3, is a method that teaches through carefully structured questions designed to involve students in problem solving about their bodies, play objects or apparatus, and the elements of movement (time, space, force, and flow). Questions must be answered with movements, not words (see Figure 15.5). There are no right or wrong answers, no demonstrations, and no recognition that one child's responses are better than another's. The emphasis is on demonstrating fluency and originality, having fun, and doing one's personal best.

Games analysis, or the **Games Design model,** discussed in Chapter 9, is a method that teaches motor creativity by involving children in problem solving about how traditional games can be changed and new games can be developed. Questions focus on game categories: players, equipment, movements, organizational pattern (formation, player positions), limitations/rules, and purpose. By changing one element in a category at a time, a game can be played in many ways. For example, dodgeball can be played with any number of players, numerous soft objects, and various kinds of throws and dodges, and in all kinds of formations, with diverse penalty and boundary rules, and with different purposes (e.g., dodge only, dodge or catch, dodge or strike). Each new version of a game can be given a new name chosen by the children.

The **Knowledge-Based Game model,** described in Chapter 21, is also a method that develops motor creativity. This method stresses problem solving as a means of enhancing

FIGURE 15.5 These girls are responding to the question "How many different shapes can you create with one partner, two noodles, and a small hoop?"

game knowledge, spontaneity, motivation, and understanding of personal capabilities. A question-and-answer approach encourages children to problem solve about all aspects of play.

Motor Creativity as Ongoing Process

Fluency, flexibility, originality, and elaboration are the abilities that enable individuals to overcome architectural, aspirational, and attitudinal barriers. Individuals with disabilities especially need these problem-solving abilities. Much of happiness, for them, may depend on discovering alternative ways of moving and succeeding. Motor creativity instruction thus leads to self-determination and self-empowerment and protects against feelings of helplessness.

Assessment of Play and Game Competence

Assessment should involve all members of the family. The leisure expectations, aspirations, and lifestyles of each person should be considered. What does the family do during leisure? What forms of play are valued? Individual and group interviews and casual conversations are the best ways to obtain this information. Leisure surveys (see Table 15.3) or books like that of Paciorek and Jones (1994) that show people with disabilities engaging in many activities can be used as props to stimulate talk. Magazines like *Sports 'N Spokes* and *Palaestra* are good also, as are scrapbooks of pictures from various sources. Professionals often must help parents understand that individuals with disabilities can participate in a wide variety of sports and games in numerous settings. During assessment interviews, parents can be helped to understand community resources and to assess their skills in accessing these resources.

Assessment of play and game competence requires an examination of how the child uses her or his free time when alone. It is essential that children have play skills for the hours when they are alone. It is important also to assess the child's play and game competence in the company of others. Play behaviors typically are different when the child is (a) with an adult or older child, (b) with a same-age child, (c) with a child who is younger, and (d) with groups of various sizes. Assess-

Table 15.3 A sport survey to assess active leisure interests and needs.

Directions: Following is a list of sports in which many people with a disability excel! Please circle the number of each sport you have tried three or more times. Then choose the five sports you would most like to be good at and underline them.

1. All-terrain vehicles	28. Powerlifting
2. Aquatics	29. Power soccer
3. Archery	30. Quad rugby
4. Basketball	31. Racquetball
5. Beep baseball	32. Road racing
6. Blowdarts	33. Roller skating
7. Boating	34. Rugball
8. Boccia	35. Scuba diving
9. Bowling	36. Shooting
10. Cross-country	37. Showdown
11. Cycling	38. Snow skiing
12. Equestrian	39. Skydiving
13. Fencing	40. Slalom
14. Field events	41. Sledge hockey
15. Fishing	42. Snowmobiling
16. Fitness programs	43. Soccer
17. Floor hockey	44. Softball
18. Flying	45. Table tennis
19. Football	46. Team handball
20. Goal ball	47. Tennis
21. Golf	48. Track
22. Gymnastics	49. Volleyball
23. Hunting	50. Waterskiing
24. Ice skating	51. Weight training
25. Ice sledding	52. Wilderness experiences
26. Lawn bowling	53. Wrestling
27. Martial arts	

ment should address each of these situations. Children who are verbal are generally eager to talk about their favorite playmates, games, and sports. Informal interviews thus serve as an excellent source of data (see Figure 15.6).

Assessment should include making a list of games and sports that the individual can play and another list of the activities that he or she would like to do. Comparing these lists against activities of same-age peers and family members helps set goals related to inclusion. Barriers to success in these activities should be examined, and action plans should be agreed upon for overcoming these barriers. Occasionally barriers are too great to be overcome, and assessment must focus on finding alternative activities that are acceptable to everyone involved. Every IEP should include specific games or sports to be mastered.

Assessment of play and game competence also requires a consideration of the skills needed to use community settings (Moon, 1994; Schleien, Meyer, Heyne, & Brandt, 1995). Assessment interviews should make families aware of the rich array of community options for leisure and give them information on how to become involved. After supplying this information and accompanying the parents to examine various facilities, professionals must ask many questions. Suppose the

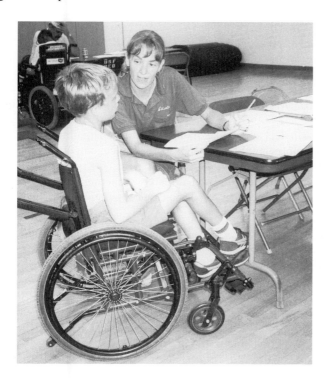

individual with a disability and her or his family decide on biweekly leisure activity at a particular bowling alley. What issues must be resolved?

1. *Transportation.* Who will supply this? Are lessons needed in using public transportation?

2. *Companionship.* Bowling is more fun when done with someone else. Are family or friends available, or should an arrangement be made for a paid or volunteer companion?

3. *Money.* How much is needed? Who will supply it? Are lessons needed in the use of money?

4. *Appropriate clothing and shoes.* Is instruction needed? Does the individual know the shoe size to ask for and have the communication skills to make himself or herself understood?

5. *Selection of ball and lane.* What instruction is needed?

6. *Game and social etiquette.* What instruction is needed?

7. *Scoring.* What kind of scoring is meaningful? What instruction is needed?

8. *Crisis management.* If problems occur, who at the bowling alley can be depended upon for understanding and help? What problems might occur? What are the protocols or plans of action to be followed?

Some communities employ recreation specialists to assist with assessment in the play and game competence area, but generally these concerns must be addressed by physical educators. Adapted physical educators especially, in relation to the transition services mandate of the law, should be sure that the assessment protocol affords opportunities to visit many types of sport and recreation settings, to engage in activity at some of

them, and to make informed decisions as to which best meets needs. This needs assessment leads to goal setting for the IEP.

Teaching Play and Game Competence

Teaching begins with agreeing on goals and objectives. This occurs at both the IEP and the classroom levels. The overall goal is usually written as follows: *To demonstrate functional competence in selected play and game behaviors*—or, for older students, *to demonstrate functional competence in active leisure behaviors required for participation in community programs.*

Game and Leisure Behaviors for Time Alone

The listing of specific play and game behaviors to be demonstrated should include some activities that can be done alone, because all individuals, especially those reared in small families, have time alone that needs to be filled with meaningful activity. Physical activities that can be done alone (e.g., shooting baskets, jumping rope, riding a bicycle, using backyard or neighborhood park apparatus) depend on available equipment and space in each individual's home. Goal setting and instruction in alone play must therefore be highly individualized. Teachers may need to visit homes to establish lesson plans with content that is realistic and generalizable. This is particularly necessary when working with individuals with severe developmental delays who will not play unless every step of the play process is carefully taught with emphasis on generalization.

Game and Leisure Behaviors for Time With Others

Most instruction for most students, however, should focus on learning the cooperation and competition behaviors essential to active leisure. Table 15.4 presents a cooperation–competition continuum to guide instruction. Most children, until about age 8, function at the egocentric and small-group game levels. Individuals with severe mental retardation or play delays might be frozen at these levels if their cognitive ability does not permit an understanding of competition. See Chapter 9 for content specifically on teaching beginning competence in game cooperation.

Until about the third grade, play and game experiences should be recreational and developmental. The emphasis should be on learning motor creativity and experiencing a wide variety of activities. Every child should be taught to swim and dance at an early age, as well as to enjoy the out-of-doors and activities that use natural resources, like hiking, camping, and boating. Games should be vehicles for having fun, learning basic play and motor skills, and reinforcing self-esteem.

Although parents tend to place children in competitive team sports like T-ball, peewee soccer, and Challenger baseball at very young ages, most professionals believe that serious competition should not be introduced until about age 8. Then the best learning progression begins with competition against a single opponent, as in track, swimming, bowling, and the like (see Table 15.4), then moves to dual or doubles competition, and finally team competition. Children should have opportunities to experience each type of game competition so that they can make informed decisions as to whether they want to become individual or team sport people. In general, how-

Table 15.4 A cooperation–competition continuum to guide instruction.

Levels	Explanation
Egocentric	1. **Individual and group play.** Thinks only of self. Lacks maturity to empathize and cooperate. Wants to be *It* all of the time. Does not share or take turns unless reminded to.
Small-Group Games	2. **Cooperative organized play.** Cooperates with others to achieve a mutual goal, like winning a relay or tagging the most persons.
Individual or Dual Competition	3. **Individual competition.** Competes with one opponent in individual sports like track, swimming, bowling, golf, and tennis. Competes against others also in trying to make the best score in fitness, track, and self-testing activities.
	4. **Dual or doubles competition.** Competes in dual sports like doubles in tennis, badminton, and table tennis. Cooperates with partner in doubles tennis, with team in bowling, and in other situations demanding a limited number of interactions.
Team Competition and Cooperation	5. **Team competition.** Cooperates with team members while concurrently competing with opponents. The smaller the team, the easier the learning progressions in cooperation and competition.

Note. The concept of personal best (self-competition) should be taught and reinforced at all levels.

ever, individual and dual sports are more accessible throughout the lifespan. Thus, individual sports are more important to teach than team sports if time does not permit instruction in all kinds of competition.

Readiness for Serious Competition

The rationale for not engaging children in serious competition until about age 8 lies mainly in human development and self-concept theory. **Serious competition** is defined as score keeping, acknowledgment of winners and losers, and coping with spectator and peer pressures. From a psychological standpoint, competition is *social comparison,* a means of judging whether you are as good as everyone else and developing opinions about your competence in various domains. This, in turn, influences self-concept, mental health, and whether or not an activity is fun.

Before age 5, most children do not understand competition because they are not yet developmentally able to make social comparisons. All sport is therefore recreational. Persons at this level of development (both the very young and the developmentally delayed) engage in sport to please parents and to feel good. Typically, they perform to the best of their ability but have no set goals other than to have fun. They do not understand winning and losing but instead base judgments of self-competence on (a) simple task mastery (either I did it or I did not, or the coach let me play or the coach did not) and (b) the feedback of significant others, mainly parents. Much of the early Special Olympics philosophy (e.g., the huggers at the finish line in track and swimming) was based on the assumption that most persons with mental retardation function at this level. Today, Special Olympics philosophy and practices have changed to emphasize assessing athletes individually and determining whether or not they understand concepts of winning.

From ages 5 to 8, children gradually achieve the cognitive capacity to make social comparisons and begin to judge their personal worth by comparing themselves to others. This strengthens the egos of children who are good at sport but weakens the self-esteem of children with motor and play deficits. Until about the age of 8, most children do not have the emotional maturity to handle losing. Exposure to serious competition should not occur until children have developed good self-esteem, are emotionally ready to enjoy the challenge of competition, and fully understand that achieving a personal best is as good as or better than beating an opponent.

The concept of personal best should be introduced in sport around age 7 or 8, with children encouraged to state **level of aspiration** before undertaking self-testing or self-competition tasks. For example, the teacher may ask each child to write his or her anticipated score (level of aspiration) on a daily contract or in a secret place before responding to such challenges as (a) "How many curl-ups can you do in 30 seconds?" (b) "How fast can you run the 50-yard dash?" and (c) "How far can you throw the softball?" By comparing aspirations with actual scores, children are helped to focus newly evolving comparison skills on a personal best rather than on the goal of being better than others.

As individuals mature, most seek both to win and to achieve a personal best. In adapted physical activity, one of the main concerns is children who seldom or never win. Almost no research is available to describe the psychosocial development of children whose social comparisons always tell them that they are performing below average. One approach to this problem is to stress competition against self instead of others and to make available activities that are recreational instead of competitive.

Basic Play and Game Skills

What, besides motor skills and an understanding of cooperation and/or competition, do individuals need to play games? To answer this question, consider the following game categories:

1. **Players**—an understanding of roles in individual, dual, and team games. Is everyone playing for individual fun as in early childhood games, or is there an obligation to help a partner or a team?

2. **Equipment**—an understanding of the use and care of play equipment and awareness of safety factors. Given a piece of play equipment, can the child show its appropriate use for a particular game?

3. **Movements**—skill in performing the motor skills in the game context and ability to have fun while performing; the use of strategy in performing motor skills and moving around the play area.

4. **Organizational pattern**—skill in getting into correct formation or going a particular space to await a turn or play a designated position.

5. **Limitations/rules**—an understanding of adherence to rules within a game context, such as stop and go, time-out, boundaries, safety zones, taking turns, making outs, direction of play, penalties, game cues or jargon, and winning points.

6. **Game purpose**—an understanding of game purposes based on one, two, or more concepts.

Children without disabilities typically learn play and game skills informally from other children in neighborhood play. In contrast, children who require adapted physical activity services often need systematic instruction and practice in each element of every game category (see Figure 15.7). Behavior management techniques (see Chapter 7) are useful in designing instruction and selecting personalized reinforcements.

Recommended First Games

If a child with a severe disability appears to have no understanding of play and games, try peek-a-boo activities or funny facial expressions and body antics that will make the child laugh. Also try coactive movements in which your arm or body moves in unison with the child's body parts. Developmentally, peek-a-boo is the first game that children without disabilities learn, and it seems to be one of the easiest to teach individuals of all ages with severe disabilities. From peek-a-boo, progress to hide-and-seek kinds of activities. Hide objects, and help the individual find them. Think of the universal appeal of Easter egg hunts and similar activities. Try to develop an easy-to-hard sequence of hide-and-seek games.

Start-and-stop games are among the easiest to teach. Remember the game called *Red Light, Green Light.* Everyone starts on the same line, moves when the teacher calls out "Green light!" and stops when the teacher calls out "Red light!" The goal is to see who can get to the opposite line first. Usually running is the mode of locomotion, but the game can use any method of movement.

Many variations of *Red Light, Green Light* are played. *Hot Potato* requires a circle formation. Usually music is the cue to pass the potato (any object) from person to person. When the music stops, the passing must stop. The goal is to not be holding the "hot potato" when the music stops. *Musical Chairs* and *Cake Walk* are similar games, both played in circle formation. Six persons, for instance, walk around five chairs set in a circle. When the music stops, everyone sits. The goal is to not be the person without a chair. In *Cake Walk,* the movement is walking or running along a pattern of squares drawn on the floor. Some of the squares have cakes drawn in them or objects placed in them. The goal is to be standing in a square with a cake when the music stops.

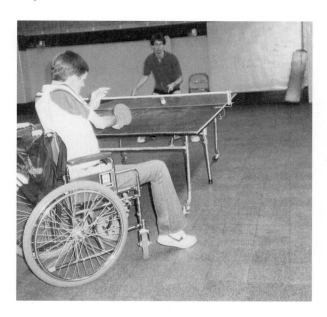

FIGURE 15.7 This individual with muscular dystrophy has been employed to give after-school lessons in table tennis to a boy with mental retardation.

Start-and-stop concepts can also be taught in games that require individuals to change places. Parachute games are among the easiest of these. The teacher can call out names of several individuals, who run under the parachute to change places. In *Squirrels in Trees,* children are in threesomes: two facing each other and holding hands to form a tree, and the third child (the squirrel) inside the tree. When given the cue to start moving, all squirrels change trees. In harder progressions, there are fewer trees than squirrels or an It tries to tag squirrels before they get to a new tree.

Games built around the theme of running home when given a particular cue (see Table 15.5) also teach start-and-stop concepts. These games typically use creative dramatics with a leader like a huntsman gathering up followers or a mother animal with her babies. Everyone follows the leader, thereby getting lots of exercise and motor skill practice, until a cue signals the need to run to the safety zone (home). The goal could be to see who can get there first or, in a more advanced progression, to see who can avoid being tagged by someone pretending to be bad or hurtful.

Table 15.5 shows how games can be taught in easy-to-hard progressions that require an understanding of an increasing number of concepts. Good teachers figure out many ways to alter games to make them easier or harder and thereby meet the needs of students. Methods books for teaching elementary school physical education provide many examples.

Recommended Easy-to-Hard Sequence for Teaching Game Concepts

Following is a recommended sequence for teaching game concepts:

1. Follow the leader
2. Start-and-stop on cues like *Red Light, Green Light*

T a b l e   1 5 . 5   **Easy-to-hard progression for teaching running game concepts.**

Step	Illustrative Games
1	*Easiest (one concept)* **Flying Dutchman** Concept: Run home on cue. Formation: Line of children holding hands. Start with circle and then break into line. Instructions: Leader pulls line in any direction around the gymnasium. On the cue "Flying Dutchman," all children run to wall or mat designated as home (safety). The term *floor spaces* may be substituted in movement education variations of this game.
2	*Medium (two concepts)* **Huntsman** Concepts: Follow leader; run home on cue. Formation: File, one student behind the other. Instructions: Teacher moves around the room and says, "I'm going to hunt the monster. Who wants to go on a hunt with me? Get in the file and follow!" This continues, with students joining file and following the leader until the cue "bang." On it, all students run independently to safety zone. Theme can be varied, as "I am a police officer. Who wants to chase robbers with me?"
3	*Harder (four concepts)* **Chickens and Fox (Run, Children, Run)** Concepts: Follow leader; run home on cue; avoid being tagged; penalty. Formation: Scattered, with safety and danger zones clearly marked. Instructions: All children (chickens, rabbits, or whatever) are at home safe with leader. Outside the safety zone is a fox or bad person either walking back and forth or pretending to be asleep. Leader says to group, "Let's take a walk" and all walk around danger zone while fox sleeps. Leader or fox can give cue to run home: "Run, chickens, run." Fox tries to tag children before they get home. Fox makes persons who are tagged do push-ups in prison (this introduces penalty concept).
4	*Very Hard (five or more concepts)* Simple One-to-One Tag Games See activity analysis in Table 9.6.

Note: In writing lesson plans, refer to Game Progression 1, Step 1, 2, 3, or 4.

3. Run-to-change-places games like *Under the Parachute* and *Squirrels in Trees*

4. Run to safety (safe vs. not safe places or people) like *Huntsman*

5. Flee (avoiding being tagged) like *Chickens and Fox*

6. Tag (learning to tag another)

7. Chase (learning to chase another)

8. Flee-tag-chase combinations with a penalty (like going to prison) for being tagged

9. Flee-tag-chase combinations involving changing roles (when tagged, you become a chaser)

How many games can you create for reinforcing each concept? Children with severe developmental delays need to always practice motor skills in relation to games in which they can be used. Early childhood games are chronologically appropriate only to about age 8.

After age 8, children should be taught basic game concepts within a sport context. The play concepts used in early childhood games, however, are the same as those incorporated into team sports like soccer, football, ice hockey, and basketball. In addition to running for safety and to change places, the game goal requires moving with a ball to an end line or goal. The person with the ball is fleeing, teammates are assisting, and opponents are chasing. Taking the ball away from the opponent is substituted for tagging.

Empowerment for Transition Into Community Sport

Children with disabilities should be involved in after-school and weekend sport at the same age as able-bodied peers in their neighborhood. This requires the teaching of sport skills and game strategies at appropriate ages. Typically the acquisition of adequate motor and social skills for acceptance by peers demands more instruction and practice than the school setting affords. Physical educators must therefore encourage the establishment of homework or neighborhood tutorial programs. Initiation of such programs often requires that physical educators supply the names and phone numbers of tutors who can be employed and/or volunteers. It is important that lists of resources include role models and individuals with disabilities similar to those of the child needing services.

Involvement of children in sport first means empowerment of parents to know how to initiate or find programs that meet their children's needs. This is one of the most important jobs of the adapted physical educator, who should plan time for frequent visits with parents. Parents need encouragement and support as much as their children do, and there is typically no one else available to assist them in concerns pertaining specifically to sports and games. Physical educators thus should see themselves as instrumental in helping parents make and execute decisions that maximize their children's involvement in appropriate, meaningful sport.

Choices should not be limited to disability or inclusive sports. Parents and children should be introduced to all of the possibilities and, if necessary, supported in creating new possibilities. A library of videotapes showing people with disabilities succeeding in various sport activities should be available for both parents and children to borrow and view. Books and magazines should also be available for loan.

Ultimately, parents must know how to empower their children to make personal choices to become involved in and stay involved in sport. This involvement should extend beyond sport participation into leadership and administrative roles in the management of sport events and organizations. Even at very young ages, children should be allowed to elect officers for their sport clubs and see themselves as responsible for many aspects of the sport experience.

Assuring the Use of Community Resources and Transition Outcomes

The use of community resources should begin as field trips that are an integral part of school physical education (see Figure 15.8). These field trips, whenever possible, should include parents or primary caretakers. Field trips should teach the role of spectator at sport events as well as the role of participant or athlete. Field trip events should include both disability and nondisability sport and should be written into the IEP as part of the coordinated set of activities related to transition.

Homework for physical education should require the use of community resources. Proof that homework was done can be in the form of journals kept, photographs taken, or signatures by facility managers on forms indicating that the student was present. It is the responsibility of the adapted physical educator to ascertain that community resources meet criteria for attitudinal and architectural accessibility.

The use of community resources is enhanced when students see teachers and their families using these resources. It is also enhanced when students see individuals with the same disabilities as their own using these resources. Community resources can be public (paid for by tax dollars) or private (managed by churches, agencies, or commercial groups). The goal should be for students to be able to independently use as many kinds of sport, recreation, and fitness facilities as possible and to continue this use after graduation from high school. IEP goals and objectives should list facilities by name and include procedures for maximizing community involvement.

The Need for Help With Relaxation

In addition to instruction in play and game competence and active leisure, some individuals want help in learning how to handle stress and hypertension through movement. In the past, tension was associated mostly with adults, but more and more children seem to need help in this area (Brandon, Eason, & Smith, 1986; Cautela & Groden, 1978). The following section covers content on assessing and teaching relaxation. People of all ages can benefit from these activities.

Assessment of Tension

Knowledge of the signs of tension enables you to assess, write specific behavioral objectives, and plan remediation. The fol-

FIGURE 15.8 Field trips should teach the role of spectator at sport events as well as the participant or athlete role.

lowing are signs of tension that should be assessed and included in the objectives you write.

1. **Hyperactivity.** Inability to remain motionless for set period of time; wriggles in chair; shifts arm or leg; plays with hair; scratches, rubs or picks at skin; makes noises with feet; drums fingers on desktop or doodles with pen; chews gum, pencil, or fingernails; fails to keep place in line or any set formation.

2. **Facial expression.** Lines in face seldom disappear; eyes frequently shift focus; lips quiver or seem abnormally tight; cheek muscles show tension; immobile expression, such as frozen smile or incessant frown; eye tic.

3. **Breathing.** Unconscious breath holding; shallow, irregular breaths; hyperventilation.

4. **Skin.** Nervous perspiration; irritations caused by picking; hives, eczema.

5. **Voice.** Two opposite patterns, the more common of which is talking too much, louder than usual, faster than usual, and with higher pitch; deep sighs indicating excessive respiratory tension; crying.

6. **Sadness.** Manifested by slouched postures, slowness in thought and action, difficulty with concentration, inability to cope, failure to laugh and enjoy activities that are designed to be fun and relaxing.

7. **Muscle tightness.** Tension and sometimes pain, usually most prevalent in face, neck, and back.

These signs are associated with acute episodes of mental illness, but they also appear in times of great stress, such as final examination periods, death or severe illness in family, impending divorce of parents, and/or incessant bickering among family members. Certain prescribed drugs, such as diet pills, and also those consumed illegally, result in overt signs of hyperactivity. Constant physical pain or discomfort is sometimes evidenced in signs of tension.

When the problems causing tension are not resolved over long periods of time, individuals slip into a state of **chronic fatigue.** They often experience insomnia. When they do sleep, they typically awaken unrested. Symptoms of chronic fatigue are (a) increase of tendon reflexes, (b) increase of muscle excitability, (c) spastic condition of smooth muscles exhibited in diarrhea and stomach upsets, (d) abnormal excitability of heart and respiratory apparatus, (e) tremors, (f) restlessness, and (g) irritability. In this stage, many persons seek the help of a physician; generally, they complain of feeling tired all of the time. They know they are not really sick, but neither do they feel well.

Testing for Excess Tension

Awareness of residual tension can be developed by instructing students to lie on their backs and release all tensions. Then you lift one body part at a time and let go. Record the degree of hypertonus present as *negative, slight, medium,* or *marked* on the right and left sides for the muscles of the wrist, elbow, shoulder, ankle, knee, hip, and neck. Hypertonus is detected by such *unconscious* muscular responses as these:

1. **Assistance.** Student assists you in lifting the body part.
2. **Posturing or set.** Student resists gravity when you remove support.
3. **Resistance.** Student tenses or resists your lifting the body part.
4. **Perseveration.** Student continues a movement after you start it.

Using Electromyography

The presence of residual tension can be assessed also through electromyography. The electromyometer, like any electromyographical apparatus, records the amount of electrical activity present in the muscle fibers. Biofeedback in the form of sound and a digital readout reinforces attempts to reduce tension, making the apparatus effective both as a teaching and an evaluation device.

Teaching Relaxation

Techniques of teaching relaxation vary with the age group, the nature of the disability, and the number of class sessions to be spent. Each of the techniques described in this section aims at lowering the tension—that is, the electrical activity of skeletal muscles. With the exception of the Jacobson techniques, few have been subjected to scientific research. Although their effectiveness might not be substantiated statistically, each of the various techniques has strong proponents and is worthy of exploration. Imagery, deep body awareness, the Jacobson techniques, static stretching exercises, yoga, and Tai Chi are considered. Breathing exercises are also important in relaxation training.

Imagery

The *imagery* or ideational approach is well received in the primary grades (see Figure 15.9). Poems and short stories are excellent to help children become rag dolls flopping, ice cream melting, merry-go-rounds stopping, balloons slowly deflating, icicles melting, faucets dripping, salt pouring from a shaker, bubbles getting smaller, and snowflakes drifting downward. For greatest effectiveness, draw the children into discussions of what relaxes them and encourage them to make up their

FIGURE 15.9 Imagery as a relaxation technique is often enhanced by giving the children props like scarves, ribbons, or towels.

own stories and poems. Asking children to develop lists of their favorite *quiet* things and *slow* activities is also enlightening. Focus on enacting things that start out fast, gradually decrease in speed, and eventually become motionless.

Some ideational approaches used to elicit relaxed movements follow:

You are a soft calico kitten lying in front of the warm fireplace. The fire is warm. You feel so-o-o good. First, you stretch your right arm—oh, that feels good. Then you stretch your left arm. Then you stretch both legs. Now you are relaxed all over. The fire is so warm and your body feels so relaxed. This must be the best place in the whole world—your own little blanket in front of your own fire. You are so-o-o relaxed that you could fall asleep right now. You are getting sleepy now—maybe you will fall asleep now.

You are the tail of a kite that is sailing gently high, oh so-o-o high in the light blue sky. The kite goes higher and so do you—very slowly and very gently in the soft breeze. Now you are going to the right. Oh, the breeze is warm and ooh so soft—it is blowing so gently that you can feel it only if you think real hard. Can you feel the soft, warm breeze blowing you to the left? It is so-o-o gentle and so-o-o soft.

You are becoming a puppet. The change starts in your feet. Slowly, each part of your body becomes lifeless and is completely relaxed, as if it were detached from you.

Let's make believe we are a bowl full of jello! Someone has left us out of the refrigerator, and we begin to dissolve slowly away. Our arms float down, and our body sinks slowly into the bowl.

Older children, no longer able to assume magically the feeling/tone of an animal or object, continue to find relaxation in the mood of certain poems and stories read aloud. They may lie in comfortable positions in a semidarkened room while listening and attempt to capture the essence of the words through consciously releasing tensions. Instrumental music may be substituted for reading if the group desires. Surburg (1989) discusses imagery techniques for special populations.

FIGURE 15.10 Two girls with Down syndrome participate in a deep body awareness relaxation activity at the close of their physical education class. This constitutes a "cool-down" time to help them make the transition from strenuous motor work to quiet academic learning.

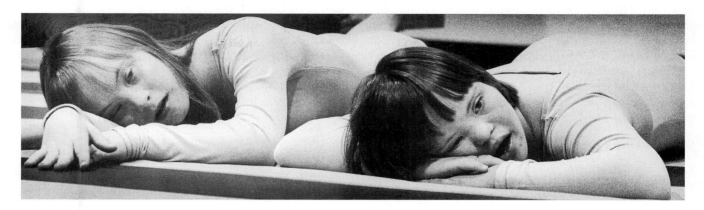

Deep Body Awareness

To facilitate deep body awareness, begin the class with everyone in a comfortable supine position (see Figure 15.10). Then direct everyone's attention to specific parts of the body, asking them to analyze and verbalize the sensations they are experiencing. If students seem reluctant to share aloud their feelings, offer such additional guidance as

1. Which parts of your arm are touching the floor? Is the floor warm or cool, smooth or rough, clean or dirty?
2. How long is your arm from the tip of the middle finger to the shoulder joint? From the tip of the middle finger to the elbow? From the tip of the middle finger to the wrist crease? How heavy is your arm? How heavy is each of its parts?
3. Can you feel the muscles loosening? If you measure the circumference of your upper arm, how many inches would you get?
4. Can you feel the blood pulsating in veins and arteries?
5. Can you feel the hairs on your arm? The creases in your wrist? Your fingernails? The cuticles? Any scars?
6. What other words come to mind when you think about *arm?*

The underlying premise in deep body awareness is that students must increase kinesthetic sensitivity before they can consciously control it. They must differentiate among parts of a whole and be able to describe these parts accurately. As deep body awareness is developed, each student discovers which thoughts and methods of releasing tension work best for him or her personally.

Deep body awareness should progress from other-directed to self-directed states. The latter is called autogenesis (self-generating). The activities described in this section are often called *autogenic training.*

Jacobson Techniques

The most widely known of the techniques of neuromuscular relaxation are those of Edmund Jacobson, a physician and physiologist who began his research in tension control at Harvard University in 1918. Jacobson's techniques, known originally as a system of *progressive conscious neuromuscular relaxation,* are referred to as *self-operations control* in his later books (Jacobson, 1970). The progression of activities is essentially the same. He suggests three steps for learning to recognize the sensations of *doing* and *not doing* in any specific muscle group:

1. tension followed by relaxation against an outside resistance, such as the teacher pushing downward on a limb that the student is trying to lift;
2. tension within the muscle group when no outside resistance is offered, followed by release of the tension; and
3. release of tension in a resting muscle group that has not been contracted.

Jacobson recommends that relaxation training begin in a supine position with arms at the sides, palms facing downward. The mastery of *differential control* of one muscle group at a time begins with hyperextension at the wrist joint only. All other joints in the body remain relaxed while the student concentrates on bending the hand backward. The resulting tension is felt in the back upper part of the forearm.

Self-operations control outlined by Jacobson is a slow procedure. Each class session is 1 hr long. During that time, a particular tension, like hyperextension of the wrist, is practiced only three times. The tension (also called the control sensation) is held 1 to 2 min, after which the student is told to *go negative* or completely relax for 3 to 4 min. After the completion of three of these tension and relaxation sequences, the student lies quietly with eyes closed for the remainder of the hour. Session 2 follows the same pattern except that the tension practiced is bending the wrist forward so as to tense the anterior muscles of the forearm. Every third session is called a zero period in that no tension is practiced. The entire body is relaxed the whole time.

In all, seven sessions are recommended for learning to relax the left arm. During the fourth session, the tension created by bending the elbow about 35° is practiced. During the fifth session, the tension created in the back part of the upper arm when the palm presses downward against a stack of books is practiced. The sixth session is a zero period. The seventh session calls for progressive tension and relaxation of the whole arm.

Detailed instructions are given for proceeding from one muscle group to the next. The completion of an entire course in relaxation in the supine position requires the following amount of time: left arm, 7 days; right arm, 7 days; left leg, 10 days; right leg, 10 days; trunk, 10 days; neck, 6 days; eye region, 12 days; visualization, 9 days; and speech region, 19 days. Then the same order and same duration of practices are followed in the sitting position. While Jacobson indicates that the course can be speeded up, he emphasizes that less thoroughness results in reduced ability to recognize tension signals and turn them off. Almost all textbooks on stress reduction describe Jacobson techniques (Girdano, Everly, & Dusek, 1990; Greenberg, 1990).

Static Stretching Exercises

To illustrate the efficacy of static stretching, try these experiments, holding each position for 60 sec or longer:

1. Let the head drop forward as far as it will go. Hold this position and feel the stretch on the neck extensors.
2. Let the body bend at the waist, as in touching the toes. When the fingertips touch the floor, hold, and feel the stretch in the back extensors and hamstrings.
3. Do a side bend to the left and hold.
4. Lie supine on a narrow bench and let your head hang over the edge.
5. Lie on a narrow bench and let the arms hang down motionless in space. They should not be able to touch the ground.

When students learn to release tension in these static positions, relaxation is achieved. Yoga, because it is based upon such static stretching, is often included in instructional units on relaxation.

Yoga

Yoga is a system of physical, mental, and spiritual development that comes from India, where it dates back several centuries before Christ (Hittleman, 1983; Isaacson, 1990). The word *yoga* is derived from the Sanskrit root *yuji,* which means "to join or bind together." Scholars recognize several branches of yoga, but in the United States, the term is used popularly to refer to a system of exercises built upon held positions or postures and breath control. More correctly, you should say *Hatha Yoga* rather than yoga when teaching aspects of this system to your students. In the word *Hatha,* the *ha* represents the sun (expression of energy) and the *tha* represents the moon (conservation of energy). In yoga exercises, these two are always interacting.

Hatha Yoga offers exercises particularly effective in teaching relaxation and slowing down the hyperactive child (Hopkins & Hopkins, 1976). The emphasis upon correct breathing in Hatha Yoga makes it especially valuable in the reconditioning of persons with asthma and other respiratory problems. Moreover, the nature of Hatha Yoga is such that it appeals to individuals whose health status prohibits participation in vigorous, strenuous physical activities.

Hatha Yoga, hereafter referred to as yoga, can be subdivided into two types of exercises: *asanas* and *pranayanas.* **Asanas** are held positions or postures like the lotus, the locust, and cobra poses. **Pranayanas** are breathing exercises. In actu-

ality, asanas and pranayanas are interrelated since correct breathing is emphasized throughout the assumption of a particular pose. Several of the asanas are identical or similar to stunts taught in elementary school physical education. The yoga *bent bow* is the same as the human rocker (a prone position with hands holding feet). The *cobra* is similar to the swan and/or the trunk lift from a prone position to test back strength. The *plough pose* resembles the paint-the-rainbow stunt (a back-lie with legs stretched up and over the head).

Differences between yoga and physical exercise as it is ordinarily taught are

1. Exercise sessions traditionally emphasize movement. *Yoga is exercise without movement.*
2. Exercises usually involve several bounces or stretches, with emphasis upon how many can be done. Yoga stresses a *single, slow* contraction of certain muscles followed by a general relaxation. Generally, an asana is not repeated. At the very most, it might be attempted two or three times.
3. Exercises usually entail some pain and discomfort since the teaching progression conforms to the overload principle. In yoga, the number of repetitions is not increased. The duration of time for which the asana is held increases in accordance with ease of performance.
4. Exercises ordinarily stress the development of strength, flexibility, and endurance. Yoga stresses relaxation, balance, and self-control.

In summary,

The gymnast's object is to make his body strong and healthy, with well-developed muscles, a broad chest, and powerful arms. The yogi will get more or less the same results; but they are not what he is looking for.

He is looking for calm, peace, the remedy for fatigue; or, better still, a certain immunity to fatigue.

He wants to quiet some inclination or other of his, his tendency to anger, or impatience—signs of disturbance in his organic or psychical life. He wants a full life, a more abundant life, but a life of which he is the master. (Dechanet, 1965, p. 18)

Tai Chi

Tai Chi Ch'uan, pronounced *tie jee chwhan* and called Tai Chi for short, is one of the many slowing-down activities found to be successful with hyperactive children (Kuo, 1991; Maisel, 1972). An increasing number of U.S. adults also practice this ancient Chinese system of exercise. In large metropolitan areas on the East and West coasts, instruction from masters, usually listed in the telephone directory, is available. Tai Chi is used by many dance therapists.

Tai Chi is a series of 108 specific learned patterns of movements called *forms* that provide exercise for every part of the body. The forms have colorful names that tend to captivate children: Grasp Bird's Tail Right, Stork Spreads Wings, Carry Tiger to Mountain, Step Back and Repulse Monkey, Needle at Sea Bottom, High Pat on Horse, Parting with Wild Horse's Mane Right. The 108 forms are based upon 37 basic movements; thus, there is much repetition in the execution of a series of forms.

Tai Chi is characterized by extreme slowness, a concentrated awareness of what one is doing, and absolute continuity of movement from one form to another. The same tempo is maintained throughout, but no musical accompaniment is provided. All movements contain circles, reinforcing the concepts of uninterrupted flow and quiet continuity. All body parts are gently curved or bent, allowing the body to give into gravity rather than working against it, as is the usual practice in Western culture. No posture or pose is ever held. As each form is approximately completed, its movement begins to melt and blend into the next form. This has been likened to the cycle of seasons, when summer blends into autumn and autumn into winter.

Although instruction by a master is desirable, Tai Chi is simple enough that it can be learned from a pictorial text. Movements can be memorized by repeatedly performing forms 1 to 20 in the same order without interruption. One form should never be practiced in isolation from others. Later, forms 21 to 57 are learned as a unity, as well as forms 58 to 108. This approach is especially beneficial for children who need practice in visual perception, matching, and sequencing. Its greatest strength, however, lies in the principle of slowness. Each time the sequence of forms is done, day after day, year after year, the goal is to perform it more slowly than before.

For persons who feel disinclined to memorize and teach preestablished forms, the essence of Tai Chi can be captured by restructuring class calisthenics as a follow-the-leader experience in which flowing, circular movements are reproduced as slowly as possible without breaking the continuity of the sequence. For real relaxation to occur, the same sequence must be repeated daily.

References

Bowe, F. (1990). Employment and people with disabilities: Challenges for the nineties. *Office of Special Education and Rehabilitative Services (OSERS) News in Print, 3*(3), 2–6.

Brandon, J. E., Eason, R. L., & Smith, T. J. (1986). Behavioral relaxation training and motor performance of learning disabled children with hyperactive behaviors. *Adapted Physical Activity Quarterly, 3*, 67–69.

Cautela, J., & Groden, J. (1978). *Relaxation: A comprehensive manual for adults, children, and children with special needs.* Champaign, IL: Research Press.

Dattilo, J. (1994). *Inclusive leisure services.* State College, PA: Venture.

DePauw, K. P., & Doll-Tepper, G. (1989). European perspectives on adapted physical activity. *Adapted Physical Activity Quarterly, 6*(2), 95–99.

Ferrara, M., Dattilo, J., & Dattilo, A. (1994). A crossdisability analysis of programming needs for athletes with disabilities. *Palaestra, 11*(1), 32–42.

Girdano, D., Everly, G., & Dusek, D. (1990). *Controlling stress and tension: A holistic approach* (3rd ed.). Englewood Cliffs, NJ: Prentice Hall.

Greenberg, J. (1990). *Comprehensive stress management* (3rd ed.). Dubuque, IA: Wm. C. Brown.

Greendorfer, S. L., & Lewko, J. H. (1978). Role of family members in sport socialization of children. *Research Quarterly, 49*, 146–153.

Hittleman, R. (1983). *Yoga for health.* New York: Ballantine.

Hopkins, H. L., & Smith, H. D. (1988). *Willard and Spackman's occupational therapy.* Philadelphia: J. B. Lippincott.

Hopkins, L. J., & Hopkins, J. T. (1976). Yoga in psychomotor training. *Academic Therapy, 11*, 461–464.

Isaacson, C. (1990). *Yoga step by step.* London: Butler & Tanner.

Ittenbach, R., Abery, B., Larson, S., Spiegel, A., & Prouty, R. (1994). Community adjustment of young adults with mental retardation: Overcoming barriers to inclusion. *Palaestra, 10*(2), 32–42.

Jacobson, E. (1970). *Modern treatment of tense patients.* Springfield, IL: Charles C Thomas.

Krebs, P. L., & Block, M. E. (1992). Transition of students with disabilities into community recreation: The role of the adapted physical educator. *Adapted Physical Activity Quarterly, 9*, 305–315.

Kuo, S. (1991). *Long life, good health through Tai Chi Chuan.* Berkeley, CA: North Atlantic Books.

Levine, P., & Edgar, E. (1994). An analysis by gender of long-term postschool outcomes for youth with and without disabilities. *Exceptional Children, 61*(3), 282–300.

Levy, J. (1978). *Play behavior.* New York: John Wiley.

Linder, T. W. (1993). *Transdisciplinary play-based assessment.* Baltimore: Paul H. Brookes.

Maisel, E. (1972). *Tai Chi for health.* New York: Holt, Rinehart & Winston.

Moon, M. S. (1994). *Making school and community recreation fun for everyone: Places and ways to integrate.* Baltimore: Paul H. Brookes.

Paciorek, M. J., & Jones, J. A. (1994). *Sports and recreation for the disabled* (2nd ed.). Carmel, IN: Cooper.

Parten, M. (1932). Social participation among preschool children. *Journal of Abnormal and Social Psychology, 27*, 243–269.

Piaget, J. (1962). *Play, dreams and imitation in childhood.* New York: W. W. Norton.

Public Law 101-476 (Individuals with Disabilities Education Act). (1990, October 30). *Education of the Handicapped Act Amendments of 1990.* Washington, DC: U.S. Government Printing Office.

Scanlan, T. K., Carpenter, P. J., Schmidt, G., Simons, J. P., & Keeler, B. (1993). An introduction to the sport commitment model. *Journal of Sport and Exercise Psychology, 15*, 1–15.

Scanlan, T. K., & Simons, J. P. (1992). The construct of sport enjoyment. In G. C. Roberts (Ed.), *Motivation in sport and exercise* (pp. 199–215). Champaign, IL: Human Kinetics.

Schleien, S. J., Meyer, L. H., Heyne, L., & Brandt, B. (1995). *Lifelong leisure skills and lifestyles for persons with developmental disabilities.* Baltimore: Paul H. Brookes.

Sherrill, C. (1986). Fostering creativity in handicapped children. *Adapted Physical Activity Quarterly, 3*, 236–249.

Sherrill, C. (1993). Women with disabilities. In G. L. Cohen (Ed.), *Women in sport: Issues and controversies* (pp. 238–248). Newbury Park, CA: Sage.

Sherrill, C., & Montelione, T. (1990). Prioritizing adapted physical activity goals: A pilot study. *Adapted Physical Activity Quarterly, 7*, 355–369.

Sherrill, C., Rainbolt, W., Montelione, T., & Pope, C. (1986). Sport socialization of blind and of cerebral palsied elite athletes. In C. Sherrill (Ed.), *Sport and disabled athletes* (pp. 189–195). Champaign, IL: Human Kinetics.

Sherrill, C., & Williams, T. (1996). Disability and sport: Psychosocial perspectives on inclusion, integration, and participation. *Sport Science Review, 5*(1), 42–64.

Surburg, P. R. (1989). Application of imagery techniques to special populations. *Adapted Physical Activity Quarterly, 6*(4), 328–337.

Torrance, E. P. (1981). *Thinking creatively in thought and action.* Bensenville, IL: Scholastic Test Service.

Wehman, P. (1977). *Helping the mentally retarded to acquire play skills.* Springfield, IL: Charles C Thomas.

Williams, T. (1994). Disability sport socialization and identity construction. *Adapted Physical Activity Quarterly, 11*(1), 14–31.

C H A P T E R

16

Adapted Dance and Dance Therapy

With Coauthor Wynelle Delaney, DTR

FIGURE 16.1 Anne Riordan of the University of Utah dances with adolescents with disabilities.

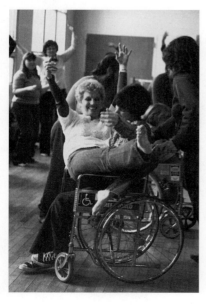

After you have studied this chapter, you should be able to do the following:

1. Discuss the similarities and differences between adapted dance and dance therapy.

2. Identify two broad pedagogical approaches and discuss the types of dance associated with each. Evaluate your experience with each type and develop a personal learning plan for enhancing knowledge and skill.

3. Explain why creative dance is recommended as a first form of movement education for children and discuss the movement and rhythm elements associated with creative dance.

4. Discuss the assessment and teaching of rhythmic patterns when persons have temporal perception problems. Design and try out activities for teaching even and uneven rhythmic patterns.

5. Identify and discuss activities especially recommended for (a) increasing body awareness, (b) improving relationships, and (c) expressing feelings. Relate your ideas to emotional disturbance and behavioral disorders.

6. Explain how dance therapy materials, principles, and tools can be used in adapted physical activity teaching and counseling. Give concrete examples.

It is beautifully apparent that dance and the child are natural companions. If, as Merleau Ponty suggests, our bodies are our way of having a world, the child is busily at home in his own body forming and shaping his own world, its inner and outer hemispheres. He is making himself up as he goes along.

—Nancy W. Smith

Perhaps no part of the physical education curriculum is as important to students with disabilities as creative rhythmic movement boldly and imaginatively taught. It can be enjoyed by the nonambulatory in beds and wheelchairs, by other health impaired persons who need mild range-of-motion exercise, and by the thousands of youngsters who find greater fulfillment in individual and dual activities than in team sports. Whereas much of physical education focuses upon cooperation, competition, and leadership-followership, creative dance offers opportunities for self-discovery and self-expression.

Children must understand and appreciate their bodies and their capacities for movement before they can cope with the world's external demands. The additional barriers to self-understanding and self-acceptance imposed by a disability intensify the need for carefully guided nonthreatening movement experiences designed to preserve ego strength, increase trust, and encourage positive human relationships. Gesture, pantomime, dance, and dance-drama can substitute for verbal communication when children lack or mistrust words to express their feelings. *Dance programming is particularly important for people with emotional disturbances, behavioral disorders, and learning disabilities.*

Distinction Between Adapted Dance and Dance Therapy

It is important to differentiate between dance as a therapeutic experience, dance therapy as a profession, and adapted dance. Prior to the formation of the American Dance Therapy Association, Inc. (ADTA), in 1966, little distinction between terms was made. Dance conducted with persons with disabilities was typically called dance therapy. Today, the term *dance therapy* is used for dance/movement conducted by persons registered as dance therapists with the ADTA. In this sense, dance therapy is like physical therapy and occupational therapy. Dance special-

ists and others who are not registered therapists may use dance with populations who are disabled and/or for therapeutic purposes, but they may not ethically describe their work as dance therapy. So what do we call dance designed to meet the educational and artistic needs of persons with special needs?

Adapted Dance

Adapted dance is a term appropriate to denote rhythmic movement instruction and/or experiences that are modified to meet the needs of persons who have significant learning, behavioral, or psychomotor problems that interfere with successful participation in programs of regular dance in education and art. *Adapt* means to make suitable, to adjust, to accommodate, or to modify in accordance with needs. These needs may be developmental or environmental. Dance specialists may *adapt* curriculum content, instructional pedagogy, assessment and evaluation approaches, and physical environment; the essence of this process of adapting is personal creativity.

Adapted dance focuses on the identification and remediation of problems within the psychomotor domain in individuals who need assistance in mainstream dance instruction and/or specially designed educational and artistic experiences. The use of adapted dance is not limited to persons with disabilities, but encompasses such special populations as the aged, juvenile delinquents and criminals, substance abusers, pregnant women, and our nation's many obese and/or unfit citizens. It also provides specialized help for clumsy persons, for whom dance instruction, in the presence of the graceful and the beautiful, is often a nightmare.

Adapted dance, like adapted physical education, is first and foremost an attitude that refuses to categorize human beings into special populations, such as the aged or the mentally retarded, and instead celebrates individual differences. Adapted dance is conceptualized especially for persons who are not comfortable and/or successful (for whatever reason) in the regular dance setting. The purpose of adapted dance, like adapted physical education, is to facilitate self-actualization, particularly as it relates to understanding and appreciation of the body and its capacity for movement. The resulting changes in psychomotor behavior eventually permit full or partial integration in regular dance as a joyous, fulfilling experience.

Adapted dance can be used to achieve any of the nine goals of adapted physical activity. A job of the specialist is to determine whether dance, sports, or aquatics is more personally meaningful to the student.

Adapted dance can be education, art, or recreation. It can also be therapeutic, but it is not therapy. The foremost pioneer in adapted dance, particularly in exploring its potential as a performing art, is Anne Riordan (see Figure 16.1), in the Modern Dance Department at the University of Utah (Fitt & Riordan, 1980). In a film titled *A Very Special Dance,* marketed by the National Dance Association, Riordan demonstrates dance as both education and art with persons who have disabilities and are members of the performing group called SUNRISE.

Dance Therapy

The official ADTA (circa 1975) definition of *dance therapy* is as follows:

> Dance therapy is the psychotherapeutic use of movement as a process which furthers the emotional and physical integration of the individual. Dance therapy is distinguished from other utilizations of dance (for example, dance education) by its focus on the nonverbal aspects of behavior and its use of movement as the process for intervention. Adaptive, expressive, and communicative behaviors are all considered in treatment, with the expressed goal of integrating these behaviors with psychological aspects of the person. Dance therapy can function as a primary treatment modality or as an integral part of an overall treatment program (p. 1).

This explanation stresses the use of dance/movement as nonverbal psychotherapy requiring a therapeutic contract between therapist and client. Thus, dance therapy is a specific treatment modality used in mental illness and emotional and behavioral problems. Dance therapy is not prescribed for other disabilities (like mental retardation and orthopedic impairment) unless the individual has emotional problems that require nonverbal psychotherapy.

Similarities of Adapted Dance and Dance Therapy

Both the dance educator and the dance therapist rely heavily on the medium of creative dance to accomplish certain objectives. Dance education can be therapeutic, just as dance therapy can be educational. Certainly, the adapted physical educator who uses creative dance as a means of helping children with disabilities to understand and appreciate their bodies and their movement capabilities is engaged in a therapeutic endeavor. But the work should not be considered dance therapy anymore than physical therapy or occupational therapy. Since the incorporation of the ADTA in May of 1966, dance therapy has gained increasing recognition as an independent profession.

Adapted Dance in the Curriculum

Dance is an integral part of physical education. As such, it must be given the same amount of time and emphasis in the curriculum as other program areas. Table 16.1 groups types of

Table 16.1 Two pedagogical approaches and types of dance.

Guided Discovery	Explanation-Demonstration-Drill
Creative or modern dance with emphasis on	*Many types of dance, including*
• Space (shape, level, size, path, focus)	Singing games
	Marching/clapping
• Time or rhythm (beat, accent pattern, phrasing)	Tap and clog
	Folk and square
• Force, effort, or weight	Social and ballroom
Heavy → Light	Aerobic
Strong → Weak	Ballet
• Flow	
Free → Bound	
Fluent → Inhibited	

dance according to teaching style. Each type teaches a set body of knowledge and skills that enrich living. Students with disabilities need exposure to dance both as a participant and observer (Boswell, 1989; Jay, 1991; Roswal, Sherrill, & Roswal, 1988; Schmitz, 1989). Field trips to dance events broaden horizons on use of leisure time and make school-based instruction more meaningful.

The method of teaching (guided discovery or explanation-demonstration-drill) determines outcomes. Guided discovery, linked with creative and modern dance, is similar to movement education (Laban, 1960; Sherborne, 1987). One goal is to develop understanding of *movement elements* (space, time, force, and flow) and ways they can be used to create compositions depicting ideas, feelings, or themes. A second goal is to develop motor skills and fitness to create and perform. Other goals (self-concept, social competence, etc.) parallel those of adapted physical activity. Creative dance is recommended as the first form of movement education for children (Fleming, 1973; Jay, 1991; Joyce, 1984). It is appropriate for children ages 3 and up who understand language. In middle school and high school, terminology changes from *creative dance to modern dance.*

With exploration-demonstration-drill pedagogy, dance can be a medium for perceptual-motor training, learning about cultural heritage, and achieving artistic excellence. It is particularly valuable in teaching relaxation, ameliorating rhythm and timing problems, and enhancing body image. Folk and square dance, properly conducted, can help slow learners with social studies. Singing games and rhythmic chants also help with academic learning (Bitcon, 1976; Sherrill, 1979).

Movement Elements

Both creative and modern dance focus upon the movement elements of space, time, force, and flow. Sally Fitt (Fitt & Riordan, 1980) proposed an excellent model for relating movement elements to dance instruction for students with disabilities (see Figure 16.2). The *element of space* can be broken down into several factors:

FIGURE 16.2 Movement improvisation in which the teacher contributes to individualized education program (IEP) goals of improving both body image and balance.

1. **Direction and shape.** Right, left, forward, backward, sideward, up, down, in, out, over, under.
2. **Level of movement or of body position.** High, low, medium; lie, sit, squat, kneel, stand.
3. **Dimension or size.** Large, small, wide, narrow, tall, short.
4. **Path of movement.** Direct (straight) or indirect (curved, zigzag, twisted, crooked).
5. **Focus of eyes.** Constant, wandering, near, far, up, down, inward, outward.

The elements of time, force, and flow are explained in Table 16.1. Excellent videotapes on how to teach the movement elements to children with disabilities are available from Dr. Boni Boswell, Physical Education Department, East Carolina University, Greenville, NC 27834.

Rhythm Elements

Rhythmic structure in dance has four aspects:

1. **Pulse beat.** The underlying beat of all rhythmic structure. Can be taught as the sounds of walk or run; the ticking of a clock, watch, or metronome; the tapping of a finger; the clapping of hands; or the stamping of feet. The beats can occur in fast, medium, or slow tempos and in constant or changing rates of speed.
2. **Accent.** An emphasis—that is, an extra loud sound or extra hard movement. Syllables of words are accented, and beats of measures are accented.
3. **Rhythmic pattern.** A short series of sounds or movements superimposed on the underlying beat and

described as even or uneven. Illustrative of *even* rhythmic patterns are the walk, run, hop, jump, leap, step-hop, schottische, and waltz. Illustrative of *uneven* rhythmic patterns are the gallop, slide, skip, two-step, polka, and bleking. Remember that the polka is a hop, step-close-step and the bleking is a heel, heel (slow), followed by heel-heel-heel-heel (fast). In rhythmic patterns, the duration of time between beats varies. The simplest patterns for children are as follows:

a. *Uneven* long-short patterns, as in the gallop, skip, and slide in 6/8 tempo:

b. *Even* twice-as-fast or twice-as-slow walking patterns in 4/4 tempo:

Walk, ♩ ♩ ♩ ♩ 4 steps to a measure.

Run, ♫ ♫ ♫ ♫ 8 steps to a measure.

Slow walk, ᓂ ᓂ 2 steps to a measure.

4. **Musical phrasing.** The natural grouping of measures to give a temporary feeling of completion. A phrase must be at least two measures long and is the expression of a complete thought or idea in music. Phrasing may help to determine the *form* of a modern dance composition, and children should be guided in the recognition of identical phrases within a piece of music. One movement sequence is created for each musical phrase; identical phrases may suggest identical movement sequences.

Rhythm Skills

Many persons with disabilities have difficulty with rhythm. Initial lessons should focus on creative movement with the teacher beating a drum to the tempo established by the student. Make an effort to determine the child's natural rhythm—whether fast, slow, or medium tempo; whether 4/4 or 3/4 phrases; whether there is a rhythmic pattern or underlying beat; whether the child responds to accents; and whether transitions from one tempo to another are made. During this period of observation, encourage the child to make up his or her own accompaniment: with a song, a nursery rhyme, a verse, hand clapping, foot stamping, or a tambourine, drum, or jingle bells. Only after the child has given evidence of moving in time to his or her own accompaniment should you introduce the next stage—conforming to an externally imposed rhythm.

Teaching Dance and Rhythm

Some children require no special help in movement to music. They do not need adapted dance. Others, who have grown up in homes without music or who have central nervous system (CNS) deficits affecting temporal perception, must be provided a carefully designed progression of experiences broken down into parts so small that success is ensured. Wearing taps on shoes is a good reinforcer. Likewise, rhythmic instruments, used as part of a dance, promote goal mastery. Music therapists often are available to help. A succession of units might include the following:

1. Creative movement without accompaniment in which an idea, feeling, or mood is expressed.

2. Creative movement, with the child encouraged to add sound effects.

3. Creative movement interspersed with discovery activities in which the child can beat a drum, clash cymbals, or use other rhythmic instruments as part of a dance-making process. No instructions are given on how to use the instruments. They are simply made available, along with the freedom to incorporate sounds as the child wishes.

4. Creative movement accompanied by the teacher or another student using a variety of interesting sounds that fit the child's dance making.

5. Discussions concerning what kind of accompaniment best supports the theme or idea of different movement sequences. Through problem solving, the child tells the teacher what kind of accompaniment he or she wants, the idea is tried, and the child evaluates whether or not it worked.

6. Introduction of the concept that a dance can be repeated over and over again. A dance has some kind of *form*—at least a beginning and an end—and both movements and accompaniment must be remembered so that they can be reproduced.

At this point, students learn the difference between dancing—that is, moving for pleasure—and making a dance. They are helped to see their creation as an art product that may endure like a painting or a musical composition. They take pride in organizing their movement sequences into an integrated whole and comparing their dance-making process and products with those of dance artists on the various films that can be rented. Since children with disabilities typically become adults with an abundance of leisure, spectator appreciation of modern dance and ballet should be developed concurrently with their first attempts at dance making. Perhaps a performing group from a local high school or college can be invited to demonstrate dance compositions. Expecting children to retain excitement about dance making (choreography) is futile unless they are exposed to the art products of others and led to believe that dance is a significant part of the cultural-entertainment world.

Only when dance experiences in which movement is primary and accompaniment is secondary prove successful should you introduce the study of rhythmic skills to children known to be weak in temporal perception. These students typically will be off the beat as often as on it. They are likely to accent the wrong beat of a measure. And they may find the recognition of musical phrases hopelessly frustrating. Dance researchers have not yet designed studies to investigate the learning problems of these students. Some dance educators seem to believe that any child can keep in time with the music if he or she tries hard enough. Such is not the case! Just as reading specialists seek alternative approaches to teaching their subject, dance educators must devise ways in which the child who is rhythmically disabled or mentally retarded can find success. Murray (1953) stressed that calling attention to inaccurate response and creating tensions through continuous drill do not solve the problem. Nothing is sadder than a child concentrating so hard on tempo that the joy of movement is lost. The child who does not keep time to the music truly may be hearing a different drumbeat.

Dance Therapy in Schools and Hospitals

The pages that follow, written by a registered dance therapist, offer specific ideas that the adapted physical educator can test in the school setting. In those parts of the country where dance therapists are available, they may be employed to work cooperatively with the adapted physical educator or to provide consultant services. Remember that people who use dance therapeutically are not dance therapists unless they have received the special extensive training that qualifies them to meet the registry standards of the ADTA.

Through the therapeutic use of rhythmic and expressive movements, children gain better perspective about themselves, their ideas, and their feelings. They come to know their bodies better. They gain skill and control as they move through space. They find ways to use body action constructively, insight is gained into the meanings implied in their body action, and a more accepting body image develops.

Therapeutic dance encourages and fosters children's faith in their own ideas and in their own ways of expressing these ideas. A sense of personal worth begins to emerge. Children begin to like themselves better as they realize that their ideas do count, are worth listening to and watching, and can be shared. Positive group relationships develop through sharing and experimenting with ideas. Children gain appreciative understanding of other people's ideas and their ways of expressing them.

The expression of feelings is interwoven in various ways into dance, both indirectly in body action at the nonverbal level and directly with words and action at a conscious level (Eddy, 1982; Riordan, 1989). It is usually characteristic of dance therapy techniques that emotional tensions are worked with indirectly by centering attention on how the muscles can be used—such as hard or fast, or slow or easy ways—rather than by speaking directly to the children's feeling-states. When children express their tensions in forceful moving-out behavior, activities are centered around aggressive-moving circle dances or controlled, slow-motion, aggressive pantomime. At other times, fast running, challenging ways of jumping-falling-rolling-pushing-spinning, or tug-of-war can reduce tensions. When tensions seem high, and forceful moving-out action seems contraindicated because the children's behaviors are expressed in depressed, turned-in movements, the action moves into gently paced rocking, swaying, swinging, controlled slow rolling, or tension-relaxation muscle isolation movements. On other occasions, when the children's tension levels are not high, activities focus on feelings directly at a conscious level. Only then do the children experiment with the different ways that feelings can be expressed through movement.

FIGURE 16.3   Reflecting the movement patterns of others.

Activities to Achieve Objectives

Persons with mental health problems typically need help with three objectives: (a) increasing body awareness, (b) improving relationships and making friends, and (c) expressing feelings.

Activities used in helping people become aware of their bodies and how their muscles work include the following:

1. **Stretches, contractions, relaxations.** Individually, with partners, and in moving circle-dance action.

2. **Opposites movements.** Experimenting with such movements as tall-short, wide-narrow, fast-slow, stiff-floppy, open-closed, heavy-light, high-low.

3. **Feeling the floor different ways with bodies.** By rolling across the floor stretched out full length at varying speeds and levels of muscle tension; rolling around in tight curled-up balls; doing front and back somersaults; crumpling body movements to effect collapsing to the floor; free-falls sideward-forward-backward.

4. **Exploring movement through space.** Making different shapes and patterns; creating geometric patterns, writing imaginary letters and numbers with their bodies stationary and/or traveling.

5. **Using different traveling styles across the floor.** Running, jumping, walking, and creeping; variations within each style; working individually, with partners, and with groups of different sizes.

6. **Muscle isolation.** Using specific parts of the body in movement patterns while the rest of the body remains immobile, or following the action of the specific set of muscles leading a movement pattern; immobilization of body parts by playing *freeze* and *statue* games that stop movement in midaction; continuing on in movement retaining the *frozen* or *statue* position; having partners arrange each other's bodies into shapes or statues.

7. **Reflection movement patterns of others** (see Figure 16.3). Moving in synchrony with a partner's movements as though looking in a mirror; moving on phrase-pattern behind a partner as though echoing his or her movements; moving in opposite patterns to partner's; reflecting similar or complementary movement patterns, yet different.

Encourage individuals' ideas to emerge in a variety of ways. At times, emphasis is on verbalization of abstract ideas, and at other times, the focus is on body movement expression. Many times, verbal and physical expression are combined. The following activities are some of the experiments and experiences that children seem to enjoy:

1. **Single-word or object stimulus.**
   a. "How many different ideas does the word *beach* remind you of?" "What kinds of ideas come to you when you hear the word *beach?*"
   b. "How many different ways can you pretend to use a popsicle stick?"

2. **Imaginary props.** "Without telling us what it is, think of one particular thing or object you could use in three different ways. Show us how you would use it. After you have finished using it three different ways, call on us and we will try to guess what object you were using." Sometimes, after the person has completed his or her turn, and the object has been guessed, the others contribute ideas orally on how the object could also be used. Stress being creatively supportive of each other's ideas.

3. **Word cues.** Words written on slips of paper are drawn in turn; the person translates the word into pantomime or dance movement. As the others think they recognize the word cue, they join in with the movement in their own ways and within their own framework of understanding. When the action is stopped, verbal comparison is made of the meanings given to the movement interpretations. Observations and comments are shared about the different ways used to express the same word-meaning in movement. Movement can then resume with everyone sharing each other's movement styles. The word cues are usually presented in categories:

   a. *Doing*—chopping, hiding, twisting, carrying, hurrying, touching, dropping, sniffing, bouncing, flying, planting, pushing
   b. *People*—old person, mailcarrier, maid, nurse, airplane pilot, cook, police officer, doctor, hunted criminal, firefighter, mother, baby
   c. *Muscle isolation dances*—shoulder, head, knee, hip, hand, elbow, foot, leg, back, finger dances
   d. *Feelings*—ashamed, surprised, sad, stuck-up, angry, worried, greedy, jealous, happy, excited, in love, afraid, disgusted
   e. *Animals*—bee, horse, alligator, lion, snake, spider, elephant, crab, butterfly, worm, monkey, gorilla, mouse
   f. *Mime dramas*—underwater adventure, a scary time, at the beach, at a bus stop, going on a picnic, climbing a mountain, a visit to the zoo, on a hike outdoors, an afternoon in the park, a baseball game
   g. *A happening story*—a siren blowing, red light flashing, thick fog, whistle blowing, fire burning, animal sounds, gun firing, child crying, dream happening, rushing water

4. **Different ways over and under a rope.** As a rope is gradually raised or lowered, everyone moves over or under it without touching it in as many ways as they can.

5. **Idea box.** Everyone puts various objects they find or like—for example, leaves, crayon bits, combs, brushes, tiny statues, clothespins, buttons, pictures, paper clips, rubber discs—into the group's idea box. Periodically, an object is taken from the box to play around with. The different ideas individuals think up about the object can be translated into creative movement, creative storytelling, or creative dramatics.

6. **Stories.** Stories are read to the children so that they can make up their own endings and/or think about the possible alternative endings. The stories and the possible endings can be translated into dramatic action, either in part or total.

When feelings are focused on directly and at a conscious level, children can experiment with different ways feelings can be expressed through movement. The following activities illustrate some of the ways children can purposefully work with feelings or feeling-tones:

1. Descriptive mime or dance movements to a stimulus word indicating a specific feeling—for example, see item 5, "Idea box," in the preceding list.

2. Descriptive mime, dance, or story reflecting the feeling-tone of a spontaneous sound made by the child.

3. Feeling-tones in music. As music is played, the children respond in their own movement styles to the feeling-quality they *hear* in the music. When the action is finished, the children compare their responses, noting difference in responses to the same music. They also *try on* each other's feeling responses or movement styles as the music is played again.

4. Stories *danced* to the feeling-quality of the music. Individuals, pairs, or several children take turns as they dance a story they have planned around the feeling-quality in the music. Sometimes, the same music is chosen for all the children; other times, the different groups of children choose different music. When the danced story is finished, the children who watched attempt to relate their observations and interpretations of the story to the dancers. After everyone has had a chance to interpret, the performer(s) describe their own story. When it seems appropriate, children share some of the movement qualities presented in the stories.

5. Feeling-tones in colors. Lightweight fabrics of different colors are placed around the floor in order of child's color preference; talk about what a specific color "makes you think about;" list ideas on paper; try on some of the ideas in movement. List ideas about what kinds of feelings might be reflected in a specific color. Experiment and show through movement how one can move to express the feelings listed, in pairs, groups, or individually. Continue on from one color fabric to another. The single feeling-action can be enlarged into pantomime or dramatizations of a story idea woven around the feeling.

6. Baseball game (or alternate sport) in different movement styles. All players work together to reflect a specific feeling in their movement styles as they "play" the game.
   a. *Sad*—The batter waits sadly for the ball to be thrown; the pitcher sadly throws the ball; the batter sadly hits at the ball. If the batter misses, everyone is sad and says so or makes sounds accordingly. The ball is sadly put back into play. If the ball is hit, the batter sadly runs to the base as the pitcher or players sadly go after the ball and try to throw the runner out. Such mood continues throughout the play around the bases until the runner sadly makes a run or is thrown out.
   b. *Happy*—Follows the same format as above. The batter is happy when he or she misses the ball or strikes out. The pitcher is happy when the batter makes a base run or a home run.
   c. *Laughing-angry*—This type of contradictory expressive behavior becomes challenging and hilarious. Different combinations of contradictory feelings/sounds demand special awareness of how one uses expressive action. This also comes close to the reality of the mixed communication many people use in less exaggerated fashion in everyday life.

FIGURE 16.4 Soft nylon has a relaxing and quieting effect.

FIGURE 16.5 Experiencing the spatial structure of soft, floating fabric.

FIGURE 16.6 Experiencing the sensation of directional change in a different way.

FIGURE 16.7 Learning trust as the hammock descends.

Materials Used in Dance Therapy

Soft materials are used in all three of the areas discussed in the previous section for stimulating a variety of safe activities that are imaginative and self-structuring. Nylon fabrics of different hues in 2.5-yard lengths aid in reducing tension and hyperactivity and in relaxing tight muscles (see Figure 16.4). In response to the floating, smooth quality of the colorful nylon, children move rhythmically—stretching, turning, reaching, and covering themselves in various ways. Their actions seem to reflect a sensuous enjoyment and an aesthetic awareness as the fabrics float and move across their bodies.

Paradoxically, the soft fabrics can become a factor in spatial structuring as well (see Figure 16.5). At times, when children feel extremely tense and seem to have a need for containment, being wrapped completely immobile in the full width of the fabric by either turning when standing or rolling when lying down has a relaxing and quieting effect. Without speaking directly to such needs, children will ask for this kind of containment by suggesting familiar activities that have included it in other movement contexts.

Nylon fabrics also provide an intermediary focus for children who find it difficult to relate directly to other persons. Spin-arounds, with partners holding opposite ends of the fab-

ric, aid in keeping distance yet staying together. Wrap-up spin-outs allow a moment's closeness with access to quick and immediate freedom from nearness.

Imaginative play and imagery are stimulated by using the fabric as clothing, costumes, bedding, housing, or light-shields to put a color glow in a darkened room. Aggressiveness is accommodated by wrapping a soft yarn ball inside one end of the fabric and throwing it as if it were a comet streaming through space. *Dodge fabric* has aggressive moments of fun and beauty combined when one or several fabrics are loosely wadded into a ball and thrown at a moving human target. The floating open of the fabric(s) while traveling in space sometimes creates unusual beauty. Children also like to lie down and be covered completely with one fabric at a time in layering fashion. As the layers of fabric increase, children typically comment on the constant change of color and the increasing dimness.

Soft, stretchy, tubular-knit fabrics approximately 3 yd long have soothing, protecting properties. The tubular fabrics make excellent *hammocks* on which to lie and be swung (see Figures 16.6 and 16.7). When persons alternate in lifting ends of the fabric, causing the body to roll from side to side, the child feels a special sensation of being moved in space. An interesting sensation of directional change is experienced when running and bouncing forward into a tautly stretched fabric that *gives* and then bounces the person off backward.

Stretch-tube fabrics also lend themselves well to nondirected dramatic play and fantasy-action. They become roads, rivers, roofs, ghosts, hooded persons, Roman togas, stuffed sausages, pickles, grass, tunnels. Playing inside stretch-tube fabrics is a way for children to shield themselves from direct observation and physical touch contact with other persons, while at the same time being able to look out through the fabric and see other persons. When working inside, the fabrics can become an open-ended tunnel to explore, or a closed and safe haven for being swung, rolled, dragged gently around the floor, or for pretending all alone in fantasy-action. Inside the fabrics can also become a place to experiment with making different shapes and forms by bending and extending body parts against the softly resilient material.

When lying outside on the fabric and being swung gently, spontaneous pantomimes of *dreams* are easily evoked. These dreams come from children's unconscious urges and needs, and the expressive body action accompanying the dream fantasies allows for safe catharsis and emotional release of tensions reflected in the dream content. The fabrics offer opportunity for rocking and swaying when children need comforting and relaxing, without those needs being openly or directly addressed. Games experienced earlier, when the children were simply exploring the use of the fabrics, can be repeated when the need for comforting arises.

Yarn balls about 6 inches in diameter permit many varieties of throwing activities for imaginative play as well as for safe release of aggressive tensions (Figure 16.8). The teacher's imaginative thinking about different ways to throw, jump with, and bat the ball stimulates alternative ways of thinking and also encourages children to risk expressing their own ideas. Warm-up stretches are executed by using different body positions to transfer the ball to the next recipient. One-to-one synchronization of full body action occurs when partners try to support a ball between them with various parts of their bodies while traveling across the room. Yarn balls can be used aggressively for bowling or dodgeball. They also can be vigorously hand-batted back and forth across the floor. More structured and functionally demanding activities are done with rhythmically synchronized toss, catch, and rolling games. Isolation of body parts can be experienced by bouncing the ball off different parts of the body or by contacting the ball with a specific body part before releasing and passing it on to another person. In dramatic play and fantasy-action, the balls become various kinds of foods, jewels, rocks, rockets, bombs, and the equipment for pretend games of baseball, kickball, touch football, and bowling.

Dance Therapy Principles

With modification, dance therapy techniques are applicable to persons of most ages and with most disabilities because dance therapy focuses on qualities of nonverbal communication in everyday life. Marian Chace (n.d.), one of the pioneers in the

FIGURE 16.8 Yarn balls permit safe release of aggressive tensions.

evolution of dance therapy as a profession, was influential in obtaining acceptance of principles that she felt were basic to dance therapy and common to all forms of therapy. These principles relate specifically to patients in a clinical setting but are applicable to students with mental health needs. Chace believed that the dance therapist should keep things simple by leading out from what is happening inside the patient, rather than imposing the action from the outside. The therapist should allow time for things to happen within the ongoing action rather than trying to *do* a lot.

Chace recommended that the dance therapist work toward enriching experiences in a nonjudgmental, neutral way, without moralizing. This is best accomplished by working *with* the patient rather than *on* him or her. The dance therapist must be secure and able to listen to what is going on at the verbal level and yet see subtle, nonverbal cues. The therapist should emanate friendliness, yet remain neutral and resist being caught up in his or her need to be liked by the patient. Patients need to relate to persons who are genuine and truthfully warm. They need relationship space that allows them to give back warmth without feeling threatened by the therapist's needs.

Therapeutic Tools

The *therapeutic tools* used by the dance therapist could be thought of as rhythm, touch, verbalization, space, and people. Activities are simply the media for the use of therapeutic tools.

The *movement of the patient,* rather than that of the therapist, is used as a means of establishing the therapeutic relationship. By tuning in and sharing a patient's movements, the therapist can very clearly and quickly relate to the patient. They can *speak* to each other in movement. The therapist then works toward transcribing patients' movements into reality-oriented and functional expressions since patients are unable to do this for themselves. The therapist also tries to influence change in patients' distorted body images through muscular action.

Basically, the *rhythmical* quality of expressive movement is what enables the patient to use body action in safe ways that hurt no one. Open use of aggressive movements has less therapeutic value than rhythmic action that focuses on body awareness. For optimal results, expressive movement must be under the patient's conscious rather than unconscious control. Rhythmic action also affords an area for relating that is outside both the patient and the dance therapist. It offers the satisfaction of sharing movement and minimizes destructiveness of action. The patient does not feel a need for the movement to be realized in its destructive form. This leaves him or her free to go on to other things, with pathological urges released rhythmically, constructively, and safely, for the moment.

All therapeutic body movement is geared toward getting in *touch* with as much of the skin's surface as possible. Tactile stimulation and muscular contraction allow the patient to regain contact with his or her body surface and to come to understand its boundaries. Direct touch by the therapist reinforces the patient's growing ability to distinguish between himself or herself and others.

Verbalization between the therapist and patient is geared to the meaning of muscular action, rather than the feeling-tone behind the action. The patient comes to realize that his or her movement qualities are reality based and that he or she is capable of purposive movement. Verbalization is not for telling the patient what to do, but for helping him or her to know where he or she is going and why.

Space is an extension and reflection of body image, so the use of space is important. A patient who is manic and hyperactive perceives his or her own space zone as wide and scattered and as having tremendous force and power. The dance therapist then uses movements far away from the patient, coming in only tentatively as the patient will allow. The patient already feels that they are *together,* even though they are actually far apart. If a patient is frozen or constricted in movement, the space zone is small and constricted. The dance therapist then moves in quite closely, but with care and awareness, because a constricted space is generally a supercharged zone. The dance therapist also uses space to encourage a *coming forward.* Such dance movements can provide safe areas for hostile body action that might have been used out of control. *Going forward* movements can provide safe areas for a withdrawn person to learn that he or she can come out and not be hurt nor hurt anybody else.

The dance therapist's ultimate goal is for patients to work in a group. Group work reduces one-to-one identifications and increases opportunities for patients to assume responsibility for their own growth and not stay dependent upon the therapist.

References

American Dance Therapy Association. (circa 1975). [Brochure]. Annual proceedings and other materials are available through the national office.

Bitcon, C. H. (1976). *Alike and different: The clinical and educational use of Orff-Schulwerk.* Santa Ana, CA: Rosha.

Boswell, B. (1989). Dance as creative expression for the disabled. *Palaestra, 6* (1), 28–30.

Chace, M. (n.d.). *Dance alone is not enough.* From mimeographed materials distributed by St. Elizabeth's Hospital and Chestnut Lodge in Washington, DC.

Eddy, J. (1982). *The music came from deep inside: Professional artists and severely handicapped children.* New York: McGraw-Hill.

Fitt, S., & Riordan, A. (Eds.). (1980). *Dance for the handicapped—Focus on dance IX.* Reston, VA: American Alliance for Health, Physical Education, Recreation and Dance.

Fleming, G. A. (Ed.). (1973). *Children's dance.* Washington, DC: American Alliance for Health, Physical Education, Recreation and Dance.

Jay, D. (1991). Effect of a dance program on the creativity of preschool handicapped children. *Adapted Physical Activity Quarterly, 8,* 305–316.

Joyce, M. (1984). *Dance technique for children.* Palo Alto, CA: Mayfield.

Laban, R. (1960). *The mastery of movement* (2nd ed.). London: MacDonald & Evans.

Murray, R. L. (1953). *Dance in elementary education.* New York: Harper & Row.

Riordan, A. (1989). Sunrise Wheels. *Journal of Physical Education, Recreation and Dance, 60*(9), 62–64.

Roswal, P. M., Sherrill, C., & Roswal, G. M. (1988). A comparison of data-based and creative dance pedagogies in teaching mentally retarded youth. *Adapted Physical Activity Quarterly, 5,* 212–222.

Schmitz, N. B. (1989). Children with learning disabilities and the dance/movement class. *Journal of Physical Education, Recreation and Dance, 60*(9), 59–61.

Sherborne, V. (1987). Movement observation and practice. In M. Berridge & G. R. Ward (Eds.), *International perspectives on adapted physical activity* (pp. 3–10). Champaign, IL: Human Kinetics.

Sherrill, C. (Ed.). (1979). *Creative arts for the severely handicapped.* Springfield, IL: Charles C Thomas.

C H A P T E R

17

Adapted Aquatics

FIGURE 17.1   Although this child is orthopedically impaired, he is not disabled in the water. (Photos by Judy Newman.)

After you have studied this chapter, you should be able to do the following:

1. Discuss the benefits of water activity for persons with different disabilities and identify adaptations that will contribute to success. List conditions for which swimming is contraindicated.

2. Discuss resources, goals, and practices for hydrotherapy, adapted aquatics, and competitive swimming.

3. Discuss similarities and differences between the Halliwick and Sherrill models and regular teaching approaches.

4. Describe activities appropriate for the explorer, advanced explorer, and floater levels. Test these activities with beginners and share your experiences.

5. Explain how different conditions affect buoyancy and describe adaptations.

6. Explain how synchronized swimming stunts and routines can be used for fun and success before stroke proficiency is achieved.

7. Discuss administrative aspects of an aquatics program for persons who are differently abled.

A mother speaks of her dyslexic son in a poignant account of learning to cope with learning disabilities:

> He might not be able to manage a tricycle, but he had the freedom of a large, safe beach, where he could run for a mile if he felt inclined. Beach balls eluded him—he could neither throw nor catch—but there was the warm sand to mess with, and the water itself. The big moment of Mike's young life came at three-and-a-half, when he learned to swim. . . . The beach baby turned into a water rat. By five, he could safely swim out of his depth, and by six, he not only had a crawl stroke, but was so at home in the water that he literally did not seem to know if he was on it or under it. (Clarke, 1973, p. 9)

When Mike grew up, he graduated from Harvard University with a doctoral degree. He still could not "read, write, nor talk too good either," but he had learned to compensate for his weaknesses and to utilize fully his strengths. Like other boys, he longed for athletic success, tried out for teams, failed. He was especially awkward in baseball and handball. As an adult, he recalled the pleasure derived from swimming and its contribution to the maintenance of some ego strength throughout a childhood characterized by very few successes.

Water can be used for physical and mental rehabilitation, fitness, relaxation, perceptual-motor remediation, self-concept enhancement, fun, and competition (see Figure 17.1). Exercises, stunts, and games traditionally done on land achieve the same goals when executed in the water.

Water activity, while beneficial for everyone, may be the program of choice for persons who are nonambulatory, unfit, obese, asthmatic, or arthritic. Because water minimizes the force of gravity, persons can often move with greater ease in a pool than on land. Water also eliminates the risk of joint damage associated with weight-bearing exercise in obesity and certain types of arthritis (Sheldahl, 1986). Swimming strokes, whether done on land or water, have long been recognized as one of the best systems of exercise.

Water also can be used to manage behaviors and change mental states. Warm water—96–98 °Fahrenheit (F), 35.5–36.5 °Celsius (C)—reduces hyperactivity, stress, and tension, whereas water of normal pool temperature—78–86 °F, 26–30 °C—increases alertness and promotes a state of "feeling good." Cold water is often used in mental health programs to snap persons out of depression and help them act out anger.

Hydrotherapy and Adapted Aquatics

Hydrotherapy (water exercise for therapeutic purposes) was systematized in the 1930s by Charles Lowman, an orthopedic physician, who today is recognized as the father of hydrotherapy (Lowman, 1937; Lowman & Roen, 1952). Although originally used primarily for persons with physical disabilities, water exercise is now recommended for everyone (Campion, 1985; Krasevec, 1989; Mayse, 1991). Water exercise may be a supplement to land exercise or an alternative.

Adapted aquatics (activities adapted to individual differences) evolved in the 1960s and 1970s as awareness increased that all persons should have opportunities to learn basic swimming skills. Leaders in this movement were Judy Newman (1976), Louise Priest, who was employed by the American Red Cross (Priest, 1979, 1987, 1990), Grace Reynolds (1973) of the YMCA, and Sue Grosse of the Milwaukee, Wisconsin, public schools (Grosse, 1985, 1987, 1993, 1996; Grosse & Gildersleeve, 1984; Grosse & McGill, 1989). The American Red Cross published *Adapted Aquatics* in 1977; it was a comprehensive source available until the 1990s when the American Red Cross (1992a, 1992b) decided to include information on disability in its regular programs rather than continuing separate adapted aquatics certification. Special Olympics International (1981) and the YMCA of the USA (1986, 1987) publish excellent adapted aquatics materials, and the Council for National Cooperation in Aquatics (CNCA), under the leadership of Louise Priest, offers consultant services.

Today, adapted aquatics philosophy has been expanded to include boating (British Sports Association for the Disabled, 1983), infant/preschool swimming (Kochen & McCabe, 1986; Langendorfer, 1989, 1990), swimming for seniors (Shea, 1986), and scuba diving (Jankowski, 1995; Robinson, 1986).

A position paper on adapted aquatics is now available from the Aquatic Council of AAALF/AAHPERD (1996). This paper defines *adapted aquatics* as a service delivery system providing appropriate aquatic instruction and recreation for participants with disabilities.

Several instructional models are available for teaching persons who are extremely fearful of water and/or who are slow learners. This chapter describes two models: (a) the Sherrill water fun and success model and (b) the Halliwick water confidence model, named for the Halliwick School for Crippled Girls in England, where James McMillan (creator of the model) taught. Both models were created in the 1950s and 1960s.

Competitive Swimming and Disability

Local, national, and international swimming competition is available for persons with disabilities through affiliation with sport organizations governed by the International Paralympic Committee and Special Olympics International (see Appendix C). Meets are conducted in the same way as for nondisabled swimmers, and similar distances are used.

Various classification systems group swimmers either by functional ability or medical status to ensure fair competition and to permit persons with severe disability the opportunity to achieve personal bests (Gehlsen & Karpuk, 1992; Richter, Adams-Mushett, Ferrara, & McCann, 1992). Competitive swimming for people with and without disabilities is governed by United States Swimming, Inc. (U.S. Swim), 1750 East Boulder Street, Colorado Springs, CO 80909. Many swimmers with disabilities train with nondisabled teams, and some compete in regular venues (Andersen, 1989).

Instructional Models for Beginners

Many persons with disabilities learn swimming through regular Red Cross and YMCA programs. The Halliwick and Sherrill models are for persons who need more help and longer time than regular programs provide. These models are similar in that both recommend (a) a one-to-one teaching ratio until swimmers gain confidence for small-group instruction; (b) teachers in the water, stimulating and supporting their swimmers; (c) learning through play and games; (d) emphasis on body awareness, movement exploration, and breathing games; (e) consideration of buoyancy principles, and (f) no use of personal flotation devices (PFDs) except for persons with severe nonambulatory conditions.

PFDs are inner tubes, arm and head floats, vests, and inflatable swimsuits that aid buoyancy. PFDs should never take the place of a one-to-one teaching ratio. Experts vary in their support of PFDs (Andersen, 1986; Grosse, 1987; Jones, 1986), but there is consensus that some persons with severe cerebral palsy need PFDs and that these devices should be carefully selected. Persons using PFDs should never be left unsupervised.

Halliwick Water Confidence Model

The *Halliwick water confidence model* is described by Kahrs (1974) and Bull et al. (1985) of Norway, by Grosse and Gildersleeve (1984) of the United States, and by Campion (1985) of Australia. The purpose of the model is to teach water buoyancy and confidence through various kinds of body rotations, floats, glides, and games. Once persons are comfortable with the buoyancy force of the water, they can learn swimming strokes by traditional methods. The Halliwick model is based on 10 points:

1. **Mental preparation.** Emphasis is on getting to know the instructor, the pool, and the dressing rooms. This is achieved through walking, talking, and showing. The goal is to have fun while learning to feel at ease in the water. Familiar land activities (games, dances, and rhythms) are adapted to water.

2. **Self-sufficiency.** Instruction begins with the teacher and student touching: (a) holding hands during locomotor activities; (b) holding hands, waist, or shoulders in face-to-face and face-to-back movement explorations; and (c) holding hands while being pulled in a horizontal position. *The head is never held because emphasis is on learning to alter body position and regulate balance through independent head movements.* As confidence is achieved, the distance between teacher and student is gradually increased by such devices as a washcloth, floatboard, and towel. Finally, there is no contact, and the teacher moves a little further away each lesson. PFDs are not sanctioned because they lessen self-sufficiency.

3. **Vertical rotation.** Mastery is achieved by learning to change from vertical to horizontal positions and vice versa. Somersaults are advanced vertical rotations.

4. **Horizontal or lateral rotation.** Mastery is achieved by learning to rotate from back to front and vice versa while in a horizontal position. Logrolls are advanced horizontal rotations.

5. **Combined rotation.** Many games that include both vertical and horizontal rotations are played.

6. **Application of buoyancy.** Games like trying to sit on the pool bottom without floating up are used to develop trust of the water's buoyancy force.

7. **Floating positions.** Movement exploration challenges are used to find different body shapes for floating.

8. **Turbulence floating and gliding.** Students learn to cope with increasing amounts of turbulence. First, confidence is gained in calm water. Then the teacher creates small, medium, and large turbulence conditions by swirling his or her hands in the water near the student's head.

9. **Simple propulsion.** Underwater, symmetrical arm movements (finning, sculling, breaststroke) are added to the back and front glides to promote simple propulsion.

10. **Development of strokes.** Swimming strokes are introduced by traditional methods after Halliwick points 1 to 9 have resulted in complete water confidence.

Sherrill Water Fun and Success Model

The *Sherrill water fun and success model* began as part of a Texas Woman's University practicum program in which university students teach children with developmental disabilities to swim. Over the years, three prebeginner swimming certificates have evolved. Initially, the levels of competency that the certificates represent were named after fish: minnows, crappies, and dolphins. The children were not as enamored of these appellations as were the adults who created them. First of all, many of them had never seen real fish, alive or dead, and to them, the names were meaningless. Some of the pupils did report firsthand knowledge of fish but remembered the unpleasant odor more than the beauty of movement. Said one, "I don't want to be a fish—ugh—they stink." Still another problem arose with respect to self-concept; heavily muscled boys, particularly from economically deprived areas, had no intention of being "sissy minnows," regardless of their dependence upon the teacher in the water.

Table 17.1 Beginning competency levels of swimming for the Sherrill model.

Level I, Explorer Movement Exploration in Water	Level II, Advanced Explorer Movement Exploration in Water	Level III, Floater Prebeginning Swimming
1. Enter and leave water alone	1. Put face in water	1. Blow bubbles (10 sec)
2. Walk across pool holding rail	2. Blow bubbles (5 sec)	2. Bracketing on front with kick
3. Walk across pool holding teacher's hand	3. Touch bottom or toes with hands	3. Change of position: stand; front-lying with support; stand
4. Stand alone	4. Retrieve objects from bottom	4. Prone float
5. Walk across pool pushing kickboard	5. Assume horizontal position with teacher's help	5. Change of position: stand; back-lying with support; stand
6. Jump or hop several steps alone	6. Hold onto kickboard pulled by teacher	6. Back float
7. Walk and do breaststroke arm movements	7. Jump into water without help	7. Flutter kick using board
8. Do various locomotor movements across the pool	8. Take rides in back-lying position	8. Jellyfish float
9. Blow bubbles through plastic tube	9. Change of level: squat to stand; stand to squat	9. Perform breaststroke arm movements
10. Blow Ping-Pong ball across pool	10. Play follow-the-leader type water games	10. Swim one-half width any style
	11. Demonstrate bracketing on back with kick (see Figure 17.5)	11. Perform at least one stunt like stand or walk on hands, front somersault, back somersault, tub, surface dive

The three certificates subsequently were designated as Explorer, Advanced Explorer, and Floater in accordance with the levels of competency achieved. These certificates were printed on cards of the same size and shape as the standard Red Cross certificates. Originally, they came in different colors, but after the year that a girl with Down syndrome sobbed all through the awards ceremony because her card was not white like her boyfriend's, it was decided to make the cards uniform in color as well as size, shape, and format.

The motor tasks required for passing each certificate are listed in Table 17.1. The major achievement at the Explorer level is to release the teacher's hand and perform basic locomotor movement patterns independently at a distance several feet away from the side of the pool. Putting the face in the water is not necessary to earn Explorer status. Many youngsters initially are so terrified of the water that several lessons are required before they will loosen their deathlike grips on the teachers. Many additional lessons pass before enough courage is developed to let go of the side of the pool and walk independently. Nevertheless, *all* students who earn the Explorer certificate take as much pride in it as their peers do in the Red Cross achievement cards.

The Advanced Explorer certificate represents two major accomplishments: putting the face in the water and willingness to lift the feet from the pool bottom, thereby assuming a horizontal position with the help of the teacher. Also at this level, the child begins experimenting with somersaults, standing on his or her head, walking on hands, and other stunts that are not based on the ability to float.

Earning the third and final prebeginner Floater certificate is dependent upon the ability to relax sufficiently to float for several seconds. At this level, children usually begin to swim. Navigation is more often under the water than on top,

and underwater swimming can be used to fulfill the requirement of one-half width. Long before the pupils learn to swim recognizable strokes, they become proficient in many basic stunts of synchronized swimming. They develop creative routines to music that are weird combinations of walks, runs, jumps, hops, standing in place and stroking with arms, and regulation synchronized swimming stunts.

Goals of Adapted Aquatics

The water can be viewed as simply another medium for refining movement patterns and exploring time-space-self relationships. The Texas Woman's University aquatics program is coordinated with lessons in movement exploration conducted in the gymnasium. Virtually every activity learned out of water is attempted also in the swimming pool. The movement exploration teaching style described in Chapter 9 (guided discovery and motor creativity) establishes the framework in which learning occurs. The three most important goals of the program are (a) to improve self-concept, (b) to increase self-confidence, and (c) to develop courage. Secondary to these goals, the teacher concentrates on dimensions of body image: (a) identification of body parts, (b) improvement of proprioception, and (c) development of such inner language concepts as bent versus straight, vertical versus horizontal, pike versus tuck, back layout versus front layout, and pull phase (application of force) versus recovery phase. As a technique for enhancing self-concept, children are drilled on the *names* of the stunts and skills they learn to perform. As they acquire a vocabulary that enables them to share their successes with others, children seem to demonstrate increased motivation for undertaking new aquatic adventures. Moreover, this emphasis on vocabulary in the swimming setting reinforces words learned in the classroom and the gymnasium, thereby contributing to transfer of learning and reducing development of splinter skills.

Adapted Aquatics Principles

Some of the differences between an adapted aquatics program and regular swimming instruction are explicit in the following principles for teachers:

1. Be in the water with the children rather than on deck (see Figure 17.2). Physical contact between teacher and student is based on the student's needs for security and affection. Although independence in the water is the ultimate goal, do not rush it.

2. Avoid saying "Put your face underwater," a task that students tend to interpret as unpleasant. Instead, introduce gamelike situations that induce the child to attempt the task without conscious realization of what he or she is doing. The following anecdote demonstrates teaching:

   I had been in the water with Charles for about 20 min and had had no success with anything I had tried to teach him. I was particularly concerned with getting him to put his entire face and head in the water. I finally decided to make a game out of it, so I borrowed the small inner tube from one of the other instructors. Without any type of explanation, I placed the inner tube between Charles and myself and ducked under water and came up with it around my neck. Charles was delighted and asked me to do it again. After repeating it I asked him if he would like to put his head through the inner tube. Without answering my question, he completely submerged his body and came up with the inner tube around his neck. I was more than pleased and had him repeat it five or six times. Then I asked him to submerge without coming up under the inner tube. I received a very blunt "no." He told me he could not put his head under water, and he did not wish to try. We continued using the inner tube for the remainder of the hour.

3. Use as few words as possible in teaching. Cues like "up," "down," "pull," "recover," and "kick 2-3-4" are substituted for sentences. A well-modulated voice helps to convey the meaning of instructions. Use a *high* voice for *up* movements and a *low* (pitch) voice for *down* movements. Use a loud and forceful voice during the pull phase and a soft and gentle voice during the recovery phase.

4. Move the child's limbs through the desired pattern of movement rather than using the explanation-demonstration technique. Some persons refer to this as the *kinesthetic* method of teaching since such input is proprioceptive.

5. Show acceptance of the child through frequent mirroring of his or her movements. Take turns *following the leader* with precise imitation of postures, arm movements, and kicks.

6. Introduce synchronized swimming, jumping, and diving much earlier than usual in swimming instruction. Emphasize the combination of stunts and locomotor movements—that is, creating sequences (routines) and remembering and executing sequences developed by others.

FIGURE 17.2 A one-to-one relationship in the water facilitates learning.

7. Modify requirements in accordance with individual differences. Plan testing on the basis of the individual's strengths, not preestablished competences that are thought to meet the needs of all beginner swimmers.

8. Encourage bilateral, unilateral, and crosslateral movement patterns, in that order, which reflects an understanding of child growth and development. Thus, the breaststroke and the elementary backstroke are the first real swimming strokes introduced. The bilateral movements of the breaststroke usually appear in underwater swimming without the benefit of instruction. Figure 17.3 compares the simplicity of bilateral strokes with the relative complexity of crosslateral strokes.

The bilateral movements of the elementary backstroke are similar to those in angels-in-the-snow and jumping jacks. Land drill is used before the children shower or after they dry and dress to ensure transfer of learning. Drill in the water can be facilitated by suspending a hammock from the ceiling, using flotation devices, and lying on a table under the water.

Figure 17.3 shows bilateral movements of the arms and legs in underwater swimming and the breaststroke and in the elementary backstroke, as well as the more difficult crosslateral swimming strokes. Six kicks of each leg are coordinated with every cycle of arm movements. As the right arm pulls, for instance, the right leg kicks *up,* down, *up.* The emphasis in the flutter kick is on the *up* beat! Arm strokes and leg kicks must be practiced in a horizontal rather than a standing position. Equally important, the teacher should demonstrate new skills in the horizontal position.

No stroke is more difficult to master than the front crawl. Although the rhythm of the flutter kick may come naturally to a few students, it is a nightmare for many others. Land drills to music in 3/4 time with a strong accent on the first beat in every measure may contribute to relaxed, effective kicking in the water; if not, the practice can be justified for its contribution to abdominal strength. Both in land drills and in the

FIGURE 17.3   Comparison of bilateral and crosslateral strokes.

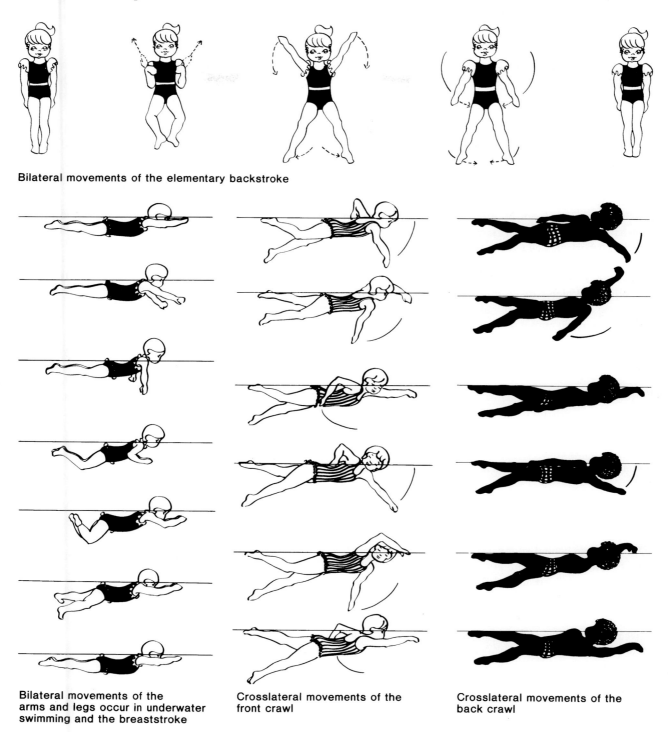

Bilateral movements of the elementary backstroke

Bilateral movements of the arms and legs occur in underwater swimming and the breaststroke

Crosslateral movements of the front crawl

Crosslateral movements of the back crawl

water, there is a tendency to collaborate with the force of gravity and accentuate the downbeat; this error must be avoided. Devising some kind of contraption 12 to 18 inches above the floor to be kicked on each upbeat may focus the student's attention on the desired accent.

The flutter kick warm-up exercise should begin in the position depicted in Figure 17.4 rather than with both legs on the floor, since at no time during the crawl stroke are the legs motionless and in the same plane. With poorly coordinated students, it is best to leave the arms motionless in the starting position until the rhythm of the kick is mastered. The verbal cues "right-arm-pull" or "left-arm-pull" can be substituted for "kick-2-3" even though the arms do not move. The first progression for this exercise is lying on the floor; the next progression is lying on a bench with arms and legs hanging over.

When a student demonstrates no progress in the flutter kick over a period of weeks, it can be safely assumed that the desired movement is not *natural* for him or her and that an

FIGURE 17.4   Ready position for flutter kick warm-up.

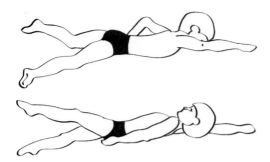

alternate method of kicking should be substituted. In such instances, the front crawl can be modified into the *trudgeon stroke* by substituting the scissors kick for the flutter kick.

The American Red Cross teaches many basic strokes. The student's ability to perform one or two of these strokes really well is the criterion for success in a program for persons with disabilities. Which stroke(s) the child chooses is not important as long as he or she feels safe in the water and enjoys swimming. One of the purposes of movement exploration is to guide the student toward personal discovery of this stroke.

Activities for the Explorer

Washcloth Games

Give each child a washcloth, and compare the swimming pool with the bathtub at home. Your relaxed patter of questions usually elicits the desired water exploration:

1. "What do you do with a washcloth? Don't tell me; show me!"
2. "What part do you wash first? Did you wring the cloth out before you started to wash? Don't you wring it out first at home?"
3. "Did you wash behind your ears? The back of your neck? Your elbows? Your knees? Your ankles? What about the soles of your feet? Are they clean?"
4. "Do you like to have someone wash your back? If you do, find a partner and take turns washing each other's back."
5. "Can you play throw and catch with your partner by using the washcloth as a ball?"
6. "What happens if you miss the catch? Can you pick the washcloth off the bottom of the pool with your toes? With some other part of your body?"
7. "Let's play steal each other's washcloth. To begin, each of you must fold your washcloth and put it neatly over your shoulder or on top of your head. When I say 'go,' move around stealing as many washcloths as you can but don't forget to protect your own. When I say 'stop,' everyone must have one hand on the railing before I count to 10; then, we will determine who is the winner."

Sponge Games

Give each child a sponge.

1. "Do you see something at the bottom of the pool? That's correct! There are plates, saucers, bowls, glasses, and

cups. Guess what your job is? That's correct! Recover the dishes any way you wish, wash them with your sponge, and set the table on the deck. Whoever finishes the most place settings wins."
2. "Have you ever scrubbed down walls? Each of you find your very own space on the wall and let's see you scrub! Have you ever washed a car? Let's pretend the wall is a car! What else can we pretend the wall is? Does anyone know how to scrub the floor? Let's see!"
3. "See this big inner tube? Let's use it to shoot baskets with our sponges. Can you make your sponge land inside the inner tube?"
4. "What other target games can we invent with the sponges?"
5. *Dodge or Catch.* This game is played like dodgeball except that the child has the option of dodging or catching. Occasionally, someone may get hit full in the face with a wet sponge. Although a sponge cannot hurt, some children feel threatened by this activity; hence, the participants should be volunteers.

The children put their sponges in the water.

1. "Who can get his or her bucket filled with water first? The only way to get water in the bucket is by squeezing out sponges."
   a. *Individual game.* "Who can recover the most sponges, squeeze them out, and toss them back in the water?"
   b. *Partner game.* One student remains in the water recovering sponges and handing them to his or her partner on deck, who squeezes the sponges and tosses them back into the water.
2. Sponges of different colors are floating in the water. Children all have one hand on the pool railing. On the signal "Go," they respond to the question, "Who can recover a blue sponge and put it on the deck first? A yellow sponge? A pink sponge?"
3. Sponges of different shapes or sizes are floating in the water. [Same instructions as before.]
4. "Who can recover two sponges and put one under each of his or her feet? How many of you are standing on sponges? Can you walk across the pool on the sponges?"

Parachute Games

In the water, a large sheet of clear plastic makes the best parachute; round tablecloths and sheets can also be used. All of the parachute activities played on land can be adapted to the water. "Who can run under the parachute?" invariably gets the face in the water. "Who can climb over the parachute?" leads to taking turns riding on the magic carpet that is pulled through the water by classmates.

Blowing Games

Blowing games can be played either in or out of the water; they are important lead-up activities to rhythmic breathing.

1. Give each child a clear plastic tube 12 to 18 inches long. Plastic tubing can be purchased in any hardware store. "Who can walk along with the plastic tube in a *vertical* position and blow bubbles in the water? Who can walk

along with the plastic tube in a *horizontal* position and blow bubbles in the water?"

2. "Who can blow a Ping-Pong ball across the water? A toy sailboat? A small sponge?"

3. "On the side of the pool are many balloons that need blowing up. The object is to blow up a balloon while you walk or run across the pool. Who can make the most trips back and forth and thus blow up the most balloons? You may take only one balloon each trip."

4. Inflatable air mattresses and rafts provide ample practice in blowing for several children. Teams of three or four children may cooperate in blowing up a mattress with the promise that they may play on it in the water after it has been sufficiently inflated.

5. Give each child a yarn ball or Ping-Pong ball suspended from a string. "Who can keep the ball in motion the longest by blowing?"

Self-Testing Activities for the Explorer

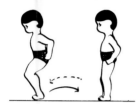

Horizontal or long jump

1. "Who can jump forward across the pool? Who can jump backward? Sideward? How many different ways can you jump? Can you carry something heavy as you jump?"

Vertical jump and reach

2. "How high can you jump?" A pole with flags of various colors provides incentive for progressively increasing the height of the jump. "Which flag did you touch when you jumped?"

Cable jump

3. "Can you jump over a stick, a scarf, or a rope? In which nursery rhyme does someone jump over a candlestick?"

Greet the toe

4. "Can you greet your toe? Can you hop while holding one foot?"

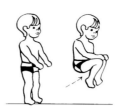

Jump and tuck

5. "Can you jump up and touch your knees? Can you jump up and touch your toes?"

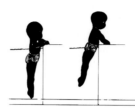

Straight arm support lean

6. "Stand in the water facing the side of the pool with both hands on deck. How many times can you lift your body up almost out of the water with your arms alone? This is like a push-up on land. Can you lift your body upward and maintain a straight-arm support?"

Aquatic sprint

7. "How many seconds does it take you to run across the pool? How many widths of the pool can you run in 3 minutes?"

Bracketing with back lean

8. "Can you hang on the pool railing (gutter) and arch your back? Can you do this with the soles of your feet on the wall instead of the floor? Can you do this with only one arm?"

Matching locomotor movements to lines and forms

9. "Can you walk a straight line drawn on the floor of the pool? A circular line? A zigzag line? Can you march on the line? Can you hop on it? Can you do these movements backward? Sideward?"

Airplane or single-foot balance

10. "How many different ways can you balance on one foot? Can you do an arabesque? A pirouette?"

Activities for the Advanced Explorer

Advanced explorers are learning to put their heads under water and to change level from up to down and vice versa. They are also experimenting with all of the possible ways to enter the water. They are not yet secure about a horizontal position in the water but will assume it when your hand is in contact with some part of their bodies.

Towel Games

1. **Taking rides.** A child who trusts you enough to hold his or her hands and allow the feet to rise from the bottom, thereby assuming a horizontal position in the water, can be taken on *rides.* These rides can be as dramatic as the child's (or your) imagination, with sound effects for a train, rocket ship, or whatever. Talk to the child, continuously maintaining eye contact and pulling him or her along while walking backward. The next step in the development of trust is to convince the child to hang onto a towel or kickboard while you pull on the other end. Thus, the rides across the pool continue, but the child is progressively farther away from you.

2. **Individual tug-of-war.** Every two children share one towel, each holding onto one end. A line on the bottom of the pool separates the two children, and the object is to see who can pull the other over the line first. As balance and body control in the water improve, teammates can be added until group tug-of-war is played. Only one teammate should be added to each side at a time.

3. **Catch the snake.** A rope about 6 ft long has a towel tied onto the end. You or an agile child pulls the rope around the pool. The object is to see who can *catch the snake* first. The winner then becomes the runner who pulls the snake around the pool.

4. **Beater goes round.** Children stand in a single circle, facing inward. The *beater* stands on the outside of the circle, facing counterclockwise and holding a small hand towel (one not big enough to hurt when a child is hit with it). A second child is running counterclockwise in front of the *beater,* trying to avoid being hit by the towel. He or she can be safe by ducking in front of any player in the circle after he or she has run around at least one-half of the circle. The player whom he or she ducked in front of must now run to avoid being beaten.

5. **Tag.** Towels on the pool bottom are safety rests.

6. **Over and under relay.** Use towels instead of a ball.

Body Shapes Used in Aquatics

The terms *tuck, pike,* and *layout* are used in synchronized swimming, diving, and gymnastics. The Advanced Explorer learns to assume these shapes on land, in shallow water, and in

the air. Movement exploration on the trampoline and the springboard in the gymnasium reinforce learning in the pool area. This aspect of aquatics training is designed specifically to improve proprioceptive awareness. The following questions elicit desired responses:

Tuck positions

1. "In how many different ways can you assume a tuck position on land? In the water? In the air?"

Pike positions

2. "In how many different ways can you assume a pike position on land? In the water? In the air?"

Layout positions

3. "How many ways can you assume a layout position on land? In the water? In the air? Can you do back layouts? Front layouts? Side layouts?"

Curved positions

4. "In how many ways can you make your body curved on land? In the water? In the air? Can you combine a front layout with a curve? A back layout with a curve? A side layout with a curve?"

Early attempts at assuming tuck, pike, and layout positions in the water often result in sinking to the bottom. Many children accidentally discover floating while concentrating on body shapes. Those who do not discover floating gain valuable practice in breath control and balance.

Ways to Enter the Water

Many children prefer a session of jumping and/or diving to swimming. In the beginning, they may wish to have you hold one or both hands and jump with them. Others prefer you to be standing or treading water and awaiting their descent with outstretched arms. Participation in some kind of creative dramatics that demands a jump into the water often subtly evokes the desired response in children who have previously demonstrated fear and reluctance. Themes that have been particularly successful in motivating children to enter the water are (a) playing firefighter and sliding down the fire pole, (b) carrying lighted candles through a dark cave or perhaps the ancient Roman catacombs, (c) going on an African safari, (d) imitating Mary

Poppins by opening an umbrella in flight, and, of course, (e) emulating space travelers through various trials and tribulations.

In response to "How many different ways can you enter the water feetfirst?" children may demonstrate the following:

1. Climb down the ladder. Most efficient method is facing ladder with back to water.
2. Sitting on edge of pool, scoot off into water: (a) freestyle (any way you wish), (b) in tuck position, (c) in pike position, and (d) with one leg straight, one bent.
3. Kneeling or half-kneeling, facing water.
4. Kneeling or half-kneeling, back to the water.
5. Squatting, facing water.
6. Squatting, back to water.
7. Standing, facing water using (a) stepoff, (b) jump and kneel in air before contacting water, (c) jump and tuck in air, (d) jump and clap hands, (e) jump and turn, (f) jump and touch toes, (g) hop, (h) leap, (i) arabesque, and (j) pike drop forward (camel walk position).
8. Standing, back to water, using: (a) stepoff, (b) jump, (c) hop, and (d) pike drop backward.

Stages in learning to dive

In response to "How many different ways can you enter the water headfirst?" children discover the various stages in learning to dive. They may also lie on the side and do a logroll into the water or accidently perform a front somersault.

Self-Testing Activities for the Advanced Explorer

Frog jump

1. "Can you jump like a frog under the water?"

Jack-in-the-box

2. "Can you squat in water over your head and then jump up and yell 'boo' like a jack-in-the-box?"

Dog walk when four limbs touch pool bottom; lame dog walk when three limbs touch bottom.

3. "Can you do a dog walk with your head under the water? A lame-dog walk?"

Mule kick

4. "Can you do a mule kick in the water?"

Seal walk

5. "Can you do a seal walk under the water?"

Camel walk

6. "Can you do a camel walk under the water? This is also called a wicket walk."

Egg sit followed by V sit

7. "Can you do an egg sit at the bottom of the pool? Can you do an egg sit near the surface and sink downward?"

Human ball bounce

8. "Can you do five bent-knee bounces at the bottom of the pool? Pretend that you are a ball being dribbled."

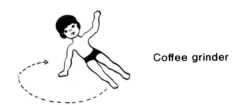

Coffee grinder

9. "Can you do the coffee grinder stunt at the bottom of the pool?"

Knee scale

10. "Can you do a balancing stunt under the water with one knee and both hands touching the bottom? Can you lift your arms and do a single-knee balance?"

Bracketing

Bracketing is the term for holding onto the gutter (rail) of the pool with one or both hands and allowing the feet to rise from the bottom of the pool so that the body is in a horizontal position (see Figure 17.5).

Retrieving Objects From the Bottom of the Pool

Advanced Explorers learn about spatial relationships within a new context as they open their eyes under water and see objects *through* the water. In the earliest stages of underwater

FIGURE 17.5   Bracketing on the front and back.

are mastered: (a) horizontal to vertical positioning, (b) floating, (c) bobbing, (d) front-to-back positioning and vice versa, and (e) simple stunts in synchronized swimming.

Horizontal to Vertical Positioning

Floaters demonstrate ease in moving from a horizontal position to a vertical one. The degree of difficulty of this task varies with amount of buoyancy, specific gravity, and absence or paralysis of limbs. Simple sequencing is introduced, as depicted in Figure 17.6.

Floating

To teach floating to persons with varying body builds and/or amputations of one type or another, you must have some understanding of the following terms: *buoyancy, specific gravity,* and *center of buoyance.*

    Buoyancy is the quality of being able to float. The buoyancy of a human being depends upon the amount of water that each body part is able to displace and the weight of the body part itself. The larger the surface of the body part, the more water it will displace. For instance, the typical woman with wide pelvis and well-rounded buttocks displaces more water than the average man with his narrow hips and flat buttocks. The lighter the weight of the body part, the less upward force is required to buoy it up. Thus, if a cork and a marble of the same surface area are dropped into water, the cork will float and the marble will sink. Adipose tissue (fat) weighs less than muscle and bone tissue. Thus, if two persons of equal surface areas try to float and one individual is fat while the other is heavily muscled, the fat person will be buoyed upward more easily than the person with well-developed musculature. Buoyancy is explained by *Archimedes' principle,* which

exploration, they may hold both of your hands and submerge with you. Under water, you and the student may establish eye contact, shake hands, and mirror each other's hand and arm movements. Later, you can challenge the student to retrieve all sorts of things from the bottom. Practice in form, size, weight, and color discrimination can be integrated with the instructions for retrieval of objects.

Activities for the Floater

The Floater is comfortable in the water and can do almost anything but swim a coordinated stroke for 20 yd to qualify for the Red Cross Beginner card. The Floater is probably more competent in underwater swimming than in performing strokes near the surface. This is the period during which the following tasks

---

FIGURE 17.6   Simple sequencing.

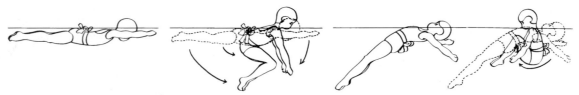

Two-part sequence to be practiced in learning change from horizontal to vertical position.

Two-part sequence to be practiced in learning to change position from a back layout to a tuck.

Back float to tight tub to back float is three-part sequence in learning to change positions.

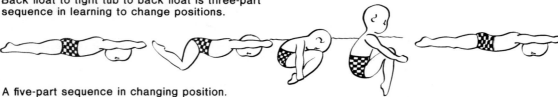

A five-part sequence in changing position.

states: A body submerged in a liquid is buoyed up by a force equal to the weight of the displaced liquid.

The *specific gravity* of a human being is her or his weight compared to the weight of an equal amount of water, as shown in this formula:

$$\text{Specific gravity} = \frac{\text{Weight of body}}{\text{Weight of equal amount of water}}$$

After full inspiration, the specific gravity of most adult human beings is slightly less than 1. This means that most adults can float with their head above the surface of the water when their lungs are filled with air. After exhalation, the specific gravity of most adults is approximately 1.02. Only when the specific gravity is above 1.02 do individuals experience difficulty in floating.

The *center of buoyancy* (CB) of a human being in water is similar in function to the center of gravity (CG) when the body is not immersed in fluid. Both are areas where weight is concentrated; both serve as fulcrums about which the body rotates.

The CB, for most persons, is located in the thoracic cavity. The more obese an individual is, the lower his or her CB is. The CB is defined as the center of gravity of the volume of the displaced water before its displacement. If an object were of uniform density, its CB and CG would coincide; this is not the case with living creatures, human or fish.

In the water, the body can be likened to a first-class lever, which, like a seesaw, totters back and forth around its fulcrum (CB) until balance is achieved. Only when the CB and the CG are in the same vertical line can a person float without motion.

Figure 17.7 shows that there is no one correct way to float. Each person must experiment until he or she discovers the position in which CB and CG are aligned vertically. The hints that follow may help students cope with problems of buoyancy.

Below-Average Buoyancy

Men, as a whole, have less buoyancy than women. Black students have less buoyancy than white students. Buoyancy can be increased by raising the CG and hence the CB. This can be done by extending the arms overhead, by bending the knees so that heels almost touch the buttocks, or by assuming a tuck or jellyfish floating position. Hyperventilating—keeping the lungs filled with air and exhaling as seldom as possible—also helps.

Students should not attempt to lift the feet and legs and attain a horizontal position since the feet and legs will only drop downward again, building up enough momentum as they do so to pull the entire body under. Many persons who believe themselves to be *sinkers* could float if they started in the vertical rather than the horizontal position.

Above-Average Buoyancy

The obese person experiences many balance problems in the water for which he or she must learn to compensate. The alternate-arm stroke on the back crawl, for instance, must be performed twice as fast as normal to prevent the body from rolling over. The hips, legs, and feet are often above water level so that no kick is possible.

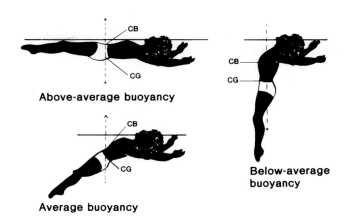

FIGURE 17.7 Effects of buoyancy on floating explain why there are many correct ways. (CB = Center of buoyancy; CG = Center of gravity.)

The most anxiety-ridden experience, however, for the obese beginning swimmer is changing from a horizontal position to a vertical stand. Try as he or she may, it is not easy to make the legs drop and the shoulders and trunk come forward so that the CG and CB are aligned over the feet.

Amputations

Amputations affect the location of the CG and the CB, which, in turn, affects buoyancy and balance. The loss of a limb causes displacement of the CG and CB to the opposite side. Thus, a student who has lost a right leg or arm has a tendency to roll to the left, where the weight of the body is centered. Most persons with amputations, whether congenital or acquired, can become excellent swimmers.

Extensive movement exploration is recommended to enable each person to discover the floating position and swimming strokes that best serve his or her needs. Most students with severe orthopedic disabilities seem to prefer swimming on the back. Specifically, the following strokes are suggested:

1. Loss of both legs—Back crawl or breaststroke.
2. Loss of one leg—Back crawl, elementary backstroke, or sidestroke.
3. Loss of both arms—Any kick that can be done on the back. This person has exceptional difficulty in changing from horizontal layout position to a stand.
4. Loss of one arm—Sidestroke or swimming on back with legs providing most of the power and the one arm finning.
5. Loss of one leg and one arm—Sidestroke with leg on the bottom; arm will create its own effective finning action.

Spasticity and Asymmetric Strength

Persons with spasticity or paralytic asymmetries tend to spin or rotate in the horizontal water position. To stabilize a float, swimmers should turn the head in the opposite direction of the body rotation. Backstrokes should be taught before front strokes, and symmetric strokes should be mastered before asymmetric strokes.

Bobbing

Bobbing is similar to several vertical jumps in place except that all the power comes from the arms. It can be done in either shallow or deep water, but traditionally is associated with water over the head.

Bobbing consists of two phases. In the *down phase,* both arms are raised simultaneously upward, causing the body to descend. The breath is exhaled. When the feet touch the bottom of the pool, the arm movement ends. The *up phase* is then initiated by both arms pressing simultaneously downward. This action pushes the body upward. The arm movements in bobbing are different from all others the child has encountered. The concept of displacing water—that is, pushing in the direction opposite from that which you wish to go—should be explained.

Down phase in bobbing   Up phase in bobbing

Bobbing accomplishes several goals: (a) improves rhythmic breathing, (b) increases vital breathing capacity—that is, tends to hyperventilate the swimmer, (c) heightens proprioceptive awareness, and (d) serves as a warm-up activity. Bobbing is recommended especially for asthmatic children. Variations of bobbing are

1. **Progressive bobbing.** The down phase is identical to that of bobbing in place. The up phase, however, is modified by using the legs to push the body off the pool bottom at approximately a 65 ° angle. The arm movement is basically the same. Progressive bobbing is a survival skill in that it can be used as a means of locomotion from the deep end of the pool to the shallow.

2. **Bobbing on one leg.**

3. **Bobbing in a tuck position.** Down phase: Arms pull upward, legs extend so that feet touch the bottom. Up phase: Arms press downward, tuck knees to chest so that full tuck is achieved at height of up phase.

4. **Seesaw bobbing with a partner.** To begin, partners face each other and hold hands. Then a rhythm is established in which one person is up while the other is down, as in partner-jumping on a trampoline.

Finning and Sculling

After students master a float, several sessions in movement exploration should focus on the arms and hands. Such problems as the following can be posed for the back layout, front layout, tuck, and pike positions:

1. "In the back layout position, how many different ways can you place your arms?"

2. "Which positions of the arms make floating easier? More difficult?"

3. "How many different kinds of movements can you perform with your arms in each position?"

4. "Which of these movements seem to make you sink? If you do sink, which of these movements can help your body rise to the surface of the water?"

5. "Which arm movements propel the body through the water headfirst?"

6. "Which arm movements enable you to execute the following position changes: (a) prone float to stand, (b) prone float to back float, (c) back float to stand, and (d) back float to prone float?"

7. "If you move only one arm, what happens? Can you propel the body directly to the right by using one arm only? Directly to the left?"

8. "In what other ways can you propel the body directly to the left? Directly to the right?"

9. "In how many different ways can you *push* the water away from you? *Pull* the water toward you?"

Ideally, creative dramatics should be combined with movement exploration so that the child can tell you and/or peers which emotions are being expressed by particular arm and hand movements: Variations of charades can be played in the water, and/or students may *act out* the feeling that a particular musical composition conveys.

Given sufficient time and encouragement, students eventually discover *finning* and *sculling* for themselves. Introduce the names of these movements and explain their usefulness in changing positions in the water. Movement exploration can then focus on how many different ways students can fin or scull.

Finning

Finning is a series of short pushes with the palms of the hands against the water in the direction *opposite* to the one in which the student wishes to move. Each push is followed by a quick, bent-arm recovery under the surface of the water.

Sculling

Many different types of *sculling* are recognized. In the standard scull, the hands are at the hips, close to the body. Movement at the shoulder joints is limited to inward and outward rotation of the arms that seems to be initiated by the hands in their execution of tiny figure-eight motions close to the water surface.

The motion of the hands and wrists consists of an inward and outward phase, each of which is performed with equal force. The palms move toward midline during the inward phase and away from midline during the outward phase so that the water is alternately scooped toward the hips and then pushed away. The thumbs are up during the inward phase and down during the outward phase. If students do not discover sculling for themselves, the movement should be introduced in the classroom and mastered before it is attempted in water. Sculling, for many swimmers, is a difficult pattern to learn through imitation.

Synchronized Swimming

The regulation stunts usually taught in units on synchronized swimming are similar to those performed in tumbling and gymnastics. Executing stunts in the water improves proprioception, enhances body awareness, and provides practice in movement imitation. The stunts described on the following pages can be mastered early in beginning swimming. The primary prerequisites are a feeling of ease in the water, the ability to scull while floating, and a keen sense of where the body is in space. Research at the Texas Woman's University has demonstrated that many slow learners can be taught to execute simple synchronized swimming stunts long before they achieve skill and endurance in regulation strokes. All stunts are begun from either the front layout position or the back layout position, as depicted below and in Figures 17.8 and 17.9.

Front layout

Back layout

Whereas skilled performers are concerned with the aesthetic appearance of a stunt, the adapted physical educator does not worry about *good form.* The stunts are introduced in a manner similar to other tasks in movement exploration. Very few verbal directions are posed; on some occasions, a casual demonstration motivates the student to attempt new positions in the water. The stunts that follow are listed in order of difficulty under their respective starting positions. *Stunts in which the body is carried in a tuck position are easier than those executed in the pike or layout positions.*

Stunts That Begin in a Back Layout Position

1. **Tub.** "Can you change from a back layout position to a tuck position with the thighs perpendicular to the surface of the water? In this position, can you use sculling to revolve the body around in a circle?"

2. **Log rolling.** "Can you roll the extended body over and over while keeping the legs motionless? This is identical to the stunt by the same name on land."

3. **Back tuck somersault.** "Can you perform a backward roll in a tuck position?"

4. **Oyster, clam, or pike up.** "Can you drop your hips as you simultaneously hyperextend and inwardly rotate the arms at the shoulder joints? When you are touching your toes in a pike position, can you sink to the bottom?"

5. **Back pike somersault.** "Can you assume a pike position with trunk under the water but parallel to the surface? Can you perform a backward roll in this pike position? Which part of this stunt is like the oyster?"

6. **Torpedo.** "Can you scull with your hands overhead so that your body is propelled in the direction of your feet? Submergence of the head and shoulders is optional."

7. **Back dolphin.** "Can you maintain a back layout position as your head leads your body around in a circle under the surface of the water? Can you perform this same stunt with one knee bent?"

8. **Single ballet leg.** "Can you scull across the pool with one leg perpendicular to the surface of the water and the other leg extended on the surface of the water?"

9. **Submarine.** "While performing a single ballet leg, can you submerge the entire body up to the ankle of the perpendicular leg and then rise to the surface?"

10. **Back walkover.** "Can you start a back dolphin but do *the splits* with the legs while they are above the surface of the water? This stunt ends in a front layout."

Stunts That Begin in a Front Layout Position

1. **Front tuck somersault.** "Can you perform a forward roll in a tuck position?"

2. **Flying porpoise.** "Can you stand on the bottom, push off, and do a surface dive that looks like a flying porpoise?"

3. **Porpoise.** "Can you bend at the waist so that the trunk is almost perpendicular to the bottom, while the thighs remain parallel to the water? From this position, can you raise both legs until the entire body is vertical and then submerge?"

4. **Front pike somersault.** "Can you assume a pike position identical to the beginning of a porpoise? From this position, can you do a forward roll?"

5. **Front walkover.** "Can you assume a pike position identical to the beginning of a porpoise? As the legs come out of the water, they do *the splits* so that you finish in a back layout position.

Rolling in the Water

Methods of rolling from back to front and vice versa in the water each have names within synchronized swimming circles. Use these terms to teach children names for the stunts that they can perform, thereby improving their communication skills.

1. **Half log roll.** "Can you change from back to front float or from front to back float?"

2. **Log roll.** "Beginning from a back layout position with arms overhead, can you execute the log roll by reaching your arm across your body, by crossing one arm over the other, or by crossing one leg over the other?"

3. **Corkscrew.** "Can you log roll from a sidestroke position to prone float or to same side on which you started? If the sidestroke is on the left, a complete roll to the left is executed."

4. **Reverse corkscrew.** "If the sidestroke is on the left, can you execute a complete roll to the *right?*"

5. **Marlin.** "Can you (a) start in a *back layout* position, arms in T position, palms down; (b) roll onto right side, moving right arm to a sidestroke position and left arm to side for a *side layout* position; (c) continue roll onto a front layout position, with both arms in T position; (d) roll onto left side, moving left arm to a sidestroke position and right arm to side for a *side layout* position; and (e) finish in a *back layout* position with arms in T position?"

FIGURE 17.8   Stunts that begin in a back layout position.

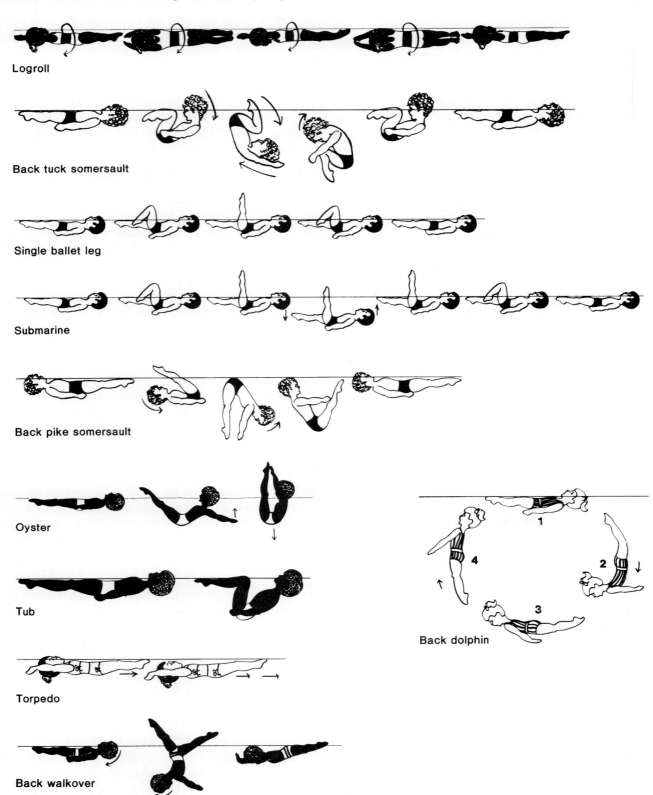

Logroll

Back tuck somersault

Single ballet leg

Submarine

Back pike somersault

Oyster

Tub

Back dolphin

Torpedo

Back walkover

FIGURE 17.9   Stunts that begin in a front layout position.

Front tuck somersault

Flying porpoise

Porpoise

Front pike somersault

Front walkover

Administrative Aspects of an Aquatics Program

Pool Recommendations

Few teachers of students with disabilities have the opportunity to design their own pool, but a community or school committed to serving *all* persons will implement adaptations recommended by a specialist. These may include construction or purchase of the following:

1. Nonskid surface for floors and decks.
2. Handrails in the shower room.
3. Several ways to turn the water off and on in the shower room, such as a button on the floor as an alternative for persons who have no use of their arms. Ideally, the water in the shower room should turn itself off automatically.
4. Doors into the locker room and the pool wide enough to allow wheelchairs through.
5. Ramps as well as stairsteps; a movable ramp for entrance into the swimming pool; ladders that telescope up and down (see Figure 17.10).
6. Flashing red and green lights at the deep and shallow ends, respectively; a metronome or radio playing at the shallow end.
7. Floating buoys extended across the pool to warn of deep water; a change in the texture (feel) of the tile along the gutter in the deep end; the depth of the pool written in braille in the tile every several feet.

FIGURE 17.10 Use of chairlift for a student with multiple disabilities.

8. A horizontal line on the wall that is the same height as the depth of the water below it. This line allows children to compare their heights with the line on the wall to ascertain that the water will not be over their heads if they jump into the pool at a certain point. The line on the wall or the wall itself may be colorcoded in terms of water depth.

9. A large storage cabinet with good ventilation to house the sponges, candles, rubber toys, Ping-Pong balls, and other accessories to movement exploration not used in ordinary swimming.

10. Hooks on the wall or plans for storage of inner tubes and other flotation devices needed in adapted physical activity.

The depth of the pool determines its expense in large part. The Olympic-size pool that provides for progressively deeper water is not recommended when instruction is the primary purpose. There is a definite trend toward building two or three separate pools rather than the multipurpose structure of the past. The instructional pool needs a depth of only 3.5 to 4 ft of water. Separate pools are constructed for diving, advanced synchronized swimming, and scuba diving.

Several public schools are now purchasing the portapool, which can be moved from school to school every several weeks. At the end of the day's instruction, a roof is pulled over the pool and securely locked in lieu of having to provide fencing and other safety measures. Nursery schools and special education units would do well to purchase the aluminum tank type pool sold by Sears and other commercial companies. Such pools are less expensive than trampolines and other pieces of playground apparatus.

The temperature of a swimming pool is normally maintained between 78 and 86 °F, 26 and 30 °C. While this temperature is invigorating, it is not geared to the needs of the beginning swimmer, who is partially out of the water when not in a horizontal position. Moreover, cold water tends to produce hypertonus and to heighten the spasticity of children with cerebral palsy.

To facilitate relaxation of muscles in the water and ensure an optimum learning environment, the water temperature for adapted physical activity should be in the low 90 °s. Increasing the temperature of the water causes two problems in pool management: (a) the chlorine evaporates in 90 ° water, and (b) the windows in the pool steam up from the evaporated water. Increasing the chlorine count is easy enough, but swimmers' complaints about the chlorine hurting their eyes appear unavoidable. Sunlamps or infrared lamps built into the ceiling tend to control evaporation.

Health Examination

Written approval of both the student's physician and parents should be on file prior to the beginning of swimming instruction. Most physicians prefer to use their own form but are willing to fill out supplementary information sheets (see Figure 17.11).

Close rapport with local physicians is essential to good adapted physical education. Mail a thank-you to the physician after receipt of the supplementary sheet and also send a list of the similarities and differences between swimming in the adapted physical education setting and the regular class. Explain such adaptations as increased pool temperature, availability of ramps and flotation devices, and individualized or small-group instruction.

Contraindications and Swimming

Swimming is universally recommended for individuals with all kinds of disabilities, with the exception of the following conditions: infectious diseases in the active stage—that is, the person still has an elevated temperature; chronic ear infections and also the months during which tubes are in the ears; chronic sinusitis; allergies to chlorine or water; skin conditions such as eczema and ringworm; open wounds and sores; osteomyelitis in the active stage; and severe cardiac conditions. Physicians will sometimes prescribe hydrotherapy for individuals with some of these conditions.

Girls who wear internal tampons should be encouraged to participate fully in regularly scheduled instruction during their menstrual periods. Pregnant women generally swim until the sixth or seventh month, depending upon the philosophy of the obstetrician.

Diving may be contraindicated for individuals with arrested hydrocephalus, hemophilia, or anomalies of the face or head that affect normal breathing. Children with spastic cerebral palsy should not be taught to dive unless instruction is requested specifically by the parents and endorsed by the physician.

FIGURE 17.11   Sample information sheet to be filled in by physician.

Name _____

Medical Diagnosis _____

Diagnosis in laymen's terms _____

_____

Which part of the body, if any, is involved:

____ Right arm   ____ Left arm   ____ Neck

____ Right leg   ____ Left leg   ____ Trunk

Other_____

What specific exercises or movements do you recommend for the involved parts?

_____

Do you recommend learning to float or swim in any particular position?

____ Front   ____ Right side   ____ Head out of water

____ Back   ____ Left side   ____ Head used normally in rhythmic
                                                  breathing

Should any special precautions be taken?

____ Needs to wear nose clip   ____ Should *not* dive

____ Needs to wear ear plug   ____ Needs to wear glasses

____ Should *not* hold breath   ____ Should *not* hyperventilate

____ Should *not* put head under water

   I recommend participation in regularly scheduled swimming lessons adapted to special needs as indicated on this sheet.

_____   _____
Date   **Name of Physician**

Time of Day for Swimming Instruction

The practice of waiting 1 or 2 hr after eating before engaging in swimming instruction is no longer viewed as valid except in the case of training for competitive swimming. Hence, swimming may be scheduled whenever it is convenient. However, conducting instruction after lunch may be better than immediately before, when the level of blood sugar characteristically reaches its daily low.

Classroom teachers report that swimming early in the day tends to exert a quieting influence upon hyperactive children. A procedure should be created whereby a student may request a pass to report to the swimming teacher in lieu of a regularly scheduled class when the child feels exceedingly aggravated or in special need of *letting off steam.*

Undressing, Showering, and Dressing

Assisting young children and individuals with severe disabilities with dressing procedures is an integral part of adapted aquatics. Be extremely careful to dry the skin and hair of children with Down syndrome since they are especially susceptible to upper respiratory infections.

Apply moisturizing cream or oil to dry skin immediately after swimming. The dry, rough skin of many children can be softened by regular applications of cream.

If a land drill is planned prior to entrance in the water, eliminate the preliminary shower. At no time should a child in a wet suit be out of the pool for more than a few seconds.

Observe swimmers closely for blueness of lips, teeth chattering, goose bumps, and other evidence of chilling. Children tend to chill more quickly than adults; the thinner the child, the shorter the time in the water she or he can endure. In accordance with the principle of individual differences, *all* students should not be scheduled for instructional periods of identical lengths. Children in wet suits should *not* be allowed to sit on the edge of the pool with a towel draped about them in the hope that they will magically warm up and return for additional instruction. A child who professes to be too cold to remain in the pool should be expected to dry off and dress fully. Activities should be planned for individuals who leave the pool early, and the dressing room should be supervised at all times.

References

American Association for Active Lifestyles and Fitness/American Alliance for Health, Physical Education, Recreation and Dance. (1996). *Adapted aquatics: A position paper.* Reston, VA: Author.

American Red Cross. (1977). *Adapted aquatics.* Garden City, NY: Doubleday.

American Red Cross. (1992a). *American Red Cross swimming and diving.* St. Louis: Mosby-Year Book.

American Red Cross. (1992b). *Water safety instructor manual.* St. Louis: Mosby-Year Book.

Andersen, L. (1986). Swimming to win. In J. A. Jones (Ed.), *Training guide to cerebral palsy sports* (3rd ed.) (pp. 161–166). Champaign, IL: Human Kinetics.

Andersen, L. (1989). *Handbook for adapted competitive swimming* (3rd ed.). Colorado Springs: United States Swimming, Inc.

British Sports Association for the Disabled. (1983). *Water sports for the disabled.* West Yorkshire, England: EP Publishing.

Bull, E., Haldorsen, J., Kahrs, N., Mathiesen, G., Mogensen, I., Torheim, A., & Uldal, M. (1985). *In the pool: Swimming instruction for the disabled.* Oslo, Norway: Ungdoms-Og Idrettsavdelingen. (Distributed in the United States by American Alliance for Health, Physical Education, Recreation, and Dance.)

Campion, M. (1985). *Hydrotherapy in pediatrics.* Rockville, MD: Aspen Systems.

Clarke, L. (1973). *Can't read, can't write, can't takl too good either.* New York: Walker & Company.

Gehlsen, G., & Karpuk, J. (1992). Analysis of the NWAA swimming classification system. *Adapted Physical Activity Quarterly, 9*(2), 141–147.

Green, J. S., & Miles, B. (1987). Use of mask, fins, snorkel, and scuba equipment in aquatics for the disabled. *Palaestra, 3*(4), 12–17.

Grosse, S. (1985). It's a wet and wonderful world. *Palaestra, 2*(1), 14–17, 40.

Grosse, S. (1987). Use and misuse of flotation devices in adapted aquatics. *Palaestra, 4*(1), 31–33, 56.

Grosse, S. (1993). *Computer information retrieval system in adapted aquatics (CIRSA): A comprehensive reference list.* Available from S. Grosse, 7252 Wabash Ave., Milwaukee, WI 53223.

Grosse, S. (1996). Aquatics for individuals with disabilities: Challenges for the 21st century. *ICHPER-SD Journal, 33*(1), 27–29.

Grosse, S., & Gildersleeve, L. (1984). *The Halliwick method: Water freedom for the handicapped.* Unpublished material available from S. Grosse, 7252 Wabash Ave., Milwaukee, WI 53223.

Grosse, S., & McGill, C. (1989). Independent swimming for children with severe physical impairments. In AAHPERD (Ed.), *The best of practical pointers I* (pp. 227–240). Reston, VA: American Alliance for Health, Physical Education, Recreation and Dance.

Jankowski, L. W. (1995). *Teaching persons with disabilities to SCUBA dive.* Montreal: Quebec Underwater Foundation.

Jones, J. A. (1986). *Training guide to cerebral palsy sports* (3rd ed.). Champaign, IL: Human Kinetics.

Kahrs, N. (1974). *Swimming teaching for the handicapped.* Oslo, Norway: Statens ungdoms-Og idrettskontor.

Kochen, C., & McCabe, J. (1986). *The baby swim book.* Champaign, IL: Human Kinetics.

Krasevec, J. (1989). *Y's way to water exercise instructor's guide.* Champaign, IL: Human Kinetics.

Langendorfer, S. (1989). Aquatics for young children with handicapping conditions. *Palaestra, 5*(3), 17–19, 37–40.

Langendorfer, S. (1990). Contemporary trends in infant/preschool aquatics. *Journal of Physical Education, Recreation and Dance, 61*(5), 36–39.

Lowman, C. L. (1937). *Techniques of underwater gymnastics.* Los Angeles: American Publications.

Lowman, C. L., & Roen, S. (1952). *Therapeutic use of pools and tanks.* Philadelphia: W. B. Saunders.

Mayse, J. (1991). Aquacise and aquafitness for adapted aquatics. *Palaestra, 7*(2), 54–56.

Newman, J. (1976). *Swimming for children with physical and sensory impairments.* Springfield, IL: Charles C Thomas.

Priest, L. (1979). Integrating the disabled into aquatics programs. *Journal of Physical Education, Recreation and Dance, 50*(2), 57–59.

Priest, L. (1987). Adapted aquatics—education and training. *Palaestra, 4*(1), 26–30.

Priest, L. (1995). Aquatics. In J. Winnick (Ed.), *Adapted physical education and sport* (2nd ed., pp. 351–364). Champaign, IL: Human Kinetics.

Reynolds, G. (Ed.). (1973). *A swimming program for the handicapped.* New York: Association Press.

Richter, K., Adams-Mushett, C., Ferrara, M., & McCann, B. C. (1992). Integrated swimming classification: A faulted system. *Adapted Physical Activity Quarterly, 9*(1), 5–13.

Robinson, J. (1986). *Scuba diving with disabilities.* Champaign, IL: Human Kinetics.

Shea, E. J. (1986). *Swimming for seniors.* Champaign, IL: Human Kinetics.

Sheldahl, L. M. (1986). Special ergometric techniques and weight reduction. *Medicine and Science in Sports and Exercise, 18*(1), 25–30.

Special Olympics International. (1981). *Special Olympics swimming and diving sports skills instructional program manual.* Washington, DC: Author.

YMCA of the USA. (1986). *YMCA progressive swimming instructor's guide.* Champaign, IL: Human Kinetics.

YMCA of the USA. (1987). *Aquatics for special populations.* Champaign, IL: Human Kinetics.

P A R T

III

Individual Differences,
With Emphasis on Sport

CHAPTER
18

Infants, Toddlers, and Young Children

FIGURE 18.1   The individualized family service plan (IFSP) goal of crawling to a desired toy is implemented for a motorically delayed 2-year-old infant with Down syndrome. The cold, slick mirror provides tactile stimulation to the bare skin, as well as visual input. The infant's primary locomotor pattern will continue to be belly crawling and/or a bunny-hop movement until he loses the symmetrical tonic neck reflex. Then the IFSP goal will be changed to creeping.

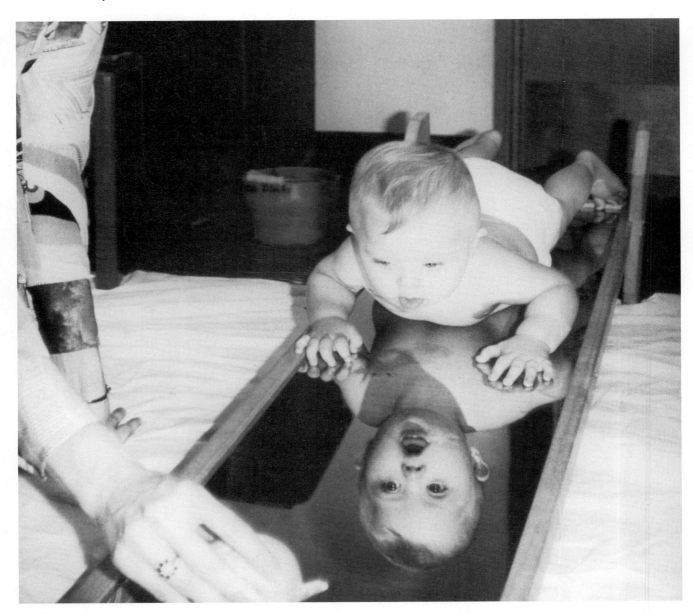

After you have studied this chapter, you should be able to do the following:

1. Describe illustrative infants, toddlers, and young children who can benefit from adapted physical activity services.

2. Discuss similarities and differences between the IFSP and the IEP.

3. Discuss assessment and programming, and describe ways to involve family members. What components in the psychomotor domain should be assessed? Why?

4. List developmental milestones in the accomplishment of various movement tasks and discuss factors that contribute to delays.

5. Identify principles of normal motor development, and give examples of how these principles can be used in explaining behavior and guiding practices.

6. Give examples of instruction and intervention approaches, and discuss their relevance in planning services to achieve specific goals.

7. Identify adapted physical activity goals and discuss programming in relation to each.

Early intervention is so important to the future of people with disabilities that federal law makes available educational services from birth onward. Two age groups are targeted for special help: (a) **infants and toddlers,** defined as individuals from birth through age 2, and (b) **early childhood,** defined as individuals aged 3 to 8 and often referred to as *young children.* Early childhood special education programs are typically conducted by schools, but infant/toddler programs are developed by various community agencies. Administrative procedures for these programs are included in the Individuals with Disabilities Education Act (IDEA), Parts C and H.

Three Diagnostic Terms

Eligibility for services is determined by an *individualized family service plan* (IFSP) for infants and toddlers and by an *individualized education program* (IEP) for young children. Diagnostic terms vary, depending upon the philosophy of local communities.

Disabled is the term used to describe children who fit into established diagnostic categories (e.g., speech and language impaired, learning disabled, mentally retarded). About 75% of young children with diagnosed disabilities fall into the speech and language impaired category.

Developmentally delayed is a generic term that permits states to establish their own criteria as to what constitutes performance significantly below average. Federal legislation indicates that developmental delays can occur in five areas: (a) cognitive, (b) physical, (c) language and speech, (d) psychosocial or emotional, and (e) self-help skills. Statistical criteria are usually established for diagnosis—for example, (a) functions at 75% or less of his or her chronological age in two or more areas, (b) scores at least 1.5 standard deviations below the mean, or (c) scores below the 30th percentile. Two or more tests, with good validity and reliability, are used to make a diagnosis. Other diagnostic procedures include documented, systematic observation by a qualified professional, parental reports, developmental checklists, and criterion-referenced instruments.

At risk for developmental delays refers to infants and toddlers who have been exposed to adverse prenatal, perinatal, or postnatal factors that are likely to cause clearly identifiable delays before age 3. Among the many factors contributing to risk are disadvantaged socioeconomic environments, prematurity and low birth weight, difficult or traumatic delivery, maternal age of under 15 or over 40, a family history of genetic disorders and/or problem pregnancies, and mothers with substance abuse or chronic health problems (Cratty, 1990; Gallahue & Ozmun, 1994; Tarr & Pyfer, 1996).

Many of these factors lead to multiple disabilities. Alcohol, for example, now recognized as the leading cause of birth defects in the United States, results in a condition called fetal alcohol syndrome (FAS), which is a combination of mental retardation, hyperactivity, attention deficit, motor incoordination, and other problems. Crack or cocaine babies manifest a similar profile. These and several other conditions are discussed in Chapter 21 on mental retardation. The term *developmental delays* is, however, a more accurate descriptor of multiple disability conditions than any one category. Figure 18.2 depicts illustrative children with developmental delays.

The Individualized Family Service Plan (IFSP)

The individualized family service plan (IFSP) is used with infants and toddlers in place of an individualized education program (IEP). The IFSP includes seven parts:

1. **Information on Child Status** (physical development, cognitive development, psychosocial development, self-help development, and language and speech development)

2. **Family Information** (family strengths and needs)

3. **Outcomes** (procedures, criteria, timelines)

4. **Early Intervention Services** (description, intensity, frequency, location, and method of service delivery)

5. **Dates** (initiation and duration of services)

6. **Case Manager** (from the profession most closely related to the child's and family's needs)

7. **Transition Plan at Age 3** (parental consent, transfer of information, future placement, and transfer preparation procedures)

This written plan is based on family/professional collaboration. Services can be delivered anywhere, including the home. Service delivery personnel work with families as well as infants and toddlers. This has implications for increased emphasis on home-based programs of adapted physical activity that are developed and monitored by professionals (Cowden, 1991).

FIGURE 18.2 How would you assess the needs of each of these children?

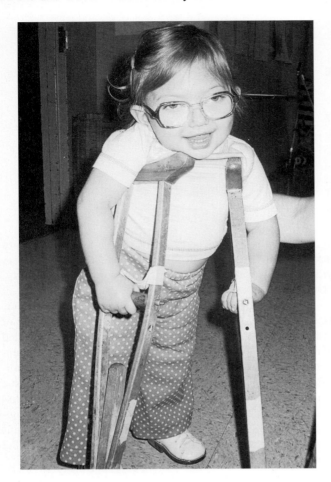

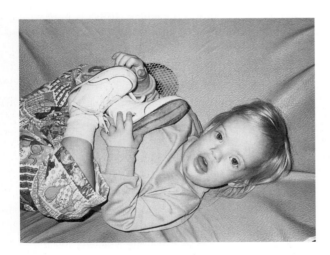

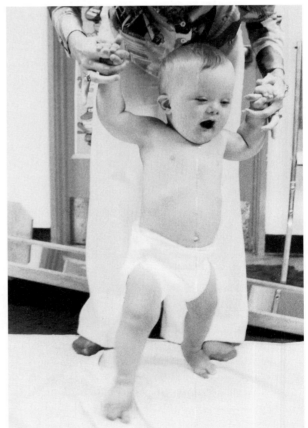

The Individualized Education Program (IEP)

The IEP, for children aged 3 or older, contains six components that can be remembered by the acronym *PAST-DE*.

P Performance, present level

A Annual goals, including short-term objectives

S Services to be provided

T Transition services

D Dates and duration

E Evaluation to determine whether objectives are achieved

    Although not required by law, family involvement is important in all aspects of writing and implementing the IEP. New assessment approaches involve family members (Linder,

FIGURE 18.3 Developmental milestones in achieving normal walking gait. Note correct terminology for *crawl* (on belly) versus *creep* (on hands and knees). Ages given are *average* time of appearance.

Fetal posture
0 month

Chin up
1 month

Chest up
2 months

Reach and miss
3 months

Sit with support
4 months

Sit on lap,
grasp object
5 months

Crawl
6–8 months

Sit alone
7 months

Stand
with help
8 months

Stand holding
furniture
9 months

Creep
10 months

Walk when
led
11 months

Pull to stand
by furniture
12 months

Climb
stair steps
13 months

Stand alone
14 months

Walk alone
15 months

1993a), and specification of services in both the IEP and the IFSP usually includes a home component and parent training.

Assessment Concerns

Assessment in the psychomotor domain is influenced by parents' concerns. These often pertain to developmental milestones and an estimation of the number of months of delay (see Figure 18.3). Many standardized instruments are available (Cowden & Torrey, 1995; Zittel, 1994), but Sherrill recommends the use of checklists and videotapes in a play-oriented, natural setting (see Chapter 6 on assessment). Three checklists in Chapter 11 present developmentally sequenced teaching/testing progressions that are particularly helpful:

Table 11.3—Walk and run skills

Table 11.7—Jumping and hopping tasks

Table 11.9—Object control skills

These checklists, however, should not be used in a formal manner with the child asked to do a particular skill and then evaluated. Instead, observe informal play in many settings (both land and water), both alone and with other children of various ages. Give priority to skills that are needed for everyday success. This includes social play skills, self-concept, and self-confidence as well as motor skills. Encourage parents to help with assessment procedures.

Use of the Test of Gross Motor Development (TGMD, Ulrich, 1985), described fully in Chapter 11, allows teachers to identify specific skill components that need work (Zittel & McCubbin, 1996). One approach to improving skills in decision making about assessment is to study protocols used in research. The July 1996 issue of *Adapted Physical Activity Quarterly,* edited by Lauriece Zittel, is devoted to delays of infants, toddlers, and young children.

If the infant, toddler, or child cannot perform age-appropriate motor milestones, then the professional must ask why. Typically there are multiple reasons, and the ecological approach to testing demands that three factors be analyzed: the task demands, the individual's functional ability, and the environment. The task demands and the environment should be systematically altered until success is achieved. For example, locomotion should be attempted on many different surfaces and inclines, with different kinds of models, motivation, and reinforcers.

Reflexes and Postural Reactions

Cerebral palsy is a factor in so many developmental delay conditions that teachers should understand reflexes and postural reactions. **Reflexes** are involuntary changes in muscle tone elicited by certain stimuli or conditions. These changes range from barely noticeable, subtle shifts in muscle tension to undesired movements of body parts (see Chapter 10 on sensorimotor integration). **Reactions** are automatic movement patterns that replace reflexes in accordance with an inborn timetable. Most reactions are lifelong and act to protect the body and/or help it maintain equilibrium.

Newborn infants have no motor control because every position change elicits reflexes. When in prone position, they are in a flexed fetal posture referred to as *flexor tone dominance* because the anterior surface muscles contract in response to the tactile stimuli from the surface (see Figure 18.4). Movement to a supine position causes the extensor muscles on the posterior surface to automatically contract. This is called *extensor tone dominance.* Any movement of the head likewise causes associated movements of other body parts. Until infants are 3 or 4 months of age, they seldom initiate voluntary, purposeful movement (see Figure 18.5).

As the central nervous system (CNS) matures, automatic reactions and voluntary spontaneous movement patterns emerge to override reflex control of muscle tone. This process is analogous to layering; it is continuous and lifelong. The more a specific voluntary act is practiced, the more the reflex activity that could have interfered is layered over or suppressed.

When the CNS is damaged (as in cerebral palsy, stroke, and traumatic brain damage), delays often occur in the integration of reflexes and the emergence of postural reactions and voluntary movement. In such cases, goals and objectives may focus on sensorimotor training.

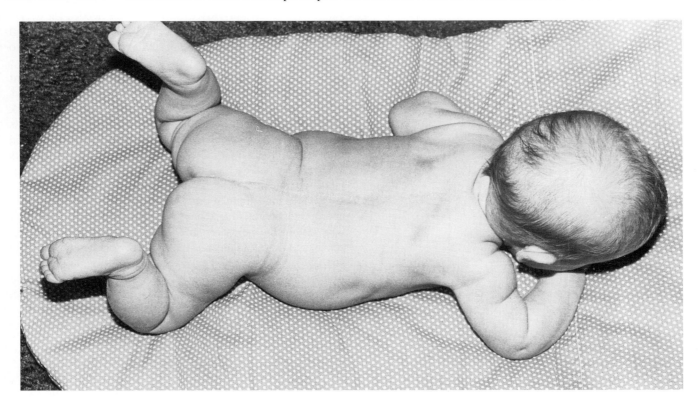

FIGURE 18.5   The same infant as in Figure 18.4 at about 6 months of age, when no longer dominated by flexor tone. Note ability to reach with one arm, while the other arm remains motionless. Arms and legs can fully extend.

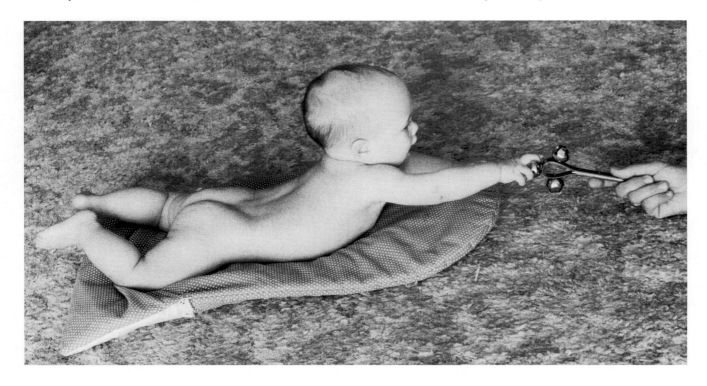

Hypotonia

Hypotonia is insufficient muscle tone, a manifestation of muscle weakness that is present in many infants, toddlers, and young children with disabilities. In particular, hypotonia is associated with Down syndrome and may be the major reason that these children are delayed in acquiring locomotor skills. Infant activity programs that utilize treadmills (Ulrich, Ulrich, & Collier, 1992) and ankle weights (Sayers, Cowden, Newton, Warren, & Eason, 1996) have been effective in helping to overcome hypotonia and related problems.

Activity-Deficit Problems

Amount of activity and opportunities for activity should be assessed through interviews with family members and other caretakers. Most individuals with severe disabilities spend more time lying or sitting than peers do, and this inactivity causes many problems. Attention to proper positioning and providing a stimulating environment may increase self-initiated movement, so assessment should include questions about where and how the individual is placed during waking hours, how many stimuli are present, and whether positioning enhances movement. For example, rolling, crawling, and creeping are easier on a hard surface than on a soft surface like a mattress. Large mirrors provide feedback. The presence of other children and/or family pets provides models and increases incentive to move.

Body Image Concerns

Body image should be assessed also. **Body image** is all of the feelings, attitudes, beliefs, and knowledge that a person has about his or her body and its capacity for movement. These include psychomotor, affective, and cognitive understandings that begin in infancy. Development of body image is fundamental to shaping a good self-concept, especially in early childhood, when most feelings about the global self stem from movement and language experiences. Consider, for example, the first praise that infants receive. This is typically directed toward physical appearance ("such a pretty baby") or achievement of motor milestones (first grasp, first steps, first playfulness).

Body image development in early childhood is synonymous with sensorimotor development. Table 18.1 shows that different terms are applied to body image constructs at different ages. Body image objectives are (a) to develop body awareness, (b) to develop pride in the body and self-confidence in using it, and (c) to develop self-initiative in moving in new and different ways. Normal children often achieve these objectives without help, but in adapted physical education, these objectives are major challenges. Progress toward these objectives should be assessed.

Body schema is the diagram of the body that evolves in the brain in response to sensorimotor input. The body schema enables the infant to feel body boundaries, identify body parts, plan and execute movements, and know where the body is in space. Figure 18.6 depicts an adult brain, showing developed potential. The motor projection areas of the brain are topographically organized, with each part controlling specific muscles that, in turn, control body movement. At birth,

Table 18.1 Terms used in different stages of body image development.

Developmental Stage	Body Image Construct
Sensorimotor (0 to 2 years)	Body schema
Preoperational (2 to 7 years)	Body awareness
	Self-awareness
Concrete operational (7 to 11 years)	Body image
	Self-concept

FIGURE 18.6   Areas of the brain related to bodily movement.

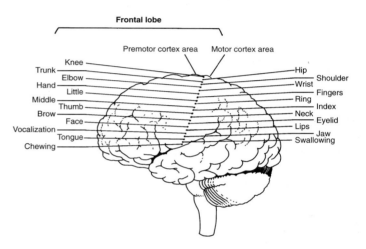

Lateral view of the adult brain, showing premotor and motor cortex strips on the frontal lobe.

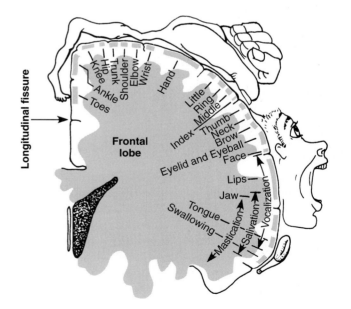

Specialized areas of the brain that evolve in response to sensorimotor input. Voluntary movements are controlled in the same area of the motor strip in all human beings.

this capacity to control movement is not yet developed. Remember the motor development principle of general-to-specific activity (i.e., generalized mass activity is replaced by specific responses of individual body parts). Each movement of the body or its parts by the infant or another provides sensorimotor input (kinesthetic, vestibular) to the brain, which causes the body schema to evolve.

Sensory input from the skin, muscles, and joints (touch, pressure, temperature, pain) also contributes to the early development of body schema. Figure 18.6 shows that the body schema develops in a *cephalocaudal (head-to-tail) direction,* with the infant first becoming aware of eating/drinking and then of seeing. Later, the infant gains control of the head/neck muscles (turning the head from side to side, lifting the head), then the shoulder and arm muscles for reaching, then the hand/finger muscles (grasping, holding toys), and finally the muscles of the lower extremities. Figure 18.6 shows also that a disproportionately large cortical area is devoted to muscle groups responsible for fine muscle control, such as that required for lips and fingers.

Body schema continues to develop and change throughout the lifespan. As the child matures, cognitive and affective dimensions are added to the psychomotor parameters. If problems occur, the body schema is affected, motor planning is damaged, and faulty movements occur. Figures 18.7 and 18.8 show body image milestones to be assessed from ages 4 to 36 months. Many of these milestones can be considered play and game skills.

During the sensorimotor period (ages 0 to 2), children learn to imitate facial expressions, limb movements, and body positions. Visual input is the most important sense modality in imitation, since seeing others motivates the child to locomotion. Needing or wanting an object (food/toy) within the visual field is another reinforcer of imitation. These facts help explain why sensorimotor development is delayed in children who are congenitally blind.

Motor planning (praxis) also emerges during the sensorimotor period as cognition develops and the child wants to manipulate objects/toys and to move from place to place. Early voluntary movement can leave the child feeling competent and loved or clumsy, scorned, and pitied. Thus, body image components in the affective domain begin to interweave with those in the psychomotor domain.

Language Development

Language development affects learning to move and concurrent development of body image and self-concept. Assessment should cover words related to the body and movement.

From birth until 2 years of age, children normally acquire a speaking vocabulary of about 300 words. Among these are names of common body parts, like hands, feet, face, tummy, nose, eyes, ears, and mouth. Self-awareness develops in a definite order: hands, feet, face, and trunk. The emergence of language for body parts and movements reinforces the growing understanding and appreciation of the body.

In the preoperational stage, speech develops rapidly (from 300 words at age 2 to several thousand words at age 7)

FIGURE 18.7 First milestones in the development of body image. Average ages are given.

4 weeks
or
1 month

Sensorimotor input from movement by another. Lifting head is first voluntary movement.

16 weeks
or
4 months

First awareness of hands. Can voluntarily bring hands to midline. Rolls over, providing sensorimotor input regarding total body in space.

28 weeks
or
7 months

First interest in mirror play and awareness of face. First awareness of feet.

40 weeks
or
10 months

Laterality is reinforced when balance is maintained in sitting, creeping. Imitation of movements begins, usually with bye-bye and shaking head yes and no.

and gradually takes precedence over movement as a means of expression. During this time span, children also begin to perceive themselves as competent and lovable, or the opposite. The way they look and move has much to do with such perceptions (see Figure 18.8).

Self-Concept

Pictorial instruments for assessment of various aspects of self-concept are recommended for ages 4 through 7 (see Chapter 8). Interviews are useful also in determining how children feel about their competence in locomotor and object control skills and their ability to play games with specific others. The richness of interview data is enhanced by showing children photographs and videotapes of themselves in game play with others.

FIGURE 18.8   Later milestones in development of body image. Average ages are given.

1 year
or
12 months

Sensorimotor input from walking and changing positions from up to down.
Competence feeling from casting balls/objects that others must retrieve.
Feelings about body as good/bad from toilet training.

1½ years
or
18 months

Understands and can say "Up," "Down" (first movement concepts).
Is learning names of body parts.
Increased competence from hurling balls/objects.
Retrieves balls for self.

2 years
or
24 months

Has about 300 words in vocabulary.
Can name body parts of doll.
Understands on-off concepts, then in-out, turn around.
Beginning imitative play with dolls, projects feeling about
self into doll play.

3 years
or
36 months

Understands over-under, front-back, big-little, short-tall/long, high-low.
Copies circles, crosses on paper, but cannot yet draw a person.
Balances on one foot.
Rides tricycle.

Principles of Motor Development

Principles of motor development help explain normal function in young children and thus serve as guides to assessment and programming (see Table 18.2). Disabilities and delays, of course, affect normal function, and professionals should pay particular attention to movement profiles that seem to violate basic principles.

The principle of *dynamic systems* is a relatively new principle, adopted from dynamic systems theory (Kugler, Kelso, & Turvey, 1982; Smith & Thelen, 1993; Ulrich & Ulrich, 1995). This principle is included as acknowledgment that all systems (e.g., skeletal, muscular, nervous, metabolic) affect motor development, are interactive, and tend to promote self-initiating and self-organizing movement behaviors. Some individuals believe that the principle of dynamic systems is antithetical to traditional motor development principles, especially those emanating from neurodevelopmental theory.

The principle of *reflex integration and reaction emergence* emphasizes that reflexes and reactions are the foundation of early movement coordination and control. Difficulty with balance relates to failure of the equilibrium reactions to fully function. Problems with coordination and control stem partly from inability to move a specific body part without undesired associated shifts of muscle tone in other parts; this occurs because reflexes have not been sufficiently integrated. Likewise, smooth, reciprocal contraction and relaxation of muscles is determined by reflex mechanisms.

The principle of reflex integration and reaction emergence supports the practice of sensorimotor training, with lots of supervised repetition to promote the emergence of mature movement patterns. The principle also supports *patterning,* taking the body parts through prescribed movements over and over again, a technique used when persons are too severely disabled to move themselves.

The principle of *uniform sequence,* often referred to as *orderly progression,* provides insight into which tasks are easiest for most persons and thus helps with task analysis. Research on thousands of infants, toddlers, and children has established normal developmental sequences like those presented in Figure 18.3. Deviance from uniform sequence, however, has been reported in infants who are blind or multiply disabled (deJong, 1990) and others who exhibit clumsiness in later years. This helps form the rationale for individual assessment rather than assuming that all children are ready for a certain task at a certain age.

The principle of *general-to-specific activity,* also called *differentiation,* explains reflex integration and motor control. The newborn responds to stimuli with generalized mass activity. With CNS maturation, children are progressively able to move specific body parts without associated overflow movement. This principle explains why early childhood physical education stresses movement exploration and imitation of total body actions (e.g., animal walks, rolls, jumps) rather than activities that require specific body parts to be used in accordance with visual and auditory input. This supports *whole-part-whole pedagogy.* General or whole body challenges are the focus until reasonable control of body parts is achieved.

T a b l e   1 8 . 2   Principles of normal motor development.

1. **Dynamic systems.** Movement is the product of many systems and subsystems that are constantly interacting and changing. When one system is delayed or injured, other systems are affected.
2. **Reflex integration and reaction emergence.** An inborn timetable is followed, whereby reflexes are suppressed and righting, protective extension, and equilibrium reactions emerge. These developments enable voluntary movement patterns to unfold and coordination and control to be acquired.
3. **General-to-specific activity.** Generalized mass activity is replaced by specific responses of individual body parts. The child learns to assemble the parts of a general pattern before altering the parts to meet specific environmental demands.
4. **Cephalocaudal direction.** Gross motor development begins with head control (strength in neck muscles) and proceeds downward.
5. **Proximodistal coordination.** Muscle groups near (*proximo-*) midline become functional before those farther away (*distal*) from midline do. For example, a child learns to catch with shoulders, upper arms, and forearms before catching with fingers. Movements performed at midline (in front of body) are easier than those that entail crossing midline (to left or right of body—i.e., more distant from midline).
6. **Bilateral-to-crosslateral motor coordination.** *Bilateral* movement patterns (both limbs moving simultaneously, as in arm movements of the breaststroke or reaching for an object at midline) are the first to occur in the human infant, followed by *unilateral* movement patterns (right arm and right leg moving simultaneously or vice versa), followed by *crosslateral* patterns (right arm and left leg moving simultaneously).
7. **Mastery or effectance motivation.** The drive to explore, master, and control the environment is *innate;* thus motor development is affected by challenges in the environment and individual capabilities in meeting challenges.

The principle of *cephalocaudal direction* explains why emphasis is placed on head control in remediation. The infant achieves control of head (*cephalus*) before control of the lower spine (generalized to *caudo,* meaning "tail"). This principle is violated by persons dominated by reflexes who learn to sit, crawl, and creep but cannot hold the head erect and motionless.

The principle of *proximodistal coordination* explains the emphasis on midline activities. The nervous system matures from the midline (spinal column) outward. Thus, muscles closer (*proximo-*) to the midline have mature innervation before those farther (distal) from midline. Muscles moving the head, neck, scapula, and trunk become coordinated to permit sitting, crawling, creeping, and standing before muscles of the arms and legs become coordinated enough for throwing, catching, and kicking. Likewise, large muscles of the shoulders and hips become coordinated before the small muscles of the hands and feet that move the digits.

The principle of *bilateral-to-crosslateral motor coordination* provides insight into developmentally appropriate exercises and games. **Bilateral movements** are arms or legs simultaneously reaching, spreading, or closing. At about 4 months of age, when voluntary movement control begins, infants bring both hands to midline and begin looking intently at them. This seems to be the beginning of awareness of body parts and cognition that parts can do something. Shortly thereafter, infants in supine or propped sitting positions reach and grasp with both hands. They also learn to hold the bottle with both hands.

By age 6 or 7 months, infants can succeed in purposeful **unilateral movements,** usually the reaching of one arm to grasp a toy. Some children with disabilities, however, cannot perform unilateral movements without undesired overflow activity in the opposite limb. Games like waving bye-bye are often used to assess early unilateral development. Imitations of single arm or leg movements are used as remediation for children who appear to be frozen at the bilateral level.

From 7 or 8 months of age onward, infants should be able to use either unilateral or bilateral movements, depending on task demands. Toddlers and young children should not be corrected when they throw with the right arm while the right foot steps forward or while the feet remain stationary. This immature movement pattern typically fades as motivation to *throw hard* increases.

Crosslateral movements are those in which the limbs work in opposition (e.g., the left leg moves forward with the right arm). These evolve naturally in walking patterns but are typically not exhibited in throwing and kicking patterns until age 5 or 6. Many adults who are clumsy still do not consistently use opposition. Crosslateral coordination is essential to good balance, and the emphasis on balancing activities in early childhood is partly to support neural maturation that will lead naturally to opposition.

The principle of *mastery or effectance motivation,* first espoused by White (1959), recognizes the innate urge to move, play, and explore the environment. Infants, toddlers, and children typically are active in shaping and changing their environment. Thus, motor development is not a passive phenomenon but instead reflects complex, continuous interactions among the individual, the environment, and the task demands. Naturally, disability affects innate urges, changing the resources available for moving, exploring, and problem solving. Concurrently, adults tend to overprotect children with disabilities and to limit their opportunities for self-initiated learning. The principle of mastery or effectance motivation reminds professionals to maximize opportunities for movement exploration and to encourage self-initiated activity.

Placement and Programming

The trend is toward placement of infants, toddlers, and children with delays/disabilities in integrated classrooms and play settings. When children cannot safely or successfully participate in an integrated environment without assistance, several options are possible. Typically, an aide is provided to assist the regular educator in meeting the child's special needs, and/or a consultant or resource teacher helps with environmental and instructional adaptations. Sometimes, a pull-out arrangement is used in which the child leaves the regular classroom for a few hours each week for special tutoring and/or therapy. Every attempt is made to keep children in integrated settings so that they can be afforded the same socializing and learning experiences as normal peers.

Instruction and Intervention Approaches

Several sources on methods and materials for teaching motor and play skills to young children with disabilities appeared in the late 1970s and early 1980s (Sherrill, 1979; Watkinson & Wall, 1982; Wessel, 1980) and remain sound. Recently, Janet Wessel, with Lauriece Zittel, has updated and expanded her work with a book called *Smart Start: Preschool Movement Curriculum Designed for Children of All Abilities* (Wessel & Zittel, 1995). The PREP play program (Watkinson & Wall, 1982), used widely in Canada, is described in Chapter 21. These early works all emphasized holistic, integrated approaches, play, creativity, and concurrent attention to language development. Following are descriptions of approaches developed specifically for early childhood.

Language-Arts-Movement Programming

The language-arts-movement programming (LAMP) model evolved from several years of federal funding in the creative arts area to Texas Woman's University and the National Committee on Arts for the Handicapped in Washington, DC. Ideas were tested in several schools and results were published as qualitative research (Eddy, 1982; Sherrill & McBride, 1984). Additionally, a book described many instructional techniques (Sherrill, 1979).

The acronym *LAMP* is intended to conjure up the vision of Aladdin's lamp and the magic of wishes that can come true (i.e., all children can learn when teachers believe in themselves and creatively use all of their resources). In this model, arts (creative drama and dance, music, story-telling, puppets, painting, drawing, and constructing) are the medium for unifying movement and language, and vice versa (see Figure 18.9).

Language, in this model, is operationally defined as speaking, singing, chanting, or signing. It may come from the teacher only, the teacher and child in unison, or the child only. Language is used to express the intent to move and/or to plan and rehearse a desired movement sequence, to describe movement as it occurs, and to praise once the action is completed. The combining of language and movement to teach concepts and develop schemas is powerful because the whole child is involved in active learning. The use of self-talk (also called verbal rehearsal) is well documented as a sound pedagogical device (Kowalski & Sherrill, 1992; Linder, 1993a, 1993b). Learning words/labels for what they are doing enhances recall. Self-talk also facilitates time-on-task because it keeps attention focused on the movement goal.

A useful strategy is to create action songs or chants to familiar tunes like "Mulberry Bush," "Farmer in the Dell," and "Looby Loo" or nursery rhyme rhythms. The words must teach the name of the movement, associated body parts, or concepts about space, time, and effort (i.e., be relevant to the

FIGURE 18.9 Pounding movements are the first object control skills developed. They are easily integrated into running and language activities.

action). For example, beam walking on a low, wide beam might inspire a "Row, Row, Row Your Boat" chant like this:

> Walk, walk, walk your feet
> Gently down the beam
> Merrily, merrily, merrily, merrily
> It is fun to walk a beam!

Or a simple repetitive chant like this:

> I am walking, I am walking
> You walk, too, You walk, too
> Walk, Walk, Walk; Walk, Walk, Walk
> And Stop, Freeze . . . Quiet, shh . . .

Young children with disabilities/delays need more repetition than normal peers. For repetition to provide the needed reinforcement, however, the child must be paying attention and receiving the kind of teacher input (eye contact, smiles, praise, pats) that makes him or her feel competent and good about self. Question and answer chants in unison with movement help to achieve this goal:

> Teacher: "Can you kick? Can you kick?"
> Child: "I can kick. I can kick."
> Teacher: "What did you kick? What did you kick?"
> Child: "A ball. I kicked a ball."
> Teacher: "Good, now go get the ball. Bring it here."

The same words are used over and over so that children develop vocabulary and improve memory for sequences. Rhythmically synchronous background music can also help young children remember movement sequences (Staum, 1988).

LAMP begins with much structure in that the goal is to simultaneously teach motor skills, language, and play concepts so that the child, in turn, develops the capacity for solitary play. When he or she begins interacting spontaneously with the environment (objects, playground apparatus, or people) in appropriate ways, this initiative is praised and reinforced. Emphasis then is on helping the child progress from solitary to parallel to interactive/cooperative play. Young children need language (both receptive and expressive) to engage in cooperative play and to benefit from small-group movement and game instruction. The LAMP model promotes integrated motor-language-cognitive development.

Activity-Based Intervention

Activity-based intervention (ABI) is an approach that emphasizes that IFSP and IEP goals should be implemented as part of activities of daily living rather than taught as isolated school subjects (Bricker & Woods-Cripe, 1992). Ulrich (1995) and Block and Davis (1996) apply ABI to adapted physical education instruction. Among the points emphasized are the following:

1. Analyze the child's activities of daily living (ADL) and select movement and social play skills needed for success in ADL. Such skills are described as *functional* and *generalizable.*

2. Establish activity centers in home and school environments with a wide variety of toys, equipment, and apparatuses that will motivate the child to engage in activities that facilitate achievement of specific goals (i.e., create environments in which IFSP/IEP goals are *embedded in activities* that children choose).

3. Emphasize child-initiated activities. Let the child choose the order of rotation from one activity center to another, and support her or his choice of specific activities. Participate in activities with individual children by imitating, mirroring, or paralleling their movements and sounds. Let the child lead!

4. Systematically use logically occurring antecedents and consequences to guide the child toward targeted goals. **Antecedents** include smiles, body language, questions, comments, imitations, and other actions that serve as prompts. **Consequences** include reinforcers that make the child feel good about movement exploration.

Transdisciplinary Play-Based Intervention

Transdisciplinary play-based assessment (TPBA) and transdisciplinary play-based intervention (TPBI), designed for children between infancy and 6 years of age and tested in the Denver public schools, are explained in books (Linder, 1993a, 1993b) and videotapes. Four areas of development are targeted: (a) cognitive, (b) social-emotional, (c) communication and language, and (d) sensorimotor. The material on sensorimotor development was written by occupational therapists and encompasses much of the content presented in Chapter 10 of this book (e.g., normalizing muscle tone, facilitating reactivity to sensory input, encouraging the emergence of equilibrium reactions and voluntary movement).

The major value of TPBA and TPBI lies in their philosophy of transdisciplinary cooperation among professionals, their involvement of family members, and their highlighting of play as the major medium for early childhood learning. According to Linder (1993b, p. 27), "Through play, the child acquires, practices, and adapts skills in all developmental areas."

FIGURE 18.10   Dr. Lauriece Zittel, coauthor of *Smart Start,* encourages a child-initiated activity.

Assessment

The TPBA is conducted in a creative play environment that includes materials and equipment that will facilitate demonstration of the full range of the child's behaviors. Although the entire team is involved in observation and subsequent data analysis, only one team member (called the play facilitator) interacts with the child. As in ABI, the child is allowed to lead the play and the facilitator imitates, models, and expands on the child's actions. After 20 to 25 minutes of this unstructured facilitation, the role of the facilitator changes slightly to entice the child to try new toys, materials, and activities.

Child–child interaction and parent/caretaker–child interaction are assessed also in both unstructured and structured facilitation. The child can be a familiar peer but should be of the same sex and have slightly higher functioning ability than the child being assessed.

The TPBA ends with 10 to 20 minutes of motor play and a snack, both of which yield additional data for full information about the child's abilities. Altogether, a total of 60 to 90 minutes are required for the TPBA.

Intervention

The philosophy of TPBI is "child-centered, family-focused, peer-oriented, culturally and developmentally relevant, and based on pleasurable play interactions" (Linder, 1993b, p. 13). TPBI is similar to ABI, in that play centers are used and children are allowed to select activities. Parents and teachers follow the child's lead and encourage self-initiated activity (see Figure 18.10). Gradually the child is helped to understand the concept of taking turns leading. The emphasis is on adults' creating environments and supplying materials that motivate children to explore and problem-solve. This approach is very similar to that used in movement exploration, creative dance, and dance therapy.

Sensorimotor Integration

Chapter 10 fully discusses sensorimotor integration. New approaches, designed specifically for infants and toddlers, include progressive interactive facilitation and dynamical systems treadmill intervention (see Figure 18.11).

Progressive Interactive Facilitation

The progressive interactive facilitation approach, proposed by Jo E. Cowden (1997) of the University of New Orleans, encompasses content presented in Chapter 10 of this text and many occupational therapy textbooks (e.g., tactile-kinesthetic-vestibular stimulation, normalization of muscle tone, repetitive patterning of movement when children cannot perform patterns without help, correct positioning, and supervised practice of activities to enhance stability and mobility). Cowden, however, refines and extends this content and adds a pediatric strength component that utilizes ankle weights and individualized resistance training. The use of this approach with infants with Down syndrome, aged 18 to 38 months, contributes to the acquisition and refinement of independent upright locomotion (Sayers, Cowden, Newton, Warren, & Eason, 1996).

Dynamical Systems Treadmill Intervention

Dale and Beverly Ulrich of Indiana University (Ulrich, Ulrich, & Collier, 1992) have completed considerable research showing that infants with Down syndrome, when supported on a motorized treadmill, can perform alternate-foot stepping patterns. Their findings indicate that muscle strength and postural stability training contribute to independent locomotion. Many factors other than neurological maturation contribute to improved motor function.

Motor Skills and Patterns

Most, but not all, children with delays/disabilities have motor skill problems. Typically, patterns like sitting, crawling, creeping, standing, and walking emerge later than in normal children.

Chapter 11 on motor performance presents developmental sequences for teaching locomotor and ball-handling skills to children ages 1 to 8. The pedagogy described in Chapter 11 is also developmental and applies to toddlers and early childhood.

Object control and toy play is an important learning objective. Children with developmental delays need instruction and practice with many kinds of objects before ball-handling skills are introduced.

Table 18.3 depicts levels in learning to manipulate play objects. Toy play is largely dependent on normal evolution of voluntary grip (about 5 months) and voluntary release (about 12 months); these abilities are often impaired in children with CP and others slow to integrate reflexes. Toy play is also dependent on visual integrity. Children who are blind are usually delayed in developing object manipulation skills. Throwing a ball is not as motivational for children who cannot see as for those reinforced by visual input.

Table 18.3 is recommended as a checklist for assessing what infants, toddlers, and young children do with objects. It can help determine amount of delay and guide program

FIGURE 18.11 *(A)* Dr. Jo Cowden applies pediatric strength intervention. *(B)* Dr. Dale Ulrich works with an infant on a treadmill.

A

B

planning. Assessment should be conducted in both free-play and imitation settings. Often, children with disabilities learn to imitate before they show initiative in free play.

If a child shows no interest and/or ability in manipulating objects, the developmental sequence in Table 18.3 may be useful in writing lesson plans. Starting with up-and-down movements, like shaking a balloon tied to the wrist or a rhythm instrument (try sewing tiny bells into gloves), may be easiest. Pounding movements, as in using a drum or hammer, come

T a b l e 1 8 . 3   Developmental levels in toy or object play.

Level	Activity	Level	Activity
1	**Repetitive manual manipulation.** Usually an up-and-down shaking movement of rattles and other noisemakers. May be an autistic behavior or blindism. All repetitive movements of this nature are described as *stereotypic behaviors.*	7	**Personalized toy play.** Occurs first as imitation, usually in conjunction with toy dishes, dolls, and stuffed animals. Pretending to feed toy or rocking it to sleep are early play behaviors. Riding a broomstick horse or using wheel-toys to get from place to place is another example. Child can respond, with gesture, to question, "What is this toy for?" These abilities emerge **between ages 1 and 2 years.**
2	**Oral contacts.** Mouthing of objects. Also considered stereotypic behaviors.		
3	**Pounding.** Developmentally, the first purposeful play movement to appear. It cannot occur until voluntary, one-handed grasp appears, usually at about **5 months of age,** and child can sit upright with support so that at least one hand is free.	8	**Manipulation of movable toy parts.** This includes all the commercial toys (dolls and trucks, for example) with parts that can be turned, pushed, or pulled without coming apart. This manipulation is purposeful, often combined with dramatic play. Also includes doorknobs, zippers, Velcro fasteners, horns, and bells. These abilities emerge **between ages 1.5 and 2.5 years.**
4	**Striking, raking a stationary object.** Normal children enjoy raking food pellets or other objects off of a table surface at **about 7 months of age.** An ulnar (toward ulna and little finger) raking movement occurs developmentally before the more mature radial (toward radius and thumb) movement. With older students who are severely disabled (especially those with cerebral palsy), striking is easier than throwing.	9	**Separation of toy parts.** This includes putting puzzles (large parts) together and taking them apart, dressing and undressing dolls, connecting and disconnecting cars of a train, building towers with blocks, and pinning tail on donkey and body parts on drawing of a person. These skills emerge **between ages 2 and 3 years.**
5	**Pulling or pushing.** This includes pulling toys by strings and pushing toys on wheels. In normal development, it occurs **at about 10 months of age** after evolution of pincer grasp (i.e., use of thumb and index finger). In older students with severe disabilities, pushing skills include box hockey and shuffleboard-type games in which a stick is used to push the object. Rolling balls back and forth to a partner is classified as a pushing activity.	10	**Combinational uses of toys.** This refers to dramatic play like tea parties, doctor/nurse, cowboys/Indians in which toys, costumes, and props are used in various combinations. **Well developed by ages 3 to 4 years,** at which time fine motor activities (drawing, printing, coloring, cutting) begin to assume dominance.
6	**Throwing.** The first two levels, according to child development theory, are called casting and hurling. *Casting* and *hurling* are often done from a sitting position. This skill cannot evolve until the child can voluntarily *release* objects—a motor milestone that occurs **at about 12 months of age.**	11	**Cards and table games.** These activities involve fine motor coordinations (i.e., moving checkers from place to place, handling dice, holding cards). These skills become functional **at about age 5.**
		12	**Active ball play.** Children are typically socialized into various kinds of ball games by **age 7 or 8 years.**

early in the developmental sequence. Children should be taught to tap the bat on home base, release the bat, and run before batting is introduced. Remember: *All children can learn if professionals use appropriate task analyses based on an awareness of which activities are developmentally the easiest to learn.*

Perceptual-Motor Learning

Chapter 12 offers ideas for teaching children who need special help in mastering motor skills and patterns. The perceptual-motor approach is more play oriented than skill oriented. Many different environments are used for increasing the child's understanding of her or his body and what it can do (see Figure 18.12).

Self-Concept

The early years are a critical period in the formation of self-concept (Wright, 1983). By ages 4 to 5 years, feelings about the self can be measured in four domains—cognitive compe-

tence, physical competence, peer acceptance, and maternal acceptance (Harter & Pike, 1984)—using an interview technique with a pictorial instrument. The child is shown two pictures at a time; the teacher interprets each picture (e.g., "This boy isn't very good at running." "This boy is pretty good at running."); and then the child is asked to point to the picture most like him or her. This and other assessment approaches show that preschoolers have begun to form definite concepts about both their acceptance and competence.

Children with orthopedic disabilities become gradually aware that they are different and/or have a disability between the ages of 3 and 7 (Dunn, McCartan, & Fuqua, 1988; Wright, 1983). However, even when aware that arms or legs are different, they tend to deny difficulty in running or problems in doing things that others do (Teplin, Howard, & O'Connor, 1981). Most children do not begin to compare themselves with others until ages 7 or 8. Self-evaluation of physical appearance and abilities thus is strongly rooted in what persons tell them. Much research is needed on how young children with disabilities perceive themselves, what shapes their beliefs, and what influences their behaviors.

FIGURE 18.12 Young children and infants with delays need careful, systematic instruction in many environments.

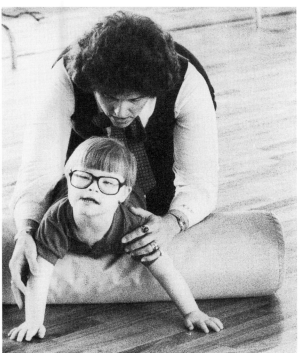

Growing awareness of self as a person with differences, disabilities, or limitations should not be left to chance, which is often both traumatic and cruel. Parents should begin providing general information to young children about their disability at age 3 or 4 (Dunn et al., 1988; Wright, 1983). Typically, children ask questions that initiate discussions or become involved in interactions with siblings or peers that require mediation. Responses should be matter-of-fact and stress assets rather than comparisons.

Wright (1983, p. 240) offers examples of good and bad answers to the question: "Do you think I'll ever be able to walk like everyone else?"

> *Good:* "Probably not, but you are learning to walk better, and that is good. And do you know that there are lots of other things you can do? Let's name some of them."

> *Bad:* "Probably not. But even if you can't walk as well as some people, there are other things that you can do better than some people."

Young children thus should be helped to understand their limitations in a friendly and caring atmosphere. As younger and younger children receive special education services, caretakers outside the family circle may have to answer first questions about being different and cope with interpersonal situations in which peers point out shortcomings.

Most children with severe disabilities/delays are inevitably exposed to discrimination and prejudice (Wright, 1983). They should therefore be prepared for difficult social encounters. Story-telling, role-playing, and discussion help with learning appropriate responses to others' thoughtless and inconsiderate behavior. A number of books are now available that feature children coping with disabilities. Among these is the "Kids on the Block" book series, available from Twenty-First Century Books, 38 South Market Street, Frederick, Maryland 21701. Each "Kids on the Block" book describes a child with a different disability (e.g., cerebral palsy, asthma, diabetes, AIDS) who copes in appropriate ways, feels good about self, and interacts with nondisabled children.

The "Kids on the Block" are also available as puppets, although somewhat expensive. Scripts and discussion guidelines come with the puppets, and over 900 community-based organizations are using these materials to increase awareness and improve attitudes (Aiello, 1988).

Young children with disabilities need access to dolls and stuffed animals with and without disabilities. This permits imaginative play comparable to real-life situations. "Hal's Pals" is a line of cabbagepatch-type dolls with different disabilities (e.g., a skier with one leg, an athlete in a wheelchair, a dancer with hearing aids) available through Jesana Ltd., P.O. Box 17, Irvington, NY 10533.

Social Competence and Inclusion

Social rejection and avoidance of children who are different begins at about age 4, unless there is intervention to promote interaction and acceptance (Siller, 1984; Weinberg, 1978). Research suggests that nondisabled children do not automatically include slow and/or different children in their activities (Jenkins, Speltz, & Odom, 1985). Early childhood educators must therefore de-

FIGURE 18.13 Young children need to see persons with disabilities in leadership roles. The teacher shown here is Don Drewry.

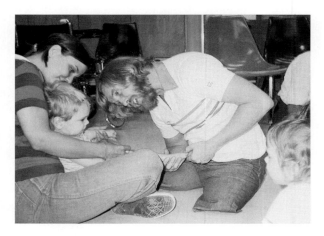

vise curriculums that systematically involve preschoolers in cooperative activities and promote caring, nurturing attitudes.

Experts favor open discussion of disabilities/differences in front of children and recommend inclusion of units covering individual differences in preschool curricula (Dunn et al., 1988). Emphasis should be on each human being's uniqueness and the importance of supporting and helping one another. Children should be helped to see that being different is not bad but simply a chance occurrence. Discussion can center on differences in eye, hair, and skin color; height and weight; the ways people walk, talk, and think; and expressions of individuality in work, play, hobbies, and leisure pursuits. Movement education and creativity training in which emphasis is on "Find another way" or "Show me all the different ways you can do something" are excellent approaches to understanding and appreciating individual differences. Likewise, good teachers stress not being afraid of people, places, foods, and other things that are different, but approaching them, assessing them, and getting acquainted.

Stories like the princess who kissed the frog and turned him into a prince can teach sensitivity. Emphasizing that appearances can be deceiving is also important. Too often, Halloween witches and storybook monsters are characterized as physically ugly or disfigured; small wonder that young children without special training begin equating being different with being bad. To counteract these influences, movement activities should feature creatures who look different but are kind, loving, and lovable. Examples are television and movie characters like Vincent in "Beauty and the Beast," Alf, ET, and the casts in *Star Wars* and *Return of the Jedi*.

Preschoolers, both with and without disabilities, need exposure to older persons with disabilities (see Figure 18.13). Research shows that children in the 3- to 6-year-old age range tend to make no verbal references to the missing leg of an interviewer; this suggests that inhibiting responses to a physical disability occurs in the early years and limits opportunities for direct learning (Somervill, Cordoba, Abbott, & Brown, 1982). Thus, when speakers with disabilities are invited to the early childhood setting, they should explain how they are similar to and different from other people and encourage questions.

Play and Game Behaviors

Children with severe delays/disabilities do not play spontaneously. Neither do they laugh and show evidence of having fun. Thus, a major goal of early childhood adapted physical activity is learning the concept of fun and responding appropriately to social and/or sensory stimulation. Normal infants smile and laugh spontaneously in response to pleasurable sights and sounds between 1 and 4 months of age. They begin reaching for objects at about 3 to 5 months and, as soon as they develop coordination, spend considerable energy working for a toy out of reach and exploring what body parts can do.

Social Play

Peek-a-boo, typically learned between 5 and 10 months of age, is the beginning of social game behaviors. Thereafter, normal infants seem to know instinctively how to imitate and respond to play activities initiated by significant others. Moreover, when left alone, they move about, explore the environment, and engage in solitary play. Gradually, without much help, they develop body control, object control, and basic movement patterns. Placed in an environment with play apparatus and equipment, most children are self-motivated to run, jump, climb, hang, slide, and balance. Movement is obviously fun, intrinsically rewarding, and inseparable from play.

In children with severe delays/disabilities, this spontaneity is often diminished or absent. Compared with nondisabled peers, they engage in fewer activities and spend much of their time sitting and lying (Linder, 1993a). Assessment of such children should begin with observations of their spontaneous interactions with the environment. Do they initiate contact with people and objects, and is their contact appropriate? How long do they sustain contact? Do they demonstrate preferences for some objects and people? If so, these preferences can guide the selection of reinforcement strategies in shaping behavior management plans.

Table 18.4 presents an inventory developed to assess play and game behaviors and guide programming. The play and game behaviors goal encompasses the following:

> to learn to play spontaneously; to progress through developmental play stages from solitary and parallel play behaviors up through cooperative and competitive play; to promote contact and interaction behaviors with toys, play apparatus, and persons; to learn basic game formations and mental operations needed for play.

No child is too severely disabled to benefit from physical education instruction. The goals, objectives, and pedagogy, however, differ from those used with nondisabled children. The major emphasis should be on the development of play and game behaviors that are movement oriented and result in good feelings about the self.

Toy and Apparatus Play

Because learning to play with toys is closely related to the development of social and motor skills, several researchers have focused on toy play, including early use of wheeled vehicles. Loovis (1985), who studied 3- to 5-year-olds with orthopedic impairments, reported that the tricycle and slide were the most preferred of 20 toys. In general, children spent considerable time using toys in inappropriate ways. Loovis noted that structured play instruction guided by an adult or older child was needed to systematically teach the proper use of toys.

Cowden and Torrey (1990), based on research with 3- to 5-year-olds with varied disabilities, reported that toy play was mostly nonsocial rather than social. Toys designed to promote social interactions failed to elicit the proper response, leading to the recommendation that toy skills must be taught. Children selected gross motor skill toys (vehicles, blocks, push toys) nearly twice as frequently as fine motor skill toys (crayon, puzzles, Play-Doh). Tricycles and riding toys were the most preferred, regardless of level of motor skills.

Little research has been conducted on the use of indoor and outdoor play apparatus, but skills in both areas are generally necessary for integration and acceptance into mainstream play. In general, the most popular pieces of playground apparatus are swings, slides, and climbers. Children must be helped to gain both motor and social skills for successful participation with others on a play apparatus.

Sport Socialization

Children with disabilities should have the same opportunities for sport socialization as peers. This means that they must see persons with conditions similar to their own in athletic roles both in integrated and nonintegrated sport settings. For attitude development, nondisabled preschoolers should also be exposed to athletes with disabilities. All young children should thus be taken to sport events like Special Olympics, wheelchair basketball and tennis, and cerebral palsy handball and boccia. Real-life experiences of this kind should be supplemented with films and videotapes (Sunderlin, 1988) and magazines like *Sports 'N Spokes* and *Palaestra* that feature athletes with disabilities. Several sport organizations that serve people with disabilities are establishing "Futures Teams" by providing recreational activities for children ages 3 and up in the same setting and at the same time that older athletes practice.

Language Development: A Concomitant Goal

Language development is so important that it is integrated into all learning activities. Authorities generally identify three areas of language development: (a) inner, (b) receptive, and (c) expressive. Physical education can contribute to each.

Inner Language

Inner language refers to thought, the ability to transform experience into meaning. Consider the infant who cries and receives attention or the toddler who touches something hot and is burned. In both cases, there may be no words, but the average infant and toddler makes a cause-and-effect linkage. Likewise, good and bad feelings derived through movement are translated into approach and avoidance thoughts.

Receptive Language

Receptive language is comprehension of gestures, postures, facial expressions, and spoken words. It is also understanding of the symbols or signs used to represent words. Receptive

T a b l e 1 8 . 4   **Sherrill Social Play Behaviors Inventory.**

	Mary	Jim	Juan
Autistic/Unoccupied			
Shows no spontaneous play.			
Makes no response to stimuli.			
Shows no object or person preference.			
Makes stereotyped/repetitive movements.			
Pounds/shakes/mouths objects without purpose.			
Self-stimulates.			
Wanders about aimlessly.			
Self-mutilates.			
Solitary/Exploratory			
Reacts to stimuli (approach/avoid).			
Reacts to persons/objects.			
Understands object permanence (peek-a-boo, hide-and-seek).			
Explores body parts.			
Explores objects/toys.			
Shows object preference.			
Shows person preference.			
Parallel			
Establishes play space near others.			
Shows awareness of others but doesn't interact.			
Plays independently with own things.			
Plays on same playground apparatus as others.			
Follows leader in imitation games and obstacle course.			
Associative/Interactive			
Initiates contact/play with others.			
Talks, signs, or gestures to others.			
Imitates others.			
Rolls/hands toy or ball to another without being asked.			
Retrieves objects for another without being asked.			
Offers to share objects/toys.			
Engages in make-believe play with others.			
Takes turns talking/listening.			
Cooperative			
Participates in small-group games.			
Sustains play in group of three or more for 5 min.			
Follows simple game rules.			
Understands stop/go.			
Understands safety zone, boundary line, base.			
Understands "It"/not "It."			
Understands game formations (circle, line, file, scattered).			
Plays games demanding one role (fleeing).			
Switches roles to achieve game goals: hide/seek, chase/flee, tag/dodge.			

T a b l e   1 8 . 5   **Words representing language concepts that can be acquired through movement lessons.**

Self	Space	Time	Force*	Flow
Body parts	**Directions**	**Speed**	**Force**	**Qualities**
Fingers	*Forward*	*Fast*	*Strong*	*Hyperactive*
Elbow	*Backward*	*Medium*	*Medium*	*Uncontrolled*
Shoulders	*Sideward*	*Slow*	*Weak*	*Free*
Knee	*Inside*	*Accelerating*	*Heavy*	*Abandoned*
Body surfaces	*Outside*	*Decelerating*	*Light*	*Exaggerated*
Front	*Up*	**Quantity**	**Qualities**	*Fluent*
Back	*Down*	*A lot (long)*	*Sudden, explosive*	*Inhibited*
Top	*Left*	*A little (short)*	*Sustained, smooth*	*Restrained*
Bottom	*Right*	*Variable*	**Creating force**	*Bound*
Inside	**Levels**	**Rhythm**	*Quick starts*	*Repressed*
Outside	*High*	*Pulse beats*	*Sustained, powerful*	*Tied up*
Body movements	*Medium*	*Accents*	*movements*	*Overcautious*
Bend/flex/curl	*Low*	*Rhythmic patterns*	*Static balances*	**Movement**
Straighten/extend	**Size/dimensions**	*Even*	**Absorbing force**	*Smooth, graceful*
Spread/abduct	*Large*	*Uneven*	*Sudden stops on balance*	*Rough, awkward*
Close/adduct	*Medium*	*Phrases*	*Gradual absorption,*	*Continuous*
Turn/rotate	*Small*	*Numbers*	*"give" as in catching*	*Staccato*
Circle	*Wide*	*Concepts*	**Imparting force**	
	Narrow	*Sequences*	*Rolling*	
	Pathways (floor or air)	*Processes*	*Bouncing*	
	Slanted		*Throwing*	
	Straight		*Kicking*	
	Curved		*Striking*	
	Zigzag			

*Some persons prefer the term *effort* or *weight.*

language presupposes integrity of memory, including the ability to remember sequences. Memory may be primarily auditory, visual, or proprioceptive, or a blending of all three.

Receptive language skills are dependent upon inner language, and vice versa. The following passage describes the interrelationship between the development of receptive language and inner language skills in Helen Keller at age 7, who was both deaf and blind:

> My teacher placed my hand under the spout. As the cool stream gushed over one hand, she spelled into the other the word water, first slowly, then rapidly. I stood still, my whole attention fixed upon the motions of her fingers. Suddenly, I felt a misty consciousness, as of something forgotten—a thrill of returning thought; and knew somehow the mystery of language was revealed to me. I knew then that "w-a-t-e-r" meant the wonderful cool something that was flowing over my hand. That living word awakened my soul, gave it light, hope, joy, set it free! There were barriers still, it is true, but barriers that could in time be swept away. I left the well-house eager to learn. Everything had a name, and each name gave birth to a new thought. (Keller, 1965, p. 14)

Until age 7, Helen Keller had neither inner language nor receptive language in the ordinary sense. The following passage, however, does show that inner language can develop without vision and audition if the child possesses sufficient intelligence to capitalize upon proprioceptive cues:

> I cannot recall what happened during the first months after my illness. I only know that I sat in my mother's lap or clung to her dress as she went about her household duties. My hands felt every object and observed every motion, and in this way, I learned to know many things. Soon, I felt the need of some communication with others and began to make crude signs. A shake of the head meant "No" and a nod, "Yes," a pull meant "Come" and a push, "Go." Was it bread that I wanted? Then I would imitate the acts of cutting the slices and buttering them. If I wanted my mother to make ice cream for dinner, I made the sign for working the freezer and shivered, indicating cold. (Keller, 1965, p. 14)

Children vary widely with respect to receptive language skills. The emphasis placed on *learning to follow directions* reveals that many teachers are not satisfied with the receptive language of their pupils. Physical educators should cooperate with classroom teachers in designing movement experiences that reinforce the meanings of words (see Table 18.5). Children should be taught the names of the things they can do, the pieces of apparatus and equipment used, and the games played.

Expressive Language

Expressive language can be verbal or nonverbal. It presupposes integrity of both receptive and inner language. The way a child speaks and writes reveals his or her memory of words, sequences, and syntactic structures. It also lends insight into the child's ability to discriminate between words and letters that sound and look alike. Nonverbal language includes sign, gesture, and facial expression. Young children with a disability often rely on nonverbal language. See Chapter 16 on adapted dance and dance therapy for more information on expressive language. Also see descriptions of movement programs designed to develop language (Connor-Kuntz & Dummer, 1996; Wessel & Zittel, 1995).

References

Aiello, B. (1988). The Kids on the Block and attitude change: A 10-year perspective. In H. E. Yuker (Ed.), *Attitudes toward persons with disabilities* (pp. 223–229). New York: Springer.

Block, M. E., & Davis, T. D. (1996). An activity-based approach to physical education for preschool children with disabilities. *Adapted Physical Activity Quarterly, 13*(3), 230–246.

Bricker, D., & Woods-Cripe, J. J. (1992). *An activity-based approach to early intervention.* Baltimore: Paul H. Brookes.

Connor-Kuntz, F., & Dummer, G. M. (1996). Teaching across the curriculum: Language-enriched physical education for preschool children. *Adapted Physical Activity Quarterly, 13*(3), 302–315.

Cowden, J. E. (1991). Critical components of the individualized family service plan. *Journal of Physical Education, Recreation and Dance, 62*(6), 38–40.

Cowden, J. E. (1997). *Pediatric adapted motor development and exercise.* Springfield, IL: Charles C Thomas.

Cowden, J. E., & Torrey, C. C. (1990). A comparison of isolate and social toys on play behaviors of handicapped preschoolers. *Adapted Physical Activity Quarterly, 7,* 170–182.

Cratty, B. J. (1990). Motor development of infants subject to maternal drug use: Current evidence and future research strategies. *Adapted Physical Activity Quarterly, 1,* 110–125.

deJong, C. G. A. (1990). The development of mobility in blind and multiply handicapped infants. In A. Vermeer (Ed.), *Motor development, adapted physical activity, and mental retardation* (pp. 56–66). Basel, Switzerland: Karger.

Dunn, L., McCartan, K., & Fugua, R. (1988). Young children with orthopedic handicaps: Self-knowledge about disability. *Exceptional Children, 55*(3), 249–252.

Eddy, J. (1982). *The music came from deep inside: Professional artists and severely handicapped children.* New York: McGraw-Hill.

Gallahue, D. L., & Ozmun, J. C. (1994). *Understanding motor development* (3rd ed.). Dubuque, IA: Brown & Benchmark.

Harter, S., & Pike, R. (1984). The pictorial scale of perceived competence and social acceptance for young children. *Child Development, 55,* 1969–1982.

Jenkins, J., Speltz, M., & Odom, S. (1985). Integrating normal and handicapped preschoolers: Effects on child development and social interaction. *Exceptional Children, 52*(1), 7–17.

Keller, H. (1965). *The story of my life.* New York: Airmont.

Kowalski, E., & Sherrill, C. (1992). Motor sequencing of learning disabled boys: Modeling and verbal rehearsal strategies. *Adapted Physical Activity Quarterly, 9*(3), 261–272.

Kugler, P., Kelso, J. A. S., & Turvey, M. (1982). On the control and coordination of naturally developing systems. In J. A. S. Kelso & J. E. Clark (Eds.). *The development of movement control and coordination* (pp. 7–78). New York: Wiley.

Linder, T. W. (1993a). *Transdisciplinary play-based assessment.* Baltimore: Paul H. Brookes.

Linder, T. W. (1993b). *Transdisciplinary play-based intervention.* Baltimore: Paul H. Brookes.

Loovis, E. M. (1985). Evaluation of toy preference and associated movement behaviors of preschool orthopedically handicapped children. *Adapted Physical Activity Quarterly, 2,* 117–126.

Sayers, L. K., Cowden, J. E., Newton, M., Warren, B., & Eason, B. (1996). Qualitative analysis of a pediatric strength intervention on the developmental stepping movements of infants with Down Syndrome. *Adapted Physical Activity Quarterly, 13*(3), 247–268.

Sherrill, C. (Ed.). (1979). *Creative arts for the severely handicapped* (2nd ed.). Springfield, IL: Charles C Thomas.

Sherrill, C., & McBride, H. (1984). An arts infusion intervention model for severely handicapped children. *Mental Retardation, 22*(6), 316–320.

Siller, J. (1984). Attitudes toward the physically disabled. In R. L. Jones (Ed.), *Attitudes and attitude change in special education: Theory and practice* (pp. 184–205). Reston, VA: Council for Exceptional Children.

Smith, L. B., & Thelen, E. (Eds.). (1993). *A dynamic systems approach to development: Applications.* Cambridge, MA: MIT Press.

Somervill, J., Cordoba, O., Abbott, R., & Brown, P. F. (1982). The origins of stigma: Reactions by male and female preschool children to a leg amputation. *American Corrective Therapy Journal, 36*(1), 14–17.

Staum, M. (1988). The effect of background music on the motor performance recall of preschool children. *Journal of Human Movement Studies, 15,* 27–35.

Sunderlin, A. (1988). Film festival: Sports and recreation videos and films, from aerobics to wilderness access. *Sports 'N Spokes, 14*(2), 51–57.

Tarr, S. J., & Pyfer, J. L. (1996). Physical and motor development of neonates/infants prenatally exposed to drugs in utero: A meta-analysis. *Adapted Physical Activity Quarterly, 13*(3), 269–287.

Teplin, S. W., Howard, J. A., & O'Connor, M. J. (1981). Self-concept of young children with cerebral palsy. *Developmental Medicine and Child Neurology, 23,* 730–738.

Ulrich, B. D., & Ulrich, D. A. (1995). Spontaneous leg movements of infants with Down Syndrome and nondisabled infants. *Child Development, 66,* 1844–1855.

Ulrich, B. D., Ulrich, D. A., & Collier, D. H. (1992). Alternating stepping patterns: Hidden abilities of 11-month-old infants with Down syndrome. *Developmental Medicine and Child Neurology, 34,* 233–239.

Ulrich, D. A. (1985). *The test of gross motor development.* Austin, TX: Pro•Ed.

Ulrich, D. A. (1995). Preschool adapted physical education. In J. P. Winnick (Ed.), *Adapted physical education and sport* (2nd ed., pp. 297–308). Champaign, IL: Human Kinetics.

Watkinson, E. J., & Wall, A. E. (1982). *The PREP play program: Play skill instruction for mentally handicapped children.* Ottawa: Canadian Association for Health, Physical Education, and Recreation.

Weinberg, N. (1978). Preschool children's perceptions of orthopedic disability. *Rehabilitation Counseling Bulletin, 21,* 183–189.

Wessel, J. A. (1980). *I CAN implementation guide for preprimary motor and play skills.* East Lansing: Michigan State University, Marketing Division, Instructional Media Center.

Wessel, J. A., & Zittel, L. L. (1995). *Smart Start: Preschool movement curriculum designed for children of all abilities.* Austin, TX: Pro•Ed.

White, R. W. (1959). Motivation reconsidered: The concept of competence. *Psychological Review, 66,* 297–333.

Wright, B. A. (1983). *Physical disability: A psychosocial approach* (2nd ed.). New York: Harper & Row.

Zittel, L. L. (1994). Gross motor assessment of preschool children with special needs: Instrument selection considerations. *Adapted Physical Activity Quarterly, 11,* 245–260.

Zittel, L. L., & McCubbin, J. A. (1996). Effect of an integrated physical education setting on motor performance of preschool children with developmental delays. *Adapted Physical Activity Quarterly, 13*(3), 316–333.

CHAPTER

19

Other Health Impaired Conditions

FIGURE 19.1 Students classified as *other health impaired* (OHI) generally look normal but have chronic or acute health problems that adversely affect their educational performance.

After you have studied this chapter, you should be able to do the following:

1. Define each of the conditions in Table 19.1, discuss causes and/or biochemical bases, and state symptoms, signs, and behaviors. Relate your discussion to persons you have known, seen on television or film, or read about.

2. Discuss the role of exercise, diet, and lifestyle in managing each condition and summarize principles/guidelines relevant to each.

3. Given any condition in Table 19.1, be able to write a physical education IEP. State age, gender, and other relevant information you used in developing the IEP. Include environmental variables to be altered.

4. Discuss the role of medication in managing OHI conditions and identify major drugs related to each. State side effects that affect exercise programming.

5. Identify and discuss contraindicated practices, activities, and environmental variables associated with OHI conditions.

6. Discuss prevention of OHI conditions. Describe some creative approaches to prevention that would be appropriate for different age groups.

Other health impairments (OHI) is an official U.S. Department of Education diagnostic category for limited strength, vitality, or alertness caused by chronic or acute health problems that adversely affect educational performance. In the lifespan approach to adapted physical activity, this definition is expanded to also include health problems that interfere with work productivity, leisure activities, and life satisfaction. **Chronic** refers to long duration, whereas **acute** means rapid onset, severe systems, and a short course. Asthma, for example, is a chronic condition that is managed by medication and healthy lifestyle. Occasionally, however, an acute episode (i.e., an asthma attack) may occur.

This chapter is an extension of Chapter 13, "Fitness and Healthy Lifestyle." Much of regular physical education is aimed toward either preventing or coping with OHI problems, especially those that pertain to weight and cardiorespiratory function. When regular physical education fails to instill the attitudes, beliefs, and habits needed for healthy lifestyle, adapted physical activity expertise and special programming are needed. People with physical and mental disabilities are at particular risk for OHI problems because of inactive lifestyles and stress related to societal barriers.

Common OHI Conditions

OHI conditions covered in this chapter are listed in Table 19.1. The incidence of these and other conditions is presented in Appendix A. Many persons cope with multiple OHI problems. Much of the time they simply do not feel good. This state of "not feeling good" affects initiative and morale. Aerobic fitness is a particular challenge, and many persons give up, exacerbating their conditions by developing negative feelings about themselves and physical activity, becoming increasingly sedentary, and gaining weight. Adapted physical activity services in school and community settings are needed to create support groups for working toward common goals (e.g., weight loss, improved breathing, a 12-min mile) and to teach ways that exercise can develop self-confidence and manage stress (see Figure 19.1). *These services should supplement rather than replace regular activity programs.*

Medication and Use of the *PDR*

Most serious OHI conditions are managed by drugs. Adherence to prescribed doses is essential to wellness, and physical educators must be able to discuss side effects and exercise

Table 19.1   OHI conditions covered in this chapter.

Condition	Page
1. Overweight/obesity syndrome	463
2. Cholesterol problems	467
3. Diabetes mellitus	467
4. Cardiovascular problems	471
Atherosclerosis	472
Heart attack	473
Stroke	473
Congestive heart disease	473
Conduction abnormalities	475
Chronotrophic incompetence	476
Sick sinus syndrome	476
Fibrillations and flutters	476
Tachycardias	476
Bradycardias	476
Heart block	476
Inflammation of the heart wall	477
Valve defects and heart murmurs	478
Rheumatic fever	478
Congenital heart defects	479
5. Hypertension	482
6. Asthma	485
7. Chronic obstructive pulmonary diseases	490
8. Bronchitis and emphysema	490
9. Cystic fibrosis	491
10. Hemophilia	492
11. Sickle-cell disease (anemia)	493
12. Anemia	493
13. Menstrual problems	493
14. Cancer	493
15. Kidney and urinary tract disorders	494
16. Convulsive disorders (epilepsy)	495
17. Environmental disorders (e.g., lead)	499
18. Tuberculosis	499
19. HIV/AIDS	500
20. Blood-borne hepatitis	502

indications and contraindications. The *Physician's Desk Reference (PDR),* which is revised annually, is the primary source of choice, but many reference books are available (e.g., Griffith, 1992; Long, 1992). Medications can be identified by family names (e.g., diuretics or thiazides), generic names (chlorothiazide), and trade or brand names (Diuril). Generally, generic names are needed to find drugs in reference books. For ease of reading, this and subsequent chapters primarily use family names. Following is a brief discussion of commonly used medications that affect exercise response.

Diuretics

Diuretics are used to manage obesity, heart disease, high blood pressure, and several other conditions. **Diuretics** are water pills that stimulate urination in order to rid the body of excess fluids and to reduce **edema** (swelling caused by a fluid accumulation). When exercisers take diuretics, professionals must allow frequent bathroom breaks and check periodically for dehydration. Diuretics, when combined with vigorous exercise and hot weather conditions, can cause adverse side effects like **hypovolemia** (excessive fluid loss) and **hypokalemia** (diminished blood volume, causing serious depletion of potassium), both of which are life-threatening conditions. Early danger signs are dizziness, weakness, and muscle cramps. These side effects can be prevented by drinking water and eating foods high in potassium (e.g., fresh fruits and vegetables). Persons taking diuretics should maintain regular fluid-intake levels.

Blood Pressure Drugs

Alpha- and beta-blocker drugs lower blood pressure and heart rates but are contraindicated in asthma and diabetes because of side effects (i.e., blockers depress functions needed to keep bronchial tubes open and to signal blood sugar changes associated with diabetes crises). Beta-blockers are frequently mentioned in exercise literature because they mask the intensity of physical activity and complicate heart rate monitoring. Hearts of persons taking beta-blockers do not respond normally to exercise; *the heart rate remains low,* giving the false impression that exercise effort is not maximum.

A common side effect of blood pressure medication is **hypotension** (dizziness or lightheadedness when changing from sitting to standing positions). Hypotension frequently causes falls and injuries in persons who are medically fragile. To minimize hypotension, teach slow pacing of position changes.

Corticosteroids for Severe Inflammation

The adrenocorticosteroids (usually called corticosteroids or steroids) mimic the hormones (glucocorticoids and mineralocorticoids) secreted by the cortex (outer covering) of the adrenal gland located above each kidney. These hormones are **systemic,** meaning that they influence the biochemistry of all body systems. Corticosteroids are typically used as a last resort, when other medications are not effective. Many persons with severe, chronic conditions that cause swelling, pain, and respiratory distress (e.g., arthritis and asthma) take corticosteroids. Cancer is also commonly treated by corticosteroids.

Even when taken only for short periods, steroids cause many side effects, like edema (excessive fluid retention), hyperactivity, increased appetite, insatiable hunger for sweets, fungus infections, and mood swings. Withdrawal results in depression, even when daily dosages are progressively decreased. Long-term prescription of the corticosteroids has such side effects as weight gain, growth retardation, diabetes, high blood pressure, and osteoporosis. Steroids are used when no other medication is effective, so persons must learn to accept and manage side effects.

Asthma Drugs

Most asthma drugs *dilate* (widen) the bronchial tubes in the lungs. An adverse side effect of these beta-2-adrenergic agonists is increased heart rate. This affects exercise prescription and requires careful study of baseline resting and exercise heart rates. Asthma drugs may be tablets or aerosols; many cause mild hyperactivity or generalized irritability.

Seizure Drugs

Drugs used in controlling seizures have side effects like poor reaction time, incoordination, attention problems, and drowsiness. Approximately 25 to 50% of people with cerebral palsy (CP) and 35% of people with severe mental retardation take seizure medication at some time during their lives. Side effects put people with these conditions at a considerable disadvantage, but many are able nonetheless to become excellent athletes.

Medication Guidelines

Most persons with chronic OHI must take medication every day at approximately the same time. Physicians prescribe medication because benefits outweigh adverse side effects. Physical activity professionals should follow these guidelines:

1. Ask for a written statement listing all medications individuals are taking and their side effects. Read about these medications, and then interview the individuals to determine their understanding of the drugs they take.

2. Ask individuals about exercise adaptations they may need, and seek to increase their awareness of drug/exercise interactions.

3. Remember that every person responds to medications differently, and responses vary from day to day. Discipline problems, mood swings, and undesirable activity levels often can be traced to medication.

Lifestyle and Risk Factors

Medication is not enough to effectively manage OHI problems. Lifestyle becomes more important when health is compromised. Physical activity professionals must emphasize good eating, sleeping, and exercise habits and promote environments and models that encourage maintenance of a healthy lifestyle. This includes zero tolerance of street drugs, tobacco, and unsafe sex practices. Today's health risks are so grave that adults must talk openly about previously taboo subjects and must set clear standards for ethical conduct. Coaches and exercise counselors often come to know all aspects of individuals' personal lives and thus have tremendous influence.

The U.S. government has revised its guidelines for weight according to age and height. In reading the weight range on the new chart, higher weights generally apply to men, who have more muscle and bone; lower weights apply to women.

Old (1985)			New (1990)		
Height Without Shoes	**Weight Without Clothes**		**Height Without Shoes**	**Weight Without Clothes**	
	Men (Pounds)	Women (Pounds)		19–34 Years	35 Years and Over
4′10″		92–121	5′	97–128	108–138
4′11″		95–124	5′1″	101–132	111–143
5′		98–127	5′2″	104–137	115–148
5′1″	105–134	101–130	5′3″	107–141	119–152
5′2″	108–137	104–134	5′4″	111–146	122–157
5′3″	111–141	107–138	5′5″	114–150	126–162
5′4″	114–145	110–142	5′6″	118–155	130–167
5′5″	117–149	114–146	5′7″	121–160	134–172
5′6″	121–154	118–150	5′8″	125–164	138–178
5′7″	125–159	122–154	5′9″	129–169	142–183
5′8″	129–163	126–159	5′10″	132–174	146–188
5′9″	133–167	130–164	5′11″	136–179	151–194
5′10″	137–172	134–169	6′	140–184	155–199
5′11″	141–177		6′1″	144–189	159–205
6′	145–182		6′2″	148–195	164–210
6′1″	149–187		6′3″	152–200	168–216
6′2″	153–192		6′4″	156–205	173–222
6′3″	157–197		6′5″	160–211	177–228
			6′6″	164–216	182–234

From a 1992 news release from the U.S. Departments of Agriculture and Health and Human Services.

OHI problems, like other kinds of disabilities, must be treated as family concerns. Families can be those of origin or of choice, but significant others should be identified and involved in all aspects of adapted physical activity.

This chapter begins with weight/obesity problems because they must be addressed first when persons make a commitment to fitness. Almost all of the other conditions listed in Table 19.1 are commonly complicated by overweight. The principles guiding exercise selection for people who are overweight are applicable to most OHI conditions.

Overweight/Obesity Syndrome

Definition of the overweight/obesity syndrome depends on assessment approach (see Chapter 13). Criteria for obesity, based on the use of skinfold calipers to determine percent body fat, are a percentage of body fat greater than 25% for males and greater than 30% for females. With height-weight tables, the traditional criterion for **overweight** is 10 to 20% above ideal weight for sex and age. The criterion for **obesity** is 20% above ideal weight. Persons over 50% of their ideal weight are considered **super obese**.

Ideal weight depends on sex, age, body type, ethnic or cultural expectations, athletic goals, and work demands. Governments issue guidelines for healthy weight, based on averages within the population (see Table 19.2). The 1990 standards of the U.S. Department of Health and Human Services,

for example, reflect research that older people can grow a little heavier without added health risks. The main concern is with fat distribution.

Importance of Fat Distribution

Fat distribution varies by age and sex. Infants and young children have a continuous layer of adipose tissue beneath the skin, often called baby fat. The amount is fairly small, 10 to 15%. As children age, the subcutaneous fat becomes thicker in some areas than others (e.g., triceps, abdomen, calf). These are the sites used in skinfold fat measurement. Hormones associated with the adolescent growth spurt cause thickening of fat deposits in different areas for females than males. In general, females have larger fat cells in the buttocks and hips, whereas the fat of males centers around the upper body. These fat distributions are popularly referred to as apple and pear shapes. *The apple shape, more common in males than in females, carries more health risk.* In general, hormones and genes influence fat distribution more than diet and exercise.

Incidence and Prevalence

Obesity affects 5 to 25% of school-age children and youth, depending on criteria used, and an even higher percentage of adults. Nearly 34 million Americans weigh 20% or more above their ideal weight, and about one third of these are severely obese. With the 10 to 20% criterion, 60 to 70 million adults and 10 to 12 million teenagers are overweight.

Causes of Obesity

Causes of obesity are endocrine, medication-induced, or nonendocrine. Typically, the physician rules out endocrine and medication-induced etiologies before delving into other possible causes.

Endocrine obesity is caused by malfunction of glands that secrete hormones. In the resulting syndromes, the fat is typically concentrated about the breasts, hips, and abdomen, and the face is moon-shaped and ruddy. **Cushing's syndrome,** or cushingoid obesity, the most common form, is recognized by (a) **hirsutism,** or excessive hair growth, (b) menstrual irregularities, (c) a buffalo hump (kyphosis condition) that progressively worsens because of related osteoporosis (bone degeneration), and (d) diabetes. Overall, less than 10% of obesity is caused by endocrine disorders.

Medication-induced obesity is caused by the corticosteroids and has the same appearance as Cushing's syndrome. The most common of these corticosteroids—prednisone and cortisone—are used to reduce inflammation and manage such severe chronic conditions as arthritis, asthma, cancer, leukemia, and kidney disease.

Nonendocrine obesity, the most common condition, is caused by interacting hereditary and environmental factors that result in an imbalance between caloric intake and output. Studies show that, when parents have normal weight, only 8 to 9% of the children are obese. When one parent is obese, 40% of the children are likewise. When both parents are obese, this percentage doubles. Eating and activity patterns learned early in childhood and passed down from generation to generation seem to be as much a factor as genetic predisposition.

Long-Term Management of Obesity

Long-term management of obesity has been likened to that of alcoholism and drug abuse. The problem can be solved temporarily, but never cured. Of the many persons who diet, only 10% achieve lifetime weight control. Clearly, new strategies must be tried, with physical educators playing a leading role in cooperative home-school-community programming. Lifestyle prescriptions must focus jointly on food intake and exercise output, and self-responsibility for monitoring behaviors and seeking help must be taught.

ACSM Guidelines

Three guidelines structure program planning (ACSM, 1995):

1. Maintain a *minimum* intake of about 1,200 calories a day.
2. Engage in a daily exercise program that expends 300 or more calories a day. For weight-loss goals, exercise of long duration/low intensity is generally best.
3. Lose no more than 2.2 lb (1 kg) a week. Gradual weight loss prevents metabolic imbalances.

Formula for Estimating Calories

The number of calories to be targeted each day depends on sex, age, height, weight, and exercise. New formulae allow more-accurate prediction of individual needs.

> **For Females:** 655.1 (a constant) + (9.6 × your weight in kilograms) + (1.8 × your height in centimeters) – (4.7 × your age in years) × (your exercise code)
>
> **For Males:** 66.5 (a constant) + (13.8 × your weight in kilograms) + (5 × your height in centimeters) – (6.8 × your age in years) × (your exercise code)

The exercise codes to be entered into the formula are as follows:

1.2—confined to bed

1.3—sedentary active

1.4—moderately active, exercises 3 to 4 times a week

1.6—very active, exercises more than 4 times a week

1.7—extremely active, exercises more than 6 times a week for more than 1 hr duration

Following is a sample calculation for a female, age 62, 144 lb, 5 ft tall, with a 1.4 exercise code:

> **Weight** = 144 lb ÷ 2.2 = 65.45 kg
>
> **Height** = 60 in. × 2.5 = 150 cm
>
> **Formula:** 655.1 + (9.6 × 65.45) + (1.8 × 150) – (4.7 × 62) = 1262 × 1.4 = 1767

To lose weight, this woman must consume fewer than 1,767 calories a day.

Lifestyle Prescription and Caloric Balance

The *FIT* acronym introduced in Chapter 13 on fitness can be modified to include both exercise and eating:

F Frequency (Three to five small meals a day at set times and places with no snacking in between; daily exercise)

I Intensity (1,200 cal distributed among the four food groups; exercise intensity great enough to expend 300 cal a day)

T Time (Each meal of long duration, with food eaten slowly, chewed well, and supplemented with pleasant conversation; exercise duration long enough to expend 300 cal a day)

The **principle of caloric balance** is extremely important in lifestyle prescription. This principle specifies that, for weight loss to occur, exercise expenditure calories must exceed food intake calories.

Principles Guiding Food Selection

The easiest way to control caloric intake is to use a system of food servings or exchanges (see Table 19.3). Several principles guide food selection:

1. **Four Foods Principle.** Eating right requires a knowledge of the four food groups and the amounts that constitute servings. To lose weight, reduce the size or number of portions but keep all meals approximately the same size.

Table 19.3   Four food groups to guide daily intake (1,300 to 1,650 calories).

Food Group	Major Nutrient Value	Number of Daily Servings	Calorie Average Each Serving
Bread/Cereal/Grain Group 1 slice or equivalent ½ cup cooked cereal, pasta, rice ¾ cup cold cereal	Carbohydrates, iron, thiamine, riboflavin, niacin	4–6	100
Fruit and Vegetable Group 1 medium size, raw 1 cup, raw ½ cup cooked or juice	Carbohydrates, iron, calcium, vitamins A, C, potassium	4–5	75
Milk and Dairy Products 8 oz milk or yogurt 1 oz cheese ½ cup cottage cheese ½ cup ice cream	Protein, fats, calcium, vitamin A, riboflavin	2	150
Meat or Protein Equivalent 2 oz lean meat 2 eggs, boiled ½ cup cottage cheese 1 cup cooked beans, peas 4 tbsp peanut butter 1 tbsp salad dressing	Protein, fats, iron, calcium, thiamin, riboflavin, potassium	2	150

Note: Children and adolescents need twice the amount in the milk and dairy product group; otherwise, recommended servings are the same. Liquid oils and margarine should be substituted for meat fats and butter in cooking.

Inclusion of these food groups in every meal assures that the six nutrients necessary for wellness are ingested. *These nutrients are carbohydrates, proteins, fats, minerals, vitamins, and water.* Only the first three generate calories.

2. **The 2:1 Food Group Principle.** This principle states that the number of servings in the bread/cereal/grain group and the fruit and vegetable group should be twice that of the milk/dairy product group and the meat or protein equivalent group. This ratio assures that the correct proportions of nutrients are eaten. The recommended daily dietary intake is 55% or more carbohydrates, 30% or less fats, and 15% or less proteins. In Table 19.3, the first two food groups provide carbohydrates, whereas the last two are the source of proteins and fats.

3. **Dietary Fat Reduction Principle.** Reducing dietary fat is especially important for weight loss. This is because 1 gram of fat is 9 cal whereas 1 gram of carbohydrates or protein is only 4.5 cal. Major sources of fat are mayonnaise, salad dressing, cooking oils, meat fats, butter, and cheese. Reducing fats also helps to control blood pressure and cholesterol problems.

Principles Guiding Exercise Selection

1. **Non-Weight-Bearing Activities Principle.** Non-weight-bearing activities minimize stress on joints and feet. Exercise modalities of choice for most obese persons are water-based exercises, cycling, and mat activities in lying and sitting positions (Sheldahl, 1986). Waterbased exercises include swimming, treading water, locomotor and stationary activities in waist-deep water, and pedaling a cycle ergometer placed in the water so that only the head and shoulders are out. Obese persons can typically perform for longer durations at higher intensities in water than on land. Heart response to exercise in water is different from that on land. Therefore, if exercise prescription is based on heart rate, assess target intensity range in the water.

2. **Walking for Long Duration Principle.** When walking is the preferred exercise, it should be done only on a level surface to minimize joint stresses. A temperature-controlled environment is recommended to keep perspiration under control. Long-duration, low-intensity walking causes weight loss more effectively than traditional aerobic exercise. *Research shows that most obese persons do not lose weight until walking time is at least 30 min a day. Two hours daily is recommended* (Sheldahl, 1986). Remember that heavy persons spend more energy per minute than light persons. An exercise leader of normal weight should perhaps wear waist or ankle weights or carry a backpack to get the feel of exertion and learn to empathize.

3. **Exercise for Enjoyment Principle.** Alternate exercise modalities and use stimulating music to reduce boredom and enhance enjoyment. Use Table 13.4 on page 355 in the fitness chapter to determine amount of exercise needed to burn 300 cal. Adapt this table to individual weights as explained in the footnote. Regardless of modality chosen, remember that the emphasis is on attitude change and on developing the habit of daily exercise.

4. **Partner and Support Group Principle.** One day of not exercising for an obese person is like falling off the wagon for an alcoholic. Teach persons how to ask for help with motivation. A buddy system generally helps. If this is not possible, create a telephone help-line that persons can call for assistance. Emphasize praising and reinforcing each other.

5. **Time Management Counseling Principle.** Help persons who are obese with time management. Weight loss is not typically achieved in a physical education or exercise class because obese persons lack the fitness to exercise at high intensity. Additional time must be committed. Teach and reinforce realistic expectations. If time cannot be found, the individual will have to settle for losing fewer pounds each week.

6. **Teach Exercise Fallacies Principle.** Teach that spot reduction is an exercise fallacy. Fat distribution depends on genetic code. Exercise may decrease the circumference of a body part by firming up the muscle, but number of fat cells remains constant. The size of fat cells is reduced only when overall energy expenditure is greater than food intake. Fat-cell size reduction seems to follow a pattern from top to bottom. Most persons notice weight loss in the face and neck first.

Implications for Physical Education

The most successful weight reduction programs are cooperative school/community endeavors that involve the entire family. Programs should be engaged in voluntarily and supported by sympathetic counseling. The approach must be nonthreatening and nonchastising. Fat persons often have emotional problems that perpetuate habits of overeating. Many psychologists believe that eating is a form of oral gratification to which persons unconsciously regress when they feel unloved or insecure. Such persons tend to nibble continuously, not because they are hungry, but to meet hidden needs and drives.

Persons must be reassured that they are loved and accepted. The self, however, is not easily separated from the body. Criticism of excessive body weight thus is often internalized as criticism of self. Many obese persons have built up elaborate defense mechanisms to preserve ego strength. Do not assume that they will be receptive to offers to help with weight loss or that they will admit openly to dissatisfaction with their bodies.

The well-proportioned physical educator often does not realize how unpleasant vigorous exercise can be for obese persons. Realistic program planning results from a consideration of the physical characteristics of obesity:

1. **Distended abdomen.** This results in anatomical differences in the position of the stomach and in the length of the intestinal tract, thereby affecting vital processes. It also creates excessive pressure on the diaphragm, which leads to difficulty in breathing and the consequent accumulation of carbon dioxide, which helps to explain patterns of drowsiness. The distended abdomen makes forward bending exercises difficult or impossible.

2. **Mobility of rolls of fat.** The bobbing up and down of breasts, abdomen, and other areas where excessive fat is deposited is uncomfortable and often painful during locomotor activities.

3. **Excessive perspiration.** Layers of fat serve as insulation, and the obese person more quickly becomes hot and sweaty than the nonobese.

4. **Galling between the thighs and other skin areas that rub together.** After perspiration begins, continued locomotion causes painful galling or chafing somewhat similar to an abrasion. Such areas heal slowly because of continuous irritation and sometimes become inflamed.

5. **Postural faults.** Obesity makes individuals vulnerable to knock-knees, pronation, flat-foot, sagging abdomen, drooped shoulders, and round back. These postural deviations all affect mechanical efficiency in even simple locomotor activities.

6. **Skeletal immaturity.** The growth centers in the long bones of obese adolescents are particularly susceptible to injury, either from cumulative daily gravitational stress or sudden traumas from such strenuous or heavy activities as contact sports, weight lifting, and pyramid building.

7. **Edema.** Obesity seems to promote fluid retention. Ankles, breasts, and wrists swell, particularly during the menstrual period. Diuretics are often prescribed.

8. **Broad base in locomotor activities.** The combination of knock-knees, tendency toward galling between thighs, and pronation results in a slow, awkward gait with feet often shoulder-width apart.

9. **Fear of falling.** Added weight makes falling from heights both painful and dangerous (see Figure 19.2).

10. **Excessive buoyancy in water.** The inability to keep most of the body submerged makes the mastery of standard swimming strokes difficult.

The need for socialization through sports and games is the same for obese students as for others. Walking and exercising done in conjunction with a special weight reduction program should not substitute for physical education activities with peers, even though participation may be limited. Others must learn to accept the obese person just as they would a person with a missing limb. Allow persons with weight problems privacy in dressing and showering if requested. Standard gymnasium clothes may be impossible to find, and long pants may be more appropriate than shorts.

The heavier a person is, the more important it is that certain activities be avoided. These activities include tasks that involve lifting his or her own weight, such as chinning and rope climbing, and those that entail lifting external weights, such as weight training, serving as the base of a pyramid, and partner tumbling stunts. The sympathetic teacher can devise many adaptations to draw the student into the group and to foster the development of favorable attitudes toward fitness.

The use of successive contracts, specifying specific goals and rewards after the loss of each 5 or 10 lb, is an effective motivational technique in weight reduction. The student is free at all times to revise the contract to allow more food and less exercise, but few take advantage of this option. Group contracts, in which several persons pledge weight losses, are particularly effective.

FIGURE 19.2 Obesity, when classified as either an *other health impaired* condition or an *orthopedic impairment,* is eligible for special education funding. Such children often need adapted physical activity more than students who are mentally retarded, blind, or deaf.

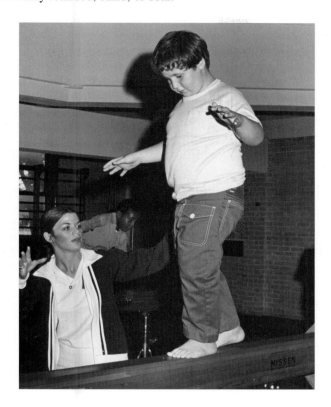

Cholesterol Problems

Total blood cholesterol levels above 180 milligrams per deciliter (mg/dl) signal borderline or high-risk status for high blood pressure and heart disease. High cholesterol is caused by (a) genetic factors, causing the liver to produce excessive amounts, (b) eating too many animal fats, or (c) a combination. Foods containing the most cholesterol (egg yolk, liver, brain, whole milk, butter, cheese, red meats) should be avoided. Dietary cholesterol intake should be less than 300 mg a day for the average person and reduced further, as needed, by persons with cholesterol problems.

Obesity is associated with high cholesterol, so a concurrent treatment is daily long-duration/low-intensity exercise to lose weight. Blood testing provides separate measures for three components of cholesterol: (a) low-density-lipoprotein cholesterol (LDL-C), (b) very-low-density-lipoprotein cholesterol (VLDL-C), and (c) high-density-lipoprotein cholesterol (HDL-C). The first two of these are bad, and the third is good. The term *lipoprotein* reminds us that fats are insoluble in water and must combine with proteins or some other substance to travel through body fluids.

LDL-C and VLDL-C are the bad components of cholesterol. LDL-C is the worst because the excess amounts attach themselves to artery walls, build up plaque, and clog passageways. LDL-C levels above 130 are borderline or risk. VLDL-C is the substance used by the liver to manufacture and transport LDL-C, so its bad effects are indirect. To remember whether LDL-C or HDL-C is bad, it helps to think: L*ousy,* L*ethargic,* L*azy* L*iving is* L*inked with* L*DL-C that* L*ikes to attach to artery walls.* LDL-C can be lowered in most persons by weight loss. However, 75% of the body's cholesterol is manufactured by the liver, and only 25% comes from food. Genes and cholesterol problems appear to be strongly linked.

HDL-C, the good cholesterol, draws fats away from artery walls, serving to counterbalance LDL-C activity. The higher the HDL-C, the better. Aerobic exercise raises HDL-C activity. The ratio between total cholesterol (TC) and HDL-C should be about 3.5. Most blood tests give this information.

Medication can lower cholesterol when caloric balance, weight loss, and exercise are not effective. Common medications are colestipol (Colestid), gembibrozil (Lopid), lovastatin (Melacor), and niacin (also called vitamin B_3 or nicotinic acid). Each has minor side effects that do not affect exercising. Illustrative side effects are constipation, increases in blood sugar, reduced absorption of vitamins, and interference with fat absorption. Certain foods, most notably oat bran, are used also but are controversial.

Diabetes Mellitus: Major Metabolic Disorder

Diabetes (meaning "passing through") is a general term for conditions characterized by excessive urination. The most common is diabetes mellitus, which derives its name from high sugar (glucose) content in the blood and urine. In common usage, diabetes mellitus is called, simply, diabetes. This condition is a disorder of carbohydrate, protein, and fat metabolism that affects vital functions, especially the conversion of foods into energy. The cause is unknown.

Diabetes is a high-incidence condition that affects from 2 to 4% of the population. Infants have a one in five chance of becoming diabetic. At least 1 of every 600 school-age children has diabetes. According to the American Diabetes Association, for every 10,000 persons, there will be 1 with diabetes under age 20, 10 between ages 20 and 50, 100 between ages 50 and 60, and 1,000 over age 60. Diabetes ranks among the leading 10 causes of death for all age groups over 14 years.

Diabetes increases the risk of blindness, coronary heart disease, amputations, and kidney and urinary conditions. Within 10 years of onset, 50% have pathological changes in the retina of the eye, called diabetic retinopathy. Between the ages of 20 and 65, diabetes is the leading cause of blindness. Diabetes is a contributing factor in 50% of all heart attacks and 75% of all strokes (Duda, 1985).

Two Types of Diabetes

Type I diabetes is insulin-dependent diabetes mellitus (IDDM) or juvenile-onset diabetes (JOD). This condition has the same incidence for males and females. Its onset is usually before age 25, and the condition is serious because the pancreatic beta cells are capable of producing little or no insulin.

Only about 10% of diabetes is Type I. Rapid weight loss, frequent urination, drowsiness, and fatigue are the classic symptoms. Type I is managed by daily insulin injections, careful monitoring of glucose, and disciplined balancing of food intake and exercise. Type I cannot be cured; it is a lifelong condition. However, research indicates that individuals with Type I

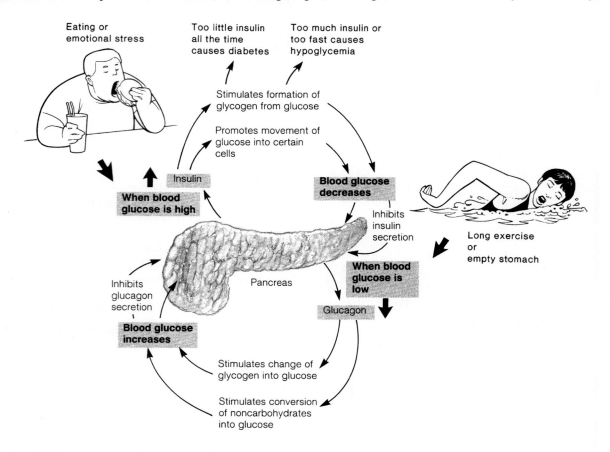

have fitness and motor profiles similar to those of their nondiabetic peers (Kertzer, Croce, Hinkle, & Janson-Sand, 1994).

Type II diabetes, which occurs mainly in overweight adults, is called non-insulin-dependent diabetes mellitus (NIDDM). More women have Type II diabetes than men. Diagnostic symptoms are the same as Type I except there is no rapid weight loss. Type II may be treated with insulin, but usually the emphasis is on diet and exercise. Often, when weight is lost and regular physical activity becomes a part of leisure, diabetic symptoms disappear. When Type II cannot be managed by diet and exercise, sulfonylurea therapy (oral tablets) is often used.

Role of Glucose and Glycogen

Glucose is a simple sugar that, through carbohydrate metabolism, is converted either to (a) cellular energy, (b) glycogen, or (c) fat. Desired concentration of glucose in the blood is 80–120 mg/dl (milligrams per deciliter). The glucose level rises slightly after meals and falls as the stomach becomes empty. The level also falls during aerobic exercise, which enhances cellular glucose intake.

Glycogen is a converted form of glucose that is stored in liver and muscle cells. When blood glucose is high, it is converted into glycogen. When blood glucose is low, glycogen is changed back to glucose.

Hormones: Insulin and Glucagon

Figure 19.3 shows how the two pancreatic hormones (insulin and glucagon) function together to maintain a relatively stable blood glucose level. These hormones are secreted by different kinds of pancreatic cells and have opposite functions. **Insulin,** secreted by beta cells, prevents blood glucose from rising too high and is most active during full stomach and after emotional stress conditions. **Glucagon,** secreted by alpha cells, prevents blood glucose from sinking too low and is most active during empty stomach and exercise conditions. Diabetes occurs when this cyclical action is inefficient. One of the first signs is frequent urination, a reaction of the kidneys to the stress of having to extract glucose from the blood.

Protein and Fat Metabolism

When glucose is not properly absorbed, cells begin to starve, causing the body to use protein as an alternative energy source. This results in protein deficiency, which is manifested by skin problems, slow healing, and infections that sometimes lead to amputations. The body also uses its stored fat to meet energy demands. In Type I diabetes, weight is lost. The person feels hungry all the time, eats more and more with no weight gain, and begins to complain of tiredness and weakness. In Type II diabetes, persons typically remain overweight because their condition is directly related to low energy and lack of exercise.

T a b l e   1 9 . 4   Information about diabetic reactions that can become crisis situations.

Focal Points	Hyperglycemia and Ketoacidosis	Hypoglycemia: An Insulin Reaction
Situation	*Unmanaged Diabetes* *Crisis Response to Stress, Infection*	*Reaction to Delayed Food,* *Insufficient Food*
Imbalance	Low insulin, high glucose	High insulin, low glucose
Onset	Within hours	Within minutes
Behavior	Lethargic to drowsy	Nervous, restless, excited, argumentative
	Sitting, lying	Moving about
	Weak, tired all day	Sudden weakness, fainting
Symptoms, signs	Excessive urination	Normal urination
	Excessive thirst, hunger	Thirst, hunger varies
	Abdominal pain	Headache
	Dry skin	Lots of perspiration
	Weak pulse	Rapid heartbeat, palpitations
	Deep, labored breathing	Normal to shallow, rapid breathing
Treatment	Insulin shot	Glucose tabs, candy, juice
	If severe, hospitalization	Glucagon shot
If no treatment	Coma, death	Coma, death

Ketone Bodies and Ketosis

Ketone bodies are the waste products that result from fat metabolism. They accumulate in the blood and urine and rely on the kidneys for disposal. When the kidneys cannot handle this extra load, the intensified spillover of ketone bodies into the blood causes *ketosis*.

Ketosis and **ketoacidosis** are imbalances between the body's acids and alkalites caused by excess ketone bodies. **Ketosis,** which results from high-fat diets as well as diabetes, affects the body in many ways: (a) muscle cramps during exercise, (b) decreased ability to fight infections, and (c) increased loss of electrolytes (sodium, potassium, calcium, and magnesium) through excess urination. As the resulting electrolyte imbalance becomes more pronounced, *ketoacidosis* ensues. **Ketoacidosis** (also called hyperglycemia) progresses from lethargy to drowsiness to diabetic coma (see Table 19.4 for signs). Immediate medical attention is required. Any condition that raises ketone levels increases the risk of ketoacidosis. Among these are (a) infection or illness; (b) diarrhea, vomiting, and stomach upsets; (c) overeating or excessive alcoholic intake; (d) emotional stress; and (e) failure to take enough insulin to offset exercise demands.

Whenever blood glucose tests show that glucose has risen to 300 mg/dl, urine should be checked for ketone bodies. A drop of urine is placed on an acetone tablet (or equivalent), and the color change caused by the presence of ketone bodies is compared against a color chart supplied with the tablets. When ketone bodies are present, adjustments are made in insulin, food intake, and diet. Most physicians want to be contacted immediately when ketones are found in the urine (Berg, 1986).

Insulin Reaction (Hypoglycemia)

Table 19.4 shows that the opposite condition of hyperglycemia/ketoacidosis is hypoglycemia. Of the two conditions, hypoglycemia is the more common. It is the reaction that persons continuously work to avoid as they carefully monitor blood glucose and balance food intake with exercise. The movie *Steel Magnolias* showed a hypoglycemic attack. The behaviors and symptoms are listed in Table 19.4. Not all persons manifest all of these, and attacks vary.

Hypoglycemic reactions are most likely to occur before meals and during strenuous exercise. Many of the behaviors, symptoms, and signs are normal outcomes of exercise (excitement, perspiration, rapid heartbeat). Physical educators and coaches must monitor these especially carefully during the hour before lunch and dinner. Despite good management, everyone with diabetes has an occasional hypoglycemic episode. The following are some accounts.

Bill Talbert, who has had diabetes since age 10, tells of having an insulin reaction during a finals tennis match with Pancho Gonzalez, then the amateur champion:

> I took the first set from the fiery Californian but lost the next two. In the fourth set, my game collapsed completely as I double-faulted, sprayed shots wildly out of court, and stumbled about. My old doubles partner, Gar Mulloy, rushed out on the court after I had lost three games in succession to Pancho.
>
> "Drink this, Willie," Gar commanded. He put a glass of sugared water into my hand, and I downed it greedily. It was the answer. Gar had realized that I was losing control of my functions and going into insulin reaction through rapid burning of sugar. In a reversal of form that baffled Pancho and the gallery, I took twelve of the next fourteen games to win the match and the Southampton trophy. (Talbert, 1971, p. 27)

Another description of an insulin reaction comes from the parents of a 6-year-old boy:

> I found him sobbing on the edge of his bed at five in the morning. I thought he was having a nightmare. He couldn't tell me what was wrong. He lay looking at his hands like someone on an LSD trip finding minuscule meanings in the texture of his skin. Then I

noticed that he was unsteady when he went for a drink of water, and I knew. It was insulin reaction.

We were frantic—preparing orange juice, jelly on bread, cookies, ice cream—but he cried hysterically and pushed away the food. We tried to force him; he fell and bumped his head. We panicked. We felt the insulin reaction was too far gone. We injected glucagon—a hormone that rapidly raises the blood sugar level.

In a few minutes, his head was clear, and he began to eat some of the sweets. But none of us was ever the same again. (Brandt, 1973, p. 36)

Monitoring of Glucose

Glucose levels should be checked several times each day. Target blood glucose levels are 60–130 mg/dl before meals, 140–180 mg/dl 1 hr after meals, 120–150 mg/dl 2 hr after meals, and 80–120 mg/dl at other times (Berg, 1986). If glucose is below target level, a carbohydrate snack is eaten. If it is above, additional insulin or sulfonylurea is taken. *Values above 240 mg/dl contraindicate aerobic exercise, and values above 300 mg/dl contraindicate all kinds of exercise.*

Glucose levels are determined by either blood or urine tests. Today, most persons use a pen-size, battery-operated device called a *glucometer.* A drop of capillary blood is obtained by pricking the side of a fingertip. The blood is placed on a paper strip that is inserted into the glucometer, which gives a precise electronic readout. This is far more accurate than the urine test, in which specially treated paper is dipped in urine and then evaluated for color change.

Management of Diabetes

Good diabetic control is based on proper diet, exercise, and insulin. A change in any one of these necessitates adjustment in the others. All persons with Type I take daily insulin injections and must acquire knowledge about insulin use and reactions that may occur if insulin dosage is miscalculated. Type II management is not as complicated. Therefore, this section focuses primarily on Type I.

Multiple Daily Insulin Shots

Insulin shots are subcutaneous—that is, under the skin but above muscle tissue. Children are taught to administer their own shots at an early age. Common injection sites are buttocks, upper arms, outer sides of thighs, and lower part of the abdomen. The injection site should be changed frequently to minimize tissue breakdown. Adjusting the injection site according to anticipated activity is also important. When the exercise is primarily lower limb, as in track, insulin should be injected into the arm. When both upper and lower extremities are involved, the preferred injection site is the abdomen.

Types of insulin vary with respect to time elapse before peak effect (2–20 hr) and duration of effect (6–36 hr). Rapid-acting insulins begin to work in about ½ hr, although peak effect is at 2 hr. Most persons take several injections daily that are mixtures of rapid- and intermediate-acting types and provide overlapping protection.

Insulin is injected before meals, with the largest dose taken before breakfast. It may not be needed before all meals. Persons learn to adjust dosages when corrective measures are needed because of unplanned changes in eating and exercising. The major principle followed for both meals and exercise, however, is consistency in time of day, duration, and amount.

Illness, infection, and emotional stress may make diabetes worse and require extra insulin injections. Medications taken for other conditions also affect insulin dosage. Among those that increase blood glucose are diuretics (water pills that promote loss of fluids), prednisone (anti-inflammatory corticosteroid medication), beta-blockers (used to manage heart and blood pressure conditions), and decongestants (for colds and sinus infections). Birth control pills inhibit insulin action and thus indirectly raise blood glucose.

Diet

Persons with diabetes typically know a lot about diet but may need support and companionship in eating correctly. The following guidelines should be emphasized:

1. Follow the consistency principle: Eat meals at the same time every day and exercise likewise.
2. Eat several small meals (about five) instead of three big ones.
3. Keep caloric intake about the same from meal to meal and day to day.
4. Identify foods that cause rapid glucose rise (have high glycemic index) and avoid them.
5. Emphasize fibers and starches (complex carbohydrates).
6. Avoid food and liquid intake when feeling nervous or anxious.
7. Balance food intake with exercise.
8. Keep glucose tablets, hard candy, or fruit juice available in case low glucose precipitates an insulin reaction.
9. Eat a carbohydrate snack about every 30 min during heavy, prolonged exercise.
10. Coordinate time and amount of food intake with exercise.

Exercise

Regular exercise is extremely important in diabetes management and may be prescribed just like medication. The prescription is typically what is good for everyone: aerobic exercise at least three times a week on alternate days, with each session lasting 45–60 min. The intensity and duration depend on initial level of fitness. Nonexercisers begin with progressive distance and speed walking programs to start attitude and habit changes. Leisure counseling helps persons to discover what is fun for them and to learn new sports (see Figure 19.4).

Blood glucose is not affected the same way by all types of exercise. Aerobic exercise lowers blood glucose and is the activity of choice if the glucose level is under 240 mg/dl. When blood glucose goes above this safety criterion, the opposite is true, and aerobics are contraindicated. Anaerobic exercises like push-ups and weight lifting do not lower glucose and should be used in moderation. They are important for strength development, but a person with diabetes should not select weight lifting as a major sport.

FIGURE 19.4 Dr. Bruce Ogilvie, the father of sport psychology, confers with an athlete who is blind. Many persons who are blind also have diabetes and need lifelong leisure and fitness counseling.

Persons with diabetes typically utilize protein and fat for energy during exercise more extensively then nondiabetics (Berg, 1986). Extra protein and carbohydrates should be eaten 15 to 30 min before exercise when planned intensity exceeds 300 cal an hour. During exercise of this intensity or greater, carbohydrate snacks are recommended every 30 min. Persons with diabetes often lose weight by exercise more quickly than nondiabetic peers.

If blood sugar is above 300 mg/dl or ketone bodies are in the urine, exercise is contraindicated. Other conditions that indicate exercise should be stopped or not initiated include (a) infection anywhere in the body, (b) high resting blood pressure, (c) severe pain in calf muscles, and (d) signs of hypoglycemia. These are all temporary problems. As soon as they are resolved, exercise programs should be resumed. For advanced reading on contraindications, see Coram and Mangum (1986).

On the day after strenuous exercise, persons with diabetes may need to decrease insulin and eat more because of a tendency toward low blood glucose. This is because muscle and liver glycogen have been depleted, and several hours are required to build up normal storage levels.

Implications for Physical Education

Emphasis should be on students with diabetes developing healthy attitudes toward exercise and body care. Students need models who have been excellent athletes despite diabetes.

Recommendations for teaching follow:

1. Ask the school nurse or appropriate person for the names of all students with diabetes and keep information readily accessible on emergency protocol, type of diabetes and medication, and special diet and snack needs. This is especially important for after-school practices and trips.
2. Meet with the school counselor or appropriate person and arrange to have students with diabetes scheduled for physical education after breakfast or lunch. Explain the importance of not exercising when blood glucose is low.
3. Create a prearranged signal that students with diabetes can use to call for a substitute or to be excused from class to respond to warning signs (i.e., to eat something or to monitor glucose because of feeling funny).
4. Provide breaks for fluid every 15 min during strenuous activity and give special attention to dehydration in hot weather.
5. Insist that students with diabetes protect themselves against sunburn, falls, blows, and the like that damage skin. This includes avoiding contact sports like boxing and football (Coram & Mangum, 1986).
6. Pay extra attention to clean, dry socks and proper shoes. Athlete's foot, blisters, and corns can become major problems for students with diabetes.
7. Treat students with diabetes with dignity and expect them to have glucose tablets, candy, or juice on hand at all times, in case of reactions. Keep a backup supply in case a student forgets. Remember that diet soda does not have enough glucose to work.
8. Do not give untrained persons with diabetes physical fitness tests that are concentrated in short time periods (Coram & Mangum, 1986). Evaluate fitness over several sessions in which duration and intensity are gradually increased.
9. Teach students with diabetes to exercise with partners who understand diabetes. Pairing persons with diabetes with those who want to lose weight is a good idea because of common interest in food and exercise.
10. Be understanding of mood swings, good and bad days, and behaviors associated with insulin reaction. Let students talk out embarrassment, frustrations, and concerns.

Cardiovascular Problems

The two causes of cardiovascular disease are acquired and congenital. *Acquired conditions,* the number one cause of death in persons aged 25 and over, primarily affect the arteries that supply oxygen to the heart and brain. In contrast, *congenital conditions* are typically defects in the structure of the heart walls and valves.

Approximately 10% of the world's population has acquired cardiovascular disease. This is typically diagnosed after age 50 or 60, but pathology begins in youth (see risk factors in Table 19.5). By age 60, one out of every five American males has coronary artery disease (CAD), the most common disorder (see Figure 19.5). Women also have CAD, but the prevalence is about six times greater in males than females.

Table 19.5   Risk factors in cardiovascular disease.

Factors That Can Be Altered

Hypertension (high blood pressure)
Elevated low-density-lipoprotein cholesterol (LDL-C) and
   triglycerides
Tobacco
Diet
Physical inactivity
Body fatness
Diabetes
Emotional stress

Factors That Cannot Be Altered

Heredity
Age
Sex
Race

FIGURE 19.5   The coronary arteries branch downward from the aorta and encircle the heart like a crown encircles the head. Disease of these arteries is the number one cause of death in persons age 25 and over.

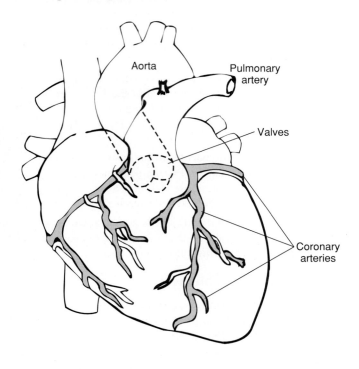

With respect to congenital heart disease, about 1% of all newborns have a heart disorder, but 20 to 60% of infants born with chromosomal defects are affected. Alcohol, tobacco, drugs, and viruses like HIV and rubella are also associated with congenital heart disease.

FIGURE 19.6   Atherosclerosis is a lifespan degenerative process that is related to known risk factors. Note how the arteries change from decade to decade when risk factors are ignored.

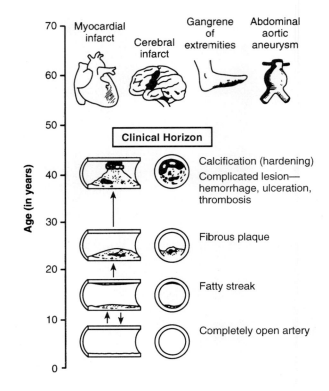

Atherosclerosis

Atherosclerosis is a degenerative process that leads to heart attacks, strokes, and circulatory problems. *Athero* is the Greek word for "gruel" (porridge or cereal) and refers to the accumulation of fatty substances resembling gruel inside the arteries. This is a lifespan process, beginning as early as age 3. *Sclerosis* means hardening of the arteries.

Atherosclerosis begins in childhood as fat streak deposits (see Figure 19.6). These are found in the aorta as early as age 3. Fat deposits subsequently appear in the coronary and peripheral arteries in late childhood and adolescence. The exact age depends on many factors. The coronary arteries are the heart's only source of oxygen. They branch downward from the aorta and encircle the heart like a crown encircles the head. Coronary is derived from the word *corona,* meaning "crown." Consider how the coronary arteries are as important to the heart as a crown is to royalty. All arteries outside of the heart are called *peripheral,* meaning "away from the center" (i.e., the heart).

By early adulthood, enough fatty substances have accumulated to be called *plaque* (see Figure 19.6). This atherosclerotic process can be happening anywhere in the body but is most dangerous in the heart and brain. Unlike soft, fatty streaks, plaque is hard with rough edges. The slow progressive buildup of plaque during the adult years not only narrows passageways but also damages surrounding cells, causing hemorrhage, ulceration, and **blood clots** known as thrombi (singular: *thrombus*) and emboli (singular: *embolus*). A **thrombus** is a blood clot that remains at its point of origin. An **embolus** is a traveling obstruction; it may be a blood clot or a bubble of gas.

The ages between 40 and 60 represent the clinical horizon for most persons when symptoms of atherosclerosis begin to be noticed (see Figure 19.6). Among the most common indicators are (a) high blood pressure, (b) discomfort or pain during strenuous exercise, and (c) blood analysis that shows high levels of triglycerides, low-density-lipoprotein cholesterol (LDL-C), and very-low-density-lipoprotein cholesterol (VLDL-C). Most persons at risk try to change their lifestyles during these years, and adapted physical activity becomes high priority.

If lifestyle change is ineffective or genetic predisposition to cardiovascular disease is overpowering, pathology is manifested in the form of heart attacks, strokes, circulatory dysfunctions, and aneurysms (see Figure 19.6). The heart, brain, and extremities are primarily damaged by **ischemia,** meaning inadequate oxygen to cells. The resulting cell death is called **infarcts** or **infarction** in the heart and brain and **gangrene** in the extremities. Thus, atherosclerosis is an *ischemic disease.*

Aneurysms are deformities of blood vessels, usually the arteries, caused by progressive, long-term weakening of the walls by atherosclerosis and/or high blood pressure. The most common site is the aorta in the abdominal region, but aneurysms can occur anywhere. The most serious aneurysms, of course, are those in the heart and brain.

The atherosclerotic process results in over 1 million deaths in the United States each year. About 60% of these come from heart attacks associated with coronary artery disease (CAD), 20% from strokes, and 20% from overall system failure related to heart muscle degeneration and high blood pressure. Heart attack and stroke usually are not fatal on first occurrence. They are, however, costly in terms of time, money, and mental health.

Heart Attack

Heart attack, called **myocardial infarction** (MI) because cells are dying, is a life-threatening crisis that occurs when the oxygen demand of the heart muscle cells is greater than the coronary arteries can supply. Inadequate oxygen is signaled by chest pain **(angina)** in the area behind the breast bone. This pain may radiate to the jaw, neck, shoulder, or arms. The pain is felt as a continuous, heavy, squeezing pressure lasting 2 or more minutes, rather than sharp or stabbing twinges. Sweating, shortness of breath, general weakness, nausea, and vomiting may also be present.

Persons of all ages have heart attacks, but most often, infarction strikes males ages 50 and above with high-risk profiles. The first 48 to 72 hr after a heart attack are critical because death of heart muscle cells and their replacement with scar tissue disrupt the rhythm of the heartbeat. This dysrhythmia often brings on a second attack. The section "Cardiac Rehabilitation for Adults," later in this chapter, discusses adapted physical activity.

Stroke

Stroke, also called cerebrovascular accident (CVA) or apoplexy, is a sudden loss of function (awareness, motor, speech, perception, memory, cognition) caused by ischemia or hemorrhage affecting brain cells. Consciousness is sometimes but not always lost. Recovery of function depends on the site and extent of brain cell death. Strokes can be massive, causing much damage, or small episodes, called **transient ischemic attacks** (TIAs), that are hardly noticed. TIAs result in muscle weakness, speech difficulty, or other mild problems that last only a few hours. These are warnings of cerebral atherosclerosis and impending major strokes.

Strokes are more common in males until about age 75, after which the incidence is equal for both sexes. Strokes can occur at any age but are most frequent after age 60. African Americans and Asian Americans are more prone to strokes than European Americans are. *Cerebral thrombosis related to atherosclerotic degeneration is the most common cause.* Visualize the four main arteries and many small branches that supply oxygen to the brain. Clogging kills brain cells by denying them oxygen, whereas hemorrhage destroys cells by issuing blood into the wrong places. Approximately one-third of stroke victims die. Others recover slowly. Additional information about stroke appears in Chapter 25 on cerebral palsy and traumatic brain injury. Stroke results in disabilities similar to these conditions.

Problems of the Extremities

Atherosclerosis can also affect arteries of the arms and legs, reducing the supply of oxygen to muscles, skin, and nails. This is one reason why the fingernails and toenails of many elderly people become abnormally thick and hard to cut. It also explains why older persons often have cold feet and hands and more frequent bruising and skin breakdown.

Legs and feet are more commonly affected by atherosclerosis than upper extremities. The first indication of an inadequate supply of oxygen to muscle is pain, aching, and cramping in the calf caused by walking short distances (e.g., half a block to a quarter mile). This pain is **claudication,** named after Emperor Claudius of ancient Rome, who walked with a limp. Claudication can be felt in any part of the hip, leg, and foot, depending on the site of arterial blockage, but the calf is most commonly affected. Pain is severe but disappears within a minute or two of rest. When walking is resumed, the pain recurs after about the same distance as before. As atherosclerosis becomes progressively worse, pain is felt even during inactivity, especially during bed rest. This is because a horizontal position prevents gravity from assisting the blood to flow down to the legs.

In advanced stages of arterial insufficiency, the extremities become increasingly susceptible to injury, disease, and temperature extremes. Open sores do not heal properly, infection sets in, and tissue death may be so great that gangrene requires amputation of affected body parts. This pathology is associated with old age; however, persons with diabetes are at high risk at all ages.

Congestive Heart Disease

A weak heart muscle can result from (a) cell death (ischemia) caused by heart attack, (b) work overload caused by structural defects, and/or (c) a sedentary lifestyle. Like other muscles, the heart must be used vigorously a few minutes each day to

Table 19.6   Review of parts of the heart and the direction of blood flow.

Function	Pumping Chamber	Upward-Flow Valves	Artery	Circulation Capillary Exchange	Venous Return	Collecting Chamber	Downward-Flow Valves
Left heart systemic circulation	Left ventricle	Aortic	Aortic	Total body	Superior and inferior vena cava	Right atrium	Tricuspid
Right heart pulmonary circulation	Right ventricle	Pulmonary	Pulmonary	Lungs	Pulmonary veins	Left atrium	Mitral or bicuspid

Note: All blood goes through both a systemic and pulmonary circuit. To trace blood flow, read from left to right.

FIGURE 19.7   The four chambers of the normal heart and the physiology of pulmonary and systemic circulation. Systemic circulation is shaded.

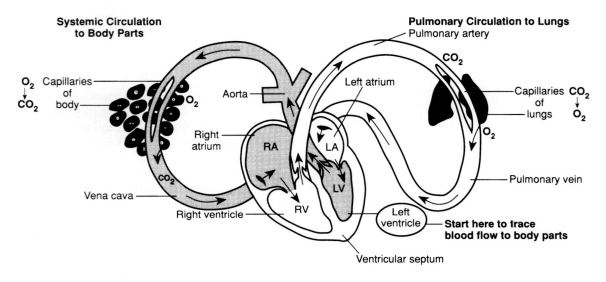

stay strong. Progressive weakness of the heart is characterized by accumulation of fluid in body parts. This is called *congestion* or *edema.*

A brief review of the parts of the heart and the direction of normal blood circulation enhances understanding of what is happening during congestive heart disease (Table 19.6 and Figure 19.7). **Systemic circulation,** initiated by contraction of the left ventricle, carries oxygenated blood to all systems of the body and returns waste-laden, oxygen-depleted blood. Weakness of the left ventricle is manifested by an inability to pump hard enough to empty the chamber; fluids begin to back up in the left atrium and lungs. **Pulmonary circulation,** initiated by contraction of the right ventricle, carries the deoxygenated blood to the lungs, where wastes are exchanged for oxygen. Insufficiency of right ventricle function causes blood to back up in the right atrium and the veins of body parts.

The left and right sides of the heart react differently to congestion. **Left heart congestion,** the most common, is characterized by fluid in the lungs, shortness of breath, wheezing, and coughing. This condition makes persons particularly susceptible to death by pneumonia (lung inflammation caused by bacteria, viruses, and chemical irritants). *Right heart congestion* causes fluid retention in the liver, legs, and feet. Edema anywhere in the body is an indication of dysfunction that is increasing blood volume and making the heart muscle work harder than normal.

Congestive heart disease may progress slowly, with no discomfort felt for years. The weak ventricular muscle, unable to squeeze strongly, simply wears out, and the blood flows too slowly to meet oxygen needs. Persons become less and less fit, eventually dying in their sleep. *This problem is particularly acute among nonambulatory persons with severe mental retardation, brain damage, or physical disabilities, who are dependent upon others to get them out of bed and provide exercise.* The primary cause of death for this population is pneumonia/heart congestion, whereas the primary cause of death for all other adult populations is coronary artery disease. Persons in nursing homes (especially the ill elderly) are at particular risk because the staff is often not able to meet their exercise needs. Congestive heart disease can be ameliorated simply by sitting upright a few hours each day so that fluids can drain, but some persons are too weak to manage this without help.

FIGURE 19.8 The electrocardiogram indicates the conduction of electrical impulses through the heart and records both the intensity of this electrical activity (in millivolts) and the time intervals involved.

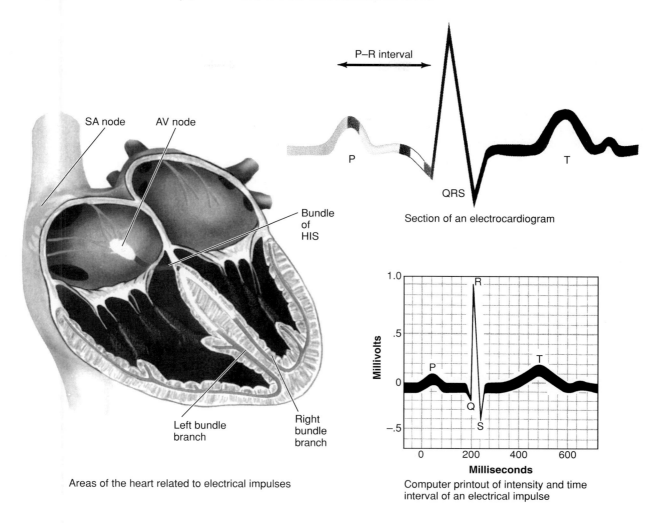

Areas of the heart related to electrical impulses

Section of an electrocardiogram

Computer printout of intensity and time interval of an electrical impulse

Breathing exercises and games (described later in the chapter discussion of asthma) are recommended also, along with gentle exercise (passive, if necessary) of all body parts.

Conduction Abnormalities and Heart Rate

Electrical impulses are what makes the heart beat. Abnormalities in the heart's electrical conduction system result in various kinds of **dysrhythmias** (fast, slow, or irregular heartbeats) and **blocks** (interruptions or delays in conduction). Many of these are important in endurance testing and exercise prescription.

The electrocardiogram (ECG) is used by physicians to identify conduction abnormalities (see Figure 19.8). Roy Shephard (1990) and ACSM literature (1995) note that lists of exercise contraindications commonly include *ST depression* and *T-wave inversion,* two ECG readings that indicate conduction abnormalities. The waves of electrical activity recorded on the ECG are designated by letters (*P, QRS, T*), which are used in describing heart function. The letters are not abbreviations for words; they were arbitrarily selected to denote up-and-down changes in the waves. Normal heartbeats display a characteristic ECG pattern with ventricular contraction beginning near the end of the *QRS*. The *T* wave represents *systole* (contraction)

and the *P* wave represents *diastole* (relaxation). Figure 19.8 shows the electrical activity of one normal heartbeat.

The structure within the heart that normally initiates the electrical impulses is the *sinus* or *sinoatrial (SA) node* (see Figure 19.8). This is the heart's natural pacemaker. Impulses travel from the sinus node to the atrioventricular (AV) node and then to the ventricles via neural pathways called the bundle of HIS, the left bundle branch, and the right bundle branch. Anything that alters these impulses affects heart function.

Sometimes, cardiac tissue other than the sinus node produces electrical impulses. When this happens, the heartbeats are called **ectopic,** meaning that they are displaced or in an abnormal position. Extra or skipped beats, also called **premature ventricular contractions** (PVC), are examples. These may indicate cardiac dysfunction but often are responses to stress or anxiety. *Repetitive or frequent ventricular ectopic activity is an exercise contraindication.*

The function of the sinus node is regulated by the hypothalamus and the autonomic nervous system. The parasympathetic system, through the vagus nerve, can lower the heart rate between 20 and 30 beats. The sympathetic system, in contrast, can speed the heart up so that it beats well over 200 times a minute. Disorders in heart rate that originate from autonomic system dysfunction are called **chronotropic** (Ellestad, 1986). These may be congenital or acquired.

Chronotropic Incompetence

Chronotropic dysfunction or incompetence is suspected when response to aerobic exercise is not normal. A slow heartbeat that fails to rise normally in response to strenuous activity makes knowing when to stop exercise difficult. This condition is relatively common in severe developmental disabilities and postoperative congenital heart defects. *Endurance activities may be contraindicated or need to be adapted to a lower-than-normal target heart rate range.*

Before birth, the parasympathetic and sympathetic systems develop at different rates, with the parasympathetic (vagal) maturing first. In premature births, chronotropic incompetence sometimes occurs because the sympathetic system is not yet mature and the heart rate is too slow (i.e., less than 100). In some persons with severe brain damage, the sympathetic system does not mature properly, and heart function remains chronotropic.

Sick Sinus Syndrome

Sick sinus syndrome (SSS) is a generic term for dysrhythmias that stem from problems of the sinus node, autonomic nervous system, and hypothalamus. This term, sometimes a synonym for chronotropic incompetence, is applied to persons with widespread, though not necessarily serious, abnormalities of rhythm (e.g., too fast or slow, or alternating fast and slow). Chronic fastness or slowness might not be noticed because the condition develops slowly or is congenital. Some sources say that SSS is most common among the elderly (NurseReview, 1987), but recently the condition has been mentioned in exercise literature pertaining to disabilities (Fernhall & Tymeson, 1987; Pitetti & Tan, 1991; Rimmer, 1993; Shephard, 1990). Fatigue, dizziness, and *syncope* (temporary unconsciousness) are exercise responses associated with SSS.

Fibrillations and Flutters

Fibrillations (rapid quivers) are incomplete contractions of heart fibers caused by conduction disturbances. **Flutters** are similar but less severe disturbances. While in fibrillation, the heart is unable to pump blood.

Ventricular fibrillation is the cause of most cardiac arrests and deaths in adults (Wilmore & Costill, 1988) and is commonly associated with coronary heart attack, electrical shock, and excess amounts of digitalis or chloroform. Electrical devices called **defibrillators** counteract fibrillation and save lives.

Atrial fibrillation also requires immediate treatment because it compromises ventricular filling. Among children and adolescents, the most common cause of atrial fibrillation is Wolff-Parkinson-White (WPW) syndrome, a condition precipitated by congenital anomalies of some of the conduction pathways. This is one of the ACSM exercise testing contraindications.

Tachycardias

Tachycardia is diagnosed when the resting heart rate in adolescents and adults is faster than 100 beats per minute. In infants and children, the criterion is much higher. There are many types of tachycardias, all caused by conduction disorders. Fast rhythms originating in the sinus node, typically between 100 to 150 beats per minute, are called **sinus tachycardias.** Alcohol, caffeine, and nicotine can trigger sinus tachycardia in healthy persons. Other causes include infection and/or disease with fever, dehydration, anemia, blood loss, hyperthyroidism, anoxia, and certain drugs used to manage asthma (theophylline) and hyperactivity (epinephrine). A fast sinus rhythm may be benign, with no exercise restrictions, or it may signal medical problems.

Fast rhythms (resting rates above 150) caused by problems arising outside the sinus node (i.e., ectopic) typically contraindicate aerobic exercise and endurance testing. In **ventricular tachycardia,** the fast rhythm originates in the ventricles, is usually associated with heart disease, and may herald ventricular fibrillation and sudden death. In **supraventricular tachycardia** (also called atrial or nodal), the abnormality is in the atria. This results in episodes of fast heartbeat (paroxysms), rather than continuous speeding, and may occur in persons with no other evidence of heart disease.

Bradycardias

Slow heartbeat can indicate either cardiovascular wellness or pathology. Chronic, slow heartbeat (**sinus bradycardia**) in athletes is an indication of excellent cardiorespiratory fitness. Resting heart rates as low as 28 beats per minute have been observed in world-class long-distance runners (Wilmore & Costill, 1988). Pathology-related causes of bradycardia are the sick sinus syndrome, acute myocardial infarction, hypothermia (prolonged coldness or freezing), hypothyroidism, complete heart blocks, anorexia nervosa, residual effects of congenital heart defects after surgery, and medications like digitalis and beta-blockers designed specifically to slow heartbeats. Slow heartbeat, as long as there is energy to complete desired tasks, is not a problem because persons generally self-select only activities that are comfortable. *Aerobic activities are contraindicated unless prescribed by a physician.*

For adults, a heart rate less than 40 beats per minute, unless the person is a trained athlete, is an indication for medication and/or an artificial pacemaker (NurseReview, 1987, p. 113). Less than 60 beats per minute is the diagnostic criterion for prepubertal persons.

Heart Block

Heart block is a pathologic interruption or delay in electrical impulse conduction that alters the rhythm of the heartbeat. Blocks may be congenital or acquired through disease or injury. There are many kinds, but only two are ACSM exercise contraindications: complete atrioventricular (AV) block and left bundle branch block.

AV blocks are interruptions between the atria and ventricles that disturb the synchrony of atrial and ventricular beats. These blocks are classified as first, second, and third degree.

The third-degree condition is the complete heart block (CHB). In most persons, the atrial rate is normal, but the ventricular rate (the one monitored by taking a pulse) is abnormally slow during both rest and exercise. Even during all-out exercise, the heart rate does not rise beyond 100 to 120 beats per minute (Bar-Or, 1983). There are many individual differences in exercise response, but fatigue and breathing difficulty are common. *In assessment of maximal aerobic power, heart rate response to standardized exercise cannot be used because it is not a valid indicator of exertion. Some persons with AV blocks can exercise normally, but physician clearance is important.*

Left bundle branch blocks (see Figure 19.8) disrupt the normal left-to-right ventricular conduction pattern, causing the ventricles to beat out of rhythm with each other. This problem is associated with myocardiac infarction but may accompany numerous other conditions.

Cardiovascular Medications

The best-known heart medications are the *nitrates* (e.g., nitroglycerin) for angina conditions and the *digitalis preparations* (e.g., digoxin) for congestive heart failure and some conduction abnormalities. Nitrates relax and dilate smooth muscles, thereby increasing heart rate and oxygen supply and decreasing blood pressure. Digitalis preparations lower heart rate but do not affect blood pressure.

Heart rhythm regulators include drugs that block or depress the sympathetic nervous system (e.g., the beta-blockers) and the transmembrane calcium flow in cardiac smooth muscle tissue (e.g., the calcium channel blockers). These drugs have variable effects on heart rates, depending on whether they manage tachycardia or bradycardia. Both beta-blockers and calcium channel blockers lower blood pressure. Alpha-blockers, also prescribed to lower blood pressure, are not heart rhythm regulators because they do not affect heart rate.

Beta-blockers lower heart rate and mask exercise effects, making the pulse an invalid indicator of effort. The main side effects of beta-blockers are early exercise fatigue and lowered maximum oxygen uptake. Some new beta-blockers have built-in sympathomimetic agents to lessen side effects. Overall, the blockers are extremely complex. Only professionals with special training should work with conditions that require SNS blockers.

When heart disease is complicated by high blood pressure, vasodilators and diuretics are typically prescribed. *Vasodilators* are drugs that lower blood pressure by increasing the size of vessels. Some vasodilators work specifically on arteries, while others work on veins. The effect of vasodilators on heart rate is therefore variable. Several cause tachycardia.

Diuretics, discussed earlier, decrease blood pressure by reducing fluid volume through urination. None of the many kinds of diuretics affect heart rate. Remember—drugs that lower blood pressure often cause hypotension.

Persons taking cardiovascular drugs can and should exercise. Graded exercise and cardiac rehabilitation programs are discussed later in this chapter. Weight loss is often the first exercise priority.

FIGURE 19.9   The heart wall.

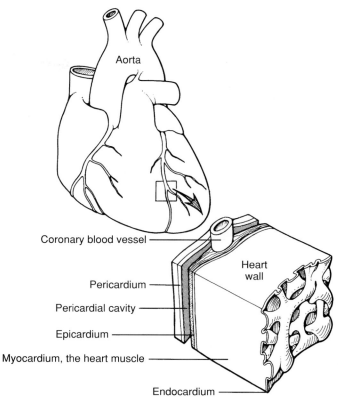

The three layers of the heart: endocardium, myocardium, and epicardium

Close-up of the middle layer of the heart, showing cardiac muscle that contracts and relaxes

Inflammation of the Heart Wall

Figure 19.9 shows the pericardium (the fibrous sac that surrounds the heart and great vessels) and the three layers that comprise the heart wall. Inflammation of these structures results in conditions called *pericarditis, myocarditis,* and *endocarditis.* Inflammation is caused by a variety of viral, bacterial, and unknown agents. Often these are introduced into the bloodstream during corrective surgery. Anything inserted into the body (e.g., tubes, shunts, or catheters) can carry a virus or bacteria. Intravenous drug users are particularly at high risk.

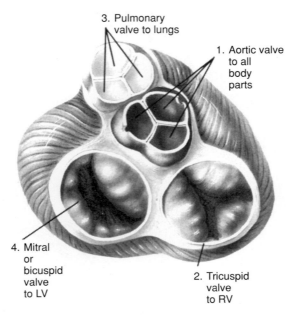

3. Pulmonary valve to lungs

1. Aortic valve to all body parts

4. Mitral or bicuspid valve to LV

2. Tricuspid valve to RV

Heart valves

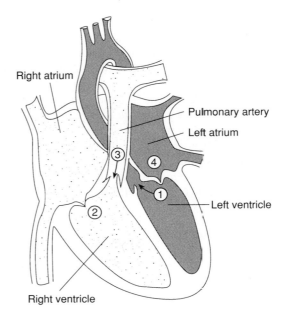

Right atrium

Pulmonary artery

Left atrium

Left ventricle

Right ventricle

Relationship of heart valves (1, 2, 3, 4) to other parts of the heart

Inflammation can also be caused by viral and bacterial diseases like influenza, diphtheria, measles, and chicken pox. Inflammation is treated by several families of anti-infective drugs (e.g., antibiotics, antimicrobials) and by corticosteroids. Exercise is contraindicated until inflammation is under control.

Valve Defects and Heart Murmurs

Valves are the membranous structures that rhythmically open and close to force the blood within the heart to flow in the right direction (see Figure 19.10). For simplicity, the mitral and tricuspid valves are called the **atrioventricular** (AV) valves because they open at the same instant to permit blood to flow downward from atria to ventricles. The closing of the AV valves is what makes the "lubb" sound in the "lubb-dupp" of the heartbeat and is the mechanism that starts constriction. Shortly thereafter, the aortic and pulmonary valves (called the **semilunar valves** for brevity) open to permit blood to be squeezed upward into the aorta and pulmonary artery. The closing of the semilunar valves marks the beginning of the rest period during which all four valves are closed.

Valvular defects typically cause heart murmurs that are heard with a stethoscope. In spite of their weird sounds, most valvular defects are mild, and some even heal themselves. About 80% of young children have a heart murmur. Most of these disappear during adolescence.

Most persons with valvular disease have few or no exercise restrictions. Ordinary physical activity does not cause shortness of breath, undue fatigue, palpitation, or chest pain. Ability to excel in vigorous activity like aerobic fitness tests and lengthy competitive games may be limited, depending on the nature and severity of the defect.

Valvular defects are of three types: (a) regurgitation, (b) stenosis, and (c) prolapse. **Regurgitation** is the backward leakage that occurs when damaged valves are unable to close tightly. This leakage places extra stress on the heart, causing the left ventricle to enlarge and the muscle wall to thicken. The ventricle gradually loses its ability to completely empty the chamber with each contraction. This results in shortness of breath and reduced exercise tolerance. **Stenosis,** or narrowing of the valves, compromises the valves' ability to open widely and permit blood to flow freely. Stenosis of the pulmonary valve causes right heart congestion. Stenosis of the aortic valve causes left heart congestion. Valvular stenosis progresses slowly and may not cause discomfort for years. *Prolapse* is the slipping or falling out of place of an organ.

The most common is **mitral valve prolapse** (MVP), in which the valve leaflets flop backward into the left atrium during the heart's squeezing action (systole). The main symptoms are arrhythmias and chest pain. MVP occurs mostly in adults and more often in Down syndrome (14% prevalence) than in the nondisabled population (Goldhaber, Brown, & St. John Sutton, 1987). MVP is also common in connective tissue disorders like osteogenesis imperfecta, Marfan syndrome, and Ehlers-Danlos syndrome (see Chapter 24 on les autres conditions).

Some heart valve disease is diagnosed at birth and corrected in early childhood, but most is not identified until late childhood or adolescence. The cause is typically unknown unless symptoms can be traced back to an infection. Among the childhood diseases most likely to cause valvular defects is rheumatic fever.

Rheumatic Fever

Rheumatic fever is the most common cause of acquired heart disease in children and adolescents. In the United States, this disease is steadily declining, but in Third World countries, rheumatic fever continues to be a major cause of illness and death. Some developing countries report an almost equal incidence of congenital and rheumatic heart disease. In sharp contrast, rheumatic fever accounts for only 1 to 3% of children's heart disease in the United States.

Rheumatic fever is an autoimmune disease in which antibodies attack tissues and cause various kinds of inflammation. The disease typically follows inadequately treated childhood streptococcal infections (e.g., strep throat or scarlet fever). Therefore, sore throats must be properly diagnosed and cared for. Fortunately, the most common sore throat is viral and does not cause rheumatic fever. A viral sore throat is characterized by a runny nose and cough; in contrast, a strep throat is very sore without these symptoms.

The onset of rheumatic fever averages about 18 days after recovery from a strep throat. Symptoms are variable. Fever and sore, swollen joints (polyarthritis) are the most common. The pain typically migrates from joint to joint, with the knees, ankles, elbows, and wrists affected most often. Shortness of breath, chest pains, and exercise intolerance are indications of inflammation of the heart (carditis), a common manifestation. **Carditis** is the term used when two or more of the heart wall layers are affected. **Chorea** or *St. Vitus Dance* (an involuntary twitching of muscles) is an indication of central nervous system involvement. Chorea, which occurs in only 8 to 10% of patients, appears much later than other symptoms, often 2 to 6 months after the strep infection.

Initial treatment is usually hospitalization and medications like aspirin and the corticosteroids to reduce inflammation, thereby relieving symptoms. The duration of this anti-inflammatory treatment varies from a few days to 3 or 4 months, depending on the tissues involved. Bed rest is recommended until symptoms disappear because inflammation anywhere in the body places extra stress on the heart. Children without carditis may return to school in 2 or 3 weeks with no restrictions other than common sense in gradually increasing exercise duration and intensity. Children with carditis recover slowly over many months.

The heart is permanently damaged in about 60% of the children who have rheumatic fever (Maurer, 1983). The mitral and aortic valves are the parts of the heart most frequently affected (see Figure 19.10).

Congenital Heart Defects

The heart problems of children are mostly congenital. The incidence of congenital heart defects is 6 to 10 per 1,000 live births. While some of these infants die during their first year, most are kept alive by surgery, often during the first few weeks of life. Ideally, this surgery is undertaken before age 6 so that the child can start school with a normal or near-normal heart and few exercise restrictions. Physical educators should be familiar with the most prevalent congenital heart defects (see Figure 19.11).

Once a congenital defect has been surgically corrected, the chances are good that the child will have no exercise restriction. Many participate in strenuous, high-level, competitive sports. The student should be allowed the freedom to decide how hard to play, since sensations are usually a reliable guide to exercise tolerance. The psychological problems stemming from parental overprotection and preoperative anxieties and fears are generally greater than residual physiological limitations.

Definitions of Terms

A review of the basic terms used in heart disease helps to make sense of the congenital disorders:

Septal—Refers to the septum, a dividing wall between two chambers. In the heart, there is an atrial septum and a ventricular septum.

Patent—From the Latin word *patens,* meaning "wide open" or "accessible."

Ductus arteriosus—A tubelike passageway in the fetus between the aorta and the main pulmonary artery.

Tetralogy—A group or series of four.

Great vessels—The aorta and pulmonary artery.

Stenosis—Constriction or narrowing of a passageway.

Coarctation—Tightening or shriveling of the walls of a vessel; compression.

Atresia—Pathological closure of a normal anatomical opening or congenital absence of the opening.

Shunt—A hole in the septum between the atria or the ventricles that permits blood from the systemic circulation to mix with that of the pulmonary circulation or vice versa.

Cyanosis—Blueness resulting from oxygen deficiency in the blood.

Three Categories of Congenital Heart Defects

Figure 19.11 shows that congenital heart defects fall into three categories: (a) left-to-right shunts, (b) obstructive lesions, and (c) right-to-left shunts. The **left-to-right shunts** are the most common, the easiest to understand, and generally the least serious. Two are holes in the heart structure, and one is a duct that fails to close. In each, oxygenated blood from the arteries seeps through a hole in the heart wall (septum) into the waste-filled blood in the right chambers. This causes a volume overload on the right ventricle and raises blood pressure, but these effects are minimal when holes are small.

Obstructive lesions narrow (a) the valves that govern upward flow of blood or (b) the aorta itself. The most serious is **aortic stenosis valvular** (ASV), which leads to left heart congestion and has been linked with sudden death syndrome. This is the only congenital heart defect in which physical exertion is considered detrimental to health (Bar-Or, 1983). The effects of coarctation of the aorta depend on the location of the narrowing, but high blood pressure is the greatest problem. **Pulmonary stenosis valvular** (PSV) leads to right heart congestion.

The **right-to-left shunts** are caused by complicated conditions, as indicated by their names. In each of these, poorly oxygenated venous blood somehow gets into the aorta, thereby reducing the oxygen being carried to all body parts. The low oxygen content causes skin, lips, and nail beds to take on a bluish tint, a characteristic known as **cyanosis.** Obviously, low oxygen limits energy and endurance. The volume overload on the left ventricle also raises blood pressure.

FIGURE 19.11 Common congenital heart defects grouped according to impairment. (From *American Heart Association Heartbook.* New York: E. P. Dutton, pp. 243–246. Reproduced with permission. © *American Heart Association Heartbook,* 1980. Copyright American Heart Association.)

Left to Right Shunts (Holes That Raise Blood Pressure)

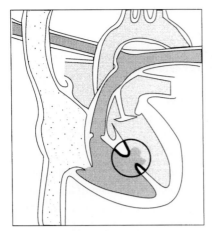

Ventricular septal defect (VSD)

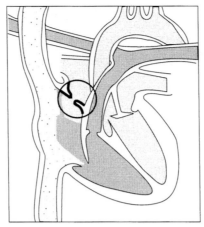

Atrial septal defect (ASD)

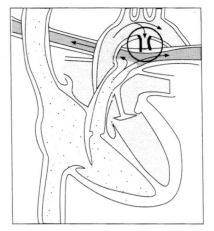

Patent ductus arteriosus (PDA)

Obstructive Lesions (Impaired Blood Flow)

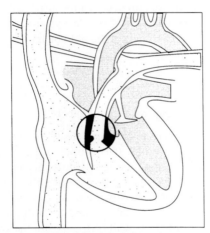

Pulmonic stenosis, valvular (PSV)

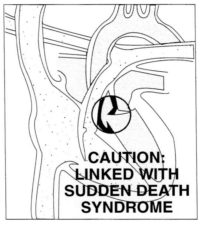

Aortic stenosis, valvular (ASV)

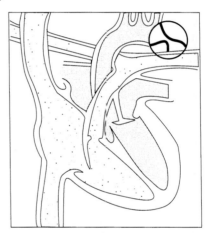

Coarctation of the aorta (COA)

Right to Left Shunts (Cyanotic Lesions)

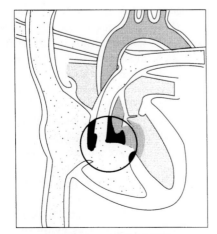

Tetralogy of Fallot (TOF)

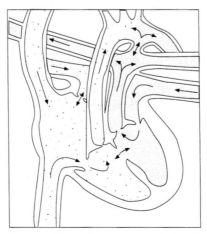

Transposition of the great vessels (TGV)

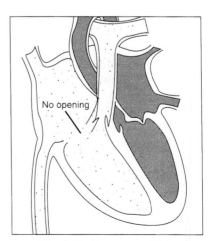

Tricuspid valve atresia (TVA)

The nine congenital heart defects shown in Figure 19.11 comprise 90% of all congenital heart defects. Ventricular septal defect (VSD) and patent ductus arteriosus (PDA) rank first and second, respectively, in prevalence estimates. Pulmonic stenosis valvular (PSV) and Tetralogy of Fallot (TOF) tie for third place, each affecting about 10% (Maurer, 1983). Together, these four defects comprise about 70% of the total.

The Four Most Common Conditions

A brief discussion of the four most common conditions follows. Other defects can best be remembered by visualization and grouping them by type (see Figure 19.11).

Ventricular Septal Defect

The severity of **ventricular septal defect** (VSD) depends on whether the hole in the ventricular septum is small or large. Small holes often close spontaneously in early childhood. Many small- and medium-sized openings that do not close are harmless. Large holes must be surgically repaired. VSD is the most common congenital heart defect. Before surgery, respiratory infections and slow physical growth are particular problems.

In the older literature (e.g., Maurer, 1983), VSD, complicated by a defect of the adjacent endocardial lining, is reported in about 40% of infants with Down syndrome (DS). However, a new source identifies the atrioventricular canal defect as the most common lesion in DS (Marino & Pueschel, 1996). The term *atrioventricular canal defect* indicates that the shunt (hole) in the ventricular wall is large enough to be called a canal, particularly when it occurs with shunting in the atrial wall in the area that normally separates the mitral and tricuspid valves. The resulting left-to-right canal causes breathing difficulty, fatigue, feeding problems, and slow growth. In most cases, surgery is performed before age 1.

Patent Ductus Arteriosus

Before birth, there is no need for blood to circulate through the lungs because the placenta takes care of oxygen needs. Therefore, the fetus has a tubelike passageway (the ductus arteriosus) between the aorta and the pulmonary artery that enables the blood to bypass the lungs. At birth, when breathing starts, reflex muscle contractions in the wall of the ductus arteriosus causes this bypass to close within a few days. When this fails to take place, normal circulation cannot be established. Part of the oxygenated blood in the aorta that should be flowing to other body parts leaks into the pulmonary artery via the open duct.

When this seepage is large, the symptoms and treatment are the same as for severe VSD. PDA occurs in about 20% of premature infants and 5% of full-term infants, making it the second most common congenital heart defect.

Tetralogy of Fallot

Tetralogy (meaning "four symptoms") is characterized by (a) VSD, (b) PSV, (c) an enlarged right ventricle, and (d) a malpositioned aorta that receives blood from both ventricles. This combination of abnormalities was discovered by a man named Fallot and thus is known as Tetralogy of Fallot. The resulting shunt is unoxygenated blood from the right ventricle leaking into the left ventricle, which pumps it throughout the

Week	Graded Exercise
1	Walk 10 min, try not to stop
2	Walk 5 min, jog 1 min
3	Walk 5 min, jog 3 min
4	Walk 4 min, jog 5 min
	Walk 4 min, jog 4 min
5	Walk 4 min, jog 5 min
6	Walk 4 min, jog 6 min
7	Walk 4 min, jog 7 min
8	Walk 4 min, jog 8 min
9	Walk 4 min, jog 9 min
10	Walk 4 min, jog 13 min
11	Walk 4 min, jog 17 min
12	Walk 4 min, jog 17 min
13	Walk 2 min, jog slowly 2 min, jog 17 min
14	Walk 1 min, jog slowly 3 min, jog 17 min
15	Jog slowly 3 min, jog 17 min

Table 19.7   Graded exercise program.

From W. B. Strong and B. S. Alpert (1982).
Note: Warm-up should consist of stretching and limbering exercises for 5 min, while cool-down should involve 3 min of walking slowly and 2 min of stretching. Check your pulse periodically to see if you are exercising within your target zone. As you become more fit, try exercising within the upper range of your target zone.

body. The unoxygenated blood, bluish in color, causes the condition known as *blue baby* or cyanosis.

TOF is usually severe, requiring surgery in infancy. Without surgery, spells of breathlessness, increased cyanosis, and loss of consciousness may occur. Breathing can be made easier by holding the child upright against an adult's shoulder, with the knees tucked up to the chest.

TOF is the most common cause of cyanosis in young children. Surgical repair may be either palliative (partial to relieve symptoms) or total. Naturally, there are more residual deficiencies in the former than the latter. The main residual is reduced maximal aerobic capability.

Pulmonic Stenosis Valvular

PSV, although relatively common, is usually mild. If blood pressure remains more-or-less normal, surgery is typically not required. In such cases, aerobic capacity is slightly reduced. The less common ASV is the valvular defect that contraindicates vigorous exercise.

Exercise and Congenital Heart Defects

For almost all moderate to severe heart conditions, corrective surgery is performed in early childhood. A healthy, active lifestyle is emphasized thereafter, with walking recommended 3 days after surgery. Children return to school within 2 to 3 weeks of surgery and soon begin a graded exercise program of walking, swimming, or cycling. Within 4 months of surgery, most children can participate in regular physical education with no restrictions (Cumming, 1987).

Table 19.7 is an example of the type of graded exercise program begun 3 days after surgery. See the table note for a description of proper warm-up and cool-down. While parents are encouraged to perform this program with their children (Strong & Alpert, 1982), school or agency personnel often are relegated responsibility. The ultimate goal is ability to exercise 30 min at least three times a week within the upper limit of the target heart rate zone recommended by the physician. See Chapter 13 (pages 356–357) for target heart rate zones.

The target heart rate zone after surgery depends on whether correction was total or partial. *In many postoperative persons, the maximal heart rate is and always will be slightly lower than normal* (see the sections "Chronotropic Incompetence" and "Sick Sinus Syndrome" earlier in this chapter). A lowered maximal heart rate seldom affects class participation because activities, with the exception of occasional aerobic testing, do not demand total exertion. Persons with postoperative conditions have a lifelong tendency to fatigue more quickly than peers. The general consensus is that teachers and coaches should allow these individuals to impose their own exercise restrictions during vigorous activity.

Most physicians recommend participation in sports. Table 19.8 presents the classifications typically used in recommending sport involvement. After completion of their graded exercise program, most postoperative persons have no restrictions except for a caution against primarily isometric activities. Isometrics increase blood pressure and risk of heart attack (Freed, 1984) because blood vessels reflexly contract during static muscle contraction.

Mild Defects, Delayed Surgery, and Restrictions

Often, no surgery is recommended for mild heart conditions because normal activity, including sport involvement, is not seriously limited. Children with mild heart conditions typically can engage in strenuous sports in an instructional or recreational setting, but high-intensity, competitive sports may be restricted. In moderate to severe defects, surgery is sometimes delayed until overall health status is improved or a certain age is reached. In the case of delayed surgery, physicians are likely to restrict children to moderately strenuous or nonstrenuous sports (see Table 19.8).

Implications for Physical Education

Many students from low socioeconomic backgrounds have mild heart defects that go undetected. Follow the ABCDEF plan in making physician referrals when symptoms are observed during vigorous activity:

A Angina, severe chest pain
B Breathing difficulty
C Color changed, bluish or pale
D Dizziness
E Edema, fluid retention and swelling of extremities
F Fatigue

Persons with disabilities, especially the various syndromes caused by chromosomal and inborn metabolic disorders, are more prone to cardiac disorders than others. The prevalence rate of heart disease for various syndromes ranges from 20 to 60%. Many of these conditions are mild and go undetected unless a teacher or coach urges vigorous activity. Particular care therefore should be taken in fitness testing and programming.

Table 19.8   Classification of sports used by physicians.

Strenuous Contact	Moderately Strenuous
Body surfing	Badminton
Diving	Baseball
Football	Curling
Ice hockey	Golf
Lacrosse (boys)	Horseback riding
Rugby	Table tennis
Surfing	**Nonstrenuous**
Wrestling	Bowling
Strenuous Limited Contact	Riflery
Basketball	**Primarily Isometric**
Field hockey	Archery
Lacrosse (girls)	Waterskiing
Skiing	Weight lifting
Soccer	Wrestling
Volleyball	
Water polo	
Strenuous Noncontact	
Climbing	
Crew	
Cross-country	
Fencing	
Gymnastics	
Swimming	
Tennis	
Track and field	

From W. B. Strong and B. S. Alpert (1982).

Use graded exercise programs like that in Table 19.7 before fitness testing, rather than the pretest-posttest models favored in research. Emphasize activities described in Chapters 13 and 15 on fitness and relaxation. Programming is similar to that for other OHI conditions in that exercise progressions are slower, and better motivation is needed because discomfort is greater and/or the persons do not yet understand their bodies and the meaning of true exertion. Guidelines for working with obese/overweight and asthmatic conditions are particularly applicable because of shared cardiorespiratory fitness problems.

Cardiac Rehabilitation for Adults

The aerobic exercise phase of cardiac rehabilitation begins about 8 to 12 weeks after a heart attack or coronary bypass surgery. Stress testing is repeated periodically and the exercise prescription revised accordingly. Persons in cardiac rehabilitation programs demonstrate achievement at the 6 MET capacity before transferring from a medically supervised, individualized program involving continuous heart monitoring to a group program conducted by exercise scientists. Refer to Chapter 13 on fitness for further information on METs and other activities appropriate in cardiac rehabilitation.

Hypertension

Hypertension, or high blood pressure, is a cardiovascular problem in which the blood exerts a greater than normal force

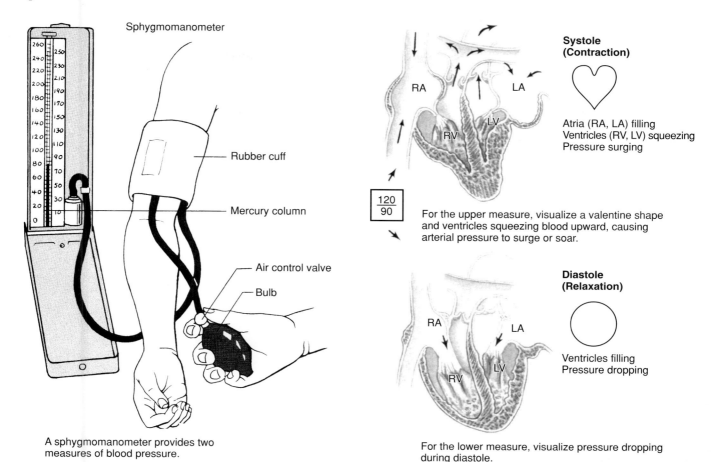

Sphygmomanometer

Rubber cuff

Mercury column

Air control valve

Bulb

A sphygmomanometer provides two measures of blood pressure.

Systole (Contraction)

Atria (RA, LA) filling
Ventricles (RV, LV) squeezing
Pressure surging

120/90

For the upper measure, visualize a valentine shape and ventricles squeezing blood upward, causing arterial pressure to surge or soar.

Diastole (Relaxation)

Ventricles filling
Pressure dropping

For the lower measure, visualize pressure dropping during diastole.

against the inner walls of the blood vessels. This excess force, in time, permanently damages organs, most often the heart, brain, kidneys, and eyes. Hypertension can be caused by atherosclerosis; certainly, anything that obstructs blood flow increases pressure. However, there are many other causes, and hypertension can exist separate from atherosclerosis.

For the population as a whole, hypertension is the leading reason for taking prescription drugs (Kaplan, 1990). Approximately 58 million persons in the United States (or about 25% of the general population) have hypertension. Of these, about 3 million are under age 17. The prevalence is greater for males than females and for blacks than other races. Prevalence increases decade by decade until about age 65 and then levels off. At age 65, approximately 50% of whites and 60% of blacks have high blood pressure.

Hypertension places persons at high risk for organ damage until the golden 70s and 80s. After ages 75 and 85 for men and women, respectively, death rate tends to be lower when blood pressure is higher. Across the lifespan, however, hypertension is a major risk factor for death by heart attack or stroke.

One reason hypertension is dangerous is that rises in blood pressure typically cause no pain or discomfort. Persons who do not have routine medical checkups are unaware of blood pressure abnormalities. When hypertension progresses to a severe stage, strenuous exercise and other forms of stress

may cause headache, visual disturbances, vomiting, and/or convulsions. On the other hand, the condition may continue to be asymptomatic. There are many individual differences.

Blood Pressure Measurement

A *sphygmomanometer* is used to measure blood pressure (see Figure 19.12). Normal blood pressure for adults is 120/90 millimeters of mercury (mm Hg) or less. A value like 120/90 indicates the pressure inside the aorta and pulmonary arteries when the ventricles of the heart contract and relax. The upper number indicates systolic or contraction pressure. The lower number indicates diastolic or relaxation pressure.

Systolic and diastolic pressure are equal in importance. Elevation of either one is cause for concern, but high blood pressure is not diagnosed until after several readings on different days. In research and clinical settings, systolic pressure can be monitored reliably during exercise on a treadmill or bicycle ergometer, but diastolic pressure cannot (Bar-Or, 1983).

Systolic and Diastolic Pressures

The heart looks like a valentine during systole, the time of greatest pressure, when the ventricles are squeezing all of their blood upward into the arteries and the atria are bulging because the atrioventricular (AV) valves have closed (see Figure 19.12). **Systole** (the contraction phase) is the beginning of the heartbeat, the loud "lubb" sound in the "lubb-dupp" heard by a stethoscope. To remember, *v*isualize *V*alentine's Day and *ven*tricles (**the 3 Vs**) with *s*queezing the blood out during *s*ystole, causing the arterial pressure to *s*urge (**the 3 Ss**).

Diastole (the relaxation phase) is easy to remember because the overall heart shape is a relaxed oval. Word derivation helps us to visualize *di-* (two chambers), *-a-* (without), *systole* (contraction). The pressure is at its lowest point when the ventricles are relaxed, the AV valves are open, and blood is filling the lower chambers. Duration of this low blood pressure phase depends upon rate of heartbeat. The slower the rate, the more relaxation and filling time.

Causes of Hypertension

For simplicity, causes of hypertension are classified in two ways: (a) primary or essential (cause unknown) and (b) secondary (cause can be linked with specific disorders or pregnancy). Among adults, 90% of all hypertension is primary.

Pregnancy is a time of particular risk. Blood volume increases to about 30% above normal during pregnancy, and many compensatory mechanisms must operate to keep blood pressure normal. This problem is especially intensified in women with spinal cord injuries (Krotoski, Nosek, & Turk, 1996). ***Preeclampsia,*** a toxemia of pregnancy condition characterized by hypertension and edema, occurs in 5 to 7% of pregnancies of able-bodied women.

Most severe childhood hypertension is associated with kidney disease, obesity, or coarctation of the aorta (a congenital heart defect that narrows the aorta). Unlike adults, the classification is seldom primary. This may be partly because hypertension is asymptomatic and many cases go undiagnosed. Early identification of children at risk for cardiovascular disease is essential. Therefore, physicians now diagnose primary hypertension in children whose blood pressure readings over time exceed the 95th percentile for their age and sex. Those with weight that exceeds the 95th percentile and a family history of hypertension are at greatest risk. Regardless of classification, the single best correlate of hypertension is large body mass (Kaplan, 1990). The best treatment for primary hypertension in children is loss of excess weight.

Classification by Severity

Adult hypertension is classified in four categories: borderline to mild (140/90), mild to moderate (150/95), moderate to severe (160/100), and uncontrolled (170/110). *Medically supervised exercise testing is contraindicated when resting values exceed 200/120.* Nonsupervised physical activity, even of low intensity, should be discontinued whenever resting rates evidence a change from normal pattern. This usually means that medication is no longer effective and that a physician needs to reassess management of the disease.

Table 19.9 shows that different criteria are used in diagnosing and classifying hypertension in children. Blood pressure in healthy persons gradually increases from infancy through adulthood. *This change results from size rather than*

T a b l e   1 9 . 9   **Classification of hypertension by age group.**

Age (in Years)	Mild/Moderate	Moderate/Severe
Infants (<2)	112/74	118/82
Children (3–5)	116/76	124/84
Children (6–9)	122/78	130/86
Children (10–12)	126/82	134/90
Adolescents (13–15)	136/86	144/92
Adolescents (16–18)	142/92	150/98
Adults	150/95	160/100

Modified from Kaplan (1990) and the Task Force on Blood Pressure Control in Children (1987).

FIGURE 19.13   Blood-pressure changes in response to vigorous big-muscle exercises in a healthy adult.

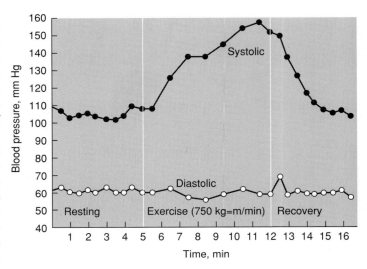

age differences. The largest increase occurs in conjunction with the adolescent growth spurt. Because blood pressure is correlated strongly with body mass, height and weight are considered in making a diagnosis.

Typically, when systolic blood pressure is elevated, the diastolic is also, and vice versa. The exception is old age, when **isolated systolic hypertension** (ISH) often occurs because atherosclerosis has decreased the elasticity of major arteries. Cardiac output shows no associated change. The diseased aorta simply cannot distend to accommodate the amount of blood ejected with each ventricular contraction.

Blood Pressure Responses to Exercise

In healthy adults, systolic blood pressure rises by 30 to 60 mm Hg during strenuous isotonic exercise. Diastolic pressure rises little or not at all (see Figure 19.13). In aerobically trained persons, diastolic pressure may even fall. In hypertension, blood pressure response to exercise is exaggerated. Monitoring values before and after exercise is a good practice. In laboratories,

FIGURE 19.14 The lungs are filled with large and small bronchial tubes, called *bronchi* and *bronchioles,* respectively, that are lined with mucous membrane. Also shown is an alveolus, or air cell.

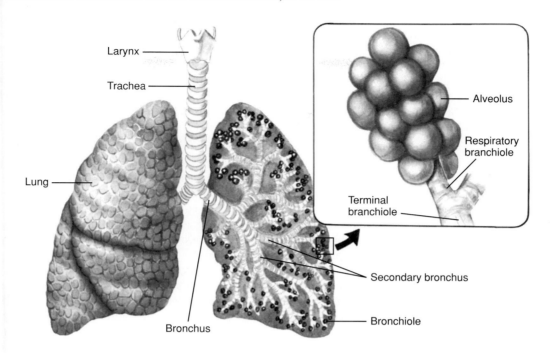

where pressure readings during exercise are possible, the criterion for stopping exercise is a value exceeding 250/120. In field settings, exercise pressures of 225/90 are considered high risk.

Isometric exercise and activities involving a Valsalva maneuver like weight lifting are controversial because they increase both systolic and diastolic blood pressures to high rates. ACSM (1995) says that isometric exercise is not strictly contraindicated in hypertension but should be used with extreme caution. High repetitions and low resistances are recommended for weight training.

Management of Hypertension

Mild hypertension is managed by accepting responsibility for healthy diet and exercise practices and acting on environmental factors that cause emotional stress. Excess weight must be lost and proper weight maintained. Salt intake, for many persons, must be reduced. This means use of fresh or frozen foods rather than canned goods, which are high in sodium, and avoidance of high-salt items like bacon, cheese, and pickles. The recommended sodium intake is 1,100 to 3,300 mg daily.

Regular aerobic exercise is beneficial because it reduces blood pressure. This occurs over time, like weight loss. Training effects, however, do not last more than 3 to 6 weeks if exercise is discontinued.

Moderate to severe hypertension requires medication in addition to healthy lifestyle. Physical activity specialists need to understand these medications because of exercise side effects. Among the major classes of antihypertensive drugs are diuretics, vasodilators, and the blocking agents.

Antihypertension drugs affect the validity of heart rate monitoring during exercise. There is no way to separate the heart's natural response to exercise from drug-induced slowness or fastness. Therefore, collect data on medications and discuss side effects before helping persons to start exercise programs.

Respiratory Problems

Most of us take breathing for granted. We squeeze air out of our lungs 20,000 times a day and seldom think about the phenomenon of respiration. Yet respiratory diseases are the fastest rising causes of death in the United States. This section is about persons who struggle to breathe. They may have *asthma, chronic obstructive pulmonary diseases,* or *cystic fibrosis.* The symptoms are similar in all conditions, and exercise is vital for the maintenance of respiratory fitness. Almost half of the chronic diseases that affect children under age 17 are respiratory in nature. Asthma, hay fever, and other allergies account for approximately 33% of all chronic disease in this age group. Bronchitis, sinusitis, and related conditions cause about 15%. Cystic fibrosis, although rare, results in death from chronic lung disorders. The physical activities for these children are the same as those for children with asthma.

Emphysema is primarily a disease of middle and old age, but its origins can often be traced to asthma and chronic bronchitis in earlier years. Over a million Americans lead restricted lives because of emphysema. The fastest growing cause of total disability in the United States, it is surpassed only by heart disease.

Asthma

Asthma recently has been redefined as a chronic lung disease characterized by airway obstruction, airway inflammation, and airway hyperreactivity (Cypcar & Lemanske, 1995). **Airway** refers to the many bronchial tubes that fill the lungs (see Figure 19.14).

Asthma is a cellular disorder, always present but only occasionally manifested as acute episodes of coughing, wheezing, and breathing difficulty. Asthma is linked with insufficient levels of theophylline in the blood and various individual factors that trigger attacks (e.g., viral infections, weather conditions, exercise, allergens, and irritants like cigarette smoke).

Persons with asthma tend to be multiply disabled in that they frequently have hay fever, allergies, sinus trouble, and upper respiratory infections. In childhood, they tend to be underweight and fragile. In adulthood, most are prone to weight problems and other side effects of an inactive lifestyle.

Prevalence

Estimates of the prevalence of asthma in the United States range from 10 to 35 million, depending on diagnostic criteria. Approximately half of all cases begin in childhood, with more males affected than females. Despite improved treatment modalities, the overall incidence is rising; this trend is particularly evident among minority children of low socioeconomic status. Asthma is the leading cause of chronic illness in children under 17 and is a special problem for physical education teachers, because 60 to 90% of individuals with asthma have conditions that are triggered by aerobic exercise. This type of asthma is called **exercise-induced asthma** (EIA). Symptoms sometimes develop during exercise but more often appear 5 to 10 min after exercise ends. Some persons experience a recurrence of symptoms 4 to 8 hr after exercise. EIA usually remits within 10 to 20 min, but it can be stopped immediately by puffs from an inhaler.

Asthma Attacks

Asthma is chronic and always present, but *attacks* occur only occasionally. Asthma attacks progress through three stages: (a) coughing, (b) dyspnea, and (c) severe bronchial obstruction.

Coughing warns of an impending attack. In this stage, the bronchial tubes are secreting mucus, which accumulates and obstructs the passage of air. Coughing is caused by the reflex action of the smooth, involuntary muscles of the bronchioles in an attempt to remove the accumulating mucus. This action is often called a *bronchospasm.*

Dyspnea, meaning breathing difficulty, occurs when the linings of the bronchioles swell, thus narrowing the air passages and diminishing the flow of air. Breathing difficulty is primarily with *exhalation,* and total emptying of air before the next inspiration is impossible.

Severe bronchial obstruction occurs as the airways continue to narrow and become clogged with mucus. Wheezing is caused by the movement of air in and out of the constricted bronchial tubes and through the accumulated mucus. If medication is not used or is ineffective, this stage progresses to **status asthmaticus,** a condition in which breathing is so labored that treatment in a hospital emergency room is needed.

A status asthmaticus condition leaves fluid in the lungs that may cause days of occasional coughing spasms. Physicians emphasize that this fluid must be coughed up and not swallowed. Part of hospital treatment is respiratory therapy to aid weak or exhausted muscles in coughing up mucus.

Persons with chronic asthma have good and bad days. Often, these are related to weather changes, high pollen counts, environmental pollutants, or an infection. A common cold, for example, usually causes the lungs to fill with fluid with a resultant mild status asthmaticus condition. On days when the lungs feel bad and breathing is harder than usual, persons with asthma must decide between slowing down and trying to keep going. Those who make the latter decision often overuse the inhaler, each time thinking that, somehow, another puff will help. It typically does not.

Causes and Medications

Pathology at the cellular level is extremely complex. Simplified, the abnormality is in the beta-adrenergic receptors of lung cells that normally maintain balance between nerve fibers that release epinephrine (adrenalin) and those that liberate acetylcholine. Alterations of this balance, whatever the causal factors, cause obstruction, inflammation, and hyperreactivity of the airways.

Most of the medications used to treat asthma are therefore bronchodilators or antiinflammatory agents. These are available in tablet, powder, liquid, or aerosol form, but the aerosol inhaler is the preferred modality. By age 6, most children can be taught to use inhalators. Some individuals take one or two puffs of aerosol only when needed; others follow prescriptions of regular use twice or more daily.

The *beta-adrenergic agonists,* named for the cell receptors they work on, are the most potent bronchodilators. The airways open almost immediately after one or two puffs. There are few side effects (mainly rapid heartbeat) for most people, unless the inhaler is overused. Beta-adrenergic agonists therefore can be used as a preventive or as direct treatment of a beginning asthma attack. Foremost among these are albuterol (Ventolin, Proventil) and metaproterenol (Alupent, Metaprel). Most individuals who are conscientious about adhering to beta-adrenergic agonist treatment have no airway problems. The secret is to use the inhalator as soon as the chest begins to feel tight and therefore prevent an attack from progressing beyond the cough stage. Although some persons can "work through" an attack without medication, this practice is not encouraged (Cypcar & Lemanske, 1995).

Sodium cromolyn (Intal) is the bronchodilator most frequently used to supplement beta-adrenergic agonists. Two puffs taken 15 to 20 min before starting exercise provides about 4 hr of protection. About 10% of the U.S. athletes in the Olympics each quadrennium have asthma and rely on sodium cromolyn (Hogshead & Couzens, 1990). It has no side effects for most persons.

Many persons with severe chronic asthma also take *theophylline* daily in liquid, tablet, or capsule form. Among its many brand names are Slophyllin, Slobid, Primatene, and Quibron. This medication is needed when the theophylline level in the blood is low, a common deficiency in persons with asthma that requires periodic blood tests and considerable experimentation to find the right drug dosage. Side effects are insomnia, nervousness, diarrhea, and stomach cramps, but these discomforts disappear over time.

The medication of last resort, used only when the others fail and/or the body is fighting an infection, is the *corticosteroids* like prednisone (Deltasone) and flunisolide (Aero-Bid). These drugs have many side effects, but their powerful anti-inflammatory properties reduce bronchial tube swelling when nothing else will. They are typically taken for only a few days, but very severe asthma may demand regular dosage.

The four types of drugs described in this section are prescription medications and should be taken according to directions. All of the drugs mentioned, except for the aerosol bronchodilators, are banned by the International Olympic Committee (IOC). Athletes taking prescribed drugs should report these to their coaches or have their physicians notify the sport governing body.

Overuse of Aerosols

Correct use of aerosols can prevent attacks, but persons often forget to use their inhalers 15 to 20 min before exercise or opt to try an activity without protection. Whatever the reason, when coughing and breathing difficulty occur, persons tend to overuse the inhaler and try to keep going.

Most inhalers carry warnings to take no more than two or three puffs every 3 hr. Overuse causes nervousness, increased heart rate, high blood pressure, and other symptoms. These side effects are often ignored because they do not seem bad compared to the oxygen deficit that is causing panic. Nevertheless, excessive use of inhalers and other asthma medications can cause death.

Exercise-Induced Asthma

Students who experience breathing problems in physical education are not yet properly managing their asthma and need to be referred to a specialist for further study. Often, considerable time is required to determine the best medication; likewise, time is needed to learn to manage both the environment and stresses related to feeling different from peers. Should the student with asthma want to give up and resume a sedentary lifestyle, the physical educator must inspire the faith and courage to keep trying alternatives. *No student should be excused from physical education because of asthma.*

Role models are particularly helpful. Among the many Olympic athletes who manage asthma with medication are track star Jackie Joyner-Kersee and swimmers Tom Dolan and Amy Van Dyken.

Persons with asthma can do low-intensity exercise for long periods without an attack. This type of exercise is good for losing weight but does not improve aerobic fitness. Once weight is lost and aerobic fitness is targeted, six basic principles should be followed to prevent attacks:

1. *Use preexercise puffs of aerosol.*
2. *Use long warm-ups of mild intensity.* A 15- to 30-min warm-up is typically needed rather than the 5 to 10 min recommended by ACSM. Wind sprints are also good. For example, seven 30-sec sprints, each 2.5 min apart, have a beneficial effect on a distance run performed 30 min later.
3. *Induce a refractory state 45 to 60 min prior to anticipated EIA.* A **refractory state** is a period of protection against further asthma attacks that can be induced by sustaining a mild EIA episode before a major exercise event (Cypcar & Lemanske, 1995). The mild EIA episode provides protection for approximately 2 hr. This practice is generally used in conjunction with the inhalator, but only 40 to 50% of individuals with asthma experience refractory states, which are not well understood. Wind sprints, used as part of the warm-up period, are often conducted specifically to induce the refractory state. A series of six 50- to 100-yd sprints is generally sufficient to induce the refractory state.
4. *Use intermittent or interval training.* When applied to EIA, this means no more than 5 min of vigorous exercise followed by 5 min or less of rest. This sequence can be repeated over and over. The 5-min criterion is based on the average amount of time that the nonmedicated person with EIA can engage in continuous vigorous exercise at target heart rate before the onset of an attack.
5. *Select appropriate climatic conditions.* Warm and humid climatic conditions are recommended. This is why swimming is an excellent sport for people with asthma. When outdoor conditions are cold and dry, opt for indoor exercise. Wear a scarf or mask over the face in cold weather to warm the air before inspiration.
6. *Specialize in sports that demand relatively short bursts of energy.* Baseball, softball, volleyball, doubles tennis, weight training, and wrestling are particularly recommended. For persons who prefer to take little or no medicine, continuous-duration sports of high intensity, such as basketball, soccer, cross-country skiing, and marathons, are contraindicated for most, but not all.

Diaphragmatic Breathing

Most persons with asthma breathe incorrectly all or most of the time, overworking the upper chest and intercostal muscles and underworking the diaphragm. A goal, therefore, is to teach them that there are two kinds of breathing and for them to feel the difference. The two kinds are (a) shallow or costal (meaning rib cage) and (b) deep or diaphragmatic. To teach this, the physiology of respiration must be explained and practice given in diaphragmatic breathing (see Figure 19.15). The ability to breathe deeply is dependent on the strength of the diaphragm during inhalation and its ability to relax during exhalation.

The **diaphragm** is the dome-shaped muscle that separates the thoracic and abdominal muscles. In inhalation, the diaphragm contracts, descends 1 to 7 cm, and creates space for the lungs to fill with air. Exhalation begins when fullness of the lungs triggers relaxation and upward recoil of the diaphragm. This squeezes the air up and out. No muscle action other than this recoiling is needed in exhalation except during vigorous exercise.

Persons with asthma have more difficulty with exhalation than inhalation. This is because the phrenic nerve that innervates the diaphragm is sensitive to anything that alters the

FIGURE 19.15   Phenomena of normal breathing.

Inhalation	Exhalation
Bronchial tubes widen.	Bronchial tubes narrow.
Diaphragm contracts and descends.	Diaphragm ascends as a result of its elastic recoil action when it relaxes.
Abdominal muscles relax (return to normal length).	Abdominal muscles shorten, particularly in forced exhalation.
Upper ribs are elevated.	Ribs are depressed.
Thoracic spine extends.	Thoracic spine tends to flex.

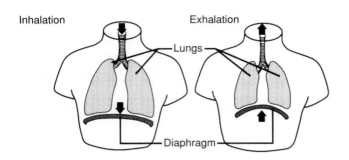

FIGURE 19.16   Child exhales into spirometer as test of pulmonary efficiency.

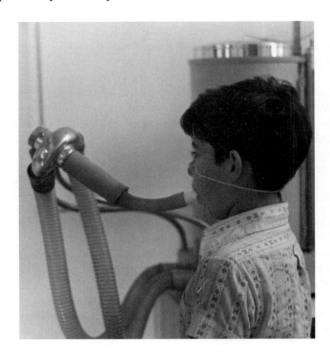

breathing pattern (wheezing, coughing, tightness, exercise, nervous tension). All of these things interfere with relaxation of the diaphragm which, in turn, decreases the amount of air pushed out. During an attack, exhalations progressively let out less and less air. The chest distends and begins to feel heavy and ache. Learning correct breathing therefore is closely related to learning to relax.

Persons who take only shallow breaths allow the diaphragm to weaken. This may not be a problem in a sedentary lifestyle unless a cold, lung infection, or asthma creates mucus or phlegm that must be coughed up. Then the reflex respiratory mechanism is inadequate, and abdominal muscle action must supplement the recoil force of the diaphragm. This explains why the abdominal muscles, especially if they are weak, are so sore after heavy coughing.

Exercise, all kinds, is easier when breathing is diaphragmatic rather than costal. Intensity of the exercise, together with fitness of the diaphragm, determine the extent that abdominal muscles must assist with exhalation. In sedentary persons with asthma, even light exercise may require abdominal activity to expel air from the lungs, whereas in fit persons, the abdominals work only during heavy exercise.

Diaphragmatic breathing is often called abdominal because persons best understand deep breathing by watching and feeling the abdomen protruding in inhalation and flattening in exhalation. Slow abdominal pumping in a supine position reinforces new understandings. Various weights (books, sandbags, etc.) can be placed on the abdomen with a challenge to watch or feel the weight go up and down. Persons may need to be reminded that normal breathing ranges from 12 to 14 breaths a minute at rest and from 40 to 50 during vigorous exercise.

Also of concern is making sure that persons with asthma breathe through the nose rather than the mouth. Many do not because of nasal congestion, but new prescription sprays eliminate this problem. Nasal breathing warms and moistens the air before it gets to the lungs, helping to maintain homeostasis. Mouth breathing does the opposite.

Changing overall pattern of breathing is as hard as permanently losing weight. Nevertheless, diaphragmatic breathing is an important goal. Activities like yoga (see Chapter 15 on relaxation) are a good way to improve breathing patterns (Nagarathna & Nagendra, 1985). During routine vigorous exercise, persons with asthma must be repeatedly reminded to breathe deeply and slowly.

Spirometers and Peak-Flow Meters

A spirometer test is periodically administered to determine status or improvement in pulmonary efficiency (see Figure 19.16). The test used most often is the FEV_1 (forced expiratory volume for 1 sec). To obtain a computer printout, the person inhales deeply and then blows air out of the mouth into the tube as hard and fast as possible.

The FEV_1 is the number of cubic centimeters of air forcefully exhaled in the first second after a deep inspiration. Normal FEV_1 values range from 500 to 4,500 cc (cubic centimeters) for boys and from 350 to 3,400 cc for girls. Any condition that causes bronchial obstruction and resistance in the airways reduces FEV_1.

The peak-flow meter is similar but less expensive, so persons can keep one at home and periodically test themselves. A scale indicating the velocity of air expelled in liters per second is on the gadget, so no computer is needed. A drop of more than 10% from one's normal reading indicates significant airflow resistance and signals the need to reevaluate one's management protocol with a physician.

Games to Improve Expiration

Breathing exercises are no longer considered a viable approach to the management of asthma. They may be used in chronic obstructive lung disease, cystic fibrosis, muscular dystrophy, and other very severe conditions that cannot be managed by medication and environmental controls. In such instances, they are commonly associated with hospitalization and inability to exercise in normal ways. Research, with one or two exceptions, has repeatedly indicated no significant values accruing from breathing exercises. Games are more effective in improving expiration and also help to clear mucus from passageways.

In ordinary expiration, no muscles are used. In vigorous exhalation, the following muscles contract: internal and external obliques, transversus abdominis, transversus thoracis, serratus posterior inferior, and posterior portions of the intercostals. Since the abdominal muscles participate vigorously in laughing, blowing, and singing, games based on these activities can be developed.

Games Using Abdominal Muscles

1. **Laugh-In.** Circle formation with "It" in center. "It" tosses a handkerchief high into the air. Everyone laughs as loudly as possible as it floats downward, but no laughter must be heard after the handkerchief contacts the floor. Anyone breaking this rule becomes the new "It." For variation, students can cough instead of laugh.
2. **Laugh Marathon.** Each student has a tape recorder. The object is to see who can make the longest-playing tape of continuous laughing.
3. **Guess Who's Laughing.** All students are blindfolded. One, who is designated as "It," laughs continuously until classmates guess who is laughing.
4. **Red Light, Green Light Laughing.** This game is played according to traditional rules except that laughing accompanies the running or is substituted for it.

All games designed to improve exhalation should be played in erect standing or running postures since the spine and pelvis must be stabilized by the lumbar extensors in order for the abdominal muscles to contract maximally.

Blowing Activities

Blowing activities are especially valuable in emphasizing the importance of reducing residual air in the lungs. Learning to play wind instruments is recommended strongly. Swimming offers a recreational setting for stressing correct exhalation. Games found to be especially popular follow:

1. **Snowflakes.** *Equipment:* A 1-inch square of tissue paper for each child. *Procedure:* Two teams with each child having one piece of paper. Each participant attempts to keep the paper above the floor after the whistle is blown.

When the paper touches the floor, the participant is disqualified. The winner is the team in which a player keeps the tissue in the air for the longest time.

2. **Ping-Pong Relay.** *Equipment:* One Ping-Pong ball for each team. *Procedure:* Two teams with one-half of the players of each team behind lines 50 ft apart. A player blows the Ping-Pong ball across the floor to his or her team member, who blows the ball back to the starting line. The relay continues until each player has blown the ball. The team that finishes first is the winner.
3. **Under the Bridge.** *Equipment:* One Ping-Pong ball for each team. *Procedure:* Teams with players standing in single file with legs spread. The last player in the file blows the ball forward between the legs of his or her team members, with additional blowing provided by the other players to move the ball quickly to the front. If the ball rolls outside the legs of the players, the last player must retrieve the ball and blow it again. When the ball reaches the front, the first player in the file picks up the ball, runs to the end of the file, and blows the ball forward again. The team finishing first is the winner.
4. **Balloon Relay.** *Equipment:* One balloon for each player. One chair for each team placed on a line 95 ft from the starting line. *Procedure:* Children on the teams line up in single file behind the starting line. Upon the signal to start, the first player of each team runs to the opposite line, blows up his or her balloon, places it on the chair, and sits on the balloon until it breaks. He or she then returns to the starting line and tags the next player, who proceeds in the same manner.
5. **Blow Out the Candle.** *Equipment:* A candle is placed on the floor between every two children. *Procedure:* Opponents lie on the floor on opposite sides 8 ft from the candle. Players attempt to blow out the candle from the greatest distance possible. The child who blows out the candle at the greatest distance is the winner.
6. **Ping-Pong Croquet.** *Equipment:* Ping-Pong balls and hoops made of milk cartons taped to the floor. *Procedure:* Each player blows the Ping-Pong ball through the series of hoops, positioned on the floor in the same manner as in a game of croquet. The ball must be moved and controlled entirely by blowing. The hands may not touch the ball at any time. The players who finish first are the winners.
7. **Self-Competition in Candle Blowing.** *Equipment:* Movable candle behind a yardstick placed opposite the mouth (see Figure 19.17A). *Procedure:* Child attempts to blow out lighted candle set at gradually lengthened distances on the yardstick.
8. **Self-Competition in Bottle Blowing.** *Equipment:* Two half-gallon bottles, half filled with water and connected with two rubber hoses and three glass pipes (see Figure 19.17B). *Procedure:* Child attempts to blow water from one bottle to another, first from sitting position and then standing position.

FIGURE 19.17   Blowing exercises.

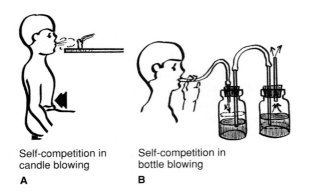

Self-competition in candle blowing

A

Self-competition in bottle blowing

B

Pursed-Lip Breathing Contests

This can be competition against self or others. Emphasize a short inspiration through the nose and long expiration through gently pursed lips, making a whistling or hissing noise. This is called *pursed-lip breathing.* Try timing the expiration phase with a stopwatch or metronome. Expiration should be at least twice as long as inspiration.

The Physical Activity Environment

Since so many persons with asthma are sensitive to pollens and dust, physical activity should be indoors at least during the seasons of peak incidence of attacks. Ideally, the room should be air-conditioned and dust-free.

Changes in weather, particularly cold, dry air, predispose persons to attacks. Alterations in body temperature—specifically, becoming overheated—seem to cause wheezing. A cold, wet towel on the forehead and/or the back of the neck between activities helps to maintain uniform body temperature.

When the chalkboard is in use, students with asthma should be stationed as far away from it as possible. Nylon-covered, allergen-free mats containing foam rubber as filler are recommended.

Most persons with asthma are extremely sensitive to cigarette smoke. Even if a cigarette is not burning, residual fumes can trigger an attack.

Whereas all children become thirsty during vigorous physical activity, they are generally encouraged to wait until the end of the period to get a drink of water. *In contrast, forcing fluids is an essential part of the total exercise program for students with asthma.* As tissues become drier during exercise, the mucus thickens and is more difficult to cough up. More than three or four consecutive coughs should be avoided, since coughing itself dries out the mucous membranes. The only means of thinning this mucus is through fluids taken by mouth or intravenously. Four or five quarts of water a day are recommended. Cold drinks are contraindicated since they may cause spasms of the bronchial tubes; hence, fluids at room temperature are recommended.

Antihistamines are not desirable for persons with asthma because they tend to dry out the mucus in the airway. If, because of hay fever or other allergies, a person is taking antihistamines, it is even more important that fluid intake be increased.

Posture Problems

Chronic asthma may result in permanent deformities of the chest—kyphosis, barrel chest, pigeon chest—and Harrison's groove (a depression along the lower edge of the thorax). These defects can be traced to an actual shortening of the muscle fibers of the diaphragm and intercostals. When maintained in the lowered position characteristic of inspiration, the diaphragm affects the position and function of the viscera, which are pushed against the abdominal wall. The person with asthma typically experiences difficulty in flattening the abdomen, which, along with the chest, may become permanently distended.

Psychological Problems

In the past, some persons believed that psychological problems caused asthma. This etiology is not valid. Asthma is a chronic lung disease that, like all illnesses and disabilities, complicates life. Different persons cope with illnesses in different ways, and some handle stress better than others.

The psychological phenomenon known as a *reaction formation* is common among persons with asthma. To prove their worth to others, they tend to establish unrealistically high levels of aspiration and then totally exhaust themselves in all-out effort to accomplish such goals. When it appears that they cannot live up to their own or the perceived expectations of others, an asthmatic attack often occurs, thereby adding more stress. "I could have made the deadline if I hadn't gotten sick!" "I would have won the match if I hadn't started wheezing." The physical educator will find many children eager to play, despite parental restrictions, and unwilling to withdraw from a game even when they evidence asthmatic symptoms. Many do not impose limitations upon themselves, refusing to accept the inevitability of an attack. Like all children, they want to be *normal.*

Chronic Obstructive Pulmonary Diseases

Chronic obstructive pulmonary diseases (COPD), including chronic bronchitis and pulmonary emphysema, now constitute the fastest growing chronic disease problem in America. The death rate has doubled every 5 years over the past 20 years.

Chronic bronchitis is a recurrent cough characterized by excessive mucus secretion in the bronchi. The three stages are (a) *simple,* in which the chief characteristic is mucoid expectoration; (b) *mucopurulent,* in which the mucus is intermittently or continuously filled with pus because of active infection; and (c) *obstruction,* in which there is narrowing of the airways in addition to expectoration. This is the stage at which the complications of emphysema and/or heart failure occur. The three stages may merge one into the other and span a period of 20 or more years.

Pulmonary emphysema is a destruction of the walls of the alveoli of the lungs. This destruction results in overdistention of the air sacs and loss of lung elasticity. *Emphysema* is a Greek word that means, literally, "to inflate or puff up." Persons with emphysema have difficulty expelling air. Whereas the normal person breathes 14 times a minute, the person with emphysema may breathe 20 to 30 times a minute and still not get enough oxygen into the bloodstream. The characteristic high carbon dioxide level in the blood causes

FIGURE 19.18 Hospital treatment for persons with asthma, cystic fibrosis, and similar conditions consists largely of special medications via a bronchodilator, chest physiotherapy done by a respiratory therapist, and postural drainage. The major purpose is to facilitate coughing to clear mucus from the clogged bronchial tubes.

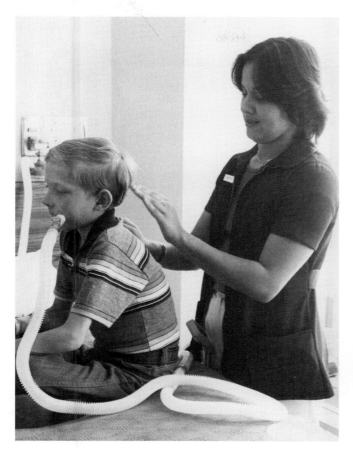 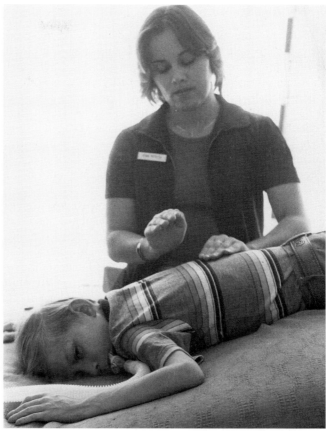

sluggishness and irritability. The heart tries to compensate for lack of oxygen by pumping harder, and possible heart failure becomes an additional hazard.

Emphysema is more common among men than women. Over 10% of the middle-aged and elderly population in America have emphysema. The specific etiology is still under study, but smoking and air pollution are causal factors.

Persons with COPD tend to restrict their activities more and more because of their fear of wheezing and dyspnea. This inactivity results in muscle deterioration, increased shortness of breath, and increasing inactivity—a vicious cycle! The activities recommended for persons with asthma are suitable also for individuals with bronchitis and emphysema.

Cystic Fibrosis

Cystic fibrosis is a genetic disorder of the secretion ability of membranes that line body organs, tubes, and passages. All organs are affected, most importantly the lungs, pancreas, intestinal mucous glands, and sweat glands. Normally, membranes secrete thin, freely moving mucus. In cystic fibrosis, the mucus is thick and sticky, creating two major problems. First, it clogs the bronchial tubes, interfering with breathing, and it lodges in the branches of the windpipe, acting as an obstruction. The resulting symptoms resemble those in asthma, bronchitis, and emphysema. Second, it plugs up the pancreatic ducts, preventing digestive enzymes from reaching the small intestine, and causing malnutrition.

Prevalence and Lifespan

Of all of the genetic diseases in the white population, cystic fibrosis is the most common life-shortening condition. In the United States, there are approximately 30,000 persons with cystic fibrosis and 10 million asymptomatic carriers. The incidence is 1 in every 2,500 live births in white Americans and 1 in every 17,000 black Americans. The condition is nonexistent in Asian Americans.

The median lifespan for persons with cystic fibrosis is now about 30 years. This is remarkable, considering that when the condition was first identified in the early 1960s, almost all children with cystic fibrosis died before reaching school age. Currently, about 35% of individuals with cystic fibrosis are age 18 or older.

Medications

Cystic fibrosis is managed by combined pulmonary, gastrointestinal, and psychological therapy. Pulmonary therapy includes daily chest physical therapy (see Figure 19.18), use of the same types of aerosols as for asthma, and relatively frequent use of corticosteroids and antibiotics to treat lung inflammation. Gastrointestinal therapy focuses on good nutrition, with emphasis on pancreatic enzyme replacement. Psychological therapy is family oriented and targets stress management.

Exercise Implications

No sports are contraindicated except scuba diving. Research indicates that people with cystic fibrosis tolerate exercise well. The same principles apply as in programming for individuals with asthma. Depending upon the severity of cystic fibrosis, the possible adverse effects of exercise are increased loss of salt and fluid through sweat, decreased tolerance for hot-weather exercise, shortness of breath, increased coughing, and lowered blood oxygen levels. Encouraging and monitoring fluid intake before, during, and after exercise is crucial. Salt tablets are not recommended, but individuals should be allowed to choose salty foods.

Exercise testing to determine the intensity of exercise needed for a personalized fitness program should be conducted by credentialed experts. The maximum heart rate used in prescribing exercise should be a measured actual maximal heart rate, not a predicted one. Lung-related factors limit exercise before the heart can achieve its maximal rate. **Desaturation,** which occurs in severe lung disease, refers to the lowering of blood oxygen (i.e., the hemoglobin count) during exercise. Testing should determine the heart rate at which this occurs, and care should be taken not to exceed this heart rate. Supplemental oxygen is used with exercise if desaturation occurs at very low heart rates. All possible accommodations are made to keep the person exercising as much as possible as the disease progresses.

Treatments for Severe Respiratory Conditions

Persons with severe asthma, chronic obstructive lung disease, and cystic fibrosis generally spend some time each year in the hospital or at home convalescing from attacks that were complicated by colds, flu, or other respiratory illness. Special treatment in hospitals includes postural drainage, thumping by a respiratory therapist, and nebulizer breathing therapy.

Postural Drainage

Postural drainage entails lying in various positions that enable gravity to help the cough drain the bronchial tree of accumulated mucus. The bronchodilator is used before the person assumes 10 different positions. The teacher, therapist, or parent taps the upper torso with his or her fingers, as depicted in Figure 19.18. Each of the positions is designed to drain a specific area of the bronchial tree; hence, the benefit derived from the position depends upon the amount of congestion present. Not all positions are required each session.

Nebulizer Breathing Therapy

While nebulizer machines can be purchased for home use, nebulizers in hospitals are more powerful and enable individuals to inhale monitored amounts of bronchodilators (see Figure 19.19). Machines are used several times daily to loosen thick mucus that accumulates in the chest. Patients are taught they *must* cough up and spit out all mucus.

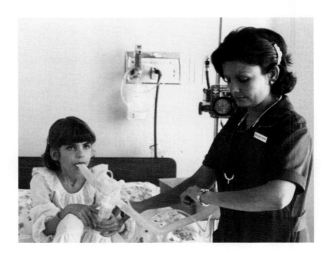

FIGURE 19.19 A young adolescent with cystic fibrosis undergoes breathing therapy several times each day during her frequent hospital confinements. Note the stunting of physical growth caused by several years of drug therapy.

Hemophilia

The term **hemophilia** encompasses at least eight different bleeding disorders caused by the lack of clotting factors in the blood. The prevalence is 1 in 10,000 persons in the United States. The physical educator who has one child with hemophilia is likely to have several since it is an inherited disorder. Historically, hemophilia has been said to appear only in males and to be transmitted through females. Recently, however, a type of hemophilia in women has been identified.

Contrary to popular belief, outward bleeding from a wound is not the major problem; rather, internal bleeding is. A stubbed toe, a bumped elbow, a violent sneeze, or a gentle tag game can be fatal. Each may cause internal bleeding that is manifested by discoloration, swelling, and other characteristics of a hematoma. The person with hemophilia tends to have many black and blue spots, swollen joints, and considerable limitation of movement. Minor internal bleeding may be present much of the time. When internal bleeding appears extensive, blood transfusions are administered.

Over a period of years, repeated hemorrhages into joints, if untreated, result in hemophilic arthritis. To minimize joint bleeding, the afflicted body part is frequently splinted. Pain is severe, and persons may avoid complete extension. This tendency, of course, results in such orthopedic complications as contractures.

Persons with hemophilia should be encouraged to engage in regular physical education and should be expected to establish their own limitations. Sports for individuals with hemophilia have been categorized from most to least safe (Beardsley, 1995). The most safe sports are swimming, walking, and table tennis. The least safe (contraindicated) sports are boxing, rugby, football, karate, weight lifting with free weights, wrestling, motorcycling, judo, hockey, and skateboarding. Additionally, adaptations are recommended for several sports, such as avoiding base sliding in baseball, heading in soccer, and jumping dismounts in gymnastics. Joint supports and pads, especially for knees and elbows, are recommended for most sports.

Sickle-Cell Disease (Anemia)

Although discovered by physician James Herrick in 1910, *sickle-cell disease* did not receive widespread attention until the early 1970s. At that time, 1 of every 400 black Americans was believed to have the disorder.

Sickle-cell disease is an inherited blood disorder that takes its name from the sickle shape the red blood cells assume when the blood's oxygen content is low. Persons with the disease are anemic, suffer crises of severe pain, are prone to infection, and often have slow-healing ulcers of the skin, especially around the ankles. Many do not live to adulthood.

Regular exercise should not be curtailed, *but tests and activities of cardiorespiratory endurance are contraindicated.* Under intense exercise stress, particularly in extreme cold or at altitudes above 10,000 ft, where the air's oxygen content is decreased, persons with sickle-cell anemia may collapse. They should also avoid becoming overheated since the normal evaporation of perspiration cools the skin and may precipitate an attack. Activities involving holding the breath, like underwater swimming, are contraindicated.

The disease develops at the time of conception, but symptoms do not usually appear until the child is 6 months or older. The first symptoms are pallor, poor appetite, early fatigue, and complaints of pain in the back, abdomen, and extremities. The child may not evidence sickle-cell anemia until he or she catches a cold or has an attack of tonsillitis; then he or she reacts worse than the normal child.

The course of the disease is marked by a sequence of physiological crises and complications that can be recognized, predicted, and treated, but not prevented. The crisis results from spasms in key blood vessels. The child experiences agonizing pain in certain muscles and joints, particularly those of the rib cage, and may run a high fever. Some crises are severe enough to require hospitalization. As the child grows older and learns limitations, the attacks become less frequent.

Anemia

Anemia is a condition of reduced oxygen-carrying capacity of the blood caused by deficiency in either red blood cells or hemoglobin, the oxygen-carrying pigment within the red blood cells. Mild anemia is not easily recognizable, but more severe conditions are characterized by loss of color in cheeks, lips, and gums; lowered activity level because of limited amount of oxygen available to burn calories; and increased heart and breathing rates.

There are many kinds of anemia. **Iron-deficiency anemia** is particularly common in females, from adolescence on, and in individuals who are dieting. Athletes at particular risk are long-distance runners and swimmers, who might become iron-deficient as a season of intensive training and competition progresses. Individuals with disabilities at particular risk are those with cerebral palsy and conditions that affect chewing or swallowing and general nutritional status. **Hereditary anemia** is

designated by many names, but exercise indications are similar. **Secondary or concomitant anemia** involves conditions that are side effects of other health impairments and/or medications. In particular, cancer, kidney disease, bleeding ulcers, and lead poisoning are typically complicated by anemia.

Anemia, depending on severity and type, is treated by iron-enriched diets, iron medications, and blood transfusions. Vitamin C supplements are also used because they improve iron absorption. Conditions are monitored by frequent blood tests to check hemoglobin and serum ferritin values. Excess iron values in the body can be dangerous, so overdosage should be avoided.

Individuals with mild to moderate anemia have no physical education restrictions except underwater swimming, but their performance levels in aerobic testing and training will generally be lower than those of peers. They are similar to individuals with asthma, in that sports that demand intermittent energy spurts are better than highly aerobic team sports like soccer, basketball, and football. Because of lowered blood oxygen levels and the tendency to fatigue quickly, aerobic conditioning will require strong internal motivation and emotional support.

Individuals with severe anemia are medically fragile, and the amount and type of exercise that can be tolerated should be individually determined. The liver, spleen, or bone marrow can be affected in severe anemia. Enlargement of the liver or spleen contraindicates all but very mild exercise.

Menstrual Problems

Three types of menstrual problems complicate exercise involvement. **Dysmenorrhea** (painful menstruation) generally occurs early in the menstrual cycle, usually before the blood begins to flow freely. This pain is often partly caused by an accumulation of gas (flatus) or by constipation. Exercises that relieve flatus, such as the bent-knee creeping position/movement, and several yoga techniques also ameliorate menstrual pain (see Figure 19.20). Severe or continued pain that cannot be relieved by aspirin and exercise signals the need to see a physician. **Menorrhagia** (excessive flow) is not normal and contraindicates exercise. The student should lie in a supine position with legs propped up and should see a physician as soon as possible. **Amenorrhea** is absence of menstruation. This condition occurs frequently in females who diet and/or exercise strenuously.

Premenstrual syndrome (PMS) is a combination of symptoms that occur 2 to 3 days before menstruation starts. Not all females have PMS, but some experience depression, edema (retention of fluids), sore and swollen breasts, lower back pain, and unexplained fatigue. These symptoms affect motivation to exercise.

Cancer

Cancer, a condition of unknown etiology in which body cells multiply in an abnormal manner and cause tumors, is second only to accidents as a cause of death in children ages 1 to 15 years. Most children who develop cancer, however, do not die; they continue to attend school while undergoing treatment.

FIGURE 19.20   Exercises for dysmenorrhea.

Knee-chest position
Lie motionless for several minutes.

Mosher abdominal pumping
Pump abdomen up and down
slowly.

Bellig pelvic stretch
Use hand to push pelvis toward
opposite side while strongly
contracting gluteal and
abdominal muscles.

Golub stretch and bend
Two parts: *On stretch*, lift leg and arm on
same side as high as possible, then relax
momentarily with arm extended at
shoulder height. *On bend*, bring feet
together and touch outside ankle with
opposite hand. Repeat both parts to
opposite side.

The incidence in children under 15 years is approximately 13 per 100,000. Each year, about 7,000 new cases are diagnosed within this age range. Table 19.10 indicates the incidence of the various types of childhood cancer.

For the population as a whole, it is estimated that one in every four persons will have cancer. Cancer, the second greatest cause of death in adults, affects more persons in middle and old age than in youth. Research shows that sport activity is a factor in preventing cancer (Grossarth-Maticek et al., 1990).

Cancer is treated by chemotherapy (drugs), radiation therapy, and surgery. Illustrative anticancer drugs are chlorambucil (Leukeran) and methotrexate (Folex). Estimates are that of every six persons with cancer, two will be saved, one will die but could have been saved if proper treatment had been received, and three cannot be saved with current knowledge. These estimates are for the total population, not children and youth whose chances for recovery are considerably higher. Over half of the cancer fatalities are over age 65.

Side effects of treatment are sometimes more difficult to manage than cancer itself. Radiation treatments are painless, but the side effects may include hair loss, nausea, vomiting, and weight loss. The side effects of chemotherapy are similar, with additional problems like anemia and associated decreased exercise tolerance, easy fatigability, and heightened susceptibility to respiratory infections. Often, low blood cell counts caused by chemotherapy result in the need for periodic blood transfusions.

The psychological effects of physical exercise and the importance of continued involvement in peer activities form the major rationale for keeping students with cancer in regular physical education, adapting instruction as needed. Exercise adaptations vary with the body part affected by cancer. Except for a few days following chemotherapy or radia-

Table 19.10   Incidence of various types of cancer in childhood.

Type	Relative Incidence (%)
Leukemias	33.8
Lymphomas, including Hodgkin's disease	10.6
Central nervous system tumors	19.2
Adrenal glands and sympathetic nervous system	7.7
Muscle, tendon, fat cancers	6.7
Kidney cancer (Wilms' tumor)	6.0
Bone cancer (sarcomas)	4.5
Eye cancer	2.7
Other	1–2.0

Note. In contrast, cancers of the lung, breast, colon, and skin are most common in adults.

tion, when the person will feel very sick, mild to moderate exercise is recommended.

Kidney and Urinary Tract Disorders

Approximately 3% of American schoolchildren have some history of a kidney or urinary tract disorder. Moreover, urinary-genital malformations account for 300,000 of the common birth defects in the United States, sharing second place in prevalence with congenital blindness and congenital deafness. Only mental retardation afflicts more newborn infants. *Vigorous exercise is contraindicated when kidney infection is present,* and the physician who has not been oriented to the possibilities of an adapted program often excuses the child from physical education.

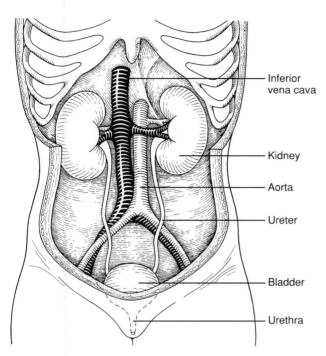

The urinary tract consists of the ureter (the tube connecting kidneys with the bladder), the bladder, and the urethra. The kidneys and urinary tract together often are called the *renal tract* or *renal system*.

A

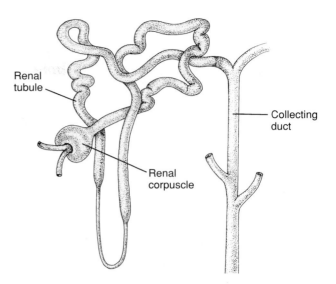

One of the million nephrons inside the kidneys

B

Biochemical Explanation

Normal functioning of the kidneys is required to excrete urine and to help regulate the water, electrolyte, and acid base content of the blood (i.e., to maintain homeostasis within the body). Problems of fluid retention (edema) and fluid depletion (dehydration) relate largely to the ability of the kidneys to alter the acidity of urine. Urination gets rid of body wastes like urea (an end product of protein metabolism). Renal failure often results in death by uremic poisoning.

Kidney and urinary disorders are many and varied. When both the kidneys and the urinary tract are involved (see Figure 19.21A), problems are often referred to as **renal disorders.** Federal law lists *nephritis* as one of its 11 examples of other health impairments. **Nephritis** (also called Bright's disease) is inflammation of the kidneys. The name is derived from *nephron,* the functional unit within the kidneys (see Figure 19.21B). Each kidney is comprised of about 1 million nephrons, each of which helps to filtrate substances from the blood and, subsequently, changes some of the resulting filtrate into urine and reabsorbs the remainder. This process results in about 45 gal (180 liters) of filtrate every 24 hr; only about 3 liters of this is voided as urine. The ability of the renal system to reabsorb the rest and maintain the balance between all its contents is obviously vital to life. The many possible disorders are too numerous to name and discuss. Approximately 55,000 deaths are kidney-related each year.

Kidney diseases often involve reduced blood flow to the kidneys. This problem, in turn, elevates blood pressure. The mechanism causing this is release of an enzyme called *renin* that stimulates production of the hormone *aldosterone* (a mineralosteroid). This hormone causes the kidneys to retain salts and water, increasing blood volume, which, in time, may overload the arterial walls and heart because of increased peripheral pressure causing elevated blood pressure.

Management of Renal Disorders

As last-resort treatments, dialysis and kidney transplants are becoming increasingly successful and affordable. Many congenital disorders are corrected through surgery, as are kidney stones and urinary tract obstructions. Routine management of less severe conditions includes antibiotics to treat infections, drugs to control hypertension, low-salt and other modified diets, and iron supplementation to control anemia.

Persons with spina bifida, spinal cord injuries, and amputations are particularly susceptible to renal disorders. Further detail on management of urinary problems appears in Chapters 23 and 24, which cover these disabilities.

Implications for Physical Education

Students with nephritis are in and out of the hospital many times. Each time they return to school, the fitness level is low. Most physicians concur that persons with kidney and urinary tract disease need moderate exercise. They are adamant, however, that such persons should not be subjected to physical fitness tests nor to actual physical stress of any kind.

Convulsive Disorders

The terms *epilepsy, seizure disorders,* and *convulsive disorders* are used interchangeably to denote a chronic condition of

FIGURE 19.22 Muscle contractions during seizures are tonic or clonic. They can affect all parts of the body.

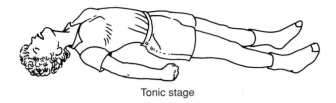

Tonic stage

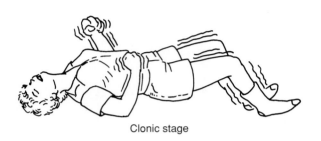

Clonic stage

FIGURE 19.23 Neurons within the cerebral cortex have synaptic knobs that release neurotransmitters that cause an increase in membrane permeability to sodium and thus trigger nerve impulses. Problems in synaptic transmission sometimes result in seizures.

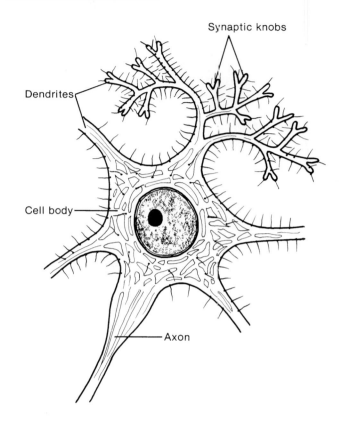

the central nervous system that is characterized by recurrent seizures. This condition is not a disease, but rather an upset in the electrical activity of neurons within the cerebral cortex.

Seizures may or may not be accompanied by **convulsions** (fits), defined as sudden, uncontrolled, and unpredictable muscle contractions and relaxations. Muscle activity in convulsions may be **clonic** (jerky or intermittent), **tonic** (continuous, stiff, or rigid), or both (tonic-clonic) (see Figure 19.22).

Most persons with epilepsy take daily medication that is 100% effective in preventing seizures. They live normal lives, and friends seldom know about their condition. A few, however, have periods of short- or long-term uncontrolled seizure activity that require restrictions on driving and exercise.

Biochemical Explanation

Seizures are caused by abnormalities in cell membrane stability. Normally, the cell membrane maintains equilibrium between sodium outside the cell and potassium inside the cell (see Figure 19.23). The balance controls **depolarization,** the cellular process that permits electrical current to be transmitted down the nerve fiber and carry messages to other nerve fibers. Epileptic cells are unable to maintain the normal balance; therefore, depolarization occurs too easily and too frequently. The resulting abnormal discharge of electrical activity spreads to the normal neurons, causing them to discharge also so that, soon, an entire area of the brain is involved.

Seizures are designated as *focal* or *generalized,* depending on how much of the brain is involved. **Focal** seizures are focused, or localized, in one specific area of the brain, such as, for instance, the motor strip of the right frontal lobe. The synonym for focal is *partial.* **Generalized seizures** involve the entire cerebral cortex (both hemispheres).

Prevalence

Prevalence of epilepsy varies from 3 to 7 per 1,000 in the nondisabled population. Among persons with brain injury, ei-

ther congenital or acquired, the incidence is much greater. From 25 to 50% of the population with cerebral palsy has seizures. About one third of everyone with severe mental retardation has seizures. Seizures are also relatively frequent in extreme old age.

Age at Time of First Seizure

The age of onset of the first seizure helps to explain why so many physical educators must cope with this problem (see Figure 19.24). Twenty percent of all persons with epilepsy have their first seizure before age 10 (see Figure 19.24). These are usually children with known or suspected neurological damage. Thirty percent of persons with epilepsy have their first seizure in the second decade, while 20% convulse initially in the third decade. The final 30% have their first seizure after age 40.

Types of Seizures

Classification of seizures varies according to whether traditional clinical symptomology serves as its basis or the international classification system adopted by the World Health Organization in 1970. The Epilepsy Foundation of America favors the latter (Gastaut, 1970), but textbooks have been slow to embrace the new system. Table 19.11 presents a comparison of

FIGURE 19.24 Ages at which various types of seizures most often occur.

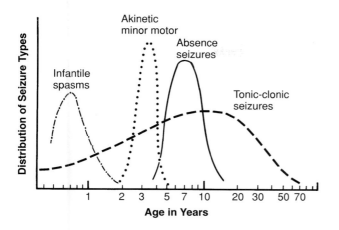

Table 19.11 Two commonly used classification systems in epilepsy: a comparison of terms.

International Classification System (Gastaut, 1970)	Traditional Clinical Classification System
I. Partial seizures	Focal epilepsy
A. Without impairment of consciousness	Motor (Jacksonian) or sensory
B. With impairment of consciousness	Psychomotor or temporal lobe epilepsy
II. Generalized seizures	
A. Absence	Petit mal
B. Tonic-clonic	Grand mal
C. Tonic only	Limited grand mal
D. Clonic only	
E. Myoclonic	Atypical petit mal *or* minor
F. Atonic	seizures *or* Lennox-Gastaut
G. Akinetic	syndrome
H. Infantile spasms	Jackknife or Salaam seizure
III. Unilateral seizures	
IV. Unclassified seizures	

the two systems. A nationwide effort is underway to educate physicians to the new terms and to convince them to discard such words as *grand mal, petit mal,* and *Jacksonian.* Different types of seizures have their first incidence at certain ages (see Figure 19.24).

Partial Seizures

Of the many kinds of partial seizures, the Jacksonian is most common. Clonic (jerky) contractions begin in one part of the body, usually a hand or foot, and from that point spread up the limb until all of the muscles are involved. This is sometimes called *march epilepsy* because the contractions march up the limb. The individual usually does not lose consciousness, although speech and other responses may be impaired.

Psychomotor epilepsy (sometimes called *automatism*) is characterized by unexplainable short-term changes in behav-

ior that later are not remembered. Automatic activity is carried on while in a state of impaired consciousness. One person may have temper tantrums, suddenly exploding for no reason, hitting another, provoking a fight, or throwing things. Another may have spells involving incoherent chatter, repetition of meaningless phrases, and inability to answer simple questions. Still another has episodes of sleepwalking or wakes the family at night with hysterical, unexplainable sobbing. Psychomotor attacks also may be confused with daydreaming or not paying attention in class.

Generalized Seizures

Absence seizures (previously called petit mal) account for about 8% of all epilepsy. Their symptoms are so subtle that the inexperienced observer seldom notices the seizure. There is an impairment of consciousness, never more than 30 sec, in which the individual seems dazed. The eyes may roll upward. If the person is talking at the time, there is a momentary silence and then continuation, with no loss of unity in thought. These seizures are rare before age 3 and often disappear after puberty. They are more common in females than males.

Tonic-clonic seizures (previously called grand mal) are the most dramatic and easily recognized. They have three or four phases.

1. **Aura.** This is a warning or premonition of the attack that is always the same for a particular person. An aura may be a certain smell, flashing of lights, vague feeling of apprehension, sinking feeling in the abdomen, or feeling of extraordinary rapture. Only about 50% of persons have auras.

2. **Tonic phase.** *Tonic* means constant, referring to the continuous contraction of muscles. The person straightens out, becomes stiff, utters a cry, and loses consciousness. If there is a tonic contraction of respiratory muscles, the person becomes cyanotic. Fortunately, this phase seldom lasts more than 30 sec.

3. **Clonic phase.** *Clonic* refers to intermittent contraction and relaxation of muscles. The clonic phase persists from a few seconds up to 2 or 3 min. The tongue may be bitten as the jaws work up and down. The sphincters around the rectum and urinary tracts relax, causing the person to urinate or defecate.

4. **Sleep or coma phase.** After a period of brief consciousness or semiconsciousness, during which the person complains of being very tired, he or she lapses into a sleep that may last several hours. Upon awakening, the person is either very clear or is dazed and confused. Usually, there is no memory of the seizure.

Occasionally, seizures occur that are entirely clonic or tonic.

Myoclonic seizures are brief, sudden, violent contractions of muscles in some part or the entire body. Often, these are manifested by a sudden head jerk, followed by jerking of arms and legs, and the trunk bending in upon itself. The individual may lose consciousness, but the duration of a myoclonic seizure is much briefer than that of tonic-clonic or tonic- or clonic-only types.

Atonic seizures are similar to absence seizures except that there is momentary diminution or abolition of postural tone. The individual tends to sag or collapse.

Akinetic seizures (also called sudden drop attacks) cause the individual to suddenly lose muscle tone and plummet to the ground, momentarily unconscious. These seizures may be sometimes purposely aborted. Sudden falling asleep (narcolepsy) may be a form of akinetic seizure.

Infantile spasms (also called jackknife seizures) are usually characterized by a "doubling up" motion of the entire body, although they may be less generalized and manifested only by head dropping and arms flexing. Infantile spasms typically occur between 3 and 9 months of age, after which other types of seizures may replace them. This problem is associated with severe mental retardation. Infantile spasms should not be confused with the generalized seizures that many normal infants and children (5 to 10%) have in conjunction with illness and high fever; these are called *febrile seizures* and typically are a once-in-a-lifetime happening.

Unilateral seizures involve only one side of the brain and, therefore, only one side of the body. These may be of any type.

Unclassified seizures are those that do not meet the criteria for any one type or those that are mixed types. About 35 to 40% of epilepsy is a combination of absence and tonic-clonic seizures.

Etiology

The etiology of epilepsy falls within two broad classifications: (a) idiopathic (genetic or endogenous) and (b) acquired (symptomatic or exogenous). **Idiopathic** means that the cause is unknown, and 80% of all epilepsy remains unexplainable. There appears to be a genetic predisposition toward epilepsy, but this is controversial. In general, the parent with epilepsy has 1 chance in 40 of giving birth to a child with epilepsy. The incidence is increased if both parents are epileptic. *Acquired* epilepsy can be traced directly to birth injuries, brain tumors, oxygen deprivation, lead poisoning, cerebral abscesses, and penetrating injuries to the brain.

Factors That Aggravate Seizures

1. Increases in alkalinity of the blood (see Figure 19.25). These changes are very subtle and minute. High alkalosis favors seizures. High acidity inhibits seizures. Diet therapy is used frequently. Acid-producing diets, high in fat content—such as cream, butter, eggs, and meat—have successfully produced a quieting effect. This kind of diet is called a **ketogenic diet** (high in fat). The accumulation of acid products in the blood as a result of exercise is also believed to help prevent seizures.

2. Hyperventilation (overbreathing) that leads to respiratory alkalosis, especially when the exercise causing hyperventilation is suddenly interrupted (Linschoten, Backx, Mulder, & Meinardi, 1990). Holding the breath as long as possible, as in distance underwater swimming, is a common form of hyperventilation that is contraindicated. Breath-holding lowers the carbon dioxide content of the

FIGURE 19.25 Most factors that aggravate seizures relate to electrolyte balance in the cellular fluids, especially the balance between acidosis and alkalosis in the pH of arterial blood. pH, an abbreviation for potential of hydrogen, is a measure used to express relative degree of acidity and alkalosis.

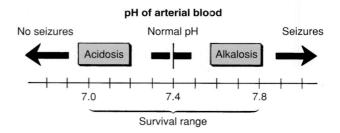

blood, which increases alkalosis. Sports that commonly induce hyperventilation are scuba diving and high-altitude climbing. Taking a deep breath and jumping into water sometimes triggers hyperventilation.

3. Hyperhydration (ingestion of too much water). This can occur during swimming, especially in beginners.

4. Hyperthermia (too much body heat) as sometimes occurs in marathons and triathlons in high temperatures under humid conditions.

5. Hypoglycemia in diabetes or in persons exercising vigorously over a long duration with no food or liquid.

6. Fatigue, especially sleep deprivation and disturbances of nocturnal rhythms.

7. Sudden emotional stress or excitement like bad news, fright, or anger.

8. Excessive alcohol and caffeine.

9. In women, menstrual periods. Many girls and women have seizures only around their periods. Edema aggravates the onset of seizures.

Seizures and Exercise

Seizures seldom, if ever, occur during vigorous physical activity. Convulsions are most likely during the cool-down after exercise and during late-night hours.

There is no evidence that intense sport competition increases the likelihood of seizures. Seizure-prone persons must, however, be conscientious in taking their medication, eating properly, and getting enough sleep. Obviously, they must minimize the factors that aggravate seizures. Within the disability sport movement, many athletes take medication to control epilepsy. Occasionally, a seizure occurs, necessitating rest for a few hours. Thereafter, training and competition are resumed. The overall philosophy is that an isolated seizure is no big deal.

Social Problems

The social problems in epilepsy are greater than the medical ones. The person regaining consciousness after a first seizure does not remember anything that happened. He or she is self-conscious and embarrassed. Who wouldn't be? First seizures in adolescence are a particular concern.

Adolescence in our culture is a time of particular sensitivity, and most teenagers with convulsive disorders confess that their greatest hang-up is what friends think. On the other hand, the peer group that has witnessed the seizure has undergone a terrifying, traumatic experience. It is probably the first seizure they have seen, and they are eager to talk about it and share perceptions. Individual responses are as variable as human beings themselves, but many persons are reluctant to continue dating or even socializing with a person who has seizures. Driver's licenses, if issued, have restrictions. Employment opportunities are reduced, and insurability under workmen's compensation may be a problem.

Medication

Phenobarbital (Luminal) and phenytoin (Dilantin), the drugs used most often in controlling *tonic-clonic seizures,* were not introduced until 1912 and 1938, respectively. Teachers who work with children from low-income families see many seizures, almost always caused because a prescription is not filled on time. Often, the problem is carelessness or ignorance rather than lack of money. When taken regularly according to directions, modern medications are almost completely effective in preventing seizures.

Epilepsy medications have a number of adverse side effects. Among these are reduced coordination and concentration, poor reaction time, drowsiness, blurred vision, and irritability. Dilantin, in particular, causes gum and teeth problems.

Management of a Seizure

Should a seizure occur, clear the area around the individual. Do not attempt to hold the body down or restrain limbs. Ascertain that the mouth and nose are clear and permit breathing. Lying in a prone or side position is best. The seizure should be allowed to run its normal course, with everyone remaining calm and accepting.

Implications for Physical Education

The American Medical Association (AMA, 1983) recommends that students with epilepsy participate fully in school physical education and athletics. Reversing its initial stand, the AMA now indicates that collision (football, ice hockey, lacrosse) sports and contact (basketball, soccer, wrestling) sports can be played by the medically balanced student. Boxing should be avoided. Activities like heading the ball in soccer, which involve repeated insults to the head, are controversial.

Activities that might result in a fall (cycling, horseback riding, rope- or tree-climbing, parallel bars, trampoline, balance beam, mountain climbing) should always be done with a partner or group. Likewise, individuals with epilepsy should not swim or engage in other water sports alone. In some students, a specific activity, for unknown reasons, may precipitate seizures. If this occurs *repeatedly,* then that one activity should be restricted.

Students whose seizures are under control are no different from their peers. They need good supervision when enrolled in beginning swimming, but so do all children! Likewise, they need a gymnastics teacher who is competent in spotting techniques. Again, this does not make them different from their peers, who also need a good spotter when undertaking activities on the high balance beam, parallel bars, and trampoline. Most important, persons with epilepsy need the acceptance and belonging that team membership ensures.

Environmental Disorders

The three most common environmental hazards to children's health are metal pollution (lead, mercury, zinc), air pollution (including cigarette smoke), and low-level radiation. Of these, the most research has been done on lead (Pueschel, Linakis, & Anderson, 1996).

Lead poisoning is a leading cause of health impairments in children ages 1 to 6 years. Elevations in blood/lead concentration are associated with cognitive and behavioral difficulties. Approximately 5 to 8% of preschool children have elevated blood lead levels. This includes 1 in 20 white children and 1 in 5 black children.

Approximately 600,000 tons of lead are released by the smelting industry into the environment annually, much of which is carried by winds and deposited in soil where children play. This lead fallout is now the leading cause of lead poisoning. In earlier decades, the main routes of exposure were leaded gasoline, ingestion of paint or paint dust, milk formulas from improperly soldered cans, and tainted drinking water. Houses built before 1960 with peeling or chipping paint continue to be a high risk factor. The federal Lead Poisoning Prevention Act of 1971 permits large-scale screening of preschool children to identify those at risk, but little else has been done (except in individual communities) to cope with this problem.

Physical educators working in blighted urban areas can expect as many as 40% of their students to carry significant lead burdens, which cause subtle health and behavior problems. Indicators of mild lead poisoning are listlessness, lethargy, irritability, clumsiness, and anemia, all of which contribute to developmental delay. Severe lead poisoning is associated with kidney disease and anemia, both of which lower exercise capabilities. Severe or persistent lead poisoning, without treatment, results in seizures, coma, and eventual death. Even with treatment, mental retardation and epilepsy often occur. Lead poisoning is treated by such drugs as edetate calcium disodium and D-penicillamine, which can be taken either orally or by intramuscular injection. The overall treatment is called **chelation therapy.** Most important, however, is removal of students from lead-tainted environments.

Tuberculosis

Tuberculosis, although no longer a common cause of death, still ranks within the top 10 reportable diseases. The incidence of reported tuberculosis is about the same as that of infectious hepatitis, measles, and rubella. Among causes of death, tuberculosis ranks 19th. A vaccine is about 80% effective in disease prevention. This vaccine, however, often is not used in poverty areas, especially those devastated by drug use and human immunodeficiency virus (HIV). In the 1990s, tuberculosis often occurs as a complication of HIV infection.

Tuberculosis, although often conceptualized as a lung disease, can affect any tissue in the body. **Tuberculosis** is an infectious disease caused by bacteria (i.e., the tubercle bacillus) and characterized by the formation of tubercles (little swellings). In this country, bone and joint tuberculosis is more likely to come to the attention of physical educators than the other types. Of the skeletal sites of tuberculosis, the most common is the spine, followed by hip and knee.

Pott's disease, or tuberculosis of the spine, is a disorder that often results in kyphosis (round upper back). This inflammation of the vertebral bodies occurs most often in children and young adults. Pott's disease is characterized by the formation of little tubercles on the vertebral bodies. Destruction and compression of the vertebral bodies affects the spinal cord and adjacent nerves to the extent that movement becomes extremely painful. The characteristic kyphotic curvature is called a *gibbus,* meaning "hump." The condition of having a humpback is *gibbosity.* A medical synonym for Pott's disease is *tuberculous spondylitis.*

Tuberculosis remains a common cause of **meningitis** (infection of the covering of the brain) during early childhood. The consequences of this disease, even with the best treatment, are severe, with some degree of intellectual deficit occurring in about 20% of children, as well as hearing and vestibular defects. Seizures, hydrocephalus, spasticity, ataxia, and incoordination are common outcomes also.

HIV/AIDS Conditions

Human immunodeficiency virus (HIV) and acquired immune deficiency syndrome (AIDS) conditions affect approximately 21.8 million persons worldwide. The epidemic continues to be most critical in Africa and South and Southeast Asia. Data released at the 11th International Conference on AIDS in 1996 indicate that about 1 in every 300 Americans carries the HIV virus, which causes AIDS. The incidence is much higher among individuals who engage in injection drug use and heterosexual or homosexual vaginal or anal sex without condoms.

The first cases of AIDS were reported in 1981, but the virus that causes it was not identified until 1984. Over the last few years, there have been many changes in terminology, prognosis, acceptance, and high-risk populations (see Figure 19.26). There is still, however, no cure or immunization.

Stages of HIV/AIDS Progression

HIV/AIDS is a global term for immune system infection, disease, and disintegration that is caused by the HIV virus group, which infects several kinds of cells but mainly targets CD4 lymphocytes. HIV/AIDS can be acquired or congenital. Acquired conditions occur through contact with the blood, semen, vaginal secretions, breast milk, and amniotic fluid of carriers. Congenital conditions occur because infected antibodies are passed on to fetuses by their HIV-infected mothers. The manifestation of symptoms is slightly different in acquired and congenital pathology.

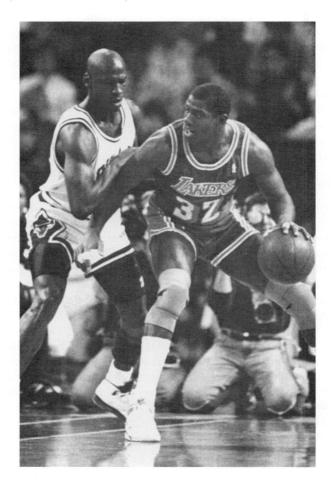

FIGURE 19.26 Magic Johnson's announcement that he has HIV increased awareness that all people are at risk. (© Reuters/Bettmann.)

Acquired HIV/AIDS

Acquired HIV/AIDS progresses through three distinct stages, and persons in each stage are carriers (Olenik & Sherrill, 1994; Seltzer, 1993).

Stage 1. HIV infection refers to a symptom-free condition lasting several years that is diagnosed by a positive antibody test that indicates HIV in the blood serum. Most persons in this latency stage do not know they are infected and thus constitute considerable risk to others if they do not practice safe sex and safe needle injection. The average latency period between infection and onset of systems is 8 to 12 years (D'Angelo, 1995).

Stage 2. HIV disease refers to all manifestations of infection prior to the onset of acute, terminal illness. Symptoms are severe weight loss, chronic diarrhea, nonproductive cough with shortness of breath, swollen lymph nodes (neck, armpit, groin), fevers of unknown origin, chronic fatigue, skin rashes, and increased susceptibility to infections. This stage formerly was called AIDS-related complex, or ARC (Surburg, 1988), but new terminology was agreed upon in the late 1980s (Gray, 1989).

Stage 3. AIDS, the terminal illness stage, refers to the final months of acute medical crises, many of which require hospitalization and/or complete bed rest. Disintegration of the immune system makes treatment of opportunistic infections and cancers ineffective. Pneumonia, Kaposi's sarcoma (cancer), and dementia caused by brain damage are associated with this stage.

Congenital HIV/AIDS

Congenital HIV/AIDS seems to follow three patterns. **Pattern 1,** which includes about 50% of infants born with HIV, is a symptom-free status. These infants test seropositive until about 2 years old because of antibodies passed on by their mothers. Thereafter, blood tests give no indication of infection, and these children are healthy. **Pattern 2,** the static form of congenital HIV, includes infants who appear healthy until age 6 to 9 months, then exhibit disease symptoms for a short period, and thereafter have a relatively long period of freedom from illness before the AIDS stage begins. Current estimates are that about 60% of these children will survive until age 5 (Diamond, 1989). **Pattern 3,** the progressive form of congenital HIV, is similar to Pattern 2 except that, once illness begins, health rapidly deteriorates; the mean survival time is 8 months.

Congenital HIV/AIDS attacks different systems in infants than in adults. Congenital etiology results in 78 to 90% of infants having central nervous system involvement as compared to 39 to 60% incidence in adults (Diamond, 1989). The most common manifestations in children are mental retardation, cerebral palsy, developmental delays, and motor abnormalities.

Motor development problems result from both HIV infection and drug-related damage. Separating what causes what is not yet possible. Spasticity, persistence of primitive reflexes, and visuomotor perceptual and organizational problems are frequently noted (Cratty, 1990; Diamond, 1989). Several kinds of cerebral palsy (spasticity, athetosis, ataxia) have been reported. The most severe viral-caused neurological changes are in the basal ganglia and pyramidal tracts of the white matter (Epstein & Sharer, 1988).

Children With AIDS, a newsletter published six times annually, is an excellent source for staying abreast of new developments. It is published by The Foundation for Children With AIDS, Inc., 77B Warren Street, Brighton, MA 02135.

Medication and Exercise

In early 1996, governmental agencies approved five new medications that interfere with HIV's ability to reproduce. Multidrug therapy, which attacks the virus in various biochemical ways, is showing tremendous promise, but research indicates that the prognosis is better if treatment begins immediately after diagnosis, long before symptoms begin to appear.

HIV/AIDS medications cause such side effects as severe diarrhea, abdominal cramps, anemia, nausea, chronic fatigue, headache, and numbness. The incidence of side effects is greater, of course, in multidrug treatment than when a single drug like AZT (zidovudine or Retrovir), the best-known medication, is used. Side effects of medications decrease the desire and ability to exercise (D'Angelo, 1995), and a major role of professionals is to provide encouragement and support to overcome barriers caused by medication side effects.

Research indicates that individuals with chronic asymptomatic HIV infections show increases in CD4 cell counts as well as in activity of natural killer (NK) cells during participation in aerobic exercise programs (LaPerriere, Fletcher, & Antoni, 1991). More research is obviously needed, but there is much empirical evidence that individuals in Stages 1 and 2 of HIV/AIDS can derive physical and mental benefits from exercise. Physicians recommend avoidance of collision sports such as boxing, wrestling, football, and rugby, to protect others, because these sports are more likely to cause blood spills.

Implications for Physical Education

As HIV-infected children increase in number, more will be attending public schools. More teachers and coworkers will also have the syndrome. These persons have the same education and employment rights as everyone else. HIV-infected students fall under the other health impairments category of federal legislation, and their physical education should be conducted accordingly.

Physical education adaptations are similar to those of other OHI children with weight loss, easy fatigue, respiratory problems, and increased susceptibility to infections. They miss more school, which creates social and learning problems. As the condition becomes more severe, children may need to carry portable oxygen tanks with them (see Figure 19.27). Books and videos that present models are essential (e.g., Schilling, 1990; White & Cunningham, 1991). The best-known child model is Ryan White, who was infected through a blood transfusion for hemophilia; he was diagnosed in 1984 and lived 6 years, during which time his battle against discrimination in an Indiana school district became national news.

Ignorance, fear, hysteria, and discrimination are probably the greatest problems to be resolved in physical education as well as in other school subjects. The American Coaching Effectiveness Program emphasizes that AIDS is *not* transmitted by the following (Landry, 1989, p. 22):

1. Competing in sports
2. Coming in contact with sweat
3. Having casual contact, such as handshaking or hugging
4. Living with someone who has AIDS and sharing eating utensils, towels, and toilets
5. Kissing
6. Swimming in a pool with someone who has AIDS

Risks and Safe Practices

HIV is often transmitted through sex without condoms and/or with multiple partners. Risk is high under these conditions, whether the relationship is heterosexual or homosexual. Condoms are not 100% safe. The best practice is obviously having sex with one mutually faithful, uninfected partner. Children who are victims of sex abuse and/or who learn about sex from the streets or television are special risk groups. Persons with

FIGURE 19.27 Jonathan, a first-grader, tells classmates how he contracted HIV from a blood transfusion during infancy. The machine in front of Jonathan is a portable oxygen tank, an adaptation used for a few months to make breathing easier but later abandoned. (Courtesy of Sharon Schilling, author of *My Name Is Jonathan (and I Have AIDS)*.)

mental retardation and other disabilities who are not provided prevention education are also at risk.

Another safe practice is to use only sterile needles or syringes. Never share a needle with another, regardless of the fluid being injected. Intravenous drug abusers are a high-risk group because so many have neither the money nor the inclination to purchase sterile needles.

First-aid and emergency care that involves blood should be rendered with rubber gloves. Even when gloves are used, hands should be washed with soap and water. If nosebleeds or injuries result in blood on the floor or equipment, wash the surface clean with a household bleach solution of 1 part bleach to 10 parts water. Towels and clothing with blood contamination are safe after hot-water/detergent washing but should be stored in tied plastic bags until laundered or trashed. These first-aid guidelines come from the U.S. Public Health Service, Centers for Disease Control (CDC).

Wounds that might seep blood should be kept covered during sport activity. Bandages not only protect the injured site but minimize the chance of blood contact by others. Care givers and teachers should maximize their own skin care and realize that they are at most risk for accidental infection when there is a skin breakdown.

Blood-Borne Hepatitis

Hepatitis B, which is transmitted by exposure to infected blood or other bodily fluids, is often grouped with HIV/AIDS conditions because of the similarity in transmission and in protocols for handling blood spills. **Hepatitis** is inflammation of the liver, the largest organ in the body, located on the right side, immediately below the diaphragm. Hepatitis B can occur with or without symptoms. Individuals with symptoms manifest these from 30 to 120 days after exposure to the hepatitis virus. Early symptoms are fever, headache, malaise, and loss of appetite. Later, **jaundice** (a yellowing of skin and body fluids) occurs along with abdominal pain or discomfort. Approximately 10 to 20% of individuals additionally experience painful joint swelling, rash, and arthritis-type symptoms. An acute disease episode usually spans 3 to 6 weeks, during which mild to moderate exercise may be beneficial.

Hepatitis B is more easily transmitted than the HIV virus, and data indicate that this disease has reached epidemic status. Approximately 10% of individuals with acute hepatitis become carriers. The fatality rate is low, but convalescence is often prolonged. Many persons have relapses of chronic illness. No specific treatment is beneficial during acute hepatitis. A hepatitis B vaccine is highly recommended for professionals who work with high-risk individuals.

References

American College of Sports Medicine. (1995). *Guidelines for exercise testing and prescription* (5th ed.). Philadelphia: Lea & Febiger.

American Medical Association. (1983). Sports and children with epilepsy. *Pediatrics, 72,* 884–885.

Bar-Or, O. (1983). *Pediatric sports medicine for the practitioner.* New York: Springer-Verlag.

Beardsley, D. S. (1995). Hemophilia. In B. Goldberg (Ed.), *Sports and exercise for children with chronic health conditions* (pp. 301–310). Champaign, IL: Human Kinetics.

Berg, K. (1986). *Diabetic's guide to health and fitness.* Champaign, IL: Life Enhancement.

Brandt, N. (1973). Your son and diabetes. *Today's Health, 51*(6), 34–37, 69–71.

Coram, S., & Mangum, M. (1986). Exercise risks and benefits for diabetic individuals: A review. *Adapted Physical Activity Quarterly, 3,* 35–37.

Cratty, B. J. (1990). Motor development of infants subject to maternal drug use: Current evidence and future research strategies. *Adapted Physical Activity Quarterly 1,* 110–125.

Cumming, G. R. (1987). Children with heart disease. In J. S. Skinner (Ed.), *Exercise testing and exercise prescription for special cases* (pp. 241–260). Philadelphia: Lea & Febiger.

Cypcar, D., & Lemanske, R. F. (1995). Exercise-induced asthma. In B. Goldberg (Ed.), *Sports and exercise for children with chronic health conditions* (pp. 149–166). Champaign, IL: Human Kinetics.

D'Angelo, L. J. (1995). Chronic blood-borne infections. In B. Goldberg (Ed.), *Sports and exercise for children with chronic health conditions* (pp. 187–196). Champaign, IL: Human Kinetics.

Diamond, G. W. (1989). Developmental problems in children with HIV infection. *Mental Retardation, 27*(4), 213–217.

Duda, M. (1985). The role of exercise in managing diabetes. *Physician and Sports Medicine, 13,* 164–170.

Ellestad, M. H. (1986). *Stress testing: Principles and practices* (3rd ed.). Philadelphia: F. A. Davis.

Epstein, L. G., & Sharer, L. R. (1988). Neurology of human immunodeficiency virus infection in children. In M. L. Rosenblum, R. M. Levy, & D. E. Bredesen (Eds.), *AIDS and the nervous system* (pp. 79–101). New York: Raven Press.

Fernhall, B., & Tymeson, G. (1987). Graded exercise testing of mentally retarded adults: A study of feasibility. *Archives of Physical Medicine and Rehabilitation, 68,* 363–365.

Freed, M. D. (1984). Recreational and sports recommendations for the child with heart disease. *Pediatric Clinics of North America, 31,* 1307–1320.

Gastaut, H. (1970). Clinical and electroencephalographic classification of epileptic seizures. *Epilepsia, 11,* 102–113.

Goldhaber, S., Brown, W. D., & St. John Sutton, M. (1987). High frequency of mitral valve prolapse and aortic regurgitation among asymptomatic adults with Down syndrome. *Journal of the American Medical Association, 258,* 1793–1795.

Gray, C. D. (1989). Opening comments on the conference on developmental disabilities and HIV infection. *Mental Retardation, 27*(4), 199–200.

Griffith, H. W. (1992). *Complete guide to prescription and nonprescription drugs.* New York: Body Press/Perigee.

Grossarth-Maticek, R., Eyesenck, H. J., Uhlenbruck, G., Rieder, H., Freesemann, C., Rakic, L., Gallasch, G., Kanazir, D., & Liesen, H. (1990). Sport activity and personality as elements in preventing cancer and coronary heart disease. *Perceptual and Motor Skills, 71,* 199–209.

Hogshead, N., & Couzens, G. S. (1990). *Asthma and exercise.* New York: Henry Holt.

Kaplan, N. M. (1990). *Clinical hypertension* (5th ed.). Baltimore: Williams & Wilkins.

Kertzer, R., Croce, R., Hinkle, R., & Janson-Sand, C. (1994). Selected fitness and motor behavior parameters for children and adolescents with insulin-dependent diabetes mellitus. *Adapted Physical Activity Quarterly, 11*(3), 284–296.

Krotoski, D. M., Nosek, M. A., & Turk, M. A. (1996). *Women with physical disabilities: Achieving and maintaining health and well-being.* Baltimore: Paul H. Brookes.

Landry, G. (1989). *AIDS in sport.* Champaign, IL: Leisure Press.

LaPerriere, A., Fletcher, M. A., & Antoni, M. H. (1991). Aerobic exercise in an AIDS risk group. *International Journal of Sports Medicine, 12,* 853–857.

Linschoten, R., Backx, F., Mulder, O., & Meinardi, H. (1990). Epilepsy and sports. *Sports Medicine, 10*(1), 9–19.

Long, J. W. (1992). *The essential guide to prescription drugs.* New York: Harper Perennial.

Marino, B., & Pueschel, S. M. (Eds.). (1996). *Heart disease in persons with Down syndrome.* Baltimore: Paul H. Brookes.

Maurer, H. M. (1983). *Pediatrics.* New York: Churchill Livingstone.

NurseReview. (1987). *Cardiac problems.* Springhouse, PA: Springhouse.

Olenik, L., & Sherrill, C. (1994). Physical education and students with HIV/AIDS. *Journal of Physical Education, Recreation and Dance, 65*(5), 49–52.

Physician's Desk Reference. (published annually). Oradell, NJ: Medical Economics.

Pitetti, K. H., & Tan, D. M. (1991). Effects of a minimally supervised exercise program for mentally retarded adults. *Medicine and Science in Sports and Exercise, 23,* 594–601.

Pueschel, S. M., Linakis, J. G., & Anderson, A. C. (Eds.). (1996). *Lead poisoning in childhood.* Baltimore: Paul H. Brookes.

Rimmer, J. (1993). *Fitness and rehabilitation programs for special populations.* Dubuque, IA: Brown & Benchmark.

Schilling, S. (1990). *My name is Jonathan (and I have AIDS): Teacher's edition.* Denver: Prickly Pair.

Seltzer, D. G. (1993). Educating athletes on HIV disease and AIDS: The team physician's role. *Physician and Sports Medicine, 2*(1), 109–115.

Sheldahl, L. M. (1986). Special ergometric techniques and weight reduction. *Medicine and Science in Sports and Exercise, 18*(1), 25–30.

Shephard, R. J. (1990). *Fitness in special populations.* Champaign, IL: Human Kinetics.

Spicer, R. L. (1984). Cardiovascular disease in Down syndrome. *Pediatric Clinics of North America, 31*(6), 1331–1344.

Strong, W. B., & Alpert, B. S. (1982). The child with heart disease: Play, recreation, and sports. *Current Problems in Pediatrics, 13*(2), 1–34.

Surburg, P. R. (1988). Are adapted physical educators ready for students with AIDS? *Adapted Physical Activity Quarterly, 5*(4), 259–263.

Talbert, W. F. (1971, February–March). Double challenge for a champion. *World Health,* 25–27.

Task Force on Blood Pressure Control in Children. (1987). Report of the task force. *Pediatrics, 79,* 271.

Thompson, K. (1990). Cystic fibrosis—Update on exercise. *Physician and Sportsmedicine, 18*(5), 103–106.

White, R., & Cunningham, A. M. (1991). *Ryan White: My own story.* New York: Dial Books.

Wilmore, J. H., & Costill, D. L. (1988). *Training for sport and activity* (3rd ed.). Dubuque, IA: Wm. C. Brown.

CHAPTER

20

Learning Disabilities, Attention Deficit Hyperactivity Disorder, and DCD

FIGURE 20.1   An alternative to beam walking is a Cratty floor grid on which every letter of the alphabet and every number can be found. Here a boy with learning disabilities leads his teacher in walking out the number 8.

After you have studied this chapter, you should be able to do the following:

1. Differentiate between learning disabilities and mental retardation. See Chapter 21, and contrast behaviors.

2. Discuss the relationship of attention deficit hyperactivity disorder (ADHD) and developmental coordination disorder (DCD) to subtypes of LD. Consider implications for programming.

3. Discuss the evolution of pedagogy for learning disabilities and the dilemma of perceptual-motor training. Differentiate between beliefs of physical and special educators.

4. Define soft signs and give examples of behavioral, perceptual, and motor soft signs. Identify tests used to elicit motor soft signs.

5. Discuss remediation for (a) perceptual-motor problems and (b) clumsiness and apraxia. Identify or create some

games, dance, and aquatics activities that would be helpful for each and explain possible adaptations.

6. Discuss instructional strategies. Make up dialogue that might occur between students and teacher when these strategies are used. Weave these together into a play that is presented to the class or try role-playing.

7. Describe illustrative behaviors and remediation for (a) inattention (b) impulsivity, (c) hyperactivity, (d) social imperception, and (e) perseveration.

8. State and discuss four principles for managing the learning environment of children with LD.

9. Describe behaviors and present level of performance and develop a physical education IEP for a student with LD.

10. Discuss available and needed research on physical education-recreation for persons with LD. Document with research published during the last 3 years.

Internationally, the term *learning disabilities (LD)* has many meanings. In the United States, LD is a separate condition from mental retardation (MR). In many other countries, and in sports governed by the International Paralympic Committee (IPC), *learning disabilities* is used interchangeably with terms like *mental handicap, learning difficulties,* and *intellectual disabilities.* This chapter presents the American viewpoint that LD is not MR. The official term used in federal legislation is *severe learning disabilities (SLD),* but this is almost universally shortened to *LD.*

This chapter also includes information on attention deficit hyperactivity disorder (ADHD) and developmental coordination disorder (DCD), conditions that are often associated with LD and were previously considered a part of LD. ADHD and DCD were recognized as independent disorders in 1980 and 1988, respectively. Assessment must determine whether an individual has only one condition (LD) or is multiply disabled by the presence of ADHD and DCD, both of which have many clinical variations.

Definition of Learning Disabilities

Specific learning disabilities (SLD) is defined by federal legislation as follows:

> a disorder in one or more of the basic psychological processes involved in understanding or in using language, spoken or written, which disorder may manifest itself in an imperfect ability to listen, think, speak, read, write, spell, or do mathematical calculations. (IDEA, 1990, Section 1401)

This part of the federal definition is typically operationalized by two criteria: (a) an IQ of 70 or higher and (b) a severe discrepancy between intellectual ability and academic achievement in one or more areas. A score that is 1.5 or more standard deviations below average on a standardized academic achievement test is generally accepted as proof of a severe discrepancy. The profiles of individuals with LD thus vary widely, ranging from below-average performance in all sub-

jects to gifted performance in all subjects but one, which is seriously below average. This tremendous diversity necessitates careful description of both strengths and weaknesses when referring to an individual diagnosed as having LD.

Historically, so many names have been used to denote LD that the federal definition includes the following statements about what can and cannot be considered LD:

> . . . Such disorders include such conditions as perceptual disabilities, brain injury, minimal brain dysfunction, dyslexia, and developmental aphasia. Such term does not include children who have learning problems which are primarily the result of visual, hearing, or motor disabilities, of mental retardation, of emotional disturbance, or of environmental, cultural, or economic disadvantage. (IDEA, 1990, Section 1401)

This definition assumes that readers are familiar with such terms as **dyslexia** (a severe reading disorder presumed to be of neurological origin) and **aphasia** (impairment of ability to communicate presumed to be of neurological origin). Other types of aphasias are **dysgraphia** (writing disorder), **dyscalculia** (math disorder), and **amnesia** (memory disorder). The most common disorders are reading and spelling, but any combination of aphasias may result in SLD.

Although the law does not recognize motor disabilities, by themselves, as sufficient for a diagnosis of LD, most authorities believe that a higher than average percentage of individuals with LD have perceptual-motor, motor coordination, and other movement-related problems that require intensive work (see Figure 20.1). It is not yet known how many of these problems can be considered a part of developmental coordination disorder (DCD).

Developmental Coordination Disorder (DCD)

DCD was officially recognized by the American Psychiatric Association (APA) and the World Health Organization in 1987 and

1989, respectively. Recognition by the APA makes treatment for conditions eligible for health insurance reimbursement consideration. In the most recent edition of the *Diagnostic and Statistical Manual of Mental Disorders (DSM-IV)*, published by the APA (1994), the diagnostic criteria for DCD are as follows:

> Performance in daily activities that require motor coordination is substantially below that expected given the person's chronological age and measured intelligence. This may be manifested by marked delays in achieving motor milestones (e.g., walking, crawling, sitting), dropping things, "clumsiness," poor performance in sports, or poor handwriting. (p. 54)

This diagnosis is made only if

1. the condition significantly interferes with academic achievement or activities of daily living, and
2. the condition is not caused by a general medical disorder (e.g., cerebral palsy, muscular dystrophy) or pervasive developmental disorder. The prevalence of this condition is estimated as 6% in the age range from 5 to 11 years.

DCD was featured in the April 1994 issue of the *Adapted Physical Activity Quarterly*, which was edited by Sheila Henderson of England, one of the developers of the Movement Assessment Battery for Children (Movement ABC), which was described in Chapter 12. This battery is recommended for diagnosis of DCD. Many of the motor problems described in this chapter may be evidence of DCD. However, it is important to note that most children with LD do not "grow out" of motor problems. DCD may therefore be a lifetime problem rather than a developmental disorder.

LD and Attention Deficit Hyperactivity Disorder (ADHD)

A higher than average percentage of individuals with LD have ADHD and related problems. This naturally complicates their learning disabilities. **ADHD** is a "persistent pattern of inattention and/or hyperactivity-impulsivity that is more frequent and severe than that typically observed in individuals at a comparable level of development" (APA, 1994, p. 78). Like DCD, ADHD is recognized by the APA but not by the IDEA. Thus, ADHD is not eligible for special education services except in conjunction with disabilities specified in the IDEA. ADHD and related disorders are discussed later in this chapter.

Prevalence of Learning Disabilities

Approximately 2 million students in the United States are classified as LD and receive special education services. This represents about 47% of all students in special education and 4 to 5% of the total school-age population. The number of students served under the LD label has been growing by 1 to 2% each year.

Educators are reluctant to assign disability classifications to young children. Therefore, infants, toddlers, and children served under IDEA-Part C and H are typically called *developmentally or language delayed*. Many of these children later are classified as LD.

Many adults with LD attend universities. A recent survey of students with disabilities in higher education revealed that 46% had LD (West et al., 1993).

Definite gender differences are evident in LD. Approximately three times as many boys as girls receive special education services for LD. Many students with other disabilities also have LD. Chief among these are individuals with cerebral palsy or severe hearing impairments.

Subtypes of LD

Movement subtypes of LD have been identified since 1976, when Rarick, Dobbins, and Broadhead published *The Motor Domain and Its Correlates in Educationally Handicapped Children*. More recently, subtypes have been described by Lazarus (1990), Hoare (1994), and Miyahara (1994).

Lazarus (1990) noted two distinct subtypes:

1. Language impaired with subtle motor difficulties, mainly in information processing. This subtype tends to prefer visual learning.
2. Visual-spatial-motor impaired with obvious perceptual-motor problems and clumsiness. This subtype mainly has problems with math, although language can be impaired also, especially in pronunciation and comprehension. Auditory input tends to be the preferred learning modality.

The identification of subtypes depends, of course, on the nature of the tests administered. Hoare (1994), after testing kinesthetic acuity, motor-free visual perception, visual-motor integration, manual dexterity, static balance, and 50-m running speed, reported five subtype clusters. Miyahara (1994) identified four subtypes, based on Bruininks-Oseretsky Test of Motor Proficiency data. Both Hoare and Miyahara reported that approximately half of their students had average or higher scores on the tests. The other students exhibited highly individual profiles of motor weaknesses. This research supports the trend away from the specification of characteristics in relation to disabilities. There are some areas in which individuals with LD seem to be at high risk, but no generalizations should be made.

Etiology of LD

The etiology of LD is biological rather than environmental, although individual ecosystems influence opportunity and ability to learn. The central nervous system is so complex that the reasons for malfunctions of specific parts are little understood. The major motor problems seem to have a cerebellar-vestibular basis (Ayres, 1972; Quiros & Schrager, 1979).

Historical Perspectives

Historically, LD has been linked with reading and speaking difficulties caused by brain damage. Accounts of individuals with congenital word blindness appear in the literature of the 1800s, but specific pedagogy was not proposed until the landmark publication of *Psychopathology and Education of the Brain-Injured Child* in 1947 by Alfred Strauss and Laura Lehtinen. This book described problems of learning, attention, and hyperactivity that subsequently became known as the **Strauss syndrome.** Four principles for managing the learning environment were stressed: (a) use optimal structure, (b) reduce space, (c) eliminate irrelevant stimuli, and (d) enhance the stimulus value of equipment or instructional material. These principles remain sound.

In addition, perceptual-motor training was widely accepted as appropriate pedagogy for remediating language and learning problems (Hallahan & Cruickshank, 1973). Much of this training was directed toward fine motor coordination and the perceptual abilities needed in reading and writing activities. By the 1980s, however, it was clearly evident that perceptual-motor training was not effective in remediating academic problems (Kavale & Mattson, 1983). The American Academy of Pediatrics Committee on Children with Learning Disabilities (Cohen et al., 1985) and the Board of Trustees, Council for Learning Disabilities (1986) were among the several groups that issued formal statements opposing perceptual-motor training.

Founding of LD Organizations

Until the 1960s, no professional organization or official nomenclature existed for LD. Dr. Samuel Kirk, a special educator at the University of Illinois, proposed the term *learning disabilities* in 1963, and a parent-professional organization called the Association for Children with Learning Disabilities (ACLD) was founded in 1964. This group was largely responsible for the recognition of LD in federal legislation and subsequent progress in theory and practice. In 1990, ACLD changed its name to Learning Disability Association of America (LDA).

Involvement of Physical Educators

Physical educators became aware of LD in the 1970s. Sherrill (1972) was the first to write a chapter on LD for an adapted physical education text; it appeared in Hollis Fait's *Special Physical Education*. Sherrill, mentored by ACLD parents and professionals, relied heavily on the works of followers of Strauss: William Cruickshank's *The Brain-Injured Child in Home, School, and Community* (1967) and Newell Kephart's *The Slow Learner in the Classroom* (1971). From Cruickshank, she learned Strauss's principles for managing the learning environment and applied them to the gymnasium setting. From Kephart, she stressed balance activities and imitation of movement games to remediate clumsiness. From association with ACLD parents and children, however, Sherrill formed the self-concept beliefs underlying her adapted physical education pedagogy.

Bryant J. Cratty, at the University of California at Los Angeles, also contributed substantially to perceptual-motor pedagogy (Cratty, 1971, 1972). Cratty rejected the special education theories that movement attributes are the basis of perceptual and intellectual development. Instead, he stressed the use of highly structured movement experiences to remediate clumsiness and improve self-control and self-concept. Cratty believed that academic abilities would be enhanced by movement only if games were developed to teach specific academic skills. He recommended that games be used to supplement classroom instruction, not to substitute for it.

Current Beliefs About Pedagogy

Special educators today focus primarily on attention, memory, and cognition and direct their instruction toward specific reading, writing, spelling, and math disabilities. Physical educators also are concerned with attention, memory, and cognition be-

cause these processes obviously are important in learning motor skills, rules, and strategies. Listening, thinking, and speaking are central to success in a gymnasium as well as to safety.

The IEP process guides both special educators and physical educators in personalizing goals and instructional strategies. When motor problems are severe, the IEP should specify maximum class size, a consultant arrangement between regular and adapted physical educators, and a class structure that emphasizes cooperative behaviors, social competence, and self-esteem. Often one-to-one tutoring and specialist help are needed. An after-school, family-movement-oriented program is typically necessary to remediate severe problems.

Neurological Soft Signs

Neurological soft signs are behavioral, perceptual, and motor indicators of central nervous system (CNS) dysfunction that cannot be substantiated through hardware technology (e.g., electroencephalogy or EEG). Research repeatedly shows that students with LD evidence neurological soft signs not present in the general population; this is why all definitions of LD emphasize its biological origin. **Behavioral soft signs** pertain to attention deficits, hyperactivity, conceptual rigidity, inappropriate reactions, emotional lability (instability), and the like. **Perceptual soft signs** include defective visual discrimination of letters (confusion of *b* and *d; p* and *q; u* and *n; b* and *h*) and words (reversals like *saw* for *was, dog* for *god*), auditory discrimination problems, and deficits in organizing, remembering, and repeating sequences. (See Chapter 12 for a review of perceptual and perceptual-motor deficits.) **Motor soft signs** include static and dynamic balance deficits, associated and choreiform (twitching) movements, awkwardness, and agnosias.

Many of the neurological tests that physicians administer are used by adapted physical educators. Table 20.1 presents tests commonly used to identify soft signs and introduces terms used in medical records. Educators often consider motor soft signs to be perceptual-motor difficulties.

Not all students exhibit soft signs, but enough do that assessment in the areas specified in Table 20.1 should be thorough. These soft signs have obvious implications for physical education performance. Research shows, however, that soft signs do not correlate highly with academic performance.

Perceptual-Motor Strengths and Weaknesses

Not all students with LD have perceptual-motor problems; many are fine athletes. But most do! One of the few prevalence studies of such problems among children diagnosed by school psychologists as LD indicated that 12% demonstrated no problems, 75% scored average on some tests but below average on others, and 13% scored 2 to 3 years below normative standards for their age group on all tests (Sherrill & Pyfer, 1985).

Many students with LD have difficulty decoding or making sense out of their bodies and space (see Figure 20.2). Assessment should identify the level at which each problem is most pronounced: (a) awareness, (b) discrimination, or (c) organization. Remember, in LD, the primary cause is neurological, but problems are often confounded by environmental conditions. Therefore, remediation must address both.

T a b l e   2 0 . 1   Examples of tests used to elicit neurological soft signs and verify neurological dysfunction.

Sign	Description	Assessment Questions
Romberg	Student stands erect with both feet together, with eyes open and then closed.	Does student sway or lose balance? In unilateral cerebellar damage, falls are toward side of lesion.
Choreiform movements	Student stands in Romberg position, but with arms held straight out in front, eyes closed, and tongue stuck out as far as possible.	Are there rotary or twitching movements of the fingers, tongue, or head?
Motor impersistence	Same as for choreiform movements.	Can student maintain this position for at least 30 sec?
Tandem stand, walk (also called Mann test sign)	Student stands in heel-toe posture, with eyes open, then closed. Also walks heel-to-toe at least six steps.	What is performance discrepancy between eyes open and eyes closed? Eyes open compensates for ataxia caused by CNS damage.
Heel walking	Student walks on heels at least six steps.	Are anterior foot and toes off the floor and the body in good control?
Stork or one-foot stand (also called one-foot Romberg) Shallow one-leg squat and rise	Student stands on one foot, with eyes open and then closed. If successful, student is asked to squat and rise (one time only), bearing the entire weight on one leg.	Can student stand on preferred leg at least 10 sec and do squat and rise with good control?
Associated movements (synkinesia—*syn* [without] and *kinesia* [movement])	Student touches thumb to index finger of same hand as rapidly as possible, at a rate of about 3 per second.	Can student keep the other hand motionless, or does it mirror the moving hand?
Dysdiadochokinesia (dis-di-ad-o-ko-ki-ne-se-a) from *dys* (bad) + *diadochos* (succeeding) + *kinesis* (movement) (also called alternating motion rate [AMR])	Student alternates pronation and supination movements of one hand as rapidly as possible, with arm bent at 90 ° angle.	Can student maintain a 90 ° angle with arms close to body while doing this, or do arms begin to flail wildly?
	If successful, student is asked to do same movement with both hands, beginning with one palm up and one palm down. This is usually done in sitting position, with hands resting on knees.	Can student maintain rapid alternating movements with hands moving in opposite directions?
Finger dexterity: Touching thumb to fingertips (also tests alternating motion rate [AMR])	Student uses thumb to rapidly touch each finger in succession, moving from little finger to index finger and then from index finger to little finger. Eyes open, then closed.	Can student perform this task in 90 sec? Alternative tests are buttoning and unbuttoning, using safety pins, and other finger patterns like pivoting thumb and index finger.
Dyssynergia or dyskinesthesia: Touching nose with index finger or touching two index fingers	From erect stand, arms extended sideward, student touches tip of index finger to tip of nose; also can bend elbows and touch tips of index fingers in front of chest.	Can the student touch precisely the place desired with eyes open, then closed? Are the movements smooth, with no tremor?
Finger agnosia: Perceptual deficit decreasing awareness of external stimuli applied to fingers	With eyes closed or hands hidden from sight, the student can identify which finger or part of the finger is being touched. Sometimes, touches are simultaneously to two or three fingers or to parts of the same finger.	Can student recognize and label touches? Can student state what part of a finger has been touched?
Right-left discriminations	Student, on command, touches right and left parts of body as well as external objects.	Can student perform both unilateral (right hand to right ear) and cross-lateral (right hand to left ear) tasks?

FIGURE 20.2 A movement lesson designed to improve hopping and jumping enhances perception of space and time.

FIGURE 20.3 Body image work with a real skeleton is exciting. Here, the child and the skeleton are taking turns leading a *Simon Says* type game (i.e., the skeleton says, "Lean to the left!").

Immature Body Image and Agnosias

As children mature, they become conscious of their bodies, internalize their perceptions, and acquire a *body image*. Children with LD, however, manifest many problems: (a) finger agnosia, (b) inability to identify body parts and surfaces, (c) inability to make right-left discriminations, and (d) difficulty in making judgments about body size, shape, and proportions. These deficits are thought to stem from brain damage.

Of the many body image deficits, **finger agnosia** (impaired perceptual awareness) has received the most attention. Table 20.1 describes the test commonly used to identify finger agnosia. This body image deficit is also evidenced in drawing, handwriting, and other fine motor tasks. The following description of a 6-year-old with high average intelligence is typical:

> He made the drawing after being instructed to draw a picture of himself and quickly drew all of the figure except the fingers. When he came to the point of wanting to put on fingers, he became confused, looked at the examiner's hands and then at his own mittens in an attempt to adapt them to the situation. Finally, in a mood of desperation, he placed his hand on the paper in the appropriate position and traced around two of his fingers; he repeated this procedure on the other side, thus putting fingers at the end of both arms. From this performance and on the basis of other evidence, we concluded that this boy had a finger agnosia. He was unable, except by highly devious routes, to visualize his own fingers. (Johnson & Myklebust, 1967, p. 237)

Remediation of immature body image problems through physical education involves the use of action songs, dances, games, and exercises that refer to body parts (see Figure 20.3). Provide opportunities for children to see themselves in the mirror, on videotape, and on film. Perceptual-motor, relaxation, dance, and aquatic activities can be used specifically to improve body image. Obstacle courses that require problem solving about body size and shape in order to squeeze under or through are especially excellent.

Poor Spatial Orientation

Closely allied to body image deficits are disturbances in spatial orientation. Children with LD are described as *lost in space*. They typically lose their way enroute to a destination and show confusion when given north-south-east-west and right-left directions. Moreover, they experience difficulty in estimating distance, height, width, and the other coordinates of space. As a result, they are forever bumping into things and misjudging the space requirements in such tasks as stepping through geometric forms, ducking under a low rope, and squeezing through a narrow opening.

To remediate, games must involve obstacle courses, mazes, and maps. Orienteering and treasure hunts are good. Risk recreation and adventure activities in an outdoor setting give meaning to this type of programming. Instruction in cue detection is important, as well as self-talk and rehearsal, both visual and verbal.

Associated or Overflow Movements

Children with LD display greater levels of overflow than peers (Lazarus, 1994). **Overflow** is the inability to keep opposite limbs motionless when performing one-arm or one-leg tasks. This phenomenon, which contributes to clumsiness, is one dimension of **disinhibition,** a generalized disorder of inhibitory control. Disinhibition is linked with impulsivity later in this chapter.

Motor Proficiency Problems

Motor proficiency refers to the underlying movement abilities measured by the Bruininks-Oseretsky Test of Motor Proficiency (BOTMP, Bruininks, 1978). See Chapter 6 for a full explanation of the BOTMP. This test appears to be particularly sensitive to differences between children with and without LD. Older research indicates that children with LD are significantly different from peers in three areas: balance, bilateral coordination, and fine motor visual control (e.g., Bruininks & Bruininks, 1977).

Current research using the BOTMP indicates that at least four distinct subtypes of movement abilities exist among

FIGURE 20.4 Profiles of children with learning disabilities, ages 8 and 14, based on Bruininks-Oseretsky Test of Motor Proficiency (BOTMP) scores in five areas. *BLC* is bilateral coordination; *ULC* is upper limb coordination. Of all children with learning disabilities tested, 44% were in Subtype 1, 25% were in Subtype 2, 24% were in Subtype 3, and 7% were in Subtype 4. (From Miyahara [1994].)

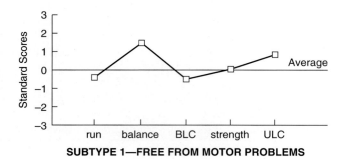

SUBTYPE 1—FREE FROM MOTOR PROBLEMS

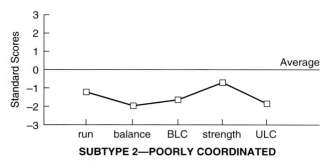

SUBTYPE 2—POORLY COORDINATED

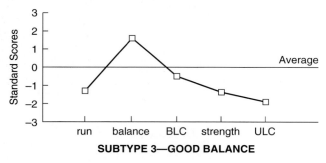

SUBTYPE 3—GOOD BALANCE

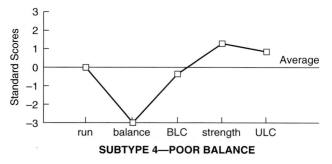

SUBTYPE 4—POOR BALANCE

children with LD (see Figure 20.4). Miyahara (1994), the researcher who developed these profiles, did not test fine motor visual control. Figure 20.4 shows that generalizations cannot be made about children with LD. Many score 1.5 or more standard deviations below average on running, balance, bilateral coordination, and upper limb coordination.

These profiles highlight the importance of providing intervention instruction in specific areas. *Running* is tested in the BOTMP by a 30-yd shuttle run, which measures both agility and speed (skills important in tag and most childhood games). *Balance* is measured by single-leg stands, heel-to-toe walking, and balance beam activities. *Bilateral coordination* is appraised by tasks that require the upper and lower limbs to work together. Examples are (a) jumping up and clapping hands, (b) jumping up and touching heels with hands, (c) tapping feet alternately while making circles with hands, and (d) maintaining the same rhythm while simultaneously tapping with foot and index finger. *Upper limb coordination* is measured by ball skills and tasks that assess dyssynergia.

Another outstanding study of underlying movement abilities revealed that the greatest motor problems were with balance, coordination, and rhythm (Levinson, 1988). This research, based on 4,000 individuals with LD, emphasized the importance of discriminating between static and dynamic balance problems. It is possible to have one without the other. Levinson reported that over half (52 to 67%, depending on age group) demonstrated static balance problems, 25 to 87% had dynamic balance difficulties, and 60 to 87% failed the finger-to-finger test of kinesthesis.

Most children diagnosed with specific movement problems do not "grow out of" their clumsiness (Cantell, Smyth, & Ahonen, 1994). As soon as specific movement weaknesses are identified, cooperative home and school community programming should be implemented. This programming should include a balance among perceptual-motor training, motor skills practice, and applications in game settings. One type of training should not precede the others; all should progress concurrently in environments carefully structured to promote success.

Clumsiness and Apraxia

Clumsiness, the inability to perform culturally normative motor activities with age-expected proficiency, is a problem for many individuals with LD. The medical term for clumsiness is *developmental coordination disorder.* The more complex an activity, game, or sport, the more likely that performance will be clumsy because of information processing and motor planning demands. **Apraxia,** one aspect of clumsiness, is a thought-organization disorder manifested in movement activities that require planning, sequencing, organizing, and remembering. Apraxia is to movement what dyslexia is to reading. There are many kinds, and none is well understood.

Louise Clarke, the mother of a boy with LD, devoted several passages to this difficulty in her excellent book:

> There was a new area of incompetence too. Mike's school was very big on athletics. All the men teachers directed at least one sport, and starting in the second grade, there was a great deal of talk about who made what team.
>
> Mike did not make any.
>
> Mr. Klein, the athletic director, was openly contemptuous, and the best Mike got from any of the

male staff was amused tolerance. He wanted very much to make a team, and during vacations he and his father threw balls back and forth, or his father would throw them for him to bat. It was an endless exercise. . . .

Mike never did get the knack of it. He would miss catches by fractions of inches, but near-misses do not count in games. His batting was so erratic that his father . . . could not field them half the time. (Clarke, 1973, p. 20)

Mike, like many other children with LD, seemed to have trouble primarily in hand-eye coordination and balance. He was an excellent swimmer, winning many ribbons in competitive events from grade school on. Moreover, his strength, cardiorespiratory endurance, and running speed enabled him to perform well on fitness tests. Having completed a PhD in science at Harvard University in his 20s, Mike recalled his physical education experiences and stated,

My hand-eye coordination was never very good, and it still isn't. But I wouldn't tell dyslexics to stay away from sports, just the competitive sports that put a premium on hand-eye coordination, like baseball or handball. Anything where the margin of error is small. Tennis and squash allow for a margin of error. They demand coordination, but you can get away with it; you don't have to hit the ball every time at dead center of the racquet. (Clarke, 1973, p. 132)

From a remediation standpoint, problems can be broken down into

1. dissociation (problems in perceiving and organizing parts into wholes),
2. motor planning and sequencing (problems in organizing parts into logical or correct order),
3. motor timing and rhythm,
4. other executive functions involved in making the body do what the mind wills, and
5. activity deficit.

Clumsiness, the combination of apraxia and specific motor deficits like balance and incoordination, can be devastating, affecting self-efficacy, self-concept, and other dimensions of life. See Chapter 8.

Dissociation and Figure-Background

Dissociation refers to problems in perceiving and organizing parts into wholes. This ability is age-related, with young children able to make sense only of wholes. Awareness that parts make up wholes develops at about age 7 (onset of concrete mental operations), but many children do not fully grasp relationships between parts and wholes until about age 9. The ability to shift back and forth between wholes and parts is prerequisite to success in tasks that require copying or imitating a model. Delays cause frustrations in integrating and coordinating movements in response to a demonstration. They also cause problems in fine motor copying, constructing, and assembly tasks that require a finished product to look like the model.

We often say that persons *do not see whole* or that they *can't see the forest for the trees.* This ability is also related to game sense, intuitively knowing where to be and what to do. The ability to process and act on several bits of information at one time is dependent on whole-part perceptions.

Dissociation is a consideration in selecting teaching methods. Problems with whole-part synthesizing and integrating generally indicate the need for whole teaching methods rather than whole-part-whole or part. Whole methodology refers to demonstration of the total pattern with no verbalization other than "Watch me." The child on the trampoline for the first time, for instance, must get the *feel* of the whole before he or she cares much about using the arms properly and landing in shoulder-width stride. Beginning instruction in throwing and striking activities should focus on the target to be hit, not on the stance, grip, backswing, release, and follow-through.

During warm-up, locomotor activities that demand the integrated working together of the whole body tend to be better than calisthenics that emphasize the movement of parts. Thus, runs, hops, jumps, animal walks, log rolls, and tumbling activities are preferable to arm flinging, side bending, toe touching, and body part circling.

When students evidence success with whole methodology, instructional strategies that teach and reinforce whole-part-whole learning can be introduced. Demonstrations can include one wrong part that students are helped to identify. Emphasis can be placed also on creative movement: "Show me everything you can do with a ball; now show me one thing you like to do best; now show me three things." Another approach is, "Show me something you can do with your whole body; now show me something you can do with one body part."

Practice in getting into different game and dance formations teaches students to see themselves as parts of a whole. Creative dance, swimming, and gymnastics in which individuals or partners devise an original stunt or movement sequence and then combine it with those of others reinforce understandings of parts versus wholes. Even a pyramid formation can be taught as a whole comprised of parts.

Figure-background and depth-perception problems are part of dissociation. **Figure-background constancy** is the ability to pick one object or figure out of a complex background. For some children, however, balls and classmates blend together or float in and out of focus. Confusions pertaining to near-far, front-back, and high-low are common.

To minimize such problems, equipment and apparatus should be brightly colored to contrast with the background. Balance beams and mats should be a different color from the floor. Masking tape figures on walls and floors should utilize reds and blues, colors that have been shown to be children's favorites (see Figure 20.5). Basketball backdrops and goal cages should stand out boldly against less relevant stimuli.

Visual and auditory games that stress the locations of objects and sounds may be directed toward remediation of figure-background problems. Illustrative of these are such guessing games as *I Bet You Can't See What I See, Who's Got My Bone?, Huckleberry Beanstalk,* and *Hot and Cold.* Scavenger hunts also demand the ability to isolate relevant stimuli from the background.

Motor Planning and Sequencing

Motor planning and sequencing is an organizational ability that includes thought and action in relation to (a) initiating movement, (b) terminating movement, and (c) putting parts in correct order. Problems typically occur when attempting to imitate something that has been seen or heard. Remediation involves games, dance, water play, and gymnastic routines in which an increasing number of movements must be remembered and chained together into sequences. Movement games like *I'm Going to Grandmother's House, Copy Cat,* and *Who Can Remember How Ted Got to the Moon?* simultaneously provide practice in movement and memory.

Temporal Organization, Rhythm, and Force

Some individuals can organize parts into wholes and get them in the right order but cannot cope with rhythm. It is difficult to know whether the underlying problem is perception, organization, or a combination. In order to look right, virtually all body movements must be timed correctly. This is especially true when accuracy, speed, and force are involved.

Another manifestation of this cluster of disorders is the inability to move or dance in time with music or externally imposed rhythms. When other adolescents are developing social and romantic relationships through dance, many youth with LD miss these experiences because rhythm does not come naturally to them, and they have received no compensatory instruction.

Bilateral coordination items in the Bruininks-Oseretsky Test of Motor Proficiency (BOTMP) measure timing. This is done by synchronized, rhythmical tapping of two body parts and imitations of hands-to-thighs rhythmical patterns. This is one of the three areas in which students with LD are weakest.

Pedagogy to remediate these problems includes early instruction in music, rhythm, and dance with teachers especially trained to understand problems (see Figure 20.6). Many students with LD profit from the use of background music or a strong percussive beat (drum or metronome) as accompaniment. The music, of course, should be carefully selected to reinforce the natural rhythm of the skill and the desired performance speed. Videotaping pairs of students (one strong, one weak) doing movement to music enables the student with LD to make visual comparisons and to develop compensatory strategies since the auditory-kinesthetic feedback circuits obviously are not working properly. Many students with LD, when dancing, do not know they are out of rhythm.

Other Executive Functions

Labeling, rehearsal, elaboration, association, organization, and chunking are among the information-processing strategies that affect academic learning, but little is known about the comparable functions in motor performance and learning (Reid, 1986, 1987). Many persons with LD say that their problem is not perception: They see, hear, and know what to do but cannot make the body perform as the mind wills.

Adults with LD, when asked to discuss motor executive functions, describe different patterns. Many say that they do not learn effectively from either demonstration or listening to instructions. Instead, they learn new motor skills best by trial and error, helped occasionally by specific, individual, corrective feedback. These people say that being labeled as impulsive or described as having attention deficits is unfair because it is natural to want the teacher to stop explaining when the words and demonstration have little meaning. The only way such individuals can achieve skill is to dig in and find out what, kinesthetically, feels right or works. Other adults with LD indicate that they think they are grasping the explanation, but something seems to happen in short-term memory. The visual and auditory input do not get encoded. Many adults with LD describe extreme difficulty with visualization of motor skills. Others insist that they learn best when one modality (visual or auditory) is used, and only one or two points are made at a time.

Activity Deficit Phenomenon

The **activity deficit phenomenon,** recently verified by research (Bouffard, Watkinson, Thompson, Dunn, & Romanow, 1996), is a sedentary lifestyle that results from avoidance coping strategies that people with movement difficulties use to preserve self-esteem and manage emotional hurts related to clumsiness. Children as young as 7 begin to manifest avoidance and withdrawal behaviors that put skill development and social-emotional growth at risk. Clumsiness is intensified as years go by and these children engage in less and less physically active play. Often, children with movement difficulties become passive learners in physical education as they use every opportunity to sit out and observe rather than participate.

Early intervention is needed before activity deficit behaviors become a permanent lifestyle. Ways must be devised to permit children with movement difficulties to have fun in physical activity despite their clumsiness. Fun is a highly individualistic feeling, with many meanings. Many individuals find fun in social relationships and will engage in an activity just to be with people they like. Teachers must find the specific reinforcers that are most effective in keeping each child intrinsically motivated to stay optimally involved in physical activity.

Instructional Strategies

Whereas adults with LD have generally given much thought to their clumsiness, children become frustrated and often give up. Spontaneous instructional strategies are not typically applied until about age 7 or 8. Children with LD show delays or absence of these strategies. Instruction must focus on how to become active learners (Bulgren & Carta, 1992; Bouffard & Wall, 1990; Vallerand & Reid, 1990).

Metacognitive Strategy Instruction

Metacognition is personal knowledge about the ways we think, move, and learn. Metacognitive strategy instruction is effective in improving academic skills of persons with LD (Harris & Pressley, 1991; Palincsar, 1986) and offers promise in motor learning. Students with LD have little insight into visualization, self-talk, spontaneous rehearsal, and the like. Metacognitive strategy instruction can make students aware of these processes and enhance problem solving about personal learning.

Use of new strategies may be tiring and fraught with uncertainty and anxiety. Thus, class instruction should offer a balance between traditional explicit learning (imitation and following verbal instruction) and movement exploration. Originality in responding to movement challenges may be a strength of children with LD (Holguin & Sherrill, 1989). Movement education, creative dance, and games that utilize original ideas and dramatic themes are especially recommended (i.e., sometimes, it is good to teach toward strengths instead of weaknesses). Instruction in relaxation is also important.

Modality-Based Instruction

Modality-based instruction is an approach for students who learn better when information is presented through one modality (visual or auditory) rather than both, as is the tradition in physical education. Research shows that most persons are mixed-modality learners by age 7 or 8. About 20 to 25% of children with LD, however, are visual preference learners, and about 10% are auditory preference learners. For these children, presenting information in the preferred modality may be better. Clinicians typically support preferred modality teaching (Dunn, 1990) whereas researchers question it (Kavale & Forness, 1987, 1990). Sherrill supports modality-based instruction.

Cognitive Style Matching

Cognitive style refers to the individual's approach to analyzing and responding to stimuli. When the student's style matches that of the teacher, there are few problems. If styles are widely divergent, however, both persons must learn tolerance. Cognitive styles are designated by bipolar adjectives: (a) field dependent, field independent, (b) global, analytical, and (c) impulsive, reflective. **Field-dependent** (FD) people are strongly influenced by the visual field. They see wholes and have trouble finding embedded figures and coping with details. Moreover, they tend to have a fast conceptual tempo, spend little time planning, and need external structure. In contrast, **field-independent** (FI) people exhibit the opposite behaviors.

Either extreme is associated with learning disabilities. The younger persons are, the more likely they are to be field dependent. This helps to explain why children typically are not much interested in details. Persons with LD are more likely to be FD than FI (Lazarus, 1990). Awareness of cognitive styles helps teachers to match instructional demands to strengths. Then, gradually, they can remediate weaknesses.

Self-Talk and Verbal Rehearsal

A self-talk and verbal rehearsal strategy is successful in helping children to learn motor sequences, improve game performance, and control impulsivity (Kowalski & Sherrill, 1992). **Self-talk** usually refers to talking oneself through an activity or sequence. It is simultaneous talking and moving. When the student does jumping jacks, for instance, he or she says *out* as the limbs spread and *in* as they return to midline. When a locomotor pattern is performed, the child says aloud *jump, jump, step, step, step, hop-2-3-4.*

Verbal rehearsal is saying aloud the parts of a planned movement before execution. This is often in response to the teacher's request, "Tell me the three things you are going to do." With guidance, students learn to ask and answer their own questions.

Motivation and Self-Concept Enhancement

Students with LD typically have lower self-concepts and more external locus of control than nondisabled peers (Switzky & Schultz, 1988; Tarnowski & Nay, 1989). This is particularly true of students with both LD and DCD (Dunn & Watkinson, 1994). The reason for this seems to be the accumulation of failure after failure and the inability of parents and teachers to help students build areas of competence that offset acknowledged weaknesses and deficits. External locus of control is manifested by low motivation and passivity. Such responses are easily understood if one considers how it must feel to visualize failure before starting each day.

Not all students with LD manifest these problems. Scores on self-concept inventories depend on **reference groups** (i.e., the significant others to whom individuals compare themselves). When students with LD attend private schools and/or use peers with LD for their social, academic, and motor comparisons, the self-concept seems to be higher than most research indicates. Only about 1% of all students with LD attend private schools, however.

Teams and partners in the integrated gymnasium should be assigned with great care, rather than left to chance. These become the new reference groups and significant others for persons with LD. Games and sports should be adapted to emphasize cooperation rather than competition. For example, volleyball can be changed to a "How long can you keep the ball in the air?" theme. Basketball can be changed to give points for number of passes completed before shooting.

Enhancement of self-concept through success-oriented movement experiences and concomitant individual and small-group counseling is the most important physical education goal for students with LD. Closely related to this goal is helping students with LD gain peer acceptance and make one or two really close friendships that carry over into leisure-time activities. Curriculum models with particular promise are cooperative games (Mender, Kerr, & Orlick, 1982), motor creativity (Sherrill, 1986), games design (Morris & Stiehl, 1989), and social-personal development (Hellison, 1985; Johnson & Johnson, 1986). See Chapters 8, 9, and 15 for a review of these models and techniques for enhancing self-concept and social competence.

Fitness and Leisure Concerns

Students with LD must be helped to find one or two lifetime physical activities that they can do well enough to feel the satisfaction needed to maintain an active, healthy lifestyle. Although research indicates that individuals with LD are inferior to nondisabled peers on fitness tasks (O'Beirne, Larkin, & Cable, 1994), such findings probably *reflect differences in experience and motivation rather than capacity deficits.* Students with LD in private schools that employ physical education specialists and provide daily physical education instruction score average or better on standardized fitness tests. There is no neurological reason why individuals with LD cannot excel in strength, cardiorespiratory endurance, and flexibility.

Teachers in LD private schools report that many of their students do well in soccer. There appear to be fewer coordination problems in foot-eye than in hand-eye ball activities. Students with LD need exposure to competitive sport in accordance with the principle of normalization. Much can be learned from carefully structured teamwork that emphasizes cooperation, sharing, and sportsmanship. Remember that children with LD are often delayed in social competence. Private schools in the Dallas-Fort Worth area have developed a soccer league for students with LD so that initial competitive sport experience is against peers with similar skills in a carefully monitored, success-oriented environment.

The play and leisure activities of individuals with LD tend to be different from that of nondisabled peers. Children with LD engage in significantly more solitary play and hold inferior sociometric status compared to others (Dunn & Watkinson, 1994; Gottlieb, Gottlieb, Berkell, & Levy, 1986). Their leisure activities tend to be passive and accompanied by feelings of loneliness (Margalit, 1984). Many demonstrate a kind of learned helplessness in regard to initiating activities with others and depend on their parents and siblings for recreational activities.

The game choices of children with LD have been studied by Cratty, Ikeda, Martin, Jennett, and Morris (1970), who concluded that clumsy children tend to avoid vigorous, active games, particularly those involving direct contact, such as football, wrestling, and boxing. Boys with movement problems seemed to prefer some type of fantasy play in which "pretend" bravery could be evidenced (spaceman, cowboy, cops and robbers). This was not true of boys of the same age representing the normal population.

Although research on the play and leisure of students with LD is sparse, there is strong indication that leisure education and counseling should be integrated into physical education instruction. School-community partnerships should utilize the expertise of therapeutic recreation specialists and foster generalization of school learning to use of community resources.

Attention Deficit Hyperactivity Disorder (ADHD)

ADHD is a combination of inattention and/or hyperactive-impulsive symptoms that are present in at least two settings

T a b l e   2 0 . 2   Diagnostic criteria for ADHD related to maladaptive behaviors that have persisted over 6 or more months.

A. **Inattention.** At least six of the following:
  1. Often fails to give close attention to details, or makes careless mistakes in schoolwork, work, or other activities.
  2. Often has difficulty sustaining attention in tasks or play activities.
  3. Often does not seem to listen when spoken to directly.
  4. Often does not follow through on instructions and fails to finish schoolwork, chores, or duties in the workplace (not due to oppositional behavior or failure to understand instructions).
  5. Often has difficulty organizing tasks and activities.
  6. Often avoids, dislikes, or is reluctant to engage in tasks that require sustained mental effort (such as schoolwork or homework).
  7. Often loses things necessary for tasks or activities (e.g., toys, school assignments, pencils, books, or tools).
  8. Often is easily distracted by extraneous stimuli.
  9. Often is forgetful in daily activities.

B. **Hyperactivity-Impulsivity.** At least six of the following:
  Hyperactivity
  1. Often fidgets with hands or feet or squirms in seat.
  2. Often leaves seat in classroom or in other situations in which remaining seated is expected.
  3. Often runs about or climbs excessively in situations in which it is inappropriate (in adolescents or adults, may be limited to subjective feelings of restlessness).
  4. Often has difficulty playing or engaging in leisure activities quietly.
  5. Often *on the go* or often acts if *driven by a motor*.
  6. Often talks excessively.

  Impulsivity
  7. Often blurts out answers before questions have been completed.
  8. Often has difficulty awaiting turn.
  9. Often interrupts or intrudes on others (e.g., butts into conversations or games).

Adapted from American Psychiatric Association (1994).

and interfere with academic, social, and occupational functioning (American Psychiatric Association, 1994). Some symptoms of ADHD must have been present before age 7 (see Table 20.2). Many individuals with LD have ADHD, but ADHD has been recognized as a separate medical diagnosis since 1980.

Three ADHD subtypes are recognized by the American Psychiatric Association (1994): ADHD, combined type; ADHD, predominantly inattention type; and ADHD, predominantly hyperactivity-impulsivity type. Remediation should be directed toward the specific indicators in Table 20.2, and physical educators should work closely with parents and school personnel in implementing behavior management programs and strategies (Bishop & Beyer, 1995; Fiore, Becker, & Nero, 1993).

Etiology and Prevalence

The etiology of ADHD is neurological with evidence implicating chemical and/or structural differences in the frontal lobes, basal ganglia, reticular activating system, and brain stem as well as the major neurotransmitter systems (Riccio, Hynd, Cohen, & Gonzalez, 1993). These differences might be inherited or caused by disease or trauma. Much research is needed to document specific etiologies, which will probably eventually be linked to subtypes of ADHD.

The prevalence of ADHD is approximately 3 to 5% in the school-age population. ADHD is more frequent in males than in females; the ratio ranges from 4:1 to 9:1, depending on the setting.

Inattention

Inattention encompasses many separate processes. Among these are **selective attention** (the ability to pick up and attend to the central or desired stimulus), **concentration** (the ability to sustain attention, presumably in an environment conducive to learning), **narrow focusing** (the ability to narrow attention to a particular task in spite of distractions), and **broad focusing** (the ability to effectively attend to many stimuli at one time). Time-on-task is often the way attention is measured.

Attention is affected by many variables. Among these are age (the younger the child, the less able to block out irrelevant detail), degree of difficulty (the harder the task, the shorter the duration of concentration), the number and intensity of distractors in the environment, the novelty and/or interest and fun features of the activity, changes in weather and humidity, and the like. Moreover, definite attentional styles appear to be related to external and internal locus of control, motivation, and incentive (Nideffer, 1977). Some persons attend well to external stimuli, whereas others concentrate better on ideas and tasks that come from within.

Stimuli overload seems to be a particular factor in ADHD. Students cannot block out irrelevant stimuli and thus seem driven to react to everything. Admonishing such pupils to *pay attention* is useless. They would if they could. Instead, such a pupil reacts to

> the grinding of the pencil sharpener, to the colors of dozens of shirts and dresses which surround him, to the movement of the child next to him across the aisle, to an announcement on the intercommunication system, to the leaves on the tree blowing in the wind outside the room, to the movement of the goldfish in the aquarium, to another child who just sneezed, to the teacher's whispers to yet a third child, to the footsteps of a group of children walking past his room in the hall, to the crack at the top of his desk into which his pencil point will just fit, to the American flag hanging in the front of the room, to the Thanksgiving Day decorations on the walls, to dozens and dozens of other unessential things in the room which prevent him from writing his name on the top line! It isn't that he refuses to cooperate with the teacher's request to "start here." It is that he simply cannot refrain from reacting to the unessential stimuli in his environment. This is, we think, the result of a neurological impairment. (Cruickshank, 1967, p. 33)

Inattention consists mainly of errors of omission rather than commission. The main problem is failure to finish tasks.

Impulsivity or Disinhibition

In contrast, impulsivity results from errors of commission. **Impulsivity** is the tendency to move without carefully considering alternatives. It is the opposite of reflectivity. Impulsive individuals finish tasks quickly, often with lots of errors. They are typically the first ones done, demanding "What do we do next?" Because they do not consider alternatives, they are sometimes perceived as conceptually rigid.

Impulsivity is also associated with **field dependence,** a perceptual-cognitive-behavioral style descriptive of persons who are dependent upon the environment (i.e., the field) rather than their own ideas and internal motivation (Lazarus, 1990). Field dependence is a lack of inhibitory control, a **forced responsiveness** to the field that leads persons to try to please significant others. Impulsivity, or field dependence, is characteristic of young children. As youth mature, they become increasingly reflective or field independent.

Impulsive children may display **catastrophic reactions** to unexpected stimuli like a sharp noise, a scary incident in a movie, or a playful jab from a teammate. They tend to fall apart, to sob uncontrollably, to scream, or to display sudden outbursts of anger or physical aggression.

Hyperactivity

The hyperactive child manifests disorders of listening, thinking, reading, writing, spelling, or arithmetic primarily because he or she cannot sit still long enough to complete a task. Such children are forever wiggling, shuffling their feet, swinging their legs, doodling, pinching, chewing gum, gritting their teeth, and talking to themselves or others. They seem never to tire and require unbelievably little sleep. They have been described as

> being up by 5:05 A.M., into the kitchen by 5:08 A.M., having the pans out of the cupboard by 5:09 A.M., mixing the flour and sugar on the floor by 5:11 A.M., walking through it in bare feet by 5:15 A.M., turning attention to the living room drapes by 5:18 A.M., and inadvertently knocking over a table lamp at 5:20 A.M. This wakens all members of the family, who individually and collectively descend on the first-floor scene, and thus begins another day of tension, discipline, and frustration. (Cruickshank, 1967, p. 34)

Hyperactivity may be worse on some days than others. Classroom teachers have been known to send the child to the playground on such days: "You take him . . . I can't teach him a thing in the classroom."

Hyperactivity should not be confused with individual differences in energy, impulse control, and enthusiasm. All toddlers exhibit problems with impulse control. This is evidenced when children of different ages are asked: "How slowly can you draw a line from this point to that point?" or "How slowly can you walk across the room?" or "How slowly can you do tasks in the Bruininks-Oseretsky tests?" The older the child is, the more easily he or she can slow down the pace and consciously determine the tempo. Impulse control may be related to hyperactive behavior, but it is not the same thing.

Other Behavioral Problems

Other behavioral problems are associated with neurological soft signs (e.g., conceptual rigidity, inappropriate reactions, perseveration) and misunderstandings that stem from deficits in listening, thinking, and speaking skills.

Social Imperception

Inadequacies of social perception—namely, the inability to recognize the meaning and significance of the behavior of others—contribute to poor social adjustment. Problems in this area occur concomitantly with both LD and ADHD.

Children with LD often have difficulty in making and keeping friends of their own age. Attention deficits, impulsivity, and hyperactivity are complicated further by their inability to deal with abstractions and double meanings. They become the butt of jokes when they cannot share the multiple meanings of such words as *screw, ball, grass, pot,* and *head.* Moreover, much of the humor in our society is abstract and entirely lost on them. Because they fail to comprehend the subtleties of facial expression, tone of voice, and body language, they do not realize that they are angering, antagonizing, or boring others until some kind of explosion erupts. They retreat with hurt feelings, wondering why the others *blew up all of a sudden* or told them *to get out and leave them alone.*

With severely involved children, play should seldom, if ever, be left unstructured. It is far better to delimit the activity with "You may play cowboys and Indians with John and Chris in Room 121 for 20 minutes" than to allow the group interaction to continue indefinitely, ultimately ending with a fight of some kind. In schools that have daily recess, the teacher should specify ahead of time names of persons who have permission to play together, the space on the playground they may occupy, and the equipment they may use. Children with social imperception are given freedom only in small degrees, as they demonstrate increasing ability to cope in social situations.

Perseveration

Often interpreted as stubbornness, **perseveration** is the inability to shift easily from one idea or activity to another. Perseveration is present when a pupil

1. Continues to grind on and on long after a pencil is sharpened.
2. Continues to bounce the ball after the signal for stopping has been given.
3. Continues to laugh or giggle after everyone else stops.
4. Repeats the same phrase over and over or gets hung up on one topic of conversation.

Perseveration is the opposite of distractibility. It contributes to a behavioral rigidity, which is evidenced in games when the student refuses to adapt rules or to test a new strategy. One approach to remediation is creativity training with emphasis on fluency and flexibility.

Another approach is to plan activities that are distinctly different from each other in formation, starting position, basic skills, rules, and strategies. A circle game, for instance, might be followed by a relay in files. In circuit training, a station stressing arm and shoulder strength might be followed by one emphasizing jumping activities. Games based upon stop-and-go concepts reinforce the ability to make transitions from one activity to another. Illustrative of these are *Red Light, Green Light, Musical Chairs, Cakewalks, Statues,* and *Squirrels in the Trees.*

Principles for Managing Environment

The concepts of Cruickshank (1967) and Strauss and Lehtinen (1947) continue to shape the educational prescriptions of students with behavioral problems. A good teaching environment is based upon four principles:

1. Establishment of a highly structured program
2. Reduction of environmental space
3. Elimination of irrelevant auditory and visual stimuli
4. Enhancement of the stimulus value of the instructional materials

Structure

The **principle of structure,** as applied to the physical education setting, requires the establishment of a routine that is repeated day after day and leaves nothing to chance. For instance, the pattern of activities should follow the same sequence each period: sitting on prescribed floor spots while waiting for class to begin, warm-ups always done in the same area and facing the same direction, introduction and practice of new skills, participation in games or dances, return to floor spots, and sitting during *cool-down* period of relaxation and discussion.

If instructional stations are used, a certain piece of apparatus should always be located in the same space and the students should always mount it from the same direction. Rotation from station to station should always be in the same direction, traditionally counterclockwise. Characteristically, after warm-ups, each student goes to his or her assigned station to start instruction, and rotation always proceeds from the same spot. Identical start, stop, and rotation signals also contribute to structure since the child knows precisely which response is appropriate for each signal.

Moreover, the composition of each squad or team should be structured in much the same fashion as are groups for play therapy or psychotherapy. A balance is maintained between the number of hyperactive and sluggish children so that one behavioral extreme tends to neutralize the other. The proportion of aggressors and nonaggressors is weighted, as are natural leaders and followers.

Structure also denotes a carefully planned system of behavior management in operation. Cues and consequences are consistent. See Chapter 7 for a review of behavior management.

Space Reduction

The **principle of space reduction** suggests the use of lane markers and partitions to delimit the vast expanse of play area considered desirable for normal children. Special emphasis must be given to boundaries and the penalties incumbent upon stepping out-of-bounds. The major value of low organized games may be learning about boundaries, baselines, and space utilization.

Space reduction necessarily limits the size of the squads, which rotate from station to station. Most elementary school children function well in groups of six to eight; children with LD often require smaller groups.

Extraneous Stimuli Control

The **principle of extraneous stimuli control** demands the maintenance of a neat, clean, well-ordered play area. No balls or equipment are in sight unless they are required for the game in progress. When several squads are each practicing different motor tasks, often on different pieces of apparatus, the student's attention may be diverted by persons at other stations. Partitions to eliminate the extraneous visual stimuli from other stations prevent problems. Similar distractions are present when physical education is held outdoors: Cars in the nearby street, neighborhood animals, leaves rustling on the trees, birds flying overhead, weeds among the grass where the ball is rolling, even the wind and sun command the child's attention. The student with severe hyperactivity should be scheduled only for indoor physical education, where environmental variables can be more easily controlled.

Instructional Stimulus Enhancement

The **principle of instructional stimulus enhancement,** as applied to the physical education setting, implies the extensive

FIGURE 20.7 Mirrors are extremely important in learning disabilities because visual input enhances kinesthetic and vestibular feedback.

and concentrated use of color to focus and hold the student's attention on a particular piece of apparatus, a target, or a ball. Sound may be used similarly. Wall-to-wall mirrors in which students can see and learn to evaluate their motor performance also seem to increase concentration (see Figure 20.7).

The principles of structure, space reduction, stimuli control, and instructional stimulus enhancement form the basis of a sound physical education program for students with LD. Freedom is increased gradually in accordance with the student's ability to cope.

Modifying Physical Education Content

Students with ADHD obviously need a different kind of physical education content than that which exists in most regular physical education settings. Emphasis should be on learning relaxation techniques (see Chapter 15), impulse control, and sport, dance, and aquatic activities that encourage reflectivity and attention to detail. Individual and small-group counseling helps students to set personal goals for managing their behavior in school and community facilities where fitness and leisure skills are pursued.

The goal, of course, is to learn self-control and self-responsibility requisite to social acceptance in afterschool and weekend youth sport. This can be achieved when teachers systematically apply the content in this chapter and related literature (Decker & Voege, 1992).

Medication

ADHD is a medical problem. Most physicians use medication only as a last resort. Nevertheless, a large number of young-

sters with ADHD are so uncontrollable that drugs are prescribed: *ritalin* (methyiphenidate), *dexedrine, benzedrine, methedrine,* and *cylert,* all of which are stimulants. These stimulants slow down the child, increase the attention span, and help with concentration (Swanson et al., 1993). Use of stimulants in hyperactivity is analogous to prescription of insulin for diabetes. Both conditions involve deficits in body chemistry for which drugs compensate.

Children do not become addicted to the drugs used in ADHD, and there are no withdrawal problems. The main side effects are depressed appetite and sleeplessness, according to medical sources. Physical educators note, however, that these medications sometimes affect balance and coordination.

References

American Psychiatric Association. (1994). *Diagnostic and statistical manual of mental disorders* (4th ed.). Washington, DC: Author.

Ayres, A. J. (1972). *Sensory integration and learning disorders.* Los Angeles: Western Psychological Services.

Bishop, P., & Beyer, R. (1995). Attention deficit hyperactivity disorder (ADHD): Implications for physical educators. *Palaestra, 11*(4), 39–46.

Board of Trustees, Council for Learning Disabilities. (1986). Measurement and training of perceptual and perceptual-motor functions. *Learning Disabilities Quarterly, 9*(3), 247.

Bouffard, M., & Wall, A. E. (1990). A problem-solving approach to movement skill acquisition: Implications for special populations. In G. Reid (Ed.), *Problems in movement control* (pp. 107–131). Amsterdam: North-Holland.

Bouffard, M., Watkinson, E. J., Thompson, L. P., Dunn, J. L. C., & Romanow, S. K. E. (1996). A test of the activity deficit hypothesis with children with movement difficulties. *Adapted Physical Activity Quarterly, 13*(1), 61–73.

Bruininks, R. H. (1978). *Bruininks-Oseretsky test of motor proficiency: Examiner's manual.* Circle Pines, MN: American Guidance Service.

Bruininks, V., & Bruininks, R. (1977). Motor proficiency of learning disabled and nondisabled students. *Perceptual and Motor Skills, 44,* 1131–1137.

Bulgren, J. A., & Carta, J. J. (1992). Examining the instructional contexts of students with learning disabilities. *Exceptional Children, 59*(3), 182–191.

Cantell, M. H., Smyth, M. M., & Ahonen, T. P. (1994). Clumsiness in adolescence: Educational, motor, and social outcomes of motor delay detected at 5 years. *Adapted Physical Activity Quarterly, 11*(2), 115–129.

Clarke, L. (1973). *Can't read, can't write, can't takl too good either.* New York: Walker & Company.

Cohen, H. J., Coker, J. W., Crain, L. S., Healy, A., Katcher, A., Openheimer, S. G., & Weisskopf, B. (1985). School-aged children with motor disabilities. *Pediatrics, 76*(4), 648–649.

Cratty, B. J. (1971). *Active learning.* Englewood Cliffs, NJ: Prentice Hall.

Cratty, B. J. (1972). *Physical expressions of intelligence.* Englewood Cliffs, NJ: Prentice Hall.

Cratty, B. J., Ikeda, N., Martin, M., Jennett, C., & Morris, M. (1970). Game choices of children with movement problems. In B. J. Cratty (Ed.), *Movement abilities, motor ability, and the education of children* (pp. 45–85). Springfield, IL: Charles C Thomas.

Cruickshank, W. (1967). *The brain-injured child in home, school, and community.* Syracuse, NY: Syracuse University Press.

Decker, J., & Voege, D. (1992). Integrating children with attention deficit disorder with hyperactivity into youth sport. *Palaestra, 8*(4), 16–20.

Dunn, J. L. C., & Watkinson, E. J. (1994). A study of the relationship between physical awkwardness and children's perceptions of physical competence. *Adapted Physical Activity Quarterly, 11*(3), 275–283.

Dunn, R. (1990). Bias over substance: A critical analysis of Kavale and Forness' report on modality-based instruction. *Exceptional Children, 56*(4), 357–361.

Fiore, T. A., Becker, E. A., & Nero, R. C. (1993). Educational interventions for students with attention deficit disorder. *Exceptional Children, 60*(2), 163–173.

Gottlieb, B. W., Gottlieb, J., Berkell, D., & Levy, L. (1986). Sociometric status and solitary play of LD boys and girls. *Journal of Learning Disabilities, 19*(10), 619–622.

Hallahan, D., & Cruickshank, W. (1973). *Psychoeducational foundations of learning disabilities.* Englewood Cliffs, NJ: Prentice Hall.

Harris, K. R., & Pressley, M. (1991). The nature of cognitive strategy instruction: Interactive strategy construction. *Exceptional Children, 57*(5), 392–404.

Hellison, D. R. (1985). *Goals and strategies for teaching physical education.* Champaign, IL: Human Kinetics.

Hoare, D. (1994). Subtypes of developmental coordination disorder. *Adapted Physical Activity Quarterly, 11*(2), 158–169.

Holguin, O., & Sherrill, C. (1989). Use of a motor creativity test with young learning disabled boys. *Perceptual and Motor Skills, 69,* 1315–1318.

Johnson, D. J., & Myklebust, H. R. (1967). *Learning disabilities.* New York: Grune & Stratton.

Johnson, D. W., & Johnson, R. T. (1986). Mainstreaming and cooperative learning strategies. *Exceptional Children, 52*(6), 553–561.

Kavale, K. A., & Forness, S. R. (1987). Substance over style: Assessing the efficacy of modality testing and teaching. *Exceptional Children, 54*(3), 228–239.

Kavale, K. A., & Forness, S. R. (1990). Substance over style: A rejoinder to Dunn's animadversions. *Exceptional Children, 56*(4), 357–361.

Kavale, K., & Mattson, P. D. (1983). One jumped off the balance beam: Meta-analysis of perceptual motor training. *Journal of Learning Disabilities, 16,* 165–173.

Kephart, N. C. (1971). *The slow learner in the classroom* (2nd ed.). Columbus, OH: Charles E. Merrill.

Kowalski, E., & Sherrill, C. (1992). Modeling and motor sequencing strategies of learning-disabled boys. *Adapted Physical Activity Quarterly, 9*(3), 261–272.

Lazarus, J. C. (1990). Factors underlying inefficient movement in learning-disabled children. In G. Reid (Ed.), *Problems in motor control: Advances in psychology series* (pp. 241–282). Amsterdam: North-Holland.

Lazarus, J. C. (1994). Evidence of disinhibition in learning disabilities: The associated movement phenomenon. *Adapted Physical Activity Quarterly, 11*(1), 57–70.

Levinson, H. N. (1988). The cerebellar-vestibular basis of learning disabilities in children, adolescents, and adults: Hypothesis and study. *Perceptual and Motor Skills, 67,* 983–1006.

Margalit, M. (1984). Leisure activities of learning disabled children as a reflection of their passive lifestyle and prolonged dependency. *Child Psychiatry and Human Development, 15*(2), 133–141.

Mender, J., Kerr, R., & Orlick, T. (1982). A cooperative games program for learning disabled children. *International Journal of Sport Psychology, 13,* 222–233.

Miyahara, M. (1994). Subtypes of students with learning disabilities based on gross motor functions. *Adapted Physical Activity Quarterly, 11*(4), 368–382.

Morris, G. S. D., & Stiehl, D. (1989). *Changing kids' games.* Champaign, IL: Human Kinetics.

Nideffer, R. M. (1977). *Test of attentional and interpersonal style.* San Diego, CA: Enhanced Performance Associates.

O'Beirne, C., Larkin, D., & Cable, T. (1994). Coordination problems and anaerobic performance in children. *Adapted Physical Activity Quarterly, 11*(2), 141–149.

Palincsar, A. S. (1986). Metacognitive strategy instruction. *Exceptional Children, 53*(2), 118–124.

Quiros, J. B., & Schrager, O. L. (1979). *Neuropsychological fundamentals in learning disabilities.* Novato, CA: Academic Therapy.

Rarick, G. L., Dobbins, D. A., & Broadhead, G. D. (1976). *The motor domain and its correlates in educationally handicapped children.* Englewood Cliffs, NJ: Prentice Hall.

Reid, G. (1986). The trainability of motor processing strategies with developmentally delayed performers. In H. A. Whiting & M. Wade (Eds.), *Themes in motor development* (pp. 93–107). Hingham, MA: Kluwer-Academic.

Reid, G. (1987). Motor behavior and psychosocial correlates in young handicapped performers. In D. Gould & M. R. Weiss (Eds.), *Advances in pediatric sport sciences* (Vol. 2, pp. 235–258). Champaign, IL: Human Kinetics.

Riccio, C. A., Hynd, G. W., Cohen, M. J., & Gonzalez, J. J. (1993). Neurological basis of attention deficit hyperactivity disorder. *Exceptional Children, 60*(2), 118–124.

Sherrill, C. (1972). Learning disabilities. In H. Fait, *Special physical education* (3rd ed., pp. 168–182). Philadelphia: W. B. Saunders.

Sherrill, C. (1986). Fostering creativity in handicapped children. *Adapted Physical Activity Quarterly, 3,* 236–249.

Sherrill, C., & Pyfer, J. (1985). Learning disabled students in physical education. *Adapted Physical Activity Quarterly, 2*(4), 283–291.

Strauss, A. A., & Lehtinen, L. (1947). *Psychopathology and education of the brain-injured child.* New York: Grune & Stratton.

Swanson, J. M., McBurnett, K., Wigal, T., Pfiffner, L. J., Lerner, M. C., & Williams, L. (1993). Effect of stimulant medication on children with attention deficit disorder: A "review of reviews." *Exceptional Children, 60*(2), 154–162.

Switzky, H. N., & Schultz, G. F. (1988). Intrinsic motivation and learning performance: Implications for individual education programming for learners with mild handicaps. *Remedial and Special Education, 9*(4), 7–14.

Tarnowski, K. J., & Nay, S. M. (1989). Locus of control in children with learning disabilities and hyperactivity: A subgroup analysis. *Journal of Learning Disabilities, 22*(6), 381–383, 391.

Vallerand, R. J., & Reid, G. (1990). Motivation and special populations: Theory, research, and implications regarding motor behavior. In G. Reid (Ed.), *Problems in movement control* (pp. 159–197). Amsterdam: North-Holland.

West, M., Kregel, J., Getzel, E., Zhu, M., Ipsen, S. M., & Martin, E. D. (1993). Beyond Section 504: Satisfaction and empowerment of students with disabilities in higher education. *Exceptional Children, 59*(5), 456–467.

CHAPTER

21

Mental Retardation, Special Olympics, and the INAS-FMH

FIGURE 21.1 Special Olympics has demonstrated the potential of persons with mental retardation to the world. *(A)* Eunice Kennedy Shriver, the founder of Special Olympics, provides encouragement. *(B)* Action from the Little Stanley Cup game, a feature event of the International Special Olympics floor hockey tournament in Toronto, Ontario.

A

B

After you have studied this chapter, you should be able to do the following:

1. State four criteria for educational diagnosis of mental retardation and discuss each part in relation to programming.

2. Summarize concepts that relate to normal curve theory, including the natural genetic distribution of IQs.

3. Discuss etiologies of MR, including syndromes.

4. Identify the three most frequently occurring syndromes associated with MR and discuss each.

5. Discuss frequently occurring medical problems that affect physical education programming.

6. Discuss motor and cognitive abilities of persons with MR. What are some implications for assessment and programming?

7. Explain how programming differs according to level of MR and give examples of models appropriate to guide programming.

8. Develop some task analyses and state cues, feedback, and reinforcement for each step.

9. Contrast and critique different programming models. (See example by Greenwood, Silliman, and French, 1990; also read Krebs and Block, 1992.)

10. Describe Special Olympics programming and discuss how you would organize and implement a year-round program.

11. Given profiles of persons with MR, write IEPs and lesson plans.

12. Contrast INAS-FMH, Special Olympics, and other opportunities for sport involvement.

Mental retardation (MR) is perhaps the best known of all disabilities because Special Olympics has given it so much visibility (see Figure 21.1). Definitions of MR, however, vary throughout the world. In the United States, mental retardation is distinguished from learning disabilities by federal law that specifies different diagnostic and funding categories. In contrast, Great Britain uses the terms *learning difficulty* and *special educational needs* instead of *mental retardation* (Sugden & Keogh, 1990).

INAS-FMH and Special Olympics Perspectives

The International Sports Federation for Persons with Mental Handicap (INAS-FMH), which is part of the Paralympic movement, uses such terms as *mental handicap, learning difficulty,* and *intellectual disability* to denote athletes with "intelligence disturbances of the rate and degree of development of cognitive functions such as perception, attention, memory, and thinking" (Atha, 1994, p. 305). The INAS-FMH was founded in Europe in 1986, and its terminology shows that much of the world prefers other terms over *mental retardation* (MR). Beginning with the World Games in Berlin in 1995, the INAS-FMH has entered its athletes into Paralympic competition, which previously was held only for athletes with physical or sensory disabilities. Several terms are used to describe INAS-FMH athletes, but the most popular seems to be *athletes with learning difficulties.*

Special Olympics International (SOI), founded in Chicago in 1968, primarily uses the term *mental retardation* (MR). It conducts its own quadrennial summer and winter games exclusively for people with MR, provides comprehensive year-round sports training, and promotes Unified Sports, a program that combines approximately equal numbers of athletes with and without disabilities on teams that compete against each other. Local Special Olympics training activities are available to anyone with MR who is age 5 or older, but rules do not permit competition until age 8.

ISO is not associated with the Paralympics. At the 1995 Summer Special Olympics World Games, approximately 7,000 athletes from more than 140 countries competed in 19 sports (Special Olympics International, 1995). Not everyone

was a winner, contrary to popular opinion, because SOI philosophy has changed over its 30-plus years of pioneer leadership. Traditional medals are awarded to athletes who win first, second, and third places. Participation ribbons are given to other athletes in recognition of their effort and accomplishments.

Adapted physical activity personnel throughout the world work with Special Olympics at many levels, local through international. The success of individual training and competition programs, typically staffed by volunteers, often largely depends upon the leadership of adapted physical activity professionals. Many school systems, therefore, expect their adapted physical educators to work with Special Olympics. Tremendous breadth of knowledge is needed, because Special Olympics is usually a community-based program that serves all age groups.

Individuals eligible to become Special Olympics athletes are persons who

1. have been identified by an agency or professional as having mental retardation; OR

2. have a cognitive delay as determined by standardized measures like intelligence tests; OR

3. have significant learning or vocational problems due to cognitive delays which require or have required specially designed instruction. (Special Olympics, 1995, p. 180)

Specially designed instruction, in this statement, refers to supportive education or remedial instruction directed at the cognitive delay. In the case of adults, involvement in specially designed programs in the workplace or home permits them to meet the criterion of specially designed instruction. Special Olympics thus serves persons with autism and serious emotional disturbances (see Chapter 22) as well as those with significant learning or vocational problems.

The Definition Dilemma

Controversy has always surrounded definitions of MR. There are many reasons for this. One reason is that definitions determine eligibility for special education and other support services. For example, a major issue today is whether the upper limit of an intelligence test quotient for diagnosing a person as mentally retarded should be 70 or 75. Parents with children who have IQs between 70 and 75 might want an upper limit of 75, while taxpayers who are conscious of the money that special services cost might want a cutoff of 70. Experts note that in a normal curve distribution there are more than twice as many cases with IQs below 75 (4.7%) as there are cases with IQs below 70 (2.3%) (MacMillan, Gresham, & Siperstein, 1995).

Since the 1950s, all definitions of MR have included the concept of **adaptive functioning** (i.e., adaptive behaviors or skills such as dressing oneself, telling time, and conveying one's needs to others). This is because many experts question the validity, reliability, and cultural fairness of IQ tests in determining an individual's performance on various tasks. **Adaptive functioning** refers to "how effectively individuals cope with common life demands and how well they meet the standards of personal independence expected of someone in their particular age group, sociocultural background, and community setting" (American Psychiatric Association, 1994, p. 40). However, there is a lack of agreement about how many adaptive behavior deficits must be present to meet the MR criterion, what the names and definitions of adaptive skill areas should be, and how adaptive skills should be assessed.

Philosophy about MR, eligibility criteria, classification, and support systems is continually changing. The American Association on Mental Retardation (AAMR) therefore periodically publishes manuals to guide professionals in staying abreast of changes and to stimulate critical thinking.

AAMR 1992 Definition and Assessment Paradigm

In 1992, the AAMR set forth a revised definition of MR and a new paradigm (model) for diagnosis (Luckasson et al., 1992). The following definition was given for **mental retardation:**

1. Refers to substantial limitations in certain personal capabilities.
2. Is manifested as significantly subaverage intellectual functioning.
3. Exists concurrently with related disabilities in two or more of the following **adaptive skill areas:**

   —Communications   —Self-care
   —Home living   —Social skills
   —Community use   —Self-direction
   —Health and safety   —Functional academics
   —Work   —Leisure

4. Begins before age 18.

This definition was an improvement over previous ones (Grossman, 1983) because it specified adaptive skill areas by name and stated that problems must be identified by age 18. See Appendix A for the federal law definition, and note similarities and differences.

The 1992 AAMR paradigm emphasizes the importance of assessing not just the person but the entire environment. A three-step process is recommended:

1. Examine IQ, adaptive skill levels, and age of onset.
2. Assess strengths and weaknesses across four dimensions:
   (a) intellectual functioning and adaptive skills,
   (b) psychological/emotional considerations,
   (c) physical/health/etiology considerations, and
   (d) environmental considerations. *Remember that strengths and weaknesses are dependent upon both individual capabilities and the environment.*
3. Develop a personal profile of the kind and intensities of supports needed for each of the four dimensions. The term **supports** refers to "an array of services, individuals, and settings that match the person's needs" (Luckasson et al., 1992, p. 7). Supports include both resources and strategies.

Supports

The AAMR assessment process substitutes the concept of supports, which requires consideration of both the person and the environment, for the tradition of classifying individuals with MR as having mild, moderate, severe, or profound conditions. The AAMR posits that emphasizing appropriate supports will encourage professionals to assess what people can actually do in particular environments rather than link preconceived behaviors and services to labels like *mild, moderate, severe,* and *profound.*

Figure 21.2 presents the supports paradigm (model) recommended by the AAMR. It is helpful to think about this model in relation to physical education instruction and leisure time use. Consider, for instance, the **support resources** that can be used in the gymnasium or in the neighborhood after school. What *personal resources* does the student bring to the setting? What kinds of consultant help are needed for teachers and parents? What kinds of paraprofessionals and/or peer helpers are needed for direct and related services? Under *technology,* what kinds of assistive devices, equipment, accommodations, and adaptations will enhance success? Under *services,* consider such needs as transportation, counseling, role modeling, and tutoring.

How can physical education contribute to the **support functions** listed in Figure 21.2? Note how these support functions relate to the adaptive skill areas in the definition. In writing goals and objectives, physical educators should consider using the terminology in the AAMR definition and model.

Support intensities vary in different life stages and situations. The adjectives in Figure 21.2 help create a uniform system of communication among educators and caretakers.

Intermittent refers to short-term support that is made available as needed (e.g., availability of a paraprofessional or resource room).

Limited refers to designated, prearranged support for short periods of time (e.g., use of an athlete role model to teach wheelchair sport skills or an after-school tutor during an instructional unit that will likely be particularly difficult).

Extensive refers to daily support in some, but not all, environments. A personal assistant (PA), for instance, might be needed when a student with multiple disabilities is enrolled in a regular physical education class. Adapted equipment might be needed in physical education but not in other classes.

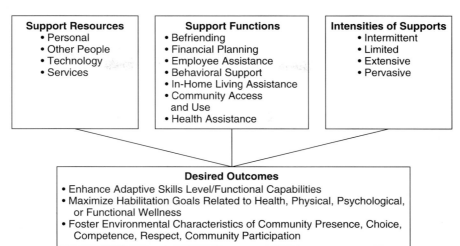

Support Resources
- Personal
- Other People
- Technology
- Services

Support Functions
- Befriending
- Financial Planning
- Employee Assistance
- Behavioral Support
- In-Home Living Assistance
- Community Access and Use
- Health Assistance

Intensities of Supports
- Intermittent
- Limited
- Extensive
- Pervasive

Desired Outcomes
- Enhance Adaptive Skills Level/Functional Capabilities
- Maximize Habilitation Goals Related to Health, Physical, Psychological, or Functional Wellness
- Foster Environmental Characteristics of Community Presence, Choice, Competence, Respect, Community Participation

Pervasive refers to constant, high-intensity, possibly life-sustaining supports. This typically involves a full-time PA and provision of such devices as ventilators, catheters, and adapted eating utensils.

Desired outcomes vary, of course, with individual needs and subject matter. The trend, however, is clearly toward instruction that will lead to increased self-direction, independent functioning in the community, and leisure skills that will enhance health and social inclusion.

Intelligence Tests

The personal capabilities that are most limited in MR are abstract thinking, concept formation, generalization, problem solving, and evaluation. **Significant subaverage intellectual functioning** is defined as an IQ lower than 70 to 75, based on assessment that includes one or more individually administered intelligence tests (Luckasson et al., 1992). Earlier references defined subaverage as any IQ that fell two or more standard deviations below the mean (see Figure 21.3). This concept continues to be accepted, although the 70 to 75 criterion is less rigid, recognizing that IQs can vary a few points from test to test.

Many standardized tests are used to assess IQ. The oldest is the Stanford-Binet Intelligence Scale (also known as the Terman-Merrill Scale), which has a mean of 100 and a standard deviation of 16. Figure 21.3 shows markers of 84, 68, 52, and so on when 16 is subtracted from 100 and each subsequent marker. Newer tests like the Wechsler Intelligence Scale for Children–Revised (WISC-R), the Kaufman Assessment Battery for Children, and the Slosson Intelligence Test all have a mean of 100 and a standard deviation of 15. Subtracting this standard deviation from 100 and subsequent markers yields 85, 70, 55, and so on. A 70 on the Wechsler is thus equivalent to a 68 on the Stanford-Binet; both IQs are 2 standard deviations below the mean and indicate that general intellectual function is lower than that of 97% of the population.

Level of Severity

Prior to the 1990s, IQs were specified for four levels of MR function: (a) mild, 52–70; (b) moderate, 36–51; (c) severe, 20–35; and (d) profound, 19 and lower. About 90% of persons with MR fell into the mild classification, 5% into the moderate, and 3.5% and 1.5%, respectively, into the severe and profound.

The 1992 policy revision recognizes only two classifications of MR: (a) mild and (b) severe. These are not based on IQ but on level of function within adaptive skill levels. Thus, IQ, if correctly used, will be relevant only in the first stage of a multidimensional classification system. The emphasis will be on assessment of disability (mild or severe) in communications, home living, community use, health and safety, work, self-care, social skills, self-direction, functional academics, and leisure.

The use of only two severity classifications is controversial. Block (1992), for example, emphasizes the need to distinguish between severe and profound function levels. **Severe** refers to persons with good levels of awareness and adequate resources to respond, learn, and function in integrated community settings when extensive support is provided. In contrast, **profound** denotes persons with very limited awareness and response repertoires.

Placement and Prevalence

Persons with MR constitute the third largest disability group receiving special education in the United States. Almost 600,000 students in the age range from 6 to 21 years receive services. Most of these students spend some part of every day in regular education.

In striking contrast to the past, few persons with MR live in large residential facilities today. Among the 6- to 21-year-old group, only 1.5% are in residential facilities. These are usually children with multiple disabilities, with IQs of less than 35, and from dysfunctional or nonexistent families. Adults with MR who used to live in institutions now mostly reside in the community in small-group homes accommodating six or fewer persons. They still receive mental health/mental retardation (MH/MR) services from a central agency, but living and learning arrangements are as close to those of nondisabled persons as possible.

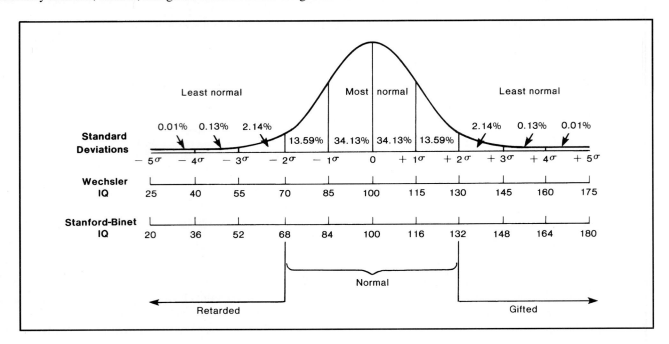

Prevalence of MR is generally estimated as 3% of the total population, a figure based partly on normal curve theory. This theory posits that 2.28% of the population has low intelligence and that an equal percentage is gifted. To understand how the estimated 2.28% is derived, look at Figure 21.3 and note the percentage of the population that falls into the third, fourth, and fifth standard deviation areas (2.14 + .13 + .01 = 2.28). To arrive at the 3% estimate, authorities add 0.72%, the percentage of the general population with known biomedical conditions that result in MR.

The United States has approximately 7.5 million citizens with MR. About 125,000 infants are born with MR each year. There are about 156 million individuals with MR in the world. Severe MR (when defined as IQ under 50) has an incidence of about 3 to 5 per 1,000 in developed countries (Sugden & Keogh, 1990).

Etiology of Mental Retardation

Most MR is caused by multiple factors, some biological and some environmental (Luckasson et al., 1992). No clear etiology can be determined for approximately 30 to 40% of individuals with MR, despite extensive laboratory testing. According to the American Psychiatric Association (1994), the predisposing factors for the other 60 to 70% are as follows:

Heredity, including normal and abnormal gene mechanisms—5%

Early alterations of embryonic development, including Down syndrome, fetal alcohol syndrome, infections—30%

Pregnancy and perinatal problems—10%

Postnatal infections, traumas, and toxins—5%

Postnatal environmental deprivation conditions and other mental disorders like autism—15–20%

The most common conditions within the combined heredity and early alterations of embryonic development categories are fetal alcohol syndrome, Down syndrome, and fragile X syndrome.

Approaches to the study of etiology are much different than in the past, when specific causes of conditions were sought. Today causes are examined primarily to aid in prevention of MR. Table 21.1 summarizes prenatal, perinatal, and postnatal causes as presented by Luckasson et al. (1992). These causes do not always result in MR; causes are included in Table 21.1 if MR can sometimes be traced to them.

Following is a brief summary of some of the more common categories of causes. Incidences of various syndromes (chromosomal and other) are given in Appendix A.

Chromosomal Abnormalities

Chromosomal abnormalities affect about 7 in every 1,000 births (Gerber, 1990). These disorders usually result from chance errors in cell division shortly after an egg and a sperm unite. With each cell division, 23 pairs of chromosomes should be passed on, each carrying the full DNA and genes to mastermind further development. Of the 23 pairs in each cell, 22 are **autosomes** (important for specific genetic markers), and one is the **sex chromosome pair,** designated as XX (female) or XY (male), which determines gender.

Abnormalities can occur in either autosomes or sex chromosomes. The most common autosomal chromosome disorder is **Down syndrome** (a short-stature MR condition, with distinguishing facial and other features). A common sex-linked chromosome disorder is **Turner syndrome,** caused by

T a b l e   2 1 . 1   Disorders in which mental retardation often occurs.

I. Prenatal causes
- A. Chromosomal disorders
  - 1. Autosomes (23 pairs in each cell)
    - a. Trisomy 21 (Down syndrome)
    - b. Translocation 21 (Down syndrome)
  - 2. Sex chromosome (1 pair in each cell)
    - a. Fragile X syndrome
    - b. Short-stature syndromes
      - 1. Turner (XO)—females only
      - 2. Noonan—males only
    - c. Tall-stature syndromes
      - 1. Klinefelter (XXY)—males only
      - 2. XYY—males only
- B. Other syndrome disorders
  Examples are Apert, Cornelia de Lange, Prader-Willi
- C. Inborn errors of metabolism
  - 1. Amino acid disorder—phenylketonuria (PKU)
  - 2. Carbohydrate disorder—galactosemia
  - 3. Nucleic acid disorder—Lesch-Nyhan syndrome
  - 4. Numerous others
- D. Brain formation disorders
  - 1. Neural tube closure disorders—spina bifida, anencephaly
  - 2. Hydrocephalus
  - 3. Microcephalus
- E. Environmental influences
  - 1. Fetal alcohol syndrome
  - 2. Cocaine and/or other drugs
  - 3. Intrauterine malnutrition
  - 4. Maternal diseases

II. Perinatal causes (from 28th week of pregnancy through 28 days following birth)
- A. Intrauterine and/or abnormal labor and delivery
- B. Neonatal
  - 1. Head trauma at birth
  - 2. Intracranial hemorrhage
  - 3. Infections
  - 4. Nutritional and late-onset metabolic disorders

III. Postnatal causes (any time before age 18)
- A. Head injuries
- B. Infections
  - 1. Encephalitis
  - 2. Meningitis
  - 3. Fungal, parasitic, or viral
- C. Degenerative disorders
  - 1. Rett syndrome
  - 2. Friedreich's ataxia
  - 3. Tay-Sachs
- D. Seizure disorders
- E. Toxic-metabolic disorders
  - 1. Lead, mercury
  - 2. Late-onset metabolic disorders
- F. Malnutrition
- G. Environmental deprivation
  - 1. Psychosocial disadvantage
  - 2. Child abuse and neglect

a division failure that results in only one X instead of the XX or XY pair in normal cells. Turner is also called XO syndrome. Some chromosomal disorders result in mental retardation (e.g., Down syndrome), but others may not (e.g., Turner syndrome). Turner syndrome, which occurs only in females, results in short stature (less than 5 ft), appearance of a short neck because of low posterior hairline and/or cervical webbing, a broad chest with widely spaced nipples, and failure to menstruate and mature sexually. A comparable condition in males is called **Noonan syndrome.**

Sex chromosome disorders occur more frequently than autosome disorders and cause less severe conditions. Most sex chromosome disorders are primarily characterized by height abnormalities (extra short or tall) and underdeveloped or overdeveloped genitalia. Any syndrome that has X or O in its name is a sex chromosome disorder. There are multiple X female (XXX, XXXX) and multiple X male (XXXY, XXXXY) syndromes; these cause short heights. Two syndromes that occur in males only (XYY and XXY) cause abnormal tallness. XXY is also called **Klinefelter syndrome.**

Fragile X Syndrome

Of particular interest is **fragile X syndrome,** a condition that is inherited rather than occurring by chance. Discovered in 1969, it could not be accurately and consistently diagnosed until the 1980s. *Fragile* refers to a gap or break in the long arm of the X chromosome. This occurs in 1 of 1,000 males and 1 of 2,000 females, but frequently goes undiagnosed. Mental function varies from severe MR to normal, with MR more common in males than in females. Behaviors are often autistic, hyperactive, and impulsive (Dykens, Hodapp, & Leckman, 1994). Physical indicators are large, narrow face, prominent ears, and large testicles.

Other Syndrome Disorders

Faces and other features of children with MR vary widely (see Figure 21.4). Some faces, however, indicate specific syndromes.

Syndromes are named for persons who first discovered them (e.g., Apert) or for distinguishing features (e.g., tuberous sclerosis) or for the causative agent (e.g., fetal alcohol). Most are rare but can easily be remembered by cranial features. **Apert syndrome** is indicated by a flat head appearance, microcephalus, defective formation of facial bones, bulging eyes, and malformed hands and feet (see Figure 21.4E). Although MR is not always present, the malformed hands and feet require physical education adaptations (Weber, 1994).

Cornelia de Lange syndrome is characterized by bushy eyebrows, long and curly eyelashes, lots of body hair, and small stature (see Figure 21.3F). *Amount of MR cannot be estimated by appearance. Occasionally a person with these syndromes has normal intelligence.* **Neurofibromatosis** (von Recklinghausen's disease) can best be remembered by the book, play, and movie about the elephant man (Montagu, 1971). It is the most common of the group of inherited disorders that affect both brain and skin. Indicators are (a) multiple *fibromas* (fibrous tumors that look like nodules) on the skin and in the central nervous system (CNS), (b) scoliosis, and (c) brown spots that look like coffee with cream (cafe au lait) stains. Neurofibromatosis usually does not become a problem until adolescence or adulthood.

In contrast, the less common **tuberous sclerosis** and **Sturge-Weber disease** are primarily neurologic disorders of infancy and childhood. To visualize tuberous sclerosis, remember that *tuber* means swelling and *sclerosis* means a hardening; the condition is characterized by hard little bumps on the nose and cheeks that resemble acne. These bumps are also scattered through the brain, heart, and other organs. Sturge-Weber disease is characterized by a large port-wine stain on parts of the face. Both conditions can cause seizures and muscle weakness (hemiparesis), and MR is common.

Prader-Willi syndrome, first identified in 1956, is diagnosed by obesity, short stature, poor development of the genital organs, small hands and feet, and an insatiable appetite. Individuals with this syndrome often have mild MR, postural defects, and motor problems, all of which require special attention from physical educators (Weber, 1993). This syndrome is also linked with diminished metabolic rates that affect activity level and weight management.

Metabolism and Brain Formation Disorders

The metabolism or nutrition category mostly includes inborn errors that cause enzyme deficiencies that interfere with food metabolism. Infants look normal at birth, but within several months evidence changes in appearance and function. Fair-skinned, fair-haired, and blue-eyed infants who begin persistent vomiting can be treated by diet therapy to manage **phenylketonuria** (PKU). If untreated, brain damage is severe. Illustrative other inborn errors of metabolism include galactosemia, Hurler's syndrome, and Tay-Sachs disease. Each is rare.

Unknown prenatal influences cause some infants to look abnormal at birth because of size and shape anomalies of the head (see Figure 21.5). Among these anomalies are **anencephaly** (partial or complete absence of the brain), **microcephalus** (abnormally small brain), **hydrocephalus** (large head caused by a cerebrospinal fluid problem), and **craniostenosis** (narrowed or flat cranium). Generally, microcephalus is associated with severe MR; it is also an indicator of specific conditions like fetal alcohol syndrome.

Hydrocephalus is described in detail in Chapter 23 because it often accompanies spina bifida. Usually, shunting procedures return head size to normal, but shunting does not always work. Hydrocephalus does not cause MR immediately. When treatment is ineffective, retardation develops slowly, as increased pressure within the cranium damages the brain.

Fetal Alcohol Syndrome

Fetal alcohol syndrome (FAS) is the most common condition within the infection, toxin, and trauma etiologies (Abel, 1987). Among pregnant women who drink heavily, the incidence of FAS is about 35%. FAS is also associated with male alcoholism. From 10 to 20% of mild MR in developed countries can be traced directly to parents' drinking. *The Broken Cord* by Dorris (1989), available as a book or videotape, chronicles growth of a child with FAS and provides an excellent bibliography.

FIGURE 21.4 Faces of mental retardation. All of the children shown here have severe MR except child with Apert syndrome. Make up a psychomotor profile for each.

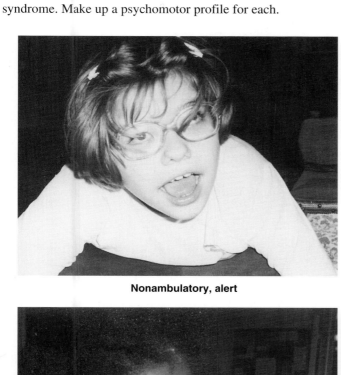

Nonambulatory, alert

Microcephalus—nonambulatory, mostly sleeps

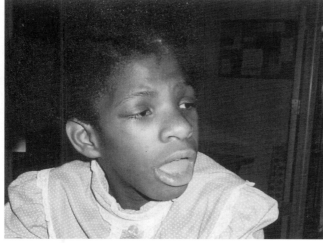

Ambulatory

Ambulatory

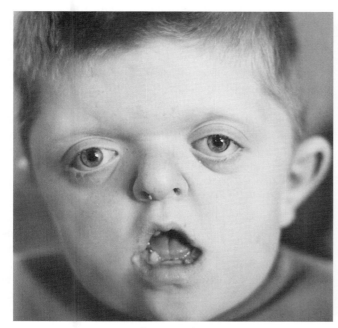

Apert syndrome

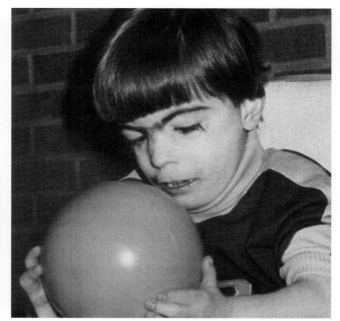

Cornelia de Lange syndrome

FIGURE 21.5 Unknown prenatal influences cause *(A)* abnormally small head (microcephalus) and *(B)* accumulation of fluid in the skull (hydrocephalus). Microcephalus is the more severe condition.

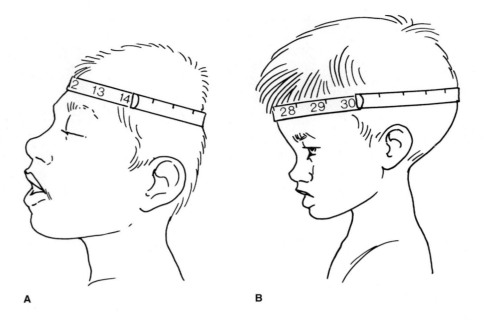

A

B

Indicators of FAS are (a) significant growth retardation before and after birth, (b) mild to moderate microcephalus (smaller than normal head), (c) altered facial features, (d) other physical and behavioral problems, and (e) diagnosis of MR, usually in the mild range. Altered facial features include almond-shaped, slanted eyes; short palpebral fissures (i.e., the opening between the eyelids); low or sunken nasal bridge; short nose; maxillary hypoplasia (small, flattened midface); thin, smooth upper lip; and indistinct philtrum (the groove between nose and upper lip). Often, there is also ptosis (dropping) of the eyelid. Most common physical and behavioral problems are fine motor incoordination, hyperactivity, stubbornness, seizures, ventricular septal defects, and mild cerebral palsy.

Study Figure 21.4. What faces most likely indicate children with FAS?

Conditions Caused by Other Toxins, Infections, and Traumas

Maternal use of crack or cocaine results in smaller than normal infants who require immediate treatment for addiction. These "crack babies" exhibit combined MR–cerebral palsy patterns as they grow. Over 10% of infants born in the United States test positive for cocaine or alcohol the first time their blood is drawn (Dorris, 1989).

Use of other drugs like marijuana, heroin, methadone, and tobacco also affects the developing embryo and fetus (Tarr & Pyfer, 1996). Drugs are commonly linked with premature births, small head circumference, low weight, delayed motor development, and failure to thrive.

Sexually transmitted diseases, including HIV/AIDS, are the main maternal infections that cause risk today, whereas *rubella* (measles) was a major factor before immunizations were developed. Childhood infection of the brain (*encephali-*

tis, meningitis) can result from common diseases like mumps, measles, and scarlet fever.

Traumas include all physical injuries and accidents that injure the brain directly or through oxygen deprivation *(anoxia, hypoxia, asphyxia)*. The risk of traumas is heightened when caretakers use drugs and alcohol.

Down Syndrome

Down syndrome (DS) is so different from other MR conditions that it warrants separate, extensive coverage. Many of the differences associated with DS affect physical education programming.

DS is an autosomal chromosomal condition that results in short stature, distinct facial features, and physical and cognitive differences that separate it from other manifestations of MR (see Figure 21.6). Intellectual function varies widely. Chris Burke as Corky on the popular ABC series "Life Goes On" demonstrates mild MR. He attends high school classes with nondisabled peers and is successful, with lots of effort, in regular education academics.

Function in DS, like that in other kinds of MR, is largely related to infant and early childhood intervention and richness of opportunity to learn in home, school, and community partnership programs. Health and freedom from severe organ defects are also important factors.

Types of Down Syndrome

Chromosomal anomalies, because they occur near the time of conception, affect growth and development of all organs. There are three types of DS: (a) trisomy 21, (b) translocation, and (c) mosaicism.

Trisomy 21 explains about 95% of DS. It is caused by **nondisjunction,** failure of chromosome pair 21 to separate properly *before or during fertilization*. The result is three chromosomes instead of two like all the others and cells that

FIGURE 21.6 *(A)* The chromosomal abnormality most common is Down syndrome, in which every cell has 47 chromosomes instead of 46. *(B)* The karyotype was made by photographing a cell nucleus under an electron microscope. Then, the chromosomes were cut out of the photograph, matched up in pairs, and numbered. Although there are several kinds of Down syndrome, the usual problem is in chromosome 21. This affects all aspects of development and function.

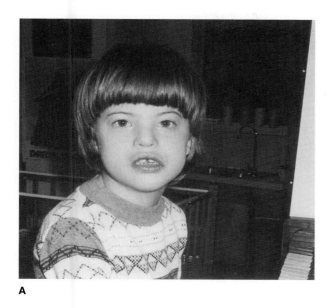

A

B

have 47 chromosomes instead of the normal 46 (see Figure 21.6B). The overall incidence is about 1 in 800 live births, but this varies with maternal age. For instance, at age 25, the risk is 1 in 1,000; over age 35, the risk is 1 in 400; over age 45, the risk is 1 in 35. Fathers are also genetically linked to occurrence of DS, but the actual cause of chromosomal nondisjunctions remains uncertain.

Translocation DS occurs when a portion of the 21st chromosome is transferred to and fused with another chromosome (usually number 14, 15, or 22). This condition has a normal chromosome count, but the extra material causes problems. About 4% of DS is of this type.

Mosaicism is very rare, accounting for less than 2% of DS. It results from a chance error in nondisjunction *after fertilization*. This causes the infant to have both normal and trisomic cells. The proportion of normal to trisomic cells varies, causing physical appearance and cognitive function to range from almost normal to classic DS (Fishler & Koch, 1991).

Physical Appearance

Persons with DS look like family members but also have many unique clinical features, including these:

- Short stature, seldom taller than 5 ft as adults.
- Short limbs, with short, broad hands and feet.
- Almond-shaped slanting eyes, often strabismic (crossed) and myopic (nearsighted).
- Flattened facial features, including bridge of nose.
- Flattened back of skull, short neck, with excess skin at nape of neck.
- Small oral cavity that contributes to mouth breathing and tongue protrusion.

- Hypotonic muscle tone in infancy that can be normalized in childhood through regular exercise.
- Joint looseness manifested by abnormal range of motion; this is caused by hypotonicity and lax ligaments. This looseness can be an advantage in gymnastics and activities requiring flexibility if muscles are strong enough to provide stability and prevent dislocation.

Sources indicate over 100 differences in physical features between people with and without DS (Sugden & Keogh, 1990). However, there is wide variation in clinical features from person to person.

Strengths and Weaknesses

Several excellent reviews of the literature summarize research on DS that relates to motor development, learning, and control (Block, 1991; Henderson, 1986; Sugden & Keogh, 1990). *In general, persons with DS tend to function motorically lower than most other persons with MR.* They do benefit, however, from infant and early childhood sensorimotor programming and intensive training in sports. Special Olympics events provide strong empirical evidence that some persons with DS can perform sports like gymnastics and swimming at high levels of proficiency. In contrast, their short heights and limbs deter success in sports like basketball and volleyball.

An area in which persons with DS seem to function higher than others with MR is rhythm (Stratford & Ching, 1983). Music and other forms of rhythmic accompaniment, imaginatively used, seem to facilitate motor learning and practice. Most persons with DS can excel in dance and rhythmic movement. Aerobic dance thus is an excellent strategy for improving fitness because it builds on this strength.

Hypotonia and Skeletal Concerns

Newborn infants with DS, like most severely neurologically involved babies, exhibit an extreme degree of *muscular hypotonia.* This fact has led to coinage of the term *floppy babies.* The muscular flabbiness decreases with age, if large-muscle exercise is stressed. The abdomen of the adolescent and the adult generally protrudes like that of a small child. Almost 90% have *umbilical hernias* in early childhood, but the condition often corrects itself. This finding suggests that abdominal exercises be selected and administered with extreme care. Other postural and/or orthopedic problems commonly associated with DS are lordosis, kyphosis, dislocated hips, funnel-shaped or pigeon-breasted chest, and clubfoot.

The lax ligaments and apparent looseness of the joints lead some authors to describe persons with DS as "double-jointed." The structural weakness of ligaments perhaps affects the function of the foot most. Many children with DS have badly pronated and/or flat feet and walk with a shuffling gait. Chapter 11 describes strategies for correcting a shuffling gait.

Motor Development Delays and Differences

Children with DS demonstrate substantial delays in emergence of postural reactions and motor milestones. Moreover, the developmental sequence is somewhat different, probably because of hypotonic muscle tone. Research on 229 children with DS in three countries showed that the rank order in which motor milestones are passed differs from that of normal babies (Dyer et al., 1990). Items passed later than expected involved balance and strength (e.g., standing, walking, throwing a ball).

The mean age for walking of children with DS is 4.2 years. This, of course, affects exploratory and social play, the major vehicle through which most children learn about themselves and the environment.

In children with DS, the development of manual control (reaching, grasping, and manipulation) is also different than in non-DS peers, possibly because of their short arms and relatively smaller hands and fingers. Other factors that can contribute to hand-eye coordination problems, including difficulty with precision grips, are vision problems, lack of motivation and practice, and neural deficits.

Balance Deficits

Balance is one of the abilities in which persons with DS are most deficient (see Figure 21.7). In this area, they tend to perform 1 to 3 years behind other persons with the same level of retardation. Many persons with DS cannot balance on one foot for more than a few seconds, and most cannot maintain balance at all with eyes closed. In general, basic movements are awkward. Deficits in balance and coordination can be explained not only by physical constraints (e.g., shortness of stature, limbs, and feet; low strength) but also by CNS dysfunction.

Balance deficits act as rate limiters in learning fundamental motor skills and patterns. This, in turn, affects involvement in games, sports, and dance and subsequent motor skill and social learning. As children with DS age, the gap between their motor performance and physical activity involvement and that of non-DS peers widens. Instruction and practice in

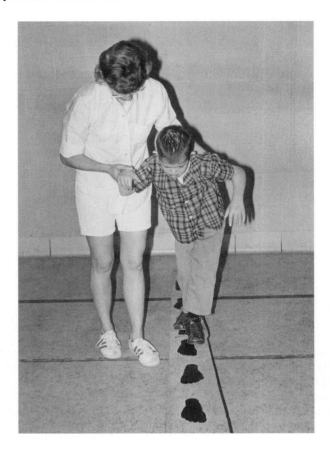

FIGURE 21.7 This preadolescent with Down syndrome exhibits balance deficits.

activities that enhance balance are particularly important. Lifetime sports like cycling, water and snow skiing, skating, and balancing games on floats in the swimming pool are recommended. Locomotor activities on uneven terrains promote extra attention to balance.

Left-Handedness and Asymmetrical Strength

A higher percentage of individuals with DS than of non-DS peers are left-handed. This fact should be remembered by persons who demonstrate activities for students to imitate. Cognitive difficulties limit the ability to transpose and copy activities of right-handed performers. In large-class instruction, left-handers should be grouped together with their own role model.

Asymmetry of strength is also common, with limbs on the left side stronger than limbs on the right (Cioni et al., 1994). This might be an expression of impairment of the left cerebral hemisphere, which is responsible for right-side movement. Asymmetry can cause problems like difficulty in swimming a straight line or awkwardness in assembling body parts to deliver the desired speed or force to a ball. Strength training should be based on assessment that examines problems of symmetry.

Visual and Hearing Concerns

Visual and visual-motor problems are rate limiters to the development of hand-eye and foot-eye coordination; this, in turn, affects success in sports that require ball handling. In general,

FIGURE 21.8 Atrioventricular canal defect in DS requires early surgery. *(A)* Heart valves affected and area where defect occurs. *(B)* Surgery to close the opening between the mitral and tricuspid valves.

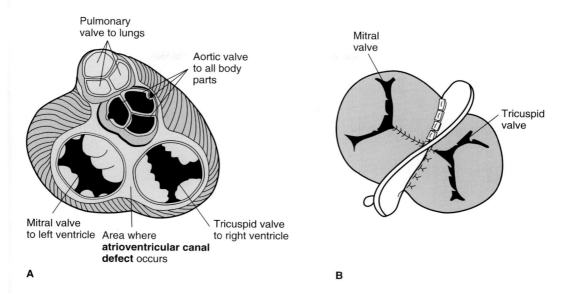

soccer is easier to learn than catching and striking activities. The most common disorders are **myopia** (nearsightedness or poor distance vision) and **strabismus** (cross eyes or squint). **Nystagmus** (constant movement of the eyeballs) is present more often in persons with DS than in non-DS peers. In adolescents and adults, **cataracts** (cloudiness of lens) occur relatively frequently.

Motor problems are, of course, intensified by the presence of visual disorders, so it is important that children with DS have eye exams as early as possible. Most visual problems can be corrected with glasses, but physical educators should routinely check that glasses are clean and properly aligned. Lens should be shatterproof, and protective goggles and sunglasses should be fitted over regular glasses as needed.

Approximately 50 to 60% of individuals with DS have significant hearing problems. Mild to moderate conductive losses in the high-frequency range are most common (see Chapter 25), causing difficulty in learning to speak, following instructions, and making and keeping friends. Often hearing losses are congenital, caused by abnormally small ear canals and/or other structural anomalies. Acquired hearing losses, which tend to occur in early childhood, are associated with the high prevalence of middle ear and respiratory infections. See Chapter 25 for adaptations that relate to hearing impairments.

Heart and Lung Problems

Approximately 40 to 60% of infants with DS have significant congenital heart disease. Older literature indicates that the **ventricular septal defect** (a hole in the septum or wall), complicated by pathology of the heart lining, is the most common congenital heart defect (Spicer, 1984), but newer literature identifies the atrioventricular canal defect as the most common lesion (Marino & Pueschel, 1996). The **atrioventricular canal defect** is an opening in the ventricular and atrial walls that normally separate the mitral and tricuspid valves. This opening causes a huge left-to-right shunt at the atrial and/or ventricular level that results in severe respiratory distress until corrected by surgery (see Figure 21.8).

In most cases, infants with atrioventricular canal defect undergo surgery before age 1. Thereafter, capacity for participation in vigorous physical activity is generally normal, except for early onset of fatigue, which compromises the ability to attain a high level of aerobic fitness. Aerobic fitness testing should be approached with care and undertaken only with a physician's approval.

Adults with DS have a 14 to 57% prevalence rate of **mitral valve prolapse** and a 11 to 14% prevalence rate of **aortic regurgitation,** both of which are attributed to the ligamentous laxity (connective tissue disorder) associated with DS (Marino & Pueschel, 1996). These heart conditions are generally asymptomatic and do not contraindicate participation in vigorous sports. However, annual cardiac checkups and careful monitoring of exercise stress testing is recommended because lab tests reveal that there is often an autonomic nervous system imbalance (i.e., reduced heart rates, parasympathetic abnormalities, chronotropic incompetence) irrespective of whether physical signs are evident during exercise. See Chapter 19 for an explanation of these conditions, and consider their implications when planning activity.

Much research is needed on the heart rate responses of persons with DS to different kinds of exercise. This research should clearly indicate whether participants have undergone surgery for congenital heart disease or presently have conditions like mitral valve prolapse that are asymptomatic. Existing research indicates that peak heart rates during treadmill protocols are low compared to those of non-DS peers. Mean peak heart rates during 300-yd sprints, however, are 191, SD = 9 (Varela & Pitetti, 1995).

Breathing during strenuous exercise, swimming lessons, and exposure to high-altitude conditions may be affected by structural abnormalities of the lungs, nasal passages, airways, and chest wall. Lungs of many individuals with DS are **hypoplastic** (underdeveloped) with a smaller than normal number of alveoli (air sacs) (Cooney & Thurlbeck, 1982). An abnormally short nasal passage, narrowed hypopharynx and bronchial tubes, and/or funnel or pigeon chest postural conditions result in chronic upper airway obstruction and diminished oxygen in all parts of the body (Marino & Pueschel, 1996). These anatomic features, coupled with hypotonia of chest and trunk muscles, make breathing particularly difficult during respiratory infections, which often develop into pneumonia. Asthma also is more stressful than in non-DS persons.

Particular care should be taken in physical education to avoid exposure to weather conditions and other factors that might cause respiratory infections. Death from respiratory infection is 124 times greater in persons with DS than in the general population (Marino & Pueschel, 1996). In addition to skeletal and muscular abnormalities, persons with DS have a higher prevalence of immunodeficiency defects that predispose them to respiratory infections.

Fitness and Obesity Concerns

Fitness of children and youth with DS has been studied extensively in Illinois, where a team of researchers led by Carl Eichstaedt collected data on over 1,000 persons with DS. Comparisons with same- or larger-sized samples of students with mild and moderate MR revealed that subjects with DS performed the poorest on all motor and physical fitness tests except the sit-and-reach test for flexibility (Eichstaedt, Wang, Polacek, & Dohrmann, 1991). Students with DS also weighed more, in spite of shorter heights, and had larger triceps and subscapular skinfolds. Girls with DS also had larger calf skinfolds. These and other findings appear in an excellent book by Eichstaedt and Lavay (1992).

The reason that individuals with DS perform more poorly on aerobic and strength tests than others with mental retardation relates to chromosomal differences that affect all of the body systems. In addition to heart and lung limitations previously described, research now suggests dysfunction of the neuromuscular system, both at the CNS level and at the joints level, that affects strength development (Cioni et al., 1994).

DS is associated with obesity and high blood cholesterol (Chad, Jobling, & Frail, 1990). This physical profile complicates health and impacts on all aspects of motor function. Sedentary lifestyle, poor eating habits, and lack of family nutritional awareness no doubt contribute to weight problems, but *research also indicates that resting metabolism rate of individuals with DS is depressed* (Chad et al., 1990). Implications are that combined exercise-nutrition programs should receive high priority in school and community programming.

Health and Temperament Concerns

The average lifespan of individuals with DS has changed from 9 years old in 1929 to over 50 in the 1990s (Eyman, Call, & White, 1991). Most closely correlated with early death are major mobility and eating problems (severe cerebral palsy). About 75% of nonambulatory persons with DS die of pneumonia. All persons with DS seem highly susceptible to upper respiratory infections. They must be protected against exposure to viruses and temperature extremes.

Self-care and cognitive abilities of adults with DS decline with age to a much greater extent than those of other people (Zigman, Schupf, Lubin, & Silverman, 1987). This is

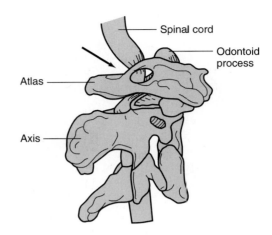

FIGURE 21.9   Atlantoaxial instability can contribute to a dislocation of the atlas, which can injure the spinal cord. It can be caused by forceful bending of the head either forward or backward.

linked with early-onset **Alzheimer-type neuropathology,** which is present from about age 40 on. Substantial regression, however, is not observed until about 50. Only 15 to 40% of older DS adults show Alzheimer behaviors. However, IQ and general motor skills of children and adolescents with DS plateau in a puzzling manner (Henderson, 1986). Children placed in regular education typically need more and more resource help as they grow older.

In general, people with DS are friendly, cheerful, mannerly, and responsible. Their social competence is much higher than would be expected. Although usually cooperative, on occasion, they exhibit extreme stubbornness. When they say, "No," professionals experience a real challenge! This occasional stubbornness appears to be a CNS deficit similar to the conceptual rigidity and perseveration associated with brain damage. Persons with DS tend to like routine; professionals need to plan strategy carefully before changing routine. On the other hand, routine can be the key to regular inclusion and practice of needed motor and game skills.

Atlantoaxial Instability

Atlantoaxial instability is an orthopedic problem present in approximately 17% of persons with DS. **Atlantoaxial** refers to the joint between the first two cervical vertebrae, the atlas and axis. Instability indicates that the ligaments and muscles surrounding this joint are lax and that the vertebrae can slip out of alignment easily. Forceful forward or backward bending of the neck, which occurs in gymnastics, swimming, and other sport events, may dislocate the atlas, causing damage to the spinal cord (Figure 21.9).

Since 1983, Special Olympics has required a physician's statement that indicates absence of this condition in persons with DS as a prerequisite for unrestricted participation in Special Olympics. This statement must be based on X rays, the cost of which is typically covered by health insurance or Medicaid. Enforcement of this requirement by school administrators would be prudent also, since contemporary physical education practice favors vigorous activity for children with DS.

If this medical clearance is not on file, physical educators should restrict students from participation in gymnastics, diving, butterfly stroke and diving start in swimming, high jump, pentathlon, soccer, and any warm-up exercise placing pressure on the head and neck muscles. This restriction should be temporary, with a time limit set for obtaining the X rays. If students with DS are diagnosed as having atlantoaxial syndrome, they are permanently restricted from these activities; there are, however, many other physical education activities in which they can safely engage.

Individuals Without DS

Individuals with MR who do not have DS vary so widely that no generalizations can be drawn. Assessment is the only way to determine strengths and weaknesses. There are no characteristics; however, each individual meets the diagnostic criteria of impaired intellectual and adaptive behaviors.

Most individuals with MR pass as normal once they have left school. They hold full-time jobs, marry, rear children, and experience the same joys and sadnesses as other people. These individuals tend to have blue-collar (physical labor) jobs that require considerable fitness but make few intellectual demands. By adulthood, persons with mild MR typically function academically somewhere between the third and the sixth grades. Cognitively, their greatest deficits are in the areas of abstract thinking, concept formation, problem solving, and evaluative activity.

Approximately 90% of individuals with MR have mild impairments, look like everyone else, and need few adaptations and supports in physical education and sport. If their parents are athletic, they probably will be also. If not, they will have the full range of individual differences in motor function and fitness exhibited by the general population. Some will participate in Special Olympics and INAS-FMH events, but most will be involved in community-based recreation and competition. Those who really love sports will probably take advantage of all opportunities in both regular and special sport programs.

Like individuals without MR, people with mild intellectual and adaptive behavior skill deficits sometimes need intermittent or limited supports and various kinds of adaptations to succeed in the physical education setting and to develop active, healthy lifestyles. They might be slow in processing instructions and learning new activities. Depending on how parents and teachers handle this slowness, individuals with MR might be teased more than non-MR peers or considered different or odd. This, in turn, can result in motivational problems and insufficient practice to keep up with classmates as skills and strategies become more advanced. Often teachers must address self-concept and social acceptance problems.

Individuals who need extensive and pervasive supports to succeed in physical education and other settings are classified as having severe MR, according to the 1992 AAMR classification system. The following pages are mostly about these people.

Associated Medical Conditions

The more severe a disability is, the more likely it is that there are associated conditions that affect motor behavior. This is particularly true when the primary etiology is chromosomal disorder or brain damage. Many of the conditions associated with DS are present also in other individuals with MR. Physical activity personnel should request access to files that describe medical history, including surgeries, and list medications. Use Chapter 19 to review side effects of medications, or consult the *Physician's Desk Reference (PDR)*.

Seizures (Epilepsy)

One of the most frequent medical problems in people with MR is seizures. About 20% of individuals with mild MR have seizures. In contrast, over 50% of individuals in the lowest ranges of MR (previously designated as profound, IQs under 20) have seizures. See Chapter 19 on seizure disorders, and be sure you know how to handle seizures. A common problem in physical education is that individuals with severe seizure disorders are often so heavily dosed with medication that they are lethargic. Medication affects attention span, balance, and other factors.

Pain Insensitivity and Indifference

Approximately 25% of individuals with developmental disabilities display signs of pain insensitivity or indifference that place them at serious medical risk (Biersdorff, 1994). Case studies describe individuals who seriously burn their hands as they take dishes, without potholders, from hot ovens, individuals who walk on broken legs and insist they feel no pain, and individuals who have died from appendicitis and bowel obstruction conditions that went undiagnosed because of no indications of pain or discomfort. Many individuals with self-injurious behaviors display no evidence of pain. Implications for physical education and sport are obvious. Teachers must carefully check body parts for injuries when accidents occur and not rely on the responses of individuals suspected to have pain insensitivity.

Dual Diagnosis

The term *dual diagnosis* can have many meanings, but in MR literature **dual diagnosis** refers to the co-occurrence of MR with psychiatric disorders. A much larger percentage of people with severe MR have serious emotional disturbances than in the general population (Borthwick-Duffy, 1994). These individuals might be taking psychotropic drugs (e.g., antipsychotics, tranquilizers) to treat **stereotypic behaviors** (i.e., repetitive, seemingly purposive behavior such as hand flapping and rocking), self-injurious behavior, aggression toward others, property destruction, social withdrawal, and many other problems. Common side effects that affect physical activity involvement are lethargy, hypersensitivity to sunlight, and balance problems.

Behavior problems at all ages have multiple causes. Most are not serious enough to warrant a dual diagnosis, but teachers should be skilled in behavior management techniques (see Chapter 7). Assessment and programming should include examination and modification of environmental factors (both social and physical) that can contribute to behavior problems. The inclusion of students with behavior problems in regular physical education requires smaller class sizes and an increased number of adult aides.

Cerebral Palsy (CP)

Many individuals with MR are nonambulatory and/or have speech difficulties because they have CP (see Chapter 25). Those with mild MR can learn to use wheelchairs and experience success in various wheelchair sports. Those with severe conditions, however, might need assistants to push their wheelchairs and assist them in getting in and out of wheelchairs. These individuals often need physical education that stresses sensory integration (see Chapter 10). Special Olympics has wheelchair events because of the large number of people with MR who also have CP or other orthopedic impairments.

Pervasive Developmental Disorders

Pervasive developmental disorders like autistic disorder (autism), Rett's disorder, and childhood degenerative disorder are associated with MR but considered separately in diagnostic manuals used by physicians (American Psychiatric Association, 1994). These disorders are described in Chapter 22 because their major clinical features are behavioral and social rather than intellectual slowness. Approximately 75% of individuals with autism function at a retarded level.

Communication and Self-Direction

Communications is the first adaptive skill area listed in the AAMR definition, presumably because receptive and expressive communications are essential to learning and to independent functioning. The more severe the MR, the lower the communication level. Teachers must present instructions slowly and clearly and be sure that students understand. Systematic experimentation with sentences of different lengths and structures should determine the best ways to communicate.

Teachers must also take time to let students respond, must provide many opportunities for choice-making, and must facilitate self-direction, another of the 10 adaptive skill areas. Choice-making should begin with two choices (would you rather play this or that; would you rather run in this direction or that; do you want a red ball or green; do you want juice or water) and then progress to multiple choices. In mainstream classes, special emphasis must be given to helping nondisabled peers learn ways to communicate with peers who have disabilities and facilitate their self-direction.

Augmentative or Alternative Communication (AAC)

Some individuals with severe MR who cannot communicate verbally learn to use manual sign or communication board/devices. This requires that teachers and at least some peers learn these communication modes. A recent trend is increased use of augmentative and alternative communication (AAC). AAC devices range from low-tech alternatives like picture boards and notebooks to high-tech devices that use synthetic or digitized speech (Datillo, 1993; Tanchak & Sawyer, 1995). AAC devices, especially computers, encourage reciprocal communication, choice-making, and self-direction.

Time Delay Interventions

Time delay interventions is the term used to describe attention to the amount of time an individual needs to initiate communi-

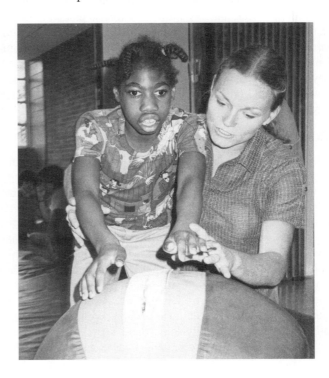

FIGURE 21.10 The one-to-one task analysis condition works best for persons with severe mental retardation.

cation. The recommended practice is to maintain eye contact with an individual with MR without prompting for up to 10 seconds. This allows individuals who are especially slow in thinking and moving the time needed to react.

Cognitive Ability Related to Motor Learning

Historically, defective mental functioning has been explained by two theories: (a) the structural difference or deficit theory and (b) the production deficiency or inappropriate strategy theory. The first theory posits structural differences and supports intervention directed toward etiological concerns (Dykens, Hodapp, & Evans, 1994). The second theory drives efforts to find strategies that will help persons with MR learn more efficiently (Bouffard & Wall, 1990; Hoover & Horgan, 1990; Reid, 1986).

Attention

Many persons with MR exhibit problems of overexclusive or overinclusive attention. **Overexclusive,** normal until about age 6, is focusing on one aspect of a task with restricted visual scanning and incidental learning. **Overinclusive,** normal from about age 6 to 12 years, is responsiveness to everything, rather than attending only to relevant cues. Either way, the attentional resources are inefficiently allocated.

This problem is largely ameliorated by shaping the environment so that there are no irrelevant cues (see Figure 21.10). The teacher then uses one particular cue to elicit the desired response (e.g., "Watch me. I roll the ball. Now you roll the ball"). The same cue is used every time, and appropriate behavior is reinforced. This approach is used when teaching persons with severe MR but does not usually generalize to ordinary settings, where many environmental stimuli compete for attention. *Eventually, the student taught in this way must be given practice under conditions with progressively more irrelevant stimuli until such time that the instructional setting is normalized.* For example, whenever other students share a room, their presence creates stimuli that must be blocked out.

For most students, therefore, the emphasis is dually on recognizing relevant cues and blocking out irrelevant ones. Teachers begin by highlighting one cue and gradually adding two or three more. Level of cognition determines the number of cues that can be attended to simultaneously. Professionals typically teach *wholes* rather than parts by starting a lesson with a demonstration. As instruction progresses, however, corrective feedback necessarily focuses on parts, and specific cues and strategies are used as attentional-getters. Attention-getters that help persons focus are

U **Unexpectedness (surprise)**

S **Size**

I **Intensity (loud, bright, heavy)**

N **Novelty (new or original)**

G **Glorious color**

N **Name (call person by name)**

E **Eye contact (a long stare)**

T **Touch**

Remember these attention-getters by the concept "USING NET to capture attention." Some applications are (a) having a student wear a colorful elbow band to remember to keep the elbow straight in racket sports; (b) shouting a key word in the middle of a quietly stated sentence; (c) showing a large flash card with the body part or action to be remembered. The "Surprise Symphony" of Hayden reminds us of how effective an unexpected change can be. Consider how the eight attention-getters can be applied to sights and sounds associated with observing and imitating a new motor skill or sequence.

Memory or Retention

Persons with MR have long-term memory equal to that of peers (Hoover & Horgan, 1990). However, they have many problems with **short-term memory** (i.e., the encoding of new information into the long-term memory store). Research indicates that we have only 30 to 60 sec to make this happen. Whereas nonretarded persons use spontaneous rehearsal strategies, persons with MR are unlikely to do so. Research shows that they can use rehearsal strategies, when carefully taught, but even then, they lag behind peers in spontaneity of application and generalization. Memory strategies from trial to trial tend to vary considerably.

Implications are that teachers should focus on rehearsal strategies and provide many, many trials. Modeling, verbal rehearsal, self-talk, and imagery are strategies commonly used. **Modeling** refers to observational learning that requires imitation. The imitation should occur within 30 sec of the observation with no intervening stimuli between visual input and imitation. Teachers should experiment to determine whether a student does better with a silent or talking model.

With talking models, much attention should be given to how much talk and when.

Verbal instruction should focus on actions or body parts rather than numbers. For example, it is better to say, "Jumping jacks, out-in, out-in, out-in, out-in, walk-walk-walk-walk" than "Jumping jacks, 1-2-3-4, walk, 1-2-3-4." When models do self-talk as they perform, students are likely to imitate this strategy and incorporate it into their unique learning style.

Verbal rehearsal and *self-talk* sometimes refer to the same thing, but a distinction is often made. **Verbal rehearsal** is talking through what we plan to do. **Self-talk** is the strategy of talking while moving. **Imagery,** also called mental practice, involves visualization before beginning an activity.

After several trials of imitating a model, students may profit from questioning that focuses attention on problem areas. For example, the teacher may ask, "What was I thinking when I moved? What was I saying? Where was I looking? Were my feet far apart or close together?" Students working as partners should also learn to ask such questions. Ultimately, students learn to ask these questions of themselves and thus begin to provide self-feedback.

Feedback

Persons with MR do not use feedback as fully as peers. Also, teachers often give lots of praise or motivational feedback but not enough **informational feedback.** *Feedback should include questioning about process as well as product.* Illustrative questions on **process** are "Did the movement *feel* good?" "Did you *tuck your head* when you did the forward roll?" "Did you *watch* the ball?" "Was your *elbow* straight?" Illustrative questions on **product** are "Did you hit the target?" "How far did you throw?" "What was your score?" Questioning is the type of feedback that involves the learner most actively, but feedback can also be passive, with the teacher telling and directing. Regardless of approach, more feedback (providing it is meaningful) leads to more success. This is the rationale for small class sizes, use of peer teachers, and availability of videotaped feedback technology.

Feedback, like input, is dependent on short-term memory. To be effective, it must be received immediately before new stimuli divert the mind from the task just completed. *A general rule is within 5 sec of task completion.* When feedback is delayed, students often need help in linking it with the antecedent. Too often, teachers move around the room saying, "Good!" without taking the time to ascertain that students understand what they are good at and why.

Task Analysis, Repetition, and Generalization

Persons with MR need more trials than peers and instruction in smaller chunks. This is the rationale underlying task analysis. The use of more trials than peers is called **overlearning** or **extended practice.** Little is known about number of successes that should be required before stopping a practice and moving on to something else.

Persons with MR have more difficulty in chaining parts into sequences than peers. Therefore, much attention should be given to practicing progressively longer sequences. Games like *Copy Cat* and *I'm Going to Grand-mother's House* (see Chapter 12) can make learning chains of gross motor activities fun (e.g., three walks, two jumps, one bend-and-reach, and sit).

Once a movement is learned, periodic practice ensures that it is remembered. This practice should be in variable environments to teach and reinforce generalization. Persons with MR have more difficulty in generalizing than peers.

Persons with MR need explicit directions. Whereas nondisabled peers learn incidentally and spontaneously, persons with MR learn best when instruction is direct, specific, and brief. The teacher should frequently ask, "What are we learning? What are we practicing? When are we going to use this"?

Crucial to generalization are field trips to parks and recreation centers where leisure skills can be practiced. Instruction must include use of public transportation, how to pay fees, and how to communicate with others who are using the facility.

Motor Performance

Traditionally, professionals have believed that children with mild MR are 2 to 4 years behind non-MR peers on measures of motor performance. This belief is based on the pioneer research of Lawrence (Larry) Rarick (1911–1995), who published extensively in the area of MR and motor behaviors. See Rarick (1980) for a review of this work. Specifically, the belief about the 2- to 4-year delay comes from data gathered in the 1950s (Francis & Rarick, 1959), before the law mandated that students with MR must receive physical education instruction like everyone else.

This belief deserves reevaluation because today the lives of children with MR are very different from in the 1950s. Except for children with chromosomal abnormalities or brain damage, the range of motor performance is probably similar to that of the non-MR population. However, there is probably a slightly larger percentage of children with MR who exhibit **developmental coordination disorder** (DCD) and below-average performance in games and sports. As rules, strategies, and motor skill demands of sports become more complex in late childhood and adolescence, the slow learner becomes increasingly disadvantaged.

Our knowledge about motor behavior typically comes from research. However, studies that report motor performance of individuals with MR need careful analysis. Individuals with DS, fragile X syndrome, and other chromosomal etiologies should not be combined with other individuals with MR, because of numerous differences. Likewise, males and females should not be grouped together, because of differences in child rearing, sport socialization, anatomy, and physiology. Moreover, studies that report motor performance become dated as accessibility to opportunity changes.

The only way to know about the motor performance of an individual is careful assessment. Remember that motor performance is multidimensional. A person might be strong in some areas and weak in others. Most individuals who process knowledge slowly do better with closed skills than with open skills. **Closed skills** are those done in a predictable environment that requires no quick body adjustments. **Open skills** are those done in unpredictable, changing environments that require rapid adjustments. Not only must motor skills be assessed under closed and open conditions, but the total ecology should be examined to determine why motor performance is as it is.

Consider the factors that affect motor performance (e.g., heredity, early instruction and practice, opportunities for continued learning and practice, cognition, motivation, self-concept, health status, medication, body composition, fitness). To learn about these factors, interview as many family members as possible. Observe the individual in as many settings as possible, including community recreation facilities and the home.

Motor Development and Delays

Depending on the severity of the disability, infants and toddlers with MR exhibit various developmental delays. Unless cerebral palsy or other kinds of brain damage cause reflex problems, the delays are typically manifested by slowness in the evolution of the righting, propping, and equilibrium postural reactions (see Chapter 10). The mean age in walking for children with MR is 3.2 years; for DS, it is 4.2 years. Slowness in development of locomotor and object control skills can cause below-average performance throughout the elementary school years, but involvement in early childhood adapted physical activity programs is believed to minimize later problems.

Influence of Physical Constraints

Some differences in motor performance between persons with MR and those with average IQs can be explained by height and body composition. Figure 21.11 shows, for example, that boys with mental retardation perform from 0.50 to about 1.50 standard deviations below the norm (see unadjusted means). When a statistical procedure is used to equate boys with and without MR on height and body composition measures, these differences become much less (see adjusted means). In fact, the boys with MR are no longer significantly different from peers on 5 of the 12 tests (sit-ups, knee extension, knee flexion, 150-yd dash, and 35-yd dash).

The research reporting these findings indicated that boys with and without MR differ significantly on height, width of hips, and skinfold measures. Boys with MR are shorter and have wider hips and more body fat (Dobbins, Garron, & Rarick, 1981). No comparable research has been conducted on girls. The implications are, however, that reducing body fat will improve motor performance.

Obesity and Overweight Problems

Persons with MR tend to be overweight or obese, and this condition affects both motor performance and predisposition to physical activity. Obesity varies with gender, severity of MR, and living arrangements (Rimmer, Braddock, & Fujiura, 1993). Females are more likely than males to be overweight. Approximately 28% of women and 19% of men in the general population are obese, whereas 59% of women and 28% of men with MR are obese (Rimmer et al., 1993). Individuals with mild/moderate MR have higher rates of obesity than individuals with severe MR. The more restrictive the living

FIGURE 21.11 An example of how deviation from average performance varies when scores of boys with mental retardation (boys ages 6 to 10, with mean IQ of 67) are statistically adjusted for height, hip width, and body fat.

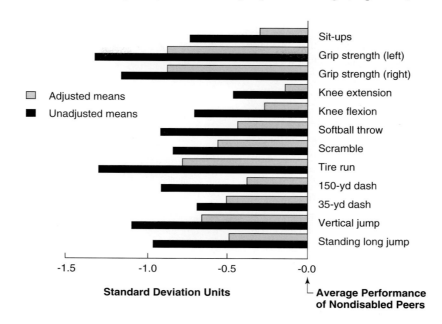

arrangement (e.g., large institution, controlled group home), the less likely individuals are to have weight problems. This might be because the few persons who remain in institutions have severe MR complicated by medical conditions like cerebral palsy that affect eating. Another reason might be that state-supported facilities employ dieticians and give high priority to nutrition, whereas individuals living with families or on their own in other housing arrangements often have little knowledge about counting calories and fat grams.

Kelly-Rimmer Equation for Computing Percent Body Fat

Professionals should understand that formulae for computing percent body weight for individuals with MR can differ from those appropriate for the general population (Kelly & Rimmer, 1987). The National Consortium for Physical Education and Recreation for Individuals with Disabilities (NCPERID, 1995), for instance, recommends knowledge of the Kelly-Rimmer equation. This equation is as follows:

% Fat = 13.545 + .48691649 (waist circum.) − .52662145 (forearm circum.) − .15504013 (height cm) + .077079958 (weight kg)

NCPERID also recommends that professionals know how to develop weight programs that emphasize nutrition, exercise, and behavioral intervention (see Chapter 19).

Physical Fitness

Studies of physical fitness of persons with MR indicate that this is a problem area that should be addressed. Even when persons are actively involved in sport programs, fitness is lower than that of peers without MR (Pitetti, Jackson, Stubbs, Campbell, & Battar, 1989). Eichstaedt et al. (1991) reported

low fitness levels for students with MR, ages 6 to 21, tested in 1980 and 1990 (N over 1,000 in both years). This cross-sectional research showed that fitness scores were lower in 1990 on all tests except abdominal and hip flexor strength.

Research thus far has focused primarily on validity and reliability of fitness test protocols (Fernhall, Tymeson, & Webster, 1988; Seidl, Reid, & Montgomery, 1987). In general, most attention centers on measurement of cardiovascular fitness. The lower the IQ, the less able persons are to understand the purpose of a distance run, concepts of speed, and discomfort like breathlessness associated with cardiovascular testing. In general, valid measures can be obtained from persons with mild MR but not from those with severe MR. The *Pacer shuttle run* is especially recommended for cardiovascular testing (NCPERID, 1995). See Chapter 13.

Chapters 13 and 19 on fitness and OHI (other health impairments) present several concerns about attempts to apply traditional test protocols to persons with severe MR. One is the increased likelihood that the heart will not respond normally to exercise because of autonomic nervous system damage; this condition is called *chronotropic incompetence* or *sick sinus syndrome* and is characterized by a slower-than-expected heartbeat. Another concern is that 20 to 60% of infants born with chromosomal defects have congenital heart disease. Others also may have undetected cardiac defects that require sophisticated technology for identification.

If persons with MR are overweight, this problem should be ameliorated before work on endurance running is begun. Chapter 19 emphasizes that low-intensity, long-duration activities achieve this goal. Walking, dance, and water activities are particularly recommended. Most persons with severe MR do not have the cognition and coordination to use regulation cycling apparatus. Apparatus can be adapted, however, so that they can pedal from a supine position.

The goal in severe MR should be **increased exercise tolerance** instead of cardiorespiratory endurance. Consideration also should be given to whether a person with severe MR will ever need the capacity to sustain a 1- or 1.5-mi run. If family members and significant others regularly run, then this may be an ecologically valid goal. Otherwise, it is probably not. Targeted cardiovascular levels should be matched to game and leisure skills. If the person with an IQ under 50 has few or no physical activity leisure competencies, then developing these competencies should, perhaps, be the primary goal.

Tests marketed by AAHPERD specifically for persons with MR in the 1970s and 1980s are no longer valid. The Prudential FITNESSGRAM is recommended for everyone. The fitness standards established for this test are generally agreed to be applicable to all populations. See Chapter 13.

The emphasis for individuals with MR, however, should be on active lifestyle, not on fitness for the sake of fitness. In most cases, this depends on developing transition-type programs that involve the home and community.

Programming for Mild Mental Retardation

Programming for persons with mild MR is typically directed toward enhancing cognition. These persons are generally in regular physical education or a resource setting designed to prepare them for the mainstream. Strategies described in the preceding section are used to help them keep up with classmates, develop some physical activity strengths, remediate weaknesses, and accept limitations. Several models described in Chapter 9 are helpful in promoting integration and inclusion. The following are additional models that have been developed specifically for persons with mild cognitive delays or slowness. These are presented to stimulate creative thinking and to motivate development of your own models.

The Knowledge-Based Model

The knowledge-based model, which focuses on movement problem solving, was developed by Marcel Bouffard, University of Alberta; Ted Wall, McGill University; and colleagues (Bouffard, 1990; Wall, Bouffard, McClements, Findlay, & Taylor, 1985). It is based on observations that movement skill lag in persons with mild MR is related to five major sources: (a) deficiencies in the knowledge base or lack of access to it, (b) failure to use spontaneous strategies, (c) inadequate metacognitive knowledge and understanding, (d) executive control and motor planning weaknesses, and (e) low motivation and inadequate practice.

The knowledge-based model emphasizes instructional process rather than activities. To improve sport, dance, and aquatics performance, instruction is directed toward three components (see Figure 21.12). **Procedural knowledge** refers to understandings about process; it is information about how to do things. **Declarative knowledge** refers to factual information; it is knowledge about the body, environmental variables, and mechanical laws. **Affective knowledge** refers to feelings about the self and ecosystem that evolve through use of procedural and declarative knowledge.

Metacognition is knowledge about what we know and do not know. For example, metacognition tells us when to

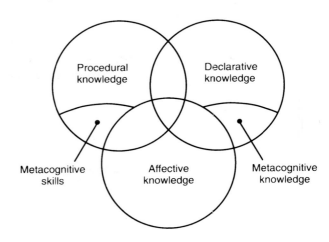

FIGURE 21.12 Types of knowledge targeted in the knowledge-based model.

stop studying or practicing. Metacognition also allows us to analyze emotion and determine what we are afraid of or angry about. Persons with MR and/or low motor skills have less metacognition than peers. They do not accurately assess abilities and therefore practice either too little or too much.

Use of the knowledge-based model to guide instruction implies careful teaching of facts and processes, with emphasis on problem solving so learners are actively involved, not just listening to someone else. Persons with MR can be successful in problem solving but require more trial-and-error opportunities than peers do. Ecological task analysis is one approach to teaching problem solving; movement education is another. Any question-and-answer teaching style will increase knowledge. Answers can be verbal, gestural, or movement.

Steps in problem solving that should be explicitly taught and practiced are these:

1. Identify the game or movement function—state what, who, where, why, and how.
2. Assess self and environmental variables. Make changes necessary for safety, comfort, and ease of motion. For instance, if facing the sun, then change position. If too hot, take off jacket. If there is an obstacle in pathway, move it.
3. Engage in motor planning. Use visual imagery, verbal rehearsal, and other strategies.
4. Use feedback from all sensory modalities as well as external sources. Use self-checking routines to regulate and oversee learning and to determine when practice should be terminated.
5. Evaluate process, product, and feeling and redefine task at set intervals like every 10 trials.

Special Olympics Sports Skills Program

Developed in the 1980s by staff at Special Olympics International (SOI) headquarters, the Special Olympics Sports Skills Program is based on an illustrated guide for each sport, mandatory training for instructors, and the rule that individuals must complete at least 8 weeks of training in a particular sport before entering competition. Each guide presents a detailed 8-week training program (3 days a week), long-term goal and short-term objectives, a criterion-referenced skills test for pre-training and posttraining assessment, and a task analysis to direct the teaching of each skill.

Although Special Olympics is usually associated with competition, *the Sports Skills program is purely instructional.* As such, it is appropriate for use in schools, homes, and after-school programs. The task analyses are as helpful in teaching regular as adapted physical education. The quality of the instruction depends, of course, on the knowledge, skills, and integrity of the teachers. Although Special Olympics attracts millions of volunteers, there are still too few professionals involved.

A basic tenet of the instructional program is that skill development is not an end in itself but rather a vehicle to an active lifestyle and access to the same sport opportunities as able-bodied peers. This is the rationale for holding local and state competitions. These are designed to enable persons to generalize skills to real-life situations and to receive intensive positive feedback for effort as well as success. Competitions are also a way of involving family members and neighbors, thereby achieving some hidden agendas relative to awareness and attitude.

Sport skills guides are available for 12 summer sports and 5 winter sports.

Summer	Winter
Aquatics	Alpine skiing
Athletics (track and field)	Cross-country skiing
Basketball	Figure skating
Bowling	Hockey
Cycling	Speed skating
Equestrian sports	
Football (soccer)	
Gymnastics	
Roller skating	
Softball	
Tennis	
Volleyball	

Figure 21.13 presents the long-term goal and short-term objectives for the track-and-field sports training program, an example of criterion-referenced assessment, and an illustrative task analysis. Under assessment, note that the *relays* test item is broken down into seven tasks. The guide provides a separate task analysis for each of these.

The goal and objectives encompass three aspects of sports: skills, social behavior, and functional knowledge of rules. **Social behavior** is operationally defined as good sportsmanship and is taught via task analysis for (a) exhibiting competitive effort and (b) exhibiting fair play at all times. The Special Olympics oath reinforces the concept of competitive effort:

Let me win
But if I cannot win
Let me be brave in the attempt.

Special Olympics Sports Skills Program guides are available from Special Olympics International, 1350 New York Avenue NW, Suite 500, Washington, DC 20005. They represent only part of a broad-based technical assistance program available through SOI.

Special Olympics Competition and Unified Sports

Special Olympics competition was begun in 1968 by Eunice Kennedy Shriver as a vehicle for awareness, attitude change, and equal opportunity. There have been many changes in policies and practices, but the underlying philosophy has remained the same:

> The mission of Special Olympics is to provide year-round sports training and athletic competition in a variety of Olympic-type sports for individuals and adults with mental retardation, giving them continuing opportunities to develop physical fitness, demonstrate courage, experience joy, and participate in a sharing of gifts, skills, and friendship with their families, other Special Olympics athletes, and the community. (SOI, 1995, p. 1)

Special Olympics is increasingly community based, with coaches encouraged to use community facilities and to attract volunteers of all ages. Many programs use a reverse mainstreaming approach, with peer tutors interacting with Special Olympics athletes. The official rules book specifically states that athletes may participate in other organized sport programs while participating in Special Olympics. Rules that govern SOI sports are the same as those for regular sports, with only a few adaptations, so generalization from one setting to another is facilitated. All that is needed is a regular education teacher or coach who is open and receptive.

To further encourage integration, SOI created the **unified sports model** in 1989. This model, which requires an equal number of persons with and without MR on the floor or field at all times, is explained in Chapter 9.

SOI has been a major force in creating a body of knowledge about curriculum planning for persons with MR. It has provided evidence that they can succeed in both team and individual sports (see issues of *Palaestra* that feature Special Olympics). In addition to official sports, SOI sponsors demonstration sports, while concurrently conducting research on their appropriateness for persons with MR. Demonstration sports currently under study are canoeing, cycling, table tennis, team handball, tennis, and power lifting.

SOI also has a list of prohibited sports that authorities believe are not appropriate for competition. These sports are

1. Javelin	7. All martial	11. Wrestling
2. Discus	arts	12. Judo
3. Hammer throw	8. Fencing	13. Karate
4. Pole vault	9. Shooting	14. Nordic jumping
5. Boxing	10. All types of	15. Trampoline
6. Platform	contact sports	
dives	(i.e., rugby,	
	American	
	football)	

SOI believes that competitive experiences are not appropriate until age 8. From this age on, all persons with MR are welcome to engage in competition. SOI recommends, however,

FIGURE 21.13   Baton pass in the relay.

Long-Term Goal for Track and Field

   The athlete will acquire basic track-and-field skills, appropriate social behavior, and functional knowledge of the rules necessary to participate successfully in athletics competitions.

Short-Term Objectives for Track and Field

1.0 Given demonstration and practice, the athlete will warm up properly before a track-and-field practice or meet.
2.0 Given demonstration and practice, the athlete will successfully perform track skills.
3.0 Given demonstration and practice, the athlete will successfully perform field skills.
4.0 Given verbal and written instruction, the athlete will comply with official athletics competition rules while participating in athletics competition.
5.0 Given an athletics practice or meet, the athlete will exhibit sportsmanship with teammates and opponents at all times.

Illustrative Assessment Checklist for Relay Race

Pre Score	Post Score	Test Item #3 Relays
☐	☐	Attempts to participate in a relay race.
☐	☐	Assumes a receiving position for a visual pass.
☐	☐	Receives the baton in a visual pass.
☐	☐	Performs an underhand baton pass.
☐	☐	Performs baton pass in exchange zone.
☐	☐	Runs designated leg of relay race in proper manner.
☐	☐	Participates in relay race competition.
☐	☐	1–2 Beginner
☐	☐	3–5 Intermediate
☐	☐	6–7 Advanced

_____ Approximate training time (hours)

Illustrative Task Analysis: Receive the Baton in a Visual Pass

Task Analysis

a. Assume proper receive position in front part of exchange zone.
b. Look back over inside shoulder for teammate (incoming runner).
c. Begin running forward when incoming runner reaches a point 4 to 5 m from exchange zone.
d. Keep left hand back with fingers pointing to the left, thumb pointing down and palm down.
e. Watch the incoming runner pass the baton underhanded into your left hand.
f. Turn to look forward, switch the baton immediately to the right hand, and continue relay.

that sport training begin at age 5. There is a Masters' Division for ages 30 and over, and occasionally, persons in their 60s and 70s participate. Competition can be serious or recreational. The important objective is active lifestyle for everyone.

Special Olympics does not use medical or functional classification to equalize abilities of persons competing against each other. Instead, it uses a system called **divisioning,** in which athletes are categorized according to their age, sex, and ability. Divisions must have at least three but no more than eight competitors or teams. The **10% rule** is followed in ability grouping. This rule states that, within any division, the top and bottom scores may not exceed each other by more than 10%. Before individuals are placed in heats or events, they must submit their best times or distances to be used in the divisioning procedure.

In team sports, divisioning is achieved by administering a battery of four or five sport-specific skills to every team member. These scores are added to create a team score that is used in divisioning.

The Stepping Out for Fitness Model

The Stepping Out for Fitness model was developed for adolescents and adults with mild to moderate MR who need programming specifically for fitness (see Figure 21.14). It is described in a book (1990) by three Canadians: Greg Reid and David Montgomery of McGill University and Christine Seidl of Summit School. This book includes 48 lessons, each 40 min long, with graded intensity designed to enable persons to reach targeted heart rates. Sessions are to be conducted two to three times a week.

A unique feature of the model is its use of music in all lessons. Several exercise sequences are presented for popular works like Michael Jackson's "Bad" and George Michael's "Faith." Lessons are built around six themes: (a) calisthenics to music, (b) exercise break package, (c) ball activities, (d) hoop and rope activities, (e) circuit training, and (f) 20-km club. The latter is a challenge for groups of 8 to collectively run 20 km within the time span of 6 lessons. During these lessons, two 10-min periods are allocated for running laps.

The instructional model includes five components: (a) assessment, (b) objectives, (c) task analysis, (d) implementation, and (e) postevaluation. Effectiveness of the model is based on a 4-month experimental study conducted by Montgomery, Reid, and Seidl (1988) with 53 subjects. The assessment used is the Canadian Standardized Test of Fitness, although any comparable test is appropriate. The model is dually based on exercise physiology principles and behavior management theory.

Each lesson includes warm-up, conditioning, and cool-down, with activities specifically for flexibility, cardiovascular improvement, and muscular endurance. Behavioral management is applied primarily in the specification of teaching cues (prompts) on lesson plans (see Figure 21.14). The code for understanding cues is

D	Demonstrate
MP	Manipulative prompt
VC	Verbal cue
MG	Minimal guidance
M	Manipulate

The book *Stepping Out for Fitness* is published by CAHPER/ACSEPL, Place R. Tait McKenzie, 1600 James Naismith Dr., Gloucester, Ontario K1B 5N4. It is appropriate for adapted or regular settings and can be followed exactly or used as an example for creating a similar program.

Programming for Young Children With MR

Children with developmental disabilities are eligible for public school intervention programs from birth on. Because children learn through play, physical educators should use play to full advantage. Many models are available for teaching motor skills. The PREP program, however, is highlighted here because it focuses on functional competence for play.

PREP Play Model

The PREP play program, used widely in Canada, was developed to guide the physical education of children with mental handicaps, ages 3 to 12 (Watkinson & Wall, 1982). This diagnostic-prescriptive model is applicable, however, to any child who needs individualized instruction in (a) locomotion, (b) large play equipment, (c) small play equipment, and (d) play vehicles. These four areas are divided into 40 specific gross motor play skills (see Figure 21.15).

A task analysis with recommended physical prompts is provided for each skill, as well as group activities for practicing and reinforcing the skills. For example, jumping down is analyzed into four steps:

1. Step down from shin height, one foot to the other foot.
2. Jump down from shin height, with a two-foot takeoff and landing.
3. Jump down from knee height, using the same pattern.
4. Jump down from hip height, using the same pattern.

Figure 21.15 also presents a sample from an instructional episode in which the teacher uses verbal and physical prompts to teach the jump-down skill (see Figure 21.16). Execution is followed by both reinforcement and information feedback. A central feature of PREP is that instruction is carried out while children are at play.

Teachers interact with one child at a time for a 1- to 5-min intervention, so that everyone receives individual attention. Brief group-teaching episodes provide practice of new skills in a group context. The length of the group session is 3 to 5 min early in the year and progresses to 15 min.

Assessment is structured through use of a free-play inventory (checklist), an individual student profile, and a daily record-monitoring form. The profile permits recording of which step in the task sequence has been completed and the type of prompt (physical, visual, verbal, none) needed.

The PREP manual includes many activities for using locomotor skills in relation to play equipment. In conjunction with each of these, children work on their knowledge base by learning names of body parts and body actions. Prior to playing a jumping game, for example, children sit on a mat and identify body parts to be used. Then they stand and review body actions, like *bend knees* and *swing arms*.

FIGURE 21.14   Examples from the Stepping Out for Fitness Model. (D = Demonstrate; MP = Manipulative prompt; VC = Verbal cue; MG = Minimal guidance.)

STEPPING OUT FOR FITNESS PROGRAM (Parts of Sample Lesson)

Lesson: 1

Major feature: Calisthenics to music
Time: 40 min

Equipment: Cassettes
Tape recorder
Mat or blanket

Activity	Teaching Cues

Introduce program:

5 min
- Value of REGULAR EXERCISE
- Proper clothing for exercising

Warm-up—Flexibility exercises:

10 min

1. 6 toe touches

D – Include demonstrations for all the following:
MP – Stand at side of person and move down together, partly manipulating at start.
VC – "Bend down SLOWLY."
"Reach as far as you can."
"Touch the floor."
"Don't bounce."

2. 12 alternate-knee raises

MG – Tap the appropriate knee to lift.
VC – "Raise (lift) your knees."
"Right, left,...."
"One, two,...."

[Warm-ups continued but not included here.]

Cardiovascular activity:

5 min

1. Jog on the spot for 30 sec

VC – "Run on the same spot."
"Faster...slower."

2. Walk one lap of the exercise area (briskly).

VC – "Now walk; breathe deeply." "Faster."

3. 10 floor jumps.

MG – Tap knees to bend prior to jump.

[Activity continued but not included here.]

Other Models for Young Children

I CAN: Preprimary emphasizes six skill areas: (a) locomotion, (b) body control, (c) object control, (d) play equipment, (e) play participation, and (f) health-fitness (Wessel, 1980). The *I CAN* acronym, created by Janet Wessel, refers to teacher competencies:

I   Individualize instruction
C   Create social leisure competence
A   Associate all learning
N   Narrow the gap between teaching and practice

Like PREP, I CAN is a diagnostic-prescriptive model that recognizes play as a vehicle for learning. Children are helped to associate preacademic skills (colors, numbers, action words) with games and activities of daily living; this narrows the gap between school and home. A **home activities** program is an integral part of I CAN, and professionals teach parents how to implement specific learning objectives.

Chapter 18 described the **Language-Arts-Movement Programming (LAMP) model,** which is highly recommended for young children with MR because it concurrently

FIGURE 21.15 Examples from the PREP play program.

Skills for Locomotion	Skills for Large Play Equipment	Skills for Small Play Equipment	Skills for Play Vehicles
Running	Ascending an inclined bench on stomach	Throwing	Riding a scooter (sitting)
Ascending stairs	Ascending an inclined bench on hands and knees	Kicking	Riding a scooter down an incline (sitting)
Descending stairs	Catching	Tummy riding on a scooter
Jumping down	Walking up an inclined bench	Bouncing	Tummy riding down an incline on a scooter
Jumping over	Jumping on a trampoline	Hitting with a baseball bat	Pulling a wagon
Hopping on one foot	Seat drop on a trampoline	Striking with a hockey stick	Riding a wagon
Forward roll	Swivel hips on a trampoline	Stopping a puck with a hockey stick	Riding a tricycle
Backward roll	Sliding down a slide	Passing a puck with a hockey stick	Riding the back of a tricycle
	Climbing on a box	Jumping a rope turned by two people	
	Swinging on a rope		
	Swinging on a bar		
	Swinging on a swing		
	Hanging from knees on a horizontal ladder		
	Rolling around a bar		
	Ascending a ladder		
	Descending a ladder		

Sample Instructional Episode

Teacher behavior	Child behavior	Teacher behavior
1. Teacher says, "Look at me." (PROMPT)	Child looks at teacher. (ATTENTION)	Teacher smiles. (REINFORCEMENT)
2. Teacher says, "Jump down," and holds child's hands. (VERBAL AND PHYSICAL PROMPTS)	Child jumps down onto two feet. (CORRECT EXECUTION)	Teacher says, "Good, let's try again." (REINFORCEMENT)
3. Teacher says, "Jump down like this," and jumps, landing on two feet. (VERBAL AND VISUAL PROMPTS)	Child steps down onto one foot, then other. (INCOMPLETE EXECUTION)	Teacher says, "Land on both feet," and touches both feet. (INFORMATION FEEDBACK)
4. Teacher says, "Try again. Jump," and holds one hand of child. (VERBAL AND PHYSICAL PROMPTS)	Child jumps down onto two feet. (CORRECT EXECUTION)	Teacher says, "Good jump. You landed on two feet." (REINFORCEMENT AND INFORMATION FEEDBACK)

teaches language and movement through play activities based in the arts (e.g., dance, music, drama). From infancy on, rhythm and music are strong aids in motor learning.

Programming for Severe Mental Retardation

Approximately 10% of people with MR fall into the severe category, which encompasses the moderate, severe, and profound levels of the old AAMR classification system. IQs associated with severe MR range from 0 to 50, but a better descriptor is low functional ability in the 10 adaptive skill areas. Typically, persons with severe MR have multiple disabilities. Their mental function may be frozen somewhere between infancy and 7 years old, or it may improve slowly up to a ceiling of about age 7.

There are many individual differences, depending on level of severity. Most individuals with severe MR, however, need a teacher-student ratio between one-to-one and one-to-three because they have little self-direction. If no one tells them what to do, they are likely to just sit or lie. Physical educators must therefore create, train, and supervise helper corps of peer tutors, teacher aides, and community volunteers. Novel approaches to this are use of older students with a higher level of MR who are training for jobs in child care and involvement of senior citizens who enjoy a foster grandparent role.

Excellent resources to help with programming are the journal and newsletter of TASH: The Association of Persons

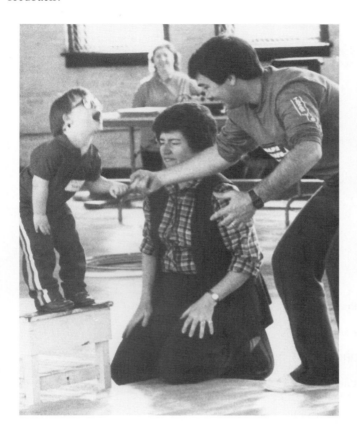

With Severe Handicaps, 29 West Susquehanna Ave., Suite 210, Baltimore, MD 21204. TASH also holds an annual conference. The *Journal of the Association for Persons With Severe Handicaps* includes many articles on leisure skill training.

Persons with severe MR mature slowly motorically as well as cognitively. Most do not learn to walk before age 3. Many learn ambulation between ages 3 and 9. Physical education in the early years thus focuses on nonambulatory locomotor activities and object control (see Chapters 10, 11, and 12). Hundreds of activities can be invented on land and in the water that use lying, sitting, and four-point positions.

Social skills and communication are major goals because they are prerequisite to game play (see Chapters 9 and 15). Persons with severe MR will typically remain in the solitary or parallel play stage unless taught to play. With good teaching, they should move into the associative and cooperative play stages between ages 9 and 12 and be able to learn simple games.

Flying Dutchman, Musical Chairs, and *Catch My Tail* are examples of beginning-level games. In *Flying Dutchman,* a line of students holding hands is walked in any direction. When the verbal cue "Flying Dutchman" is called out by the teacher, the students drop hands and run back to a mat that has been established as home base. *Musical Chairs* can be played without modification, but the students may need help in finding their chairs. In *Catch My Tail,* one corner of a scarf is tucked into the back of the belt of one student, who runs about the room, with the others trying to grab the scarf.

Examples of games not usually successful are *Chicken, Come Home; Cat and Rat;* dodgeball; and relays. In *Chicken, Come Home* and similar activities, the students cannot remember which role they are playing or which direction to run. Only a few seem to understand the concepts of tagging, dodging, and catching. In *Cat and Rat,* there seems to be no idea about who is chasing whom, that one should get away, or that the circle should either help or hinder the players. In dodgeball, they fail to grasp the idea of the game and wander away from the circle. These students can be forced through the motions of a relay but have no idea of its purpose, of winning and losing, or of belonging to a team.

By adolescence, many persons with severe MR are interested in the opposite sex and activities that support romantic interests. Although mental age is delayed, social and recreational interests tend to parallel those they see on television and in the world around them. Many learn individual sports, although they seldom can handle the rules and strategies of unmodified team sports.

Criteria to guide programming include (a) valid and reliable assessment procedures, (b) clearly identified goals and objectives, and (c) activities that are specialized, practical, age-appropriate, developmental, and functional (Greenwood, Silliman, & French, 1990). Underlying these criteria are the principles of normalization and ecological or social validity. Block

(1992) favors the term *life-skills curriculum* to emphasize that age-appropriate, functional activities should be taught in natural environments and based on students' preferences. The following are curriculum models recommended for persons with severe MR. Goals and objectives vary widely, but pedagogy almost always incorporates behavior management with careful analysis, consistent cues and reinforcements, good correction protocols, and variable practice to aid generalization.

Sensorimotor Models

Among the earliest sensorimotor models developed specifically for persons with severe MR is the one by Ruth Webb and associates at Glenwood State Hospital-School in Iowa (Webb & Koller, 1979). Table 21.2 summarizes this model, which focuses on four goals. The actions can be easily stated as objectives (e.g., *Show awareness of tactile stimulation by smile and/or approach-type body movements that last 3 or more sec; Reach for an attractive object and sustain reaching behavior for at least 5 sec*).

The first two goal areas in Table 21.2 are directed toward persons who are nonambulatory, have no language, and seem to be unaware of their environment. They represent the lowest level of function. Only a small percentage of persons with MR fit this description, but under law, they must receive some kind of physical education. The last two goal areas are applicable to many persons with severe MR.

Given a 30-min class period three times a week and five nonambulatory students, ages 5 to 10, use the activities in Table 21.2 to guide development of some lesson plans. Visualize the students arriving in wheelchairs; some can talk and some cannot. All need as much gross motor activity as possible. Before developing lesson plans, remember to describe present level of psychomotor performance and write goals and objectives. Chapters 10, 11, and 12 will help.

Data-Based Gymnasium Model

The data-based gymnasium model is the application of special education technology developed by a group called Teaching Research in Monmouth, Oregon, to physical education. The model is fully described in a book by John Dunn, physical education professor, and colleagues (Dunn, Morehouse, & Fredericks, 1986). Behavior management techniques emphasized are cueing, consequating (reinforcers, punishers, time-out), shaping, fading, and chaining. The teaching approach is task analysis with skills broken down into phases and steps.

A unique aspect of this model is the development of a clipboard of programming management for each student. Seven pages on every clipboard enable anyone trained in the data-based pedagogy to work with and keep a student on task. For every additional skill sequence targeted, there are 4 additional pages (i.e., motor task sequence sheet, program cover sheet, data sheet, and maintenance file). Thus, some persons' clipboards have 15 or 20 pages.

Another unique feature of the data-based model is its systematic plan for training and using volunteers and parents. The same protocol is used at home as at school, and the data

sheet is passed back and forth daily to keep everyone informed of progress.

The data-based model offers task analyses in four areas: (a) movement concepts, (b) motor skills, (c) physical fitness, and (d) leisure skills. It is designed for one-to-one teaching and testing and is appropriate for all age groups. Task analyses focus on ambulatory persons. To use this model, formal training must be completed. Its value, however, is great in stimulating professionals to apply data-based protocol when creating their own models.

Project Transition Model

The project transition behavior management model encompasses task-analyzed sequences for teaching and testing five hygiene areas (face washing, teeth brushing, hand washing, deodorant use, and overall appearance) and five fitness areas (upper body strength, cardiovascular endurance, abdominal strength, trunk flexibility, and grip strength). Tests used to measure the latter are bench press, 300-yd run/walk, bent-knee sit-ups for 60 sec, sit-and-reach, and dynamometer. This model was created by Paul Jansma, a physical education professor at Ohio State University, and colleagues (Jansma, Decker, Ersing, McCubbin, & Combs, 1988).

A particular strength of this model is an assessment system that yields both qualitative and quantitative data. The qualitative data pertain to level of independence, and the quantitative data are traditional performance scores. Knowledge about this model reinforces the importance of recording the amount of assistance needed when teaching persons with severe MR. The fitness tests used in this model provide insights into problems relative to cardiovascular endurance. Valid scores could not be obtained on distances greater than 300 yd. This means that **exercise tolerance** is being measured, not fitness of the heart and lungs.

Special Olympics Motor Activities Training Program

The Special Olympics Motor Activities Training Program (MATP) was instituted in 1989 as a replacement for the Special Olympics Developmental Program that previously served persons with severe MR. The excellent *MATP Guide* focuses on four types of activities, so there is something for everyone, regardless of severity of condition (see Table 21.3). Information is provided so that the MATP fits into the IEP model. The long-range goal is:

> The participant will demonstrate motor and sensory-
> motor skills, appropriate behavior, and an
> understanding of the skills and rules of the MATP
> that will enable him/her to successfully take part in
> Training Day activities and official Special Olympics
> sports. (SOI, 1989, p. 6)

Twelve illustrative short-term objectives are stated with the recommendation that volunteers select two to four of the objectives to guide an 8- to 16-week training program. The MATP is designed to supplement (not replace) existing programs and curricula used by parents, teachers, and therapists.

T a b l e 2 1 . 2   **Techniques of sensorimotor training for persons with severe mental retardation.**

Goal	Action	Materials Required
To increase body awareness	1. Toweling, brushing, icing, stroking, tapping, contact with textures	1. Towels, brushes (light), ice bags, textured fabrics
	2. Applying restraints for short periods, promoting body awareness by cuddling and holding tightly	2. Sandbags; splint jackets; strong, gentle arms
	3. Following flashlight, hanging ball, colored toys, camera flashes	3. Flashlight, ball hanging from ceiling, blocks, balls, dolls, camera with flash
	4. Calling name of child; naming objects used, nearby persons, and actions; shaking ball, rattle; presenting music and commands	4. Wrist and ankle bells; noisemakers; tape recorders; nursery rhymes and records with varying loudness, pitch, and tempo
	5. Exposing child to extreme tastes	5. Sweet, sour, bitter, salty substances (honey, lemon, alum, salt)
	6. Exposing child to extreme odors	6. Pungent substances (coffee, cinnamon, vinegar), scented candles, incense, aerosol sprays
	7. Exposing child to extreme temperatures	7. Two basins with warm and cold water, ice bags, heating pads
	8. Mirror play	8. Full mirror, small mirrors that can be moved horizontally
	9. Wind movements	9. Fans to create wind tunnels, blowing air, fanning
	10. Vibration	10. Hand vibrators, mattress vibrators
To improve prelocomotion movement skills	1. Rolling	1. Mats with rough, smooth, hard, soft surfaces
	2. Rocking	2. Rocking chairs and horses, large beach balls
	3. Bouncing	3. Air mattress, trampoline, jump-up seat
	4. Swinging	4. Hammocks, suspended seats
	5. Coactive movements	5. Physical guidance of body or limbs (Chapter 10)
To improve object manipulation skills	1. Reaching	1. Toys with various textures, colors, and sounds; water play; sticky clay; sand; finger paint; punching balls
	2. Grasping	2. Same as 1, yarn balls, Nerf balls
	3. Holding	3. Same as 1 and 2
	4. Releasing	4. Small balls
	5. Throwing	5. Balls, praise, food treats, affection
	6. Responding to social cues	6. Same as 5
	7. Developing relationship to one person	7. Individual teacher
To develop posture and locomotion skills and patterns	1. Lifting head while prone	1. Chest support
	2. Sitting	2. Rubber tube
	3. Crawling and creeping	3. Crawler, scooterboard, creep up padded stairs, inclined mats
	4. Standing	4. Standing tables, human support
	5. Riding tricycle	5. Tricycle with or without seat support and feet straps
	6. Walking	6. Parallel bars, human support, pushing weighted cart, coactive movement
	7. Stair climbing	7. Practice stairs

T a b l e 2 1 . 3   Activities included in the Special Olympics Motor Activities Training program for persons with severe mental retardation.

1.0 Warm-Up Activities
  1.1 Breathing
  1.2 Tactile stimulation
  1.3 Relaxation activities
  1.4 Range of motion
2.0 Strength and Conditioning Activities
  2.1 Exercise bands
  2.2 Continuous walking
  2.3 Toe touches
  2.4 Sit-ups
  2.5 Aerobic dance
3.0 Sensory-Motor Awareness Activities
  3.1 Visual stimulation
  3.2 Auditory stimulation
  3.3 Tactile stimulation
4.0 Motor Activities
  4.1 Mobility leading to gymnastics
  4.2 Dexterity leading to athletics
  4.3 Striking leading to softball
  4.4 Kicking leading to soccer
  4.5 Manual wheelchair leading to athletics
  4.6 Electric wheelchair leading to athletics
  4.7 Aquatics

The MATP philosophy encompasses seven points:

1. Training should be fun and teach participants to ultimately self-initiate and choose these activities during their leisure time.

2. Activities should be age-appropriate.

3. Training, not competition, is the emphasis. This training may lead to competition, but 8 to 16 weeks of training should come first.

4. After completion of MATP, every person should have the opportunity to show new skills to significant others in a Training Day program.

5. The **principle of functionality** should guide activity selection. Criteria to be used are (a) high probability of opportunity to use skills in home, school, and community environments and (b) skills will increase self-sufficiency and acceptance.

6. The **principle of partial participation** shall be followed. This means that persons with severe MR who lack capability for independent function are given whatever assistance and adapted equipment are needed (i.e., their partial participation is supplemented to permit full inclusion). See Block (1992) and Krebs and Block (1992) for further explanation.

7. Volunteers should be creative in providing community-based sports and recreational opportunities. They should think integration first, rather than isolation.

The MATP begins with assessment of present level of performance. A task analysis assessment sheet is provided for each of the seven motor activities, with directions to chart the amount of assistance needed for 15 weeks. Codes used are *P,* for physical; *G,* for gestural; *V,* for verbal or visual; and *I,* for independent.

Training techniques emphasize setting objectives that match assessment data, utilizing behavior management techniques like shaping and reinforcing, and charting performance. Several task analyses are presented to guide teaching of each motor activity. For example, kicking is broken down into three subtasks:

1. Participant will touch ball with foot.
2. Participant will push ball forward with foot.
3. Participant will kick ball forward.

A separate task analysis is provided for each subtask, as well as general teaching suggestions that emphasize variability of practice conditions and application of skills in lead-up games.

SOI believes that competition, properly conducted and individualized, should be available to everyone who can meet three criteria:

1. Cognitively demonstrate awareness of competing against other athletes
2. Physically demonstrate the ability to perform the movements required by a particular event
3. Adhere to the rules and regulations of the particular sport

This belief is based largely on the **principle of normalization** (i.e., that persons with MR should have available the same opportunities as normal peers). Competition, when every participant is made to feel like a winner, provides conditions conducive to building good self-concepts (Gibbons & Bushakra, 1989; Wright & Cowden, 1986). The number of persons who watch, applaud, and praise are important aspects of the self-concept effect. Also important is the emphasis on personal best rather than social comparison.

Table 21.4 lists official Special Olympics events designed specifically for persons with severe MR and multiple disabilities. These are conducted as **individual skill tests** and should be practiced many times in the school setting before being administered in the competitive milieu. Often, Special Olympics meets are the only time that the general public sees persons with severe MR. Philosophy supports the right of these persons to be seen and heard. This is a first step toward societal acceptance and toward inclusion of sport events for persons with severe MR in regular school and community track meets.

T a b l e   2 1 . 4　　**Special Olympics Sports Skills competitive events for persons with severe mental retardation.**

Aquatics
10-m assisted swim
15-m walk
15-m flotation race
15-m unassisted swim

Athletics (Track and Field)
10-m assisted walk
25-m walk
10-m wheelchair event
25-m wheelchair race
30-m motorized wheelchair slalom
25-m motorized wheelchair obstacle race
Ball throw for distance (tennis ball)

Basketball
10-m basketball dribble
Speed dribble
Target pass
Spot shot
Team skills basketball

Bowling
Section B, rules of competition (see use of ramps)
Target bowl
Frame bowl

Gymnastics
Level A wide beam
Level A floor exercise
Level A tumbling
Level A all-around

Soccer (called football in many countries)
Kick and score
Dribble, turn, and shoot
Team skills soccer

Softball
Bat for distance
Base race
Team skills softball

Volleyball
Volleyball pass

Team Handball
Spot shot
Team skills handball

Weight Lifting
Bench press
Modified push-ups
Sit-ups
Exercycle
One-arm curl
Chin-ups

References

Abel, E. L. (1987). *Fetal alcohol syndrome and fetal alcohol effects.* New York: Plenum Press.

American Psychiatric Association. (1994). *Diagnostic and statistical manual of mental disorders* (4th ed.). Washington, DC: Author.

Atha, B. (1994). Issues in classification in sport for the mentally handicapped. In R. D. Steadward, E. R. Nelson, & G. D. Wheeler (Eds.), *Vista 93—The outlook* (pp. 304–309) Edmonton, Canada: University of Alberta.

Biersdorff, K. K. (1994). Incidence of significantly altered pain experience among individuals with developmental disabilities. *American Journal on Mental Retardation, 98*(5), 619–631.

Block, M. E. (1991). Motor development in children with Down syndrome: A review of the literature. *Adapted Physical Activity Quarterly, 8*(3), 179–209.

Block, M. E. (1992). What is appropriate physical education for students with profound disabilities? *Adapted Physical Activity Quarterly, 9*(3), 197–213.

Borthwick-Duffy, S. A. (1994). Epidemiology and prevalence of psychopathology in people with mental retardation. *Journal of Consulting and Clinical Psychology, 62,* 17–27.

Bouffard, M. (1990). Movement problem solutions for educable mentally handicapped individuals. *Adapted Physical Activity Quarterly, 7,* 183–197.

Bouffard, M., & Wall, A. E. (1990). A problem-solving approach to movement skill acquisition: Implications for special populations. In G. Reid (Ed.), *Problems in movement control* (pp. 107–131). Amsterdam: North-Holland.

Chad, K., Jobling, A., & Frail, H. (1990). Metabolic rate: A factor in developing obesity in children with Down syndrome. *American Journal on Mental Retardation, 95*(2), 228–235.

Cioni, M., Cocilovo, A., DiPasquale, F., Rillo Araujo, M. B., Rodriguez Siqueira, C., & Bianco, M. (1994). Strength deficit of knee extensor muscles of individuals with Down syndrome from childhood to adolescence. *American Journal on Mental Retardation, 99*(2), 166–174.

Cooney, T. P., & Thurlbeck, W. M. (1982). Pulmonary hypoplasia in Down syndrome. *New England Journal of Medicine, 307*(19), 1170–1173.

Datillo, J. (1993). Reciprocal communication for individuals with severe communication disorders: Implications to leisure participation. *Palaestra, 10*(1), 39–47.

Dobbins, D. A., Garron, R., & Rarick, G. L. (1981). The motor performance of educable mentally retarded and intellectually normal boys after covariate control for difference in body size. *Research Quarterly for Exercise and Sport, 52,* 1–8.

Dorris, M. (1989). *The broken cord.* New York: Harper & Row.

Dunn, J. M., Morehouse, J., & Fredericks, H. (1986). *Physical education for the severely handicapped: A systematic approach to a data-based gymnasium.* Austin, TX: Pro•Ed.

Dyer, S., Gunn, P., Rauh, H., & Berry, P. (1990). Motor development in Down syndrome children: An analysis of the motor scale of the Bayley Scales of Infant Development. In A. Vermeer (Ed.), *Motor development, adapted physical activity, and mental retardation,* (pp. 7–20). Basel, Switzerland: Karger.

Dykens, E. M., Hodapp, R. M., & Evans, D. W. (1994). Profiles and development of adaptive behavior in children with Down syndrome. *American Journal on Mental Retardation, 98*(5), 580–587.

Dykens, E. M., Hodapp, R. M., & Leckman, J. F. (1994). *Behavior and development in fragile X syndrome.* Thousand Oaks, CA: Sage.

Eichstaedt, C., & Lavay, B. (1992). *Physical activity for individuals with mental retardation: Infant to adult.* Champaign, IL: Human Kinetics.

Eichstaedt, C., Wang, P., Polacek, J., & Dohrmann, P. (1991). *Physical fitness and motor skill levels of individuals with mental retardation, ages 6–21.* Normal, IL: Illinois State University.

Eyman, R. K., Call, T., & White, J. F. (1991). Life expectancy of persons with Down syndrome. *American Journal on Mental Retardation, 95*(6), 603–612.

Fernhall, B., Tymeson, G., & Webster, G. (1988). Cardiovascular fitness of mentally retarded individuals. *Adapted Physical Activity Quarterly, 5,* 12–18.

Fishler, K., & Koch, R. (1991). Mental development in Down syndrome mosaicism. *American Journal on Mental Retardation, 96*(3), 345–351.

Francis, R. J., & Rarick, G. L. (1959). Motor characteristics of the mentally retarded. *American Journal of Mental Deficiency, 63,* 792–811.

Gibbons, S. L., & Bushakra, F. (1989). Effects of Special Olympics participation on the perceived competence and social acceptance of mentally retarded children. *Adapted Physical Activity Quarterly, 6*(1), 40–51.

Greenwood, M., Silliman, L. M., & French, R. (1990). Comparisons of physical activity programs for severely/profoundly mentally retarded persons. *Palaestra, 6*(4), 38–47.

Grossman, H. J. (Ed.). (1983). *Classification in mental retardation.* Washington, DC: American Association on Mental Deficiency.

Henderson, S. E. (1986). Some aspects of the development of motor control in Down's syndrome. In H. T. A. Whiting & M. G. Wade (Eds.), *Themes in motor development* (pp. 69–92). Boston: Martinus Nijhoff.

Hoover, J. H., & Horgan, J. S. (1990). Short-term memory for motor skills in mentally retarded persons: Training and research issues. In G. Reid (Ed.), *Problems in movement control* (pp. 217–239). Amsterdam: North-Holland.

Jansma, P., Decker, J., Ersing, W., McCubbin, J., & Combs, S. (1988). A fitness assessment system for individuals with severe mental retardation. *Adapted Physical Activity Quarterly, 5,* 223–232.

Kelly, L. E., & Rimmer, J. (1987). A practical method for estimating percent body fat of adult mentally retarded males. *Adapted Physical Activity Quarterly, 4,* 117–125.

Krebs, P., & Block, M. E. (1992). Transition of students with disabilities into community recreation: The role of the adapted physical educator. *Adapted Physical Activity Quarterly, 9*(4), 305–315.

Luckasson, R., Coulter, D., Polloway, E., Deiss, S., Schalock, R., Snell, M., Spitalnik, D., & Stark, J. (1992). *Mental retardation: Definition, classification, and systems of supports* (9th ed.). Washington, DC: American Association on Mental Retardation.

MacMillan, D. L., Gresham, F. M., & Siperstein, G. N. (1995). Heightened concerns over the 1992 AAMR definition: Advocacy versus precision. *American Journal on Mental Retardation, 100*(1), 87–97.

Marino, B., & Pueschel, S. M. (Eds.). (1996). *Heart disease in persons with Down syndrome.* Baltimore: Paul H. Brookes.

Montagu, A. (1971). *The elephant man.* New York: Ballantine.

Montgomery, D. L., Reid, G., & Seidl, C. (1988). The effects of two physical fitness programs designed for mentally retarded adults. *Canadian Journal of Sport Sciences, 13*(1), 73–78.

National Consortium for Physical Education and Recreation for Individuals with Disabilities. (1995). *Adapted physical education national standards.* Champaign, IL: Human Kinetics.

Pitetti, K., Jackson, J., Stubbs, N., Campbell, K., & Battar, S. (1989). Fitness levels of adult Special Olympics participants. *Adapted Physical Activity Quarterly, 6,* 354–370.

Rarick, G. L. (1980). Cognitive-motor relationships in the growing years. *Research Quarterly for Exercise and Sport, 51,* 174–192.

Reid, G. (1986). The trainability of motor processing strategies with developmentally delayed performers. In H. T. A. Whiting & M. G. Wade (Eds.), *Themes in motor development* (pp. 93–107). Dordrecht, Holland: Martinus Nijhoff.

Reid, G., Montgomery, D. L., & Seidl, C. (1990). *Stepping out for fitness: A program for adults who are intellectually handicapped.* Gloucester, Ontario: Canadian Association for Health, Physical Education, and Recreation.

Rimmer, J. H., Braddock, D., & Fujiura, G. (1993). Prevalence of obesity in adults with mental retardation: Implications for health promotion and disease prevention. *Mental Retardation, 31*(2), 105–110.

Seidl, C., Reid, G., & Montgomery, D. L. (1987). A critique of cardiovascular fitness testing with mentally retarded persons. *Adapted Physical Activity Quarterly, 2,* 106–116.

Special Olympics International (1995). *Special Olympics World Games Connecticut 1995 official handbook.* New Haven, CT: 1995 Special Olympics World Games Organizing Committee.

Special Olympics International. (1989). *Special Olympics motor activities training guide.* Washington, DC: Author.

Spicer, R. L. (1984). Cardiovascular disease in Down syndrome. *Pediatric Clinics of North America, 31*(6), 1331–1344.

Stratford, B., & Ching, E. (1983). Rhythm and time in the perception of Down syndrome children. *Journal of Mental Deficiency Research, 27,* 23–38.

Sugden, D. A., & Keogh, J. F. (1990). *Problems in movement skill development.* Columbia: University of South Carolina Press.

Tanchak, T. L., & Sawyer, C. (1995). Augmentative communication. In K. M. Flippo, K. J. Inge, & J. M. Barcus (Eds.), *Assistive technology. A resource for school work and community* (pp. 57–85). Baltimore: Paul H. Brookes.

Tarr, S., & Pyfer, J. L. (1996). Physical and motor development of neonates/infants prenatally exposed to drugs in utero: A meta-analysis. *Adapted Physical Activity Quarterly, 13*(3), 269–287.

Varela, A. M., & Pitetti, K. H. (1995). Heart rate response to two field exercise tests by adolescents and young adults with Down syndrome. *Adapted Physical Activity Quarterly, 12*(1), 43–51.

Wall, A. E., Bouffard, M., McClements, J., Findlay, H., & Taylor, M. J. (1985). A knowledge-based approach to motor development: Implications for the physically awkward. *Adapted Physical Activity Quarterly, 2*(1), 21–43.

Watkinson, E. J., & Wall, A. E. (1982). *PREP: The PREP play program: Play skill instruction for mentally handicapped children.* Gloucester, Ontario: Canadian Association for Health, Physical Education, and Recreation.

Webb, R., & Koller, J. (1979). Effects of sensorimotor training on intellectual and adaptive skills of profoundly retarded adults. *American Journal of Mental Deficiency, 83,* 490–496.

Weber, R. C. (1993). Physical education for children with Prader-Willi syndrome. *Palaestra, 9*(3), 41–47.

Weber, R. C. (1994). Physical activity for children with Apert syndrome. *Palaestra, 10*(2), 13–18.

Wessel, J. (1980). *I CAN implementation guide for preprimary motor and play skills.* East Lansing: Michigan State University, Marketing Division, Instructional Media Center.

Wright, J., & Cowden, J. (1986). Changes in self-concept and cardiovascular endurance of mentally retarded youth in a Special Olympics swimming program. *Adapted Physical Activity Quarterly, 3,* 177–184.

Zigman, W. G., Schupf, N., Lubin, R., & Silverman, W. (1987). Premature regression of adults with Down syndrome. *American Journal of Mental Deficiency, 92*(2), 161–168.

C H A P T E R

22

Serious Emotional Disturbance and Autism

FIGURE 22.1 The child with serious emotional disturbance must be taught how to channel aggression. Behavior disorders are a common problem in public schools.

After you have studied this chapter, you should be able to do the following:

1. Contrast different types of serious emotional disturbance with each other and with autism. What are the similarities and differences in behaviors and in physical education pedagogy?

2. Explain why autism was recognized as a separate diagnostic category in 1990. Observe some classes with students with serious emotional disturbance and with autism and discuss similarities and differences in programming.

3. Compare definitions of emotional disturbance used by the federal government, the Council for Exceptional Children (CEC), and the American Psychiatric Association (APA). Why are definitions different?

4. Make a list of persons that you have known or read about with serious emotional disturbance or autism. Assess your knowledge and personal experience with each of the conditions in this chapter. Make plans for further learning by selecting autobiographies to read, videotapes to view, and programs to visit.

5. Select three persons with different conditions and discuss the role of medication, psychotherapy and/or counseling, and cooperative home-school-community intervention in the life of each.

6. Know how to use the *Physician's Desk Reference (PDR)* and similar reference books to learn about medications and their side effects. Discuss how specific medications change behaviors and how professionals need to adapt the ecosystem for specific side effects.

7. Describe ways to assess specific behaviors in the physical education setting and write some goals and objectives to guide intervention in reducing undesirable behaviors.

8. Give examples of specific instructional strategies that will help students achieve physical education goals and objectives.

Everyone, at one time or another, has emotional problems that are serious enough to benefit from professional help. Only a few of the individuals in need, however, have the financial resources, knowledge, and inclination to seek counseling from qualified mental health personnel. Teachers are therefore often the major source of help to individuals and families at risk. Teachers and others who serve individuals with disabilities should take counseling courses and learn as much as possible about various helping techniques. In particular, they need to learn how to work with families, because children's behavior is generally rooted in social problems. Consider the following statistics that place many individuals *at risk* for serious emotional disturbance:

- Over 2.9 million children are reported annually to social agencies as being abused or neglected.
- Every 30 seconds an infant is born into poverty; approximately 15% of the American population (about 1 in 7) are living in poverty.
- Every 59 seconds an infant is born to a teenage mother.
- Every 2 minutes a baby is born to a mother who had late or no prenatal care.
- Every 5 minutes a child is arrested for a violent crime.
- Every 2 hours a child is murdered.
- From 20 to 60% of children live in one-parent households.
- From 35 to 50% of adults report illicit drug use at some time in their lives; an estimated 4.5 million women of childbearing age are current users of illicit drugs.
- Over 3 million children each year witness domestic violence, ranging from hitting and punching to fatal assaults.
- Violence also is prevalent in television, movies, and newspapers. Most families permit toys that allow children to model behaviors seen on television. Almost all children today need to be taught appropriate ways to express emotions (see Figure 22.1).

Statistics vary, of course, by socioeconomic level, ethnic group, cultural background, family structure, and neighborhood. Family pressures are intensified by the birth and rearing of a child with a disability, as they are by disability or illness in any family member at any time. The aging and gradual debilitation of grandparents, many of whom live to be 90 or older, can also add stress. Mental illness also is sometimes present in families, adding to the uniqueness of the complex set of everyday variables that affect behaviors.

A key concept of this chapter is that behavior is caused by a multitude of factors—some environmental, some genetic, and some biological. Team approaches (multidisciplinary, interdisciplinary, crossdisciplinary), with family involvement, should be used to analyze the causes of inappropriate behaviors and to determine interventions. Physical activity personnel are an important part of the team, because individuals often behave differently in activity settings than in academic or workplace sites. This different behavior can be more positive or more negative.

Prevalence of Serious Emotional Disorders

Prevalence statistics for serious emotional disorders vary widely because of differing definitions and diagnostic criteria. The diagnosis of mental disorders is difficult, and most psychiatrists prefer not to attach a label. The prevalence of behavior disorders in the school population ranges from 2 to 22%, depending upon the criterion of behavior disorders used. The ratio of boys to girls with mental disorders is approximately 4 to 1. The U.S. Department of Education estimates very consecutively that approximately 7 to 8% of the school-age population is so seriously emotionally disturbed that special education provisions are required.

Suicide increasingly is a problem of childhood and adolescence, ranking as the third leading cause of death in the 15-to-24 age bracket. Statistics for all age groups combined reveal over 25,000 suicides each year. Approximately 2 million Americans have made one or more attempts at suicide.

Delinquency, a legal term reserved for youngsters whose behavior results in arrest and court action, is another manifestation of emotional problems. The crime rate among young persons has increased steadily during the past decade. Long before their initial arrest, many delinquents are described by teachers as defiant, impertinent, uncooperative, irritable, bullying, attention seeking, negative, and restless. Other delinquents are seen as shy, lacking in self-confidence, hypersensitive, fearful, and excessively anxious. A greater than average incidence of delinquency occurs among students who rank lowest in school performance and social standing. This includes many individuals with mental retardation and/or attention deficit disorders.

A trend of the 1990s is recognition that many individuals with developmental disabilities have mental illness or severe behavioral disorders (Borthwick-Duffy, 1994). Some estimates suggest that up to 60% of individuals with developmental disabilities also manifest mental illness or a severe behavioral disorder (Shoham-Vardi et al., 1996). **Dual diagnosis,** the co-occurrence of mental retardation and psychiatric disorders, is made with increasing frequency so as to obtain needed resources and support services. Approximately 26 to 40% of residents in community-based small-group homes and 35% of residents in state institutions currently receive drugs for behavior problems (Schaal & Hackenberg, 1994).

Individuals with disabilities are also at greater risk than the nondisabled population for experiencing violence and abuse (Sobsey, 1994). In particular, people with developmental disabilities are at an increased risk for **sexual assault** and **sexual abuse** (Sundram & Stavis, 1994). Most do not receive adequate training to enable them to say no to sex, drugs, and partner or gang involvement in crime. The trend toward community placement and inclusive settings has intensified these problems, because individuals with mental retardation now daily come into contact with more people, some of whom tease, hurt, and exploit them. Professionals must be increasingly aware of risks and problems and know how to handle them.

Definitions of Serious Emotional Disturbance

Definitions of serious emotional disturbance come from several sources. The three most frequently used are those of federal law, the Council for Exceptional Children (CEC), and the American Psychiatric Association (APA).

Federal Law Terminology

The federal term used in determining eligibility for special education services is **seriously emotionally disturbed.** This term means

a condition exhibiting one or more of the following characteristics over a long period of time and to a marked degree, which adversely affects educational performance:
(A) An inability to learn which cannot be explained by intellectual, sensory, or health factors;
(B) An inability to build or maintain satisfactory interpersonal relationships with peers and teachers;

(C) Inappropriate types of behavior or feelings under normal circumstances;
(D) A general pervasive mood of unhappiness or depression; or
(E) A tendency to develop physical symptoms or fears associated with personal or school problems. (*Federal Register,* September 1992, p. 44802)

Originally, this definition included **autism.** In 1981, however, students with autism were included instead in the official definition of *other health impaired.* Finally, in 1990, autism was recognized as an independent diagnostic category. Autism is discussed at the end of this chapter.

CEC Terminology

Many special educators use the term *behavior disorders* rather than *emotional or mental illness.* In 1962, the Council for Exceptional Children (CEC) formed the Council for Children with Behavioral Disorders (CCBD). This organization publishes a quarterly journal called *Behavioral Disorders* and influences special education practices.

APA Terminology

The American Psychiatric Association (APA) is the professional organization that assumes responsibility for publishing the reference book on mental disorders that is used by all of the disciplines that follow the medical model, by courts of law, and by insurance companies. This book, entitled *The Diagnostic and Statistical Manual of Mental Disorders (DSM),* is the definitive source of knowledge about mental disorders, terminology, diagnostic features, prevalence, and course. The content of *DSM* is consistent with *International Classification of Diseases (ICD)* published by the World Health Organization (1989).

DSM-IV (APA, 1994) identifies 16 major diagnostic classes and has one additional section, "Other Conditions That May Be a Focus of Clinical Attention." The terminology of several conditions has changed since the publication of the earlier edition, *DSM-III.* For example, affective disorders are now called *mood disorders.* Substance-use disorders are now called *substance-related disorders.* The concept of organic mental disorders has been replaced with more-specific conditions designated as *delirium, dementia, and amnesia.* Following is a brief discussion of some of the classic mental disorders covered by *DSM-IV* and a more detailed discussion of disorders usually first diagnosed in infancy, childhood, or adolescence.

Classic *DSM* Mental Disorders

The most common of the 16 *DSM-IV* diagnostic categories are described in this section. Children and youth, as well as adults, may be diagnosed as having these disorders. The behaviors are essentially the same, regardless of age.

Substance-Related Disorders

Use of substances like coffee, alcohol, and caffeine soft drinks to modify mood or behavior under certain circumstances is generally considered normal and appropriate. There are, however, widespread cultural and religious variations in what is considered appropriate.

When more or less regular substance use results in behavioral changes that negatively affect work and leisure productivity, social functioning, or the happiness and welfare of family or friends, substance use is labeled a mental disorder. **Substance-related disorders** can be manifested as either *abuse* or *dependence*. Substances can be either *legal* (coffee, tobacco) or *illegal* (marijuana, cocaine, amphetamines). Likewise, they may be medically prescribed to control a chronic health problem or available on the open market. The nature of the substance is not relevant; the diagnostic criteria include inability to reduce or stop use and episodes of overuse.

Schizophrenia and Other Psychotic Disorders

Schizophrenia is a psychotic disturbance that lasts for at least 6 months and includes at least 1 month of two or more of the following: **delusions** (interpreting ideas and events in unrealistic, inappropriate ways), **hallucinations** (perceiving things that do not exist), disorganized speech, grossly disorganized or catatonic behavior, and negative symptoms. **Catatonic** refers to motor extremes, either purposeless hyperactivity or stupor-like hypoactivity. **Negative symptoms** include **affective flattening** (immobile and unresponsive face, poor eye contact, and reduced body language), **alogia** (poverty of speech, as in brief, empty replies), and **avolition** (inability to initiate and persist in goal-directed activities).

Although the word *schizophrenia* is derived from *schizein* (to split) and *phren* (mind), schizophrenic disorders are no longer described as split personality. Following are five distinct types of schizophrenia:

1. **Disordered type.** Marked incoherence and dull, silly, or inappropriate affect, but no delusions.
2. **Catatonic type.** Marked psychomotor disturbance that can range from stupor to purposeless hyperactivity. *Catatonic rigidity* is the maintenance of a rigid posture against efforts to be moved. *Catatonic posturing* refers to inappropriate or bizarre postures.
3. **Paranoid type.** Delusions and/or hallucinations.
4. **Undifferentiated type.** Prominent delusions, hallucinations, incoherence, or grossly disorganized behavior. Meets criteria for more than one type of schizophrenia or for none.
5. **Residual type.** Such chronic signs as social withdrawal, eccentric behavior, dull affect, and illogical thinking, but without prominence of delusions or hallucinations.

Of the mental conditions that require hospitalization, schizophrenic disorders are the most common. Half of all mental patients are schizophrenic. Moreover, 1 of every 100 persons in the world has schizophrenia at some time or another.

DSM-IV states that the onset of schizophrenia is usually in adolescence or adulthood. Nevertheless, estimates of the number of cases of childhood schizophrenia currently in the United States range from 100,000 to 500,000. There are approximately 4,000 children with psychotic disorders in state hospitals, close to 2,500 in residential treatment and day-care centers, and at least 3,000 children with schizophrenia in day-care clinics.

Psychotic disorders is a broad term that refers to manifestation of delusions, hallucinations, or other serious symptoms that grossly interfere with the capacity to meet the ordinary demands of life but that do not meet the diagnostic criteria for schizophrenia or other mental disorders. The term **psychotic** is used in many ways, but its most common use is to denote the onset of the active phase of serious mental illness (e.g., an acute psychotic episode), which typically requires hospitalization. During this active phase, individuals can be dangerous to themselves or others.

Schizophrenia and psychotic disorders can usually be managed by daily medication. Failure to take this medication results in **acute psychotic episodes** or active-phase illness. Individuals with schizophrenia typically have motor abnormalities related to the side effects from treatment with antipsychotic medications (APA, 1994). The most common motor abnormality is **tardive dyskinesia,** the presence of involuntary movements of the tongue, jaw, trunk, or extremities (e.g., tongue thrusting, clicking, grunting). These involuntary movements may occur in any of the following patterns: *choreiform* (rapid, jerky, nonrepetitive), *athetoid* (slow, continual), or *rhythmic* (various stereotypies). Tardive dyskinesia is usually mild and is considered a small price to pay for management of serious illness.

Mood Disorders

Mood disorders, formerly called affective disorders, can be **bipolar** (mood shifts from mania to depression and vice versa) or **unipolar** (usually episodes of extreme depression). **Manic episodes** are defined as the presence (for at least 1 week) of such behaviors as hyperactivity and restlessness; decreased need for sleep; unusual talkativeness; distractibility manifested as abrupt, rapid changes in activity or topics of speech; inflated self-esteem; and excessive involvement in such high-risk activity as reckless driving, buying sprees, sexual indiscretions, and quick business investments. **Depressive episodes** include loss of interest or pleasure in all or almost all usual activities; too much sleep or insomnia; poor appetite and significant weight loss; low self-esteem; chronic fatigue; diminished ability to think, concentrate, and make decisions; and recurrent thoughts of death and suicide. Children with depression tend to withdraw and must be coaxed into activity (see Figure 22.2).

Individuals with bipolar conditions can have rapid cycling (four or more mood episodes during the previous 12 months) or slower transitions with relatively long periods of normalcy between episodes. Individuals with mania usually do not want to take medication and typically deny problems because they like the feeling of being high. There are all degrees of mania, with symptoms peaking and then smoothing out. Some individuals channel their mania into intense periods of productivity. Illustrative of this are many famous musicians, writers, and artists with manic-depressive symptomatology (Jamison, 1993, 1995). Others get their families deeply in debt or alienate close associates with behaviors that are chaotic, embarrassing, or hurtful. The depressive episodes that follow are intensified by acknowledgment of all the problems caused by

FIGURE 22.2 Depression is associated with withdrawal. Here, Dr. Karen DePauw guides a rhythmic activity and encourages involvement.

mania. However, during depression there is no physical or mental energy to cope with anything; this is a time of total fatigue.

Bipolar and major depressive disorders are relatively common. About 1 person in 100 has severe manic-depressive illness, and an equal number have milder variants. The average age of onset is 18, and both sexes are affected equally. In contrast, major depressive illness is twice as likely to affect women. The average age of onset of serious unipolar depression is 27. About 1 person in 20 experiences a major depressive illness at least once during his or her lifetime. Medications are highly effective in treating both conditions. Lithium is the drug of choice in manic-depressive illness, and a wide variety of antidepressants are used for depression. Psychotherapy is typically needed along with medication to help individuals cope with the repercussions of past episodes and understand the importance of staying on medication.

Anxiety Disorders

Anxiety disorders is the broad diagnostic category that includes panic attacks, panic disorders, phobias, obsessive-compulsive disorders, and other conditions of excessive worry and unease. Each of these is relatively common, with a prevalence of 1 in 100 or greater. Treatment consists of medication in conjunction with outpatient counseling and psychotherapy.

Panic attacks, which occur in several anxiety disorders, are periods of intense fear or discomfort accompanied by a sense of imminent danger or impending doom and an urge to escape. Symptoms vary but can include a pounding heart, sweating, trembling or shaking, shortness of breath, a feeling of choking, chest pain or discomfort, nausea or abdominal distress, chills or hot flashes, and the like. **Panic disorder** is the recurrence of unexpected panic attacks.

Phobias are intense, persistent, and unreasonable fears in relation to specific objects or situations that cause avoidance behaviors. **Agoraphobia** is extreme anxiety about being in places or situations from which escape might be difficult or embarrassing; individuals with severe agoraphobia typically refuse to leave home. Phobias should not be confused with **situational fears,** which many individuals feel when confronted with new and unfamiliar situations or demands like learning to swim or use gymnastic apparatus.

Obsessive-compulsive disorders are conditions in which anxiety is expressed through **obsessions** (recurrent and persistent thoughts, images, or impulses that cause worry or distress) and **compulsions** (repetitive behaviors or mental acts that a person feels driven to perform in response to an obsession). Usually the compulsions are performed to prevent some dreaded event or situation that in reality is not likely to occur.

Dementia

Dementia is a broad diagnostic term for multiple cognitive deficits, including impairment in memory, that are a significant change from a previous level of functioning and can be attributed to a medical condition and/or a substance. The most common dementias are those caused by **Alzheimer's disease** (degeneration of the brain associated primarily with old age), head trauma, Parkinson's disease, human immunodeficiency virus (HIV) disease, and long-term substance abuse.

Eating Disorders

The eating disorders category includes gross disturbances in eating behaviors. Most common are anorexia nervosa and bulimia. Although these can occur at any age, their first manifestation is usually in adolescence.

Anorexia nervosa is a condition characterized by significant weight loss, refusal to maintain normal body weight, disturbance of body image, and intense fear of becoming obese. In females, it is accompanied by **amenorrhea** (cessation of menstrual periods). The disorder occurs primarily (95%) in females. The prevalence rate for females in the 12-to-18-year-old age range is about 1 of every 250. This condition leads to death by starvation in about 15 to 21% of the treated cases. Hospitalization is generally required to prevent starvation. The major diagnostic criterion is permanent weight loss of at least 25% of original body weight.

Bulimia is characterized by recurrent episodes of binge eating (the consumption of huge quantities in 2 hr or less), awareness that the eating pattern is abnormal, fear of being unable to stop eating voluntarily, and depressed mood following eating binges. The disorder is more common in females than males and typically begins in adolescence or early adulthood. Persons with bulimia are usually within a normal weight range, but they exhibit frequent weight fluctuations because of alternating binges and fasts. They try to control weight by dieting, self-induced vomiting, or the use of laxatives and medicines. Bulimia is seldom totally incapacitating, although it may affect social, leisure, and vocational functioning. Unlike anorexia nervosa, it does not result in death when untreated. It is, in fact, very much like alcohol and substance abuse.

Implications of Adult Mental Disorders for Children

The disorders described thus far (substance-related disorders, schizophrenia and other psychotic disorders, mood disorders, anxiety disorders, dementia, and eating disorders) are primarily adult disorders but occur occasionally in children and adolescents. The presence of any of these conditions in family members, especially parents, has a profound effect on children and adolescents. These conditions can alter child-rearing patterns and practices, change the emotional climate of the home, and cause much anxiety to children, who lack full understanding of why events or behaviors are happening. Moreover, considerable prejudice against mental illness still exists in our society, and families often attempt to keep such conditions secret. Children are therefore cautioned not to talk about the illness outside the home and thus can be denied needed emotional support. Children also are often fearful of inheriting these conditions. This anxiety is not totally unfounded, because a genetic predisposition exists for many types of mental illness.

DSM Disorders in Children and Adolescents

DSM-IV lists 10 conditions that are usually first diagnosed in infancy, childhood, or adolescence (see Table 22.1). Several of these conditions are discussed elsewhere in this book: (a) mental retardation in Chapters 18 and 21, and (b) learning disor-

ders, developmental coordination disorder, and attention deficit hyperactivity disorder (ADHD) in Chapter 20. *DSM* conditions not yet covered that relate to school-age children are disruptive behavior disorders not caused by ADHD (conduct disorder and oppositional defiant disorder), tic disorders, stereotypic movement disorders, and pervasive developmental disorders.

Conduct Disorder

Conduct disorder is a pattern of persistent and repetitive behaviors that violate the basic rights of others and/or major age-appropriate societal norms or rules. According to the APA (1994), these behaviors fall into four main groups: (a) aggressive conduct that causes or threatens physical harm to other people or animals; (b) destruction of property; (c) deceitfulness, lying, or theft; and (d) serious violations of major rules (e.g., truancy from school, running away from home, ignoring curfews).

Conduct disorder is one of the most frequently diagnosed conditions in late childhood and adolescence. The prevalence rates for males range from 6 to 16%; those for females range from 2 to 9%. Individuals with conduct disorder are considered at risk for several adult disorders, including substance-related abuse, mood disorders, and anxiety disorders. Moreover, conduct disorder occurs most frequently in children who have parents with mental illness. Without effective interventions, many individuals with conduct disorder become juvenile delinquents.

Oppositional Defiant Disorder

Oppositional defiant disorder is a recurrent pattern of hostile and disobedient behavior toward authority figures that is manifested by at least four of the following behaviors: losing one's temper, arguing with adults, actively defying the requests or rules of adults, deliberately annoying others, blaming others for one's own misbehavior or mistakes, being touchy or easily annoyed by others, being angry and resentful, and being spiteful and vindictive. In general, the disruptive behaviors associated with oppositional disorder are less serious that those exhibited in conduct disorder. Before puberty, oppositional defiant disorder occurs more frequently in males than in females; thereafter it affects the sexes equally. The overall prevalence rate ranges from 2 to 16%.

Tic Disorders and Tourette's Disorder

DSM-IV defines a **tic** as a "sudden, rapid, recurrent, nonrhythmic, stereotyped motor movement or vocalization" (APA, 1994, p. 101) and identifies tic disorders as one of the 10 mental disorders usually first diagnosed in childhood. Tics are involuntary, occur frequently during daytime hours, and are diminished or absent during sleep. Illustrative tics are eye blinking, neck jerking, arm flinging, facial grimacing, throat clearing, grunting, barking, jumping, squatting, touching, sniffing, repeating words or phrases, and using obscenities. The latter, called **coprolalia,** is present in only about 10% of individuals with tic disorders.

Tourette's disorder, the best known of the tic disorders, occurs in 4 to 5 children per 10,000 and affects three to four times as many males as females. Age of onset is between 2 and 18 years, but over 60% of affected children exhibit their first tics between ages 5 to 8. Vulnerability to this nervous system disorder is transmitted genetically and expressed in many ways. Some individuals show no symptoms, others have forms of obsessive-compulsive or attention deficit hyperactivity disorder (ADHD), and still others manifest tic patterns that vary in severity. Associated mental disorders, especially obsessions, compulsions, and ADHD, are relatively common.

Despite recent attention (Berecz, 1992; Cumings, 1990; Sacks, 1995), Tourette's disorder often is not diagnosed until children have undergone years of admonitions and various forms of behavior management to try to control their "nervous habits." Family support and acceptance vary, but most children develop self-concept problems as they realize that the tics make them different from others. In school, their tics distract others from learning and require that peers and teachers learn to ignore the unusual behaviors. Social acceptance is typically the major problem to be addressed. Medications (e.g., Ritalin, haloperidol, Prozac) are often prescribed, and teachers should be aware of side effects.

Individuals with Tourette's disorder are often drawn to athletics, partly because they have good speed, accuracy, and reaction time (Sacks, 1995). By definition, tics are very fast, and children learn early to accommodate their visual-motor coordination and body movements to the tics so that they interfere minimally with other activity. Often during rhythmic activities like swimming, running, and singing such children are free of tics. Adults with severe tic disorders drive cars, fly planes, and succeed in many professions, including surgery (Sacks, 1995). Occasionally, there are tic-free periods, but never for more than 3 consecutive months. Type of tic, severity, and frequency vary from month to month, and severity of the condition often diminishes in adolescence and adulthood. Most individuals with tic disorders have average or better intelligence.

Stereotypic Movement Disorders

DSM-IV places stereotypies in a different diagnostic category from tics. **Stereotypic movement disorders** (often called *self-stimulatory behaviors*) are repetitive, seemingly driven, non-functional motor behaviors that markedly interfere with normal activities or result in self-inflicted bodily injury (APA, 1994). These can be independent disorders, but typically they coexist with such conditions as severe mental retardation, autism, deaf-blindness or blindness.

Self-injurious behaviors (SIBs) occur most frequently in medical conditions associated with severe mental retardation (e.g., Lesch-Nyham syndrome, fragile X syndrome, and Cornelia de Lange syndrome). In Lesch-Nyham syndrome, for example, severe self-biting often leads to loss of fingers. In other syndromes, head banging or hitting can result in anemia from loss of blood, infections, retinal detachment, and blindness. Pinching and scratching can lead to chronic skin irritations, bruises, and calluses. The prevalence of SIBs is 2 to 3% in individuals in community housing and 25% in individuals in institutions. Restraints, medication, and behavior management are often ineffective in controlling SIBs.

Less severe stereotypies are often rhythmic (e.g., body rocking, head thrusting, hand waving or flicking). The major problem associated with these is social acceptance. Behavior management programs are applied to minimize time spent in stereotypic movement, but some experts believe that ignoring the stereotypy and accepting the person in spite of it is a viable alternative.

Pervasive Developmental Disorders

This *DSM-IV* category is discussed at the end of this chapter because in federal law and school policy **autism** is treated as a separate disability from serious emotional disturbance.

Treatment of Serious Emotional Disturbance

Treatment of serious emotional disturbance typically requires medication, psychotherapy and/or counseling, and cooperative home-school-community intervention programs. Lasting improvement seldom occurs unless all three of these programs are skillfully conducted and coordinated. The ecosystem must be changed as well as the individual. Serious emotional disturbance, like other kinds of disability, has acute phases or episodes and periods of remission. During the acute phase, individuals typically do not go to school or work. Instead, most are referred to mental health hospitals or outpatient clinics for diagnostic services or crisis management. Today's prescription medications are so effective that hospital stays seldom last more than a few days. Individuals who refuse medication or are careless in taking daily dosages tend to develop dysfunctional lifestyles that gradually alienate them from family and friends.

Medication (Drug Therapy or Pharmacotherapy)

Table 22.2 presents four categories of drugs commonly used in managing attention deficit hyperactivity disorder (ADHD) and serious emotional disturbance. These drugs, taken in various dosages, enable most persons to lead relatively normal lives. The main difficulty in drug therapy is determining the best drug and the appropriate dosage to manage the condition. This usually requires considerable trial and error and a willingness to cope with various side effects. *Most side effects are greatest during the first few weeks,* while the body is adjusting to the drug, and eventually disappear. Occasionally the side effect is violent illness similar to food poisoning or severe flu. Individuals vary considerably in the number and severity of side effects they experience and in their willingness to cope with these side effects.

Professionals need to understand side effects and offer support to individuals involved in drug therapy. For *ADHD drugs,* the common side effects are insomnia, loss of appetite, and weight loss. For *antianxiety drugs,* the common side effects are diminished mental alertness and motor coordination, drowsiness, feelings of fatigue, dry mouth, nausea, loss of appetite, forgetfulness, and headaches. For most *antidepressant drugs,* the common side effects are dry mouth, drowsiness, rapid heartbeat, dizziness, constipation, and weight gain.

Lithium, used as both an antidepressant and an antipsychotic drug, is considered the drug of choice for rapid reversal of acute mania and for stabilization of mood in bipolar illness. However, individuals taking lithium are at risk for more side effects than with other drugs, must take regular blood

Table 22.2 Illustrative medications used in managing hyperactivity and serious emotional disorders (trade names).

Hyperactivity and ADHD management drugs
Ritalin
Dexedrine
Cylert
Antianxiety drugs (minor tranquilizers)
Valium
Librium
Xanax
Prozac
Antidepressant drugs
Prozac
Lithium, Lithobid
Elavil
Tofranil
Antipsychotic drugs (neuroleptic, also known as major tranquilizers)
Thorazine
Haldol
Lithium, Lithobid

tests, and must avoid excessive sweating that might cause loss of body salt. Common side effects are skin rashes, generalized itching, hair loss, headache, dizziness, weakness, blurred vision, fine hand tremor, unsteadiness, nausea, and diarrhea.

Prozac, hailed as the new miracle drug and recommended for both anxiety disorders and depression, causes fewer side effects than other drugs. Approximately 3 to 4% of the people who try Prozac discontinue it because of nausea, its main side effect; another 2 to 3% discontinue it because of nervousness and insomnia. These statistics are far lower than those cited for other drugs.

Thorazine generally is the drug of choice in managing schizophrenia and other severe aggressive, self-injurious, and agitated behaviors. It is widely prescribed for individuals with a co-diagnosis of mental retardation and mental illness in residential facilities (Schaal & Hackenberg, 1994). Side effects of Thorazine and other antipsychotic drugs are sedation, orthostatic hypotension (dizziness when rising from a sitting position), skin rashes, dry mouth, sensitivity to sunlight, constipation, stuffy nose, and lack of responsiveness to temperature changes. Of greater concern are long-term side effects. Among these are **tardive dyskinesia** (tongue thrusting, lip smacking, and other abnormal movements of the mouth, jaw, and extremities), **parkinsonism** (tremor, slowed movement, "mask-like" facial expressions), and **acute dystonic reactions** (grimacing, upward gazing of the eyes, eyelid tics, and unusual movements).

Drug therapy, in summary, often results in side effects that alter appearance and movement and are uncomfortable or embarrassing. The classic source of information on medications and side effects is the *Physician's Desk Reference* (published annually), referred to by its abbreviation, the *PDR*. Good physicians monitor dosage carefully to minimize side effects. Physical activity personnel should assist with this monitoring, because effects of medication are sometimes altered by exercise. Most individuals with schizophrenia and

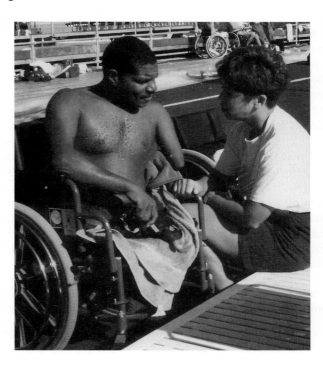

FIGURE 22.3 Counseling often occurs in informal settings when staff know how to actively listen and are willing to get involved.

major mood disorders require continual drug therapy for long periods, often for life. Less is known about the drug requirements of individuals with mental retardation and severe behavior problems. Concern has been expressed that drugs are overprescribed and undermonitored in residential facilities (Schaal & Hackenberg, 1994).

Psychotherapy and Counseling

Psychotherapy is the combined use of drugs and other helping techniques that are prescribed and monitored by a physician who specializes in psychiatry. Psychotherapy is generally carried out by psychologists or counselors in a medical setting. Most psychotherapy follows one of the cognitive psychology systems and relies primarily on verbal strategies. However, **dance therapy** (explained in Chapter 16) is a form of psychotherapy that uses movement as a change agent.

Counseling has many meanings. In this text, **counseling** is psychological help through interactive verbal communication that is guided by mental health specialists certified in counseling and by teachers and peer counselors who have completed counseling courses and workshops. Techniques of counseling were covered in Chapter 7, because the philosophy underlying this textbook is that good teaching is interwoven with counseling. A prerequisite to counseling is establishing trust so that the individual with problems is willing to share problems and learn to assume initiative and self-responsibility. Strategies for establishing trust vary widely, but counselor behaviors should include active listening, empathy, acceptance, willingness to get involved, and knowledge of when and how to make referrals (see Figure 22.3).

A growing number of schools have **peer counseling programs** because of the tendency for many children and adolescents to trust individuals of their own age more than adults. A certified adult counselor is typically responsible for carefully selecting, training, and mentoring peer counselors who work one-on-one or in small groups. Peer counseling is often interwoven with challenging physical activity programs like ropes courses and wilderness camping that help develop trust, cooperation, and positive interdependence. Peer counseling may also involve cooperative care of animals, horseback riding, or frisbee activities with a dog, because some individuals initially relate better to animals than to people.

Involvement in small-group sharing sessions and support networks with others who have similar problems is another counseling technique. A good example of this approach is the Alcoholics Anonymous program, which has been adapted to many kinds of dependency and special needs. Strategies of particular value are helping persons to understand and share their problems (e.g., to stand in front of peers, admit a problem, and ask for help) and providing mentors who give one-on-one help and support.

Cooperative Home-School-Community Intervention Programs

The ecological approach of home-school-community programs is built on recognition that behavior, even serious emotional disturbance, is affected by interaction with many specific factors in the social and physical environment. For optimal progress in managing problems, all of the human beings in an individual's life must work as a team. Turnbull and Ruef (1996) state six major challenges in providing support for individuals with severe emotional disturbance:

1. **Assessing problem behaviors.** Family members and school personnel should work together to cooperatively identify specific problem behaviors and decide on strategies for coping and change that will work at home and at school. Often school personnel must provide parents with formal training in behavior management if strategies are to succeed. See Chapter 7. Of particular importance is **consistency** in preventing and handling specific problem behaviors. It is also important to refrain from blaming individuals and/or families (i.e., remember that many factors interact to cause behaviors).

2. **Incorporating structure in routines. Structure** is a behavior management strategy that emphasizes sameness in (a) sequence of daily activities, (b) social and physical environment, (c) teaching or parenting style, (d) rules, and (e) consequences of behavior. Structure is discussed in detail in Chapter 7 (see Table 7.8) and Chapter 20. The principle of structure, which is associated with the **command teaching style,** is implemented when an individual has extreme difficulty in coping with change or handling personal freedom. Such individuals often display **catastrophic reactions** (temper tantrums, uncontrollable sobbing, aggressive acts) in response to new or unexpected stimuli, such as a different food at mealtime or a chance happening that alters the day's schedule.

Inappropriate behaviors are minimized when routines, menus, and the like are written out or indicated by pictures on a bulletin board; everyone knows what to expect, and necessary deviations are carefully explained well ahead of time. Contracts that everyone signs can help clarify the roles of various individuals (including the child) in creating and maintaining structure.

3. **Enhancing communication.** This challenge involves teaching everyone ways to improve verbal and nonverbal communication. Especially important is the use of gesture and body language in expressing positive emotion. See Chapters 8, 9, 15, and 16. Dance therapy often focuses on this concern.

4. **Expanding relationships.** Most individuals with severe problems have few emotionally connected, reciprocal relationships with others outside the family. School and community personnel should help families find trained individuals who will assume friend or companion roles on a volunteer or paid basis. Ideally, inclusion strategies at school lead to the development of genuine friendships, but much work is needed for these to generalize to home and community activities. See Chapters 8, 9, and 15.

5. **Increasing choice-making.** Significant others need to create increased opportunities for individuals with serious emotional disturbance to learn to make choices, to recognize good and bad alternatives, and to face the consequences of their choices. See Chapter 9. First offer individuals a choice between only two alternatives, then between three alternatives, and later more. Carefully structure the way choice-making is handled.

6. **Reducing stress.** Individuals with problem behaviors and associates who are affected by these behaviors all need to learn stress management and relaxation techniques. See Chapter 15. There should also be voluntary time-out places, where individuals can go to be alone and draw upon inner resources. Likewise, crisis telephone service and special counselors should be easily accessible.

Exercise and Serious Emotional Disturbance

Research indicates that exercise is an effective means of reducing depression, anger, disruptive behaviors, and stereotypies (Allen, 1980; Berger, 1994; Elliott, Dobbin, Rose, & Soper, 1994; Levinson & Reid, 1993; Yell, 1988). Jogging and other forms of aerobic exercise tend to yield better results than less vigorous activity, although as little as 5 minutes of walking can elevate mood (see Figure 22.4). In general, exercise as an intervention for emotional disturbance should be:

1. perceived as pleasant and enjoyable;
2. aerobic or as close to aerobic as the individual can tolerate with ease;
3. noncompetitive;
4. nonthreatening (i.e., a closed motor activity that is predictable, repetitive, and routine);
5. of moderate intensity for at least 20 to 30 minutes; and
6. used two or three times a day or as often daily as an individual feels the exercise is beneficial.

The criterion of exercising two, three, or more times a day is based on the assumptions that persons want to exercise and that exercise can serve as a voluntary time-out or a time of reflection and relaxation. Individuals should not be required to exercise as part of treatment or therapy, but many options (e.g., swimming, cycling, walking, horseback riding, skating) should be available. The criterion of wanting to exercise is probably the most important, in that an activity must feel good to have mental health benefits.

When possible, exercise should be accompanied by **music** of the individual's choice. This principle requires the availability of headphones. Individuals with manic, aggressive, or hyperactive conditions should be permitted to choose from several selections of slow, quiet music, whereas individuals with depression should be encouraged to choose from fast, energizing music.

Schools, hospitals, and centers designed for treatment of serious emotional disturbance typically have good exercise programs. Most public schools, in contrast, must restructure facilities and rules to create opportunities for exercise to be used as a time-out or a counseling time when a trained adult or peer counselor can exercise with the person needing help and create the informal setting needed by many individuals to develop trust and share problems. Consideration should also be given to where individuals can safely exercise in their apartment buildings, homes, and neighborhoods.

Adapting the Public School Program

Students whose behavior problems are so severe that they meet federal law eligibility requirements for special services are often assigned to separate, adapted physical education instruction because their behaviors pose a safety threat to others or severely disrupt regular class activities. A class size not larger than 12 students is strongly recommended because behaviors of such children are extremely hard to manage. Additionally, paraprofessionals should be assigned to individual students, as needed, and supports like portable phones to call for help in case of emergency should be provided.

Occasionally a student with serious emotional disturbance will be integrated into regular physical education; in such cases, class size should be reduced and peer counselors or partners should be assigned. The physical educator should negotiate for whatever supports are needed to assure everyone's safety.

General Guidelines for Conducting Class

General guidelines for conducting a class of students with serious emotional disturbance are as follows:

1. Display appropriate authority. Let students know you are competent to handle any situation that might arise, but that you expect and will reward good behavior.
2. Explain the class goals on the first day, and describe the routine to be followed during class periods. Provide the amount of structure needed to minimize discipline problems.
3. Meet individually as often as necessary with each student, discuss goals, and cooperatively develop a **contract** that states what each of you must do for the student to achieve each goal. When appropriate, include the student's peer counselor or paraprofessional in these meetings. Help the student see how her or his goals fit with the group goals.
4. Keep class rules simple, and set as few rules as possible. An illustrative set of rules is as follows:
   Follow directions.
   Keep hands, feet, and objects to yourself.
   Do NOT leave the room without permission.
   No swearing or teasing.
   No yelling or screaming.
5. Clearly explain the consequences of following and breaking rules. The consequences of following rules are typically individual or group rewards. The consequences of breaking rules typically depend on whether the misbehavior was **aggressive** (e.g., hitting, biting, verbal threat) or **noncompliant** (e.g., failure to stay on task or give personal best).
6. Involve the students in setting the consequences, posting these on the wall, and helping to enforce them. Agreement on consequences should occur early in the semester, when a contract is signed by students and teacher, indicating that everyone understands the system. Usually the consequence for **aggressive behavior** is some kind of punishment, whereas the consequence for **noncompliant behavior** depends on its underlying cause.

If noncompliance is a form of acting out and trying to get attention, it is ignored. If noncompliance is an indicator of anxiety or confusion, the teacher should ask, "Do you need help?" and then respond accordingly.

7. Demonstrate consistency in enforcing rules and providing positive feedback. Aim for a 5:1 praise/criticism ratio.

Applied Behavior Analysis (ABA) Principles

According to the National Consortium for Physical Education and Recreation for Individuals with Disabilities (NCPERID, 1995) standards, physical educators should apply applied behavior analysis (ABA) principles when teaching students with serious emotional disturbance. These principles include the following:

1. Target specific behaviors that need to be changed and carefully define all components of these behaviors.

2. Observe, chart, and analyze the behaviors to be changed.

3. Select and apply specific strategies to achieve behavior changes. Consider the following when selecting strategies:
    - Signals for getting attention, starting, and stopping activities
    - Routines for making transition from one activity to another
    - Techniques for organizing small groups and game formations
    - Strategies for coping with disruptive behaviors
    - Methods of teaching individual goal setting
    - Pedagogy for enhancing self-management and maintenance

4. Periodically evaluate progress toward changing an individual's behaviors and revise her or his behavior change plan.

More detail about behavior management appears in Chapter 7. Also see the section on principles for managing environment in Chapter 20. Pedagogy concerning individual goal setting, self-management, and maintenance appears in Chapters 8 and 9, which focus on assessment and pedagogy particularly relevant for students with serious emotional disturbance.

Transitions From Activity to Activity

Transitions from one activity to another are particularly difficult for many children with serious ED. In classes where all students have serious ED, *the use of teaching stations might be contraindicated* until children can handle such change. A progression should be used when introducing children to the routine of rotating from station to station. At first only two stations should be used, then three, and then more when students are ready. Rotation from station to station should always be in the same direction, traditionally counterclockwise. A time limitation (usually 10 seconds) should be given for rotation from station to station. This can be enacted by the cue, "Ready, change stations, 1-2-3-4-5-6-7-8-9-10." By the time the teacher counts aloud to 10, all students should be at their next station. When a student with serious ED is integrated into regular physical education, a partner is often needed to get her or him from station to station.

Lesson plans in physical education usually have three distinct parts: introductory activities (roll call, warm-up), lesson body, and summary (cool-down). The lesson body often has several subparts (e.g., different games or practice of different motor skills). Transitions from one part of the lesson to another should be carefully structured. Whereas non-ED children thrive on change and the goal is to teach them as many games or drills as possible, children with serious ED need more time on each activity. They also need specific instruction on getting into game formations and changing game formations (see Chapter 12, pages 333–337). Assessment and, subsequently, individual learning objectives should include such activities as "Given a setting with 11 classmates, demonstrate ability to move from a circle formation to a line formation in 10 seconds."

Behavior Management Techniques

Behavior management, also called **contingency management,** is the major pedagogy used in most physical education classes. When a class contains several students with serious ED, much creativity is needed to find effective rewards and punishments. Following are brief descriptions of some techniques.

Time-Outs

The most frequently used punishment is the **isolation time-out,** the exclusion of the student from the activities of the group for a specified number of minutes. Usually this involves going to a corner or bench that is as distant as possible from the group and facing away from the group. The rationale behind the use of time-out as a punishment is that students want to be involved in the activity and therefore a time-out will decrease the frequency of misbehaviors. This rationale often is not sound for individuals with serious ED who lack the social competency to care about being with their peers and being involved in the activity like everyone else. It has been argued that time-outs are overused, causing students to annually miss many minutes of instruction (Costenbrader & Reading-Brown, 1995). Teachers therefore need to consider alternatives to time-outs or ways to make time-outs a positive learning experience.

Students with serious ED who receive many time-outs probably are not ready for group recreational activities. A viable alternative is to change the curriculum (Ferro, Foster-Johnson, & Dunlap, 1996). Availability of a paraprofessional or peer counselor enables the teacher to help the student choose to learn another activity that he or she will find more reinforcing.

Time-outs can be used to teach **self-management skills** rather than as punishment. When used for self-management, time-outs can involve (a) imposing a time lapse between an upsetting incident and the expression of emotion by counting and/or walking a short distance away or (b) voluntarily withdrawing for several minutes from an environment that is upsetting. Teachers should model the time-lapse type of time-out (e.g., counting aloud to 10) as a means of delaying their reactions to some misbehaviors and explain this procedure to the students. Individuals with serious ED need to learn that everyone gets angry and this is OK; the important thing is learning how to control anger.

Special time-out areas both at school and at home should be made available for students to go to during voluntary withdrawal. Assuming that the purpose of voluntary withdrawal is to get control of emotions, the time-out area can be a quiet, darkened room where relaxation techniques are performed or a room where aerobic exercise equipment permits tension reduction. Use of voluntary time-out assumes that students have received instruction in relaxation and tension control (see Chapter 15). In the school setting special time-out areas require monitoring by a trained counselor or paraprofessional.

The Good Behavior Game

The *Good Behavior Game* is a behavior management technique that helps students to help each other conform to on-task behavior (Vogler & French, 1983). Tokens in the form of frowny faces are given to class squads (six students in size) for each student who is not on task. Squads with the fewest tokens are rewarded with free time. The *Good Behavior Game* involves everyone on a squad helping and monitoring each other so as to achieve a desired reward; thus, it teaches caring behaviors.

Group Evaluation Systems

Whereas in the *Good Behavior Game* the teacher traditionally makes decisions about whose behavior is good and bad, the trend is toward group self-evaluation systems that are collaborative and peer-mediated (Salend, Whittaker, & Reeder, 1992). The group evaluation system involves several steps:

1. Divide the group into teams of three or four students each.
2. Select a target behavior that everyone needs to work on. Our example will be talkouts—verbalizations without permission. Tell the students that they will be evaluating their team on talkout misbehavior, and acquaint them with the 5-point rating scale to be used.
3. Give the team 2 min to discuss the team's talkout misbehavior and agree on a team rating.
4. Compare each team's rating with the teacher's and award points or tokens for (a) the accuracy of the team's rating, defined as how closely it matches the teacher's rating, and (b) low misbehavior scores.
5. Arrange for teams to exchange their points or tokens for sport-oriented rewards like tickets to a sport event, sport equipment or magazines, or extra class time on their favorite sport.

Cognitive Psychology/Humanistic Techniques

Cognitive psychology/humanistic techniques emphasize counseling approaches to helping students learn to think through problems, assume responsibility for their own actions and for how these affect others' behavior, and improve their self-concepts. Research indicates that children with serious ED have poor self-concepts and poor attitudes toward physical activity (Politino & Smith, 1989). Illustrative of physical education programs that use the humanistic approach is the **social development or social responsibility model** of Don Hellison (1978, 1984). Use of this model begins with assessment to determine level of social development; the goal then is to provide curriculum that will enable students to advance from level to level (DeBusk & Hellison, 1989).

Hellison posits six levels of social development. Level 0, *Irresponsibility,* is characterized by disruptive behaviors, abuse, and refusal to participate and cooperate. Level 1, *Self-Control,* is beginning awareness of the importance of accepting responsibility for one's actions; the student is no longer disruptive, but neither is he or she prepared, productive, or fully participating. Level 2, *Involvement,* is characterized by genuine efforts to follow instructions and to cooperate with others; behavior is inconsistent, however, and students need frequent prompts and rewards. Level 3, *Self-Responsibility,* is evidenced by ability to work independently, set personal goals, and stay on task with minimal or no assistance. Level 4, *Caring,* is characterized by self-initiative in helping and supporting others; students are able to empathize and sustain caring relationships. Level 5, *Going Beyond,* is the social maturity to accept leadership responsibilities.

Curriculum to advance movement toward self-responsibility and leadership is built on humanistic philosophy and pedagogy. Emphasis is on students learning to make choices and accept responsibility. First, the teacher develops **contracts** that students sign. Gradually, students assume responsibility for their own contracts. Initially, contracts are for short periods, like 5 or 10 min, but later, they may structure several days or weeks.

In addition to contracting, students are taught social skills like negotiation and compromise.

Ecological Concerns and Specific Conditions

Serious behavior problems can be reduced by **changing the content of curricular activities** to better meet student interests and needs (Ferro et al., 1996). Illustrative changes include modifying the difficulty of an activity, offering students choices of activities and modifiers, and taking students on field trips to reinforce their understanding that activities being learned in class are transferable to community programs.

In summary, physical education instruction of students with serious ED is extremely demanding and requires **small class sizes** and the availability of **many supports.** Time must be made available for home visits and involvement in cooperative home-school-community intervention programs if teaching is to be effective and result in achievement of transition goals and lifespan healthy lifestyle. Following are brief discussions of how physical educators can cope with or manage specific serious ED conditions.

Strategies for Schizophrenia

Students with schizophrenia generally do not respond well to firm discipline, particularly if they have paranoid tendencies or fear authority figures. The presence of schizophrenic behaviors depends largely on whether medication is working properly. Environmental factors sometimes affect the way prescription drugs work, resulting in good and bad days from a behavioral perspective. High-stress situations, such as competitive sport and challenges to learn new motor tasks that the individual perceives as hard, dangerous, or threatening, should be avoided. Instructional objectives related to the content in Chapter 8 (self-concept), Chapter 9 (social competence), and Chapter 15 (play and recreation) should guide class activities.

Students often seem out of contact with reality or sometimes talk about hallucinations. The best teacher responses to such behaviors are "You know that is not true" or "That doesn't make sense." The teacher should not *play along* with hallucinations or ask questions pertaining to them, thereby appearing to be interested.

In students with schizophrenia, even small bits of criticism can elicit destructive behavior. The physical educator should understand that hostility is basically a **protective reaction.** Some students feel endangered by criticism or even by helpful suggestions. Yet such students must be given firm limits. They must also learn that there are adults who do not get angry when they misbehave. The physical educator must combine friendliness and warmth with consistent enforcement of limits. Should a temper tantrum occur, it is better not to try to talk over the noise. A student driven by panic or rage is out of contact with reality, and reasoning will not help. Sometimes, the only alternative for stopping aggressive behavior is physical restraint.

The following suggestions may help:

1. Prevent conflict that might cause temper tantrums. Overlook minor transgressions. Each temper tantrum is a step backward.

2. If the student becomes aggressive, try to distract him or her. Introduce some new toy or game. Use humor.

3. Should a student strike or bite you, do not become ruffled or angry. In a cool, calculated manner, say something like, "Ouch, that hurt! What in the world did I do to cause you to bite me?"

4. Do not show fear or confusion about a behavior. Students with schizophrenia tend to be extrasensitive to the feelings of teachers and might use such information to manipulate the adult. Never say, for instance, "I just don't understand you" or "I don't know what to do with you."

5. Do not use threats of physical violence or abandonment. Avoid all forms of physical punishment, because such punishment reinforces paranoid beliefs.

6. Reward good behavior and structure the situation to avoid bad behavior.

7. Create situations for learning to relate socially to others in movement exploration (see Figure 22.5), dance, and individual and dual sports before pushing the student into the complex human relationships of team sport strategy.

8. Structure play groups and/or class squads very carefully, maintaining a balance between the number of aggressive and the number of passive persons. The school psychologist may help with this endeavor.

Strategies for Anger and Aggression

Most of the guidelines for working with schizophrenia apply to working with anger and aggression. The major difference is that traditional behavior management strategies (see Chapter 7) are more successful when schizophrenia or other biochemical conditions are not present. Adult and peer counseling should help children identify sources of anger and learn to avoid or minimize contact with the persons or situations that make

FIGURE 22.5 Sharing a piece of tubular jersey during a guided movement exploration lesson helps two children to begin to relate to each other socially in a nonthreatening setting.

them angry. The **talking-bench strategy** is used when two persons get into an argument. The individuals go to a designated area, remain seated until differences are resolved, and then report the outcome to the teacher. Time missed from physical activity is made up.

Physical education should include activities that permit students to express hostility in socially acceptable ways (see Figure 22.6): punching a bag, jumping, leaping, throwing, pushing, and pulling. Offensive skills like the smash and volleyball spike can be practiced when tension is especially great. It sometimes helps to paint faces on the balls and punching bags. The teacher can join in stomping empty food cans, paper cups turned upside down, and balloons. The making of noise itself relieves tension.

Students must learn that it is acceptable to take out aggressions on things but never on persons or animals. Thus, boxing or wrestling is contraindicated for some students with serious ED. Aggressive persons often can be developed into good squad leaders. Always, they demand special attention—a personal "Hello, John" at the *first* of the period and the frequent use of their names throughout class instruction.

School-based anger management programs for adolescents with serious ED teach the physiology, triggers, and consequences of anger as well as coping strategies for managing anger (Kellner & Tutin, 1995). Students are taught to keep a **hassle log.** This self-monitoring device allows he or she to record (a) incidents that trigger anger, (b) ways he or she handled each incident, (c) self-appraisal of the degree of anger experienced, and (d) self-appraisal of skill in handling the

incident. Considerable emphasis is placed on helping students identify the signs of anger in their own and others' bodies (e.g., red and twisted face, quickly beating heart, sweaty palms, raised voice). Physical education incidents that cause anger are role-played, with students making up scripts for right and wrong ways to manage anger.

The underlying assumption is that students want to control their anger but lack coping skills. A part of each lesson is therefore spent in teaching and practicing specific skills such as relaxation, assertion, self-instruction, thinking ahead, self-evaluation, and problem solving (see Chapters 9 and 15). An occasional display of uncontrolled anger is not punished but treated as a relapse. Small group size permits everyone to be involved in discussing the incident and suggesting ways they can work together to prevent further relapses.

Strategies for Depression and Withdrawal

Depression is manifested by social withdrawal, loss of initiative, a decrease in appetite, and difficulty in sleeping. Persons with depression generally have a self-depreciating attitude, be-lieve that they are bad, and wish to punish themselves. Suicide, truancy, self-destructive behaviors like head banging, and disobedience may all be behavioral equivalents of depression.

More than anything else, persons who are depressed need to be kept active. Yet, they often refuse to participate in physical activity. They have no desire to learn new skills since life is not worth living and they intend to kill themselves anyway. Some persons will sit for days, crying and thinking of methods of suicide. Whereas most of us are inclined to sympathize with anyone who cries, displaying a rough, noncommittal exterior to individuals who are depressed is best. For instance, the person may be asked, "Do you play golf?" The typical response is a self-depreciating, "I'm not any good" or "I'm not good enough to play with so-and-so." Instead of trying to build up the person's ego, as a teacher might do with a well person, it is best to agree and make a statement like "That's probably true!" In other words, the teacher should **mirror** or restate the person's thoughts rather than contradict him or her. Psychologists concur that praise and compliments only make persons who are depressed feel more unworthy.

They feel guilty when others say good things about them and/or are nice to them.

Severe depression is treated with antidepressant medications. Persons who are depressed generally follow instructions but will not engage in activities voluntarily. They often must be taken gently by the arm, pulled to an upright position, and accompanied to the activity site.

Strategies for Anxiety, Fear, and Withdrawal

Most authorities concur that students should not be forced to participate in activities that they fear or intensely dislike. Swimming, tumbling, and apparatus seem to evoke withdrawal reactions more often than do other physical education activities. In most persons, these fears gradually subside when it becomes obvious that the peer group is having fun. Coaxing, cajoling, and reasoning accomplish little. In the case of actual behavior disorders, psychotherapy and other specialized techniques are generally needed.

Desensitization, for example, is a behavior management strategy that uses a carefully planned progression of activities to gradually reduce fear reactions to a stimulus. The underlying assumption is that a stimulus like a snake, climbing apparatus, or swimming setting becomes less frightening when exposure to it occurs in small chunks with continuous reassurance about safety. The following desensitization steps might be used with a child who fears heights and refuses to try activities on a climbing apparatus.

1. The child looks at pictures of other children playing on the climbing apparatus and tells the teacher what she or he sees. The child plays with dolls on a miniature replica of the apparatus and observes other children playing on the apparatus.
2. The child walks in a circle around the apparatus while holding the teacher's hand.
3. The child and teacher take walks that each time come closer to the apparatus, until child is willing to reach out and touch the apparatus with various body parts.
4. The child sits or stands on low rungs of the apparatus while the teacher supports the child's body; duration of time in contact with apparatus is increased gradually.
5. The child makes transitions from one part of the apparatus to another while the teacher supports the child; the child agrees to allow the teacher to reduce or eliminate physical support for increasingly longer durations of time.

Other techniques for helping individuals to manage anxiety and fear are embedded in Bandura's (1977) **self-efficacy theory,** which was originally posited as a framework for changing fearful or avoidant behaviors. Bandura recommended reduction of fear by improving **situation-specific self-confidence** through one of the following four strategies:

1. Enable individuals to feel safe by task-analyzing and structuring activities to assure personal mastery.
2. Promote vicarious feelings of mastery by watching and listening to models who look successful and appear to be having fun.

3. Use personal persuasion by significant others.
4. Provide counseling or psychotherapy that teaches cognitive control of anxiety and fear.

Pervasive Developmental Disorders, Including Autism

Pervasive developmental disorders (PDD) is a broad diagnostic category for severe impairment in reciprocal social interaction or communication skills and/or the presence of stereotyped behavior, interests, and activities. This category includes such conditions as autism (called autistic disorders in *DSM-IV*), Asperger's disorder, and Rett's disorder.

Types of Pervasive Developmental Disorders

In each of the PDDs, infants develop normally for several months, after which delays or abnormal function become **pervasive,** affecting every aspect of life and seriously limiting the children's ability to learn in the same ways as their peers. Often, specific diagnosis is difficult. Some experts consider all or most forms of PDD to be a part of an autism continuum. However, professionals should be able to define and discuss each disorder as a separate condition.

Autistic Disorder

Autistic disorder is a severe, lifelong developmental disability that is diagnosed by abnormal functioning, with onset before age 3 years, in (a) social interaction, (b) language as used in social communication, (c) imaginative or social imitative play, and (d) repetitive, stereotyped patterns of behavior. Degree of autism varies from child to child; descriptors indicate level of functioning (e.g., high, low). Synonyms include *Kanner's autism, classic autism, childhood autism,* and *early infantile autism.*

The term *autism* comes from the Greek word *autos,* meaning "self," and refers specifically to self-absorption and withdrawal (i.e., lack of responsiveness to other people). Leo Kanner (1943) was the first to describe autism as a syndrome.

Autism is also associated with mental retardation, fragile X syndrome, epilepsy, and other disorders that affect brain function. About 20% of people with autism have IQs above 70; 20% have IQs between 50 and 70; and 60% have IQs below 50. Determining intellectual function is difficult because people with autism tend to score low on tasks demanding verbal skills and abstract reasoning but high on tasks requiring memory and visual-spatial or manipulative skills. From 20 to 40% of children with autism have seizures before age 10. Of these, 75% have psychomotor seizures (see Chapter 19, p. 497).

Asperger's Disorder

Asperger's disorder is a severe and sustained impairment in social interaction, coupled with repetitive, stereotyped patterns of behavior, that seriously impacts function. Unlike autistic disorder, there are no clinically significant delays in language, cognitive function, self-help skills, adaptive behaviors (except for social interaction), or curiosity about the environment. The major *DSM-IV* criterion for delay in language is inability to use single words by age 2 and to speak in phrases by age 3.

Hans Asperger (1944), of Vienna, was the first to ~~his~~ disorder, but his work did not impact PDD diagno- ~~atment~~ in English-speaking countries until its transla- ~~al~~ decades later. Today, Asperger's disorder is often ~~-functioning autism.~~ Some individuals diagnosed as ~~erger's~~ disorder as adults had classic autism in early ~~ut~~ responded well to early intervention.

~~rder~~

~~rder,~~ which affects only females, is a severe de- ~~condition~~ diagnosed by deceleration of head growth ~~ges~~ 5 and 48 months, loss of previously acquired ~~between~~ 5 and 30 months, loss of interest in the so- ~~onment,~~ appearance of stereotyped hand-wringing ~~nts~~ and gait and coordination problems, and subse- ~~development~~ of severe impairment in language and psy- ~~motor~~ function.

Incidence of Pervasive Developmental Disorders

Incidence statistics vary according to the specific diagnostic criteria used. The incidence of autism is about 15 in 10,000 births; this is about the same as the incidence of Down syndrome (see Appendix B). Autism is about four times more common in males than in females. The incidence of Asperger's disorder is about 3 in 10,000 births. The incidence of Rett's syndrome is about 1 in 10,000 female births.

Autism and the Federal Law

Autism was considered a form of emotional disturbance until 1981, when federal law reclassified it under *other health impairments.* In 1990, the Individuals with Disabilities Education Act (IDEA) recognized autism as a separate diagnostic category. In school settings, however, students with autism are generally placed with students who have common problems that require behavior management.

IDEA defined *autism* as follows:

a developmental disability significantly affecting verbal and nonverbal communication and social interaction, generally evident before age 3, that adversely affects a child's educational performance. Other behaviors often associated with autism are engagement in repetitive activities and stereotyped movements, resistance to environmental change or change in daily routines, and unusual responses to sensory experiences. The term does not apply if a child's educational performance is adversely affected primarily because the child has a serious emotional disturbance. (*Federal Register,* September 29, 1992, p. 44801)

The law does not yet distinguish between autistic disorder and other forms of PDD. Autism is considered the broad diagnostic category that encompasses all forms of PDD that adversely affect educational performance.

Causes of Autism

The causes of autism are **neurobiological,** not environmental as first posited by Kanner (1943). In some cases the cause ap-

pears to be **genetic,** because the incidence of autism within families is greater than would be expected by chance occurrence. However, a specific gene for autism has not yet been identified. Autism occurs more frequently than chance would dictate in families with a history of mood disorders, attention deficit disorder, Tourette's disorder, and obsessive-compulsive disorder (Sacks, 1995). Autism also sometimes appears to be **acquired** and is linked to childhood diseases (e.g., rubella, encephalitis), metabolic problems, and brain injury. However, the specific nature of the link is not well understood.

Savantism and Autism

Savantism is the ability to spontaneously perform musical, artistic, computational, athletic, or other kinds of skills at exceptional levels without benefit of instruction or practice. **Savant talents** usually appear at a very young age. Oliver Sacks, a neurologist, provides good coverage of savants (prodigies) in his book of case studies *An Anthropologist on Mars* (1995). The 1988 movie *Rain Man,* now available on video, provides an excellent portrayal of savantism combined with autism. Dustin Hoffman, as the savant, Raymond, demonstrated genius-level calculational and memory skills but was unable to relate meaningfully to his brother or other human beings.

The incidence of savantism in autism (about 10%) is about 200 times its incidence in the population with mental retardation and thousands of times its incidence in the population at large (Sacks, 1995). J. Langdon Down, one of the first observers of the prodigious memory powers of savants, coined the term *idiot savant* in 1887, but today we call such persons *savants with autism* or *savants with mental retardation.* Although savants perform remarkable feats, they typically lack an understanding of what they are doing. For example, some are able to read and memorize hundreds of pages but have no clue as to the meaning of the content.

Illustrative People With Autism and Intervention Programs

About one third of persons with autism are able to live and work fairly independently by adulthood. The other two thirds remain severely disabled. Traditionally, autism has been considered a lifelong condition, but an increasing number of books by parents describe partial or total recovery from classic autism as a result of intensive, structured early childhood intervention programs (e.g., Kaufman, 1994; Maurice, 1993).

Undoubtedly, the best-known person with autism who lives and works independently is Temple Grandin, who has a doctoral degree and works as an assistant professor in the Animal Sciences Department at Colorado State University. Grandin has published numerous books, including her autobiography *Emergence: Labeled Autistic* (1986), observations about her life entitled *Thinking in Pictures* (1995), and more than 100 professional papers divided between her two major interests, autism and animal behavior. Sacks (1995) has written an extensive case study of Grandin. It is entitled "An Anthropologist on Mars" because this is the phrase she uses to describe her inability to understand and relate to human beings and her intense study of human behavior in an effort to make sense of the world. Grandin (1995) states that today she would be diagnosed as having Asperger's disorder, but as a 2-year-old she demonstrated signs of classic Kanner's autism.

A well-known individual who has recovered from autism is Raun Kaufman, who recently graduated from Brown University, in Rhode Island. As a young child, Raun was featured in a book and a television movie, both entitled *Son-Rise* (Kaufman, 1994), which are well worth reviewing. Raun's parents established a private institute in Sheffield, Massachusetts, in the early 1980s that continues to be a popular training center for parents of children with autism. This center is noteworthy in that it does not subscribe to classic behavior management, which aims to extinguish autistic behaviors, but instead emphasizes a psychotherapy approach (i.e., acceptance and imitation **[mirroring]** of the child's autistic behaviors until she or he is ready to give them up or replace them with other more age-appropriate activities). Central to this approach is the presence of an adult in a one-to-one therapeutic relationship almost every hour of the day. Much of the intervention used is dance or movement therapy.

In contrast, Catherine Maurice (1993), a parent using a pseudonym, writes about the gradual recovery of her two children with autism and others who are following the behavior management curriculum of Ivar Lovaas at UCLA. Maurice recommends that parents and teachers read *The Me Book* (Lovaas, 1981) and other materials by Lovaas available through Pro•Ed (see Appendix E). The Lovaas program is used in many public schools and follows classic behavior management principles (see Chapter 7).

Whereas the Lovaas program emphasizes direct compliance, the North Carolina TEACCH program uses a cognitive approach that manages behavior by addressing it as indirectly as possible. **TEACCH** is the acronym for Treatment and Education of Autistic and related Communication-Handicapped Children (Landrus & Mesibov, 1985). TEACCH includes both assessment instruments and instructional strategies. Emphasis is on the use of structure, involvement of parents as co-teachers in the classroom, and the development of functional skills that will enhance community integration.

New Program Trends Involving Parents

Children with severe autism perhaps present a greater challenge to public school personnel than children with any other disability. Progress, which tends to be slow and inconsistent, requires comprehensive, structured programming across all of the student's environments all 52 weeks of the year. State education agencies (SEAs) are therefore implementing plans for in-home training, parent training, and extended, school day, year-round services (EYS). These services are now written into the IEP or IFSP and monitored carefully.

In-home training is service delivery to the child in the home, community, or other natural environments to assist the child in generalizing skills learned at school to other environments. The designated in-home providers conduct a specific number of sessions and hours each week as determined by the IEP or IFSP committee. Training is guided by specific goals and objectives that promote maximum independent performance of skills in all environments. For example:

Goal: Tony will develop, generalize, and maintain appropriate behaviors that are socially acceptable in all environments.

Objective: Tony will demonstrate appropriate toilet search and use behaviors in all kinds of settings 100% of the time.

Objective: Tony will use a bicycle in all kinds of settings, 100% of the time, in ways that are safe to himself and others.

Parent training is similar to in-home training except that it focuses on changing the behaviors of parents and other family members so that they can more effectively generalize behavior management and other instructional programs conducted at school to home and community environments. The specific number of sessions and hours each week are written into the IEP or IFSP. Parent training is conducted in the home.

Extended, school day, year-round services (EYS) are addressed in IEPs and IFSPs because research shows that most children with autism substantially regress if their structured programming lapses for even brief periods of time. One hearing officer in Texas required that the daily written schedule for a student with autism cover 24 hours a day, 7 days a week, including holidays (*Andrew T.K. v. Houston ISD,* reported by Martin, 1996). Time increments in daily schedules should be based on assessed attention spans in performing specific activities. Schedules should be designed so that there is minimal "down time" for engaging in self-stimulating stereotypical movements, commonly called *stimming*. Furthermore, schedules should not include unstructured play or leisure time unless specific objectives require children to learn to use unstructured time. In such cases, the unstructured time is carefully supervised to assure that progress is being made toward achievement of the objective.

Motor Clumsiness and Generalization Problems in Autism

Students with autism typically evidence motor clumsiness (Morin & Reid, 1985; Reid, Collier, & Morin, 1983). *DSM-IV* specifically notes that motor clumsiness is often observed in individuals with Asperger's disorder (APA, 1994), but motor incoordination is widespread at all levels of autism. Approximately 50% of children with Asperger's disorder and 67% of children with high-functioning autism (IQs in the normal or near-normal range) demonstrate a clinically significant level of motor impairment (Manjiviona & Prior, 1995). Formal assessment data collected in conjunction with research, however, is often misleading, in that students with autism often will not respond to test directions and can actually perform better than scores indicate. It is important therefore to observe, and document with videotapes, their motor and fitness performance in informal, natural settings.

Goals and objectives should focus on functional motor competence that permits physical activity for fun and fitness in many settings, not just the acquisition of isolated skills. For example:

Goal: Jim will develop, generalize, and maintain appropriate behaviors for participation in Challenger baseball practices and games in different settings with different buddies.

Objective: Jim will drop the bat and run at full speed from home plate to first base 100% of the time on five different playing fields in different locations.

Objective: On signal, Jim will run to his assigned position on the baseball diamond, assume an alert stance, and focus his eyes on the batter and then on the batted ball.

Objective: On the field, in his assigned place, Jim will run to meet an oncoming batted ground ball in the area he is supposed to cover, stoop to field the ball, and then stand and wait for directions on where to throw the ball.

These illustrative objectives indicate three different contexts for practicing running fast. Running should always be linked to a sport situation or an activity of daily living (ADL) in which running is appropriate. When severe autism is present, the student will need to hold onto the hand of a buddy or onto a short contact **tether** (a rope or towel) that connects her or him to a buddy who also runs. The length of this tether is gradually increased until the tether is no longer needed.

Autistic Behaviors and Pedagogy

Every individual with autism has a different constellation of autistic behaviors, and this constellation changes with age and environment. Assessment of autistic behaviors should therefore be conducted in each of the environments in which the student is expected to function. Furthermore, because autistic behaviors occur on a continuum from mild to severe, the degree of each behavior should be quantified by using a 5-point rating scale.

Physical activity settings are so different from other learning environments that special care is needed in assessment, instructional design, and pedagogy. Following are behaviors that some individuals with autism display and recommendations for intervention. In most instances, the recommendations are for a behavior in the **severe range** of the continuum.

Social Interaction and Social Learning Impairments

Most individuals with autism need intense behavior management programs to learn appropriate nonverbal social behaviors (e.g., eye contact, facial expressions, body postures, gestures). Without these social skills, it is difficult for them to relate to family members, teachers, and peers. Likewise, their lack of interest in the social world means that these children seldom learn through the normal processes of imitation and listening to instructions or advice. Many children with autism appear to be **functionally deaf,** in that they do not seem to hear noises or speech. The only way to get their attention is through firmly taking hold of one or both shoulders. **Firm pressure** is better than light touch because many children are tactile defensive to light touch stimuli.

Most behavior management programs require that the teacher insist on eye contact during one-to-one interactions. This usually means physically holding the child's head in a position opposite one's own head (usually with one hand under her or his chin), giving a specific prompt, "Look at me," and providing a reinforcer for the correct response. Often, in the early stages of learning, the reinforcer must be held up at eye level.

FIGURE 22.7 Partners must be carefully trained before they are assigned to work with a child with autism. Emphasis must be on helping, not competing.

Impairment in social interaction is also manifested by a lack of awareness of appropriate behavior in a gymnasium. Instead of listening to instructions or watching others for cues about what to do and where to go, the child with autism often wanders aimlessly from space to space until taught a particular **floor spot,** which serves as her or his personal space at the beginning of each class and at designated times during class when the teacher calls out, "Floor Spots." Because the child's social learning skills are weak, the teacher must provide specific rules that encourage cognition about what to do in different situations. These rules need to be posted in both pictorial and written word formats.

Traditional punishments like time-outs are seldom effective because the child with autism prefers to be alone. The emphasis therefore must be on reinforcers that are personally meaningful enough to motivate compliance with the teacher's requests. Food is used more often as a reinforcer with children with autism than with other children because social reinforcers tend not to be effective.

After children develop beginning social interaction skills, the content in Chapter 9 should be used to guide physical education instruction. Partners or buddies are extremely important, but such individuals need careful training to understand their partner's social interaction impairments (see Figure 22.7).

Language Impairments

About 50% of children with autism do not talk. Many were using words before the onset of autism. Loss of language and failure to learn to speak are major features of autism that are addressed immediately upon diagnosis by regular, intensive speech therapy. With help, about 50% of children with autism slowly learn to talk and use language more or less appropriately. Many, however, use stereotyped and repetitive phrases. Problems of echolalia and pronoun reversal are common. **Echolalia** (echoing) is involuntary repetition of words spoken by others. **Pronominal reversal** is generally avoidance of "I" by saying "you." For example, the teacher might say, "Do you want to jump on the trampoline?" The person with pronoun reversal would answer, "You want to jump," meaning "I want to jump." The avoidance of "I" is either a denial of selfhood or an absence of awareness of self, while the substitution of "you" shows some awareness of others. In the gymnasium setting, teachers should follow the child's behavior management plan for responding to inappropriate language. Many different approaches are used. Some ignore inappropriate speech, some repeat the phrase correctly, and some use specific extinction procedures.

Among higher-functioning people with autism, communication idiosyncracies like the "Who's on base" scenario in *Rain Man* are common. Speech is often used essentially to talk to oneself, not to others. Individuals with Asperger's disorder have no language problems per se, but their social interaction impairment affects their ability to initiate and sustain meaningful conversations with others. Videotapes that depict physical education or sport incidents with appropriate verbal exchanges give these children models to study and follow. Role playing is also recommended (see Chapter 9).

Difficulty Thinking in Words and Responding Appropriately

Many individuals with autism have difficulty processing auditory input. They are visual thinkers. Grandin (1995), for instance, states that pictures are her first language and words are her second language. Grandin translates both spoken and written words into full-color movies, complete with sound, that run like a videotape in her head. Words representing concrete concepts are easier to translate than words representing abstract concepts. Physical educators should teach to a person's preferred modality (see Chapter 20) and use visualization skills like Grandin's as strengths to help master content. For a visual thinker, demonstrations are more helpful than verbal directions.

Motor Planning and Executive Control Problems

Research indicates that motor planning, sequencing, and other aspects of executive control (i.e., central processing) are deficient in individuals with autism (Hughes, 1996; Pennington & Ozonoff, 1996). In particular, **verbal working memory** seems limited. This means that teachers should match length and duration of verbal instructions to individual capabilities. Temple Grandin points out that she can remember only three steps at a time. She has difficulty remembering phone numbers and other things that she cannot translate into mental pictures.

Pedagogy for executive control problems depends, of course, on the severity of autism. In physical education, **memory games** should be used that involve imitating the teacher's movement and receiving reinforcement. Instruction should begin with imitating single movements and progress to imitating increasingly longer sequences of movement. Early childhood singing games (e.g., *Hokey-Pokey, Mulberry Bush*) provide good structure for memory games; some children with autism seem to respond better when words and sentences are sung to them (Grandin, 1995). Chants that teachers make up to teach a particular concept are helpful also, when used over and over. The chants should be simple, and the child should be encouraged to join the teacher in saying the chant. In small-group instruction, this practice is implemented through choral responding (Kamps, Dugan, Leonard, & Daoust, 1994). Imitation and choral responding activities help to remediate social interaction problems.

Self-talk, verbal rehearsal, and visualization activities are also recommended for remediation of executive control problems. **Self-talk,** out loud or silent, is a means of cueing oneself through a sequence of tasks or movements. Self-talk occurs during the movement. In contrast, **verbal rehearsal** is saying aloud the parts of a planned movement before execution. **Visualization** is making the mind see pictures of a planned movement before execution. The teacher should routinely cue children to remember to use these strategies. Figure 22.8 shows children performing a sequence on a climbing apparatus.

Unusual Responses to Sensory Input, Including Stimming

Individuals with autism respond in unusual or bizarre ways to input from one or more sense modalities: sight, hearing, touch, smell, taste, pain, kinesthetic, vestibular. Sometimes the children appear unaware of stimuli (e.g., functionally deaf or blind), but more often their responses are exaggerated. High-pitched, shrill noises that are mildly unpleasant for ordinary people are extremely painful to some children with autism and thus result in anxiety, fear, and anger reactions, such as screaming, crying, or rocking with their hands over their ears. Sounds that should be minimized in physical education settings are school bells, whistles, PA systems, buzzers on scoreboards, chairs or objects scraping on the floor, and echos. Mainstream physical education with large classes and noisy activities are contraindicated for children with catastrophic responses to certain sounds.

Children with extreme sound sensitivity respond better to individuals who talk in quiet tones or whispers. Whereas increasing the loudness of one's voice to impose discipline or emphasize a point is effective with ordinary children, teachers should decrease the loudness of their speech to a whisper when exerting control over a child with sound sensitivity problems.

Visual stimuli like bright colors and moving objects seem to excessively stimulate some children with autism. The stimulations sometimes are serious distractions that prevent attending to the lesson; more often they cause stereotyped behaviors (stimming) like extended gazing or twirling, spinning, or tapping stimming behaviors. The extreme pleasure derived from certain visual stimuli and concurrent body response to stimming is similar to what many people feel during sexual

FIGURE 22.8 A climbing apparatus is often used to teach memory of sequences (e.g., crawl through hoop, then arm-walk across ladder, then go to X-point and stand, then climb to top). Some children can practice two-part sequences while others practice three- or four-part sequences.

orgasm, except that the pleasure seems to continue for hours or until the child is stopped from stimming. Stopping a child from stimming usually results in screaming, so behavior management protocols for each type of stimming should be written into the IEP and IFSP and followed. Sometimes self-stimulation behaviors are targeted for elimination, and other times they are modified into acceptable behaviors. A child who stands and rocks, for instance, can be taught to use a rocking chair.

Vigorous aerobic exercise on a motorized treadmill is sometimes effective in preventing stereotypic and hyperactive behaviors (Elliott et al., 1994; Grandin, 1995). More research is needed on the prevention of stereotypic behaviors and the duration of time that such behaviors can be prevented by various forms of aerobic exercise.

Many children with autism dislike being hugged. Grandin (1995, p. 62) describes her dislike of hugging as follows: "I wanted to experience the good feeling of being hugged, but it was just too overwhelming. It was like an all-engulfing tidal wave of stimulation. . . . I was overloaded and would have to escape, often by jerking away suddenly." Children who react negatively to hugging and other forms of physical contact are not expressing dislike for the persons who are trying to show affection. Research indicates that children with autism do develop attachment behaviors, but they demonstrate these differently than other children do (Dissanayake & Cross-

ley, 1996). **Sensorimotor integration** techniques (see Chapter 10) are recommended for children who are **tactile defensive.**

Pathological Resistance to Change

Pathological resistance to change is another manifestation of bizarre responses. Emotional outbursts are common when sameness of environment is threatened. Persons with autism want to do the same things every day in precisely the same way. To start a student on a new activity or to make a transition from one activity to another, a hierarchy of prompts is often needed in combination with reinforcements. Achievement of objectives is recorded by writing the number indicating the type of prompt needed (see Table 22.3).

Physically guiding a person with autism through a new movement pattern has traditionally been the pedagogy of choice, but comparison of verbal/visual and verbal/physical teaching models shows equivalent results (Reid, Collier, & Cauchon, 1991). Many persons with autism are **tactile defensive** and thus respond better to verbal/visual input than to verbal/physical.

Making transitions from one activity station to another is particularly difficult and is contraindicated for some students. When several students with autism are in the same class, they may be taught to walk in chainlike file formations with one or both hands on the shoulders of the person in front of them. For other suggestions on making transitions, see p. 560.

Table 22.3 A hierarchy of extrastimulus prompts and independent functions with numbers for recording student's performance level.

1. Full physical prompt met with resistance
2. Full physical prompt
3. Partial physical prompt
4. Light touch reminder
5. Pointing prompt
6. Direct verbal prompt (e.g., "Throw the ball")—this can be words or signs
7. Indirect verbal prompt (e.g., "What do you need to do now?" or "Try again")
8. Independent function when in same setting with same teacher and same materials
9. Independent function when in same setting with different teacher and similar materials
10. Independent function when in a variety of similar settings with a variety of people and materials

Adherence to the *principle of structure,* reviewed earlier in this chapter, makes classes run smoothly. However, structure should be gradually and systematically reduced as an instructional strategy for eliminating pathological resistance to change. **Fading,** the gradual removal of guidance through the use of a hierarchy of prompts, also serves as intervention.

Stimulus Overselectivity and Attention Problems

Abnormally limited attentional scope, often called **stimulus overselectivity** or overselective attention, is the basis of much bizarre behavior. Inability to select relevant cues and to see whole naturally results in learning problems. An example of stimulus overselectivity is discriminating between two people solely on the basis of shoe color or a piece of jewelry. Teachers should adapt for stimulus overselectivity by (a) wearing plain, simple clothing (preferably all the same color), (b) avoiding whistles hanging from lanyards and jewelry, and (c) removing all distractors from the teaching environment.

Cues (often called **prompts** in autism literature) must be matched to a student's specific assessed needs. Assessment should determine, for a particular task and setting, whether the student needs extrastimulus prompts, within-stimulus prompts, or both. **Extrastimulus prompts,** a hierarchy extending from a full physical prompt to no prompt needed across a variety of settings, are illustrated in Table 22.3. The term **within-stimulus prompts** (called "instructional stimulus enhancement" in Chapter 20) refers to increasing the stimulus appeal of instructional materials, as in creating special lighting and auditory effects or altering the size or color so that the object requiring attention stands out. Physical education research is limited but thus far supports extrastimulus prompting (Collier & Reid, 1987), whereas research on academic teaching supports within-stimulus prompts.

Summary of Teaching Suggestions

Specific teaching suggestions recommended by Connor (1990) include (a) teach to the preferred modality, (b) minimize un-

necessary external stimuli, (c) limit the amount of relevant stimuli presented at one time, (d) limit the use of prompts, and (e) teach in a gamelike environment to facilitate generalization. Research by Collier and Reid (1987) does not support limiting prompts. *Reinforcement, task analysis, and physical prompting are the three keys* to motor skill improvement for most persons with autism according to Reid et al. (1991). Sensory stimulation like that provided by music, dance, and water activities is especially successful in broadening attentional scope and providing substitutes and alternatives for self-stimulations. Children with autism proceed through the same aquatic skill levels of water orientation as nondisabled peers (Killian, Joyce-Petrovich, Menna, & Arena, 1984).

Special Olympics and Transition Into Community Sports

Most persons with autism are eligible for Special Olympics training and competition (see Chapter 21 on mental retardation). The estimated 80% of people with autism who have IQs under 70 can profit from the same kinds of programming as people with mental retardation. Preoccupation with sameness is a strength in fitness and sport training, and persons with autism often become models of schedule adherence and hard work.

An increasing number of Special Olympics programs are community-based and serve all ages. Involvement in these programs should be supplemented with other activities that support transition to independent use of community sport and fitness facilities.

References

Allen, J. (1980). Jogging can decrease disruptive behaviors. *Teaching Exceptional Children, 12*(2), 22–29.

American Psychiatric Association. (1994). *Diagnostic and statistical manual of mental disorders* (4th ed.). Washington, DC: Author.

Asperger, H. (1994). Autistic psychopathology in childhood. Translated by U. Frith. In U. Frith (Ed.). (1991), *Autism and Asperger's syndrome* (pp. 37–92). Cambridge, England: Cambridge University Press.

Berecz, J. M. (1992). *Understanding Tourette syndrome, obsessive compulsive disorder, and related problems.* New York: Springer.

Berger, B. G. (1994). Coping with stress: The effectiveness of exercise and other techniques. *Quest, 46*(1), 100–119.

Borthwick-Duffy, S. A. (1994). Epidemiology and prevalence of psychopathology in people with mental retardation. *Journal of Consulting and Clinical Psychology, 62,* 17–27.

Collier, D., & Reid, G. (1987). A comparison of two models designed to teach autistic children a motor task. *Adapted Physical Activity Quarterly, 4,* 226–236.

Connor, F. (1990). Physical education for children with autism. *Teaching Exceptional Children, 23,* 30–33.

Costenbrader, V., & Reading-Brown, M. (1995). Isolation time-out used with students with emotional disturbance. *Exceptional Children, 61*(4), 353–363.

Cumings, D. E. (1990). *Tourette syndrome and human behavior.* Duarte, CA: Hope Press.

DeBusk, M., & Hellison, D. (1989). Implementing a physical education self-responsibility model for delinquency-prone youth. *Journal of Teaching Physical Education, 8,* 104–112.

Dissanayake, C., & Crossley, S. A. (1996). Proximity and sociable behaviors in autism: Evidence for attachment. *Journal of Child Psychology and Psychiatry, 37*(2), 149–156.

Elliott, R. O., Dobbin, A. R., Rose, G. D., & Soper, H. V. (1994). Vigorous, aerobic exercise versus general motor training activities: Effects on maladaptive and stereotypic behaviors of adults with both autism and mental retardation. *Journal of Autism and Developmental Disorders, 24*(5), 565–576.

Federal Register. (September 1992). The Individuals with Disabilities Education Act.

Ferro, J., Foster-Johnson, & Dunlap, G. (1996). Relation between curricular activities and problem behaviors of students with mental retardation. *American Journal on Mental Retardation, 101*(2), 184–194.

Grandin, T. (1995). *Thinking in pictures.* New York: Vintage.

Grandin, T., & Scariano, M. (1986). *Emergence: Labeled autistic.* Navato, CA: Arena.

Hellison, D. (1978). *Beyond balls and bats: Alienated youth in the gym.* Washington, DC: American Alliance for Health, Physical Education and Recreation.

Hellison, D. (1984). *Goals and strategies for teaching physical education.* Champaign, IL: Human Kinetics.

Hughes, C. (1996). Planning problems in autism at the level of motor control. *Journal of Autism and Developmental Disorders, 26*(1) 99.

Jamison, K. R. (1993). *Touched with fire: Manic-depressive illness and the artistic temperament.* New York: Free Press.

Jamison, K. R. (1995). *An unquiet mind: A memoir of moodness and madness.* New York: Alfred A. Knopf.

Kamps, D. M., Dugan, E. P., Leonard, B. R., & Daoust, P. M. (1994). Enhanced small group instruction using choral responding and student interaction for children with autism and developmental disabilities. *American Journal on Mental Retardation, 99*(1), 60–73.

Kanner, L. (1943). Autistic disturbances of affective contact. *Nervous Child 2,* 217–250.

Kauffman, B. (1994). *Son-rise: The miracle continues.* Tiburon, CA: H. J. Kramer.

Kellner, M. H., & Tutin, J. (1995). A school-based anger management program for developmentally and emotionally disabled high school students. *Adolescence, 30*(120), 813–825.

Killian, K., Joyce-Petrovich, R., Menna, L., & Arena, S. (1984). Measuring water orientation and beginner swim skills of autistic individuals. *Adapted Physical Activity Quarterly, 1*(4), 287–295.

Landrus, R., & Mesibov, G. (1985). *Preparing autistic students for community living: A functional and sequential approach to training.* Chapel Hill, NC: University of North Carolina, Department of Psychiatry, Division TEACCH.

Levinson, L. L., & Reid, G. (1993). The effects of exercise intensity on the stereotypic behaviors of individuals with autism. *Adapted Physical Activity Quarterly, 10*(3), 255–268.

Lovaas, I. (1981). *The me book.* Austin, TX: Pro•Ed.

Manjiviona, J., & Prior, M. (1995). Comparison of Asperger syndrome and high-functioning autistic children on a test of motor impairment. *Journal of Autism and Developmental Disorders, 25*(1), 23–39.

Martin, J. L. (1996). *Overview of legal issues involved in educating students with autism and PDD under IDEA.* Paper presented at the Fifth Annual State Conference on Autism, Corpus Christi, TX.

Maurice, C. (1993). *Let me hear your voice: A family's triumph over autism.* New York: Fawcett Columbine.

Morin, B., & Reid, G. (1985). A quantitative and qualitative assessment of autistic individuals on selected motor tasks. *Adapted Physical Activity Quarterly, 2*(1), 43–55.

National Consortium for Physical Education and Recreation for Individuals with Disabilities. (1995). *Adapted physical education national standards.* Champaign, IL: Human Kinetics.

Pennington, B. F., & Ozonoff, S. (1996). Executive functions and developmental psychology. *Journal of Child Psychology and Psychiatry, 37*(1), 51–87.

Physician's desk reference. (published annually). Oradell, NJ: Medical Economics.

Politino, V., & Smith, S. L. (1989). Attitude toward physical activity and self-concept of emotionally disturbed and normal children. *Adapted Physical Activity Quarterly, 6,* 371–378.

Reid, G., Collier, D., & Cauchon, M. (1991). Skill acquisition by children with autism: Influence of prompts. *Adapted Physical Activity Quarterly, 8,* 357–366.

Reid, G., Collier, D., & Morin, B. (1983). The motor performance of autistic individuals. In R. Eason, T. Smith, & F. Caron (Eds.), *Adapted physical activity* (pp. 201–218). Champaign, IL: Human Kinetics.

Sacks, O. (1995). *An anthropologist on Mars.* New York: Vintage.

Salend, S. J., Whittaker, C., & Reeder, E. (1992). Group evaluation: A collaborative, peer-mediated behavior management system. *Exceptional Children, 59*(3), 203–209.

Schaal, D. W., & Hackenberg, T. (1994). Toward a functional analysis of drug treatment for behavior problems of people with developmental disabilities. *American Journal on Mental Retardation, 99*(2), 123–140.

Shoham-Vardi, I., Davison, P. W., Cain, N. N., Sloane-Reeves, J., Giesow, V., Quaijano, L. E., & Houser, K. D. (1996). Factors predicting re-referral following crisis intervention for community-based persons with developmental disabilities and behavioral and psychiatric disorders. *American Journal on Mental Retardation, 101*(2), 109–117.

Sobsey, D. (1994). *Violence and abuse in the lives of people with disabilities: The end of silent acceptance.* Baltimore: Paul H. Brookes.

Sundram, C. J., & Stavis, P. F. (1994). Sexuality and mental retardation: Unmet challenges. *Mental Retardation, 32*(4), 255–264.

Turnbull, A. P., & Ruef, M. (1996). Family perspectives on problem behavior. *Mental Retardation, 34*(5), 280–293.

Vogler, E. W., & French, R. (1983). The effects of a group contingency strategy on behaviorally disordered students in physical education. *Research Quarterly for Exercise and Sport, 54*(3), 273–277.

World Health Organization. (1989). *International classification of diseases* (10th ed.). Geneva, Switzerland: Author.

Yell, M. L. (1988). The effects of jogging on the rates of selected target behaviors of behaviorally disordered students. *Behavior Disorders, 13,* 273–279.

C H A P T E R

23

Wheelchair Sports and Orthopedic Impairments

FIGURE 23.1   Schools should provide opportunities to learn wheelchair sports. (Photo courtesy of Candy Jackson, Courage Center, Golden Valley, MN.)

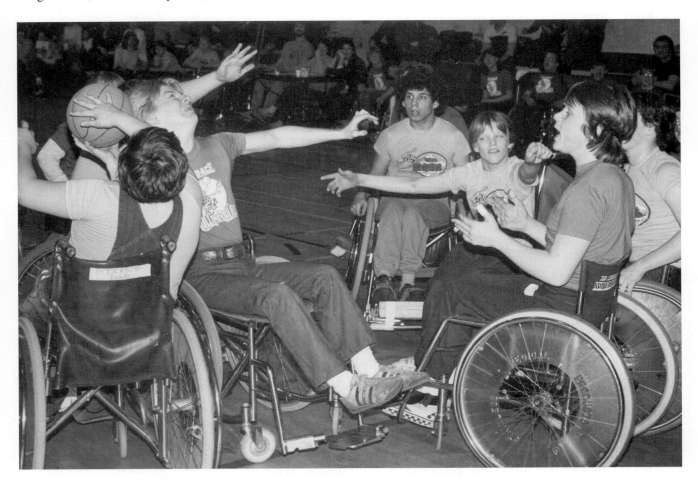

After you have studied this chapter, you should be able to do the following:

1. Define orthopedic impairments, identify sport organizations associated with each, and discuss how these organizations can be used by public school personnel.

2. Discuss wheelchair sport philosophy and the inclusion of wheelchair sports in school and community programs, both integrated and separate.

3. Explain how nerves emerge from the spinal cord and how lesion levels determine severity of condition, walking potential, and physical activity programming.

4. Describe and discuss the three conditions featured in this chapter: (a) spina bifida, (b) spinal cord injury, and (c) poliomyelitis and postpolio syndrome. Include physical activity recommendations for each.

5. Identify common concerns in paralysis and discuss their implications for teaching and coaching.

6. Discuss assessment to guide programming in locomotor and ball-handling activities.

7. Given age, gender, lesion level, and condition, be able to write a physical education IEP and substantiate physical education placement.

8. Differentiate between types of wheelchairs and explain similarities and differences in parts.

9. Discuss wheelchair sports, rules and chair adaptations, and resources for learning more.

10. Know names and background on several famous wheelchair athletes and discuss how this information can be used in teaching, coaching, and advocacy.

Orthopedic impairments are so diverse that separate sport organizations have evolved to meet different needs. Because a major goal of physical education is to develop lifetime leisure sport skills, the next three chapters are organized around the clusters of disability served by major U.S. sport organizations.

The following definition of **orthopedically impaired** (OI) appears in federal legislation:

> **Orthopedically impaired** means a severe orthopedic impairment that adversely affects a child's educational performance. The term includes impairments caused by congenital anomaly (e.g., clubfoot, absence of some member, etc.), impairments caused by disease (e.g., poliomyelitis, bone tuberculosis, etc.), and impairments from other causes (e.g., cerebral palsy, amputations, and fractures or burns that cause contractures). (*Federal Register,* September 29, 1992.)

Most orthopedic impairments do not adversely affect academic classroom performance. They do, however, require adaptations for safe and successful integrated physical education. Moreover, to learn wheelchair sports, students need some instruction each year built around their specific needs (see Figure 23.1). Wheelchair sport instruction, practice, and competition should be written into the individualized education programs (IEPs) of individuals eligible to play in wheelchairs. The IEP should also address transition and integrated community recreation (Axelson, 1986).

This chapter focuses on **spinal paralysis** (spina bifida, spinal cord injuries, and poliomyelitis/postpolio syndrome). These impairments historically have been grouped together and are served respectively by two multisport organizations: Wheelchair Sports, USA (WS, USA) and Disabled Sports/USA (DS/USA).

Chapters 24 and 25 are also about orthopedic impairments. Chapter 24 focuses on people served by the U.S. Les Autres Sports Association (USLASA) and Disabled Sports/USA (DS/USA). **Les autres** is the French term for "the others" and refers to all physical disabilities not governed by Wheelchair Sports, USA (WS, USA) and the U.S. Cerebral Palsy Athletic Association (USCPAA). Chapter 25 focuses on people served by the USCPAA.

Sport Organizations

Sport organizations are the best source of help in planning and conducting activities for persons with orthopedic impairments. Table 23.1 summarizes the disabilities associated with each of the five multisport organizations. WS, USA requires that all sports be played in wheelchairs. In contrast, DS/USA, USCPAA, and USLASA offer both wheelchair and ambulatory sports.

Table 23.1   Orthopedic impairments served by major multisport organizations.

Wheelchair Sports, USA (WS, USA)
Spinal cord injuries
Spina bifida
Poliomyelitis and postpolio syndrome
Disabled Sports/USA (DS/USA)
Winter sports for everyone
Summer sports for amputees
Paralympic competition for les autres
U.S. Cerebral Palsy Athletic Association (USCPAA)
Cerebral palsy
Stroke
Traumatic brain injury
U.S. Les Autres Sports Association (USLASA)
Muscular dystrophies
Arthritis
Multiple sclerosis
Arthrogryposis
Osteogenesis imperfecta
Muscle weakness conditions
Burns
Nonparalytic skeletal disorders
 Congenital disorders (e.g., clubfoot)
 Acquired disorders (e.g., hip degeneration)
Dwarf Athletic Association of America
Achondroplasia
Other short stature syndromes

Note. Prior to 1991, sports for persons with amputations were governed by the U.S. Amputee Athletic Association. This organization dissolved in 1990.

In addition to the five multisport organizations are many single-sport organizations like the National Wheelchair Basketball Association (NWBA), the U.S. Quad Rugby Association (USQRA), and the National Foundation of Wheelchair Tennis (NFWT). These organizations, unlike the multisport structures, are open to people with all kinds of orthopedic impairments. This includes people who are ambulatory in activities of daily living (ADL) but who use wheelchairs for sport recreation and competition.

Wheelchair Sports, USA

First organized in 1956, WS, USA (formerly called the National Wheelchair Athletic Association, NWAA) used to be associated primarily with track and field. It now is the umbrella organization for several national governing bodies (NGBs). Among these are Wheelchair Athletics of the USA (track and field), U.S. Wheelchair Swimming, U.S. Wheelchair Weightlifting Federation, American Wheelchair Table Tennis Association, National Wheelchair Shooting Federation, National Wheelchair Basketball Association, U.S. Quad Rugby Association, and Wheelchair Archery, USA. These are the main Paralympic sports for persons with spinal paralysis. Addresses of these and other sport organizations appear in Appendix C.

Persons, age 16 and over, compete with adults in most wheelchair sports. Junior competition is increasingly available for ages 5 to 15. Several large cities, usually through the cooperation of sport organizations, school systems, and municipal parks and recreation associations, offer youth sport competitions. Illustrative of these are the Junior Orange Bowl Sports Ability Games in Coral Gables, Florida, begun in 1982. The first national junior wheelchair championship conducted by NWAA (now WS, USA) was held at the University of Delaware in July 1984.

Internationally, WS, USA is associated with the International Stoke Mandeville Wheelchair Sports Federation (ISMWSF), named for the famous Stoke Mandeville Sport Centre near London, England, and the International Paralympic Committee (IPC), which has an office in the Rick Hansen Centre at the University of Alberta in Canada. Thus, WS, USA sport rules and classifications are similar to (but not always identical with) those of ISMGF and IPC.

Disabled Sports/USA

DS/USA (previously named National Handicapped Sports) governs winter sports and facilitates fitness for everyone, regardless of type of OI condition. *Sports 'N Spokes* and *Palaestra* include many articles on winter sports (Axelson, 1988). DS/USA is the governing body for athletes with amputations. In Paralympic events, it also serves les autres athletes.

Normal Mental Function and Wheelchair Sports

The term **wheelchair sports** should be preceded by WS, USA USCPAA, or DS/USA to denote the population served. These organizations limit their sports to persons with normal intellectual functioning. Special Olympics offers wheelchair activities for persons with mental handicaps. The widespread asso-

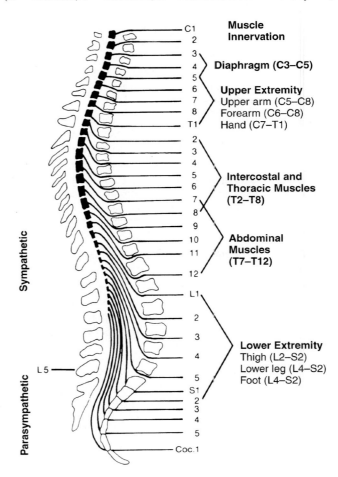

FIGURE 23.2   Thirty-one pairs of spinal nerves issue from the spinal cord and innervate groups of muscles as shown. (C = Cervical; T = Thoracic; L = Lumbar; Coc. 1 = Coccyx 1.)

ciation of the word *special* with mental retardation makes this word unacceptable to most persons with other disabilities. Terminology like *Special Physical Education* or *Special Events Day* should therefore be avoided.

Anatomy of Spinal Paralysis

Spinal paralysis is a broad term for conditions caused by injury or disease to the spinal cord and/or spinal nerves. Paralysis can be complete (total) or incomplete (partial). **Paresis** is muscle weakness in incomplete paralysis.

Spinal paralysis involves both the central and autonomic nervous systems. The **central nervous system** (spinal cord and nerves) governs movement and sensation. The **autonomic nervous system** governs vital functions like heart rate, blood pressure, temperature control, and bladder, bowel, and sexual activity.

Figure 23.2 shows how 31 pairs of spinal nerves issue from segments of the spinal cord and exit from the spinal column. The nerves are named, not for the segment of the cord they come from, but for their associated vertebrae. The exception is the eighth cervical nerve (C8); there are only seven cervical vertebrae.

Nerves are specified by stating region first (cervical, thoracic, lumbar, sacral) and number second. Thus, Figure 23.2 shows that the diaphragm (muscle that enables breathing) is innervated by C3 to C5, the upper arm is innervated by C5 to C8, and so on. Persons with spinal paralysis typically know their lesion level(s)—for example, C5/6 or T12/L1.

Physical activity personnel should be familiar with the body parts innervated by various nerve groups. In general, cervical nerve dysfunction affects arm and hand movements. Thoracic nerve dysfunction affects ability to (a) maintain balance in a sitting position and (b) breathe forcefully in aerobic endurance activities that cause respiratory distress. Lumbar nerve dysfunction affects leg and foot movements. Sacral nerve dysfunction affects bladder, bowel, and sexual function.

Severity of Condition

Severity of spinal paralysis depends on (a) the level of the lesion and (b) whether it is complete or incomplete. The higher the lesion, the more loss of function. *Quadriplegia* and *paraplegia* are terms used in many medical conditions to indicate level of severity.

Quadriplegia (also called tetraplegia) means involvement of all four limbs and the trunk. About half of the persons with quadriplegia have incomplete lesions, meaning that they are able to walk. The disability caused by incomplete lesions is difficult to predict. Schack (1991) presents an excellent case study of a college-age male with an incomplete C1/2 lesion who is ambulatory and jogs. **High-level quads** are those with complete C1 to C4 lesions. These persons are dependent upon motorized chairs for ambulation. They are not eligible for WS, USA sports because WS, USA offers activities only for manual chairs. C1 to C4 quads and some C5 quads are encouraged to affiliate with the USLASA. Persons with complete lesions at C3 and above cannot breathe independently and must carry portable oxygen tanks.

Paraplegia means involvement of the legs but often includes trunk balance as well. *Para-* comes from the Latin *par,* meaning "equal" or "a pair." For sport programming, **trunk balance** is the most useful criterion in determining level of severity. Persons with complete T1 to T6 lesions have no useful sitting balance and must be strapped in their chairs. A complete T7 to L1 lesion allows some useful sitting balance, whereas from L2 on there is normal trunk control. Persons with low-level lesions can walk without assistance (except for braces) but are still classified as paraplegics.

Walking Potential

Many persons judge severity of disability in terms of walking potential. Four classifications, based on complete lesions, are used:

> T2 and above—Nonambulators
> T3 to T11—Walking used only as therapy
> T12 to L1—Household ambulators
> L2 and below—Community ambulators

A **community ambulator** is defined as someone who can walk 1,000 yd nonstop, ascend and descend stairs, and function independently, with or without braces, in activities of daily living (ADL).

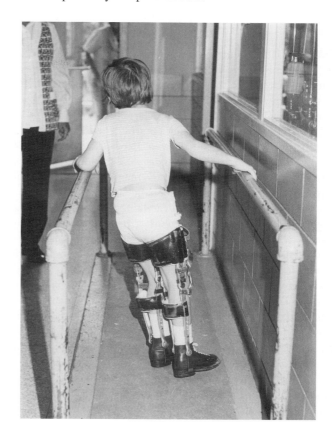

Except for persons with very low lesions, walking requires braces. T3 to T11 ambulators primarily use parallel bars for walking exercise; they wear long leg braces, and persons with the lower lesions can take a few steps with crutches (see Figure 23.3). Most household ambulators wear long leg braces and use crutches. In contrast, community ambulators usually have knee joint control (the quadriceps work) and wear only short leg braces. Persons with ankle joint control (the tibialis anterior and posterior work) may or may not use short leg braces.

Regardless of ambulation classification, people with spinal paralysis are not able to engage in integrated competitive sports safely and successfully from a standing position. This is why the WS, USA promotes only wheelchair sports. Community ambulators may be able to perform some of the skills and exercises in an integrated class (i.e., upper extremity activities) but require adaptations and support services for full integration.

Functional Electrical Stimulation

Technological advances offer the promise of more people walking in the future, but electrically stimulated walking ability is not likely to affect sport potential. **Functional electrical stimulation** (FES) is the computerized application of electrical current to paralyzed muscles to enhance functions like walking, stationary cycling, and hand control. FES machines can be used in physical therapy settings or purchased for home use. This rehabilitation modality, however, continues to be quite expensive. FES is heralded as rebuilding paralyzed muscles, providing neuromuscular reeducation, and helping regain functions like bladder control, hand use, and walking (Petrofsky, Brown, & Cerrel-Bazo, 1992).

Transfers and Rotator Cuff Injuries

Transfers is the generic term for how persons in wheelchairs or on crutches move from one position to another. Ability to transfer back and forth between chair, bed, toilet, automobile, swimming pool, and the like obviously influences capacity for independent living. Transfers are largely dependent on arm and shoulder strength and trunk control. They are categorized broadly as independent and assisted. *Persons with complete lesions above C6 typically need assistance.* C6 function (characterized by almost all shoulder movement, elbow flexion, and wrist extension) makes many independent transfers possible.

Efficient transfers are facilitated by weight management and disciplined development of residual muscle ability. Persons who need assistance with transfers are vulnerable to injury when unskilled persons try to help. Particularly at risk are the **four rotator cuff muscles** that stabilize the shoulder joint. These are known by the acronym SITS, referring to the first letter of each muscle (supraspinatus, infraspinatus, teres minor, and subscapularis). The SITS muscles are often injured when persons are lifted by their arms, as in downward transfers to a mat or swimming pool. Learning correct ways to assist is usually a part of orientation or on-the-job in-service. The best approach is always to ask people if they want help. If they say "yes," then ask for a description of how to provide it.

Congenital and Acquired Paralysis

Time of onset, of course, is an important factor in physical activity programming. Two types of spinal paralysis—congenital and acquired—have vastly different impacts on development. The child born with paralysis is shaped by life events very different from those that surround disability in later life by accident, disease, or war.

The hurt and disappointment of parents coping with a birth defect are often passed onto the child, influencing self-concept and personality development. Overprotection tends to lower self-expectation and achievement motivation. Children with congenital paralysis generally are not socialized into sport unless parents are athletes or adapted physical activity is provided early in life.

Acquired paralysis is associated more with sport success than congenital paralysis. This is because many persons with acquired disabilities have already been socialized into sport. **Age of onset** in acquired disability is extremely important in this regard. Research shows that acquired disability does not change personality and self-concept in adults (Sherrill, 1990). Less is known about children and adolescents.

In general, physical education and recreation programming is the same for congenital and acquired conditions. Problems to be resolved and pedagogy depend mainly on age, level of lesion, and complete or incomplete paralysis. The sections that follow describe the three most common spinal paralysis conditions. Thereafter, the content of the chapter is applicable to each.

FIGURE 23.4 *(A)* Parts of a single vertebra viewed from the top. *(B)* Spina bifida in a newborn infant.

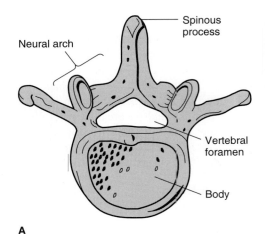

A

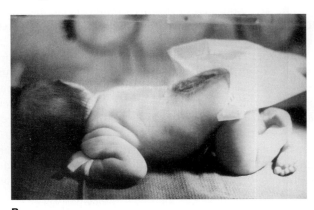

B

Spina Bifida

Spina bifida is a congenital defect of the spinal column caused by failure of the neural arch of a vertebra to properly develop and enclose the spinal cord (see Figure 23.4). This developmental anomaly occurs between the fourth and sixth week of pregnancy, when the embryo is less than an inch long. **Bifida** comes from the Latin word *bifid,* meaning "cleft" or "split into two parts." As yet, there is no understanding of why this anomaly occurs.

Gender, race, geographical location, and socioeconomic status all relate significantly to spina bifida. More girls than boys are affected. Whites have higher rates of spina bifida than other races. In Great Britain and Ireland, about 4 of every 1,000 newborns have spina bifida. In the United States, the incidence is 1 to 2 per 1,000 (about 11,000 newborns each year). Poverty is associated with many of these births, but not all. Families with one child with spina bifida have a 1 in 20 (5%) risk of reoccurrence in subsequent births.

Next to cerebral palsy, spina bifida is the cause of more orthopedic defects in school-age children than any other condition. Whereas the survival rate of spina bifida used to be less than 50%, it is now 90% with aggressive treatment. Corrective surgery is generally undertaken within 24 hr of birth, although some physicians prefer to wait 9 or 10 days.

FIGURE 23.5   Three types of spina bifida.

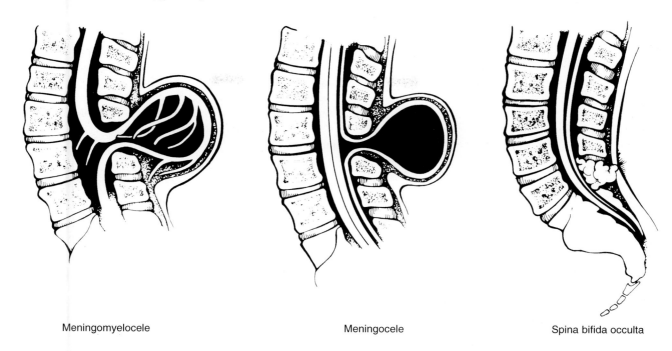

Meningomyelocele   Meningocele   Spina bifida occulta

Types of Spina Bifida

From most to least severe, the types of spina bifida are (a) meningomyelocele, (b) meningocele, and (c) spina bifida occulta (see Figure 23.5). **Meningomyelocele** (often shortened to MM) is by far the most common, and incidence rates (1 to 2 in 1,000) typically refer to it. The derivation of this word is *meningo-* (referring to membrane or covering of spinal cord), *myelo* (denoting involvement of the cord), and *cele* (meaning "tumor"). Figure 23.5 shows how the spinal cord and nerve roots exit through a vertebral cleft and fill a tumorous sac in MM. In **meningocele,** only the spinal cord covering (meninges) pooches out into the sac; the cord and nerves are not displaced. In both conditions, the spinal cord fluid leaks into the sac. Both must be corrected by surgery.

       Spina bifida occulta is so named because the condition is concealed under the skin. The occult, as in magic, astrology, and the supernatural, is hidden or secret. The occulta condition does not cause paralysis or muscle weakness, although it is associated with adult back problems. On some people, a tuft of hair, birthmark, or dimple mark the occulta, but most are not diagnosed unless X rays are taken for other problems.

Nonprogressive Condition

Spina bifida is nonprogressive—that is, it remains the same, never becoming worse. As explained in the section "Anatomy of Spinal Paralysis," the higher the location of MM on the spinal column, the more nerves are affected. Most MM occurs from T12 downward.

       As with other types of paralysis, there is no cure. After surgery, MM is managed by passive range-of-motion (ROM) exercises done twice daily by family until the child learns to creep/crawl and engages in enough activity that ROM therapy is not needed. Also important in infancy and early childhood is lots of handling and activity in the prone,

FIGURE 23.6   Scooterboard activities offer young children with spina bifida easy mobility while building arm and shoulder strength.

side, and upright positions. The emphasis is on establishing **equilibrium reactions** and normalizing, as much as possible, visual and other kinds of input. This is to counteract the tendency of parents to leave babies in supine.

Developmental Activities

Development of head, trunk, shoulder, arm, and hand control is obviously important for persons with spina bifida. Pushing, pulling, and lifting with the arms are major goals because upper extremity strength must compensate for leg paralysis. Push-and-pull toys, scooterboards, parachute and towel activities, apparatus climbing and hanging, and weight lifting are high priority (see Figure 23.6).

Table 23.2 Relationship among location of spina bifida, loss of muscle control, and type of ambulation.

Approximate Location of Vertebral Defect	Point Below Which Control Is Lost	Prognosis for Ambulation	Equipment Used for Ambulation	WS, USA Classification
12th thoracic	Trunk	Nonambulatory	Wheelchair, standing brace	Probable Class IV
1st lumbar	Pelvis	Exercise ambulation	Wheelchair, long leg braces, and crutches	
3rd lumbar	Hip	Household ambulation	Long leg braces and crutches	Probable Class V
5th lumbar	Knee	Community ambulation	Short leg braces and crutches	

Note. Table supplied by Dennis Brunt, who has his doctoral degree in adapted physical education and is certified also in physical therapy. (WS, USA = Wheelchair Sports, USA.)

Orthotics (splinting and bracing) is begun in infancy to facilitate upright positioning as close to the normal age as possible. Brief periods of supported standing from infancy onward aid blood circulation and other functions. Many preambulation devices help children learn to stand and walk at about the same age as peers. Crutches are introduced as early as age 2 or 3. See Chapter 11 for different kinds of crutchwalking and gaits. Whereas physical therapists focus on walking, physical educators teach play and game skills, creative expression, and fitness.

Appraisal of nonlocomotor movement capabilities lends insight into program planning. The following are questions to guide movement exploration. They can lead to games on land and in the water.

1. What body parts can you bend and straighten? What *combination* of body parts can you bend and straighten? What body parts can you swing?

2. What body parts can you stretch? In which directions can you stretch?

3. What body parts can you twist? What *combination* of body parts can you twist? Can you twist at different rates of speed? Can you combine twists with other basic movements?

4. What body parts can you circle? What *combination* of body parts can you circle?

5. Can you rock forward in the wheelchair and bend over to recover an object on the floor? If lying or curled up on a mat, can you rock backward and forward? Can this rocking movement provide impetus for changing positions? For instance, when sitting on a mat, can you rock over to a four-point creeping position?

6. Do you have enough arm strength to lift and replace the body in the wheelchair in a bouncing action? Can you relax and bounce on a mattress, a trampoline, or a moon walk?

7. What body parts can you shake? What combination of body parts? Can you shake rhythm instruments?

8. Can you sway from side to side? Can you sway back and forth while hanging onto a rope or maintaining contact with a piece of apparatus?

9. Can you push objects away from the body? Do you have the potential to succeed in games based on pushing skills, like box hockey and shuffleboard? Can you maneuver a scooterboard? A tricycle? A wagon? Can you walk while holding onto or pushing a wheelchair? Can you push off from the side of the swimming pool? Can some part of your body push off from a mat?

10. Can you pull objects toward yourself? In which directions can you pull? Can you use a hand-over-hand motion to pull yourself along a rope, bar, or ladder? Can you manipulate weighted pulleys?

11. Can you change levels? For instance, can you move from a lying position to a sitting, squatting, or kneeling position or vice versa? How do you get from a bed, sofa, chair, or toilet to the wheelchair and vice versa?

12. Can you demonstrate safe techniques for falling? When you lose balance, in which direction do you usually fall?

Table 23.2 reviews ambulation goals for persons with spina bifida. Most children with high-level lesions are fitted with wheelchairs before age 5 because long leg braces are too cumbersome for easy walking. Thus, physical education emphasizes wheelchair games and sports and activities performed in sitting or lying positions. Most of these can be done in an integrated setting. Swimming is particularly good, although some persons are hesitant about exposing withered limbs.

Hydrocephalus

Approximately 90% of infants with MM have **hydrocephalus** (increased cerebrospinal fluid in ventricles of brain). About 25% are born with this condition, and the rest develop it shortly after surgery for spina bifida. Closure of the spinal lesion means that there is no longer an outlet for excessive fluid, which subsequently backs up in the ventricles and causes intracranial pressure and increased head circumference.

Hydrocephalus is surgically relieved by a shunting procedure (see Figure 23.7). **Shunts** (also called tubes or catheters) sometimes become clogged or malfunction and must be replaced. Common symptoms of shunt problems are frequent headaches, vomiting, seizures, lethargy, irritability, swelling, redness along the shunt tract, and changes in personality or school performance. Persons with shunts typically have no activity restrictions except avoidance of trauma to

FIGURE 23.7 Sometimes, hydrocephalus can be corrected through a surgical procedure called *shunting*. The ventriculo-peritoneal (VP) shunt involves inserting a tube into the ventricles. This tube has a one-way valve that lets fluid flow out of the brain and into another tube that is threaded just under the skin down to the abdomen, where it is reabsorbed by the blood vessels in the membranes surrounding internal organs. A less-often used procedure is to thread the tube into the heart instead of the abdomen. Children with shunts typically have no activity restrictions except avoidance of blows to the head.

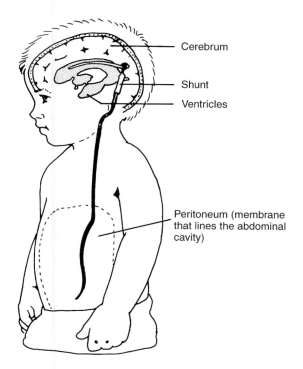

Cerebrum

Shunt

Ventricles

Peritoneum (membrane that lines the abdominal cavity)

head (e.g., soccer heading, boxing, headstands, forward rolls). Diving is controversial. The only visible evidence of a shunt is a small scar behind the ear.

Hydrocephalus in spina bifida is associated with the **Arnold-Chiari malformation,** also called Chiari II. This is a congenital defect of the hindbrain in which the posterior cerebellum herniates downward, displacing the medulla into the cervical spinal canal and obstructing the normal flow of cerebral spinal fluid. Chiari II varies in severity and is managed by shunting. There are many causes of hydrocephalus, but in MM, the Chiari II is the most common.

Cognitive Function and Strabismus

The IQs of most persons with spina bifida are average. However, a large percentage have perceptual-motor deficits, specific learning disabilities, and attention deficits. Content presented in Chapter 20 on learning disabilities therefore applies. **Strabismus** (cross-eyes) is relatively common and may partially explain visual perception problems. The restricted mobility lifestyle in early childhood no doubt limits spontaneous learning about space and figure-ground relationships, so sensorimotor deprivation is another explanation.

Cognitive function may be damaged before birth or before shunting is undertaken. In the past, complications aris-

ing from shunt-related infections caused subtle brain damage, but improved medical technology is reducing this problem.

Posture and Orthopedic Defects

Paralysis causes an imbalance between muscle groups that further complicates the orthopedic problems of growing children. Incorrect positioning and/or inadequate splinting and bracing create additional defects. For example, **plantar flexion deformities** often occur because, without movement, the ankle joint freezes in the toes-pointed-downward position. This makes fitting shoes and braces difficult. In high lumbar paralysis, the hip flexors and abductors are normal, but the extensors and abductors are weak or paralyzed. This imbalance often leads to **hip dislocation.** For children who can crutch-walk, this imbalance causes **toeing inward** (pigeon toes).

Posture problems vary with lesion level. Persons with T12 to L3 involvement often develop scoliosis. Also, the lower extremities of these persons fail to grow properly, so legs are small and frail. In contrast, children with L4 to L5 paralysis tend to develop hyperlordosis as they learn to walk. Without crutches, their gait is a side-to-side **gluteus medius lurch** (see walking gaits in Chapter 11). Persons with sacral-level paralysis walk unassisted but may develop a hip-and-knee flexion **crouched gait** because of weak ankle plantar flexors.

The activities presented in Chapter 14 on postures are helpful for these conditions. In most cases, however, problems are aggressively treated by splinting, bracing, casting, and surgery. These modalities remove children from normal movement and play for weeks at a time and further explain skill, fitness, and perceptual-motor problems associated with spina bifida. Adapted physical activity programming must be aggressive also in teaching these children to appreciate and use their motor strengths and to maintain body parts in good alignment.

Other Problems

Persons with spina bifida experience many problems common to all forms of spinal paralysis. These include bladder and bowel function, sexuality concerns, skin lesions, and obesity, all of which are discussed later in the chapter. Problems are greater for children—especially young ones who lack cause-and-effect understandings—than adults. Children, for example, often play with abandon, disregarding bruises and blows. Without sensation in the lower limbs, children with MM might not notice and report skin breakdown until serious infection sets in. Children also are more likely to be wearing splints and braces than adults, and many skin problems result from poorly fitted orthoses.

Sport and Active Lifestyle Socialization

Persons with spina bifida have the potential to become fine wheelchair athletes. They are not likely to be able to compete safely and successfully in ambulatory sports without adaptations. Integrated physical education should be supplemented with intensive training in wheelchair sports so that lifetime leisure options are available. A growing body of literature is available on physical education needs (Connor-Kuntz, Dummer, & Paciorek, 1995).

Models are especially important because children who frequent medical clinics and have a history of surgery and orthotics often perceive themselves as sickly and unathletic. Jean Driscoll, who has won the Boston Marathon the last 7 years, is illustrative of athletes with spina bifida who can inspire children. Her story and others can be found in *Palaestra* (Huber, 1966) and in *Sports 'N Spokes, TeamRehab,* and *New Mobility.*

Spinal Cord Injuries

Spinal cord injuries (SCI) are quadriplegia and paraplegia acquired through some kind of trauma. Estimated causes of SCI are 48% motor vehicles, 21% falls, 14% violence (including war), 14% sport injuries, and 3% other. Diving causes 10 times more SCI than any other sport. Next highest in risk are football and snow skiing.

Industrialized countries report an incidence of 13 to 50 per million. Approximately 10,000 persons in the United States sustain SCI each year. About 80% are males, and most range in age between 16 and 30 years. Age of onset for about half of all SCI persons is under 25.

With improved roadside emergency service and medical technology, incomplete lesions are increasingly the trend. Of the estimated 200,000 to 500,000 Americans with SCI, the division between complete and incomplete lesions is about equal. Incomplete lesions, of course, are more conducive to sport success than complete lesions. This is particularly true in quadriplegia. In the sport world, these athletes are called *walking quads.* The first question to be asked when programming for SCI is whether the lesion is complete or incomplete. If incomplete, the potential is unpredictable and can be learned only by trial and error.

Most Common Injuries

The most common injury is quadriplegia—specifically, the middle-to-low lesion (C5 to C6). The individual with a C5/6 injury has little or no hand control without adaptive devices, little or no control of the triceps (elbow extensors), and almost no trunk control and mobility. Without good triceps, a person cannot effectively push a manual wheelchair. Therefore, this person is likely to use a motorized chair in activities of daily living.

In sports, however, a properly fitted high-back manual wheelchair permits competition in many activities, especially if the lesion is incomplete. Success in quad rugby is more realistic than in wheelchair basketball, where teams prefer lower level quads with more functional ability. Achievement depends largely on a properly designed chair and motivation. Some persons with quadriplegia have completed marathons (26.2 mi). Many play tennis (Moore & Snow, 1994). In relearning how to swim, they initially need flotation devices but have the ability to swim independently.

The second most common site of injury is the thoracolumbar junction (T12/L1). Persons with this injury can learn all gaits and typically use Lofstrand (forearm) crutches for activities of daily living. They can learn almost any wheelchair sport and, with special apparatus, can stand while snow skiing.

Learning About SCI

The best way to learn about SCI is to attend a wheelchair tennis or basketball game or watch wheelchair track and field and other sports (see Figure 23.8). Almost all marathons include some racers in wheelchairs. Films also increase awareness, particularly in regard to rehabilitation and emotional growth. Films about war veterans usually depict paraplegia, as in *Coming Home* and *Born on the Fourth of July,* both of which illustrate T11 to L2 injuries. Quadriplegia is shown in *Whose Life Is It Anyway* (depicting an architect with a C4/5-level injury caused by an automobile accident) and *The Other Side of the Mountain* (depicting an athlete with a C5/6-level injury caused by a skiing accident). The books and plays on which these films are based, as well as many excellent autobiographies, also may be read. Especially recommended are those of Brooklyn Dodger Roy Campanella (1959) and marathoner Rick Hansen (Hansen & Taylor, 1987).

Adapted Physical Activity for Individuals With SCI

Physical activity for individuals with SCI generally centers on strengthening and using the upper extremities. Concurrently, the person must learn to use and care for a wheelchair. The best approach with a school-age person is to introduce him or her to models who are wheelchair athletes and to affiliate the individual with a team. These persons also should be instructed in upper extremity activities that can be done in an integrated setting.

Students with SCI should be *asked* what they can do and encouraged to help plan their own physical education and recreation activities. Most important is motivation, optimal involvement with peers, and group problem solving about architectural barriers and transportation. Their problems are similar to those of other wheelchair users: a tendency for the hip, knee, and ankle flexors to become too tight, with resulting **contractures** (abnormal shortening of muscles) from extended sitting; **ulcers or pressure sores** from remaining in one position too long; bruises and friction burns from rubbing body parts that lack sensation and give no pain warnings; and tendency toward obesity because of low energy expenditure.

Poliomyelitis and Postpolio Syndrome

Poliomyelitis is a viral infection that causes quadriplegia or paraplegia. The name is derived from the part of the spine attacked by the virus. *Polio* means "gray," referring to the color of the nerve cell bodies it attacks. *Myelitis* indicates infection of the protective covering around the nerve fibers. Specifically, the polio virus destroys only motor nerve cells, which are found in the anterior part of the spinal cord and in the brain. Polio is similar to SCI and spina bifida in that muscles are paralyzed. It is dissimilar in that sensation is intact because the virus does not attack sensory nerve fibers. For this reason, athletes with polio are often perceived to have an advantage when playing wheelchair sports.

Polio epidemics from 1915 through the 1950s left thousands paralyzed. Degree of disability varied according to whether the medulla or upper or lower spinal cord was affected. There are three types of polio virus: bulbar, spinal, and bulbarspinal. The bulbar types affected the breathing centers in the medulla, leaving survivors dependent upon iron lungs

FIGURE 23.8 Attending wheelchair tennis tournaments is a good way to learn about spinal cord injury and other orthopedic impairments. Note the two different types of wheelchairs.

(now called ventilators) for respiration. Today, in industrial countries, polio is almost entirely eradicated. In Third World countries, however, it continues to cause paralysis. Worldwide, about 5 million new cases appear each year.

In the United States, there are approximately 300,000 polio survivors with some degree of disability. In the 1980s, about 25% of these persons began to experience new joint and muscle pain, muscle weakness at old and new sites, severe fatigue, profound sensitivity to cold, and new respiratory problems. This combination of symptoms has been named the **postpolio syndrome.** Its cause is not yet understood. The postpolio weakness progresses very slowly over many years, requiring gradual lifestyle adjustments.

Franklin D. Roosevelt, U.S. president from 1932 to 1945, is the most famous person to have had polio. Paralyzed early in his political career, Roosevelt could stand and walk only with long leg braces and crutches. Until the 1950s, polio was the leading cause of orthopedic impairments in the United States.

Activity adaptations for polio are similar to those of other types of spinal paralysis. However, paralysis is often incomplete, and judging level of lesion is difficult. Because people with polio have sensation, pain is a concern. Muscle and joint pain are particularly aggravated by cold temperature and exces-

sive exercise. **Overuse syndrome** is pain and muscle weakness associated with diminished function after strenuous use.

Common Concerns in Paralysis

Concerns common to all types of spinal paralysis include (a) sensation and skin breakdown, (b) temperature control, (c) contractures and injury prevention, (d) spasms, (e) atrophy of limbs, (f) urination and defecation, (g) sexuality, (h) heart and circulatory function, (i) blood pressure and autonomic dysreflexia, and (j) weight management and osteoporosis. The exception to this generalization is polio, which affects only motor nerve fibers and leaves sensation intact. In polio, paralysis is usually incomplete, and no assumptions should be made. Polio does not impair genitourinary function, so all body elimination processes and sexual activity are unaffected. Each of these concerns has implications for physical activity programming.

Sensation and Skin Breakdown

Feelings of touch, pressure, heat, cold, and pain are impaired by spinal cord lesions. In complete lesions, all sensation below the

FIGURE 23.9 Spinal nerve dermatomes, showing innervation of sensation.

CUTANEOUS DISTRIBUTION OF SPINAL NERVES

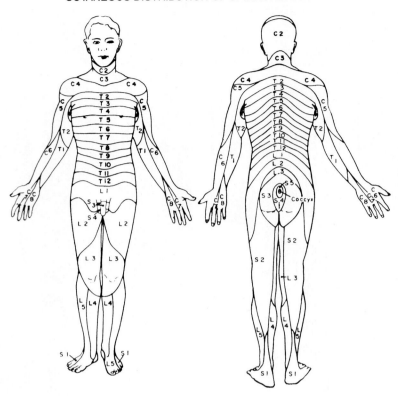

injury is lost. In incomplete lesions, there is no rhyme or reason to the pattern. **Spinal nerve dermatomes** are used to enable persons to point to areas of lost sensation or pain (see Figure 23.9). Whereas movement is innervated by impulses that travel the anterior part of the spinal cord, sensation is innervated by impulses that travel the posterior part of the spinal cord.

A person can have motor paralysis and no loss of sensation or vice versa. Usually, however, both are present. The exception is polio. Figure 23.9 shows which nerves innervate sensation of different body segments. Touch, pressure (light and deep), heat, cold, and pain each have different sensory receptors and their own specific tracts in the spinal cord. It is therefore possible to lose some sensations but not others.

Inability to feel sensation makes persons particularly vulnerable to injury and skin breakdown. Wrinkles in socks and poorly fitted shoes or braces cause blisters that become infected. Scooting across the floor on buttocks (ambulation often used by children) and crawling/creeping may cause scuff burns and bruises that go undetected. Lack of cleanliness in relation to urination, defecation, and menstruation causes itching in able-bodied (AB) persons but, when itching cannot be felt, rashes and infection result.

Persons with spinal paralysis should be taught to inspect their body parts regularly to see that all sores, however minor, are cared for. Skin should be kept dry also, with care given to remove perspiration after heavy exercise and to towel properly after swimming and bathing. Circulation problems related to paralysis increase the danger of infection and make healing slow. Infection can cause severe problems (see the section on autonomic dysreflexia later in the chapter).

Of particular concern are pressure sores caused by sitting or lying in one position for a long time. **Pressure sores** (also called *decubitus ulcers* or *ischemic ulcers*) often result in hospitalization. They heal very slowly. To prevent pressure sores, seat cushions are used and persons are taught to frequently change positions.

Sunburn is a special problem because persons with spinal paralysis cannot feel discomfort caused by sun on skin when there is no sensation. Clothes with long sleeves and pants are recommended.

Temperature Control

Spinal paralysis above T8 renders the body incapable of adapting to temperature changes. **Poikilothermy** is the name for the condition in which the body assumes the same temperature as the environment. To prevent poikilothermy, special attention must be given to appropriate clothing, heating, and air-conditioning. Whereas AB persons often do some vigorous movements to warm up, paralyzed individuals cannot. Teachers must be sensitive to signs of overexposure, especially in swimming pools and during weather extremes.

Fluid intake is closely related to temperature regulation. Hot and cold drinks are recommended aids. Additionally, persons engaging in activity and/or sitting in the sun should be encouraged to drink water about every 30 min.

Contractures and Injury Prevention

A **contracture** is a permanent shortening and tightening of a muscle or muscle group caused by spasticity, paralysis, or disuse. It is felt as a stiffened joint that impairs normal range of motion (ROM). Contractures should be prevented by ROM exercises twice daily. Once a contracture occurs, the treatment is typically splinting, casting, or surgery. Among persons who spend most of their time in wheelchairs, hip, knee, and ankle flexors tend to become too tight. This is true also of AB people who sit a lot.

Stretches should slowly move the body part to the extreme of its ROM, where it is held 10 to 30 sec (Curtis, 1981). These can be done by self, family, or friends. A physical therapist usually teaches technique, after which others assume responsibility. Gentle warm-up exercises should be done before ROM stretches. Stretching is also important prior to sport and dance activity to prevent injury. The same stretches are used as in AB sports.

Spasms of Spinal Origin

Paralyzed muscles in people with lesions above L1 often jerk involuntarily. This is caused by excessive reflex activity below the lesion level. Ordinarily, reflex activity is coordinated by the brain, but in spinal paralysis, impulse transmission is impaired. The stimuli causing spasms vary by person but include sensory input (touch, hot, cold), pathology (bladder infections, skin breakdown), and menstrual period.

Spasms are frustrating and sometimes embarrassing because they draw attention and interfere with activities of daily living. Occasional spasms are good for circulation and help with retention of muscle shape. When spasms are too severe, several treatment options are available: (a) physical therapy, mainly stretching; (b) drug therapy (baclofen, dantrolene, valium, diazepine), (c) nerve blocks, and (d) surgery.

Athletes who use medication should report this to coaches. Use of drugs banned by the International Olympic Committee results in disqualification and loss of medals.

Atrophy of Limbs

Over time, paralyzed limbs decrease in size and lose the attractive shapes associated with good muscle tone. This withering is called **atrophy.** Many persons with lower limb paralysis are self-conscious about this and do not like to wear shorts and swimsuits around AB peers. Trousers should be accepted as sport and dance attire until these individuals are able to accept and appreciate the body as it is.

Persons do tend to stare at atrophied limbs unless sensitized. Prospective teachers should visit rehabilitation and sport settings to see limbs of all sizes and shapes. **Contact theory** posits that repeated contact, combined with attitudinal guidance, decreases discomfort.

Urination and Defecation

All persons with spinal paralysis above S2 (except those with polio) have some kind of bladder dysfunction, requiring that they urinate in a different way. The most common alternative is **intermittent catheterization,** a procedure of inserting a tube into the urethra for a few seconds and draining urine into

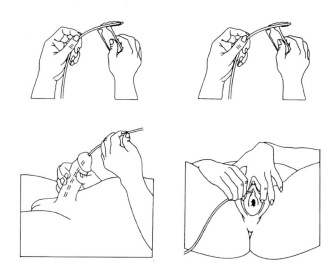

FIGURE 23.10   Catheterization as a means of withdrawing urine from the bladder is used by persons with spina bifida, spinal cord injuries, and other conditions that cause urinary incontinence. The catheter is lubricated and then inserted into the penis about 6 inches or into the female opening about 3 inches. Parents can generally instruct teachers in the correct procedure.

a small, disposable plastic bag (see Figure 23.10). Intermittent catheterization is performed several times a day on a rigid schedule to keep the bladder empty and prevent accidents. Persons with incomplete lesions may feel sensation and use catheterization only in response to need. Many of these persons have hyperactive bladders and urinate more frequently than AB peers. *Holding urine is contraindicated.* Architecturally accessible restrooms should be located near activity areas, and time planned for use.

In early childhood, catheterization must be done by the teacher or an aide, but later, persons learn to perform this simple, nonsterile procedure for themselves. Alternatives to catheterization are the **Crede maneuver** (exerting manual pressure on the lower abdomen to initiate urination), the wearing of urinary leg bags, and the use of an indwelling internal catheter (Foley) that remains inside the urethra.

Whatever the procedure, frequent emptying of the bladder is important. Retention of urine leads to **urinary and kidney infections,** a major cause of illness and death among persons with spinal paralysis. Should signs of infection (flushed face, elevated temperature) be noted, no exercise should be allowed without physician clearance. Any changes in urination frequency or in other practices related to urination should be noted.

Defecation is managed by scheduling time and amount of eating as well as by regulating time of bowel movements. If defecation becomes too great a problem, surgical procedures (**ileostomy** or **colostomy**) create an opening (**stoma**) in the abdomen. A tube inserted in this opening connects the intestine with a bag that fills up with fecal matter and must be emptied and cleaned periodically. These bags are not worn during swimming; the stoma is covered with a watertight bandage.

Sexuality

Sexual function is innervated by the same nerves as urinary function (S2 to S4). Lesions above the sacral region (except in polio) may make it necessary to alter roles, methods, and positions for lovemaking, depending on whether the lesions are complete or incomplete. Capacity for erection, ejaculation, and orgasm must be evaluated individually because both parasympathetic stimulation and reflex patterns are involved. Women with spinal paralysis can bear children (Krotoski, Nosek, & Turk, 1996). Menstruation is not affected.

Heart and Circulatory Concerns

Persons with quadriplegia and high-level paraplegia have abnormally low resting heart rates (Shephard, 1990). This condition is called **chronotropic incompetence** or sick sinus syndrome. Likewise, their heart rate response to aerobic exercise is sluggish because of sympathetic nervous system impairment. Lesions at or above T5 affect heart rate response to arm exercise, whereas lesions at or below T10 affect cardiac responses to leg exercises.

Obviously, maximum heart rates and target zones used in aerobic exercise programs for AB persons are not appropriate in high-level spinal paralysis. Instead, baseline data are collected and individual goals set.

A major circulatory problem is the pooling of blood in the veins of paralyzed body parts. This is called *venous pooling* or *venous insufficiency* and is caused mainly by sympathetic nervous system dysfunction. Specifically, the **vasoconstrictor function** is impaired, meaning that the vessels cannot constrict and force the blood through the venous valves and back to the heart. Two problems result. First, the sluggish return of blood to the heart lowers stroke volume which, in turn, limits the amount of blood available to carry oxygen to working body parts. Inadequate oxygen (also called *arterial insufficiency*) results in early fatigue and/or limited aerobic endurance. Second, venous pooling increases the cross-sectional area of the veins, creating stress on the vascular walls that is relieved by some of the fluid in the blood leaking into the surrounding tissue. This results in swelling (edema).

AB persons have similar problems in jobs that require motionless standing and during pregnancy. We all know the importance of shifting from foot to foot when standing for long periods. People in wheelchairs must use their arms to move paralyzed legs and/or must prop the legs up from time to time. Also recommended is the wearing of **jobst pressure garments** (sometimes called *jobsts*). Recently, many wheelchair racing clothes have been made of tight-fitting elastic fabric that presumably serves to ameliorate venous pooling. Excessive constriction about the abdomen and upper thighs should be avoided, however, because this is associated with the development of blood clots in the extremities.

Blood Pressure, Autonomic Dysreflexia, and Boosting

The baseline blood pressure of persons with lesions above T6 is typically low. Whereas normal blood pressure for adults is 120/90 mm Hg (millimeters of mercury), the baseline in quadriplegia may be as low as 90/60 mm Hg. Blood pressure responses to exercise (see Chapter 13) must be interpreted in light of this fact.

Autonomic dysreflexia (AD), also called *hyperreflexia,* is a life-threatening pathology that sometimes occurs in lesions above T6. The pathology is characterized by sudden-onset high blood pressure/slowed heartbeat, sweating, severe headache, and goose bumps. AD is triggered by a stimulus within the body below the lesion level, usually by a distended bladder or colon because urination or defecation needs have been ignored.

In AB persons, the need to empty an organ is relayed up the spinal cord, but in individuals with spinal paralysis, the nerve impulses are blocked. This sets off a sympathetic nervous system reflex action that causes blood vessels below the lesion level to constrict, thereby raising blood pressure. Eventually and indirectly, the brain picks up signals and activates the parasympathetic system to bring the sympathetic system under control. It does this by dilating the blood vessels and slowing the heart rate but lacks capacity to act on the high blood pressure.

This physiology is important to understand because many elite wheelchair athletes purposely induce AD states to maximize blood circulation during track and swimming events. This practice, called **boosting,** is obviously very dangerous and should be discouraged (Burnham et al., 1994). AD states are induced by drinking huge quantities of water before a race or by sitting on a sharp object like a tack.

Anytime a person with a lesion above T6 vomits, loses consciousness, or appears sick during or after an athletic event, AD should be suspected. Usually, the cause is simply forgetfulness or carelessness about urine needs. AD may, however, be caused by infections or irritations like pressure sores, ingrown toenails, or burns below lesion level. First aid is simple. First, raise the head to a 90° angle or put the person in a sitting position; this helps lower the blood pressure. Next, drain the bladder or evacuate the fecal matter. If neither bladder nor colon are full, check for other causes. Obviously, there should be no physical activity until blood pressure is normalized. Typically, a physician is consulted.

Weight Management and Osteoporosis

Sedentary lifestyles usually lead to weight problems. Nonathletic persons in wheelchairs are at particular risk. Obesity is a health threat to all of us but is more dangerous to persons whose lean muscle mass is reduced by paralysis. Consider the size difference in leg and arm muscles. AB persons use the big muscles of the lower extremities to move their fat around, whereas persons in wheelchairs and on crutches are dependent on the strength of arm and shoulder muscles. These individuals also have less oxygen available to working muscles because of venous insufficiency. For many reasons, the hearts of persons with spinal paralysis are more stressed by obesity than those of AB peers.

Sedentary lifestyles also lead to **osteoporosis,** the gradual loss of calcium in bone tissue. This makes bones more vulnerable to fracture. The fatter one is, the more stress is placed on weight-bearing bones.

FIGURE 23.11 Medical and functional classifications for wheelchair sports. NWBA refers to National Wheelchair Basketball Association.

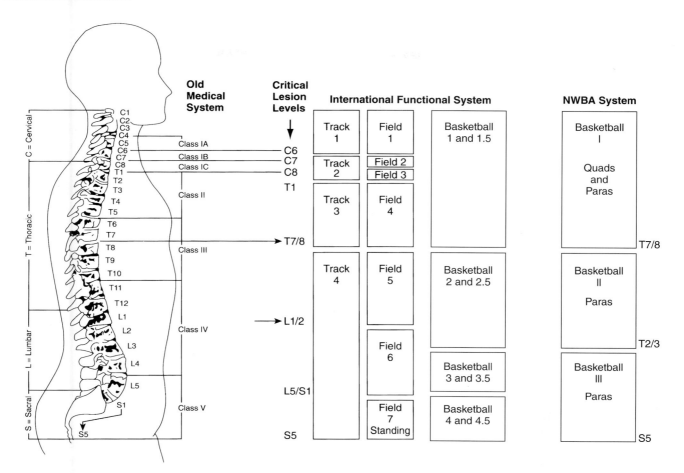

Sport Classification

Sport classification is an assessment system that (a) guides programming and (b) equalizes opportunity in competition. Each sport organization has its own classification system, and there is much controversy about fairness (Curtis, 1991; Davis & Ferrara, 1996; Steadward, Nelson, & Wheeler, 1994).

The **medical classification system,** which developed in the 1940s when competitive sports were begun in England for people with spinal paralysis, dominated worldwide until recently. In this system, three quadriplegic classes (IA, IB, IC) and four paraplegic classes (II, III, IV, V) were assigned to track-and-field competitors on the basis of muscle strength tests and observations of trunk balance. In basketball, a similar system involved only three classes (see Figure 23.11).

A **sport-specific functional system** was adopted in the early 1990s to guide international competition (Curtis, 1991). Whether the United States will adopt this system or continue with medical classification is not yet known. In a functional system, classifiers observe what persons can and cannot do in a particular sport. Assignment is based on a functional profile.

Figure 23.11 shows classifications for the three sports most popular among people in wheelchairs. The number of functional profiles varies for each sport. For example, there

are four for track, seven for field, three for basketball in the USA, and eight for international basketball. Each profile is matched with expected function when there is a *complete* lesion at a designated neurological level.

The basketball classification systems also involve assignment of a point value to each player to equalize competing teams. The points of the five players cannot exceed 12 in NWBA play and 14 in international play.

Critical Lesion Levels for Sports

Of the 31 possible lesion levels, only eight are deemed critical for learning about sport potential. Simplified, each is associated with one or two performance criteria that describe highest function. Persons with **complete quadriplegia** have no trunk control or sitting balance. They use higher back chairs and are strapped in for safety. Progressive use of arm, hand, and finger muscles is what distinguishes between classes. The critical lesion levels are

C6—Have elbow flexion and wrist extension

C7—Have triceps (i.e., elbow extension)

C8—Have some finger control

T1—Have all arm, hand, and finger movement

Persons with paraplegia have full use of upper extremities but vary widely on trunk control and sitting balance. Those with lesions above T7/8 typically must hold onto the chair with one hand whenever they reach downward or sideward for a ball. They have some shoulder rotation that can be used in steering but lack the full trunk rotation needed in most sport activities. Progressive trunk control and balance are what distinguish between the first three paraplegic classes. The critical lesion levels are

T7/8—Have trunk rotation and fair-to-good sitting balance

L1/2—Have trunk extension from a bent-over position

L3—Have sideward bend and return capacity; trunk moves freely in all planes

L5/S1—Can throw while standing

Assessment of Sport Function and Skill

Few skill tests are available for people in wheelchairs (Brasile, 1984, 1986; Yilla, 1993). A good way for beginning teachers and coaches to become familiar with sport function is to learn to administer the *Strohkendl Basketball Function Tests*. This assessment system was created in the early 1980s by Dr. Horst Strohkendl (1986) of the University of Cologne in Germany. This system led directly to functional assessment.

Test 1: Trunk Rotation and Sitting Stability

Give the following directions: "Rotate your trunk as far to the right as possible; then bounce and catch the ball. Repeat to the left." Individuals who complete this test with no balance problems are assigned to Basketball Class II (see Figures 23.11 and 23.12). Individuals with sitting stability problems are assigned to Class I.

Test 2: Chair Sit-Up, Using Abdominal Muscles Only

Give the following directions: "Clasp your hands behind your neck, and lean forward until your trunk touches your thighs. From this position, do a slow, controlled sit-up back to erect sitting position. Use only your abdominal muscles to do this sit-up." Individuals who complete this test are assigned to Basketball Class III (see Figures 23.11 and 23.12).

Test 3: Sideward Bend and Lift Ball Over Head

Give the following instructions: "Place the ball to the side of your chair. Then do a sideward bend, pick up the ball with both hands, raise the ball overhead, and then place it on the floor on the opposite side of your chair." Individuals who complete this test are assigned to Basketball Class IV in the international system or are considered an advanced Class III in the USA system (see Figures 23.11 and 23.12).

Programming for Quadriplegia

Use of the Strohkendl Basketball Function Tests (Strohkendl, 1986) enables professionals to understand that a major difference in sport function between quadriplegia and paraplegia is

sitting stability and ability to rotate the trunk to throw, catch, and dribble balls. Individuals with complete quadriplegic lesions fail all of the Strohkendl tests. They seldom are given much playing time on wheelchair basketball teams because of their inability to maintain balance while rotating their trunk and difficulty in raising their arms above the head. Therefore, most athletes with quadriplegia prefer quad rugby, a team sport developed specifically to meet their needs.

Quad Rugby

Quad rugby (also called murderball and wheelchair rugby) is the team game that most persons with lesions from C6 through T1 enjoy (Hooper, 1991). Played on a regulation basketball court with a four-person team and a volleyball, the game combines elements of basketball, football, and ice hockey. The object is to score points by carrying the ball over the opponents' goal line. The ball is passed from player to player and advanced down the floor by whatever movement patterns that individual abilities allow. There must be one bounce every 10 sec (Yilla & Sherrill, 1994).

Figure 23.13 shows the difficulty that people with quadriplegia have in fully extending their arms. Note also that the players use waist bands to strap themselves into their chairs and often hold on to the chair with one hand while controlling the ball or reaching with the other. Arm splints and specially designed gloves compensate for forearm and hand weakness. A classification system ensures an equitable balance between teams of players with C6, C7, and C8 lesions.

Other Sports for C6, C7, and C8 Lesions

Individuals with C6 and above lesions can engage in all kinds of sport activities (see Table 23.3). This is because there is (a) sufficient elbow flexion to propel a manual chair and (b) enough wrist extension to enable a crude grasp. Propelling a chair with only elbow flexion is slow and awkward, but it works. The hands remain in contact with or close to the handrim. They are placed either (a) with the back of the wrist behind the handrim or (b) with the palm pushing down on top of the handrim in a forward position. Obviously, gloves are worn. Some athletes have completed marathons, but realistic distances to be conquered in a physical education class appear in Table 23.3. The **club** is the **easiest field event** for C6 function, although some persons like the challenge of a discus.

A C7 lesion means that the triceps are intact, allowing elbow extension, a mechanically efficient way to push a chair and give impetus to field implements. Grasp and release is still a problem because there is little finger use.

C8 represents the breakthrough for throwing and striking activities. A **good fist** can be made, and the fingers can be spread. Hand and finger power is not normal but sufficient for fairly good distance with the shot, discus, and javelin. Many persons with C8 lesions enjoy wheelchair tennis.

Remember that many individuals with quadriplegia have incomplete lesions and might therefore perform above expectations. Some can walk and are called *walking quads*. Never place limits on a person.

FIGURE 23.12 The Strohkendl Basketball Function Tests.

Test 1. Trunk rotation and good sitting stability

Test 2. Chair sit-up, using abdominal muscles

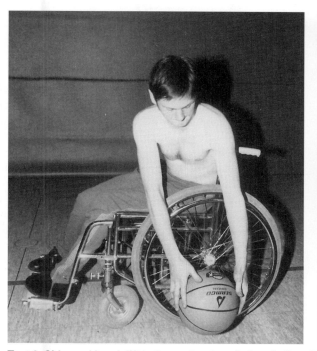

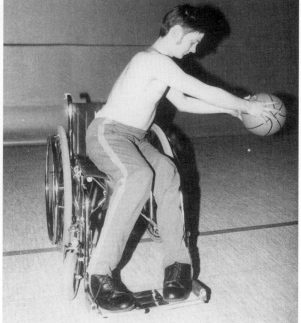

Test 3. Sideward bend; lift ball over head, and place ball on floor on opposite side

FIGURE 23.13 Quad rugby, played by four-person teams and a volleyball, is an exciting contact sport in which players crash into each other's chairs and make the most of residual arm and hand function. (Photo courtesy of Mary Carol Peterson, TOP END by Action.)

Activities for C5 and Above Lesions

Individuals with C5 and above complete lesions lack the arm and shoulder strength to use a manual chair in sport events, so activities must be devised that can be done from a motorized chair. The **slalom,** a race against time in which persons follow an obstacle course, encourages mastery of the hand or mouth device used to guide the chair. **Personal floatation devices** (PFDs) make swimming an achievable goal; see Appendix E for companies that sell PFDs. For individuals who cannot move their limbs independently, assistants must provide therapeutic exercises that take body parts through their full range of motion one or more times a day.

Christopher Reeve, the movie star who gained fame as Superman, is now the best-known person to survive a C1-C2 injury. Watching him in TV appearances lends insight into the abilities of individuals at this level. In medical lingo, Reeve is known as a **vent-quad,** meaning he is dependent upon a ventilator (also called a respirator) to breathe. The amount of air the lungs can take in with each breath influences speech. Reeve uses a **sip-and-puff tube** to control his motorized chair. Little independent movement is possible below head level, so round-the-clock medical personnel must be available.

Individuals with lesions at C5 and above have partially or fully paralyzed diaphragms, the muscle responsible for forceful breathing. Current estimates indicate that between 700 and 2,000 school-age children require **ventilator assistance** either full or part-time. Many attend school, and physical educators must devise meaningful physical education experiences to supplement their physical therapy. Not all of these individuals are spinal cord injured; many are in advanced stages of muscular dystrophy, but their programming needs are similar. Games that use residual respiratory abilities are recommended; see Chapter 19 on asthma. How many games can you devise that utilize blowing skills (e.g., blowing bubbles, darts, table tennis balls)?

Individuals with C1 to C5 lesions exhibit many individual differences. Those with complete lesions above C4 have no appreciable movement of body parts other than eyes, ears, and mouth; they can, however, play computer games with eye movements and move their motorized chairs via mouth devices. Persons with lesions at the C4 level can do head movements, and those with lesions at the C5 level can perform shoulder joint actions and weak elbow flexion. Striking games that use balloons and other lightweight objects are possible, especially when forearm braces are worn.

Table 23.3 **Goals for persons with complete quadriplegic lesions.**

Spinal Cord Level	OT Goals *Self-Care and* *ADL Skills*	PT Goals *Wheelchair and* *Ambulation Skills*	PE and R Goals *Sports, Dance, and* *Aquatics Skills*
Incomplete C5	Type, feed self Use assistive devices	Push on flat surface Manipulate brakes Stand at tilt table	Power chair activities, games, dance Basic sport skills Swimming with flotation devices
C6	Drink Wash, shave Brush hair Dress upper half Sit up/lie down in bed Write, draw Crafts, hobbies	Push on sloping surface Turn wheelchair Remove armrests/foot plates Transfer chair to bed, chair to car Stand in bars	Manual chair activities, games, and dance 60-, 100-, 200-, 400-, 800-m track events Slalom Club throw, 2-k shot put, discus Weight lifting 25-m front and back freestyle, breast, and butterfly 100-m freestyle swim Archery, air weapons, table tennis Sit-skiing (snow events)
C7	Turn in bed Dress lower half Skin care Bladder and bowel control Crafts, hobbies	Wheel over uneven surface Bounce over small elevations Pick up objects from floor Negotiate curbs Perform almost all transfers Swing-to in bars Drive automobile with manual controls	1500-m track events Shot put, discus, javelin (no club) Swimming same, except 100-m individual medley (4×25), with butterfly as fourth stroke
C8	Same as C7, except more finger control	Same as C7, except more finger control	Same as C7, except 200-m distance freestyle

Note. OT = Occupational therapy; ADL = Activities of daily living; PT = Physical therapy; PE and R = Physical education and recreation.

Programming for Paraplegia

Programming depends on sport classifications, which provide general guidance about what people can and cannot do (see Figure 23.11 and Table 23.4), assuming the lesions are complete. If lesions are incomplete, only trial and error can determine sport capabilities. Almost every sport can be played in a wheelchair (Adams & McCubbin, 1991; Paciorek & Jones, 1994). Professionals should begin by introducing individuals to *Sports 'N Spokes* and *Palaestra* so that they can see what is possible. Likewise the stories of models in these magazines and/or the opportunity to see models live or on television is of prime importance.

Models

The best-known athletes with paraplegia include the following:

David Kiley, stellar basketball player, who is now commissioner of the National Wheelchair Basketball Association (NWBA)

Sharon Rahn Hedrick, outstanding basketball player, the first woman to complete the Boston Marathon in a

wheelchair (in 1977), and the first woman to win a gold in the 800-m wheelchair exhibition events for the Olympics (in 1984)

Rick Hansen, who wheeled 24,901 miles on an around-the-world trip and has a disability sport center named for him at the University of Alberta in Canada (Hansen & Taylor, 1987)

George Murray, the first wheelchair athlete to break the 4-min mile, and one of the first to wheel across the United States (McBee & Ballinger, 1984)

Bob Hall, the first sanctioned wheelchair entrant in the Boston Marathon (in 1975), who finished with a time of 2:58, who now runs a wheelchair design company called Hall's Wheels (Huber, 1996)

Candace Cable-Brookes, who has won the Boston Marathon six times

Jean Driscoll, who has won the Boston Marathon seven consecutive times from 1990 through 1996; best time was 1:34:22 (Huber, 1996)

T a b l e   2 3 . 4   **Goals for persons with complete paraplegic lesions.**

Spinal Cord Level	OT Goals *Self-Care and* *ADL Skills*	PT Goals *Wheelchair and* *Ambulation Skills*	PE and R Goals *Sports, Dance, and* *Aquatics Skills*

T1 to T6	Trunk, leg, foot
	Vocational rehabilitation
		Do wheelies
		Transfer chair to floor
		Walk in bars or with walker
			Same as C8 (see Table 23.3),
			  except: 3-k shot put
			50-m front and back freestyle,
			  breast
			Class 2 wheelchair basketball

T7/8 to L1	Same as above	Swing-to on crutches Transfer chair to crutches Use stairs	Same as T1 to T5, except: 400- and 1600-m track relay 50-m butterfly 400-m distance freestyle Snow skiing (upright with special apparatus)
L1/2 to L5/S1	———	All gaits on crutches All transfers	Class 2 wheelchair basketball Same as T6 to T10, except: 200-m individual medley 500-m distance freestyle

L2/3 and below	———	Functional walking without
		  crutches—may use cane,
		  braces
			Class 3 wheelchair basketball
			Standing events

Note. OT = Occupational therapy; ADL = Activities of daily living; PT = Physical therapy; PE and R = Physical education and recreation.

Peter Axelson, who excels in winter and various recreational sports and is owner-manager of Beneficial Designs, a company that specializes in the design of recreational systems and devices for persons with disabilities (Axelson, 1986)

Mark Wellman, mountain climber and forest ranger, who used his powerful arms to climb up a high rope and light the Paralympic flame at Opening Ceremonies of the 1996 Paralympics in Atlanta (Wellman & Flinn, 1995)

Track and Racing Events for Paraplegia

Only two sport classifications are needed to guide instruction, recreation, and competition in track and racing events. Individuals with T1 to T7/8 lesions (Track Class 3) are significantly different from those with lower lesions (Track Class 4). This difference is primarily in sitting stability, trunk rotation, and the ability to assume the **flexed trunk position** that minimizes aerodynamic drag in racing (see Figure 23.14).

Individuals with lesions above T6 are at risk for autonomic dysreflexia (AD), sluggish heart rate response to exercise, and venous pooling. Those with lesions above T8 have problems regulating body temperature. These limitations are not constraints to sport participation but are reminders to watch carefully for signs of physiological distress. In contrast, individuals with lesions below T7/8 are relatively free of medical risk.

Track and racing chairs, customized to the individual's body build and capabilities, are major factors in success. Professionals should help parents and others realize the importance of buying the right chair for each sporting event and of replacing chairs as technological advances occur. Wheelchair athletes can serve as consultants in helping to make decisions with regard to chairs.

All-Terrain Vehicles and Cycling

The development of all terrain vehicles (ATVs) has contributed to sport, as well as to trail riding and other off-road adventures (Axelson & Castellano, 1990). ATVs typically have three or four wheels, low-set seats, and increased distance between front and back wheels.

On-the-road hand cycling is also becoming popular. David Cornelsen (1991), for example, reports that he regularly rides with members of an AB club. The rides are usually 35 to 55 mi of hilly terrain, averaging 15 mi an hour.

Field Events for Paraplegia

Four sport classifications are needed to meet the needs of varying functional capacities within paraplegia. Consider how each of the following influences the way you would teach object propulsion (ball, frisbee, discus, shot put, javelin).

Field Class 4 (T1 to T7/8) includes persons who must hold on to the chair while throwing because of their impaired sitting balance and inability to rotate the trunk.

Field Class 5 (T7/8 to L1/2) includes persons who can rotate their trunks but do not have full backward, forward, and sideward trunk mobility and power in generating force.

Field Class 6 (L1/2 to L5/S1) includes persons who have the functional capacity to lift their thighs off of the chair, thereby imparting more force to the throw. Some individuals also have leg function, such as pressing the knees together, straightening the knees, and bending the knees, that enhances object propulsion.

Field Class 7 (S1 and below) includes persons who have the functional capacity to stand while throwing.

Wheelchair Basketball

Wheelchair basketball, the world's most popular team sport for persons with disabilities, was developed by war veterans in the late 1940s (Strohkendl, 1996). Only a few of the rules are different from those of able-bodied basketball:

1. Five, rather than 3 sec, are allowed in the lane.
2. When dribbling or holding the ball in the lap, the player can only make two thrusts of the wheels, after which he or she must dribble, pass, or shoot.
3. There is no double-dribble rule in wheelchair basketball.
4. A player raising his or her buttocks off the chair is a physical advantage foul. This counts as a technical foul.

Several books are available on coaching wheelchair basketball (Hedrick, Byrnes, & Shaver, 1989; Owen, 1982; Shaver, 1981). Obviously, good performance is dependent upon learning wheelchair- and ball-handling skills. Quad rugby, although designed for persons with quadriplegia, can serve as a lead-up game to wheelchair basketball. Many of the same skills are used. Anyone with a permanent lower limb disability may compete in wheelchair basketball.

Rules for wheelchair basketball are governed by the International Wheelchair Basketball Federation (IWBF). Since 1992, IWBF has used eight classifications to equalize team abilities. Each classification is assigned points (1, 1.5, 2, 2.5, 3, 3.5, 4, 4.5), and equity is achieved by requiring that the classifications of the players on the floor cannot exceed 14 points. Players in Classes 1 and 1.5 cannot pass any of Strohkendl's Basketball Function Tests and generally have T1 to T7/8 lesion levels or disabilities with comparable ability levels. In contrast, players in Classes 4 and 4.5 can pass all tests, have very minor lower limb disabilities, and generally do not use wheelchairs except for basketball.

In national competition, countries can choose to use their own classification systems rather than that of IWBF. The United States uses three classifications (see Figure 23.11), with a numerical value of 1, 2, or 3 assigned to players. Players on the floor, according to U.S. rules, cannot total more than 12 points. The two combinations used most often in game play are five players with the following classifications:

3	3
3	3
3	2
2	2
1	2
12	12

Women's basketball tournaments are conducted separately from men's at both national and international levels, but

FIGURE 23.15 Randy Snow, wheelchair tennis champ, conducts workshops around the country. See his life story in the January/February 1990 *Sports 'N Spokes* (Crase, 1990).

in local and regional play women sometimes play on teams with men because there are not enough women players in their geographical region to field an all-female team. Some wheelchair basketball teams invite able-bodied (AB) athletes to learn wheelchair techniques and join them for local game play or practice (Brasile, 1992). Some countries permit AB athletes in national competitions, but the USA does not.

Wheelchair Tennis

With the exception of track, field, and swimming, wheelchair tennis is the most popular individual sport (see Figure 23.15). Individuals with quadriplegia, paraplegia, and other orthopedic disabilities can play (Moore & Snow, 1994). Wheelchair tennis has few modifications. The main rule change is two bounces instead of one. Persons with limited grip strength can use elastic, tape, or special orthotic devices to bind the racquet to the hand. If an overarm serve is not possible, the player uses a bounce-drop serve. The back wheels of the chair must remain behind the service line until contact with the ball is made.

Instead of a classification system, **division play** is used to ensure fairness. There are five divisions for men and three for women. These are designated as Open (for the best players), A, B, C, and D. Players move from division to division by winning in regional and then national tournaments; each knows his or her rank or standing within a division. Individuals with quadriplegia compete in a separate division.

Wheelchair tennis officially began in 1976, with the founding of the National Foundation of Wheelchair Tennis (NFWT) by Brad Parks, a wheelchair user. Over 6,000 people worldwide play wheelchair tennis (Carhill, 1991). Many are children because Brad and his wife Wendy, a physical therapist, attach high priority to junior competition and sport camps. Many AB persons play doubles and singles with wheelchair athletes. Tennis uses community facilities and facilitates integration.

Sport Wheelchairs

The many types of sport wheelchairs were first introduced in this textbook in Chapter 2 (see Figure 2.12) because an understanding of chairs is essential to becoming a good spectator and advocate of disability sport. Teachers and coaches should strive for a high level of knowledge in this area, because success in sports depends largely on appropriateness and fit of chair. An excellent resource in this regard is the annual review of wheelchairs published by *Sports 'N Spokes*. Relatively new magazines like *TeamRehab* and *New Mobility* also feature many articles on wheelchair technology (see addresses in Appendix E).

People with the disabilities covered in this chapter (spina bifida, spinal cord injury, and polio) are more likely to be using everyday, sport, or racing chairs than the medical model chair, which better meets the needs of individuals with severe, multidisabling conditions (e.g., cerebral palsy, stroke, traumatic brain injury). The medical model chair, discussed therefore in Chapter 25, is one that has handles for an assistant to push, removable armrests and foot plates, and a structure that enables it to be easily folded and transported. In contrast, chairs used for sport have rigid frames and do not fold. They can, however, be disassembled easily and quickly by pushing a **quick-release button on the axle tube** of the main wheel.

Sport chairs traditionally have had four wheels (two large, two small), but three-wheeled chairs are becoming increasingly popular for tennis and basketball. The T-frame design, with one wheel (a caster) in front, is advertised as minimizing drag, thereby allowing for easier, faster turning. Use of the T-frame design, however, requires relatively good balance.

Figure 23.16 shows the parts of a traditional basketball chair and how the camber tube, chair frame, and foot plate are adjusted in the manufacture of the T-frame chair. In order to communicate with people who use chairs, professionals should know the following facts.

The **height of the chair back** is usually an indication of the severity of the disability. Usually, the higher the chair back, the greater the disability.

Camber tubes or bars, near the center of the large wheels, permit adjustment of the angle of the wheels from 0° (no camber) to 15° (maximum camber). **Camber** is the degree to which the tops of the wheels slant inward (i.e., the bottoms are farther apart than the tops). Camber makes pushing more efficient, lessens the chance that the arm will bump against the wheel, and permits a natural, relaxed position for the elbows.

The small front wheels are called **casters,** and the large wheels are called **main wheels.** The main wheel tires are air-filled (pneumatic), similar to those on bicycles, which requires knowing how to fix flat tires. There are two types of pneumatic tire: (a) the clincher, which has a separate tire and inner tube, and (b) the tubular, in which the tire is sewn around the inner tube.

Handrims or **pushrims,** the part of the chair stroked by the hands, are comparable to gearshifts on bicycles. Relatively large handrims, similar to low gears, are used on sport chairs, enabling them to start and stop quickly. In contrast, racing chairs have small handrims that enable top speeds on the road but are slow in initial acceleration.

Adjustable seat inclinations and heights are made possible by **axle tubes or plates** in the center of the large or

FIGURE 23.16   Parts of a sport chair. Both four-wheeled and three-wheeled chairs are used for basketball and tennis. (Photo courtesy of Mary Carol Peterson, TOP END by Action.)

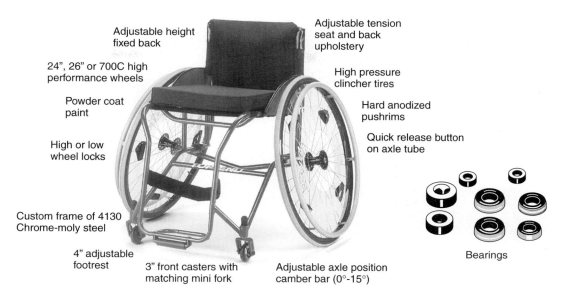

Adjustable height fixed back

Adjustable tension seat and back upholstery

24", 26" or 700C high performance wheels

High pressure clincher tires

Powder coat paint

Hard anodized pushrims

High or low wheel locks

Quick release button on axle tube

Custom frame of 4130 Chrome-moly steel

4" adjustable footrest

3" front casters with matching mini fork

Adjustable axle position camber bar (0°-15°)

Bearings

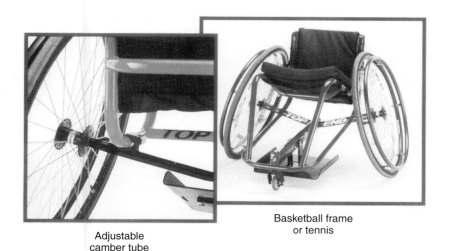

Adjustable camber tube

Basketball frame or tennis

Adjustable foot plate

main wheels. Relatively flat seats (no inclination) are used by people with low-level lesions, but people with high-level lesions who need help with balance adjust their seats to slope backward. This keeps their knees relatively high and their buttocks low, and therefore more stable, in the chair. Axle mechanisms allow basketball players to sit as high as rules allow, with the main wheels adjusted backward for greater stability. In contrast, tennis players sit as low as possible, with the main wheels adjusted forward so that the chair can spin around faster and be more maneuverable.

A **bearing** is the outermost part of an axle (see Figure 23.16). Bearings affect the rolling resistance of a wheel (i.e., tightening the axle toward the frame makes wheel revolution more difficult; loosening too much causes wheels to wobble). Bearings may be sealed or not sealed. Teachers should know how to adjust and/or lubricate bearings.

Quad rugby chairs, while similar to basketball chairs, are recognized by a heavier, reinforced front framework to permit the chairs to crash into each other. They also have an additional structure at foot level called the offensive or defensive front end to help absorb the shock of purposeful crashes. The footrest is recessed to give more leg and foot protection.

Track and Racing Chairs

Track and racing chairs differ from sport and everyday models primarily in number of wheels, size of wheels (larger) and handrims (smaller), lowered seat position, longer wheelbase (distance from front to back), and much camber (vertical angle of the main wheels). Figure 23.17 depicts these characteristics.

There are many kinds of racing chairs, each personalized to individual needs. Special cage designs allow athletes to lean forward by kneeling with their legs behind them or to tie their legs in a forward position, with knees high, and chest touching thighs. LeAnn Shannon, the 13-year-old who set a world record of 16.62 seconds in the 1996 Paralympic 100-m race, illustrates the kneeling position in Figure 23.17; Claude Issarot illustrates the legs-forward position. The cages of most

FIGURE 23.17 LeAnn Shannon and Claude Issarot demonstrate different body positions in personalized racing chairs. (Photos courtesy of Mary Carol Peterson, TOP END by Action.)

FIGURE 23.18   Wheelchair arm techniques.

Short propulsion thrusts in ADL activities, basketball, tennis, and most sports except racing. In this technique, the athlete pushes forward and downward (i.e., applies force from A to B) while simultaneously inclining the trunk forward. The handrims are released at point B, the trunk returns to its upright position, and the arms are lifted and repositioned for the next downward and forward push.

Forward, downward   Beginning of   End of
thrust   recovery   recovery

Long-duration, circular-propulsion thrust in track and marathon racing. In this technique, which requires small-diameter handrims and correct positioning of the wheelchair seat and back, the athlete maintains hands in contact with the handrims through approximately three-fourths of a circle, applying force the entire time. The grip on the handrim is never released, only loosened to allow repositioning. Shoulder joint extension is especially important in providing final propulsive thrust. The lower the seat, the more important the ability of the arms to lift backward.

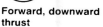

Forward, downward   Force continues   Beginning of
thrust   recovery

racing chairs are very narrow and uncomfortable, so athletes use these chairs only for racing. Travel with athletes requires careful planning for carrying extra chairs.

Wheelchair Sport Techniques

Technique varies according to sport, degree of disability, and type of wheelchair (Axelson & Castellano, 1990; Cooper, 1988; Higgs, 1995). The following are important points.

1. **Arm Propulsion.** The arm movement is different in track and marathon racing from that in most sports and activities of daily living (ADL). Figure 23.18 shows these differences. In athletes with good trunk control, the trunk alternately inclines forward and back during the thrust and recovery phases of the arm in all sports but track.

2. **High Knee Position.** Most athletes race with the knees as high as possible and the center of gravity as low as possible. This position permits optimal forward lean of the trunk, which, in turn, offers (a) lowered wind resistance, (b) better driving position for arms, and (c) increased trunk stability.

3. **Flexed Trunk Position.** Most athletes race with the trunk flexed and as close to the legs as possible. This position minimizes aerodynamic drag. Whereas in early racing history, persons with high-level lesions could not lean over because of trunk instability, new wheelchair technology enables them to assume desired positions. Increasing the sag in the seat and seat back is one way this is achieved.

Wheelchairs in Integrated School Physical Education

All schools with an enrollment of 300 or more should have at least two sport wheelchairs as part of their permanent physical education equipment. These chairs should be used in regular and separate physical education settings by students with and without disabilities. In practice and competition, one chair can be assigned to each team; who is in the chair is relatively unimportant, since all students can benefit from exposure to wheelchair sports. The student with a physical disability, however, has no opportunity to develop locomotor sport skills generalizable to adulthood unless wheelchairs are provided. Wheelchairs can be integrated into all physical education instruction: dance, individual sport relays, challenge courses, and adventure activities. Equal learning opportunity can be ensured only through the provision of wheelchairs (Brasile, 1992). This aspect of instruction should therefore be written into the IEP.

The alternative to providing wheelchair instruction is to limit the physical education curriculum to upper extremity activities done from a stationary position (archery, riflery, table tennis, horseshoes, bowling), swimming, and horseback riding. No student should be forced to sit on the sidelines or serve as scorekeeper or official because an activity in which he or she cannot participate fully is being taught. If wheelchair integration is not deemed appropriate, students with orthopedic problems should be rotated into separate, adapted physical education.

Winter Sports

Persons in wheelchairs enjoy winter sports like everyone else. For mobility on the snow, special apparatus called sit-skis and mono-skis have been invented (Axelson, 1988). The **sit-ski,** similar to a sled with a bucket seat affixed, was invented first and is still used for learning basic skills and playing games like ice and sledge hockey. The sit-ski is propelled by poles or **picks** (special short sticks for pushing). To learn downhill skiing, the beginner practices direction and control while the sit-ski is tethered to an AB skier who stays behind, pulling on the **tether** to assist with control.

In the 1980s, mono-skis were invented for use in downhill skiing, especially racing. Whereas the sit-ski is close to the snow, the **mono-ski** is essentially a trunk-seat-leg orthosis suspended via a linkage system about 10 to 18 inches above a single ski (see Figure 23.19). Hand-held **outriggers** (forearm crutches with short ski tips attached to the ends) are used for control, including braking.

Sledge and pulk sports for persons with disabilities can be traced to Norway in the 1960s. **Sledge** means fishermen's sleigh, and the first racing was cross-country with dog

FIGURE 23.19 Winter sports. *(A)* Sit-ski or pulk used in downhill skiing in the 1970s and 1980s. Peter Axelson is shown in sled he designed. *(B)* Mono-ski for downhill skiing in the 1990s. *(C)* Sledge hockey players from Beitostølen, Norway.

A. Sit-ski or pulk

B. Mono-ski with outriggers

C. Sledge hockey players from Beitostølen, Norway

teams and sledge toboggans. Shortly thereafter, special sledges with very thin metal runners were created. **Pulks** (originally, reindeer-drawn sleighs in Lapland) are similar to sit-skis; they have solid bottoms. Sledge and pulk events can be animal- or self-propelled, using poles or picks. Independent ambulation is often called *pulk poling* or *ice picking.*

Sledge or ice hockey is played on a regulation-size ice rink with a puck or small playground ball. Six players on each team play offense and defense similar to stand-up hockey, using picks that double as hockey sticks. Regulation padding, helmets, and gloves are important. A mask is optional. Persons with weak grips use Velcro strips on the gloves and picks (Paciorek & Jones, 1994).

Other popular winter sports that can be adapted for persons in wheelchairs are ice fishing, ice tubing, snowmobiling, snow camping, and cross-country sit-skiing. Just moving from place to place on snow- or ice-covered surfaces, like going out to get the mail, can be a challenge. Use of poles, called **wheelchair poling,** can be an activity of daily living (ADL) or an organized race for time and distance.

A major consideration in winter sports is appropriate warm clothing because of the temperature regulation problems in spinal paralysis above T6. Layered clothing and waterproof gloves are very important.

Winter sports are governed by Disabled Sports/USA in affiliation with the U.S. Ski Association (USSA) and the International Ski Federation (ISF). Clinics are regularly held for learning to ski and for instructor training and certification. The Winter Park Handicapped Ski Association and Breckenridge Outdoor Education Center, both in Colorado, historically have pioneered training. Internationally, the famous Beitostølen Health Sports Center in Norway is best known. Addresses to write for further information follow:

Inge Morisbak
Beitostølen
Helsesportsenter
2953 Beitostølen
Norway

Disabled Sports/USA
451 Hungerford Drive
Suite 100
Rockville, MD 20850
(301) 217-0960

Winter Park
Handicapped Ski Association
Box 36
Winter Park, CO 80482
(303) 726-4101

Breckenridge Outdoor
  Education Center
P.O. Box 721
Breckenridge, CO 80424
(303) 453-6422

Fitness Programming

To date, the only published fitness research on youth with orthopedic impairments is that of Winnick and Short (1984) in conjunction with Project UNIQUE (see Chapter 13 on fitness). Their subjects included 141 youths, ages 10 to 17 years, with paraplegic spinoneuromuscular conditions. Eleven tests (triceps, abdominal, and subscapular skinfolds; right and left hand-grip strength; arm hang; pull-ups; 50-yd dash; shuttle run; long-distance run; and softball distance throws) were administered.

Comparisons between AB students and students with disabilities showed that the latter were inferior on all measures.

Moreover, the normally expected improvements from age to age did not appear in the youth with disabilities. Boys performed better than girls only on the softball throw. There were no significant test differences between sport classifications. Norms, based on these subjects, and testing procedures appear in a Project UNIQUE manual (Winnick & Short, 1985). This research demonstrates the need for better fitness programming and more active lifestyles.

Research on adults with spinal paralysis also indicates the need for increased fitness. Excellent reviews of literature and training programs appear periodically (Shephard, 1990; Wells & Hooker, 1990). Athletically active persons in wheelchairs have fewer kidney infections, skin breakdowns, and other medical complications than sedentary persons (Stotts, 1986). Athletes tend also to be self-actualized and happy (Sherrill, 1990; Sherrill, Silliman, Gench, & Hinson, 1990). In general, it is not disability that affects wellness but, rather, poor attitudes toward exercise and lack of discipline.

Activity specialists should focus on making exercise fun, changing lifestyles, and promoting social support networks. One approach is to develop community-based programs in which wheelchair users can exercise with family, spouse, and friends (Lasko-McCarthey & Aufsesser, 1990). Another is to plan attractive risk recreation and/or strenuous outdoor ventures that motivate persons to develop the fitness levels needed for participation (Axelson, 1986). For example, wanting to ride a horse is motivation for developing the arm and shoulder strength to mount and dismount. Likewise, sailboat racing, kayaking, canoeing, rock climbing, and the like require a commitment to strength and endurance training.

Fun means different things to different people. Often, it is associated with inclusion, friendship, and respect. Fitness activities done with partners or in small support groups help meet this need, especially if incentives are provided for out-of-class cooperative work toward shared goals. Points, rewards, or recognition should be given for both process (effort/time spent) and product (improved scores). A shared cooperative goal in weight management might be three people losing a grand total of 30 lb rather than each individual losing a certain amount. The same principle can be applied to pull-ups, grip strength, and other upper extremity goals.

Disability tends to isolate people. Children and youth, in particular, do not need further isolation at hand-cranking and arm-cycling machines. Partners can be assigned to face each other and talk while doing distinctly different fitness activities. Unless some kind of positive contact/sharing is assigned and reinforced, it may not happen.

Arm Cranking and Wheelchair Ergometry

Facilities that serve people with physical disabilities (integrated and other) need specialized equipment for assessment and training. Among these are various kinds of arm exercise machines (DeGraff, 1989; Glaser, 1989) and hand cycles (Cornelsen, 1991). Different kinds of handgrip designs must be available to help people with quadriplegia (see Figure 23.20).

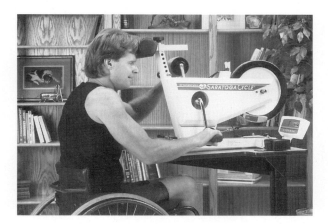

FIGURE 23.20 Hand-cranking apparatus must be available to develop cardiorespiratory endurance. (Photos courtesy of Saratoga Access & Fitness, Inc.)

Heart and circulatory limitations discussed earlier affect training protocol and outcomes. Additionally, the smaller muscle mass of the arms cannot produce the training effects associated with leg work. In individuals with high lesions, arm cranking often cannot raise the heart rate above 120 beats a minute. Goals should be individualized and comparisons with others avoided. Arm exercise done in an upright, sitting position may be so limited by blood pooling in the leg veins that apparatus must be adapted to allow hand-cranking from a supine position (Glaser, 1989).

When the purpose of fitness training is to prepare for athletic excellence, the principle of specificity is important. **Wheelchair ergometry** (the use of rollers) is preferred over arm cranking by most coaches. Rollers are to wheelchair users what treadmills are to ambulatory runners (see Figure 23.21). Hedrick and Morse (1991), coaches at the University of Illinois, describe roller training and the importance of a fan for ventilation and periodic fluid intake to prevent dehydration. Wheelchair ergometry results in a higher maximum heart rate than arm cranking and thus contributes more to fitness.

Shoulder Joint Injury

Reliance on upper extremities for fitness training makes wheelchair users especially vulnerable to shoulder joint injury

FIGURE 23.21   Rollers are to wheelchair users what treadmills are to ambulatory runners. (© The State Journal Register, Springfield, IL.)

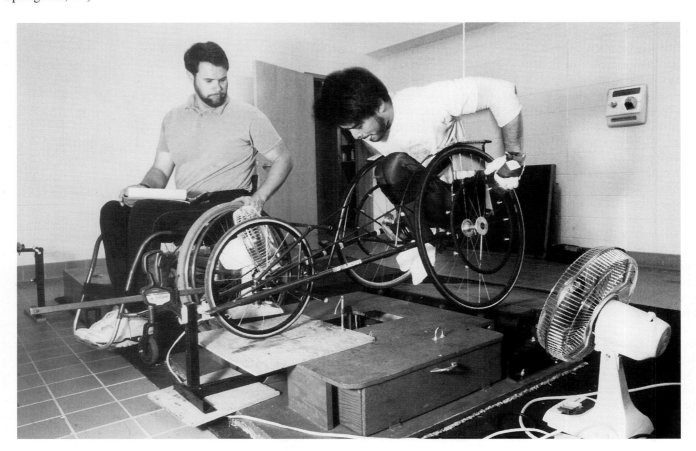

(Millikan, Morse, & Hedrick, 1991). Pushing activities tend to overdevelop anterior arm and shoulder muscles and cause an imbalance in strength between anterior and posterior musculature. Clinical signs are round shoulders, decreased flexibility, discomfort in the muscles between the shoulder blades, and increased risk of straining the rotator-cuff muscle group and/or dislocating the joint. Prevention focuses on stretching the anterior muscles and strengthening the posterior ones. For further information, see Chapters 13 and 14 on fitness and postures.

References

Adams, R. C., & McCubbin, J. (1991). *Games, sports, and exercises for the physically disabled* (4th ed.). Philadelphia: Lea & Febiger.

Axelson, P. (1986). Facilitation of integrated recreation. In C. Sherrill (Ed.), *Sport and disabled athletes* (pp. 81–89). Champaign, IL: Human Kinetics.

Axelson, P. (1988). Hitting the slopes . . . Everything you ever wanted to know about mono-skis and mono-skiing. *Sports 'N Spokes, 14*(4), 22–34.

Axelson, P., & Castellano, J. (1990). Take to the trail . . . Everything you ever wanted to know about off-road wheelchairs. *Sports 'N Spokes, 16*(2), 20–24.

Brasile, F. (1984). A wheelchair basketball skills test. *Sports 'N Spokes, 9*(7), 36–40.

Brasile, F. (1986). Do you measure up? *Sports 'N Spokes, 12*(4), 42–47.

Brasile, F. (1992). Inclusion: A developmental perspective. A rejoinder to "Examining the Concept of Reverse Integration." *Adapted Physical Activity Quarterly, 9*(4), 293–304.

Burnham, R., Wheeler, G., Bhambhari, Y., Belanger, M., Eriksson, P., & Steadward, R. (1994). Intentional induction of autonomic dysreflexia among quadriplegic athletes for performance enhancement. In R. D. Steadward, E. R. Nelson, & G. D. Wheeler (Eds.), *Vista '93—The outlook* (pp. 224–241). Edmonton, Canada: Rick Hansen Centre.

Campanella, R. (1959). *It's good to be alive.* New York: Little, Brown.

Carhill, M. E. (1991). People in sports: Brad and Wendy Parks—Making the dream come true. *Sports 'N Spokes, 17*(1), 42–45.

Connor-Kuntz, F. J., Dummer, G. M., & Paciorek, M. J. (1995). Physical education and sport participation of children and youth with spina bifida myelomeningocele. *Adapted Physical Activity Quarterly, 12*(3), 228–238.

Cooper, R. (1988). Racing chair lingo . . . or how to order a racing wheelchair. *Sports 'N Spokes, 13*(6), 29–32.

Cornelsen, D. (1991). The wonderful world of hand cycling. *Sports 'N Spokes, 17*(2), 10–12.

Crase, N. (1990). Winning: Randy Snow. *Sports 'N Spokes, 15*(5), 8–12.

Curtis, K. A. (1981). Stretching routines. *Sports 'N Spokes, 7*(3), 16–18.

Curtis, K. A. (1991). Sport-specific functional classification for wheelchair athletes. *Sports 'N Spokes, 17*(2), 45–48.

Davis, R., & Ferrara, M. (1996). Athlete classification: An explanation of process. *Palaestra, 12*(2), 38–44.

DeGraff, A. H. (1989). Accessible aerobic exercise: The Saratoga cycle. *Palaestra, 5*(3), 30–33.

Glaser, R. (1989). Arm exercise training for wheelchair users. *Medicine and Science in Sports and Exercise, 21*(5, Suppl.), S149–S153.

Hansen, R., & Taylor, J. (1987). *Rick Hansen: Man in motion.* Vancouver, British Columbia: Douglas & McIntyre.

Hedrick, B., Byrnes, D., & Shaver, L. (1989). *Wheelchair basketball.* Washington, DC: Paralyzed Veterans of America.

Hedrick, B., & Morse, M. (1991). Getting the most from roller training. *Sports 'N Spokes, 16*(6), 81–83.

Higgs, C. (1995). Enhancing wheelchair performance. In J. P. Winnick (Ed.), *Adapted physical education and sport* (2nd ed., pp. 421–432). Champaign, IL: Human Kinetics.

Hooper, E. (1991). Quad rugby: The chance to compete. *Sports 'N Spokes, 16*(6), 70–71.

Huber, J. H. (1996). Boston: The 100th marathon and the wheelchair athlete. *Palaestra, 12*(2), 33–37.

Krotoski, D. M., Nosek, M. A., & Turk, M. A. (Eds.). (1996). *Women with physical disabilities: Achieving and maintaining health and well-being.* Baltimore: Paul H. Brookes.

Lasko-McCarthey, P., & Aufsesser, P. (1990). Guidelines for a community-based physical fitness program for adults with physical disabilities. *Palaestra, 6*(5), 18–29.

McBee, F., & Ballinger, J. (1984). *The continental quest.* Tampa, FL: Overland Press.

Millikan, T., Morse, M., & Hedrick, B. (1991). Prevention of shoulder injuries. *Sports 'N Spokes, 17*(2), 35–38.

Moore, B., & Snow, R. (1994). *Wheelchair tennis: Myth to reality.* Dubuque, IA: Kendall/Hunt.

Owen, E. (1982). *Playing and coaching wheelchair basketball.* Champaign, IL: University of Illinois Press.

Paciorek, M., & Jones, J. A. (1994). *Sports and recreation for the disabled: A resource manual* (2nd ed.). Indianapolis: Cooper.

Petrofsky, J. S., Brown, S. W., Cerrel-Bazo, H. (1992). Active physical therapy and its benefits in rehabilitation. *Palaestra, 8*(3), 23–27, 61–62.

Schack, F. (1991). Effects of exercise on selected physical fitness components of an ambulatory quadriplegic. *Palaestra, 7*(3), 18–23.

Shaver, L. (1981). *Wheelchair basketball: Concepts and techniques.* Marshall, MN: Southwest State University Press.

Shephard, R. J. (1990). *Fitness in special populations.* Champaign, IL: Human Kinetics.

Sherrill, C. (1990). Psychosocial status of disabled athletes. In G. Reid (Ed.), *Problems in motor control* (pp. 339–364). Amsterdam: North-Holland.

Sherrill, C., Silliman, L., Gench, B., & Hinson, M. (1990). Self-actualization of elite wheelchair athletes. *Paraplegia, 28,* 252–260.

Steadward, R. D., Nelson, E. R., & Wheeler, G. D. (Eds.). (1994). *Vista '93—The outlook.* Edmonton, Canada: Rick Hansen Centre.

Stotts, K. M. (1986). Health maintenance: Paraplegic athletes and nonathletes. *Archives of Physical Medicine Rehabilitation, 67,* 109–114.

Strohkendl, H. (1986). The new classification system for wheelchair basketball. In C. Sherrill (Ed.), *Sport and disabled athletes* (pp. 101–112). Champaign, IL: Human Kinetics.

Strohkendl, H. (1996). *The 50th anniversary of wheelchair basketball: A history.* New York: Waxmann.

Wellman, M., & Flinn, J. (1995). *Climbing back* [book] and *No barriers* [videotape]. Available from Eric Perlman Productions, P.O. Box 8636, Truckee, CA 96162. Phone 800-726-7003.

Wells, C., & Hooker, S. (1990). The spinal injured athlete. *Adapted Physical Activity Quarterly, 7,* 265–285.

Winnick, J., & Short, F. (1984). Test item selection for the Project UNIQUE physical fitness test. *Adapted Physical Activity Quarterly, 1*(4), 296–314.

Winnick, J., & Short, F. (1985). *Physical fitness testing of the disabled: Project UNIQUE.* Champaign, IL: Human Kinetics.

Yilla, A. (1993). *Development of a quad rugby skill test.* Unpublished thesis, Texas Woman's University, Denton.

Yilla, A., & Sherrill, C. (1994). Quad rugby illustrated. *Palaestra, 10*(4), 25–31.

CHAPTER

24

Les Autres Conditions and Amputations

FIGURE 24.1   *Les autres,* meaning "the others," is a sport team referring to all persons with physical disabilities who are not eligible to compete with persons who have spinal paralysis, cerebral palsy, stroke, or traumatic brain injury.

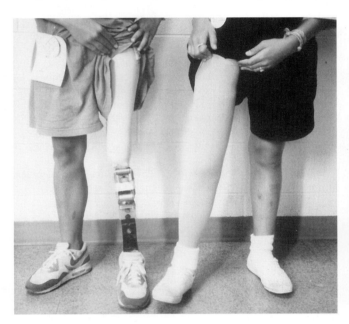
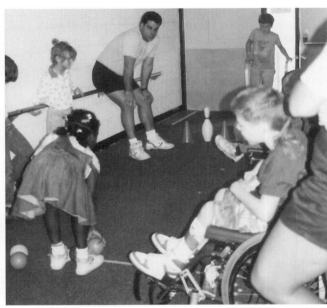
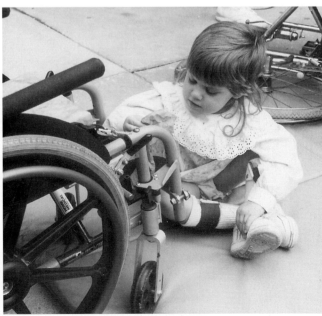

After you have studied this chapter, you should be able to do the following:

1. Discuss sports for les autres conditions and amputations. Include governing bodies, recommended activities, and your personal experience with these conditions.

2. Describe assessment to guide programming in locomotor and ball handling activities for les autres conditions and amputations.

3. Describe and discuss each condition in this chapter (see Table 24.1). Include physical activity recommendations for each.

4. Be able to spell names of conditions and on a test to match descriptions with names. Be able also to classify each condition as mostly muscular or mostly skeletal.

5. Be able to recognize and name these conditions in real life or when shown films, videotapes, and slides.

6. Given age, gender, and condition, be able to write a physical education IEP. Substantiate physical education placement. Be sure to include contraindications and to consider inclusion.

Les autres conditions and amputations are grouped together in this chapter because, historically, they have been governed by the International Sports Organization for the Disabled (ISOD). *Les autres,* the French term for "the others," is used in sport to denote the *other locomotor disabilities,* namely those not eligible to compete as spinally paralyzed or cerebral palsied (see Figure 24.1). Les autres conditions covered in this chapter are listed in Table 24.1.

Individuals with les autres conditions differ enormously. Some require activities in motorized chairs, some can compete in wheelchair sports described in Chapter 23, and some can participate in ambulatory activities adapted to particular needs. This chapter begins with conditions of progressive muscle weakness. Some of these, like the muscular dystrophies, have an unknown cause. Others can be classified as neuromuscular in that they are caused by degeneration of motor and/or sensory nerves. The chapter continues with thermal injuries (burns), a high incidence condition, that often results in contractures or amputations. Burns limit range of motion (ROM) and can be linked with both the muscular and skeletal systems.

The second half of the chapter presents conditions that affect bones and joints. First, conditions that can involve any body part or the entire body are described. These include arthritis, osteomyelitis, arthrogryposis, dwarfism, and osteogenesis imperfecta. Next, congenital and growth disorders that affect only one body part are described. The chapter concludes with a discussion of limb deficiencies and amputations.

Sport Governing Bodies

The disability sports organizations (DSOs) in the United States that govern amputations and les autres conditions are in constant flux. From 1981 to 1990, the U.S. Amputee Athletic Association (USAAA) conducted sport activities. Now amputees are the responsibility of Disabled Sports/USA, formerly National Handicapped Sports. Originally, the cerebral palsy sport organization conducted les autres events, but the U.S. Les Autres Sports Association (USLASA) was organized in 1986 and continues to serve all conditions except dwarfism. The Dwarf Athletic Association of America (DAAA), also founded in 1986, sponsors its own events. For Paralympic sport events, Disabled Sports/USA serves as the coordinating body for all disabilities in this chapter.

Table 24.1   Conditions covered in this chapter.

Individuals with skeletal disorders are more likely to become involved in competitive sport than are individuals with muscular weakness conditions. Success depends largely on selecting appropriate sports for one's height, body build, and functional capabilities. Creating an equitable sport classification system is difficult, but the trend within the Paralympic movement is toward sport-specific, functional classifications

that include individuals with different medical conditions who appear to have comparable performance capabilities. The sport classifications for track and field described in Chapter 23 are therefore applied to athletes with les autres conditions who use wheelchairs. Experts in each Paralympic sport are endeavoring to create fair, functional classification systems specific to their sports.

Wheelchair Use

Programming for persons with severe degenerative muscle conditions requires knowledge of motorized chairs and medical model chairs with push handles. Motorized chair sport events like **slaloms** (obstacle courses) and sprints should be part of physical education programming (see Figure 24.2).

Motorized Chairs

Motorized chairs (sometimes incorrectly called electric chairs) give persons with severe disabilities considerable independence. They move at high and low speeds and are generally capable of about 5 mi an hour. Most can climb inclines of at least 10°. Families/agencies that can afford to do so provide children who have little arm and shoulder strength with motorized chairs at a very young age.

The battery-powered chair is the most common, with two 12-volt batteries mounted on a carrier at the back of the chair below seat level. These batteries must be recharged each night to supply power for approximately 8 hr of continuous use. Regular automobile batteries are used on most chairs.

Motorized chairs, which must have sturdy frames to support the weight of batteries and other special equipment, are very heavy. Without the batteries, a chair typically weighs 75 to 80 lb. Folding the chair is impossible without battery removal. Problems in portability generally lead users of motorized chairs to purchase a second vehicle (manual) for travel.

Medical Model Chairs

For persons with severe disabilities who cannot push their own chair or have minimal arm function, the **medical model chair** is typically prescribed. This model is seen in residential facilities, nursing homes, rental agencies, schools, and recreation centers. Following are skills that professionals should learn.

Handling Brakes

Brakes are used to lock the main wheels, thereby immobilizing the chair and providing needed stability for making transfers, engaging in field events, and playing stationary games like shuffleboard. Brakes may be placed partially on to reduce acceleration in going down a steep ramp. Many sport and racing chairs do not have brakes.

Removing Armrests and Foot Plates

Armrests and foot plates should be removed before engaging in sport events and before transfers to and from the wheelchair. Armrests are removed by lifting the tubular frames of the arm out of the tubing on the wheelchair. Removable foot plates are swinging or nonswinging. In the swinging type, the front rigging is released and swung to the side, after which it is removed. In nonswinging foot plates, a button-type or hook-in-place lock is released to permit removal.

Pushing a Person in a Chair

When pushing an individual in a wheelchair, the most important thing to remember is the safest direction for the rider to face. The rest (e.g., the use of the tipping levers) is common sense. Guidelines include the following:

Descending curb or steep ramp: Turn self and wheelchair backward.

Descending stairs: Go down forward with chair tilted backward.

Ascending curb: Go forward.

Ascending stairs: Back up the stairs.

In managing stairs, two adults are best, one in back and one in front. The stronger adult should be in back since he or she has the heavier load. The person in back tilts the chair backward and lifts with the push handles. The person in front lifts the frame (never the foot plates, which might accidentally come off).

Opening and Closing the Chair

To open a wheelchair, *push down* on the two seat rails (outermost surfaces of seat). Do not try to open the chair by pulling it apart because this damages the telescoping parts of removable armrests.

To close the chair, lift up the foot plates. Then grasp the seat at its front and back and pull upward. If you intend to lift the folded chair into a vehicle, remove all detachable parts before closing it. *The best position to stand in while opening or closing a chair is to the side (i.e., facing the wheel).*

Sport Chairs

Individuals with muscular dystrophy, multiple sclerosis, and similar conditions should use sport chairs (described in Chapter 23) as long as they have the muscle strength to propel them. Sport chairs are lighter and have many advantages. Professionals often must advise parents concerning the type of chair needed.

Crutches, Canes, and Walkers

Individuals might come to class with assistive devices like crutches, canes, and walkers. Various gaits used with crutches and canes are described in Chapter 11 on motor skills and patterns. The use of crutches requires considerable arm and shoulder strength, so crutches are seldom used by people with conditions described in the first half of this chapter. Crutches are often used, however, by persons with skeletal conditions. Canes and walkers are often used by persons who have had strokes or traumatic brain injury.

Note the type of crutches used: (a) axillary, which fit under the armpits, or (b) forearm, also called Lofstrand or Canadian. Individuals with only axillary crutches cannot be programmed for ambulatory track because forceful pressure against the armpits, as in a race, cuts off circulation from the nerves and/or causes other kinds of nerve damage. An orthopedist should be consulted to see if the axillary crutches can be replaced with forearm ones.

Muscular Dystrophies

The **muscular dystrophies** are a group of genetically determined conditions in which **progressive muscular weakness** is attributed to pathological, biochemical, and electrical changes that occur in the muscle fibers. The causes of these changes remain unknown. The muscular dystrophies are common in school-age children and rank with cerebral palsy and spina bifida as important conditions for physical educators to learn about.

Several different types have been identified since 1850, many of which are rare. The three muscular dystrophies having the highest incidence are Duchenne, facio-scapular-humeral, and limb girdle types. Approximately 250,000 persons in the United States have muscular dystrophy. Of this number, 50,000 use a wheelchair. Most persons with Duchenne muscular dystrophy fall between the ages of 3 and 13 and attend public school. Of these, few live beyond early adulthood. Specifically, 1 of every 500 U.S. children will get or has muscular dystrophy. Boys are affected five or six times more often than girls.

Muscular dystrophy in itself is not fatal, but the secondary complications of immobilization heighten the effects of respiratory disorders and heart disease. With the weakening of respiratory muscles and the reduction in vital capacity, the child may succumb to a simple respiratory infection. **Dystrophic changes** in cardiac muscle increase susceptibility to heart disease. The dilemma confronting the physical educator is how to increase and/or maintain cardiovascular fitness when muscle weakness makes running and other endurance-type activities increasingly difficult (Croce, 1987). Breathing exercises and games are recommended.

Duchenne Muscular Dystrophy

The *Duchenne type* of muscular dystrophy is the most common and most severe. Its onset is usually before age 3, but symptoms may appear as late as age 10 or 11. Males are affected more frequently than females. The condition is caused by a sex-linked trait that is transmitted through females to

FIGURE 24.3 Walking posture and Gower's sign in muscular dystrophy. *Gower's sign* refers to the peculiar method of rise to stand.

males. The sister of an affected male has a 50% chance of being a carrier and will pass the defective gene on to 50% of her sons. Persons with muscular dystrophy seldom live long enough to marry. Indicators of Duchenne muscular dystrophy include the following:

1. Awkward side-to-side waddling gait.
2. Difficulty in running, tricycling, climbing stairs, and rising from chairs.
3. Tendency to fall frequently.
4. Peculiar way of rising from a fall. From a supine position, children turn onto their face, put hands and feet on the floor, and then climb up their legs with their hands. This means of rising is called the **Gower's sign** (see Figure 24.3).
5. Lordosis.
6. Hypertrophy of calf muscles and, occasionally, of deltoid, infraspinatus, and lateral quadriceps.

The **hypertrophy** (sometimes called pseudohypertrophy) occurs when quantities of fat and connective tissue replace degenerating muscle fibers, which progressively become smaller, fragment, and then disappear. The hypertrophy gives the mistaken impression of extremely well-developed healthy musculature. In actuality, the muscles are quite weak.

The initial areas of muscular weakness, however, are the **gluteals, abdominals, erector spinae** of the back, and **anterior tibials.** The first three of these explain lordosis and difficulty in rising, while the last explains the frequent falls. Weakness of the anterior tibials results in a **foot drop** (pes equinovarus), which causes children to trip over their own feet. See Chapter 11 for illustrations of the muscular dystrophy and steppage (foot drop) gaits.

Within 7 to 10 years after the initial onset of symptoms, contractures begin to form in the ankle, knee, and hip joints. **Contractures** of the Achilles tendons force children to walk on their toes and increase still further the incidence of falling. Stretching exercises are very important in preventing and minimizing contractures. Between ages 10 and 15, most children with dystrophy lose the capacity to walk, progressively spending more and more time in the wheelchair and/or bed. This enforced inactivity leads to severe distortions of the chest wall, kyphoscoliosis, and respiratory problems.

Facio-Scapular-Humeral Type

The *facio-scapular-humeral type* is the most common form of muscular dystrophy in adults. It affects both genders equally. Symptoms generally do not appear until adolescence and often are not recognized until adulthood. The prognosis is good, compared with that of the other dystrophies, and life span is normal. The condition may arrest itself at any stage. Indicators include

1. Progressive weakness of the shoulder and arm muscles, beginning with the trapezius and pectoralis major and sequentially involving the biceps, triceps, deltoid, and erector spinae.
2. Progressive weakness of the face muscles, causing drooping cheeks, pouting lips, and inability to close the eyes completely. The face takes on an immobile quality, since muscles lack the strength to express emotion.
3. Hip and thigh muscles are affected less often. When involvement does occur, it is manifested by a waddling side-to-side gait and the tendency to fall easily.

Limb Girdle Type

The *limb girdle type* of muscular dystrophy can occur at any time from age 10 or after. The onset, however, is usually the second decade. Both genders are affected equally. The earliest symptom is usually difficulty in raising the arms above shoulder level or awkwardness in climbing stairs. Weakness manifests itself initially in either the shoulder girdle muscles or the hip and thigh muscles, but eventually, both the upper and lower extremities are involved. Muscle degeneration progresses slowly.

Progressive Muscle Weakness

Daily exercise slows the incapacitating aspects of muscular dystrophy. As long as the child is helped to stand upright a few minutes each day and to walk short distances, contractures do not appear. Once the individual becomes a wheelchair user, however, functional ability tends to deteriorate rapidly. Stretching exercises become imperative at this point, as do breathing games and exercises.

Eight stages of disability are delineated by the Muscular Dystrophy Associations of America:

1. Ambulate with mild waddling gait and lordosis. Elevation activities adequate (climb stairs and curbs without assistance).
2. Ambulate with moderate waddling gait and lordosis. Elevation activities deficient (need support for curbs and stairs).
3. Ambulate with moderately severe waddling gait and lordosis. Cannot negotiate curbs or stairs but can achieve erect posture from standard-height chair.
4. Ambulate with severe waddling gait and lordosis. Unable to rise from a standard-height chair.
5. Wheelchair independence. Good posture in the chair; can perform all activities of daily living (ADL) from the chair.
6. Wheelchair with dependence. Can roll the chair but need assistance in bed and wheelchair activities.
7. Wheelchair with dependence and back support. Can roll the chair only a short distance but need back support for good chair position.
8. Bed patient. Can do no ADL without maximum assistance.

Even in Stage 8, some time each day is planned for standing upright by use of a tilt table or appropriate braces. Children should attend regular public school and engage in adapted physical education as long as possible, with emphasis upon the social values of individual and small-group games, dance, and aquatics. In the later stages, they may attend school only a small part of each day.

Full participation in games and athletics while the condition is in the early stages may enable the child to form close friends who will stick by as he or she becomes increasingly helpless. The child with muscular dystrophy and his or her friends also should receive instruction in some sedentary recreational activities that will carry over into the wheelchair years. Rifle shooting, dart throwing, archery, bowling, fishing, and other individual sports are recommended. The parents may wish to build a rifle or archery range in their basement or backyard to attract neighborhood children in for a visit as well as to provide recreation for their own child. Unusual pets, such

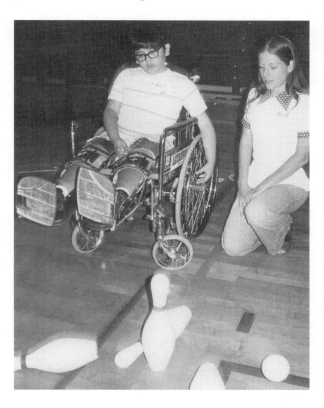

FIGURE 24.4 This boy in stage 5 of muscular dystrophy has such limited strength that bowling must be with a light ball and close to the pins.

as snakes, skunks, and raccoons, also have a way of attracting preadolescent children. Swimming is recommended, with emphasis upon developing powerful arm strokes to substitute for the increasing loss of leg strength.

Children with dystrophy are learning to adjust to life in a wheelchair just when their peers are experiencing the joys of competitive sports (see Figure 24.4). They are easily forgotten unless helped to develop skills like scorekeeping and umpiring, which keep them valued members of the group. The physical educator should not wait until disability sets in to build such skills, but should begin in the early grades, congratulating them on good visual acuity, knowledge of the rules, decision-making skills, and other competencies requisite to scorekeeping and umpiring. *These integrated activities should not, however, substitute for adapted physical education.*

Multiple Sclerosis

Multiple sclerosis (MS) is an inflammatory disease of the central nervous system (CNS) with variable symptoms and highly unpredictable periods of acute illness (called an attack, exacerbation, bout, or relapse) interspersed with periods of remission. Some individuals with MS have only one or two attacks in a lifetime, recover well, and never become disabled (Shuman & Schwartz, 1994; Sibley, 1992). About 25% have frequent attacks but recover sufficiently to consider themselves nondisabled, ordinary people. Others become more and more disabled with each attack, and eventually become wheelchair users with highly individual profiles of motor and sensory disturbances, pain, fatigue, and bladder/bowel disorders.

The cause of MS is unknown, but recent research indicates that 30 to 60% of new clinical attacks occur shortly after a cold, influenza, or other viral illness. Therefore, the theory currently favored is that MS is an immune system disorder in which the body mistakes portions of nerve covering (myelin) for a virus and therefore releases substances that cause myelin to disintegrate. Symptoms vary with each individual and with each attack, depending on which part of the CNS is affected. The name *multiple sclerosis* derives from the Greek word *sklerosis,* which means "hardening," and refers to the scar tissue that replaces the disintegrating myelin. The resulting lesions throughout the white matter of the brain and spinal cord vary from the size of a pinpoint to more than 1 cm in diameter. The cause of the demyelination is unknown.

The availability of magnetic resonance imaging (MRI) has greatly enhanced diagnostic procedures, and the prevalence of MS is now believed to be two to three times greater than previous estimates. This is largely because mild cases can now be identified. Estimates vary, with 1 out of 600 persons having MS in some communities (Sibley, 1992). Roughly twice as many individuals have MS as have one of the muscular dystrophies. MS occurs more frequently in women than men (about a 2:1 ratio) and is most common in whites, especially those of northern European ancestry. Age of onset is typically between 20 and 40.

MS symptoms usually last 4 to 12 weeks and then gradually disappear, leaving various degrees of disability. During periods of exacerbation, **nerve impulse conduction** through affected areas is abnormal, being either slow or blocked, producing such symptoms as weakness, numbness and tingling, dimness of vision, double vision, slurred speech, fatigue, pain, and urinary incontinence or urgency. In the progressive type of MS, spasticity, tremors, and paralysis can occur in the later stages. Symptoms are treated primarily with medications and the prescription of canes, crutches, walkers, and wheelchairs as needed. Appropriate exercise during periods of exacerbation is slow gentle stretching, walking, and water exercise in relatively cold temperatures.

Case Study

The following description of MS over an 8-year period was written by Sherry Rogers, who developed MS while a junior physical education major in college:

• *Now with the diagnosis starts the story of the most demanding years of my life. The pain I experienced was tremendous. It was more localized now. It was mostly on my right side and the lower part of my back, especially the sciatic nerve of my right leg.*

After about a month of medication every day, I could see some improvement. Then the physician started me on cold showers to stimulate my circulation. All of this and my prayers worked for me. Physical therapy, mainly to exercise my legs, was given me also. I had not moved much of my

body for about a year, and the therapy was designed to stimulate the muscles. I continued to progressively get better control of myself.

Then blindness, seeing only a narrow vision of light, appeared, lasting for about three weeks. Seeing double lasted for about another month. Then my vision progressively got better until it seems normal at present except that I now need glasses to read or do any close work.

I lost my voice for a while. I was told that the only thing to do for my disease was to rest and walk very much. Because of this, I rest each day for about an hour or more. I walk some distance each day, depending upon how I feel.

The effects of multiple sclerosis on me can best be described as weakening. There are days when I need crutches to walk and other days when I feel fine and can walk without any assistance. The muscle groups affected the most were all of the voluntary muscles of my right side. The most noticeable to me has been my right hand, which feels like it is asleep all of the time. I again was fortunate because I am left-handed. Endurance was the most noticeable change in fitness. I have to rest after any strenuous exercise. My strength is about one fourth of what it used to be. My posture has been very much affected. I bend forward from my waist some days when I stand. This is more apparent on some days than others, depending upon my strength. I was paralyzed for about a year. Gradually, I improved until now I walk almost normally.

My handwriting is not as legible as it was, and there are times when MS recurs slightly and affects portions of my right side. This sometimes lasts for days but always returns to what is now normal for me.

In spite of my disability, I returned to college and received my Bachelor of Science degree in physical education and was presented the most representative woman physical education major award from Delta Psi Kappa. All of this has impressed upon me the fact that the bodies of men are truly temples of God and should be cared for as such. If there is one thing I could tell you, it is that nothing is certain in this life and it is not to be taken for granted. Make certain that you live to the fullest because you never know what the future holds for you. •

Course of the Disease

In the most advanced stages of MS, loss of bladder or bowel control occurs as well as difficulties of speech and swallowing. Progressively severe **intention tremors** interfere with writing, using eating utensils, and motor tasks. The prognosis for MS varies. Many individuals have long periods of remission, during which their lives are essentially normal.

Program Implications

Type of physical activity depends on the extent of demyelination and the presence of pain, spasticity, tremors, muscle weakness, ataxia, impaired sensation, chronic fatigue, and heat intolerance (Lockette & Keyes, 1994). Movements are often slow and seem to require great energy expenditure. Some individuals with MS, however, are active in wheelchair basketball and tennis. Others try to swim, cycle, or walk daily and routinely perform stretching exercises. College students with MS should engage in regular physical education to the greatest extent possible. Swimming in cool water is particularly recommended. After graduation, individuals should join a fitness or sport club and/or establish a support group that will help them to stay motivated to exercise daily.

A unique aspect of MS is **heat intolerance.** Exposure to heat and humidity intensifies problems caused by demyelination and results in rapid fatigue. Any activity that substantially raises the body's core temperature is contraindicated. Morning exercise is recommended because the body temperature is normally lowest in the morning and higher in the afternoon.

Friedreich's Ataxia

Friedreich's ataxia is an inherited condition in which there is progressive degeneration of the sensory nerves of the limbs and trunk, which results in **diminished kinesthetic input.** The most common of the spinocerebellar degenerations, Friedreich's ataxia first occurs between ages 5 and 15 years. The primary indicators are **ataxia** (poor balance), clumsiness, and lack of agility. Many associated defects (slurred speech, diminished fine motor control, discoordination and tremor of the upper extremities, vision abnormalities, cardiac involvement, and skeletal deformities) may also develop and affect sport performance. Degeneration may be slow or rapid. Many persons become wheelchair users by their late teens; others manifest only one or two clinical signs and remain minimally affected throughout their life cycle. The incidence of Friedreich's ataxia is about 2 per 100,000. Several persons with this condition compete in Paralympic-level sport.

Guillain-Barré Syndrome

Guillain-Barré syndrome is a transient condition of progressive muscle weakness caused by inflammation of the spinal and cranial nerves **(polyneuritis).** Weakness, sometimes followed by paralysis, first affects the feet and lower legs, then the upper legs and trunk, and eventually the facial muscles. Some individuals die, and some are left with muscle and respiratory weakness. Most, however, make a complete recovery. Rehabilitation may require many months of bracing and therapy. The incidence is 1 per 100,000. Equal numbers of males and females are affected.

Charcot-Marie-Tooth Syndrome

Also called peroneal muscular atrophy, **Charcot-Marie-Tooth syndrome** is a relatively common hereditary disorder that appears between ages 5 and 30 years. It begins as weakness in the **peroneal muscles,** which are on the anterolateral lower leg, and gradually spreads to the posterior leg and small muscles of the hand. Weakness and atrophy of the peroneal muscles causes **foot drop,** which characterizes the **steppage gait** (see Chapter 11). The condition, which is caused by demyelination of spinal nerves and motor neurons in the spinal cord, is progressive but sometimes arrests itself. Persons with

Charcot-Marie-Tooth syndrome may be active for years, limited only by impaired gait and hand weakness.

Spinal Muscle Atrophies of Childhood

Several **spinal muscle atrophies** (SMA) have been identified: Werdnig-Hoffman disease (see Figure 24.5). Kugelberg-Welander disease, and Oppenheim's disease, among others. In school settings, however, these are usually called the *floppy baby syndromes* or *congenital hypotonia* since the major indicator is **flaccid muscle tone.** Most of these atrophies are present at birth or occur shortly thereafter. They are caused by progressive degeneration of the spinal cord's motor neurons.

The conditions vary in severity, with some leveling off, arresting themselves, and leaving the child with chronic, nonprogressive muscle weakness. Others are fatal within 2 or 3 years of onset. Typically, in severe cases, there is a loss of muscle strength, followed by tightening of muscles, then contractures, and finally nonuse. Stretching exercises are particularly important to combat contractures. SMA is sometimes impossible to distinguish from muscular dystrophy. It can be differentiated from cerebral palsy because there is no spasticity, no ataxia, no seizures, and no associated dysfunctions. Sensation remains intact.

Progressive Muscle Weakness of Middle and Old Age

Among the progressive muscle weakness conditions that occur in late adulthood are **Parkinson's disease,** recently associated with Muhammad Ali, Janet Reno, and Billy Graham; **Huntington's disease,** made well known by Woody Guthrie; and **amyotrophic lateral sclerosis** (ALS), also known as Lou Gehrig's disease. By far the most common, Parkinson's disease (a disorder of the basal ganglia) affects over 1 million adults, causing stiffness, weakness, and tremors in the early stages and more serious disability in the later stages (see the propulsion or **festination shuffling-type gait** in Chapter 11).

Programming for Muscular Weakness Conditions

Individuals with muscular dystrophy, multiple sclerosis, and similar conditions require adaptations that accommodate progressive loss of strength, endurance, and speed. Principles to guide adaptation include the following:

1. Avoid activities that cause fatigue or pain. Remember that the goal of exercise is to maintain function as long as possible, not to increase it. Ignore the overload principle (Lockette & Keyes, 1994).
2. Increase rest periods during activity. Remember that people with muscle weakness use more energy when exercising than peers do.
3. Use interval training rather than aerobic activities.
4. Create activities that allow personal choice of sport equipment. Make available lightweight bats, rackets, balls, and other sport equipment.

FIGURE 24.5 This 10-year-old boy has spinal muscular atrophy, Werdnig-Hoffman type. He has normal intelligence and attends a special school for children with orthopedic disabilities. Note how scoliosis limits breathing.

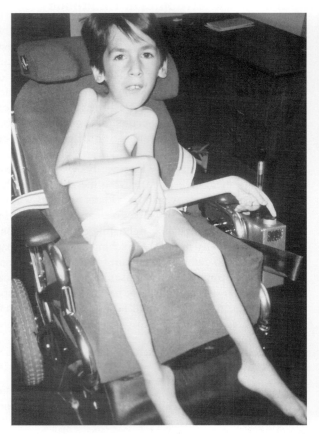 

5. Create activities that allow personal selection of distances and speeds in both locomotion and propulsion of activities.

6. Allow choices concerning which time of day seems best for exercise.

7. Arrange for exercise areas where temperature and humidity can be controlled.

8. Be patient. Allow extra time for initiating movement, getting into a comfortable position, and adjusting straps.

9. Introduce wheelchair sports and dance activities before wheelchairs are needed for activities of daily living (ADL). Create a positive attitude about wheelchair use.

10. Use lots of partner activities. Be sure individuals have partners to talk with during rest periods. Promote the development of friendships.

Thermal Injuries

Approximately 300,000 Americans annually suffer disfiguring injuries from fires. Another 12,000 die each year. The mortality rate is greatest among persons under age 5 and over age 65. No other type of accident permanently affects as many school-age children. Many thermal injuries result in amputations. As more persons are kept alive, physical educators must become increasingly adept at coping with all aspects of thermal injuries.

During past decades, children with more than 60% of their skin destroyed seldom survived. Now, increasing numbers of individuals are returning to society scarred and disfigured. What kind of physical education should be provided for the young child with extensive scar tissue? How can we help such children find social acceptance? What are the effects of disfiguring thermal injuries upon self-concept? An account of a child with third-degree burns over 90% of his body helps to answer these questions (see Rothenberg & White, 1985).

Thermal injury can be caused by fire, chemicals, electricity, or prolonged contact with extreme degrees of hot or cold liquids. Children who have sustained disfiguring thermal injuries, upon entering school, frequently recognize for the first time that they are deviates from the *normal*. They have been known to describe themselves as monsters. Typically, they have no scalp hair and no eyebrows or eyelashes, and scar tissue covers the face.

Scar Tissue

Scar tissue is an inevitable outcome of severe burns. Wound coverage is attained by the growth of scar tissue from the periphery to the center of the wound. Thick scar tissue forms **contractures** across joints, limits ROM, causes scoliosis of the spine, and shortens underlying muscles. The severity of

FIGURE 24.6 Hypertrophic scarring of healed burn on lateral aspect of trunk 2 years after burn occurred.

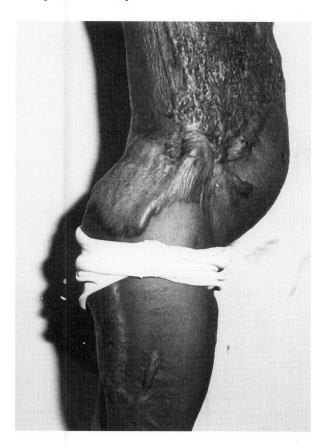

FIGURE 24.7 Jobsts elastic support jackets applied to arm and hand.

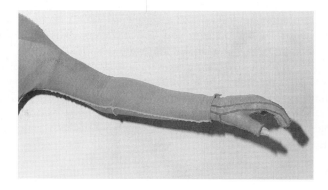

FIGURE 24.8 Jobsts elastic face mask and isoprene splint applied to the junction of the nose and cheek.

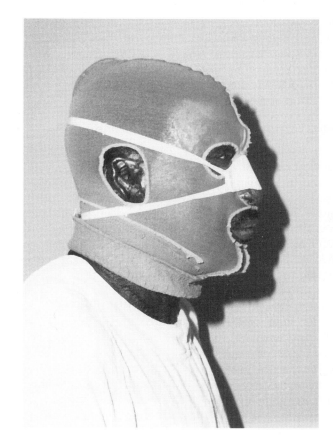

hypertrophic scarring (see Figure 24.6) and scar contracture may be decreased by early splinting, pressure, and therapeutic exercise.

Jobsts, elastic supports made to fit a specified portion of the body, may be prescribed as a means of reducing scar hypertrophy (see Figure 24.7). The purpose of the jobst is to apply constant pressure to the healed areas that are presenting signs of thickening scar tissue. The elastic supports achieve the best results when worn 24 hr daily. Therefore, as the child is returned to the classroom, he or she is expected to wear these supports under clothing.

Isoprene splints or *braces* may be applied to areas where the jobsts do not provide adequate pressure to the scar tissue. The elastic face mask, although helpful, does not apply significant pressure to the junction of the nose and cheek, which frequently fills with scars (see Figure 24.8). Isoprene splints require frequent removal for cleansing of the splint and application of lotion to prevent skin dryness. A child might be required to wear one of various types of hand splints for abduction of the thumb during daily activities. The student wearing such splints should be encouraged to use the hands normally in physical education activities and should be given no restrictions. Hence, the student is encouraged to increase **pain tolerance.** The physical educator might need to assist the child in proper cleaning and reapplication of the splint after vigorous exercise.

Program Implications

Several years of rehabilitation are required for persons with severe burns. They must not be excused from physical education because they are wearing jobsts, braces, or splints. Each student must learn the tolerance of new skin tissue to such elements as direct sunlight and chlorine in freshwater pools. They must expose themselves to the sun for a progressively longer period each day. PE-R personnel may wish to confer with a specialist in thermal injuries.

The young tissue of healed burns is delicate. It quickly becomes dry when exposed to sunlight for an extended period of time. Full thickness burns have a tendency to dry and irritate easily because of the absence or impairment of sweat ducts, hair follicles, and sebaceous glands. Itching occurs with drying and irritation of healed burn wounds. Frequent applications of a lanolin lotion are recommended.

Indoor physical education is preferable to activities in the direct sunlight. Since contractures are a major problem, emphasis should be upon flexibility or ROM exercises. Dance and aquatic activities are especially recommended. Many thermal injuries result in amputations, which are discussed later in the chapter.

Arthritis

Over 37 million Americans have some form of arthritis or rheumatic disease. The terms *rheumatism* and *arthritis* are sometimes used synonymously, but technically they are separate entities. **Rheumatism** refers to a whole group of inflammatory disorders affecting muscles and joints. It includes all forms of arthritis, myositis, myalgia, bursitis, fibromyosis, and other conditions characterized by soreness, stiffness, and pain in joints and associated structures. *Arthritis* means, literally, "inflammation of the joints." Rheumatoid arthritis is also completely different from rheumatic fever, although it can be a side effect of rheumatic fever.

Adult Rheumatoid Arthritis and Osteoarthritis

Over 100 causes of joint inflammation have been identified, but most cases fall within two categories: (a) rheumatoid arthritis and (b) osteoarthritis, often called degenerative joint disease. **Rheumatoid arthritis** affects all ages, with the usual onset between 20 and 50 years. It is three times more common in women than men until age 50, when the gender distribution becomes equal. **Osteoarthritis** mainly affects persons age 50 and over and has the same incidence in men and women. Osteoarthritis is the major cause of disability in the older population; advanced cases are aggressively treated with joint replacements that permit full range of motion (ROM) with no pain.

Joint problems in arthritis are pain, swelling, heat, redness (symptoms of inflammation), decreased ROM, and related muscle weakness. In advanced cases, the affected joint becomes unstable and deformed. Rheumatoid arthritis is most troublesome early in the day, and its characteristic aching and stiffness are relieved by gentle exercise. In contrast, pain in osteoarthritis is associated with use or weight bearing and worsens as the day goes on. Medication is prescribed to reduce inflammation and pain. **Nonsteroidal anti-inflammatory drugs** (NSAIDs) like aspirin and fenoprofere are favored.

Exercise is strongly recommended, with the **2-hr pain principle** serving as the guide to activity intensity. This principle states that any pain continuing 2 hr after exercise is an indicator that the exercise was too intense or inappropriate (Samples, 1990). Isometric strength exercises can be used when pain prevents other kinds. Low-impact activities that are smooth and repetitive are recommended (e.g., swimming, walking, cycling, ice skating, cross country skiing). When osteoarthritis affects lower limbs, weight-bearing exercises may be contraindicated; swimming, water exercise, and cycling therefore are often the activities of choice.

The Arthritis Foundation YMCA Aquatic Program (AFYAP) is the best-known program for persons with arthritis. Recommended water temperature is 83° to 88°F. Information about AFYAP and other programs can be obtained from the Arthritis Foundation, Box 19000, Atlanta, GA 30326 and from YMCAs.

Juvenile Rheumatoid Arthritis

The average age of onset of juvenile rheumatoid arthritis is 6 years, with two peaks of incidence occurring between ages 2 and 4 and between ages 8 and 11. Rheumatoid arthritis affects three to five times as many girls as boys. The specific etiology is generally unknown. Because young children seldom complain of pain, a slight limp is often the only manifestation of the condition. More than 70,000 U.S. children and youth have juvenile rheumatoid arthritis.

Mode of Onset

The onset of juvenile rheumatoid arthritis is capricious, sometimes affecting only one joint and other times involving several joints. In about 30% of the initial episodes, only one joint, usually the knee, is involved, but within a few weeks or months, many more joints may swell. The onset of arthritis may be sudden, characterized by severe pain, or progressive, with symptoms appearing almost imperceptibly over a long period of time. In the latter situation, joint pain is not a major problem.

Systemic and Peripheral Effects

Rheumatoid arthritis may be *systemic,* affecting the entire body, or *peripheral,* affecting only the joints. When the disease is systemic, the joint inflammation is accompanied by such symptoms as fever, rash, malaise, pallor, enlargement of lymph nodes, enlargement of liver and spleen, and pericarditis. Systemic rheumatoid arthritis in children is sometimes called **Still's disease,** deriving its name from George F. Still, a London physician who first described the condition in 1896.

Knee

The knee is involved more often than other joints, causing a slight limp as the child walks. The characteristic swelling gives the appearance of **knock-knees** (genu valva). Swelling makes knee extension difficult or impossible. Knee flexion deteriorates from its normal range of 120° to 80 or 90°. Flexion contraction usually develops.

Ankle

Involvement of the ankle joint results in a ducklike, flat-footed gait similar to that of the toddler. Muscles of the lower leg tend to atrophy, and the Achilles tendon becomes excessively tight. Limitation of motion and pain occur most often in dorsiflexion.

Foot

Swelling within the foot joints makes wearing shoes uncomfortable. Characteristic arthritic defects are pronation, flatfoot, *calcaneal valgus* (outward bending), and a cock-up position of the metatarsal phalangeal joints, especially the big toe.

FIGURE 24.9 Swollen fingers and hands require special attention.

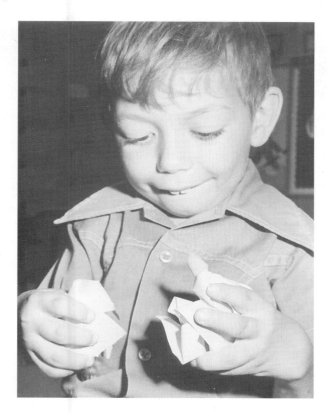

FIGURE 24.10 (A) The first half of logroll demands an all-out effort. (B) The second half shows characteristic flexion.

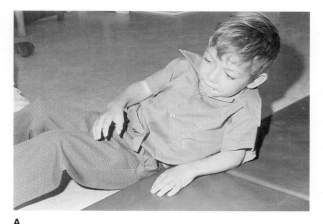

A

B

Wrist, Hand, and Arm

Wrist, hand, and arm extension is limited by many factors (see Figure 24.9). A common late manifestation is **ankylosis.** This is an abnormal union of bones whose surfaces come into contact because the interjacent cartilages have been destroyed. Normal grip strength is lessened by the combination of muscular atrophy, contracture, and pain on motion.

Hip

Over one third of the children with juvenile rheumatoid arthritis favor one hip over the other. All ROMs are limited, but the flexion contracture is most troublesome.

Spinal Column

Juvenile rheumatoid arthritis tends to limit motion in the cervical spine (see Figure 24.10). There may be spasms of the upper trapezius muscle and local tenderness along the spine. The thoracic and lumbar spine are seldom involved. In young males, a form of rheumatoid arthritis, classified as **rheumatoid spondylitis**, causes pain and stiffness in the back. This condition is also called *Marie-Strumpell disease.*

Course of the Disease

In spite of enlargement of the liver and spleen, pericarditis, and other side effects, rheumatoid arthritis is rarely fatal. It does cause severe disability in about 25% of the cases and mild to moderate disability in 30%. Complete functional recovery is reported in 30 to 70% of the cases. When the disease affects the entire body, the period of acute illness lasts from 1 week to several months. During this time, children may be confined to home. They require frequent rest periods and daily ROM exercise. When joint swelling is significantly reduced and other symptoms disappear, the disease is said to be in partial or total remission. Unfortunately, periods of remission are interspersed with weeks of acute illness and maximum joint involvement.

Program Implications

The purposes of movement for the child with rheumatoid arthritis are (a) relief of pain and spasm, (b) prevention of flexion contractures and other deformities, (c) maintenance of normal ROMs for each joint, and (d) maintenance of strength, particularly in the extensor muscles (Tecklin, 1989). *Daily exercise must begin as soon as the acute inflammation start to subside.* At this time, even gentle, passive movement may be painful, but every day of inactivity increases joint stiffness and the probability of permanent deformity. Physical activity personnel should work with parents in establishing a home exercise program. In addition, children should participate in a school physical education program adapted to their needs.

FIGURE 24.11   Cortisone and other drugs used in arthritis tend to inhibit normal growth. This 8-year-old boy is so disabled that he uses a quadricycle in lieu of walking.

Physical activity personnel must plan exercise sequences that will strengthen the extensors, the abductors, the internal rotators, and the pronators. *Most authorities agree that flexion strength exercises are contraindicated.* Activities of daily living (ADL) provide adequate flexion, and there is no danger that the joints will stiffen in flexion.

In the early stages of remission, most of the exercises should be performed in water or in a lying position to minimize the pull of gravity. Stretching exercises to minimize contractures are essential. When exercise tolerance is built up sufficiently, activities in a sitting position can be initiated. Riding a bicycle or tricycle affords a means of transportation as well as good exercise. Sitting for long periods of time, however, is contraindicated since it results in stiffness.

Some children, such as the 8-year-old boy depicted in Figure 24.11, are left so disabled that they cannot walk. The gait of the child with severe arthritis is slow and halting. The child has difficulty ascending and descending steps. Any accidental bumping or pushing in the hallway or while standing in lines is especially painful. Older students who change rooms should be released from each class early so that they can get to the next location before the bustle of activity begins. Occasionally, their schedule of courses must be adjusted so that all classrooms are on the same floor and/or in close proximity.

Physical activity personnel should know the normal ROM in degrees for each joint and be proficient in the use of the goniometer. The number of degrees through which each body part can move is recorded and serves as an index against which progress can be measured. Each body part, even the individual fingers and toes, should be taken through its full range of motion two or three times daily. These stretching exercises may be either active or partner-assisted as in proprioceptive neuromuscular facilitation (PNF).

Contraindicated Activities

The following activities are contraindicated for individuals with arthritis because of trauma to the joints:

1. All jumping activities, including jump rope and trampoline work
2. Activities in which falls might be frequent, such as roller skating, skiing, and gymnastics
3. Contact sports, particularly football, soccer, and volleyball
4. Hopping, leaping, and movement exploration activities in which the body leaves the floor
5. Diving
6. Horseback riding
7. Sitting for long periods

Recommended Activities

During periods of remission, persons with arthritis who can participate in an activity *without pain* should be encouraged, but not forced, to do so. Because of the weeks and/or months of enforced rest during acute attacks, circulorespiratory endurance is likely to be subaverage. Hence, frequent rest periods are needed.

Swimming and creative or modern dance are among the best activities. The front crawl and other strokes that emphasize extension are especially recommended. Water must be maintained at as warm a temperature as is feasible. Creative dance also stresses extension in its many stretching techniques and affords opportunities for learning to relate to others. Group choreography and performance can provide as many positive experiences as the team sports that are denied youngsters with arthritis. Quiet recreational games include croquet, ring or ball tossing, miniature golf, horseshoes, shuffleboard, and pool. Throwing activities are better than striking and catching activities.

Medication Side Effects

Cortisone and other steroids are prescribed when NSAIDs like aspirin are not effective. Unfortunately, one of the major side effects of steroids is the inhibition of normal growth, causing children to look several years younger than they really are. Alterations in body growth occur as the direct result of severe rheumatoid arthritis. This stunting of growth, coupled with the overprotection of parents, may contribute to serious problems in peer adjustment. See Chapter 19 for other side effects of steroids.

Arthrogryposis

Approximately 500 infants are born with *arthrogryposis* (pronounced ar-throw-gry-pó-sis) each year in the United States.

FIGURE 24.12 Arthrogryposis, overweight, and poor fitness combine to make batting a real chore for this 11-year-old. Arms show the characteristic increase of subcutaneous fat and loss of skin flexion creases, which result in a tubular appearance sometimes described as wooden and doll-like. Despite the awkwardness of joint positions and mechanics, no pain is felt.

FIGURE 24.13 This lively 7-year-old with arthrogryposis demonstrates his best posture.

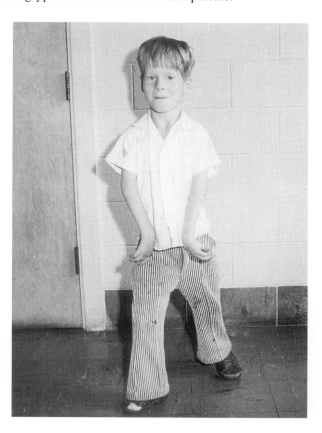

The incidence is 3 per 10,000 births. **Arthrogryposis** multiplex congenital (AMC) is a nonprogressive **congenital contracture syndrome** usually characterized by internal rotation at the shoulder joints, elbow extension, pronated forearms, radial flexion of wrists, flexion and outward rotation at the hip joint, and abnormal positions of knees and feet. This birth defect varies tremendously in severity, with some persons in wheelchairs and others only minimally affected. The contracture syndrome is characterized by dominance of fatty and connective tissue at joints in place of normal muscle tissue. Some or all joints may be involved.

The major disability is restricted ROM. Many persons with AMC have almost no arm and shoulder movement. They can, however, excel in track activities in a motorized chair. Figures 24.12 and 24.13 depict two boys, ages 11 and 7 and from the same school system, who have arthrogryposis. Although both boys have some limb involvement, their greatest problem is the fixed medial rotation of the shoulder joints (see Figure 24.14). Both have normal intelligence, as is almost always the case in arthrogryposis. Until recently, the older boy walked without the use of crutches. His present reliance on them is believed to be somewhat psychosomatic, although articular surfaces do tend to deteriorate with age.

Major physical education goals are to increase ROM (flexibility) and to teach sports and games for leisure use. Activities discussed under arthritis are appropriate in most cases, as are those in Chapter 25 on cerebral palsy. Programming

FIGURE 24.14 Medial rotation at the shoulder joints complicates fine muscle coordination.

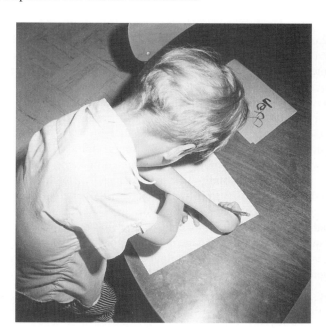

FIGURE 24.15 Water activities provide range-of-motion exercises for young child with arthrogryposis.

FIGURE 24.16 Individual differences in stature and body proportions in three children, age 10 years.

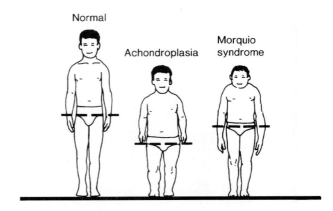

depends, of course, upon sport classification. Swimming is particularly recommended in that it fulfills both goals. It teaches a leisure skill and stretches muscle groups.

Dr. Jo Cowden (1985), at the University of New Orleans, reported movement work with a 4-year-old AMC child over a 2-year period and emphasized the importance of early intervention (see Figure 24.15). Periodic videotapes show that levels of mobility have been obtained that were once not believed possible. When the child began the program, she used her chin to pull herself across the mat, rolled from place to place, or used a wheelchair. Now she can crawl and creep through obstacle courses and walk using reciprocal braces with a walker. Like many children with spina bifida, she was taught first to use a **parapodium** (standing apparatus) with a walker and then progressed to reciprocal braces. Surgery, casting, and bracing have characterized much of her early life. As a potential les autres athlete, this child can swim competitively with flotation devices and engage in slalom, track, and soccer activities in a wheelchair. As important as increasing ROM is developing attitudes and habits favorable to physical recreation.

Dwarfism and Short-Stature Syndromes

Since 1985, the date of the founding of the Dwarf Athletic Association of America (DAAA), persons who meet the medical criteria for short-stature syndrome have preferred to be called dwarfs. Earlier, the preferred terminology was "little people," as indicated by the formation of the Little People of America (LPA), an organization with about 5,000 members that meets annually. Today, both *dwarf* and *little people* are acceptable terms. The term *midget,* however, is offensive and should never be used. Dwarfs consider themselves normal and call nondwarfs *average-sized people* rather than "normal."

The medical criteria for dwarfism varies. The height standard for membership of adults in LPA is 4 ft, 10 inches or less, but DAAA uses a 5 ft or less criterion. In general, dwarfs are at least 3 standard deviations below the mean height of the general population and shorter than 98% of their peers (see Figure 24.16). Short stature in dwarfs is caused by a genetic condition or some kind of pathology.

Disproportionate and Proportionate Dwarfs

Over 250 types of dwarfism affect about 100,000 persons (Ablon, 1988). In general, dwarfs are classified into two categories: disproportionate and proportionate (Scott, 1988). The disproportionate category is more common.

Disproportionate dwarfs typically have average-sized torsos but unusually short arms and legs. The major cause of disproportionate dwarfism is **skeletal dysplasia** or chondrodystrophy, the failure of cartilage (*chondro*) to develop into bone. This is either inherited or caused by spontaneous gene mutations.

Proportionate dwarfs are persons whose body parts are proportionate but abnormally short. The main cause of this is pituitary gland dysfunction, also known as growth hormone (GH) deficiency. In addition to endocrine etiologies, there are numerous other causes. Many of these conditions can now be treated so that prevalence within this category is decreasing.

Achondroplasia and Hypoachondroplasia

Achondroplasia, the most common form of dwarfism, is a disproportionate body structure with an average-size trunk, short limbs, and, in many cases, a relatively large head (see Figure 24.17A). The name is more easily remembered if we consider

A. Achondroplasia

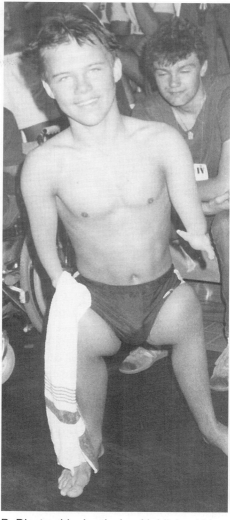

B. Diastrophic dysplasia with bilateral hip dislocation

C. Spondyloepiphyseal dysplasia (SED)

the meaning of each of its parts. First of all, remember that skeletal bones begin as cartilage in the embryo. The Latin word for cartilage is *chondro* (pronounced kon-dro). **Chondroplasia** thus refers to normal formation of cartilage because *plasia* means "to mold or form." **Achondroplasia** is simply the prefix *a-* (meaning "without") attached to *chondroplasia.*

Incidence figures for achondroplasia vary from 1 in 10,000 (Ablon, 1988) to 1 in 40,000 births (Scott, 1988). Associated problems are lumbar lordosis, waddling gait caused by abnormally short femoral heads, restricted elbow extension, and bowed legs. The latter is generally corrected by surgery. Other than lordosis, there are no spinal problems. Aerobic fitness may be limited by small chest size and narrow nasal passages. In general, however, persons with achondroplasia can be excellent athletes.

Hypoachondroplasia is the term for the tallest dwarfs, individuals who are actively recruited into sport as soon as they are discovered. The prefix *hypo-* indicates less achondroplasia and thus greater height.

Diastrophic Dysplasia

Diastrophic dysplasia is the most disabling of the common forms of dwarfism (see Figure 24.17B). This condition, which often requires crutches or wheelchairs for ambulation, typically involves spinal deformity (usually scoliosis), clubfoot (talipes equinovarus), hand deformities, and frequent hip and knee dislocations. These anomalies are resistant to corrective surgery. Figure 24.17B shows bilateral hip dislocation.

The name *diastrophic dysplasia* is derived from Latin terms for two (*di-, dia-*) problems: failure of nourishment (*trophy* or *trophic*) during prenatal bone growth and *dystrophy,* failure of nerve centers that innervate and/or failure of blood supply that carries nutrients.

Spondyloepiphyseal Dysplasia (SED)

SED is mainly abnormal development of the growth plates (*epiphyses*) within the vertebrae (*spondylo*) (see Figure 24.17C). This causes a **disproportionately short trunk** with various spinal and limb irregularities. The arms typically look abnormally long. The face and skull in SED are normal, but eye complications are common. Many persons with SED are excellent athletes.

Program Implications

Profound shortness is obviously a disadvantage in most sports. Moreover, disproportionately short limbs are a limitation in ball handling, racquet sports, and track. However, in some sports, such as powerlifting and tumbling, average trunk size and short limbs are advantageous (Low, Knudsen, & Sherrill, 1996).

DAAA promotes several sports. Especially popular are basketball, volleyball, powerlifting, track, field, swimming, bowling, and boccia. Basketball is played with baskets set at the standard height. The court size is regulation, and the ball size is that used by average-sized women. In volleyball, the net is lowered slightly so dwarfs can spike. Work is underway to create a sport classification system for track, field, and swimming so that competition among persons of different heights and proportions can be more fair (Low, 1992). Boccia is an accuracy sport in which players take turns throwing small balls toward a target ball.

Nonachondroplasia dwarfism is associated with **atlantoaxial instability** (see Chapter 21). Individuals with these forms of dwarfism are required to submit neck x-rays prior to sport participation. Contraindicated activities when atlantoaxial instability is suspected are diving, jumping, gymnastics, heading soccer balls, and contact sports.

Several other joint defects limit ROM and contribute to a high incidence of dislocations and trauma. Especially affected are the shoulder, elbow, hip, and knee joints (Knudsen, 1993). The inability to completely straighten the elbow causes difficulty with respect to the regulations that govern powerlifting. Thrusting the head forward to gain the advantage when crossing the finish line in track may cause muscle strain if the head is disproportionately large. Strenuous training in track and/or distance running may lead to hip and knee joint trauma. Swimming may be the best lifetime sport to promote because it does not stress joints.

Internationally, dwarfs compete with les autres. The classification system used is considered unfair by many dwarfs (Sawisch, 1990), and an international sport organization for dwarfs has been founded so that, in addition to Paralympic sport, dwarfs can compete against one another.

In school settings, adaptations are necessary for dwarfs as well as for nondwarf short people. Class teams, formed to practice basketball and volleyball skills, should be equated on heights or a system whereby the shorter team starts with a set number of points. No one likes to feel that he or she is a handicap to the team; the teacher's role is to prevent such feelings by adapting game rules and strategies.

Short Stature and Normal Intelligence

Intelligence and mental functioning of dwarfs are the same as in the average-sized population. Several other short stature conditions, in which intelligence is usually normal, warrant mention. Three conditions are characterized by a disproportionally short neck: (a) **Turner syndrome** (females only), (b) **Noonan syndrome** (males only), and (c) **Morquio syndrome** (both sexes).

Turner and Noonan syndromes are chromosomal, whereas Morquio syndrome is metabolic. Turner and Noonan syndromes have several common features: (a) necks often webbed as well as short, (b) broad chests with widely spaced nipples, (c) low posterior hairline, and (d) various other deviations. Most persons with Turner and Noonan syndromes are not sexually fertile; males have an abnormally small penis, whereas the ovaries in females fail to develop properly. In Morquio syndrome, the trunk and neck are abnormally short, causing the arms to look disproportionately long (see Figure 24.16). Usually, severe kyphosis, knock-knees, and bone growth irregularity limit hip and joint flexibility.

Short Stature and Mental Retardation

Several mental retardation syndromes are characterized by short stature. These include Down syndrome (1 per 2,000 incidence), Cornelia de Lange syndrome (1 per 10,000 incidence), fetal alcohol syndrome (3 to 6 per 1,000 incidence), Hurler's syndrome (1 per 100,000 incidence), and rubella syndrome (1 per 10,000 incidence). These conditions obviously require physical education adaptations for short stature and short limbs. They are discussed more fully, however, in Chapter 21 on mental retardation since the primary adaptations relate to mental functioning (i.e., task analysis and behavior management).

Osteogenesis Imperfecta

Word derivation is also helpful in visualizing **osteogenesis imperfecta** *(OI). Os* and *osteo* refer to "bone." *Genesis* means "origin." *Imperfecta* clearly indicates that something is wrong with bone formation. The basic defect of OI (pronounced os-tee-oh-gen′-e-sis im-per-fect′-ah) is in the **collagen fibers** (a type of protein) found in **connective tissue** (bone, ligaments, cartilage, and skin). The defect makes bone and cartilage soft and brittle, while causing skin and ligaments to be overly elastic and hyperextensible.

OI is an inherited condition that is present at birth. Bone breaks peak between 2 and 15 years of age, after which the incidence of fractures decreases. Indicators are **short stature** and small limbs that are bowed in various distortions from repetitive fractures. Joints are hyperextensible, with predisposition for dislocation. Most persons with OI are in wheelchairs.

Chest defects (barrel and pigeon shapes) limit respiratory capacity and aerobic endurance, and spinal defects are common (see Figure 24.18). These are partly from **osteoporosis** (bone degeneration) caused by lack of exercise. Clearly, adapted physical activity, especially swimming and ROM games, is important. Until the condition arrests itself, usually in adolescence, motorized chairs permit the challenge and thrill of track and slalom events. Use of a 5-oz **soft shot** (beanbag) or discus seldom causes fractures, whereas regulation balls might. Shuffleboard and ramp bowling add variety.

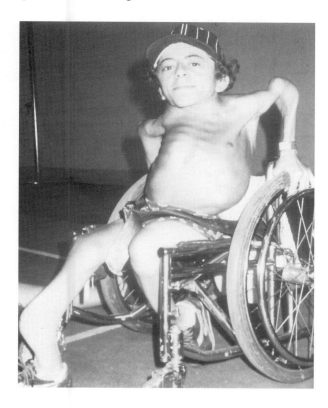

After the condition arrests itself, the person can engage in almost any sport. Wayne Washington, who weighs 112 lb, is a world-class weight lifter with a 290-lb record; he began weight lifting at age 18 (see Figure 24.19). Bill Lehr, a world-class track and swimming star, also plays wheelchair basketball and has completed the Boston Marathon in 2 hr and 50 min (see Figure 24.20). He has done the 100 m in 18.8, the 400 in 1:16.8, and the 800 in 2:34.

About his childhood, Bill says,

I was born with a broken collarbone, my knees were bent in a way a baby's knees aren't supposed to bend, and in the first 12 years of my life, I must have spent half the time in surgery. . . . When I was growing, I could walk and even run a few yards at a time. Then a bone would break in one of my legs, and they'd have to put a cast on me. I'd be laid up for a few weeks, get out of the cast, but that would only last a week or two before I'd break another bone and have to be put back in a cast again.

Before Bill's condition arrested itself, he had over 40 fractures. From age 7 onward, he was a wheelchair user; he began wheelchair basketball and track at age 12. Telling OI children about world class athletes like Bill Lehr and Wayne Washington and showing them photos and videotapes opens new horizons; this is an important part of the physical educator's job.

The incidence of OI is 1 in 50,000 births for congenital OI and 1 in 25,000 for a later appearing, less serious form called OI tarda. These medical statistics may be inaccurate in that OI students can easily be spotted in every large school system. OI makes persons eligible to compete either with the dwarf or les autres organizations.

Ehlers-Danlos Syndrome

Several collagen defects are similar to OI but do not cause bones to break. **Ehlers-Danlos syndrome** is an inherited condition characterized by hyperextensibility of joints, with predisposition for dislocation at shoulder girdle, shoulder, elbow, hip, and knee joints. Other features are loose and/or hyperextensible skin, slow wound healing with inadequate scar tissue, and fragility of blood vessel walls. Sports with a high risk of injury are therefore contraindicated. Special emphasis is given to blister prevention (e.g., properly fitted shoes) and hand protection (e.g., gloves). The best sport is probably swimming.

Childhood Growth Disorders

The physical educator working with junior high or middle school youngsters is confronted with a high incidence of **osteochondroses** or growth plate disorders. Such diagnoses as *Perthes' disease, Osgood-Schlatter disease, Kohler's disease,*

FIGURE 24.21   Common sites of osteochondroses.

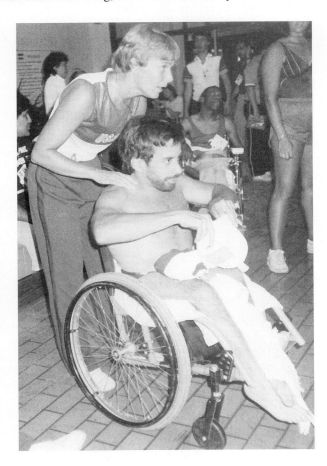

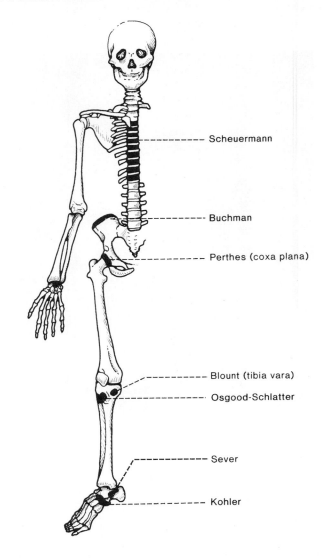

Calve's disease, and *Scheuermann's disease* all fall within this category and demand adaptations in physical education.

An *osteochondrosis* is an abnormality of an **epiphysis** (growth plate) in which normal growth or ossification is disturbed. Disorders of the growth plate include premature closure, delayed closure, and interruption in the growth process. **Epiphyseal closure** occurs at different ages. Bones of the upper limbs and scapulae become completely ossified at ages 17 to 20 years. Bones of the lower limbs become completely ossified at 18 to 23 years. Bones of the vertebrae, sternum, and clavicle are the last to ossify (ages 23 to 25) and thus are the most vulnerable to growth disorders.

Bone growth and subsequent closure are affected by heredity, diet, hormones, general health status, and trauma. Ill health and malnutrition generally delay overall growth plate closure. Obese children are particularly susceptible to disorders of the growth plate.

Some of the most common sites of growth plate disorders are depicted in Figure 24.21 and listed in Table 24.2. Over 70% of the osteochondroses are found at the first four sites mentioned in Table 24.2. The pathology in all of the osteochondroses is similar. For unknown reasons, cells within the bony center of the epiphysis undergo partial **necrosis** (death), probably from interference with the blood supply. The

necrotic tissue is removed by special cells called osteoclasts, and the bony center is temporarily softened and liable to **shape deformation,** which may become permanent. In time, the condition arrests itself. New, healthy bone cells replace the dead tissue, and the bones return to normal.

This cycle of changes may take as long as 2 years, during which time the youngster must be kept off the affected limb. Enforcing this rule of no weight bearing on an athletic child is not easy since the child experiences no symptoms of illness and only occasional pain. The primary danger in osteochondroses is not in the present, but rather in the deformity, limp, and predisposition to arthritis that may occur later if rules are not followed.

Osgood-Schlatter Condition

Osgood-Schlatter disease is a temporary degenerative condition of the **tibial tuberosity** that causes pain and swelling where the patellar tendon inserts on the tibia (see Figure 24.22). It is caused by a partial separation of the growth plate from the tibia, typically brought on by overuse or

Table 24.2 Common sites of growth plate disorders.

Bony Part Affected	Name of Disorder
Tibial tuberosity	Osgood-Schlatter
Calcaneus	Sever
Vertebra	Scheuermann
Head of femur	Perthes (Legg-Calve-Perthes)
Tibia	Blount
Tarsal, navicular	Kohler
Iliac crest	Buchman

FIGURE 24.22 Site of Osgood-Schlatter disorder.

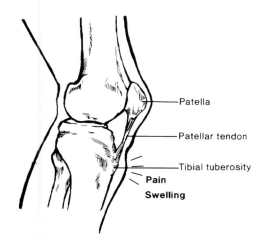

FIGURE 24.23 Common hip joint growth disorders.

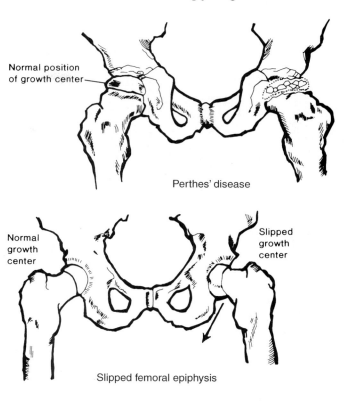

trauma. Adolescents who are active in strenuous sports involving the knee joint are the most vulnerable. Continuous rope jumping or kicking, for example, places much stress on the knee. Teachers who use contraindicated exercises like repeated squats and the duck walk may contribute to the onset of this condition.

Diagnosis is made by X ray, and treatment varies, depending on severity and the philosophy of the physician. The knee may be immobilized in a brace or cast for several weeks, after which activity is restricted for 3 to 6 months. *In most cases, students are told to avoid explosive knee extension or all knee extension.* Nonweight-bearing isometric exercises that strengthen the quadriceps and stretch the hamstrings may be prescribed.

Perthes' Condition (Legg-Calve-Perthes)

Perthes' condition, the destruction of the growth center of the hip joint, occurs between the ages of 4 and 8 (see Figure 24.23). Its incidence is 1 per 18,000, and approximately four to five times more boys than girls are affected. Typically, the condition lasts 2 to 4 years, during which the child may need adapted physical education—most likely in the mainstream setting. Adapting is needed in choice of activities that can be done while wearing a splint and/or using a wheelchair. If the hip joint is not protected (i.e., kept in non-weight-bearing status) during the body's natural repair process, the femoral head

becomes flattened and irregular **(coxa plana),** which makes the joint surface incongruent and leads to hip joint degenerate arthritis. Sometimes, despite the best care, permanent damage (usually a slight limp) occurs. Champion wheelchair tennis and basketball player Steve Welch is illustrative of adults who have residual effects from Perthes' condition.

Slipped Femoral Epiphysis

Also called adolescent *coxa vara* or epiphysiolysis, **slipped femoral epiphysis (SFE)** is a hip joint disorder diagnosed by a waddling gait or a limp that favors one leg. Typically, the head of the femur is outwardly rotated. This is caused by a **downward-backward-medial slippage** of the growth center on the femoral head (see Figure 24.23). Attributed to trauma, stress, or overuse, the condition typically occurs in adolescence and is associated with obesity. The incidence is 2 to 13 per 100,000. SFE is more common in males (2.2 to 1) than females and in blacks than whites. It may also occur in younger children as a result of falls from great heights or abuse and in newborns as a result of difficult deliveries.

The groin, buttock, and lateral hip are the major pain centers. If the condition is not corrected, the affected leg becomes shorter, and adduction contractures result (Chung, 1981). These decrease the angulation of the neck of the femur, making it more horizontal, and causing an inward inclination (vara position) of the femur. During exercise, persons with SFE show limited hip joint inward rotation and abduction.

Once diagnosed, SFE is usually corrected surgically by pinning the epiphysis in place. More conservative treatment

FIGURE 24.24   Hip joint dislocation and slippage.

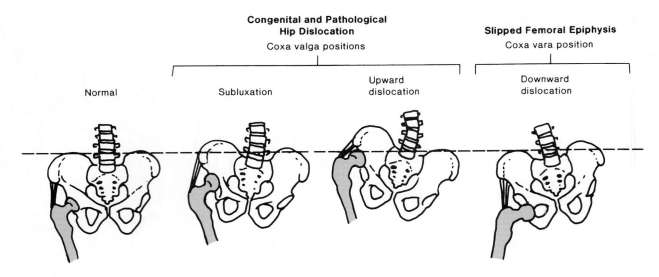

is use of short-leg casts with a crossbar to prevent weight bearing and to hold the femoral head in abduction and inward rotation. *Students are usually restricted from vigorous weight-bearing physical education for about a year.* Adaptation entails arranging for swimming and/or upper extremity sports and exercises in place of the regular curriculum.

Scheuermann's Disease

Juvenile kyphosis, or ***Scheuermann's disease,*** is a disturbance in growth of the thoracic vertebrae. It results from *epiphysitis* (inflammation of an epiphysis) and/or *osteochondritis* (inflammation of cartilage), either of which may cause fragmentation of vertebral bodies. One or several vertebrae are involved. The etiology is generally unknown. *During the active phase, forward flexion is contraindicated.* The student should be protected from all flexion movements by a hyperextension brace, which places the weight on the neural arches rather than on the defective vertebral bodies.

Although there is some discomfort, the pain is not great enough to impose limitation of natural movement; sometimes, the condition is pain-free. In such instances, convincing the student to refrain from activity may be difficult. Unfortunately, if bracing and nonactivity are not enforced, the resulting kyphotic hump may be both severe and persistent. When X rays reveal the healing of fragmented areas, class participation is resumed with no restrictions. Occasionally, the student will continue to wear a back brace, body jacket, or cast for a number of months after the disease is arrested.

Scoliosis and Chest Deformity

Lateral curvature of the spine is discussed fully in Chapter 14 on postures. Severe conditions are treated by surgery, casting, and braces. As in Scheuermann's disease, vigorous forward flexion of the trunk may be contraindicated. Otherwise, physical activity is seldom restricted unless the condition is caused by concurrent disabilities.

Many of the conditions in this chapter are associated with scoliosis and chest deformities that limit respiration and aerobic fitness. Breathing and ROM exercises and games are important.

Congenital Dislocation of the Hip

Congenital dislocation of the hip (CDH) encompasses various degrees of **dysplasia,** or abnormal development, of the hip socket (acetabulum) and/or head of the femur. This condition is the fourth most common congenital defect. It is more common among girls than boys and usually occurs in one hip rather than both. Its incidence is approximately 1 to 3 per 1,000 births.

Subluxation and *luxation* are synonyms for dislocation, describing the position of the femoral head in relation to a **shallow, dysplasic acetabulum** (see Figure 24.24). In subluxation, the femur is only partially displaced, whereas in luxation, the femoral head is completely dislocated above the acetabulum rim. These aberrations often are not recognized until the child begins to walk. Nonsurgical treatment involves repositioning, traction, and casting. In the majority of cases in which the child is over age 3, surgical reduction (repositioning) is used. After age 6, more complicated operative procedures, such as **osteotomy** (dividing a bone or cutting out a portion) and **arthroplasty** (reconstructing a joint), are applied.

Reference to congenital hip dislocation on a child's record usually means that he or she has undergone long periods of hospitalization and immobilization in splints or casts extending from waist to toes. Generally, the child has had fewer opportunities to learn social and motor skills through informal play than have normal peers. As in other congenital anomalies, any problems the child manifests are more likely to be psychological than physical.

Pathological Dislocation of the Hip

Dislocation of the hip is a problem commonly associated with persons unable to stand because of severe paralytic or neurological conditions (polio, spina bifida, cerebral palsy). The

FIGURE 24.25 Abnormalities of foot alignment. Varus positions are frequently seen in hemiplegic spastic cerebral palsy and in uncorrected congenital bone and joint defects. Valgus positions are seen in association with flat and/or pronated feet. The cavus position is rare.

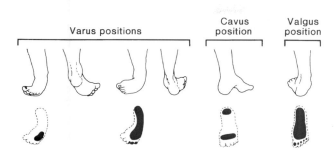

FIGURE 24.26 Surgically corrected clubfeet of preadolescent boy.

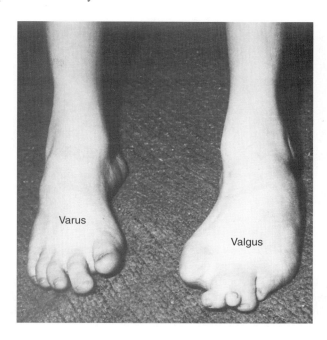

incidence of dislocation in severely disabled nonambulatory persons is 25%. The average age of dislocation is 7 years, but the range of frequent occurrence varies from 2 to 10 years. Like CDH, the condition is corrected by surgery.

Pathological dislocation may occur at any age. In most cases, the head of the femur becomes **displaced upward and anteriorly.** Pathological dislocation appears mostly in persons with **coxa valga** (increased neck-shaft angle of femur) and hip **adduction contracture.** Coxa valga is present in most normal infants before weight bearing begins; a gradual change in neck-shaft femoral angle accompanies normal motor development. Childhood coxa valga and associated hip dislocation thus sometimes characterize delayed or abnormal motor development.

Clubfoot (Talipes)

Talipes equinovarus, or *congenital clubfoot,* is the most common of all orthopedic defects, with an incidence of 1 out of approximately 700 births (see Figure 24.25). **Talipes** comes from two Latin words: *talus,* meaning "ankle" and *pes,* meaning "foot." *Equinovarus* (stemming from *equus,* meaning "horse," and *varus,* meaning "bent in") is an adjective specifying a position in which the entire foot is inverted, the heel is drawn up, and the forefoot is adducted. This forces the child to walk on the outer border of the foot. Although bracing, casting, and surgery may correct clubfoot, the child reverts to supinated walking when especially tired or upon first awakening.

Children who have undergone casting and splinting for clubfoot are generally required to wear *corrective shoes.* Extremely expensive, these shoes are often unattractive high-top, leather shoes with many laces. Many children, sensitive about this prescription, refuse to wear their corrective shoes as they grow older. Or they may ask to wear tennis shoes, at least in physical education, in order to be like their friends. Permission should be tactfully denied unless written instructions from the physician indicate that the child need not wear the corrective shoes during physical education.

Types of Talipes

Talipes equinovarus varies in degree of severity. Changes in the tendons and ligaments result mostly from contractures. The Achilles and tibial tendons are always shortened, causing a tendency to walk on the toes or forefoot. Bony changes occur chiefly in the talus, calcaneus, navicular, and cuboid. Tibial torsion is usually present.

Several other types of talipes are recognized (see Figure 24.25):

1. **Talipes cavus.** Hollow foot or arch so high as to be disabling.
2. **Talipes calcaneus.** Contracture of foot in dorsiflexed position.
3. **Talipes equinus.** Contracture of foot in plantar-flexed position.
4. **Talipes varus.** Contracture of foot with toes and sole of foot turned inward. Associated with **spastic** hemiplegic cerebral palsy and/or scissors gait.
5. **Talipes valgus.** Contracture of foot with toes and sole of foot turned outward. Associated with **athetoid** cerebral palsy, arthritis, and flat or pronated feet.

Just as *talipes equinovarus,* the most common form, is a combination of two types, so any two types can coexist as calcaneovarus, calcaneovalgus, or equinovalgus.

Program Implications

Figure 24.26 shows the clubfoot of a preadolescent boy who has undergone several operations and spent months in casts and braces. He is an enthusiastic athlete and in the starting lineup of his Little League baseball team. His slight limp is noticeably worse during cold winter days and rainy seasons, when he can hardly walk the first hour or so after awakening. As the day wears on, his gait becomes almost normal, enabling him to run fast enough to hold his own in athletic feats with peers.

FIGURE 24.27 The Denis-Browne splint used to correct clubfoot and other problems.

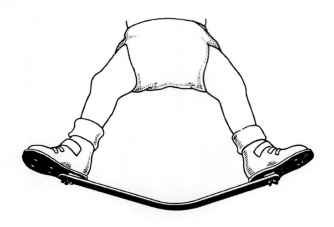

Metatarsus varus is a frequent congenital defect similar to clubfoot except that only the forefoot or metatarsal area is affected. The treatment for talipes and metatarsus varus is similar, beginning preferably within the first 2 weeks of life with casting that may continue for many months. The weight of a cast prevents normal mobility of the infant and may delay the accomplishment of such motor tasks as rolling over, standing alone, and walking.

The Denis-Browne splint is used for correcting clubfoot and other defects (see Figure 24.27). It may be worn nights only or both day and night. Although it does not permit standing, the splint allows vigorous activities that utilize crawling, creeping, and scooterboards.

Congenital defects of the feet, legs, and hips are generally corrected by surgery, bracing, or casting in infancy or early childhood. In spite of the correction, the gait may continue to be impaired so that persons do not have a fair chance in competitive activities with peers. *Such persons are eligible for wheelchair basketball and tennis.* Swimming is also good.

Limb Deficiencies and Amputations

International sport classifications distinguish between *limb deficiencies* (congenital amputations) and *acquired amputations.* Limb deficiencies are considered les autres conditions.

Prevalence of amputations in the United States ranges from 300,000 to over 500,000. This is probably because some estimates include both congenital and acquired amputations, while others include only the acquired. Statistics might be affected also by the fact that many individuals born with limb deficiencies have malformed body parts amputated at an early age so that prostheses can be fitted (Krementz, 1992). Limb deficiencies are much more common than acquired amputations, with a 2:1 ratio usually given. Most sources agree that lower limb amputations are more common than upper limb amputations.

Types of Limb Deficiencies

There are many types of limb deficiencies and malformations, each with its own name (e.g., thrombocytopenia absent radius,

proximal focal femoral deficiency). For simplicity, however, two categories can be used to encompass the many individual differences: **dysmelia** (absence of arms or legs) and **phocomelia** (absence of middle segment of limb, but with intact proximal and distal portions). In the latter, hands or feet are attached directly to shoulders or hips, respectively. In phocomelia (*phoco* means "seal-like" and *melos* means "limb"), the hand or foot is often removed surgically within the first few months after birth. Absence of the fibula, with a congenitally deformed foot, is also a common condition that is corrected surgically.

Joey Lipski, world-class swimmer and track star, is illustrative of a person with dysmelia (see Figure 24.28). Born without arms, he does not wear prostheses in competition. Joey learned to swim at age 8 and at age 15 set world records for his classification in the 100-m freestyle event (2:05.6) and in the 50-m backstroke (57.0). He runs the 100-m dash in 19.5 sec and the 200-m event in 41.42 sec.

Karen Farmer, world-class athlete in discus, javelin, and shot put, was born with a clubfoot and missing fibula. These were surgically removed when she was 18 months old, and a prosthesis was fitted soon afterward. Her shot put and discus records are 10.02 and 32.36 m, respectively. Almost all of Karen's competitive experience has been against AB athletes; she attended Washington State University on an athletic scholarship and says she has never found a sport she could not master.

The cause of limb deficiencies is seldom known. In the 1960s the drug *thalidomide,* used as a sedative and sleeping pill, was identified as having caused hundreds of birth defects and immediately removed from the market. Since then, drugs have been tested more carefully before they are placed on the market. Nevertheless, each year many individuals are born with limb deficiencies. Most develop considerable manual dexterity with upper limb body parts and opt not to use artificial limbs (see Figure 24.28). With help, they can find many sports that do not require arms for success (e.g., soccer, track, field, swimming). Individuals with lower limb deficiencies have many choices: wheelchair sports, ambulatory sports with prostheses like the popular Flex-Foot, or activities that can be done without prostheses like swimming and high jumping.

Prostheses

A *prosthesis* (plural: *prostheses*) is a substitute for a missing body part. A **prosthesis** contains several parts: (a) the socket, (b) a connection mechanism (e.g., harness, straps, suspension device, suction apparatus, clamp), and a terminal device, which is either cosmetic or mechanically efficient. Age of prosthetic fitting is obviously very important in subsequent development of motor skills. Upper extremity prostheses are fitted when the child develops good sitting balance, usually between 8 and 10 months of age. Lower extremity prostheses are fitted when the child begins to pull up to a stand, usually between 10 and 15 months. As the child grows, the prostheses must be periodically replaced: every 15 to 18 months for an upper extremity prosthesis and about every 12 months for a lower extremity prosthesis.

FIGURE 24.28   Examples of limb deficiencies.

Dysmelia: absence of limbs

Phocomelia: middle limb portions missing with digits extending from upper arms

Since 1964, immediate postsurgical prosthetic fitting has gradually become the trend. This practice offers several advantages. First, particularly in a person with cancer, a prosthesis and early ambulation contributes to a positive psychological outlook. Second, amputation stumps in children do not usually shrink, and there is no physical reason for delaying fitting. Third, phantom pain has become almost nonexistent because of improved surgical techniques. Fourth, edema (swelling) is best controlled and wound healing facilitated by an immediate postsurgical socket.

After surgery, individuals go to rehabilitation centers, where they are provided with training in use of the prosthesis by physical therapists and occupational therapists. Ideally, this training includes exposure to playground equipment and recreational activities. If the child does not appear secure in class activities utilizing gymnastic and playground equipment, the adapted physical educator may need to supplement the hospital training.

The usefulness of lower limb prostheses has improved tremendously since 1982, when a **prosthetist** named Van Phillips created the Flex-Foot, a lightweight, energy-efficient prosthesis made of carbon fiber composite, the material used extensively in the aerospace industry for its superior strength and flexibility. Carbon fiber is impervious to heat, cold, water, corrosion, and stress. Many models of Flex-Foot are available, enabling individuals to select the type best suited to a specific sport or activity (see Figure 24.29). Flex-Foot has revolutionized amputee track-and-field events, enabling athletes to achieve times and distances comparable to those of able-bodied athletes. Information about Flex-Foot Inc. and other companies that manufacture prosthetic devices appears in Appendix E.

Case Study: World's Fastest Leg-Amputee

Tony Volpentest, born with short malformed arms and legs, is currently the world's fastest leg-amputee. He began track as a high school sophomore, working out and running with the able-bodied team, but initially was able to run the 100 in only 16.9 seconds, way behind peers. In one season, he bettered his time to 14.3. A year later Tony participated in his first disability sport meet, won all of his races, and learned about Flex-Foot. Today, wearing Flex-Foot, Tony runs the 100 in about 11.26 and the 200 in about 22.67, times that often enable him to beat able-bodied competitors.

Many factors contribute to the success of athletes with amputations. First is hard work. Like most Paralympic athletes, Tony trains 2 to 3 hr a day, splitting his time between track practice and strength training. Technology is also important, and athletes must be helped to find sponsors to cover the cost of prosthetic devices. For example, Tony's prostheses cost about $20,000. If an athlete shows outstanding potential, companies like Flex-Foot Inc. will often donate prostheses. Tony also had the full support of family and coaches, who urged him to get involved in mainstream sport as early as possible. These individuals helped him also with creative solutions to problems

FIGURE 24.29 Many models of Flex-Foot enable choices to meet specific activity needs.

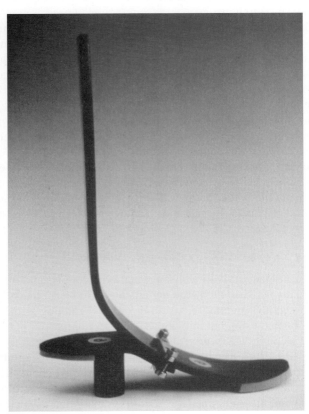

like his inability to assume the track starting position because he has abnormally short arms. The solution to this is using two paint cans topped with padding (see Figure 24.30A,B).

Gaits and Movement Patterns

Individuals with lower limb amputations use many movement patterns. Those with **double-leg amputations** often walk on their stumps when at home or forced to do so by architectural barriers that make wheelchair use impossible. For sports most use a wheelchair, although some prefer the new lightweight prosthetic devices. Those with **single-leg amputations** often use crutches for everyday activity but switch to a wheelchair or Flex-Foot for sports.

FIGURE 24.30 Individuals with limb deficiencies can be outstanding athletes. *(A)* Tony Volpentest running the 100 in about 11.26 seconds. *(B)* The adaptation needed at the starting blocks for runners with short arms.

A

B

Gaits used by people with prostheses are called hop-skip running and leg-over-leg running. **Hop-skip running** entails the following sequence: (a) stepping forward on the sound leg, (b) hopping on the sound leg while swinging through the prosthetic leg, (c) switching weight to the prosthetic side, and (d) immediately transferring weight to the sound side. Flex-Foot and other new lightweight prosthetic devices permit **leg-over-leg running** that looks like the able-bodied reciprocal running pattern, except for a slight asymmetry in stride length and time spent on each foot.

Children who have not yet been fitted for prostheses often prefer to use crutches in racing and other physical education activities. Professionals should encourage participation but watch closely for fatigue signs, in that crutch-racing and hop-skip gaits with older types of prostheses put much strain on the hip joints. *Racing should be done only with forearm crutches, never axillary crutches.*

PE Adaptations for Persons With Amputations

A main adaptation pertains to dressing and shower rules. Girls and boys should be allowed to wear long pants or the type of clothing in which they feel most comfortable. Shower rules should be waived. The person who is sensitive about changing clothes in the locker room should be given a place of his or her own, and classmates should be encouraged to allow the desired privacy.

The general attitude among physicians is that persons with an amputation can do anything if the prostheses are well fitted.

Balance

Balance is probably the one aspect of motor performance that gives the most trouble. The sound limb is used for kicking balls while the prosthetic limb maintains the weight of the body. In ascending stairs, the child should be taught to lead with the sound limb; in descending, to lead with the prosthesis in the stable extended position. The bilateral above-knee amputee has more difficulty with steps and often requires a railing and crutch. He or she typically climbs and descends stairs in a sideward manner. The weight of a bowling ball or tennis racquet in a unilateral upper-limb amputation may cause balance problems. This problem, at least in bowling, can be overcome by developing a scissors step, crossing the leg on the good arm side over the other, and taking the weight of the ball in stride.

Reduced Cooling Surfaces and Perspiration

Amputation or a limb deficiency reduces skin surface area and hence affects the normal heat dissipation process by which the body cools itself. Perspiration is therefore increased in the rest of the body, necessitating special attention to exercise clothing, room temperature, and stump and prosthesis hygiene. Use of a prosthesis increases energy expenditure, which further exacerbates sweating. Perspiration of the stump inside a socket predisposes the skin to bacterial and fungal infections. Adaptations include monitoring individuals for heat-related illness, encouraging the drinking of extra fluids before, during, and after exercise, and checking that stumps are kept dry.

Skin Breakdown on Stump

Skin irritations and ulcerations on the stump must be prevented by proper socket fit and by reasonable care when individuals choose to exercise or ambulate without a prosthesis. Socks and gloves covering stumps should be made of porous, absorbent materials. Sunburn should be prevented. Stumps should be washed and dried thoroughly daily or more often, depending on the amount of perspiration.

Muscle Atrophy, Contractures, and Posture Problems

Muscle atrophy and contractures around the stump or limb deficiency should be prevented by daily strength and range-of-motion (ROM) exercises. Hip joint muscles are prone to flexion, abduction, and outward rotation contractures, and knee joint muscles are prone to flexion contractions. These are the muscle groups that should be stretched. Strength exercises should focus on their antagonists.

Unequal leg length and/or use of one side more than the other can contribute to scoliosis and to hip or knee degeneration. **Early-onset arthritis** is a common side effect of mechanical inefficiency. Correct postures should be emphasized. Individuals typically stand with their weight on their good leg rather than distributing their weight equally.

Increased Energy Expenditure

Although the Flex-Foot featured in this chapter is lightweight, many prostheses (especially those for double amputations) are relatively heavy and increase energy requirements. Loss of muscle mass through an amputation also decreases the number of muscles available to move the body. Obesity further complicates this problem, because the heavier a person is, the heavier the prosthesis must be. The use of crutches with prostheses increases energy expenditure still more. Individuals might therefore fatigue early and require much motivation and support to continue in exercise programs that will increase their strength, flexibility, and aerobic endurance. Many persons choose to use wheelchairs instead of prostheses because most wheelchairs require less energy expenditure than prostheses.

Acquired Amputations

Acquired amputations occur more often in adults than in children. Diabetes and various circulatory problems associated with heart disease often necessitate amputations in middle and old age. War injuries and vehicular accidents are major causes also.

The etiologies of acquired amputations in children in order of incidence are trauma, cancer, infection, and vascular conditions like gangrene. Under trauma, the leading causes of amputations are farm and power tool accidents, vehicular accidents, and gunshot explosions. Most of these occur in the age group from 12 to 21. Children who lose limbs because of malignancy are also primarily within this age group.

Arnie Boldt, the one-legged world champion high jumper, is illustrative of a person with an acquired amputation (see Figure 24.31). Raised on a farm, he lost his lower leg in a farm accident at 3 years of age. Much of his competitive experience has been against AB athletes.

Terry Fox, who died of cancer, is perhaps the best-known individual with an amputation. He devoted the last months of his life to running (with one leg) across Canada to raise money for cancer and increase awareness. His story, available on videotape, is well worth watching.

Degree of Severity

The number of limbs missing and the level of the amputation determine, to a large extent, motor performance. Compared with other lower extremity disabilities, amputees are considered minimally disabled unless both femurs are amputated at the hip joint (bilateral hip amputee). With the exception of these persons, for instance, all amputees are in Class III (least disabled) in wheelchair basketball; this means that their abilities are equivalent to Class 7 and 8 athletes with cerebral palsy and persons with spinal cord injuries who can walk, but with a limp.

Amputee Sport Classifications

By the time children with amputations reach adolescence, many want opportunities for vigorous competition against others with comparable disabilities. To ensure fair competition, ISOD and Disabled Sport/USA enforce a strict classification

FIGURE 24.31 Canadian Arnie Boldt, world champion high jumper.

system, with nine classifications (see Table 24.3). Some of these are presented in Figures 24.32 and 24.33. Note that the odd numbers (1, 3, 5, 7, 9) denote the greater disability.

Track and Field

Individuals have a choice between ambulatory and wheelchair track. The usual practice is for Classes A1 and A3 to use wheelchairs and for Classes A2 and A4 to compete standing, using a Flex-Foot.

In field events, fewer classifications are used. In field, double arm amputees compete together in one class, whether the amputation is above or below the elbow, and single arm amputees likewise form one class. More severely

Table 24.3   Nine general sport classifications for persons with amputations.

Class A1 = Double AK	Class A7 = Double BE
Class A2 = Single AK	Class A8 = Single BE
Class A3 = Double BK	Class A9 = Combined
Class A4 = Single BK	lower plus
Class A5 = Double AE	upper limb
Class A6 = Single AE	amputations

Note. AK = Above or through the knee joint; BK = Below the knee, but through or above the ankle joint; AE = Above or through the elbow joint; BE = Below the elbow, but through or above the wrist joint.

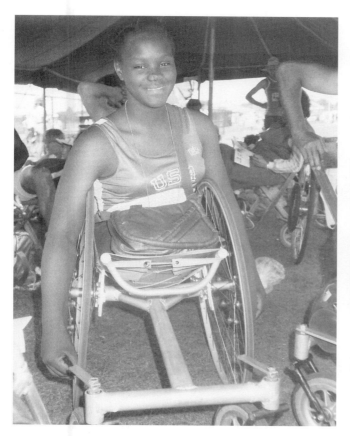

Classification A1, double AK

Classification A2, single AK

Classification A3, double BK

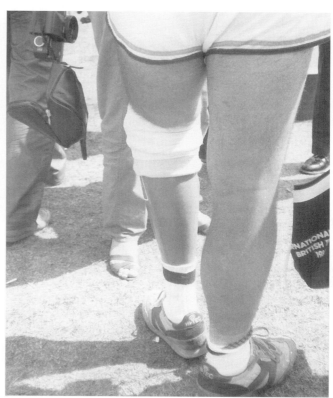

Classification A4, single BK

Classification A6, single AE

Classification A5 (double AE) with girlfriend who has A2 (single AK)

involved lower extremity amputees use wheelchairs, whereas less involved ones throw from a standing position.

Both long and high jump events are popular. For high jumps, athletes seldom use prostheses. For long jumps, the Flex-Foot is preferred. This prosthesis makes jumping possible for individuals with double amputations, a feat unheard of a few years ago.

Sitting and Standing Volleyball

Volleyball is governed by the ISOD and, at the Paralympic level, considered an amputee sport. Lower limb prostheses and orthoses are permitted but not upper limb.

In volleyball, a point system similar to that in wheelchair basketball is used to ensure equal distribution of abilities on opposing teams. Persons are assigned 1, 2, 3, or 4 points, depending upon two criteria: A1 to A9 classification and muscle strength score determined by certified testers. At all times, players on the floor must total 13 or more points. Like regular volleyball, six players comprise a team. *Sitting volleyball* allows all classes to compete, whereas *standing volleyball* is open only to Classes A2 to A4 and A6 to A9.

Swimming

Persons with limb deficiencies and amputations race against individuals with various other kinds of disabilities in the Paralympic functional swimming classification system and often win. Prostheses are not permitted in competition. Professionals should know that loss of a body part causes displacement of the center of gravity and center of buoyancy to the opposite side. The intact side tends to sink. Loss of a right arm or leg thus creates a tendency to roll to the left, which can usually be overcome by turning the head toward the affected side. Think about performing a log roll in the water; this is the lateral rotation that persons with missing limbs must learn to control.

Double-leg amputation increases trunk buoyancy but causes the head to lie low. Stretching the arms out behind the head tends to cause vertical rotation (a back somersault), so considerable movement exploration is needed to decide on a preferred stroke. For instructional and recreational swimming, fins or plexiglass paddles can be attached to stumps (Summerford, 1993).

Horseback Riding, Cycles, and Other Vehicles

Recreational and competitive riding is popular. Many individuals propel cycles with one leg. All-terrain vehicles make camping, hunting, and fishing possible. Specially made saddles and other kinds of equipment are often needed in horseback riding (see Figure 24.34).

FIGURE 24.34 Therapeutic horseback riding was initiated in England in the 1950s. The first established program in the United States began in 1968, when the Cheff Center in Augusta, Michigan, opened. Don Drewry *(in the photos)* was taught riding by a Cheff Center graduate. Note the specially made saddle.

 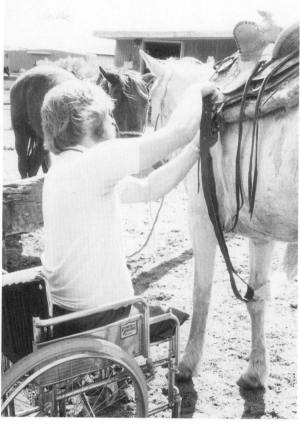

Other Sports

Use of prostheses and orthoses is regulated. In air pistol, air rifle, and swimming, for instance, prostheses and orthoses are not permitted. In archery, the draw may be made with a prosthesis or orthosis, and a releasing aid may be used by Classes A6, A8, and A9. These classes may also receive help with loading arrows into the bow. In lawn bowling, Classes A5 and A7 may use prostheses or orthoses if they wish. In table tennis, however, these are not allowed. Persons who are unable to perform a regulation serve because of their disability are allowed to bounce the ball on the table and then smash it across the net. Physical educators need a lot of information to help students with amputations prepare for high-level competition.

References

Ablon, J. (1988). *Living with difference: Families with dwarf children.* New York: Praeger.

Chung S. M. K. (1981). *Hip disorders in infants and children.* Philadelphia: Lea & Febiger.

Cowden, J. (1985). *Arthrogryposis: A case study approach for adapted physical education.* Unpublished manuscript, University of New Orleans.

Croce, R. (1987). Exercise and physical activity in managing progressive muscular dystrophy: A review for practitioners. *Palaestra, 3*(3), 9–14, 15.

Krementz, J. (1992). *How it feels to live with a physical disability.* New York: Simon & Schuster.

Knudsen, M. (1993). *Flexibility and range of motion of dwarfs with achondroplasia.* Unpublished thesis, Texas Woman's University, Denton.

Lockette, K. F., & Keyes, A. M. (1994). *Conditioning with physical disabilities.* Champaign, IL: Human Kinetics.

Low, L. (1992). *Prediction of selected track, field, and swimming performance of dwarf athletes by anthropometry.* Unpublished doctoral study, Texas Woman's University, Denton.

Low, L., Knudsen, M. J., & Sherrill, C. (1996). Dwarfism: New interest area for adapted physical activity. *Adapted Physical Activity Quarterly, 13*(1), 1–15.

Rothenberg, M., & White, M. (1985). *David: Severely burned by father.* Old Tappen, NJ: Fleming H. Revell.

Samples, P. (1990). Exercise encouraged for people with arthritis. *Physician and Sportsmedicine, 18*(1), 122–127.

Sawisch, L. (1990). Strategic positioning in the disabled sports community: A perspective from the New Kids on the Block. *Palaestra, 6*(5), 52–54.

Scott, C. I. (1988). Dwarfism. *Clinical Symposia, 40*(1), 2–32.

Shuman, R., & Schwartz, J. (1994). *Living with multiple sclerosis: A handbook for families* (2nd ed.). New York: Macmillan.

Sibley, W. A. (1992). *Therapeutic claims in multiple sclerosis* (3rd ed.). New York: Demos.

Summerford, C. (1993). Apparatus used in teaching swimming to quadriplegic amputees. *Palaestra, 9*(3), 54–57.

CHAPTER
25

Cerebral Palsy, Stroke, and Traumatic Brain Injury

FIGURE 25.1 Widespread individual differences exist within cerebral palsy. *(A)* Class 7 and 8 athletes play soccer. *(B)* Class 1 athlete plays indoor wheelchair soccer. *(C)* Class 2 athletes use their feet to propel specially designed chairs.

A

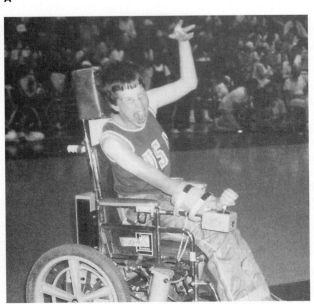

B

C

After you have studied this chapter, you should be able to do the following:

1. Define and discuss etiology, prevalence, and incidence of (a) cerebral palsy (CP), (b) stroke, and (c) traumatic brain injury (TBI). Explain why they are grouped together in this chapter.

2. Contrast associated dysfunctions of the general CP population with U.S. Cerebral Palsy Athletic Association (USCPAA) athletes. Explain the importance of not making generalizations.

3. Explain four types of motor disorders: (a) spasticity, (b) athetosis, (c) ataxia, and (d) hypotonia. Discuss motor remediation for each.

4. Describe eight profiles that can be used for physical education-recreation assessment and programming for individuals with CP, stroke, and TBI. Given descriptions of functional ability, be able to correctly assign the profiles, discuss programming, and write IEPs.

5. Identify and discuss special problems that complicate programming for CP, stroke, and TBI.

6. Discuss USCPAA and other resources in terms of their roles in sport socialization and in lifelong sport interest and activity. Describe sports especially designed for CP.

Cerebral palsy (CP), stroke, and traumatic brain injury (TBI) are grouped together in this chapter because individuals with these conditions have many common needs. CP, by definition, is primarily a motor disorder, whereas stroke and TBI usually (but not always) affect motor function. Often multiple parts of the brain are damaged, and sensory, perceptual, and cognitive disorders of varying degrees of severity coexist with motor problems. Despite multiple disabilities, most individuals with these conditions can participate in a wide range of sport activities (see Figure 25.1).

Cognitive ability is the variable that determines physical activity programming. When motor impairment occurs *without mental retardation,* individuals are served by the Cerebral Palsy–International Sports and Recreation Association (CP-ISRA) and affiliated national organizations like the Canadian Cerebral Palsy Sports Association (CCPSA) and the United States Cerebral Palsy Athletic Association (USCPAA). When a dual diagnosis of mental retardation and motor impairment is made, individuals are served by Special Olympics and the International Sports Federation for Persons with Mental Handicaps (INAS-FMH).

This chapter focuses on CP-ISRA programming because many individuals who are eligible to benefit from CP sports are not being identified in the public schools and provided with the kind of instruction needed to develop lifespan healthy, active lifestyles. Programming for individuals with CP, stroke, and TBI is challenging because of the many individual differences that occur when the brain is damaged. This requires knowledge of eight sport classifications to guide programming decisions as well as background information on reflexes (see Chapter 10), neurological soft signs and attention deficits (see Chapter 20), and wheelchair technology (see Chapter 23 for sport chairs and Chapter 24 for motorized chairs).

Definitions, Etiologies, and Incidence

Two conditions discussed in this chapter—cerebral palsy (CP) and stroke—are classified by the U.S. federal government as orthopedic impairments. The third condition—traumatic brain injury (TBI)—was recognized as a separate diagnostic category by PL 101-476, IDEA, enacted in 1990. Prior to this, TBI in children was associated with CP and learning disabilities.

Cerebral Palsy

Cerebral palsy (CP) is a chronic neurologic disorder of movement and posture caused by a lesion of the immature brain and accompanied by associated dysfunctions (Sugden & Keogh, 1990). It is not hereditary, contagious, or progressive. The disorder varies from mild (generalized clumsiness or a slight limp) to severe (dominated by reflexes, unable to ambulate except in motorized chair, inability to speak, and almost no control of motor function).

The etiology of CP is varied, including everything that can cause damage to the immature brain. About 90% of such brain damage occurs before or during birth. Common prenatal causes are maternal infections (e.g., AIDS, rubella, herpes), chemical toxins (e.g., alcohol, tobacco, prescribed and nonprescribed drugs), and injuries to the mother that affect fetal development. Maternal age is associated with CP, with the risk increased for mothers under age 20 or over age 34. Prematurity and low birth weight both increase the incidence of CP. Direct damage to the brain can occur during difficult deliveries or under conditions that cause oxygen deprivation (anoxia, hypoxia, asphyxia).

About 10% of CP occurs postnatally, with estimates ranging from 6 to 25% (Stanley & Blair, 1984). Sources vary with regard to definition of immature brain, with most requiring manifestation of a movement problem before age 2 years but some accepting age 5 as the diagnostic cutoff. Brain infections (encephalitis, meningitis), cranial traumas from accidents and child abuse, chemical toxins (airborne or ingested), and oxygen deprivation are the most common causes of acquired CP.

Because diagnostic criteria are controversial, CP incidence and prevalence rates vary. The incidence is approximately 7 per 1,000 live births, and the prevalence is 500 cases in every 100,000 persons. The 1990 census figures for the U.S. population (250 million) are the basis for the estimate that 1,250,000 Americans have CP. The condition is more common among males than females and also among firstborn. *CP is the orthopedic impairment most often found in the public schools.*

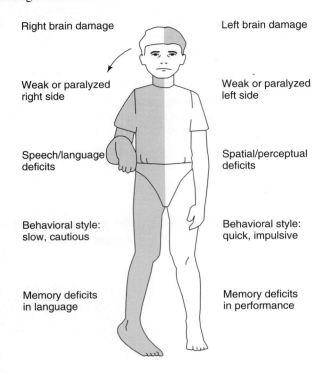

Right brain damage

Left brain damage

Weak or paralyzed right side

Weak or paralyzed left side

Speech/language deficits

Spatial/perceptual deficits

Behavioral style: slow, cautious

Behavioral style: quick, impulsive

Memory deficits in language

Memory deficits in performance

Stroke

Stroke, also called cerebrovascular accident (CVA) or disease, is the sudden onset of neurological impairment (awareness, motor, speech, perception, memory, cognition) that occurs when the flow of oxygen and nutrients to the brain is disrupted by blood clot blockage (ischemia) or hemorrhage (bleeding). Strokes can occur at any age, although they are most common after age 60. **Ischemic strokes** are associated with heart disease and high cholesterol levels, whereas **hemorrhagic strokes** are linked with high blood pressure, weak or malformed arteries and veins within the brain, and leukemia. Approximately 80% of strokes are ischemic.

Figure 25.2 shows that strokes affect many functions. **Left-brain strokes** result in weakness or paralysis of the right side, speech/language deficits, a slow, cautious behavioral style, and memory deficits that affect speech. **Right-brain strokes** impair movement on the left side of the body. Recovery of muscle function, including speech, can progress for several months or stop abruptly, leaving the individual permanently disabled. Typically, muscle function gradually progresses from a state of flaccidity (hypotonus) to spasticity, to flexor and extensor stereotypic patterns called **synergies,** to return of voluntary movement. The *synergies* look and act like primitive reflexes. Most persons with complete stroke have difficulty with both sitting and standing balance (Kottke & Lehmann, 1990), and postural reactions must be relearned. During the spasticity stage, contractures must be prevented by daily range of motion (ROM) exercises.

Over 2 million Americans are coping with the residual effects of stroke. This is about 1 of every 125 persons. Strokes are more common in males until about age 75, after which the incidence is equal for both sexes. The incidence of strokes in children is about 2.3 cases per 100,000 population per year, much more common than most people realize. In the past, **early childhood strokes** that resulted in motor impairment were often mistakenly considered CP and called infant hemiplegia. *The major difference is that stroke is followed by gradual improvement, whereas CP is nonprogressive.*

Children show more improvement after strokes than adults with similar-sized lesions, and young children show more recovery than older ones. Nevertheless, the *sequelae* (the conditions following or resulting from brain damage) often include **hemiparesis** (weakness on one side), seizure disorders, learning disabilities, visual perception problems, memory deficits, speech deficits, and mental retardation. These children are prime candidates for adapted physical education and USCPAA sports.

Incomplete strokes, also called **transient ischemic attacks (TIAs),** occur in both children and adults. These strokes are characterized by total recovery (Kottke & Lehmann, 1990) but cause several hours of dysfunction in varied areas (e.g., muscle weakness, speech difficulty, memory and perception problems). Often, TIAs are warnings of severe cerebral pathology and impending major strokes.

Traumatic Brain Injury

Traumatic brain injury (TBI) refers to permanent damage caused by concussion, contusion, or hemorrhage sustained in vehicular accidents, assaults, falls, and other kinds of traumas. Most of these are **closed-head injuries** in that the skin is not broken. Collectively, these injuries are the leading cause of death and disability for persons under age 35. Each year, over 500,000 persons (about 1 out of 500) sustain TBI. Of these, approximately 100,000 die, 50,000 to 100,000 survive with severe impairments that prevent independent living, and the others learn to live with various **sequelae** that alter sensation, perception, emotion, cognition, and motor function.

Sequelae vary widely, depending on the site and extent of damage. The response of the brain to trauma also varies with age. Some research indicates that children recover more completely than adults, but this is controversial. Generally, recovery spans many years. Often, it appears to be complete, but professionals can detect minor deviations from normal, particularly in behaviors. Residual brain injury is also expressed by neurological *soft signs,* discussed in the next section.

Males sustain twice as many TBIs as females. Presumably, this is because males drive under the influence of alcohol more and are more involved in risk recreation and work activities than females. Over half of TBIs occur in motor vehicular accidents.

The major concern after injury is prediction of amount of recovery. Since 1974, the Glasgow Coma Scale (GCS) has been the major clinical assessment for this purpose. Possible scores on this scale range from 3 to 15 points. Death or a vegetative state is the prognosis of over 50% of persons who score in the 5 to 7 range. The closer the score is to 15, the better the prognosis. The scale is based on three types of response: (a) eye opening, (b) motor, and (c) verbal. Patients who are conscious respond to commands ("Open your eyes." "Show me two fingers." "Tell me what day this is.") and obviously make the highest scores. The motor responses of unconscious persons to stimuli like pinpricks include withdrawal, abnormal flexion, abnormal extension or rigidity, and no reaction. Medical files almost always include a GCS score.

A GCS score of 8 or less indicates coma. The longer a person is comatose, the worse the prognosis. Research indicates that children in a coma for more than 24 hr are likely to have IQs less than 85 when tested 6 months after injury (Ylvisaker, 1985). Posttraumatic amnesia (PTA) is also a good predictor of future function. Recovery is better when PTA lasts only a few minutes. Often, PTA persists for many months. In fact, permanent memory deficits are common sequelae.

Attention, memory, and visuomotor difficulties are the predominant sequelae in school-age persons. Recovery from motor involvement is better than from cognitive and behavioral sequelae. Typically, however, over one half of children with TBI have some degree of permanent spasticity and/or ataxia. Percentages are somewhat higher for adults. The similarity of their motor profiles to those of persons with CP explains why USCPAA serves persons with TBI.

Soft Signs and Associated Dysfunctions

Persons described in this chapter are multidisabled. **Neurological soft signs** complicate behavioral, perceptual, and motor performance and interfere with learning. **Soft signs** are indicators of central nervous system (CNS) dysfunction that cannot be substantiated by electroencephalogy (see Chapter 20). Common behavioral indicators of brain damage are attention deficits, hyperexcitability, perseveration, conceptual rigidity, emotional lability, and hyperactivity. Interpretation of sensory input is altered by brain damage, resulting in many kinds of perceptual problems (see Chapter 10). Particularly affected is **sensorimotor integration** of tactile, kinesthetic, vestibular, and visual input. Reflex, balance, and muscle-tone disorders are also considered soft signs. Soft signs and other diagnostic criteria indicate many associated dysfunctions in persons with upper motor neuron disorders (see Table 25.1).

In the remainder of this chapter, the abbreviation CP is used to encompass the motor sequelae and associated dysfunctions of stroke and TBI. Physical educators must assess carefully to determine whether students can best be served by a Special Olympics or a USCPAA sport-oriented curriculum. The major difference is in intellectual functioning. USCPAA specifies average or better intelligence as an eligibility criterion, although some athletes (5 to 15%) are perceived as borderline by coaches.

Table 25.1 describes differences between the general CP population and those served by USCPAA. Textbooks cite prevalence rates for coexisting CP and mental retardation (MR) as between 30 and 70%. Recognition that speech, lan-

Table 25.1 Associated dysfunctions of general CP population as compared to USCPAA athletes.

Associated Dysfunctions	General CP Population (%)	USCPAA Athletes (%)
Mental retardation	30–70	10–20
Speech problems	35–75	25–35
Learning disabilities	80–90	45–55
Visual problems	55–60	20–30
Hearing problems	6–16	10–20
Perceptual deficits	25–50	60–70
Seizures	25–50	25–35
Reflex problems	80–90	65–75

Note. Estimates for the general population come from published sources (Bleck & Nagel, 1982). Estimates for USCPAA athletes come from the author's research.

guage, and motor impairments make valid evaluation difficult is resulting in more learning disability (LD) diagnoses and less classification as MR. When associated dysfunctions make placement uncertain, it is better to assume LD and introduce the family to USCPAA activities. Many adults with CP describe lifetime academic achievement and self-concept problems that result from incorrect school placement and early exposure to curricula for MR rather than LD.

Electronic communication devices like the Canon communicator and the use of computers to teach language have demonstrated that many persons with CP, previously believed to be MR, have intact intelligence. The speech of many athletes who qualify for international competition cannot be understood without much practice. Interpreters are often used, just as with individuals who speak in sign or a foreign language. A person without intelligible speech should never be assumed to be MR.

Almost all children with CP need speech therapy. Even with intensive training, however, only about 50% improve to the degree that they communicate primarily by talking. Many use communication boards with words or symbols, as depicted in Figure 25.3. Others learn sign language. Teachers must take the time to listen to persons with CP, stroke, and TBI and to allow them to make as many of their own decisions as possible.

Inadequate communication skills lead to problems in socialization and delays in social development. Consider the leisure activities of able-bodied (AB) persons. Almost all require ability to use the hands (cards, board games, arts and crafts, cooking), to converse and/or sing, or to drive a car. About 50% of persons with upper motor neuron disorders do not have these abilities; their leisure and social functioning is therefore very different from that of peers. They can, however, excel in sports designed for their specific ability classification.

Visual defects affect over 50% of people with CP, stroke, and TBI. **Strabismus,** the inability to focus both eyes

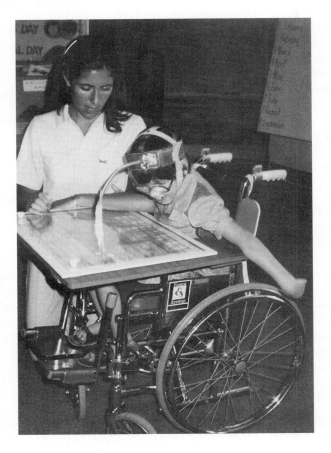

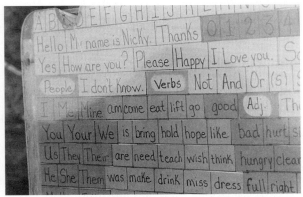

simultaneously on the same object, is the most common problem—not surprisingly, considering that focus requires six pairs of muscles to move each eyeball. Imbalances in strength cause squinting, poor binocular vision, and inefficiencies in depth perception, pattern discrimination, and figure-background detection. These deficits naturally affect motor learning and success in sports.

Seizures are relatively common occurrences for individuals with upper motor neuron disorders but do not contraindicate sport participation (Adams-Mushett, Wyeth, & Richter, 1995). Over 25% of USCPAA athletes regularly take medication to control seizures. Travel and excitement inevitably result in some persons forgetting to take medication. An evening seizure, however, seldom prevents competition cn the following day.

Of all the dysfunctions in Table 25.1, reflex problems concern physical educators the most. These prevent maturation of the balance reactions needed for stable sitting and for learning to walk. About half of USCPAA athletes are in wheelchairs because of reflex and reaction abnormalities. An additional 20 to 35% have coordination problems related to reflexes, even though the individuals are ambulatory.

In summary, associated dysfunctions explain why USCPAA needs a different sport classification system from that of other disabilities. Upper motor neuron disorders typically

FIGURE 25.4 Spasticity in some persons may be so great that limbs need to be strapped down during physical activity. Here, Tom Cush, international Class 2 athlete with cerebral palsy, has both arms strapped to chair while he competes in indoor wheelchair soccer. In throwing and striking activities, only one arm is strapped down.

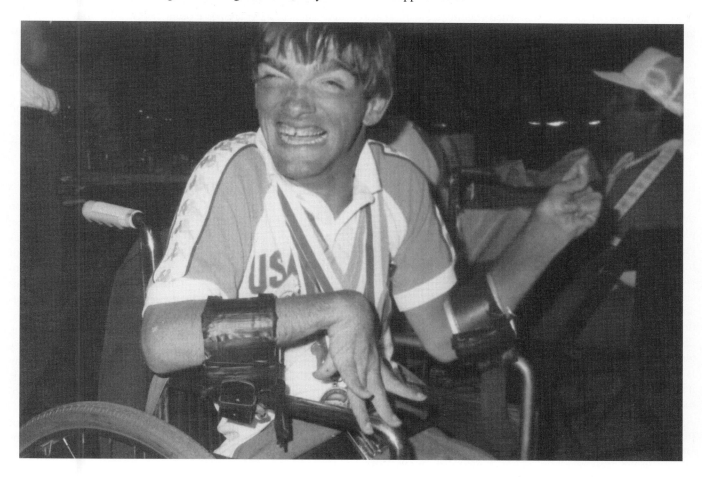

involve two or more limbs, causing abnormal muscle tone and postures that are worsened by perceptual and reflex problems. For example, few persons with CP are able to excel in wheelchair basketball. To compensate, USCPAA has devised alternative sports like **boccia** and **indoor wheelchair soccer,** formerly known as team handball.

Number of Limbs Involved

Number of limbs involved is typically specified on IEPs and other records to help with programming. The terms used, except for *paraplegia,* are the same as those in Chapters 23 and 24.

1. **Diplegia.** Lower extremities are much more involved than upper ones. This term is preferred over *paraplegia.*
2. **Quadriplegia.** All four extremities are involved. In international sports, a synonym is *tetraplegia.*
3. **Hemiplegia.** The entire right side or left side is involved.
4. **Triplegia.** Three extremities, usually both legs and one arm, are involved.

These terms permit description of and programming for functional abilities. Such terms as *mild* and *severe* indicate degree of involvement.

Types of Motor Disorders

Motor disorder in CP, stroke, and TBI is described in terms of abnormal muscle tone and postures (Bobath, 1980; Levitt, 1995; Sugden & Keogh, 1990). The old (1956) neuromuscular classifications of the American Academy for Cerebral Palsy are no longer used. *Instead, three types of CP are recognized: (a) spasticity, (b) athetosis, and (c) ataxia.* Most persons have mixed types, and diagnosis indicates which is most prominent. **Hypotonia** is a temporary diagnosis associated with floppy baby syndrome and coma.

Spasticity of Cerebral Origin

Spasticity, the most common type of motor disorder, is abnormal muscle tightness and stiffness characterized by **hypertonic muscle tone** during voluntary movement. About 65% of people with CP have this as their predominant type. Spasticity is mainly caused by damage to the motor cortex and the cortical tracts that carry motor commands downward through the brain. Damage to the basal ganglia and cerebellum further exacerbates spasticity.

The resulting **hypertonic state** causes muscles to feel and look stiff (see fingers in Figure 25.4). Normally, muscles on one surface relax when those on the opposite surface contract (the reciprocal innervation principle), but hypertonicity results in **cocontraction** or stiffness. This, in turn, makes release of objects difficult or impossible, an obvious problem in learning to throw or to let go of the pool side when wanting to swim. It also interferes with ability to make precise movements.

Associated with spasticity is the **exaggerated stretch** or **myotatic reflex.** This reflex normally serves a protective purpose because it instantaneously withdraws a body part from hurtful stimuli. Damage to the cerebellum results in exaggerated response (recoil, withdrawal, flexion) to stretch receptor input that ranges in intensity from a subtle timing problem to a violent recoil like a jackknife closing. All stretches do not activate exaggerated responses, and intensity varies from time to time. In some persons, the stretch reflex is so disruptive that limbs are strapped down (see Figure 25.4).

Among the abnormal postures associated with spasticity are the scissors gait (both legs involved) and the hemiplegic gait (arm and leg on same side involved). The **scissors gait** is a pigeon-toed walk caused by abnormal tightness of the hip joint flexors, adductors, and inward rotators that is associated with retention of the positive support and crossed extension reflexes. Also tight are the knee joint flexors (hamstrings) and ankle joint plantar flexors (calf muscles and Achilles tendon) that keep knees bent and weight on toes (see Figure 25.5). If arms are involved, the tightness follows the same pattern (flexors, adductors, and inward rotators). The spastic arm is bent and pronated, carried close to the body, with a fisted hand. The **hemiplegic gait** is a limp caused by asymmetry in extension (see Figure 25.5).

Abnormal postures are also caused by retention of primitive reflexes and immaturity of postural reactions. Inability to move the head without associated muscle tension in the arms results in many abnormal postures. When reflex disturbances are severe, persons with spasticity remain nonambulatory.

Athetosis

Athetosis, the second most common type of motor disorder, is constant, unpredictable, and purposeless (CUP) movement caused by **fluctuating muscle tone** that is sometimes hypertonic and sometimes hypotonic. Damage to the basal ganglia in the cerebral white matter is the primary cause of this involuntary **overflow disorder.** Most persons with athetosis are quadriplegic. About 25% of CP is primarily athetosis.

Constant movement is most troublesome to the head and upper extremities. Facial expression, eating, and speaking are major problems. The head is usually drawn back but may roll unpredictably from side to side; the tongue may protrude and saliva drool down the chin. Lack of head control causes problems of visual pursuit and focus that impair ability to read and perform hand-eye accuracy tasks. Constant movement of the fingers and wrist render handwriting and fine muscle coordinations almost impossible.

Many persons with athetosis use wheelchairs, but some have enough motor control to walk. Their gait is typically unsteady or staggering. They walk with trunk and shoulder girdle leaning backward, reinforcing extensor tonus, to prevent collapsing. Hips and knees tend to be hyperextended, the back in lordosis, and the feet kept dorsiflexed, pronated, and everted (a **valgus** position). Steps are short to help maintain balance. Falls are more often backward than forward. Persons with such gaits compete in track but wear knee and elbow pads and gloves.

There are many types of athetosis: (a) **dystonia,** with fluctuating muscle tone; (b) mixed with spasticity, in which muscle tone is mostly hypertonic; (c) mixed with floppy baby syndrome, in which muscle tone is primarily hypotonic; and (d) mixed with ataxia. Changes from one type to another sometimes occur with age, particularly from floppy baby to dystonic children. Generally, *athetosis* and *dystonia* are synonyms.

Ataxia

Ataxia is a combined disturbance of balance and coordination generally characterized by hypotonia or low postural tone. Ataxia can result from disorders of the spinal cord as well as the brain. In CP, stroke, and TBI, however, the ataxia is of **cerebellar-vestibular origin.** Ataxia is diagnosed only in people who can walk unaided. To compensate for extreme unsteadiness of gait, the arms are typically overactive in balance-saving movements. Falls are frequent.

When persons can maintain balance with eyes open, but not closed, ataxia is usually the diagnosis. Voluntary movements are clumsy and uncoordinated with underreaching and overreaching common. Uneven or unlevel ground, stairs, and stepping over objects are particular problems because of cerebellar-vestibular body awareness deficits.

Ataxia varies from mild to severe. A diagnosis of pure ataxia is made in only about 10% of CP. Many persons not diagnosed as disabled probably have ataxia. Combined disturbances of balance and coordination are common among low-skilled persons.

Flaccidity/Hypotonia

The terms *flaccidity* and *hypotonia* refer to low muscle tone. Infants and young children are sometimes assigned a diagnosis of flaccidity/hypotonia until type of CP (spasticity, athetosis, ataxia) becomes clear. Adults, however, can have this condition also. Persons in comas are hypotonic. After a severe stroke, the first stage in motor recovery is flaccidity.

Problems in persons with hypotonia are (a) poor head and trunk control, (b) absent postural and protective reactions, (c) shallow breathing, and (d) joint laxity or hypermobility. Hypotonia may be so severe that persons cannot sit or move unaided (i.e., they are in a vegetative state). Hypotonia is associated with damage of nuclei deep in the cerebellum that, in turn, affect motor cortex and brain stem action. In time, the motor cortex may compensate by increasing facilitatory impulses.

Profiles to Guide Assessment and Programming

Sport classifications should be used to write individualized education programs (IEPs) and individualized family service plans (IFSPs). There are eight classes or profiles, four for the

FIGURE 25.5   Abnormal gaits associated with spasticity and ataxia.

Scissors gait.
The legs are flexed and adducted at the hip joint, causing them to cross alternately in front of each other with the knees scraping together. The knees may be flexed to a greater degree than normal, and the weight of the body may be taken primarily on the toes. The gait is characterized by a narrow walking base. Scissoring may be caused by retention of the positive supporting reflex or the crossed extension reflex. Toe walking may be caused also by the positive supporting reflex.

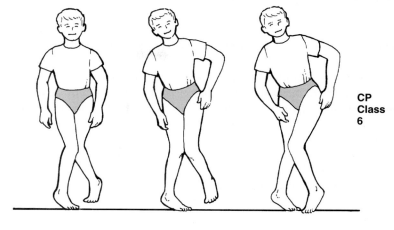

CP
Class
6

Hemiplegic gait.
Both arm and leg on the same side are involved. Tends to occur with any disorder producing an immobile hip or knee. Affected leg is rigid and swung from the hip joint in a semicircle by muscle action of the trunk. Individual leans to the affected side, and arm on that side is held in a rigid, semiflexed position.

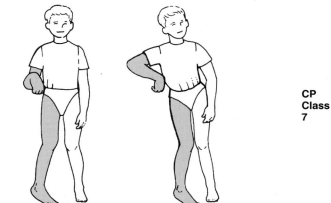

CP
Class
7

Cerebellar gait/kinesthetic defect.
Irregularity of steps, unsteadiness, tendency to reel to one side. Individual seems to experience difficulty in judging how high to lift legs when climbing stairs. Problems are increased when the ground is uneven. Note the similarity between this and the immature walk of early childhood before CNS has matured.

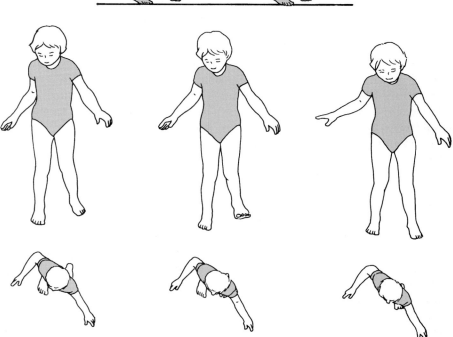

nonambulatory and four for the ambulatory. Classes 1, 2, 3, and 6 designate persons who are the most severely involved.

Assessment begins with determining whether a person is nonambulatory (Classes 1 to 4) or ambulatory (Classes 5 to 8). This requires careful questioning because many persons who use wheelchairs do not need them. This is particularly true of persons who (a) must navigate hills and other barriers in a school or work environment that demands speed in moving from place to place and (b) are overweight or have low fitness. Assessment for movement and sport programming places emphasis on abilities (i.e., how many steps can be taken without a wheelchair). Persons who cannot ambulate across the room, even with crutches or canes, are assigned to Classes 1 to 4. Those who need crutches or canes (called assistive devices) are placed in Class 5. All others are assigned to Classes 6 to 8.

Class 1—Motorized Chair

Class 1 includes everyone without the ROM and power to push a manual wheelchair. Such persons have severe involvement in all four limbs and little head and trunk control. They typically are dominated by reflexes, are unable to maintain body parts in good alignment without help, and have limited ROM. When placed in a lying position, they may be unable to initiate a roll, sit-up, or other voluntary movement. Usually, the motor disorder is primarily hypotonic (especially ages 0 to 7) or spastic.

Chapter 10 describes physical education programming for these persons in early childhood. Emphasis is on total body movement activities on mats, in the water, and in apparatus that can be pushed, pulled, or tilted by the teacher. **Coactive movement** is used to normalize muscle tone and prevent contractures. If the child is dominated by extensor muscle tone, then flexion activities are stressed as normalizers. If flexor tone dominates, then extensor activities are emphasized.

If the child has the mental function to learn use of a motorized chair, all kinds of activities are possible. By age 7 or 8, physical education goals should stress track and field. Whether the chair is powered by hand, foot, or mouth switch, speed and control must be learned. Racing for speed can be on straightaways or around obstacles like cones (see Figure 25.6). The child needs to learn how to weave around obstacles, make circles around them, and manage a ramp.

Appropriate field activities are those using soft implements that can be easily handled, like a soft shot or discus. Throws for distance and height should be practiced, as well as tosses at ground targets like those used in archery. If the hand grasp reflex is still present, release is difficult. It can, however, be overridden by higher cortical levels with much concentration and practice. Games should be devised that give points regardless of the direction the object flies.

Class 1 students can succeed in many game, sport, and aquatic activities if teachers are creative. Because release is so difficult, striking patterns are often emphasized. Inclined boards called *chutes* permit striking to activate a ball in bowling-type games. Suspended ball and tabletop activities are also good. Lying sideways or prone on mats, persons can use body parts to knock over strategically set bowling pins (Miller &

Schaumberg, 1988) and hit or kick objects. In the motorized chair, a game goal may be moving around the room and knocking down pins with the hand. Similar games can be played in the water while lying on floating mats or being coactively moved in a vertical position. A personal flotation device (PFD) should be worn. Many water games should be played before swimming is introduced.

Class 1 persons often require one-on-one assistance. Principals may need to be convinced to supply aides. A record should be kept of each student's time on task (i.e., actual physical activity) or number of trials completed. No child is too disabled to benefit from physical education.

Class 2—Athetosis; 2L or 2U

Class 2 persons can propel a manual chair but have moderate to severe involvement in all four limbs and trunk. Individual differences at this level are so great that Class 2 is subdivided into uppers (U) and lowers (L), with the adjective denoting the limbs with greater functional ability. The 2L propels a chair with feet, with speed and control varying widely (see Figure 25.6). The 2L often is able to do everything with feet (i.e., eating, writing, turning pages) that ordinary people do with hands. Physical education for a 2L emphasizes kicking events and ball handling that is done with the feet. The toes can grasp a soft shot or discus and toss it in various ways. The 2L can learn to tricycle, swim, and do other activities that do not require upper extremities.

In contrast, the 2U relies on arms and learns traditional wheelchair track-and-field activities. Propulsion is weak and slow, however, so that even adult events require short distances (i.e., between 20 and 200 m). Early throwing activities may feature the soft discus and shot, but the 2U, as an adult, must use a regulation (but lightweight) club, shot, and discus. The sooner this equipment is introduced, the better. The legs of a 2U are relatively useless, but the arm stroke can generate enough power for swimming success with and occasionally without a PFD (see Figure 25.6).

Class 2 persons typically have more athetosis than spasticity. Control in accuracy tasks is a challenge, but both 2L and 2U persons engage in bowling and other games similar to those played by Class 1 individuals. Bowling balls with retractable handles are available from several equipment companies (see Appendix E). Class 2 individuals also must cope with major reflex and postural reaction problems.

Class 3—Moderate Triplegic or Quadriplegic

Class 3 is similar to a 2U except that involvement is less and motor disorder is usually predominantly spastic. There is moderate involvement in three or four limbs and trunk. Class 3 individuals propel the chair with short, choppy arm pushes but generate fairly good speed. They can take a few steps with assistive devices, but this ambulatory mode is not functional. Some have enough leg control to learn tricycling events.

All wheelchair activities and swim strokes (except butterfly) are possible. Reflex and postural reaction problems affect performance, so wheelchair basketball and tennis are not games of choice because of their speed-distance-accuracy

FIGURE 25.6 Both Class 1 and Class 2 can use personal flotation devices in USCPAA swimming but not in international events. See Davis, Gehlsen, and Wilkerson (1990) for information on the Class 2 foot-pushing technique.

Class 1 in motorized chair

Class 2, propelling with feet

Class 1, all limbs flexed

Class 2, some extension possible

demands. Sports like indoor wheelchair soccer and quad rugby are better suited to abilities. In general, physical education should stress sports, dance, and aquatics, with as few adaptations as possible.

Class 4—Diplegic

Class 4 individuals use a wheelchair with the same skill, precision, and speed as people with spinal cord injury and spina bifida. They propel the chair with forceful, continuous pushes, have good strength in trunk and upper extremities, and minimal control problems. Some succeed at wheelchair basketball, but subtle associated dysfunctions like visual perception deficits often interfere with aspirations to be on the starting

five. They are not eligible for quad rugby, so indoor wheelchair soccer is the game of choice. They can perform all swim strokes.

Class 4 persons are considered mildly disabled. Unlike others in wheelchairs, their associated dysfunctions are minimal and subtle. They are good candidates for integrated physical education but also need separate instruction in wheelchair sports.

Class 5—Assistive Devices

Class 5 is the only profile that includes persons who use crutches, canes, and walkers (see Figure 25.7). The motor disorder is primarily spastic, and involvement is either hemiplegic or diplegic. Spasticity is moderate to severe.

FIGURE 25.7 Class 5 persons use assistive devices.

Many activities offer success. Track events include 100- to 400-m distances run on foot. The only contraindication is use of **axillary crutches** (those that touch armpits) because pressure in this area can cause nerve damage. In field events, the major problem is balance. Throws can be from either a standing or seated position. Some persons prefer the tricycle, but others use a bicycle. Class 5 persons are eligible to play indoor wheelchair soccer and need wheelchair skills to make the team. They are also eligible to play USCPAA soccer and are groomed particularly for goalkeeper and defensive positions.

In some countries, Class 5 people compete in wheelchairs. Although USCPAA rules do not encourage this type of skill development, Class 5 is eligible for wheelchair sports like tennis and handball that are sponsored by other organizations.

Class 6—Athetosis, Ambulatory

Class 6 individuals are primarily affected by athetosis, and associated dysfunctions are severe. They have moderate to severe involvement of three or four limbs, with severe balance and coordination problems. These are less prominent when running and throwing than walking.

In terms of overall severity of condition, Class 6 is often grouped with Classes 1, 2, and 3. Unsteadiness of gait, balance, and reflex problems vary widely. All physical education, however, is ambulatory, with elbow and knee pads recommended because of frequent falls. When mainstreamed, these persons are helped by the presence of a bar or chair to provide support during calisthenics and other activities that require good balance. In USCPAA competition, Class 6 persons have a choice between tricycle and bicycle. Like Class 3 individuals, they can do all swim strokes except the butterfly.

Class 7—Hemiplegic

Class 7 includes only persons with hemiplegia. Spasticity ranges from mild to moderate. Class 7 persons ambulate with a slight limp and are able to pump effectively only with the noninvolved arm; the spastic arm is somewhat conspicuous because of its bent, pronated position (see Figure 25.8). The spastic leg is noticeably smaller than the normal one.

Class 7 persons are typically in integrated physical education and able to do everything that peers do, except with more effort. Sue Moucha, an international Class 7 athlete, states:

> I have biked 100 mi in one day, run a marathon, and have successfully completed an able-bodied Outward Bound course, which included rock climbing, rappelling, canoeing, and a mini-marathon. Sports acts as a benchmark. I enjoy physical activities and am eager to do something new. (Moucha, 1991, p. 38)

Class 8—Minimal Involvement

Class 8 persons run and jump freely without a noticeable limp (see Figure 25.9). Their gait is symmetrical in both walking and running. They demonstrate good balance but have noticeable (although minimal) coordination problems. This is usually seen in the hands or in a lack of power or coordination in one limb. Sometimes, associated dysfunctions are more disabling than the motor involvement.

Coping With Special Problems

Among the motor problems that require special attention are (a) delayed development, (b) reflex and postural reaction abnormalities, (c) abnormal muscle tone, (d) contractures, and (e) additional orthopedic defects. Attitudinal barriers constitute a major social problem.

Delayed Motor Development

Children in Classes 7 and 8 often learn to walk by age 2, but others are delayed several years or never learn. All aspects of motor development are typically delayed, which limits the physical, mental, and emotional stimulation that children need. To compensate, early intervention should involve several hours of big muscle activity daily. Chapter 10 presents content to guide programming of nonambulatory children from birth until age 7.

The type of motor performance that a child with CP has at age 7 is predictive of performance as an adult (Bleck & Nagel, 1982). Most children who are going to learn to walk have done so by age 7. Bleck and Nagel (1982, p. 79) emphasize, "Physical therapy to improve the child's walking once he or she has reached 7 or 8 years is unlikely to be worth the time and effort expended, and other areas of function (like play and sports) should take precedence." These and other physicians agree that emphasis on integration of reflexes should change to instruction in sports, dance, and aquatics at about age 7. *Persons*

FIGURE 25.8   Class 7 athletes are hemiplegic and run with a slight limp.

FIGURE 25.9   Class 8 athletes run freely without a noticeable limp.

who have not lost reflexes by age 7 will probably have them for-ever and can be taught to compensate or to use reflexes to en-hance performance. Turning the head to the right, for example, can increase the power of a right-handed movement via the asymmetrical tonic neck reflex. Hyperextending the head can extend arms and flex legs, making the exit from a pool easier via the symmetrical tonic neck reflex (see Figure 25.10).

Postural Reactions

Sports, dance, and aquatics can be used to enhance postural reactions. Emphasis on protective extension of arms during falls (the parachute reactions) and on development of equilib-rium should continue. Some sports should be selected for working on weaknesses (e.g., balance beam routines, horse-back riding, gymnastics, roller and ice skating, dance, wrestling, and judo), whereas others should build on strengths and the desire to participate in the same activities as peers. Most sport skills, done in correct form, normalize muscle tone. The more difficult principle to implement is avoidance of abnormal postures and stereotyped patterns that may cause injury, contribute to posture deviations, and further so-cial rejection. These are associated with reflexes and muscle

FIGURE 25.10 Different manifestations of tonic neck reflexes.

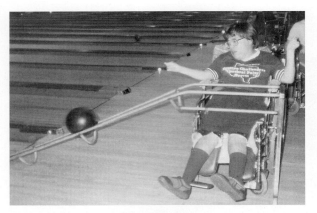

The ATNR causes increased extensor tone in the arm on the face side and increased flexor tone in the arm on the scalp side.

The STNR extends arms and flexes legs.

tone abnormalities. Hence, work continues in these areas but for different reasons.

Reflexes and Abnormal Postures

Chapter 10 describes the 10 reflexes that are most troublesome, principles to guide integration, and activities. This section therefore focuses on proper holding, carrying, and positioning.

Holding and Carrying

Class 1 and 2 people, regardless of age, need help in making transfers. Unless body weight prohibits carrying children from place to place, it is both efficient and therapeutic to do so. Figure 25.11 shows several correct ways for carrying on land and in water activities. Many games like airplane and Batman can be played from these positions. Children dominated by **extensor tone** (i.e., stiff all over) should be held close to the body in tucked positions that maintain their head and limbs in flexion. Children dominated by **flexor tone** (i.e., bent or curled) should be held in ways that maintain head and limbs in extension. Thus, the commonsense principle of keeping body parts in good alignment is followed.

When apparatus is used, much Velcro, padding, and cushioning is needed to achieve proper alignment. Often, each body part must be strapped in place. Many sources provide ideas for adapting equipment (Farber, 1982; Finnie, 1974; Robinault, 1973). Such equipment is also available from commercial companies like Preston (see Appendix E).

Strapping and Positioning

Good alignment in sitting requires that (a) the hips are at 90° flexion and in contact with the back of the chair, (b) thighs are slightly abducted and in contact with the seat, and (c) knees, ankles, and elbows are positioned at 90° flexion. There should be at least 1 inch of space between the knees and the seat to avoid pressure on the tender area behind the knees. The feet should be in contact with a firm, flat surface. The head and neck must be held in midline and kept in extension. Often, strapping is the only way to meet these criteria for a good sitting posture.

Strapping traditionally has been associated with occupational therapy and physical therapy, but the new emphasis on wheelchair sports in school physical education requires learning strapping techniques to assure safety and maximize performance (Burd & Grass, 1987). All-out effort in a wheelchair, without

FIGURE 25.11 Correct ways to carry children with cerebral palsy.

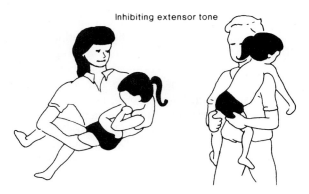

Inhibiting extensor tone

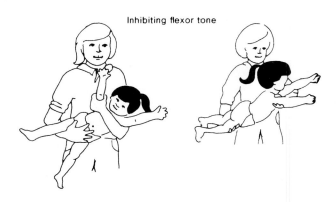

Inhibiting flexor tone

proper strapping, often elicits an **extensor pattern** that tends to pull the body down and out of the chair. This is characterized by spinal, hip, and knee extension and toe pointing (plantar flexion). In conjunction with this, scissoring is a problem.

To control the extensor pattern, a strap should come forward from the rear-underneath portion of the chair, where it is secured to the frame. The strap angle should be about 45°, with the fastening mechanism in front. This type of lap belt holds the hips in place much better than a traditional seat belt at waist level. Some persons, however, may need an H strap arrangement that holds both upper back and hips in place.

Knee flexion and the adduction/inward rotation pattern caused by scissoring are controlled by straps placed around each thigh and pulled tight. A single strap across the thighs may be sufficient. Experimentation is important.

The feet and lower legs may need to be strapped in similar fashion. Often, a strap is also placed beneath the feet as a means of elevating the footrests and increasing knee flexion. Regardless of body part strapped, wide, 2-inch Velcro or webbing should be used to reduce the possibility of circulation and irritation problems. If swelling or redness occurs or the athlete complains of discomfort, adjust the straps. Extremities should not be strapped for long periods. As soon as competition or the activity ends, straps should be loosened.

Figure 25.12 shows how strapping and positioning inhibit reflexes. A bolster between the thighs inhibits the **crossed extension reflex** that causes scissoring. The extensor pattern can be prevented by positioning self at eye level rather than forcing the student to look upward. Hyperextension of the head can elicit either the extension pattern or the symmetrical tonic neck reflex. In general, both should be avoided. This calls for proper placement of suspended balls and visual aids. Also depicted in Figure 25.12 is use of a bolster, wedge, and inclined board to correctly position a child in prone and inhibit flexor tone dominance.

During the time that no one is interacting with a severely involved person, positioning is very important. *For the person who cannot initiate voluntary movement, side-lying with the head propped up on a pillow is considered best.* Foam cushions maintain correct position. The individual should be facing the action, a television, or a source of stimulation. If a person can hold up the head and use arms, a prone position is better. Mirrors on the wall and floor reinforce voluntary movement. Supine-lying is avoided because of the helplessness it causes; propped sitting is better.

Severely involved persons spend so much time in wheelchairs that mat work is an important part of physical education. Ideally, the mat area should be an elevated platform about the same height as the wheelchair seat to facilitate transfers. Bolsters and wedges must be available if students wait turns.

Contraindicated Activities

Activities that elicit or reinforce abnormal movement patterns are contraindicated. **Creeping on all-fours,** for example, may be contraindicated in quadriplegia and diplegia if it increases flexor spasticity. The **frog or W sitting position** (resting on the buttocks between the heels of the feet) should be avoided because it worsens the hip joint adduction-inward rotation-flexion pattern that needs to be eliminated. **Bridging in supine** (pushing down with feet and lifting pelvis from mat), which

often occurs in athetosis, should not be allowed because it worsens abnormal neck extension and scapulae retraction. Movement education challenges to walk on tiptoe or to point the toes are contraindicated for persons with tight calf muscles.

Spasticity Problems

Abnormal postures are often corrected manually, especially in young children. In particular, adduction-inward rotation-flexion patterns of the shoulder and hip joints must be corrected. In general, this is achieved by applying an inhibitory pattern that is the opposite of the spastic posture. To correct scissoring in supine, grasp the thighs and gently spread the legs while outwardly rotating and flexing the hip joint. This corrective pattern also decreases plantar flexion at the ankle joint and makes it easier to put on shoes and socks. To correct abnormal arm position, grasp the upper arm and lift it over the head while gently outwardly rotating.

Three principles underlie handling techniques. The first is to *maintain symmetry* (i.e., strive to keep body parts in midline). The second is to *use inhibitory actions that are the opposite of the undesired pattern.* The third is to *work from designated key points of central control* (i.e., grasp body parts as close to the joint as possible). Key points are (a) the shoulder joint for abnormal arm positions, (b) the hip joint for scissoring, and (c) the head and neck for the arched back extensor spasm.

The fisted hand, a common problem, is worsened by wrist hyperextension. When an activity calls for releasing an object or maintaining an open hand, use both shoulder joint and radioulnar rotation to relax the wrist and fingers. Do not try to pry fingers open.

Overall spasticity of the body is decreased by rotation of the trunk. This forms the rationale for r**hythmic rolling activities** on a stationary or moving surface (i.e., large therapy ball) and gentle **rocking movements** on lap, ball, or tiltboard. Horseback riding is also helpful, and many therapeutic programs are available. Rotation and rocking activities also create weight-shifting situations that promote development of equilibrium reactions.

Active exercises, for persons able to initiate independent movement, should follow the three principles of correct handling. Rotatory and rocking movements are important for warm-up and relaxation to minimize spasticity. Chapters 16 and 17 on dance and swimming present many good activities. Water play and exercises in a warm pool (about 90°) are excellent. Swim fins are helpful in minimizing the stretch reflex. Sport is strongly recommended for people with spasticity (Richter, Gaebler-Spira, & Adams-Mushett, 1996).

Daily stretching exercises can help prevent contractures. These should be slow, static stretches as described in Chapter 13 on fitness. Participation in sport also prevents contractures.

Athetosis Problems

Class 2 and 6 persons exhibit more athetosis than spasticity, but both conditions are often present. Although constant, unpredictable, purposeless (CUP) movement would seem a hindrance

FIGURE 25.12 Methods of inhibiting primitive reflexes. *(A)* Strapping the thighs and lower legs to wheelchair prevents extensor thrust. *(B)* A hard roll or bolster between the thighs maintains the legs in abduction and inhibits scissoring. *(C)* The position of the teacher influences extensor pattern. *(D–F)* Use of bolster, wedge, and inclined board for correct positioning in prone.

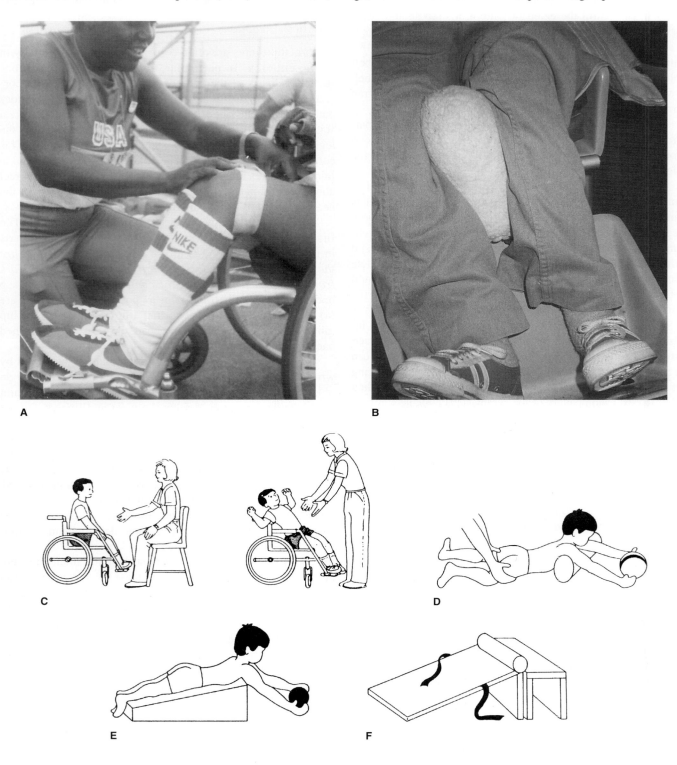

FIGURE 25.13 Apparatus to help children with cerebral palsy stand is built with straps to keep body parts centered in midline and thus inhibit asymmetrical tonic neck reflex.

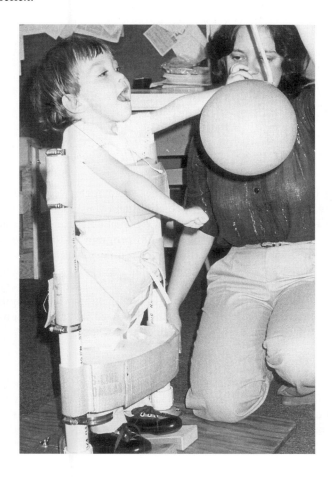

in aiming activities, persons with athetosis can succeed in bowling, tennis, and golf. USCPAA also has accumulated evidence that Class 2 people can excel in aiming activities and recommends bowling and boccia.

USCPAA promotes proper warm-up for persons with athetosis. Previous beliefs that athetoid movements provide a natural state of readiness have not been subjected to research and thus have no base for support.

Early childhood positioning and exercise goals are different for athetosis and spasticity. The main goal in athetosis is head and trunk control (proximal stability), which, in turn, tends to decrease undesired limb movement. To promote midline control, infants and toddlers are placed quite early in sitting, kneeling, and standing positions (see Figure 25.13). Upright rather than prone activities are stressed in mat work. Knee walking (wearing pads) is recommended, as well as walking using parallel bars for support. Tricycling and bicycling (both stationary and moving) reinforce midline control, as does horseback riding.

Surgery and Braces

Several surgical procedures correct or relieve problems caused by severe spasticity. A **tenotomy** is surgical sectioning of a tendon. It is primarily used to lengthen the Achilles tendon, thereby reducing toe-walking caused by abnormal tightness. In about 6 weeks, the cutout sections are filled in by new tendon growth. Tenotomy is also used to lengthen the iliopsoas tendon to relieve hip flexion contractures and to lengthen hamstring tendons to relieve knee flexion deformities.

A **myotomy** is a similar procedure except it is applied to muscles, mainly the tight adductor muscles of the hip joint. A **neurectomy** is a cutting (partial or total) of nerves that supply spastic muscles. A **tendon transplant** is surgical relocation of the origin of a muscle, also a technique to ameliorate adduction and flexion deformities.

Arthrodesis is the surgical immobilization of a joint; it is sometimes done at the ankle joint to relieve severe **pes valgus** (combined eversion, plantar flexion, and adduction) caused by contractures. **Valgus deformities** occur commonly in ambulatory spastic diplegia. Arthrodesis causes feet to remain in a fixed dorsiflexion position, which gives more stability than pathological plantar flexion.

Braces (orthoses) are also used to control spasticity and to provide needed stability. Figure 25.14 shows some of these, which are typically referred to by their initials: AFOs (ankle-foot orthoses), KAFOs (knee-ankle-foot orthoses), or HKAFOs (hip-knee-ankle-foot orthoses). Orthoses are not considered assistive devices and are allowed in all USCPAA events. The **parapodium** and other standing devices are primarily used in early childhood, before independent standing is possible.

Hip Dislocation, Scoliosis, and Foot Deformities

Nonambulatory children with CP are at high risk for hip dislocation. In approximately 25%, the head of the femur becomes displaced in an upward direction. The average age of dislocation is 7 years. Correction is by surgery. This propensity for hip dislocation explains why learning to properly handle scissored legs is so important.

Abnormal muscle tone, reflex problems, and improper positioning result in a high percentage of scoliosis. Approximately one third have scoliosis and can benefit from the exercises and bracing described in Chapter 14 on postures. Nonambulatory persons are at greatest risk.

Foot deformities are common, presumably because insufficient attention is given to stretching the tight calf muscles and Achilles tendon (heel cord). **Equinovalgus** (abnormal plantar flexion, eversion, and pronation) is associated with ambulatory spastic diplegia, whereas **equinovarus** (abnormal plantar flexion, inversion, and supination) occurs most often in hemiplegia and nonambulatory persons with total involvement. *In both conditions, activities requiring toe pointing are contraindicated.* Dorsiflexion games like walking up (but not down) steep, inclined boards and hills should be devised. In contrast, ambulatory persons with athetosis tend to have a **dorsiflexed valgus foot position.**

Attitudinal Barriers

The multidisabled profiles of persons with CP result in attitudinal barriers that make social acceptance especially difficult. Research shows that persons with CP are ranked last or next to last as friendship choices when several disabilities are compared (Mastro, Burton, Rosendahl, & Sherrill, 1996; Tripp, 1988). This affects success in mainstream activities,

FIGURE 25.14 Illustrative orthoses.

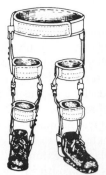
Hip-knee-ankle-foot orthosis (HKAFO)

Parapodium

Metal KAFO

Metal AFO

Plastic AFO

self-concept, and motivation. Educational programming must therefore focus on attitudes and seek to ameliorate social delays and associated deficits in play and game knowledges and strategies (Brown, 1987).

Fitness and CP

Little is known about fitness of individuals with CP because widespread differences in Classes 1 to 8 tend to mask results when research is undertaken. As part of Project UNIQUE (see Chapter 13), Short and Winnick (1986) compared 309 individuals with CP to 1,192 AB adolescents, ages 10 to 17 years, and reported significant differences on all test items except skinfold measures. Items included sit-ups, leg raises, trunk raises, grip strength, flexed arm hang, pull-ups, standing broad jumps, and sit-and-reach. Interestingly, the subjects with CP generally did not improve with age, as is the expected developmental trend. Also, expected gender differences were not found on many of the items. Follow-up research, which compared persons with CP/MR dual diagnosis with CP-only diagnosis, indicated no significant difference (Winnick & Short, 1991).

Body build differences may affect fitness measures. Children with CP tend to be short for their age and to have reduced body cell mass and increased body water (Shephard, 1990). Allowance for these differences indicates that the aerobic power of well-trained persons with CP may be essentially normal, even though it is typically reported as 10 to 30% below normal standards.

Spasticity, athetosis, and exaggerated reflex action are associated with **mechanical inefficiency** and tremendous expenditure of energy, even on easy motor tasks. This helps to explain why weight is not typically a problem. Because persons with CP require more time than average to perform activities of daily living (ADL) and to travel to school or work, little time or energy is left at the end of the day for strenuous activities. When asked to prioritize physical education goals, many persons with CP select motor and leisure skills. Once such skills are learned and people are socialized into sport, fitness training becomes more meaningful.

Flexibility has long been the most important fitness goal in CP, but athletes are interested also in strength and aerobic training (Jones, 1988). USCPAA sanctions powerlifting

as one of its competitive sports and encourages weight training, especially free weights, Nautilus, and Universal (Lockette & Keyes, 1994). Research indicates that athletes can engage in a 10-week circuit-training strength program (2 to 3 days a week), supplemented by flexibility training, with no loss of ROM except at wrist and ankle joints, areas not given attention (Holland & Steadward, 1990). Muscle groups of every joint should be stretched daily in conjunction with strength training. This includes muscles not involved in strength training because spasticity is a total body response.

Sports and Aquatics

The first international games for persons with CP were held in 1968 in France. Sport groups have been testing activities and identifying those in which persons with CP have the most opportunity for success for over 30 years. In general, persons with CP perform better in individual sports than in team activities.

Team Sports

Only three team sports are conducted by USCPAA: soccer, indoor wheelchair soccer, and boccia. Classes 6 to 8 are eligible to compete in *ambulatory soccer,* which is played (with only a few exceptions) according to the rules of AB soccer. The game is coed, with seven players on a team; these must include at least one Class 6 and no more than four Class 8 athletes. The game consists of two equal periods of 25 min each.

In 1997, indoor wheelchair soccer (IWCS) replaced team handball as a USCPAA sport especially designed for Classes 1 to 6. However, the new sport is open to Classes 1 to 8 and to all physical disabilities. IWCS uses six-person teams (3 quads and 3 paras), with one motorized chair on the floor at all times. The goal is to get a 10-inch playground ball into the opponents' goal cage, a structure 5 ft in width, 4 ft in depth, and 5 ft, 6 inches in height. The playing area is a regulation basketball court. Basketball skills are used for both offense and defense, except that players with 2L or 6L classifications may kick the ball. The ball must be passed or bounced every 3 sec.

Boccia, played with leather balls of about baseball size, can be either a team or an individual sport. Balls can be given impetus by throwing, rolling, kicking, or assistive

FIGURE 25.15 Boccia is a bowling-type game specifically for Class 1 and 2 athletes. A team is comprised of three members, one of whom must be Class 1. The object is to give impetus to the ball so that it lands as close as possible to the white target ball. Each player has two balls per round. A team game is six rounds.

Class 1 athlete with no functional use of arms or legs uses head pointer to give impetus to the ball.

Class 2 athletes either kick or throw the ball into play, depending upon whether they are 2L or 2U.

Table 25.2   Swimming events for USCPAA.

Event	Nonambulatory Classes				Ambulatory Classes			
	1	*2*	*3*	*4*	*5*	*6*	*7*	*8*
25-m freestyle	×	×						
25-m backstroke	×	×						
50-m freestyle	×	×	×	×	×	×	×	×
50-m backstroke	×	×	×	×	×	×	×	
50-m breaststroke			×	×	×	×	×	
50-m butterfly				×	×			
100-m freestyle			×	×	×	×	×	×
100-m backstroke			×	×	×	×	×	×
100-m breaststroke			×	×	×	×	×	×
100-m butterfly								×
200-m freestyle			×	×	×	×	×	×
200-m backstroke					×			×
400-m freestyle				×	×		×	×
800-m freestyle				×	×	×	×	×
1500-m freestyle				×	×	×	×	×
3 × 50 individual medley		×				×	×	
4 × 50 individual medley				×	×			×

Note. In the United States, Class 1 and 2 can compete with and without personal flotation devices (PFDs). International rules do not allow a PFD.

device. Figure 25.15 illustrates this game. Although popular in Europe, boccia is just beginning to be known in the United States. Indoor adapted boccia sets, with game rules, can be ordered through USCPAA. All balls except the target ball (which is smaller) weigh 275 g and are 26.5 cm in diameter.

Individual Sports

Individual sports in which persons with CP do well include archery, bowling, bicycling and tricycling, track and field, horseback riding, swimming, rifle shooting, slalom, table tennis,

and powerlifting (Jones, 1988). Tables 25.2 and 25.3 indicate distances that must be achieved in swimming, slalom, track, and cycling events before persons are eligible for USCPAA adult competition. School physical education should use these distances as goals. These tables also summarize events appropriate for the different classes.

Use of PFDs is permitted when teaching persons with CP to swim. Most Class 1 and 2 athletes, because of severe spasticity, need PFDs throughout their lives, regardless of how well they learn to swim. A few internationally ranked swimmers

T a b l e 2 5 . 3   Slalom, track, and cycling events for USCPAA.

Event	Nonambulatory Classes					Ambulatory Classes			
	1	2L	2U	3	4	5	6	7	8
Slalom	×	×	×	×	×				
60-m weave	×								
20-m			×						
60-m			×						
100-m		×	×	×	×	×	×	×	×
200-m		×	×	×	×	×	×	×	×
400-m		×		×	×	×	×	×	×
800-m		×			×		×	×	×
1,500-m					×			×	×
Cross country, 3,000-m							×	×	×
4 × 100		×	×	×	×		×	×	×
Tricycle									
1,500-m		×		×		×	×		
3,000-m						×	×		
5,000-m						×	×		
Bicycle									
1,500-m						×	×		
3,000-m						×	×		
5,000-m						×	×	×	×
10,000-m								×	×
20,000-m								×	×
Total	2	7	6	6	7	9	12	10	10

Note. All wheelchairs are manual except Class 1.

are exceptions to this generalization, but independence from PFDs is not a realistic goal for most Class 1 and 2 athletes. *Speed* is the goal rather than good form, although increasing ROM improves form as well as speed. Flippers are not allowed. Team relays are popular.

Tricycles, bicycles, and horses offer a chance for freedom not possible in wheelchairs. Stationary tricycles and bicycles should be available in adapted physical education resource rooms and for winter use. Three-wheeled adult cycles are available through Sears and other popular chain stores. Like AB students, every child with CP should own his or her cycle and master this means of locomotion. Often, adaptations must be made to tricycles and bicycles; special seats can be used, and feet can be attached to pedals with Velcro straps.

The **slalom,** a wheelchair race against time in which persons follow a clearly marked obstacle course, is a good school activity. Four components of the slalom course are (a) one 360° circle around a cone, (b) one 360° gate and three reverse gates, (c) one figure eight around three cones, and (d) one ramp. These components can be combined in various ways, or USCPAA can be contacted for a copy of official slalom courses.

Field events are more popular in USCPAA than any other activity. These also offer great promise in school physical education. In early childhood, beanbags are typically used. By age 7, terminology changes to **soft shot.** This is because of the normalization principle; beanbag activities are not appropriate

for older children. Regulation-size soft shots are available through USCPAA. For Class 3 and above, instruction should focus on the club, shot put, and discus. The javelin is appropriate for Class 4 and above (see Figures 25.16 and 25.17). Of the official implements, the club is the easiest to handle.

Softball throwing and catching are deemphasized except for Classes 7 and 8 because these are not official events. Classes 7 and 8, when in integrated physical education instruction, may have limited success in softball games. In general, however, catching is difficult to teach (Rintala, Lytinen, & Dunn, 1990) and takes away time better spent on activities more suited to functional ability. Recreational sports that offer success are adaptations using clubs, sticks, and paddles.

Bowling, like field events, is a sport of choice because it permits many adaptations. The ball can be delivered from a sitting or standing position. Persons with fisted hands can use a ramp (also called a chute), with or without an assistant. The assistant does nothing but follow instructions (voice, gesture, head nod) on how to position the ramp or ball. Many bowlers use balls with retractable handles (see Appendix E).

Tables 25.4 and 25.5 summarize events that require equipment and describe adaptations. Parents should be encouraged to begin taking children to USCPAA events at ages 3 to 4 because parents then learn about equipment and begin home programs. The national headquarters for USCPAA moved in 1995 to 200 Harrison Ave, Newport, RI 02840.

FIGURE 25.16 Throwing events for Classes 3–4 are the same as for Classes 5–8 except for the javelin, which is inappropriate for Class 3. Note that Class 3 athletes need waist and leg straps for support and hold onto their chairs during the release. Class 4 athletes do not need straps or arm support.

Class 3 Shotput

Class 3 Club throw

Class 4 Javelin throw

Class 4 Club throw

FIGURE 25.17   Class 6 athletes have more motor control problems than Classes 4–5. Class 6 ambulates without assistive devices but typically has much athetoid movement, which causes balance and accuracy problems.

Class 6 Discus throw

Class 6 Shot put

Paralympics and International Issues

Since 1978, athletes with CP have competed internationally against each other, using a functional classification system that assured equity of opportunity. At the 1992 Paralympics in Barcelona, however, the new integrated, functional classification system (see Chapter 23) required athletes with CP to compete against athletes with spinal paralysis and les autres conditions. Many experts believe that this new system is unfair to people with CP because it does not adequately address associated dysfunctions that are unique to upper neuron disorders (Richter, Adams-Mushett, Ferrara, & McCann, 1992). Few athletes with CP won medals in track, field, or swimming at the 1992 and 1996 Paralympics. What are possible solutions? Should we accept the new, integrated system or seek to change it?

Another international issue is the social acceptance of people with CP as elite athletes. Although the Paralympics movement began in 1960, athletes with CP were excluded until 1980, when ambulatory athletes were invited to Arnhem, Holland. In 1984, nonambulatory athletes with CP finally gained access to Paralympic competition. Many countries still do not enter athletes with CP into the Paralympics. As a result women and nonambulatory athletes are severely underrepresented.

Table 25.4   Boccia, bowling, and field events for USCPAA.

Event	Nonambulatory Classes				Ambulatory Classes			
	1	2	3	4	5	6	7	8
Boccia	×	×						
Chute bowling with assistant	×	×						
Chute bowling, no assistant			×			×		
Regulation bowling				×	×		×	×
Soft discus	×							
Precision throw	×							
Distance soft shot	×							
High toss	×							
Distance kick		×						
Thrust kick		×						
Shot put		×	×	×	×	×	×	×
Club throw		×	×	×	×	×		
Discus		×	×	×	×	×	×	×
Javelin				×	×	×	×	×
Long jump							×	×

Note. Class 2L do the two kicking events; 2U do the throws.

Table 25.5 Official equipment for sports for individuals with cerebral palsy.

Event	Implement	Weight or Design
Distance, precision, and high throws	Soft shot	5 oz (150 g)
Thrust kick	Medicine ball	6 lb (3 kg)
Distance kick	Playground ball	13 inches
Club throw	Club	1 lb, 14 inches long
Discus	Standard women's discus	2 lb (1 kg), 180 mm diameter
Shot put	Shot put	4, 6, or 8 lb, depending on classification
Javelin	Standard women's javelin except for Class 8 males	
Boccia	Leather-covered boccia ball	275 g, 26.5 cm diameter
Ambulatory soccer	Regulation soccer ball	14 to 16 oz
Wheelchair soccer	Playground ball	10 inches
Weight lifting	Universal weight machine, nonprogressive bench	
Bowling	With or without retractable handle chute (ramp)	Varies; 10 lb for Classes 1 and 2

Note. The soft-shot *precision throw* uses a ground target with eight concentric rings. The athlete has six throws from a distance of 6 ft from the center of the bull's-eye. The bull's-eye counts 16 points. Each ring away from it counts 2 points less than the previous. The soft-shot *high throw* uses high-jump standards, with the bar set at 3 ft and raised 6 inches at a time. The competitor is at least 1 mm from the bar and has three throws per height. See Chapter 11, page 306.

To combat this problem, more efforts must be directed all over the world to socializing children with CP into sport and providing lifespan opportunities for self-actualization through both competitive and recreational sport (Lugo, Sherrill, & Pizarro, 1992; Sherrill & Rainbolt, 1986, 1988). Also, more serious efforts must be directed toward fitness training that generalizes to sport (Pitetti, Fernandez, & Lanciault, 1991). How can you help?

References

Adams-Mushett, C., Wyeth, D. O., & Richter, K. H. (1995). Cerebral palsy. In B. Goldberg (Ed.), *Sports and exercise for children with chronic health conditions* (pp. 123–133). Champaign, IL: Human Kinetics.

Bleck, E., & Nagel, D. (Eds.). (1982). *Physically handicapped children: A medical atlas for teachers* (2nd ed.). New York: Grune & Stratton.

Bobath, K. (1980). *A neurophysiological basis for the treatment of cerebral palsy.* Philadelphia: J. B. Lippincott.

Brown, A. (1987). *Active games for children with movement problems.* London: Harper & Row.

Burd, R., & Grass, K. (1987). Strapping to enhance athletic performance of wheelchair competitors with cerebral palsy. *Palaestra, 3*(2), 28–32.

Farber, S. D. (1982). *Neurorehabilitation: A multisensory approach.* Philadelphia: W. B. Saunders.

Finnie, N. R. (1974). *Handling the young cerebral palsied child at home* (2nd ed.). New York: E. P. Dutton.

Holland, L. J., & Steadward, R. D. (1990). Effects of resistance and flexibility training on strength, spasticity/muscle tone, and range of motion of elite athletes with cerebral palsy. *Palaestra, 6*(4), 27–31.

Jones, J. A. (1988). *Training guide to cerebral palsy sports* (3rd ed.). Champaign, IL: Human Kinetics.

Kottke, F. J., & Lehmann, J. (1990). *Krusen's handbook of physical medicine and rehabilitation* (4th ed.). Philadelphia: W. B. Saunders.

Levitt, S. (1995). *Treatment of cerebral palsy and motor delay* (3rd ed.). Boston: Blackwell Scientific.

Lockette, K. F., & Keyes, A. M. (1994). *Conditioning with physical disabilities.* Champaign, IL: Human Kinetics.

Lugo, A. A., Sherrill, C., & Pizarro, A. L. (1992). Use of a sport socialization inventory with cerebral palsied youth. *Perceptual and Motor Skills, 74,* 203–208.

Mastro, J., Burton, A. W., Rosendahl, M., & Sherrill, C. (1996). Attitudes of elite athletes with impairments toward one another: A hierarchy of preference. *Adapted Physical Activity Quarterly, 13*(2), 197–210.

Miller, S. E., & Schaumberg, K. (1988). Physical education activities for children with severe cerebral palsy. *Teaching Exceptional Children, 20*(2), 9–11.

Moucha, S. (1991). The disabled female athlete as role model. *Journal of Physical Education, Recreation, and Dance, 62*(3), 37–38.

Pitetti, K., Fernandez, J., & Lanciault, M. (1991). Feasibility of an exercise program for adults with cerebral palsy: A pilot study. *Adapted Physical Activity Quarterly, 8*(4), 333–341.

Richter, K., Adams-Mushett, C., Ferrara, M., & McCann, B. C. (1992). Integrated swimming classification: A faulted system. *Adapted Physical Activity Quarterly, 9*(1), 5–13.

Richter, K. J., Gaebler-Spira, & Adams-Mushett, C. (1996). Sport and the person with spasticity of cerebral origin. *Developmental Medicine and Child Neurology, 38,* 867–870.

Rintala, P., Lytinen, H., & Dunn, J. M. (1990). Influence of a physical activity program on children with cerebral palsy: A single subject design. *Pediatric Exercise Science, 2,* 46–56.

Robinault, I. (1973). *Functional aids for the multiply handicapped.* New York: Harper & Row.

Shephard, R. J. (1990). *Fitness in special populations.* Champaign, IL: Human Kinetics.

Sherrill, C., & Rainbolt, W. (1986). Sociological perspectives of cerebral palsy sports. *Palaestra, 2*(4), 20–26, 50.

Sherrill, C., & Rainbolt, W. (1988). Self-actualization profiles of male able-bodied and cerebral palsied athletes. *Adapted Physical Activity Quarterly, 5*(2), 108–119.

Short, F. X., & Winnick, J. P. (1986). The performance of adolescents with cerebral palsy on measures of physical fitness. In C. Sherrill (Ed.), *Sport and disabled athletes* (pp. 239–244). Champaign, IL: Human Kinetics.

Stanley, F., & Blair, E. (1984). Postnatal risk factors in the cerebral palsies. In F. Stanley & E. Alberman (Eds.), *The epidemiology of the cerebral palsies* (pp. 135–149). Philadelphia: J. B. Lippincott.

Sugden, D. A., & Keogh, J. (1990). *Problems in movement skill development.* Columbia, SC: University of South Carolina Press.

Tripp, A. (1988). Comparison of attitudes of regular and adapted physical educators toward disabled individuals. *Perceptual and Motor Skills, 66,* 425–426.

Winnick, J. P., & Short, F. X. (1991). A comparison of the physical fitness of nonretarded and mildly mentally retarded adolescents with cerebral palsy. *Adapted Physical Activity Quarterly, 8,* 43–56.

C H A P T E R

26

Deaf and Hard-of-Hearing Conditions

FIGURE 26.1   The Rome School for the Deaf has its own style of sideline conversation. The deaf community does not use first-person terminology, because deaf people consider deafness a linguistic difference, not a disability.

After you have studied this chapter, you should be able to do the following:

1. Describe Gallaudet University, deaf sport, and the deaf community. Identify organizations for the deaf and outstanding deaf persons and discuss their relevance to teaching physical education-recreation.

2. Differentiate between deafness and hard-of-hearing conditions. Discuss language and communication in relation to each, with an emphasis on the age that hearing loss was sustained and other factors that affect decision making.

3. Identify three approaches to teaching communication skills, discuss controversy, and state your own beliefs.

4. Explain hearing loss in terms of the three attributes of sound. Relate your explanation to understanding test results and adapting physical education instruction for different hearing loss classifications.

5. Develop three make-believe case studies in which you demonstrate understanding of (a) classification of hearing loss in decibels, (b) causes of hearing loss, (c) congenital and acquired conditions, (d) role of parents in development, and (e) probable physical education performance level.

6. Create two games for teaching persons the parts of the ear, how hearing loss occurs, and/or other concepts in this chapter.

7. Using your case studies or those assigned, write physical education IEPs. State and justify placement, goals, and objectives.

8. Develop an instructional unit or lesson plans to guide improvement of vestibular dysfunction and balance.

9. Explain speechreading, cued speech, different kinds of sign language, personal hearing aids, assistive listening devices and systems, and telecommunication devices for the deaf.

10. Discuss existing and needed research. Show evidence of reading research published in the last 3 years.

Deaf and hard-of-hearing (HH) students often excel in physical education. At Gallaudet University in Washington, DC, the only liberal arts college in the world for persons who are deaf, student interest in athletics is so high that men and women engage in several intercollegiate sports. This university, founded in 1864, is recognized worldwide for its leadership in sports, education, and sign language. The football huddle was invented at Gallaudet so opponents could not see the game strategies being communicated through sign. Here, too, was the famous revolt of March 1988, when students refused to attend classes until the Board of Regents appointed a deaf president who could use sign and would advocate for rights (Sacks, 1989). I. King Jordan, the new president, simultaneously signed and spoke his acceptance speech:

> The world has watched the deaf community come of age. We will no longer accept limits on what we can achieve. . . . We know that deaf people can do anything hearing people can except hear.

The Gallaudet Modern Dance Group has performed in Europe and throughout the United States. Says Peter Wisher, founder of the group, "The majority of audiences are composed of hearing people, but they soon forget the dancers are deaf. They become tremendously involved with the kids, especially during the numbers using abstracted sign language" (Carney, 1971, p. 21).

Some deaf persons, like Denver Broncos football player Kenny Walker (previously University of Nebraska) and baseball player William "Dummy" Hoy (1862–1961) have gained recognition as outstanding members of hearing teams. Hoy played with both American and National leagues and instigated the development of umpire hand signals. More and more people who are deaf or HH are in mainstream physical education and sports. Some, however, opt to participate in deaf sport only, where most athletes sign (see Figure 26.1).

Deaf Sport and Deaf Community

Deaf sport, a team created by individuals who are deaf, is explained by David Stewart (1991) in his excellent book *Deaf Sport: The Impact of Sports Within the Deaf Community:*

> Deaf sport is a social institution within which Deaf people exercise their right to self-determination, competition, and socialization surrounding Deaf sport activities. The magnitude and the complexity of Deaf sport reflects many of the dimensions of being deaf in a hearing society. In this sense, Deaf sport is a microcosm of the Deaf community (p. 2). . . . Deaf sport emphasizes the honor of being Deaf, whereas society tends to focus on the adversity of deafness. (p. 1)

Stewart, by birth a Canadian, is a professor at Michigan State University. See Chapter 2 for more information on Stewart.

Deaf sport refers to all of the sport opportunities provided by the **deaf community,** a term coined by people who are deaf to describe their cultural and linguistic separateness from the hearing, speaking world. Over the centuries, deaf persons have tended to cluster together and to take care of one another's needs. Their language is sign, and until recently, few hearing persons knew much about them. Deaf persons do not advocate person-first terminology. That is why this chapter refers to deaf people rather than people with deafness.

The rules, strategies, and skills of deaf sport are not adapted except for communication modes. Modifications are made only in starting and stopping signals and in the ways officials communicate with players. Deaf sport internationally is governed by the Comite International des Sports des Sourds (CISS), founded in France in 1924. The English translation of this is International Committee on Silent Sports, but the commonly used abbreviation (CISS) is derived from the French name. Summer World Games for the Deaf began in 1924, almost a quarter of a century before international competition

Table 26.1 Summer sports in which deaf persons compete internationally.

Individual	Team
Cycling (men)	Soccer (men)
Wrestling, Greco Roman and freestyle (men)	Water polo (men)
Swimming (men and women)	Handball (men)
Track and field (men and women)	Volleyball (men and women)
Tennis (men and women)	Basketball (men and women
Table tennis (men and women)	
Badminton (men and women)	
Shooting (men and women)	

was initiated for other special populations. The American Athletic Association for the Deaf (AAAD) was founded at the end of World War II (1945), long before organizations for athletes with disabilities were conceived. Every nation has a deaf community and deaf sport (e.g., the Canadian Deaf Sports Association, 1987).

Although affiliated for a short time with the Paralympic movement in the early 1990s, deaf sport has chosen to dissociate itself from disability sport. World Games for the Deaf, like the Olympics, are held every 2 years. Summer Games are held on a schedule that runs 1997, 2001, and so on, and Winter Games are held on a schedule that runs 1999, 2003, and so on. Summer games typically attract around 2,500 athletes from over 30 nations.

To be eligible for participation in deaf sport, athletes must have a hearing loss of 55 decibels (dB) or greater in the better ear. Deaf athletes are not classified according to severity of hearing loss. Hearing aids are not permitted during competition.

Table 26.1 presents the eight individual and five team summer sports in which deaf athletes can compete internationally. Competition in the Winter World Games includes alpine and nordic skiing, speed skating, and ice hockey. Additionally, deaf athletes have regional and national competitions. News about deaf sports is regularly published in magazines called *The Deaf American* and *Deaf Sports Review*. There is also a growing body of research (Stewart, McCarthy, & Robinson, 1988; Stewart, Robinson, & McCarthy, 1991).

In addition to AAAD, there are many other sport organizations for persons who are deaf. The oldest of these are the National Deaf Bowling Association and the U.S. Deaf Skiers Association, established in 1963 and 1968, respectively. Illustrative other organizations are the World Recreation Association of the Deaf (WRAD), American Deaf Volleyball Association, American Hearing Impaired Hockey Association, Deaf Athletic Federation of the United States, and National Racquetball Association of the Deaf. In Canada, there are several ice hockey organizations, and winter sports like curling are emphasized. Addresses of these organizations change frequently. For information, contact the Athletic Department at Gallaudet University or the National Association of the Deaf, 814 Thayer Avenue, Silver Spring, MD 20910.

Definitions and Concepts

What do we call persons with a hearing loss? Many such individuals do not consider themselves disabled and prefer to be thought of as a cultural and linguistic minority (Butterfield, 1991; Stewart, 1991). They are often proficient in both sign and English and wonder why so much of the world can communicate only in one way. In particular, most world-class athletes who are deaf take this stance. In contrast, adults adjusting to a hearing impairment may mourn their loss in ways similar to persons with physical disabilities. Obviously, there are many individual differences.

Hearing loss is correctly termed *deaf* or *hard of hearing,* mainly depending on the degree of loss but sometimes on the communication ability of an individual. These are categories specified by both federal legislation and policy-making organizations. The term *deaf* may be used to encompass all conditions in which the loss is significant, as in the name of the American Athletic Association for the Deaf (AAAD) and the Canadian Deaf Sports Association (CDSA). Or a sharp distinction can be made, usually for funding or school purposes. **Deaf** describes a person who is unable to understand speech through use of the ears alone, with or without hearing aids. **Hard of hearing** (HH) is a condition that makes difficult, but does not prevent, the understanding of speech through use of the ears alone, with or without hearing aids. The generic term *hearing impairment* is losing favor.

The practice of linking auditory and visual deficits and discussing them in the same chapter or context as sensory impairments is now outdated. The conditions are much more different than alike. Blindness is primarily a disability of mobility, whereas deafness, if it is considered a disability, is a matter of communication and social acceptance.

Deafness is associated more closely with speech impairment and specific learning disability than other special education categories. About 6 to 8% of deaf and HH children have diagnosed learning disabilities (Cherow, 1985; Martin, 1991). In general, deaf persons have normal intelligence and perform as well on tasks that measure thinking as their hearing peers. Academic achievement depends largely on educational opportunity. Many deaf and HH people have problems with reading and writing beyond the fifth-grade level.

Language and Communication

The terms *language* and *communication* should not be used interchangeably. Language can be (a) inner, (b) receptive, or (c) expressive (see Chapter 18). Communication is typically described as verbal or nonverbal. Verbal methods are (a) oral, (b) written, and (c) sign (i.e., any modality that uses words). Nonverbal methods are facial expressions, postures, body language, or gestures. Nonverbal also refers to silent demonstrations.

Persons who are deaf or HH communicate in many ways, depending on (a) the age that the loss was sustained, (b) training, (c) ability, and (d) cultural affiliation. They might read lips, a skill called *speechreading,* or rely on *sign language,* a manual communication system in which fingers, hands, facial expressions, and body movements are used to convey meaning (see Figure 26.2). There are many forms of

FIGURE 26.2 Dr. Stephen Butterfield, well-known researcher at the University of Maine, signs test instructions to a child.

signing: American Sign Language (ASL), also called Ames-lan; Pidgin Sign English (PSE), also called Siglish; and Manu-ally Coded English (MCE). Of these, ASL is the recognized language of deaf and HH people who communicate manually. ASL has its own grammar and syntax, so sentences are not constructed in the same way that words are ordered in English.

Fingerspelling is a system in which a particular hand position is used for each letter of the alphabet. Each word is spelled letter by letter; because it is slower than signing, it is rarely used by itself. Fingerspelling may be the communica-tion system of choice with hearing persons who do not know sign or with deaf-blind persons who cannot see sign. With the latter, the hand positions are made in the palm of the recipi-ent's hand.

When hearing loss occurs before age 3, learning to speak English is slow and laborious. In older children, who lose the ability to hear their own speech and monitor pronunci-ation of new words, speaking may gradually become less easy. Problems occur because many listeners will not take the time to become familiar with a different speech pattern. This is the same kind of discrimination experienced by foreigners who speak English with an accent (or poorly).

Approaches to Communication

Three approaches to teaching communication skills are (a) manual, which includes fingerspelling and signing; (b) oral or speech only; and (c) total communication, which combines the best of manual and oral methods. Most school systems today use total communication. In the past, however, deaf edu-cation was characterized by bitter controversy over the better method, oral or manual. This intensified in the late 1800s, with Alexander Graham Bell (the inventor of the telephone) cham-pioning the oral method and Edward Gallaudet (founder and director of Gallaudet University) advocating the manual method. Both of these men had deaf mothers, but different at-titudes prevailed in their households. Eventually, the oral method won, and sign was not taught in most classrooms until the 1970s, when total communication became the accepted philosophical approach.

Although sign was not allowed in the classroom, it continued to be used in everyday life. Many deaf people have always regarded sign as their major language, and today sign is widely accepted as a language. Many movies and video-tapes depict communication and other issues. Among these, *Children of a Lesser God* (originally a play) is perhaps best known because Marlee Matlin, who is deaf, won an Oscar in 1987 as best actress for her role. Matlin signed her acceptance speech but later used her voice in various public appearances, thereby drawing criticism from some deaf persons. Since 1991 Matlin has starred in various television movies (e.g., *Reason-able Doubt*). In contrast, Kitty O'Neal, who holds the world speed records for women in water skiing and various car rac-ing events, defends the oral method in the video presenting her life story.

Sound and Vibration

Sound waves are really vibrations. They start at a particular point and spread, much like a rock tossed into a pond makes circles of waves. Most people both hear and feel vibrations. Total deafness means vibrations can only be felt. Consider a rock concert, especially the bass tones. Sounds are conducted to the inner ear through both air and bone conduction. Vibra-tions, however, are felt by the whole body and convey a basic beat or rhythm.

Central to the understanding of hearing loss are the three attributes of sound: intensity, frequency, and timbre or tone. Figure 26.3 depicts an audiogram that shows how inten-sity (the vertical axis) and frequency (the horizontal axis) are used to describe hearing loss. Perfect hearing would be noted by shading the 0 line across all frequencies. The loss depicted is a mild conductive one that can be simulated by placing your fingers in both ears. Figure 26.3 shows that the speech sounds *f, s,* and *th* at high frequencies (pitches) are the first to be lost, along with *p, h, z,* and *v* at lower frequencies. To better under-stand audiograms and hearing classifications, let's consider the attributes of sound.

Intensity

Intensity refers to the perception of loudness and softness. The unit of measurement that expresses the intensity of a sound is the *decibel* (dB). This term is named for Alexander Graham Bell and literally means one tenth of a bell. A sound at 0 level is barely audible. Speech can be heard from a dis-tance of 10 to 20 ft when the loudness is 35 to 65 dB, depend-ing on the pitch. When the intensity of sound ranges above 100 dB, the sound may become painful.

Frequency

Frequency refers to the perception of high and low pitch. It is measured in terms of hertz (Hz). Most human beings can per-ceive frequencies from about 20 to 20,000 Hz. The audiogram includes only the frequencies between 125 and 8,000, since these are the most important in daily communication.

Three of these frequencies—500, 1,000, and 2,000 Hz—are emphasized in hearing tests. For instance, persons who do not hear frequencies above 2,000 Hz have difficulty in

FIGURE 26.3   Audiogram findings for mild conductive loss superimposed on illustration of various environmental and speech sounds at different frequencies and intensities.

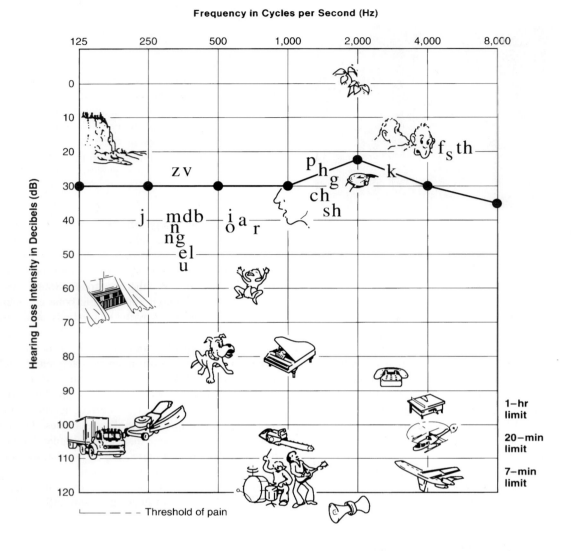

recognizing such high-frequency sounds as the letters *s, z, sh, zh, th* as in *think*, *th* as in *that*, *ch* as in *chair*, *j* as in *Joe*, *p, b, t, d, f, v*, and *h*.

Check your understanding of pitch on a piano. The lowest note on the keyboard *(A)* is 30 Hz. Middle *C* is 256 Hz. The highest *C* on the keyboard is 4,000 Hz.

Timbre or Tone

Timbre refers to all of the qualities besides intensity and frequency that enable us to distinguish between sounds, voices, and musical instruments. It is sometimes conceptualized as the resonance quality of a sound because it depends on the number and character of the vibrating body's overtones. Hearing persons deficient in this area are called *tone deaf*. They can distinguish between some tones but not others. Vowel and vowel combinations (diphthongs) have more easily distinguished tones than consonants.

Testing and Classifying Hearing Loss

Formal hearing tests are conducted by an audiologist or speech and hearing therapist using an instrument called an audiometer. Table 26.2 presents the most widely used system for classifying hearing loss. In general, the first three classes (slight, mild, moderate) are considered HH, and the last two (severe, profound) are considered deaf.

Hearing loss is so complex that there are many individual differences in how persons with each classification function. Table 26.2 offers generalizations about hearing and speaking limitations. There are, of course, exceptions to the rule. Many persons with a 25- to 40-dB loss can benefit from hearing aids (Roeser & Downs, 1988), but 40 dB is the more traditional criterion.

A 3- to 5-ft criterion is useful in making classroom adaptations for slight and mild losses. Students farther away than this may miss as much as 50% of class instruction if they cannot see lips. Consider how this affects learning in various physical education settings.

Table 26.2   Classification of hearing loss.

Degree of Loss	Loss in Decibels	Difficulty With
Slight	25–40	Whispered speech
Mild	41–54	Normal speech at distance greater than 3 to 5 ft
Marked or moderate	55–69	Understanding loud or shouted speech at close range; group discussions
Severe	70–89	Understanding speech at close range, even when amplified
Profound	90+	Hearing most sounds, including telephone rings and musical instruments (see Figure 26.3)

Note. 55 dB or worse in one ear is the criterion for sport eligibility in AAAD.

The moderate classification (55 to 69 dB) is of particular interest because 55 dB is the minimum criterion for eligibility to participate in AAAD activities. The 55-dB and greater loss is associated with difficulty in following and contributing to small-group conversations and class discussions. Loud or shouted speech at close range may be heard but not totally understood because of distortions and background noise. Speech training becomes imperative at this level for correct pronunciation.

The 70-dB level is the accepted criterion for distinguishing between HH and deafness. Persons partially hear speech sounds within 1 ft, but they cannot understand most of them, even with amplification. Individuals at both the severe and profound levels may need intensive training in total communication. Interpreters and/or buddy systems are helpful in communicating with hearing people, especially in group settings.

Congenital and Acquired Conditions

Ability to communicate in conventional spoken English is largely dependent upon age that hearing loss occurs. Therefore, time of onset (congenital or acquired) must be considered in both education and research. A synonym for *acquired* is *adventitiously deaf.* The terms *prelingual* and *postlingual* further specify whether loss was sustained before or after the development of language.

With congenital hearing losses, knowing whether parents are hearing or deaf and what language (sign or spoken English) dominates in the home is critical. This affects all aspects of development, especially self-esteem. Deaf children born to deaf parents typically have significantly higher self-esteem than those born to hearing parents because they are immediately accepted and begin learning language (sign) at a very young age.

Only about 10% of deaf children have deaf parents. Illustrative of such persons among the leaders in deaf sport is Donalda Ammons (1986, 1990), who has served for many years as chairperson of the U.S. World Games for the Deaf Team Committee. Ammons is Director of Foreign Study Programs at Gallaudet. Her best sports are basketball and swimming.

Hearing children are often born of deaf parents. The excellent novel *In This Sign* by Greenberg (1970) is one of several that explore relationships in families and describe growing up deaf. In it, Abel and Janice Ryder (both born deaf) marry and have hearing children and grandchildren. The television presentation of this book—*Love Is Never Silent*—is well worth renting.

Acquired hearing losses vary in severity, depending on the degree of loss and age of onset. Among the many persons with acquired hearing losses are Ludwig van Beethoven, Bernard Baruch, and Thomas Alva Edison. The last 25 years of Beethoven's life were spent in almost total deafness. His famous Ninth Symphony, the *Missa Solemnis,* and many of his piano sonatas and string quartets were composed after he became totally deaf. At his last appearance at a public concert, in 1824, Beethoven was completely oblivious to the applause of the audience acclaiming his ninth and final symphony.

Deaf-Blind Conditions

Discussion of combined deaf-blind losses, covered in this chapter in earlier editions of this book, has been moved to Chapter 27 on blindness. This is because persons who are deaf-blind typically engage in sports under the auspices of the U.S. Association for Blind Athletes (USABA) rather than AAAD. Sight and hearing are seldom both totally lost. With regard to educational placement, knowing which loss is the greater and when each occurred is important. If the condition is prelingual, training in speech and language (i.e., deaf education) will probably be given more emphasis than mobility.

Types and Causes of Hearing Loss

There are three types of hearing loss: (a) conductive, (b) sensorineural, and (c) mixed. Visualizing the three parts of the ear and the causes of disorders in each part is helpful (see Figure 26.4). The Greek word for ear is *otos,* so inflammation of the ear is **otitis**. The instrument used in an ear examination is an *otoscope.*

Conductive Loss

Conductive loss is diminished sound traveling through the air passages of the external and middle ear. Putting your finger in your ear canal creates about a 25-dB conductive loss. You can still hear, but not as well. A conductive loss results in an HH condition, not deafness.

Disorders of the external ear center around the size and shape of the ear canal. Occasionally, infants are born without a canal (**atresia**) or with one that is abnormally narrow. Usually, however, problems are caused by obstruction (impacted earwax), injury, or infection (external otitis) and respond well to treatment.

Disorders of the middle ear are more serious, often resulting in permanent damage. The middle ear is the small space between the eardrum (tympanic membrane) and the bony capsule of the inner ear. It includes the ossicles (malleus, incus, stapes), the small bones shaped, respectively, like a hammer, anvil, and stirrup that transmit sound waves to the inner ear much like a blacksmith once worked on horseshoes

FIGURE 26.4 Three parts of the ear shown in relation to locations of disorder. Descriptors for air conduction and sensorineural losses are summarized.

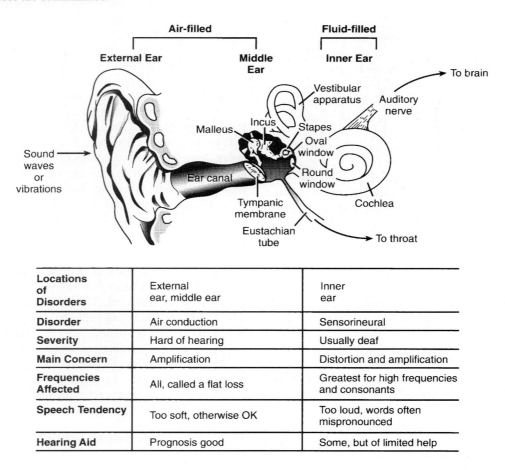

Locations of Disorders	External ear, middle ear	Inner ear
Disorder	Air conduction	Sensorineural
Severity	Hard of hearing	Usually deaf
Main Concern	Amplification	Distortion and amplification
Frequencies Affected	All, called a flat loss	Greatest for high frequencies and consonants
Speech Tendency	Too soft, otherwise OK	Too loud, words often mispronounced
Hearing Aid	Prognosis good	Some, but of limited help

with a hammer. The middle ear also contains the Eustachian tube, which connects the nasopharynx passageway with the throat, and is much affected by colds, sinus infections, and allergies.

Inflammation of the middle ear, called **otitis media,** accounts for more conductive disorders than any other condition. Young children are especially at risk, because 76 to 95% have at least one ear infection before age 2. There are several kinds of otitis media. Some are *acute,* characterized by severe pain and swelling. Others are *chronic,* with persons adjusting to the discomfort and hardly aware of the fluid accumulation behind the eardrum. Many adults with a childhood history of colds, asthma, and respiratory infections do not realize the danger of this fluid until too late.

Otitis media (or any condition that causes the tubes to swell or clog) prevents the Eustachian tubes from performing their functions: (a) ventilating and keeping dry the middle ear cavity and (b) equalizing air pressure on the two sides of the eardrum. If corrective measures are not taken, damage occurs. Antibiotics and other medications sometimes require several days to take effect.

When Eustachian tubes are clogged, flying and activities that involve changes in altitude (e.g., mountain climbing, biking) and pressure (swimming, diving, snorkeling) should be

avoided. Obviously, colds and infections should be treated promptly to avoid or minimize Eustachian tube clogging.

Middle ear ventilation tubes are used when Eustachian tubes are chronically blocked or infected, a condition more prevalent in younger than older children. These tubes are surgically inserted, under local or general anesthesia, with one end in the middle ear and the other just outside the eardrum. During the months that a tube is in place, swimming is contraindicated.

Sensorineural Loss

Sensorineural loss occurs in the inner ear, where sensory receptors convert sound waves into neural impulses that travel to the brain for translation. The hearing apparatus within the inner ear is the *cochlea,* so named because it resembles a snail shell in appearance. The oval and round windows are the passages through which sound waves enter the inner ear and disrupt the fluid and hair cells in the cochlea, the mechanism central to sensory reception. Also housed in the inner ear is the *vestibular apparatus* (semicircular canals) that governs balance. This explains why sensorineural hearing loss and balance deficits sometimes occur together (see Figure 26.5).

Sensorineural loss not only reduces sound but also causes distortions in residual hearing. In young children, this

FIGURE 26.5 Sensorineural loss is linked to balance deficits.

makes learning to speak a real challenge and delays development of language concepts. If loss is total, there is no need for a hearing aid because no amount of amplification will help. If loss is partial, hearing aids will help but not as much as in a conductive loss. Often, hearing aids are used only for auditory and speech training in a structured setting.

Most persons who are born deaf have sensorineural loss. Over 60 types of hereditary hearing loss have been identified, with **autosomal recessive genes** accounting for about 40% of childhood deafness (Kottke & Lehmann, 1990). Often, persons do not know they are carrying these genes. Only about 10% of deaf infants are born to parents who are deaf. Of these, about half have one parent who is hearing.

About 50% of all hearing losses in children have an unknown (idiopathic) etiology (Batshaw & Perret, 1986; Schildroth & Karchmer, 1986). This is largely because hearing losses are often not discovered until language delays are noted. Many of these losses may be genetic.

Among young children, **meningitis** (usually a bacterial infection) and various viral infections (e.g., mumps, scarlet fever, encephalitis, measles) often dramatically wipe out both hearing and balance. Meningitis carries a 1 in 5 risk of hearing loss. An infection of the meninges (coverings) surrounding the spinal cord and brain, meningitis is characterized by high fever, vomiting, and stiff neck. From 30 to 50% of its survivors have multiple disabilities.

Maternal illnesses during pregnancy often result in deafness. Many of these, like measles, are controlled by vaccines so widespread epidemics no longer occur. Herpes viruses and **toxoplasmosis** (infection caused by protozoa found in animals and birds) continue to produce serious hearing defects.

Among adolescents and adults, noise is the main cause of new cases of hearing loss (Kottke & Lehmann, 1990). Several million Americans work in occupations with potentially hazardous noise levels (i.e., above 85 dB). Federal laws govern the number of hours that persons can work at high decibel levels and require the wearing of hearing-protection devices, but these laws are not always followed. Additionally, life in big cities is increasingly noisy, especially time spent in travel. Some sports create noise levels that persons mask by wearing **hearing-protection devices** (e.g., shooting, snowmobiling, motorcycles). Rock concerts and personal earphones attached to stereo devices are also sources of hearing damage.

Lastly, parts of the sensorineural hearing mechanism deteriorate with age, just like other body parts. Reasons for the high prevalence of hearing loss with aging are not clear, but noise is believed to be a major factor. Parts of the conductive system may deteriorate also, but it is sensorineural loss that causes the problems widely associated with biological aging.

Mixed Loss and Tinnitus

Many persons have mixed (combined) conductive and sensorineural losses. This is particularly true of senior citizens.

Tinnitus is a sound sensation in one or both ears that affects about 6% of the population. Associated with both conductive and sensorineural losses, it is experienced as a whistling, hissing, buzzing, roaring, throbbing, or whining sound. It can be sporadic but is continuous for many people. Medical management is sometimes effective, but most persons simply learn to block out their tinnitus.

Prevalence and Incidence of Hearing Loss

Most sources indicate that 7 to 15% of the population have significant hearing losses. Over 17 million Americans have hearing losses, of whom 2 million (about 1 person in 8) are profoundly deaf (Kottke & Lehmann, 1990). At all ages, hearing loss predominates in males.

Prevalence varies sharply, however, by age group, with senior citizens affected the most. Profound hearing loss is present in about 1 in 1,000 newborns (Roeser & Downs, 1988). Approximately 3 in every 1,000 children below age 6 have a moderate or greater sensorineural loss in both ears (Blackman, 1983). The rate is increased 15 to 30 times when mild sensorineural loss is included. Conductive losses are more difficult to track because mild conditions often remain undetected; all children who have had middle ear infections are at risk. Those with Down syndrome, cleft palate, and face/head malformations are at particular risk because of abnormally narrow ear canals. Numbers increase as disease, injury, and environmental noise take their toll. Among school-age children, about 5 to 7% could benefit from special education services for hearing losses.

The prevalence of hearing loss for the 45- to 64-year-old age group is about 11%, whereas that for the 65- to 74-year-old age group is 30%. By age 75, approximately 50% of the population has a significant loss. This is usually for the

FIGURE 26.6 Presbycusis is degeneration of hearing with age. It mostly causes sensorineural losses. (© Thomas Braise/The Stock Market.)

higher frequencies (i.e., consonants and high-pitched voices and sounds). Background noise (including music) intensifies problems. Speech discrimination is typically more of a problem than loudness; this means that hearing aids are of limited value.

Presbycusis is the term for degeneration of hearing with age. Although all parts of the auditory apparatus are subject to breakdown, presbycusic changes are primarily sensorineural rather than conductive (see Figure 26.6).

In summary, hearing loss is a high-prevalence condition when older age groups are included. It affects more persons than heart conditions, arthritis, blindness, and any chronic physical disability (Kottke & Lehmann, 1990).

Educational Placement

Of the special education conditions recognized by legislation, deafness was the first, historically, to receive attention. The first residential schools in the United States, founded in 1817 and 1818, respectively, were for deaf students (see Appendix G). Thomas Gallaudet, father of Edward (who founded Gallaudet University), started the first residential school. By the late 1800s, almost every state had a school for deaf students. Most of these had excellent physical education programs and encouraged sport competition. Historically, deaf sport has drawn most of its athletes from these schools (Stewart, 1991). This is partly because sport-inclined deaf students in public schools are typically coached by persons who know little or nothing about deaf sport.

Patterns of educating deaf children have varied, of course, from family to family. Some children have always lived at home while attending public or private schools. With the enactment of federal legislation in 1975 has come a definite trend away from residential school placement. Local communities are required to provide the services that deaf children need in regular public schools. Interpretation of need and compliance with law vary widely, however. Particularly underserved are over 4,000 students in small schools where they are the only persons who are deaf or HH (Butterfield, 1991).

Much debate currently centers on the question of what is the least restrictive educational environment for students who are deaf or HH. Where and how can they best learn total communication—in a special school, a special class within a regular school, a resource room pull-out arrangement, or the regular class with a tutor or interpreter? Who will be the leaders in resolving issues?

When a student who is deaf or HH attends a regular school, regardless of academic placement, he or she is likely to be assigned to regular physical education. This is because many persons on individualized education program (IEP) teams believe that physical education is a good place to work on socialization skills. In addition, conventional wisdom suggests that motor performance and fitness are not limited by hearing loss. The exception is the student with inner ear damage that has affected balance.

Some deaf students, like hearing ones, can benefit from adapted physical education services. Whenever assessment indicates that a student is functioning at a lower level than classmates and/or needs special assistance to succeed, adapted physical education services should be written into the IEP. These services do not necessarily mean separate or pull-out settings. Services are often consultant in nature, with a specialist supplying information to the regular educator and facilitating attitude change. Many adapted physical activity personnel take sign classes so that they can use total communication and help others to learn basic sign.

Assessment of Performance

Federal law states that assessment, for purposes of placement, must be in the student's native language. For many deaf students, this is American Sign Language (ASL). Others, who rely mainly on speechreading, should have optimal lighting and a speaker they can understand. In some instances, an interpreter may be needed. Deaf students may demonstrate delays or perform below average simply because they do not understand test instructions. Dunn and Ponticelli (1988) statistically examined the effect of two communication modes (ASL and Signing Exact English) on the motor performance of prelingually deaf students and reported that ASL produced higher scores. Dummer, Haubenstricker, and Stewart (1996) indicated that communication difficulties (both instructional and motivational) affected scores of their 210 subjects. Stewart, Dummer, and Haubenstricker (1990) critically reviewed physical education research on deaf and HH persons and pointed out test administration weaknesses (see Figure 26.7).

Deaf and HH persons rely on a variety of communication modes. In both teaching and research, individual preferences should be honored. Rapport with the tester should be established before formal evaluation, with interpreters used as needed. Motivational cues (e.g., "good," "run faster," "throw harder") should be carefully planned, as should preliminary instructions. In reporting findings, a thorough description of communication methodology permits replication as well as valid comparisons of performance from year to year. It is not enough to say *total communication* because this term refers to a wide range of communication behaviors.

FIGURE 26.7 Three leading researchers from Michigan State University work together in data collection. From left to right: John Haubenstricker, David Stewart, and Gail Dummer.

Physical Education Instruction

Instruction, regardless of setting, should be based on assessed needs in the nine physical education goal areas. The following presents research and pedagogy related to each goal for deaf and HH individuals.

Self-Concept

Feeling good about self in a particular domain determines amount of effort expended and, ultimately, success. Underachievement may occur in mainstream physical education (Garrison & Tesch, 1978; Hopper, 1988), where deaf and HH students experience communication difficulties and related problems of social acceptance. **Perceived athletic competence** varies, therefore, with the setting, with many persons preferring deaf sports. If assessment indicates low athletic self-concept in mainstream physical education, possible reasons should be carefully studied. The quality and frequency of communication should be examined and plans for improvement developed cooperatively. In particular, teacher and peers should make sure that praise and encouragement are heard, speechread, and seen (signed) to the same extent as other students.

Other reasons for low athletic self-concept are a school, community, or family that does not value abilities and/or a perception that significant others hold low expectations. Some parents are so concerned with language, speech, and hearing training that they feel there is not time for after-school sports. Other parents may be overprotective. Some schools may stress academics so much that students feel nothing else is really important. In such cases, little energy is put into sports.

Little research has been conducted on athletic self-concept of deaf and HH persons. Hopper (1988) studied children ages 10 to 14 at Washington State School for the Deaf and reported a relatively low athletic self-concept. Scores were highest in the scholastic domain and lowest in the social acceptance domain. The pattern of self-concepts in different domains may relate specifically to the school attended. Much research is needed in this area.

Socialization and Social Acceptance

An important goal of physical education is to help students make friends who will carry over into after-school leisure activities. Research shows that socialization occurs only when there is planned intervention that requires communication and cooperation. The noise level in most sport settings requires careful planning in this regard. Ideally, when a deaf student is being integrated for the first time, teacher and classmates should learn basic signs. A partner or buddy assures that class instructions are understood.

The IEP team that specifies socialization as a goal should ensure that the integrated setting has a class size and a curriculum that enables communication and cooperation. Obviously, the smaller the class, the less noise and the more opportunity for getting to know each other. Maximum class size (about 20) should be written into the IEP. The curriculum most conducive to communication and cooperation includes individual and dual sports, dance, movement education, aquatics, and cooperative games. These are activities that demand partners. The deaf student must be equal to or better than his or her hearing partner in motor skill and fitness to make the relationship one of mutual respect.

Deaf persons with good sport skills can also make lasting friends in team sport settings if the teacher monitors communication and ascertains inclusion. Research shows that members of winning teams like each other better than those on losing teams. The teacher should therefore see that deaf students are assigned to teams that are likely to win.

Some deaf students are shy about talking and may not take the initiative in making friends. They may tend to withdraw and not want to take their turn in leading class exercises. Such individuals need support and incentive systems. A friend who regularly asks, "What do you think?" is helpful. Socialization requires considerable empathy on the part of both hearing and deaf persons.

Fun/Tension Release

A goal of fun/tension release in physical education is especially important because speechreading and sign require tremendous concentration. Background noise creates tension in persons wearing hearing aids as well as in those who speechread without aids. Poor lighting conditions and other environmental barriers also raise frustrations.

Appropriate goals of physical education and sport on some days are (a) to relax and have fun and/or (b) to channel frustrations, tensions, and hostilities into the healthy outlet of physical activity. The former may be accomplished best by cooperative activities, whereas the latter may be best served by competitive sports. Fun is defined in many ways, and teachers should ascertain what is fun for each individual.

Motor Skills and Patterns

Performance in motor skills and patterns is the same as for hearing persons except when inner ear balance deficits exist. Experts widely agree that much of the published research on motor development and performance of deaf and HH groups is inaccurate. Reasons include (a) etiology was not considered,

(b) communication of test instructions was not optimal, and (c) learning opportunities were not examined. Reviews of research literature (Goodman & Hopper, 1992; Savelsbergh & Netelenbos, 1992; Schmidt, 1985) thus indicate contradictory findings, with most experts concluding that nonvestibular impaired deaf and hearing persons perform similarly when opportunities are equal.

That opportunities are not equal is shown in recent studies that report motor delays. Stephen Butterfield, University of Maine, and David Stewart, Michigan State University, are researchers with many years of experience in deaf and HH sport. Studies spearheaded by them show delayed motor development in catching, kicking, jumping, and hopping (Butterfield, 1986) when assessed by the Ohio State University Scale of Intra Gross Motor Development (OSU-SIGMA) and in the hop, horizontal jump, leap, skip, and all object control skills (Dummer et al., 1996) when assessed by Ulrich's Test of Gross Motor Development (TGMD). Both SIGMA and TGMD (see Chapters 6 and 11) are qualitative tests that assess maturity of form, rather than distance, speed, and accuracy. This suggests communication difficulty in comprehending good form and emulating it. Communication is a two-way street, so the problem may be the expressive language of the teacher, the receptive language of the child, or both.

Butterfield, after examining the influence of age, sex, hearing loss, and balance on mature form, concluded that most skills are affected primarily by age and balance. Static balance and dynamic balance were examined separately (the correct procedure) and contributed in different amounts to skill (Butterfield, 1987, 1989, 1990; Butterfield & Ersing, 1988).

Static and dynamic balances of deaf and HH students should be thoroughly tested. When problems are identified, balance should become the targeted area of supplementary instruction. Gymnastics, trampoline, tumbling, dance, and movement exploration are particularly helpful (Butterfield, 1988). Physical education programming, however, should be balanced between using strengths and remediating weaknesses.

Leisure-Time Skills

Persons in the deaf community seem to participate more in deaf sports than those in integrated settings. This is closely linked to ease of communication and social acceptance.

Many deaf/HH persons watch lots of television, despite their hearing loss, and receive little encouragement from parents to develop active leisure lifestyles (Hattin, Fraser, Ward, & Shephard, 1986). An important role of physical activity personnel is to acquaint deaf/HH persons with the many available options and to help them get to know role models. This may entail going with them to various sport events, making introductions, and creating buddy and support systems (Stewart, 1984, 1991).

Physical Fitness

The most comprehensive study of the fitness of deaf ($N = 892$) and HH ($N = 153$) students, ages 10 to 17, showed that deaf/HH and hearing peers are similar in body composition, grip strength, sit-and-reach flexibility, 50-yd dash times, and 9- or 12-min endurance runs (Winnick & Short, 1986). Only on abdominal strength (sit-ups) are hearing students superior. This finding has not been explained and needs further research.

Studies with smaller sample sizes present conflicting evidence. Some report that deaf students are less fit than hearing peers (Campbell, 1983; Shephard, Ward, & Lee, 1987). In general, research on fitness of deaf/HH individuals has the same weaknesses as that on motor performance. Etiology and balance function require more attention because these factors affect running efficiency in endurance items, sit-ups, and other exercises.

Play and Game Behaviors

Young deaf children particularly need instruction in play and game behaviors because this area is closely associated with language concepts. Hearing peers pick up game rules, strategies, and behaviors in incidental ways and spontaneous neighborhood play. Opportunities for deaf children are limited, not only because of communication and social acceptance, but because speech, hearing, and language training may cut into the hours that others play.

Perceptual-Motor Function and Sensory Integration

Balance is probably the most important component in the area of perceptual-motor function and sensory integration. Research shows a tendency for postural and body awareness activities to improve balance function in deaf and HH individuals (Effgen, 1981; Lewis, Higham, & Cherry, 1985). The damaged vestibular system cannot be cured, but compensatory measures are learned.

Body image training is essential for young children who can learn signs for body parts and actions through movement. *Tap dance* teaches sounds the feet can make. The teacher may tap the rhythm lightly on the child's head so that he or she can perceive it via bone conduction while moving the feet. Another possibility is positioning the child so that his or her hand is on the record player, piano, or drum. A system of flashing lights can also be devised to convey rhythmic patterns.

Perceptual-motor activities also can be used to teach language and academics (see Figures 26.8 and 26.9). Training in prepositions (*up, down, toward, away from, in, out*) and other speech forms is made fun by movement. Charades in which partners move like different animals while class members try to guess which animal are fun when signs and words are learned simultaneously.

Creative Expression

Much of deaf education is extremely structured. In particular, young children are repeatedly reinforced on the right and wrong ways to form sounds with the mouth and signs with the hands. The end results must be identical to the adult they are imitating. There is little time for movement exploration and dance unless these are woven into physical education instruction. Several researchers show that creativity, movement skill, and language can be improved when total communication is used in movement exploration on climbing apparatus (Lubin & Sherrill, 1980) and in dance instruction (Reber & Sherrill, 1981).

FIGURE 26.8 Language concepts are reinforced through movement education challenges given by sign.

FIGURE 26.9 Games should be invented to reinforce classroom learnings in such subjects as geography and social studies. "How fast and how accurately can you trace the boundaries of the states I call out [sign]?" is the challenge issued by the teacher.

Vestibular Dysfunction and Balance Training

The inner ear governs both hearing and balance. If the vestibular apparatus is damaged, static and/or dynamic balances are impaired. Balance is not a general ability that can be measured by one or two tests. Balance is specific to task requirements and body positions. It is particularly affected by head movements and body righting reactions. *Thus, static and dynamic balances should be assessed in many ways and trained under variable conditions.*

Vestibular dysfunction is almost always present in persons who have recovered from meningitis. Minor damage, undiagnosed, may affect many persons whose inner ear deafness is not hereditary. With increasing age, when there are lots of movement opportunities, people learn to compensate for balance deficits. Balance normally improves from childhood through adolescence, when performance plateaus. Then, in old age, when the inner ear mechanisms begin to degenerate, balance again becomes a problem. This explains why research that combines many ages seldom yields useful information about balance deficits.

Balance is also dependent upon good vision. Persons with vestibular deficits particularly need training in using the eyes. Balance beam walking, for example, is made easier by keeping the eyes focused on a wall spot. Activities performed with eyes closed or blindfolded obviously complicate balance problems and typically are contraindicated for deaf persons who need vision to enable communication.

Individuals, deaf or otherwise, who have balance problems should be given special instruction on the principles of equilibrium. Movement exploration sessions may be developed around the following themes:

1. **Center of gravity.** "What is it? How do your movements affect it? In what movements can you keep the center of gravity centered over its supporting base? Can your hands be used as a supporting base? What happens when your center of gravity moves in front of the supporting base? In back of it? To the side of it? What activities lower your center of gravity? Raise it?"

2. **Broad base.** "How can you adapt different exercises so that the supporting base is larger than normal? In what directions can you enlarge your base—that is, how many stances can you assume? In which direction should you enlarge your base when throwing? Batting? Serving a volleyball? Shooting baskets?"

Persons learn quickly to compensate for poor balance by maintaining the body in a mechanically favorable position. Games and relays on skates, stilts, or using novel apparatus (sack races) teach compensation (see Figure 26.10). Activities should be planned to enhance vision and kinesthesis. All forms of dance and gymnastics increase body awareness. The increasingly popular Oriental exercise systems and martial arts—karate, kung fu, and Tai Chi—also contribute to this objective.

Speechreading and Cued Speech

Speechreading, formerly called lipreading, is a difficult skill because many sounds look identical. For example, *b, p,* and *m* are produced by bringing the lips together. *L, t,* and *d* are

formed with the tongue on the roof of the mouth behind the front teeth. Words like *mama, papa, man, mat, mad, bat, bad, ban, pan, pad,* and *pat* look the same and can be understood only if the general idea or context of the speech is followed.

Several trap sentences illustrate the problem of speechreading: "What's that big loud noise?" looks the same as "What's that pig outdoors?" the title of an excellent autobiography by deaf journalist Henry Kisor (1990). Try saying "It rate ferry aren't hadn't for that reason high knit donned co" to someone with earplugs. Chances are that he or she will think you said, "It rained very hard and for that reason I didn't go." According to Kisor (1990), much of speechreading is guesswork. About 30 to 40% is understanding words, and the rest is *context guessing* to fill in the gaps.

Cued speech is a system whereby spoken words are supplemented with hand signs near the face to help persons interpret words that look the same, like *son/sun* and *bat/pat.* Eight specific hand shapes presented in four positions near the face provide a multitude of cues. This system was created by Cornett (1967).

Naturally, it is easier to speechread familiar acquaintances than strangers. During initial meetings, 50% or sometimes less is understood. With continued contact, comprehension increases. However, occasionally, there are persons

(about 10%) who are impossible to speechread. These are typically people who move their lips very little, speak fast, show little expression and emotion, chew gum, or have a mustache.

Speechreading is particularly difficult in group conversations or discussions in which the speaker is frequently changing. Obviously, the deaf or HH individual must be able to see the lips of everyone talking but also be fast in determining which new person is talking. Discussions seldom elicit much talk from speechreaders because they tend to be uncertain about when pauses occur for them to jump in and about the exact time a topic or focus changes. To facilitate involvement, restating the topic and asking the speechreader what he or she thinks is helpful.

Speechreading is much more fatiguing than ordinary auditory processing of words. Most persons speak over 120 words a minute. A cough, sneeze, or other distraction disrupts understanding. Success in speechreading demands high concentration. Young children, of course, focus for shorter periods than older ones. Instruction should be adapted to individual differences.

Proper lighting conditions facilitate speechreading. Care should be taken that deaf persons are not facing into the sun. This is also important in sign language. What other environmental adaptations should be made?

American Sign Language and Other Forms of Sign

American Sign Language (ASL) is a bona fide language like Spanish and French, with its own grammar and syntax. Much practice is necessary before communication level reaches the sophistication expected of adults. ASL can express abstract as well as concrete thoughts. It is the dominant language of the deaf community in the United States and Canada and has regional variations and dialects. Other countries have sign languages comparable to ASL (e.g., British and French sign). ASL is the fourth most commonly used language in the United States (Flodin, 1991). Only English, Spanish, and Italian rank ahead of it.

ASL sentence structure is different from that of English. For example, in English, we might say, "Have you been to Texas?" In ASL, this would be TOUCH FINISH TEXAS YOU QUESTION, with *you* and *question* signed simultaneously.

Most hearing people do not take the time to learn ASL syntax and grammar. Instead, they link signs together in the same order they speak words in English. The result is a form of **signed English** or English signing. In contrast, **Pidgin sign** refers to a mixture of English and ASL. When enrolling in sign language classes, it is wise to ask which kind of sign will be taught.

ASL generally is not the language used in total communication classes in public schools. Signed English permits signs to be presented in the same order that English is spoken and thus enhances the improvement of speechreading skills. Signed English has educational appeal because it may help deaf persons learn to speak, read, and write English. Some deaf persons are therefore bilingual in sign. They use ASL in the deaf community and signed English at school. Additionally, they learn to speak, read, and write English and other languages.

In becoming multilingual, deaf persons experience the frustrations common to learning foreign languages. Proficiency in English may not be as strong as that of persons who are unilingual. This affects academic achievement. Books and videotapes that teach and/or use ASL in exercise can be ordered from Gallaudet University Press, 800 Florida Avenue NE, Washington, DC 20002-3695 (Phone 800–451–1073). Particularly appropriate for physical education is an aerobic workout tape called "Sign 'n Sweat." This tape features a deaf instructor, Gina Oliva (1989), using total communication.

Learning Some Signs

Signs are useful substitutes for whistles and shouts in noisy physical education environments. An increasing number of teachers are weaving sign into sport and dance instruction. Many students cannot hear over the background noise, and so sign is a viable instructional supplement.

Signs are easily worked into early childhood games, creative dramatics, and action songs. They enrich the perspective of hearing children who, in the next decade, will be learning sign in elementary school, just as they do Spanish and French.

Learning sign often begins with fingerspelling (see Figure 26.11). Persons generally master their name first and

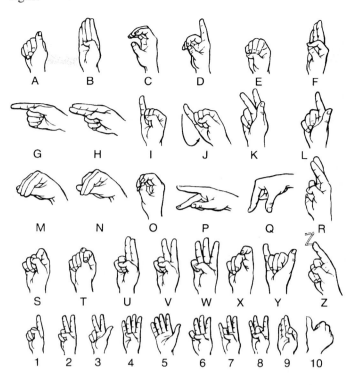

FIGURE 26.11 Standard fingerspelling and number signs.

then add signs for "Hi, my name is _____ ." See Figures 26.12, 26.13, and 26.14. Note that the explanation of *name* in Figure 26.12 refers to the *H* finger. The better we know the manual alphabet, the easier sign is. When instructions say to move clockwise or counterclockwise, this is from the viewpoint of the signer, not the watcher. Note that signs in instructional manuals are shown as they are seen by the watcher. The type of sign used by most beginners is **manually coded English** (MCE). Much formal instruction is needed to use systems like ASL and pidgin sign language (PSE).

Among the many books and articles that teach sign are the following:

Butterworth, R. R., & Flodin, M. (1989). *Signing made easy.* New York: Putnam.

Costello, E. (1983). *Signing: How to speak with your hands.* New York: Bantam.

Fant, L. (1983). *The American Sign Language phrase book.* Chicago: Contemporary Books.

Flodin, M. (1991). *Signing for kids.* New York: Putnam.

Riekehof, L. (1987). *The joy of signing* (2nd ed.). Springfield, MO: Gospel Publishing House.

Robinson, J., & Stewart, D. (1987). *Coaching deaf athletes.* Ontario: Canadian Deaf Sports Association.

Signing can be viewed on television when church services for deaf persons are broadcast. It is also used by the National Theatre of the Deaf, which has toured both Europe and the United States since its establishment in 1967. Most of the company's professional actors are alumni of Gallaudet University. The National Theatre of the Deaf is housed in Waterford, Connecticut.

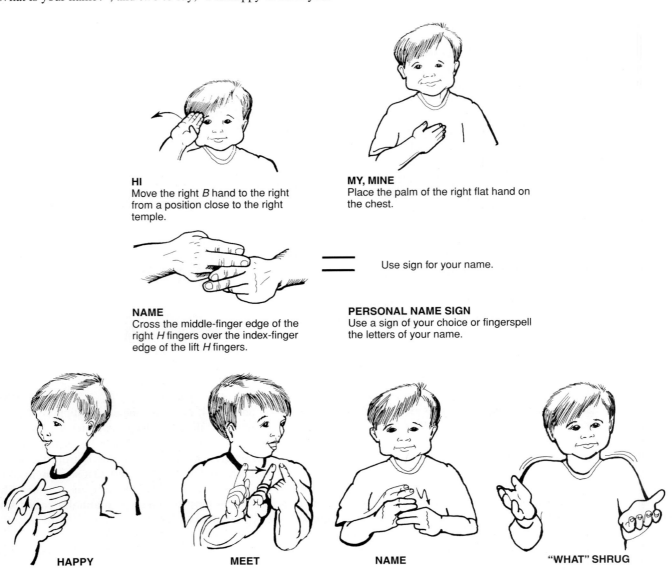

HI
Move the right *B* hand to the right
from a position close to the right
temple.

MY, MINE
Place the palm of the right flat hand on
the chest.

NAME
Cross the middle-finger edge of the
right *H* fingers over the index-finger
edge of the lift *H* fingers.

PERSONAL NAME SIGN
Use a sign of your choice or fingerspell
the letters of your name.

= Use sign for your name.

HAPPY   **MEET**   **NAME**   **"WHAT" SHRUG**

"I'm happy to meet you" in American Sign Language   "What is your name?" in American Sign Language

Interpreters and Transliteration

Transliteration is the process of transmitting information from English to ASL and vice versa. Persons trained to do this are called interpreters and can be located through speech and hearing personnel in schools and universities. Interpreters expect to be paid, just like other professionals. Transliteration is an exhausting activity, so several interpreters take turns when sessions are long.

Personal Hearing Aids

Who can benefit from a hearing aid? The 40-dB loss is the traditional criterion, but there is a trend toward prescribing them for 25- to 40-dB losses, especially in young children who need help in learning speech and language. Hearing aids amplify sound but do not ameliorate distortions. They are therefore used more in conductive than in sensorineural conditions. Losses over 90 dB typically leave too little residual hearing for amplification to be of help in communication. Hearing aids are not allowed in deaf sport competition.

Hearing aids work best when the listening environment is quiet and structured and the speaker is relatively close (not more than 4 or 5 ft away) or wearing a special device to transmit sound waves. Hearing aids have the same components as public address systems and amplify in the same way. Their five main parts are (a) input microphone, (b) amplifier, (c) earphone or output receiver, (d) battery, and (e) on/off switch.

Hearing aids are available in four styles, named according to their location: (a) chest or body-worn, (b) behind the ear, (c) eyeglass, and (d) in the ear. The chest style is worn primarily by young children or by persons with multiple disabilities. The behind-the-ear style is used mostly by school-age individuals, whereas adults may opt for any of the latter three.

FIGURE 26.13   Signs to play start-stop games like *Red Light, Green Light*. Note that many games are played with only two signs. These signs are also important for classroom discipline.

Play Start, Stop Games Like *Red Light, Green Light*

START, BEGIN
Hold the left flat hand forward with the palm facing right. Place the tip of the right index finger between the left index and middle finger; then twist the right index in a *clockwise direction once or twice.*

STOP
Bring the little-finger side of the right flat hand down sharply at right angles on the left palm.

FIGURE 26.14   Signs to reinforce students. These signs should be used frequently in teaching and coaching.

Learn Reinforcers!

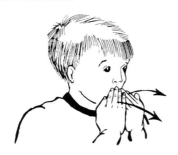

THANKS, THANK YOU, YOU'RE WELCOME
Touch the lips with the fingertips of one or both flat hands; then move the hands forward until the palms are facing up. It is natural to smile and nod the head while making this sign.

GOOD
Place the fingers of the right flat hand at the lips; then move the right hand down into the palm of the left, with both palms facing up.

Regardless of style, proper maintenance is a daily concern because parts are prone to breakdown. Most malfunctions are caused by dead or weak batteries, corrosion on battery contacts, or improper battery replacement. Other problems include clogged earmolds, frayed cords, cracked tubing, excessive distortion, and poor frequency response. Teachers should not automatically assume that hearing aids are working correctly. Research shows that 30 to 50% of hearing aids of school-age children are not performing adequately on any given day (Roeser & Downs, 1988).

Moisture is a particular problem, especially for persons who perspire heavily during activity. Hearing aids can be dried with hair blowers. Swimming settings usually contraindicate use of aids. Contact sports, where there is danger to the aid or to the wearer, may also be contraindicated.

Deaf and HH persons have personal preferences about wearing aids in physical activity settings. These should be honored. A hearing aid amplifies *all* noise, not just word sounds. As a result, persons wearing aids may react negatively to prolonged noise and have frequent tension headaches. What implications does this have for integrated physical education and sport?

Assistive Listening Devices and Systems

Assistive listening devices and systems (ALDS) include all electronic and electromechanical devices except the personal hearing aid. Over 200 devices are available to amplify sounds, convert them to light or vibration systems, or in some way transmit meaning (e.g., closed-captioned television). Among the sounds relayed are the ring of the telephone, the buzz of an alarm clock, the chime of a doorbell, the warning of a fire alarm or smoke detector, and the cry of an infant.

Think about adaptations that might make housing safer, entertainment (television, theatre, sports) more enjoyable, and learning in a large lecture hall or gymnasium more effective! For the latter, AM and FM radio frequencies can transmit voice sounds when the speaker wears a special device. Decoders are now being built into all television sets so that they have the capacity for closed-captioning. New devices are available every day.

Telecommunication Device for the Deaf

A **telecommunication device for the deaf** (TDD) permits telephone communication between two deaf persons or a deaf and hearing person. The TDD has three parts: (a) a portable typewriter, (b) a screen that displays one line of text at a time, and (c) two rubber cups into which a telephone handset can fit. The TDD is wired to a regular telephone that makes distinctive beeps when a TDD caller is on the line.

To send a TDD message, simply place the telephone handset on the rubber cups and type your first sentence. The message is converted into tones that are conveyed over the phone line to another TDD, which transforms the tones into words on the screen. The receiver then types back a message. TDDs can be powered by either batteries or household current. In many ways, they resemble computers, but TDDs use the Baudot code to transmit information, whereas most computers use the ASCII code.

TTY, an abbreviation for teletypewriter, correctly refers to the early models of TDDs, first created in the late 1950s by a deaf Bell Telephone engineer. Some persons, however, continue to use TDD and TTY interchangeably. The important thing is that government, public, and private offices have available a device that permits communication with deaf persons. Letterhead stationary, advertisements, and public announcements should include TDD numbers. Where on your campus and in your community can you make TDD calls?

General Guidelines for Deaf and HH Conditions

1. When first meeting a deaf/HH person, ask if he or she can understand your speech. If not, find someone to help or use paper/pencil communication.

2. Remember that short sentences are easier to speechread than long ones.

3. Speak normally and remember that only 3 to 4 of every 10 words are distinguishable on the lips. Use facial expressions and body language to help convey meaning.

4. When a sentence is not understood, repeat it. If one repetition does not help, then rephrase, using different words. Remember that some words are harder to speechread than others. Many words look the same. Find alternatives.

5. If you do not understand the other person's speech, do not pretend. Ask for as many repetitions as you need. Suggest, "Tell me again in a different way."

6. Empty your mouth before speaking. This applies to chewing gum, food, tobacco, cigarettes, straws, and anything else that distorts sights and sounds.

7. Keep your lips fully visible. Avoid mustaches, hands in front of face, and Halloween masks. Do not talk while writing on the chalkboard unless your face is visible.

8. Keep lighting conditions optimal.

9. Avoid standing in front of a window or bright light that forces a deaf/HH person to cope with a glare.

10. When outdoors, position yourself so that you, rather than the deaf/HH person, face the sun.

11. Minimize background noise and distractions.

12. Do not raise your voice when speaking to a person with a hearing aid.

13. When teaching, use lots of visual aids and demonstrations. Have order of events and class rules posted.

14. When behavior problems occur, consider whether students are seeing and hearing adequately. Note that restlessness often signals fatigue.

15. Encourage students with hearing losses to move freely around the gymnasium in order to be within seeing and hearing ranges.

16. Learn basic signs and weave them into the class structure. Give attention to signs that praise performance and motivate personal bests. Use these signs concurrently with speech with all students, not just those with hearing losses.

17. Be aware that head and neck positions that enable persons to see starting signals may affect speed. Read the excellent article by Bressler (1990) on the deaf sprinter. Communication needs may also affect the way persons want to swim (face out of water) and other activities.

References

Ammons, D. A. (1986). World games for the deaf. In C. Sherrill (Ed.), *Sport and disabled athletes* (pp. 65–72). Champaign, IL: Human Kinetics.

Ammons, D. A. (1990). Unique identity of the world games for the deaf. *Palaestra, 6*(2), 40–43.

Batshaw, M. L., & Perret, Y. (1986). *Children with handicaps: A medical primer* (2nd ed.). Baltimore: Paul H. Brookes.

Blackman, J. A. (1983). *Medical aspects of developmental disabilities in children birth to three.* Iowa City, IA: University of Iowa Press.

Butterfield, S. A. (1986). Gross motor profiles of deaf children. *Perceptual and Motor Skills, 62,* 68–70.

Butterfield, S. A. (1987). The influence of age, sex, hearing loss, etiology, and balance ability on the fundamental motor skills of deaf children. In M. E. Berridge & G. R. Ward (Eds.), *International perspectives on adapted physical activity* (pp. 43–51). Champaign, IL: Human Kinetics.

Butterfield, S. A. (1988). Deaf children in physical education. *Palaestra, 4*(3), 28–30, 52.

Butterfield, S. A. (1989). Influence of age, sex, hearing loss, and balance on development of throwing by deaf children. *Perceptual and Motor Skills, 69,* 448–450.

Butterfield, S. A. (1990). Influence of age, sex, hearing loss, and balance on development of sidearm striking by deaf children. *Perceptual and Motor Skills, 70,* 361–362.

Butterfield, S. A. (1991). Physical education and sport for the deaf: Rethinking the least restrictive environment. *Adapted Physical Activity Quarterly, 8*(2), 95–102.

Butterfield, S. A., & Ersing, W. F. (1988). Influence of age, sex, hearing loss, and balance on development of catching by deaf children. *Perceptual and Motor Skills, 66,* 997–998.

Campbell, M. E. (1983). *Motor fitness characteristics of hearing impaired and normal hearing children.* Unpublished master's thesis, Northeastern University, Boston.

Canadian Deaf Sports Association. (1987). *Coaching deaf athletes.* Ontario: Author.

Carney, E. (Ed.). (Spring, 1971). Beat of a different drum. *Gallaudet Today,* p. 21.

Cherow, E. (Ed.). (1985). *Hearing-impaired children and youth with developmental disabilities.* Washington, DC: Gallaudet University Press.

Cornett, R. O. (1967). Cued speech. *American Annals of the Deaf, 112,* 3–13.

Dummer, G., Haubenstricker, J., & Stewart, D. A. (1996). Motor skill performances of children who are deaf. *Adapted Physical Activity Quarterly, 13*(4), 400–414.

Dunn, J., & Ponticelli, J. (1988). The effect of two different communication modes on motor performance test scores of hearing impaired children. In *Abstracts: Research Papers, 1988 AAHPERD Convention.* Reston, VA: American Alliance for Health, Physical Education, Recreation, and Dance.

Effgen, S. K. (1981). Effect of an exercise program on the static balance of deaf children. *Physical Therapy, 61,* 873–877.

Flodin, M. (1991). *Signing for kids.* New York: Putnam.

Garrison, W. M., & Tesch, S. C. (1978). Self-concept and deafness: A review of research literature. *Volta Review, 80,* 457–466.

Goodman, J., & Hopper, C. (1992). Hearing impaired children and youth: A review of psychomotor behavior. *Adapted Physical Activity Quarterly, 9*(3), 214–236.

Greenberg, J. (1970). *In this sign.* New York: Holt, Rinehart & Winston.

Hattin, H., Fraser, M., Ward, G. R., & Shephard, R. J. (1986). Are deaf children unusually fit? A comparison of fitness between deaf and blind children. *Adapted Physical Activity Quarterly, 3*(3), 268–275.

Hopper, C. (1988). Self-concept and motor performance of hearing impaired boys and girls. *Adapted Physical Activity Quarterly, 5*(4), 293–304.

Kisor, H. (1990). *What's that pig outdoors? A memoir of deafness.* New York: Penguin Books.

Kottke, F., & Lehmann, J. (1990). *Krusen's handbook of physical medicine and rehabilitation* (4th ed.). Philadelphia: W. B. Saunders.

Lewis, S., Higham, L., & Cherry, D. (1985). Development of an exercise program to improve the static and dynamic balance of profoundly hearing-impaired children. *American Annals of the Deaf, 130*(4), 278–284.

Lubin, E., & Sherrill, C. (1980). Motor creativity of preschool deaf children. *American Annals of the Deaf, 125,* 460–466.

Martin, D. S. (Ed.). (1991). *Advances in cognition, education, and deafness.* Washington, DC: Gallaudet University Press.

Oliva, G. A. (1989). Advocacy: Evolution or revolution? *Palaestra, 6*(1), 49–51, 59.

Reber, R., & Sherrill, C. (1981). Creative thinking and dance/movement skills of hearing impaired youth: An experimental study. *American Annals of the Deaf, 26*(9), 1004–1009.

Roeser, R., & Downs, M. (1988). *Auditory disorders in school children* (2nd ed.). New York: Thieme Medical.

Sacks, O. (1989). *Seeing voices: A journey into the world of the deaf.* Berkeley: University of California Press.

Savelsbergh, G., & Netelenbos, J. B. (1992). Can the developmental lag in motor abilities of deaf children be partly attributed to localization problems? *Adapted Physical Activity Quarterly, 9*(4), 343–352.

Schildroth, A. N., & Karchmer, M. (1986). *Deaf children in America.* Boston: Little, Brown.

Schmidt, S. (1985). Hearing impaired students in physical education. *Adapted Physical Activity Quarterly, 2*(4), 300–306.

Shephard, R., Ward, R., & Lee, M. (1987). Physical ability of deaf and blind children. In M. E. Berridge & G. R. Ward (Eds.), *International perspectives on adapted physical activity* (pp. 355–362). Champaign, IL: Human Kinetics.

Stewart, D. A. (1984). The hearing impaired student in physical education. *Palaestra, 1*(1), 35–37.

Stewart, D. A. (1991). *Deaf sport: The impact of sports within the deaf community.* Washington, DC: Gallaudet University Press.

Stewart, D. A., Dummer, G., & Haubenstricker, J. (1990). Review of administration procedures used to assess the motor skills of deaf children and youth. *Adapted Physical Activity Quarterly, 7,* 231–239.

Stewart, D. A., McCarthy, D., & Robinson, J. (1988). Participation in deaf sport: Characteristics of deaf sport directors. *Adapted Physical Activity Quarterly, 5*(3), 233–244.

Stewart, D. A., Robinson, J., & McCarthy, D. (1991). Participation in deaf sport: Characteristics of elite deaf athletes. *Adapted Physical Activity Quarterly, 8*(2), 136–145.

Winnick, J., & Short, F. (1986). Physical fitness of adolescents with auditory impairments. *Adapted Physical Activity Quarterly, 3,* 58–66.

CHAPTER

27

Blindness and Visual Impairments

FIGURE 27.1 Charles Buell (1912–1992) gives a child with visual impairment and his sighted opponent a first lesson in wrestling.

After you have studied this chapter you should be able to do the following:

1. Differentiate between legal blindness, travel vision, motion perception, light perception, and total blindness. Explain deaf-blindness. Discuss physical education programming for each.

2. Identify some of the concerns, aspirations, and behaviors associated with blindness. Discuss implications for physical education.

3. Discuss the following in relation to assessment and instruction: (a) haptic perception, (b) spatial awareness, (c) trust and courage, (d) sound usage, (e) physical fitness, (f) orientation and mobility, and (g) adaptations of equipment and facilities.

4. Contrast public and residential facilities in the education of blind students.

5. Discuss the U.S. Association for Blind Athletes (USABA) and opportunities for competition.

6. Explain the three USABA classifications and discuss similarities and differences in the sport events recommended for each.

7. Describe the games of goal ball and beep baseball.

8. Discuss existing and needed research concerning vision loss and physical education. Review the contributions of such researchers as Charles Buell, Joseph Winnick, and James Mastro.

Never check the actions of the blind child; follow him, and watch him to prevent any serious accidents, but do not interfere unnecessarily; do not even remove obstacles which he would learn to avoid by tumbling over them a few times. Teach him to jump rope, to swing weights, to raise his body by his arms, and to mingle, as far as possible, in the rough sports of the older students. . . . Do not too much regard bumps upon the forehead, rough scratches, or bloody noses, even these may have their good influences. At the worst, they affect only the bark, and do not injure the system, like the rust of inaction.

—Samuel Gridley Howe (1841)

The previous statement was made by the first director of Perkins Institution in Boston, a residential school founded in the early 1800s for children who were blind. Perkins is known for its training of Anne Sullivan Macy, the teacher of Helen Keller, and for its outstanding physical education and sport program. Most states have a residential school for children who are blind, and a field trip to this facility is a good way to learn about physical education programming, which historically has been excellent (Buell, 1984). The trend today, however, is for children to live at home and to be educated in public schools, where resource room help is available.

Charles Buell (1912–1992), the best-known pioneer in blind sport, emphasized that children with visual impairments (VI) should be taught in mainstream settings and held to the same achievement standards as their sighted peers. Buell (1982, 1986) particularly recommended wrestling as a sport in which youth with VI can compete equitably with sighted peers (see Figure 27.1). Buell, legally blind himself, held a doctorate from the University of California and was recognized worldwide as an athlete, physical educator, coach, researcher, and a founder of the United States Association for Blind Athletes (USABA).

Founded in 1976, the USABA has proven to the world that individuals with blindness (total or partial) can be outstanding athletes. They compete in the summer and winter Paralympics, the World Games for the Blind (held every 3 years), the National Games for the Blind (held alternate years, 1997, 1999, and so on), and many able-bodied marathons and sport events.

Definitions and Basic Concepts

Blindness and *visual impairment* are often used as synonyms, particularly in the sport world. The International Blind Sports Association (IBSA) and the U.S. Association for Blind Athletes (USABA) serve persons whose vision varies from 20/200 ft (6/18 m) to total blindness. Table 27.1 shows the three sport classifications, which are based on a **Snellen chart measure** of **acuity** (sharpness of vision) and assessment of field of vision.

Field of vision refers to the area within which objects can be seen when the eyes are fixed straight ahead. A severely limited field of vision is called **tunnel vision.** To understand limitations of field of vision, look through a straw (equivalent to a 5° field of vision) or larger tubes for progressively greater fields of vision. A normal field of vision is about 180°.

Educators often use different terminology than sport people to denote degrees of visual acuity. Following is an explanation of how the educational and sport classifications relate.

Table 27.1 Sport classifications for USABA and IBSA.

Classification	Description
B1	No light perception in either eye up to light perception and inability to recognize the shape of a hand in any direction and at any distance
B2	Ability to recognize the shape of a hand up to a visual acuity of 2/60 and/or a limitation of field of vision of 5°
B3	2/60 to 6/60 (20/200) vision and/or field of vision between 5 and 20°

Note. In 1982, this system was adopted in place of the system that used Classes A, B, C.

B1 Classification

B1 encompasses two educational classifications:

> **Total Blindness (lack of visual perception).** Inability to recognize a strong light shown directly into the eye.
>
> **Light Perception (less than 3/200).** Ability to distinguish a strong light at a distance of 3 ft from the eye, but inability to detect movement of a hand at the same distance.

B1s, as they are called in sport events, do some sports like swimming, judo, and wrestling independently. In track events, they typically run side by side with a guide. The athlete maintains contact with the guide by means of a **tether** (a rope or shoestring no more than 50 cm in length) held by each by the inside hand (see Figure 27.2). In snow skiing, a longer tether allows a person who is blind to follow his or her guide. In water skiing, the rope between the boat and the skier serves as the tether.

B2 Classification

B2 encompasses two educational classifications:

> **Motion Perception (3/200 to 5/200).** Ability to see at 3 to 5 ft what the normal eye sees at 200 ft. This ability is limited almost entirely to motion.
>
> **Travel Vision (5/200 to 10/200).** Ability to see at 5 to 10 ft what the normal eye sees at 200 ft.

B2s can do many activities independently when the sunlight or indoor lights are bright. In track events, they have the option of running independently or using a guide. Tethers are optional. Obviously, individuals with travel vision have greater acuity than those with only motion vision, but the low prevalence of blindness among youth and young adults requires that these two abilities be grouped together in order to have enough competitors to hold a track meet. B2s typically wear thick glasses and can read large print with the aid of magnifying devices.

B3 Classification

B3 is the same as legal blindness, the minimal disability condition specified by law that permits special services:

> **Legal Blindness (20/200).** Ability to see at 20 ft what the normal eye sees at 200 ft (i.e., 1/10 or less of normal vision).

B3s do not use guides, but they might require verbal assistance during night or low-vision conditions. They wear thick glasses and can read large print without magnifying devices. Some can read regular-size print by placing their faces very close to the page.

Guidelines for Interactions

At least 80% of people who are blind have some residual vision. Given good light conditions to use residual vision, their sport performance is similar to that of sighted peers when instruction and practice are equal. They are most disadvantaged by weather (dark, rainy days) and scheduling of early or late practices when the sun is not overhead. Persons often profess to see more than they do, partly because of the desire for nor-

FIGURE 27.2 *(A)* Harry Cordellos *(left)* with sighted partner, Randy Foederer. Note that both will take first step with inside foot. *(B)* Both hold onto a *contact tether* no more than 50 cm in length.

A

B

malcy and partly because they have no experience upon which to judge normal vision. Some persons, although legally blind, are very sensitive about being called *blind*.

In general, the following guidelines will help fully sighted individuals with interacting with people with visual impairments (VI) in social and instructional settings.

1. When starting an interaction, always state your name. Do not expect to be recognized by the sound of your voice. This is especially important in noisy settings.

2. Ask if help is needed with mobility. Do not grab the person's arm. The appropriate protocol is for the person with VI to grasp your upper arm and walk with you, side by side, unless the passage is too narrow. Give verbal cues, indicating steps (up or down), changes in surface (holes, inclines), and doors to be opened (in, out; push, pull). Ask for feedback on how you can improve your technique.

3. When suggesting places to go, indicate the anticipated level of noise. When the goal is conversation, it is essential to select quiet settings where you can be heard.

4. When serving food, indicate the location of food on the plate (e.g., meat at 12 o'clock, salad at 3 o'clock, potatoes at 6 o'clock). Provide bread or a cracker to be used as a pusher.

5. When providing learning material, ask whether the person prefers large print, braille, or audiotapes. Check the technology offered by your library or other nearby resources in terms of talking machines that can read print.

Prevalence of Blindness and Visual Impairment

Blindness and VI are largely problems of old age. Approximately a half-million persons in the United States are legally blind, and countless others have serious visual problems. At least two thirds of these persons are over 65 years of age.

The statistics concerning VI among school-age children vary with the definition used. Approximately 23,000 children with VI between the ages of 3 and 21 are receiving special education services. However, VI affects fewer children than any other disability, with the exception of the deaf-blind classification.

Causes of Blindness and Activity Contraindications

Most blindness in school-age persons is attributed to birth defects (congenital cataracts, optic nerve disease, retinopathy) or retinopathy of prematurity (ROP), previously called retrolental fibroplasia. **ROP** occurs when oxygen is poorly regulated in incubators. Excessive oxygen damages the retina and sometimes causes mild brain damage and learning problems.

Most VI conditions have no activity contraindications, but three conditions require particular attention: retinal detachment, retinitis pigmentosa, and glaucoma. The **retina,** or inner lining of the eyeball, is an expansion of the optic nerve that contains the sensory receptors for light rays. **Retinal detachment** is a break or tear in the retina that causes fluid to seep between the retina and the cells that supply its nutrition (see Figure 27.3). As cells die, vision is lost. No pain is involved. The presence of a retinal tear or detachment contraindicates contact sports and other activities that might jar the head and increase damage.

Retinitis pigmentosa is a degenerative condition of the retinal cells, which are replaced by pigmented tissue that looks like footprints of a bird. The degeneration gradually restricts the vision field, eventually causing tunnel vision and night blindness. The condition most often occurs in childhood and adolescence, and individuals must be monitored to prevent

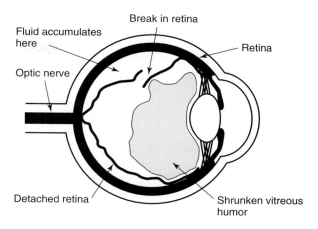

FIGURE 27.3 Retinal detachment, which can be corrected by surgery, contraindicates contact sports.

their continued participation in sports that require good peripheral vision for safety. Sport participation in low-light conditions is contraindicated.

Glaucoma is a condition in which the pressure inside the eyeball rises to a point where it damages the optic nerve, first affecting peripheral vision and later causing central vision blindness. An early sign is complaints that lights appear to have halos around them. There are several types, some of which cause considerable pain. Contraindications are isometric activities, swimming under water, inverted body positions, excess fluid intake, use of antihistamines, and other practices that may increase eye pressure.

About 4% of visual disorders in children are caused by a genetic disorder called **albinism,** a congenital absence of pigment in the skin, hair, and eyes. These persons have very fair skin, platinum blond hair, and blue eyes. Related visual problems are myopia, predisposition to sunburn, photophobia (unusual intolerance of light), astigmatism, and nystagmus. Many persons with albinism compete as Class B3 athletes in USABA.

Infectious diseases, tumors, and injuries are minor causes of blindness. In older persons, cataracts and diabetes are leading causes. **Cataracts** are clouded or opaque spots on the lens that gradually increase in size and diminish vision, particularly in low-light conditions. Within 10 years of the onset of diabetes, 50% of individuals have pathological changes of the retina, called **diabetic retinopathy.** Between the ages of 20 and 65, diabetes is the leading cause of blindness.

Motor Development and Performance

Motor development is delayed in blind infants, particularly in mobility- and locomotion-related behaviors (Adelson & Fraiberg, 1974; Fraiberg, 1977; Jong, 1990). The median age of walking is about 20 months. Mastery of motor milestones is in a different order from that of sighted infants, with milestones that require vision for motivation delayed most (e.g., raising the head from prone, reaching, crawling, creeping, and walking). Object control and manipulation tend to be delayed 3 to 6 months. This, in turn, prevents proper emergence of tactile perception abilities and related problem-solving skills.

Early intervention is beneficial but does not completely remediate delays (Levine, Carey, Crocker, & Gross, 1983; Norris, Spaulding, & Brodie, 1957). Of particular concern are delays in development of play and social skills. Children with VI cannot progress without help to parallel or cooperative play because of lack of awareness of others' presence.

Research on the motor performance of individuals with VI reveals lower levels than sighted classmates (Skaggs & Hopper, 1996). Generally, persons with partial sight perform better than those with total blindness.

Time of Onset

VI is typically designated as **congenital** (born with) or **adventitious** (diagnosed at age 2 or 3 or later). Congenital VI is often not recognized until motor or cognitive delays appear. Age of onset should always be indicated because it gives insight into amount of time the child had for developing space and form perception, visualization skills, and locomotor and object control patterns. The younger children are when they develop blindness, the more likely they are to be overprotected.

Overemphasis on Academics

Reading and other academic skills require more time than average for individuals with VI. As a result, such children often spend time in study that others use for leisure and large muscle activity. This not only deprives them of skill and fitness but also interferes with making and keeping friends. With age, deficits in social competence become more and more obvious.

Unless helped with social development, the life experiences of persons with VI differ considerably from those of peers. This eventually may interfere with job success. Most jobs are lost, not because of inadequate vocational skills, but because of inability to get along with other workers.

Stereotyped Behaviors and Appearance

Stereotyped behaviors or **stereotypies** (previously called blindisms) are mannerisms like rocking backward and forward, putting fist or fingers into eyes (see Figure 27.4), waving fingers in front of face, whirling rapidly round and round, and bending the head forward. These same behaviors may be observed among sighted persons with emotional problems, autism, or limited opportunities to move. They can be prevented or at least minimized through the provision of vigorous daily exercise. Some persons like Ray Charles become quite successful in spite of stereotypies, but most need help in making appearance as normal as possible. Verbal correction often causes anxiousness and self-consciousness. A good approach is to agree on a tactile cue like a hand on the shoulder as a reminder to stop.

Persons with VI should be taught self-monitoring in relation to appearance, postures, and facial expressions. VI limits ability to imitate, thereby spontaneously learning appropriate behaviors and responses as do sighted persons. Verbal instructions are needed in many areas that individuals with normal vision take for granted.

FIGURE 27.4 Rubbing the eye is a stereotypy that should be called to the child's attention and extinguished.

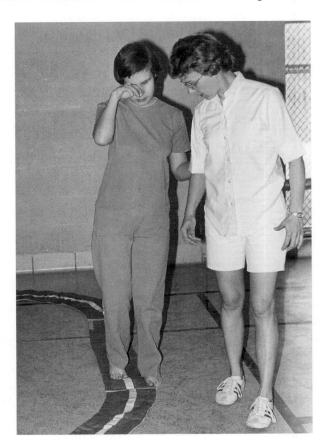

Physical and Motor Fitness

Most research shows that persons with VI have lower fitness than sighted peers (Shephard, 1990; Skaggs & Hopper, 1996; Winnick, 1985). This is generally attributed to lack of instruction and practice, inactive lifestyles, and overprotection. Degree of VI, age, and sex affect fitness scores. The more severe the VI, the lower the fitness; this is probably because overprotection increases with severity. The performance gap between males and females with VI is greater than for sighted peers; presumably this is because girls are more overprotected than boys. Boys improve steadily from ages 6 to 17, whereas girls plateau at about age 13 or 14.

Of the 14 items used in Project UNIQUE (see Chapter 13), the greatest discrepancy between blind and sighted youth was in throwing, running, and jumping (Winnick, 1985). These findings partially support the work of Buell (1982), which showed greatest weakness in running and throwing events.

Most research also shows that persons with VI have greater skinfold thicknesses than sighted peers (Hopkins, Gaeta, Thomas, & Hill, 1987; Winnick, 1985). There is also a tendency toward shorter heights (Lee, Ward, & Shephard, 1985).

In general, youth with VI should take the same fitness tests as sighted peers. In health-related fitness, distance runs require a partner. Otherwise, few adaptations are needed except in motivation. Whereas sighted persons are challenged to personal bests by seeing others succeed, VI limits the motivational value of social comparison. Verbal input should be substituted.

VI also limits social comparisons of height and weight, the amount that others are eating, and exercise habits. Whereas we may see someone jogging on the other side of the street and be motivated to follow suit, persons with VI are more dependent on internal motivation. Whereas we can run, cycle, or drive to an exercise site at will, persons with VI must be assertive in finding companions.

Studies on cardiorespiratory fitness of persons with VI have shown fitness levels either equal to sighted persons or low fitness levels that significantly improve as a result of treadmill and bicycle ergometer training. Harry Cordellos, marathon runner who is blind and American Alliance for Health, Physical Education, Recreation, and Dance (AAH-PERD) honor award recipient, has such outstanding fitness that he is the subject of an ongoing longitudinal study at the Cooper Aerobic Institute in Dallas. A film featuring Cordellos, entitled *Survival Run,* is available (Cordellos, 1983).

When persons with VI are navigating unfamiliar areas, gaits become mechanically less efficient. This, in turn, contributes to early fatigue. Good fitness is needed to combat both fatigue and stress. Research shows that B1 and B2 sprinting patterns are less mechanically efficient than those of B3 (Gorton & Gavron, 1987; Pope, McGrain, & Arnhold, 1986). Long-distance runs that require a sighted partner heighten stress because of the required adjustment to new people.

Role Models

Models with VI help individuals with VI to realize what is possible. For sighted persons, models with VI help to change attitudes and dispel misconceptions. While live models are best, books and videotapes are also helpful.

The autobiographies of such persons as Harold Krents (1972) and Tomi Keitlen (1960) emphasize the importance of sport participation in making friends and gaining self-confidence. Krents recalls step-by-step how his brother taught him to catch a regulation football and to bat a 10-inch playground ball—skills he could have been taught by a physical educator but was not. In high school physical education, he was allowed to play touch football with his sighted classmates but was admonished to "Keep out of the way." The anecdotes leading to his acquisition of the nickname "Cannonball" make the book well worth reading. Tomi Keitlen describes in detail her first attempts at swimming, golf, horseback riding, fencing, and skiing after becoming totally blind at age 33. In addition to valuable accounts of how such sports can be learned and enjoyed without sight, Keitlen describes the problems of adjusting to blindness. The greatest battle, she stresses, is to avoid being segregated and labeled as different from sighted persons.

James Mastro, a B1 international athlete, has been active in USABA since its inception in 1976, repeatedly winning gold medals in wrestling, judo, shot put, and discus.

FIGURE 27.5 Dr. James Mastro *(left),* U.S. Association for Blind Athletes (USABA) gold medalist, conducts workshop on wrestling.

Mastro was born with one eye sightless and injured the other while fencing with curtain rods in late childhood. In spite of countless surgeries, he lost all vision but light perception by age 18. This did not deter his becoming a member of the university wrestling team and eventually becoming an Olympic wrestler. A broken arm in the last qualifying bout kept him from winning and becoming a member of the U.S. Olympic Team, but he was named an alternate.

Since completing his doctorate in adapted physical education at Texas Woman's University, Dr. Mastro has taught at the University of Minnesota, been president of the National Beep Baseball Association, and conducted workshops throughout the world (see Figure 27.5). He is also a prolific researcher (see Sherrill, 1990, for a review of his work). Dr. Mastro is the first totally blind person to earn a doctorate in physical education and is a strong model for others.

Harry Cordellos (1976, 1981, 1993) is another strong model whose autobiographies *Breaking Through* and *No Limits* are filled with sport stories (see Figure 27.6). Cordellos, born with glaucoma and a heart murmur, was partially sighted throughout childhood but so overprotected by his parents and teachers that he never engaged in vigorous play. In spite of 14 operations, he was totally blind by age 20. Fortunately, he outgrew his heart problems. At age 20, he was

FIGURE 27.7 Harry Cordellos performing on one ski.

can volunteer to serve as partners in long-distance runs, provide transportation, and the like.

Physical Education Instruction

introduced to sports via water skiing (see Figure 27.7), and subsequently he dedicated his life to athletic training and educating the sighted world about the potential of persons with VI. Cordellos has run over 100 marathons; he does this with a sighted partner. His best time in the Boston Marathon is 2 hr, 57 min, 42 sec. Cordellos has run 50 mi in less than 8 hr and has competed in the Iron Man Triathlon in Hawaii (swimming 2.4 mi, biking 112 mi, and running 26.2 mi). He has demonstrated that there is no physiological reason why persons with VI cannot excel in sports.

Erling Stordahl, of Norway, now deceased, is also an outstanding model. The creator of the world-famous sport center (Helsesportsenter) in Beitostølen, he broadened the horizons of persons with and without disabilities. He was particularly known for leadership in winter sports and innovations that permit persons with VI to ski.

Charles Buell, described in the opening section of this chapter, is another model. Until age 80, he continued to work out daily and to encourage mainstream acceptance of people with VI.

Find persons with VI, support their involvement in sports, and ask them to lecture in public schools and universities. Exposure to models is one of the best ways of ameliorating the problem of overprotection. University students

Regular class physical education placement is recommended for students with VI (Nixon, 1988, 1989), but consultant help is often needed. Except for ball-handling activities, students with VI can participate with few adaptations. Their success depends in large part on the ability of the physical educator to give precise verbal instructions. Like other students, they strive to fulfill their teacher's expectations. Falls, scratches, and bruises should be disregarded as much as possible to allow the dignity of recovering without oversolicitous help.

When activities are practiced in small groups, the teacher should ascertain that students with VI know the names of their classmates, the approximate space allocated to each, their place in the order of rotation if turns are being taken, and the direction of movement. Sight is not required for success on the trampoline, parallel bars, and other pieces of apparatus; for tumbling, free exercise, and dance; for weight lifting, fitness activities, swimming; or for many other sports.

Especially recommended activities for persons with VI are wrestling, tumbling, gymnastics, bowling, swimming, weight training, judo, dart throwing, dance, roller skating, ice skating, shuffleboard, horseback riding, tandem cycling, hiking, camping, fishing, rowing, waterskiing, and surfing. These sports require little or no adaptation for students with VI to participate with the sighted (see Figure 27.8).

FIGURE 27.9   Standard English braille alphabet.

A study of the memories and opinions of adults with VI about physical education found that their favorite childhood outdoor sport was baseball/softball (Sherrill, Rainbolt, & Ervin, 1984). Respondents did not mention adaptations. Tying for second place were swimming, football, and horseback riding. Two thirds of the sample had been reared in residential schools. These persons expressed positive opinions about school-based physical education, but negative feelings about both past and present community, church, and family physical education and recreation—indicating that usually there were none.

Community facilities, like schools, need to make materials available in braille (see Figure 27.9), in large-size print, and on audiotapes. Physical educators are responsible for promoting the use of community resources and encouraging better communication.

Adaptations of Equipment and Facilities

Teachers and parents of children with VI should write to the American Foundation for the Blind for catalogs of special equipment. Each year, improvements are made in sound-source balls and audible goal locators that facilitate the teaching of ball skills. Electronic balls with beepers are gradually replacing balls with bells. *Balls should be painted orange or yellow for persons with partial sight.* In most primary school activities, beanbags with bells sewn inside are preferred over balls, which are harder to recover.

Outside softball diamonds should be of grass with mowed baselines or should have wide asphalt paths from base to base and from the pitcher's mound to the catcher. Inside, guidewires can be constructed from base to base. Boundaries for various games are marked by a change in floor or ground surfaces that can be perceived by the soles of the feet. Tumbling mats, for instance, can be placed around the outside periphery of the playing area to mark its dimensions.

Braille can be used on the swimming pool walls to designate the changing water depths. It can also be used on gymnasium floors and walls as aids in determining the colors, shapes, and sizes of targets.

Portable aluminum bowling rails 9 ft long and 3 ft high are available through the American Foundation for the Blind. These rails are easily assembled and broken down for transportation to different bowling alleys.

For the most part, however, equipment does not need to be adapted for individuals with VI. The play area should be quiet enough to facilitate use of sound and well lighted to enhance use of residual vision.

Guidewires and Sighted Partners

Students with VI and blindfolded friends should be provided with a **guidewire** stretched from one end of the playfield or gymnasium to the other to enable them to meet such challenges as "Run as fast as you can," "Roller skate as fast as you can," or "Ride a tricycle or bicycle as fast as you can." The students can hold onto a short rope looped around the guidewire. *Gliding fingers directly over the wire can cause burns.* Window-sash cord stretched at *hip height* is probably best for running practice. A knot at the far end of the rope warns the runner of the finish line. Students can improve their running efficiency or master a new locomotor skill *by grasping the upper arm of a sighted partner,* but the ultimate goal should always be self-confidence in independent travel.

Spatial Awareness and Body Image Training

In spatial awareness training, objectives are tactile identification of objects, orientation to stable and moving sounds, spatial orientation, improvement of movement efficiency, and mobility training. **Brailling** is the term for tactile inspection of an object (see Figure 27.10).

Children with VI need special training in recognizing the right-left dimensions of objects that are facing them (Cratty, 1971). Not capable of seeing, they have never received a mirror image; hence, the concept of someone facing them is especially difficult.

Children with VI must be provided with opportunities for learning about their own body parts as well as about those of animals and other human beings. This can be accomplished,

FIGURE 27.10 Child with B1 classification brailles her medal.

at least partially, by tactual inspection. Three-dimensional figures must be available to teach similarities and differences between different body builds, male and female physical characteristics, and postural deviations. Movement exploration based on modifications of the dog walk, seal crawl, mule kick, and the like is meaningless unless the child can feel, smell, and hear the animal about to be imitated.

The following are other activities that help individuals with VI to organize and learn about space:

1. Practice walking a straight line. Without sight, persons tend to veer about 1.25 inches per step or walk a spiral-shaped pathway.

2. Practice facing sounds or following instructions to make quarter, half, three-quarter, and full turns.

3. Practice reproducing the exact distance and pathway just taken with a partner.

4. Take a short walk with a partner and practice finding the way back to the starting point alone.

5. Outside, where the rays of the sun can be felt, practice facing north, south, east, west. Relate these to goal cages and the direction of play in various games.

6. Practice determining whether the walking surface is uphill or downhill or tilted to the left or right; relate this to the principles of stability and efficient movement.
7. Practice walking different floor patterns. Originate novel patterns and then try to reproduce the same movement.

These and other space explorations offer fun and excitement for sighted youngsters who are blindfolded as well as for children with VI. Remember, however, that the blindfolded child is at a greater disadvantage than persons who have had several years to cope with spatial problems.

Sound Usage in Locomotion and Sports

Students with VI can be grouped with individuals who have auditory perception deficits for special training in recognizing and following sounds. A continuous sound is better than intermittent ones. Whenever possible, the sound source should be placed in front of the student so that he or she is moving directly toward it. The next best position is behind the person so that he or she can proceed in a straight line away from it. Most difficult to perceive and follow are sounds to the side. A progression from simple to difficult should be developed. After success with a single sound source, students should be exposed to several simultaneous sounds, with instructions to pick out and follow only the relevant one.

Try the following activities, using a blindfold, to get an idea of competencies that must be developed for success in sport:

1. Discriminate between the bouncing of a small rubber ball for playing jacks, a tennis ball, a basketball, and a cageball.
2. Judge the height of the rebound of a basketball from its sound and thus be able to catch a ball bounced by you or by another.
3. Perceive the direction of a ground ball and thus be able to field or kick one being rolled toward your left, right, or center.
4. Discriminate, in bowling, the difference between sounds of a ball rolling down the gutter as opposed to the lane and also the difference between one bowling pin versus several falling.
5. Recognize, in archery, the sound of a balloon bursting when it is hit by an arrow or of an arrow penetrating a target made of a sound-producing material (see Figure 27.11).
6. Recognize the difference between the center of the trampoline and its outer areas by the sound of a ball attached to its undersurface.
7. Walk a nature trail or participate in a treasure hunt by following sounds from several tape cassettes located about the area.
8. Follow a voice or bell as you swim and dive in an open area.
9. Perceive the rhythm of a long rope alternately touching the ground and turning in the air so that you know when to run under and jump the rope.

Orientation and Mobility Training

Comprehensive physical education programs include units on orientation and mobility (O and M). Many children with VI are overprotected prior to entering school and hence need

FIGURE 27.11   Balloons attached to the target enable the child who is blind to hear a bull's-eye.

immediate help in adjusting to travel within the school environment. The physical educator must orient young children to the playground equipment as well as to space. Bells may be attached to the supporting chains of swings to warn of danger. Children who are blind often excel in climbing and hanging feats. Unable to see their distance from the ground, they seem fearless in the conquering of great heights and enjoy the wonder and praise of sighted classmates.

The following are illustrative objectives for a unit on the use of playground equipment for students with VI. Students should

1. Demonstrate how to play safely on all equipment.
2. Tell safety rules and reasons for each.
3. Display a cooperative attitude and express a willingness to learn.

4. Walk a hand ladder (arm-swing from rung to rung).

5. Use the legs to pump while swinging (in a sitting position).

6. Climb to the top of both 8- and 14-ft slides alone and slide down feet first.

7. Perpetuate a tilted merry-go-round by swinging out on the downside and leaning in on the upside.

8. Play simple games on the jungle gym.

9. Use a seesaw safely with a companion.

Haptic Perception Teaching Model

In general, the pedagogy in this section can be conceptualized as a *haptic teaching model*. **Haptic perception** refers to the combined use of tactile sensations and kinesthesis.

When planning movement exploration activities, the physical educator must realize that space is interpreted unconventionally by haptic-minded persons. Whereas the visually oriented child perceives distant objects as smaller than those nearby, the child with VI does not differentiate between foreground and background. The size of objects is not determined by nearness and farness, but rather by the objects' emotional significance and the child's imagination.

Children with VI experience difficulty in conceptualizing boundaries. Having no visual field to restrict them, their space is as large as their imagination. They tend, however, to think in parts rather than wholes since concepts are limited to the amount of surface they can touch at any given time. To familiarize themselves with the gymnasium, they may move from one piece of apparatus to another, feel the walls, discover windows and doors, and creep on the floor. They are, however, never completely certain how the unified whole feels or looks.

Three-dimensional models (similar to dollhouses) of the gymnasium, swimming pool, playground, campsite, and other areas are helpful. Miniature figures can be arranged on the simulated playground to acquaint students with playing positions, rules, and strategies. Dolls can also be used to teach spatial relationships among dancers in a group composition, cheerleaders in a pep squad demonstration, and swimmers in the assigned lanes of a meet. Unless dolls with movable joints are taken through such movements as forward rolls, cartwheels, and skin-the-snake on a parallel bar, the student with VI has no way of conceptualizing the whole prior to attempting a new activity.

USABA and Sport Competition

An understanding of national and international sport opportunities gives insight into programming for individuals with VI. While persons with VI can participate in many integrated activities, they should be given optimal training in areas where they are most likely to excel.

While sports have been well organized within the residential school network for years, the movement gained new impetus with the formation of USABA in 1976. In 1977, USABA sponsored its first national championships. Summer games are now held on alternate years (1997, 1999, etc.). Winter sports are held annually. Sanctioned sports for the national games include powerlifting, judo, swimming, track and field, wrestling, goal

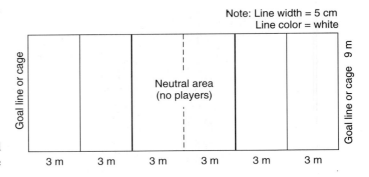

FIGURE 27.12   Playing area for goal ball (18 × 9 m).

ball, women's gymnastics, winter sports (downhill and cross-country skiing), tandem cycling, and others as selected by the USABA board. Under consideration are crew rowing, sailing, archery, and competitive diving. The rules for these sports are based on those used by such national governing bodies as the U.S. Gymnastics Federation (USGF), the National Collegiate Athletic Association (NCAA), and the National Federation of State High School Associations (NFSHSA).

Track-and-Field Events

Three systems enable individuals to excel in track: guide runners with tethers, callers, and guidewires. In the United States, guide runners are favored. Track events include 100, 200, 400, 800, 1500, 3000 (women) 5000 (men) 10,000 meters 4 × 100 Relay, 4 × 400 Relay, and the Marathon conducted separately for B1, B2, and B3 athletes. B1 runners must use guide runners, B2 runners may or may not use guide runners, and the use of a tether is optional. B3 runners require no assistance. When guides are used, the person with VI must always precede the sighted partner.

Field events include the long jump, triple jump, high jump, shot put, javelin, pentathlon, and discus. Regulation throwing implements are used. Callers at the end of a runway may help athletes jump in the right direction.

Goal Ball

A game created in Europe especially for veterans blinded in World War II, goal ball is played under the rules of the International Blind Sport Association (IBSA). The only required equipment is a bell ball. Each team consists of three players wearing knee and elbow pads and blindfolds. The playing area is the same for males and females (see Figure 27.12). Very important is the regulation that all field markings be 5 cm in width and made of a distinctive texture for easy player orientation.

Games are 14 min in duration, with 5-min halves and 2 min between halves. Each team tries to roll the ball across the opponent's goal while the other team tries to stop them (see Figure 27.13). A thrown ball may bounce, but it must be rolling before it reaches the opponent's throwing area or it becomes an infraction. The entire team helps with defense. The arriving ball can be warded off in a standing, kneeling, or lying position with any body part or the whole body (see Figure 27.14).

FIGURE 27.13 Starting positions for the offensive team in goal ball.

FIGURE 27.14 In goal ball, any part of the body or the whole body can be used to prevent the bell ball from rolling across the goal line.

FIGURE 27.15 Playing field for beep baseball. The
circular foul line between 1st and 3rd bases is a constant
distance of 40 ft from home plate. A batted ball must travel
over this line to be considered *fair*. The pitcher stands 20 ft
from home plate. The distance between home plate and each
base location is 90 ft. The base is 10 ft outside the baseline.

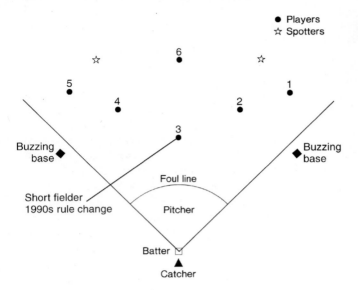

FIGURE 27.16 Dr. Lauren Lieberman, coauthor of
Games for People With Sensory Impairments, communicates
at the 1996 Paralympics with an athlete who is deaf-blind.

team is up to bat and act as spotters when their team is in the
field. As spotters, their role is to call out the fielder's name to
whom the hit ball is coming closest. Only one name is called,
for obvious safety reasons.

Batters are allowed four strikes and one ball (1991
rule change). Except on the last strike, fouls are considered
strikes. Batters must attempt to hit all pitched balls, with the
option of letting one go by without penalty. When a fair ball is
hit, the umpire designates which one of the two buzzing bases
shall be activated. A run is scored if the batter gets to the designated base before the ball is fielded. Games are six innings,
with three outs an inning. Teams have both male and female
players.

Other Games and Sports

Many other excellent activities are described in a book by
Lieberman and Cowart (1996). Lieberman, now at the State
University of New York at Brockport, spent many years teaching at Perkins, possesses skills for working with all kinds of
sensory impairments, and is available as a consultant (see Figure 27.16).

Deaf-Blindness

Deaf-blind means a combination of auditory and visual impairments that results in severe communication and other
needs that require supplementary educational assistance beyond that provided in special education for one disability.

Athletes who are deaf-blind compete under the
auspices of the USABA. Illustrative of such athletes is the
16-year-old boy in Figure 27.17 A & B, who lost his vision as
a toddler and then progressively lost all hearing by the age of
15. He was, however, an excellent competitive swimmer and
practiced with a local swim team. At a recent Paralympics, he
carried a small, portable TDD (a **telecommunication device
for the deaf,** see Chapter 26) with him so that persons could
type in communication, which he read via a braille tape output
and then answered. He also could understand fingerspelling

Because all team members are required to wear a
blindfold, goal ball places persons with VI on equal terms with
sighted peers and thus can be used in mainstream physical education. Rules are available through USABA (see Appendix
C), or from physical educators at residential schools. Many
adapted games and drills of this nature can be designed to give
mainstream students a novel experience as well as excellent
training in auditory perception. Goal ball is suitable for all age
groups, beginning in about the third or fourth grade.

Beep Baseball

Although not a USABA regulation sport, beep baseball is
played by many persons with VI (Montelione & Mastro,
1985). Its rules are governed by the National Beep Baseball
Association, which was founded in 1976. These rules are different from the original game, invented by Charlie Fairbanks
in 1964.

Current rules call for a regulation-size baseball diamond with grass mowed to an approximate height of 2 inches
(see Figure 27.15). Grassy areas are used because they provide
optimal safety and comfort for players who often dive onto the
ground to field balls. The ball, which is available through the
Telephone Pioneers (see the list of organizations in
Appendix D), is a regulation softball 16 inches in circumference, with a battery-operated electronic sound device inside. A
regulation bat is used. Bases are 48 inches tall, with the bottom part made of a 36-inch tall pliable plastic cone and the top
part made of a long cylinder of foam rubber. An electronic
buzzer is installed in each base.

A team is comprised of six blindfolded players and
two sighted players who act as pitcher and catcher when their

FIGURE 27.17 Two ways to converse with a person who is deaf-blind. *(A)* Fingerspelling in palm of hand. *(B)* Use of a telecommunication device for the deaf (TDD) with braille output.

A

B

when hand positions for the various letters were made in the palm of his hand (see Figure 27.17). Unfortunately, few team and staff members had fingerspelling skills of sufficient speed to maintain his interest. His greatest problem thus was communication. Embedded in this was the need for sensory stimulation and companionship, especially for people to take the time to talk to him via the TDD or fingerspelling.

A considerable body of literature on physical education and recreation for deaf-blindness was developed in the

1960s and 1970s, and the pedagogy therein remains relevant. A newer source is Kratz, Tutt, & Black (1987). Information can be accessed through the ERIC computer network or by contacting one of the 10 regional offices of the Helen Keller National Center for Deaf-Blind Youths and Adults (see list in April 1988 *American Annals of the Deaf*).

Deaf-blindness, of course, seldom results in total loss. Diagnosis aims at determining amount of residual vision and hearing and prescribing education, eyeglasses, hearing aids, and communication devices that will enable optimal function.

Prevalence and Causes

Approximately 1,600 students, ages 6 to 21, are documented as receiving special education services for deaf-blindness. Because the widespread rubella epidemics of the early 1960s resulted in more deaf-blindness than any other factor, most persons with this condition are adults (an estimated 8,000).

Deaf-blindness can be hereditary or acquired. Prenatal and perinatal conditions that affect the nervous system often damage both vision and hearing. Drug and alcohol abuse, sexually transmitted diseases, and maternal infections are associated with multiple disability. Childhood diseases linked with deaf-blindness are meningitis, rubella, and scarlet fever. In the hereditary category, **Usher's syndrome** is the leading cause. It is a genetic condition resulting in congenital deafness and a progressive blindness known as **retinitis pigmentosa,** which first appears in the early thirties. Usher's syndrome affects 3 of every 100,000 persons.

Coactive Movement Model

The coactive movement model is an instructional model that works well with toddlers and young children who are blind or deaf-blind and was popularized by Van Dijk of the Netherlands in the 1960s and incorporated into instructional programs throughout the world. The purpose of this model is to develop communication skills through movement instruction that progresses through several stages (Leuw, 1972; Van Dijk, 1966).

In the initial stage, the teacher sits with legs extended on the floor, places the child on his or her lap, and seat-scoots across the floor. Arms, legs, and trunks of the teacher and child touch so that body part movements are in unison. This **coactive movement pattern** is used also for creeping, with the teacher's chest touching the child's back and all eight limbs plastered against one another.

Surfaces of the two bodies are in as much contact as possible as new patterns (knee-walking, walking, rise-to-stand, stair climbing, and the like) are tried in a variety of environments: on mats, water beds, moon walks, trampolines, floors with carpets of various textures, grass, and wading pools. The teacher talks, sings, hums, or whistles the name of the activity throughout the coactive movement. If there is no residual hearing, fingerspelling or a tactual cue is used before, during, and after the movement.

In the second stage, the child and teacher cooperatively move together, but the distance between their bodies is gradually increased so that the action becomes mirroring or imitation. When the child links language with movement, then cues can be given to promote independent body action. Subsequent stages resemble **perceptual-motor programming,** with emphasis on imitation of total body movements, then limb actions, then hand gestures, and finally, fingerspelling and sign language. For children who have residual hearing, learning to follow verbal commands is stressed.

Deaf-Blind Role Models

The best known of persons with deaf-blindness was Helen Keller (1880–1968), who was disabled by an illness at 19 months of age. Helen Keller graduated *cum laude* from Radcliffe, mastered five languages, and wrote three books. Her autobiography (Keller, 1965) is among the classics that everyone should read. Her story has also been immortalized in a play and film called *The Miracle Worker.*

Still another deaf-blind person, Robert J. Smithdas, who suffered cerebral spinal meningitis at age 5, has gained recognition via an autobiography and his work as a public relations counselor and lecturer. At age 32, after completing a master of arts degree at New York University and working in a salaried position for several years, Smithdas wrote,

> Loneliness was continually present in my life after I became deaf and blind. And even now, in adulthood, I find it with me despite all my adjustments to social living. Loneliness is a hunger for increasing human companionship, a need to be part of the activity that I know is constantly going on about me. . . . To share my moments of joy with someone else, to have others sympathize with my failures, appreciate my accomplishments, understand my moods, and value my intelligence—these are the essential conditions that are needed for happiness. (Smithdas, 1958, p. 259)

References

Adelson, E., & Fraiberg, S. (1974). Gross motor development in infants blind from birth. *Child Development, 45,* 114–126.

Buell, C. (1982). *Physical education and recreation for the visually handicapped* (2nd ed.). Washington, DC: American Alliance for Health, Physical Education, Recreation and Dance.

Buell, C. (1984). *Physical education for blind children* (2nd ed.). Springfield, IL: Charles C Thomas.

Buell, C. (1986). Blind athletes successfully compete against able-bodied opponents. In C. Sherrill (Ed.), *Sport and disabled athletes* (pp. 217–223). Champaign, IL: Human Kinetics.

Cordellos, H. (1976). *Aquatic recreation for the blind.* Washington, DC: American Alliance for Health, Physical Education and Recreation.

Cordellos, H. (1981). *Breaking through.* Mountain View, CA: Anderson World.

Cordellos, H. (1983). *Survival run.* Videotape available through Harry Cordellos, 1021 Second Street, Unit B, Novato, CA 94945.

Cordellos, H. C. (1993). *No limits.* Waco, TX: WRS Publishing.

Cratty, B. (1971). *Movement and spatial awareness in blind children and youth.* Springfield, IL: Charles C Thomas.

Fraiberg, S. (1977). *Insights from the blind: Comparative studies of blind and sighted infants.* New York: New American Library.

Gorton, B., & Gavron, S. (1987). A biomechanical analysis of the running pattern of blind athletes in the 100-m dash. *Adapted Physical Activity Quarterly, 4,* 192–203.

Hopkins, W. G., Gaeta, H., Thomas, A. C., & Hill, P. M. (1987). Physical fitness of blind and sighted children. *European Journal of Applied Physiology, 56,* 69–73.

Howe, S. G. (1841). *Perkins report.* Watertown, MA: Perkins Institute for the Blind.

Jong, C. G. A. (1990). The development of mobility in blind and multiply handicapped infants. In A. Vermeer (Ed.), *Motor development, adapted physical activity, and mental retardation* (pp. 56–66). Basel, Switzerland: Karger.

Keitlen, T. (1960). *Farewell to fear.* New York: Avon Books.

Keller, H. (1965). *The story of my life.* New York: Airmont.

Kratz, L. E., Tutt, L., & Black, D. A. (1987). *Movement and fundamental motor skills for sensory deprived children.* Springfield, IL: Charles C Thomas.

Krents, H. (1972). *To race the wind.* New York: Putnam.

Lee, M., Ward, G., & Shephard, R. J. (1985). Physical capacities of sightless adolescents. *Developmental Medicine and Child Neurology, 27,* 767–774.

Leuw, L. (1972). *Co-active movement with deaf-blind children: The Van Dijk model.* Videotape made at Michigan School for Blind. Available through many regional centers for deaf-blind.

Levine, M. D., Carey, W., Crocker, A., & Gross, R. (1983). *Developmental-behavioral pediatrics.* Philadelphia: W. B. Saunders.

Lieberman, L. J., & Cowart, J. F. (1996). *Games for people with sensory impairments.* Champaign, IL: Human Kinetics.

Montelione, T., & Mastro, J. (August, 1985). Beep baseball. *Journal of Physical Education, Recreation and Dance,* pp. 60–61, 65.

Norris, M., Spaulding, P., & Brodie, F. (1957). *Blindness in children.* Chicago: University of Chicago Press.

Nixon, H. L. (1988). Getting over the worry hurdle: Parental encouragement and the sports involvement of visually impaired children and youths. *Adapted Physical Activity Quarterly, 5*(1), 29–43.

Nixon, H. L. (1989). Integration of disabled people in mainstream sports: Case study of a partially sighted child. *Adapted Physical Activity Quarterly, 6,* 17–31.

Pope, C., McGrain, P., & Arnhold, R. (1986). Running gait of the blind: A kinematic analysis. In C. Sherrill (Ed.), *Sport and disabled athletes* (pp. 173–180). Champaign, IL: Human Kinetics.

Shephard, R. J. (1990). *Fitness in special populations.* Champaign, IL: Human Kinetics.

Sherrill, C. (1990). Psychosocial status of disabled athletes. In G. Reid (Ed.), *Problems in movement control* (pp. 339–364). Amsterdam: North-Holland.

Sherrill, C., Rainbolt, W., & Ervin, S. (1984). Attitudes of blind persons toward physical education and recreation. *Adapted Physical Activity Quarterly, 1*(1), 3–11.

Skaggs, S., & Hopper, C. (1996). Individuals with visual impairments: A review of psychomotor behavior. *Adapted Physical Activity Quarterly, 13*(1), 16–26.

Smithdas, R. J. (1958). *Life at my fingertips.* New York: Doubleday.

Van Dijk, J. (1966). The first steps of the deaf-blind child towards language. *International Journal for the Education of the Blind, 15*(1), 112–115.

Winnick, J. (1985). The performance of visually impaired youngsters in physical education activities: Implications for mainstreaming. *Adapted Physical Activity Quarterly, 2*(4), 292–299.

Federal Law Definitions of Disabilities

1. **"Autism"** means a developmental disability significantly affecting verbal and nonverbal communication and social interaction, generally evident before age 3, that adversely affects a child's educational performance. Other characteristics often associated with autism are engagement in repetitive activities and stereotyped movements, resistance to environmental change or change in daily routines, and unusual responses to sensory experiences. The term does not apply if a child's educational performance is adversely affected primarily because the child has a serious emotional disturbance.

2. **"Deaf-blindness"** means concomitant hearing and visual impairments the combination of which causes such severe communication and other developmental and educational problems that they cannot be accommodated in special education programs solely for children with deafness or children with blindness.

3. **"Deafness"** means a hearing impairment that is so severe that the child is impaired in processing linguistic information through hearing, with or without amplification, and this adversely affects a child's educational performance.

4. **"Hearing impairment"** means an impairment in hearing, whether permanent or fluctuating, that adversely affects a child's educational performance but that is not included under the definition of deafness in this section.

5. **"Mental retardation"** means significantly subaverage general intellectual functioning existing concurrently with deficits in adaptive behavior and manifested during the developmental period that adversely affects a child's educational performance.

6. **"Multiple disabilities"** means concomitant impairments (such as mental retardation–blindness, mental retardation–orthopedic impairment, etc.) the combination of which causes such severe educational problems that they cannot be accommodated in special education programs solely for one of the impairments. The term does not include deaf-blindness.

7. **"Orthopedic impairment"** means a severe orthopedic impairment that adversely affects a child's educational performance. The term includes impairments caused by congenital anomaly (e.g., clubfoot, absence of some member, etc.), impairments caused by disease (e.g., poliomyelitis, bone tuberculosis, etc.), and impairments from other causes (e.g., cerebral palsy, amputations, and fractures or burns that cause contractures).

8. **"Other health impairment"** means having limited strength, vitality, or alertness, as due to chronic or acute health problems such as a heart condition, tuberculosis, rheumatic fever, nephritis, asthma, sickle-cell anemia, hemophilia, epilepsy, lead poisoning, leukemia, or diabetes that adversely affects a child's educational performance.

9. **"Serious emotional disturbance"** is defined as follows: (i) The term means a condition exhibiting one or more of the following characteristics over a long period of time and to a marked degree that adversely affects a child's educational performance:
   A. An inability to learn that cannot be explained by intellectual, sensory, or health factors
   B. An inability to build or maintain satisfactory interpersonal relationships with peers and teachers
   C. Inappropriate types of behavior or feelings under normal circumstances
   D. A general pervasive mood of unhappiness or depression
   E. A tendency to develop physical symptoms or fears associated with personal or school problems
   (ii) The term includes schizophrenia. The term does not necessarily apply to children who are socially maladjusted, unless it is determined that they have a serious emotional disturbance.

10. **"Specific learning disability"** means a disorder in one or more of the basic psychological processes involved in understanding or in using language, spoken or written, that may manifest itself in an imperfect ability to listen, think, speak, read, write, spell, or do mathematical calculations. The term includes such conditions as perceptual disabilities, brain injury, minimal brain dysfunction, dyslexia, and developmental aphasia. The term does not apply to children who have learning problems that are primarily the result of visual, hearing, or motor disabilities, mental retardation, emotional disturbance, or environmental, cultural, or economic disadvantage.

11. **"Speech or language impairment"** means a communication disorder such as stuttering, impaired articulation, a language impairment, or a voice impairment that adversely affects a child's educational performance.

12. **"Traumatic brain injury"** means acquired injury to the brain caused by an external physical force, resulting in total or partial functional disability or psychosocial impairment, or both, that adversely affects a child's educational performance. The term applies to open or closed head injuries resulting in impairments in one or more areas, such as cognition; language; memory; attention; reasoning; abstract thinking; judgment; problem solving; sensory, perceptual, and motor abilities; psychosocial behavior; physical functions; information processing; and speech. The term does not apply to brain injuries that are congenital or degenerative, or brain injuries induced by birth trauma.

13. **"Visual impairment including blindness"** means an impairment in vision that, even with correction, adversely affects a child's educational performance. The term includes both partial sight and blindness.

Source: Federal Register, September 29, 1992.

Prevalence and Incidence Information

Prevalence

Prevalence is the number of cases with a specific condition in the population at a given time. For prevalence statistics to be meaningful, we must know the total number of people in the population. Consider the following:

1. The United States population is 250 million. Of this total, 43 million individuals (17%) have disabilities.

2. Of this 43 million, about 10% are children and adolescents, about 30% are young and middle-aged adults, and about 50% are persons over the age of 65.

3. The U.S. Department of Education, Office of Special Education Programs, documents services to about 5 million individuals from birth through age 21. This is only about 2% of this age group, although most sources indicate that 10 to 12% of individuals in the birth-to-age-21 group have disabilities and could benefit from special education services, including physical education.

Incidence

Incidence is the frequency of occurrence of a condition in relation to the population. Incidence varies by age groups (e.g., muscular dystrophy affects 1 out of 500 children but only 3 out of 100,000 persons when all age groups are combined).

Table B.1 gives insight into conditions of high, moderate, and low incidence. Sources vary considerably on incidence statistics, so remember that the figures in the table are estimates.

T a b l e   B . 1   Incidence of selected conditions for all age groups combined.

High-Incidence Conditions (Based on 1,000 Persons)		Moderate-Incidence Conditions (Based on 10,000 Persons)		Low-Incidence Conditions (Based on 100,000 Persons)	
Amputations	2	Achondroplasia	1	Apert's syndrome	0.5
Anorexia nervosa	4[a]	Arthrogryposis	3	Cri-du-chat	5
Arthritis	150	Asperger's syndrome	3	Friedreich's ataxia	2
Asthma	3–6	Blindness	2	Galactosemia	2.2
Autism	1.5	Cooley's anemia	9	Guillain-Barré	1
Cancer	250	Cornelia de Lange syndrome	1	Huntington's disease	6.5
Cerebral palsy	3.5	Cretinism	1.7	Hurler's syndrome	1
Cleft palate and/or lip	1	Hemophilia	1	Marfan's syndrome	5
Clubfoot (Talipes)	1.5	Neurofibromatosis	3	Muscular dystrophy	3
Congenital heart defects	6–10	Prader-Willi	1–2	Osteogenesis imperfecta	3
Congenital hip dislocation	1–3	Rett's syndrome	1	Perthes' condition	4–5
Convulsive disorders	5	Rubella syndrome	1	Phenylketonuria	7
Cystic fibrosis	1	Tourette's syndrome	4–5	Reye's syndrome	1
Deafness	9	Trisomy 18	3	Spinal cord injury	5
Depression	120	Turner's syndrome	1[a]	Tuberous sclerosis	1
Diabetes	10				
Down syndrome	1				
Fetal alcohol syndrome	2				
Fragile X syndrome	1				
Hard of hearing	32				
Klinefelter syndrome	1[b]				
Learning disabilities	3–20				
Mental illness	200				
Mental retardation	30				
Multiple sclerosis	1				
Noonan syndrome	1				
Obesity	150				
Parkinson's disease	4				
Schizophrenia	10				
Sickle-cell anemia	2[c]				
Spina bifida	1–3				

[a]Females only
[b]Males only
[c]Blacks only

APPENDIX C
Addresses of Sport Organizations

Table C.1   Multisport governing bodies and programs.

International Paralympic Committee (IPC)
Dr. Robert Steadward, President
Rick Hansen Centre
W1-67 Van Vliet Centre
University of Alberta
Edmonton, Alberta T6G 2H9, Canada
(403) 492-3182
Fax: (403) 492-7161
E-mail: rsteadwa@per.ualberta.ca

IPC Sport Science Committee
Dr. Gudrun Doll-Tepper
Freie Universität Berlin
Schwendenerstrasse 8
Institute of Sport Science
Berlin, Germany 14195
49-30-824-3731
Fax: 49-30-824-1136
E-mail: gudrunolt@ledat.fu-berlin.de

Canadian Wheelchair Sports Association
1600 James Naismith Drive
Gloucester, Ontario K1B 5N4, Canada
(613) 748-5685
Fax: (613) 748-5722

Bachman Recreation Center
2750 Bachman Drive
Dallas, TX 75220
(214) 670-6266

Casa Collina Outdoor Adventures
2850 North Garey Avenue
Pomona, CA 91767
(909) 596-7733

Committee on Sports for Disabled (COSD)
Mark Shepherd, COSD Chair
United States Olympic Committee (USOC)
1750 East Boulder Street
Colorado Springs, CO 80909-5760
(719) 578-4818

Courage Center
3915 Golden Valley Road
Golden Valley, MN 55422
(612) 588-0811

Rehabilitation Institute of Chicago (RIC) Center
  for Health and Fitness
710 North Lake Shore Drive, 3rd Floor
Chicago, IL 60611
(312) 908-4292
Fax: (312) 908-1051

United States Organization for Disabled Athletes
  (USODA)
143 California Avenue
Uniondale, NY 11553
(800) 25-USODA

Table C.2   Major disability sport organizations by disability.

Amputations and Les Autres Conditions
Disabled Sports/USA
Kirk Bauer, Executive Director
451 Hungerford Drive, Suite 100
Rockville, MD 20850
(301) 217-0960
Fax: (301) 217-0968
TDD: (301) 217-0963
E-mail: dsusa@dsusa.org
http://www.dsusa.org/~dsusa/dsusa.html

United States Les Autres Sports Association
Dave Stephenson, Executive Director
National Office
1475 West Gray, Suite 165
Houston, TX 77019-4926
National Program Office
200 Harrison Avenue
Newport, RI 02840
(401) 848-2460

International Sports Organization for the Disabled
Idrottens Hus
Storforsplan 44
12387, Farsta
Sweden

Blindness and Visual Impairment
U.S. Association for Blind Athletes
Charlie Huebner, Executive Director
33 North Institute Street
Colorado Springs, CO 80903
(719) 630-0422
Fax: (719) 630-0616
E-mail: usaba@usa.net

International Blind Sports Association
Hybratenveien No. 7C
Oslo 10, Norway

Enrique Sanz Jimenez, IBSA President
c/o Quevedo 1
28014 Madrid, Spain
34-1-589-4533
Fax: 34-1-589-4537

Canadian Blind Sport Association
1600 James Naismith Drive
Gloucester, Ontario K1B 5N4, Canada
(613) 748-5609

Ski for Light
1400 Carole Lane
Green Bay, WI 54313
(414) 494-5572

Cerebral Palsy and Traumatic Brain Injury
U.S. Cerebral Palsy Athletic Association
Jerry McCole, Executive Director
200 Harrison Avenue
Newport, RI 02840
(401) 848-2460
Fax: (401) 848-5280
E-mail: uscpaa@mail.bbsnet.com
http://www.uscpaa.org

Jeffrey A. Jones, President USCPAA
RIC Center for Health and Fitness
710 North Lake Shore Drive, 3rd Floor
Chicago, IL 60611
(312) 908-4292
Fax: (312) 908-1051
E-mail: ric-sports@nwu.edu

Cerebral Palsy–International Sports and
  Recreation Association (CP-ISRA)
Miss Elizabeth Dendy, President
9, Kingswood Road
London, W4 5EU
United Kingdom
44-181-994-4262
Fax: 44-181-994-4262

Trudie Rombouts
Secretariat CP-ISRA
6666 ZG HETEREN
The Netherlands
Tel & Fax: 31-26-472-25-93

Canadian Cerebral Palsy Sports Association
1600 James Naismith Drive
Gloucester, Ontario K1B 5N4, Canada
(613) 748-5725

Deafness
American Athletic Association of the Deaf
3607 Washington Boulevard, Suite 4
Ogden, Utah 84403-1737
(801) 393-8710
Fax: (801) 393-2263

National Information Center on Deafness
Gallaudet University
800 Florida Avenue NE
Washington, DC 20002-3625
(202) 651-5000

Canadian Deaf Sports Association
333 River Road
Ottawa, Ontario K1L 8H9, Canada

Dwarf
Dwarf Athletic Association of America
Janet Brown, Executive Director
418 Willow Way
Lewisville, TX 75067
(972) 317-8630

Mental Retardation
Special Olympics International
Eunice Kennedy-Shriver, Founder-Director
Timothy Shriver, CEO
Dr. Tom Songster, VP for Sports Policy and
    Research
1325 G Street, NW, Suite 500
Washington, DC 20005-3104
(202) 628-3630

International Sports Federation for Persons with
    Mental Handicap (INAS-FMH)
Bernard Atha, Executive Director
13-27 Brunswick Place
London N1 6DX
United Kingdom
44-171-250-1100
Fax: 44-171-250-0110

Spinal Paralysis
Wheelchair Sports, USA
3595 East Fountain Boulevard, Suite L-1
Colorado Springs, CO 80910
(719) 574-1150
Fax: (719) 574-9840

International Stoke Mandeville Wheelchair Sports
    Federation
Stoke Mandeville Sports Stadium
Harvey Road
Aylesbury, Bucks HP 21 8PP
United Kingdom

Canadian Wheelchair Sports Association
1600 James Naismith Drive
Gloucester, Ontario K1B 5N4, Canada
(613) 748-5685
Fax: (613) 748-5722

T a b l e C . 3   **Sport organizations/contacts for one sport.**

Basketball
National Wheelchair Basketball Association
David Kiley, Commissioner
Charlotte Institute for Rehabilitation
1100 Blythe Boulevard
Charlotte, NC 28203
(704) 355-1064
Fax: (704) 446-4999

Canadian Wheelchair Basketball Association
1600 James Naismith Drive
Gloucester, Ontario K1B 5N4, Canada
(613) 748-5888
Fax: (613) 748-5889

Boccia
Cathy Shea
Capper Foundation
3500 SW 10th Avenue
Topeka, KS 66604-1995
(913) 272-4060
Fax: (913) 272-7912

Howard Bailey
CP-ISRA Boccia Chair
Dept of Kinesiology and Health
Georgia State University
Atlanta, GA 30303-3083

Golf
Association of Disabled American Golfers
7700 East Arapahoe Road, Suite 350
Englewood, CO 80112
(303) 220-0921
Fax: (303) 843-9284

Bowling
American Wheelchair Bowling Association
6264 North Andrews Avenue
Ft. Lauderdale, FL 33309
(954) 491-2886

American Blind Bowling Association/
    Alice Hoover
411 Sheriff
Mercer, PA 16137
(412) 662-5748

Horseback Riding
North American Riding for the Handicapped
    Association (NARHA)
P.O. Box 33150
Denver, CO 80233
(800) 369-RIDE

Quad Rugby
United States Quad Rugby Association
309 Stoney Ford Road
Holland, PA 18966
(215) 504-0443
Fax: (215) 504-0445

Racquet Sports
National Foundation of Wheelchair Tennis
Brad Parks, Director
940 Calle Amanecer, Suite B
San Clemente, CA 92672
(714) 361-3663
Fax: (714) 361-6603

National Wheelchair Racquetball Association
2380 McGinley Road
Monroeville, PA 15146
(412) 856-2468

Road Racing
International Wheelchair Road Racers Club, Inc.
30 Myano Lane
Stamford, CT 06902
(203) 967-2231

Shooting
NRA Disabled Shooting Services
11250 Waples Mill Road
Fairfax, VA 22030
(703) 267-1495

Swimming/Aquatics
Aquatics Council/AAHPERD
c/o Sue Grosse
7252 Wabash Avenue
Milwaukee, WI 53223
(414) 354-8717

Council for National Cooperation in Aquatics
c/o Louise Priest
901 W. New York Street
Indianapolis, IN 46202
(317) 638-4238

United States Swimming, Inc.
1750 East Boulder Street
Colorado Springs, CO 80909

Table C.3   Continued.

Softball/Baseball

National Wheelchair Softball Association
1616 Todd Court
Hastings, MN 55033
(612) 437-1792

Challenger Baseball
Little League Baseball Headquarters
P.O. Box 3485
Williamsport, PA 17701

National Beep Baseball Association
c/o Jeanette Bigger
2231 West 1st Street
Topeka, KS 66606-1304
(913) 234-2156

Weightlifting/Powerlifting

U.S. Wheelchair Weightlifting Federation
39 Michael Place
Levittown, PA 19057
(215) 945-1964

USCPAA Powerlifting
Michael McDevitt
8420 West Chester Pike
Upper Darby, PA 19082

Winter Sports

Disabled Sports/USA
451 Hungerford Drive, Suite 100
Rockville, MD 20850
(301) 217-0960

Ski for Light, Inc.
1400 Carole Lane
Green Bay, WI 54313
(414) 494-5572/492-5821

U.S. Disabled Ski Team
P.O. Box 100
Park City, UT 84060
(801) 649-9090

American Sledge Hockey Association
10933 Johnson Avenue, South
Bloomington, MN 55437
(612) 644-2666

APPENDIX D

Addresses of Other Organizations and Agencies

Table D.1   Professional associations.

Adapted Physical Activity Council, AAHPERD

American Association for Active Lifestyles and
   Fitness (AAALF)
c/o Dr. Janet Seaman
1900 Association Drive
Reston, VA 22091
(800) 213-7193, ext. 431
Fax: (703) 476-9527

Adapted Physical Education National Standards
   (APENS); National Certification Exam
Dr. Luke E. Kelly
University of Virginia, Department of Human
   Services
Charlottesville, VA 22903
(804) 924-6194

American College of Sports Medicine
P.O. Box 1440
Indianapolis, IN 46206-1440
(317) 637-9200
Fax: (317) 634-7817

American Dance Therapy Association
2000 Century Plaza, Suite 108
Columbia, MD 21044
(410) 997-4040

American Occupational Therapy Association
4720 Montgomery Lane
P.O. Box 31220
Bethesda, MD 20824-1220
(800) 377-8555

American Kinesiotherapy Association
P.O. Box 614
Wheeling, IL 60090-0614
(800) 296-AKTA

American Physical Therapy Association
1111 North Fairfax Street
Alexandria, VA 22314
(800) 999-2782

American Psychological Association
750 First Street NE
Washington, DC 20002

American Therapeutic Recreation Association
P.O. Box 15215
Hattiesburg, MS 93404-5215
(800) 553-0304

Canadian Association for Health, Physical
   Education, and Recreation (Suite 606)
1600 James Naismith Drive
Gloucester, Ontario K1B 5N4, Canada

Canadian Association of Sport Sciences (Suite 311)
1600 James Naismith Drive
Gloucester, Ontario K1B 5N4, Canada

Canadian Fitness and Lifestyle Research Institute
   (Suite 313)
1600 James Naismith Drive
Gloucester, Ontario K1B 5N4, Canada

Council for Exceptional Children (CEC)
1920 Association Drive
Reston, VA 22091
(703) 620-1589

International Federation of Adapted Physical
   Activity (IFAPA)
Contact Dr. Claudine Sherrill
11168 Windjammer Drive
Frisco, TX 75034

National Association of State Directors of Special
   Education
1800 Diagonal Road, Suite 320
Alexandria, VA 22314
(703) 519-3800

National Consortium for Physical Education and
   Recreation for Individuals with Disabilities
   (NCPERID)
(Address changes every 2 years with new
   president)
Contact Dr. Claudine Sherrill
11168 Windjammer Drive
Frisco, TX 75034

National Dance Association
1900 Association Drive
Reston, VA 22091

National Rehabilitation Association
633 S. Washington Street
Alexandria, VA 22314

National Therapeutic Recreation Society
2775 S. Quincy Street, Suite 300
Arlington, VA 22206
(800) 626-6772

Rehabilitation International USA
25 East 21st Street
New York, NY 10010

Very Special Arts
John F. Kennedy Center for Performing Arts
1300 Connecticut Avenue NW, Suite 700
Washington, DC 20036
(800) 933-8721

Table D.2 Associations related to disabilities.

Autism
Autism Society of America
7910 Woodmont Avenue, Suite 650
Bethesda, MD 20814
(800) 3-AUTISM

Blind
American Foundation for the Blind
11 Penn Plaza, Suite 300
New York, NY 10001
(800) 232-5463

Association for the Education and Rehabilitation
   of the Blind and Visually Impaired—Bulletin
   for Physical Educators
206 N. Washington Street, Suite 320
Alexandria, VA 22314

Cerebral Palsy and Traumatic Brain Injury
American Academy for Cerebral Palsy and
   Developmental Medicine
6300 N. River Road, Suite 727
Rosemont, IL 60018
(708) 698-1635

Brain Injury Association
1776 Massachusetts Avenue NW, Suite 100
Washington, DC 20036-1904
(202) 296-6443

National Easter Seal Society, Inc.
230 West Monroe Street, Suite 1800
Chicago, IL 60606
(800) 221-6827

United Cerebral Palsy Associations
1660 L Street NW, Suite 700
Washington, DC 20036
(800) 872-5827

Dwarf
Little People of America
P.O. Box 9897
Washington, DC 20016
(800) 24-DWARF

Deaf
Alexander Graham Bell Association for the Deaf
3417 Volta Place NW
Washington, DC 20007

Gallaudet College
800 Florida Avenue NE
Washington, DC 20002-3625
(202) 651-5000

Helen Keller National Center for Deaf-Blind
   Youths and Adults
111 Middle Neck Road
Sands Point, NY 11050

National Association of the Deaf
814 Thayer Avenue
Silver Spring, MD 20910
(301) 587-1788

Learning Disabilities
Council for Learning Disabilities
P.O. Box 40303
Overland Park, KS 66204
(913) 492-8755

Learning Disability Association of America (LDA)
(formerly ACLD)
4156 Library Road
Pittsburgh, PA 15234
(412) 341-1515

Mental Retardation
American Association on Mental Retardation
444 N. Capitol Street NW, Suite 846
Washington, DC 20001-1512

The ARC (formerly Association for Retarded
   Citizens)
500 East Border Street, Suite 300
Arlington, TX 76010
(800) 433-5255

National Down Syndrome Congress
1605 Chantilly Drive, Suite 250
Atlanta, GA 30324
(800) 232-6372

National Down Syndrome Society
666 Broadway
New York, NY 10012
(800) 221-4602

National Fragile X Foundation
1441 York St., Ste. 303
Denver, CO 80206
(800) 688-8765

The Association for Persons with Severe
   Handicaps (TASH)
(formerly AAESPH)
29 West Susquehanna Avenue, Suite 210
Baltimore, MD 21204
(800) 482-8274

Physical Disabilities
Muscular Dystrophy Association (MDA)
3300 East Sunrise Drive
Tucson, AZ 85718
(520) 529-2000

National Spinal Cord Injury Association
545 Concord Avenue, No. 29
Cambridge, MA 02138
(800) 962-9629

Paralyzed Veterans of America
801 18th Street NW
Washington, DC 20006
(800) 424-8200

Spina Bifida Association of America
4590 MacArthur Boulevard NW, Suite 250
Washington, DC 20007
(800) 621-3141

Table D.3 Voluntary health organizations.

American Cancer Society
1599 Clifton Road NE
Atlanta, GA 30329

American Diabetes Association
P.O. Box 25757
1660 Duke Street
Alexandria, VA 22314

American Heart Association
7272 Greenville Avenue
Dallas, TX 75231-4596
(214) 373-6300

American Lung Association
1740 Broadway
New York, NY 10019

American Red Cross
17th and D Streets NW
Washington, DC 20006

Arthritis Foundation
1314 Spring Street NW
Atlanta, GA 30309

Asthma and Allergy Foundation of America
1125 15th Street NW, Suite 502
Washington, DC 20005
(800) 7-ASTHMA

Cystic Fibrosis Foundation
6931 Arlington Road, No. 200
Bethesda, MD 20814

Epilepsy Foundation of America
4351 Garden City Drive
Lancover, MD 20785

National Hemophilia Foundation
110 Greene Street, Room 406
New York, NY 10012

National Multiple Sclerosis Society
733 Third Avenue
New York, NY 10017

Table D.4 Government offices/agencies.

American Disabilities Act
For information: (800) 949-4232

Clearinghouse on Disability Information
Office of Special Education and Rehabilitative
Services
Room 3132, Switzer Building
330 C Street SW
Washington, DC 20262-2524
(202) 205-8241

DB-LINK
National Information Clearinghouse on Children
Who Are Deaf-Blind
345 North Monmouth Avenue
Monmouth, OR 97361
(800) 438-9376

ERIC Clearinghouse on Disabilities and Gifted
Education
Council for Exceptional Children (CEC)
1920 Association Drive
Reston, VA 22091-1589
(800) 328-0272

National Diffusion Network (NDN)
Office of Educational Research and Improvement
555 New Jersey Avenue NW
Washington, DC 20208-5645
(202) 219-2134

National Information Center for Children and
Youth with Disabilities (NICHCY)
P.O. Box 1492
Washington, DC 20013
(800) 695-0285

National Rehabilitation Information Center
(NARIC) and ABLEDATA
330 C Street SW
Washington, DC 20202
(800) 346-2742

President's Committee on Employment of
People with Disabilities (PCEPD)
1331 F Street NW
Washington, DC 20004-1107
(202) 376-6200

President's Council on Physical Fitness and
Sports
701 Pennsylvania Avenue NW, Suite 205
Washington, DC 20004
(202) 272-3421

State agencies and information on
disability—Contact NICHCY (see
previously listed address)

U.S. Government Printing Office
Superintendent of Documents
P.O. Box 371954
Pittsburgh, PA 15250-7954
(202) 512-1800

APPENDIX E

Addresses for Purchasing Journals and Materials

Table E.1 Books, journals, and videos.

McGraw-Hill Higher Education
2460 Kerper Boulevard
Dubuque, IA 52001
(800) 338-5578
Publishes several textbooks

Challenge Publications
P.O. Box 508
Macomb, IL 61455
(309) 833-1902
Publishes **Palaestra**

Human Kinetics Publishers
Box 5076
Champaign, IL 61820
(800) 747-4457
Publishes **Adapted Physical Activity Quarterly**
and several textbooks

Paralyzed Veterans of America/Sports 'N Spokes
211 East Highland, Suite 180
Phoenix, AZ 85016
(602) 224-0500
Publishes **Sports 'N Spokes,** which is a major
information source for purchase of wheelchairs
and products used by people in wheelchairs

Pro•Ed
8700 Shoal Creek Boulevard
Austin, TX 78757-6897
(512) 451-3246
Publishes **Academic Therapy, Focus on Autism
and Other Disabilities, Journal of Learning
Disabilities, Topics in Early Childhood
Special Education,** and other journals

SPORT Database
1600 James Naismith Drive
Gloucester, Ontario K1B 5N4, Canada
(613) 748-5658
Produces comprehensive reference lists and
computerized data

The Message Makers
Disability Sport Videos
Terry N. Terry, CEO
1217 Turner Street
Lansing, MI 48906
(517) 482-3333

Research Press
Behavior Management Videos
Box 31775
Champaign, IL 60820

Miramar Communications, Inc.
23815 Stuart Ranch Road
P.O. Box 8987
Malibu, CA 90265-8987
(800) 543-4116
Publishes **TeamRehab, New Mobility, Spinal
Network**

Table E.2 Equipment.

Cosom/Mantua Industries, Inc.
Grandview Avenue
Woodbury Heights, NJ 08097
(609) 853-0300

Communication Aids for Children & Adults
Crestwood Company
6625 North Sidney Place
Milwaukee, WI 53209-3259

Flaghouse, Inc.
601 Route 46 West
Hasbrouck, NJ 07604
(800) 793-7922

GSC/BSN Sports
P.O. Box 7726
Dallas, TX 75209
(800) 525-7510

Jayfro Corporation
976 Hartford Turnpike
Waterford, CT 06385
(203) 447-3001

J. A. Preston Corporation
744 West Michigan Avenue
Jackson, MI 49204
(800) 631-7277

LS & S Products for Visually Impaired
P.O. Box 673
Northbrook, IL 60065
(800) 468-4789

Rifton for People With Disabilities
Box 901
Rifton, NY 12471
(800) 374-3866

Sportime
One Sportime Way
Atlanta, GA 30340-1402
(800) 444-5700

Wolverine Sports
745 State Circle
Ann Arbor, MI 48108
(800) 521-2832

Table E.3 Personal flotation devices.

Danmar Products, Inc.
2390 Winewood
Ann Arbor, MI 48102

Excel Sports Science, Inc.
P.O. Box 5612
Eugene, OR 97405

Flaghouse, Inc.
601 Route 46 West
Hasbrouck, NJ 07604
(800) 793-7922

J & B Foam Fabricators, Inc.
P.O. Box 144
Ludington, MI 49431

Table E.4 Test and curriculum materials.

American Guidance Service (AGS)
P.O. Box 99
Circle Pines, MN 55014-1796
(800) 323-2560
**Bruininks-Oseretsky Test and Body Skills: A
Motor Development Curriculum**

Paul H. Brookes Publishing Company
P.O. Box 10624
Baltimore, MD 21285
(800) 638-3775
**Bricker's Assessment, Evaluation, and
Programming System; Carolina Curriculum;
Transdisciplinary Play-Based Assessment
and Curriculum**

Council for Exceptional Children (CEC)
1920 Association Drive
Reston, VA 20191-1589
(800) 232-7323
Special education assessment materials and
curricula

Canadian Association for Health, Physical
Education, and Recreation
1600 James Naismith Drive
Gloucester, Ontario K1B 5N4, Canada
(613) 748-5639
Moving to Inclusion Curriculum; PREP
materials

Cooper Institute for Aerobics Research
12330 Preston Road
Dallas, TX 75230
(800) 635-7050
Prudential FITNESSGRAM materials; **You Stay
Active Curriculum**

Denver Developmental Materials, Inc.
P.O. Box 6919
Denver, CO 86202-0919
**Denver Developmental Screening Test;
Denver II**

Pro•Ed
8700 Shoal Creek Boulevard
Austin, TX 78757-6897
(512) 451-3246
I CAN physical education materials, **Test of
Gross Motor Development (TGMD),** data-
based gymnasium materials, behavior
management and social skills curricula

Psychological Corporation
555 Academic Corporation
San Antonio, TX 78204-2498
(800) 228-0752
Movement ABC; TOMI revisions; **Bayley
Scales II**

Special Olympics International
Sports Training Curricula
Attn: Finance/Publications
1325 G Street NW, Suite 500
Washington, DC 20005-4709
(202) 628-3630
Sports skills program guides for all major summer
and winter sports, applicable to all disabilities

Western Psychological Services (WPS)
12031 Wilshire Boulevard
Los Angeles, CA 90025
(800) 222-2670
Self-concept and personality inventories; counseling
materials; Ayres sensory integration tests

Important Events in Adapted Physical Activity

1817 The first residential schools established in the United States were for deaf students: the American School for the Deaf in Hartford, CT, and the New York School for the Deaf in White Plains, NY, founded in 1817 and 1818, respectively. Thomas Hopkins Gallaudet is credited with founding the school in Connecticut. In 1856, the institution now known as Gallaudet University, Washington, DC, evolved through the efforts of philanthropist Amos Kendall.

1830 The first residential schools for individuals with blindness were founded between 1830 and 1833 in Boston, New York, and Philadelphia. Only one of the early residential facilities, the Perkins Institution in Boston, provided physical education for its students.

1847 *The American Annals of the Deaf,* first published in 1847, is the oldest educational journal in the United States still in existence.

1848 The first residential institution for persons with mental retardation in the United States was organized in Massachusetts.

1863 The earliest residential facilities for persons with physical disabilities bore such names as Hospital of the New York Society for the Relief of the Ruptured and Crippled (1863) and the Home for Incurables in Philadelphia (1877).

1864 Edouard Seguin's classic book *Idiocy and Its Diagnoses and Treatment by the Physiological Method* was translated into English. This book provided the framework for the earliest attempts to train persons with mental retardation. Seguin was a student and protégé of Jean-Marc Itard, known for his work with Victor, the "Wild Boy of Aveyron," in the early 1800s.

1876 Establishment of the American Association on Mental Deficiency (AAMD). First president was Edouard Seguin. One of its original goals was to promote the development of residential facilities. During the first decade of AAMD's existence, 20 states created residential schools for persons with MR.

1885 Formation of the Association for the Advancement of Physical Education, the forerunner of AAHPERD. First president was Edward Hitchcock, MD. Almost all the early members were physicians.

1885 Baron Nils Posse of Sweden introduced Per Henrik Ling's medical gymnastics into the United States. This was the beginning of adapted physical activity service delivery.

1895 The National Education Association (NEA) organized a Department of Physical Education.

1899 Public schooling for persons with disabilities had begun, with the earliest documentation citing 100 large cities with special education classes. Among these were Boston, Chicago, Cleveland, Detroit, New York, and Milwaukee.

1902 The National Education Association organized a Department of Special Education. Alexander Graham Bell, pioneer in deaf education, spearheaded this recognition.

1905 Therapeutic Section of the American Physical Education Association (APEA) began with Baroness Rose Posse as chair. This date is often used to mark the beginning of the adapted physical activity profession.

1906 Formation of the Playground Association of America, the forerunner of National Recreation and Park Association (NRPA), of which the National Therapeutic Recreation Society (NTRS) is a subdivision. First president was Dr. Luther Halsey Gulick.

1912 Establishment of Children's Bureau in Washington, DC, to promote the welfare of children and to prevent their exploitation in industry.

1917 Origin of the National Society for the Promotion of Occupational Therapy, the forerunner of the American Occupational Therapy Association (1921). First president was William Rush Dunton, Jr., now considered the "father of OT."

1919 National Easter Seals Society for Crippled Children and Adults founded.

1920 The National Civilian Vocational Rehabilitation Act, a forerunner of the Social Security Act, passed.

1921 Origin of forerunner of American Physical Therapy Association. First president was Mary McMillan, who strongly influenced early leaders in corrective physical education who were also physical therapists: George Stafford and Josephine Rathbone.

1922 Establishment of Council for Exceptional Children (CEC), the first organization to advocate for all groups with disabilities. First president was Elizabeth Farrell.

1928 First textbooks to use the term *corrective physical education* were published:
  Stafford, G. T. (1928). *Preventive and corrective physical education.* New York: A. S. Barnes.
  Lowman, C., Colestock, C., & Cooper, H. (1928). *Corrective physical education for groups.* New York: A. S. Barnes.

1930 Historic White House Conference on Child Health and Protection. The Committee on the Physically and Mentally Handicapped wrote the often-quoted Bill of Rights for Handicapped Children.

1935 Social Security Act passed.

1944, 1952, also **1915–17** Major epidemics of poliomyelitis, which left thousands of persons paralyzed. In 1952 alone, 57,628 cases of polio were reported.

1944 Sir Ludwig Guttmann, a neurosurgeon, established the Stoke-Mandeville Hospital for treatment of spinal cord injuries and began experimenting with sport as rehabilitation.

1945 Formation of the American Athletic Association for the Deaf (AAAD). This was the first special population in the United States to form its own sport organization.

1946 Association for Physical and Mental Rehabilitation (APMR) established, the forerunner of American Kinesiotherapy Association (AKA). Name changed to American Corrective Therapy Association in 1967 and to AKA in 1983.

1949 Formation of the National Wheelchair Basketball Association (NWBA). Founder and first commissioner was Timothy Nugent, University of Illinois.

1950 The National Association for Music Therapy, Inc. (NAMT) formed.

1950 The National Association for Retarded Citizens (NARC) founded. Name changed in 1979 to Association for Retarded Citizens (ARC). In 1992, ARC became the name rather than the initials for words.

1952 Terminology officially changed from *corrective physical education* to *adapted physical education.* First definition of adapted physical education published by AAHPER.

1954 First textbook entitled *Adapted Physical Education* published. Author was Arthur Daniels of the Ohio State University.

1955 Salk vaccine recognized as 80 to 90% effective against paralytic polio.

1956 Formation of National Wheelchair Athletic Association (NWAA). Name changed to Wheelchair Sports, USA in 1994.

1958 National Foundation for Infantile Paralysis became The National Foundation—March of Dimes and turned attention to birth defects and genetic counseling.

1958 PL 85-926 was passed, authorizing grants for training personnel in mental retardation. This legislation represents the beginning of the federal government's commitment to the rights of persons with disabilities.

1959 Pioneer research on mental retardation and motor development by Francis and Rarick published, which reported that children with MR were 2 to 4 years behind nondisabled peers.

1960 First Paralympic Games held in Rome. This was the first time that the International Stoke-Mandeville Games were held in conjunction with Olympic Games.

1961 Kennedy appointed the first President's Panel on Mental Retardation.

1963 PL 88-164 amended 1958 legislation to encompass all handicapped groups that required special education.

1964 Civil rights legislation (PL 88-352) passed.

1964 Association for Children with Learning Disabilities (ACLD) formed. Name changed in 1980 to ACLD, Inc. (An Association for Children and Adults with Learning Disabilities) and in 1990 to LDA (Learning Disability of America).

1965 PL 89-10, the Elementary and Secondary Education Act (ESEA), passed. Included Titles I to IV. Illustrative funded programs were Vodola's Project ACTIVE in New Jersey and Long's Project PEOPEL in Arizona.

1965 Eunice Kennedy Shriver was keynote speaker at AAHPER conference in Dallas. Her challenge to professionals was the beginning of awareness of needs of people with mental retardation.

1965 The AAHPER Project on Recreation and Fitness for the Mentally Retarded was formed with a grant from the Joseph P. Kennedy, Jr. Foundation. This project was the forerunner of the Unit on Programs for the Handicapped, which served AAHPERD members from 1968 to 1981.

1966 American Dance Therapy Association, Inc. (ADTA) founded in New York City.

1966 Bureau of Education for the Handicapped (BEH) created by PL 89-750 within the Office of Education of HEW. BEH, which became the Office of Special Education Programs (OSEP) in 1980, is the agency that funds university training programs in physical education and recreation for persons with disabilities.

1966 Hollis Fait began battle concerning name of the profession by changing title of his textbook from *Adapted Physical Education* (1st ed., 1960) to *Special Physical Education.* This battle ended in late 1980s. Fait lost the battle.

1967 Formation of the National Handicapped Sports and Recreation Association (NHSRA), which governs winter and amputee sports. Name changed to National Handicapped Sports (NHS) in 1992 and to Disabled Sports/USA in 1995.

1967 ESEA amended under PL 90-170, Title V, Section 502, to support training, research, and demonstration projects in physical education and recreation for individuals with disabilities.

1967 National Therapeutic Recreation Society (NTRS) created as a branch of the National Recreation and Park Association.

1968 AAHPER Unit on Programs for the Handicapped approved. This replaced Project on Recreation and Fitness for the Mentally Retarded. Director until 1981 was Julian Stein.

1968 Special Olympics founded by Eunice Kennedy Shriver. AAHPER-Kennedy Foundation Special Fitness Awards established. First director of Special Olympics was Frank Hayden of Canada.

1968 First master's degree specialization in adapted physical education established by Joseph Winnick at State University of New York (SUNY) at Brockport.

1969 First doctoral programs in adapted physical education established at several universities with help of federal funding (PL 90-170).

1970 Title VI, Public Law 91-230, Education of the Handicapped Act (EHA), passed. This was the first major legislation leading to the subsequent passage of PL 94-142 in 1975.

1970 Series of institutes sponsored by BEH held on the Development of AAHPER Guidelines for Professional Preparation Programs for Personnel Involved in Physical Education and Recreation for the Handicapped. Report published by AAHPER in 1973.

1972 Information and Research Utilization Center (IRUC) in Physical Education and Recreation for the Handicapped funded by BEH and established in conjunction with AAHPER Unit on Programs for the Handicapped. Julian Stein was director.

1972 Title IX legislation (PL 92-318) passed.

1972 AC/FMR (Accreditation Council for Facilities for the Mentally Retarded) issued standards, including recreation services, which all residential and intermediate care facilities must implement in order to receive accreditation. New AC/FMR standards are issued periodically.

1973 Section 504 of Rehabilitation Act (PL 93-112) enacted, mandating nondiscrimination in programs and facilities receiving federal funds. Not implemented, however, until 1977, when rules and regulations were published in the *Federal Register.*

1973 National Ad Hoc Committee on Physical Education and Recreation for the Handicapped formed by BEH project directors at Minneapolis (AAHPER) conference. This was the forerunner of the National Consortium (see 1975).

1973 International Federation of Adapted Physical Activity founded. First symposium held in Montreal in 1977.

1974 At the annual conference in Anaheim, California, AAHPER was reorganized as the American Alliance for Health, Physical Education, and Recreation with seven independent associations. Three of these included programs for people with disabilities: ARAPCS (Association for Research, Administration, Professional Councils and Societies), NASPE (National Association for Sport and Physical Education), and AALR (American Association for Leisure and Recreation).

1974 Formation of the American Association for the Education of the Severely/Profoundly Handicapped (AAESPH). In 1980, the name of this organization changed to The Association for the Severely Handicapped (TASH) and the title of its journal became *JASH, Journal of Association for Severely Handicapped.*

1975 National Consortium on Physical Education and Recreation for the Handicapped (NCPERH) evolved from National Ad Hoc Committee. First president was Leon Johnson, University of Missouri. Name changed in 1992 to National Consortium for Physical Education and Recreation for Individuals With Disabilities (NCPERID).

1975 PL 94-142 enacted. Called the "Education for All Handicapped Children Act," it stated specifically that *instruction in physical education* shall be provided for all children with disabilities.

1976 Formation of the U.S. Association for Blind Athletes (USABA).

1976 The Olympiad for the Physically Handicapped held in Canada in conjunction with the Olympic Games. This was the first time that athletes with blindness and amputations were recognized and allowed to participate.

1976 White House Conference on Handicapped Individuals (WHCHI) held. The final report included 420 recommendations, several of which pertained to recreation and leisure.

1977 First National Championships, U.S. Association for Blind Athletes.

1977 Regulations to implement Section 504 of PL 93-112, the Rehabilitation Act of 1973, published in May 4 issue of *Federal Register.*

1977 Regulations to implement PL 94-142 published in the August 23 issue of the *Federal Register.* (See Chapter 4.)

1977 First Annual National Wheelchair Marathon held in conjunction with the Boston Marathon (26.2 mi).

1978 Formation of the National Association of Sports for Cerebral Palsy (NASCP). Name changed in 1986 to U.S. Cerebral Palsy Athletic Association.

1978 PL 95-606, the Amateur Sports Act, recognized the sport organizations of athletes with disabilities as part of the U.S. Olympic Committee structure.

1979 The U.S. Olympic Committee (USOC) organized a Committee for the Handicapped in Sports, with Kathryn Sallade Barclift elected as its first chairperson. This committee brought together for the first time representatives from the five major sport organizations for athletes with disabilities. Now named Committee on Sports for the Disabled (COSD).

1979 PL 96-88 changed the status of the old U.S. Office of Education within the Department of Health, Education, and Welfare (HEW) to a Department of Education. Shirley M. Hufstedler was appointed its first secretary. HEW was disbanded.

1979 AAHPER's name officially changed to AAHPERD (American Alliance for Health, Physical Education, Recreation, and Dance), thereby giving recognition to dance as a discipline separate from physical education.

1980 Reorganization completed for the two new departments replacing HEW. These new structures are the Department of Education (ED) and the Department of Health and Human Services (HHS). Within ED's seven principal program offices, the Office of Special Education and Rehabilitative Services (OSERS) relates to people with disabilities. Principal components of OSERS are Office of Special Education Progams (OSEP), which replaces BEH; Rehabilitation Services Administration (RSA); and National Institute of Handicapped Research.

1981 New AAHPERD guidelines (competencies) on adapted physical education published.

1981 Declared the "International Year of the Disabled" by the United Nations.

1981 January 19 issue of *Federal Register* (Vol. 46, No. 12) devoted to IEPs, including clarifications for physical education.

1981 Formation of the U.S. Amputee Athletic Association (USAAA). Dissolved in 1990.

1982 First UNESCO-sponsored international symposium on physical education and sport programs for persons with physical and mental disabilities. Leader was Julian Stein.

1984 International Games for the Disabled (blind, cerebral palsied, amputee, and les autres) held in Long Island, NY, with approximately 2,500 athletes competing. Seventh World Wheelchair Games (spinally paralyzed) held in England.

1984 *Adapted Physical Activity Quarterly* first published. This was first professional journal to be devoted specifically to adapted physical education. Geoffrey Broadhead was founding editor.

1984 *Palaestra* first published. This was a specialized journal for adapted physical activity, sport, and recreation. David Beaver was owner/editor.

1985 Merger completed within AAHPERD of NASPE Adapted Physical Education Academy and ARAPCS Therapeutic Council. The new structure was called the Adapted Physical Activity Council and was housed within ARAPCS. See 1993 for current names.

1986 Canadian adapted physical activity movement was stimulated by Jasper Conference on Strategies for Change.

1986 *Sport and Disabled Athletes,* the proceedings of the Olympic Scientific Congress, published by Human Kinetics. This was the first published source of information on all disability sports. Editor was Claudine Sherrill.

1988 Paralympics held in Korea. This was the first time that all athletes with physical disabilities competed at the same venue.

1989 Revitalization of International Federation of Adapted Physical Activity (IFAPA) with symposium in Berlin directed by Gudrun Doll-Tepper. Marks beginning of international era.

1990 Americans with Disabilities Act (PL 101-336) enacted.

1990 Individuals With Disabilities Education Act (PL 101-476) enacted. Person-first philosophy and terminology established. Rules and regulations published in September 29, 1992, *Federal Register.*

1991 European Master's Degree Program in Adapted Physical Activity (EMDAPA) established in Leuven, Belgium. First director was Herman Van Coppenolle.

1992 Montreal Symposium on Adapted Physical Activity conducted by Greg Reid. Planning for a North American regional affiliate of IFAPA began.

1992 National Consortium on Physical Education and Recreation for Individuals with Disabilities (NCPERID) received 5-year grant from federal government to develop adapted physical education national standards and a national certification exam. Project director was Luke Kelly.

1992 Paralympics held in Barcelona. This was the first time that integrated classifications were used.

1993 First quadrennial International Special Olympics Meet held outside of USA. World Winter Games in Salzburg, Austria.

1993 AAHPERD's ARAPCS was changed to the American Association for Active Lifestyles and Fitness (AAALF). This is the AAHPERD structure that adapted physical activity personnel join because it contains the Adapted Physical Activity Council (APAC). Janet Seaman is director.

1994 *Adapted Physical Activity Quarterly* became the official journal of the International Federation of Adapted Physical Activity (IFAPA).

1994 North American Federation of Adapted Physical Activity (NAFAPA) founded as a regional affiliate of IFAPA at symposium directed by Gail Dummer at Michigan State University. Dale Ulrich was first president.

1995 Adapted Physical Education National Standards (APENS) published by Human Kinetics. APENS specifies knowledge related to 15 standards to be tested by the national certification exam.

1995 Deaf sport group withdrew from Paralympic movement.

1996 Paralympics held in Atlanta. This was first Paralympics to include athletes with mental retardation at the same competition site and events.

1996 Gudrun Doll-Tepper elected president of the International Council of Sport Science and Physical Education (ICSSPE), an indicator of acceptance of adapted physical activity by the other sport science associations.

1997 Adapted physical activity included as one of the nine basic sport science disciplines in textbook, *The History of Exercise and Sport Science,* edited by John Massengale and Richard Swanson.

CREDITS

LINE ART, TABLES, TEXT

2

Figure 2.1. Adapted from unpublished work of Duncan Wyeth, Michigan Dept. of Education.
Song on p. 26 by Nancy Anderson. From videotape *Look at Me.* By permission of Terry N. Terry, President, The Message Makers, 1217 Turner, Lansing, MI 48906.
Excerpt, p. 29. Leo Buscaglia. *The Disabled and Their Parents: A Counseling Challenge.* (Thorofare, NJ: Charles B. Slack, Inc., 1975), pp. 19–20.
Excerpt, p. 30. *Guidelines for Writing and Speaking About People With Disabilities,* Research and Training Center on Independent Living, University of Kansas, Lawrence.
Poem on p. 32 by Jean Caywood, Richardson, TX.

4

Figure 4.1. Adapted from table (p. 3) in *NICHCY News Digest, 1* (1), 1991.

5

Figure 5.3. Developed from concepts on pp. 15–51, A. Maslow (1970). *Motivation and personality* (2nd ed.). New York: Harper & Row.
Figure 5.6. Based on concepts presented in A. Bandura (1977). Self-efficacy: Toward a unifying theory of behavioral change. *Psychological Review, 84* (7), 191–215.
Tables 5.9 and 5.10. Concepts from Janet Wessel's I CAN and ABC federally funded projects. Also included in J. Wessel and L. Kelly (1986). *Achievement-Based Curriculum Development in Physical Education.* Philadelphia: Lea & Febiger.

6

Table 6.2. From *AAHPER: Youth Fitness Test Manual* (American Alliance for Health, Physical Education, and Recreation, 1976).
Table 6.3. © The Cooper Institute for Aerobics.
Table 6.4. Content from Test of Gross Motor Development, 1985, by Dale A. Ulrich. PRO•ED, 8700 Shoal Creek Blvd., Austin, TX 78758.
Figure 6.7. From G. S. D. Morris (1980). *How to Change the Games Children Play,* 2nd ed., Minneapolis: Burgess.
Figure 6.8. Reproduced with the permission of American Guidance Service, Inc. *Bruininks-Oseretsky Test of Motor Proficiency* by Robert N. Bruininks. Copyright 1978. All rights reserved.
Table 6.11. Based on content in Denver Developmental Screening Test Manual published by Denver Developmental Materials, Inc., P.O. Box 6919, Denver, CO 80206–0919.

7

Figure 7.10. Based on concepts of Muska Mosston, Teaching Physical Education—From Command to Discovery. Columbus, OH: Charles E. Merrill, 1966, 1981.

Table 7.12. Based on unpublished dissertation of Nancy Megginson, 1982, Texas Woman's University, Denton.

8

Figure 8.3. From "Testing the Validity of the Griffin/Keogh Model for Movement Confidence by Analyzing Self-Report Playground Involvement Decisions of Elementary School Children," by M. E. Crawford & N. S. Griffin. This article is reprinted with permission from the *Research Quarterly for Exercise and Sport, vol. 57.* no. 1 (1986).
Figure 8.4. From "The Self-Esteem Complex and Youth Fitness" by K. R. Fox, 1988, *Quest,* 40, pp. 233 and 237.
Figure 8.6. Reprinted with permission of Psychologists and Educators Inc., P.O. Box 513, Chesterfield, MO 63006.
Tables 8.4 and 8.5. From S. Harter, *Manual for the Self-Perception Profile for Adolescents,* 1988. Reprinted with permission.
Figure 8.7. Reprinted with permission of Dr. Dale Ulrich, Physical Education Dept., Indiana University, Bloomington, IN 47405.
Table 8.7. From K. R. Fox, 1990, *The Physical Self-Perception Profile Manual,* Office of Health Promotion, Northern Illinois University, DeKalb, IL 60115.
Figure 8.12. Based on content in M. R. Weiss, B. Bredemeier, & R. Shewchuk (1985). An intrinsic/extrinsic motivation scale for the youth sport setting. *Journal of Sport Psychology, 7,* 75–91.
Figure 8.13. From "Attributions of Athletes with Cerebral Palsy" by G. Dummer, M. Ewing, R. Habeck, & S. Overton, 1987, *Adapted Physical Activity Quarterly, 4* (4), p. 282. Reprinted with modification with permission.

9

Figure 9.5. From *Cowstails and Cobras* (pp. 34, 36, 41, and 43) by Karl Rohnke, 1977, Hamilton, MA: Project Adventure. Copyright 1977 by Project Adventure. Reprinted by permission.
Poem on p. 223–224. From Dave Compton, "OK Being Different" in *Proceedings of Special Populations Institute,* March 28–29, 1974. Ogleby Park, Wheeling, West Virginia: Northern Community College.
Table 9.8. From G. N. Siperstein (1980). *Instruments for measuring children's attitudes toward the handicapped.* University of Massachusetts Center for the Study of Social Acceptance, Boston.

10

Figure 10.5. Adapted from G. Sage (1977). *Introduction to Motor Behavior: A Neuropsychological Approach,* p. 106. Reading, MA: Addison-Wesley Publishing Co.
Figure 10.24. Reprinted by permission of A. Milani-Comparetti and E. A. Gidoni, Italy. Reproduced by permission from Norris G. Haring,

Developing Effective Individualized Education Programs for Severely Handicapped Children and Youth (Columbus, OH: Special Press, 1977, p. 79). Available for purchase from Crace Rossa Italiana, Comitato Provinciale De Firenze, Centro Di Educazione Motoria, "Anna Torrigiani," via Di Comerata 8, 50133 Firenze.
Figures 10.6, 10.28(a), 10.28(b), 10.29, 10.31. From John W. Hole, Jr., *Human Anatomy and Physiology,* 2d ed. Copyright © 1981 Wm. C. Brown Communications, Inc., Dubuque, Iowa. All Rights Reserved. Reprinted by permission.
Figure 10.32. From Sylvia S. Mader, *Inquiry Into Life,* 4th ed. Copyright © 1985 Wm. C. Brown Communications, Inc., Dubuque, Iowa. All Rights Reserved. Reprinted by permission.
Figure 10.34. Redrawn from "Rhythmical Stereotypes in Normal Infants" by E. Thelen, 1979, *Animal Behavior, 27* pp. 703, 706.

11

Figure 11.17. Adapted from *Fundamental Movement: A Developmental and Remedial Approach,* by Bruce A. McClenaghan and David L. Gallahue. Copyright © 1978 by W. B. Saunders Company.
Figures 11.18 (c) and (d) and 11.19 (d) and (e). Courtesy of Mr. Jeffrey A. Jones, Rehabilitation Institute of Chicago.
Figure 11.20. Adapted from M. Wild, *Research Quarterly,* AAHPERD, 1938; redrawing from C. Corbin, *A Textbook of Motor Development,* 2d ed. Copyright © 1980 Wm. C. Brown Publishers, Dubuque, Iowa. All Rights Reserved. Reprinted by permission.
Figure 11.22. Table portion from G. S. D. Morris (1980). *How to Change the Games Children Play,* 2nd ed., Minneapolis: Burgess.
Excerpts from Test of Gross Motor Development, 1985, by Dale A. Ulrich. PRO•ED, 8700 Shoal Creek Blvd., Austin, TX 78758.

13

Figure 13.3. © Cooper Institute for Aerobics Research.
Figure 13.5. Adapted from R. Detrano & V. F. Froelicher (1988). Exercise testing: Uses and limitations considering recent studies. *Progress in Cardiovascular Diseases, 31* (3), 173–204. Figure on p. 178.
Figure 13.9(b). From Carl C. Seltzer and Jean Mayer, "A Simple Criterion of Obesity," *Postgraduate Medicine 38* (August, 1965): A101–107.
Figure 13.12(a). Courtesy of Mr. Jeffery A. Jones, Rehabilitation Institute of Chicago.
Figure 13.14. From Edward L. Fox, Richard W. Bowers, and Merle L. Foss, *The Physiological Basis of Physical Education and Athletics,* 4th ed. Copyright © 1989 Wm. C. Brown Communications, Inc., Dubuque, Iowa. All Rights Reserved. Reprinted by permission.

14

Figure 14.2. Reprinted by permission of Reedco Incorporated.

18

Figure 18.3. Redrawn from Shirley, M. M. "The First Two Years" in *Child Welfare Monograph 7,* 1933. © 1933, renewed 1960, University of Minnesota Press, Minneapolis.
Figure 18.6. From *The Cerebral Cortex of Man,* by Penfield and Rasmussen © 1985 by MacMillan Publishing Co.

19

Figure 19.6. From "Natural History of Human Atherosclerotic Lesions" by H. L. McGill, J. C. Geer, and J. P. Strong. In *Atherosclerosis and Its Origins* (p. 42) by M. Sandler and G. H. Bourne (Eds.), 1963, New York: Academic Press. Copyright 1963 by Academic Press. Reprinted by permission.
Figure 19.3 (center), 19.7, 19.8 (graph) 19.9 (left), 19.10, 19.14, 19.23, and 19.25. From John W. Hole, Jr., *Human Anatomy and Physiology,* 5th ed. Copyright © 1990 Wm. C. Brown Communications, Inc., Dubuque, Iowa. All Rights Reserved. Reprinted by permission.
Figure 19.3 (top left/bottom right). From Charles B. Corbin and Ruth Lindsey, *Concepts of Physical Fitness,* 7th ed. Copyright © 1990 Wm. C. Brown Communications, Inc., Dubuque, Iowa. All Rights Reserved. Reprinted by permission.
Figure 19.5. From *American Heart Association Heartbook.* New York: E. P. Dutton, p. 176. Reproduced with permission. *American Heart Association Heartbook,* 1980. Copyright American Heart Association.
Figure 19.8(a). From Kent M. Van De Graaff and Stuart Ira Fox, *Concepts of Human Anatomy and Physiology,* 2d ed. Copyright © 1989 Wm. C. Brown Communications, Inc., Dubuque, Iowa. All Rights Reserved. Reprinted by permission.
Figures 19.10 (right side) and 19.11. From *American Heart Association Heartbook.* New York: E. P. Dutton, pp. 243–246. Reproduced with permission. *American Heart Association Heartbook,* 1980. Copyright American Heart Association.
Figure 19.12 (left). From Stuart Ira Fox, *Laboratory Guide to Human Physiology,* 5th ed. Copyright © 1990 Wm. C. Brown Communications, Inc., Dubuque, Iowa. All Rights Reserved. Reprinted by permission.
Figure 19.13. From Herbert A. de Vries, *Physiology of Exercise for Physical Education and Athletics,* 4th ed. Copyright © 1986 Wm. C. Brown Communications, Inc., Dubuque, Iowa. All Rights Reserved. Reprinted by permission.
Figure 19.21. From Sylvia S. Mader, *Inquiry Into Life,* 4th ed. Copyright © 1985 Wm. C. Brown Communications, Inc., Dubuque, Iowa. All Rights Reserved. Reprinted by permission.

20

Figure 20.4. From M. Miyahara (1994). Subtypes of students with learning disabilities based on gross motor functions. *Adapted Physical Activity Quarterly,* 11 (4), p. 374.
Table 20.2. From American Psychiatric Association (1994) *Diagnostic and Statistical Manual IV,* pp. 83–84.

21

Table 21.2. From American Association on Mental Retardation (1992). *Mental retardation: Definition, classification, and systems of supports,* p. 102.
Figure 21.8(a). From John W. Hole, Jr., *Human Anatomy and Physiology,* 5th ed. Copyright © 1990 Wm. C. Brown Communications, Inc., Dubuque, Iowa. All Rights Reserved. Reprinted by permission.
Figure 21.9. From John W. Hole, Jr., *Human Anatomy and Physiology,* 5th ed. Copyright © 1990 Wm. C. Brown Communications, Inc., Dubuque, Iowa. All Rights Reserved. Reprinted by permission.
Figure 21.11. From D. A. Sugden and J. F. Keogh (1990). *Problems in Movement Skill Development.* Columbia, South Carolina: University of South Carolina Press, p. 87. Redrawn from Dobbins, D. A., Garron, R., & Rarick, G. L. (1981). The motor performance of educable mentally retarded and intellectually normal boys after covariate control for differences in body size. *Research Quarterly for Exercise and Sport, 58,* 1–8.
Figure 21.12. From A. E. Wall, M. Bouffard, J. McClements, H. Findlay, & M. J. Taylor (1985). A knowledge-based approach to motor development: Implications for the physically awkward, p. 32, *Adapted Physical Activity Quarterly, 2* (1), 21–42.
Figure 12.13. From Special Olympics International. *Athletics Sports Skills Program.* Reprinted with permission.
Figure 21.14. From G. Reid, D. Montgomery, & C. Seidl, *Stepping Out for Fitness,* pp. 31–33. Copyright 1990 by Canadian Association for Health, Physical Education, and Recreation.
Table 21.15. From E. J. Watkinson and A. E. Wall, *PREP: The Play Program: Play Skill Instruction for Mentally Handicapped Children,* pp. 14 & 21. Copyright 1982 by Canadian Association for Health, Physical Education, and Recreation.
Table 21.2. Adapted from Ruth C. Webb, "Sensory-Motor Training of the Profoundly Retarded," *American Journal of Mental Deficiency, 74* (September, 1969): 287.
Tables 21.3 and 21.4. From Special Olympics International (1989). *Special Olympics Motor Activities Training Guide.* Reprinted with permission.

23

Figure 23.4(a). From John W. Hole, Jr., *Human Anatomy and Physiology,* 5th ed. Copyright © 1990 Wm. C. Brown Communications, Inc., Dubuque, Iowa. All Rights Reserved. Reprinted by permission.
Figure 23.5. From G. G. Williamson (1987). *Children with Spina Bifida: Early Intervention and Preschool Programs* (p. 2). Baltimore, MD: Paul H. Brookes Publishing Co.; reprinted with permission.
Figure 23.9. From M. L. Barr & J. A. Kiernan (1988). *The Human Nervous System: A Medical Viewpoint* (5th ed.). Hagerstown, MD: Harper & Row. By permission of J. P. Lippincott, Philadelphia.

25

Figure 25.11. Redrawn from *Handling the Young Cerebral Palsied Child at Home,* 2nd edition, by Nancy R. Finnie. Copyright © 1974 by Nancy R. Finnie, F.C.S.P., additions for U.S. edition, copyright © by E. P. Dutton and Company, Inc.

26

Figure 26.3. From J. L. Northern & M. P. Downs (1991). *Hearing in Children* (4th ed.). Baltimore: Williams & Wilkins Co., p. 17. © Williams & Wilkins Co.

PHOTOGRAPHS

1

Figure 1.5. Deborah Buswell

2

Figure 2.7. Barron Ludlum, *Denton Record Chronicle*

Figure 2.12. Mary Carol Peterson, Action Top End, Invacare Corporation
Figure 2.16(a, b, c, d). Deborah Buswell

4

Figure 4.4. U.S. Cerebral Palsy Athletic Association

5

Figure 5.5. Top End Wheelchair Sports, Inc.
Figure 5.8. B. Cadden, Valdez Public Schools in Alaska
Figure 5.9. Joe Nolan
Figure 5.13. Deborah Buswell

6

Figure 6.6. Cosom Games and Athletic Goods Company, Minneapolis, MN

7

Figure 7.1. Rae Allen
Figure 7.2. DeKalb Public Schools, Georgia
Figure 7.5. Dr. Garth Tymeson, now at University of Wisconsin at LaCrosse
Figure 7.9. Deborah Buswell

8

Figure 8.8. Joe Nolan
Figure 8.11. Deborah Buswell

9

Figure 9.2. Deborah Buswell

10

Figure 10.3. Joe Nolan

12

Figure 12.1. Sharon Schmidt
Figure 12.10. Ernest Bundschuh, retired from University of Georgia

13

Figure 13.1. Deborah Buswell
Figure 13.2. Deborah Buswell

15

Figure 15.1. Mary Carol Peterson, Action Top End, Invacare Corporation
Figure 15.10. Barron Ludlum, *Denton Record Chronicle*

17

Figure 17.1. Judy Newman
Figure 17.10. Longview, WA YMCA

18

Figure 18.11(a). Dr. Jo Cowden
Figure 18.11(b). Dr. Dale Ulrich, Indiana University

19

Figure 19.1. Rae Allen
Figure 19.2. Fonda Johnstone

22

Figure 22.2. Ross Photos
Figure 22.3. Jim Estes
Figure 22.4. Joe Nolan

23

Figure 23.1. Candy Jackson, Courage Center, Golden Valley, MN
Figure 23.12. Dr. Horst Strohkendl, Universidat Koln, W. Germany
Figure 23.13. Mary Carol Peterson, Action Top End, Invacare Corporation
Figure 23.14. Mary Carol Peterson, Action Top End, Invacare Corporation
Figure 23.15. Paralyzed Veterans of America/*Sports 'n Spokes*
Figures 23.16 and 23.17. Mary Carol Peterson, Action Top End, Invacare Corporation
Figure 23.19(a). Beneficial Designs, Inc., Santa Cruz, CA
Figure 23.19(b). Deborah Buswell
Figure 23.19(c). Inge Morisbak

24

Figure 24.5. Marilyn Butt, adapted physical education consultant from Ontario, Canada
Figures 24.6–24.8. University of Texas SWMS–Dallas, Department of Medical Art
Figure 24.15. Dr. Jo Cowden, University of New Orleans

27

Figure 27.1. Steve Edmonds
Figures 27.8–27.10, 27.11. Christian Record Braille Foundation. Photo by Robert L. Sheldon
Figures 27.13 and 27.14. Provided by Rosanna Copeland, Parkview School for the Blind in Oklahoma

NAME INDEX

SUBJECT INDEX